new dictionary of the history of ideas

EDITORIAL BOARD

new dictionary of the history of ideas

maryanne cline horowitz, editor in chief

volume 2

Communication of Ideas to Futurology

CHARLES SCRIBNER'S SONS
An imprint of Thomson Gale, a part of The Thomson Corporation

Detroit • New York • San Francisco • San Diego • New Haven, Conn. • Waterville, Maine • London • Munich

New Dictionary of the History of Ideas
Maryanne Cline Horowitz, Editor in Chief

LIBRARY OF CONGRESS CATALOGING-IN-PUBLICATION DATA

New dictionary of the history of ideas / edited by Maryanne Cline Horowitz.
    p. cm.
  Includes bibliographical references and index.
  ISBN 0-684-31377-4 (set hardcover : alk. paper) — ISBN 0-684-31378-2 (v. 1) — ISBN 0-684-31379-0 (v. 2) — ISBN 0-684-31380-4 (v. 3) — ISBN 0-684-31381-2 (v. 4) — ISBN 0-684-31382-0 (v. 5) — ISBN 0-684-31383-9 (v. 6) — ISBN 0-684-31452-5 (e-book)
  1. Civilization—History—Dictionaries. 2. Intellectual life—History—Dictionaries.
  I. Horowitz, Maryanne Cline, 1945–

CB9.N49 2005
903—dc22
                                                    2004014731

This title is also available as an e-book.
ISBN 0-684-31452-5
Contact your Thomson Gale sales representative for ordering information.

Printed in the United States of America
10 9 8 7 6 5 4 3

CONTENTS

Volume 1

List of Articles

Preface

Historiography

Reader's Guide

NEW DICTIONARY OF THE HISTORY OF IDEAS
Abolitionism–Common Sense

Volume 2

Reader's Guide

Communication of Ideas–Futurology

Volume 3

Reader's Guide

Game Theory–Lysenkoism

Volume 4

Reader's Guide

Machiavellism–Phrenology

Volume 5

Reader's Guide

Physics–Syncretism

Volume 6

Reader's Guide

Taste–Zionism

List of Contributors

Index

EDITORIAL AND PRODUCTION STAFF

Project Editors
Mark LaFlaur, Scot Peacock, Jennifer Wisinski

Editorial Support
Kelly Baiseley, Andrew Claps, Alja Collar, Mark Drouillard,
Kenneth Mondschein, Sarah Turner, Ken Wachsberger,
Rachel Widawsky, Christopher Verdesi

Art Editor
Scot Peacock

Chief Manuscript Editor
Georgia S. Maas

Manuscript Editors
Jonathan G. Aretakis, John Barclay, Sylvia Cannizzaro,
Melissa A. Dobson, Ted Gilley, Gretchen Gordon,
Ellen Hawley, Archibald Hobson, Elizabeth B. Inserra,
Jean Fortune Kaplan, Christine Kelley, John Krol,
Julia Penelope, Richard Rothschild, David E. Salamie,
Linda Sanders, Alan Thwaits, Jane Marie Todd

Proofreaders
Beth Fhaner, Carol Holmes, Melodie Monahan,
Laura Specht Patchkofsky, Hilary White

Cartographer
XNR Productions, Madison, Wisconsin

Caption Writer
Shannon Kelly

Indexer
Cynthia Crippen, AEIOU, Inc.

Design
Jennifer Wahi

Imaging
Dean Dauphinais, Lezlie Light, Mary Grimes

Permissions
Margaret Abendroth, Peggie Ashlevitz, Lori Hines

Compositor
GGS Information Services, York, Pennsylvania

Manager, Composition
Mary Beth Trimper

Assistant Manager, Composition
Evi Seoud

Manufacturing
Wendy Blurton

Senior Development Editor
Nathalie Duval

Editorial Director
John Fitzpatrick

Publisher
Frank Menchaca

READER'S GUIDE

This Reader's Guide was compiled by the editors to provide a systematic outline of the contents of the New Dictionary of the History of Ideas, *thereby offering teachers, scholars, and the general reader a way to organize their reading according to their preferences. The Reader's Guide is divided into four sections: Communication of Ideas, Geographical Areas, Chronological Periods, and Liberal Arts Disciplines and Professions, as indicated in the outline below.*

COMMUNICATION OF IDEAS

Introduction to History of Communication of Ideas

Communication Media

GEOGRAPHICAL AREAS

Global Entries

Africa

Asia

Europe

Middle East

North America

Latin and South America

CHRONOLOGICAL PERIODS

Ancient

Dynastic (400 C.E.–1400 C.E.)

Early Modern (1400–1800 C.E.)

Modern (1800–1945)

Contemporary

LIBERAL ARTS DISCIPLINES AND PROFESSIONS

Fine Arts

Humanities

Social Sciences

Sciences

Professions

Multidisciplinary Practices

Especially Interdisciplinary Entries

COMMUNICATION OF IDEAS

This category is the newest aspect of the *New Dictionary of the History of Ideas*; cultural studies, communications studies, and cultural history are moving the disciplines in this direction.

Introduction to History of Communication of Ideas

The following entries focus on the media humans have used to communicate with one another.

Absolute Music
Aesthetics: Asia
Architecture: Overview
Architecture: Asia
Arts: Overview
Astronomy, Pre-Columbian and Latin American
Bilingualism and Multilingualism
Borders, Borderlands, and Frontiers, Global
Calendar
Cinema
City, The: The City as a Cultural Center
City, The: The City as Political Center
Communication of Ideas: Africa and Its Influence
Communication of Ideas: Asia and Its Influence
Communication of Ideas: Europe and Its Influence
Communication of Ideas: Middle East and Abroad
Communication of Ideas: Orality and Advent of Writing
Communication of Ideas: Southeast Asia
Communication of Ideas: The Americas and Their Influence
Consumerism
Cultural Revivals
Cultural Studies
Dance
Diffusion, Cultural
Dress
Dualism
Education: Asia, Traditional and Modern
Education: Global Education
Emotions
Experiment
Garden
Gesture
Humor
Iconography
Images, Icons, and Idols
Japanese Philosophy, Japanese Thought
Language and Linguistics
Language, Linguistics, and Literacy
Learning and Memory, Contemporary Views
Mathematics
Media, History of
Metaphor
Migration: United States
Modernity: Africa
Museums
Music, Anthropology of

Musical Performance and Audiences
Oral Traditions: Overview
Oral Traditions: Telling, Sharing
Political Protest, U.S.
Practices
Protest, Political
Reading
Realism: Africa
Reflexivity
Relativism
Representation: Mental Representation
Resistance
Resistance and Accommodation
Rhetoric: Overview
Rhetoric: Ancient and Medieval
Ritual: Public Ritual
Ritual: Religion
Sacred Places
Text/Textuality
Textiles and Fiber Arts as Catalysts for Ideas
Theater and Performance
Third Cinema
Totems
Tradition
Translation
Virtual Reality
Visual Culture
Visual Order to Organizing Collections

Communication Media

This is a listing of the types of historical evidence the author used in writing the entry. While entries in the original Dictionary of the History of Ideas were to a great extent the history of texts, the entries in the New Dictionary of the History of Ideas are generally the cultural history of ideas, making use of the records of oral communication, visual communication, and communication through practices, as well as the history of texts, in order to show the impact of the idea on a wide variety of people.

ORAL

The selective list below contains the entries that give the most coverage to historical examples of the oral transmission and transformation of ideas.

Civil Disobedience
Civil Society: Europe and the United States
Communication of Ideas: Orality and Advent of Writing
Cosmopolitanism
Cultural Capital
Determinism
Dialogue and Dialectics: Socratic
Dialogue and Dialectics: Talmudic
Dream
Emotions
Empire and Imperialism: Europe
Equality: Overview
Etiquette
Fascism
Harmony
Magic
Masks
Media, History of
Millenarianism: Latin America and Native North America

Music, Anthropology of
Musical Performance and Audiences
Musicology
Nomadism
Oral Traditions: Overview
Oral Traditions: Telling, Sharing
Populism: United States
Psychoanalysis
Public Sphere
Republicanism: Republic
Rhetoric: Overview
Ritual: Public Ritual
Ritual: Religion
Slavery
Theater and Performance
Tragedy and Comedy
Trope
Wisdom, Human

COMMUNICATION THROUGH HIGH TECHNOL-
OGY MEDIA (radio, television, film, computer, etc.)
Absolute Music
Africa, Idea of
Alienation
Americanization, U.S.
Anticolonialism: Africa
Anti-Semitism: Islamic Anti-Semitism
Architecture: Overview
Avant-Garde: Overview
Bilingualism and Multilingualism
Bioethics
Calculation and Computation
Capitalism: Overview
Capitalism: Africa
Censorship
Chicano Movement
Cinema
City, The: The City as a Cultural Center
City, The: The City as Political Center
Colonialism: Southeast Asia
Communication of Ideas: Africa and Its Influence
Communication of Ideas: Asia and Its Influence
Communication of Ideas: Europe and Its Influence
Communication of Ideas: Middle East and Abroad
Communication of Ideas: Orality and Advent of Writing
Communication of Ideas: Southeast Asia
Communism: Latin America
Composition, Musical
Computer Science
Consciousness: Overview
Consumerism
Cosmopolitanism
Creativity in the Arts and Sciences
Critical Theory
Cultural Studies
Death
Demography
Development
Dream
Dress
Dystopia
Empire and Imperialism: United States
Environmental History
Expressionism
Fascism
Fetishism: Fetishism in Literature and Cultural Studies

Field Theories
Futurology
Game Theory
Gay Studies
Gender: Gender in the Middle East
Gender in Art
Genetics: Contemporary
Genetics: History of
Genocide
Genre
Geography
Globalization: General
Harmony
Hinduism
History, Economic
Human Capital
Iconography
Intelligentsia
Jihad
Jouissance
Judaism: Modern Judaism
Language and Linguistics
Law
Learning and Memory, Contemporary Views
Life
Life Cycle: Elders/Old Age
Literary Criticism
Literature: Overview
Literature: African Literature
Loyalties, Dual
Lysenkoism
Maps and the Ideas They Express
Masks
Mathematics
Media, History of
Medicine: Europe and the United States
Medicine: Islamic Medicine
Meme
Memory
Modernism: Overview
Modernism: Latin America
Modernity: East Asia
Motherhood and Maternity
Motif: Motif in Music
Music, Anthropology of
Musical Performance and Audiences
Musicology
Nuclear Age
Occidentalism
Pan-Arabism
Parties, Political
Physics
Political Protest, U.S.
Political Science
Postmodernism
Power
Presentism
Privacy
Probability
Progress, Idea of
Propaganda
Property
Protest, Political
Public Sphere
Quantum

Reading
Reform: Europe and the United States
Reform: Islamic Reform
Relativity
Representation: Mental Representation
Resistance
Rhetoric: Overview
Science Fiction
Sexuality: Overview
Social History, U.S.
Society
State, The: Overview
Symbolism
Taste
Technology
Third Cinema
Third World
Totalitarianism
Victorianism
Virtual Reality
Visual Culture
War and Peace in the Arts
Westernization: Africa
Westernization: Middle East
Women and Femininity in U.S. Popular Culture
Work
World Systems Theory, Latin America

VISUAL

Each of the following entries in the *NDHI* either evocatively describes ideas, includes a visual image of an idea, or provides historical examples of societies visually transmitting and transforming ideas.

Abolitionism
Aesthetics: Africa
Aesthetics: Asia
Aesthetics: Europe and the Americas
Alienation
Altruism
Ambiguity
Americanization, U.S.
Ancestor Worship
Animism
Anti-Semitism: Overview
Apartheid
Architecture: Overview
Architecture: Africa
Architecture: Asia
Arts: Overview
Arts: Africa
Asceticism: Hindu and Buddhist Asceticism
Asceticism: Western Asceticism
Asian-American Ideas (Cultural Migration)
Assimilation
Astrology: Overview
Astronomy, Pre-Columbian and Latin American
Authoritarianism: Latin America
Autobiography
Avant-Garde: Militancy
Aztlán
Barbarism and Civilization
Beauty and Ugliness
Behaviorism

Bioethics
Black Atlantic
Black Consciousness
Body, The
Bushido
Calculation and Computation
Calendar
Cannibalism
Capitalism: Overview
Capitalism: Africa
Causation
Censorship
Change
Chemistry
Childhood and Child Rearing
Cinema
City, The: Latin America
City, The: The City as a Cultural Center
City, The: The City as Political Center
City, The: The Islamic and Byzantine City
Civil Disobedience
Classicism
Classification of Arts and Sciences, Early Modern
Colonialism: Southeast Asia
Common Sense
Communication of Ideas: The Americas and Their Influence
Communication of Ideas: Asia and Its Influence
Communication of Ideas: Europe and Its Influence
Communication of Ideas: Orality and Advent of Writing
Communication of Ideas: Southeast Asia
Composition, Musical
Computer Science
Consciousness: Overview
Consumerism
Continental Philosophy
Cosmology: Asia
Cosmopolitanism
Creativity in the Arts and Sciences
Critical Race Theory
Critical Theory
Cultural Capital
Cultural History
Cultural Revivals
Cultural Studies
Cycles
Cynicism
Dada
Dance
Death
Death and Afterlife, Islamic Understanding of
Demography
Demonology
Determinism
Development
Diasporas: African Diaspora
Diasporas: Jewish Diaspora
Dictatorship in Latin America
Discrimination
Diversity
Dream
Dress
Dystopia
Ecology

Education: Europe
Education: Islamic Education
Emotions
Empire and Imperialism: Europe
Empire and Imperialism: United States
Empiricism
Encyclopedism
Enlightenment
Environment
Environmental History
Epistemology: Ancient
Epistemology: Early Modern
Equality: Overview
Equality: Racial Equality
Essentialism
Ethnicity and Race: Anthropology
Ethnicity and Race: Islamic Views
Ethnocentrism
Etiquette
Eugenics
Europe, Idea of
Everyday Life
Evil
Expressionism
Extirpation
Family Planning
Fascism
Fatalism
Feminism: Overview
Feminism: Chicana Feminisms
Feminism: Third World U.S. Movement
Fetishism: Overview
Fetishism: Fetishism in Literature and Cultural Studies
Feudalism, European
Field Theories
Form, Metaphysical, in Ancient and Medieval Thought
Foundationalism
Friendship
Futurology
Game Theory
Garden
Gender: Overview
Gender: Gender in the Middle East
Gender in Art
Genetics: Contemporary
Genetics: History of
Genius
Genocide
Geography
Geometry
Gesture
Ghetto
Globalization: Asia
Globalization: General
Greek Science
Harmony
Hate
Health and Disease
Heaven and Hell
Heaven and Hell (Asian Focus)
Hedonism in European Thought
Heresy and Apostasy
Hinduism
History, Economic
History, Idea of

Honor
Honor, Middle Eastern Notions of
Humanism: Chinese Conception of
Humanity: African Thought
Humanity: European Thought
Humanity in the Arts
Humor
Hygiene
Iconography
Idealism
Ideas, History of
Identity: Identity of Persons
Identity, Multiple: Overview
Identity, Multiple: Jewish Multiple Identity
Images, Icons, and Idols
Imagination
Impressionism
Intentionality
Interdisciplinarity
Islam: Shii
Islamic Science
Jainism
Jihad
Jouissance
Knowledge
Landscape in the Arts
Language, Linguistics, and Literacy
Law, Islamic
Leadership
Learning and Memory, Contemporary Views
Liberty
Life Cycle: Overview
Life Cycle: Elders/Old Age
Literary History
Love, Western Notions of
Machismo
Magic
Maps and the Ideas They Express
Masks
Mathematics
Matriarchy
Mechanical Philosophy
Media, History of
Medicine: Europe and the United States
Medicine: Islamic Medicine
Memory
Men and Masculinity
Mestizaje
Metaphor
Microcosm and Macrocosm
Migration: United States
Millenarianism: Islamic
Millenarianism: Latin America and Native North
  America
Minority
Miracles
Modernism: Overview
Modernism: Latin America
Modernity: Overview
Modernity: Africa
Monarchy: Overview
Monasticism
Motherhood and Maternity
Motif: Motif in Music
Museums

Musical Performance and Audiences
Musicology
Mysticism: Chinese Mysticism
Mysticism: Christian Mysticism
Myth
Nation
Nationalism: Overview
Natural History
Naturalism
Naturalism in Art and Literature
Naturphilosophie
Negritude
Newtonianism
Nomadism
Nuclear Age
Nude, The
Occidentalism
Organicism
Orthodoxy
Pacifism
Pan-Asianism
Paradigm
Paradise on Earth
Periodization of the Arts
Person, Idea of the
Perspective
Philosophies: American
Philosophies: Feminist, Twentieth-Century
Philosophy: Relations to Other Intellectual Realms
Phrenology
Physics
Political Protest, U.S.
Population
Postmodernism
Practices
Pre-Columbian Civilization
Prejudice
Privacy
Property
Protest, Political
Psychoanalysis
Public Sphere
Pythagoreanism
Queer Theory
Race and Racism: United States
Reading
Realism
Relativism
Religion: Indigenous Peoples' View, South America
Religion and Science
Religion and the State: Latin America
Renaissance
Representation: Mental Representation
Representation: Political Representation
Republicanism: Republic
Resistance
Resistance and Accommodation
Responsibility
Ritual: Public Ritual
Ritual: Religion
Romanticism in Literature and Politics
Sacred and Profane
Sacred Places
Science, History of
Science Fiction

Scientific Revolution
Sexuality: Overview
Sexuality: Sexual Orientation
Shinto
Slavery
Social History, U.S.
Sophists, The
Sport
Subjectivism
Superstition
Surrealism
Symbolism
Syncretism
Taste
Terror
Text/Textuality
Theater and Performance
Theodicy
Third Cinema
Third World Literature
Toleration
Totalitarianism
Totems
Trade
Tragedy and Comedy
Treaty
Untouchability: Menstrual Taboos
Utilitarianism
Utopia
Victorianism
Virtual Reality
Visual Culture
Visual Order to Organizing Collections
Volunteerism, U.S.
War
War and Peace in the Arts
Westernization: Southeast Asia
Witchcraft
Witchcraft, African Studies of
Women and Femininity in U.S. Popular Culture
Women's History: Africa
World Systems Theory, Latin America
Yin and Yang

PRACTICES

Most of the entries in the *NDHI* discuss how specific societies habituated people to specific ideas. This selective list includes the entries on schools of thought and practice, religions, and political movements, as well as the entries on distinctive practices.

Abolitionism
Afropessimism
Agnosticism
Alchemy: China
Alchemy: Europe and the Middle East
Anarchism
Ancestor Worship
Animism
Anticolonialism: Africa
Anticolonialism: Latin America
Anticolonialism: Middle East
Anticolonialism: Southeast Asia
Anticommunism: Latin America
Antifeminism

Anti-Semitism: Overview
Anti-Semitism: Islamic Anti-Semitism
Apartheid
Aristotelianism
Asceticism: Hindu and Buddhist Asceticism
Asceticism: Western Asceticism
Astrology: Overview
Astrology: China
Atheism
Avant-Garde: Militancy
Behaviorism
Black Consciousness
Buddhism
Bureaucracy
Bushido
Cannibalism
Capitalism: Overview
Capitalism: Africa
Cartesianism
Character
Chicano Movement
Chinese Thought
Christianity: Overview
Christianity: Asia
Cinema
Citizenship: Naturalization
Civil Disobedience
Classicism
Classification of Arts and Sciences, Early Modern
Colonialism: Africa
Colonialism: Latin America
Colonialism: Southeast Asia
Communication of Ideas: Orality and Advent of Writing
Communism: Europe
Communism: Latin America
Communitarianism in African Thought
Computer Science
Confucianism
Conservatism
Constitutionalism
Cosmopolitanism
Creationism
Critical Theory
Cultural Capital
Cultural Studies
Cynicism
Dance
Daoism
Deism
Dialogue and Dialectics: Socratic
Dialogue and Dialectics: Talmudic
Discrimination
Diversity
Eclecticism
Ecumenism
Empire and Imperialism: Overview
Empire and Imperialism: Americas
Empire and Imperialism: Asia
Empire and Imperialism: Europe
Empire and Imperialism: Middle East
Empire and Imperialism: United States
Empiricism
Epicureanism
Equality: Overview
Etiquette

Eugenics
Everyday Life
Existentialism
Extirpation
Fascism
Fatalism
Feminism: Overview
Feminism: Africa and African Diaspora
Feminism: Chicana Feminisms
Feminism: Islamic Feminism
Feminism: Third World U.S. Movement
Fetishism: Overview
Feudalism, European
Game Theory
Genocide
Ghetto
Gift, The
Gnosticism
Health and Disease
Hegelianism
Hinduism
Humanism: Renaissance
Humanism: Secular Humanism in the United States
Human Rights: Overview
Human Rights: Women's Rights
Interpretation
Islam: Africa
Islam: Shii
Islam: Southeast Asia
Islam: Sunni
Jainism
Japanese Philosophy, Japanese Thought
Jihad
Judaism: Judaism to 1800
Judaism: Modern Judaism
Kantianism
Law
Leadership
Legalism, Ancient China
Liberalism
Liberation Theology
Machiavellism
Magic
Manichaeism
Maoism
Marxism: Overview
Marxism: Asia
Marxism: Latin America
Masks
Mechanical Philosophy
Medicine: China
Medicine: Europe and the United States
Medicine: India
Medicine: Islamic Medicine
Migration: Migration in World History
Monarchy: Overview
Monasticism
Multiculturalism, Africa
Museums
Music, Anthropology of
Musical Performance and Audiences
Musicology
Myth
Nationalism: Overview
Nationalism: Africa

Nationalism: Cultural Nationalism
Nationalism: Middle East
Neoplatonism
Nihilism
Nomadism
Nonviolence
Orthodoxy
Orthopraxy: Asia
Orthopraxy: Western Orthopraxy
Pacifism
Pan-Africanism
Pan-Arabism
Pan-Asianism
Pan-Islamism
Pan-Turkism
Paradigm
Phrenology
Physics
Platonism
Political Protest, U.S.
Polytheism
Population
Populism: Latin America
Positivism
Practices
Pragmatism
Pseudoscience
Psychoanalysis
Psychology and Psychiatry
Public Sphere
Punishment
Race and Racism: Asia
Race and Racism: Europe
Race and Racism: United States
Radicals/Radicalism
Rational Choice
Reading
Realism: Africa
Reflexivity
Reform: Europe and the United States
Relativism
Religion: Overview
Religion: Africa
Religion: African Diaspora
Religion: East and Southeast Asia
Religion: Indigenous Peoples' View, South America
Religion: Latin America
Religion: Middle East
Republicanism: Latin America
Republicanism: Republic
Resistance
Resistance and Accommodation
Responsibility
Revolution
Ritual: Public Ritual
Ritual: Religion
Romanticism in Literature and Politics
Sacred and Profane
Scholasticism
Science: Overview
Scientific Revolution
Secularization and Secularism
Segregation
Skepticism
Slavery

Socialism
Socialisms, African
Sophists, The
Sport
Stoicism
Subjectivism
Suicide
Superstition
Symbolism
Syncretism
Temperance
Terror
Theater and Performance
Time: Traditional and Utilitarian
Totalitarianism
Totems
Trade
Tradition
Tragedy and Comedy
Tribalism, Middle East
Untouchability: Overview
Untouchability: Menstrual Taboos
Untouchability: Taboos
Utilitarianism
Visual Order to Organizing Collections
Volunteerism, U.S.
Westernization: Africa
Westernization: Middle East
Westernization: Southeast Asia
Witchcraft
Witchcraft, African Studies of
Work
Yoga
Zionism

TEXTUAL

Every entry in the *New Dictionary of the History of Ideas* used texts. The following is a list of entries that focused mainly on the history of a succession of texts. Each academic discipline has a succession of major authors with whom later practitioners of the discipline build upon and respond to creatively. The historian of a discipline—such as the history of political philosophy, literary history, or the history of science—considers the responses of thinkers and practitioners of a discipline to the major earlier texts in the discipline. In tracing the origin, development, and transformation of an idea, the historian of ideas considers thinkers' responses to texts from a variety of disciplines.

Agnosticism
Alchemy: Europe and the Middle East
Algebras
Altruism
America
Analytical Philosophy
Aristotelianism
Asceticism: Hindu and Buddhist Asceticism
Autobiography
Autonomy
Biography
Bureaucracy
Capitalism: Overview
Cartesianism
Casuistry

Causality
Censorship
Change
Chinese Thought
Civil Disobedience
Class
Communitarianism in African Thought
Conservatism
Continental Philosophy
Cosmology: Cosmology and Astronomy
Creolization, Caribbean
Crisis
Cycles
Death and Afterlife, Islamic Understanding of
Deism
Dialogue and Dialectics: Socratic
Dialogue and Dialectics: Talmudic
Eclecticism
Encyclopedism
Epistemology: Ancient
Epistemology: Early Modern
Equality: Gender Equality
Eschatology
Essentialism
Existentialism
Experiment
Falsifiability
Fatalism
Fetishism: Fetishism in Literature and Cultural Studies
Form, Metaphysical, in Ancient and Medieval Thought
Free Will, Determinism, and Predestination
General Will
Generation
Genius
Genre
Geometry
Gift, The
Globalization: Asia
Gnosticism
Good
Greek Science
Happiness and Pleasure in European Thought
Heaven and Hell
Hegelianism
Hermeneutics
Hierarchy and Order
Hinduism
Historical and Dialectical Materialism
Historicism
Historiography
History, Idea of
Humanism: Africa
Humanism: Chinese Conception of
Humanism: Renaissance
Humanity: Asian Thought
Human Rights: Overview
Idealism
Ideas, History of
Identity, Multiple: Overview
Identity: Identity of Persons
Imagination
Immortality and the Afterlife
Individualism
Intelligentsia
Jouissance

Judaism: Judaism to 1800
Justice: Overview
Justice: Justice in American Thought
Justice: Justice in East Asian Thought
Kantianism
Knowledge
Language, Philosophy of: Ancient and Medieval
Language, Philosophy of: Modern
Legalism, Ancient China
Liberalism
Liberty
Literature: African Literature
Materialism in Eighteenth-Century European Thought
Mechanical Philosophy
Medicine: China
Metaphor
Metaphysics: Ancient and Medieval
Metaphysics: Renaissance to the Present
Microcosm and Macrocosm
Mind
Modernity: East Asia
Mohism
Moral Sense
Motif: Motif in Literature
Mysticism: Chinese Mysticism
Mysticism: Christian Mysticism
Mysticism: Kabbalah
Natural Law
Natural Theology
Naturalism
Naturphilosophie
Negritude
Neocolonialism
New Criticism
Nihilism
Organicism
Orientalism: Overview
Orthopraxy: Western Orthopraxy
Paradigm
Phenomenology
Philosophies: African
Philosophies: Islamic
Philosophy: Historical Overview and Recent Develop-
    ments
Philosophy, History of
Philosophy, Moral: Ancient
Philosophy, Moral: Medieval and Renaissance
Philosophy, Moral: Modern
Philosophy and Religion in Western Thought
Philosophy of Mind: Ancient and Medieval
Philosophy of Religion
Pietism
Platonism
Poetry and Poetics
Political, The
Postcolonial Theory and Literature
Practices
Pragmatism
Prehistory, Rise of
Progress, Idea of
Psychoanalysis
Queer Theory
Race and Racism: Overview
Rationalism
Reading

Realism: Africa
Reflexivity
Relativity
Religion: Overview
Representation: Political Representation
Republicanism: Republic
Romanticism in Literature and Politics
Sacred Texts: Asia
Science: East Asia
Science, History of
Science Fiction
Social Capital
Social Contract
State of Nature
Stoicism
Structuralism and Poststructuralism: Overview
Structuralism and Poststructuralism: Anthropology
Taste
Text/Textuality
Toleration
Treaty
Truth
Universalism
Utopia
Virtue Ethics
Wealth
World Systems Theory, Latin America

GEOGRAPHICAL AREAS

Global Entries

EXEMPLARY GLOBAL ENTRIES
    Anthropology
    Atheism
    Bilingualism and Multilingualism
    Black Atlantic
    Christianity: Overview
    Communication of Ideas: Orality and the Advent of
        Writing
    Constitutionalism
    Critical Theory
    Dance
    Environmental History
    Eurocentrism
    Feminism: Overview
    Fundamentalism
    Garden
    Historiography
    History, Economic
    Humanity in the Arts
    Identity, Multiple: Jewish Multiple Identity
    International Order
    Islam: Shii
    Islam: Sunni
    Life Cycle: Elders/Old Age
    Magic
    Maps and the Ideas They Express
    Marxism: Overview
    Mathematics
    Migration: Africa
    Migration: Migration in World History
    Migration: United States
    Monasticism
    Music, Anthropology of

Musical Performance and Audiences
Nuclear Age
Pan-Africanism
Peasants and Peasantry
Person, Idea of the
Polytheism
Postcolonial Theory and Literature
Property
Protest, Political
Religion and the State: Africa
Resistance and Accommodation
Ritual: Religion
Sacred Places
Secularization and Secularism
Slavery
Sovereignty
Superstition
Syncretism
Temperance
Third Cinema
Third World Literature
Tradition
Treaty
Witchcraft
Women's Studies

ENTRIES ON AT LEAST THREE GEOGRAPHIC
AREAS OR A GLOBAL TOPIC
Abolitionism
Aesthetics: Africa
Africa, Idea of
Alchemy: China
Alienation
Animism
Anthropology
Anticolonialism: Africa
Anticolonialism: Latin America
Anticolonialism: Southeast Asia
Antifeminism
Architecture: Overview
Arts: Overview
Arts: Africa
Asceticism: Hindu and Buddhist Asceticism
Astrology: Overview
Atheism
Authoritarianism: Overview
Authority
Autobiography
Barbarism and Civilization
Bilingualism and Multilingualism
Bioethics
Biography
Black Atlantic
Body, The
Borders, Borderlands, and Frontiers, Global
Buddhism
Calculation and Computation
Calendar
Cannibalism
Capitalism: Overview
Capitalism: Africa
Censorship
Childhood and Child Rearing
Cinema
Citizenship: Overview
City, The: The City as a Cultural Center

Civil Disobedience
Civil Society: Europe and the United States
Colonialism: Africa
Colonialism: Southeast Asia
Communication of Ideas: Africa and Its Influence
Communication of Ideas: Middle East and Abroad
Communication of Ideas: Orality and the Advent of
    Writing
Computer Science
Consciousness: Overview
Corruption in Developed and Developing Countries
Cosmology: Asia
Cosmopolitanism
Creativity in the Arts and Sciences
Creolization, Caribbean
Critical Theory
Cultural Capital
Cultural Studies
Dance
Death
Deism
Democracy
Demography
Demonology
Dependency
Diasporas: African Diaspora
Diasporas: Jewish Diaspora
Discrimination
Diversity
Dream
Dress
Dualism
Ecology
Economics
Ecumenism
Education: Global Education
Education: Islamic Education
Empire and Imperialism: Overview
Empire and Imperialism: Asia
Empire and Imperialism: Europe
Empire and Imperialism: Middle East
Empire and Imperialism: United States
Environment
Equality: Overview
Equality: Gender Equality
Equality: Racial Equality
Ethnicity and Race: Anthropology
Ethnocentrism
Ethnography
Evil
Family: Family in Anthropology since 1980
Family Planning
Fascism
Feminism: Africa and African Diaspora
Feminism: Islamic Feminism
Feminism: Third World U.S. Movement
Fetishism: Overview
Friendship
Futurology
Gay Studies
Gender: Overview
Gender: Gender in the Middle East
Gender in Art
Gender Studies: Anthropology
Generation

Genius
Genocide
Geography
Ghetto
Globalization: General
Hate
Heaven and Hell
Honor
Human Capital
Humanism: Chinese Conception of
Humanity: African Thought
Human Rights: Overview
Human Rights: Women's Rights
Iconography
Identity, Multiple: Overview
Images, Icons, and Idols
Immortality and the Afterlife
Intelligentsia
Islam: Africa
Islamic Science
Jihad
Judaism: Modern Judaism
Justice: Overview
Kinship
Landscape in the Arts
Language, Linguistics, and Literacy
Law
Liberation Theology
Liberty
Life Cycle: Overview
Life Cycle: Adolescence
Literature: Overview
Machiavellism
Masks
Matriarchy
Media, History of
Medicine: China
Meditation: Eastern Meditation
Men and Masculinity
Millenarianism: Overview
Millenarianism: Latin America and Native North
  America
Minority
Miracles
Modernism: Overview
Modernism: Latin America
Modernity: Overview
Modernity: Africa
Modernization Theory
Monarchy: Overview
Motif: Motif in Music
Museums
Musicology
Mysticism: Chinese Mysticism
Myth
Nation
Nationalism: Overview
Nationalism: Africa
Native Policy
Negritude
Neocolonialism
Nihilism
Nomadism
Nonviolence
Occidentalism

Oral Traditions: Overview
Organicism
Orientalism: Overview
Orientalism: African and Black Orientalism
Orthodoxy
Orthopraxy: Asia
Other, The, European Views of
Pacifism
Paradise on Earth
Peace
Periodization
Periodization of the Arts
Perspective
Philosophies: African
Philosophy: Historical Overview and Recent Develop-
  ments
Philosophy: Relations to Other Intellectual Realms
Philosophy, Moral: Africa
Political Science
Population
Postcolonial Studies
Practices
Prehistory, Rise of
Prejudice
Presentism
Privatization
Pseudoscience
Race and Racism: Overview
Reading
Reflexivity
Religion: Overview
Religion: East and Southeast Asia
Religion: Latin America
Religion and the State: United States
Representation: Political Representation
Republicanism: Republic
Rhetoric: Overview
Ritual: Public Ritual
Sacred and Profane
Scarcity and Abundance, Latin America
Science: Overview
Segregation
Sexuality: Overview
Social Capital
Society
Sport
State, The: Overview
Structuralism and Poststructuralism: Anthropology
Symbolism
Third World
Time: China
Toleration
Totalitarianism
Totems
Trade
Translation
Travel: Travel from Europe and the Middle East
University: Overview
University: Postcolonial
Untouchability: Overview
Untouchability: Menstrual Taboos
Untouchability: Taboos
Victorianism
Visual Order to Organizing Collections
War

War and Peace in the Arts
Westernization: Africa
Westernization: Southeast Asia
Wisdom, Human
Work
World Systems Theory, Latin America

Africa
ENTRIES FOCUSING ON AFRICA
Aesthetics: Africa
Anticolonialism: Africa
Architecture: Africa
Arts: Africa
Authenticity: Africa
Black Atlantic
Capitalism: Africa
Colonialism: Africa
Communication of Ideas: Africa and Its Influence
Communitarianism in African Thought
Democracy, Africa
Diasporas: African Diaspora
Ethnicity and Race: Africa
Feminism: Africa and African Diaspora
Globalization: Africa
Humanism: Africa
Humanity: African Thought
Islam: Africa
Literature: African Literature
Migration: Africa
Modernity: Africa
Multiculturalism, Africa
Mysticism: Mysticism in African Thought
Nationalism: Africa
Pan-Africanism
Personhood in African Thought
Philosophies: African
Philosophy, Moral: Africa
Realism: Africa
Religion: Africa
Religion: African Diaspora
Religion and the State: Africa
Sociability in African Thought
Socialisms, African
Sufism
Westernization: Africa
Women's History: Africa
Witchcraft, African Studies of
ENTRIES THAT CONSIDER AFRICA
Abolitionism
Africa, Idea of
African-American Ideas
Afrocentricity
Afropessimism
Ancestor Worship
Anthropology
Apartheid
Arts: Overview
Bilingualism and Multilingualism
Black Consciousness
Buddhism
Christianity: Overview
Civil Disobedience
Civil Society: Responses in Africa and the Middle East
Communication of Ideas: Orality and Advent of Writing

Creolization, Caribbean
Critical Theory
Dance
Demography
Dependency
Diasporas: Jewish Diaspora
Discrimination
Dress
Ecology
Empire and Imperialism: Europe
Empire and Imperialism: Middle East
Environmental History
Equality: Racial Equality
Ethnography
Eurocentrism
Family: Modernist Anthropological Theory
Fascism
Feminism: Overview
Feminism: Islamic Feminism
Fetishism: Overview
Genocide
Globalization: General
Historiography
History, Economic
Humanity in the Arts
Identity, Multiple: Jewish Multiple Identity
International Order
Islam: Shii
Islam: Sunni
Jainism
Kinship
Law
Liberation Theology
Life Cycle: Elders/Old Age
Machiavellism
Magic
Maps and the Ideas They Express
Masks
Mathematics
Men and Masculinity
Migration: Migration in World History
Migration: United States
Minority
Modernism: Overview
Motherhood and Maternity
Museums
Music, Anthropology of
Negritude
Neocolonialism
Nomadism
Oral Traditions: Overview
Orientalism: African and Black Orientalism
Pacifism
Peasants and Peasantry
Person, Idea of the
Philosophies: Islamic
Polytheism
Postcolonial Studies
Postcolonial Theory and Literature
Property
Protest, Political
Race and Racism: Overview
Religion: Latin America
Religion and the State: United States
Resistance and Accommodation

Ritual: Religion
Sacred and Profane
Sage Philosophy
Segregation
Slavery
State, The: The Postcolonial State
Syncretism
Temperance
Third Cinema
Third World
Third World Literature
Time: Traditional and Utilitarian
Toleration
Totems
Treaty
Tribalism, Middle East
University: Postcolonial
Untouchability: Menstrual Taboos
Victorianism
War
Wisdom, Human
Witchcraft
Womanism
Women's Studies
Work
World Systems Theory, Latin America

Asia

ENTRIES FOCUSING ON ASIA
Aesthetics: Asia
Alchemy: China
Anticolonialism: Southeast Asia
Architecture: Asia
Authoritarianism: East Asia
Buddhism
Causation in East Asian and Southeast Asian Philosophy
Chinese Thought
Chinese Warlordism
Christianity: Asia
Colonialism: Southeast Asia
Communication of Ideas: Asia and Its Influence
Communication of Ideas: Southeast Asia and Its Influence
Confucianism
Consciousness: Chinese Thought
Consciousness: Indian Thought
Cosmology: Asia
Daoism
Education: Asia, Traditional and Modern
Education: China
Education: India
Education: Japan
Empire and Imperialism: Asia
Examination Systems, China
Globalization: Asia
Heaven and Hell (Asian Focus)
Hinduism
Humanism: Chinese Conception of
Humanity: Asian Thought
Islam: Southeast Asia
Jainism
Japanese Philosophy, Japanese Thought
Justice: Justice in East Asian Thought
Landscape in the Arts

Legalism, Ancient China
Literature: Overview
Maoism
Marxism: Asia
Medicine: China
Medicine: India
Meditation: Eastern Meditation
Modernity: East Asia
Mysticism: Chinese Mysticism
Mysticism: Islamic Mysticism in Asia
Orthopraxy: Asia
Pan-Asianism
Pan-Turkism
Philosophy: Historical Overview and Recent Developments
Race and Racism: Asia
Religion: East and Southeast Asia
Sacred Texts: Asia
Science: East Asia
Time: China
Time: India
Westernization: Southeast Asia
Women's History: Asia
ENTRIES THAT CONSIDER ASIA
Algebras
Ancestor Worship
Anthropology
Anticolonialism: Africa
Architecture: Overview
Arts: Overview
Asceticism: Hindu and Buddhist Asceticism
Asian-American Ideas (Cultural Migration)
Astrology: China
Astronomy, Pre-Columbian and Latin American
Atheism
Autobiography
Barbarism and Civilization
Beauty and Ugliness
Bilingualism and Multilingualism
Biography
Body, The
Borders, Borderlands, and Frontiers, Global
Bushido
Calculation and Computation
Cannibalism
Censorship
Childhood and Child Rearing
Christianity: Overview
Cinema
Civil Disobedience
Civil Society: Responses in Africa and the Middle East
Communication of Ideas: Middle East and Abroad
Communication of Ideas: Orality and the Advent of Writing
Constitutionalism
Cosmopolitanism
Creativity in the Arts and Sciences
Critical Theory
Cultural Revivals
Cycles
Dance
Deism
Demography
Demonology
Dependency

Diasporas: African Diaspora
Diffusion, Cultural
Dream
Dress
Dualism
Ecumenism
Education: Global Education
Education: Islamic Education
Empire and Imperialism: Europe
Empire and Imperialism: Middle East
Empire and Imperialism: United States
Environment
Environmental History
Ethnography
Eurocentrism
Evil
Family: Family in Anthropology since 1980
Family Planning
Fascism
Feminism: Overview
Field Theories
Friendship
Fundamentalism
Garden
Gay Studies
Gender Studies: Anthropology
Generation
Genetics: Contemporary
Genocide
Globalization: General
Health and Disease
Heaven and Hell
Historiography
History, Economic
Human Capital
Humanity in the Arts
Hygiene
Iconography
Identity, Multiple: Asian-Americans
Identity, Multiple: Jewish Multiple Identity
Images, Icons, and Idols
Imagination
Immortality and the Afterlife
Individualism
Intelligentsia
International Order
Islam: Shii
Islam: Sunni
Islamic Science
Kinship
Language, Linguistics, and Literacy
Liberty
Life Cycle: Overview
Life Cycle: Adolescence
Life Cycle: Elders/Old Age
Machiavellism
Magic
Maps and the Ideas They Express
Marxism: Overview
Masks
Mathematics
Matriarchy
Migration: Migration in World History
Migration: United States
Miracles

Modernism: Latin America
Modernity: Africa
Modernization Theory
Mohism
Monarchy: Overview
Monasticism
Monism
Motherhood and Maternity
Motif: Motif in Music
Museums
Musical Performance and Audiences
Musicology
Nation
Neoliberalism
Nomadism
Nonviolence
Nuclear Age
Nude, The
Occidentalism
Organicism
Orientalism: Overview
Orthodoxy
Pacifism
Paradise on Earth
Peace
Peasants and Peasantry
Periodization
Person, Idea of the
Perspective
Philosophy: Relations to Other Intellectual Realms
Political Science
Population
Postcolonial Studies
Postcolonial Theory and Literature
Practices
Prehistory, Rise of
Privacy
Property
Protest, Political
Race and Racism: United States
Reading
Religion: Overview
Religion and the State: United States
Resistance and Accommodation
Revolution
Rhetoric: Overview
Ritual: Public Ritual
Ritual: Religion
Sacred and Profane
Sacred Places
Secularization and Secularism
Sexual Harassment
Sexuality: Sexual Orientation
Shinto
Slavery
Society
Sovereignty
Sport
Suicide
Superstition
Syncretism
Taste
Temperance
Terror
Textiles and Fiber Arts as Catalysts for Ideas

Third Cinema
Third World
Third World Literature
Toleration
Totems
Trade
Translation
Treaty
University: Postcolonial
Untouchability: Overview
Untouchability: Menstrual Taboos
Untouchability: Taboos
Victorianism
Virtue Ethics
Visual Order to Organizing Collections
War and Peace in the Arts
Wisdom, Human
Witchcraft
Women's Studies
Work
World Systems Theory, Latin America
Yin and Yang
Yoga
Zen

Europe

ENTRIES FOCUSING ON EUROPE
Architecture: Overview
Capitalism: Overview
Christianity: Overview
Classification of Arts and Sciences, Early Modern
Colonialism: Africa
Colonialism: Latin America
Colonialism: Southeast Asia
Communication of Ideas: Europe and Its Influence
Communism: Europe
Consumerism
Dada
Democracy
Dialogue and Dialectics: Socratic
Dialogue and Dialectics: Talmudic
Education: Europe
Empire and Imperialism: Overview
Empire and Imperialism: Europe
Encyclopedism
Enlightenment
Epistemology: Ancient
Epistemology: Early Modern
Epistemology: Modern
Eurocentrism
Europe, Idea of
Existentialism
Expressionism
Fascism
Feudalism, European
Greek Science
Happiness and Pleasure in European Thought
Hedonism in European Thought
Historical and Dialectical Materialism
Humanism: Europe and the Middle East
Humanism: Renaissance
Humanity: European Thought
Judaism: Judaism to 1800
Judaism: Modern Judaism
Landscape in the Arts

Literature: Overview
Love, Western Notions of
Marxism: Overview
Materialism in Eighteenth-Century European Thought
Mechanical Philosophy
Medicine: Europe and the United States
Metaphysics: Ancient and Medieval
Metaphysics: Renaissance to the Present
Monarchy: Overview
National History
Orthopraxy: Western Orthopraxy
Other, The, European Views of
Pan-Turkism
Philosophy: Historical Overview and Recent Developments
Philosophy, Moral: Ancient
Philosophy, Moral: Medieval and Renaissance
Philosophy, Moral: Modern
Philosophy and Religion in Western Thought
Philosophy of Mind: Ancient and Medieval
Pythagoreanism
Race and Racism: Europe
Regions and Regionalism, Eastern Europe
Religion and the State: Europe
Scientific Revolution
Victorianism
ENTRIES THAT CONSIDER EUROPE
Abolitionism
Absolute Music
Aesthetics: Europe and the Americas
Africa, Idea of
Afrocentricity
Agnosticism
Alchemy: Europe and the Middle East
Algebras
Alienation
Altruism
Ambiguity
America
Americanization, U.S.
Analytical Philosophy
Anarchism
Animism
Anthropology
Anticolonialism: Africa
Anticolonialism: Latin America
Anticolonialism: Middle East
Anticolonialism: Southeast Asia
Antifeminism
Anti-Semitism: Overview
Anti-Semitism: Islamic Anti-Semitism
Apartheid
Architecture: Africa
Aristotelianism
Arts: Overview
Arts: Africa
Asceticism: Western Asceticism
Assimilation
Astrology: Overview
Atheism
Authoritarianism: Overview
Authority
Autobiography
Autonomy
Avant-Garde: Overview

Avant-Garde: Militancy
Barbarism and Civilization
Beauty and Ugliness
Behaviorism
Bilingualism and Multilingualism
Biography
Biology
Black Atlantic
Body, The
Borders, Borderlands, and Frontiers, Global
Buddhism
Bureaucracy
Calculation and Computation
Calendar
Cannibalism
Cartesianism
Casuistry
Causality
Causation
Censorship
Change
Character
Chemistry
Childhood and Child Rearing
Christianity: Asia
Cinema
Citizenship: Overview
Citizenship: Naturalization
City, The: The City as a Cultural Center
City, The: The Islamic and Byzantine City
Civil Disobedience
Civil Society: Europe and the United States
Civil Society: Responses in Africa and the Middle East
Class
Classicism
Common Sense
Communication of Ideas: Africa and Its Influence
Communication of Ideas: Middle East and Abroad
Communication of Ideas: Orality and the Advent of
  Writing
Communication of Ideas: Southeast Asia
Composition, Musical
Computer Science
Consciousness: Overview
Conservatism
Consilience
Constitutionalism
Continental Philosophy
Corruption
Cosmology: Cosmology and Astronomy
Cosmopolitanism
Creationism
Creativity in the Arts and Sciences
Creolization, Caribbean
Crisis
Critical Theory
Cultural Capital
Cultural History
Cultural Revivals
Cultural Studies
Cycles
Cynicism
Dance
Deism
Demography

Demonology
Dependency
Determinism
Development
Diasporas: African Diaspora
Diasporas: Jewish Diaspora
Diversity
Dream
Dress
Dystopia
Eclecticism
Ecology
Economics
Ecumenism
Education: Global Education
Education: India
Education: Islamic Education
Emotions
Empire and Imperialism: Asia
Empire and Imperialism: Middle East
Empire and Imperialism: United States
Empiricism
Environment
Environmental Ethics
Environmental History
Epicureanism
Equality: Overview
Equality: Gender Equality
Equality: Racial Equality
Essentialism
Ethnicity and Race: Africa
Ethnicity and Race: Anthropology
Ethnocentrism
Etiquette
Eugenics
Everyday Life
Evil
Evolution
Experiment
Extirpation
Fallacy, Logical
Falsifiability
Family: Modernist Anthropological Theory
Family: Family in Anthropology since 1980
Family Planning
Fatalism
Feminism: Overview
Feminism: Africa and African Diaspora
Feminism: Islamic Feminism
Fetishism: Overview
Fetishism: Fetishism in Literature and Cultural Studies
Field Theories
Form, Metaphysical, in Ancient and Medieval Thought
Formalism
Foundationalism
Free Will, Determinism, and Predestination
Friendship
Fundamentalism
Garden
Gay Studies
Gender: Gender in the Middle East
Gender in Art
Gender Studies: Anthropology
General Will
Generation

Genetics: Contemporary
Genetics: History of
Genius
Genocide
Geography
Geometry
Gesture
Ghetto
Gift, The
Globalization: Africa
Globalization: Asia
Globalization: General
Good
Harmony
Hate
Health and Disease
Heaven and Hell
Hegelianism
Hegemony
Heresy and Apostasy
Hermeneutics
Hierarchy and Order
Hinduism
Historicism
Historiography
History, Economic
History, Idea of
Honor
Human Capital
Humanity in the Arts
Human Rights: Overview
Humor
Hygiene
Iconography
Idealism
Ideas, History of
Identity: Identity of Persons
Identity, Multiple: Overview
Identity, Multiple: Jewish Multiple Identity
Images, Icons, and Idols
Immortality and the Afterlife
Impressionism
Individualism
Intelligentsia
Intentionality
Interdisciplinarity
International Order
Interpretation
Islam: Africa
Islam: Shii
Islam: Sunni
Islamic Science
Jainism
Jouissance
Justice: Overview
Kantianism
Kinship
Knowledge
Language and Linguistics
Language, Linguistics, and Literacy
Language, Philosophy of: Ancient and Medieval
Language, Philosophy of: Modern
Law
Leadership
Learning and Memory, Contemporary Views

Liberalism
Liberation Theology
Liberty
Life
Life Cycle: Overview
Life Cycle: Elders/Old Age
Linguistic Turn
Literary Criticism
Literary History
Logic
Logic and Philosophy of Mathematics, Modern
Loyalties, Dual
Lysenkoism
Machiavellism
Magic
Manichaeism
Maoism
Maps and the Ideas They Express
Masks
Mathematics
Matriarchy
Media, History of
Medicine: Islamic Medicine
Meme
Memory
Men and Masculinity
Metaphor
Microcosm and Macrocosm
Migration: Africa
Migration: Migration in World History
Migration: United States
Millenarianism: Overview
Millenarianism: Islamic
Millenarianism: Latin America and Native North America
Mind
Miracles
Modernism: Overview
Modernism: Latin America
Modernity: Overview
Modernity: Africa
Modernity: East Asia
Modernization
Modernization Theory
Monasticism
Monism
Moral Sense
Motherhood and Maternity
Motif: Motif in Literature
Motif: Motif in Music
Museums
Music, Anthropology of
Musical Performance and Audiences
Musicology
Mysticism: Christian Mysticism
Mysticism: Kabbalah
Mysticism: Mysticism in African Thought
Myth
Narrative
Nation
Nationalism: Overview
Nationalism: Africa
Nationalism: Cultural Nationalism
Nationalism: Middle East
Native Policy

Natural History
Natural Theology
Naturalism
Naturalism in Art and Literature
Nature
Naturphilosophie
Negritude
Neocolonialism
Neoliberalism
Neoplatonism
New Criticism
Newtonianism
Nihilism
Nonviolence
Nuclear Age
Nude, The
Objectivity
Obligation
Occidentalism
Organicism
Orientalism: Overview
Orthodoxy
Pacifism
Pan-Africanism
Pan-Asianism
Pan-Islamism
Paradigm
Paradise on Earth
Parties, Political
Patriotism
Peace
Peasants and Peasantry
Periodization
Periodization of the Arts
Person, Idea of the
Perspective
Phenomenology
Philosophies: African
Philosophies: Feminist, Twentieth-Century
Philosophies: Islamic
Philosophy: Relations to Other Intellectual Realms
Philosophy, History of
Philosophy, Moral: Africa
Philosophy of Mind: Overview
Phrenology
Physics
Platonism
Pluralism
Poetry and Poetics
Political, The
Political Science
Polytheism
Population
Positivism
Postcolonial Studies
Postcolonial Theory and Literature
Postmodernism
Poverty
Power
Practices
Pragmatism
Pre-Columbian Civilization
Prehistory, Rise of
Prejudice
Presentism

Privacy
Probability
Progress, Idea of
Propaganda
Property
Prophecy
Protest, Political
Pseudoscience
Psychology and Psychiatry
Public Sphere
Punishment
Puritanism
Quantum
Queer Theory
Radicals/Radicalism
Rational Choice
Rationalism
Reading
Realism
Realism: Africa
Reason, Practical and Theoretical
Reform: Europe and the United States
Reform: Islamic Reform
Reformation
Relativism
Relativity
Religion: Overview
Religion: East and Southeast Asia
Religion: Latin America
Religion: Middle East
Religion and Science
Religion and the State: Latin America
Religion and the State: United States
Renaissance
Representation: Mental Representation
Representation: Political Representation
Republicanism: Latin America
Republicanism: Republic
Resistance
Resistance and Accommodation
Responsibility
Revolution
Rhetoric: Overview
Rhetoric: Ancient and Medieval
Ritual: Public Ritual
Ritual: Religion
Romanticism in Literature and Politics
Sacred and Profane
Sacred Places
Sage Philosophy
Scarcity and Abundance, Latin America
Scholasticism
Science: Overview
Science, History of
Science Fiction
Secularization and Secularism
Sexuality: Overview
Skepticism
Slavery
Social Capital
Social Contract
Social Darwinism
Socialism
Socialisms, African
Society

Sophists, The
Sovereignty
Sport
State, The: Overview
Stoicism
Structuralism and Poststructuralism: Overview
Structuralism and Poststructuralism: Anthropology
Subjectivism
Suicide
Superstition
Surrealism
Symbolism
Taste
Technology
Temperance
Terror
Terrorism, Middle East
Textiles and Fiber Arts as Catalysts for Ideas
Theodicy
Third Cinema
Time: Traditional and Utilitarian
Toleration
Totalitarianism
Trade
Tragedy and Comedy
Translation
Travel: Travel from Europe and the Middle East
Treaty
Trope
Truth
Universalism
University: Overview
University: Postcolonial
Untouchability: Overview
Untouchability: Menstrual Taboos
Untouchability: Taboos
Utilitarianism
Utopia
Virtue Ethics
Visual Order to Organizing Collections
Volksgeist
Volunteerism, U.S.
War
War and Peace in the Arts
Wealth
Westernization: Africa
Westernization: Middle East
Westernization: Southeast Asia
Wildlife
Wisdom, Human
Witchcraft
Witchcraft, African Studies of
Women's History: Africa
Women's Studies
Work
World Systems Theory, Latin America
Zionism

Middle East

ENTRIES FOCUSING ON THE MIDDLE EAST
Alchemy: Europe and the Middle East
Anticolonialism: Middle East
Civil Society: Responses in Africa and the Middle East
Communication of Ideas: Middle East and Abroad
Death and Afterlife, Islamic Understanding of

Dialogue and Dialectics: Talmudic
Education: Islamic Education
Empire and Imperialism: Middle East
Feminism: Islamic Feminism
Gender: Gender in the Middle East
Honor, Middle Eastern Notions of
Humanism: Europe and the Middle East
Intercession in Middle Eastern Society
Islam: Shii
Islam: Sunni
Islamic Science
Judaism: Judaism to 1800
Judaism: Modern Judaism
Law, Islamic
Literature: Overview
Medicine: Islamic Medicine
Monarchy: Islamic Monarchy
Nationalism: Middle East
Pan-Arabism
Pan-Islamism
Pan-Turkism
Philosophies: Islamic
Religion: Middle East
Religion and the State: Middle East
Sufism
Terrorism, Middle East
Tribalism, Middle East
Westernization: Middle East
Zionism
ENTRIES THAT CONSIDER THE MIDDLE EAST
Africa, Idea of
Algebras
Anthropology
Antifeminism
Anti-Semitism: Overview
Anti-Semitism: Islamic Anti-Semitism
Architecture: Overview
Architecture: Africa
Aristotelianism
Arts: Africa
Astrology: Overview
Astrology: China
Atheism
Authoritarianism: Overview
Authority
Barbarism and Civilization
Bilingualism and Multilingualism
Biography
Calendar
Childhood and Child Rearing
Christianity: Overview
City, The: The Islamic and Byzantine City
Class
Communication of Ideas: Africa and Its Influence
Communication of Ideas: Europe and Its Influence
Communication of Ideas: Orality and the Advent of
  Writing
Computer Science
Constitutionalism
Cosmopolitanism
Creativity in the Arts and Sciences
Critical Theory
Dance
Deism
Demography

Demonology
Dependency
Diasporas: African Diaspora
Diasporas: Jewish Diaspora
Dream
Dualism
Ecumenism
Empire and Imperialism: Europe
Environment
Ethnicity and Race: Islamic Views
Eurocentrism
Evil
Family Planning
Feminism: Overview
Feminism: Africa and African Diaspora
Free Will, Determinism, and Predestination
Friendship
Fundamentalism
Garden
Gay Studies
Gender in Art
Ghetto
Gift, The
Gnosticism
Hate
Health and Disease
Heaven and Hell
Heresy and Apostasy
Historiography
Humanity in the Arts
Iconography
Identity, Multiple: Jewish Multiple Identity
Images, Icons, and Idols
Imagination
Immortality and the Afterlife
Intelligentsia
International Order
Islam: Africa
Jihad
Language, Linguistics, and Literacy
Language, Philosophy of: Ancient and Medieval
Liberty
Life Cycle: Elders/Old Age
Literature: African Literature
Logic
Manichaeism
Maps and the Ideas They Express
Mathematics
Matriarchy
Microcosm and Macrocosm
Migration: Africa
Migration: Migration in World History
Millenarianism: Overview
Millenarianism: Islamic
Minority
Miracles
Monarchy: Overview
Motherhood and Maternity
Museums
Musicology
Mysticism: Islamic Mysticism
Mysticism: Islamic Mysticism in Asia
Mysticism: Kabbalah
Mysticism: Mysticism in African Thought
Nation

Nationalism: Cultural Nationalism
Nihilism
Nomadism
Nonviolence
Nuclear Age
Organicism
Orientalism: Overview
Orientalism: African and Black Orientalism
Orthodoxy
Orthopraxy: Western Orthopraxy
Pan-Africanism
Paradise on Earth
Peace
Perspective
Philosophies: African
Philosophy, Moral: Medieval and Renaissance
Philosophy of Mind: Ancient and Medieval
Political Science
Polytheism
Postcolonial Studies
Postcolonial Theory and Literature
Property
Prophecy
Protest, Political
Pythagoreanism
Reform: Islamic Reform
Religion: East and Southeast Asia
Religion and Science
Religion and the State: Africa
Religion and the State: Europe
Religion and the State: United States
Resistance and Accommodation
Rhetoric: Overview
Sacred Places
Sacred Texts: Koran
Science, History of
Scientific Revolution
Secularization and Secularism
Sexual Harassment
Sexuality: Islamic Views
Slavery
Sovereignty
Suicide
Superstition
Syncretism
Temperance
Textiles and Fiber Arts as Catalysts for Ideas
Theodicy
Third Cinema
Third World Literature
Toleration
Totalitarianism
Totems
Travel: Travel from Europe and the Middle East
Treaty
University: Overview
Untouchability: Menstrual Taboos
Untouchability: Taboos
Visual Order to Organizing Collections
Westernization: Africa
Westernization: Southeast Asia
Wisdom, Human
Women's History: Africa
Women's Studies
World Systems Theory, Latin America

North America
  ENTRIES FOCUSING ON NORTH AMERICA
    African-American Ideas
    America
    Asian-American Ideas (Cultural Migration)
    Black Atlantic
    Chicano Movement
    Christianity: Overview
    Civil Society: Europe and the United States
    Communication of Ideas: The Americas and Their Influence
    Consumerism
    Democracy
    Education: North America
    Empire and Imperialism: Americas
    Empire and Imperialism: United States
    Ethnohistory, U.S.
    Feminism: Chicana Feminisms
    Feminism: Third World U.S. Movement
    Humanism: Secular Humanism in the United States
    Identity, Multiple: Asian-Americans
    Judaism: Modern Judaism
    Justice: Justice in American Thought
    Landscape in the Arts
    Medicine: Europe and the United States
    Migration: United States
    Millenarianism: Latin America and Native North America
    Native Policy
    Philosophies: American
    Political Protest, U.S.
    Populism: United States
    Race and Racism: United States
    Reform: Europe and the United States
    Religion and the State: United States
    Volunteerism, U.S.
  ENTRIES THAT CONSIDER NORTH AMERICA
    Abolitionism
    Aesthetics: Europe and the Americas
    Africa, Idea of
    Afrocentricity
    Altruism
    Americanization, U.S.
    Analytical Philosophy
    Anthropology
    Anticolonialism: Latin America
    Anticolonialism: Southeast Asia
    Antifeminism
    Asceticism: Western Asceticism
    Assimilation
    Astronomy, Pre-Columbian and Latin American
    Atheism
    Authoritarianism: Latin America
    Authority
    Autobiography
    Aztlán
    Beauty and Ugliness
    Behaviorism
    Bilingualism and Multilingualism
    Bioethics
    Biology
    Body, The
    Borders, Borderlands, and Frontiers, Global
    Buddhism
    Calculation and Computation

    Cannibalism
    Causation
    Censorship
    Childhood and Child Rearing
    Cinema
    Citizenship: Overview
    Citizenship: Cultural Citizenship
    Citizenship: Naturalization
    City, The: The City as a Cultural Center
    Civil Disobedience
    Colonialism: Latin America
    Communication of Ideas: Africa and Its Influence
    Communism: Latin America
    Computer Science
    Conservatism
    Consilience
    Constitutionalism
    Continental Philosophy
    Cosmopolitanism
    Creationism
    Critical Race Theory
    Critical Theory
    Cultural Capital
    Cultural Revivals
    Cultural Studies
    Dance
    Death
    Deism
    Demography
    Diasporas: African Diaspora
    Diasporas: Jewish Diaspora
    Discrimination
    Diversity
    Dream
    Dress
    Dualism
    Dystopia
    Ecology
    Economics
    Ecumenism
    Education: Global Education
    Emotions
    Empire and Imperialism: Asia
    Empiricism
    Enlightenment
    Environment
    Environmental Ethics
    Environmental History
    Equality: Overview
    Equality: Gender Equality
    Equality: Racial Equality
    Essentialism
    Ethnicity and Race: Anthropology
    Ethnocentrism
    Ethnography
    Eugenics
    Eurocentrism
    Everyday Life
    Evil
    Evolution
    Family: Modernist Anthropological Theory
    Family: Family in Anthropology since 1980
    Family Planning
    Feminism: Overview
    Feminism: Africa and African Diaspora

Feminism: Islamic Feminism
Fetishism: Overview
Fetishism: Fetishism in Literature and Cultural Studies
Field Theories
Foundationalism
Friendship
Fundamentalism
Game Theory
Garden
Gay Studies
Gender: Overview
Gender: Gender in the Middle East
Gender in Art
Gender Studies: Anthropology
Generation
Genetics: Contemporary
Genetics: History of
Genius
Genocide
Ghetto
Globalization: Asia
Globalization: General
Hate
Hegelianism
Historiography
History, Economic
Human Capital
Humanity: European Thought
Humanity in the Arts
Human Rights: Overview
Ideas, History of
Identity: Identity of Persons
Identity: Personal and Social Identity
Identity, Multiple: Overview
Identity, Multiple: Jewish Multiple Identity
Impressionism
Intentionality
Interdisciplinarity
Internal Colonialism
International Order
Interpretation
Islam: Shii
Jainism
Justice: Overview
Kantianism
Language and Linguistics
Language, Philosophy of: Modern
Law
Leadership
Learning and Memory, Contemporary Views
Liberation Theology
Life
Life Cycle: Adolescence
Life Cycle: Elders/Old Age
Linguistic Turn
Literary Criticism
Literary History
Loyalties, Dual
Machismo
Magic
Maps and the Ideas They Express
Marxism: Overview
Marxism: Latin America
Masks
Mathematics

Matriarchy
Media, History of
Meme
Men and Masculinity
Mestizaje
Migration: Africa
Migration: Migration in World History
Millenarianism: Overview
Mind
Minority
Modernism: Latin America
Modernity: Overview
Monasticism
Motif: Motif in Music
Museums
Music, Anthropology of
Musical Performance and Audiences
Myth
Narrative
Nation
Nationalism: Overview
Nationalism: Africa
Natural History
Natural Theology
Naturalism
Neocolonialism
Neoliberalism
New Criticism
Nihilism
Nuclear Age
Objectivity
Obligation
Occidentalism
Orientalism: African and Black Orientalism
Orthodoxy
Other, The, European Views of
Pacifism
Pan-Africanism
Paradigm
Parties, Political
Periodization
Person, Idea of the
Philosophies: Feminist, Twentieth-Century
Philosophy: Relations to Other Intellectual Realms
Philosophy of Mind: Overview
Pluralism
Political Science
Population
Positivism
Postcolonial Studies
Postcolonial Theory and Literature
Postmodernism
Practices
Pragmatism
Prehistory, Rise of
Prejudice
Presentism
Privacy
Probability
Progress, Idea of
Property
Protest, Political
Pseudoscience
Psychology and Psychiatry
Quantum

Queer Theory
Race and Racism: Overview
Rational Choice
Reading
Reflexivity
Relativism
Relativity
Religion: Latin America
Religion and Science
Renaissance
Representation: Mental Representation
Representation: Political Representation
Resistance
Resistance and Accommodation
Responsibility
Rhetoric: Overview
Ritual: Religion
Scarcity and Abundance, Latin America
Science, History of
Science Fiction
Secularization and Secularism
Segregation
Sexual Harassment
Sexuality: Overview
Sexuality: Sexual Orientation
Slavery
Social History, U.S.
Sovereignty
Sport
State, The: Overview
Subjectivism
Suicide
Superstition
Syncretism
Taste
Technology
Temperance
Terrorism, Middle East
Time: Traditional and Utilitarian
Totems
Trade
Treaty
Trope
Truth
University: Postcolonial
Utilitarianism
Victorianism
Visual Culture
Visual Order to Organizing Collections
War
War and Peace in the Arts
Westernization: Southeast Asia
Wildlife
Witchcraft
Womanism
Women and Femininity in U.S. Popular Culture
Women's Studies
World Systems Theory, Latin America

Latin and South America

ENTRIES FOCUSING ON LATIN AND SOUTH AMERICA
Anticolonialism: Latin America
Astronomy, Pre-Columbian and Latin American
Authoritarianism: Latin America

Black Atlantic
Colonialism: Latin America
Communication of Ideas: The Americas and Their Influence
Communism: Latin America
Creolization, Caribbean
Empire and Imperialism: Americas
Marxism: Latin America
Millenarianism: Latin America and Native North America
Modernism: Latin America
Native Policy
Populism: Latin America
Pre-Columbian Civilization
Religion: Indigenous Peoples' View, South America
Religion: Latin America
Religion and the State: Latin America
Republicanism: Latin America
Scarcity and Abundance, Latin America
World Systems Theory, Latin America
ENTRIES THAT CONSIDER LATIN AND SOUTH AMERICA
Abolitionism
Aesthetics: Africa
Africa, Idea of
America
Ancestor Worship
Animism
Anthropology
Arts: Overview
Atheism
Authenticity: Africa
Authoritarianism: Overview
Autobiography
Aztlán
Bilingualism and Multilingualism
Borders, Borderlands, and Frontiers, Global
Calculation and Computation
Cannibalism
Chicano Movement
Christianity: Overview
Cinema
Citizenship: Overview
Citizenship: Cultural Citizenship
Citizenship: Naturalization
Critical Theory
Cultural Capital
Dance
Demography
Demonology
Dependency
Diasporas: African Diaspora
Diffusion, Cultural
Discrimination
Diversity
Empire and Imperialism: United States
Environmental History
Ethnohistory, U.S.
Evil
Extirpation
Family Planning
Fascism
Feminism: Overview
Feminism: Africa and African Diaspora
Feminism: Chicana Feminisms

Fetishism: Overview
Friendship
Gender in Art
Genetics: Contemporary
Historiography
History, Economic
Honor
Humanity in the Arts
Identity, Multiple: Overview
Identity, Multiple: Jewish Multiple Identity
Indigenismo
Internal Colonialism
International Order
Liberation Theology
Life Cycle: Overview
Life Cycle: Elders/Old Age
Machiavellism
Machismo
Magic
Maps and the Ideas They Express
Masks
Mathematics
Matriarchy
Media, History of
Men and Masculinity
Mestizaje
Migration: Africa
Migration: Migration in World History
Migration: United States
Minority
Modernism: Overview
Modernization Theory
Motherhood and Maternity
Motif: Motif in Music
Museums
Music, Anthropology of
Nationalism: Africa
Negritude
Orthopraxy: Western Orthopraxy
Pan-Africanism
Peasants and Peasantry
Periodization of the Arts
Perspective
Phrenology
Political Protest, U.S.
Polytheism
Population
Postcolonial Studies
Postcolonial Theory and Literature
Practices
Prehistory, Rise of
Property
Protest, Political
Race and Racism: Overview
Religion: African Diaspora
Resistance and Accommodation
Revolution
Rhetoric: Overview
Ritual: Public Ritual
Ritual: Religion
Secularization and Secularism
Segregation
Slavery
Sport
State, The: Overview

Structuralism and Poststructuralism: Anthropology
Surrealism
Syncretism
Temperance
Third Cinema
Third World
Third World Literature
Trade
Treaty
University: Overview
University: Postcolonial
Visual Order to Organizing Collections
Witchcraft
Women's Studies
Work

CHRONOLOGICAL PERIODS

This section is divided according to five periods in world history: Ancient, Dynastic, Early Modern, Modern, and Contemporary. Use this section together with the section on Geographical Areas.

Ancient (before 400 C.E.)

ENTRIES FOCUSED ON THE PERIOD
Buddhism
Consciousness: Chinese Thought
Consciousness: Indian Thought
Democracy
Dialogue and Dialectics: Socratic
Epicureanism
Gnosticism
Greek Science
Hinduism
Justice: Justice in East Asian Thought
Language, Linguistics, and Literacy
Microcosm and Macrocosm
Orthopraxy: Asia
Orthopraxy: Western Orthopraxy
Poetry and Poetics
Sacred Places
Sacred Texts: Asia
Sophists, The
Textiles and Fiber Arts as Catalysts for Ideas
Time: China
Time: India
Yin and Yang

ENTRIES WITH EXAMPLES FROM BEFORE 400 C.E.

Generally the examples in this category are from the ancient Middle East, Europe, or Asia.

Aesthetics: Asia
Aesthetics: Europe and the Americas
Africa, Idea of
Alchemy: China
Alchemy: Europe and the Middle East
Algebras
Ambiguity
Anarchism
Anthropology
Anti-Semitism: Overview
Architecture: Overview

Architecture: Africa
Architecture: Asia
Aristotelianism
Arts: Overview
Asceticism: Western Asceticism
Astrology: Overview
Astrology: China
Atheism
Authority
Autobiography
Barbarism and Civilization
Beauty and Ugliness
Biography
Biology
Body, The
Borders, Borderlands, and Frontiers, Global
Bureaucracy
Calendar
Casuistry
Causality
Causation
Causation in East Asian and Southeast Asian Philosophy
Censorship
Change
Character
Childhood and Child Rearing
Chinese Thought
Christianity: Overview
Christianity: Asia
City, The: The City as a Cultural Center
City, The: The City as Political Center
City, The: The Islamic and Byzantine City
Civil Society: Europe and the United States
Class
Classicism
Classification of Arts and Sciences, Early Modern
Communication of Ideas: Asia and Its Influence
Communication of Ideas: Europe and Its Influence
Communication of Ideas: Middle East and Abroad
Communication of Ideas: Orality and Advent of Writing
Communication of Ideas: Southeast Asia
Communication of Ideas: The Americas and Their Influence
Composition, Musical
Confucianism
Constitutionalism
Corruption
Cosmology: Asia
Cosmology: Cosmology and Astronomy
Cosmopolitanism
Creationism
Creativity in the Arts and Sciences
Creolization, Caribbean
Cycles
Cynicism
Dance
Daoism
Death
Demonology
Development
Diasporas: Jewish Diaspora
Dream
Dress
Dualism

Eclecticism
Ecumenism
Education: Asia, Traditional and Modern
Education: China
Education: Europe
Education: India
Emotions
Empire and Imperialism: Overview
Empire and Imperialism: Asia
Environment
Epistemology: Ancient
Equality: Overview
Eschatology
Essentialism
Etiquette
Eurocentrism
Europe, Idea of
Evil
Evolution
Experiment
Fallacy, Logical
Fatalism
Form, Metaphysical, in Ancient and Medieval Thought
Foundationalism
Free Will, Determinism, and Predestination
Friendship
Fundamentalism
Garden
Gay Studies
Gender in Art
Generation
Genre
Geography
Geometry
Gesture
Gift, The
Good
Happiness and Pleasure in European Thought
Harmony
Health and Disease
Heaven and Hell
Heaven and Hell (Asian Focus)
Hedonism in European Thought
Hegemony
Heresy and Apostasy
Hierarchy and Order
Historiography
History, Idea of
Humanism: Chinese Conception of
Humanism: Europe and the Middle East
Humanity: African Thought
Humanity: Asian Thought
Humanity: European Thought
Humanity in the Arts
Human Rights: Overview
Humor
Hygiene
Ideas, History of
Identity, Multiple: Jewish Multiple Identity
Images, Icons, and Idols
Imagination
Immortality and the Afterlife
Individualism
International Order
Interpretation

Jainism
Judaism: Judaism to 1800
Justice: Overview
Knowledge
Landscape in the Arts
Language, Philosophy of: Ancient and Medieval
Leadership
Legalism, Ancient China
Liberty
Life
Literary History
Literature: Overview
Literature: African Literature
Logic
Love, Western Notions of
Loyalties, Dual
Machiavellism
Manichaeism
Maps and the Ideas They Express
Marriage and Fertility, European Views
Mathematics
Matriarchy
Mechanical Philosophy
Media, History of
Medicine: China
Medicine: Europe and the United States
Medicine: India
Medicine: Islamic Medicine
Meditation: Eastern Meditation
Memory
Men and Masculinity
Metaphor
Metaphysics: Ancient and Medieval
Migration: Migration in World History
Millenarianism: Overview
Miracles
Mohism
Monarchy: Overview
Monasticism
Monism
Motherhood and Maternity
Museums
Music, Anthropology of
Musical Performance and Audiences
Mysticism: Chinese Mysticism
Mysticism: Christian Mysticism
Narrative
Nation
Natural Law
Nature
Neoplatonism
Nomadism
Nonviolence
Nude, The
Organicism
Orthodoxy
Other, The, European Views of
Pacifism
Paradigm
Paradise on Earth
Patriotism
Peace
Periodization
Periodization of the Arts
Perspective

Philanthropy
Philosophies: African
Philosophies: Islamic
Philosophy: Historical Overview and Recent Developments
Philosophy: Relations to Other Intellectual Realms
Philosophy, Moral: Ancient
Philosophy, Moral: Medieval and Renaissance
Philosophy and Religion in Western Thought
Philosophy of Mind: Ancient and Medieval
Physics
Platonism
Pluralism
Political, The
Political Science
Poverty
Prehistory, Rise of
Presentism
Prophecy
Punishment
Pythagoreanism
Rationalism
Reading
Reason, Practical and Theoretical
Reform: Europe and the United States
Reformation
Religion: Overview
Religion: Africa
Religion: East and Southeast Asia
Religion and the State: Europe
Renaissance
Representation: Political Representation
Republicanism: Republic
Resistance
Responsibility
Revolution
Rhetoric: Overview
Rhetoric: Ancient and Medieval
Ritual: Public Ritual
Science: East Asia
Scientific Revolution
Shinto
Skepticism
Slavery
Society
Sovereignty
Sport
State of Nature
Stoicism
Suicide
Superstition
Syncretism
Taste
Text/Textuality
Toleration
Totalitarianism
Tragedy and Comedy
Translation
Travel: Travel from Europe and the Middle East
Treaty
Trope
Truth
University: Overview
Untouchability: Overview
Untouchability: Menstrual Taboos

New Dictionary of the History of Ideas

Virtual Reality
Virtue Ethics
Visual Order to Organizing Collections
War and Peace in the Arts
Wealth
Wildlife
Witchcraft
Work
Yoga
Zen

Dynastic (400 C.E.–1400 C.E.)
  ENTRIES FOCUSED ON THE PERIOD
    Astronomy, Pre-Columbian and Latin American
    Buddhism
    Death and Afterlife, Islamic Understanding of
    Dialogue and Dialectics: Talmudic
    Feudalism, European
    Heresy and Apostasy
    Motif: Motif in Literature
    Orthopraxy: Western Orthopraxy
    Sacred Places
    Sacred Texts: Asia
    Sacred Texts: Koran
    Scholasticism
    Textiles and Fiber Arts as Catalysts for Ideas
  ENTRIES WITH EXAMPLES FROM THE PERIOD
  400 C.E.–1400 C.E.
    Aesthetics: Asia
    Africa, Idea of
    Alchemy: China
    Alchemy: Europe and the Middle East
    Algebras
    America
    Anti-Semitism: Overview
    Anti-Semitism: Islamic Anti-Semitism
    Architecture: Overview
    Architecture: Africa
    Architecture: Asia
    Aristotelianism
    Arts: Overview
    Asceticism: Western Asceticism
    Astrology: Overview
    Astrology: China
    Authority
    Autobiography
    Aztlán
    Barbarism and Civilization
    Beauty and Ugliness
    Biography
    Biology
    Body, The
    Borders, Borderlands, and Frontiers, Global
    Bureaucracy
    Bushido
    Calculation and Computation
    Calendar
    Casuistry
    Causality
    Causation in East Asian and Southeast Asian Philosophy
    Change
    Childhood and Child Rearing
    Chinese Thought
    Christianity: Overview
    Christianity: Asia

City, The: The City as a Cultural Center
City, The: The Islamic and Byzantine City
Civil Disobedience
Civil Society: Europe and the United States
Class
Classicism
Classification of Arts and Sciences, Early Modern
Communication of Ideas: Africa and Its Influence
Communication of Ideas: Asia and Its Influence
Communication of Ideas: Europe and Its Influence
Communication of Ideas: Middle East and Abroad
Communication of Ideas: Orality and Advent of Writing
Communication of Ideas: Southeast Asia
Communication of Ideas: The Americas and Their
  Influence
Composition, Musical
Confucianism
Consciousness: Indian Thought
Consilience
Constitutionalism
Corruption
Cosmology: Asia
Cosmopolitanism
Creationism
Creativity in the Arts and Sciences
Daoism
Death
Democracy
Demonology
Diasporas: Jewish Diaspora
Dream
Dualism
Eclecticism
Ecumenism
Education: Asia, Traditional and Modern
Education: China
Education: Europe
Education: India
Education: Islamic Education
Education: Japan
Empire and Imperialism: Overview
Empire and Imperialism: Asia
Encyclopedism
Equality: Overview
Eschatology
Ethnicity and Race: Islamic Views
Etiquette
Eurocentrism
Europe, Idea of
Evil
Examination Systems, China
Experiment
Fallacy, Logical
Feminism: Islamic Feminism
Form, Metaphysical, in Ancient and Medieval Thought
Free Will, Determinism, and Predestination
Friendship
Garden
Gay Studies
Gender: Gender in the Middle East
Gender in Art
Gesture
Gift, The
Globalization: Asia
Good

Happiness and Pleasure in European Thought
Harmony
Health and Disease
Heaven and Hell
Hegemony
Hierarchy and Order
Hinduism
Historiography
History, Idea of
Honor, Middle Eastern Notions of
Humanism: Africa
Humanism: Chinese Conception of
Humanism: Europe and the Middle East
Humanity: Asian Thought
Humanity: European Thought
Humanity in the Arts
Human Rights: Overview
Hygiene
Iconography
Identity, Multiple: Jewish Multiple Identity
Images, Icons, and Idols
Imagination
Immortality and the Afterlife
Individualism
Intentionality
International Order
Interpretation
Islam: Africa
Islam: Shii
Islam: Sunni
Islamic Science
Jainism
Japanese Philosophy, Japanese Thought
Jihad
Judaism: Judaism to 1800
Knowledge
Landscape in the Arts
Language, Philosophy of: Ancient and Medieval
Law, Islamic
Liberty
Literary History
Literature: Overview
Logic
Love, Western Notions of
Loyalties, Dual
Manichaeism
Maps and the Ideas They Express
Marriage and Fertility, European Views
Mathematics
Medicine: China
Medicine: Europe and the United States
Medicine: Islamic Medicine
Metaphor
Metaphysics: Ancient and Medieval
Microcosm and Macrocosm
Migration: Africa
Migration: Migration in World History
Millenarianism: Overview
Millenarianism: Islamic
Millenarianism: Latin America and Native North America
Miracles
Monarchy: Islamic Monarchy
Monarchy: Overview
Monasticism

Monism
Motif: Motif in Music
Musical Performance and Audiences
Mysticism: Chinese Mysticism
Mysticism: Christian Mysticism
Mysticism: Islamic Mysticism
Mysticism: Islamic Mysticism in Asia
Mysticism: Kabbalah
Nation
Natural Law
Natural Theology
Neoplatonism
Nomadism
Nude, The
Objectivity
Organicism
Orthodoxy
Other, The, European Views of
Paradigm
Paradise on Earth
Patriotism
Peace
Peasants and Peasantry
Periodization
Periodization of the Arts
Perspective
Philanthropy
Philosophies: African
Philosophies: Islamic
Philosophy: Historical Overview and Recent Developments
Philosophy, Moral: Medieval and Renaissance
Philosophy and Religion in Western Thought
Philosophy of Mind: Ancient and Medieval
Physics
Platonism
Poverty
Pre-Columbian Civilization
Prophecy
Protest, Political
Race and Racism: Asia
Reform: Islamic Reform
Religion: Africa
Religion: East and Southeast Asia
Religion: Middle East
Religion and the State: Europe
Religion and the State: Middle East
Religion and the State: United States Renaissance
Representation: Political Representation
Republicanism: Republic
Responsibility
Revolution
Rhetoric: Overview
Rhetoric: Ancient and Medieval
Ritual: Public Ritual
Scientific Revolution
Sexuality: Islamic Views
Shinto
Skepticism
Sophists, The
Sovereignty
Stoicism
Sufism
Suicide
Superstition

Syncretism
Taste
Terror
Time: Traditional and Utilitarian
Toleration
Totalitarianism
Tragedy and Comedy
Translation
Travel: Travel from Europe and the Middle East
Tribalism, Middle East
University: Overview
Untouchability: Menstrual Taboos
Virtual Reality
Virtue Ethics
Visual Order to Organizing Collections
War
War and Peace in the Arts
Wealth
Women's History: Asia
Work
Yoga
Zen

Early Modern (1400–1800 C.E.)
   ENTRIES FOCUSED ON THE PERIOD
     Astronomy, Pre-Columbian and Latin American
     Cartesianism
     Casuistry
     Empiricism
     Humanism: Renaissance
     Idealism
     Identity: Identity of Persons
     Kantianism
     Materialism in Eighteenth-Century European Thought
     Mechanical Philosophy
     Moral Sense
     Naturphilosophie
     Newtonianism
     Phrenology
     Protest, Political
     Reformation
     Renaissance
     Scientific Revolution
     Theodicy
     Time: Traditional and Utilitarian
     Westernization: Middle East
   ENTRIES WITH EXAMPLES FROM THE PERIOD
   1400–1800 C.E.
     Abolitionism
     Aesthetics: Africa
     Aesthetics: Asia
     Aesthetics: Europe and the Americas
     Africa, Idea of
     African-American Ideas
     Agnosticism
     Alchemy: Europe and the Middle East
     Algebras
     Ambiguity
     America
     Ancestor Worship
     Anticolonialism: Latin America
     Antifeminism
     Anti-Semitism: Overview
     Apartheid
     Architecture: Overview

Architecture: Asia
Aristotelianism
Arts: Overview
Arts: Africa
Asceticism: Western Asceticism
Astrology: Overview
Atheism
Authoritarianism: Latin America
Authority
Autobiography
Autonomy
Aztlán
Barbarism and Civilization
Beauty and Ugliness
Biography
Biology
Body, The
Borders, Borderlands, and Frontiers, Global
Buddhism
Bureaucracy
Bushido
Calculation and Computation
Calendar
Cannibalism
Capitalism: Overview
Capitalism: Africa
Causality
Causation
Causation in East Asian and Southeast Asian Philosophy
Censorship
Change
Character
Chemistry
Childhood and Child Rearing
Chinese Thought
Christianity: Asia
Christianity: Overview
City, The: The City as a Cultural Center
City, The: Latin America
Civil Disobedience
Civil Society: Europe and the United States
Civil Society: Responses in Africa and the Middle East
Class
Classicism
Classification of Arts and Sciences, Early Modern
Colonialism: Africa
Colonialism: Latin America
Colonialism: Southeast Asia
Common Sense
Communication of Ideas: Africa and Its Influence
Communication of Ideas: The Americas and Their Influence
Communication of Ideas: Asia and Its Influence
Communication of Ideas: Europe and Its Influence
Communication of Ideas: Middle East and Abroad
Communication of Ideas: Orality and Advent of Writing
Communication of Ideas: Southeast Asia
Communism: Europe
Composition, Musical
Computer Science
Confucianism
Consciousness: Overview
Conservatism
Constitutionalism

Consumerism
Context
Continental Philosophy
Corruption
Cosmology: Asia
Cosmology: Cosmology and Astronomy
Cosmopolitanism
Creationism
Creativity in the Arts and Sciences
Creolization, Caribbean
Crisis
Critical Theory
Cultural History
Cycles
Death and Afterlife, Islamic Understanding of
Deism
Democracy
Dependency
Determinism
Development
Diasporas: African Diaspora
Diasporas: Jewish Diaspora
Dictatorship in Latin America
Dream
Dress
Dualism
Dystopia
Eclecticism
Ecology
Economics
Education: Asia, Traditional and Modern
Education: China
Education: Europe
Education: India
Education: Islamic Education
Education: Japan
Education: North America
Empire and Imperialism: Americas
Empire and Imperialism: Asia
Empire and Imperialism: Middle East
Encyclopedism
Enlightenment
Epistemology: Early Modern
Equality: Overview
Equality: Gender Equality
Equality: Racial Equality
Eschatology
Essentialism
Etiquette
Eurocentrism
Europe, Idea of
Everyday Life
Evil
Evolution
Examination Systems, China
Experiment
Extirpation
Fascism
Fetishism: Overview
Field Theories
Foundationalism
Free Will, Determinism, and Predestination
Friendship
Garden
Gay Studies

Gender in Art
General Will
Genius
Genre
Geography
Geometry
Gesture
Ghetto
Gift, The
Globalization: Africa
Globalization: Asia
Globalization: General
Gnosticism
Good
Harmony
Health and Disease
Hedonism in European Thought
Hierarchy and Order
Historiography
History, Idea of
Honor
Honor, Middle Eastern Notions of
Human Capital
Humanism: Africa
Humanism: Chinese Conception of
Humanism: Europe and the Middle East
Humanism: Secular Humanism in the United States
Humanity: African Thought
Humanity: Asian Thought
Humanity: European Thought
Humanity in the Arts
Human Rights: Overview
Humor
Hygiene
Iconography
Identity, Multiple: Overview
Identity, Multiple: Jewish Multiple Identity
Imagination
Immortality and the Afterlife
Indigenismo
Individualism
International Order
Interpretation
Islam: Africa
Islam: Shii
Islam: Southeast Asia
Islam: Sunni
Islamic Science
Japanese Philosophy, Japanese Thought
Judaism: Judaism to 1800
Judaism: Modern Judaism
Justice: Overview
Justice: Justice in American Thought
Knowledge
Landscape in the Arts
Language, Linguistics, and Literacy
Leadership
Liberalism
Liberty
Life
Life Cycle: Overview
Literary History
Literature: Overview
Logic
Love, Western Notions of

Loyalties, Dual
Machiavellism
Magic
Maps and the Ideas They Express
Marriage and Fertility, European Views
Mathematics
Medicine: Europe and the United States
Medicine: Islamic Medicine
Men and Masculinity
Mestizaje
Metaphor
Metaphysics: Renaissance to the Present
Microcosm and Macrocosm
Migration: Africa
Migration: Migration in World History
Migration: United States
Millenarianism: Overview
Millenarianism: Islamic
Millenarianism: Latin America and Native North
    America
Mind
Modernity: Africa
Monarchy: Overview
Monarchy: Islamic Monarchy
Monasticism
Monism
Motif: Motif in Literature
Motif: Motif in Music
Museums
Mysticism: Christian Mysticism
Mysticism: Kabbalah
Nation
National History
Native Policy
Natural History
Natural Law
Natural Theology
Nature
Neoplatonism
Nomadism
Nude, The
Objectivity
Obligation
Oral Traditions: Overview
Organicism
Orientalism: Overview
Orthodoxy
Orthopraxy: Western Orthopraxy
Other, The, European Views of
Paradigm
Paradise on Earth
Patriotism
Peace
Periodization
Periodization of the Arts
Perspective
Philanthropy
Philosophies: American
Philosophies: Feminist, Twentieth-Century
Philosophy: Historical Overview and Recent Develop-
    ments
Philosophy: Relations to Other Intellectual Realms
Philosophy, History of
Philosophy, Moral: Africa
Philosophy, Moral: Medieval and Renaissance

Philosophy, Moral: Modern
Philosophy and Religion in Western Thought
Philosophy of Mind: Overview
Philosophy of Religion
Physics
Pietism
Platonism
Pluralism
Poetry and Poetics
Political Protest, U.S.
Political Science
Polytheism
Poverty
Power
Pre-Columbian Civilization
Prehistory, Rise of
Presentism
Probability
Progress, Idea of
Propaganda
Property
Prophecy
Punishment
Puritanism
Pythagoreanism
Race and Racism: Asia
Race and Racism: Europe
Radicals/Radicalism
Rationalism
Reason, Practical and Theoretical
Reform: Europe and the United States
Reform: Islamic Reform
Relativity
Religion: Africa
Religion: African Diaspora
Religion: East and Southeast Asia
Religion: Indigenous Peoples' View, South America
Religion: Latin America
Religion and Science
Religion and the State: Europe
Religion and the State: Latin America
Religion and the State: Middle East
Religion and the State: United States
Representation: Political Representation
Republicanism: Latin America
Republicanism: Republic
Resistance
Resistance and Accommodation
Responsibility
Revolution
Rhetoric: Overview
Ritual: Public Ritual
Ritual: Religion
Romanticism in Literature and Politics
Scarcity and Abundance, Latin America
Scholasticism
Science: Overview
Science, History of
Secularization and Secularism
Sexuality: Overview
Sexuality: Islamic Views
Shinto
Skepticism
Slavery
Social Contract

Society
Sovereignty
Sport
State of Nature
Stoicism
Sufism
Suicide
Superstition
Syncretism
Taste
Temperance
Terror
Text/Textuality
Toleration
Totalitarianism
Tradition
Tragedy and Comedy
Translation
Travel: Travel from Europe and the Middle East
Treaty
Tribalism, Middle East
Trope
Truth
Universalism
University: Overview
Untouchability: Taboos
Utopia
Virtue Ethics
Visual Order to Organizing Collections
Volksgeist
Volunteerism, U.S.
War and Peace in the Arts
Wealth
Westernization: Middle East
Westernization: Southeast Asia
Witchcraft
Women's History: Africa
Work
World Systems Theory, Latin America

Modern (1800–1945)

ENTRIES FOCUSED ON THE PERIOD
Alienation
Altruism
Americanization, U.S.
Analytical Philosophy
Avant-Garde: Overview
Avant-Garde: Militancy
Black Atlantic
Bureaucracy
Chicano Movement
City, The: Latin America
Civil Disobedience
Consumerism
Continental Philosophy
Democracy
Empire and Imperialism: Europe
Eugenics
Evolution
Existentialism
Expressionism
Fascism
Field Theories
Fundamentalism
Futurology

Globalization: Africa
Globalization: Asia
Globalization: General
Hegelianism
Hegemony
Historicism
Humanism: Secular Humanism in the United States
Impressionism
Internal Colonialism
Kantianism
Life
Linguistic Turn
Literary History
Logic and Philosophy of Mathematics, Modern
Maoism
Marxism: Overview
Marxism: Asia
Marxism: Latin America
Media, History of
Modernism: Overview
Modernism: Latin America
Modernity: Overview
Modernity: Africa
Modernity: East Asia
Modernization
Modernization Theory
National History
Nationalism: Overview
Nationalism: Africa
Nationalism: Cultural Nationalism
Nationalism: Middle East
Naturalism
Naturalism in Art and Literature
Naturphilosophie
Neocolonialism
Neoliberalism
Orientalism: African and Black Orientalism
Pan-Africanism
Pan-Arabism
Pan-Asianism
Pan-Islamism
Pan-Turkism
Parties, Political
Phenomenology
Philosophies: Feminist, Twentieth-Century
Phrenology
Populism: Latin America
Populism: United States
Positivism
Pragmatism
Protest, Political
Psychoanalysis
Psychology and Psychiatry
Quantum
Realism
Realism: Africa
Relativism
Relativity
Science Fiction
Secularization and Secularism
Segregation
Sexuality: Sexual Orientation
Sociability in African Thought
Social Darwinism
Socialism

Socialisms, African
Structuralism and Poststructuralism: Overview
Structuralism and Poststructuralism: Anthropology
Subjectivism
Surrealism
Technology
Third World
Time: Traditional and Utilitarian
Totalitarianism
Utilitarianism
Victorianism
Westernization: Africa
Westernization: Middle East
Westernization: Southeast Asia
Work
Zionism

ENTRIES WITH EXAMPLES FROM THE PERIOD
1800–1945

Abolitionism
Absolute Music
Aesthetics: Africa
Aesthetics: Asia
Aesthetics: Europe and the Americas
Africa, Idea of
African-American Ideas
Agnosticism
Alchemy: China
Alchemy: Europe and the Middle East
Algebras
Ambiguity
America
Anarchism
Ancestor Worship
Animism
Anthropology
Anticolonialism: Africa
Anticolonialism: Latin America
Anticolonialism: Middle East
Anticolonialism: Southeast Asia
Antifeminism
Anti-Semitism: Overview
Anti-Semitism: Islamic Anti-Semitism
Apartheid
Architecture: Overview
Aristotelianism
Arts: Overview
Arts: Africa
Asceticism: Western Asceticism
Asian-American Ideas (Cultural Migration)
Assimilation
Atheism
Authenticity: Africa
Authoritarianism: Overview
Authoritarianism: East Asia
Authoritarianism: Latin America
Authority
Autobiography
Barbarism and Civilization
Beauty and Ugliness
Behaviorism
Bilingualism and Multilingualism
Bioethics
Biography
Biology
Body, The
Borders, Borderlands, and Frontiers, Global
Buddhism
Bushido
Calculation and Computation
Capitalism: Overview
Capitalism: Africa
Cartesianism
Casuistry
Causality
Censorship
Change
Character
Chemistry
Childhood and Child Rearing
Chinese Warlordism
Christianity: Overview
Christianity: Asia
Cinema
Citizenship: Overview
Citizenship: Naturalization
City, The: The City as a Cultural Center
City, The: The Islamic and Byzantine City
Civil Society: Europe and the United States
Civil Society: Responses in Africa and the Middle East
Class
Classicism
Colonialism: Africa
Colonialism: Latin America
Colonialism: Southeast Asia
Common Sense
Communication of Ideas: Africa and Its Influence
Communication of Ideas: The Americas and Their Influence
Communication of Ideas: Asia and Its Influence
Communication of Ideas: Europe and Its Influence
Communication of Ideas: Middle East and Abroad
Communication of Ideas: Orality and Advent of Writing
Communication of Ideas: Southeast Asia
Communism: Europe
Communism: Latin America
Composition, Musical
Computer Science
Confucianism
Consciousness: Overview
Conservatism
Constitutionalism
Context
Corruption
Corruption in Developed and Developing Countries
Cosmology: Asia
Cosmology: Cosmology and Astronomy
Cosmopolitanism
Creationism
Creativity in the Arts and Sciences
Creolization, Caribbean
Crisis
Critical Theory
Cultural Capital
Cultural History
Cultural Revivals
Cycles
Dada
Dance
Death
Death and Afterlife, Islamic Understanding of

Deism
Democracy: Africa
Dependency
Determinism
Development
Diasporas: African Diaspora
Diasporas: Jewish Diaspora
Dictatorship in Latin America
Diffusion, Cultural
Discrimination
Diversity
Dream
Dress
Dystopia
Ecology
Economics
Education: Asia, Traditional and Modern
Education: China
Education: Europe
Education: Global Education
Education: India
Education: Islamic Education
Education: Japan
Education: North America
Emotions
Empire and Imperialism: Asia
Empire and Imperialism: Middle East
Empire and Imperialism: United States
Empiricism
Environmental Ethics
Environmental History
Epistemology: Modern
Equality: Overview
Equality: Gender Equality
Equality: Racial Equality
Eschatology
Essentialism
Ethnicity and Race: Africa
Ethnicity and Race: Anthropology
Ethnicity and Race: Islamic Views
Ethnography
Etiquette
Eurocentrism
Europe, Idea of
Everyday Life
Evil
Examination Systems, China
Experiment
Falsifiability
Family: Modernist Anthropological Theory
Family Planning
Feminism: Overview
Feminism: Africa and African Diaspora
Feminism: Chicana Feminisms
Feminism: Third World U.S. Movement
Fetishism: Overview
Fetishism: Fetishism in Literature and Cultural Studies
Formalism
Foundationalism
Friendship
Game Theory
Gay Studies
Gender: Gender in the Middle East
Gender in Art
Gender Studies: Anthropology

General Will
Generation
Genetics: Contemporary
Genetics: History of
Genius
Genocide
Genre
Geography
Geometry
Gesture
Ghetto
Gift, The
Gnosticism
Good
Happiness and Pleasure in European Thought
Harmony
Health and Disease
Hermeneutics
Historical and Dialectical Materialism
Historiography
History, Economic
History, Idea of
Honor, Middle Eastern Notions of
Human Capital
Humanism: Africa
Humanism: Chinese Conception of
Humanism: Europe and the Middle East
Humanity: African Thought
Humanity: Asian Thought
Humanity: European Thought
Humanity in the Arts
Human Rights: Overview
Humor
Hygiene
Iconography
Idealism
Ideas, History of
Identity: Identity of Persons
Identity, Multiple: Overview
Identity, Multiple: Asian-Americans
Identity, Multiple: Jewish Multiple Identity
Imagination
Immortality and the Afterlife
Indigenismo
Individualism
Intelligentsia
Intentionality
Intercession in Middle Eastern Society
International Order
Interpretation
Islam: Africa
Islam: Shii
Islam: Southeast Asia
Islamic Science
Japanese Philosophy, Japanese Thought
Jihad
Jouissance
Judaism: Modern Judaism
Justice: Overview
Justice: Justice in American Thought
Justice: Justice in East Asian Thought
Kinship
Knowledge
Landscape in the Arts
Language and Linguistics

Language, Linguistics, and Literacy
Language, Philosophy of: Modern
Law
Law, Islamic
Leadership
Learning and Memory, Contemporary Views
Liberalism
Liberty
Life Cycle: Adolescence
Life Cycle: Elders/Old Age
Literary Criticism
Literature: Overview
Literature: African Literature
Love, Western Notions of
Loyalties, Dual
Lysenkoism
Magic
Maps and the Ideas They Express
Marriage and Fertility, European Views
Masks
Mathematics
Matriarchy
Medicine: Europe and the United States
Medicine: India
Medicine: Islamic Medicine
Memory
Men and Masculinity
Mestizaje
Metaphor
Metaphysics: Renaissance to the Present
Microcosm and Macrocosm
Migration: Africa
Migration: Migration in World History
Migration: United States
Millenarianism: Overview
Millenarianism: Latin America and Native North
  America
Mind
Minority
Monarchy: Overview
Monarchy: Islamic Monarchy
Monasticism
Monism
Motherhood and Maternity
Motif: Motif in Literature
Motif: Motif in Music
Multiculturalism, Africa
Museums
Music, Anthropology of
Musical Performance and Audiences
Musicology
Mysticism: Kabbalah
Mysticism: Mysticism in African Thought
Myth
Narrative
Nation
Native Policy
Natural History
Natural Theology
Nature
Negritude
New Criticism
Nihilism
Nonviolence
Nude, The

Objectivity
Obligation
Occidentalism
Oral Traditions: Overview
Organicism
Orientalism: Overview
Orthodoxy
Orthopraxy: Western Orthopraxy
Other, The, European Views of
Pacifism
Paradigm
Patriotism
Peace
Peasants and Peasantry
Periodization
Periodization of the Arts
Person, Idea of the
Philanthropy
Philosophies: African
Philosophies: American
Philosophy: Historical Overview and Recent Develop-
  ments
Philosophy: Relations to Other Intellectual Realms
Philosophy, History of
Philosophy, Moral: Africa
Philosophy, Moral: Modern
Philosophy and Religion in Western Thought
Philosophy of Mind: Overview
Philosophy of Religion
Physics
Platonism
Pluralism
Poetry and Poetics
Political Protest, U.S.
Political Science
Political, The
Polytheism
Population
Postcolonial Studies
Poverty
Power
Practices
Prehistory, Rise of
Prejudice
Presentism
Privacy
Probability
Progress, Idea of
Propaganda
Property
Pseudoscience
Punishment
Puritanism
Queer Theory
Race and Racism: Overview
Race and Racism: Asia
Race and Racism: Europe
Race and Racism: United States
Radicals/Radicalism
Rational Choice
Rationalism
Reading
Reason, Practical and Theoretical
Reflexivity
Reform: Europe and the United States

Reform: Islamic Reform
Regions and Regionalism, Eastern Europe
Religion: Overview
Religion: Africa
Religion: African Diaspora
Religion: East and Southeast Asia
Religion: Indigenous Peoples' View, South America
Religion: Latin America
Religion: Middle East Religion and the State: Africa
Religion and Science
Religion and the State: Europe
Religion and the State: Latin America
Religion and the State: Middle East
Religion and the State: United States
Renaissance
Republicanism: Latin America
Republicanism: Republic
Resistance
Resistance and Accommodation
Responsibility
Revolution
Rhetoric: Overview
Ritual: Public Ritual
Ritual: Religion
Romanticism in Literature and Politics
Sacred and Profane
Sacred Places
Sage Philosophy
Scarcity and Abundance, Latin America
Science: Overview
Science, History of
Sexuality: Overview
Sexuality: Islamic Views
Shinto
Skepticism
Slavery
Social Capital
Social History, U.S.
Society
Sophists, The
Sovereignty
Sport
State of Nature
State, The: Overview
Sufism
Suicide
Superstition
Symbolism
Syncretism
Temperance
Terror
Text/Textuality
Toleration
Totems
Trade
Tradition
Translation
Travel: Travel from Europe and the Middle East
Treaty
Trope
Truth
Universalism
University: Overview
Untouchability: Overview
Untouchability: Menstrual Taboos
Untouchability: Taboos
Utopia
Virtual Reality
Visual Culture
Visual Order to Organizing Collections
Volksgeist
Volunteerism, U.S.
War
War and Peace in the Arts
Wealth
Wildlife
Wisdom, Human
Witchcraft
Witchcraft, African Studies of
Women's History: Africa
Women's History: Asia
World Systems Theory, Latin America

Contemporary
ENTRIES FOCUSED ON THE PERIOD

African-American Ideas
Americanization, U.S.
Anticolonialism: Africa
Anticolonialism: Latin America
Anticolonialism: Middle East
Anticolonialism: Southeast Asia
Anti-Semitism: Islamic Anti-Semitism
Apartheid
Bioethics
Black Atlantic
Black Consciousness
Buddhism
Bureaucracy
Capitalism: Africa
Chicano Movement
Citizenship: Naturalization
Civil Disobedience
Communitarianism in African Thought
Consumerism
Continental Philosophy
Creationism
Critical Race Theory
Critical Theory
Cultural Studies
Democracy
Dress
Dystopia
Empire and Imperialism: Europe
Empiricism
Eugenics
Field Theories
Fundamentalism
Futurology
Gay Studies
Gender: Overview
Genetics: Contemporary
Globalization: Africa
Globalization: Asia
Globalization: General
Historicism
Humanity: African Thought
Human Rights: Overview
Human Rights: Women's Rights
Internal Colonialism
International Order

Jihad
Liberation Theology
Liberty
Life
Linguistic Turn
Literary History
Logic and Philosophy of Mathematics, Modern
Maoism
Marxism: Overview
Marxism: Asia
Marxism: Latin America
Media, History of
Modernization
Modernization Theory
Nationalism: Overview
Nationalism: Africa
Nationalism: Cultural Nationalism
Nationalism: Middle East
Neocolonialism
Neoliberalism
Nuclear Age
Orientalism: African and Black Orientalism
Pan-Africanism
Pan-Arabism
Pan-Asianism
Pan-Islamism
Pan-Turkism
Paradigm
Parties, Political
Personhood in African Thought
Phenomenology
Philosophies: Feminist, Twentieth-Century
Poetry and Poetics
Populism: Latin America
Populism: United States
Positivism
Postcolonial Studies
Postcolonial Theory and Literature
Postmodernism
Pragmatism
Presentism
Privatization
Protest, Political
Psychoanalysis
Psychology and Psychiatry
Quantum
Queer Theory
Realism: Africa
Relativism
Relativity
Science Fiction
Segregation
Sexual Harassment
Sexuality: Sexual Orientation
Sociability in African Thought
Social Darwinism
Socialisms, African
Structuralism and Poststructuralism: Overview
Structuralism and Poststructuralism: Anthropology
Subjectivism
Technology
Terrorism, Middle East
Text/Textuality
Theater and Performance
Third Cinema

Third World
Totalitarianism
Virtual Reality
Virtue Ethics
War
Westernization: Africa
Westernization: Southeast Asia
Witchcraft
Womanism
Women and Femininity in U.S. Popular Culture
Women's Studies
Zionism

ENTRIES WITH EXAMPLES FROM THE PERIOD
SINCE 1945 (especially since the 1970s)
Absolute Music
Aesthetics: Africa
Aesthetics: Asia
Aesthetics: Europe and the Americas
Africa, Idea of
Afrocentricity
Afropessimism
Agnosticism
Algebras
Alienation
Altruism
Ambiguity
America
Analytical Philosophy
Anarchism
Animism
Anthropology
Antifeminism
Anti-Semitism: Overview
Architecture: Overview
Architecture: Africa
Arts: Overview
Arts: Africa
Asceticism: Western Asceticism
Asian-American Ideas (Cultural Migration)
Assimilation
Atheism
Authenticity: Africa
Authoritarianism: Overview
Authoritarianism: East Asia
Authoritarianism: Latin America
Authority
Autobiography
Autonomy
Avant-Garde: Overview
Aztlán
Barbarism and Civilization
Beauty and Ugliness
Behaviorism
Bilingualism and Multilingualism
Biography
Biology
Body, The
Bushido
Calculation and Computation
Cannibalism
Capitalism: Overview
Cartesianism
Casuistry
Causality
Causation

Censorship
Change
Character
Childhood and Child Rearing
Christianity: Overview
Christianity: Asia
Cinema
Citizenship: Overview
Citizenship: Cultural Citizenship
City, The: The City as a Cultural Center
City, The: The City as Political Center
City, The: The Islamic and Byzantine City
Civil Society: Europe and the United States
Civil Society: Responses in Africa and the Middle East
Classicism
Colonialism: Africa
Colonialism: Southeast Asia
Communication of Ideas: Africa and Its Influence
Communication of Ideas: Asia and Its Influence
Communication of Ideas: Southeast Asia
Communism: Europe
Communism: Latin America
Composition, Musical
Computer Science
Confucianism
Consciousness: Overview
Conservatism
Consilience
Context
Corruption
Corruption in Developed and Developing Countries
Cosmopolitanism
Creolization, Caribbean
Crisis
Cultural Capital
Cultural History
Cultural Revivals
Cycles
Dada
Dance
Death
Death and Afterlife, Islamic Understanding of
Deism
Democracy: Africa
Demography
Demonology
Dependency
Determinism
Development
Diasporas: African Diaspora
Diasporas: Jewish Diaspora
Dictatorship in Latin America
Diffusion, Cultural
Discrimination
Diversity
Dream
Dualism
Ecology
Economics
Ecumenism
Education: Europe
Education: Global Education
Education: Islamic Education
Education: North America
Emotions

Empire and Imperialism: Middle East
Empire and Imperialism: United States
Enlightenment
Environment
Environmental Ethics
Environmental History
Epistemology: Modern
Equality: Overview
Equality: Gender Equality
Equality: Racial Equality
Essentialism
Ethnicity and Race: Africa
Ethnicity and Race: Anthropology
Ethnicity and Race: Islamic Views
Ethnocentrism
Ethnography
Ethnohistory, U.S.
Etiquette
Eurocentrism
Europe, Idea of
Evil
Existentialism
Experiment
Falsifiability
Family: Modernist Anthropological Theory
Family: Family in Anthropology since 1980
Family Planning
Fascism
Fatalism
Feminism: Overview
Feminism: Africa and African Diaspora
Feminism: Chicana Feminisms
Feminism: Islamic Feminism
Feminism: Third World U.S. Movement
Fetishism: Overview
Fetishism: Fetishism in Literature and Cultural Studies
Formalism
Foundationalism
Free Will, Determinism, and Predestination
Friendship
Game Theory
Gender: Gender in the Middle East
Gender in Art
Gender Studies: Anthropology
Generation
Genetics: History of
Genius
Genocide
Geography
Ghetto
Gift, The
Gnosticism
Good
Happiness and Pleasure in European Thought
Harmony
Hate
Health and Disease
Hegelianism
Hermeneutics
Hierarchy and Order
Hinduism
Historical and Dialectical Materialism
Historiography
History, Economic
History, Idea of

Honor, Middle Eastern Notions of
Human Capital
Humanism: Africa
Humanism: Europe and the Middle East
Humanism: Secular Humanism in the United States
Humanity: European Thought
Humanity in the Arts
Humor
Ideas, History of
Identity: Identity of Persons
Identity: Personal and Social Identity
Identity, Multiple: Overview
Identity, Multiple: Asian-Americans
Identity, Multiple: Jewish Multiple Identity
Imagination
Immortality and the Afterlife
Impressionism
Intelligentsia
Intentionality
Intercession in Middle Eastern Society
Interdisciplinarity
Islam: Shii
Islam: Southeast Asia
Jainism
Japanese Philosophy, Japanese Thought
Jouissance
Judaism: Modern Judaism
Justice: Overview
Justice: Justice in American Thought
Kantianism
Kinship
Knowledge
Landscape in the Arts
Language and Linguistics
Language, Philosophy of: Modern
Law
Law, Islamic
Leadership
Learning and Memory, Contemporary Views
Liberalism
Life Cycle: Adolescence
Life Cycle: Elders/Old Age
Literary Criticism
Literature: African Literature
Lysenkoism
Machiavellism
Machismo
Magic
Maps and the Ideas They Express
Marriage and Fertility, European Views
Masks
Mathematics
Matriarchy
Medicine: China
Medicine: Europe and the United States
Medicine: Islamic Medicine
Meditation: Eastern Meditation
Meme
Memory
Men and Masculinity
Mestizaje
Metaphor
Metaphysics: Renaissance to the Present
Migration: Africa
Migration: Migration in World History

Migration: United States
Millenarianism: Overview
Millenarianism: Islamic
Millenarianism: Latin America and Native North America
Mind
Minority
Modernism: Latin America
Modernity: Overview
Modernity: Africa
Modernity: East Asia
Monarchy: Overview
Monasticism
Monism
Moral Sense
Motherhood and Maternity
Motif: Motif in Literature
Motif: Motif in Music
Multiculturalism, Africa
Museums
Music, Anthropology of
Musical Performance and Audiences
Musicology
Mysticism: Mysticism in African Thought
Narrative
Nation
Native Policy
Natural Law
Natural Theology
Nature
Negritude
New Criticism
Nihilism
Nomadism
Nonviolence
Objectivity
Obligation
Occidentalism
Oral Traditions: Overview
Organicism
Orientalism: Overview
Orthodoxy
Pacifism
Patriotism
Peace
Peasants and Peasantry
Periodization of the Arts
Person, Idea of the
Perspective
Philanthropy
Philosophies: American
Philosophy, History of
Philosophy, Moral: Africa
Philosophy, Moral: Modern
Philosophy and Religion in Western Thought
Philosophy of Mind: Overview
Philosophy of Religion
Pluralism
Political Protest, U.S.
Political Science
Population
Poverty
Power
Practices
Prejudice

Privacy
Probability
Progress, Idea of
Propaganda
Property
Pseudoscience
Public Sphere
Punishment
Race and Racism: Overview
Race and Racism: Asia
Race and Racism: Europe
Race and Racism: United States
Radicals/Radicalism
Rational Choice
Reading
Reason, Practical and Theoretical
Reflexivity
Reform: Europe and the United States
Reform: Islamic Reform
Regions and Regionalism, Eastern Europe
Religion: Africa
Religion: African Diaspora
Religion: Indigenous Peoples' View, South America
Religion: Latin America
Religion: Middle East
Religion and Science
Religion and the State: Africa
Religion and the State: Latin America
Religion and the State: Middle East
Religion and the State: United States
Renaissance
Representation: Mental Representation
Representation: Political Representation
Resistance
Resistance and Accommodation
Responsibility
Ritual: Public Ritual
Ritual: Religion
Sacred Places
Sacred Texts: Koran
Sage Philosophy
Science: Overview
Science: East Asia
Science, History of
Scientific Revolution
Secularization and Secularism
Sexuality: Overview
Sexuality: Islamic Views
Shinto
Skepticism
Slavery
Social Capital
Social Contract
Social History, U.S.
Society
Sophists, The
Sovereignty
Sport
State, The: Overview
State, The: The Postcolonial State
State of Nature
Superstition
Surrealism
Symbolism
Syncretism

Taste
Terror
Third World Literature
Toleration
Totems
Trade
Tradition
Translation
Treaty
Tribalism, Middle East
Trope
Truth
Universalism
University: Overview
University: Postcolonial
Untouchability: Overview
Untouchability: Menstrual Taboos
Untouchability: Taboos
Utilitarianism
Utopia
Visual Culture
Visual Order to Organizing Collections
War and Peace in the Arts
Wealth
Wildlife
Wisdom, Human
Witchcraft, African Studies of
Women's History: Africa
Women's History: Asia
Work
World Systems Theory, Latin America

LIBERAL ARTS DISCIPLINES AND PROFESSIONS

This section is in accord with the university divisions of the Liberal Arts into Fine Arts, Humanities, Social Sciences, and Sciences and the graduate programs of the professions of Law, Medicine, and Engineering. The sample of Interdisciplinary Programs are listed under their most common university grouping. For example, Fine Arts includes Performance Arts; Social Sciences includes Women's Studies and Gender Studies, as well as Ethnic Studies; Sciences includes Ecology and Geology, as well as Computer Sciences; Humanities includes programs of Communication, Language, and Linguistics. Meanwhile, the growth of interdisciplinary programs reflects the increasing overlap between studies listed under the labels of Fine Arts, Humanities, Social Sciences, and Sciences. A discipline or interdisciplinary program only appears once, but an entry may appear under the several disciplines and interdisciplinary programs that influenced the scholarship of the article. Titles that appear in bold indicate entries that are especially suited as a introduction to the discipline.

Under the category Multidisciplinary Practices, there are entries on the many methods, techniques, theories, and approaches that have spread across the disciplines. The Multidisciplinary Practices help explain the contemporary trend of interdisciplinarity for which the history of ideas has long been known. At the end of this Reader's Guide is a listing of a number of entries that overlap three of the four divisions and a listing of entries that overlap all four divisions.

Fine Arts
  VISUAL STUDIES
    Absolute Music
    Aesthetics: Africa
    Aesthetics: Asia
    Aesthetics: Europe and the Americas
    Ambiguity
    Anthropology
    Architecture: Overview
    Architecture: Africa
    Architecture: Asia
    Arts: Overview
    Arts: Africa
    Asceticism: Hindu and Buddhist Asceticism
    Asceticism: Western Asceticism
    Avant-Garde: Overview
    Avant-Garde: Militancy
    Aztlán
    Beauty and Ugliness
    Body, The
    Buddhism
    Change
    Chinese Thought
    Cinema
    City, The: Latin America
    City, The: The City as a Cultural Center
    City, The: The Islamic and Byzantine City
    Classicism
    Classification of Arts and Sciences, Early Modern
    Communication of Ideas: Asia and Its Influence
    Composition, Musical
    Consumerism
    Context
    Cosmopolitanism
    Creativity in the Arts and Sciences
    Cultural History
    Dada
    Death
    Dream
    Dress
    Dystopia
    Environmental Ethics
    Environmental History
    Everyday Life
    Expressionism
    Extirpation
    Fascism
    Fetishism: Overview
    Garden
    Gay Studies
    Gender in Art
    Genre
    Geography
    Geometry
    Gesture
    Ghetto
    Globalization: Asia
    Heaven and Hell (Asian Focus)
    Hinduism
    History, Idea of
    Humanity: European Thought
    Humanity in the Arts
    Humor
    Iconography
    Ideas, History of

    Images, Icons, and Idols
    Imagination
    Impressionism
    Islamic Science
    Kantianism
    Knowledge
    Landscape in the Arts
    Life Cycle: Overview
    Literary History
    Literature: Overview
    Maps and the Ideas They Express
    Masks
    Matriarchy
    Media, History of
    Medicine: Europe and the United States
    Mestizaje
    Modernism: Overview
    Modernism: Latin America
    Modernity: Africa
    Modernity: East Asia
    Monarchy: Overview
    Motherhood and Maternity
    Museums
    Musical Performance and Audiences
    Musicology
    Mysticism: Chinese Mysticism
    Mysticism: Christian Mysticism
    Naturalism in Art and Literature
    Negritude
    Nude, The
    Occidentalism
    Organicism
    Pan-Africanism
    Paradise on Earth
    Periodization of the Arts
    Perspective
    Philosophy: Historical Overview and Recent Developments
    Political Protest, U.S.
    Postmodernism
    Pre-Columbian Civilization
    Protest, Political
    Psychoanalysis
    Pythagoreanism
    Realism
    Realism: Africa
    Religion: Africa
    Renaissance
    Representation: Mental Representation
    Ritual: Public Ritual
    Sacred Places
    Sacred Texts: Asia
    Science: East Asia
    Science, History of
    Science Fiction
    Social History, U.S.
    Sport
    Surrealism
    Symbolism
    Syncretism
    Taste
    Text/Textuality
    Textiles and Fiber Arts as Catalysts for Ideas
    Third Cinema
    Victorianism

Virtual Reality
Visual Culture
Visual Order to Organizing Collections
War and Peace in the Arts
Westernization: Southeast Asia
Women and Femininity in U.S. Popular Culture
Yin and Yang
MUSIC
Absolute Music
Aesthetics: Africa
Aesthetics: Asia
Authenticity: Africa
Avant-Garde: Overview
Cinema
Classicism
Classification of Arts and Sciences, Early Modern
Communication of Ideas: Africa and Its Influence
Composition, Musical
Context
Cosmopolitanism
Dada
Dance
Empire and Imperialism: United States
Formalism
Generation
Genre
Harmony
Hinduism
Humanism: Africa
Humanism: Chinese Conception of
Humor
Iconography
Identity, Multiple: Jewish Multiple Identity
Judaism: Judaism to 1800
Knowledge
Learning and Memory, Contemporary Views
Love, Western Notions of
Modernism: Overview
Motif: Motif in Music
Music, Anthropology of
Musical Performance and Audiences
Musicology
Mysticism: Chinese Mysticism
Orientalism: Overview
Pan-Asianism
Pietism
Political Protest, U.S.
Postmodernism
Protest, Political
Pythagoreanism
Realism: Africa
Religion: Africa
Religion: African Diaspora
Resistance
Resistance and Accommodation
Society
Sophists, The
Symbolism
Taste
Text/Textuality
Third Cinema
Virtual Reality
Visual Order to Organizing Collections
Westernization: Africa

PERFORMANCE ARTS (includes drama, dance, oratory, ritual, and ceremony)
Absolute Music
Aesthetics: Africa
Aesthetics: Asia
Alienation
Americanization, U.S.
Ancestor Worship
Anthropology
Arts: Overview
Asceticism: Hindu and Buddhist Asceticism
Asceticism: Western Asceticism
Astronomy, Pre-Columbian and Latin American
Authenticity: Africa
Autobiography
Avant-Garde: Overview
Body, The
Cannibalism
Censorship
Cinema
Civil Disobedience
Civil Society: Europe and the United States
Communication of Ideas: Africa and Its Influence
Communication of Ideas: Asia and Its Influence
Communication of Ideas: Orality and Advent of Writing
Communication of Ideas: Southeast Asia
Composition, Musical
Confucianism
Context
Cosmopolitanism
Creolization, Caribbean
Cultural Capital
Cynicism
Dada
Dance
Determinism
Dialogue and Dialectics: Socratic
Dialogue and Dialectics: Talmudic
Dictatorship in Latin America
Dream
Dress
Emotions
Empire and Imperialism: Europe
Environment
Equality: Overview
Ethnicity and Race: Anthropology
Etiquette
Everyday Life
Expressionism
Extirpation
Fascism
Feminism: Chicana Feminisms
Fetishism: Overview
Fetishism: Fetishism in Literature and Cultural Studies
Game Theory
Gay Studies
Gender: Overview
Gender in Art
Generation
Genre
Gesture
Harmony
Hinduism
History, Economic

History, Idea of
Honor
Humanism: Africa
Humanism: Chinese Conception of
Humanity: African Thought
Humor
Ideas, History of
Identity, Multiple: Jewish Multiple Identity
Images, Icons, and Idols
Intelligentsia
Islam: Shii
Islam: Sunni
Jouissance
Judaism: Judaism to 1800
Knowledge
Language and Linguistics
Language, Philosophy of: Modern
Law, Islamic
Leadership
Learning and Memory, Contemporary Views
Life Cycle: Overview
Literary Criticism
Literary History
Literature: African Literature
Love, Western Notions of
Magic
Manichaeism
Masks
Media, History of
Medicine: China
Medicine: Islamic Medicine
Meditation: Eastern Meditation
Men and Masculinity
Metaphor
Millenarianism: Islamic
Millenarianism: Latin America and Native North
  America
Modernism: Overview
Modernity: Overview
Modernity: Africa
Motif: Motif in Music
Music, Anthropology of
Musical Performance and Audiences
Musicology
Mysticism: Chinese Mysticism
Mysticism: Islamic Mysticism in Asia
Mysticism: Kabbalah
Myth
Narrative
Nation
Nationalism: Middle East
New Criticism
Nomadism
Nuclear Age
Oral Traditions: Overview
Orientalism: Overview
Orthodoxy
Orthopraxy: Asia
Pan-Turkism
Periodization of the Arts
Person, Idea of the
Philosophies: African
Philosophies: American
Philosophies: Feminist, Twentieth-Century
Philosophies: Islamic

Philosophy: Historical Overview and Recent Develop-
  ments
Philosophy, Moral: Ancient
Philosophy of Mind: Ancient and Medieval
Pietism
Poetry and Poetics
Political Protest, U.S.
Populism: United States
Postmodernism
Practices
Pre-Columbian Civilization
Propaganda
Protest, Political
Psychoanalysis
Punishment
Queer Theory
Reading
Realism: Africa
Reflexivity
Reform: Europe and the United States
Relativism
Religion: Africa
Religion: African Diaspora
Religion: East and Southeast Asia
Religion: Indigenous Peoples' View, South America
Religion: Latin America
Religion: Middle East
Religion and the State: United States
Republicanism: Republic
Resistance
Resistance and Accommodation
Responsibility
Rhetoric: Overview
Rhetoric: Ancient and Medieval
Ritual: Public Ritual
Ritual: Religion
Romanticism in Literature and Politics
Sacred Places
Sacred Texts: Asia
Sexuality: Overview
Shinto
Slavery
Society
Sophists, The
Sport
Stoicism
Subjectivism
Superstition
Surrealism
Symbolism
Syncretism
Taste
Temperance
Text/Textuality
Theater and Performance
Third Cinema
Third World Literature
Time: China
Time: India
Toleration
Totalitarianism
Totems
Tragedy and Comedy
Translation
Trope

Untouchability: Menstrual Taboos
Utilitarianism
Victorianism
Virtual Reality
Volunteerism, U.S.
Westernization: Middle East
Westernization: Southeast Asia
Wisdom, Human
Witchcraft
Witchcraft, African Studies of
Yin and Yang
Yoga

Humanities

COMMUNICATION, LANGUAGE, AND LINGUISTICS

Aesthetics: Africa
Aesthetics: Asia
Africa, Idea of
Afrocentricity
Agnosticism
Algebras
Americanization, U.S.
Analytical Philosophy
Anthropology
Anticolonialism: Africa
Asceticism: Hindu and Buddhist Asceticism
Asceticism: Western Asceticism
Astronomy, Pre-Columbian and Latin American
Authenticity: Africa
Avant-Garde: Overview
Avant-Garde: Militancy
Aztlán
Barbarism and Civilization
Beauty and Ugliness
Behaviorism
Bilingualism and Multilingualism
Body, The
Borders, Borderlands, and Frontiers, Global
Buddhism
Calculation and Computation
Calendar
Cannibalism
Casuistry
Censorship
Chinese Thought
Cinema
Civil Disobedience
Classification of Arts and Sciences, Early Modern
Colonialism: Southeast Asia
Communication of Ideas: Africa and Its Influence
Communication of Ideas: The Americas and Their Influence
Communication of Ideas: Asia and Its Influence
Communication of Ideas: Europe and Its Influence
Communication of Ideas: Middle East and Abroad
Communication of Ideas: Orality and Advent of Writing
Communication of Ideas: Southeast Asia
Computer Science
Consumerism
Context
Continental Philosophy
Cosmopolitanism
Creolization, Caribbean
Critical Theory
Cultural Capital

Cultural History
Cultural Revivals
Cultural Studies
Cynicism
Dance
Democracy
Determinism
Dialogue and Dialectics: Socratic
Diasporas: Jewish Diaspora
Dictatorship in Latin America
Diffusion, Cultural
Discrimination
Diversity
Dream
Dress
Ecumenism
Education: Asia, Traditional and Modern
Empire and Imperialism: Asia
Empire and Imperialism: Europe
Empire and Imperialism: United States
Empiricism
Encyclopedism
Epistemology: Ancient
Epistemology: Early Modern
Epistemology: Modern
Ethnicity and Race: Africa
Ethnicity and Race: Anthropology
Ethnicity and Race: Islamic Views
Etiquette
Eurocentrism
Everyday Life
Examination Systems, China
Extirpation
Fallacy, Logical
Feminism: Overview
Feminism: Chicana Feminisms
Fetishism: Overview
Fetishism: Fetishism in Literature and Cultural Studies
Feudalism, European
Formalism
Gender: Gender in the Middle East
Gender in Art
Geometry
Gesture
Globalization: Asia
Globalization: General
Greek Science
Harmony
Hegemony
Hermeneutics
Hinduism
History, Economic
History, Idea of
Humanism: Africa
Humanism: Chinese Conception of
Humanism: Europe and the Middle East
Humanism: Renaissance
Humanity: African Thought
Human Rights: Overview
Idealism
Ideas, History of
Identity: Identity of Persons
Identity, Multiple: Overview
Identity, Multiple: Jewish Multiple Identity
Indigenismo

Intelligentsia
Interdisciplinarity
Interpretation
Islam: Africa
Islam: Southeast Asia
Islam: Sunni
Islamic Science
Japanese Philosophy, Japanese Thought
Jihad
Jouissance
Judaism: Judaism to 1800
Kantianism
Kinship
Knowledge
Language and Linguistics
Language, Linguistics, and Literacy
Language, Philosophy of: Ancient and Medieval
Language, Philosophy of: Modern
Law
Liberty
Life Cycle: Overview
Linguistic Turn
Literary Criticism
Literary History
Literature: Overview
Literature: African Literature
Machismo
Magic
Maps and the Ideas They Express
Masks
Materialism in Eighteenth-Century European Thought
Mathematics
Matriarchy
Media, History of
Medicine: Europe and the United States
Medicine: India
Meme
Mestizaje
Metaphor
Metaphysics: Renaissance to the Present
Migration: Africa
Migration: United States
Millenarianism: Latin America and Native North
  America
Mind
Minority
Modernism: Overview
Modernity: Overview
Modernity: Africa
Monarchy: Overview
Motherhood and Maternity
Motif: Motif in Literature
Motif: Motif in Music
Multiculturalism, Africa
Music, Anthropology of
Musical Performance and Audiences
Musicology
Mysticism: Chinese Mysticism
Mysticism: Christian Mysticism
Mysticism: Islamic Mysticism in Asia
Mysticism: Kabbalah
Mysticism: Mysticism in African Thought
Narrative
Nation
Nationalism: Overview

Nationalism: Middle East
Native Policy
Natural History
New Criticism
Nomadism
Objectivity
Occidentalism
Oral Traditions: Overview
Organicism
Orientalism: Overview
Orthodoxy
Pacifism
Pan-Africanism
Pan-Arabism
Pan-Asianism
Pan-Turkism
Paradigm
Patriotism
Periodization of the Arts
Person, Idea of the
Personhood in African Thought
Philosophies: African
Philosophies: American
Philosophies: Feminist, Twentieth-Century
Philosophies: Islamic
Philosophy: Historical Overview and Recent Develop-
  ments
Philosophy of Mind: Overview
Philosophy of Mind: Ancient and Medieval
Philosophy of Religion
Poetry and Poetics
Political Protest, U.S.
Positivism
Practices
Pre-Columbian Civilization
Prejudice
Presentism
Privacy
Probability
Progress, Idea of
Propaganda
Protest, Political
Pseudoscience
Psychology and Psychiatry
Public Sphere
Punishment
Pythagoreanism
Quantum
Queer Theory
Race and Racism: Asia
Race and Racism: Europe
Race and Racism: United States
Reading
Realism
Realism: Africa
Reflexivity
Relativism
Relativity
Religion: Africa
Religion: African Diaspora
Religion: East and Southeast Asia
Religion: Indigenous Peoples' View, South America
Religion: Latin America
Religion: Middle East
Religion and the State: Latin America

Religion and the State: Middle East
Representation: Mental Representation
Republicanism: Republic
Resistance
Resistance and Accommodation
Responsibility
Rhetoric: Overview
Ritual: Public Ritual
Ritual: Religion
Romanticism in Literature and Politics
Sacred and Profane
Sacred Places
Sacred Texts: Asia
Sacred Texts: Koran
Sage Philosophy
Science: East Asia
Science, History of
Sexual Harassment
Sexuality: Overview
Sexuality: Sexual Orientation
Shinto
Slavery
Social History, U.S.
Society
Sophists, The
Sport
State, The: Overview
Stoicism
Structuralism and Poststructuralism: Overview
Structuralism and Poststructuralism: Anthropology
Subjectivism
Superstition
Surrealism
Symbolism
Syncretism
Technology
Temperance
Text/Textuality
Textiles and Fiber Arts as Catalysts for Ideas
Theater and Performance
Third Cinema
Third World Literature
Time: India
Time: Traditional and Utilitarian
Toleration
Totalitarianism
Totems
Trade
Tragedy and Comedy
Translation
Travel: Travel from Europe and the Middle East
Treaty
Trope
Truth
Untouchability: Taboos
Utilitarianism
Victorianism
Virtual Reality
Visual Culture
Visual Order to Organizing Collections
Westernization: Middle East
Westernization: Southeast Asia
Wisdom, Human
Witchcraft
Witchcraft, African Studies of

Womanism
Women and Femininity in U.S. Popular Culture
Yin and Yang
LITERATURE
Absolute Music
Aesthetics: Africa
Aesthetics: Asia
Aesthetics: Europe and the Americas
Africa, Idea of
African-American Ideas
Alienation
America
Anticolonialism: Africa
Anti-Semitism: Overview
Architecture: Asia
Asceticism: Hindu and Buddhist Asceticism
Authenticity: Africa
Autobiography
Avant-Garde: Overview
Aztlán
Biography
Buddhism
Bushido
Casuistry
Chinese Thought
Cinema
Classicism
Classification of Arts and Sciences, Early Modern
Colonialism: Africa
Communication of Ideas: Africa and Its Influence
Communication of Ideas: Asia and Its Influence
Communication of Ideas: Europe and Its Influence
Communication of Ideas: Middle East and Abroad
Communication of Ideas: Orality and Advent of Writing
Communication of Ideas: Southeast Asia
Consciousness: Overview
Continental Philosophy
Corruption
Cosmopolitanism
Creativity in the Arts and Sciences
Critical Race Theory
Critical Theory
Cultural Studies
Dada
Dialogue and Dialectics: Socratic
Dream
Dystopia
Education: Islamic Education
Empire and Imperialism: Europe
Enlightenment
Etiquette
Europe, Idea of
Evil
Examination Systems, China
Existentialism
Expressionism
Extirpation
Fascism
Feminism: Overview
Feminism: Chicana Feminisms
Feminism: Third World U.S. Movement
Fetishism: Fetishism in Literature and Cultural Studies
Formalism
Friendship
Futurology

Game Theory
Gay Studies
Gender: Overview
Gender: Gender in the Middle East
Generation
Genius
Genre
Globalization: Asia
Gnosticism
Heaven and Hell
Heaven and Hell (Asian Focus)
Hedonism in European Thought
Hermeneutics
Hinduism
Historiography
History, Economic
History, Idea of
Honor, Middle Eastern Notions of
Humanism: Africa
Humanism: Chinese Conception of
Humanism: Renaissance
Humanity: African Thought
Humor
Ideas, History of
Identity, Multiple: Jewish Multiple Identity
Imagination
Indigenismo
Individualism
Intelligentsia
Interdisciplinarity
Interpretation
Islam: Africa
Islam: Shii
Islam: Sunni
Islamic Science
Japanese Philosophy, Japanese Thought
Jouissance
Judaism: Judaism to 1800
Judaism: Modern Judaism
Language and Linguistics
Language, Philosophy of: Ancient and Medieval
Language, Philosophy of: Modern
Law, Islamic
Leadership
Life Cycle: Overview
Linguistic Turn
Literary Criticism
Literary History
Literature: Overview
Literature: African Literature
Love, Western Notions of
Magic
Manichaeism
Marxism: Overview
Marxism: Latin America
Masks
Matriarchy
Medicine: China
Medicine: Islamic Medicine
Memory
Men and Masculinity
Mestizaje
Metaphor
Metaphysics: Renaissance to the Present
Microcosm and Macrocosm

Millenarianism: Overview
Millenarianism: Islamic
Millenarianism: Latin America and Native North
  America
Modernism: Overview
Modernism: Latin America
Modernity: Overview
Modernity: East Asia
Mohism
Monarchy: Overview
Motherhood and Maternity
Motif: Motif in Literature
Motif: Motif in Music
Musicology
Mysticism: Chinese Mysticism
Mysticism: Christian Mysticism
Myth
Narrative
Nation
Nationalism: Africa
Naturalism
Naturalism in Art and Literature
Nature
Negritude
New Criticism
Occidentalism
Oral Traditions: Overview
Organicism
Orientalism: Overview
Orientalism: African and Black Orientalism
Pan-Africanism
Pan-Asianism
Person, Idea of the
Phenomenology
Philosophies: African
Philosophies: American
Philosophies: Feminist, Twentieth-Century
Philosophies: Islamic
Philosophy: Historical Overview and Recent Develop-
  ments
Philosophy, Moral: Ancient
Philosophy, Moral: Medieval and Renaissance
Pietism
Platonism
Poetry and Poetics
Political Protest, U.S.
Postcolonial Studies
Postcolonial Theory and Literature
Postmodernism
Practices
Privacy
Property
Prophecy
Protest, Political
Psychoanalysis
Queer Theory
Race and Racism: Europe
Reading
Realism: Africa
Religion: Africa
Religion: African Diaspora
Religion: East and Southeast Asia
Religion: Indigenous Peoples' View, South America
Religion: Latin America
Religion: Middle East

Religion and the State: United States
Renaissance
Republicanism: Republic
Resistance and Accommodation
Rhetoric: Overview
Rhetoric: Ancient and Medieval
Ritual: Public Ritual
Romanticism in Literature and Politics
Sacred Texts: Asia
Sacred Texts: Koran
Sage Philosophy
Scholasticism
Science Fiction
Science: Overview
Sexuality: Overview
Slavery
Social History, U.S.
Society
Sophists, The
State of Nature
Stoicism
Structuralism and Poststructuralism: Overview
Surrealism
Symbolism
Syncretism
Text/Textuality
Theater and Performance
Third World Literature
Toleration
Totalitarianism
Tragedy and Comedy
Translation
Travel: Travel from Europe and the Middle East
Trope
Utopia
Victorianism
Virtue Ethics
Visual Order to Organizing Collections
War and Peace in the Arts
Wisdom, Human

RELIGION
Abolitionism
Aesthetics: Africa
Aesthetics: Asia
Africa, Idea of
Agnosticism
Alchemy: China
Alchemy: Europe and the Middle East
Alienation
Altruism
Americanization, U.S.
Ancestor Worship
Animism
Antifeminism
Anti-Semitism: Overview
Anti-Semitism: Islamic Anti-Semitism
Architecture: Overview
Architecture: Asia
Aristotelianism
Arts: Overview
Arts: Africa
Asceticism: Hindu and Buddhist Asceticism
Asceticism: Western Asceticism
Assimilation
Astrology: Overview

Astrology: China
Astronomy, Pre-Columbian and Latin American
Atheism
Authority
Autonomy
Bioethics
Body, The
Buddhism
Calendar
Cannibalism
Capitalism: Overview
Cartesianism
Casuistry
Causality
Causation in East Asian and Southeast Asian Philosophy
Censorship
Change
Chinese Thought
Christianity: Overview
Christianity: Asia
City, The: Latin America
City, The: The Islamic and Byzantine City
Civil Disobedience
Civil Society: Europe and the United States
Classification of Arts and Sciences, Early Modern
Colonialism: Southeast Asia
Communication of Ideas: Africa and Its Influence
Communication of Ideas: Asia and Its Influence
Communication of Ideas: Middle East and Abroad
Communication of Ideas: Orality and Advent of Writing
Communication of Ideas: Southeast Asia
Composition, Musical
Confucianism
Consciousness: Indian Thought
Conservatism
Continental Philosophy
Corruption
Cosmology: Asia
Cosmology: Cosmology and Astronomy
Cosmopolitanism
Creationism
Cultural History
Dance
Daoism
Death
Death and Afterlife, Islamic Understanding of
Deism
Demonology
Dialogue and Dialectics: Talmudic
Diasporas: Jewish Diaspora
Dictatorship in Latin America
Diversity
Dream
Dress
Dualism
Ecology
Ecumenism
Education: Asia, Traditional and Modern
Education: Europe
Education: Islamic Education
Education: Japan
Empire and Imperialism: Overview
Empire and Imperialism: Americas
Empire and Imperialism: Europe
Enlightenment

Environment
Environmental Ethics
Environmental History
Epicureanism
Epistemology: Early Modern
Epistemology: Modern
Equality: Overview
Eschatology
Ethnicity and Race: Islamic Views
Etiquette
Europe, Idea of
Everyday Life
Evil
Evolution
Existentialism
Expressionism
Extirpation
Family: Family in Anthropology since 1980
Fascism
Fatalism
Feminism: Overview
Feminism: Africa and African Diaspora
Feminism: Chicana Feminisms
Feminism: Islamic Feminism
Fetishism: Overview
Form, Metaphysical, in Ancient and Medieval Thought
Free Will, Determinism, and Predestination
Friendship
Fundamentalism
Gay Studies
Gender: Gender in the Middle East
Gender in Art
General Will
Genetics: Contemporary
Genocide
Ghetto
Gift, The
Globalization: Asia
Gnosticism
Good
Harmony
Health and Disease
Heaven and Hell
Heaven and Hell (Asian Focus)
Hedonism in European Thought
Heresy and Apostasy
Hermeneutics
Hierarchy and Order
Hinduism
Historicism
Historiography
History, Idea of
Honor
Honor, Middle Eastern Notions of
Humanism: Africa
Humanism: Chinese Conception of
Humanism: Renaissance
Humanism: Secular Humanism in the United States
Humanity: African Thought
Humanity: Asian Thought
Humanity: European Thought
Humanity in the Arts
Human Rights: Overview
Iconography
Ideas, History of

Identity: Identity of Persons
Identity, Multiple: Jewish Multiple Identity
Images, Icons, and Idols
Imagination
Immortality and the Afterlife
Individualism
Intelligentsia
Intentionality
Intercession in Middle Eastern Society
Interdisciplinarity
Islam: Africa
Islam: Shii
Islam: Southeast Asia
Islam: Sunni
Islamic Science
Jainism
Japanese Philosophy, Japanese Thought
Jihad
Jouissance
Judaism: Judaism to 1800
Judaism: Modern Judaism
Kantianism
Kinship
Knowledge
Language and Linguistics
Language, Philosophy of: Ancient and Medieval
Law, Islamic
Liberation Theology
Life
Literary History
Love, Western Notions of
Magic
Manichaeism
Marriage and Fertility, European Views
Marxism: Overview
Marxism: Latin America
Masks
Materialism in Eighteenth-Century European Thought
Matriarchy
Medicine: Europe and the United States
Medicine: Islamic Medicine
Meditation: Eastern Meditation
Men and Masculinity
Metaphor
Millenarianism: Overview
Millenarianism: Islamic
Millenarianism: Latin America and Native North
   America
Minority
Miracles
Modernity: Overview
Mohism
Monarchy: Overview
Monarchy: Islamic Monarchy
Monasticism
Monism
Motherhood and Maternity
Motif: Motif in Music
Multiculturalism, Africa
Museums
Music, Anthropology of
Musical Performance and Audiences
Mysticism: Chinese Mysticism
Mysticism: Christian Mysticism
Mysticism: Islamic Mysticism

Mysticism: Islamic Mysticism in Asia
Mysticism: Kabbalah
Mysticism: Mysticism in African Thought
Myth
Nation
Nationalism: Cultural Nationalism
Nationalism: Middle East
Naturalism
Natural Law
Natural Theology
Newtonianism
Nomadism
Nonviolence
Nude, The
Obligation
Organicism
Orientalism: Overview
Orientalism: African and Black Orientalism
Orthodoxy
Orthopraxy: Asia
Orthopraxy: Western Orthopraxy
Other, The, European Views of
Pacifism
Paradise on Earth
Parties, Political
Peace
Periodization of the Arts
Person, Idea of the
Personhood in African Thought
Perspective
Philanthropy
Philosophies: African
Philosophies: American
Philosophies: Feminist, Twentieth-Century
Philosophies: Islamic
Philosophy: Historical Overview and Recent Developments
Philosophy: Relations to Other Intellectual Realms
Philosophy, Moral: Africa
Philosophy, Moral: Medieval and Renaissance
Philosophy, Moral: Modern
Philosophy and Religion in Western Thought
Philosophy of Mind: Ancient and Medieval
Philosophy of Religion
Physics
Pietism
Platonism
Political Protest, U.S.
Polytheism
Population
Poverty
Practices
Pre-Columbian Civilization
Privacy
Propaganda
Prophecy
Protest, Political
Pseudoscience
Psychoanalysis
Punishment
Puritanism
Pythagoreanism
Race and Racism: Europe
Rationalism
Reading

Reflexivity
Reform: Islamic Reform
Reformation
Relativism
Religion: Overview
Religion: Africa
Religion: African Diaspora
Religion: East and Southeast Asia
Religion: Latin America
Religion: Middle East
Religion and Science
Religion and the State: Africa
Religion and the State: Europe
Religion and the State: Latin America
Religion and the State: Middle East
Religion and the State: United States
Renaissance
Representation: Political Representation
Republicanism: Latin America
Resistance and Accommodation
Responsibility
Rhetoric: Ancient and Medieval
Ritual: Religion
Romanticism in Literature and Politics
Sacred and Profane
Sacred Places
Sacred Texts: Asia
Sacred Texts: Koran
Scholasticism
Secularization and Secularism
Sexuality: Islamic Views
Shinto
Skepticism
Slavery
Sophists, The
Subjectivism
Sufism
Suicide
Superstition
Symbolism
Syncretism
Temperance
Theodicy
Time: China
Time: India
Time: Traditional and Utilitarian
Toleration
Totalitarianism
Totems
University: Overview
Untouchability: Overview
Untouchability: Menstrual Taboos
Untouchability: Taboos
Utilitarianism
Victorianism
Visual Order to Organizing Collections
Volunteerism, U.S.
War
War and Peace in the Arts
Westernization: Africa
Westernization: Middle East
Westernization: Southeast Asia
Witchcraft
Witchcraft, African Studies of
Yin and Yang

Yoga
Zen
Zionism
PHILOSOPHY
Absolute Music
Aesthetics: Asia
Aesthetics: Europe and the Americas
Africa, Idea of
African-American Ideas
Afrocentricity
Agnosticism
Alchemy: China
Algebras
Alienation
Altruism
Ambiguity
Analytical Philosophy
Anticolonialism: Africa
Antifeminism
Architecture: Overview
Architecture: Asia
Aristotelianism
Asceticism: Hindu and Buddhist Asceticism
Asceticism: Western Asceticism
Astronomy, Pre-Columbian and Latin American
Atheism
Authenticity: Africa
Autonomy
Avant-Garde: Militancy
Bioethics
Black Consciousness
Body, The
Buddhism
Cartesianism
Casuistry
Causality
Causation
Causation in East Asian and Southeast Asian Philosophy
Censorship
Change
Character
Chemistry
Chinese Thought
Christianity: Overview
Civil Disobedience
Civil Society: Europe and the United States
Civil Society: Responses in Africa and the Middle East
Class
Classification of Arts and Sciences, Early Modern
Common Sense
Communitarianism in African Thought
Confucianism
Consciousness: Overview
Consciousness: Chinese Thought
Consciousness: Indian Thought
Conservatism
Consilience
Context
Continental Philosophy
Corruption
Corruption in Developed and Developing Countries
Cosmology: Asia
Cosmopolitanism
Creationism
Critical Race Theory
Critical Theory
Cultural History
Cycles
Cynicism
Dance
Daoism
Death
Deism
Democracy
Democracy: Africa
Determinism
Dialogue and Dialectics: Socratic
Dream
Dress
Dualism
Dystopia
Eclecticism
Education: China
Education: Global Education
Education: Japan
Emotions
Empiricism
Enlightenment
Environment
Environmental Ethics
Environmental History
Epicureanism
Epistemology: Ancient
Epistemology: Early Modern
Epistemology: Modern
Equality: Overview
Equality: Gender Equality
Equality: Racial Equality
Essentialism
Ethnocentrism
Eugenics
Everyday Life
Evil
Existentialism
Expressionism
Fallacy, Logical
Falsifiability
Family Planning
Fascism
Fatalism
Feminism: Overview
Feminism: Africa and African Diaspora
Feminism: Chicana Feminisms
Feminism: Islamic Feminism
Field Theories
Form, Metaphysical, in Ancient and Medieval Thought
Foundationalism
Free Will, Determinism, and Predestination
Friendship
Gender: Gender in the Middle East
Gender in Art
General Will
Genetics: Contemporary
Genetics: History of
Geometry
Gift, The
Globalization: Asia
Gnosticism
Good
Greek Science

Happiness and Pleasure in European Thought
Harmony
Health and Disease
Heaven and Hell (Asian Focus)
Hedonism in European Thought
Hegelianism
Hegemony
Hermeneutics
Hierarchy and Order
Hinduism
Historical and Dialectical Materialism
Historicism
Historiography
History, Idea of
Humanism: Africa
Humanism: Chinese Conception of
Humanism: Europe and the Middle East
Humanism: Secular Humanism in the United States
Humanity: African Thought
Humanity: Asian Thought
Humanity: European Thought
Human Rights: Overview
Human Rights: Women's Rights
Idealism
Ideas, History of
Identity: Identity of Persons
Identity, Multiple: Overview
Identity, Multiple: Jewish Multiple Identity
Immortality and the Afterlife
Impressionism
Individualism
Intelligentsia
Intentionality
Interdisciplinarity
International Order
Islam: Africa
Islam: Sunni
Islamic Science
Jainism
Japanese Philosophy, Japanese Thought
Jouissance
Judaism: Modern Judaism
Justice: Overview
Justice: Justice in American Thought
Justice: Justice in East Asian Thought
Kantianism
Knowledge
Language and Linguistics
Language, Philosophy of: Ancient and Medieval
Language, Philosophy of: Modern
Law
Liberalism
Liberty
Life
Linguistic Turn
Literary Criticism
Literary History
Logic
Logic and Philosophy of Mathematics, Modern
Magic
Manichaeism
Maoism
Marxism: Overview
Marxism: Latin America
Materialism in Eighteenth-Century European Thought

Mathematics
Mechanical Philosophy
Medicine: China
Medicine: Europe and the United States
Meditation: Eastern Meditation
Memory
Metaphor
Metaphysics: Ancient and Medieval
Metaphysics: Renaissance to the Present
Microcosm and Macrocosm
Mind
Modernism: Latin America
Modernity: Overview
Mohism
Monism
Moral Sense
Music, Anthropology of
Musicology
Mysticism: Chinese Mysticism
Myth
Narrative
Natural History
Natural Law
Natural Theology
Naturalism
Nature
Naturphilosophie
Neoplatonism
Newtonianism
Nihilism
Nonviolence
Nuclear Age
Objectivity
Obligation
Occidentalism
Organicism
Orientalism: Overview
Orthopraxy: Asia
Other, The, European Views of
Pacifism
Pan-Africanism
Paradigm
Parties, Political
Peace
Person, Idea of the
Personhood in African Thought
Phenomenology
Philanthropy
Philosophies: African
Philosophies: American
Philosophies: Feminist, Twentieth-Century
Philosophies: Islamic
Philosophy: Historical Overview and Recent Developments
Philosophy: Relations to Other Intellectual Realms
Philosophy, History of
Philosophy, Moral: Africa
Philosophy, Moral: Ancient
Philosophy, Moral: Medieval and Renaissance
Philosophy, Moral: Modern
Philosophy and Religion in Western Thought
Philosophy of Mind: Overview
Philosophy of Mind: Ancient and Medieval
Philosophy of Religion
Physics

Pietism
Platonism
Pluralism
Poetry and Poetics
Political Protest, U.S.
Political Science
Population
Populism: United States
Positivism
Postcolonial Studies
Postmodernism
Poverty
Practices
Pragmatism
Presentism
Privacy
Probability
Progress, Idea of
Protest, Political
Pseudoscience
Punishment
Pythagoreanism
Quantum
Queer Theory
Race and Racism: Overview
Radicals/Radicalism
Rational Choice
Rationalism
Reading
Realism: Africa
Reason, Practical and Theoretical
Reflexivity
Reform: Europe and the United States
Relativism
Relativity
Religion: Overview
Religion: East and Southeast Asia
Religion: Middle East
Religion and Science
Religion and the State: United States
Renaissance
Representation: Political Representation
Resistance
Responsibility
Rhetoric: Overview
Romanticism in Literature and Politics
Sacred Texts: Asia
Sage Philosophy
Scholasticism
Science: Overview
Science: East Asia
Science, History of
Scientific Revolution
Secularization and Secularism
Sexual Harassment
Sexuality: Overview
Skepticism
Sociability in African Thought
Social Darwinism
Socialisms, African
Society
Sophists, The
State of Nature
Stoicism
Structuralism and Poststructuralism: Overview

Subjectivism
Suicide
Surrealism
Symbolism
Taste
Text/Textuality
Theodicy
Time: China
Time: India
Toleration
Totalitarianism
Translation
Truth
Universalism
Utilitarianism
Victorianism
Virtue Ethics
Visual Culture
Visual Order to Organizing Collections
Volksgeist
Volunteerism, U.S.
War
Wildlife
Wisdom, Human
Witchcraft
Witchcraft, African Studies of
Womanism
Yin and Yang
Yoga
Zen
EDUCATION
Abolitionism
Aesthetics: Africa
Aesthetics: Asia
Afrocentricity
Altruism
Americanization, U.S.
Anthropology
Anticolonialism: Africa
Anticolonialism: Southeast Asia
Antifeminism
Anti-Semitism: Overview
Apartheid
Architecture: Overview
Aristotelianism
Asceticism: Hindu and Buddhist Asceticism
Authenticity: Africa
Authoritarianism: Latin America
Behaviorism
Bilingualism and Multilingualism
Biology
Black Consciousness
Body, The
Buddhism
Bushido
Calculation and Computation
Capitalism: Overview
Capitalism: Africa
Character
Childhood and Child Rearing
Chinese Thought
Christianity: Asia
Citizenship: Naturalization
City, The: The City as a Cultural Center
Civil Society: Europe and the United States

Classification of Arts and Sciences, Early Modern
Communication of Ideas: Africa and Its Influence
Communication of Ideas: Asia and Its Influence
Communication of Ideas: Europe and Its Influence
Communication of Ideas: Southeast Asia
Composition, Musical
Confucianism
Consciousness: Chinese Thought
Consciousness: Indian Thought
Cosmopolitanism
Creationism
Creolization, Caribbean
Cultural Capital
Cultural Revivals
Cultural Studies
Dance
Daoism
Death and Afterlife, Islamic Understanding of
Democracy: Africa
Dialogue and Dialectics: Socratic
Dialogue and Dialectics: Talmudic
Diasporas: Jewish Diaspora
Diffusion, Cultural
Discrimination
Diversity
Dress
Eclecticism
Education: Asia, Traditional and Modern
Education: China
Education: Europe
Education: Global Education
Education: India
Education: Islamic Education
Education: Japan
Education: North America
Emotion
Empire and Imperialism: Asia
Empire and Imperialism: Europe
Empire and Imperialism: United States
Enlightenment
Environmental Ethics
Environmental History
Epicureanism
Epistemology: Ancient
Epistemology: Early Modern
Epistemology: Modern
Equality: Overview
Ethnicity and Race: Anthropology
Etiquette
Examination Systems, China
Experiment
Extirpation
Family Planning
Fascism
Feminism: Overview
Feminism: Africa and African Diaspora
Feminism: Chicana Feminisms
Feminism: Islamic Feminism
Gender: Gender in the Middle East
Generation
Globalization: Asia
Good
Greek Science
Harmony
Health and Disease

Hermeneutics
Hinduism
Historical and Dialectical Materialism
Historiography
History, Economic
Human Capital
Humanism: Chinese Conception of
Humanism: Europe and the Middle East
Humanism: Renaissance
Humanity: Asian Thought
Hygiene
Ideas, History of
Identity, Multiple: Jewish Multiple Identity
Individualism
Interdisciplinarity
Interpretation
Islam: Africa
Islam: Southeast Asia
Islam: Sunni
Islamic Science
Japanese Philosophy, Japanese Thought
Jihad
Jouissance
Judaism: Judaism to 1800
Judaism: Modern Judaism
Justice: Justice in East Asian Thought
Kantianism
Kinship
Knowledge
Language and Linguistics
Language, Linguistics, and Literacy
Learning and Memory, Contemporary Views
Life Cycle: Overview
Life Cycle: Adolescence
Life Cycle: Elders/Old Age
Literary Criticism
Loyalties, Dual
Maoism
Maps and the Ideas They Express
Marxism: Overview
Masks
Matriarchy
Medicine: Europe and the United States
Men and Masculinity
Mestizaje
Metaphor
Minority
Modernity: Overview
Modernity: Africa
Modernity: East Asia
Modernization Theory
Mohism
Motherhood and Maternity
Multiculturalism, Africa
Museums
Music, Anthropology of
Musical Performance and Audiences
Musicology
Mysticism: Chinese Mysticism
Mysticism: Islamic Mysticism in Asia
Mysticism: Kabbalah
Nation
Nationalism: Africa
Natural History
Negritude

Neoplatonism
Newtonianism
Nuclear Age
Nude, The
Objectivity
Occidentalism
Oral Traditions: Overview
Organicism
Orientalism: Overview
Orthodoxy
Pan-Arabism
Pan-Asianism
Paradigm
Periodization of the Arts
Philosophies: American
Philosophies: Feminist, Twentieth-Century
Philosophies: Islamic
Philosophy: Historical Overview and Recent Developments
Philosophy, History of
Philosophy, Moral: Ancient
Philosophy, Moral: Medieval and Renaissance
Philosophy, Moral: Modern
Philosophy of Mind: Ancient and Medieval
Physics
Platonism
Political Protest, U.S.
Population
Populism: United States
Practices
Pragmatism
Prejudice
Privacy
Propaganda
Protest, Political
Pseudoscience
Psychoanalysis
Punishment
Queer Theory
Reading
Realism: Africa
Reason, Practical and Theoretical
Reflexivity
Reform: Islamic Reform
Reformation
Relativism
Religion: East and Southeast Asia
Religion: Middle East
Religion and the State: Europe
Religion and the State: Latin America
Religion and the State: Middle East
Religion and the State: United States
Renaissance
Representation: Political Representation
Republicanism: Republic
Resistance
Rhetoric: Overview
Rhetoric: Ancient and Medieval
Ritual: Public Ritual
Sacred Places
Sacred Texts: Asia
Sage Philosophy
Scholasticism
Science: East Asia
Segregation

Sexuality: Overview
Skepticism
Slavery
Sociability in African Thought
Social Capital
Social History, U.S.
Sophists, The
Sport
State, The: Overview
Stoicism
Subjectivism
Sufism
Superstition
Temperance
Theater and Performance
Third Cinema
Third World Literature
Time: China
Totalitarianism
Tragedy and Comedy
University: Overview
University: Postcolonial
Untouchability: Menstrual Taboos
Untouchability: Taboos
Utilitarianism
Utopia
Victorianism
Visual Order to Organizing Collections
Volunteerism, U.S.
War and Peace in the Arts
Westernization: Africa
Westernization: Middle East
Westernization: Southeast Asia
Wisdom, Human
Women's History: Africa
Women's Studies
Yoga
Zen

Social Sciences
    WOMEN'S STUDIES AND GENDER STUDIES
        Abolitionism
        Aesthetics: Asia
        African-American Ideas
        Anarchism
        Anthropology
        Antifeminism
        Asceticism: Western Asceticism
        Autobiography
        Beauty and Ugliness
        Biography
        Black Atlantic
        Body, The
        Capitalism: Africa
        Censorship
        Chicano Movement
        Childhood and Child Rearing
        Christianity: Overview
        Cinema
        Class
        Colonialism: Africa
        Colonialism: Southeast Asia
        Communication of Ideas: Southeast Asia
        Composition, Musical
        Confucianism

Consumerism
Continental Philosophy
Creativity in the Arts and Sciences
Critical Race Theory
Critical Theory
Cultural Studies
Dance
Death
Death and Afterlife, Islamic Understanding of
Democracy: Africa
Demography
Diversity
Dress
Dystopia
Economics
Education: Asia, Traditional and Modern
Education: China
Education: Europe
Education: Islamic Education
Education: North America
Emotions
Environmental History
Equality: Overview
Equality: Gender Equality
Essentialism
Etiquette
Eugenics
Eurocentrism
Everyday Life
Existentialism
Family: Modernist Anthropological Theory
Family: Family in Anthropology since 1980
Family Planning
Fascism
Feminism: Overview
Feminism: Africa and African Diaspora
Feminism: Chicana Feminisms
Feminism: Third World U.S. Movement
Fetishism: Overview
Fetishism: Fetishism in Literature and Cultural Studies
Friendship
Gay Studies
Gender: Overview
Gender: Gender in the Middle East
Gender in Art
Gender Studies: Anthropology
Genius
Genre
Hate
Historiography
History, Economic
Honor
Honor, Middle Eastern Notions of
Human Capital
Humanism: Renaissance
Humanity: Asian Thought
Humanity: European Thought
Human Rights: Women's Rights
Humor
Iconography
Identity: Identity of Persons
Identity, Multiple: Overview
Impressionism
Intelligentsia
Interdisciplinarity

Internal Colonialism
Interpretation
Islam: Shii
Jouissance
Justice: Overview
Kinship
Knowledge
Law
Law, Islamic
Legalism, Ancient China
Liberalism
Liberation Theology
Life Cycle: Adolescence
Literary History
Literature: African Literature
Love, Western Notions of
Machismo
Marriage and Fertility, European Views
Masks
Matriarchy
Medicine: Europe and the United States
Men and Masculinity
Mestizaje
Minority
Modernism: Overview
Motherhood and Maternity
Music, Anthropology of
Musicology
Mysticism: Christian Mysticism
Narrative
Nude, The
Orientalism: African and Black Orientalism
Orthodoxy
Pan-Africanism
Periodization of the Arts
Philosophies: African
Philosophies: American
Philosophies: Feminist, Twentieth-Century
Philosophy: Historical Overview and Recent Developments
Poetry and Poetics
Political Protest, U.S.
Population
Postcolonial Studies
Postcolonial Theory and Literature
Postmodernism
Pre-Columbian Civilization
Privacy
Progress, Idea of
Propaganda
Prophecy
Protest, Political
Psychoanalysis
Public Sphere
Queer Theory
Radicals/Radicalism
Reading
Reflexivity
Relativism
Religion: Africa
Religion: African Diaspora
Renaissance
Republicanism: Latin America
Resistance and Accommodation
Rhetoric: Ancient and Medieval

Ritual: Public Ritual
Ritual: Religion
Romanticism in Literature and Politics
Science: Overview
Science, History of
Science Fiction
Scientific Revolution
Secularization and Secularism
Sexual Harassment
Sexuality: Overview
Sexuality: Islamic Views
Sexuality: Sexual Orientation
Shinto
Slavery
Social Contract
Social History, U.S.
Sport
State, The: The Postcolonial State
Structuralism and Poststructuralism: Overview
Subjectivism
Symbolism
Universalism
University: Overview
Untouchability: Menstrual Taboos
Utopia
Victorianism
Virtue Ethics
Visual Culture
Visual Order to Organizing Collections
Volunteerism, U.S.
War
Witchcraft
Witchcraft, African Studies of
Womanism
Women and Femininity in U.S. Popular Culture
Women's History: Africa
Women's History: Asia
Women's Studies
Work
ETHNIC STUDIES
Abolitionism
Absolute Music
Africa, Idea of
African-American Ideas
Afrocentricity
America
Americanization, U.S.
Ancestor Worship
Anthropology
Anticolonialism: Africa
Anticolonialism: Southeast Asia
Anti-Semitism: Overview
Anti-Semitism: Islamic Anti-Semitism
Apartheid
Architecture: Africa
Arts: Overview
Assimilation
Astronomy, Pre-Columbian and Latin American
Authenticity: Africa
Autobiography
Aztlán
Barbarism and Civilization
Bilingualism and Multilingualism
Black Atlantic
Black Consciousness

Body, The
Borders, Borderlands, and Frontiers, Global
Cannibalism
Capitalism: Overview
Capitalism: Africa
Chicano Movement
Cinema
Citizenship: Cultural Citizenship
City, The: Latin America
City, The: The City as a Cultural Center
City, The: The City as Political Center
Civil Disobedience
Class
Colonialism: Africa
Colonialism: Latin America
Colonialism: Southeast Asia
Communication of Ideas: Southeast Asia
Communitarianism in African Thought
Composition, Musical
Consumerism
Context
Cosmopolitanism
Creolization, Caribbean
Critical Race Theory
Critical Theory
Cultural Capital
Cultural Revivals
Cultural Studies
Dance
Death
Demography
Diasporas: African Diaspora
Diasporas: Jewish Diaspora
Diffusion, Cultural
Discrimination
Diversity
Dress
Education: North America
Empire and Imperialism: Europe
Empire and Imperialism: Middle East
Environmental History
Equality: Overview
Equality: Racial Equality
Essentialism
Ethnicity and Race: Africa
Ethnicity and Race: Anthropology
Ethnicity and Race: Islamic Views
Ethnocentrism
Ethnography
Ethnohistory, U.S.
Eugenics
Eurocentrism
Extirpation
Family Planning
Fascism
Feminism: Overview
Feminism: Africa and African Diaspora
Feminism: Chicana Feminisms
Feminism: Third World U.S. Movement
Fetishism: Overview
Fetishism: Fetishism in Literature and Cultural Studies
Gender Studies: Anthropology
Generation
Genetics: Contemporary
Genocide

Gesture
Ghetto
Gift, The
Hate
Hinduism
History, Economic
Honor
Humanity: European Thought
Humor
Hygiene
Iconography
Identity, Multiple: Overview
Identity, Multiple: Asian-Americans
Identity, Multiple: Jewish Multiple Identity
Indigenismo
Intelligentsia
Interdisciplinarity
Internal Colonialism
Islam: Africa
Jouissance
Judaism: Modern Judaism
Kinship
Law
Liberation Theology
Life Cycle: Adolescence
Literary History
Literature: African Literature
Loyalties, Dual
Machismo
Marxism: Latin America
Mathematics
Matriarchy
Men and Masculinity
Mestizaje
Migration: Africa
Migration: Migration in World History
Migration: United States
Minority
Modernism: Overview
Modernity: Africa
Motherhood and Maternity
Multiculturalism, Africa
Music, Anthropology of
Musical Performance and Audiences
Mysticism: Kabbalah
Nation
Nationalism: Overview
Nationalism: Africa
Nationalism: Cultural Nationalism
Nationalism: Middle East
Native Policy
Naturalism
Negritude
Nomadism
Nuclear Age
Occidentalism
Orientalism: Overview
Orientalism: African and Black Orientalism
Orthodoxy
Other, The, European Views of
Pan-Africanism
Pan-Asianism
Pan-Islamism
Pan-Turkism
Patriotism

Periodization of the Arts
Person, Idea of the
Philosophies: African
Philosophies: American
Political Protest, U.S.
Population
Populism: United States
Postcolonial Studies
Postcolonial Theory and Literature
Postmodernism
Practices
Pre-Columbian Civilization
Prehistory, Rise of
Prejudice
Privacy
Protest, Political
Psychoanalysis
Queer Theory
Race and Racism: Overview
Race and Racism: Asia
Race and Racism: Europe
Race and Racism: United States
Reading
Realism: Africa
Reflexivity
Regions and Regionalism, Eastern Europe
Relativism
Religion: African Diaspora
Religion: Indigenous Peoples' View, South America
Religion: Latin America
Religion: Middle East
Republicanism: Latin America
Resistance and Accommodation
Ritual: Religion
Sage Philosophy
Scarcity and Abundance, Latin America
Secularization and Secularism
Segregation
Sexuality: Overview
Shinto
Slavery
Socialisms, African
Sport
State, The: The Postcolonial State
Superstition
Symbolism
Syncretism
Terror
Third Cinema
Third World
Third World Literature
Time: Traditional and Utilitarian
Totalitarianism
Totems
Trade
Translation
Treaty
Untouchability: Menstrual Taboos
Untouchability: Taboos
Utopia
Victorianism
Visual Culture
Volksgeist
Volunteerism, U.S.
War

New Dictionary of the History of Ideas

Westernization: Africa
Westernization: Southeast Asia
Wisdom, Human
Witchcraft, African Studies of
Womanism
Women and Femininity in U.S. Popular Culture
Women's History: Africa
Women's Studies
Work
World Systems Theory, Latin America
Zionism

HISTORY

Aesthetics: Europe and the Americas
Afrocentricity
Afropessimism
Altruism
Americanization, U.S.
Anthropology
Anticolonialism: Latin America
Anticolonialism: Southeast Asia
Anti-Semitism: Overview
Architecture: Overview
Architecture: Africa
Asceticism: Hindu and Buddhist Asceticism
Authoritarianism: Latin America
Autobiography
Autonomy
Aztlán
Barbarism and Civilization
Biography
Buddhism
Capitalism: Overview
Change
Childhood and Child Rearing
Chinese Thought
City, The: The City as a Cultural Center
Classification of Arts and Sciences, Early Modern
Colonialism: Africa
Colonialism: Latin America
Colonialism: Southeast Asia
Consciousness: Overview
Conservatism
Context
Continental Philosophy
Cosmology: Asia
Creolization, Caribbean
Crisis
Cultural History
Cultural Revivals
Cultural Studies
Cycles
Dance
Determinism
Diasporas: African Diaspora
Diasporas: Jewish Diaspora
Dictatorship in Latin America
Diffusion, Cultural
Dress
Ecology
Economics
Education: Europe
Empire and Imperialism: Overview
Empire and Imperialism: United States
Enlightenment
Environmental History

Ethnography
Ethnohistory, U.S.
Eurocentrism
Everyday Life
Evil
Extirpation
Fascism
Fatalism
Feminism: Overview
Feminism: Third World U.S. Movement
Feudalism, European
Futurology
Gender in Art
Generation
Genius
Genre
Geography
Globalization: Asia
Hegelianism
Hermeneutics
Historical and Dialectical Materialism
Historicism
Historiography
History, Economic
History, Idea of
Honor
Iconography
Ideas, History of
Identity, Multiple: Jewish Multiple Identity
Intelligentsia
Intentionality
Interdisciplinarity
Internal Colonialism
International Order
Interpretation
Islamic Science
Japanese Philosophy, Japanese Thought
Jihad
Judaism: Judaism to 1800
Knowledge
Language and Linguistics
Leadership
Learning and Memory, Contemporary Views
Life Cycle: Elders/Old Age
Linguistic Turn
Literary Criticism
Literary History
Literature: African Literature
Love, Western Notions of
Machiavellism
Maoism
Marxism: Overview
Marxism: Asia
Marxism: Latin America
Matriarchy
Media, History of
Memory
Mestizaje
Metaphor
Migration: Africa
Migration: Migration in World History
Millenarianism: Overview
Millenarianism: Islamic
Millenarianism: Latin America and Native North
    America

Modernism: Latin America
Modernity: Overview
Modernity: Africa
Modernity: East Asia
Modernization
Modernization Theory
Motif: Motif in Literature
Music, Anthropology of
Musicology
Narrative
Nation
Nationalism: Overview
Nationalism: Africa
Native Policy
Negritude
Nomadism
Nuclear Age
Occidentalism
Oral Traditions: Overview
Pan-Asianism
Paradigm
Patriotism
Peasants and Peasantry
Periodization
Periodization of the Arts
Philosophies: Feminist, Twentieth-Century
Philosophy: Historical Overview and Recent Developments
Philosophy, History of
Philosophy of Religion
Poetry and Poetics
Political Protest, U.S.
Polytheism
Postcolonial Theory and Literature
Postmodernism
Power
Practices
Pragmatism
Pre-Columbian Civilization
Presentism
Privacy
Progress, Idea of
Protest, Political
Public Sphere
Queer Theory
Race and Racism: Asia
Reading
Realism: Africa
Reflexivity
Reform: Europe and the United States
Reformation
Regions and Regionalism, Eastern Europe
Relativism
Religion: East and Southeast Asia
Religion: Indigenous Peoples' View, South America
Religion: Middle East
Religion and the State: United States
Renaissance
Republicanism: Latin America
Republicanism: Republic
Resistance
Responsibility
Revolution
Ritual: Public Ritual
Sacred Texts: Asia

Scarcity and Abundance, Latin America
Science: Overview
Science, History of
Scientific Revolution
Sexuality: Overview
Skepticism
Slavery
Social Capital
Social Darwinism
Social History, U.S.
Society
Sophists, The
Sport
State of Nature
Structuralism and Poststructuralism: Overview
Subjectivism
Surrealism
Syncretism
Technology
Theater and Performance
Theodicy
Third World
Time: China
Time: India
Time: Traditional and Utilitarian
Toleration
Totalitarianism
Trade
Treaty
Trope
Utopia
Victorianism
Visual Order to Organizing Collections
Volksgeist
War
War and Peace in the Arts
Westernization: Middle East
Westernization: Southeast Asia
Witchcraft
Witchcraft, African Studies of
Women's History: Africa
Women's History: Asia
World Systems Theory, Latin America

ANTHROPOLOGY AND SOCIOLOGY
Aesthetics: Asia
Aesthetics: Europe and the Americas
Africa, Idea of
Alienation
Altruism
Americanization, U.S.
Ancestor Worship
Anthropology
Anti-Semitism: Overview
Architecture: Overview
Architecture: Africa
Asceticism: Hindu and Buddhist Asceticism
Asceticism: Western Asceticism
Astronomy, Pre-Columbian and Latin American
Aztlán
Barbarism and Civilization
Beauty and Ugliness
Bilingualism and Multilingualism
Body, The
Borders, Borderlands, and Frontiers, Global
Buddhism

Calendar
Cannibalism
Capitalism: Overview
Character
Childhood and Child Rearing
Chinese Thought
Cinema
Citizenship: Cultural Citizenship
City, The: The City as a Cultural Center
Civil Society: Europe and the United States
Colonialism: Latin America
Colonialism: Southeast Asia
Communication of Ideas: Orality and Advent of Writing
Communication of Ideas: Southeast Asia
Communitarianism in African Thought
Composition, Musical
Context
Continental Philosophy
Cosmopolitanism
Creativity in the Arts and Sciences
Creolization, Caribbean
Cultural Capital
Cultural History
Cultural Revivals
Cultural Studies
Dance
Death
Death and Afterlife, Islamic Understanding of
Demography
Demonology
Development
Diasporas: African Diaspora
Diasporas: Jewish Diaspora
Diffusion, Cultural
Discrimination
Diversity
Dream
Dress
Ecology
Environment
Environmental Ethics
Environmental History
Ethnicity and Race: Africa
Ethnicity and Race: Anthropology
Ethnocentrism
Ethnography
Ethnohistory, U.S.
Etiquette
Eugenics
Eurocentrism
Europe, Idea of
Everyday Life
Extirpation
Family: Modernist Anthropological Theory
Family: Family in Anthropology since 1980
Family Planning
Fascism
Feminism: Overview
Feminism: Third World U.S. Movement
Fetishism: Overview
Gender Studies: Anthropology
Generation
Genetics: Contemporary
Genetics: History of
Gesture

Ghetto
Gift, The
Globalization: Asia
Hinduism
Historiography
History, Economic
History, Idea of
Honor
Honor, Middle Eastern Notions of
Humanism: Chinese Conception of
Humanity: African Thought
Humanity: European Thought
Humor
Ideas, History of
Identity: Personal and Social Identity
Identity, Multiple: Asian-Americans
Identity, Multiple: Jewish Multiple Identity
Intelligentsia
Intentionality
Interdisciplinarity
Interpretation
Jouissance
Judaism: Modern Judaism
Kinship
Knowledge
Language and Linguistics
Life Cycle: Overview
Life Cycle: Adolescence
Life Cycle: Elders/Old Age
Linguistic Turn
Literary Criticism
Machiavellism
Magic
Manichaeism
Marriage and Fertility, European Views
Marxism: Overview
Masks
Matriarchy
Meditation: Eastern Meditation
Memory
Men and Masculinity
Mestizaje
Metaphor
Migration: Migration in World History
Migration: United States
Minority
Motherhood and Maternity
Motif: Motif in Music
Music, Anthropology of
Musical Performance and Audiences
Musicology
Mysticism: Chinese Mysticism
Myth
Nation
Native Policy
Natural History
Occidentalism
Oral Traditions: Overview
Organicism
Orientalism: African and Black Orientalism
Orthodoxy
Orthopraxy: Asia
Other, The, European Views of
Peasants and Peasantry
Person, Idea of the

Philosophies: Feminist, Twentieth-Century
Philosophy, Moral: Africa
Phrenology
Pluralism
Polytheism
Postcolonial Theory and Literature
Postmodernism
Power
Practices
Pre-Columbian Civilization
Prehistory, Rise of
Prejudice
Presentism
Privacy
Psychoanalysis
Public Sphere
Queer Theory
Race and Racism: Asia
Reading
Reflexivity
Reform: Europe and the United States
Relativism
Religion: Overview
Religion: Africa
Religion: African Diaspora
Religion: Latin America
Religion: Middle East
Representation: Mental Representation
Resistance
Resistance and Accommodation
Ritual: Public Ritual
Ritual: Religion
Sacred and Profane
Scarcity and Abundance, Latin America
Sexuality: Overview
Sexuality: Sexual Orientation
Social Capital
Social Darwinism
Social History, U.S.
Society
Sport
State of Nature
Structuralism and Poststructuralism: Overview
Structuralism and Poststructuralism: Anthropology
Subjectivism
Superstition
Surrealism
Symbolism
Syncretism
Textiles and Fiber Arts as Catalysts for Ideas
Theater and Performance
Time: Traditional and Utilitarian
Toleration
Totalitarianism
Totems
Trade
Tradition
Tragedy and Comedy
Tribalism, Middle East
Trope
Untouchability: Menstrual Taboos
Untouchability: Taboos
Utilitarianism
Victorianism
Virtue Ethics

War and Peace in the Arts
Westernization: Southeast Asia
Wisdom, Human
Witchcraft
Witchcraft, African Studies of
Women's History: Africa
Work
World Systems Theory, Latin America
Yin and Yang
POLITICAL SCIENCE (emphasizing political philosophy)
Abolitionism
Absolute Music
Africa, Idea of
African-American Ideas
Afrocentricity
Afropessimism
Alienation
Altruism
America
Americanization, U.S.
Anarchism
Anthropology
Anticolonialism: Africa
Anticolonialism: Latin America
Anticolonialism: Middle East
Anticolonialism: Southeast Asia
Anti-Semitism: Overview
Anti-Semitism: Islamic Anti-Semitism
Apartheid
Architecture: Overview
Architecture: Africa
Architecture: Asia
Asceticism: Western Asceticism
Asian-American Ideas (Cultural Migration)
Assimilation
Astronomy, Pre-Columbian and Latin American
Authoritarianism: Overview
Authoritarianism: East Asia
Authoritarianism: Latin America
Authority
Autobiography
Avant-Garde: Militancy
Aztlán
Barbarism and Civilization
Bilingualism and Multilingualism
Bioethics
Black Atlantic
Black Consciousness
Borders, Borderlands, and Frontiers, Global
Bureaucracy
Bushido
Calculation and Computation
Cannibalism
Capitalism: Overview
Capitalism: Africa
Casuistry
Censorship
Chicano Movement
Childhood and Child Rearing
Chinese Warlordism
Christianity: Overview
Christianity: Asia
Citizenship: Overview
Citizenship: Cultural Citizenship
Citizenship: Naturalization

City, The: Latin America
City, The: The City as a Cultural Center
City, The: The City as Political Center
Civil Disobedience
Civil Society: Europe and the United States
Civil Society: Responses in Africa and the Middle East
Class
Colonialism: Africa
Colonialism: Latin America
Colonialism: Southeast Asia
Common Sense
Communication of Ideas: Europe and Its Influence
Communication of Ideas: Middle East and Abroad
Communication of Ideas: Southeast Asia
Communication of Ideas: The Americas and Their Influence
Communism: Latin America
Communism: Europe
Communitarianism in African Thought
Composition, Musical
Computer Science
Confucianism
Consciousness: Overview
Consciousness: Chinese Thought
Conservatism
Constitutionalism
Continental Philosophy
Corruption
Corruption in Developed and Developing Countries
Cosmopolitanism
Creolization, Caribbean
Critical Race Theory
Cultural Studies
Cycles
Cynicism
Dada
Dance
Daoism
Democracy
Democracy, Africa
Demography
Dependency
Determinism
Dialogue and Dialectics: Socratic
Diasporas: African Diaspora
Diasporas: Jewish Diaspora
Dictatorship in Latin America
Discrimination
Diversity
Dress
Dystopia
Ecology
Economics
Education: China
Education: Global Education
Education: India
Education: Japan
Education: North America
Empire and Imperialism: Overview
Empire and Imperialism: Americas
Empire and Imperialism: Asia
Empire and Imperialism: Europe
Empire and Imperialism: Middle East
Empire and Imperialism: United States
Environmental Ethics

Environmental History
Equality: Overview
Equality: Gender Equality
Equality: Racial Equality
Ethnicity and Race: Africa
Ethnicity and Race: Anthropology
Ethnicity and Race: Islamic Views
Etiquette
Eugenics
Eurocentrism
Europe, Idea of
Evil
Examination Systems, China
Existentialism
Expressionism
Extirpation
Fallacy, Logical
Family Planning
Fascism
Feminism: Overview
Feminism: Africa and African Diaspora
Feminism: Chicana Feminisms
Feminism: Islamic Feminism
Feminism: Third World U.S. Movement
Fetishism: Overview
Feudalism, European
Friendship
Fundamentalism
Futurology
Game Theory
Garden
Gay Studies
Gender: Gender in the Middle East
Gender in Art
General Will
Generation
Genetics: Contemporary
Genocide
Ghetto
Globalization: Africa
Globalization: Asia
Globalization: General
Good
Happiness and Pleasure in European Thought
Heaven and Hell
Heaven and Hell (Asian Focus)
Hegelianism
Hegemony
Hinduism
Historical and Dialectical Materialism
Historiography
History, Economic
History, Idea of
Honor
Honor, Middle Eastern Notions of
Human Capital
Humanism: Chinese Conception of
Humanism: Europe and the Middle East
Humanism: Renaissance
Humanism: Secular Humanism in the United States
Humanity: African Thought
Human Rights: Overview
Human Rights: Women's Rights
Hygiene
Ideas, History of

Identity, Multiple: Overview
Identity, Multiple: Asian-Americans
Identity, Multiple: Jewish Multiple Identity
Individualism
Intelligentsia
Intentionality
Intercession in Middle Eastern Society
Interdisciplinarity
Internal Colonialism
International Order
Islam: Africa
Islam: Shii
Islam: Southeast Asia
Islam: Sunni
Islamic Science
Japanese Philosophy, Japanese Thought
Jihad
Jouissance
Justice: Overview
Justice: Justice in American Thought
Justice: Justice in East Asian Thought
Kantianism
Kinship
Knowledge
Language and Linguistics
Law
Law, Islamic
Leadership
Legalism, Ancient China
Liberalism
Liberation Theology
Liberty
Life Cycle: Elders/Old Age
Literary Criticism
Literary History
Literature: Overview
Literature: African Literature
Lysenkoism
Machiavellism
Machismo
Maoism
Maps and the Ideas They Express
Marriage and Fertility, European Views
Marxism: Overview
Marxism: Asia
Marxism: Latin America
Masks
Mathematics
Matriarchy
Medicine: Europe and the United States
Meme
Men and Masculinity
Mestizaje
Migration: Migration in World History
Migration: United States
Millenarianism: Islamic
Millenarianism: Latin America and Native North
    America
Minority
Modernism: Overview
Modernism: Latin America
Modernity: Overview
Modernity: Africa
Modernity: East Asia
Modernization

Modernization Theory
Mohism
Monarchy: Overview
Monarchy: Islamic Monarchy
Motherhood and Maternity
Motif: Motif in Literature
Multiculturalism, Africa
Music, Anthropology of
Musical Performance and Audiences
Musicology
Mysticism: Chinese Mysticism
Myth
Narrative
Nation
Nationalism: Overview
Nationalism: Africa
Nationalism: Cultural Nationalism
Nationalism: Middle East
Native Policy
Natural Law
Naturalism
Negritude
Neocolonialism
Neoliberalism
New Criticism
Newtonianism
Nihilism
Nomadism
Nonviolence
Nuclear Age
Objectivity
Obligation
Occidentalism
Organicism
Orientalism: Overview
Orientalism: African and Black Orientalism
Orthodoxy
Orthopraxy: Asia
Pacifism
Pan-Africanism
Pan-Arabism
Pan-Asianism
Pan-Islamism
Pan-Turkism
Paradigm
Parties, Political
Patriotism
Peace
Periodization of the Arts
Person, Idea of the
Personhood in African Thought
Philanthropy
Philosophies: American
Philosophies: Feminist, Twentieth-Century
Philosophies: Islamic
Philosophy: Historical Overview and Recent Develop-
    ments
Philosophy, History of
Philosophy, Moral: Africa
Philosophy, Moral: Ancient
Philosophy, Moral: Modern
Philosophy of Religion
Phrenology
Pluralism
Political Protest, U.S.

Political Science
Political, The
Population
Populism: Latin America
Populism: United States
Postcolonial Studies
Poverty
Power
Practices
Pre-Columbian Civilization
Prejudice
Presentism
Privacy
Privatization
Probability
Progress, Idea of
Propaganda
Property
Protest, Political
Pseudoscience
Psychoanalysis
Public Sphere
Punishment
Puritanism
Pythagoreanism
Quantum
Queer Theory
Race and Racism: Overview
Race and Racism: Asia
Race and Racism: United States
Radicals/Radicalism
Rational Choice
Reading
Realism
Realism: Africa
Reason, Practical and Theoretical
Reflexivity
Reform: Europe and the United States
Reform: Islamic Reform
Regions and Regionalism, Eastern Europe
Relativism
Religion: Africa
Religion: African Diaspora
Religion: East and Southeast Asia
Religion: Latin America
Religion: Middle East
Religion and the State: Africa
Religion and the State: Europe
Religion and the State: Latin America
Religion and the State: Middle East
Religion and the State: United States
Renaissance
Representation: Political Representation
Republicanism: Latin America
Republicanism: Republic
Resistance
Resistance and Accommodation
Responsibility
Revolution
Rhetoric: Ancient and Medieval
Ritual: Public Ritual
Romanticism in Literature and Politics
Sacred and Profane
Scarcity and Abundance, Latin America
Science, History of

Science Fiction
Secularization and Secularism
Segregation
Sexual Harassment
Sexuality: Overview
Sexuality: Islamic Views
Sexuality: Sexual Orientation
Shinto
Skepticism
Slavery
Sociability in African Thought
Social Capital
Social Contract
Social History, U.S.
Socialism
Socialisms, African
Society
Sophists, The
Sovereignty
Sport
State, The: Overview
State, The: The Postcolonial State
State of Nature
Stoicism
Subjectivism
Sufism
Suicide
Superstition
Surrealism
Symbolism
Syncretism
Technology
Temperance
Terror
Terrorism, Middle East
Third Cinema
Third World
Third World Literature
Time: China
Time: Traditional and Utilitarian
Toleration
Totalitarianism
Trade
Translation
Treaty
Tribalism, Middle East
University: Postcolonial
Untouchability: Menstrual Taboos
Untouchability: Taboos
Utilitarianism
Utopia
Victorianism
Virtue Ethics
Visual Order to Organizing Collections
Volksgeist
Volunteerism, U.S.
War
War and Peace in the Arts
Wealth
Westernization: Africa
Westernization: Middle East
Westernization: Southeast Asia
Wildlife
Witchcraft
Witchcraft, African Studies of

Women's History: Africa
Work
World Systems Theory, Latin America
Zionism
ECONOMICS
Abolitionism
Africa, Idea of
African-American Ideas
Afropessimism
Alienation
Altruism
Anarchism
Anthropology
Anticolonialism: Africa
Anticolonialism: Latin America
Anticolonialism: Middle East
Anticolonialism: Southeast Asia
Anti-Semitism: Islamic Anti-Semitism
Apartheid
Architecture: Africa
Arts: Africa
Asceticism: Western Asceticism
Asian-American Ideas (Cultural Migration)
Assimilation
Astronomy, Pre-Columbian and Latin American
Authoritarianism: East Asia
Authoritarianism: Latin America
Avant-Garde: Militancy
Bioethics
Black Atlantic
Black Consciousness
Bureaucracy
Bushido
Calculation and Computation
Capitalism: Overview
Capitalism: Africa
Chicano Movement
Cinema
City, The: The City as a Cultural Center
City, The: The City as Political Center
City, The: The Islamic and Byzantine City
Civil Society: Europe and the United States
Civil Society: Responses in Africa and the Middle East
Class
Colonialism: Africa
Colonialism: Southeast Asia
Communication of Ideas: Africa and Its Influence
Communication of Ideas: Middle East and Abroad
Communication of Ideas: Southeast Asia
Communism: Europe
Communism: Latin America
Composition, Musical
Confucianism
Consumerism
Corruption in Developed and Developing Countries
Critical Race Theory
Cultural Capital
Cultural History
Cultural Studies
Democracy: Africa
Demography
Dependency
Diasporas: African Diaspora
Diasporas: Jewish Diaspora
Dictatorship in Latin America
Diffusion, Cultural
Discrimination
Diversity
Dress
Dystopia
Economics
Education: China
Education: Global Education
Empire and Imperialism: Americas
Empire and Imperialism: Asia
Empire and Imperialism: Europe
Empire and Imperialism: Middle East
Empire and Imperialism: United States
Environmental Ethics
Environmental History
Equality: Overview
Equality: Gender Equality
Equality: Racial Equality
Eugenics
Eurocentrism
Europe, Idea of
Everyday Life
Examination Systems, China
Family: Modernist Anthropological Theory
Family Planning
Fascism
Feminism: Overview
Feminism: Africa and African Diaspora
Feminism: Chicana Feminisms
Feminism: Islamic Feminism
Feminism: Third World U.S. Movement
Fetishism: Overview
Fetishism: Fetishism in Literature and Cultural Studies
Feudalism, European
Futurology
Game Theory
Generation
Genetics: Contemporary
Ghetto
Gift, The
Globalization: Africa
Globalization: Asia
Globalization: General
Good
Hegelianism
Hegemony
Hinduism
Historical and Dialectical Materialism
Historicism
Historiography
History, Economic
History, Idea of
Human Capital
Human Rights: Women's Rights
Ideas, History of
Identity, Multiple: Asian-Americans
Indigenismo
Individualism
Intelligentsia
Intentionality
Internal Colonialism
Interpretation
Islam: Africa
Islam: Sunni
Islamic Science

Jainism
Japanese Philosophy, Japanese Thought
Jihad
Justice: Overview
Justice: Justice in American Thought
Law, Islamic
Leadership
Liberalism
Liberation Theology
Life Cycle: Elders/Old Age
Literary Criticism
Maoism
Maps and the Ideas They Express
Marriage and Fertility, European Views
Marxism: Overview
Marxism: Asia
Marxism: Latin America
Mathematics
Migration: Africa
Migration: Migration in World History
Migration: United States
Minority
Modernity: Africa
Modernity: East Asia
Modernization
Modernization Theory
Motherhood and Maternity
Nationalism: Africa
Native Policy
Naturalism
Neocolonialism
Neoliberalism
Nomadism
Nuclear Age
Occidentalism
Orthopraxy: Asia
Pan-Africanism
Pan-Asianism
Parties, Political
Peasants and Peasantry
Philanthropy
Philosophies: American
Philosophy, History of
Political Protest, U.S.
Political Science
Population
Populism: Latin America
Populism: United States
Postcolonial Studies
Poverty
Practices
Pre-Columbian Civilization
Presentism
Privacy
Privatization
Probability
Progress, Idea of
Property
Protest, Political
Pseudoscience
Public Sphere
Punishment
Puritanism
Race and Racism: United States
Radicals/Radicalism

Reason, Practical and Theoretical
Reform: Europe and the United States
Religion and the State: Africa
Religion and the State: Latin America
Renaissance
Representation: Political Representation
Republicanism: Republic
Resistance
Resistance and Accommodation
Responsibility
Ritual: Public Ritual
Ritual: Religion
Scarcity and Abundance, Latin America
Secularization and Secularism
Segregation
Sexual Harassment
Sexuality: Islamic Views
Slavery
Social Capital
Social Darwinism
Social History, U.S.
Socialism
Sport
State, The: Overview
State, The: The Postcolonial State
Technology
Terrorism, Middle East
Third Cinema
Third World
Third World Literature
Time: China
Time: Traditional and Utilitarian
Totalitarianism
Trade
Translation
Travel: Travel from Europe and the Middle East
Treaty
Untouchability: Taboos
Utilitarianism
Victorianism
Visual Culture
Volunteerism, U.S.
War and Peace in the Arts
Wealth
Westernization: Africa
Westernization: Middle East
Westernization: Southeast Asia
Women and Femininity in U.S. Popular Culture
Women's History: Africa
Work
World Systems Theory, Latin America
Zen
Zionism
GEOGRAPHY
Africa, Idea of
America
Anthropology
Architecture: Overview
Barbarism and Civilization
Borders, Borderlands, and Frontiers, Global
Capitalism: Overview
Chinese Warlordism
Cultural Studies
Diffusion, Cultural
Economics

Environment
Environmental History
Ethnicity and Race: Anthropology
Ethnicity and Race: Islamic Views
Eurocentrism
Feudalism, European
Geography
Ghetto
Globalization: Asia
Globalization: General
History, Economic
History, Idea of
Identity, Multiple: Jewish Multiple Identity
Islamic Science
Maps and the Ideas They Express
Mathematics
Migration: Africa
Migration: Migration in World History
Migration: United States
Minority
Nation
Nationalism: Africa
Natural History
Nomadism
Occidentalism
Orientalism: Overview
Pan-Africanism
Pan-Asianism
Perspective
Population
Privacy
Race and Racism: Asia
Race and Racism: United States
Regions and Regionalism, Eastern Europe
Religion: Indigenous Peoples' View, South America
Sacred Places
Scarcity and Abundance, Latin America
Third Cinema
Third World
Travel: Travel from Europe and the Middle East
Victorianism
Westernization: Southeast Asia
World Systems Theory, Latin America

Harmony
Hierarchy and Order
Hinduism
Humanism: Chinese Conception of
Humanity: African Thought
Ideas, History of
Lysenkoism
Magic
Manichaeism
Medicine: China
Medicine: India
Metaphysics: Ancient and Medieval
Mysticism: Chinese Mysticism
Myth
Natural Theology
Naturphilosophie
Organicism
Paradigm
Person, Idea of the
Philosophies: Islamic
Philosophy: Historical Overview and Recent Developments
Philosophy of Religion
Phrenology
Pseudoscience
Race and Racism: Europe
Race and Racism: United States
Religion: Indigenous Peoples' View, South America
Religion and Science
Ritual: Religion
Sacred Places
Science: East Asia
Segregation
Sexuality: Sexual Orientation
Slavery
Superstition
Syncretism
Time: China
Time: India
Untouchability: Menstrual Taboos
Witchcraft
Yin and Yang

Sciences

HISTORY OF SCIENCE, EARLY (entries focused on early ideas about nature and the human relationship with nature)
Alchemy: China
Alchemy: Europe and the Middle East
Anthropology
Aristotelianism
Asceticism: Hindu and Buddhist Asceticism
Astrology: Overview
Astrology: China
Astronomy, Pre-Columbian and Latin American
Change
Confucianism
Consciousness: Chinese Thought
Cosmology: Asia
Daoism
Ethnicity and Race: Africa
Ethnicity and Race: Anthropology
Ethnicity and Race: Islamic Views
Greek Science

HISTORY OF SCIENCE, MODERN AND CONTEMPORARY (entries focused on the origins of modern or contemporary ideas in the physical, chemical, biological, mathematical, or earth sciences)
Agnosticism
Algebras
Behaviorism
Body, The
Calendar
Cartesianism
Causation
Causation in East Asian and Southeast Asian Philosophy
Chemistry
Communication of Ideas: Middle East and Abroad
Computer Science
Context
Continental Philosophy
Cosmology: Cosmology and Astronomy
Creationism
Creativity in the Arts and Sciences
Cultural History
Demonology
Determinism

Development
Ecology
Education: Islamic Education
Empiricism
Enlightenment
Environment
Environmental History
Epistemology: Early Modern
Equality: Racial Equality
Everyday Life
Experiment
Falsifiability
Free Will, Determinism, and Predestination
Health and Disease
History, Economic
Idealism
Islamic Science
Kantianism
Knowledge
Life
Linguistic Turn
Mathematics
Mechanical Philosophy
Medicine: Europe and the United States
Medicine: Islamic Medicine
Metaphor
Museums
Nature
Newtonianism
Nuclear Age
Objectivity
Philosophies: African
Philosophies: Feminist, Twentieth-Century
Philosophy, History of
Philosophy of Mind: Overview
Philosophy of Mind: Ancient and Medieval
Physics
Platonism
Poetry and Poetics
Positivism
Prehistory, Rise of
Probability
Progress, Idea of
Pythagoreanism
Quantum
Race and Racism: Asia
Rationalism
Reason, Practical and Theoretical
Reflexivity
Reform: Europe and the United States
Relativity
Renaissance
Scholasticism
Science: Overview
Science, History of
Scientific Revolution
Sexuality: Overview
Social Darwinism
Social History, U.S.
Technology
Victorianism
Visual Order to Organizing Collections
PSYCHOLOGY
Absolute Music
Aesthetics: Asia

Aesthetics: Europe and the Americas
Alchemy: Europe and the Middle East
Alienation
Altruism
Ambiguity
Ancestor Worship
Animism
Anthropology
Anti-Semitism: Overview
Asceticism: Hindu and Buddhist Asceticism
Asceticism: Western Asceticism
Authoritarianism: East Asia
Beauty and Ugliness
Behaviorism
Bioethics
Biography
Biology
Body, The
Buddhism
Cartesianism
Character
Cinema
Communitarianism in African Thought
Composition, Musical
Computer Science
Consciousness: Overview
Consciousness: Chinese Thought
Consciousness: Indian Thought
Consumerism
Context
Continental Philosophy
Creativity in the Arts and Sciences
Cultural Studies
Dada
Dance
Daoism
Death
Demonology
Determinism
Diffusion, Cultural
Discrimination
Dream
Emotions
Empiricism
Epistemology: Early Modern
Epistemology: Modern
Ethnicity and Race: Africa
Eugenics
Everyday Life
Existentialism
Feminism: Overview
Fetishism: Overview
Fetishism: Fetishism in Literature and Cultural Studies
Form, Metaphysical, in Ancient and Medieval Thought
Foundationalism
Friendship
Gay Studies
Gender: Overview
Gender: Gender in the Middle East
Gender in Art
Gender Studies: Anthropology
Gesture
Harmony
Hate
Health and Disease

Heaven and Hell
Hinduism
Humanism: Secular Humanism in the United States
Humanity: African Thought
Humanity: European Thought
Identity: Identity of Persons
Identity: Personal and Social Identity
Identity, Multiple: Overview
Identity, Multiple: Asian-Americans
Images, Icons, and Idols
Imagination
Immortality and the Afterlife
Impressionism
Indigenismo
Intentionality
Jainism
Jouissance
Kinship
Knowledge
Language and Linguistics
Learning and Memory, Contemporary Views
Life
Life Cycle: Elders/Old Age
Literary Criticism
Love, Western Notions of
Machismo
Magic
Manichaeism
Masks
Medicine: China
Medicine: Europe and the United States
Meditation: Eastern Meditation
Memory
Men and Masculinity
Metaphor
Metaphysics: Renaissance to the Present
Mind
Modernism: Overview
Modernity: Overview
Modernity: Africa
Modernity: East Asia
Monarchy: Overview
Monism
Motherhood and Maternity
Musical Performance and Audiences
Mysticism: Chinese Mysticism
Mysticism: Islamic Mysticism in Asia
Myth
Narrative
National History
Nationalism: Overview
Naturphilosophie
Negritude
Objectivity
Person, Idea of the
Personhood in African Thought
Philosophies: Islamic
Philosophy, Moral: Modern
Philosophy of Mind: Overview
Philosophy of Mind: Ancient and Medieval
Philosophy of Religion
Phrenology
Political Science
Prejudice
Presentism

Privacy
Probability
Progress, Idea of
Protest, Political
Psychoanalysis
Psychology and Psychiatry
Punishment
Queer Theory
Realism: Africa
Reflexivity
Religion: Africa
Religion: African Diaspora
Religion: Indigenous Peoples' View, South America
Religion: Latin America
Religion and Science
Representation: Mental Representation
Resistance and Accommodation
Responsibility
Ritual: Public Ritual
Sexuality: Overview
Sexuality: Sexual Orientation
Slavery
State of Nature
Structuralism and Poststructuralism: Overview
Subjectivism
Superstition
Surrealism
Symbolism
Syncretism
Temperance
Text/Textuality
Third Cinema
Toleration
Totalitarianism
Tragedy and Comedy
Untouchability: Menstrual Taboos
Untouchability: Taboos
Utilitarianism
War and Peace in the Arts
Witchcraft
Witchcraft, African Studies of
Womanism
Women and Femininity in U.S. Popular Culture
BIOLOGICAL SCIENCES
Agnosticism
Altruism
Ancestor Worship
Anthropology
Antifeminism
Asceticism: Hindu and Buddhist Asceticism
Asceticism: Western Asceticism
Beauty and Ugliness
Behaviorism
Bioethics
Biology
Body, The
Buddhism
Cannibalism
Cartesianism
Casuistry
Classification of Arts and Sciences, Early Modern
Composition, Musical
Computer Science
Consciousness: Overview
Consilience

Creationism
Critical Race Theory
Death
Demography
Determinism
Development
Dystopia
Ecology
Emotions
Environmental Ethics
Environmental History
Epistemology: Early Modern
Equality: Racial Equality
Ethnohistory, U.S.
Eugenics
Evolution
Family: Modernist Anthropological Theory
Family: Family in Anthropology since 1980
Family Planning
Feminism: Overview
Game Theory
Garden
Gender: Overview
Gender: Gender in the Middle East
Gender in Art
Gender Studies: Anthropology
Genetics: Contemporary
Genetics: History of
Genocide
Gesture
Greek Science
Health and Disease
Heaven and Hell
History, Idea of
Humanism: Secular Humanism in the United States
Humanity: African Thought
Hygiene
Identity: Identity of Persons
Immortality and the Afterlife
Intentionality
Islamic Science
Jainism
Jouissance
Kinship
Learning and Memory, Contemporary Views
Life
Life Cycle: Adolescence
Life Cycle: Elders/Old Age
Lysenkoism
Machiavellism
Marriage and Fertility, European Views
Masks
Materialism in Eighteenth-Century European Thought
Mechanical Philosophy
Medicine: China
Medicine: Europe and the United States
Medicine: Islamic Medicine
Meme
Memory
Men and Masculinity
Mestizaje
Monarchy: Overview
Motherhood and Maternity
Musical Performance and Audiences
Natural History

Naturalism
Natural Theology
Nature
Naturphilosophie
Negritude
Organicism
Other, The, European Views of
Periodization of the Arts
Person, Idea of the
Perspective
Philosophies: Islamic
Philosophy of Mind: Ancient and Medieval
Phrenology
Population
Prehistory, Rise of
Probability
Progress, Idea of
Psychoanalysis
Psychology and Psychiatry
Punishment
Queer Theory
Religion: Indigenous Peoples' View, South America
Representation: Mental Representation
Science: East Asia
Science, History of
Sexuality: Overview
Sexuality: Sexual Orientation
Sociability in African Thought
Social Darwinism
Sport
State of Nature
Subjectivism
Superstition
Temperance
Terror
Text/Textuality
Totems
Untouchability: Menstrual Taboos
Utilitarianism
Victorianism
Visual Order to Organizing Collections
War and Peace in the Arts
Wildlife
Women and Femininity in U.S. Popular Culture
PHYSICAL SCIENCES
Agnosticism
Alchemy: China
Astrology: China
Astronomy, Pre-Columbian and Latin American
Calculation and Computation
Calendar
Causality
Causation
Causation in East Asian and Southeast Asian Philoso-
  phy
Change
Chemistry
Classification of Arts and Sciences, Early Modern
Computer Science
Consciousness: Overview
Consilience
Cosmology: Asia
Cosmology: Cosmology and Astronomy
Creationism
Cycles

Ecology
Empiricism
Environmental Ethics
Environmental History
Epistemology: Early Modern
Ethnohistory, U.S.
Experiment
Falsifiability
Field Theories
Form, Metaphysical, in Ancient and Medieval Thought
Geography
Geometry
Greek Science
Harmony
Hinduism
History, Economic
Islam: Sunni
Islamic Science
Japanese Philosophy, Japanese Thought
Knowledge
Language, Philosophy of: Modern
Life
Literary History
Logic and Philosophy of Mathematics, Modern
Maps and the Ideas They Express
Materialism in Eighteenth-Century European Thought
Mathematics
Mechanical Philosophy
Metaphysics: Renaissance to the Present
Microcosm and Macrocosm
Monism
Myth
Natural Theology
Naturalism
Nature
Naturphilosophie
Newtonianism
Nuclear Age
Paradigm
Periodization of the Arts
Philosophies: Islamic
Philosophy: Historical Overview and Recent Developments
Philosophy, History of
Physics
Positivism
Power
Pragmatism
Probability
Progress, Idea of
Psychoanalysis
Pythagoreanism
Quantum
Rationalism
Realism: Africa
Reason, Practical and Theoretical
Relativity
Religion: East and Southeast Asia
Religion: Indigenous Peoples' View, South America
Religion and Science
Science: Overview
Science: East Asia
Science, History of
Scientific Revolution
Sophists, The

Stoicism
Subjectivism
Superstition
Time: China
Time: India
Victorianism

ECOLOGY AND GEOLOGY
Aesthetics: Asia
Anthropology
Architecture: Overview
Architecture: Asia
Astronomy, Pre-Columbian and Latin American
Authoritarianism: Overview
Bioethics
Biology
Borders, Borderlands, and Frontiers, Global
Calendar
Capitalism: Overview
City, The: Latin America
City, The: The City as a Cultural Center
City, The: The Islamic and Byzantine City
Creationism
Death
Dystopia
Ecology
Education: Global Education
Environment
Environmental Ethics
Environmental History
Evolution
Feminism: Overview
Garden
Genetics: Contemporary
Genetics: History of
Genocide
Geography
History, Economic
History, Idea of
Hygiene
Impressionism
Landscape in the Arts
Life
Life Cycle: Elders/Old Age
Lysenkoism
Machiavellism
Maps and the Ideas They Express
Matriarchy
Medicine: Islamic Medicine
Memory
Migration: Migration in World History
Natural History
Nuclear Age
Organicism
Periodization of the Arts
Political Protest, U.S.
Prehistory, Rise of
Presentism
Protest, Political
Religion: Latin America
Ritual: Religion
Scarcity and Abundance, Latin America
Science, History of
Social Darwinism
Totems
Untouchability: Menstrual Taboos

Utopia
Visual Order to Organizing Collections
Wildlife
Witchcraft
Witchcraft, African Studies of
World Systems Theory, Latin America
CHEMISTRY
  Alchemy: China
  Alchemy: Europe and the Middle East
  Biology
  Chemistry
  Classification of Arts and Sciences, Early Modern
  Computer Science
  Consciousness: Overview
  Development
  Experiment
  Genetics: Contemporary
  Genetics: History of
  Health and Disease
  Islamic Science
  Life
  Materialism in Eighteenth-Century European Thought
  Mechanical Philosophy
  Medicine: Europe and the United States
  Mysticism: Chinese Mysticism
  Paradigm
  Philosophies: Islamic
  Physics
  Quantum
  Science: East Asia
  Science, History of
MATHEMATICS
  Absolute Music
  Aesthetics: Europe and the Americas
  Algebras
  Analytical Philosophy
  Astronomy, Pre-Columbian and Latin American
  Beauty and Ugliness
  Calculation and Computation
  Causation
  Causation in East Asian and Southeast Asian Philosophy
  Chemistry
  Classification of Arts and Sciences, Early Modern
  Computer Science
  Cosmology: Cosmology and Astronomy
  Death
  Demography
  Economics
  Empiricism
  Environmental History
  Equality: Overview
  Experiment
  Fallacy, Logical
  Falsifiability
  Foundationalism
  Futurology
  Game Theory
  Generation
  Genetics: Contemporary
  Genetics: History of
  Genocide
  Geometry
  Harmony
  History, Economic
  Humanism: Chinese Conception of

Islamic Science
Knowledge
Language, Philosophy of: Ancient and Medieval
Language, Philosophy of: Modern
Language and Linguistics
Logic and Philosophy of Mathematics, Modern
Mathematics
Newtonianism
Perspective
Philosophies: Islamic
Philosophy: Historical Overview and Recent Developments
Physics
Political Science
Positivism
Prejudice
Probability
Pythagoreanism
Quantum
Rationalism
Reading
Reason, Practical and Theoretical
Relativism
Relativity
Representation: Mental Representation
Scientific Revolution
Social History, U.S.
Sophists, The
Truth
COMPUTER SCIENCE
  Calculation and Computation
  Computer Science
  Consciousness: Overview
  Futurology
  Game Theory
  Genetics: Contemporary
  Genetics: History of
  Geography
  History, Economic
  Interdisciplinarity
  Language and Linguistics
  Learning and Memory, Contemporary Views
  Maps and the Ideas They Express
  Mathematics
  Privacy
  Probability
  Social History, U.S.
  Virtual Reality

Professions
  MEDICINE
    Alchemy: China
    Alchemy: Europe and the Middle East
    Americanization, U.S.
    Ancestor Worship
    Anthropology
    Asceticism: Hindu and Buddhist Asceticism
    Asceticism: Western Asceticism
    Astrology: China
    Bioethics
    Biology
    Body, The
    Casuistry
    Chemistry
    Childhood and Child Rearing

Computer Science
Creativity in the Arts and Sciences
Death
Demography
Determinism
Diversity
Environment
Environmental History
Eugenics
Feminism: Overview
Feminism: Third World U.S. Movement
Gay Studies
Gender: Overview
Gender Studies: Anthropology
Genetics: Contemporary
Genetics: History of
Greek Science
Health and Disease
Hinduism
Humanity: African Thought
Humor
Hygiene
Iconography
Islam: Sunni
Islamic Science
Life
Life Cycle: Elders/Old Age
Literary Criticism
Magic
Mathematics
Medicine: China
Medicine: Europe and the United States
Medicine: India
Medicine: Islamic Medicine
Meditation: Eastern Meditation
Miracles
Motherhood and Maternity
Music, Anthropology of
Mysticism: Chinese Mysticism
Narrative
Naturphilosophie
Philosophies: Feminist, Twentieth-Century
Philosophies: Islamic
Phrenology
Population
Privacy
Psychoanalysis
Psychology and Psychiatry
Pythagoreanism
Queer Theory
Religion: Africa
Religion: African Diaspora
Religion: East and Southeast Asia
Religion: Indigenous Peoples' View, South America
Ritual: Religion
Science: East Asia
Science, History of
Sexuality: Overview
Skepticism
Superstition
University: Overview
Untouchability: Menstrual Taboos
Utilitarianism
Victorianism
Visual Culture

Visual Order to Organizing Collections
Volunteerism, U.S.
Westernization: Africa
Witchcraft
Women and Femininity in U.S. Popular Culture
Yin and Yang
LAW
Abolitionism
African-American Ideas
Altruism
Anticolonialism: Africa
Anticolonialism: Latin America
Anticolonialism: Southeast Asia
Antifeminism
Anti-Semitism: Islamic Anti-Semitism
Apartheid
Asian-American Ideas (Cultural Migration)
Assimilation
Authoritarianism: Overview
Authoritarianism: East Asia
Barbarism and Civilization
Bioethics
Black Consciousness
Cannibalism
Capitalism: Overview
Capitalism: Africa
Casuistry
Censorship
Citizenship: Overview
Citizenship: Cultural Citizenship
Citizenship: Naturalization
City, The: The Islamic and Byzantine City
Civil Disobedience
Civil Society: Europe and the United States
Colonialism: Southeast Asia
Consciousness: Chinese Thought
Constitutionalism
Context
Corruption in Developed and Developing Countries
Creationism
Critical Race Theory
Cultural History
Cultural Revivals
Deism
Democracy
Democracy: Africa
Dialogue and Dialectics: Socratic
Dialogue and Dialectics: Talmudic
Dictatorship in Latin America
Discrimination
Diversity
Education: Islamic Education
Empire and Imperialism: Overview
Empire and Imperialism: Europe
Empire and Imperialism: United States
Environmental History
Equality: Overview
Equality: Racial Equality
Ethnicity and Race: Anthropology
Ethnicity and Race: Islamic Views
Europe, Idea of
Extirpation
Fallacy, Logical
Falsifiability
Family Planning

Fascism
Feminism: Overview
Feminism: Africa and African Diaspora
Feminism: Islamic Feminism
Feudalism, European
Gender: Gender in the Middle East
General Will
Genetics: Contemporary
Genetics: History of
Genocide
Ghetto
Globalization: Africa
Good
Hate
Heresy and Apostasy
Hinduism
Honor, Middle Eastern Notions of
Human Rights: Overview
Humanism: Secular Humanism in the United States
Iconography
Identity, Multiple: Jewish Multiple Identity
Indigenismo
Individualism
Intentionality
Interdisciplinarity
International Order
Islam: Africa
Islam: Shii
Islam: Southeast Asia
Islam: Sunni
Jihad
Judaism: Judaism to 1800
Justice: Overview
Justice: Justice in American Thought
Justice: Justice in East Asian Thought
Kinship
Language and Linguistics
Law
Law, Islamic
Learning and Memory, Contemporary Views
Legalism, Ancient China
Liberalism
Liberty
Life Cycle: Elders/Old Age
Literary Criticism
Loyalties, Dual
Marriage and Fertility, European Views
Masks
Matriarchy
Migration: United States
Minority
Modernity: Overview
Monarchy: Overview
Monarchy: Islamic Monarchy
Motherhood and Maternity
Mysticism: Islamic Mysticism
Narrative
Nation
Nationalism: Cultural Nationalism
Nationalism: Middle East
Native Policy
Natural Law
Nonviolence
Nuclear Age
Obligation

Person, Idea of the
Philanthropy
Philosophies: American
Philosophies: Feminist, Twentieth-Century
Philosophies: Islamic
Philosophy: Historical Overview and Recent Developments
Philosophy, Moral: Ancient
Political Protest, U.S.
Population
Postcolonial Studies
Power
Privacy
Progress, Idea of
Property
Protest, Political
Punishment
Queer Theory
Race and Racism: United States
Reason, Practical and Theoretical
Reform: Europe and the United States
Regions and Regionalism, Eastern Europe
Relativism
Religion: African Diaspora
Religion: Middle East
Religion and the State: Africa
Religion and the State: Europe
Religion and the State: Middle East
Religion and the State: United States
Representation: Political Representation
Republicanism: Republic
Resistance
Responsibility
Rhetoric: Ancient and Medieval
Ritual: Public Ritual
Sacred Texts: Koran
Segregation
Sexual Harassment
Sexuality: Overview
Sexuality: Islamic Views
Sexuality: Sexual Orientation
Skepticism
Slavery
Sociability in African Thought
Social Contract
Socialisms, African
Society
State, The: Overview
State, The: The Postcolonial State
State of Nature
Stoicism
Subjectivism
Sufism
Suicide
Temperance
Toleration
Totalitarianism
Treaty
University: Overview
Untouchability: Taboos
Utilitarianism
Victorianism
Virtue Ethics
Visual Order to Organizing Collections
Volunteerism, U.S.
War and Peace in the Arts

Westernization: Africa
Westernization: Middle East
Westernization: Southeast Asia
Wildlife
Witchcraft
ENGINEERING
Alchemy: China
Alchemy: Europe and the Middle East
Architecture: Overview
Architecture: Africa
Architecture: Asia
Beauty and Ugliness
Biology
Calculation and Computation
Capitalism: Overview
Capitalism: Africa
Cinema
City, The: Latin America
City, The: The City as a Cultural Center
City, The: The City as Political Center
City, The: The Islamic and Byzantine City
Communication of Ideas: Southeast Asia
Computer Science
Diffusion, Cultural
Dystopia
Ecology
Empire and Imperialism: Europe
Environmental History
Epistemology: Early Modern
Experiment
Futurology
Gender Studies: Anthropology
Genetics: Contemporary
Genetics: History of
Genocide
Geometry
Globalization: General
Greek Science
Harmony
Historical and Dialectical Materialism
History, Economic
Humanism: Secular Humanism in the United States
Interdisciplinarity
Japanese Philosophy, Japanese Thought
Knowledge
Literary Criticism
Maps and the Ideas They Express
Mathematics
Mechanical Philosophy
Meme
Modernity: Overview
Modernity: Africa
Modernity: East Asia
Modernization
Modernization Theory
Motherhood and Maternity
Music, Anthropology of
Musical Performance and Audiences
Mysticism: Chinese Mysticism
Newtonianism
Nomadism
Nuclear Age
Occidentalism
Perspective
Power

Presentism
Privacy
Progress, Idea of
Protest, Political
Reform: Europe and the United States
Relativity
Science, History of
Science Fiction
Technology
Textiles and Fiber Arts as Catalysts for Ideas
Totalitarianism
Victorianism
Virtual Reality
Visual Culture
War and Peace in the Arts
Westernization: Middle East
Westernization: Southeast Asia
World Systems Theory, Latin America

Multidisciplinary Practices

The *New Dictionary of the History of Ideas* has many entries that discuss the methods by which scholars and researchers pursue knowledge. The entries below discuss approaches, methods, and practices that have influenced many disciplines.

ENTRIES ON MULTIDISCIPLINARY PRACTICES
THAT ORIGINATED IN ANCIENT TIMES
Aesthetics: Asia
Africa, Idea of
Algebras
Anthropology
Architecture: Overview
Architecture: Asia
Aristotelianism
Astrology: Overview
Biology
Body, The
Buddhism
Casuistry
Causality
Censorship
Classicism
Classification of Arts and Sciences, Early Modern
Composition, Musical
Cosmology: Asia
Creationism
Creativity in the Arts and Sciences
Daoism
Development
Dialogue and Dialectics: Socratic
Dualism
Eclecticism
Education: China
Education: Europe
Epistemology: Ancient
Equality: Overview
Essentialism
Eurocentrism
Experiment
Fallacy, Logical
Fetishism: Fetishism in Literature and Cultural Studies
Form, Metaphysical, in Ancient and Medieval Thought
Fundamentalism
Gender in Art
Genre

Geometry
Greek Science
Harmony
Health and Disease
Hierarchy and Order
Hinduism
History, Idea of
Humanism: Europe and the Middle East
Humor
Ideas, History of
Imagination
Interpretation
Knowledge
Language, Philosophy of: Ancient and Medieval
Life
Literary History
Literature: African Literature
Logic
Maps and the Ideas They Express
Mathematics
Medicine: China
Medicine: Europe and the United States
Medicine: India
Memory
Metaphor
Metaphysics: Ancient and Medieval
Monism
Museums
Music, Anthropology of
Musical Performance and Audiences
Mysticism: Chinese Mysticism
Narrative
Nature
Orthodoxy
Orthopraxy: Asia
Orthopraxy: Western Orthopraxy
Paradigm
Periodization
Perspective
Philosophies: African
Philosophies: Islamic
Philosophy: Historical Overview and Recent Develop-
     ments
Philosophy and Religion in Western Thought
Physics
Platonism
Presentism
Progress, Idea of
Pythagoreanism
Rationalism
Reading
Reason, Practical and Theoretical
Religion: Overview
Responsibility
Rhetoric: Overview
Rhetoric: Ancient and Medieval
Sacred Places
Sacred Texts: Asia
Science: East Asia
Scientific Revolution
Skepticism
Sophists, The
Syncretism
Taste
Text/Textuality

Toleration
Translation
Trope
Truth
Virtual Reality
Wisdom, Human
Yin and Yang

ENTRIES ON MULTIDISCIPLINARY PRACTICES OF
   MORE RECENT ORIGIN
Absolute Music
Aesthetics: Africa
African-American Ideas
Afrocentricity
Analytical Philosophy
Astronomy, Pre-Columbian and Latin American
Avant-Garde: Militancy
Behaviorism
Bilingualism and Multilingualism
Bioethics
Black Atlantic
Calculation and Computation
Class
Conservatism
Consilience
Continental Philosophy
Critical Race Theory
Critical Theory
Cultural Studies
Dada
Dialogue and Dialectics: Talmudic
Dream
Dystopia
Economics
Education: Global Education
Education: Islamic Education
Empiricism
Encyclopedism
Environmental Ethics
Environmental History
Epistemology: Early Modern
Epistemology: Modern
Ethnicity and Race: Anthropology
Ethnocentrism
Ethnography
Ethnohistory, U.S.
Examination Systems, China
Expressionism
Family: Modernist Anthropological Theory
Feminism: Overview
Fetishism: Overview
Field Theories
Formalism
Futurology
Game Theory
Gender: Gender in the Middle East
Generation
Genetics: Contemporary
Genetics: History of
Geography
Hegelianism
Hermeneutics
Historicism
Humanism: Africa
Humanism: Renaissance
Iconography

Idealism
Identity: Identity of Persons
Intentionality
Interdisciplinarity
Japanese Philosophy, Japanese Thought
Language, Philosophy of: Modern
Language and Linguistics
Law, Islamic
Learning and Memory, Contemporary Views
Linguistic Turn
Literary Criticism
Logic and Philosophy of Mathematics, Modern
Masks
Metaphysics: Renaissance to the Present
Mind
Modernism: Overview
Modernism: Latin America
Modernization
Modernization Theory
Motif: Motif in Literature
Motif: Motif in Music
Mysticism: Kabbalah
Myth
Naturalism
Naturalism in Art and Literature
Naturphilosophie
Newtonianism
Objectivity
Oral Traditions: Overview
Orientalism: Overview
Philosophies: Feminist, Twentieth-Century
Philosophy, Moral: Africa
Philosophy of Religion
Phrenology
Poetry and Poetics
Polytheism
Positivism
Postcolonial Studies
Postmodernism
Power
Practices
Pragmatism
Prejudice
Probability
Pseudoscience
Psychoanalysis
Queer Theory
Realism
Realism: Africa
Reflexivity
Regions and Regionalism, Eastern Europe
Relativism
Relativity
Religion: Indigenous Peoples' View, South America
Religion and Science
Representation: Mental Representation
Romanticism in Literature and Politics
Sacred Texts: Koran
Sage Philosophy
Scholasticism
Science: Overview
Science, History of
Science Fiction
Secularization and Secularism
Social Capital

Social History, U.S.
State, The: Overview
Structuralism and Poststructuralism: Overview
Structuralism and Poststructuralism: Anthropology
Subjectivism
Symbolism
Third Cinema
Totems
Tradition
Universalism
Utilitarianism
Visual Culture
Volksgeist
Women's Studies

Especially Interdisciplinary Entries

The most interdisciplinary entries synthesized knowledge by using the methods and focusing on the topics of practitioners of several disciplines. Very few entries listed below are in only one division. Common pairs for the history of ideas are social sciences and humanities, social sciences and sciences, and humanities and sciences. In the early twenty-first century there is generally a recognition of the common overlap of the social sciences with the humanities; social scientists may take ethical and literary factors into consideration and humanists may incorporate societal contexts into their work. The presence of psychology in the sciences, as well as the quantitative nature of some social sciences work, creates an overlap of social sciences with sciences. Another interesting overlap is between humanities and sciences—topics that in antiquity were treated as philosophy or religion are now investigated by those following scientific methods.

SOCIAL SCIENCES, SCIENCES, AND FINE ARTS
  Architecture: Africa
  Geography
  Phrenology
  Virtual Reality
SCIENCES, FINE ARTS, AND HUMANITIES
  Enlightenment
  Epistemology: Early Modern
  Feminism: Third World U.S. Movement
  Field Theories
  Geometry
  Globalization: Asia
  Text/Textuality
FINE ARTS, HUMANITIES, AND SOCIAL SCIENCES
  Aesthetics: Africa
  Alienation
  Americanization, U.S.
  Anticolonialism: Africa
  Arts: Overview
  Arts: Africa
  Authenticity: Africa
  Autobiography
  Avant-Garde: Overview
  Aztlán
  Censorship
  Chinese Thought
  City, The: The Islamic and Byzantine City
  Civil Disobedience
  Civil Society: Europe and the United States
  Colonialism: Southeast Asia
  Communication of Ideas: Africa and Its Influence
  Communication of Ideas: The Americas and Their Influence

Communication of Ideas: Asia and Its Influence
Communication of Ideas: Orality and Advent of Writing
Cultural Capital
Cultural History
Cynicism
Dialogue and Dialectics: Socratic
Dialogue and Dialectics: Talmudic
Diasporas: Jewish Diaspora
Dictatorship in Latin America
Etiquette
Everyday Life
Expressionism
Extirpation
Fascism
Feminism: Chicana Feminisms
Gay Studies
Gender Studies: Anthropology
Genre
Ghetto
Honor
Humanity in the Arts
Humor
Identity, Multiple: Jewish Multiple Identity
Images, Icons, and Idols
Islam: Shii
Landscape in the Arts
Leadership
Life Cycle: Overview
Linguistic Turn
Literature: African Literature
Maoism
Millenarianism: Islamic
Millenarianism: Latin America and Native North
    America
Minority
Modernism: Latin America
Musicology
Mysticism: Christian Mysticism
Mysticism: Islamic Mysticism in Asia
Mysticism: Kabbalah
Mysticism: Mysticism in African Thought
Nation
New Criticism
Nude, The
Oral Traditions: Overview
Orientalism: Overview
Orthodoxy
Orthopraxy: Asia
Pan-Africanism
Pan-Asianism
Pan-Turkism
Philosophies: African
Philosophies: American
Philosophy, Moral: Ancient
Populism: United States
Postmodernism
Practices
Pre-Columbian Civilization
Realism
Religion: Africa
Religion: Middle East
Religion and the State: United States
Renaissance
Resistance

Romanticism in Literature and Politics
Sage Philosophy
Shinto
Society
Taste
Theater and Performance
Theodicy
Third World Literature
Wisdom, Human
HUMANITIES, SOCIAL SCIENCES, AND SCIENCES
Afropessimism
Alchemy: China
Alchemy: Europe and the Middle East
Altruism
Antifeminism
Asceticism: Hindu and Buddhist Asceticism
Asceticism: Western Asceticism
Astrology: China
Astrology: Overview
Borders, Borderlands, and Frontiers, Global
Calculation and Computation
Calendar
Capitalism: Overview
Capitalism: Africa
Cartesianism
Casuistry
Causality
Causation
Causation in East Asian and Southeast Asian Philosophy
Character
Chicano Movement
Childhood and Child Rearing
Confucianism
Consciousness: Chinese Thought
Consciousness: Indian Thought
Consilience
Cosmology: Asia
Cycles
Daoism
Demography
Demonology
Discrimination
Dress
Dualism
Education: Islamic Education
Empiricism
Equality: Racial Equality
Ethnicity and Race: Africa
Ethnohistory, U.S.
Fallacy, Logical
Foundationalism
Futurology
Genetics: Contemporary
Genetics: History of
Genocide
Health and Disease
Hermeneutics
Historical and Dialectical Materialism
Hygiene
Intelligentsia
Internal Colonialism
Islam: Africa
Jainism
Japanese Philosophy, Japanese Thought
Kinship

Law, Islamic
Machiavellism
Machismo
Medicine: China
Medicine: India
Meme
Memory
Mestizaje
Modernization Theory
Motif: Motif in Music
Museums
Music, Anthropology of
Nationalism: Africa
Natural History
Naturalism
Negritude
Objectivity
Philosophy, History of
Philosophy, Moral: Modern
Philosophy of Religion
Population
Positivism
Pragmatism
Prejudice
Presentism
Privacy
Probability
Quantum
Race and Racism: Overview
Race and Racism: Asia
Race and Racism: Europe
Reason, Practical and Theoretical
Religion: Overview
Religion and Science
Science: Overview
Scientific Revolution
Segregation
Sexuality: Islamic Views
Sexuality: Sexual Orientation
Skepticism
State of Nature
Structuralism and Poststructuralism: Overview
Time: China
Time: India
Truth
Universalism
University: Overview
Wildlife
World Systems Theory, Latin America
FINE ARTS, HUMANITIES, SOCIAL SCIENCES, AND
SCIENCES
Absolute Music
Aesthetics: Asia
Aesthetics: Europe and the Americas
Ancestor Worship
Anthropology
Architecture: Overview
Architecture: Asia
Astronomy, Pre-Columbian and Latin American
Beauty and Ugliness
Bilingualism and Multilingualism
Bioethics
Body, The
Cannibalism
Change

Chemistry
Cinema
City, The: The City as a Cultural Center
City, The: The City as Political Center
Classification of Arts and Sciences, Early Modern
Communication of Ideas: Southeast Asia
Composition, Musical
Computer Science
Consciousness: Overview
Consumerism
Context
Continental Philosophy
Cosmopolitanism
Creationism
Critical Theory
Cultural Studies
Dance
Death
Determinism
Dream
Dystopia
Ecology
Emotions
Empire and Imperialism: Europe
Environment
Environmental Ethics
Environmental History
Equality: Overview
Equality: Gender Equality
Ethnicity and Race: Islamic Views
Eugenics
Examination Systems, China
Feminism: Overview
Fetishism: Overview
Fetishism: Fetishism in Literature and Cultural Studies
Friendship
Game Theory
Gender: Gender in the Middle East
Gender in Art
Generation
Greek Science
Harmony
Heaven and Hell
Hinduism
History, Economic
History, Idea of
Humanity: African Thought
Ideas, History of
Identity, Multiple: Overview
Intentionality
Interdisciplinarity
Islam: Sunni
Islamic Science
Kantianism
Knowledge
Language and Linguistics
Learning and Memory, Contemporary Views
Life
Literary Criticism
Literary History
Love, Western Notions of
Magic
Manichaeism
Maps and the Ideas They Express
Masks

Mathematics
Matriarchy
Medicine: Europe and the United States
Medicine: Islamic Medicine
Meditation: Eastern Meditation
Men and Masculinity
Metaphor
Modernism: Overview
Monarchy: Overview
Modernity: Africa
Modernity: East Asia
Motherhood and Maternity
Musical Performance and Audiences
Mysticism: Chinese Mysticism
Myth
Narrative
Newtonianism
Nomadism
Nuclear Age
Occidentalism
Organicism
Paradigm
Periodization of the Arts
Person, Idea of the
Philosophies: Feminist, Twentieth-Century
Philosophies: Islamic
Philosophy: Historical Overview and Recent Developments
Poetry and Poetics
Political Protest, U.S.
Progress, Idea of
Property
Protest, Political
Pseudoscience
Psychoanalysis
Punishment
Pythagoreanism
Queer Theory
Reading
Realism: Africa
Reflexivity
Reform: Europe and the United States
Relativism

Religion: East and Southeast Asia
Religion: Indigenous Peoples' View, South America
Religion: Latin America
Representation: Mental Representation
Resistance and Accommodation
Responsibility
Ritual: Public Ritual
Ritual: Religion
Sacred Places
Science: East Asia
Science, History of
Science Fiction
Sexuality: Overview
Social History, U.S.
Sophists, The
Sport
Stoicism
Subjectivism
Superstition
Surrealism
Symbolism
Syncretism
Temperance
Third Cinema
Toleration
Totalitarianism
Totems
Tragedy and Comedy
Untouchability: Menstrual Taboos
Untouchability: Taboos
Utilitarianism
Utopia
Victorianism
Visual Culture
Visual Order to Organizing Collections
Volunteerism, U.S.
War and Peace in the Arts
Westernization: Middle East
Westernization: Southeast Asia
Witchcraft
Witchcraft, African Studies of
Yin and Yang

CONTINUED

COMMUNICATION OF IDEAS.

This entry includes seven subentries:

Africa and Its Influence
The Americas and Their Influence
Asia and Its Influence
Europe and Its Influence
Middle East and Abroad
Orality and the Advent of Writing
Southeast Asia and Its Influence

AFRICA AND ITS INFLUENCE

The communication of ideas in and from Africa is characterized by enormous changes over time and variations among societies. Historically, as might be expected for such a large and ancient continent—the second largest in the world and the one where humanity originated—African societies have exhibited high levels of cultural diversity, uneven patterns of political and socioeconomic development, and different forms of engagement with other world regions. Africa is home to hundreds of cultural groups and languages that have influenced each other in complex ways. It has given rise to advanced societies, such as the ancient civilizations of Egypt and West Africa, which existed alongside simpler societies. Many parts of the continent in the northern and northeastern subregions, and later the western coastal regions, were integrated into extracontinental cultural and commercial traffic, while some parts in the interior were relatively isolated. It was in the zones of intensive intercultural communication that ideas from Africa were transmitted to the outside world and ideas from other regions entered Africa. Needless to say, modern African countries are at different stages of industrialization and development, and unequally integrated into the global circuits of ideas and information.

Understanding these disparities is crucial to analyzing and mapping out the changing processes and patterns in the communication of ideas in and from Africa. For one thing, it underscores the difficulty of, indeed the need to avoid, simple generalizations. The development and connections between the various modes of communication—oral, textual, visual, and performance—have manifested themselves in multiple ways across the continent at different times. Similarly diverse are the institutional forms, and their patterns of growth, through which ideas have been expressed, ranging from educational and religious institutions to civic and professional bodies and mass media outlets. As an interactive process, the communication of ideas has a spatial dynamic that entails not only the travel of the ideas themselves from one place to another through several media, but also their transmission by human agents who move and settle in different places.

In this context, for example, the conquest of Spain by the Moors from northwestern Africa, which they ruled for nearly eight centuries, was crucial to the diffusion of ideas from Africa and other parts of the ancient world to Western Europe. So was the forced migration of enslaved Africans across the Atlantic important for the spread of countless African ideas to the Americas. Likewise, European invasions of Africa, most crucially colonization (both the ancient Roman colonization of North Africa and the nineteenth-century European colonization of the continent as a whole), played a profound role in the spread of ideas from Europe, some of which were, as is true of Christianity, ideas that previous generations of African thinkers, such as the Egyptian Gnostics and St. Augustine from the Maghreb, had contributed to their development, and that the newly converted Africans proceeded to further transform. This back-and-forth process typifies the complex flows of ideas in world history and the dangers of ethnocentric claims of exclusive cultural authorship.

Orality and Performance

Looking at the span of human history in its entirety, orality clearly antedates literacy, so deciphering the origins and development of oral and textual forms of communication in Africa, and their relationships, is not an easy task. Many Africanists used to claim that Africa, by which they often meant "sub-Saharan Africa," was defined by oral modes of expression and communication before the intrusion of European influences from the fifteenth century and especially following colonization in the nineteenth. The contention that Africa was ontologically oral and Europe literary had both positive and negative implications. On the positive side, it led to the valorization of oral sources in reconstructions of African history and of oral narratives—what came to be known as oral literature, or orature—in African literature. On the negative side, it oversimplified both African histories and narrative traditions and reinforced the age-old analytical dichotomies in the conceptualization of African and European phenomena.

Undoubtedly, oral communication and traditions have been important modes of social dialogue and transmitting history in African societies for a long time. Oral traditions include oral narratives (epics, legends, and explanatory tales), poetry (praise poetry, chants, and songs), and epigrams (proverbs, riddles, puns, and tongue twisters). Combined, they served to link the past and the present, construct collective worldviews and identity, educate the youth, express political views, and provide entertainment and aesthetic pleasure. The production of oral traditions often involved performance based on a participatory ethic. In many societies, there were highly trained and esteemed custodians of oral tradition. Among the Mande of West Africa, for example, they were known as *griots,* a word that acquired popularity in the United States following the 1977 airing of the acclaimed television miniseries *Roots,* based on the 1976 book in which Haley reputedly traced his African ancestry to a village in the Gambia with the help of a griot.

From Thomas Hale's fascinating history, it is clear that griots had many other functions besides being genealogists. They were historians, advisers to rulers, patrons, and other members of society, spokespersons, diplomats, mediators, interpreters and translators, musicians, composers, teachers, exhorters, warriors, witnesses, praise-singers, and ceremony participants during namings, initiations, courtship, marriages, installations, and funerals. Griots first emerged at least a thousand years ago; since then their role has changed, and so have interpretations of their history in the oral accounts themselves and in written accounts by locals and outsiders. In more recent times, the griots have taken advantage of twentieth-century technologies including radio, television, audiocassettes, and CDs to spread their knowledge to new audiences locally and globally. Also, many griot epics, such as the renowned *Epic of Sundiata,* about the legendary king of the Mali Empire, have been committed to print. While the literature has mostly discussed male griots, recent scholarship has demonstrated that there were female griots, or *griottes,* as Hale refers to them.

The case of the griots demonstrates the intricate connections between orality and performance. As a medium for the construction, dissemination, and consumption of ideas, performance in the forms of drama and music and dance were particularly important in African societies. According to Modupe Olaogun, African drama dates back to ancient times and includes pantomimes, dance-drama, mask, shadow, and court theaters, heroic recitations, praise-poetry, and market comedy by itinerant troupes, which use, in various combinations and with different degrees of sophistication, role-playing, dialogue, mime, movement, dance, song, puppetry, costume, and scenic spectacle. In the late eighteenth century, African theater entered a new era as contacts with Europe increased and European theater motifs and practices were introduced, elements of which were creatively appropriated and used to further diversify African theatrical expression. Most important was the incorporation of scripted text and reorganization of theatrical space to separate performers and spectators. In Egypt, Ya'qub Sannu (1839–1912) founded modern Egyptian theater with distinct European influences.

Syncretized performances emerged. For example, the black township music theater of South Africa combined the indigenous dramatic modes of storytelling (the isiZulu's *ingoma* or the isiXhosa's *ntsomi*) with Western choral and vaudeville forms to create a popular theater, which from the 1930s became a powerful vehicle for antiapartheid resistance. In West Africa, where European settler influence was negligible, new theatrical practices were largely developed through educational institutions. In the 1920s, there emerged in countries such as Ghana

and Nigeria itinerant indigenous language theater. By the mid-twentieth century, European influences had waned and Africa's vibrant theater could be divided into distinct forms: literary, popular, and theater for development, each with its own styles, aesthetics, themes, messages, languages, and audiences.

Similarly, music as a mode of cultural production and communication underwent significant changes over the centuries. As with theater, different musical forms developed across the continent, depending on the performance contexts of location and audience, the nature of the performers (spontaneous groups, popular musicians, or specialized musicians), the instruments used (ranging from idiophones to membranophones including drums, aerophones, and chordophones), and their functions (whether entertainment, political, religious, and educational, work-related, or mnemonically to recall past events). According to Turino (2003), despite their obvious differences, music in African societies tended to share a participatory ethic rather than a presentational one (except for music specialists at royal courts), and music and dance were conceptualized as part of the same art form and as social processes rather than as set items or products.

Dance not only included music, but was a complex interactive affair involving movement, theater, sculpture, and religion, whose styles and organization served as social metaphors that communicated aesthetic preferences, issues of kinship, gender, status, and age. Different African societies influenced each other, and from the nineteenth century they began to feel European influences, not least missionary attacks against African dance as "lewd" or "lascivious." In the course of the twentieth century, numerous old dances were reconfigured and recontextualized and new ones emerged. In the 1950s and 1960s, formal dance companies and national dance ensembles practicing traditional dance were created in many countries. In the meantime, new dances such as highlife and rhumba had emerged in Africa's rapidly expanding cities. All this demonstrates, argues Oforiwaa, the continent's remarkable cultural flexibility, capability, and creativity.

Many of the new music and dance styles were adapted from the African diaspora in the Americas. Rhumba, for example, was an Afro-Cuban dance genre created by slaves after emancipation in the 1880s. While African music was exported to the Americas during the era of the Atlantic slave trade, where it was further developed and transformed, as cultural contacts between Africa and the African diaspora grew from the late nineteenth-century diasporan music—from jazz, rhumba, and reggae to pop music and hip hop—it was re-exported back to Africa, where it was reappropriated and converted. In the twentieth century, African music and dance became a powerful medium to express Pan-African, cosmopolitan, and nationalist consciousness, in addition to performing gender, class, and religious ideas and identities.

Written Communication
It is quite evident that African "traditional" cultures and modes of communication have demonstrated a capacity to use new communication technologies and, in the process, to transform both themselves and those technologies. This challenges many

of the simplistic generalizations and dichotomies about African cultural and intellectual history. Writing specifically about literacy and orality, Eileen Julien is critical of those who regard orality and writing as exclusive domains and successive moments in which the oral represents Africa's authentic expressive form. She argues that there is nothing intrinsically oral about Africa, that orality and writing have continually influenced each other for a long time, as Albert Gérard (1981) and Harold Scheub have shown in their exhaustive studies. This intertextuality can be seen in the works of contemporary African writers who deliberately appropriate oral forms to serve literary artistic ends.

Among the earliest African societies to develop writing as a method of recording and transmitting knowledge and information were Egypt, Nubia (whose Meroitic script [2nd century B.C.E.–5th century C.E.] has yet to be deciphered), and Ethiopia. In these early literary traditions, writing and reading were confined to a tiny religious and political elite. In Egypt, hieroglyphic writing began about 3000 B.C.E. The literature of the Old Kingdom (2650–2152 B.C.E.) was largely didactic, dominated by the "wisdom" genre. Literary genres multiplied during the Middle Kingdom (2040–1640 B.C.E.) to include more intricate literary forms such as novels, satires, and autobiographies, as well as political and social commentaries and philosophical discourses. During the New Kingdom (1539–1069 B.C.E.) a new literary genre emerged—the love poem—and writers began to abandon classical language and to write in the colloquial language of their time. Later, a new literature known as Demotic (meaning "of the people") developed, and, after large numbers of Egyptians had converted to Christianity, a Coptic literature emerged emphasizing religious themes.

Ethiopian writing (in a language called Ge'ez) began in about 500 B.C.E. It grew when the Kingdom of Axum became Christianized (c. 400 C.E.), following the conversion of King Ezana in 330 C.E. The Bible was translated from Greek into Ge'ez and other religious translations were produced. The "golden age" of Ge'ez literature, according to Gérard (1981), was between 1270 and 1520, during which both religious and secular writing flourished. Between 1314 and 1322, the clergy, in support of a new dynasty, wrote the *Kabra Nagast* (Glory of Kings), reportedly the most venerated book in Ethiopian history. Royal chronicles, in fact, were an important genre of Ethiopian writing until the beginning of the twentieth century. In the fifteenth century, local hagiographies began to appear as nationalist homage to the holy men of the Ethiopian Church. Ge'ez writing waned from the sixteenth century, to be followed three centuries later by the development of writing in Amharic, the commonly spoken language in Ethiopia, which flowered in the twentieth century, incorporating new literary and intellectual trends.

The Arab conquest of North Africa (661–750 C.E.) ushered in a new period in African political, religious, and cultural history. It brought Islam and the Arabic language and script, which altered the modes of communication of ideas and Africa's links to the wider world. Muslim North Africa gave the continent and the world its first universities, the mosque universities of Ez-Zitouna in Tunis (founded in 732),

Quaraouiyine in Fez (founded in 859), and Al-Azhar (founded in Cairo in 969). Lulat argues that these universities influenced the development of the modern European university, which acquired five elements from the Muslims: (1) a large corpus of knowledge; (2) rationalism and the secular investigative approach of natural science; (3) division of knowledge into academic subjects; (4) the notion of the university as a community of individual scholars; and (5) the idea of the college. He concludes that "the modern university that was brought to Africa by the colonial powers is as much Western in origin as it is Islamic" (p. 16).

North African intellectuals produced a vast body of scholarship in a wide range of fields, from the natural sciences to poetry and history, and some of the world's most renowned minds including Ibn Batuta of Tangier (1304?–1377?), the traveler who visited numerous countries in Asia, Europe, and Africa and wrote extensively on his explorations, and Ibn Khaldun of Tunis (1332–1406), the historian who pioneered secular history in his monumental *Kitab-al-'Ibar* (Universal History) and three-volume *Muqaddimah* (Introduction to History).

Through trans-Saharan trade, Islam spread from North Africa to West Africa, where it began to make significant inroads in the eleventh century. Centers of Islamic learning emerged, including the mosque university of Tombouctou established in the twelfth century, where numerous works were produced, such as *Ta'rikh al-Fattash* (Chronicle of the Researcher) and *Ta'rikh al-Sudan* (History of the Sudan), written by Mahmud Ka'ti (b. 1468) and Abd al-Rahman al-Sa'di (1596–1656), respectively. In addition to writing in Arabic, West African scholars also wrote in African languages using Arabic script, writings that are called *Ajami*. Examples include the *Kano Chronicle* and the *Gonja Chronicle,* produced in modern-day Ghana in the eighteenth century. Arabic and *ajami* writing flourished in nineteenth-century Hausaland. Usman dan Fodio (1754–1817), the leader of the Islamic reform movement that created the Sokoto Caliphate, the largest state in nineteenth-century West Africa, and his brother and daughter, wrote hundreds of books and treatises on law, theology, politics, finance, history, and poetry. Senegal also produced illustrious scholars and religious leaders, among them the legendary Amadou Bamba (1850–1927), whose works remain popular to this day.

Arabic and *ajami* writing also spread to the east African coast and Madagascar. Malagasy *ajami* writing was well established by the time the first Europeans arrived in the early seventeenth century, although it did not achieve the status it did in West Africa or among the Swahili along the east African coast. *Ajami* was gradually supplanted by Roman script from the 1820s as part of the Merina kingdom's (1787–1896) ambitious modernization drive. Swahili writing, whose origins have been dated to the thirteenth century (if not earlier), produced a vigorous literature, mostly poetry and historical chronicles, such as the sixteenth-century *Kilwa Chronicle*. Classical Swahili literature entered its golden age between the mid-eighteenth and mid-nineteenth centuries, during which the work of several writers stands out: Saiyid Abdallah b. Nassar (1720–1820), Muyaka bin Haji al-Ghassaniy (1776–1840), Muhyi 'l-Din

(1789–1869), and Umar b. Amin (1798–1870), who wrote religious and epic poetry. From the second half of the nineteenth century, Swahili writing was confronted with a new challenge in the form of European imperialism.

The vast corpus of African writings in Arabic and *ajami* (much of the latter is scattered in private holdings) across the continent contains important records of African contributions to human knowledge in general and Islamic scholarship in particular. As with early and contemporary Christianity, Africans have made significant contributions to Islamic thought almost from its emergence in the Arabian peninsula in the seventh century.

The coming of Europeans in the fifteenth century, during the infamous Atlantic slave trade, crystallizing into colonization from the mid-nineteenth century, marked yet another watershed in the development of African writing and in the technologies of the communication of ideas. European Christianity was especially critical in the introduction of new cultural practices and writing to many languages that had previously had no written tradition. In Southern Africa, for example, the written literature of the Zulu and Xhosa dates to the early nineteenth century, and most of the works were initially religious in tone, including translations of the Bible and books such as *Pilgrim's Progress*. Later, a more secular and anticolonial literature emerged, especially in journals and newspapers. Dictionaries and historical works were also produced. A vibrant local language literature also developed in West Africa, especially in Ghana and Nigeria. Particularly impressive was writing in Yoruba, consisting mostly of fiction, drama, poetry, journalism, and historical works, such as Samuel Johnson's (1846–1901) landmark *History of the Yorubas* (1921).

The nineteenth century also witnessed the development of new African scripts, especially in West Africa, the most famous being the Vai script invented by Duwalu Bukele (1810–1850). Even more consequential in the long run was the development of African writing in the European languages, especially English and French, a subject that is exhaustively discussed in the edited collections by Albert Gérard (1986) and Oyekan Owomoyela (1993), among others. Initially, African writings in the European languages concentrated on autobiographies such as Olaudah Equiano's (1745–1797) *The Interesting Narrative of the Life of Olaudah Equiano, or, Gustavus Vassa, the African* (1789). In the nineteenth century, scholarly works began to be produced by such intellectuals as Edward William Blyden (1832–1912), author of tomes like *A Vindication of the African Race* (1857) and *Christianity, Islam, and the Negro Race* (1887), which had a permanent influence on African thought.

In the twentieth century, as colonialism became entrenched, European language writing and communication spread to all aspects of African cultural and social life and became a definitive part of African literature, scholarship, education, and public discourse. The use of European languages continued after independence, a period that saw an explosion in education at all levels. For example, the number of universities increased from forty-two in 1960 (many of which were in North Africa and in South Africa) to more than four hundred, enrolling about five million students, by the beginning of the new century. Although a vast improvement compared to the colonial era, this still represented a relatively low enrollment ratio of less than 5 percent.

The mastery of the European languages by Africans can be seen in the fact that several have won the Nobel Prize for Literature and other prestigious international awards, and many African academics are among the leading figures in their respective fields. In fact, claim the authors of *Africa and the Disciplines,* "research in Africa has shaped the disciplines and thereby shaped our convictions as to what may be universally true" (Bates, Mudimbe, and O'Barr, p. xiv). Some see the European languages as a force for cultural unification, national integration, administrative efficiency, modernization, and globalization, while others contend that the dominance of these languages erodes Africa's linguistic and epistemic autonomy and its ability to define itself, pursue development, and entrench democratic rights in a situation where the languages of tuition, government, and business are not indigenous and spoken by the masses in daily life.

The Development of Modern Media

Besides educational institutions and religious institutions, the modern media have been critical channels for spreading ideas. The modern printed press dates to the turn of the nineteenth century. The first newspapers, in both African and European languages, appeared in Egypt in 1798, in South Africa in 1800, in Sierra Leone in 1801, in Ghana in 1822, in Liberia in 1826, and in Nigeria in 1859. The most important Egyptian paper in the first half of the nineteenth century was *al-Waqa'ie Al-Misriyya* (Egyptian events), founded in 1828, and from the second half of the nineteenth century until the twentieth century it was *al-Ahram* (The pyramids), founded in 1875. After the British occupation of 1882, Egyptian newspapers became vehicles of nationalist protest. Between 1900 and 1914, 250 newspapers appeared, although many did not survive. The Egyptian press entered its "golden age" after independence in 1922, and by 1937, according to Amy Ayalon, there were 250 Arabic and 65 foreign-language papers.

In West Africa, members of the Western educated elite established newspapers as vehicles to express incipient nationalism in the face of European colonial encroachment. Among the most influential papers were the *Accra Herald*, later renamed the *West Africa Herald*, established by Charles Bannerman in 1858, and the *Iwe Ihorin,* founded in 1859 by African missionaries in Abeokuta, Nigeria, and written in Yoruba. During the first half of the twentieth century, when colonialism was firmly entrenched, a host of private newspapers were established by African businessmen and nationalists, from Herbert Macaulay (1864–1946), who founded the *Lagos Daily News* in 1925, to Nnandi Azikiwe (b. 1904), the first president of independent Nigeria, who founded *West African Pilot* in 1937, and whose party, the National Council of Nigeria and the Cameroons, came to control ten newspapers by the 1950s.

In the French colonies, the first African-run papers did not emerge until the 1920s, although before 1900 Senegal had three settler papers. The press expanded rapidly after World

War II: some 365 newspapers were established between 1945 and 1960, when the French colonies attained their independence. In Southern, Central, and Eastern Africa, the press was largely a European creation to serve the information, education, and entertainment needs of the European settler communities, leaving the African readership in search of alternative channels of communication. After World War II some nationalists founded their own papers—for example, *Muigwithamia* (Work and play) and *Nyanza Times,* established by Jomo Kenyatta and Oginga Odinga, who later became independent Kenya's first president and vice president, respectively.

After independence the print media faced new opportunities and challenges. The growth of education and literacy levels expanded their readership base, but the emergence of authoritarian one-party states and military regimes undermined press freedom and led to the closure or imprisonment and harassment of many journalists. National news agencies were established and many of the new governments either bought existing papers or established new ones. A few governments were more concerned about the role of foreign ownership and tried to encourage local private media ownership, as was the case, for example, in Nigeria, where Moshood Abiola (1955–1998), later elected president in the annulled elections of 1992, and the Ibru Group established vast media empires. Concerns about the role of the international media— its excessive control of global news flows and misrepresentations of events in the global South—soon translated into international demands in the 1970s by African, Asian, and Latin American countries for the establishment of a New World Information Order (NWIO).

The demands for NWIO were not heeded. In any case, the prodemocracy movement that arose across Africa in the mid-1980s soon transformed Africa's media landscape. These movements were fueled by, and in turn facilitated, the rapid growth of newspapers, so that countries that had a handful of tightly controlled papers suddenly had several dozen vociferous tabloids. Another development was the creation of the Internet, which opened new possibilities for the African press to reach new audiences at home and abroad. By 2000, all African countries had access to the Internet and hundreds of African newspapers were available online.

The Internet is the latest in a long line of telecommunication technologies to be appropriated by African countries. Previously there had been the telegraph, then telephony, cinema, radio, and television, all of which, except radio, grew relatively slowly during the colonial period. The transistor radio played a major role as a vehicle of nationalist mobilization during the struggle for independence. But many countries did not have direct telephone connections with each other and it often took years to get a phone installation, a situation that persisted well after independence. Colonial Africa was generally excluded from the international agencies that regulate global telecommunications, a situation that changed as independent governments joined these organizations, such as the International Telecommunication Union and the International Telecommunications Satellite Organization, and tried to make up for lost time.

The emergence of the so-called information society and knowledge economies, fueled by the forces of global market integration and the emergence and convergence of new information technologies—what came to be known collectively as "globalization"—compelled African governments to accelerate the pace of telecommunications infrastructure development and to liberalize that sector. In pursuit of this agenda, attempts were made to forge more effective government policies, create regional telecommunication initiatives, and leapfrog old technologies by acquiring the latest technologies such as cell phones and satellites. The use of cell phones across the continent skyrocketed. In 1998, the Afristar satellite was launched, the first of its kind in the world designed to broadcast directly to consumer radio receivers.

These initiatives have borne some fruit. Numerous African institutions from governments to universities use Internet services and Africa is more connected to the rest of the world than it has ever been. Yet, many challenges remain. While the number of Internet users on the continent more than quadrupled in the 1990s, reaching 3.1 million by the beginning of 2001, this represented less than 1 percent of worldwide users, which then numbered 407.1 million. The challenge is not only to close the digital divides—within Africa and between Africa and the developed world—but also for Africa to increase its production of the technologies themselves and the content of information on the global information highway.

Thus, by the beginning of the twenty-first century, Africa's postcolonial mediascape was a dynamic and multifaceted blend of traditions, influences, and technologies. The most modern forms of communications technologies coexisted with the indigenous media, electronic outlets lived side by side with street information and rumor mills, known under various names in different regions such as *radio trottoir* in Francophone Africa, *radio boca a boca* in Lusophone (Portuguese-speaking) Africa, and *bush telegraph,* or *pavement radio,* in Anglophone Africa.

Africa and Its Influence

Through the various modes of communication identified above, ideas have been and continue to be transmitted within, from, and into Africa—ideas about religion, culture, politics, and the arts, as well as ideologies, iconographies, and images, not to mention academic theories, concepts, and methodologies. Discourses on African influences tend to be dominated by the tropes of origination, contestation, recipiency, hybridity, and agency. *Origination* emphasizes Africa's authenticity and as the source of Western civilization associated with the work of Cheikh Anta Diop and the Afrocentricists. *Contestation* refers to Ali Mazrui's notion of counterpenetration or counterconquest, celebrating Africa's capacities to contest other civilizations at home and abroad (2002).

Recipiency portrays Africa largely as a recipient of external influences, whether negatively, as in Walter Rodney's *How Europe Underdeveloped Africa,* or positively as in the numerous works that discuss the benefits of external interventions for Africa from colonialism and Christianity to foreign aid and globalization. *Hybridity* is inspired by postcolonial theory and, as in Kwame Anthony Appiah's *In My Father's House,* dismisses any African essence and sees Africa as a constellation of hybrid cultures and identities. The *agency* paradigm is beloved by nationalist and radical historians who seek to show how Africans have actively fashioned their material, mental, and moral lives from the complex ebbs and flows of internal and external forces and influences.

In reality, Africa has not been constituted only from within but also from without. Indeed, it is fair to say that Africa has been constituted by the world as much as it has constituted the world in all its ramifications—historical, demographic, cultural, economic, political, and discursive.

See also **African-American Ideas; Afrocentricity; Arts: Africa; Colonialism: Africa; Diasporas: African Diaspora; Diffusion, Cultural; Humanism: Africa; Humanity: African Thought; Literature: African Literature; Modernity: Africa; Mysticism: Mysticism in African Thought; Negritude; Orientalism: African and Black Orientalism; Pan-Africanism; Personhood in African Thought; Philosophies: African; Philosophy, Moral: Africa; Realism, Africa; Sociability in African Thought; University: Postcolonial; Westernization: Africa; Women's History: Africa.**

BIBLIOGRAPHY

Ajayi, Omofolabo S. *Yoruba Dance: The Semiotics of Movement and Body Attitude in Nigerian Culture.* Trenton, N.J.: Africa World Press, 1998.

Al-Khozai, Mohamed A. *The Development of Early Arabic Drama (1847–1900).* London and New York: Longman, 1984.

Amanze, J. N. *A History of the Ecumenical Movement in Africa.* Gaborone, Botswana: Pula Press, 1999.

Appiah, Kwame Anthony. *In My Father's House: Africa in the Philosophy of Culture.* New York: Oxford University Press, 1992.

Asante, Molefi Kete. *The Afrocentric Idea.* Rev. ed. Philadelphia: Temple University Press, 1998.

Ayalon, Ami. *The Press in the Arab Middle East: A History.* New York: Oxford University Press, 1995.

Ayegboyin, Deji, and S. Ademola Ishola. *African Indigenous Churches: An Historical Perspective.* Lagos, Nigeria: Greater Heights, 1997.

Banham, Martin, James Gibbs, and Femi Osofisan, eds. *African Theater in Development.* Oxford: James Currey; Bloomington: Indiana University Press, 1999.

Barber, Karin, John Collins, and Alain Ricard. *West African Popular Theater.* Bloomington: Indiana University Press; Oxford: James Currey, 1997.

Bates, Robert H., V. Y. Mudimbe, and Jean O'Barr, eds. *Africa and the Disciplines: The Contribution of African Research in Africa to the Social Sciences and Humanities.* Chicago: University of Chicago Press, 1993.

Beebe, Maria, K. Kouakou, and Banji Magliore. *Africa Dot Edu: IT Opportunities and Higher Education in Africa.* New Delhi: Tata McGraw-Hill, 2003.

Bernal, Martin. *Black Athena: The Afroasiatic Roots of Classical Civilization.* 2 vols. New Brunswick, N.J.: Rutgers University Press, 1987.

Blyden, Edward Wilmot. *Christianity, Islam, and the Negro Race.* London: W. B. Whittingham, 1887.

———. *A Vindication of the African Race; Being a Brief Examination of the Arguments in Favor of African Inferiority.* Monrovia, Liberia: G. Killian, 1857.

Bourgault, Louise M. *Mass Media in Sub-Saharan Africa.* Bloomington: Indiana University Press, 1995.

Charry, Eric S. *Mande Music: Traditional and Modern Music of the Maninka and Mandinka of Western Africa.* Chicago: University of Chicago Press, 2000.

Chernoff, John H. *African Rhythm and African Sensibility: Aesthetics and Social Action in African Musical Idioms.* Chicago: University of Chicago Press, 1979.

Conteh-Morgan, John. *Theater and Drama in Francophone Africa: A Critical Introduction.* Cambridge, U.K.: Cambridge University Press, 1994.

Diop, Cheikh Anta. *The African Origin of Civilization: Myth or Reality.* Translated by Mercer Cook. Chicago: L. Hill, 1974.

Ejiaga, Romanus, and Paul Tiyambe Zeleza. "Education: Postindependence." In *Encyclopedia of Twentieth-Century African History,* edited by Paul T. Zeleza and Dickson Eyoh. London and New York: Routledge, 2003.

Equiano, Olaudah. *The Interesting Narrative of the Life of Olaudah Equiano, or, Gustavus Vassa, the African,* edited by Werner Sollors. New York: Norton, 2001. Originally published in 1789.

Falola, Toyin, and Christian Jennings. *Sources and Methods in African History: Spoken, Written, Unearthed.* Rochester, N.Y.: University of Rochester Press, 2003.

Gérard, Albert S. *African Language Literatures: An Introduction to the Literary History of Sub-Saharan Africa.* Harlow, U.K.: Longman, 1981.

———, ed. *European-Language Writing in Sub-Saharan Africa.* 2 vols. Budapest: Akadémiai Kiadó, 1986.

Hale, Thomas A. *Griots and Griottes: Masters of Words and Music.* Bloomington: Indiana University Press, 1998.

Hyden, Goran, Michael Leslie, and Foulu F. Ogundimu, eds. *Media and Democracy in Africa.* New Brunswick, N.J., and London: Transaction, 2002.

Isichei, Elizabeth A. *A History of Christianity in Africa: From Antiquity to the Present.* Lawrenceville, N.J.: Africa World Press, 1995.

Jeyifo, Biodun. *The Truthful Lie: Essays in a Sociology of African Drama.* London: New Beacon Books, 1985.

Julien, Eileen. *African Novels and the Question of Orality.* Bloomington: Indiana University Press, 1992.

Kruger, Loren. *The Drama of South Africa: Plays, Pageants, and Publics since 1910.* London and New York: Routledge, 1999.

Levtzion, Nehemia, and L. Randall Pouwels, eds. *The History of Islam in Africa.* Athens: Ohio University Press, 2000.

Lulat, Y. G.-M. "The Development of Higher Education in Africa: A Historical Survey." In *African Higher Education: An International Handbook,* edited by Damtew Teferra and Philip Altbach, 15–31. Bloomington: Indiana University Press, 2003.

Magubane, Zine. "The Influence of African-American Cultural Practices on South Africa, 1890–1990." In *Leisure in Urban Africa,* edited by Paul Tiyambe Zeleza and Cassandra Rachel Veney. Trenton, N.J.: Africa World Press, 2003.

Martin, Phyllis. *Leisure and Society in Colonial Brazzaville.* New York: Cambridge University Press, 1995.

Mazrui, Alamin. "Globalization and Some Linguistic Dimensions of Human Rights in Africa." In *Human Rights, the Rule of Law and Development in Africa,* edited by Paul T. Zeleza and Philip J. McConnaughay, 52–70. Philadelphia: University of Pennsylvania Press, 2004.

Mazrui, Ali A. *Africa and Other Civilizations: Conquest and Counter-Conquest.* Edited by Ricardo René Laremont and Fouad Kalouche. Trenton, N.J.: Africa World Press, 2002.

Mazrui, Ali A., and Alamin Mazrui. *The Power of Babel: Language and Governance in the African Experience.* Chicago: University of Chicago Press, 1998.

Miller, Ivor L. "A Secret Society Goes Public: The Relationship between Abakua and Cuban Popular Culture." *African Studies Review* 43, no. 1 (2000): 161–188.

Modupe, Olaogun. "Theater." In *Encyclopedia of Twentieth-Century African History,* edited by Paul T. Zeleza and Dickson Eyoh, 548–555. London and New York: Routledge, 2003.

Monson, Ingrid T., ed. *The African Diaspora: A Musical Perspective.* New York: Garland, 2000.

Mudimbe, Valentin Y. *The Invention of Africa: Gnosis, Philosophy, and the Order of Knowledge.* Bloomington: Indiana University Press, 1988.

Ngugi wa Thiong'o. *Decolonising the Mind: The Politics of Language in African Literature.* Nairobi, Kenya: Heinemann, 1986.

Nketia, J. H. Kwabena. *The Music of Africa.* New York: Norton, 1974.

Noam, Eli M., ed. *Telecommunications in Africa.* New York: Oxford University Press, 1999.

Oforiwaa, Aduonum. "Dance." In *Encyclopedia of Twentieth-Century African History,* edited by Paul T. Zeleza and Dickson Eyoh, 124–130. London and New York: Routledge, 2003.

Okpewho, Isidore. *African Oral Literature: Backgrounds, Character, and Continuity.* Bloomington: Indiana University Press, 1992.

Owomoyela, Oyekan, ed. *A History of Twentieth-Century African Literatures.* Lincoln: University of Nebraska Press, 1993.

Ranger, Terence O. *Dance and Society in Eastern Africa, 1890–1970: The Beni Ngoma.* London: Heinemann, 1975.

Riverson, L. Kwabena. *Telecommunications Development: The Case of Africa.* Lanham, Md.: University Press of America, 1993.

Robinson, David. *Muslim Societies in African History.* Cambridge, U.K.: Cambridge University Press, 2004.

Rodney, Walter. *How Europe Underdeveloped Africa.* Washington, D.C.: Howard University Press, 1982.

Rosander, Eva E., and David Westerlund, eds. *African Islam and Islam in Africa: Encounters between Sufis and Islamists.* Athens: Ohio University Press, 1997.

Sanneh, Lamin O. *The African Transformation of Christianity: Comparative Reflections on Ethnicity and Religious Mobilization in Africa.* Tempe: Arizona State University Press, 1998.

Scheub, Harold. "A Review of African Oral Traditions and Literature." *African Studies Review* 28, nos. 2/3 (1985): 1–72.

Teferra, Damtew, and Philip Altbach. "Trends and Perspectives in African Higher Education." In *African Higher Education: An International Reference Book,* edited by Damtew Teferra and Philip Altbach, 3–14. Bloomington: Indiana University Press, 2003.

Turino, Thomas. "Music." In *Encyclopedia of Twentieth-Century African History,* edited by Paul T. Zeleza and Dickson Eyoh, 371–378. London and New York: Routledge, 2003.

———. *Nationalists, Cosmopolitans, and Popular Music in Zimbabwe.* Chicago: University of Chicago Press, 2000.

Vansina, Jan. *Oral Tradition as History.* Madison: University of Wisconsin Press, 1985.

Warren, Lee. *The Dance of Africa: An Introduction.* Englewood Cliffs, N.J.: Prentice-Hall, 1972.

Waterman, Christopher A. *Juju: A Social History and Ethnography of an African Popular Music.* Chicago: University of Chicago Press, 1990.

White, Luise, Stephan F. Miescher, and David William Cohen. *African Words, African Words: Critical Practices in Oral History.* Bloomington: Indiana University Press, 2001.

Zeleza, Paul T., and Ibulaimu Kakoma, eds. *In Search of Modernity: Science and Technology in Africa.* Trenton, N.J.: Africa World Press, 2003.

Paul Tiyambe Zeleza

THE AMERICAS AND THEIR INFLUENCE

The Americas were first settled from Asia by successive waves of migrants who crossed the Bering Sea from Siberia to Alaska during the last Ice Age using a land bridge, the frozen sea, and possibly open boats. Estimates as to when this began range from twenty thousand to one hundred thousand years ago. By 8000 B.C.E. settlements had reached the southern tip of South America. The new arrivals came as hunter-gatherers, but over the millennia many adopted agriculture and a few groups built civilizations comparable to what had developed earlier in ancient Mesopotamia, Egypt, and the Indus Valley.

Pre-European Communication

Anthropological research suggests a rich and historically deep tradition of oral communication among early Amerindian people in which linguistic diversity appears to have been considerable. Even within the usually accepted language groupings of North America—Eskimo-Aleut; Athabascan, or Na-Dene; Algonquian-Wakashan; Aztec-Tanoan; Hokan-Siouan; Penutian; and Arawakan—many dialects existed, a consequence of regional diversity and the linguistic fluidity of primary oral cultures.

The communication of ideas among the first Americans, however, was not limited to spoken language. Smoke signals and the tom-toms, immortalized in Hollywood film, actually existed. The latter could transmit a variety of messages via rhythmic signatures in ways that resemble how bugle calls have been used by military groups in more recent history. The result was a form of communication over distance whereby messages could travel faster than messengers, an accomplishment often first attributed to telegraphy. Another form of long-distance communication developed by Native Americans, although they were probably not the first to come up with the idea, emerged in the nineteenth century when mirrors acquired in trade were used to flash messages across the plains. This practice inspired the United States Army to develop the heliograph, in which the signal mirrors were adapted to transmit Morse code.

One of the more remarkable achievements in communication developed by Native Americans is Plains Sign Language (PSL). It served as a lingua franca, enabling communication between tribes speaking different dialects and in some cases completely different languages. PSL is not a series of rudimentary gestures, but a full-fledged semantically open system capable of sending a virtually infinite variety of messages—it has even been used to recount episodes from the Bible. Most PSL signs are, to use the classic semiotic categories, either iconic (resembling what they represent, such as crossed fingers standing for a tepee) or indexical (where, metonymically, a part stands for the whole, as when a continuous circular motion of the index finger represents a wagon). Although the third semiotic category, the symbolic or arbitrary sign (the dominant one for spoken language), is rare in PSL, it is not altogether absent; we find it, for example, when a part of the body such as the knee or elbow is used to represent a concept. PSL's exploration of the interface between spoken language and the nonverbal communication of gestures has prompted wide and enduring fascination—it has been studied by philosophers of language and appropriated by Boy Scouts.

New World Civilizations

It was once believed that to have civilization—a political state with a centralized government, ruling bureaucracy, complex division of labor, agricultural surplus, and monumental public works—writing had to be in use. The Americas have yielded a major exception to this rule: the empire of the Incas. Centered in Peru, this extended in a north-south direction from Ecuador to Chile, and eastward into part of the Amazon Basin. Keeping track of this enormous social experiment depended not on writing but on a communication medium capable of doing some of the same things. The Incas used the quipu, a series of woolen or cotton cords of different length, thickness, and color that could be braided and knotted in various ways. Each of these elements represented information. This enabled the quipu to be used for a variety of complex tasks, such as the recording of a census or the calculation of economic output, tribute obligations, and taxes. In conjunction with the Incan oral tradition, quipus were even used as mnemonic devices, to assist in recounting aspects of historical succession.

In contrast to the Incas, the two great Mesoamerican civilizations, the Aztecs and the Maya, developed writing. More specifically, they created a form of writing similar to, but not as elaborate as, Egyptian hieroglyphics. Numerous images and occasionally abstract signs (as opposed to the more streamlined and economical characters of an alphabet) were used to represent parts of speech rather than—as is the case with Chinese script, for example—objects and concepts. It could be argued that precursors of writing in the Americas can be found in rock art (petroglyphs) and in images (pictograms) drawn on animal skins; several buffalo hide inscriptions actually tell a story. However, the possibilities inherent in freeing writing from purely iconic representation allowed it to be used for much more elaborate forms of communication. Nowhere in the Americas has this been demonstrated more than in the case of the Maya.

Mayan history spans roughly the first millennium C.E. The Maya wrote on durable media—stone and parchment (animal skins). Although lacking metal tools, the wheel, or domestic draft animals, Mayan culture nonetheless developed ideas of considerable sophistication. Their mathematical and astronomical knowledge rivaled that of the Babylonians and surpassed that of the Egyptians. One result is a calendar of staggering complexity and accuracy. The lunar month was calculated at 29.53020 days, which compares favorably with our current reckoning of 29.53059 days. Mayans viewed world history in terms of cycles of creation and destruction. (The current cycle, or long count, places the next destruction of the world on 23 December 2012.)

For reasons that remain a source for much archaeological speculation, classic Mayan civilization collapsed dramatically in the ninth century, whereas the fall of the Incas and Aztecs did not occur until the Spanish conquest. Although this appears to have been a case of self-destruction—an environmental degradation hypothesis has gained increasing support—the Spanish did administer a coup de grace of sorts. Under the auspices of the Catholic Church, almost all the surviving Mayan codices (parchment books) were destroyed. The few that remain, such as the famous Dresden Codex, provide a revealing, if only partial, view of Mayan thought and culture.

Colonial America

Whether the quest was for riches, as in the Spanish incursion into the New World, or for a life free from the constraints of the homeland, which motivated the settlement of most of Anglophone North America, religion played an important role. When the Spanish decided to follow plunder with colonization, taming the indigenous peoples through religious conversion became an imperative. In 1539, less than one hundred years after Gutenberg's invention of moveable-type printing, the bishop of Mexico established the first printing office in the New World. Books of religious instruction helped Franciscans and Jesuits spread Catholicism. They made religious conversions at a rate that far surpassed the later efforts of Protestants in North America, largely because of Catholicism's greater capacity to accommodate indigenous beliefs. The teaching of literacy was not a high priority in Catholic proselytizing at this time, except for those natives destined for ordination.

The seventeenth-century Puritans, in contrast, attempted to teach peoples under their purview to read various religious texts translated into the languages of the tribes in question, but the project was eventually abandoned. The Latin alphabet has only limited phonetic utility when used to transcribe non–Indo-European languages. In 1821, however, the Cherokee Sequoya devised an indigenous writing system by modifying the Latin alphabet to represent syllables of the Cherokee language. Often referred to as an alphabet, this eighty-five-character script is, technically speaking, a syllabary. At one point it was even used for newspapers; after falling into disuse, it is now enjoying renewed interest. Other Native American groups, such as the Cree and Inuit, have also developed syllabaries.

Whether brought by Puritans, Quakers, Mennonites, or any of the other Protestant groups that settled North America, the influence of the Reformation was profound. Idolatry was rejected and vernacular literacy was encouraged so that all could have direct access to the word of God. Imported Epistles were soon supplanted by Bibles, psalm books, and catechisms minted in America after print shops were set up (1640) in Boston and Cambridge. The literacy rate in colonial New England at this time has been estimated at about 60 percent for adult males, with a figure of about half that for women. It was somewhat less in the southern colonies—50 percent for males and 25 percent for females—given the more agrarian (and, in some places, Catholic) nature of the South, where the education system tended, apart from the segment that catered to the elite, to be less well developed.

The eighteenth century saw a gradual rise in colonial literacy, along with the publication of texts besides those relating to religion—schoolbooks, professional and technical manuals, and eventually the political tracts that would inspire the American Revolution. By 1790 American editions of English works began to appear, to be followed in several decades by a national tradition of fiction and poetry. Throughout the eighteenth century, books were relatively costly. Access to them was abetted by the establishment of subscription libraries, the prototype being the Philadelphia Library Company, established in 1731, largely through the efforts of Benjamin Franklin. Newspapers also facilitated the dissemination of ideas throughout the century, beginning in 1700 with Boston postmaster John Campbell's hand-copied news sheet, which went to print in 1704 as the *Boston News-Letter.* Within a generation a dozen such publications were available, and throughout the remainder of the century growth would be exponential.

In the decades leading up to 1776, a growing volume of printed matter urged resistance to British authority. Perhaps the most notorious document in this regard is Thomas Paine's *Common Sense,* published as the revolution began, on 9 January 1776. Although the ideals of those advocating independence included free speech and a free press, pro-British newspapers expressing Loyalist sentiments were often suppressed. By the time of the revolution there was near universal literacy in the northern colonies. Nevertheless, the importance of the oral tradition cannot be discounted. What was read was discussed and augmented by speeches in taverns, meeting halls, and other public places.

The Penny Press

In the 1830s American newspapers began their emergence as a true mass medium—one that disseminates the same information to large numbers of people. In the colonies or early republic a successful newspaper attracted only a few thousand readers at most. After the revolution, advertising helped finance newspapers, and many, if not most, had the word *Advertiser* in their title. Circulation was dependent on subscription. Early in the nineteenth century, partisan politics began to play an increasingly important role as papers aligned themselves with political parties in response to the debate between Federalists and Anti-Federalists. No matter what political constituency these journals served, the associated business interests determined their emphasis. Subscribers were generally well-off and had to sign on for a year at a cost of six cents an issue.

The arrival of the penny papers changed the industry. The idea began in New York and within a decade had spread to other metropolitan areas. Benjamin Day's *New York Sun* (1833), James Gordon Bennett's *New York Herald* (1835), and Horace Greeley's *New York Tribune* (1841) were sold on the street for a penny and reached a readership many times that of the partisan press. Many readers were immigrants, members of the traditional middle class, or from a nascent literate working class. These papers were not without political leanings, but they were not party-funded (advertising revenue helped defray costs) and were quite capable of shifting an allegiance if a candidate's platform displeased them. Local news, along with crime—the more sensational the better—human interest stories, and coverage of late-breaking events such as the war with Mexico made the penny papers immediate as well

as informative. Journalistic practice shifted from the interpretation of an event, in some cases long after the fact, to speedy, descriptive reporting. Eventually the penny papers added coverage of the arts, theater, sports, and general entertainment.

Several theories have been put forth to explain the success of the penny press. On the technological side, steam power and the rotary press facilitated mass production. The use of steam in rail and ship transportation and improved roads speeded the movement of news. By the mid-1840s that movement was no longer limited to the available means of transportation, given the advent of the electric telegraph, which prompted the formation of news agencies such as the Associated Press (1849). News was becoming a commodity—the fresher the better. Nevertheless, it must be noted that the advent of the penny press itself preceded technological influences that contributed so greatly to its success. On the human side, a literate urban population was expanding and was feeling a greater sense of empowerment through the electoral process. Being informed through regular access to news helped give direction to that empowerment.

Yellow Journalism

Penny papers dominated news reporting until the end of the nineteenth century, when they were outdone at their own game by the journalistic innovations of Joseph Pulitzer and William Randolph Hearst. Beginning in midcentury, though, there were alternative visions of what a newspaper should be. The most notable such experiment was Henry Raymond's *New York Times,* sometimes referred to as an example of the "information press." Beginning in 1851, the *Times* eschewed the base populism of the penny press and used a matter-of-fact style to report urban news, public-interest stories, and business activities. On the eve of the Civil War the *Times* became associated with the Republican Party and its antislavery position. Perhaps the paper's finest hour in its first half-century of operation occurred in the 1870s, when it helped expose the infamous New York municipal corruption ring headed by William Marcy "Boss" Tweed.

The challenge to the penny press and the information press posed by Pulitzer and Hearst gave rise to what became known as "yellow journalism." The term itself, which evokes notions of sensationalism and scandalmongering, derives from a cartoon character bent on exposing corruption, the Yellow Kid, drawn by Richard Outcault for Pulitzer's *New York World.* Pulitzer, a Hungarian immigrant, took over the paper in 1885. His numerous innovations included a populist, pro-labor and pro-union position; campaigns to expose municipal corruption and injustice; advocacy of an increased tax burden for the wealthy; investigative journalism that tackled everything from phony psychics to the dire conditions in a mental hospital; and publicity-seeking stunts to improve circulation, such as sending Nellie Bly on her legendary seventy-two-day trip around the world in 1888–1889.

Pulitzer also streamlined the prose style of his papers (he would acquire a chain of them) by avoiding colloquial and esoteric terms and shortening paragraphs and sentences. Headlines, barely discernible in the penny papers, now spanned columns. Visuals—diagrams, cartoons, along with the reproduction of photographs using the new halftone process—earned a prominent place. This helped make Pulitzer's papers appealing, especially to immigrants for whom English was a second language.

Hearst admired these innovations but believed they could and should be extended further. In 1895 he took over the *New York Journal* and began a battle for circulation supremacy with Pulitzer that has been described as fiercer than the Spanish-American War that both papers would cover three years later. Hearst's moneyed background allowed him to hire away part of Pulitzer's staff, including Outcault and his Yellow Kid.

Hearst's journalistic exposés were not always limited to stories relating to the public interest. Sensationalism was omnipresent. Lurid scandals that we associate today with tabloid journalism sometimes made the front page, accompanied by massive, attention-getting headlines. Hearst also had a reputation for newsmaking when mere reporting would not suffice. His most famous foray in this direction occurred when he drummed up sentiment for a reluctant U.S. government to declare war on Spain. Hearst's quip to artist Frederick Remington, who had cabled from Cuba that there was little fighting to report—"You furnish the pictures and I'll furnish the war"— is humorously dramatized in Orson Welles's 1941 film based on Hearst's life, *Citizen Kane.*

Book Publishing

In addition to religious publications, a major type of book emerging from the colonial press was the almanac. Benjamin Franklin's *Poor Richard's Almanac* (1732), blending self-help advice with humor, became a best-seller. Book production was centered at first in Boston and Cambridge, but by the early eighteenth century Philadelphia (where Franklin was based) became a major player. Censorship limited the variety of books that could be published, and there was no enforcement of copyright. By the early nineteenth century the industry had diversified its output, and the burgeoning commercial center of the new nation, New York, had become the center of publishing as well.

In the United States, modern book publishing—featuring a diverse general list and home-grown authors—began in 1817, when James and John Harper established the firm bearing their name. They were soon followed by John Wiley, who took over his father's fledgling business in 1826. The house scored a major coup when it signed a then-unknown James Fenimore Cooper—later referred to as "America's Sir Walter Scott"— who went on to become the country's first literary celebrity. In 1840 Wiley went into partnership with George Putnam, who would eventually leave to establish his own firm in 1849. In 1846 Wiley and Putnam published Herman Melville's first novel, *Typee,* which in turn passed to Harper's in 1849. (Melville was never a big seller during his lifetime.)

Harper's went on to become the largest publisher in America, earning considerable sums from pirating English favorites including the Bröntes, Thackeray, and Dickens. The house also produced textbooks and a magazine that bore its name, which emerged as the medium to which many people turned

for Civil War coverage, especially owing to impressive visuals (woodcut illustrations). Other well-known firms that emerged during this time include Appleton (1831), Scribner's (1846), and D. Van Nostrand (1848). However, it was a small Boston publisher, John P. Jewett, working in the shadow of Little, Brown (1847) and Houghton (1848), who scored the century's biggest publishing coup. After Phillips, Sampson and Company (1850) turned down the novel rights to Harriet Beecher Stowe's serialized (in the *National Era*) story *Uncle Tom's Cabin,* Jewett published it in 1852. The book became the biggest-selling hardcover in nineteenth-century America and had an enormous impact on the (northern) public's attitude toward slavery and its rising antipathy toward the South.

The second half of the century saw the country secure, both in its publishing industry and in the literary ability of American authors. The old houses grew and new ones sprang up as reading tastes diversified. Harper's even signed the once-pirated Dickens in 1867. In 1895, during a decade that saw a boom in American fiction publishing, Harper's secured the rights to sixteen books by Mark Twain (Samuel Clemens). Twain and several other prominent writers successfully promoted their work through a series of highly entertaining public readings—performances, in the case of Twain—that recaptured, at least in spirit, the oral tradition of storytelling that had been so integral to the cultural life of both Native Americans and African-Americans.

See also **Censorship; Literature; Media, History of.**

BIBLIOGRAPHY

Amory, Hugh, and David D. Hall, eds. *The History of the Book in America.* Vol. 1: *The Colonial Book in the Atlantic World.* New York: Cambridge University Press, 2000.
Ascher, Marcia, and Robert Ascher. *Code of the Quipu: A Study in Media, Mathematics, and Culture.* Ann Arbor: University of Michigan Press, 1981.
Carey, James W. *Communication as Culture: Essays on Media and Society.* Boston: Unwin Hyman, 1989.
Coe, Michael D. *The Maya.* London: Thames and Hudson, 1980.
Crowley, David, and Paul Heyer, eds. *Communication in History: Technology, Culture, Society.* Boston: Allyn and Bacon, 2003.
Czitrom, Daniel. *Media and the American Mind: From Morse to McLuhan.* Chapel Hill: University of North Carolina Press, 1982.
Peters, John Durham. *Speaking into the Air: A History of the Idea of Communication.* Chicago: University of Chicago Press, 1999.
Pfeiffer, John E. *The Emergence of Society: A Pre-history of the Establishment.* New York: McGraw-Hill, 1977.
Robinson, Andrew. *The Story of Writing: Alphabets, Hieroglyphics, and Pictograms.* London and New York: Thames and Hudson, 1995.
Ruhlen, Merritt. *The Origin of Language: Tracing the Evolution of the Mother Tongue.* New York: Wiley, 1994.
Schudson, Michael. *Discovering the News: A Social History of American Newspapers.* New York: Basic Books, 1978.
Stephens, Mitchell. *A History of News: From the Drum to the Satellite.* New York: Viking, 1988.
Tebbel, John. *Between Covers: The Rise and Transformation of Book Publishing in America.* New York: Oxford University Press, 1987.

Tebbel, John, and Mary Ellen Zuckerman. *The Magazine in America: 1741–1990.* New York: Oxford University Press, 1991.

Umiker-Sebeok, D. Jean. "Aboriginal Sign 'Languages' from a Semiotic Point of View." In *The Sign and its Masters,* by Thomas A. Sebeok. Lanham, Md.: University Press of America, 1989.

Paul Heyer

ASIA AND ITS INFLUENCE

Asia comprises a vast amount of land divided into numerous countries, many of which have civilizations dating back thousands of years. Due to the huge scope of this topic, this entry will focus on India as an important hub for the transmission of ideas throughout Asia and how other Asian countries influenced the development of Indian civilization.

When India became independent in 1947, the new government faced the daunting task of convincing a large and highly disparate population that the various peoples of India constituted one nation. The populace was divided among a variety of religious groups, the majority of whom were Hindus (more than 80 percent). Hindus are divided into more than two thousand endogamous castes (*jati*), each of which considers itself to be different from all the others. In the early twenty-first century there are over 800 million Hindus, 81 million Muslims, 20 million Christians, 14 million Sikhs, 6 million Buddhists, 3 million Jains, and about 600,000 Zoroastrians in India. In addition, there is enormous linguistic diversity: the 1971 census (the most recent containing a survey of languages) listed thirty-three languages with more than one million speakers, and there are numerous smaller languages and dialects, many of which are mutually incomprehensible. Since independence, the government has made great strides in promoting education, but more than half of the population remains illiterate.

In this situation, oral and visual texts play a central role in communicating ideas among India's population, which currently numbers over one billion. The ideals of nationhood and government initiatives are often disseminated orally or symbolically, and this is also true of religious ideas. Public performances of religious tales are widely popular all over India, and the annual Ramlila ("Sport of Rama") plays generally draw huge crowds. These are based on Tulsidas's (1543?–1623) version of the Hindu epic *Ramayana,* which tells the story of the mythical king Rama, an incarnation of the god Vishnu. When the *Ramayana* was serialized on television in the 1980s, it became a major national event, and the country came to a standstill every week when it was showing. This was followed by serialization of the *Mahabharata,* the other major religious epic of India, which was equally well received. Due to the continuing popularity of public performances and mass media presentations of religious themes, religious narratives and the ideas they convey are widely diffused in India. The spread of Internet access and growing expertise in software development in India have increased this process, at least among those who are able to use computers. It is now possible to make virtual pilgrimages to Hindu holy sites and to perform virtual *puja* (offerings and prayers) at several popular Hindu cultural Internet sites. These generally use English, the language of elite communication in India, and they appeal particularly to Indians living overseas.

Language Issues

Even after fifty years as an independent country, there is no real national language, despite government attempts to promote Hindi, which is spoken in the northern part of the country. Linguistically related to Sanskrit, Hindi is the single most spoken language in India, but even so it falls well short of a majority. In 1971 there were 153,792,062 Hindi speakers listed, but even though it is widely spoken (and linguistically related to other languages in the so-called Hindi Belt of north India), there was significant resistance to a government proposal to make it the national language.

The main opposition came from speakers of the Dravidian languages of the south and tribal groups, who felt that they would be disadvantaged if Hindi became the language of government examinations, higher education, and interstate communication. People in the north who speak either Hindi or a linguistically related language would have a significant edge, while speakers of other languages would have to become proficient in Hindi to compete. In response to these concerns, the Indian government first mandated that both English and Hindi would be national languages until 1965, after which English would be dropped, but continued pressure forced the government to retain English for an indefinite period until it could be replaced by Hindi. Many Indian nationalists deplore this situation and feel that the continued use of the language of India's colonizers is an affront to national dignity, but the situation seems likely to continue for the foreseeable future.

A complex system of center-state communication has been devised. Most of India's states are organized along linguistic lines, and those states in which Hindi is dominant must communicate with the central government in Hindi. Others may communicate in either Hindi or English. In India, language is closely linked to cultural identity, and there are concerted efforts in many parts of India to ensure that traditional tongues are maintained.

English and Sanskrit

The use of English as a national medium proved to be an important aspect of India's rise to prominence in science and technology in the late twentieth century, particularly the development of computer software. Hindi and other Indian languages are poorly suited to communication of modern scientific ideas and terminology. The development of vernacular equivalents is still in its infancy, and so the widespread use of English in elite education, tertiary institutions, and the government-sponsored Indian Institutes of Technology (IITs)—which turn out the majority of Indian information technology workers—has helped India to become an international powerhouse in software technology. English also functions as a marker of elite status in India and is seen as a sign of education and upward mobility among the middle classes. Despite this, according to government estimates, only 11 percent of Indians are fluent in English, and its use is mainly confined to the educated elite.

The use of English as an elite lingua franca has parallels to the position of Sanskrit in ancient and classical India. As with Latin in medieval Europe, Sanskrit was the language of philosophers, writers, and religious teachers, who used it to bridge the linguistic diversity of the subcontinent. The Vedas, the earliest sacred texts of Hinduism, were composed in Sanskrit, probably between 2000 and 400 B.C.E. Most of India's great classical literature, philosophy, and religious works were written in Sanskrit, and it functioned as a means for communicating ideas across the subcontinent for millennia. Despite the widespread use of writing, oral transmission has always been predominant. The main religious duty of the priestly caste of Brahmans is to memorize and transmit the Vedas to their descendants, a process that continues in the early 2000s.

The use of Sanskrit by the elite facilitated the communication of ideas within the areas that adopted it as the lingua franca. One example of its use in communication of ideas was the tradition of public philosophical debate (*vadavidya*) among rival philosophical factions. From at least the time of the Buddha (c. 563–c. 483 B.C.E.) and Mahavira (c. 599–527 B.C.E.) such debates were common. Reports of the time indicate that they were generally sponsored by rulers and often attracted large crowds. The stakes were quite high in these contests: the winners received financial rewards, government patronage, and increased status, but the losers had to publicly acknowledge their defeat and leave the area. Thus it is not surprising that underhanded techniques were commonly used to win debates, and by the first century C.E. there were several manuals outlining the rules and proper conduct for philosophical disputes. According to Akshapada, there are three types of debate: (1) honest debate (*vada*), in which both sides seek the truth and try to establish the correct view; (2) sneaky debate (*jalpa*), in which one tries to win by any means; and (3) destructive debate (*vitanda*), in which one side merely tries to demolish the opponent's position without putting forward an alternative. The most famous practitioner of the third type was the Buddhist philosopher Nagarjuna (fl. c. 150–250 C.E.). By all accounts, because the stakes were so high, the first type of debate generally was confined to members of the same philosophical school, and the primary objective in encounters with rival traditions was to defeat them and establish one's own school as dominant.

Some of the common concerns of oral philosophical debates were: What is the meaning or purpose of life? Should one pursue sensual pleasures, or does asceticism lead to better results? Is the world eternal? Is there an individual soul, and if so, is it eternal? In ancient India there was an enormous diversity of philosophical schools, and one of the key focal points of debate concerned what should function as valid means of knowledge (*pramana*). There were a number of commonly accepted *pramanas,* such as direct perception (*pratyaksa*), inference (*anumana*), verbal testimony (or scripture, *sabda*), and analogy (*upamana*). Some of the most vigorous intersectarian debates centered on issues of validity; some schools accepted all of the *pramanas,* some orthodox Brahmanical schools relied ultimately on scriptural testimony, and the Buddhists only accepted direct perception and inference. These philosophical debates were waged for millennia between rival philosophical factions, and the interchange of ideas they fostered led to significant developments within all major philosophical traditions.

Trade and the Exchange of Ideas

Because India was a major cultural and commercial center, it had widespread influence in the region. Sanskrit was not only the language of ruling elites in India but also extended into neighboring countries. Sanskrit was adopted as the language of statecraft and a symbol of royal legitimacy in Angkor (whose name derives from the Sanskrit word *nagara,* city), and was used by ruling elites ranging from Prambanam in central Java to Annam (modern-day Vietnam) to Peshawar in Gandhara (modern-day Pakistan). The languages of neighboring countries such as Ceylon (Sri Lanka), Thailand, Indonesia, and Malaysia are strongly influenced by Sanskrit and contain many cognate words. Versions of the *Ramayana* and *Mahabharata* are found all over South and Southeast Asia and continue to be widely performed, and Indian thought, myth, and cultural themes pervade the region.

In addition to being a hub of ideas and technology, India was the nexus of trade in the region. Early records indicate that guilds run by Brahmans dominated regional commerce and document commercial interactions with Thailand, Alexandria, Lebanon, Burma, island and mainland Southeast Asia, China, Vietnam, and the Philippines. India's major international trade routes began at Patna in the north and went on to Taxila, through the Hindu Kush mountains to Bactria and Seleucia, and west toward Damascus and the seaports of Ionia. Trade with China is documented as early as the first century C.E., when embassies were sent between the two countries, and a major expansion of trade took place during the Tang dynasty (618–907). The most important avenues of trade were the silk routes, which brought goods and technology by sea and overland through Central Asia. The overland trade routes from northern India went to the north and south of the Tarim Basin and met at the Chinese frontier at the Jade Gate near the oasis city of Dunhuang. The famous caves of Dunhuang were constructed between the fifth and eighth centuries and were used to store texts and images. Dunhuang became a major center of interchange between Indian and Chinese culture, and during the period that it was annexed by the expanding Tibetan empire (ninth century) it also served as a conduit for Buddhist learning and literature from Tibet, Central Asia, and China.

Beginning in the second century C.E., Buddhist missionaries began to follow the trade routes through Central Asia and made their way into China. In 142 a group of monks led by An Shigao established a translation bureau in Loyang to render Sanskrit Buddhist texts into Chinese. For several centuries interest in Buddhism was largely confined to émigrés from Central Asia, but in the fourth century significant numbers of Chinese began to convert. This led to increased importation of texts and ideas from India as well as increased pilgrimage by Chinese Buddhists to India. Among the most famous of these intrepid travelers was Faxian, who traveled overland to India in 399, and Xuanzang, who journeyed overland through Central Asia to India. Xuanzang spent a total of sixteen years there (629–645) and traveled all over the subcontinent, chronicling Buddhist institutions and schools. He brought back numerous texts and spent most of the rest of his life translating and interpreting them.

During the Tang dynasty there were reportedly thousands of Indians in China's major cities. Some were traders and others were Buddhist missionaries. Some, such as Bodhiruchi (fl. 508–537), brought more than just Buddhist learning: Bodhiruchi was born into a Brahman family and was learned in Samkhya philosophy, astrology, mathematics, medicine, and grammar. He translated fifty-three volumes of the Buddhist canon under the patronage of the emperor and was also influential in introducing the court to other aspects of Indian learning and technology. Pilgrims and traders who returned to India brought peaches, pears, vermilion, and Chinese silk with them, and many also studied Chinese medicine, astrology, and mathematics during their stay.

Conquest, Invasion, and Emigration

In addition to these generally amicable trade relations, conquest and invasion played major roles in the transmission of ideas into India. India is geologically separated from the rest of Asia; the Himalayas—the world's highest mountains—constitute its northern border, but their passes have been crossed by innumerable invaders, migrants, and travelers. One important early group of migrants was the Aryans, who probably originated in Europe and arrived in India in the second millennium B.C.E. They spoke a proto-Sanskrit language and brought their sacred texts, the Vedas. Over the course of centuries they became predominant in northern India, but their culture probably absorbed elements from India's indigenous inhabitants.

Alexander the Great crossed the Indus River in 326 B.C.E. and easily conquered the divided kingdoms of northern India, but his troops revolted at the Beas River and refused to advance, so his expansion into the subcontinent was halted. In the political vacuum left by Alexander's withdrawal, an Indian dynasty, the Mauryas (321–185 B.C.E.), conquered the Gangetic plain and the Indus River valley, but the dynasty fell apart several decades after the death of the great emperor Ashoka (r. 269–232 B.C.E.). After this there were some small dynasties, such as the Shungas and Kanvas, but none were able to match the Mauryas' power. In the following centuries there were invasions by several groups of foreigners, including Bactrian military commanders of Alexander's frontier provinces. They were followed by Persians, Scythians, and Central Asian barbarian tribes.

The Bactrians carved out small kingdoms in the northern parts of the subcontinent, and their rule was a time of cultural exchange between the Greek cultural world and India. There is evidence of transmission of technology and literature as well as medical and astrological knowledge. The works of Plato were brought to India, and the *Mahabharata* was read by some Greeks. In one famous example of intercultural exchange, the Bactrian king Menander (fl. 160–135 B.C.E.) reportedly had a series of philosophical dialogues with the Buddhist sage Nagasena, which are preserved in the *Questions of King Milinda* (*Milindapanho*). This became one of the classics of Buddhist philosophy and was translated into Chinese as early as the fourth century C.E. In this text, Menander poses questions from the perspective of classical Greek philosophy, and Nagasena answers from a Buddhist perspective. Menander is presented as

an admirer of the Buddha and his doctrine, and he seems to be familiar with Buddhist philosophy.

Buddhist thought and culture were also spread into Southeast Asia beginning in the third century B.C.E. The first successful Buddhist mission was reportedly sponsored by Ashoka, who sent his son Mahinda, a Theravada Buddhist monk, to Ceylon. After becoming established there, Theravada spread to other areas of Southeast Asia and became the dominant religion in Thailand, Burma, Cambodia, and Laos. Beginning in the seventh century, Mahayana Buddhism was adopted by the kings of Tibet, who began a process of importation of Indian Buddhist culture and learning. They sponsored Tibetan scholars to study in the great monastic universities of north India, and Indian scholars were brought to Tibet to spread their religion and to translate the Buddhist canon into Tibetan.

Beginning in the eighth century, a series of Islamic invaders penetrated into India from the north. One of these, Mahmud of Ghazni (971–1030), conquered large areas of northern India and also engaged in widespread destruction and looting of religious sites. As a result of the depredations of his armies and later Muslim invaders, the Buddhist monastic universities were destroyed, and by the thirteenth century Buddhism had largely disappeared in India. In the thirteenth century, the Ghurids from Central Asia established the Delhi sultanate, which ruled much of northern India until 1526. They in turn were defeated by the armies of Babur (1483–1530), a descendant of Genghis Khan and Timur, who established the Mughal dynasty, which ruled most of India until 1856. The Delhi Sultanate and the Mughal Empire established a prolific trade in both ideas and commerce between India and the Islamic world. Persian was the language of the Mughal court, which patronized the arts and philosophy. The height of the Mughal dynasty was a period of cultural flourishing in India, and ideas, literature, and technology circulated among India, Persia, and the Middle East as well as the rest of Asia.

In 1656 the Mughal emperor Dara Shukoh had sections of the Upanishads translated into Persian, believing that they were secret scriptures referred to in the Koran. Sufi writings and teachers also exercised significant influence in India, and this continues in the early twenty-first century. The great emperor Akbar (r. 1556–1605) was highly influential in the interchange of ideas in India and is reported to have held philosophical and religious discussions with representatives of a range of religions and traditions. Following an expansion of the empire under Aurangzeb (r. 1658–1707), internal pressures weakened it, and local hegemons began to carve out small states.

European traders began to arrive in the sixteenth century. The first were the Portuguese, who established Goa as their trading base in 1510. In 1608 the British East India Company founded its first trade headquarters in Surat, followed by Madras in 1641 and Calcutta in 1691. During the next century, the East India Company gradually extended its control and by the eighteenth century had overcome most of its rivals. Following General Robert Clive's defeat of French forces at Plassey in Bengal 1757, Britain became the dominant power in the subcontinent and began to create rail and communications networks. In the early 1850s the East India Company spent £110,250 on telegraph lines linking the presidencies of India (the areas under direct British rule), which along with the railways and a postal service created by the British allowed for transport of goods and ideas all over the subcontinent. In 1865 a cable link was established between Britain and India.

Indians at first perceived the British as low-caste invaders, but gradually elites began to recognize the benefits of British education and started sending their children to study abroad. At the same time, the British established English-medium schools in India for their children and those of Indian elites. As British scholars began to explore India, interest in its classical literature increased dramatically. Chairs for the study of Sanskrit and Indian culture were established at leading British universities, and religious, philosophical, and literary classics were translated into European languages. Initially the main emphasis was on classical studies, and German scholars were at the forefront of this movement. The pioneering Indologist Max Müller published the first printed versions of the Vedas in Oxford between 1849 and 1873. A French translation of the Upanishads (from the Persian translation sponsored by Dara Shukhoh) was published in 1801–1802.

At the same time, European humanism and political philosophy were widely disseminated among British-educated Indians. The most influential leader of India's independence movement, Mohandas K. (Mahatma) Gandhi (1869–1948), first read the *Bhagavad Gita* in Sir Edwin Arnold's English translation after joining the London Vegetarian Society while studying law in London. His writings indicate that in addition to the *Gita,* he was profoundly influenced by Leo Tolstoy, the Sermon on the Mount, and Henry David Thoreau. As with many other Indians educated in British schools, his thought was a mixture of traditional Hinduism and Western thought.

During their study in British schools, India's independence leaders learned about Western notions of democracy and used these against their colonizers. In addition, the British-built railroads enabled activists to travel all over the subcontinent and to speak with like-minded people in distant areas. This, along with the availability of instant communications via telegraph and, later, telephone and wireless, facilitated the process of learning to imagine themselves as constituting one people belonging to a unified nation.

Because of India's diversity, the process of nation-building and the task of fostering nationalist consciousness among its various religious, linguistic, racial, and tribal groups continues in the early twenty-first century. The growing penetration of telephone service, television, radio, and other forms of mass communication is part of this process. Probably the most pervasive and influential medium for the dissemination of ideas is "Bollywood" films, which are produced en masse and are widely popular not only in India but also Nepal, Tibet, and Southeast Asia. Most of these use a simplified version of Hindi (often referred to as Hindustani), and they function as cultural markers that contain lessons about morality, behavioral norms, courtship and marriage, political issues, and religious themes. The plots are generally thin, characters tend to be stereotypical, and the acting is mediocre at best, but they are enormously

popular and are important texts for both Indians and outsiders in regard to popular attitudes and current ideas. They also have helped to spread oral comprehension of Hindi throughout the subcontinent and even beyond, which may in time aid the government's goal of making it the national language. As it continues to define itself in the aftermath of its colonial period, India is once again emerging as a major center for the development and dissemination of ideas in Asia, and Indian thought and technology have become part of the global inheritance of humanity.

See also **Aesthetics: Asia; Asceticism: Hindu and Buddhist Asceticism; Chinese Thought; Consciousness: Indian Thought; Cosmology: Asia; Education: Asia, Traditional and Modern; Empire and Imperialism: Asia; Hinduism; Jainism; Sufism.**

BIBLIOGRAPHY

Brass, Paul R. *Language, Religion, and Politics in North India.* London and New York: Cambridge University Press, 1974.

Goody, Jack. *The East in the West.* Cambridge, U.K., and New York: Cambridge University Press, 1996.

Hartmann, Paul, B. R. Patil, and Anita Dighe. *The Mass Media and Village Life: An Indian Study.* New Delhi: Sage, 1989.

Hein, Norvin. *The Miracle Plays of Mathurā.* New Haven, Conn., and London: Yale University Press, 1972.

Kersenboom, Saskia. *Word, Sound, Image: The Life of a Tamil Text.* Oxford and Washington, D.C.: Berg, 1995.

Kuppuswamy, B. *Communication and Social Development in India.* New Delhi: Sterling, 1976.

Lopez, Donald S., Jr., ed. *Curators of the Buddha: The Study of Buddhism under Colonialism.* Chicago: University of Chicago Press, 1995.

Matilal, Bimal Krishna. *The Character of Logic in India.* Edited by Jonardon Ganerit and Heeraman Tiwari. Oxford: Oxford University Press, 1998.

Pollock, Sheldon. "The Sanskrit Cosmopolis, A.D. 300–1300: Transculturation, Vernacularization, and the Question of Ideology." In *Ideology and Status of Sanskrit,* edited by Jan E. M. Houben, 197–248. Leiden, Netherlands, and New York: E. J. Brill, 1996.

Pollock, Sheldon, ed. *Literary Cultures in History: Reconstructions from South Asia.* Berkeley: University of California Press, 2003.

Smith, David. *Hinduism and Modernity.* Oxford: Blackwell, 2003.

Wang, Georgette, ed. *Treading Different Paths: Informatization in Asian Nations.* Norwood, N.J.: Ablex, 1994.

Yadava, J. S., and Vinayshil Gautam, eds. *The Communication of Ideas.* New Delhi: Concept, 1980.

John Powers

EUROPE AND ITS INFLUENCE

By the first millennium B.C.E., major world civilizations were flourishing in Mesopotamia, Egypt, the Indus Valley, and China. Each had developed a distinct form of writing, along with urban centers for administration and record keeping. In contrast, Europe was largely a series of diverse nonliterate village farming communities steeped in the conventions of primary oral communication. The eventual emergence of a literate tradition in Europe took place in Greece—at its cusp, one of the most celebrated works in the history of Western civilization.

Orality and Literacy in Greece

Homer's *Iliad* and *Odyssey* occupy an important early niche in the history of European literature. It has been argued, however, that the Homeric epics, strictly speaking, are not even literature. In *An Essay of the Original Genius and Writings of Homer* (1775), the English diplomat and archaeologist Robert Wood initiated a continuing debate by arguing that Homer could not read or write and that the poetic character of the epics facilitated memorization and therefore oral transmission. More recent research has shown that these narratives share important characteristics with the oral histories of nonliterate societies around the world. Their aural resonance results from the use of devices such as hyperbolic turns of phrase, metrically patterned formulae, and extensive clichés.

Sometime between 700 and 550 B.C.E., the Homeric epics were committed to writing, using an alphabet the Greeks had recently adapted from the twenty-two-character Phoenician consonantal alphabet, which some scholars insist should be called rather a syllabary or consonantal syllabary. The Greek variant modified the original characters and added several new ones in order to represent a series of independent vowel sounds. This made writing easier to learn, a more complete approximation of speech, and a medium capable of transcribing different dialects and even other languages—such as Coptic, an Egyptian language recorded using modified Greek characters. Within a hundred years the convention of writing left to right displaced the right-to-left Phoenician (and Semitic) tradition. Before this conversion the Greeks briefly experimented with boustrophedon, the seemingly logical but ultimately impractical style of alternating the direction of the script in each line.

The literacy revolution in Greece had significant cultural consequences, but it must be remembered that at first what was transcribed reflected the extant oral tradition, as in the poetics of Homer. Over the next several centuries, writing would gradually take a less flowery and more prosaic turn. This evolution, in which the content of a new medium is at first that of the previous mode of communication, is a central tenet in the communication theory of Marshall McLuhan. It recurs throughout the cultural history of Europe. In the fifteenth century, for example, the incunabula, or first wave of printed books, replicated not only the content but the calligraphic style of the earlier manuscripts—the Gutenberg Bible was even printed on parchment, the preferred medium for manuscripts—and before the rise of newspapers in the seventeenth century, during the period when reports of major news events were printed in pamphlets and broadsides, they were often written in verse. Eventually, more efficacious ways of using a new medium change the forms of discourse conveyed by that medium, and so it was with alphabetic literacy in Greece.

Until the fifth century B.C.E., a teacher in Greece taught from transcribed texts that were steeped in the conventions of the spoken word. Students were expected to commit the information conveyed to memory (similarly, in the Middle Ages, a scribe might read a manuscript passage aloud in order to

ensconce it in auditory memory). By the end of the fifth century, in the period coinciding with Plato's early education, what had been recited was now read by students schooled in the new mode of communication. How widespread literacy was at this time—it was limited in theory to free male citizens—is still subject to debate. Nevertheless, its influence on institutions, such as the law, as well as on philosophy and knowledge in general, was profound. Learning the new alphabetic script was facilitated through the use of several easily accessible media—sand, slate, and waxed tablets. More permanent texts were inscribed on papyrus (imported from Egypt) and parchment (obtained from the skins of domestic animals).

Plato's Critique

Standing on the cusp of this information revolution, Plato saw benefits and liabilities in the transformation. In the utopian vision of his *Republic,* he has harsh words for both the oral tradition of Homeric verse and the later legacy of dramatists such as Aeschylus, whose writings have poetic overtones. Their emotionality, heavy reliance on sensory experience in describing the world (a signature trait of primary oral languages), imprecise use of language, and ambivalent portraits of the world and the gods Plato saw as exerting a corrupting influence on youth. On the other hand, he did not hold the new literate education, capable of circumventing these conceits, to be without its own limitations. In his *Phaedrus,* Plato uses a dialogue with Socrates—not a recorded conversation but literary prose imitating speech—to lament the attenuation of memory that is a consequence of literacy. He argues that dependency on an external source, such as writing, will diminish the internal resources of thought and memory and thereby weaken the mind. Also, since the written text is passive, a dialogic give-and-take is not possible. Yet despite these reservations it was writing—phonetic literacy, to be precise—that would facilitate the type of abstractions underlying Plato's philosophy and much of subsequent Western thought.

Alphabetic literacy fostered the gathering of a wide variety of data that would be difficult to retain using the relevance structure of primary oral communication. That this data could be analyzed and preserved for posterity is attested to by numerous texts that have come to us from ancient Greece, among them the geography of Anaximander (610–547 B.C.E.), characterized by a visionary cartographic impulse; the histories of Herodotus (c. 484–c. 420 B.C.E.); Hippocrates' (fl. c. 600 B.C.E.) treatises on medicine; the philosophy of Aristotle (384–322 B.C.E.); and the geometry of Euclid (fl. c. 300 B.C.E.), with its verbal arguments as well as figures. To this list must be added the imperial legacy of Alexander the Great (ruled 336–323 B.C.E.), abetted as it was by literate administrators.

Rome

The legacy of Hellenic culture would eventually and selectively pass to Rome. It was preceded by the art of writing itself. The Roman alphabet, nearly identical to the one we employ but limited at the time to block capitals, resulted from the modification of a Greek variant sometimes known as the Euboean or Western Greek alphabet. This diffused into the Italian peninsula under the auspices of the Etruscans, who eventually ceded it to Rome, where it was modified into the alphabet used in most of western Europe, sub-Saharan Africa, Australasia, and the Americas. The contrasting Ionian or Eastern Greek alphabet became the standard for written communication in the fifth-century B.C.E. Athens and the model for the modern Greek alphabet; it also provided inspiration for the later Cyrillic alphabet, used to write Russian and several other Slavic languages.

Many historians contend that the intellectual and artistic achievements of Rome failed to surpass the legacy of Hellenic civilization. However, it appears that in both the Roman Republic (fifth to first centuries B.C.E.) and Roman Empire (first century B.C.E. to fifth century C.E.) the literacy rate was higher—yet oratorical eloquence was just as prized and cultivated as it had been in Greece. Earlier views suggesting that mass literacy might have existed in Rome have been tempered by recent estimates restricting it to anywhere from 5 to 20 percent of the population. Nevertheless, writing, in the form of signage and inscriptions on altars and monuments, was widespread. The ruins of Pompeii even reveal electoral posters, along with graffiti drawing on the poetry of Ovid and Propertius, which suggests that even some members of the underclass must have been able to read and write. In wealthier homes slaves were sometimes taught to be household scribes. Literacy was also not unknown among the gladiators.

The book trade, in the form of papyrus scrolls, flourished under the empire. Teams of scribes were able to produce hundreds of copies and occasionally revised "editions" of a given work—a feat usually linked with the printing revolution. Bookstores were established, and even advertised. Papyrus was, however, expensive (ordinary correspondence usually employed wax tablets) and many private libraries accumulated written materials more for status—conspicuous consumption, to use Thorstein Veblen's term—than for the sake of having a repository of knowledge.

More so than in Greece, the communication of ideas in Rome emphasized practical arts such as the building of roads, aqueducts, bridges, and mills. Literacy also served administration and law, especially in rationalizing the transition from republic to empire. The growing body of law regarding contract and property rights and other legal obligations further inflated a growing bureaucracy. Communication over distance was accomplished through an efficient imperial postal system and an early forerunner of the newspaper, the *acta*—a sheet of relevant news that would be distributed, copied, redistributed, and when necessary, read aloud to those who were not literate. Coordinating events in time was expedited through the calendrical reforms overseen by Julius Caesar (100–44 B.C.E.), which laid the foundations of the calendar we use today. The variable (against the solar year) 12-month lunar calendar, in which the year starts in March, was displaced by a 365.2-day, (366 every fourth year), 12-month year starting in January, with the number of days in each month adjusted accordingly.

The Middle Ages
The usually accepted date for the fall of the Roman Empire and dawn of the Middle Ages is 476 C.E., when the Teutonic prince Odoacer deposed the youthful figurehead Romulus Augustulus, thus ending the imperial succession. However, as the historian Henri-Jean Martin insists, the death throes of classical culture had begun before and continued for several centuries after that date. Earlier barbarian invasions, crippling taxes, corrupt administration, and, most likely, food shortages and epidemics all contributed to the collapse of Rome. In the fourth century, in the face of growing instability, the emperor Constantine had adopted Christianity, and Rome had eventually followed suit. Constantine had also established Constantinople as the capital of the Eastern (Byzantine) Empire, which would outlast the Western Empire by almost a thousand years.

The Middle Ages saw a more limited and ecclesiastical form of written communication than was the case in classical antiquity. The parchment codex, or *pergamenum,* displaced the papyrus scroll. Its form resembles that of the modern book, with facing pages written on both sides. The codex manuscript began appearing in the first century C.E., became common in the third and fourth centuries, and then established itself as the dominant medium for written knowledge until the advent of the printed book in the fifteenth century. The codex could compress more information into a smaller space than the scroll. Parchment is also far more durable than papyrus and has the advantage of reusability when washed, resulting in a palimpsest that often reveals traces of the original text; and although costly, it could be produced locally at a time when trade with Egypt was being curtailed.

The Roman Catholic Church assumed administrative leadership in postimperial Rome, with popes replacing emperors. Europe became a decentralized, largely nonliterate patchwork of feudal estates based on rural agriculture. The centuries that followed are usually seen as a period of cultural decline, often referred to as the Dark Ages—a term now dismissed, however, by many historians; Lynn White, for example, has argued that while classical learning may have been eclipsed, significant developments were occurring in agricultural practice (the plow and crop rotation), the mechanical arts (accurate clocks), and technology (multipurpose water-powered mills).

Monastic Expansion
By the end of the sixth century, under the auspices of Pope Gregory the Great (reigned 590–604), another invasion of Europe from Rome began. The monastic tradition, founded by St. Benedict (c. 480–547) and originally dedicated to prayer and asceticism, now formed itself into a proselytizing militia. When the churchmen moved north they were met with accommodation more than resistance as local rulers availed themselves of the literacy-based administrative skills the monks could provide. None were more appreciative or proactive in accepting what the newcomers brought than the Frankish king Charlemagne (742–814). Although his capacity to read and write is debated by historians—apparently he sought to acquire the skill as an adult—he promoted the cause assiduously, overseeing the creation of written legal charters and of schools for the teaching and standardizing of Latin, which had become plagued with inconsistent usage. This Carolingian Renaissance, as it is called, although short-lived (his empire fragmented in

the ninth century), left a profound imprint on subsequent European communication. It also yielded a new script, Carolingian miniscule, using lower-case characters with clean lines and improved punctuation.

Written knowledge became ensconced in monastic libraries that might contain several hundred to a thousand manuscripts. In contrast, however, libraries in Damascus, Cairo, and Córdoba, when Spain came under Moorish occupation in the tenth century, had upward of one hundred thousand volumes. These collections, fully employing the new medium of paper, evidenced far greater intellectual diversity than was permitted in Christendom, where the Catholic Church aggressively censored what was copied and knowledge was steeped in theological assumptions. When the church did allow secular classics from antiquity to become available, they were subject to revisionist interpretation—thus, for example, Plato was appreciated for the otherworldliness of his philosophy and his disavowal of sensory experience. Medieval texts were usually read aloud; although silent reading would begin to appear in the later Middle Ages and became the norm after printing, for most of the era it was the exception. In his *Confessions* (c. 400), St. Augustine of Hippo expresses both bewilderment and admiration when he observes St. Ambrose reading silently.

Sacred vs. Secular

The worldview of the churchmen, sometimes referred to as a cosmography, regarded nature as a book to be interpreted, not a domain amenable to empirical discovery or rational analysis. However, with new ideas entering Europe from the Crusades and through the Islamic presence in Spain, as well as from the newly emergent church-founded universities, some accommodation became necessary. In response, Thomas Aquinas (1225–1274) argued for a partial application of rational methods to an understanding of the world, provided scriptural revelation remained the final arbiter. The Franciscan Roger Bacon (1214–1294) abused this license with a series of experiments, most notably in optics, that resulted in his imprisonment. The fate of others who transgressed Catholic ideology is chronicled in the history of the Inquisition.

In communicating its teachings to the mostly nonliterate masses, the church employed a rich iconography. Cathedrals were texts to be read; each image told a story. By the thirteenth century, clerics, drafting voluminous contracts, charters, and wills, began to increasingly serve the needs of both secular rulers and a merchant class that had been growing since the emergence of towns two centuries earlier. Still, in this mostly oral world, the language of everyday life remained poetic. Rhymes were used to remember everything from agricultural practice to accountancy, and newsworthy events were conveyed in song by traveling troubadours. The period also saw the beginnings of writing in local languages, or vernaculars, facilitated through the spread of paper, which had initially entered Europe via trade and by the fourteenth century was increasingly being manufactured there. Vernacular literatures emerged, as evidenced in the writings of Dante (1265–1321), Petrarch (1304–1374), and Chaucer (c. 1342–1400).

The Print Revolution

Although few scholars would argue that any single technology merits the label "historical prime mover," moveable-type printing is certainly one of the few likely candidates. It gave new impetus to the Renaissance already underway, opened the door to modernity, and offered a technique for mass production that would proliferate during the industrial revolution. Johannes Gutenberg, a goldsmith from Mainz whose forty-two-line Bible was printed in 1455, is usually deemed the creator of the new medium. It must be remembered, however, that printing from wooden blocks had begun seven hundred years earlier in China, and that by the eleventh century the Chinese were experimenting with moveable type using baked clay characters. Since Chinese print shops required thousands of such characters, given China's nonalphabetic script, and since the results were less aesthetically appealing than block books, the experiment had not endured. By the late fourteenth century Korea had developed both an alphabetic script and moveable-type printing using bronze characters. This remained a temporary development. It was the European variant of the technology that would eventually sweep the world.

By 1501, European printers had turned out twenty-seven thousand known publications totaling over ten million copies. Further growth would be exponential. Early print runs produced from two hundred to a thousand copies of a book at a cost far below that of scribal labor, not to mention the greater affordability of paper versus parchment. Although literacy rates rose steadily, nothing approaching mass literacy would emerge until the nineteenth century. Churchmen and scholars were the first to avail themselves of the new printed texts, with Bibles, prayer books, and the Latin and Greek classics having priority. By the sixteenth and seventeenth centuries, however, dictionaries and treatises on philosophy, science, and medicine, often with woodcut illustrations, became widespread. Practical manuals in the technological arts also proliferated, diminishing a dependency on face-to-face apprenticeship in a number of fields.

The printed book assumed a look that was clearly different from that of the medieval manuscript. Printers such as the Venetian Aldus Manutius (Aldo Mannucci; 1449–1515) reduced its size (his Aldine editions prefigure the contemporary pocket book), streamlined the font, and made many Greco-Roman classics available in translation at a relatively low cost to the Renaissance consumer. Other features that we often take for granted began to appear: a regularized title page indicating the date and place of publication, improved punctuation, and layouts that made silent reading the norm. The index, once an oddity in manuscript culture, was now often used to make reference works easier to use.

The spread of knowledge brought about through printing increasingly drove a wedge between the world of the theologians and the views of both secular scholars and an emerging bourgeoisie with vested commercial interests. Print also abetted a schism within the church itself, when religious leaders saw it as a way of expediting the reproduction and sale of papal indulgences. This, along other church "indulgences," led a German theologian, Martin Luther, to nail to a Wittenberg church door ninety-five theses (1517) advocating reform. His grievances were soon printed and the church responded in kind, resulting in a full-scale war of words and, ultimately, the Protestant Reformation.

Philosophy and Literature

Although Luther oversaw the first vernacular edition of the Bible, in German—only to be perturbed by how some in his flock interpreted various passages—the first two centuries of the print revolution saw Latin still used for most scholarly publications. But it was a language on the wane, as was the influence of theology on both natural science and the newly emerging human sciences. Nicolaus Copernicus (1473–1543) and Galileo Galilei (1564–1642), the former somewhat reluctantly (he was averse to seeing his work in print) and the latter stridently, challenged theological orthodoxy in scientific matters. By the eighteenth century in France, the Enlightenment philosophes demanded the removal of theological explanations from the realm of history. They also sought a science of man based on the models and methods of the natural sciences. Many were inspired by and participated in one of the great book publishing ventures in history, the French *Encylopédie,* edited (1751–1772) by Denis Diderot and Jean d'Alembert. The seventeen volumes (eleven volumes of plates) identified its contributors, defied government and church attempts at censorship, and symbolized the age more than any other writing project.

Print also brought into wider circulation the vernacular literatures of Europe. At first this did not require widespread literacy, as broadsheet ballads and chapbooks could be read aloud to the nonliterate. Authors were usually funded by a patron. The eighteenth century also saw an increase in the literacy rate, though, with writers now becoming dependent on the whims of the marketplace. Book purchase was often beyond the means of an expanding audience of readers; rental from a growing number of circulating libraries, however, became a viable option.

The nineteenth century, sometimes referred to as "the age of the novel," saw a series of changes that made books less costly and would by its end usher in nearly universal literacy. The making of linen rag paper moved into the world of industrial mass production as waterpower replaced manpower, and was in turn replaced by steam. Early beneficiaries included Walter Scott, whose *Waverley* (1814) became a best-seller, as did Charles Dickens's *Pickwick Papers* (1836). The last quarter of the century witnessed a further drop in the cost of books resulting from the process of manufacturing paper from wood pulp rather than rag. This served to make not only novels but also works dealing with travel, adventure, and popular science affordable. Small personal libraries, once the preserve of the aristocracy, gentry, and later the bourgeoisie, now became an aspect of many working-class homes.

News

Orators in antiquity, the Roman *acta,* medieval troubadours, and handwritten and early printed broadsides were some of the ways through which news had circulated in premodern Europe. The first true newspapers, defined by a regular publication schedule, were weeklies that began in Germany in the first decade of the seventeenth century. Other countries quickly embraced the idea. Written in the vernacular, these publications were in part a response to the rise of nation-states and their growing economic interdependence. Freedom of the press was virtually nonexistent. In most countries a government license was required to publish newspapers as well as books, which meant submitting to censorship and high taxes. Circulation was limited to a few thousand readers at best. Domestic news was minimal and any critique of the government could lead to a charge of treasonous libel, for which several printer/publishers were executed. "Safe" domestic stories included the occasional and usually sensationalized account of a gruesome murder—an intriguing link with contemporary tabloids.

Beginning in London in the first decade of the eighteenth century, the daily newspaper became a fact of life in many large European cities. Greater public access to information, coupled with the ideals of the Enlightenment, especially free speech, led to laws guaranteeing freedom of the press. The first of these was passed in Sweden in 1766, and by the end of the next century most European countries had followed suit. During this period newspapers became a true mass medium. Contributing factors included the rotary steam-driven press, which reduced production time; the viability of engraved illustrations, a feature popularized by the *Illustrated London News* when it began in 1842; and the spectacular increase in the speed of information movement the electric telegraph brought to news gathering—demonstrated dramatically in coverage of the Crimean War (1853–1856). By the turn of the century, wood-pulp paper, the linotype machine (invented in the United States), the half-tone process for reproducing photographs, and increased advertising allowed newspapers to expand their size and scope without a substantial increase in price. These changes also helped give them a look that would endure well into the twentieth century.

See also **Censorship; Education; Encyclopedism; Literature; Maps and the Ideas They Express; Media, History of; Propaganda.**

BIBLIOGRAPHY

Burke, James. *The Day the Universe Changed.* Boston: Little, Brown, 1985.

Clanchy, Michael. *From Memory to Written Record in England, 1066–1307.* Cambridge, Mass.: Harvard University Press, 1979.

Crowley, David, and Paul Heyer, eds. *Communication in History: Technology, Culture, Society.* Boston: Allyn and Bacon, 2003.

Drucker, Johanna. *The Alphabetic Labyrinth.* New York: Thames and Hudson, 1995.

Eisenstein, Elizabeth. *The Printing Press as an Agent of Change: Communications and Cultural Transformations in Early Modern Europe.* New York: Cambridge University Press, 1979.

Feather, John. *A History of British Publishing.* London and New York: Routledge, 1991.

Harris, William V. *Ancient Literacy.* Cambridge, Mass.: Harvard University Press, 1989.

Havelock, Eric, and Jackson P. Hershbell, eds. *Communication Arts in the Ancient World.* New York: Hastings House, 1978.

Illich, Ivan, and Barry Sanders. *A B C: The Alphabetization of the Popular Mind.* New York: Vintage, 1989.

Le Goff, Jacques, ed. *Medieval Callings.* Chicago: University of Chicago Press, 1990.

Logan, Robert. *The Alphabet Effect.* New York: Morrow, 1986.

Lovejoy, Arthur O. *The Great Chain of Being.* New York: Harper and Row, 1960.

McLuhan, Marshall. *The Gutenberg Galaxy.* New York: Signet, 1969.

Manguel, Alberto. *A History of Reading.* New York: Viking, 1996.

Martin, Henri-Jean. *The History and Power of Writing.* Chicago: University of Chicago Press, 1994.

Menache, Sophia. *The Vox Dei: Communication in the Middle Ages.* New York: Oxford University Press, 1990.

Ong, Walter J. *Orality and Literacy: The Technologizing of the Word.* London and New York: Methuen, 1982.

Peters, John Durham. *Speaking into the Air: A History of the Idea of Communication.* Chicago: University of Chicago Press, 1999.

Stephens, Mitchell. *A History of News: From the Drum to the Satellite.* New York: Viking, 1988.

White, Lynn Townsend, Jr. *Medieval Technology and Social Change.* New York: Oxford University Press, 1978.

Paul Heyer

MIDDLE EAST AND ABROAD

The great continental Eurasian landmass, with its vast steppes stretching east to west in a more or less uniform climatic belt, has been a useful path for the transit of ideas and techniques throughout history, with what is now the Arab world as the fulcrum of the exchange between China and Europe. Over roughly the first thirteen or fourteen centuries of the Common Era, there was a slow, steady diffusion of ideas and, particularly, technology from East to West.

The Ancient Near East

The administration of large political entities, whether kingdoms or empires, required skills in writing and numeracy for administrative purposes, so that the ruler's writ could be understood by his officials and communicated throughout the land. In ancient empires there was a priestly monopoly on secular, as well as esoteric, knowledge. In societies whose cultural "memory" was limited by their inability to store large quantities of data in archives, the centralization of all knowledge was no doubt functional. Monopoly of knowledge was based on stone (later papyrus) and pictographs in Egypt, clay tablets and cuneiform in Mesopotamia. Difficult scripts were ultimately a constraint on both governance and trade, so expanding empires required conventionalization of the written language.

Conquest, in turn, involved the mixing of languages and writing systems. The Sumerians had a word-value writing system, while that of the Akkadians was based on syllable values. Simplification of writing was paired with the adoption of the sexagesimal counting system in the centralized bureaucracy established by Hammurabi (1792–1750 B.C.E.; Old Assyrian Empire, 1800–1375 B.C.E.). The sexagesimal system had been passed on after 2000 B.C.E. from the Sumerians to the Babylonians and Assyrians, "together with their cuneiform script, which they adapted to their Semitic languages" (van der Waerden, p. 667).

The alphabet was invented by Semitic peoples, possibly in Palestine, on the fringes of the Babylonian and Egyptian empires before 1500 B.C.E., and perfected along the Phoenician coast. The alphabet formed part of an integrated writing system that came to include papyrus and the reed pen. Two families of script emerged: one Phoenician (reflecting demands of maritime trade and an alphabet that could be used with papyrus), the other Aramaic (responding to demands of land-based trade and, possibly, the use of parchment). The alphabet was flexible, and it favored the growth of trade and the rise of cities. Extensive oral traditions of the ancient Jews and Egyptians now could be written down. The written letter replaced the graven image. The ban on graven images in Judaism (and, later, in Islam) may well reflect ancient rivalries with peoples whose writing systems were based on pictographs.

The centralization of power (Assyrians, then Persians) involved problems of communication and transportation, both of which were reflected in administrative capacity (the ability to move documents over space) and continuity (the ability to store documents over time). Laws and edicts had to be delivered to provincial governors and also stored over time in a central archive to promote continuity and stability, both in administration and in law.

Conquest has always been a powerful means of cultural diffusion. When the Persians conquered Egypt in 525 B.C.E., they set off a century of intense cultural exchange. Babylonian astrology may have first reached Egypt then (Parker, p. 723). Conquest also had systemic effects on language use. The Roman conquest (and doubtless that of the Arabs later on) had the effect of destroying oral cultures and replacing them by a more standardized written one. This has been a constant of Middle Eastern history.

Ease of communication meant that there were continuous or intermittent cultural exchanges over long periods of time between the same places, in both directions. Thus, Indian mathematical astronomy received a constant infusion of new ideas from the West: in the fifth century B.C.E. from Mesopotamia via Persia; in the second and third century C.E. from Mesopotamia via Greece; in the fourth century C.E. directly from Greece; in the tenth through the eighteenth centuries from Persia; in the nineteenth century from England. In the first three transmissions, the Indians got theory that was either out-of-date in its country of origin or else was deviant, so there was virtually no reflection of Ptolemaic astronomy in India until the seventeenth century (Pingree, p. 533). At the same time that elements of Greek astronomy reached India, the Arabs introduced Indian astronomical tables in the Middle East and adopted their format.

Medieval Communication and Transportation

The East-to-West process of diffusion picked up pace subsequent to the Islamic conquests, when the Islamic world acquired (in the words of Joseph Needham) "a focal character in the process of diffusion." The innovations diffused included a package of Indian crops and the irrigation technologies needed to grow them in arid or semiarid environments that the Arabs recognized as comprising a distinctively Indian style of agriculture, which they called *filaha hindiyya* (Indian agriculture). The package included the *noria* (an animal-powered water-lifting wheel), and a whole roster of crops including sugar cane, rice, citrus trees, and the watermelon. From Persia came the *qanat* or filtration gallery (a way of tapping water for irrigation that became attached to the Indian package), perhaps the windmill, the artichoke, and the eggplant. China was the most fecund source of technological innovation (paper, block printing with a press, the compass, gunpowder, to name only the most salient). The agents of diffusion were varied, mostly merchants and soldiers fulfilling their characteristic historical role as bearers of new ideas, but agricultural innovations were typically borne by folk migrations of tribal segments or clans, such as those who left Arabia in the seventh century and whose children and grandchildren settled in Islamic Spain, where they introduced Indian-style agriculture.

The Silk Road was an overland caravan system (with a number of auxiliary sea routes via India) that brought silk from China to Mesopotamia or the Roman frontier around the first century C.E., and to Baghdad after the Arab conquests. Not much merchandise besides silk was carried because there was little demand in China for Western products, with some exceptions such as Roman glassware. However, once established, the route became a conduit for the spread of ideas and techniques. Medieval Arab and European travelers (for example, ibn Battuta [1304–1365] and Marco Polo [1254–1324]) used it, as did merchants, and some specific Chinese techniques, such as textile machinery, are known to have reached Europe via the Silk Road. Chess is thought to have been a diversion perfected by Muslim Silk Road merchants. Persian merchants bore ideas to and from China to Persia from the fifth through the tenth centuries.

Richard Bulliet describes a reciprocal relationship between the decline of Roman roads and the introduction of the camel. Camels do not need paved roads. The Muslim conquest represented, in its early centuries, the dominance of nomads over settled areas, made possible by the adoption of the North Arabian camel saddle. Once the dominance was established, a decisive cost factor (20 percent) over shipping by wagon quickly led to the disappearance of wheeled vehicles in most areas of the Islamic world. Roman roads were already in decline and the caravan routes that replaced them were shortened long-distance overland trade routes because wheeled vehicles required fairly gentle gradients (following the crest lines of ridges rather than heading straight across valleys). With respect to trade, caravan routes were linked to overseas trading networks, forming a great web for the transportation of goods that knit together the "world economy" of the Islamic Empire. Trade over long distances led to the invention in the Islamic world of methods of business organization and credit that later were adopted, first in Italian commercial ventures, then those of other European countries: the partnership among merchants, called *commenda* in medieval Europe, was known in the Arab world of Muhammad (Arabic, *shirka*, "partnership") and the European bill of exchange was modeled on the Arabic *suftaya*, the check on Arabic *sakk* (both conceptually and etymologically). The Muslim world economy functioned as a kind of free-trade zone (propitious as well for the transfer of ideas and techniques), powered by the gold *dinar* and the silver *dirham.*

Medieval Translation Movements

The great translation movement that began in ninth-century Baghdad displays an overall pattern quite similar to that of the westward movement of technology from China, India, and Persia. The movement began through an internal mechanism: the Sassanid kings of Persia (224–651 C.E.), whose mantle of authority and legitimation the Arab Abbasid caliphs (750–1256 C.E.) sought, had maintained a palace library and manuscript copying office whose task was to carry out an ideological precept of the Sassanid state, which was that Persian and other ancient lore should be preserved in a central place. One of Persian kingship's claims to legitimation was that it was the guardian of knowledge. Under Arab rule, this palace library, with the same task, was known as the Dar al-Hikma (House of Wisdom). The Abbasids clothed this preexisting rationale with a geopolitical cloak: its message to both the Persian elites to the East of Baghdad and the Greek-speaking masses to the West was that the caliphate was the only legitimate heir to their respective cultural traditions. Thus did the entire extant corpus of Greek wisdom come to be translated into Arabic; to it were added, in particular, Persian and Indian components. Among the latter was a family of celestial charts that, when coupled with Ptolemy's theoretical astronomy, laid the basis for medieval Arab, and later Latin, astronomy, which, along with Indian numerals (including the zero) and the place-value system, formed the core of the medieval scientific achievement.

This scientific movement, based at first on translation and the retrieval of ancient lore, was an epiphenomenon of the ease of communication within the Eurasian landmass, facilitated by the political unity provided by the Islamic empire of the early Middle Ages. Travel for the sake of knowledge (Arabic, *al-rihla fi-talab al-'ilm*) was characteristic of both Muslim and Jewish scholars, who traveled from one end of the Islamic world to the other in order to study the religious and secular sciences with famous teachers.

The assimilation of knowledge originating in cultures different from that of the core society always involves not only a range of linguistic problems associated with translation but also culturally rooted conceptual problems. Among all the peoples involved in medieval "translation movements" (Greek and Persian into Arabic, Arabic into Latin, Hebrew, Chinese, and European vernacular languages), there was a fairly standard debate about the relative merits of literal versus free translation (Latin, *ad verbum* and *ad sensum,* respectively). In some cases, defective texts bearing alien conceptions were passed along in the most literal fashion possible in order to preserve what sense there was. Such was the case of Aristotle's *Posterior Analytics* (350 B.C.E.), which survived in the form of student notes and which, having passed through an Arabic translation, became one of the keystones of scientific method in both medieval Islam and Europe. The Arabs also had conceptual difficulties with Aristotle's *Poetics* (350 B.C.E.), much of which presumes familiarity with drama, because there was no such literary tradition in their culture. In the case of alchemy, a series of translation errors that confused the color gold with the metal, dating to classical antiquity, led to an increasingly esoteric body of knowledge that, at each successive step, compounded the error.

Once a core of science existed in Arabic, it was then diffused again in both directions from Islamic civilization through the Eurasian plain, eastward to China and westward, through Sicily and Spain, to Latin Europe. Arab astronomy (and its practical side, astrology) reached Latin Europe in the early twelfth century, several decades after the Christian conquest of Toledo (1085), and reached China about a century later. The Chinese founded observatories and staffed them with Muslim personnel. Interest in both East and West was preeminently practical: astronomical calculation of calendars and the practice of "political astrology," the assessment of favorable times for military, political, and economic activities.

When one considers the relative importance of oral versus written culture in the communication of knowledge, perhaps one can profitably begin with the case of mathematics (which has the advantage of reducing ideological issues to a minimum). Even after the reception of Indian calculation (*hisab al-hind*) in the Arabic-speaking world, calculation (among merchants, for example) continued to utilize hand signals. If the intermediate steps were written, a dust board (the original sense of *abacus*) was used, then erased, and the results were often written down in alphanumeric form. So in mathematics and commerce there was always a range of media available and, in practice, they were mixed according to various utilitarian principles. Similar mixes of oral and written culture were probably equally useful in other areas of human experience.

The game of chess originated in India, and was then cultivated in Persia, the immediate sources of the Arabic game *al-Shatranj.* It followed the same path of diffusion westward as did Indian astronomy and mathematics and had the same audience, namely educated people attracted to mathematics and logic. The first technical treatises on chess in Arabic appeared in the ninth century. There was also a popular variant of the game that was astronomical in nature, played on a round board divided into the twelve houses of the zodiac. Part of the reason that chess was popular among Muslims and Jews is that gambling was forbidden by both religions, an example of a cultural stimulus to the adoption of an innovation.

Paper and Literacy

The culturewide significance of media of communication can be appreciated from the example of paper. Paper reached the Arabs in 751 C.E. when they conquered Turkistan and found Chinese papermakers there: "It is stated that craftsmen from China made [paper] in Khurasan like the form of Chinese paper" (Ibn al-Nadim, I, 39–40). The technique reached Iraq in the precise moment that the Abbasids were consolidating power, with administrative as well as cultural consequences. The caliph Harun al-Rashid (r. 786–809 C.E.) instituted the first of several bureaucratic reforms based on the use of paper. The chemistry associated with the fabrication and use of paper and inks reflects a characteristic mix of Indian, Persian, Greek, and Babylonian elements that appears in the movement of translation, especially early Arab alchemy. With an administrative reform of the early tenth century, all Abbasid edicts had to be copied on paper for provincial governors and for preservation in registers. Thus, paper was crucial to administrative expansion and bureaucratic consolidation, giving the

Abbasids an augmented capacity for governing far-flung provinces effectively.

Paper was associated with a vertical mill, whereby a water wheel turns a horizontal axis fitted with hammers. Paper was one element in a unified set of Chinese technologies that diffused simultaneously westward along with the mill type: preparation of different kinds of oil, paper, sugar, indigo, lacquer, and tea—all of which require pounding or maceration (Daniels, pp. 30–39)—bringing the paper and sugar industries to the Middle East simultaneously. The names *al-Warraq* (papermaker) and *al-Sukkari* (sugar maker) appear in ninth-century Iraq.

It is thought that, because of the democratizing effect of paper, literacy was more widespread in the Islamic world than in medieval Europe, where both writing (on parchment) and reading were the province of a small, mainly clerical elite. But the definition of literacy has recently broadened somewhat: a person may well have a piece of paper (a deed, a horoscope, a prescription) that cannot be completely read, but the contents are generally understood. There was a great deal of what might be called partial literacy, and many people who could read (at whatever level) could not write. The two skills were not as tightly linked as they have been in recent centuries. Among Muslims and Jews, reading in particular and, to a lesser degree, writing, were skills that were required for an ordinary religious life, dependent on mastery of scriptural and other religious texts (hadith, Talmud). The Cairo *Geniza* (a repository of tenth-century documents written in Hebrew and Judeo-Arabic) shows a certain democratization of ideas: almanacs, amulets, horoscopes, prescriptions, and other such quasi-scientific paraphernalia were widely circulated.

Sacred objects were visualized in different ways. Judaism and Islam were iconoclastic, the Persians less so, thus human figures adorn their manuscripts. But the Muslims liked other kinds of representations such as huge, ornately lettered Korans.

The Ottomans and Early Modernization

There was an eastward reflux of technological diffusion when Jews and Muslims were expelled from Spain, the Jews in 1492 and the Moriscos, in a steady flow of emigrants from 1492 through the definitive expulsion of 1610. The Moriscos took back to North Africa a version of Indian agriculture (Arabic, *filaha hindiyya*) updated especially with New World crops (maize, tomatoes, American beans, chili pepper, *opuntia* [cactus], and tobacco). The Ottomans (and the Mamlukes before them) received firearms from different sources, but the Moriscos diffused the Spanish approach to artillery. Ibrahim ibn Ahmad ibn Ghanim, a Morisco who had been an artilleryman in Spain, arrived in Tunis in 1609–1610 and wrote an influential artillery manual in Arabic, in great part paraphrased or translated from Luis Collado's *Plática manual de artillería.*

Spanish Jews introduced a new, modern textile industry, that of broadcloth, into the Ottoman Empire, the new cloth being the result of the introduction, from Spain, of a fulling mill that made for a stronger, cheaper brand of textile. A French traveler in Istanbul in the mid-sixteenth century remarked that the Marranos "were the men who have taught the

Turks how to trade and to deal with those things that we use mechanically." In Cristóbal de Villalón's pseudonymous sixteenth-century *Viaje de Turquia,* the author explains that the Turkish artillery corps

> had no masters to teach them (particularly how to mount pieces on carriages) until the Jews were thrown out of Spain. They showed them how, as well as how to fire muskets, to make forts and trenches, and whatever devices and strategies there are in war, because before they [the Turks] were no better than animals.

The report is exaggerated, but all the crafts of the Renaissance military engineer are represented. Giovanni Soranzo (doge of Venice, r. 1312–28) is said to have prevented the expulsion of the Jews from Venice in 1571 on the grounds that Jewish refugees from Spain had taught the Turks how to make cannons, cannonballs, and other armaments. That Jews had modernized medicine in the Ottoman Empire had become a cliché in European commentary by the eighteenth century. Villalón, referring to Jewish physicians in the Ottoman court, says they practiced there "almost by inheritance." Those physicians diffused a kind of compendium of late medieval European medicine.

The traditional culture of the Middle East also offered ample resistance to innovations: some opposed the telegraph because they supposed that spirits inhabited the wires. Jews or Christians generally established the first printing presses in the Ottoman Empire or Islamic world because Muslims had long opposed printing on religious grounds. The first government gazette in the Ottoman Empire appeared in Turkish and Arabic in 1867, the first newspaper, the following year (the first newspaper did not appear in Persia until 1935).

Modernization

The predominant pattern of innovation in the nineteenth century was that the Ottomans filtered the European model of modernization and diffused specific techniques to selected sites in their empire. Centralization was the dominant political ideal associated with modernization. In terms of Arab society, this translated into bringing tribes under central control, which, in turn, involved a stepped-up military capacity and favored spatially unifying technologies such as the telegraph and the railroad. Bedouins realistically viewed the telegraph as an unwelcome government intrusion. The first Ottoman telegraph lines were built in 1855. Beirut was linked to Damascus in 1861 and to Istanbul two years later. Then Iraq was linked by telegraph to Istanbul, but also to India, a move that was thought to enhance the economic stability of the country (England pushed for this to enhance its control over India after the Mutiny of 1857–1859). Istanbul was linked to Arabia in 1901, complementing the Hijaz railroad, which linked Syria to Arabia. The telegraph and railroads were a unifying force economically (because they increased the volume of commerce in the towns and districts along their routes and in their termini) and politically. Because the Hijaz railroad carried pilgrims, it became a visible, material symbol of Pan-Islamism.

The telegraph and railroad were designed to reduce the time and distance factors across the great Eurasian landmass.

Ottoman imperial administration differed in places that had the telegraph, where communication was instantaneous, and those that didn't, where it took days for dispatches to arrive, with palpable results in law enforcement, tax collection, price and wage regulation, and so forth. The telegraph was also a spur to democratization, as citizens used telegrams to petition the central government directly. As a result, the pace of innovation may have quickened, at least in cities, and selected rural economies certainly benefited. However, the deeper cultural manifestations of such technologies have yet to be explored.

Darwinian evolution illustrates how acceptance or resistance to modern scientific ideas was channeled along religious lines. The Syrian Protestant College in Beirut (later American University of Beirut) was famously a node of diffusion of Darwinism. The chief backer of Darwin there, Edwin Lewis, was fired for his efforts, but not before having passed the idea to students, mostly secular writers of Christian origin who continued their advocacy of Darwin in Lebanon and Egypt. Among Muslims, interestingly, Shiite theologians tended to have a more moderate view of evolution than did their Sunni counterparts. Religious opposition was uniformly based on scriptural authority, although moderate (generally Shiite) commentators stressed that there was no specific Koranic warrant to oppose the theory.

What explains the receptivity to innovation in the early Islamic world and the rejection of innovation in the modern Islamic world? Under what circumstances did Islam itself become a barrier to the diffusion of ideas and techniques? In the broadest possible terms, so long as a minority of Muslims ruled a majority of non-Muslims (a garrison state model), it was to the advantage of the rulers to be open to whatever innovations might increase their power and augment their prestige. Once Muslims were in a majority, a kind of cultural self-sufficiency set in, which turned the interests of the elite inward, toward refining the Islamic system, which was (in theory, at least) a kind of theocracy in which no distinction was made between religious and civil (legal) spheres and in which religious law regulated all aspects of daily life. Innovation was viewed as arbitrary, having no basis in recognized tenets of Islam. The traditional education system, mosque-based schools (*madrasas*), never evolved into a system that could encompass exogenous elements. In such a cultural system, innovation is irrelevant. *Bid'a* (Arabic, "innovation") was held to be both good and bad, betraying ambivalence (at the least) toward innovation, and was invoked selectively against, for example, tobacco, coffee, and various aspects of modern science.

See also **Diffusion, Cultural; Education: Islamic Education; Empire and Imperialism: Middle East; Islam; Islamic Science; Trade.**

BIBLIOGRAPHY

Allsen, Thomas T. *Culture and Conquest in Mongol Eurasia.* Cambridge, U.K.: Cambridge University Press, 2001.

Bloom, Jonathan M. *Paper before Print: The History and Impact of Paper in the Islamic World.* New Haven, Conn.: Yale University Press, 2001.

Bulliet, Richard W. *The Camel and the Wheel.* Cambridge, Mass.: Harvard University Press, 1975.

Daniels, Christian. "Sugarcane Technology." In *Science and Civilisation in China*, edited by Joseph Needham, vol. 6, part 3, 5–539. Cambridge, U.K.: Cambridge University Press, 1996.

Diamond, Jared M. *Guns, Germs, and Steel: The Fates of Human Societies.* New York: Norton, 1997.

Glick, Thomas F. "Moriscos and Marranos as Agents of Technological Diffusion." *History of Technology* 17 (1995): 113–125.

Glick, Thomas F., and Helena Kirchner. "Hydraulic Systems and Technologies of Islamic Spain: History and Archeology." In *Working with Water in Medieval Europe: Technology and Resource-Use,* edited by P. Squatriti, 267–329. Leiden, Netherlands: Brill, 2000.

Gutas, Dmitri. *Greek Thought, Arabic Culture: The Graeco-Arabic Translation Movement in Baghdad and Early Abbasid Society.* New York: Routledge, 1998.

Ibn al-Nadim. *The Fihrist of al-Nadim: A Tenth-Century Survey of Muslim Culture.* 2 vols. Edited by Bayard Dodge. New York: Columbia University Press, 1970.

Innis, Harold A. *The Bias of Communication.* Toronto: University of Toronto Press, 1964.

Issawi, Charles. *The Fertile Crescent, 1800–1914: A Documentary Economic History.* New York: Oxford University Press, 1988.

Needham, Joseph. *Science and Civilisation in China, Volume 1: Introductory Orientations.* Cambridge, U.K.: Cambridge University Press, 1954.

Parker, Richard A. "Egyptian Astronomy, Astrology, and Calendrical Reckoning." In *Dictionary of Scientific Biography,* edited by Charles C. Gillespie, vol. 15, 706–727. New York: Scribners, 1970–1978.

Pingree, David. "History of Mathematical Astronomy in India." In *Dictionary of Scientific Biography,* edited by Charles C. Gillespie, vol. 15, 531–633. New York: Scribners, 1970–1978.

Rogan, Eugene. "Instant Communication: The Impact of the Telegraph in Ottoman Syria." In *The Syrian Land: Processes of Integration and Fragmentation,* edited by Thomas Philipp and Birgit Schaebler, 113–128. Stuttgart: F. Steiner, 1998.

van der Waerden, B. L. "Mathematics and Astronomy in Mesopotamia." In *Dictionary of Scientific Biography,* edited by Charles C. Gillespie, vol. 15, 667–680. New York: Scribners, 1970–1978.

Ziadet, Adel A. *Western Science in the Arab World: The Impact of Darwinism, 1860–1930.* New York: St. Martin's, 1986.

Thomas F. Glick

ORALITY AND THE ADVENT OF WRITING

The communication of ideas is not basically different from any other type of human communication. It is founded on the unique human skill of speech, a highly developed and formalized system of audio communication, which links with animal sounds and other forms of the communicative act but is infinitely more sophisticated. The jury is still out on the question of the genetic component in spoken language, but that need not affect this analysis of its consequences.

Communication of Ideas in Oral Cultures

The development of human society over the long term is affected by the speed and accuracy with which ideas are transferred from one individual or group to another. In the Old Stone Age, or Paleolithic period, such a process was slow since communication in the sense of physical movement was slow. And with oral communication, virtually all transfer had to be face-to-face, a matter of constant conversations over time. Nevertheless, ideas were exchanged and human life slowly changed, for example, from using one type of stone tool to another in parallel ways throughout the world. Of course, one reason for this commonality could be the intrinsic logic of development, in which intergenerational communication would also be important, but the intergroup transfer of ideas has been of overwhelming significance in much of human history.

How is it that nonutilitarian ideas, for example, even about witchcraft and sorcery, about mystical aggression, are so similar in preindustrial societies in many parts of the world? The standard answer would be phrased by reference to some version of the idea of "primitive mentality," that these ideas were appropriate to "primitive societies." At a very general level, such a contention may be valid but circular. It follows a line of thinking that sees similar environmental conditions (for example, in hunting and gathering economies) as producing similar sets of ideas. That is a tenable position. But the degree of similarity is the crucial issue. These ideas of witchcraft, like the idea of the alphabet, seem very close to one another in contexts where the possibility of alternative conceptions seems to be wide open. So there is not simply the question of the general appropriateness of ideas to a particular set of socioeconomic circumstances but of the communication of more specific notions over time, possibly in this case internally from a common source.

A clearer case is that of the folktale. The collections of Stith Thompson trace distinct thematic similarities over many parts of the world, some of which, like the Cinderella stories, show considerable resemblances over wide areas. It is highly unlikely that such tales have emerged independently, given the common features, nor yet that their distribution reflects some early wanderings of peoples. Rather it is surmised that they represent the transmission of particular stories from one community to another by travelers or by itinerant storytellers, who provide a precise mechanism for their circulation. Naturally such stories have to be "acceptable" to the recipients, but acceptability does not mean that they have to reflect in any precise way the sociocultural conditions of those who listen and adapt the stories. In northern Ghana, folktales incorporated the notion of chiefship (*nalo*) even among chiefless groups who had never had, or had rejected, the institution but who knew that it existed in neighboring states. One aspect of the folktale was therefore "imaginary" in some communities, embodying ideas of authority that they did not accept as part of their own way of life. So such tales were unlikely to have arisen independently but rather by some process of intergroup communication since their thematic content was not functionally or structurally integrated with the cultures themselves. In this case intercultural communication occurred in oral cultures by means of a specific mechanism, the traveler or the wandering "teller of tales."

That process continues to be of great significance in the spread of ideas and information even in written cultures, where wandering scholars, past and present, are important elements in the process of communication. Physical movement is still of great significance in the early twenty-first century. Despite electronic means of communication that supplement and could perhaps eliminate them, conferences proliferate, not simply as an excuse for academic tourism; in certain fields at least they are seen as ways of gaining access to the latest ideas, or perhaps to the creators of those ideas. In other words they are seen as contributing to the exchange of knowledge. Above all they serve to set up personalized networks that have the function of leading to collaboration between individuals and groups working on similar topics, contacts that serve to facilitate the flow of ideas by establishing informal (oral) communication to supplement the more formal and more widespread type made possible by the use of the written word.

Such international conferences, involving an increased tempo and range of contact, depend upon the development of new modes of transport, especially relatively cheap air travel that is changing ways of life in other less formal ways. Whatever doubts may be expressed about travel broadening the mind, it has certainly led to some shifts in terms of everyday behavior, such as food and drink. Even if mass tourism has not led to any very evident changes of a more conceptual kind, it seems likely that the opportunities for the youth of Europe to travel to India or Nepal has resulted in an increased interest in the religions of those areas, and hence in Buddhist, Islamic, or Hindu philosophical notions. Vegetarianism and a different attitude toward the slaughter of animals, and to the nature of the boundary between "us" and "them," becomes an important part of the belief systems of the Western world that had hitherto been largely characterized by its addiction to the eating of meat. For such persons the notion of animal rights includes their right to stay alive.

Written Communication of Ideas

The communication of ideas took on somewhat greater possibilities when humankind moved into the graphic age in the Upper Paleolithic, with the elaboration of cave art and the use of signs, such as the palms of hands and what have been called "traces" by Jacques Derrida, though under this rubric he includes not only graphic marks but also the memory traces of speech. However, these were not "writing" in the full sense since they did not systematically represent the spoken word externally, but they did mean that visual signs with restricted meanings, as in the North American wampum belts, could be communicated to others at a distant destination. Obviously there had to be some community of understanding, for example, that an arrow meant danger, but a full linguistic code came only with the invention of writing in the Fertile Crescent of the Near East around 3000 B.C.E. Then a whole sentence or conversation could be transferred over space and over time with greater speed and accuracy given that it was preserved in a relatively permanent form, on tablets or on papyrus, as "visible language." As a result, ideas could be transmitted from the past, from earlier civilizations (in the strict sense of that word) without any human intermediaries. The works of Aristotle might be forgotten, lost for a while, by Europeans and then brought back into circulation by way of Arabic translations some thousand years later. So his ideas never disappeared in the way they

did in oral cultures of which the Senegalese author Amadou Hampaté Bâ wrote that "when an old man dies, a whole library is burnt." With writing, the previous generation is no longer the only or main source of cultural ideas. They can now be bypassed by reference to books that form a quite independent source of knowledge. One is no longer limited to folk wisdom, to the sayings of the elders; one can refer to the works of Plato, of Moses ben Maimon (Maimonides), of Mencius, or of Indian philosophers, which one's teacher, either in the family or outside, may have never read or possibly even heard of. Intellectually and in other ways, the relationship with one's family is dramatically changed. The death of an old man is of less account since his ideas are already recorded or irrelevant. The educational process takes on a totally different character.

Turning speech into a visual, material object also makes possible the communication of ideas and information at a distance. An individual can send a message far away without being involved face-to-face. That has had disadvantages as well as advantages. The former mean that verbal messages became divorced from the wider context of speech, so that one misses the accompanying gestures and tonality and moves to a great decontextualization of language and a certain depersonalization of the process of communication. But the great advantage lay not only in giving linguistic communication a permanent frame but at the same time in making it more "abstract." It did not, of course, introduce abstraction but it did increase the resort to more abstract notions; nouns were often preferred to verbs; what had been implicit speech became more explicit in the written register. The latter, being visible, enabled a more detailed examination of linguistic expressions by the eye, which could range back and forth over the page, reappraising and reviewing the ideas that had been formulated there. Once again such a considered approach to what was being said was not impossible in oral intercourse, but it was not easy and inevitable as it became with the written word, which then saw the virtual birth of activities that were later to be named "philosophy" or "theology." Both the "sophia" and the "logos" were stimulated by the use of writing, subsequently giving birth to a whole range of topics that had remained only implicit in purely oral cultures. It is true that then one can speak of ethnosciences such as ethnogeography or ethnobotany. All societies have concepts of space and time, and all resort to some classification of the animals and plants that surround them. But those fields of enquiry are significantly advanced by the use of written lists that impose a beginning and an end on particular sequences and hence give rise to explicit questions of inclusion and exclusion that probe the nature of categories.

In some written languages, the category is even shown in the way a word is constructed. In Mesopotamian cuneiform, for example, a certain suffix may indicate whether one is referring to a god or a town to which the god is attached. That is one of the advantages of nonphonetic scripts; they can point to the range of phenomena or ideas in which one can search whereas phonetic scripts such as alphabets are necessarily limited to the information contained in the oral forms.

This attempt to classify ideas and information was promoted by the development of schools, which were necessary to teach the techniques of reading and writing, so that the system could be passed down from one generation to the next. Unlike other innovations, that transfer could not be achieved within the family. It was now useful for pupils to be segregated from the family and to have lists of plants and animals as exercises, a process that led to the consolidation of lists in encyclopedias, such as the Onomastica of Egypt, as well as to the emergence of distinct fields of enquiry, such as zoology, and to the development of more integrated, more precise, more "scientific" sets of ideas, which became more readily communicated to those who had studied a particular field than to the public in general. As such sets of ideas developed, they were more readily communicated to a specialist audience, except in a watered-down, "popular" form. Since some ideas became more difficult to communicate unless to an "educated" audience, the relative unity of knowledge in oral cultures with memory storage became shattered into particular spheres with writing.

Literate and Illiterate Communication

The greatest division of this kind was between those who could read and those who could not, a division that applied not only to cultures, literate and nonliterate, but to individuals within societies, literate and illiterate. For the first five thousand years of the history of writing until the end of the nineteenth century, writing was (with a few, marginal exceptions) acquired only by a minority of the population. In many ways, the literate minority made most of the running intellectually. They were responsible for the written religion, for the schools, the administration, the written works of literature, drama, music, and poetry, producing and communicating many of the dominant ideas. The rest of the population were, of course, affected by these developments, for example, by way of the "Bible of the Poor," through images; their intellectual apparatus was also influenced by techniques such as "oral arithmetic," which it took writing to invent. And they had their own, often vigorous, "popular" culture that was in turn affected by the narratives produced by the literates and in turn impinged upon the latter's achievements. But as far as most literate activities were concerned, they played very much a subordinate role. Only with the gradual extension of education, based on learning to read and write, was this situation largely changed.

It has been claimed by some recent writers, unwilling to accept the absence of writing in, for example, Africa, that any visual signs, even memory traces, represent writing. Such a position is held by certain well-meaning persons who wish to play down intellectual differences of the kind that are embodied in Levy-Bruhl's notion of a "primitive mentality" that failed to perceive contradiction, were prelogical, and resorted to mystical participation. Such notions need to be set aside, as was done by the anthropologist Evans-Pritchard in the work on Azande witchcraft where he tried to demonstrate that their ideas about witchcraft were in fact "logical." One specific case he took was the Azande explanation for why a man was killed by a brick falling off a wall as he passed underneath; the Azande would not accept the notion of an accident, insisting that some person or force had mystically caused the brick to drop at that particular time.

Certainly his position could not be considered "prelogical" in Levy-Bruhl's terms. On the other hand, that logic had in turn to be differentiated from the "logic" of Greek philosophers and others, which depended critically on developments in the written sphere, in the formality that characterizes the treatment and composition of written statements such as the syllogism. While embryonic forms may exist in oral discourse, the syllogism itself, a is to b and so on, must be considered as a product of writing that in this way extends and elaborates the range of "technologies of the intellect" available to humans. Equally one can posit that many notions of mathematics, anything except simple multiplication and division, are, unlike addition and subtraction, dependent upon the written mode. So the advent of writing does not simply allow the communication of ideas but strongly influences the nature of the ideas to be communicated.

Paper and Communication

Not only the advent of writing but the use of cheaper and more flexible writing materials helped the communication of ideas and the democratization of knowledge through the spread of education. An important stage was reached with the use of paper. Previously the media for visible language consisted of clay tablets (as in Mesopotamia), of other solid materials, of wax tablets, of papyrus, and in the West of parchment (of skins). Papyrus gave Egypt a considerable advantage for the sending of messages and recording of information, but in the West that material had to be imported at considerable expense and the local use of parchment meant that a manuscript of 150 pages required the skins of a dozen sheep, only possible in a "carnivorous society" (Braudel, p. 497). Paper was cheap and could be manufactured out of local vegetable or waste material. But it was a long time coming to the West and when it did so, like writing and later printing, represented "the conquest of the East." Invented in China at the beginning of the common era, it was adopted throughout the Islamic world from Central Asia, to Baghdad around 1000 C.E., to Spain where paper mills were turning in the twelfth century. In Christian Europe, paper was first manufactured in Italy two hundred years later. The enormous advantage this gave to Islamic cultures in the communication of ideas is illustrated by the fact that the library of the caliph of Cordoba in the twelfth century consisted of 400,000 volumes, while the number in the monastery of St. Gall in Switzerland, one of the largest in the north, was six hundred. The discrepancy was enormous and represented the great lag in Western knowledge systems before the Renaissance and the advent of the printing press, also probably from China, at the end of the fifteenth century.

In Asia, the expense of communication was in copying (and creation) rather than materials; the use of paper enabled ideas and information to be communicated rapidly from East to West. The notion of zero and Arabic numerals that made such a difference to mathematical calculation were just part of a transfer that paved the way for the Renaissance and the "scientific revolution," including the revival of interest in the classical civilizations. Hence the rush of Western scholars to Palermo (such as Adelard of Bath) or to Toledo (the mathematician Gerbert of Aurillac) in search of what the Islamic world had to offer.

Gutenberg printing press. Johannes Gutenberg (c. 1395–1468) invented the printing press sometime in the mid-fifteenth century. The moveable printing blocks it employed made it far simpler to operate than the complicated machinery of the Far East, allowing Europe to gain an intellectual foothold in the world. © ERICH LESSING / ART RESOURCE, NY

Printing

The balance of intellectual power partly shifted to Europe with the advent of printing following Gutenburg. Its success was partly due to the great advantage of the alphabet, which enabled movable type to be used with a minimum number of units, unlike the more complex logographic scripts of the Far East. Paper was essential in this shift since it provided a flexible, smooth, and inexpensive surface for the press; it was then that the milling of paper really took off in the West. In the Islamic world, which had diffused the production of paper from China to Europe, the acceptance of printing was very different; scriptures sacred to Muslims had at first to be written, not printed. In contrast to earlier times, with the mechanization of writing, the circulation of ideas and information became much less costly and more rapid in Europe than elsewhere. The value of rapid exchange of ideas at a distance can be seen in the correspondence of members of the Royal Society in Britain, where the impetus of the scientific revolution was certainly supported by such communication between scholars in various fields and countries, in the same way, but much faster than had earlier happened in the vast Islamic world as a result of the use of paper as a writing material. Now it was possible to send printed versions of scientific papers to a wide range of people known to be interested in the same topic.

Mass Media

The speed and openness of the communication of ideas and information generally is increased even more by the appearance of the mass media, including electronic ones. In a sense mass media began in the early days of printing with broadsheets and newsletters. Indeed printing itself eventually enabled the large-scale production of almanacs as well as of textbooks for schools, as the price decreased. That process developed yet further with the coming of the roller press in the nineteenth century, which ensured the wider distribution of newspapers and magazines whose contents ranged from the sports and leisure activities to more serious ideas of a popular kind; but academic discussion, too, increasingly took place in journals that were taken by the growing number of libraries, established earlier in monasteries, and later in universities, colleges, schools, and eventually in towns and even villages.

Electronic media further speeded up the process of transmissions, through the telephone from the 1880s for brief individual messages, to more substantial broadcasts through the radio, the cinema, and television. But for scholarly purposes the great breakthrough came with the development of communication by means of interconnected computers that enable immediate access to huge stores of information throughout the world. Those living in remote areas, away from libraries, can download material from the latest journals worldwide and keep up with the most recent developments in their topic. Indeed in some scientific fields, research workers are expected to post their findings without waiting for formal publication. The rapidity of the access to and the flow of scientific ideas promotes their application and hence the "innovativeness" of human society. The problem then becomes one of finding a way around this mass of information, for which purpose a number of "search engines" have appeared to assist with enquiries.

See also **Diffusion, Cultural; Language, Linguistics, and Literacy; Oral Traditions.**

BIBLIOGRAPHY

Ballestini, Simon. *Ecriture et texte: contribution africaine.* Quebec: Presses de l'Universitè Laval, 1997.

Braudel, Fernand. *The Structures of Everyday Life.* Vol. 1: *Civilization and Capitalism 15th–18th Century.* Berkeley: University of California Press, 1992.

Cox, Marian Roalfe. *Cinderella: Three Hundred and Forty-Five Variants of Cinderella.* Folklore Society Monograph 31. London: Folklore Society, 1893.

Derrida, Jacques. *Of Grammatology.* Translated by Gayatri Chakravorty Spivak. Baltimore: John Hopkins University Press, 1977. First published in 1967.

Evans-Pritchard, E. E. *Witchcraft, Oracles, and Magic among the Azande.* Oxford: Clarendon, 1976.

Goody, Jack. "Animals, Men and Gods in Northern Ghana." *Cambridge Anthropology* 16, no. 3 (1992–1993): 46–60.

———. *The Domestication of the Savage Mind.* Cambridge, U.K.: Cambridge University Press, 1977.

Lévy-Bruhl, Lucien. *L'Ame primitive.* Paris: Presses Universitaires de France, 1963.

Thompson, Stith A. *Motif-Index of Folk-Literature.* 6 vols. Rev. and enlarged ed. Bloomington: Indiana University Press, 1955–1958.

Tsien, Tsuen-hseuin. *Science and Civilization in China.* Vol. 5: *Chemistry and Chemical Technology.* Part 1: Paper and Printing. Cambridge, U.K.: Cambridge University Press, 1988.

Jack Goody

SOUTHEAST ASIA AND ITS INFLUENCE

Trade has always accompanied the spread of knowledge throughout Southeast Asia. From ancient times, exchange networks linked the mainland's coast with the Red, Mekong, and Chao Phraya Rivers, while by the second half of the first millennium B.C.E. Indian traders had arrived with goods and religiously based concepts of government.

Precolonial Southeast Asia

The Lao-Thai culture area, encompassing modern Thailand, Laos, Cambodia, and Burma (present-day Myanmar), has a common history of Hinduized states and Theravada Buddhism. Pali (the language of early Buddhist texts) and Sanskrit (the language of early Hinduism) are also Indian in origin. Vietnam, while sharing aspects of mainland Southeast Asian culture and society, represents the cultural influence of Han Chinese and Confucianism overlying indigenous traditions.

The major language groups of Southeast Asia include Austronesian (Cham on the mainland and many languages throughout the islands of contemporary Malaysia and Indonesia), Mon-Khmer, Burman, Tai (Thai/Lao), and Vietnamese. Of these, Mon-Khmer, Burman, Thai, and Lao have Indian-derived writing systems. In the case of societies influenced by Hindu and Buddhist cultures, the primary purpose of text was to convey religious knowledge. However, the role of written text and its use in everyday life varied significantly among Southeast Asian societies, as discussed below. The Hindu-Buddhist states possessed rich oral traditions, passed down through dramatic performances and shadow-puppet plays featuring the *Ramayana* and other Indian epics, with the *Ramayana* in particular presenting models not only of the ideal ruler but of ideal male and female roles in society. Buddhism is an important religious tradition throughout much of Southeast Asia in the early twenty-first century.

The Age of Commerce

With the advent of Muslim traders in the thirteenth century and Europeans in the sixteenth, Southeast Asia encountered a new set of cultures and languages as Islam and Christianity exerted their influence. Europeans came seeking Asia's fabled wealth, particularly spices essential for preserving meat, but later trade gave way to conquest and settlement. By 1900 Europeans had divided the region among themselves, introducing a new set of languages: Spanish in the Philippines, French in Indochina (present-day Laos, Cambodia, and Vietnam), English in Burma, and Dutch in the Dutch East Indies. Spanish control of the Philippines effectively ended the eastward spread of Muslim influence. Many English loanwords from Southeast Asian languages (e.g., godown, gong) date from this period.

Anthony Reid suggests that despite ideas of male superiority entrenched among courts and urban elites due to the male-dominated written traditions of Hinduism, Buddhism, Confucianism, and Islam, women played a surprisingly influential role in society during the period of early European exploration. Because they were heavily involved in trade, including long-distance and wholesale marketing, women often knew multiple languages. European visitors left numerous accounts of female merchants who translated for them and acted as diplomats and negotiators for indigenous governments.

European traders also reported a high level of literacy among women as well as men in several locations. Reid suggests that literacy in Southeast Asia may actually have declined between the sixteenth century and the early twentieth century as Islamic and Christian education systems displaced a different, older

Hindu temple of Angkor Wat, erected in the twelfth century in Cambodia. Much of the communication in Hindu and Buddhist cultures involved the sharing of religious or historical knowledge. The facade of the temple at Angkor Wat depicts scenes from Hindu epics and events in the life of King Suryavarman II. © DAVID BALL/CORBIS

type of literacy. In the Lampung districts of southern Sumatra, the Philippines, southern Sulawesi, and the island of Sumbawa, the old Indonesian *ka-ga-nga* alphabet was written on bamboo or palm leaf, and women actively perpetuated the writing tradition by teaching it to household members. Literacy in these areas apparently existed for the sole purpose of courtship, that is, the composition of love poetry. Visitors also noted high literacy in Java and Bali. When Muslims began to dominate a region, the traditions were quickly stamped out, and women's literacy was discouraged. In contrast to these early reports, recent accounts of Southeast Asian Buddhist societies describe a disadvantaged position for women with regard to literacy. Because Buddhist texts were written in the Pali language and only males became monks and received their education in temples, women's education during the last century lagged behind that of men. In Laos, for example, which received little in the way of development resources from its French occupiers, few women became literate in Lao until the late-twentieth-century generation.

Colonial Society

By the late nineteenth century and early twentieth century, colonial rulers in Malaya, Burma, Indochina, and the Dutch East Indies were introducing formal Western education. Colonial governments established schools, teacher-training institutions, medical colleges, and universities. Where colonizers wanted to develop a class of indigenous civil servants, instruction was given in European languages. In the Dutch East Indies, for example, Malay and Dutch were both taught in Roman characters, and in Vietnam instruction was in French. In Laos, however, which had already been staffed with French-speaking Vietnamese ad-

ministrators, the colonial government of 1941 to 1945 actively encouraged Lao language standardization and the creation of a distinct Lao identity to enlist local support for French rule.

Daniel Marr notes that "among all the countries of Southeast Asia, Vietnam probably enjoyed the most favorable conditions for meaningful intellectual activity" (pp. 32–33). For one thing, 85 percent of Vietnamese spoke the same language. Literacy, however, was a major issue. At the beginning of the twentieth century, four different writing systems were available: (1) Chinese characters; (2) nom (demotic characters); (3) French; and (4) *quoc-ngu* (romanized script developed by seventeenth-century French missionaries). Chinese knowledge had been important for civil exams in the nineteenth century but declined in the twentieth. Although only about 5 percent of the Vietnamese population could read by the mid-1920s, school enrollment increased, and people learned *quoc-ngu* informally after that. The French established the University of Indochina (now the University of Hanoi) and upgraded it in the 1930s because too many Vietnamese were going to France and learning anticolonial ideas. Both government and private Vietnamese schools expanded in the 1930s, while French works were translated into *quoc-ngu*.

The French conquerors brought the first modern printing press to Vietnam, and French-language bulletins were published in Saigon as early as 1861; the first Vietnamese (French-language) newspaper went to press in 1917. By the 1930s, however, both Vietnamese nationalism and *quoc-ngu* were developing together. Intellectuals sought to use the script as a vehicle to modernize Vietnamese culture, while revolutionaries, particularly after the founding of the Democratic Republic of Vietnam in 1945, made the elimination of illiteracy a top priority. Vietnamese publication was remarkably prolific, unparalleled by any other Southeast Asian country: roughly fifteen million bound publications were produced in the two decades before the August 1945 revolution (about eight or nine books or pamphlets per literate individual).

The most important European concepts to influence Southeast Asia were probably nationalism and the idea of the nation-state, made possible by growing literacy in indigenous languages and the development of the local press. Prenationalist movements grew not only because of direct experience with colonial injustice but also as the result of influences from abroad, including the Meiji Revolution in Japan and the 1911 Chinese Revolution of Sun Yat-sen. The 1917 Russian Revolution led to the establishment of Communist Parties in Southeast Asia. Young men (including the Vietnamese leader Ho Chi Minh) were attracted to the Communist Party abroad because of its anticolonialism. Marxist ideas, such as nationalization and state-controlled economies, kept their popularity in several Southeast Asian countries after independence.

Postcolonial Society

The introduction of secular education and a Western curriculum in the twentieth century had profound effects on Southeast Asian language and culture. Necessary skills for preserving and transcribing old texts have been lost, while Western cultural traits have become a source of status. After publishing houses were es-

TIMELINE—SOUTHEAST ASIA

Mainland Southeast Asia consists of the present-day states of Myanmar (Burma), Thailand, Cambodia, Laos, and Vietnam. Maritime or island Southeast Asia includes the Malay part of the peninsula and a large archipelago divided between Indonesia and the Philippines.

PRECOLONIAL ERA

c. 500 B.C.E. Indian trade with mainland Southeast Asia begins, leading to the spread of Hindu-Buddhist ideology and the influence of Sanskrit and Pali on local languages.

c. 1 C.E. With the spread of trade into the islands, west and central maritime Southeast Asia comes under the influence of Hindu and Buddhist traditions.

1st millennium C.E. Mon-Khmer people settle Irawaddy Valley, Bangkok Plain, and Mekong Delta; Khmer site of Angkor Wat (ninth century) typifies court of Hinduized Southeast Asian state. Red River Valley (southernmost extent of Chinese Empire) occupied by Vietnamese. Chams (Malayo-Polynesian language group) inhabit coast from the Red River Valley to the Mekong Delta.

Early 2nd millennium C.E. Burmans move into the Shan Hills from the eastern Himalayas; conquer Mon-dominated Irawaddy River Valley. Thai and related Lao move into what is now Laos and Thailand from Southeast China.

1300 C.E. Islam expands into island Southeast Asia from the Indian Ocean, following trade routes; Muslims introduce Arabic as they convert local populations.

14th–18th centuries. Vietnamese push south, dominating Chams and taking the Mekong Delta from the Khmers.

16th century. Spain annexes the Philippines, bringing Christianity and Spanish and blocking the eastward spread of Muslim conversions. Portuguese and then the Dutch occupy the Spice Islands.

18th century. Four ethnic groups dominate mainland Southeast Asia by this time: Burmans (Irawaddy River Valley), Thais (Bangkok Plain), Lao (northern and central Mekong Valley), and Vietnamese (eastern lowlands). The contemporary states of Myanmar (Burma), Thailand, Laos, and Vietnam take their names from these ethnic groups.

COLONIAL ERA

1824–1885. British acquire Burma, which becomes an Indian province in 1885.

1858–1885. French take over the Nguyen dynasty of Vietnam; French becomes the language of administration in French Indochina (present-day Vietnam, Laos, and Cambodia). French introduce the printing press to Vietnam; the first French-language bulletins appear in 1861. Malay (later the Indonesian national language) develops a popular literature, spreading ideas of modernization and nationalism from the late nineteenth century on.

1885–1945. Western schools rapidly expand by the early twentieth century. First Vietnamese (French-language) newspaper is printed in 1917. First Thai publishing houses are established in the 1930s. In Vietnam a remarkable expansion of literacy in *quoc-ngu,* romanized Vietnamese script, takes place between the 1920s and 1940s. Early nationalist movements develop throughout Southeast Asia in response to colonialism and the introduction of Western thought.

1945–1954. Most of Southeast Asia is decolonized in the aftermath of World War II.

POSTCOLONIAL ERA

1954–1975. The expansion of radio in the 1960s and 1970s creates a community of listeners in Southeast Asian countries for the first time. The Vietnam War, ending in 1975 with the fall of Saigon, results in massive devastation, population loss, and displacement within mainland Southeast Asia as well as an unprecedented international refugee flow.

Mid-1980s. Television is introduced to Laos and Bali. The refugee diaspora stimulates use of new media, such as video. Literary analysis and the first women scholars emerge in Laos during the late twentieth century.

1990s. Television viewing greatly expands with the advent of satellite television.

2000. Cell phones, fax machines, computers, and cybercafes permeate city life. The Thai language, in both spoken and written forms, increasingly dominates neighboring Laos.

tablished in Laos and Northeast Thailand in the 1930s, writing on palm leaves became obsolete. In the late twentieth century a new field of Lao literary analysis emerged in which female as well as male Lao scholars participate.

The last two decades of the twentieth century brought modern mass media within reach of most Southeast Asians, though access varies. Television first appeared in Thailand during the 1950s but was not available outside the capital until rural electrification took place in the late 1970s. During the 1980s color television sets and then videocassette recorders became common, and by the next decade television viewing had greatly increased. In Bali (Indonesia), famous for its popular theater, the effect of television on live theater was so great that eight out of ten theater troupes vanished during the 1980s. Siam's (present-day Thailand) confrontation with Western colonialism in the nineteenth century led to a concern with boundaries and remodeling of the Siamese administration system after the model of Dutch and British colonial practice. One of the first Asian countries to use new media to further national development, Thailand has promoted an "official" national cultural identity for at least ninety years through its public education system and mass literacy in Central Thai. By the late 1980s television programming was used to introduce new, nonindigenous patterns of consumption, such as the presentation of Christmas gifts. Due to Thai control of modern mass media, the Thai language in both spoken and written forms increasingly dominates neighboring Laos. Whereas Thai and Lao are closely related, the Thai language modernized more rapidly; Lao scholars are still debating the standardization of its writing system.

Communication of ideas on the popular level in mainland Southeast Asia in the early twenty-first century is largely within an Asian sphere of influence; for example, Thai boxing and beauty contests, Hong Kong dramas dubbed into Vietnamese or Thai. Foreign ideas and the English language have begun to enter Thailand to some extent as a result of the increase in tourism after 1987. The influence of Southeast Asian refugees on both their host countries and countries of origin should not be ignored, particularly now that former refugees can visit or even return permanently to Southeast Asia; new ideas include more rights for women, increased individualism, and democracy. The political legacy of the Vietnam War remains a part of global, particularly U.S., consciousness.

See also **Colonialism: Southeast Asia; Globalization: Asia; Westernization: Southeast Asia.**

BIBLIOGRAPHY

Bellwood, Peter. "The Prehistory of Island Southeast Asia: A Multidisciplinary Review of Recent Research." *Journal of World History* 1 (1987): 171–224. Useful background on prehistory of region.

Chandler, David P. *A History of Cambodia.* 2nd ed. Boulder, Colo.: Westview, 1992.

Christie, Clive J. *A Modern History of Southeast Asia: Decolonization, Nationalism, and Separatism.* London and New York: Tauris Academic Studies, 1996.

Ebihara, May M., Carol A. Mortland, and Judy Ledgerwood. *Cambodian Culture since 1975: Homeland and Exile.* Ithaca, N.Y.: Cornell University Press, 1994.

Evans, Grant, ed. *Laos: Culture and Society.* Chiang Mai, Thailand: Silkworm Books, 1999. This is a useful collection of essays on Lao language and culture.

Ginsburg, Faye D., Lila Abu-Lughod, and Brian Larkin, eds. *Media Worlds: Anthropology on New Terrain.* Berkeley: University of California Press, 2002. See particularly essays by Annette Hamilton, Mark Hobart, Rosalind C. Morris, and Louisa Schein.

Higham, Charles. "The Later Prehistory of Mainland Southeast Asia." *Journal of World Prehistory* 3 (1989): 235–282. Useful for overview of ethnic groups and languages.

Marr, David G. *Vietnamese Tradition on Trial, 1920–1945.* Berkeley: University of California Press, 1981. Fascinating discussion of how romanized Vietnamese script became the vehicle for literacy and popular debate between the 1920s and the 1940s, developing along with the nationalist movement. Has an excellent chapter on women.

McDaniel, Drew. *Electronic Tigers of Southeast Asia: The Politics of Media, Technology, and National Development.* Ames: Iowa State University Press, 2002.

Reid, Anthony. *Southeast Asia in the Age of Commerce, 1450–1680.* 2 vols. New Haven, Conn.: Yale University Press, 1988–1993.

Somers Heidhues, Mary. *Southeast Asia: A Concise History.* New York: Thames and Hudson, 2000.

Janet E. Benson

COMMUNISM.

This entry includes two subentries:

Europe
Latin America

EUROPE

"A spectre is haunting Europe—the spectre of Communism." The famous opening line to *The Communist Manifesto* evokes the expectations and fears that have been associated with European communism. Published in 1848 amid a tumultuous period of political unrest across the continent, this polemical pamphlet was an idealistic call to arms directed at an emerging male working class ("the proletariat") that was identified with the growth of industrial capitalism. The authors, Karl Marx and Friedrich Engels, predicted that this new class would become the agent of a revolutionary transformation of the existing social order and that they would in turn create a new form of society in their own image: communism. This they foresaw would be an egalitarian proletarian civilization that abolished divisions based upon private property and the market and in which oppressive states would disappear to be replaced by "an association, in which the free development of each is the condition for the free development of all." All other social groups would disappear, in particular the industrial middle class ("the bourgeoisie"), which they identified as the dominant force in the modern world. The struggle to create this new form of equal society, as close to perfect freedom as possible, would be one of the most titanic and final in human history.

Karl Marx and the Origins of Modern Communism

In articulating this powerful vision of a future society, the authors of the *Manifesto* appropriated the concept of communism to themselves—so much so that communism and Marxism have often been taken as inseparable, if not synonymous, establishing a line of political thinkers and activists from Marx onward who contributed to the development of both. This link was strengthened further after the Bolshevik revolution of 1917 and the establishment of the Soviet regime (U.S.S.R.) in Russia, which claimed to be creating an authentic communist society in direct connection with Marx's ideas, and by political movements that sought to spread that revolution worldwide. Communism seemed to become an established feature of European political culture and conflict. Its significant impact on European societies was deepened yet further by the spread of Soviet-style regimes to most of Eastern Europe after 1945, which suggested that the most significant political choice of modern times was between accepting and rejecting communism. However, the reality of life under these dictatorships was increasingly at odds with the ideals that they supposedly stood for. Any sense of permanence was then shattered in the period from 1989 to 1991 by the complete collapse of these states and of most of the communist movements elsewhere in Europe. From the perspective of the early twenty-first century the whole conception of Marxist communism in its European context appears redundant as a form of political theory and practice.

The above description serves as a useful starting point, reflecting an image of communism that has dominated current understanding of it. But not all communists have been Marxists, and not all Marxists have been communists. In reality communism has been a more complex and contested doctrine, as was evident even when *The Communist Manifesto* was written.

In fact, hardly any single element of the *Manifesto*'s conceptualization of communism was truly novel—including the use of the term itself. It was already used by a variety of minority groups across Europe, religious as well as political, to indicate an egalitarian, communally organized society. Marx and Engels took it from socialism, which developed from Enlightenment thinking as a rejection of liberalism and in reaction to the failure of the French Revolution of 1789 to produce a more complete social transformation. From Gracchus Babeuf's ill-fated *Conspiracy of the Equals* in 1796 and his attempt to produce a "commune," *communism* became a term indicating the most extreme end of the spectrum of French socialist thought. It indicated those groups most committed to the complete rejection of existing society and a belief that violent means were needed to achieve this goal. As such Marx and Engels's use of *communist* derived from their attempt to identify their own particular brand of thinking within the socialist market. More particularly, the *Manifesto* was published as the badge of a tiny organization they had founded, the German Communist League. At the same time, other groups, such as that of Louis-Auguste Blanqui, also described themselves as communist.

Other ideas in the *Manifesto* also predated Marx and Engels in socialist thinking: that industrialization was transforming human relations; the identification of the working class as agents of change; the idea of a class struggle and that a "dictatorship of the proletariat" would be required before communism could be achieved. Nor was their very brief and generalized description of the nature of a future communist society particularly novel. They also included a series of immediate demands made by the league, including universal male suffrage, that were even less unusual. As it turned out, Marx and Engels had misread the immediate prospects for revolutions of the type they predicted. The year 1848 did not mark the start of the final crisis of capitalism as they conceived of it; in fact capitalism was only just developing, and that crisis was to be endlessly postponed.

What made Marx's version of communism distinctive was his bold claim that it embraced a "scientific" worldview and the fact that he placed his analysis of communism in a much broader context. The latter reflected his major preoccupation in life, which was the analysis of contemporary society and of trends in its development. He engaged with the most significant intellectual movements of his age. In addition to French socialism, he brought German philosophy, British political economy, and above all the new methods and language of the natural sciences into a brilliant synthesis. Marx described the result as "scientific socialism," which he distinguished from the "utopianism" of his many forebears and rivals. His aim was to unify theory and practice, to marry the analysis of society to political action. This was what made Marx and Engels's analysis of the coming communist society so powerful: their brand of socialism would succeed not because of mere striving and wishful thinking but because it was based in scientific study and represented the culmination of an inevitable trend in the modern world. Accordingly the *Manifesto* contained little discussion of political organization or revolutionary activity. Instead it presented communism as the direct product of a process of historical change involving a class struggle that was rooted in the effects of industrialization. The working class was destined to become a majority in society, and it would be bound, in the face of obvious economic oppression, to demand change, which could only be achieved by seizing economic and political power. In this view societies passed through great epochs: as feudalism had given way to capitalism, so capitalism would give way to communism. It was this faith in the inevitability of communism, as predicted by scientific socialism, that was Marx's great contribution. From it the possibility of communism as a political ideology in its own right and as a secular religion could be fashioned, but this did not happen immediately.

Non-Marxist Communism

Ironically, after the collapse of the German Communist League in 1850 *The Communist Manifesto* remained largely unread until rediscovered later as a prophetic work. No new political creed and form of political organization followed its publication, nor did Marx or Engels wish to separate themselves from other revolutionary currents. In fact, no other movements describing themselves as "communist" appeared again for seventy years. Nevertheless, the use of the term *communism* did resurface, but it was largely used by individuals and movements that were unconnected with Marx's ideas. The Russian anarchist thinker Mikhail Bakunin had used the term as part of his early political lexicon. Again he used *communism* rather loosely to indicate a future form of egalitarian society; decentralized and communally organized, it would be free from domination by the propertied classes and above all from a dictatorial state. Bakunin argued that the peasantry, and not just the working class, could be revolutionary agents and that communism could be based on peasant institutions. However, by the time the International Working Men's Association (IWMA, 1864–1876) was formed, Bakunin had changed his views. The First International, as it became known, was an attempt to create cooperation between all the European political groups that claimed to speak on behalf of the working class, but within a few years the organization foundered in a welter of internal disputes.

By the 1880s, however, a fully fledged version of anarchist or "libertarian" communism had appeared that was most closely associated with another Russian revolutionary, Peter Kropotkin. As well as expanding the theoretical basis of anarchist thinking, Kropotkin also provided a critique of the state-centered approach of socialist communism to revolution. He argued that the state must be destroyed for a communist society to exist, as the state in any form was always an oppressive force. In contrast, Marx and Engels, and their later followers, asserted that the state needed to be captured and used by the workers in the "dictatorship of the proletariat" of the revolution. It would then "wither away" as the emergence of communism made it either completely or partly redundant. Other non-Marxist socialist movements also espoused forms of communism, most notably the Socialist Revolutionaries (SRs), who appeared in Russia in 1902. Following in the footsteps of the Russian Populists of the 1860s and 1870s and writers such as Alexander Herzen, who had again argued that the peasantry could be the basis of a revolutionary society, the SRs proposed an agrarian form of socialism that would be based upon village communes. Once again, a perfect society was the aim, though the nature of that society and the means to achieve it were quite distinct from Marxist communism.

Marxism and European Socialism

If not all communists were Marxists by the 1880s, more strangely, hardly any Marxists actually called themselves communists at this time. Most mainstream socialists began to describe themselves as Marxists, but hardly any labeled themselves as "communists." From 1850 until his death in 1883, Marx himself never again felt the need to distinguish his notion of socialism as communist. This reflected the passing of a particular moment in the late 1840s but also the way in which socialism was developing. Though falsely welcomed, by Marx as well as many others, as the first genuinely "proletarian revolution," the horrific aftermath of the Paris Commune of 1871 largely dealt a death blow to the idea of "spontaneous" insurrection as a path to socialism. There was also the realization that the vaguely defined working class would not automatically opt for socialism and that organization was required to win over workers to a cause previously espoused by small groups of intellectuals. Accordingly European socialists created permanent political bodies that could attract mass support and campaign for change. By the late 1880s the most influential model was provided by the German Social Democratic Party (SPD), first formed in 1875. And by the 1890s social democrat movements had appeared in every major European country. Although formed on national lines—reflecting the consolidation of nation-states and of national economies in Europe—they also joined together in the Second International. This was formed in 1889, during a conference to celebrate and examine the achievements of the French Revolution of 1789, as a confederation of socialist parties. Every party was officially committed to a revolutionary Marxist analysis and theoretically to the notion that socialism would lead to a society without classes, private property, and the oppressive state. Whatever appearances might suggest, however, this did not represent the triumph of a communist version of socialism.

Marxist orthodoxy in the International was adapted for everyday purposes by a series of interpreters and popularizers, the most prominent of whom were Engels (until his death in 1895), August Bebel, G. V. Plekhanov, and Karl Kautsky. Indeed Kautsky's *The Class Struggle* was the bible for social democrat activity, though it is doubtful to what degree the rank and file of these movements was really aware of the nuances of even this version of Marxism. The analysis of capitalist society, the revolutionary mission of the proletariat, the role of class struggle in causing change, and the inevitable triumph of socialism were all there, as was the language of science in which the whole was couched. Also present was the "stages" view of historical and economic development, but here Marx's essentially economic analysis was qualified by a more practical political approach. The leading spokesmen of the Second International believed that not just a capitalist society but a liberal democratic ("bourgeois democratic") political system was required before real socialism could be achieved. Within such a system the workers' movement could develop and gain influence and eventually power. The state could be conquered by essentially peaceful means, using the growing numerical superiority of the working class, and the socialist stage could then be attempted. This downplayed the need for a seizure of power by force and reformulated the notion of a dictatorship of the proletariat. The aim was still a socialist revolution and eventually a communist society, but these were now longer-term aims that awaited a crisis of capitalism. The immediate priority was to organize politically and economically, to campaign for liberal democratic reforms, and to obtain immediate improvements in the lives of workers. The centrality of class struggle was further qualified by other issues. European imperialism and the threat of war became major preoccupations. In fact, the desire to prevent war through working-class solidarity across national boundaries became the major preoccupation of the Second International. And for the first time, equality between the sexes also became a significant issue for mainstream Marxists. Both August Bebel and Engels wrote tracts on the "woman question," and an increasing number of socialist-feminist women followed suit. In 1907 Clara Zetkin, the leading socialist-feminist of the SPD, organized the Socialist Women's International to campaign for working women's rights and female suffrage. However, insistence on the primacy of class over gender also divided social democrats. Some parties, led by the Austrians, rejected separate organizations for women and resisted the call for women to receive the vote. Many female activists, such as Rosa Luxemburg, also argued that revolution would automatically bring gender equality and that campaigns on women's issues were simply a diversion.

Small groups of dissenters within social democracy took different elements of Kautsky's ideas and pursued them to different conclusions. Revisionists within the SPD, particularly Eduard Bernstein, questioned the very possibility of revolution, let alone its inevitability in modern industrial capitalism, proposing as a consequence that socialists should abandon the rhetoric of a revolutionary transformation, accept the permanence of capitalism, seek legality, and participate in existing institutions with the aim of securing democracy and improvements for workers. Socialism would come through the success of capitalism, as a means to redistribute its products more fairly, rather than through its collapse. These were still radical aims for the time, and the growth of social democrat representation in western European countries with parliamentary institutions and a working-class franchise lent plausibility to this strategy. Even so, revisionism was rejected by the mainstream as a heresy and even more vigorously by other factions that took seriously the revolutionary rhetoric of social democracy. For them, socialists should make revolution a reality by taking more active immediate steps to take power and overturn capitalist society. What they really rejected was the deterministic idea that revolution would come about through a process of inevitable historical change; instead it had to be made by revolutionary activists. A variety of factions and leaders became associated with this more forceful approach, the best known being the German Spartacists led by Rosa Luxemburg and Karl Liebknecht and the Russian Bolsheviks headed by Vladimir Ilich Lenin. But none designated themselves as "Communists" or sought separation from social democracy. Even in Russia, where the social democrats divided into two separate Bolshevik and Menshevik factions in 1903, both groups maintained their adherence to the International, and the ideological differences between them were far less than they were later to be presented. What was distinctive was the Bolsheviks' approach to organization and revolutionary activity. Lenin believed that conventional parties, particularly in the conditions of the tsarist autocracy, were futile and that workers had to be led by a "revolutionary vanguard" of tightly organized revolutionary professionals—the conspiratorial and military overtones were striking and prophetic.

In 1902 Lenin published *What Is To Be Done,* in which he laid out his ideas relating to the role of the party and party organization in the revolutionary movement. Little read at the time, it was to become a founding work of Leninism, the most significant ideological expression of twentieth-century communism. But while social democracy remained united, it served to constrain these more radical and revolutionary voices on the fringe of European socialism.

Splits in the European Social Democratic Movement

World War I and its aftermath shattered the delicate unity of the International. With the outbreak of war the overwhelming majority of socialists abandoned their pacifist and antinationalist stance. With the exception of the Serbian and both

Russian movements, all the parties pledged themselves to their respective war efforts and in many cases joined governments of national unity. They gained respectability, a new status, and shared responsibility for government actions. But as the war progressed and antiwar sentiment grew, they also faced growing dissent from within their own ranks. War deprivation, inflation, labor disputes, and growing social and political unrest in many European states divided socialists. In Germany an antiwar group broke away from the SPD to form the Independent Social Democratic Party (USPD, 1916). As the war dragged on to its close in late 1918, uncoordinated social and political unrest broke out in much of Europe, starting in Russia in February 1917 when the tsar abdicated and was replaced by a weak liberal government supported by the Mensheviks. Governments also collapsed in much of central and eastern Europe and were weakened elsewhere, including in states such as Spain that had been neutral in the war, creating power vacuums that were often filled by a plethora of ad hoc committees. Many of those involved in this so-called council communism in countries such as Austria, Germany, Hungary, and Italy were dissident socialists, but militants from other political movements, radicalized soldiers, and the previously uncommitted also participated. Women were also prominent in many of the activities of these committees, which challenged state authority and became a chief feature of the revolutionary unrest that gripped parts of Europe until 1921. They were heterogeneous in both their participants and in their political outlook, taking different forms in different places and at different times. In Austria, Germany, and Hungary during 1919 to 1921 workers and soldiers' councils became the basis for revolutionary insurrections that were suppressed by counterrevolutionary force. Elsewhere protest was essentially syndicalist in nature, with workplace committees formed as part of economic activities. These were significant in Britain, France, and Belgium and most widespread in northern Italy, where a wave of factory occupations spread across northern cities in late 1920. Revolutionary activists were galvanized by these events, even where they fell far short of an outright seizure of power. Once again the long-awaited crisis of capitalism seemed at hand. It was out of this chaotic situation that self-proclaimed communist movements and ideas appeared once more.

Bolshevism and the Emergence of the Communist International

It was Bolshevism that self-consciously promoted itself as a model for a new kind of revolutionary Marxist party and ideology. After February 1917 and considerable discussion within the movement, the Bolsheviks declared their opposition to the liberal government. While the Mensheviks concentrated on the liberal-democratic phase of revolution, Lenin declared that this could be skipped and that a "workers and peasants state" could be established. In an agrarian country, the Bolsheviks substituted the revolutionary party for the working class as the agent of revolutionary change. Never a mass movement, the Bolsheviks gathered support among soldiers and civilians disillusioned with the war and, crucially, in the committees (soviets) that sprang up in the major cities. Converts to the Bolshevik cause included the

Menshevik leader Leon Trotsky. With less success they also tried to extend their influence into those parts of the countryside where peasants had seized control of the land and their localities. By October 1917, with the government discredited by its own failures to end the war and carry out social reforms, the Bolsheviks were able to seize control in the main cities by force.

This was really only the beginning of the Bolsheviks' struggle to secure power, let alone to fulfilling their declared aim of creating a communist society and a world revolution. This process was accompanied by the creation of a mythology that legitimized the violent revolutionary methods of the Bolsheviks as the only path to communism. Lenin's main theoretical contribution was laid out in two works, *The April Theses* and *The State and Revolution,* both published in 1917. Once again theory and practice were unified. Bolshevik leaders, particularly Lenin, were lauded as the only true revolutionaries and interpreters of Marxist thought, farsighted and infallible in their judgments. In that sense successful revolution represented the triumph of the will of these leaders, and an authentic socialist revolution leading to communism could be carried out only by Bolsheviks. Similarly the party they led was the only representative of the interests of the working class. Indeed the party was needed to make up for the deficiencies of workers, who, left to their own devices, would not develop a "revolutionary consciousness." The path to true communism was through true bolshevism, and all other claims to revolutionary status were therefore fraudulent. Bolshevism's minority status and tenuous links to mainstream Marxism and socialism were glossed over, as was the fact that other groups within Russia—as elsewhere—also claimed revolutionary status as "communists": particularly the Socialist Revolutionaries and anarchist communists who rejected a centralized state and were supported by sections of the peasantry. By March 1918 the Bolsheviks began to describe themselves as the Communist Party.

In fact, the real route to power came through pragmatic compromises and a bloody civil war that lasted until 1921 in which the real instrument that established Bolshevik rule was not the party but the Red Army. The result was that opponents of all political persuasions, from the ultraleft to the tsarist right, were either crushed or marginalized. The main claim to the primacy of what after Lenin's death in 1924 became called the Marxist-Leninist approach to revolutionary communism came from the success of the Bolsheviks in seizing power in Russia and retaining it. Not surprisingly, all interpretations of communism had to contend with Lenin's ideas and the Soviet regime. However, there was no unquestioning acceptance of Bolshevik ideology and practice; far from it. From the start, questions abounded as to whether Leninism was Marxism or even socialism, and whether the Soviet Union was evolving as a communist society. For a majority of European Marxists, who continued to call themselves socialists, and for many who called themselves communists, the answers to these questions were negative. Kautsky, for example, was quick to condemn both Leninism and the Soviet Union as perversions of Marxism and socialism. Likewise, as a witness to the destruction of Russian anarchist communism at the hands of the Bolsheviks, Kropotkin wrote to Lenin denouncing the regime as a betrayal of communist ideas of freedom and humanity. Lenin's response to these critics, at home and abroad, was to denounce them as utopians in *"Left-Wing" Communism: An Infantile Disorder,* published in 1920.

Paradoxically, the international attractions of Leninism as a universal ideology were increased by the fact that the Bolshevik revolution proved to be an exception. Short-lived Soviet governments were proclaimed in Munich and Hungary, but Bolshevik-style revolution was defeated everywhere outside Russia. Mainstream social democrats often played a pivotal role in this process, eschewing violence and opting instead to secure liberal-democratic regimes in power. The result was a deep and enduring division between the majority of social democrats and the dissenters. It was institutionalized in 1919 by the formation of a new Communist International (Comintern) based in Moscow. Its creation was based on the notion that Bolshevik-style revolution had failed not because developments in Russia were a peculiar case but because other countries lacked a proper Bolshevik party. Therefore the Comintern was to be a world Communist Party organized on Bolshevik lines, with different sections in each country, which aimed to spread Bolshevism beyond the borders of Soviet Russia. Adherents in each country were required to agree to a twenty-one-point charter based on Leninist principles of organization and activity. Between 1919 and 1921 Communist Parties of this "new type" were created in most European countries, drawing in mostly dissident socialists but also others who saw Bolshevism as the path to revolution.

Leninism offered a path to power, but what to do with it was a more difficult matter. The formulations of Lenin and other leading Bolsheviks such as Leon Trotsky on how communism was to be created or what it would look like in practice had been as vague as those of all the preceding generations of Marxists who assumed that it would emerge out of an advanced industrial society rather than a rural one. In reality, they had no blueprint. The regime that emerged in Russia called itself a Soviet democracy with a constitutional apparatus. Significantly, neither the U.S.S.R. nor later Communist states actually claimed to be communist societies. Their governments argued that they were living through a socialist stage, "the dictatorship of the proletariat" again, and were in the process of building communism. In practice this meant the permanent dictatorship of the party and the creation of a party-bureaucratic state that, in theory if not in practice, subsumed all aspects of society to it. Nor could any rivals—not just political but also religious—be tolerated. Throughout all the considerable changes, conflicts, and real debates about policy that took place in Soviet society and government, this was to be the constant reality that inhibited pluralism and independence, even during the genuinely radical early phase of Bolshevism, with its cultural and social experimentation. Symptomatic of the trend that set in was the case of Alexandra Kollontai, a strong advocate of the equality that the Soviet regime promised to women. Though initially prominent in the party and government, she and her writings were gradually marginalized, as was the question of real equality.

After Lenin's death in 1924 the question of how to create a communist society in a country that lacked an industrial working class was at the heart of the struggle for the party leadership. Although a political and personality dispute as well, the three main contenders—Nikolai Bukharin, Leon Trotsky, and Joseph Stalin—all shared this basic goal but differed over how it was to be achieved. Bukharin favored a gradualist approach, while Trotsky argued that a "permanent revolution" was required—a swift transformation and a determined effort to secure the spread of the revolution worldwide. Rather than contributing wholly new ideas to these disputes, Stalin maneuvered between them and emerged triumphant. His approach was domestic and sought to create a specifically Russian version of communism, "socialism in one country." However, the second revolution that he announced in 1928 borrowed heavily from Trotsky's ideas in terms of the elimination of the peasantry through the collectivization of agriculture and rapid industrialization. The application of state power to centralize economic and social control that followed could only be achieved through considerable force and at the cost of millions of lives and was accompanied by a Stalinist terror that eliminated political enemies both real and imagined. Ideological conformity to Marxism-Leninism, as now defined by Stalin, became a prerequisite for survival. Nonconformist communists were accordingly particular targets, usually labeled as "Trotskyists" whether they were followers of Trotsky or not. This created a permanent division among Marxist communists, all of whom saw themselves as the heirs of Lenin and Bolshevism, between those who accepted the Soviet Union as it developed under Stalin and those who did not.

These disputes and developments in the Soviet Union inevitably impacted on the wider international communist movement. Stalin was mostly contemptuous of the Comintern, seeing foreign communists as inadequate and other communist parties as failures and sources of dissent. And in terms of recreating Bolshevik success this was a correct assessment, as no other successful revolution occurred in Europe despite some serious efforts in the early 1920s. The International went through various strategic twists and turns until it was finally dissolved in 1943, all of which proved futile and, for Stalin, simply proved his point. Individual parties did often play a prominent political role, particularly in liberal-democratic conditions. But for the most part international communism provided a threat and a justification for the authoritarian and Fascist movements that rose in Europe in the 1920s and 1930s—a threat that was without any real substance. After 1928, developments in the Soviet Union increasingly divided communists. On the one hand, many were appalled at the excesses of Stalinism and either became dissenters or abandoned communism completely. But on the other hand, the apparent achievements of collectivization and industrialization could also be a matter of pride and an example that communism offered a real alternative to the unemployment and economic depression that gripped Europe after 1929. As a result, and encouraged by the Comintern, Communist Parties turned in on themselves in pursuit of dissidents—many of whom were expelled as Trotskyists. Some formed small rival Communist groups, and Trotsky himself, in exile until his murder by Soviet agents in 1940, attempted to form a rival International.

For non-Russian communists questions about why the Bolshevik revolution could not be repeated and of the direction taken by Soviet communism became central preoccupations. Most of the discourse of the orthodox Communist Parties simply aped that of the Soviet government and the International. In particular, the idea that the Bolshevik path was simply unrepeatable in the conditions in the more economically and socially advanced societies in the rest of Europe was officially unacceptable. Even so, some creative intellectuals, often called the Western Marxists, did flourish. Chief among them were Antonio Gramsci, Karl Korsch, György Lukács, and some members of the so-called Frankfurt School (particularly Herbert Marcuse). They were active in the first flood of revolutionary enthusiasm for the Soviet experiment, when there was more space for creative thinking within communist movements. Questions about the significance of culture and aesthetics in Marxist analysis concerned them as much as, if not more than, economics and politics. They were aware that cultural and social circumstances often conditioned political possibilities. Often implicitly, rather than explicitly, they offered a critique of Leninism in all its variations (including Trotsky's). Gramsci in particular, without ever rejecting the Soviet model, suggested a path to revolution that contained the same sense of human agency as Lenin's views but rejected its insurrectionary and conspiratorial strategy as well as the primacy placed on the material conditions necessary for revolutionary change. In complex Western societies, Gramsci argued, revolution was intimately bound up with a competition or struggle for cultural dominance (*egemonia*). In order for socialism to be established it had to be as consensual as possible—more akin to the triumph of the Italian Renaissance. Such thinking remained a minority concern and was decisively marginalized after 1928 in the drive to impose Stalinist orthodoxy on all communists. Either purged from their parties, recanting their views, exiled or imprisoned by their governments, they were silenced and their writings ignored by contemporaries.

In many respects, the fund of genuinely new ideas about communism, in Europe at least, began to dry up by the 1940s. The consolidation of Soviet rule under Stalin and the failure of communism outside of Russia contributed to that feeling. But once again a world war transformed the fortunes of communism in Europe. The war effort allowed Stalin to combine Soviet rule and Russian nationalism—a potent combination that was also to be successful outside of Europe after 1945. The isolation of the Soviet Union was also ended between 1945 and 1949, when Soviet rule spread to Eastern Europe under military occupation by the Red Army, and Yugoslavia was liberated by Communist partisans under Marshall Tito. In Western Europe as well, Communists also gained greater respectability and popularity as a result of the prominent role they played in the civilian resistance movements in parts of occupied Europe. Powerful and popular parties developed in France, Greece, and Italy. After 1945 Communists even participated in governments, though they were ejected by 1947 as the Cold War developed and political divisions hardened. Increasingly, political choices were dominated by attitudes toward communism, both domestically and internationally. This was, in fact, to mark the highpoint of communist success and, though not clearly perceivable at the time, the trend was from then on to be decline. Both within the Soviet-style regime and within the Western Communist Parties, as well as in the wider world of communist thinking, communism ossified. And the search for renewal, and the recycling of old ideas, began to dominate.

Without World War II it is extremely unlikely that Soviet-style regimes would ever have emerged in this region. Even so, communism was not established overnight. By 1949, however, Communist Party rule prevailed throughout Eastern and Central Europe. At first many elements of Stalinist policies were imposed on the newly formed regimes: collectivization of agriculture, state economic control, the suppression of religion and class differences. But by the time of Stalin's death in 1953 it had become apparent that, due to the distinctive social, economic, and cultural conditions that existed in each of these countries, attempts to create systems in the likeness of the Soviet Union could never be completely successful. Yugoslavia was the one country in the communized part of Europe that completely escaped Soviet domination. Thanks in large measure to the partisan leader, Josip Broz, or Tito, from 1948 on Yugoslavia followed an independent course of Communist development. However, this extension of Communist rule also marked the beginnings of decline and the eventual destruction of communism as a state ideology in Europe. Following Stalin's death the problems of cultural, economic, and social stagnation steadily mounted. Opposition to Communist dictatorship also grew, including from intellectuals within party ranks who used the tools of official Marxism to dissect the failings of their own societies. The growth of dissent and the rejection of the regimes by many of their own supporters were to be key features of decline.

The central, unsolvable problem for all the Communist states became how to liberalize and renew themselves without rejecting party rule. The first serious attempt to do so came in the Soviet Union during the mid-1950s when a new premier, Nikita Khrushchev, surprised the world by denouncing the crimes of Stalinism and promising a renewal of communist ideals. The slogan "communism within a generation" was accompanied by attempts at economic reform and political liberalization. However, a conservative backlash unseated Khrushchev and destroyed the drive for reform. Similar experiments under Imre Nagy in Hungary in late 1956 and in Czechoslovakia under Alexander Dubcek in the spring of 1968 resulted in military intervention by the Soviet Union and Warsaw Pact countries. By the 1980s all the Communist states suffered from "stagnation" (zastoy), the term used by Russians to describe conditions under the leadership of Leonid Brezhnev. Any serious belief that communism could renew itself as a state ideology had finally passed. In Poland a powerful independent trade union organization, Solidarity, emerged in the early 1980s and soon posed a serious challenge to the regime. It contained a coalition of ideas ranging from Catholicism to dissident Marxism. Only direct military rule was able temporarily to contain it.

The End of Communism

What would turn out to be a significant shift in Soviet leadership occurred in 1985, when the reform-minded and relatively youthful Mikhail Gorbachev became head of state. His plans for more open debate (glasnost) about new ideas and policies

were accompanied by an attempt at restructuring (perestroika) the Soviet economic system. Gorbachev also made waves on the foreign policy front. Early in his administration he made it clear that the Soviet Union was no longer going to impose its policies over Communist regimes in Eastern and Central Europe, which set in motion the dissolution of the political, economic, and military ties that had formerly bound these countries to the Soviet Union. By 1989 nearly all the Communist regimes had imploded, and the fall of the Berlin Wall reunited Germany, effectively ending the Cold War. The Soviet Union was, once again, isolated as the only Communist state. However, in 1991 a failed military coup by conservative hard-liners, dismayed at Gorbachev's reforms and the loss of the Eastern European regimes, precipitated a final crisis. Gorbachev was sidelined, and more radical groups within the Soviet Communist Party, led by Boris Yeltsin, announced the dissolution of the regime.

Developments in Western communism took a parallel but distinctive course. After 1949 the hopes of spreading revolution to the West became ever more remote, confirmed by the defeat of the Greek Communists in the civil war of 1944–1949. Though still linked to the Soviet Union, the trend in Western parties was for increasing independence and a search for a more distinctively "Western" approach to communism. During the 1940s and 1950s, the atmosphere of the Cold War and the political restrictions it brought about inhibited free discussion of Marxist ideas in Europe—ironically paralleling the situation in the Soviet bloc. But by the late 1950s and 1960s, when de-Stalinization in the Soviet Union eased the Cold War, many Western parties adopted a policy of National Communism in an attempt to adapt themselves to specific conditions in different countries. This was due to a number of reasons, including rejection of many of the tenets of Leninism as unsuitable, and a reaction to many of the aspects of Soviet rule and to the failure of liberalization. Western parties also faced competition from dissenting communist movements—Trotskyites and also new models derived from the Third World (Maoism, Castroism). Communists also found themselves radically out of step with the long economic boom that transformed Western European capitalism from the early 1960s onwards. Many orthodox Communists embraced Eurocommunism, which broke entirely with the Soviets and was particularly influential in Italy and Spain. This involved the frantic rediscovery of many of the Western Marxists of the 1920s, particularly Antonio Gramsci, who was particularly promoted by the leader of the Italian Communist Party, Palmiro Togliatti, in a search for distinctive ideas. However, these developments came too late and only tended to divide Western Communists. By the 1980s the trend in all parties was toward decline and, in many cases, eventual disappearance.

Beyond some very basic ideas, there has never been a consensus about communism, nor a fixed body of doctrine that has underpinned it. Historically it has been a concept in a constant state of redefinition, used and interpreted in a diversity of ways. Even the appropriation of the term by Soviet-style regimes was but one definition of what communism could mean. It would now seem to have exhausted the possibilities for further renewal. The remaining standard-bearers for communism in Europe reflect this eclectic heritage. So-called unreconstructed Stalinists remain as a dying breed. Where communist parties remain they have tended to downplay their Marxist-Leninist credentials and have embraced the broader agendas of the feminist, ecological, and antiglobalization movements. It has been their erstwhile opponents on the dissident Far Left, anarchist communists, and "Trotskyites" who have retained their revolutionary purity on their own terms. All these are vestiges of the past. Whether a new form of thought that calls itself "communist" can ever emerge in Europe remains an unknown.

See also **Anarchism; Authoritarianism; Communism: Latin America; Marxism.**

BIBLIOGRAPHY

PRIMARY SOURCES

Alexander, Robert J. *International Trotskyism 1929–1985: A Documentary Analysis of the Movement.* Durham, N.C.: Duke University Press, 1991.

Bebel, August. *Women and Socialism.* London: Zwan Books, 1988.

Gramsci, Antonio. *Selections from the Prison Notebooks.* Edited and translated by Quinton Hoare and Geoffrey Nowell Smith. London: Lawrence and Wishart, 1971.

Kautsky, Karl. *The Class Struggle (Erfut Program).* New York: Norton, 1971.

Kollantai, Alexandra. *Selected Writings.* Translated by Alix Holt. London: Alison and Busby, 1977.

Korsch, Karl. *Karl Korsch: Revolutionary Theory,* edited by Douglas Kellner. Austin: University of Texas Press, 1977.

Kropotkin, Peter. *Anarchist Communism,* edited by Nicolas Walter. London: Freedom Press, 1987.

Lenin, Vladimir I. *Selected Works.* 3 vols. Moscow: Progress, 1977.

Lukács, György. *Political Writings, 1919–1929.* Translated by Michael McColgan. London: New Left Books, 1972.

Marx, Karl, and Friedrich Engels. *The Communist Manifesto.* New York: St. Martin's Press, 1999.

Marxists Internet Archive. Available from www.marxists.org. A wide range of texts in English translation and other information.

Stalin, Joseph. *Selected Works.* Edited by Lightning Source Inc. Honolulu: University Press of the Pacific, 2002.

SECONDARY SOURCES

Berger, Stefan, and David Broughton, eds. *The Force of Labour: The Western European Labour Movement and the Working Class in the Twentieth Century.* Oxford: Berg, 1995.

Blackburn, Robin. *After the Fall: The Failure of Communism and the Future of Socialism.* London: Verso, 1991.

Bull, Martin J., and Paul Heywood, eds. *West European Communist Parties after the Revolutions of 1989.* London: Macmillan, 1994.

Cahm, Caroline. *Kropotkin and the Rise of Revolutionary Anarchism, 1872–86.* Cambridge, U.K., and New York: Cambridge University Press, 1989.

Carey Hunt, R. N. *The Theory and Practice of Communism.* Rev. ed. London: Penguin, 1963.

Claudín, Fernando. *The Communist Movement: From Comintern to Cominform.* London: Cox and Wyman, 1975.

Cowling, Mark, ed. *The Communist Manifesto: New Interpretations.* Edinburgh: Edinburgh University Press, 1998.

Donald, Moira, and Tim Rees, eds. *Reinterpreting Revolution in Twentieth Century Europe.* New York: St. Martin's Press, 2001.

Eley, Geoff. *Forging Democracy: The History of the Left in Europe, 1850–2000.* Oxford: Oxford University Press, 2002.

Fowkes, Ben. *The Rise and Fall of Communism in Eastern Europe.* London: Macmillan, 1983.

Furet, François. *The Passing of an Illusion: The Idea of Communism in the Twentieth Century.* Translated by Deborah Furet. Chicago: University of Chicago Press, 1999.

Harding, Neil. *Leninism.* London: Macmillan, 1996.

Haupt, Georges. *Aspects of International Socialism, 1871–1914.* Cambridge, U.K., and New York: Cambridge University Press, 1986.

Joll, James. *The Second International, 1889–1914.* 2nd ed. London: Routledge, 1974.

Kindersley, Richard, ed. *In Search of Eurocommunism.* London: Macmillan, 1981.

Laqueur, Walter. *The Dream That Failed: Reflections on the Soviet Union.* Oxford and New York: Oxford University Press, 1994.

Lichtheim, George. *A Short History of Socialism.* London: Weidenfeld and Nicholson, 1980.

McDermott, Kevin, and Jeremy Agnew. *The Comintern: A History of International Communism from Lenin to Stalin.* New York: St. Martin's Press, 1996.

Millar, James R., and Sharon L. Wolchik, eds. *The Social Legacy of Communism.* Cambridge, U.K., and New York: Cambridge University Press, 1994.

Naimark, Norman, and Leonid Gibianskii, eds. *The Establishment of Communist Regimes in Eastern Europe, 1944–1949.* Boulder, Colo.: Westview Press, 1997.

Rose, R. B. Rose. *Gracchus Babeuf: The First Revolutionary Communist.* Stanford, Calif.: Stanford University Press, 1978.

Sassoon, Donald. *One Hundred Years of Socialism: The West European Left in the Twentieth Century.* New York: I. B. Tauris, 1996.

Stern, Geoffrey. *The Rise and Decline of International Communism.* Aldershot, U.K.: Edward Elgar, 1990.

Westoby, Adam. *The Evolution of Communism.* Cambridge, U.K.: Polity Press, 1989.

Woodcock, George, and Ivan Avakumovic. *The Anarchist Prince: A Biographical Study of Peter Kropotkin.* New York: Schocken, 1971.

Tim Rees

LATIN AMERICA

Latin America in the 1890s was a society primed for the dissemination of socialist ideologies. It was ruled by autocrats and oligarchs who were exploiting an increasingly discontented peasant populace and perpetuating a sharply divided two-class social structure. During this time, increased productivity and foreign investment ushered in the earlier stages of exploitative capitalism as well as a wave of European immigrants advocating the Marxist philosophies upon which socialist and communist movements were being built in Europe. The spread of this ideology was acutely evidenced by its recurrent presence in Latin American literature and art, most notably in the Mexican mural movement in the 1920s and 1930s. Led by famous artists such as Diego Rivera (1886–1957), José Clemente Orozco (1883–1949), and David Alfaro Siqueiros (1896–1974), the mural movement initiated decades of controversial

---

ANTICOMMUNISM IN LATIN AMERICA

A period of increased productivity and foreign investment in Latin America during the latter part of the nineteenth century attracted a wave of Italian, German, and Spanish immigrants who spread Marxist ideas throughout Latin America. This feudal, medieval, Catholic, and patrimonial region translated these ideas into a movement against its hierarchical two-class agrarian-based system. Following the Great Depression of the 1930s, leftist political parties emerged that promoted a strong role for the state in directing change, a leftist ideology, and anti-American nationalism. The next two decades were marked by instability and conflict as authoritarian, democratic, and communist groups vied for power.

In 1954 the United States intervened in Guatemala to overthrow a leftist regime that the United States said was communist. Four years later Fidel Castro led the successful Cuban Revolution. Cuba became the first openly socialist country in Latin America, the first to ally itself with the Soviet Union, and the first to openly turn its back on the United States. As a result, anticommunism in the region gained powerful U.S. military, political, and covert backing. Cuba added a new Marxist-Leninist "model" for Latin America and consequently made the prevention of "another Cuba" the central focus of United States policy. The United States chose time and again to support anticommunist military regimes over unstable democracies that believed in freedom for leftists. As workers, peasants, and guerrillas mobilized throughout the region, the traditional elite power-holders turned to their armies for support and received the backing of the United States, thereby ushering in twenty years of conflict and military–authoritarian rule.

The most famous U.S. anticommunist engagements in Latin America included the 1961 Bay of Pigs fiasco, in which the CIA trained and financed 1,400 Cuban exiles who were supposed to incite a popular revolt against Castro, but were instead arrested upon arrival. In 1962, the Cuban Missile Crisis brought the world to the brink of nuclear war, when the United States discovered that the Soviet Union was attempting to assemble nuclear missiles in Cuba. In 1965, the United States intervened in the Dominican Republic to prevent what it thought was a communist uprising.

Internal anticommunist movements also emerged throughout the region. One notable example of this was in Chile. In 1973 General Augusto Pinochet, head of the Chilean army, overthrew democratically elected, but Marxist, Salvador Allende in an attempt to save the country from communism. Leftist parties were banned and their supporters exiled, tortured, or killed. Pinochet subsequently shut down the old political system and established a personalist dictatorship that maintained power through violent repression for more than a decade.

In Nicaragua, a Marxist guerrilla movement known as the Sandinista Liberation Front gained much domestic and international support by the late 1970s. It forced the powerful Somoza family from power and established the second openly socialist regime in Latin America. The *contras* emerged as an armed anti-Sandinista resistance movement and were strongly supported by the United States. The *contras'* resistance, combined with a U.S. boycott that devastated the economy, undermined Sandinista control. Internationally supervised elections were held in 1991. As in the majority of Latin American states that had democratized since the 1970s, the Marxists did not win a majority of the vote in Nicaragua but continued to participate as a significant player in the democratic political process.

---

socialist and revolutionary expressions in art and culture throughout the continent.

Revolutionary socialism seemed to "fit" Latin America's two-class society, but it was strongly opposed by the Roman Catholic Church, the armed forces, and the oligarchy.

Meanwhile, the Great Depression ushered in a series of revolutions that placed power in the hands of the middle class, began an era of organized labor's political influence, and fostered the emergence of Marxist-socialist political movements and parties. The twenty years that followed were plagued with instability as communist, authoritarian, and democratic groups vied for power.

The Cuban Model
In 1959 the Cuban Revolution, led by Fidel Castro, established the first Marxist-Leninist regime in Latin America and set an example for like-minded movements throughout the region. Cuba became an active participant in regional politics and engaged in extensive revolutionary activism abroad. Its alliance with the Soviet Union led to the Cuban Missile Crisis of 1962, with the American discovery of Soviet nuclear missiles being assembled in Cuba leading to the brink of nuclear war.

Like other Latin strongman leaders (caudillos) of his generation, Castro, a socialist caudillo, claimed to personify his country, led through repression, and had no tolerance for political dissidence. He ushered in attractive changes in health, education, and social mobilization, but his administrative mistakes, combined with the fall of communism abroad and a continued American boycott, have left Cuba's increasingly declining economy with little prospects for recovery. What began as a popular revolution deteriorated into the last communist dictatorship in the region, one mired in poverty and oppression.

Guerrilla Insurgents
However, in the 1960s, at the height of its regional influence and revolutionary appeal, Cuba joined with the Soviet Union in funding and training Marxist guerrilla groups throughout Latin America. Following Cuba's lead, these movements chose armed conflict over electoral competition as a means to their deliverance from exploitation. What followed in many countries were two decades of civil wars and military-authoritarian rule as powerful elites turned to their armies, as well as to the anticommunist strategies of the United States, to repress the guerrilla insurgents. The most successful guerrilla insurrection was the Sandinista Liberation Front in Nicaragua, which eventually established the second officially socialist regime in Latin America. Although this regime was ousted through elections in 1991 with the help of an economic boycott and support of anticommunist Contra forces by the United States, Marxists remained a powerful force in the newly democratic system. As a wave of democracy began to overtake the continent by the late 1970s, many communist and guerrilla movements transitioned into political parties and contested for power through the democratic process.

Diverse forms of Marxism and communism developed in other countries, reflecting their diverse histories, sociologies, and levels of development. Indeed that was a major problem for Marxist movements, how to adapt a quite rigid ideological formula to different nations and circumstances. In Peru the socialist Aprista movement and the more rigid communist groups were bitter enemies for decades. Nicaragua had Christian socialists as well as independent Marxists and Leninists. Colombia has four different Marxist and guerrilla movements. Throughout the continent, rivalries between socialists and communists, and various types of each, have been intense.

Democratic Transition
As the twentieth century came to a close, a phenomenal shift occurred in Latin America from authoritarian and—in the case of Nicaragua but not yet Cuba—communist regimes to incomplete democracies. With the fall of the Soviet Union and the poor economic and social conditions of the four remaining communist states in the world (China, North Korea, Vietnam, and Cuba), the Marxist-Leninist model was less appealing than ever. The nineteen Latin American democratic states, with Cuba remaining the only nondemocratic one, each had a unique experience with a liberal transition, but the region as a whole changed from a rural peasant-agricultural society to a modern, urban, industrial, and diversified one. While it experienced improved economic conditions, better human rights records, and political liberalization after its transition from authoritarianism, Latin America was still far from stable in the early 2000s.

The gap between rich and poor was the largest in the world and still widening. Economic development was continuing at a slow pace, with major collapses in several states. Political participation and civic engagement were not entirely free; patrimonialism, cronyism, and corruption continued, with most governments closely monitoring and regulating political parties and associational life. In the view of most Latin Americans, democracy had yet to deliver on its promises, and polls indicated declining support for it. This disillusionment, exacerbated by the continued two-class system and the dire straits of the poverty-stricken masses, made a return to authoritarianism increasingly appealing to many Latin Americans and led to a revival of Marxist language, but a resurgence of communism or communist parties is highly unlikely. With globalization, new openings in free trade, and numerous successful models of liberal economic and political systems worldwide, it is unlikely that Marxism-Leninism will be revived or that even the Cuban regime will remain communist for long after the eventual passing of the resilient Fidel Castro.

Conclusion
While the turn of the nineteenth century ushered in a wave of socialist ideology that gained much momentum in the art, culture, and politics of Latin America, with the new millennium came a waning tide for socialist ideals and movements. The twentieth century witnessed varieties of communist movements in Latin America, including international Marxists, Fidelistas, guerrilla insurgents, and communist parties participating in the political process. Although democracy seems to have outlasted the alternatives, the book is not closed on the future of the partially consolidated and still transitioning democratic regimes of the region. With continued economic and political instability and an exceptionally large income gap, Latin America might be ripe for renewed Marxist appeals, as it was in the late nineteenth century. Although guerrilla insurgents and socialist parties remain and leftist coalitions may be securing power in states such as El Salvador, the future may likely see a rise in new forms of statism and authoritarianism, but a return to the failed model of Marxist-Leninism or even a resurgence of strong Marxist movements is unlikely.

See also **Authoritarianism; Democracy; Dictatorship in Latin America; Marxism.**

BIBLIOGRAPHY

Alexiev, Alexander A. *Marxism and Resistance in the Third World.* Santa Monica, Calif.: Rand Corporation, 1989.

Huntington, Samuel P. *The Third Wave: Democratization in the Late Twentieth Century.* Norman: University of Oklahoma Press, 1991.

Kryzanek, Michael J. *U.S.–Latin American Relations.* Westport, Conn.: Praeger, 1996.

Löwy, Michael, ed. *Marxism in Latin America from 1909 to the Present: An Anthology.* Atlantic Highlands, N.J.: Humanities Press, 1992.

Wiarda, Howard J. *Comparative Democracy and Democratization.* Fort Worth, Tex.: Harcourt College Publishers, 2002.

Wiarda, Howard J., and Harvey F. Kline, eds. *Latin American Politics and Development.* Boulder, Colo.: Westview, 2000.

Howard J. Wiarda
Esther M. Skelley

COMMUNITARIANISM IN AFRICAN THOUGHT.

This essay explores representative Africanist thought on personhood and community, highlighting especially the debate between Ifeanyi Menkiti and Kwame Gyekye on communitarianism, defined generally as relating to social organization in small, cooperative, partially collectivist communities. The general debate on these issues in Africa can be traced to important studies of personhood and psychology in African life and thought championed by French ethnologists and British and American social anthropologists as well as African scholars in different fields. The groundbreaking work, *La notion de personne en Afrique noire,* edited by Germaine Dieterlen (1973), which grew out of the French ethnological tradition, inaugurated a vigorous debate on personhood that has bearing on questions of individualism and communitarianism. In his insightful 1986 essay, "The Person and the Life Cycle in African Social Life and Thought," Paul Riesman explored Africanist literature relevant to personhood, individuality, and community. Riesman argued that the Marcel Griaule school developed interest in personhood and community and that scholars such as Griaule and Dieterlen underscored concepts of individuality and community. In British social anthropology, Meyer Fortes grounded his studies of personhood in customs, behavior, and personality. Other scholars focused on the powers of a person's obligations and social roles as well as on conflicts, legal systems, and individual responsibility.

The 1987 Uppsala symposium "African Folk Models and Their Application" also addressed personhood and personal experiences. Introducing the book published after this conference, Ivan Karp argued: "Quite simply, persons sometimes experience themselves in a human way, sometimes in a Lockean way, and sometimes, as in the case of positivist social scientists, as Kantian transcendentalists. However, these modalities of experience should not be reified and then debated as competing epistemologies. Rather they should be seen as descriptive of the varying ways human beings experience the world according to widely varying needs and interests" (Jackson and Karp, p. 17). Victor Turner's studies also called attention to individuality. Jean Comaroff argued that there was widespread

conception of an "essence" of the person, whose soul was not a privatized interiority but a being-in-the-world. Ellen Corin argued that societies do not always overshadow individuals because certain modalities allowed an individual to particularize to defend himself or herself from "'collectivizing' pressure of the clanic image" (p. 146). Michael Jackson also highlighted individuality in the phenomenological approaches, and V. Y. Mudimbe approached the subject from the viewpoint of inequality of power.

Since 1950 the Africanists Elinore Bowen, Mary Smith, Sarah LeVine, and Marjorie Shostak have articulated personhood, individuality, self-consciousness, and self-identity in community. Philosophers Ifeanyi Menkiti of Nigeria and Kwame Gyekye of Ghana have brought the debate into sharp relief by articulating positions on individualism and communitarianism. Menkiti has articulated a communitarian ethos, while Gyekye has defended a balanced perspective, which he calls moderate communitarianism. Gyekye has pointed out that the debate on individualism and the community in Africa affects the way people think of philosophical and moral issues. Philosophically, the debate probes whether an individual stands on his or her own and does not depend on the community or the individual is naturally embedded in social relations and a community. The moral concerns explore whether individual rights are primary and cannot be violated for any reason or people should instead pursue the common good.

Menkiti on Communitarianism

In "Person and Community in African Traditional Thought" (1984), Menkiti argued that, in Africa, the community had priority over the individual. He distinguished between Western views, which generally hold that a person is a lone individual, and African views, in which a person is defined "by reference to the environing community," quoting John Mbiti's statement, "I am because we are, and since we are, therefore I am," to support his thesis (p. 171). According to Menkiti, "as far as Africans are concerned, the reality of the communal world takes precedence over the reality of individual life histories" (p. 171). Thus the communal ethos has ontological and epistemological precedence. Menkiti also defended the communitarian view on biological and social grounds because the individual comes from a common gene pool and belongs to a linguistic community: "Just as the navel points men to umbilical linkage with generations preceding them, so also does language and its associated social rules point them to a mental commonwealth with others whose life histories encompass the past, present, and future" (p. 172). Menkiti stated emphatically that personhood is defined by community and not by qualities such as rationality, will, or memory.

Menkiti underscored his views of personhood by affirming a *processual,* or procedural, mode of being in African thought in which an individual becomes a person through social and ritual incorporation. Menkiti conflates the facticity of personhood with quality. He does this by distinguishing between *muntu mutupu* (a man of middling importance) and *muntu mukulumpe* (a powerful man, a man with a great deal of force). It is not clear why both persons cannot hold the status of "person," even though one is "middling" and the other is already great. Menkiti rejects the Western minimalist definition of a person, "whoever has a soul, or rationality, or will, or memory; the African view is 'maximal'." Menkiti uses the word *maximal* to indicate that the African view of personhood includes other criteria and is not limited to soul, rationality, or will. Since personhood is achieved, not endowed, in Africa, one could fail at achieving it. There are rules governing social rituals of incorporation that are designed to help the individual attain selfhood. The older an individual becomes, the more of a person that individual becomes. Menkiti quoted an Igbo proverb, "What an old man sees sitting down, a young man cannot see standing up," to support his claim that personhood is a quality acquired as one gets older. While this proverb hints at differences of perspective between older and younger individuals, it is not implicit that personhood is an acquired quality. Opponents might agree with Menkiti that a youth has a different point of view from that of an older individual but might also affirm, in contrast with Menkiti's views, that both are persons.

Menkiti defended the communitarian ethos by arguing that people use the neuter pronoun *it* to refer to a child rather than the personal pronouns *him* or *her* because the child has not yet attained personhood. He also stated that when a child dies, the funeral ceremonies are brief. However, when an older person dies, elaborate funeral celebrations take place because the older individual has achieved personhood and has now become an ancestor who lives among the people. In general, when one dies, he or she ceases to be a person. At the beginning of life, an individual who has no name will work toward personhood, and at the end of life, that individual loses personhood because he or she has departed for the next world. The departed ones may be referred to with the neuter pronoun *it* because their contact with the human community has been severed.

Thus it is clear that people at both ends of life are not persons because the young have yet to attain personhood while the dead have completed their development. "It is the carrying out . . . [of] obligations that transforms one from the "it"-status of early childhood, marked by an absence of moral function, into the person-status of later years, marked by a widened maturity of ethical sense—an ethical maturity without which personhood is conceived as eluding one" (Menkiti, p. 176). Meyer Fortes also argued that, among the Tallensi, "No one can be certainly known to have been a full human person until he is shown, at the time of his death, to have been slain by his ancestors and therefore to deserve a proper funeral" (1987, p. 257).

But Menkiti's view that brief mourning periods indicate the degree of personhood of the deceased is contested. Elias Bongmba has argued that funeral rites of children among the Wimbum are brief and sad for reasons that do not reflect a child's status as a person but because the Wimbum people mourn the fact that the young person has not lived life fully. They take personhood for granted but consider the death of a young person *rkwi bipsi shu,* meaning "death that has spoiled the mouth." This means that the death of a young person shocks and numbs the appetite for food or drink, which people consume when an elderly person dies (Bongmba).

Menkiti cited John Rawls, who argued that justice is owed a moral personality, "a potentiality that is ordinarily realized in due course," to support his claims that individuals acquire personhood as they carry out their obligations (Rawls, pp. 505–506). However, one could argue that Rawls emphasized moral potential and not personality. Whereas for Menkiti personhood is acquired when one develops and carries out moral acts, Rawls's position is that an individual who is already a person has the potential of becoming a moral person. Menkiti rejected Jean-Paul Sartre's definition of individualism because it stipulated unconditioned freedom and choice, which Sartre assumed was available to all. The African view is that such an idea of freedom is wrong because it ignores the community, which plays an important role in the life of the individual. According to the Africanist view, Sartre was wrong to place children and adults on the same level of choice. Finally, Menkiti rejected Western views that the community is a collectivity of self-interested individuals. This makes the community an aggregation of separate individuals. In Mbiti's phrase "I am because we are," the "we" is not additive "but a thoroughly fused collective we" (Menkiti, p. 179). African societies thus emphasize duty, while Western societies emphasize rights.

Gyekye on Moderate Communitarianism

Gyekye has argued that Menkiti overstated claims and that his views are misleading. Other factors, such as rationality, virtue, evaluation of moral judgments, and choice are important in determining personhood in Africa. People are born into community and have an orientation toward others. The Akan proverb, "A person is not a palm tree to survive alone," summarizes human interdependence. Individual capacities, talents, dispositions, goals, and needs are met in interaction with others in society. Gyekye has also argued that it is a mistake to conclude that there are no individual dimensions to personhood in Africa. He cites another Akan proverb in which the view that individuals exist prior to community is implicit: "One tree does not make a forest." "Community existentially derives from the individual and the relationships that would exist between them" (Gyekye, p. 38). Thus the reality of the community is derivative, not primary, and individuals choose whether they want to belong to a community or not. The community allows an individual to actualize his or her potential and develop personality in the social world without destroying his or her own will.

Gyekye quoted another Akan proverb to support his views of individuality. "A clan is like a cluster of trees which, when seen from afar, appear huddled together, but which would seem to stand individually when closely approached." Two other Akan proverbs underscore individuality: "One does not fan [the hot food] that another may eat," and "The lizard does not eat pepper for the frog to sweat." Individuals have particular attributes, which they often exercise in contrast to the community. In opposition to Menkiti's position that one earns personhood, Gyekye has argued that the term *person* is ambiguous. For example, what is implied in the expression *onye onipa*—"He is not a person"—is that the person does not display the norms of human behavior such as kindness, generosity, compassion, benevolence, and respect for other people. The Akan also say of someone, "He is a person," meaning the person fulfills his or her obligations. Personhood also involves responsible action that leads to success.

Exercising one's potential cannot be seen as the process of becoming a person in the sense in which Menkiti describes it. Individuals have a rational, moral sense and a capacity for virtue and judgment that the community nurtures. Individuals can also question what they do not agree with. Individuals are self-directing and self-determining and for that reason possess autonomy. Individual autonomy should not be equated with morality; instead, a moral agent must have the capacity to distinguish between good and evil. Although there is no conceptual link between autonomy and morality, there is a link between autonomy and freedom. Actions that result from a person's vision (visionary acts) concretize individuality because visionaries are always ahead of the public. Individuals who have visions can come up with innovative things to do even though such innovation might draw from the past history and narrative of the community.

Gyekye also has advocated moderate communitarianism because communities are more than associations of individuals; communities share values and obligations, and members of the community often express a desire to promote communal interests. Thus members of the community often invest intellectual, ideological, and emotional attachment to the community and engage in reciprocal social relations within the family, clan, village, ethnic group, neighborhood, city, and nation. Community, in this sense, refers to a cultural community, one that shares values and practices, not simply to a language group. The idea of community implies a common good, which is not merely the combination of individual interests but shared values, working together to meet the necessities of life and a common humanity, and not merely a surrogate of total individual goods. Thus "the common good" refers to all the values a community shares: peace, freedom, respect, dignity, security, and satisfaction.

Gyekye has argued that Western communitarians like Alasdair MacIntyre and Michael Sandel, who argue that individuals are only part of a community because they inherit their narratives from the community in which they are embedded, have overstated their case. One may indeed start from a certain narrative, but the fact that one can also reject sections of the narrative or practice one finds immoral is an indication that an individual person is not entirely constituted by the social. Radical communitarians thus exaggerate the impact of history and communal structures on individual autonomy. Furthermore, communitarians have rejected the construction of political thought solely from a foundation of individual rights. According to MacIntyre, "the truth is plain: there are no such rights, and belief in them is one with the belief in witches and in unicorns" (1984, p. 69). Communitarians would want to replace the politics of right with the idea of common good. By contrast, Gyekye has argued that rights are indispensable to self-assertion and the evaluative process. The idea of rights strengthens human dignity. Advocates of rights anchor their beliefs in the theistic perspective that human beings have intrinsic value because God created them.

Finally, rights can also be derived from nature because an individual has a rational faculty that allows him or her to strive to be the best he or she can be. Therefore a community cannot disregard individual rights. Moderate communitarianism, however, is not obsessed with rights alone but also emphasizes, according to Gyekye, social values such as peace, harmony, stability, solidarity, mutuality, and reciprocity. Individual rights should be matched with responsibility. A sense of responsibility implies that supererogation is not necessary to morality, but that morality should be open, with no limits placed on individual self-sacrifice.

This view of personhood allows for consideration of, among other things, human rights in the African context. Postcolonial leaders stressed communitarian views, assuming that this kind of communal spirit would easily translate into the more complex needs of a nation-state. Politicians were eager to champion socialism and communal essentialism, and their preference for a communitarian ethos has compromised the debate on human rights in Africa. The human rights question suggests and implies that individuals have certain rights and should therefore possess self-determination. Strengthening individuality cannot be seen then as a concession to Western values because the Western tradition also supports communitarian perspectives. Moderate communitarianism is appealing because a radical communal thesis paints only a partial portrait of the dialectic between individualism and communitarianism.

See also **Africa, Idea of; Humanity: African Thought; Identity: Personal and Social Identity; Life Cycle: Overview; Person, Idea of the.**

BIBLIOGRAPHY

Bongmba, Elias Kifon. *African Witchcraft and Otherness: A Philosophical and Theological Critique of Intersubjective Relations.* Albany: State University of New York Press, 2001.

Comaroff, Jean. *Body of Power, Spirit of Resistance: The Culture and History of a South African People.* Chicago: University of Chicago Press, 1985.

Corin, Ellen. "Vers une réappropriation de la dimension individuelle en psychologie africaine." *Revue canadienne des etudes africaines* 14, no. 1 (1980): 135–156.

Dieterlen, Germaine. *Les âmes des dogon.* Paris: Institut d'ethnologie, 1941.

Dieterlen, Germaine, ed. *La notion de personne en Afrique noire.* Paris: Éditions du centre cational de la recherche scientifique, 1973.

Donnelly, Jack. "Human Rights and Western Liberalism." In *Human Rights in Africa: Cross-Cultural Perspectives,* edited by Abdullahi Ahmed An-Nai'im and Francis Deng. Washington, D.C.: Brookings Institution, 1990.

Evans-Pritchard, E. E. *Witchcraft, Oracles and Magic among the Azande.* Oxford: Clarendon, 1937.

Fortes, Meyer. *The Dynamics of Clanship among the Tallensi.* London: Oxford University Press, 1945.

———. *Religion, Morality, and the Person: Essays on Tallensi Religion.* Cambridge, U.K.: Cambridge University Press, 1987.

———. *The Web of Kinship among the Tallensi.* London: Oxford University Press, 1949.

Gluckman, Max, ed. *The Allocation of Responsibility.* Manchester, U.K.: Manchester University Press, 1972.

Griaule, Marcel. *Dieu d'eau: Entretiens avec Ogotemmêli.* Paris: Editions du Chêne, 1948.

Gyekye, Kwame. *Tradition and Modernity: Philosophical Reflections on the African Experience.* New York: Oxford University Press, 1997.

Hallen, Barry, and J. O. Sodipo. *Knowledge, Belief, and Witchcraft: Analytic Experiments in African Philosophy.* London: Ethnographica, 1986.

Jackson, Michael, and Ivan Karp, eds. *Personhood and Agency: The Experience of Self and Other in African Cultures.* Washington, D.C.: Smithsonian Institution Press, 1990.

Jacobson-Widding, Anita. "The Shadow as an Expression of Individuality in Congolese Conceptions of Personhood." In *Personhood and Agency: The Experience of Self and Other in African Cultures,* edited by Michael Jackson and Ivan Karp, 31–58. Washington, D.C.: Smithsonian Institution Press, 1990.

LeVine, Sarah. *Mothers and Wives: Gusii Women of East Africa.* Chicago: University of Chicago Press, 1979.

MacIntyre, Alasdair. *After Virtue: A Study in Moral Theory.* Notre Dame, Ind.: University of Notre Dame Press, 1984.

———. *Whose Justice? Which Rationality?* Notre Dame, Ind.: University of Notre Dame Press, 1988.

Menkiti, Ifeanyi A. "Person and Community in African Traditional Thought." In *African Philosophy, an Introduction,* edited by Richard Wright, 171–182. Lanham, Md.: University Press of America, 1984.

Rawls, John. *A Theory of Justice.* Cambridge, Mass.: Harvard University Press, 1971.

Riesman, Paul. *Freedom in Fulani Social Life: An Introspective Ethnography.* Translated by Martha Fuller. Chicago: University of Chicago Press, 1977.

———. "The Person and the Life Cycle in African Social Life and Thought." *African Studies Review* 29, no. 3 (June 1986): 71–138.

Senghor, Léopold S. *On African Socialism.* Translated by Mercer Cook. New York: Praeger, 1964.

Shostak, Marjorie. *Nisa: The Life and Words of a Kung Woman.* Cambridge, Mass.: Harvard University Press, 1981.

Smith, Mary. *Baba of Karo [Kro].* Introduction and notes by M. G. Smith. New York: Philosophical Library, 1955.

Turner, Victor. *The Forest of Symbols: Aspects of Ndembu Ritual.* Ithaca, N.Y.: Cornell University Press, 1957.

Wiredu, Kwasi. *Cultural Universals and Particulars: An African Perspective.* Bloomington: Indiana University Press, 1996.

———. "Person and Community in Akan Thought." In *Person and Community,* edited by Kwasi Wiredu and Kwame Gyekye. Washington, D.C.: Council for Research in Values and Philosophy, 1992.

Wiredu, Kwasi, and Kwame Gyekye, eds. *Person and Community.* Washington, D.C.: Council for Research in Values and Philosophy, 1992.

Elias K. Bongmba

COMMUNITY. *See* **Society.**

COMPLEMENTARITY. *See* **Quantum.**

COMPOSITION, MUSICAL. The term *composition* (from the Latin *com,* together, and *ponere,* to put) is commonly applied in Western music to a notated work, and in non-Western systems to a consistently united progression or organization of sounds. Although Western music compositions have been defined by their narrative structure (i.e., progression toward a climax, etc.) a more accurate definition, encompassing modern Western experimental music and much non-Western music, is that of music composition as an alteration of a listener's "normal" acoustic environment through the creation of an artificially created acoustic environment by the joint activities of a composer and performer—movement through time rather than specifically narrative. In the field of music perception, composition is described scientifically, as a combination of linguistic elements (grammar, syntax, communication), the brain's bias toward finding pattern and regularity, and psychoacoustic factors (the physical limitations of the human senses). The details of this article on music composition will largely focus on Western classical music, but as necessary with such a wide-ranging term, other countries and styles are included in a limited form as well.

Cultural Roles

Music compositions are not constructed in a vacuum, but fill a cultural role in society. Composers provide music for many activities, including entertainment, social ritual, religious enlightenment, educational study, accompaniment to drama, and healing, both emotional and physical. These artificial social divisions are of course not inflexible, as music written for entertainment can be used in a learning environment and religious music has entered the concert hall. Entertainment music includes the immense diversity of Western art music composed for the concert performance, from Gustav Mahler's (1860–1911) *Symphony of a Thousand* to John Cage's short silent work *4'33",* and also incorporates the many uses of background music. Music compositions used for religious purposes are diverse, including chant from all religions (most without attribution), hymns, spirituals (also without attribution), complex polyphony for Christian services, both Catholic and Protestant, and the mbira compositions improvised upon by Shona performers to aid in spirit possession ceremonies, or *bira.* Educational music is seldom attributed to specific composers, despite its universal nature and scope—from nursery chants and simple teaching songs to the extensive historical sagas found in eastern Europe consisting of thousands of stanzas. Music for drama is subsidiary to text and plot, and includes incidental music for plays, Broadway show tunes, opera, and Japanese Noh theater. Composition is often altered through improvisation during performances of folk music, jazz, many types of non-Western music, and Western art music of the Baroque and Classical periods.

Composers have a societal function as well. In many eras and cultures, composers have a well-defined job—providing music to those who can pay within the limitations set by the occasion. The importance of a composer's work, however, is directly dependent on the distinction between composer and performer, so in cultures that focus on improvisation, composers have little to no place. For example, in religious chant and much folk music, composers are unspecified and therefore receive no recognition. In the twenty-first century, however, composers have a clear and important place in Western society—Beethoven's name makes the comic pages in *Peanuts,* and Mozart is the subject of the award-winning movie and musical *Amadeus.*

Despite the common perception that musical skill or talent is the major factor in their success, composers have attained high positions as artists because of social factors such as rank, race, political connections, heredity, and gender. Until the twentieth century, for example, women were not accepted as major composers of Western art music. In south India, the Brahman caste is traditionally associated with music. Composers' financial status in the West is determined by payments from performers and organizations for new works, sales of music of existing works and fees from concert performances, and royalties from recordings and broadcasts on radio. Composers also teach and perform music—passing on the ability to compose and perform their works to the next generation.

Changing Definitions

The transformation of the definition of composition can be seen through a study of changes in music over time. Although musical composition was obviously a part of earlier Greek, Egyptian, and Roman society, based on evidence from the visual arts and literature, the lack of musical notation makes it impossible to reconstruct the works, as only texts survive to earlier compositions. The earliest pitch notation in Western compositions is found in the eighth century, in notation for Gregorian chant. Gregorian chant, however, did not have composer attribution; Pope Gregory I (r. 590–604) received it from heaven, according to legend. As the medieval period drew to a close, composer's names became attached to works and compositions became more elaborate, incorporating greater rhythmic complexity (syncopation, hocket, meter changes) and harmonic subtlety (use of modes, polyphony, use of cantus firmus, greater use of triads, thirds, and dissonance).

In late-medieval and Renaissance music (1500–1650) compositional rules and techniques became codified. The enormous outpouring of musical composition based on these rules included lively dance works, simple songs, and complex vocal works organized by strict pitch rules (counterpoint). Renaissance composers such as Josquin des Prez (c. 1440–1521) and Giovanni da Palestrina (c. 1525–1594) were respected members of the art world of the Renaissance just as their counterparts Shakespeare, Rembrandt, and Leonardo da Vinci were. As a reaction to the complexity of music from the high Renaissance, works in the Baroque period (1600–1750), such as Claudio Monteverdi's (1567–1643) *Orfeo* (1607), focused on the relative simplicity of solo lines accompanied by clearly stated harmonic progressions. These harmonies were delineated by realizations of a "figured bass" by two instruments, one low melodic instrument (cello, trombone, bassoon) playing the bass line, and the other chordal instrument (harpsichord, guitar, lute, harp, organ) presenting harmonic realizations. This method of composition—open for improvisation in the harmony part and closely linked to the emotions of a specific text—was so controversial it became known as the "second practice." Balancing the freedom and textual expression of the early Baroque with tightly structured counterpoint was an achievement of late Baroque (1700–1750) composers such as

Johann Sebastian Bach (1685–1750) and George Frideric Handel (1685–1759).

In the Classical period (1750–1820), Wolfgang Amadeus Mozart (1756–1791) and Franz Joseph Haydn (1732–1809) explored abstraction and the expression of Enlightenment ideals in music through a combination of carefully balanced structures with graceful expression. Ludwig van Beethoven's (1770–1827) early works are in the simpler, balanced style of the Classical period, but the power, intensity, emotionalism, and unconstrained attitude toward Classical-era forms place much of his work closer to the Romantic style. Extramusical inspirations from such sources as patriotic fervor, literature, and the visual arts became tools for Romantic period (1820–1900) composers to use in mining emotional depths. They sought extremes in emotions expressed through extended dissonances, and unique structures such as the tone poem.

Tonality was still used in a large part of music in the Modern epoch; as the basis of pop, rock, film, and jazz music as well as many works of Western art music by composers such as Aaron Copland (1900–1990), Leonard Bernstein (1918–1990), Dmitry Shostakovich (1906–1975), Sergey Prokofiev (1891–1953), and Igor Stravinsky (1882–1971). Those composers using tonality in the twentieth century, however, did so with a strong awareness of historical precedent. In the late Romantic–early Modern environment, tonality had become so extended as to seem, to Arnold Schoenberg (1874–1951) and his students Alban Berg (1885–1935) and Anton Webern (1883–1945), irrelevant as an organizational system, especially in the explorations of atonality. In Schoenberg's alternative to tonality, serialism, each piece begins with a series—a group of equally important tones. This system, dependent on mathematics and democracy instead of tonality's traditions and hierarchy, was a complete break with part pitch organization and musical traditions. Serialism became one of the predominant compositional forces of the twentieth century, expanded after World War II to include the organization of rhythms, dynamics, and note length as well and as reviled by audiences as it was embraced in academic environments. The twentieth century also fostered a strong community of compositional rebels, including Charles Ives (1874–1954) and John Cage (1912–1992), as composers experimented with unusual combinations of sounds, extended silences, and chance procedures as compositional tools.

Throughout the twentieth century and continuing in the twenty-first century, the music world has splintered into factions with contradictory compositional outlooks. Although Western music focuses largely on pitch distinctions, as seen above, distinguishing features of compositions can vary. In other cultures, folk, pop, and jazz, text changes, phrase alterations, or changes in usage also can be seen as defining features for distinguishing individual compositions.

Conclusion

Musical compositions all have a common foundation—the acoustic and physiological realities of the human body. Composers combine these physical realities with an awareness of the sociocultural context and the emotional and aesthetic ramifications of patterns, acoustics, and language. The inability of defining such a complex process, a delicate balancing act between the physical, emotional, spiritual, and intellectual is at the heart of Frederic Rzewski's description of composition as seen by a composer: "Composition is a constant search for reproducible patterns in the sound-universe and for rational symbols to describe them. It is a mystery how deep unconscious processes can somehow be expressed in a symbolic form, which makes them comprehensible to other minds" (Lecture at the Hochschule der Künste Berlin, 21 June 1994).

See also **Absolute Music; Music, Anthropology of; Musical Performance and Audiences; Musicology.**

BIBLIOGRAPHY

Becker, Howard S. *Art Worlds.* Berkeley: University of California Press, 1982.

Berry, Wallace. *Structural Functions in Music.* Englewood Cliffs, N.J.: Prentice-Hall, 1976.

Hindemith, Paul. *The Craft of Musical Composition.* Vol. 1. New York: Associated Music, 1945.

Kerman, Joseph. *Contemplating Music: Challenges to Musicology.* Cambridge, Mass.: Harvard University Press, 1985.

Kunst, Jos. *Making Sense in Music: An Enquiry into the Formal Pragmatics of Art.* Ghent, Belgium: Communication and Cognition XVI, 1978.

Shelemay, Kay Kaufman, ed. *Ethnomusicology: History, Definition, and Scope.* Garland, 1992.

Kathryn Pisaro

COMPUTER SCIENCE.

Computer science is often defined as "the systematic study of algorithmic processes, their theory, design, analysis, implementation and application." An algorithm is a precise method usable by a computer for the solution of a problem. The term *algorithm* comes from the last name of a Persian author, Abu Ja'far Mohammed ibn Musa al Khowarizmi (c. 825 C.E.), who wrote an early textbook on mathematics. Some computer scientists study broad classes of algorithms, while others study algorithms for a specific task. Algorithms must be written down in some notation. Often the notation used is a programming language, as algorithms written in a programming language can be transformed and executed on a digital computer. Such algorithms are called computer software. Computer science is also concerned with large software systems, collections of thousands of algorithms, whose combination produces a significantly complex application. For these systems new issues become prominent: reliability, security, dependability, scalability, and modifiability of both the computer software and hardware. Another aspect of computer science is the impact it has had on other disciplines. Computer science "thinking," namely the modeling of processes by algorithms, has had a major impact on researchers in other fields.

Early History

The field called computer science was born in the 1940s, though its roots extend back to the nineteenth century and even earlier. One of the early founders of the field was Alan Turing (1912–1954), a citizen of Great Britain, who in 1937 published his famous paper entitled "On Computable Numbers with an Application to the Entscheidungsproblem." In this paper he introduced the concept of an abstract computing device, later dubbed a Turing machine. It was precisely the simplicity of his model that permitted scientists to ask, and answer, fundamental questions about the nature of computation. Any computer can be simulated by a Turing machine, and the converse is also true. Moreover, the complexity of Turing machine computations yields insights into the efficiency of computations on real computers. Two other famous mathematical logicians who made early contributions to computer science were Alonzo Church (1903–1995) and Kurt Gödel (1906–1978). Church developed a system called the lambda calculus, which makes possible logically precise expressions of mathematical propositions. The lambda calculus proved to be a model for functional programming, and the popular LISP programming language used the lambda calculus as its theoretical base. Of equal import was the so-called Church thesis, which states that every effectively calculable number-theoretic function is lambda-definable. The importance of this result is that it ties numerical computation to string manipulation, an initially surprising result. Kurt Gödel is best known for his proof of "Gödel's Incompleteness Theorems." As early as 1931 he proved fundamental results about axiomatic systems, showing that in any axiomatic mathematical system there are propositions that cannot be proved or disproved within the axioms of the system. In particular the consistency of the axioms cannot be proved.

Computer science was not founded solely by mathematicians. An equally important group was electrical engineers, who focused on actually building a computing machine. World War II identified and spurred a need for computing devices, machines that could help carry on the mechanics of war. Enlisted into this cause were some of the greatest scientists of the day. One of these was Howard Aiken (1900–1973), who in 1944 built the Automatic Sequence Control Calculator (Mark I) at Harvard University. Another groundbreaking effort was the development of the ENIAC computer by John Mauchly and John Presper Eckert at the Moore School of Electrical Engineering of the University of Pennsylvania. Mauchly and Eckert were in turn influenced by John Vincent Atanasoff (1903–1995), who is now widely recognized as the inventor of the world's first electronic computer, the so-called Atanasoff-Berry computer (ABC machine). The ABC machine employed all of the basic units of a modern digital computer, including binary arithmetic, a separate arithmetic unit, and vacuum tubes for emulating logical switching circuits such as adders. The mathematician-turned-computer-scientist John von Neumann (1903–1957) worked closely with Mauchly and Eckert, and among many results he is usually credited with the idea of the stored program computer, the idea that a computer would contain within it both a program for processing the data as well as the data itself.

Computer Science Chronology

During the early period (1950s–1960s), a great deal of computer science work focused on understanding and refining essential elements of a computer system. Operating-systems software was developed to facilitate the control of the functional units of a computer: the processor and the input and output devices. Programming languages were devised so programmers could more easily express the computations they wished to accomplish. FORTRAN (Formula Translation), developed by John Backus and a team at IBM around 1954, was the first popular, high-level programming language. Its focus was on efficient numerical calculation. LISP (LISt Processor), developed by John McCarthy at MIT around 1956, focused on symbolic programming. Both languages had major impacts and, though less popular, were still in use in the early twenty-first century.

The study of algorithms. As the definition of computer science is the systematic study of algorithms, it is not surprising that the decade of the 1970s was a period when the study of algorithms was dominant. One aspect of this research was the development of a theory of algorithms. Building on the theories of Church and Turing, computer scientists asked questions such as "Is there an algorithm for any Turing machine such that it decides whether or not the machine eventually stops if it is started in some initial state?" This is termed the Halting Problem. The Halting Problem has been shown to be unsolvable. Another aspect of the theory of algorithms has to do with problem reducibility. For example, it has been shown that if an algorithm did exist for the Halting Problem, then it would be possible to solve Hilbert's "tenth problem"—namely, given a Diophantine equation, determine a procedure that decides in a finite number of steps if the equation has an integer solution. Computer scientists have shown that Hilbert's problem is reducible to the Halting Problem and is therefore unsolvable.

A second aspect of algorithm studies concerns the development of new algorithmic solutions for specific problems. Topics such as sorting, searching, and graph theory were closely studied from an algorithmic point of view. Many new and efficient algorithms for these topics have been produced—for example, Hoare's Quicksort algorithm for sorting, hashing as a technique for searching, and Tarjan's algorithm for determining graph planarity, to name just a few. As the search for new algorithms proceeded, new techniques for analyzing the performance of these algorithms were developed. Methodologically, worst-case, best-case, and average-case analysis have become standard questions to address when presenting an algorithm. There are standard mathematical notations for presenting these results. Algorithm design techniques were identified, for example, divide-and-conquer, depth-first search, greedy method, and dynamic programming.

No discussion of computer science would be complete without a discussion of its most famous problem, "Does P = NP?" P is the set of problems that can be solved in deterministic polynomial time. That means that for a problem with inputs of size N, there must be some way to solve the problem in F(N) steps for some polynomial F. F can be any polynomial, even N to a very high power. For example, sorting a set of N numbers can be done in polynomial time. This problem is in the set P. NP is the set of problems one can solve in

Difference Engine No. 1, a differential calculating machine invented by Charles Babbage (1792–1871). In the early nineteenth century, British mathematician Babbage constructed machines to perform basic numerical computations. True computer science, however, did not exist until the mid-twentieth century. © BETTMANN/CORBIS

nondeterministic polynomial time. That means for a problem with inputs of size N, there must be some way to solve the problem in F(N) steps for some polynomial F just as before. In NP, however, the program is allowed to make lucky guesses, though it must prove the solution is correct. Many problems are in NP—for example, the traveling salesman, finding a Hamiltonian cycle, satisfiability of propositional expressions, finding a maximum clique, integer knapsack problem, and the optimal scheduling problem.

All problems in P are also in NP. You do not need to use nondeterministic guesses in an NP program if you do not want to. But does P = NP? This problem was first posed by Steven Cook (1971). No one has ever proven that they are equal and no one has ever proven they are not. But despite this failure, the "P = NP?" problem has contributed a great deal to our understanding of algorithms. This has come about because computer scientists have been able to identify a large class of problems, all of which are reducible to each other, that is, solving one of these problems will immediately lead to a solution for the others. This class is called the NP-complete problems. The fact that NP-complete problems are (intuitively) the most difficult in NP follows from the fact that we may prove P equals NP if and only if some NP-complete problem has a polynomial-time algorithm. In his original formulation of the "P = NP?"

Mark I computer, built in 1944 by Howard Aiken (1900–1973). Aiken's calculator replaced mechanical components with electromagnetic ones and responded to instructions it was fed from punched cards. Aiken later introduced a computer science program to Harvard University, the first of its kind. THE LIBRARY OF CONGRESS

problem, Cook showed that the satisfiability problem (find an assignment of values to Boolean variables in a logical statement to make it true) was a member of the NP-complete problems (this is called Cook's Theorem). However, despite many efforts, no one has ever shown that an NP-complete problem is also in P. Because no one has found such an example, many researchers believe that P is not equal to NP. And yet computer science is relatively new, and lots of other difficult problems have remained unsolved for centuries before someone came up with a solution, so perhaps this one just needs more time.

Artificial intelligence. The 1980s saw a great deal of work in the field of artificial intelligence (AI). AI is the subfield of computer science that is concerned with the computational understanding of intelligent behavior and with the creation of systems that produce such behaviors. One approach has been to develop computer programs that mimic the way humans behave. A second approach is to produce a computational model of some intelligent behavior, regardless of whether the model imitates human processes or not. One of the earliest examples of the latter approach was James Slagle's SAINT program for performing symbolic integration at the level of a college freshman. AI researchers early on emphasized heuristics as a problem-solving approach. Heuristics differ from algorithms in that they may not converge (or produce) the correct or exact answer, but experience shows that they often produce acceptable answers. For example, computers that play chess must evaluate the worth of their position at every step. Since it is computationally infeasible to work out the worth of all of the possible moves, researchers have developed heuristics that return a numerical assessment of the worth of a future move.

Returning to Alan Turing, in an article he published in 1950 he described a game in which a human interrogator

attempts to determine, solely on the basis of a written interrogation, whether the identity of the "person" answering his questions is in fact a person or a computer. This has come to be known as the Turing test. This challenge inspired a great deal of AI research. Of special mention is the ELIZA program developed by Joseph Weizenbaum, which appears to emulate a nondirective therapist. If the person being interrogated says "I am very happy," ELIZA might respond with "Why are you very happy?" and so it goes. Other researchers attempted to develop computer programs that would exhibit behaviors that were believed to be signs of human intelligence. Playing chess or proving mathematical theorems were two such areas of intense study. There are many subareas of artificial intelligence, including natural language understanding, general problem solving, knowledge representation and reasoning, learning, machine vision, robotics, and autonomous agents.

Personal computers and the Internet. An important phenomenon of the 1980s was the success of industry in producing a low-cost, miniaturized computer processor. This brought about the personal computer. Initially these machines might include 640,000 bytes of memory, no disk (only a floppy drive), and a processor whose speed might be 1 KHz (kilohertz) or less. The cost of such a machine was approximately $5,000. As technology improved, prices steadily dropped while capabilities were enhanced, and computers moved from the exclusive domain of the government and large corporations into the home and small business arena. A personal computer in 2004 might have 1 billion bytes of memory, a disk with a capacity of 100 gigabytes, and a processor whose speed is 10 MHz (megahertz) and might cost less than $2,000. Word processing and accounting (spreadsheets) became dominant applications. But this had little effect on computer science per se.

SOME EXAMPLES OF COMPUTER SCIENCE MERGING WITH OTHER FIELDS

Library science, which is concerned with the archiving of texts into digital libraries so the information can be efficiently and accurately retrieved. With the advent of the Internet, digital libraries are causing major changes to the traditional bricks-and-mortar library.

Management science, which is concerned with the development of computer models to help businesses perform their planning and forecasting functions. It also uses computer databases to store business transactions and to mine those transactions to better understand the critical elements of the company.

Economics, which uses computer models to forecast economic conditions and to evaluate the effects of varying strategies.

Medicine and biology, which use computer models to diagnose and treat disease. Modern imaging methods such as magnetic resonance imaging (MRI) critically rely on computers, graphics algorithms, and software.

Psychology and cognitive science, which are concerned with understanding human thought and emotion. Computer models are used to gain insight into the operation of the human mind and nervous system.

Linguistics, which is concerned with the use of computers for speech recognition and synthesis and for machine translation between languages.

In the 1990s research that had started back in 1969 with the U.S. Department of Defense, and that led to the digital network of computers called the ARPAnet, became accessible to everyone as the Internet. Research on packet switching and network protocols led to the development of TCP/IP (transmission control protocol/Internet protocol), the standard that now enables any pair of connected computers to communicate. As the number of Internet users grew, computer scientists began to study how best to exchange information between them. This culminated in the development of the World Wide Web by Tim Berners-Lee (c. 1990).

In the early twenty-first century new issues challenged computer researchers. People studied how digital sensors by the thousands can be coordinated to do things like predict the weather. Others developed methods for connecting thousands of idle personal computers together to work on a single problem (GRID computing). And simulations of physical processes down to the atomic level could be achieved, as digital computer speeds reached Teraflop level (a thousand billion instructions per second).

Basic Methodologies of the Field

The digital computer is the center of computer science. Abstract models are developed in the hope of capturing essential elements, but the models need sufficient accuracy so conclusions reflect what will actually occur on a real digital computer. Algorithmic thinking requires one to express solutions to problems as a sequence of steps, each one sufficiently precise that it could be translated into the elemental steps of a digital computer, and then to analyze the efficiency of these steps.

Another fundamental mode of thinking for a computer scientist is representation—namely, the way in which data is stored so that algorithms making use of the data will compute efficiently. For example, a phone book is organized alphabetically so we can easily locate a person's phone number if we know his or her name. On the other hand, if we know a phone number and want to know the name of the person who has that number, the phone book is useless. Organizing the data so questions can be answered efficiently is the end goal of data representation. Representation does not only refer to ways to organize data but also ways to encode data. For example, how does one represent a mathematical expression that needs to be differentiated or integrated, or how should one encode speech, sound, or a movie so that it is compact yet is able to be faithfully rendered? Compression algorithms have succeeded in reducing the size of popular songs to approximately 3 megabytes (3 million characters), but a full-length feature movie, using the best encoding scheme of the day, requires approximately 1,000 megabytes. The former can be transferred across the Internet in a matter of minutes, while the latter requires several hours or more. Computer scientists are researching both sides of the problem, studying how to increase the bandwidth of the network while also improving the degree to which compression algorithms work.

Computer scientists have differing approaches to problems. Theoreticians aim to bring order to rapidly emerging subfields.

They attempt to develop models or analytic methods to help understand what is going on. In some computer science areas formal models exist, such as automata theory, switching theory, graph theory, and formal languages. However, for some fields, such as operating systems, programming languages, and compilers, theory has had a limited impact. Experimenters build systems and then use them to test out a variety of questions. Performance analysis and comparisons of different architectures are often the results of such experimentation.

Relationships to Other Disciplines

Computer science originated within mathematics, mainly through mathematical logic, and through electrical engineering with the use of Boolean algebra and switching theory to describe electronic circuitry. Conversely, computer science has strongly influenced mathematics. In some cases computers have been used to help prove theorems. One example is the question of whether four colors are sufficient for coloring any planar map, called the Four Color problem. This problem remained unsolved for more than one hundred years until the Four Color Theorem was proven by Kenneth Appel and Wolfgang Haken in 1976. As part of the Appel-Haken proof that four colors are sufficient, they use a computer to investigate a large but finite number of potential counterexamples.

Computer science has an equally strong connection with engineering, and in many ways the connection is much stronger than with mathematics. Computers are now indispensable when it comes to designing and building any complex structure, from a skyscraper or submarine to a computer. CAD/CAM systems (computer-aided design/computer-aided manufacturing) rely on a combination of computer graphics, specialized algorithms, and a complex of supporting software to provide the engineer with a set of tools by which one can master the complexity involved.

In the late 1990s and early 2000s a new bond grew between the physical sciences and computer science. The fields of physics, chemistry, biology, geology, and astronomy posed grand challenge experiments, problems that require massive high-speed computations. Human-genome sequencing is one such problem. Biologists view DNA as an encoding of information needed to generate a unique organism. The international effort to sequence the 3 billion DNA letters in the human genome, accomplished on 14 April 2003, was considered by many to be one of the most ambitious scientific undertakings of all time. Computer science played a pivotal role. All of the sequence data generated by the Human Genome Project has been deposited into public databases and made freely available to scientists around the world. Assembling and interpreting this data has required new levels of coordination and collaboration of computer scientists and biologists to formulate the necessary computing algorithms, data-management approaches, and visualization systems. In short, high-performance computing has fundamentally changed the way biologists do science; parallel computing systems have enabled high-throughput genome analysis; and modern search engines are allowing access to unprecedented amounts of biological data.

Another grand challenge is the Human Brain Project. This is a broad-based effort involving neuroscientists and information scientists (computer scientists, engineers, physicists, and mathematicians). The goal is to produce new digital capabilities providing a World Wide Web (WWW)–based information management system in the form of interoperable databases and associated data management tools. Tools include graphical interfaces, information retrieval and data analysis, visualization and manipulation, and biological modeling and simulation. It is expected that the neuroscience databases will be interoperable with other databases, such as genomic and protein databases. From these two examples and many more one sees that researchers from many fields are now regarding computation as a third paradigm of scientific investigation, alongside theory and experimentation.

See also **Calculation and Computation; Logic; Mathematics.**

BIBLIOGRAPHY

Barr, Avron, and Edward A. Feigenbaum, eds. *The Handbook of Artificial Intelligence.* Vol. 4. Reading, Mass.: Addison Wesley, 1990.

Denning, Peter J., et al. "Computing as a Discipline." *Communications of the ACM* 32, no. 1 (January 1989): 9–23.

Denning, Peter J., and Robert M. Metcalfe, eds. *Beyond Calculation: The Next Fifty Years of Computing.* New York: Copernicus, 1997.

Hartmanis, Juris, and Herbert Lin, eds. *Computing the Future: A Broader Agenda for Computer Science and Engineering.* Washington, D.C.: National Academy, 1992.

Knuth, Donald E. *The Art of Computer Programming.* 3 vols. Reading, Mass.: Addison Wesley, 1997–1998.

Ralston, Anthony, Edwin D. Reilly, and David Hemmendinger, eds. *Encyclopedia of Computer Science.* 4th ed. London: Nature Publishing Group, 2000.

Ellis Horowitz

CONFUCIANISM.

The word *Confucianism* implies the existence of a philosophy, a religion, or a worldview that goes by the name. "Confucian" ideas or attributes are assumed to have roots in ancient China, to be part of the common heritage of people of Chinese ancestry in other parts of the world, and to be shared by the peoples of Korea, Japan, and Vietnam, who have been heavily influenced by Chinese culture. *Confucianism* has been used to identify an ideology of benevolent kingship used by empires to legitimize themselves in various parts of eastern Asia. It is often applied to the practice of ancestor worship or simple respect for family elders. Yet, although there was an ancient Chinese word for "scholar" (*ru*), referring to those who studied ancient texts, the term *Confucianism* has no precise equivalent in Chinese. In order to understand why so many different phenomena have gotten lumped together in this fashion, we had better start with Confucius, or "the master," whose name was Kong (551–479 B.C.E.).

Confucius

The master speaks to us in the *Lunyu* (Analects), which contains brief, disconnected sayings attributed to him, conversations he had with disciples, and additional sayings or comments by some of those disciples. The text portrays Confucius as mentor and patron to a group of younger men who sought to serve in the government of a small state called Lu between 510 and 479 B.C.E. It is from their questions and answers that the notion of Confucian "learning" derives. Confucius describes himself simply as one who loves to learn and as a transmitter of wisdom from the ancient past. That he also learns from his students demonstrates that learning, knowing, and holding to the truth were considered parts of a continuous process, which was at once intellectual, practical, and spiritual. Learning was essential to knowing, knowing was essential to doing, doing was essential to spiritual fulfillment, and spiritual fulfillment was essential to learning. This process was held up as a standard against which the corrupting influences of wealth and power could be measured. After his death, it was the learning of Confucius that his disciples sought to emulate, and the standards he set were what students in later times struggled to achieve.

The concepts the learners used were appropriated from the pre-Confucian discourse of a broad class of warriors across the North China Plain. In this discourse power and virtue ideally were one (*de*). The worlds of men and of spirits (*gui* or *shen*) were separate but communication between the two was possible, and so was mutual intervention. Shamans and oracles were the agents of communication, while the warriors' sacrificial rites (*li*) were intended to mollify the spirits and to prevent their capricious intervention in the affairs of men. Five hundred years before the time of Confucius, astrologers in the service of a particular coalition of warrior clans called Zhou had interpreted the movements of stars and planets as signs of the movement of spiritual forces in an ordered cosmos. From this they had extrapolated the overarching idea of a Mandate of Heaven (*Tian Ming*), which legitimated the Zhou claim to order the world under heaven (*tianxia*) with a clarification of the ritual duties of all the warrior clans, in accordance with their rank. At the apex of this ritual hierarchy was the head of the house of Zhou, who alone among men bore the title of king (*wang*), but who by the time of Confucius no longer had any real political power.

The wisdom that Confucius sought to transmit was expressed in the language of Zhou texts and embodied in the performance of the rites as codified by the original Zhou patriarchs. But in the absence of Zhou power, the wisdom of the ancients with respect to bringing peace and order to the world could only be validated by the conscience, or benevolence (*ren*), of especially virtuous "gentlemen" (*junzi*) who rejoiced in the prospect of placing duty, or righteousness (*yi*), above personal gain. Resisting the temptation to validate the Mandate of Heaven by appealing to revealed truth, the early Confucians held that human virtue, without reference to spiritual intervention, was both necessary and sufficient for bringing order to a world fraught with conflicts over wealth and power.

Warring States Confucianism

Until the time of Mencius (Mengzi; c. 371–c. 289 B.C.E.) the principal proponents of Confucian learning resided in Lu, where they studied and taught the ancient texts and proper performance of the rites. The text that bears the name Mencius confirms historians' judgments that this era, the height of

the Warring States period, witnessed a rapid change in the ethos of the ruling class. The rulers of the larger states all appropriated the title of king for themselves. They accelerated the development of institutions of direct taxation and conscription within their borders and belligerently applied new technologies in their efforts to expand beyond these borders. They actively sought advice on how to develop, defend, and expand their states, inviting scholars from throughout the known world to participate. Two opposing tendencies appear to have defined a new discourse involving a "Hundred Schools of Thought." On the one side were ideas that reflected and further encouraged the standardization of institutions and laws, the simplification and clarification of administrative methods, and the realistic pursuit of political goals. On the other side were ideas that reflected and further encouraged belief in divine retribution, spiritual intervention, and the Mandate of Heaven. Mencius revived the early Confucians' concepts of conscience, duty, ritual performance, and wisdom within this discourse.

The Confucius of the *Analects* answered a question about the meaning of wisdom by advising the questioner to "revere the spirits but keep them at a distance." He had very little to say about heaven. The Warring States discourse defines the domain of man as the space between heaven and earth. In this domain there is a Way (*dao*)—a set of principles and/or activities—that parallels, follows, approximates, resonates with, or reflects the "Way of Heaven and Earth." In Mencius the "Way of Man" is moral and the "gentleman" is its agent. The Warring States discourse also anticipates a reappearance of the spiritual forces that were manifest in the Zhou Mandate of Heaven. In Mencius the Mandate of Heaven appears at two levels. At one level Mencius advises kings and lesser rulers as to how they must act if they expect to receive the mandate and become a "true" king. At another level the text defines the "gentleman" as one who is able to grasp and hold onto the original moral "mind," or "heart" (*xin*), which was heaven's mandate to each individual human, and thereby to "transform the environment through which he passes and invest with spirituality (*shen*) the place in which he resides." At both levels, the idea of the Mandate of Heaven is inseparable from the idea that in the mind of every person originally there are the seeds both of benevolence and of the duty to spread it in the domain of humanity.

In political thinking the idea of a world ordered by ritual was being displaced by the idea of a world ordered by law, or rewards and punishments. Yet proper performance of the rites remained important to the ruling elite, who still sought to legitimize their status by showing respect for their dead parents and ancestors as well as reverence for the gods of local communities over which they ruled. Mencius included the rites among the four virtues that were seeded by heaven in the human mind, but the Legalists—those who would reform the world by enforcing new laws—dismissed them as artifacts of a world that was no more, while the Daoists, for whom the Way was not moral but natural, regarded them as the last means of moral suasion before a ruler resorted to force. In the middle of the next century, as the powerful state of Qin mounted its conquest of the world, Xunzi (c. 298–c. 230 B.C.E.)—the last of the great Warring States scholars to apply the early Confucians' concepts—revived the concept of ritual with a stunning attack on the Legalists, the Daoists, and Mencius alike.

Xunzi argued that in the absence of benevolent rulers, it was the principles inherent in the performance of the rites that preserved the wisdom of the ancients and provided the means by which the "gentleman" could transform the world. The Daoists were right about heaven; it was neither moral nor responsive to human pleas for help. But, in addition, it was the origin of all life, and it provided man with a mind capable of learning by observing nature and by moderating the natural drive toward self-gratification. Human nature could not be distinguished from animal nature by its goodness, as Mencius had argued. Humans could understand the meaning of the word "good" because humans had invented it to contrast with the natural urge to gratify their desires. This natural urge was enhanced by emotions that, if allowed to prevail, led to ever increasing conflict and ultimate self-destruction. Social order, in short, was invented by the sages, and the rites were their means of channeling the emotions between the extremes that would destroy that order. For Xunzi, ordinary men find benevolence unattractive because they are naturally inclined to pursue pleasure and profit, leaving benevolence to the sages, but everyone benefits from a social order that keeps our angry and acquisitive urges at bay.

Xunzi replaces the moral mind of Mencius with a mind that is "empty, unified, and still." Like the Daoists, Xunzi argues that reasoning—moving the mind, filling it with things, and analyzing them—forces us to make distinctions that lead us away from first principles and into petty disputes. Because the "gentleman" understands the principles behind the rites, an understanding that guides him to the middle ground between keeping to form and releasing the feelings, he finds comfort in carrying them out. Officials only maintain them, while ordinary people perform them because they are customary and believe they have something to do with spirits. As for laws and regulations, or rewards and punishments, these are necessary but not sufficient tools for governing. "Although there can be disorder where the laws are good, I have never heard of a case of disorder where the ruler was a 'gentleman.'"

Han Confucianism

With the successful completion of the Qin conquest (221 B.C.E.) and gradual development of imperial rule under the Han by the time of the emperor Wudi (141–86 B.C.E.) came another shift in political and cosmological discourse within the ruling class. The unique title of the emperor (august lord; *huangdi*) placed him above the warriors, scholars, magistrates, and economic managers who ran the state, and also above the complex array of magicians, shamans, and religious cults that made up the spiritual landscape. The ruler now occupied the position of cosmic pivot. The cosmos was explained as constantly changing, its primordial energy, or the psychophysical stuff of which all things are made (*qi*), being differentiated by the complementary interaction of bipolar valences (yin and yang). Every part of the cosmos resonated with the changes occurring in the others. Small changes in climate, ecology, production, and administrative policy were related to a larger process that moved in grand cycles through five phases. Scholars gathered at the imperial academy

and many lesser academies across the realm to improve their understanding of heaven, earth, and human sciences based on this cosmology. Dong Zhongshu (c. 179–c. 104) is credited with the revival of early Confucian textual studies and the Mencian idea of "moral mind" within this context.

What modern scholars have called "Han Confucianism" comprised a broad spectrum of beliefs, social practices, and textual scholarship. The Five Classics on which imperial academy scholars based their interpretations were the *Changes, Documents, Odes,* and *Rites*—all purported to be Zhou classics— and *Spring and Autumn Annals of Lu,* an extremely spare text attributed to Confucius. Dong Zhongshu used the *Spring and Autumn Annals* as a prophetic text, giving it more power in imperial academic discussions. One commentary on this text, the *Gongyang zhuan,* imagined in it cryptic references to a past and future age of "great peace," which readily fit into the discussions of continuous cycles of change and cosmic resonance. Dong advocated studying the past to prepare for the future. He interpreted specific natural disasters that damaged symbolic imperial structures as warnings to the emperor that corruption and dishonesty at court were moving the human world away from the "great peace" and toward cosmic disorder. Although contemporary scholars increasingly conclude that this version of "Han Confucianism" never subsumed the larger cosmology of which these moral arguments were a part, the image of Confucius as a sage continued and the idea of a Confucian vision of a utopian future reappeared in the nineteenth century. The radical reformer Kang Youwei (1858–1927) applied it to the modern world.

As the male educated elite of the Later Han period (25–220 C.E.) found themselves dependent more on large landed estates, inherited titles, and marriage ties than on official positions with the Han state, they found other uses for the texts. The families of the titled elite used the *Rites* as their guide to social relations. Confucius had become something like a patron saint of scholars (*ru*), and education in the classics had become a necessary part of elite status. An early Han text called *Filial Piety* preached devotion to parents and ancestors. If education for men had carried with it the obligation to serve both one's parents and the public good, education for women entailed the obligation to serve both the family of one's birth and the family of one's marriage in their roles as daughters, wives, and mothers. The rituals of ancestor worship distinguished elite male lines of descent, while the rituals of marriage and childbirth defined the passage of women from one line to another. Ban Zhao (c. 48–c. 119), an educated woman of the highest status during this period, has been celebrated for her literary talents and exemplary role in further propagating these family values in her essays *Admonitions to Women*. With this text also begins a discussion of gender using Confucian concepts, as the author reminds her male readers that if a "gentleman" owes his status not to conditions of birth but to "Confucian" learning, then the same must be true of the exemplary woman.

Neo-Confucianism

For nearly a thousand years after the disintegration of the Han empire, the maintenance of elite family rituals and repeated invocation of filial duty were the only distinctively "Confucian" markers of the political elite in China. The classics, now labeled "New Texts," were replaced by more recently discovered "Old Texts," which joined Buddhist scriptures and imperial institutions as the eclectic markers of civilization. This was the civilization that spread to the Korean Peninsula and the Yamato Plain of Japan. The great Tang state of the seventh century left the elite families and their self-defined hierarchy in place. The Tang model resonated with the interests of great families in Korea and Japan. But not until the eleventh century, in an East Asian world that was divided among shifting imperial states but increasingly integrated by an expanding commercial economy, did another new ethos invite the recasting of early Confucian ideas.

The recasting, which has led Western scholars to coin the term "Neo-Confucianism" in an effort to define it, developed at the intersection of three social-intellectual trends. First, in the great Song empire of the eleventh century an emergent scholar-official elite, in their discussions of statecraft, tended to support their arguments on all sides with appeals to "native" precedents and values, in contrast to "imported" religious values and the imputed values of a rising commercial class. This nativist trend produced "moral learning" (*daoxue*), which centered on early Confucian ideas of the Way and self-cultivation. Second, with the development of woodblock printing, the growth of unprecedentedly large commercial urban centers, and the appearance of private academies, there emerged a new metaphysical discussion that subsumed Buddhist and Daoist philosophy. This metaphysical trend was labeled "principle learning" (*lixue*). Third, as an increasing number of scholar-official families relocated in rural areas in central, eastern, and southern China where they could invest in land and form strategic alliances with other locally prominent families, they began to appropriate the genealogical rules, forms of record keeping, contracts for incorporating property, and family rituals of the old hereditary elite as part of their localist social strategies. This localist trend led to the reinvention of the rites to suit their needs, while raising new problems for those scholar-officials who were engaged in "moral learning."

Zhu Xi (1130–1200), the great master of Song "principle learning," brought these three trends together in his copious writings on learning, statecraft, family rituals, cosmology, and the sciences. Philosophers of the previous century, especially Cheng Yi (1033–1107), had challenged the Buddhist view that prior to something (i.e., prior to the mind's effort to distinguish one thing from another) there is nothing (*wu*). They turned to the cosmology of the *Changes,* according to which all things come into being with the movement of the complementary valences of yin and yang. Their movement is limited only by the finite amount of *qi* in the cosmos, and this limit (*ji*) is called the "great ultimate" (*taiji*). In other words, they argued, prior to something there is a principle (*li*), which is best understood as both the ultimate limit and that which has no limit (*wuji*). The mind's awareness of principles in things is not, as the Buddhists argued, something that it invents and confuses with reality but, rather, the completion of the process by which something simultaneously comes to exist and becomes knowable as principle. In the words of Zhu Xi, the "investigation of things," which, according to one ancient

text, the *Great Learning,* was the first step in the process of learning that led to self-cultivation and world peace, meant the "exhaustive comprehension of principle." Drawing on this and another ancient text called the *Doctrine of the Mean,* he also argued that the unity of principle and mind was a manifestation of the Mandate of Heaven, which could only be understood as good, thereby merging the moralist with the metaphysical trend. He wrote commentaries on these two texts along with the *Analects* and *Mencius,* supplementing the commentaries by Cheng Yi, and advocated their study as a unit called the Four Books.

The moralist trend intersected the localist trend as the rites of upwardly mobile families began to change and the value of women in marriage arrangements began to rise. In the commercial world, especially in the households of urban and geographically mobile small traders and shopkeepers, a woman's value could easily depend more on the talents and abilities she brought to the trade than on her conformity to Ban Zhao's model. For a landowning scholar-official family, on the other hand, a woman's value was determined primarily by the family's rank, wealth, and local status. As daughters tended to marry upward on the social scale, dowries rose to a level that moralists regarded as grotesque. Concurrently, scholar-official families began to perform ceremonies at gravesites and to include in their ancestral rites greater generational depth. To further enhance their pedigrees, they began compiling genealogical records, which then became the currency of social relations locally, regionally, and empire-wide as time went on. When appeals to moral principles proved insufficient to counter these trends, scholars adapted the ancient texts and traditions to the setting of official standards for the new practices. Zhu Xi himself wrote copiously on issues of the family rituals that were the tools, or the cultural capital, of this class. Marriages, deaths, burials, ancestral rites, genealogical record keeping, and patterns of descent group formation were all contributing to a new discussion, the vocabulary of which derived from ancient ritual texts and concurrent discussions of learning and morality among the scholar-official elite.

After the Mongol expansion and domination of Asia, the texts and commentaries of Song "Neo-Confucianism" emerged as the orthodoxy on which success in the examination system of the Ming and Qing imperial civil service depended. A broadening stratum of educated elites in rural and urban communities throughout China drew on this tradition of learning to construct the nexus of power between the imperial state and local society. At the same time, the tradition's dual focus on self-cultivation and public duty defined a new debate on the role of individuals quite apart from the state. By the mid-sixteenth century a newly vibrant urban culture, based in part on global trade and silver flows, challenged the scholar-officials' nexus of power. An alternative reading of the ancient texts proposed by Wang Yangming (1472–1529) produced an array of new traditions that differed from the Song moralist trend. Wang argued that the "exhaustive comprehension of principle" could not occur in the first stage of learning because knowledge of principles was inseparable from the act of knowing. Learning entailed the "unity of knowledge and action," so that only when the mind actively applied itself to something could the principle be

According to Confucius, the point of "learning" was to attain confidence in one's own understanding of the Way, which also entailed the duty to restore virtue to power through benevolence and the use of ritual. One who understood this was called a "gentleman," to be distinguished from a "petty man," who did not. The core of this teaching can be found in a few pithy quotations from book 4 of the *Analects*:

The benevolent man is attracted to benevolence because he feels at home in it; the wise man is attracted to benevolence because he finds it to his advantage (4:2).

There is no point in seeking the counsel of an officer who sets his mind on the Way, if he is ashamed of poor food and poor clothes (4:9).

The gentleman cherishes virtue in power; the petty man cherishes his native land. The gentleman cherishes justice; the petty man cherishes mercy (4:11).

The gentleman understands what is right; the petty man understands what is profitable (4:16).

When you meet someone better than yourself, turn your thoughts to becoming his equal. When you meet someone not as good as you are, look within and examine your own self (4:17).

If one is able to run the state with rites and deference, then what is the difficulty? If one is unable to run the state with rites and deference, then what good are the rites? (4:13).

Mencius believed that humans were inclined to goodness by nature and that this original goodness could be found by looking into one's heart (or mind), which heaven had made sensitive to the suffering of others: "Suppose one were, all of a sudden, to see a young child on the verge of falling into a well. One would certainly be moved to compassion. . . . The heart of compassion is the germ of benevolence; the heart of shame is the germ of duty; the heart of deference is the germ of the rites; the heart of right and wrong is the germ of wisdom. Having these four germs is like having four limbs. To say that one cannot use them is to cripple oneself; to say that one's ruler cannot use them is to cripple one's ruler."

Mencius also counseled rulers of states on how to recover and apply the compassion that was in their hearts. The key was to "take this very heart here and apply it to what is over there. . . . Why is it that your bounty is sufficient to reach animals yet the benefits of your government fail to reach the people? . . . The people will not have constant hearts if they are without constant means. Lacking constant hearts, they will go astray and fall into excesses, stopping at nothing. To punish them after they have fallen foul of the law is to set a trap for the people. How can a benevolent man in authority allow himself to set a trap for the people?"

Xunzi believed that humans were inclined to selfishness and that goodness was the result of the conscious activity of the mind (or heart). Neither "goodness" nor the rites were mandated by heaven; both were created by men who understood that ritual and deference were necessary for social order and the collective good. "The former kings looked up and took their model from Heaven, looked down and took their model from the earth, looked about and took their rules from mankind. Such rules represent the ultimate principle of community harmony and unity. . . . Hence the sacrificial rites originate in the emotions of remembrance and longing, express the highest degree of loyalty, love, and reverence, and embody what is finest in ritual conduct and formal bearing." Man shares energy, life, and intelligence with the animals; why is man superior? "Because he is able to organize himself in society and they are not. Why is he able to organize himself in society? Because he sets up hierarchical divisions. And how is he able to set up hierarchical divisions? Because he has a sense of duty."

Zhu Xi believed that one could be said to have learned something only when the principle in a text had revealed to one the principle that was buried in one's mind: "When one's original mind has been submerged for a long time, and the moral principle in it hasn't been fully penetrated, it's best to read books and probe principle without any interruption; then the mind of human desire will naturally be incapable of winning out, and the moral

(continued on the next page)

(continued from previous page)

principle in the original mind will naturally become safe and secure. . . . In reading, we cannot seek moral principle solely from the text. We must turn the process around and look for it in ourselves. . . . We have yet to discover for ourselves what the sages previously explained in their texts—only through their words will we find it in ourselves."

Wang Yangming believed that "learning" required both knowing and acting, and it was not necessarily aided by reading books. "In all the world, nothing can be considered learning that does not involve action. Thus the very beginning of learning is already action. To be earnest in practice means to be genuine and sincere. This is already action." "In the basic structure of mind there is neither good nor evil; when the mind moves purposively, then there is good and evil; knowing good and evil is what is meant by 'moral knowledge'; doing good and destroying evil is what is meant by 'the investigation of things.'"

---

known. By the same token, insofar as the substance of mind was empty and still, it was neither good nor evil, but a clarified mind in action "naturally" or "intuitively" conformed to what was "good." This, he argued, is what Mencius had meant by "moral knowledge" (*liang zhi*). Some of the new traditions developed closer affinities with Buddhist and Daoist enlightenment. Some gave a much higher priority to individual enlightenment than to educational status. Some made it a duty to convert wealth into charity or to spread the enlightenment attained through self-cultivation to women and to social classes that were outside the nexus of power. Some even pointed out the ways in which the structures of family, lineage, and state impeded the learning process for men and women alike.

Ming challenges to Song Neo-Confucian orthodoxy continued to influence the personal moral choices of educated Chinese during the Ming decline and Qing conquest in the seventeenth century, but they did not displace that orthodoxy in the examination system. Nor did they prevent the Qing from using Confucian state ideology, demanding loyalty and compliance with prescribed norms in regular readings of the emperor's "Sacred Edict," or providing official support for patriarchal lineage institutions throughout the empire. On the other hand, a new trend of "evidential scholarship" (*kaozheng*) emerged to challenge the antiquity of the pre-Han texts on which the orthodox commentaries depended. By the mid-eighteenth century, philological studies of ancient texts had developed into a science known as "Han learning" that complemented the learning imported by Jesuits into the Qing court's bureau of astronomy, weakening the cosmological underpinnings of the imperial state without challenging its political dominance. As Han learning gradually eroded the validity of the "Old Texts" of the Confucian tradition, new champions of the early Han "New Texts" also appeared. When alternative cosmologies and political philosophies arrived along with British gunboats and opium in the early nineteenth century, Chinese scholars and reformers responded not simply by reinforcing imperial Confucian ideology, but by drawing on current evidential scholarship and renewed debates over ethics that were strikingly relevant to the modern age.

In Korea the Chosŏn dynasty officially implemented Confucian rituals for local control using texts propagated by Zhu Xi, whose commentaries also remained orthodoxy in imperial examinations. By the eighteenth century Chosŏn state power had declined but a thoroughly ensconced local elite maintained a strict social hierarchy using Confucian family and community rituals, prescribed by law. In Tokugawa Japan, on the other hand, Confucian scholars found it difficult to reconcile Neo-Confucian ideas with *bakufu* military governance, as distinct from imperial authority, and the strict social distinction between a *samurai* class and common folks. Ogyū Sorai (1666–1728) and his successors in "Ancient studies" (*kogaku*) challenged the Neo-Confucian worldview with observations akin to Xunzi's about the need to implement rites that are appropriate in time and place. A school of "National learning" (*kokugaku*) arose and went even further, blaming Chinese learning in general for corrupting the native traditions of Shinto and the idea of imperial power. In response, Japanese "Han learning" promoted the study of the literary products of Chinese civilization as a valuable tradition in its own right. In the nineteenth century the Mito school devised a new formula, according to which the Chinese sages, as understood by the Duke of Zhou and Confucius, had formulated for China a philosophy whose principles were intrinsic in the Japanese imperial cult and original Shinto practice. Holding to the idea that Chinese civilization reflected universally true ideas, they concluded that the Way of the sages and the Way of the gods (Shinto) were actually one.

Modern Confucianism

After 1868 the Meiji leaders of Japan reinvented Shinto as a state religion in the effort to create a Japanese nation that could compete in a world dominated by modern imperialist powers. In its new imperial discourse it would also claim righteousness and demand loyalty of Korean and Chinese subjects in Confucian terms. In China, moderate reformers tried to combine Confucian traditions of education, political unity, and social order with modern technology and institutional reforms to enable the Qing empire to compete as well. With its capture of Taiwan in 1895 the Japanese empire emerged as both the greatest threat to China and the most obvious model for inventing

---

a Chinese nation. Kang Youwei, a visionary who captured the imagination of a younger generation of reformers, drew on the "New Text" tradition to reinvent the image of Confucius himself as a radical reformer who envisioned an egalitarian world without political or cultural borders. The eras of "great peace" and, eventually, "great unity" would be China's contribution to a world that would eventually emerge from this era of imperialist expansion. At the same time, Kang and the other radical reformers hoped to place the young Guangxu emperor in a position analogous to that of the Meiji emperor in Japan, as the symbolic head of an empire strong enough to resist demolition at the hands of foreign powers.

In the revolutionary tide that engulfed China over the century after the failure of the Qing reforms, Kang's vision was dismissed as an artifact of a world swept away by modern change. But the very way in which it was dismissed demonstrates the role Confucianism has played in revolutionary discourse. The reformers' adaptation of ideals of self-cultivation, family loyalty, and Confucian education to a modern national identity galvanized support for the effort to save China among overseas Chinese in Southeast Asia and elsewhere, contributing to a culturally specific style of engaging the modern world that is still thriving. As educated Japanese increasingly distanced themselves from the "backward" cultures of East Asia, blaming the failures of Neo-Confucian idealism in large part, educated Chinese increasingly identified themselves with humanistic Confucian traditions to combat the rampant "superstition" of popular religious culture and the "backwardness" of the imperial state. Liang Qichao (1873–1929), who was the most influential of Kang Youwei's followers, forced into exile in 1898 after the failed reform effort, tried to meld Xunzi's realistic concepts of a social order based on group obligations with German authoritarian notions of law in order to overcome both the impractical idealism of the Song tradition and the disintegrative effects that a more liberal political philosophy would likely have had on China. By the 1920s he was urging politically dispossessed students to learn from Wang Yangming's philosophy of *liang zhi* and the unity of knowledge and action. The Communist revolutionary leader Liu Shaoqi, on the other hand, urged the educated cadre to apply the unflagging selflessness of Confucian learning to the socialist cause. To combat Communism, the Nationalist regime appropriated the image of Confucius as authoritative teacher, lover of tradition, and counselor of respect for parents, elders, and rulers—the very opposite of the radical, visionary Confucius imagined by Kang Youwei.

More recently Confucian cultural norms have been credited for the Asian "economic miracle," the political stability and unprecedented economic development of China since the fall of the Soviet Union, and the educational success of East Asians in general. The same norms have been shamelessly invoked by dictators and blamed for the relative weakness of opposition politics, cronyism, and persistent gender inequality. Samuel Huntington has claimed that "Confucian civilization" provides a set of norms and symbols that opponents of the progressive ideas and institutions of "Western civilization" can use to maintain power in their own countries. Such a view represents a powerful position on the geopolitical struggles of the post–Cold War world, but it does not reflect the complex history or diversity of the ideas and practices associated with the Confucian tradition.

Other scholars have tried to understand the ways in which new traditions of Confucian learning appeared over time as economic and social conditions changed. Much postwar Japanese scholarship on Confucianism has focused on the libertarian and communitarian tendencies in China and Japan since the time of Wang Yangming. The same tendencies have led others to focus on tensions related to social mobility, increasing literacy, and shifting gender roles. Tu Wei-ming has argued that Chinese on the intellectual and geographic periphery have been the most creative in adapting Confucian learning to modern change. He believes that others will benefit from the lessons learned by those on the periphery and continue to develop new modern identities while renewing their Confucian roots. Chinese scholars of Confucianism in Hong Kong, Singapore, and more recently Taiwan and China have turned their focus to arguments about the balance between human rights and political authority, pressing politicians and entrepreneurs to attend to grievances, provide for education and welfare, value the law, and share the wealth. In a postcolonial, postrevolutionary world, the future of Confucian learning can hardly be predicted, but it seems unlikely that it will cease.

See also **Chinese Thought; Daoism; Education: China; Legalism, Ancient China.**

BIBLIOGRAPHY

PRIMARY SOURCES

Confucius. *Confucius: The Analects (Lun Yü).* Translated with an introduction by D. C. Lau. Harmondsworth, U.K., and New York: Penguin, 1979.

———. *The Original Analects: Sayings of Confucius and His Successors.* Translated with commentary by E. Bruce Brooks and A. Taeko Brooks. New York: Columbia University Press, c. 1998.

Mencius. *Mencius.* Translated with an introduction by D. C. Lau. Harmondsworth, U.K.: Penguin Books, 1970.

Wang Yang-ming. *Instructions for Practical Living, and Other Neo-Confucian Writing.* Translated by Wing-tsit Chan. New York: Columbia University Press, 1963.

Xunzi. *Xunzi: Basic Writings.* Translated by Burton Watson. New York: Columbia University Press, 1963.

———. *Xunzi.* Translated by John Knoblock. 3 vols. Stanford, Calif.: Stanford University Press, 1988–1994.

Zhu, Xi. *Chu Hsi's Family Rituals: A Twelfth-Century Chinese Manual for the Performance of Cappings, Weddings, Funerals, and Ancestral Rites.* Translated by Patricia Buckley Ebrey. Princeton, N.J.: Princeton University Press, 1991.

———. *Learning to Be a Sage: Selections from the Conversations of Master Chu, Arranged Topically.* Translated with a commentary by Daniel K. Gardner. Berkeley: University of California Press, 1990.

SECONDARY SOURCES

Chang, Hao. *Liang Ch'i-ch'ao and Intellectual Transition in China, 1890–1907.* Cambridge, Mass.: Harvard University Press, 1971.

Ching, Julia. *To Acquire Wisdom: The Way of Wang Yang-ming.* New York: Columbia University Press, 1976.

Chow, Kai-wing. *The Rise of Confucian Ritualism in Late Imperial China: Ethics, Classics, and Lineage Discourse.* Stanford, Calif.: Stanford University Press, 1994.

De Bary, William Theodore, and John W. Chaffee, eds. *Neo-Confucian Education: The Formative Stage.* Berkeley: University of California Press, 1989.

De Bary, William Theodore, and Tu Wei-ming, eds. *Confucianism and Human Rights.* New York: Columbia University Press, 1998.

Ebrey, Patricia Buckley. *Confucianism and Family Rituals in Imperial China: A Social History of Writing about Rites.* Princeton, N.J.: Princeton University Press, 1991.

Elman, Benjamin A. *Classicism, Politics, and Kinship: The Ch'ang-chou School of New Text Confucianism in Late Imperial China.* Berkeley: University of California Press, 1990.

Elman, Benjamin A., John B. Duncan, and Herman Ooms, eds. *Rethinking Confucianism: Past and Present in China, Japan, Korea, and Vietnam.* Los Angeles: University of California Press, 2002.

Goldin, Paul Rakita. *Rituals of the Way: The Philosophy of Xunzi.* Chicago: Open Court, 1999.

Hsiao, Kung Chuan. *A Modern China and a New World: K'ang Yu-wei, Reformer and Utopian, 1858–1927.* Seattle: University of Washington Press, 1975.

Queen, Sarah A. *From Chronicle to Canon: The Hermeneutics of the Spring and Autumn, According to Tung Chung-shu.* Cambridge, U.K.: Cambridge University Press, 1996.

Tillman, Hoyt Cleveland. *Confucian Discourse and Chu Hsi's Ascendency.* Honolulu: University of Hawaii Press, 1992.

Tu, Wei-ming. *Centrality and Commonality: An Essay on Confucian Religiousness.* Albany: State University of New York Press, 1989.

———. *Neo-Confucian Thought in Action: Wang Yang-ming's Youth (1472–1509).* Berkeley: University of California Press, 1976.

Tu, Wei-ming, ed. *Confucian Traditions in East Asian Modernity: Moral Education and Economic Culture in Japan and the Four Mini-dragons.* Cambridge, Mass.: Harvard University Press, 1996.

Yao, Xinzhong. *An Introduction to Confucianism.* Cambridge, U.K., and New York: Cambridge University Press, 2000.

Jerry Dennerline

CONSCIOUSNESS.

This entry includes three subentries:

Overview
Chinese Thought
Indian Thought

OVERVIEW

Consciousness has three distinct meanings in the modern world. First it refers to immediate subjective experience. Second, it is the source of immediate and certain knowledge of mental states. For example, if I am in pain, I am conscious of pain and certain of this knowledge of my mental state. Third, it is self-consciousness, a concept of the self that answers the question "Who am I"?

From the seventeenth to the later part of the nineteenth century, the first two meanings of *consciousness* were indistinguishable and often joined by the third meaning: The presence of immediate private experience was assumed, and infallible truths about states of mind and personal or collective identities were derived from it. Since the later nineteenth century, these three ideas of consciousness have been distinguished from each other and subjected separately to criticisms and doubts.

The etymology of *consciousness* is derived from the Latin *con* (with, together) and *scire* (to know). When Romans shared particular knowledge, they had con-sciousness. Sharing knowledge with oneself is the etymological source of *conscience*. In medieval Latin, for example in the works of St. Thomas Aquinas (c. 1224–1274), *consciousness* came to mean a knowing subject, as distinct from an unconscious person or a plant. However, the first two modern senses of *consciousness* were introduced largely by René Descartes (1596–1650).

Consciousness in Modern Philosophy

Since its inception in the seventeenth century, the history of the modern idea of consciousness is intertwined with the history of the idea of science and the scientific worldview. Consciousness has been on the rims of the scientific worldview, at once a challenge to the applicability of the scientific method for understanding consciousness, and an alternative possible source of knowledge, more certain than scientific empirical knowledge that must rely on the senses.

The Cartesian revolution. When Descartes initiated the discussion of consciousness in Europe, it was against the backdrop of the scientific revolution of the seventeenth century. Science presented then a materialist and mechanistic worldview. Pre-Newtonian science considered the universe to be composed of material particles that generate motion and change by direct physical interaction and transmission of force, much like clockwork or a billiard game. Descartes proposed to distinguish humans from artificial or organic machines (brutes) by the presence of mind, language, reason, and consciousness. Descartes believed that consciousness provides an intimate and certain source of knowledge, superior to empirical knowledge that is founded on the fallible and often misleading evidence of the senses. What we take as our sensory input may be a dream; we may be "brains in a vat," as later epistemologists put it. But conscious introspection can provide sure knowledge about ourselves that is independent of the senses. For example, Descartes's famous saying, *cogito ergo sum,* "I think, therefore I am," suggests that any act of thinking implies the presence of a thinker, a person, and therefore self-knowledge of personal existence is certain. Descartes then divided the universe into material things, *res extensa,* that exist in space, and *res cogitas,* consciousness, a mind that thinks but has no material extension. The resulting duality of mind and body came to be known as dualism. Dualists must explain how mind and body interact in the person despite their qualitative differences, and respond to attempts to reunify mind and body in monistic philosophic systems that consider everything to be either ideal, part of immaterial consciousness, or material, so that consciousness is part of the material world that science describes—brain states, for example.

The phenomenological tradition.
Immanuel Kant (1724–1804) revolutionized philosophy by distinguishing the introspective study of the structure of pure consciousness as the subject matter of philosophy, distinct from the study of nature, the subject matter of science. Kant studied how any sensory input must appear in consciousness, in what he called the categories such as time, space, and causal order. However, Kant also concluded that while philosophical introspection may offer an infallible knowledge of the structure of consciousness, there could never be knowledge of the world as it is independent of consciousness.

Georg Wilhelm Friedrich Hegel (1770–1831) attempted to reunify consciousness with the world in an idealist monistic scheme according to which the world is a spirit, and our consciousness is that part of the world that can achieve self-consciousness. Consciousness, then, is what determines being, what happens to exist materially at any moment.

In his 1874 *Psychology from an Empirical Standpoint,* Franz Brentano (1838–1917) introduced the thesis that all conscious states are intentional. We experience the world against the background of our intentions, manifested in a sense of meaningfulness or meaninglessness. For example, my current conscious state includes my thoughts about this entry, vision of a computer screen, the sounds of a Mahler symphony in the background, and so forth. All these experiences are imbued with meaning against my intentions, to write a comprehensive and informative entry, to enjoy listening to my favorite composer, and so on. Had my intentions been different, say to earn a lot of money and to become better acquainted with contemporary rap, my state of consciousness, though including the same sights and sounds, would have been different and the experience much less meaningful.

Brentano taught at the University of Vienna. Among his most remarkable students were both Edmund Husserl (1859–1938) and Sigmund Freud (1856–1939). The first founded the philosophical school of phenomenology, the culmination of the tradition that considered consciousness to be the subject matter of philosophy and direct introspection the sure method. The second extended intentionality to unconscious states, but also shifted the focus of intellectual discourse from consciousness to the unconscious.

Husserl's phenomenology is the last great school of philosophy to attempt to found certain knowledge on introspection of our consciousness. Husserl thought that with the scientific revolution, people lost awareness of pristine and immediate consciousness, which has been emptied of meaning because they objectify, abstract, and conceptualize. Husserl sought to recapture and philosophically analyze this immediate consciousness. Husserl called his method *epoché,* the suspension of belief in the distinction between subjective and objective phenomena that allows immediate consciousness to "appear." Within *epoché,* consciousness appears full of meaning, prior to conceptualization, and so the philosopher who

follows Husserl's method will be able to analyze the universal aspects of consciousness. Husserl called what should appear to anybody who goes through *epoché* the "life-world." Husserl's description of the life-world he discovered may be interpreted as a reaction against increasing modernity, urbanization, and loss of traditions and security in Europe in the early twentieth century; against the loss of a pristine bucolic world of farmers rooted in their land; and against the growing gap between the scientific worldview of matter and energy, galaxies and atoms, and the human perspective on the world of earth and sky, flowers and friends. Husserl's method of *epoché* proved susceptible to personal biases and so generated accounts as different from each other as those of Martin Heidegger and Emmanuel Levinas (1906–1995). Husserl was also criticized for not considering possible differences between human consciousness in different historical eras or cultures, though such philosophical anthropology has never been his purpose.

The gap between the modern scientific worldview and human point of view also spurred the explorations of the French philosopher Henri-Louis Bergson (1859–1941). Bergson was particularly interested in our consciousness of time. Physics (except for Newton's law of entropy, which stipulates increasing disorder in the universe in the direction of time) is indifferent to the direction of time from past to future. Einsteinian relativity considers time as a dimension that can be stretched or compressed in relation to gravity and velocity. Our conscious experience of time is quite different. Bergson attempted to distinguish our conscious experience of time as a continuous duration from its scientific divisibility into moments.

At the same time, "stream of consciousness" novelists such as Henry James, Arthur Schnitzler, Virginia Woolf, and especially James Joyce in *Ulysses* explored consciousness and time through a narrative method that attempted to record everything that goes through their protagonist's minds.

The Unconscious
Freud broke with the philosophic tradition that had identified the mental, the mind, with consciousness and consequently considered the introspective study of consciousness as the source of certain knowledge. Freud divided our mental lives into the conscious and the unconscious. Freud's unconscious is composed of desires that are suppressed, expelled from the conscious self because they are unacceptable or too painful especially in connection with suppressed memories of traumas suffered especially during early childhood. Still, though unconscious, these motives and memories express themselves in dreams, neurotic obsessive symptoms, phobias, slips, jokes, sublimated art, and under hypnosis. It is impossible to learn of the content of the unconscious by direct introspection, but indirectly, through free association and the symbolic interpretation of dreams.

Freudian psychoanalysis offered to cure neurotics through recollection of the suppressed memories of the events that caused the suppression of desires. This "catharsis" should increase consciousness at the expense of the unconscious. Since the suppressed memories are painful, people devise a variety of defense mechanisms to avoid confronting them consciously.

Consequently, the Cartesian tradition of gaining certain knowledge through introspection collapsed: introspection is useless for gaining access to the unconscious, indeed it may be misleading because of defense mechanisms. The correspondence between one's thought and thoughts about thoughts (self-consciousness) has come under even greater criticism since Freud. For example, Gilbert Ryle in his *Concept of Mind* (1949) argued that introspection, inward perception of mental entities, is fallible and incomplete.

In a larger historical context, Freud responded to the rise of irrational political forces in Europe that appealed to unconscious, uncontrolled, and ultimately destructive mental forces that eventually dominated the middle of the twentieth century in Europe. Freud wished to devise a method that would bring the unconscious under the control of the rational conscious. Other trends within depth psychology, art, and politics sought quite on the contrary to release the unconscious powers, dreams, and nightmares and allow them to dominate the conscious. Younger psychoanalysts like Carl Jung (1875–1961) and Jacques Lacan (1901–1981) offered alternative characterizations of the conscious and the unconscious.

Contemporary Philosophy of Mind

The middle of the twentieth century witnessed a decline in discussion of consciousness. The research programs associated with the chief intellectual trends of the time had no fruitful implications for our understanding of consciousness: Martin Heidegger (1889–1976) directed phenomenology toward ontology and hermeneutics; structuralism and poststructuralism studied texts and languages; Marxism considered subjective consciousness to be derived from the more basic and objective material relations of production; in psychology, behaviorism ignored consciousness, while in philosophy logical positivism ignored in principle what cannot have immediate operational, empirical, effects. Behaviorism and positivism, the dominant schools respectively in academic psychology and philosophy until the sixties, ignored the study of consciousness because it could not be reduced to observable behavior or empirically verified. Since the study of private consciousness was beyond the methods associated with the research programs of either school, it was left to literature and mysticism.

In the last few decades of the twentieth century several intellectual developments led to refocusing of philosophy, especially in English-speaking countries, on the problem of consciousness. The failure of philosophical positivism to explain actual scientific theories that contain nonobservable concepts such as *energy*, and the uselessness of behaviorism for the solution of many problems in psychology in comparison with alternative research programs, spurred an academic search for more fruitful research programs and a return to the problem of consciousness.

Advances in neurology; the physical study of the brain, using brain scanning, rare cases of localized brain damage, and so forth; the discovery of genetic causes for a variety of mental illnesses; and research into the effects of drugs on the brain allowed scientists for the first time to offer physiological, material explanations to a variety of states of consciousness. At the same time, advances in computer technology generated advanced forms of artificial intelligence. For the first time, humans created artifacts that appeared more intelligent than themselves. This led to a reexamination of popular conceptions of the distinctive essence of humanity. If not intelligence, perhaps consciousness could distinguish us from our machines?

Philosophers, scientists, and writers wondered about the prospects for conscious artificial intelligence, and hence about the meaning of consciousness. The knowledge acquired about complex information processing through the analysis of systems, such as those of artificial intelligence, prepared expectations for attempting to understand the mind as a complex information-processing system, and consciousness in those terms. These developments have led to the founding of the new, yet controversial, "cognitive science"—"cognitive silence" for its detractors.

The discussion of consciousness in recent philosophy of mind may be traced to Thomas Nagel's (1974) groundbreaking reformulation of the mind-body problem, the relation between the physical and the mental. Nagel asked whether the physical-material external description of brain states could ever explain the mental internal experience of consciousness. Nagel argued that there is and always will be an "explanatory gap" between our consciousnesses and what a science of the mind may explain, however sophisticated it becomes. It will never be able to explain "what it is like" to have specific points of view, for example, what it is like to be a bat, hang upside down from the ceiling, and sense radar rays.

Much of the subsequent debate centered on reasons for affirming or denying the existence of the explanatory gap. Dualists like Nagel and John Searle suggested that though consciousness is a natural phenomenon, we lack the concepts and theories to close the explanatory gap. Eliminativism claims that there is no explanatory gap because consciousness does not exist; it "eliminates" the explanatory gap by eliminating consciousness. Daniel C. Dennett (1991), following Julian Jaynes (1976), claimed that consciousness is a cultural construct that emerged in ancient Greece.

Functionalists such as Australian philosopher D. M. Armstrong and Hilary Putnam proposed to characterize states of consciousness by their causes and effects, rather than by their internal properties. Physicalists claim that ultimate reality is material and described by physics. Both consider the explanatory gap as a problem of reduction of the mental to the physical. They recognize that there is at present an explanatory gap, but they believe that it may be possible to close it through a successful scientific reduction of the mental to physical theories. Some advocated that such a reduction will prove that a type of conscious state such as being in love or seeing red will be reduced to a physical or chemical description of a brain state. Others, such as Patricia and Paul Churchland, envisioned the reduction of what they call "folk psychology" to an advanced neuroscience along the lines of the reduction by chemical theories of ordinary descriptions of chemical interactions to a small number of types of basic elements and the laws that govern their interactions. Such a reduction may demonstrate correspondence between several types of physical interaction and the same conscious state, as the same tune may be played by a variety of different orchestral arrangements.

Frank Jackson (1982) and David Chalmers (1996) argued that scientific material external explanations cannot explain consciousness, since it is possible to conceive of a universe where the descriptions of material states of affairs that explain consciousness are true, but people do not develop consciousness, a world of zombies that act in response to stimuli without being conscious. For example, people may react to hunger by eating and to danger by defending themselves without being conscious of dining or fighting. Such a problem does not exist when scientists reduce water to two atoms of hydrogen and one atom of oxygen. Colin McGinn (1991) went further by suggesting that human beings are forever blocked from knowing the link between physical brain states and consciousness because introspective consciousness provides no immediate knowledge of brains, while neuroscientific knowledge of brains provides no access to consciousness.

Frank Jackson (1982) further attacked physicalism by demonstrating that some qualia, the subjective qualities of conscious experience, cannot be reduced to physical facts. Jackson introduced the following thought experiment: Suppose that a scientist named Mary was locked all her life in a room where everything was in black and white but had access to the world outside through black and white books and television. Mary could learn everything that science can teach us about colors, optics, and wavelengths, how they interact with the eye and transmitted to the brain, and so forth. Still, though Mary would be familiar with the physicalist-scientific explanation of color, it would not prepare her for anything like the actual experience of red, because it is irreducible to scientific physical descriptions.

Physicalist responses to Jackson's thought experiment claimed that Mary's new experience of red would not add to the number of facts she knows, rather it would represent knowledge of old facts in a new way, or a broadening of Mary's imagination. The description and explanation of mental causation of physical effects is a major problem for dualists like Jackson. Eliminativists do not think there is consciousness, only perceptions of it, no qualia, properties of experience, but perceptions of qualia "as if" there were mental objects. So, mental causation of physical events is not a problem for them because they deny the mental. Jackson advocated epiphenomenalism; he considers consciousness to be a side effect of physical processes that connects physical causes with effects. Consciousness is irrelevant for the generation of physical events. Consciousness emerges then from physical interactions, has properties that are irreducible to those of a physical lower level, and so is more than the sum of its parts. A related question is whether the emergence of consciousness may be explained by Darwinian evolution as conveying some sort of adaptationist advantage.

Historical Self-Consciousness

Self-conscious introspection was presented as a source for certain knowledge of history as well as the person. Philosophies of history presented themselves as that part of the historical process

that is conscious of itself. As Nathan Rotenstreich has suggested, Giambattista Vico (1668–1744), Hegel, Marx, Benedetto Croce (1866–1952), and Robin George Collingwood (1889–1943) tried to base the very possibility of historical knowledge on the identity of subject and object. They constructed metaphysical entities like "ideal eternal history," "the spirit," "organic civilizations," "clashing civilizations," and so forth, to designate what they took to be the essence of history. If a philosophy of history is the self-consciousness of history, not just a consciousness of history, how history appeared to people who lived at a place and time, philosophers of history must occupy a privileged position within the historical process, at its end, the end of history. From the temporal vantage point of the end of a process, whether it is linear or cyclical, it is possible to discern its direction and meaning. Therefore philosophies of history from Vico to Francis Fukuyama, through Hegel, Marx, and Arnold Joseph Toynbee, have had to include apocalyptic themes in their philosophy to justify their claim to be conscious of the whole historical process. Still, mutually inconsistent philosophies of history seem to have been reflecting the consciousnesses of their particular eras rather than of the whole of history.

Self-Consciousness and Identity

Consciousness may refer to self-identity. As Locke put it in his *Essay Concerning Human Understanding,* "as far as . . . consciousness can be extended backwards to any past action or thought, so far reaches the identity of that person."

Hegel, Marx, György Lukács, Heidegger, and Jean-Paul Sartre (1905–1980) elaborated on the extent to which one's self-consciousness may not depend on introspection, but on how others conceive of oneself. Hegel introduced the master-slave dialectics, where the master's consciousness depends on the slave, since without the recognition of the slave, the master is not a master. Marx interpreted ideology as false consciousness, self-identity that does not conform to objective class interests, derived of relations to the means of production as owners or laborers. The Hungarian György Lukács (1885–1971) combined Hegel's phenomenology with Marx's materialism to present a theory of class-consciousness that became influential among European Marxists and emphasized reification and alienation. Heidegger analyzed alienation in modern mass societies where self-consciousness is imposed from without by the mass media and mass society, molding all people to become identical and anonymous. Sartre criticized the reduction of persons to roles, the promotion of essence above existence.

Under these influences, especially through the writings of Michel Foucault (1926–1984), historians have been tracing the history of such constructed and imposed self-consciousnesses, of sexual identities, madness, deviance and crime, ethnic and national identities, and so forth. These contributions to the history of consciousness have an emancipatory as well as a scholarly purpose, they intend to discover the history of self-consciousness as well as liberate groups from identities that were imposed on them from without to control and dominate.

Another debate within the writing of history and social sciences is about the primacy of consciousness and human intellect over being, material conditions and especially economic structures, in history. Materialists attempt to explain historical changes in consciousness including scientific theories and new religions and artistic styles, as resulting from economic changes, whereas idealists attempt to show the opposite. As the new president of free Czechoslovakia and a former political prisoner, playwright Václav Havel put it in his speech to the joint houses of Congress in February 1990: "The experience [of totalitarianism] has given me one great certainty: Consciousness precedes Being!"

See also **Cartesianism; Dualism; Idealism; Materialism in Eighteenth-Century European Thought; Monism.**

BIBLIOGRAPHY

Brentano, Franz Clemens. *Psychology from an Empirical Standpoint.* Translated by Antos C. Rancurello, D. B. Terrell, and Linda L. McAlister. London: Routledge, 1973.

Chalmers, David. *The Conscious Mind.* Oxford: Oxford University Press, 1996.

Churchland, Patricia Smith. *Neurophilosophy: Toward a Unified Science of the Mind-Brain.* Cambridge, Mass.: MIT Press, 1986.

Churchland, Paul M. *The Engine of Reason, the Seat of the Soul: A Philosophical Journey into the Brain.* Cambridge, Mass.: MIT Press, 1995.

Dennett, Daniel C. *Consciousness Explained.* Boston: Little, Brown, 1991.

Jackson, Frank. "Epiphenomenal Qualia." *The Philosophical Quarterly* 32 (1982): 127–136.

Jaynes, Julian. *The Origin of Consciousness in the Breakdown of the Bicameral Mind.* Boston: Houghton Mifflin, 1982.

Lukács, Gregor. *History and Class Consciousness: Studies in Marxist Dialectics.* Translated by Rodney Livingstone. Cambridge, Mass.: MIT Press, 1971.

McGinn, Colin. *The Problem of Consciousness.* Cambridge, U.K.: Blackwell, 1991.

Nagel, Thomas. "What Is It Like to Be a Bat?" *The Philosophical Review* 83 (1974): 435–450.

Rotenstreich, Nathan. *Between Past and Presence: An Essay on History.* New Haven, Conn.: Yale University Press, 1958.

Velmans, Max. *Understanding Consciousness.* Philadelphia: Routledge, 2000.

Aviezer Tucker

CHINESE THOUGHT

Human consciousness in Chinese thought may be seen in three layers, each of which requires the other two for both development and understanding. While these three layers of consciousness are constructed for analytical purposes, in reality they are interconnected. Psychologically, they represent different frames of reference, but they are also different dimensions of the same individual and/or collective human consciousness. The first layer, cosmological consciousness, defines the objective world of being and becoming for the human person. The second layer, consciousness of the human self, provides a world of human distinction based on the self-reflection of the human mind and heart in which a human self can be uniquely identified in the life-world of humanity. The third layer, political consciousness, is where the human self projects or reconstructs an ideal political and practical world of reality in which the human self could realize its desires for power, creativity, and freedom of action. Hence we may regard the three layers as forming an integral part of each other so that any human action and human language could impart and receive meaning relative to these three layers.

Cosmological Consciousness

Chinese cosmological consciousness was first described in the texts of *Zhouyi* (also called *Yijing*). The symbolic realism of the *Zhouyi* presents a world of changes that are embodied in symbolic forms of what may be called an onto-cosmological consciousness. Later, in the sixth to fifth century B.C.E., the Daoist text *Dao de jing* presented the development of a cosmogony from the reality as void.

The Chinese metaphysical tradition is distinguished from the Western tradition by a dialectical understanding of reality as a dynamic presentation of events and things in a context of universal and profound interconnectedness. The central idea is creative change (*yi, shengsheng*), which manifests itself in the generation of life, in the transformation of states of being, and in the two modes of becoming referred to as yin and yang, the invisible and the visible, the formless and the formed, the soft and the firm, the creative and the receptive. Transformation (*hua*) of things in these two modes of becoming is the subtle creative movement of reality in growth and decline, in an interchange of vital forces (*qi*), which also embodies relevant forms and principles (*li*). Hence any event-thing in reality is both concrete and principled, both phenomenal and noumenal. The phenomenal and the noumenal cannot be separated and their unity is realized in a cosmological process that is also ontologically understood. There is no way to speak of the ontological except by referring to it as the ultimate creative source and origin of the cosmological, the *taiji*. Based on this understanding, we may observe several features of this onto-cosmological consciousness.

Onto-cosmological reality as a process. Onto-cosmological reality is a process that has a primordial origin and source of abundant creativity because all the ten thousand things are generated from it by way of yin-yang interaction. This reality is exhibited in the phenomenon of heaven and earth and forms a space-time in which all things take place in the contexts or in the form of a situation: all situations are portents of future development and embody a history. The development of situations follows an implicit ordering of yin-yang interaction, difference, conflict, balance, and harmony.

In this process of onto-cosmology, the human person is conceived to be generated as arising from the best spirits of heaven and earth and thus embodies a nature of goodness of cosmic creativity, which matches heaven and earth by development of culture and morality. The thesis of unity of heaven and man (*tianren heyi*) is given an actual meaning and an ideal meaning: a human being is endowed with a nature and a function from heaven and earth in his birth and thus is capable of producing and creating like heaven and earth on the higher level of mind and intelligence. The ultimate goal of human life is to strive for self-realization in moral cultural creativity derived from the onto-cosmological creativity of heaven and earth.

Indeterminate and boundless creativity. It should be noted that the onto-cosmology of *yi* (change) is not theological. Unlike the Greeks, who sought a creative force and a motivating value ending in a transcendent deity or power, the Chinese view of reality is creation from an internal creative source called the *taiji* or the Dao, not an external God. It is also unlike the Hebrew religion, which conceived God as personal and spiritual and absolutely transcendent over and above the human person, in that the ultimate reality is conceived as a spontaneous process called the Dao, and its creative indeterminateness is not confined to any personal qualities.

Perhaps it is because of the early presence of this notion of the indeterminate and boundless creativity that no personalistic religion ever came to predominate. The Chinese believer may take any and all religions as compatible and contributing to a whole of human goodness. It is also due to the early presence of this onto-cosmology that there is a lack of mythology in the early history of Chinese consciousness. This is indeed noteworthy, because almost all main cultural traditions in the world have a rich repertoire of mythological figures.

Although the Chinese onto-cosmological consciousness is not about a god, it can be described as a divine consciousness in so far as the divine (*shen*) suggests creativity from what is given to what is not given and from what is not to what is. It is in this sense that the Chinese notion of heaven and the *taiji* could also be said to be transcendent, either continuously or noncontinuously. Continuous transcendence is creativity based on what is given to produce what is not given, without excluding what is given in the new states of being. As it always links the created to the source of the creative, it is both internal and inclusive. Noncontinuous transcendence is external and exclusive in the sense that it creates things from a prior unrelated source and supervises what is created without being an integral part of it.

This may lead to the question of creation from the nonbeing and void, which is explicitly developed in the Daoist texts. It must be pointed out that the development of the Daoist cosmo-ontology in the *Dao de jing* is not separable from the *Yijing* onto-cosmology. In so far as the *Yijing* stresses the movement from the internal ontology of creativity to a dynamic and harmonious cosmology of universe, the Daoist sees the process of creative change as a comprehensive way of balancing all things and forces and as a process of return to the origin. This process and totality is called the Way (the Dao). The first Daoists were motivated by a desire to seek peace and tranquility of mind and spirit in the human person after witnessing the corruption of human cultures and morality and the destructiveness of wars. They wished to go back to a starting point where desires and greed in the human person had not yet been provoked and where people could appreciate the value in taking no action. For them, natural and spontaneous action embodied a morality, which is creative and harmonious for human life. It is in this light that they came to see the importance of understanding the void (*wu*). The void is without determinateness of being and is yet full of creativity of being.

It is also the formless source from which all things will return. With this notion of the void, we can see how the void gives rise to being by nonaction or spontaneous action (*ziran*) in so far as being can be seen to arise out of spontaneity.

We must of course distinguish this view of nonbeing giving rise to being from the argument *creatio ex nihilo* in Christian theology on one hand and from the argument of dependent co-origination (*yuanqi*) from emptiness (*sunyata*) in Buddhist philosophy. The *nihilo* is absolute nothingness, and God simply creates everything from this absolute nothingness by his powerful act of creation. The *sunyata* is not absolute nothingness but a state of nonclinging and no-desires in the human mind. The formation of mind is from delusion of mind, so that all things we come to know come from a co-origination, which needs to be dissolved in *sunyata*.

Natural realism. Compared with these two forms of creation, we must recognize in the *Yijing* and in Daoism a sense of natural realism that stresses different aspects of the creativity of a natural reality. The Chinese concept of consciousness is radically different from the Western scientific materialism, which reduces mind to matter, and from the Western transcendent dualism, which bifurcates the human from the divine and which separates the bodily from the spiritual. In the Chinese onto-cosmology there is no reduction but holistic correlation, no dualism but comprehensive organicism. The cosmic consciousness is not separable from the human consciousness but exists as a part of it. There is a sense of the origin and a sense of the way of development and return. There is also a sense of a potentiality for creative development from internal creativity that is both transcending and inclusive, both transforming and harmonizing. This natural realism is to be experienced as a result of comprehensive experience based on both observation and reflection. This experience is also practical and pragmatic, as what one has experienced could be applied for furthering one's life and enhancing one's pragmatic and moral actions.

Consciousness of Human Self

The development of morality in Confucianism and Mohism heightened the development of human consciousness of humanity as both individual and community. We can explain this first in terms of the formation of the *li* (ritual) as an institution that links the human individual development to the development of a society or community and to the state.

Li serves to maintain a social order founded on family relations. It is therefore a particularistic and concrete practice of relating people so that the society not only becomes ordered but also becomes affectively consolidated. In a deeper sense *li* is the sentiment showing practical care for concrete people in particular contexts and thus becomes a matter of *ren* (benevolence, humanity, human-heartedness, human goodness). But when *li* becomes merely a form without the concern or the feeling, it loses its meaning. This is the background against which the Confucian *Analects* and *Records of Li* (*Liji*) called for the reform of *li* and an awakening to *ren*.

Ren is the deep feeling of a person beyond desires, a feeling of the unity of humanity, and a consciousness of an underlying bond among human persons that would lead to the love, care, and regard of one for the other. This deep feeling of unity is experienced as inherent in human existence. Confucius (551–479 B.C.E.) believed that the practice of *li* based on the feeling of *ren* would render *li* a meaningful and living force that would both regulate oneself inside and harmonize human relationships outside. On this basis, the world would be ordered, and the well-being of people would be secured.

Confucius thus suggests that *li* can be restored and instituted as part of social and community life. With *ren,* old forms could be modified and new forms of conduct could be adjusted and made to fit particular relationships and situations. The individuating principle of *yi* (righteousness/rightness) enables us to see how differences in situations and relationships exhibit a need for relating, which is only fulfilled by the formation of the concrete rules of *li.*

Hence, Confucius proposed three sets of virtuous relationships: the relationship between *ren* and *yi* is one of generalization and particularization; the relationship between *ren* practice and *li* is one of a general content and general form; the relationship between *li* and *yi* is one of concrete form and particular content. These three relationships represent a challenge to the old order of morality that depended exclusively on the particular forms of *li.* The principles of these relationships also form an endowment for the human mind to define its own forms of understanding and conduct. The power of seeing right and acting right is wisdom (*zhi*), which is native but which needs to be refined by practice and experience. Having attained *zhi,* a person will not be perplexed, just as having attained *ren,* a person will not have anxiety. Confucius also speaks of moral courage (*yong*) as absence of fear. When one acts right with genuine heart for *ren,* there is natural absence of fear, and there is moral courage.

Ethics and morality. Confucius takes *ren* as the basis of both ethics and morality. If *ethics* means norms governing human relationships, it is clearly founded on *ren* in consideration of human relationships. It is *ren* embodied in *yi* (righteousness) and *li* (propriety) as guided by *zhi* (wisdom). There is a dimension of *ren* that reveals the deep bond of universal humanity with heaven conceived as the ultimate metaphysical source of humanity. Confucius says the ultimate truth, or Dao, may be found in light of the experience of this ultimate source.

This deepened and heightened sense of *ren* as a vertical and uplifting force contrasts with the horizontal and expanding sense of *ren,* which includes a family, a clan, a community, and a whole world of people. We can see *ren* in either sense as a form of transcendence, a transcendence of inclusion and absorption as earlier described. In the ideal state the vertical uplifting sense of *ren* may even include the horizontal and expanding sense of *ren* (while the latter may not include the former). It is in this ideal state that we can see how the moral consciousness in Confucianism comes to a full realization of the humanity in a person.

Mencius and Zhongyong, Daxue and Xunxi. Confucianism developed in two distinct ways: Mencius (Mengzi;

c. 371–c. 289 B.C.E.) and Zhongyong emphatically expounded the upward-transcending aspect of *ren* (or *ren* in a vertical uplifting sense), while Daxue and Xunxi (c. 298–c. 230) expounded the across-transcending aspect of the Confucian *ren* (or *ren* in a horizontal expanding sense).

The uplifting sense of *ren* leads Mencius to explicitly define the essence of a human being as a moral being,with four root feelings of morality: sympathetic care, self-restraint, reverence, and distinction between the right and wrong. Zhongyong explicitly recognizes human nature as derived from heaven or from the mandate of heaven (*tianming*) and hence capable of participating in the creative and ceaseless creation and preservation of being. Zhongyong further identifies the uplifting sense of *ren* as a sense of reality by holding that if one is sincere (in the sense of having full reflection of oneself without self-deception and without withholding oneself to the openness to reality) one's mind will become illuminated.

Unlike Zhongyong, who relates the self to ultimate reality, Daxue confronts the self with the extended world of things, so that the self has to have an experiential understanding of the real world before one can relate to things and then relate to other people. Whereas the bright virtue (*mingde*) of Daxue focuses on one's ability to love and renovate people with one's self-cultivation and the cultivation of moral relations, the *daqingming* (great purity and clarity) of Xunzi focuses on renovating people with institutional design for education and governmental organization. In other words, Xunzi's approach to renovation of the people is political and economical rather than merely moral and moralistic.

It is obvious that classical Confucianism developed a system of morality that integrates humanities, education, and even religion. It is a unique system based not on a single idea of value, but on a unity of principles and ideas of *ren* and *li.* This system is truly both knowledge and value. It includes both the theoretical and the practical. As this system is continuous and coterminal with the onto-cosmology described in the first section, it can be regarded as a human development of the onto-cosmology, which leads to the unity of the heaven and the human (*tianren heyi*) through a unified process of self-reflection, self-cultivation, and self-practice (*zhixing heyi*).

Philosophical Daoism and Mohism. Two alternative systems exhibit equivalent consciousness of totality and human action. Both are critical of the Confucian system: the Daoist system rejects the practice of *li* and together the invention and development of culture and knowledge. The Mohist philosophy sought to redefine *yi* in order to achieve a standard of social justice.

Two great classical Daoists who respectively represent the initiation and development of the school of philosophical Daoism were Laozi and Zhuangzi. Laozi presents the Dao as a source of being from which things rise and to which they would return. He urges a simple style of living that is consistent with the primordial dao. His vision of reality is in fact a partial adaptation from the *Yijing*'s onto-cosmology with an emphasis on the principle of receptivity and passivity as the ground and as reason for the natural creation of the world. Hence he sees human culture as a blocking of the Dao. But for Zhuangzi (c. 369–c. 286 B.C.E.), the emphasis is not on a variant of onto-cosmology, but on how one may practice the nonseparation between oneself and the Dao where the Dao is to be embodied in all things in the world, large or small. The whole world of being is to be understood by an open and creative mind, which would link the out-world of nature to the inner world of human spirit.

The Mohist philosophy as represented by Mozi (468?–376 B.C.E.) criticizes Confucianism for its excessive engagement with *li* and thus for lacking a sense of universality and a sense of productivity. In the spirit of *li*, the Confucians practice *ren* as self-control and graded love, which Mozi sees as leading to a society of hierarchy of difference and circles of dissension. Further, Mozi sees Confucianism as dividing social classes into the ruled and the ruling, which lack a common base for solidarity. He sees the continuous wars of his time as an inevitable result of an inequitable society that lacks a sense of social justice. What then is social justice? According to Mozi, social justice must be founded on one identical standard. He uses the same word, *yi,* that Confucius used, but he intends a meaning that is objective. To establish this identity and objectivity of *yi,* Mozi appeals to the will of the heaven (*tianzhi*), with which everyone should comply. But his doctrine of identity compliance (*shangtong*) is also hierarchical, as he assumes a hierarchy of ranks that enforce the compliance. This would amount to enforcing the ideology of those upper-class leaders in the name of the *tianzhi* and this no doubt assumes or leads to a political dictatorship or totalitarianism that Mozi would build on the foundation of selection/election of the talented who are devoted to the government and consequent meritocracy.

Mozi diagnoses the cause of continuous wars as the lack of love among people. In order to reach peace among warring states, he advocates the doctrine of universal love (*jian-ai*). Love is universal (*jian*) if it can be shared on an equal basis. Thus one should love other people's family as one loves one's own family. The point is that we should not love our own family to the exclusion of other families in consideration of benefits to be shared. (But later Mencius misinterprets this as meaning treating another's father as one's own father and thus denies the unique status of one's own father). The doctrine of universal love if universally practiced would eliminate wars because it allows each group of people or state to care for its own land and property without trying to ravage lands of other states and other groups of people. There is also the more desirable consequence of this doctrine: namely the mutual benefit of states and peoples. This leads to the ultimate ideal of Mozi: every person, every people, and every state would live on an equitable basis, and a society of human life would flourish just as a society of natural life flourishes under the compassionate will of heaven.

This social idealism of Mozi is criticized for its unrealistic and utopian projections. But a more serious difficulty is the contradiction between his prescription for social justice on the basis of identity compliance and his argument for equitable love of mutual benefit. The problem results from his lack of consideration of the feelings and moral freedom of the individual, which the Confucians make great efforts to evince as the natural basis of society and government.

Political Consciousness

Since the Daoist and the Mohist philosophies did not become the guiding principles for the development of political governance in Chinese history after the Warring States period (475–221 B.C.E.), one may ask why Confucianism became the dominating and received political ideology in the early Han period, and hence the mainstream moral and political axiology in post-Qin Chinese history. In order to answer this question, we have to understand how Legalism (*fajia*) and legalist politics failed during the Qin period, which preceded the Han. *Legalism* refers to a trend of thought focused on administrative power and punitive laws and regulations that culminated in Han Fei Zi (c. 280–233 B.C.E.). In this system the notion of law (*fa*) as a tool of punishment is too narrow a representation of the actual use of law, which was generally to the exclusion and at the expense of social morality. Legalism was based on an understanding and manipulation of human desire for reward and fear of punishment, with total disregard for human needs for freedom and trust. Because of this narrow instrumentation of the law, Legalism is identified with strict authoritarianism, which is couched in laws and regulations set by the ruler's own desire for power and wealth. Its failure to address equally fundamental and important needs in human nature doomed the Qin power to a short span despite its great work in unifying China. It also laid the foundation for a need and desire to return to Confucianism as a tradition of human nature in the trust of moral virtues.

Return to Confucianism. The return to Confucianism and especially to the political consciousness of Confucianism in the early Han period thus is not surprising, especially as there were no better alternatives as far as political governance is concerned. Confucianism more than any system presented an axiology of well-related and integrated values that were rooted in history and that could be defined or redefined as norms of a political ideology to be used to regulate the behavior of the people. Dong Zhongshu (179–104 B.C.E.) developed the Confucian justification and promotion of political ideology for political rule. Dong speaks of the harmonization and preservation of humanity and community as the primary concern of a ruler, who should extend his *ren* from the moral to the political domain. Thus Dong transforms the values of five virtuous relationships into three basic norms of organization and leadership: the people obey the ruler, the son obeys the father, and the wife obeys the husband.

This set of norms, based on Confucian virtues and a vision of a grand unity and harmony among different groups of people, worked in Chinese society for the next 2,000 years but collapsed confronting the demands for openness, equality, and individual freedom in the beginning of the twentieth century. Yet, the rejection of the three norms did not lead to the rejection of the five virtuous relationships among people. Instead there arose the opportunity to examine the political significance of the primordial Confucian proposition on the unity of inner sageliness (*neisheng*) and outer kingliness (*waiwang*) as a core of political consciousness in Confucianism and hence as the everlasting feature in Chinese philosophy.

Righteousness and the ability to rule. To rule or to govern (*zhi*) is to have power to cause others to follow or obey an order. To be aware of and practice *ren* is the first and foremost requirement for a self-cultivating person to be able to rule or to govern. A good ruler must know both what the people want and what is really good for them, and he must be worthy of their trust. The second requirement is that a ruler be led by *zhi* (wisdom) to make enlightened decisions and policies and avoid mistakes of ignorance and short-sightedness. A man of *ren* of course further requires ritual (*li*) to make his action sustainable, but this must be made on the basis of the presence of *ren*. To have *ren* and to conduct oneself right in terms of wisdom and the moral form of appropriateness, one can be said to set a good example for people to follow and emulate so that people can be satisfied with their leaders.

Rectification of names. Another essential requirement of successful governance is the Confucian doctrine of rectification of names. In the Zilu chapter of the *Analects* Confucius says:

> If names are not rectified, then language will not be smooth, if language is not smooth, things will not be done. If things are not done, then rituals and music will not flourish. If rituals and music will not flourish, then punishments will not meet their target. If punishments will not meet their targets, then people do not know what to do.

Thus, names and language reflect reality but they also determine what reality is, particularly with regard to social and political matters. One may interpret this observation of Confucius as requiring a system of correct names and language that would order social and political relationships as the basis for political administration.

Once basic moral and social relationships among people are set in order, a political order should ensue. In order to reach such a state, the ruler has to set things right beginning with himself as a moral example. This does not preclude the institution of laws of punishment to ensure the moral order. However, the Confucian vision is that once basic order is established, then political order will be easily implemented without necessarily appealing to laws of punishment.

This point needs to be made clear: Confucius is not opposed to laws for any state. Rather, he holds that we should aim at going above the requirement of law and reach for the Dao. The political consciousness of a moral ruler is to hold oneself to the standard of the Dao so that one would not deviate from the Dao. Of course, one could still find that what one does with the intention to do good may still be wrong-doing. Rather than an intentional wrong, that would be a factual mistake, which one must conscientiously be willing to correct.

Compatibility with democracy. It has often been asked whether Confucianism is compatible with the modern Western concept of democracy, or rule by the people. The answer can be ambiguous depending on what is perceived as the goal of political rule. If the goal is social and moral order, in so far as modern democracy will lead to such a desirable state of society, democracy is compatible with the Confucian moral patriarchy. On the other hand, if democracy is geared toward achievement of basic freedom of the people to decide how to rule themselves, then the moral patriarchy of Confucian political consciousness is indeed a problem. The basic assumption of Confucianism is often that people are incapable of making such decisions and therefore require a wise and benevolent leader to take care of them and to put their lives in order. Hence the ruler is given the whole and sole responsibility to take care of the people for the benefit of the people. On the other hand, it is believed that people can tell a good ruler from a bad ruler and that people could complain about their rule and even rise up to remove a ruler, as Mencius makes clear.

This implies that the people can also rise to choose a new ruler. The morally superior person (*junzi*) can be said to be a potential candidate for becoming a ruler. It may be argued that if he continues to develop himself in moral superiority by acquiring all the moral powers of relating to all people, he could be elected to the position of ruler. Since Confucius urges and educates all people to be morally superior persons, it logically follows that everyone can become a candidate for political rulership and could be considered engaged in a competition for successful development of oneself as a moral person in order to be eventually selected or elected to be the ruler. We must note that for the implicit mandate of the people to develop into the democratic consciousness of a modern nation-state, the major step of entrusting people to make a popular election must be made.

We may also note that the Confucian idea of the moral cultivation of a *junzi* suggests the presence of a potential democracy, because the *junzi* must win the people's trust as a good ruler. The moral requirement for political rectitude suggests that a rational understanding is needed to transform the implicit moral democracy into an explicit political practice. This transformation would represent a new development of the moral-political philosophy of Confucianism. This would amount to a revolution in the Confucian political consciousness by way of a deep rational reflection.

Two further observations of the Confucian political consciousness can be made. First, in comparison with the Greek city-state, where people were more actively concerned with the political affairs of the community, the Chinese society was primarily based on agriculture, and the people, having little time for self-governance, relied on their leaders to impose order. Once China became industrialized and people became better educated, the demand for democratic government was greater, and democracy will eventually prevail. Historically, China as a political entity has been involved in a process of consolidation of political power and integration of large groups of people for purposes of defense, so that the demand for democracy did not even arise. There is also a lack of rational reflection and understanding on the process of succession of political power to the extent that the inevitability of dynastic cycling by way of intrigue or force has become a historically conditioned belief among the large mass of people.

Second, when Confucius wrote his historical *Annals of Lu* (*Lu Chunjiu*) in which he praises moral and condemns immoral actions of dukes and ministers, he established a tradition of moral critique of political figures in light of their individual actions instead of their institutional practice. This suggests that the political consciousness of Confucianism subjected a rational consideration of institutions to a moral consideration of personal action. But we do, however, see in Confucius a critical awareness of a need for adaptiveness of a ritual system and hence a critical awareness of the question of appropriateness and timeliness of a given ritual system or institution in the governance and personal action of a ruler.

Conclusion

We have dealt with the mainstream schools of Chinese philosophy in the classical period and their contributions to human consciousness in a threefold structure. In the development of these schools a fundamental consciousness of reality emerges as the leading force of influence, namely the consciousness of the ultimate reality that is the incessant source and foundation for the building of a system of morality and a system of politics in later times. But this consciousness of the ultimate that is rooted in a human person can also be described as an original consciousness of reality as a body of truths or a system of truths (*benti*) as experienced by self-conscious individuals. This idea of *benti* has its own inner logic of development as described on the three levels of human consciousness in Chinese philosophy. In later history we see projects of realizing emptiness and achieving enlightenment in Chinese Buddhism. We also witness efforts to incorporate Buddhist insight into a Confucian framework as well as efforts to integrate various strains of thought in new syntheses and formulations of the world and the self. These efforts have continued into the twenty-first century while facing a still larger challenge: the integration of the Chinese and the Western.

See also **Chinese Thought; Confucianism; Cosmology: Asia; Daoism; Humanism: Chinese Conception of; Humanity: Asian Thought; Justice: Justice in East Asian Thought; Legalism, Ancient China; Mysticism: Chinese Mysticism; Religion: East and Southeast Asia.**

BIBLIOGRAPHY

Chan, Wing-tsit, trans. and ed. *A Source Book in Chinese Philosophy.* Princeton, N.J.: Princeton University Press, 1963.

Cheng, Chung-ying, and Nick Bunnin, eds. *Contemporary Chinese Philosophy.* Malden, Mass.: Blackwell, 2002.

Cua, Antonio S., ed. *Encyclopedia of Chinese Philosophy.* New York and London: Routledge, 2003.

Feng, Youlan. *A History of Chinese Philosophy by Fung Yu-lan.* 2 vols. Translated by Derk Bodde. Princeton, N.J.: Princeton University Press, 1983.

Hsiao, Kung-chuan. *History of Chinese Political Thought.* Translated by F. W. Mote. Princeton, N.J.: Princeton University Press, 1979.

Chung-ying Cheng

INDIAN THOUGHT

There is enormous diversity among the various traditions of classical Indian philosophy concerning the nature of consciousness and the place of humanity in the cosmos, but there are a number of presuppositions that are shared by many of India's great thinkers. Most classical Indian philosophical schools agree, for example, that living beings are reborn over and over again in a beginningless cycle (*samsara*) and that one's present situation is determined by past actions (*karma*). The final goal of most of these systems is also the same: liberation (*moksa*) from the cycle of birth, death, and rebirth.

Brahmanical Systems

In the Brahmanical systems, karmic actions are closely related to one's social duty (*dharma*), which is determined by the endogamous group (*varna*) into which one is born. Morality is not individual, but collective, and in making decisions one is not expected to decide for oneself what is and is not moral; rather, one determines what people of one's type ought to do in particular situations, and one group's morality might differ significantly from another's. For example, while killing is characterized as immoral for most groups, it is the duty of a member of the warrior caste (*ksatriya*) to slay enemies in a just war. The tension between the demands of dharma and the dictates of conventional morality is highlighted in the *Song of God* (*Bhagavad Gita*) in which the warrior Arjuna balks at the idea that in an immanent battle he will be required to kill relatives and teachers—people with whom he has intimate karmic obligations—and he decides to escape his dharma by becoming a world renouncer (*samnyasin*). The god Krishna informs him that this is not a viable option and that it would lead to ridicule from his fellow *ksatriyas* in this life and negative karmic consequences in future lives.

Atman. The *Bhagavad Gita* upholds a notion that is found in most Brahmanical systems: that every being has a permanent, unchanging essence or soul (*atman*) that transmigrates from life to life, appropriating bodies and life situations that are directly concordant with past karma. According to the *Upanishads*, however, the atman is not directly affected by the vicissitudes of one's rebirths; although in some texts it is described as being pure consciousness, it is not directly aware of, or affected by, change. It moves from body to body, but the individual is normally unaware of it. All beings have an intellect (*buddhi*), which when trained leads one toward direct understanding of the atman, but actual perception of it is the result of yogic training, in which one learns to control the senses and look within, differentiating the apparently real phenomena of perception and the truly real atman.

The search for the atman figures prominently in several Upanishads. In the *Katha Upanishad,* for example, a Brahman boy named Naciketas asks Yama, the lord of death, to reveal the truth of what becomes of the individual after the body dies. Yama first tests him to see if he is psychologically ready to learn the truth and, after Naciketas rejects offers of riches and fame as merely transitory, Yama decides that he has no interest in the material world and tells him of the eternal, unchanging atman. At the culmination of his speech, Yama pronounces the famous "great statement" (*mahavakya*), "You are that" (*tat tvam asi*), indicating that the individual atman is the same as the ultimate reality, referred to as *Brahman.* Brahman is described in the Upanishads as pure being (*sat*); it never changes, and it is the sole reality. All the phenomena of existence are merely projections of Brahman, and when a sage learns to perceive reality as it is, everything other than Brahman is revealed as illusion.

According to the *Katha Upanishad,* the sufferings of ordinary beings are due to their lack of control over their senses (*indriya*). Yama states that the intellect is like the reins of a chariot, which the charioteer uses to control his horses. The horses are compared to the senses. Without the restraint of a firm charioteer, the horses will run rampant, just as unrestrained senses pursue fleeting sense objects. A skilled charioteer gains control over his horses in the same way that a yogi restrains his senses through meditation. The chariot is compared to the body, which is motivated to pursue attractive things by unrestrained senses but attains a state of peace through meditative practice. The atman is like a passenger who travels along with the chariot, but exercises no control over it. Liberation is attained by those who directly perceive the atman. When one recognizes that individual existence is merely illusion, all sense of separateness from Brahman is transcended, and the individual atman is merged with it, like a wave that is absorbed into the ocean.

The world of appearances. In the Non-dualist (*Advaita*) Vedanta system of shankara (c. 8th century C.E.), the world of appearances is said to be merely the sport of Brahman (*brahmalila*). Brahman projects the illusion of ordinary reality for its own enjoyment, but ultimately none of it is real. On the conventional level, phenomena operate according to laws, and so conventionally shankara accepts the validity of direct perception (*pratyaksa*). From the ultimate perspective the multiplicity of appearance is false, however, and so in seeking the truth one should learn to overlook the evidence of one's senses and initially rely on the Vedic scriptures (of which the Upanishads are a part), which reveal the way things really are. Scriptural statements are later confirmed by introspective meditation.

Arguments regarding valid means of knowledge (*pramana*) figure prominently in intersectarian disputes among Indian philosophers. Most schools of classical Indian philosophy accept the primacy of direct perception, as well as inference (*anumana*) based on sense experience. For shankara, however, the evidence of the senses is false, and so ultimately only scriptural testimony (*sabda*) is valid. The scriptures themselves require no validation, because they "are like the sun which reveals itself while revealing colors." The Vedas are part of the very fabric of reality and are eternally true. They have no author (*apauruseya*) and are directly perceived by "seers" (*rsi*), who reveal them, but do not alter their content.

The Nyaya school—which like Vedanta is regarded as one of the six "orthodox" (*astika*) traditions of Brahmanical philosophy—takes issue with several of these ideas. According to Nyaya, it is ridiculous to claim that the Vedic texts have no author; instead, the Naiyayikas hold that they are composed by God, who is omniscient. God's position as the being who knows all things serves to validate the truth of Vedic statements. In addition, God is also the author of the medical texts of the *ayurveda*, and the fact of their effectiveness serves as an analogical proof that Vedic statements that cannot be verified

by ordinary humans are also true. They are further corroborated by the testimony of trustworthy persons (*apta*), and so ordinary humans can accept them with confidence.

Like the Advaita Vedantins, the Naiyayikas assert the existence of an eternal atman, which is the locus of each individual's karma, but unlike shankara, they claim that the atman is able to acquire knowledge, feeling, and volition. It is not the sort of spiritual entity postulated by Advaita Vedanta, and each atman has its own mind (*manas*), which is connected with it until it reaches liberation. At that point, the atman becomes completely liberated from everything, including mind. The path to liberation for Nyaya begins with reasoning, which brings correct knowledge.

In common with other Indian classical philosophical systems, the Nyaya asserts that living beings are caught up in transmigration as a result of ignorance (*avidya*), which manifests in the form of mistaken ideas. Correct reasoning, guided by scripture, is an essential prerequisite for liberation. It eliminates wrong ideas and reveals the truth of things, and thus serves to overcome ignorance. One does not engage in argument for its own sake; correct reasoning leads to certainty, and is in accord with Vedic statements. On this basis, one can engage in introspective meditation, by means of which one is able to directly validate the truth of scripture. Liberation in this system is not conceived of as bliss, as in some other Indian traditions, but rather as absence of pain. Bliss requires its opposite, but in the liberated state one transcends all qualities and dichotomies. In liberation the atman is separated from the physical body—and all other physicality—and attains a state of absolute neutrality.

Buddhist Systems

The Buddhists, while accepting the notions of *karma, samsara,* and *moksa* (or *nirvana* in common Buddhist parlance), reject many of the core assumptions of the Naiyayikas, as well as important doctrines of the Upanishads and Advaita Vedanta. One of the cornerstones of Indian Buddhist schools is the doctrine of "no-self" (*anatman*), which rejects the Brahmanical belief in a permanent, unchanging soul. The Buddhists rely mainly on the *pramanas* of direct perception and inference, and reject the atman as a conceptual construct that is unfindable either by the senses or by reasoning. The Buddha pointed out that the central reality of all existence is change. All phenomena come into being as a result of causes and conditions, they change in every moment, and eventually they pass away. If there were some disembodied, unchanging entity, it would have no relation to any individual, and because it lies beyond the world of the senses it could never be perceived.

Epistomological tradition. The "Epistemological" (Pramana) tradition, whose most influential exponent was Dharmakirti (c. 530–600), further contends that an unchanging entity would have no causal efficacy, and so it would be entirely unrelated to the world. Dharmakirti's approach is pragmatic and empirical: he asserts that there is no point in discussing things that can never be verified by sense experience and that have no impact on the physical world. In his pragmatist system, all statements and cognitions are subject to falsifiability: a statement is true only as long as subsequent perceptions and analysis do not show it to be false. In addition, Dharmakirti believes that there is no point in discussing merely theoretical topics (such as the atman) and that an essential test of validity is the possibility of effective activity (*artha-kriya*). Practical application is one of the conditions of valid knowledge. In his system, statements become true through a process of verification: they must be able to withstand subsequent analysis and be corroborated by relevant perceptions. Those that meet this test may be accepted as true, while others (even statements contained in Buddhist scriptures) should be rejected.

In his major work, the *Commentary on [Dignaga's] Compendium of Valid Cognition* (*Pramana-varttika*), Dharmakirti only accepts the *pramana*s of direct perception and inference, and rejects others that are accepted by the Naiyayikas, such as comparison (*upamana*) and scriptural testimony. The former is unreliable because it is not based on direct experience, and the latter only convinces those who already accept the cited scriptures as normative. Dharmakirti asserts that any truth claim must be verifiable by analytical reasoning and direct perception. Direct perception is defined as being "free from conceptuality and incontrovertible." In his system, only the first moment of perception counts as direct perception, and subsequent moments are overlaid with conceptuality. They are not produced by cognition of a directly perceived sign, but instead are merely based on the initial perception and interpreted by the mind.

The epistemological tradition also claims that the nonexistence of the atman can be confirmed by developing a special cognitive capacity called "yogic direct perception" (*yogi-pratyaksa*), which allows meditators to directly perceive truths that are hidden from ordinary beings. In most Indian philosophical traditions, there is a close link between meditative practice and philosophy, and the training regimens of the various schools begin with study of doctrine, which is reinforced by yoga. The paths of Indian philosophical/religious traditions are intended to ensure that meditators directly perceive the tenets of the system in which they are training, and philosophy is often a reflexive exercise that uses reasoning to argue for the insights gained in meditation. Doctrine is derived from practice, and those whose experiences differ from the tradition's doctrines are either brought into line or expelled (and sometimes they become founders of new schools).

Transmigration and liberation. In rejecting the atman, the Buddhists were widely seen as being vulnerable on the question of what transmigrates from life to life. The Buddha is said to have taught that the belief in a permanent self is shared by all ordinary people, but despite its universality it is a false concept, and one that leads to grasping after material things and mistaken notions about reality. Those who seek liberation must overcome the innate belief in a self, and this requires meditative training. In searching for the atman through introspective meditation, Buddhists find that there is no enduring essence (either atman or Brahman), and that instead individuals are composites of five "aggregates" (*skandha*): form,

feelings, discriminations, consciousness, and compositional factors. The first refers to physical form, and the second comprises one's emotional responses to phenomena. These are discriminated into positive, negative, and neutral, and this process leads to desire for certain phenomena and aversion toward others. The aggregate of consciousness encompasses one's mental events and includes phenomena that are generally regarded as part of the unconscious in Western psychology. Compositional factors are other elements that are part of the innate sense of self, and mainly consist of karmic factors.

According to most Buddhist schools, consciousness is the aggregate that transmigrates from life to life. It is commonly described as being of the nature of "clear light" (*prabhasvara*), and all defilements are said to be adventitious (*agantuka*). One's volitional actions produce karmas, which move consciousness in certain directions and determine the nature of one's rebirth, but consciousness, unlike the atman, changes in every moment and is directly affected by the vicissitudes of one's life. Meditative training aims to remove mental defilements like anger, desire, and obscuration, while simultaneously cultivating good qualities like patience, morality, and wisdom.

In classical Indian philosophy, Buddhism was one of the main "heterodox" (*nastika*) systems. The Buddhists rejected the authoritativeness of the Vedas and claimed that their own scriptures contained correct doctrines and the only truly effective path to liberation. They asserted that the core existential problem is suffering (*duhkha*) and that it is caused by ignorance. Because beings misunderstand the true nature of reality, they make choices that lead to suffering and result in continuing transmigration. Since the problem is a cognitive one, the solution is also cognitive: liberation requires that one overcome mistaken ideas and acquire correct understanding. One of the most basic misconceptions, according to the Buddhists, is the notion of the atman. They assert that anyone who clings to a permanent self or to an ultimate reality (whether conceived as God or Brahman) will inevitably continue to transmigrate from life to life, and they hold that only those who free themselves from such false notions are able to attain liberation.

For all of the traditions discussed in this essay, the central concern of philosophy should be liberation. Indian philosophical texts commonly state in their introductions that the purpose of composition is to aid others in the pursuit of *moksa*, which indicates that philosophy is not viewed as an exercise in discussing semantic problems, but ideally should be a matter of profound concern for anyone seeking to comprehend reality as it is and thus attain the ultimate goal.

See also **Cosmology: Asia; Philosophy; Religion: East and Southeast Asia.**

BIBLIOGRAPHY

Chakrabarti, Kisor K. *Classical Indian Philosophy of Mind: The Nyaya Dualist Tradition.* Albany: State University of New York Press, 1999.

Dreyfus, Georges B. J. *Recognizing Reality: Dharmakirti's Philosophy and Its Tibetan Interpretations.* Albany: State University of New York Press, 1997.

Griffiths, Paul J. "Pure Consciousness and Indian Buddhism." In *The Problem of Pure Consciousness: Mysticism and Philosophy,* edited by Robert K. C. Forman, 71–97. New York: Oxford University Press, 1990.

Gupta, Bina. *CIT: Consciousness.* New Delhi: Oxford University Press, 2003.

Matilal, Bimal K. *Perception: An Essay on Classical Indian Theories of Knowledge.* Oxford: Clarendon, 1986.

Mohanty, J. N. "Understanding Some Ontological Differences in Indian Philosophy." *Journal of Indian Philosophy* 8, no. 3 (1980): 205–217.

Potter, Karl H. *Presuppositions of India's Philosophies.* Westport, Conn.: Greenwood, 1972.

John Powers

CONSERVATISM. *Conservatism* lends itself to misunderstanding because its political designation is easily confused with popular usage. To be conservative in the sense of preferring the familiar to the unfamiliar is a common form of behavior. Since this attitude toward life is universal, it issues from no necessary political commitment. For any person, even the most bohemian, not to develop a settled habit or a lingering attachment would be almost inconceivable. However, it is possible to conceive of persons having such habits and attachments and yet being radical in his or her politics. That would have been true, for instance, of Adolf Hitler. Equally, to be conservative in the sense of wishing to maintain a position of authority, privilege, reverence, or wealth is another universally recognizable form of behavior that issues from no necessary political commitment. It would be exceptional for someone who has achieved or inherited such powerful status not to want to secure it. This would have been true, for instance, of Joseph Stalin. Both of these popular meanings of conservatism—as shorthand for individual or social characteristics—are inadequate to understanding conservatism in politics. Both of them are primordial in their instincts, general in their applications, and empty of content.

Conservatism in politics, on the other hand, is a relatively recent historical phenomenon, particular in its significance, and as a consequence has a distinctive, if differentiated, character. Conservatism is best understood as a set of propositions about the activity of governing, defined against those radical ideologies with roots in eighteenth-century speculation, like liberalism and socialism, that were to have such a profound effect on world history in the course of the nineteenth and twentieth centuries. It is opposed to grand schemes for the political emancipation or salvation of humankind to which such radical speculation can lead. Conservatism advocates limited ambitions in politics, argues that the aspiration of government should be modest, and emphasizes the value of continuity in the state. Conservatives believe that government can be authoritative only when it is limited, modest, and continuous. If it were possible to identify a distinctive desire uniting all forms of conservatism, it would be the desire to be left alone to enjoy the benefits of a well-ordered society. As the nineteenth-century British prime minister Lord Salisbury (Robert Arthur Talbot Gascoyne-Cecil) once put it, conservatism is like a policeman: if there were no (radical) criminals to protect against, there would be no need for it. However, conservatives will not be left alone.

Origins of Conservatism: Britain, France, and Germany

Restricting the scope of politics in this manner has made conservatism appear at odds with the promise of modernity. Certainly, any political project to remove evil from the world is for the religious conservative an act of impiety, just as any project to perfect humankind is for the secular conservative an act of dangerous folly. The difficulty remains that these fundamental criticisms of modern hubris are easily dismissed as nostalgic, self-interested, and most damning of all, irrationally prejudiced. If conservative irrationalism can be ascribed to any particular failing, it is thought to be the presumption of resisting historical progress. In this view, conservatism and modernization are antithetical, since to be modern is to assume history to be linear and its meaning to be emancipation from ignorant custom. That is an audacious concept of politics that understands traditional restraints to be obstacles to manifest destiny.

Conventional historical wisdom has been that the event that transformed these terms of political argument was the French Revolution. That convention is a sound one. The main currents of European intellectual life were drawn into the revolution, and out of it emerged the modern narrative of progress versus reaction, improvement versus obstruction, and reason versus tradition that was to shape political reflection in the course of the following two centuries. This has been an influential narrative and a persuasive one. In its light, conservatism at best serves as a prudential brake on the wheels of change, at worst as an insufferable denial of human development. In neither case is it thought to involve anything of substantial value or intellectual significance. Nevertheless, the temptation to interpret conservatism as "antimodern" should be resisted, for to be conservative does not entail a passive acceptance of the status quo. Rather it involves a critical encounter with what exists. *Conservatism* was itself a nineteenth-century neologism for a modern, novel, self-conscious disposition in politics and as such is a contemporary of *socialism, liberalism,* and *nationalism.* Its meaning has been given by modern experience and its content by the recurring expression of certain principles in the work of thinkers alarmed into reflection by revolutionary activity. Conservatism, in other words, has a history, not a nature, and that is an insight owed to the Irish "philosopher in action," Edmund Burke (1729–1797).

Britain. If Burke is taken to be paradigmatic of conservative thought, it is by attribution rather than by design. Burke drew on a large repertoire of ideas, such as the social-contract tradition of Thomas Hobbes (1588–1679) and John Locke (1632–1704) and the skeptical conventionalism of David Hume (1711–1776), and marshaled them like a great melodist to challenge the abstract "speculatism" of the French revolutionaries. Writing from within a culture of constitutional monarchy that had only recently and precariously secured its legitimacy (albeit with the loss of the American colonies), Burke's intent in *Reflections on the Revolution in France* (1790) is to warn against the implications of revolutionary principles, which he thinks are as subversive of good government as they are of bad. If society is indeed a social contract, it is a contract "between those who are living, those who are dead, and those who are to be born," and in that formulation Burke tries to make safe two of the potentially radical loose ends bequeathed by Locke. Political society, Burke argues, is not dissolvable according to demands made by the present generation, and the "tacit" consent of contemporaries is assumed because of their inherited obligations and future responsibilities. Burke does refer these obligations and responsibilities to laws of nature, but he is aware that nature can be a false friend. It is those very "natural" rights, so beloved by revolutionaries in France, that he dismisses as being incompatible with the "real" rights of political society. For Burke, to "follow nature" is not a radical invitation to rebel against society but an injunction to accept one's "second nature" as a dutiful member of a historically achieved political order. Since history is a record of experience and since all practical knowledge is a product of experience, history supplies a sufficient guide to political activity. From that empiricist rather than natural-law premise, Burke proposes that prudence, circumstance, utility, convenience, and respect for order provide the proper conditions for liberty, while abstract theorizing delivers the condition of "rational despotism."

For some, this committed Burke (and conservatism) to an "organic" theory of society. That is an understandable interpretation, but a degree of caution is required because the argument is more subtle and the content less mysterious than the expression "organic" sometimes implies. Burke's notion of the constitution assumes an arrangement in which order and liberty presuppose one another. It assumes that the individual is part of and has meaning within a social order of classes or estates and that the state is an authoritative expression of that social order. The "little platoons" of immediate identity are functional to stability because their education in local and social affection forms the basis of patriotism. On the one hand, the state cannot be absolute, for its existence depends on the life of its parts and it has a duty to secure them. On the other hand, reasons of state cannot be reduced alone to the protection of the rights of individuals. If revolutionary theorizing would dissolve these historical associations into dust and make social relationships as evanescent as the "flies of summer," Burke's model was not an alternative blueprint. Unlike the revolutionary's vision of France as "nothing but *carte blanche,* upon which he may scribble anything he pleases," Burke is defending what he takes to be the actual life of the British state, monarchical, aristocratic, and constitutional.

The paradigmatic conservatism of Burke's thought lies in its evocation of sympathy for what is enduring in a political association. While revolutionary politics proclaim a profound incompatability between the values of the people and the principles of traditional structures of government, Burke proclaims a deep congruence. Tradition, which is shorthand for a politics of congruence, emerges from his work as an important value in conservative politics. Conservatism puts the idea of tradition to work in defense of the political order. It seeks to encourage people to accept the world around them, for it just

happens to be the world in which we do live and it is one that sets limits to political change. In the British case, the ability of the political order to secure its authority through prolonged periods of economic and social change appeared to confirm Burke's maxim that a state without the means of reform is without the means of its own conservation. It also appeared to confirm his assumption that the advancement of civilization owes more to the advantages of stability than it does to the pursuit of abstract rights. In the conduct of reform, continuity is secured because improvements are never wholly new and what is retained is never wholly obsolete. Of course, the reconciled condition that conservatism proposes is reconciliation within the ideology itself and not necessarily reconciliation in experience. It is possible to conceive of reality as being seriously at odds with the ideology.

France. This was the case for conservatives in France, where, unlike the happy condition of Britain, the experience and effect of revolution had disconnected the state from what they believed to be the true spirit of society. This compelled thinking through with passionate intensity questions of order and legitimacy, and it fostered a politics that made fundamental distinctions between what is true and what exists. In this case what mattered was the fractured rather than the coherent relationship between political structures and spiritual truth. The legitimacy of those who had usurped power in the name of reason could never be secure against the consecrated authority they had displaced. The task of conservative political argument was to recall people to their true allegiance by clarifying the principles that had been forsaken.

For Joseph-Marie de Maistre (1753–1821), the French Revolution represents divine retribution for the sins of the godless Enlightenment and the "century of blasphemy" that had preceded it. One consequence of that blasphemy is the rationalist misconception involved in the creation of a written constitution. The true constitution is not to be found in the fine words of such a document but in the public spirit that should animate it. For de Maistre, "what is written is nothing." The constitution is divine in origin, and only when one acts in harmony with God can his or her actions be creative. Once separated from the Creator, people's actions are rendered negative and destructive. The rule of number, implied by popular sovereignty, has nothing to do with the rule of justice and would ultimately prove to be self-destructive. This is what the course of revolutionary history reveals to conservatives—a succession of failed constitutions of increasing perniciousness and impiety. That disastrous history is as much the fault of the internal corruption of the ancien régime as of the arguments of the philosophes. Ironically then, the revolution will serve as a necessary purgative and will lead to the inevitable, because divinely ordained, restoration of monarchy, religion, and nation. That dissociation between the social and the political as well as the theocratic justification for the restoration of the ancien régime is also found in the work of Louis de Bonald (1754–1840). Monarchy and church, throne and altar, will together bring back into harmony the body and spirit of the nation that the French political revolution had willfully divided. It will, moreover, defeat secular nationalism and replace it with ultramontane Catholicism.

CONSERVATISM

Like Burke, de Maistre and de Bonald associated the terror and the chaos in France with the new, rapacious, self-seeking, revolutionary elite, and they formulated a sociology as well as a pathology of revolution to account for it. They recall to attention the monstrosity of humankind when liberals may prefer to flatter humanity, and they remind one that original sin may be a better guide to modern history than natural goodness. Nevertheless, there are a number of problems with their denunciation of revolutionary presumption. Like radicalism, their thought conveys a profound alienation between what is and what ought to be and, like radicalism, presents itself as a science of politics with a blueprint of restoration as grandiose as the Declaration of the Rights of Man and Citizen. Moreover, de Maistre's celebrated recommendation that if "you wish to *conserve* all, *consecrate* all" is a proposition that transforms the sacred into human artifice, as impious to the true faith as the revolutionary consecration of the cult of the Supreme Being. The intelligent reflection necessary to make the case for conserving all tends to corrode the myths upon which traditions depend and collapses conservatism into very unconservative reaction.

Germany. If conservatism in Britain defended the congruence and conservatism in France demanded the restoration of harmony between the social and political orders, then conservatism in nineteenth-century Germany aspired to bring together an idea of the social and an idea of the political. Here revolutionary France in all its horrible fascination was instructive, demonstrating not only the radical dangers of popular sovereignty but also the military effectiveness of national unity. A romantic evocation of the cultural and racial characteristics of the *Volk* existed alongside a statist philosophy of realpolitik. Both were to contribute to an aggressive nationalism favored by those who thought German culture threatened by alien influences and by those who thought its state insufficiently powerful. If these tendencies are present in some measure in all conservative politics, they were to take a radical and racist turn in twentieth-century German history when combined in the detraditionalized, de-Christianized, alienated, genocidal (and so unconservative) shape of National Socialism.

A very different sort of reconciliation is provided by Georg Wilhelm Friedrich Hegel (1770–1831), whose philosophy courageously addresses the central problem of modernity—the idea of progress—that conservative thought either chose to veil (like Burke) or to deny (like de Maistre). The conservative suspicion of progress is that it denies the present in pursuit of the future. A restless and limitless ambition for change, based on an abstract model of human experience, makes modernity into a political *project* to be implemented rather than a *process* (for good and ill) to be understood. The French Revolution was such a political project, and Hegel attempts to map the lineage and the lineaments of the modern state in order to contain the destructive potential of the ideal of emancipation (that Hegelianism was not the *project* of modernity, the fulfillment of which demanded a new science of revolution, was well understood by that most insightful student, Karl Marx). On the conviction that the rational is actual and the actual is rational, Hegel argues in *The Philosophy of Right* (1821), the "plain man like the philosopher takes his stand." The task of the philosopher is to reveal the rationality of the common-sense intuition of the plain person. Hegel does not approve an institution on the basis of Burkean prescription—that its survival alone is sufficient justification of its rationality—but on the basis of its conformity with the rational self-understanding of the age. Such rationalism and historicism sit uneasily with conservative traditionalism, which often despises the self-understanding of the age and believes that the best reason for a practice is that no reason need be given. Despite his philosophical ambivalence, Hegel's appeal to the conservative is twofold. His reflections satisfy the need to feel that the enjoyment of present liberties is meaningful and should not be sacrificed to some abstract "ought to be." They also satisfy that deep desire to arrest the disturbing uncertainties of modern life within stable political institutions. Ironically, it has been these emotional satisfactions rather than his rational metaphysical system that constitute Hegel's enduring attraction to conservative thinkers.

The Challenge of the Modern
If there has been a specter haunting conservatism in modern times, it is the specter of "mass society." The fear of mass society is a product of two related possibilities. The first is the disintegration of traditional allegiances in the name of liberation and personal freedom. Since conservatives hold that such allegiances are the condition of identity, the consequence would be the loss of individuality. Liberalism, ironically, promotes the death of liberty. The second fear concerns the manipulation of that disintegration by ideologies that promise material satisfaction in return for absolute political power. Having destroyed individuality, mass society would demand abasement before the secular image of its collective power, the state. Socialism, ironically, promotes the death of the social.

In the nineteenth century and for much of the twentieth century, conservatism defended property, religion, and family as bulwarks against the feared drift to "mass" society in which the decencies of civilized life would be subverted by popular barbarism. This disposition helps to capture what is distinctive about the conservative idea of the nation, the one form of popular politics to which it not only adapted but which it also helped to define. For conservatives, the nation is understood as a political community united in acceptance of the legitimacy of traditional political arrangements. The "people" is not some abstract category but the historic nation in its regional and social variety, with its traditional beliefs, particular affections, and long-standing prejudices. To be conservative is another way of professing one's sympathy for the "real" character of the nation, and like de Maistre, conservatives would agree that they have met the French, English, Germans, or Americans but have yet to meet "Humanity."

In rejecting the universal claims of radical politics, conservatism has been compelled to identify exactly what it is that makes the nation distinctive. What differentiates conservatism from right-wing ideologies is the nature of that distinctiveness. In right-wing thought the idea of the nation serves to mobilize the people in order to assert its distinctive purity, honor, and greatness. In conservative thought, the idea of the nation serves to foster piety toward its distinctive social and political institutions. This differentiation has nothing to do with the intensity of national feeling. It has to do with the source of national feeling. Right-wing thought locates it in the will of the people. Conservatism locates it in the inherited practices of a way of life and has been concerned to limit the popular will in the name of tradition and order. In Europe between the two world wars, conservatism was outflanked by radical right-wing movements because an appeal to tradition and order appeared irrelevant in conditions of economic collapse and social disintegration. The sense of political decadence made an ideology of popular salvation, like fascism, a powerful alternative to traditional conservative patriotism. Britain was the exception, and the experience of British conservatism was thought to illustrate the distinction between the politics of the moderate right and the politics of the extreme right.

While the drama of modern European history has been taken to be exemplary of this difference, an American illustration is more appropriate. Harvey C. Mansfield Jr. considered that the great achievement of American politics has been the replacement of the idea of the sovereign people with the idea of the constitutional people. "The warmth of their republican genius must somehow be cooled; the confidence in their own sovereignty, which is responsible for the factiousness of democratic majorities, must be restrained" (Mansfield, p. 57). The practice of constitutional politics educates democracy in the responsibilities of government, in particular the need to limit power in order to enjoy life, liberty, and happiness. All elements of government "are derived *from* the people but none of them *is* the people," and populism, with its tendency to deny limit and constitutional constraint, is just as subversive of good government as any other species of radicalism (Mansfield, p. 55). This does not imply that there are no elements of populism in conservatism or that conservative politics has not appealed to its prejudices against innovation. However, conservatism's suspicion of political enthusiasm of all kinds makes it uncomfortable with the fickleness as well as the hubris of popular opinion, especially when it proclaims itself to be "the moral majority."

Resisting democracy, defending tradition. Of course, resisting the claims of democracy in the name of limited constitutional politics can be interpreted as an offense to modern sensibility, and defending tradition in a world of rapid change can be seen as either irrelevant or willfully ignorant. Conservatism always faces an enormous challenge in making these ideas persuasive in a world of programmatic politics. It appears insufficiently purposeful to those who are seeking a political faith and insufficiently principled to those who are seeking an alternative to radicalism. To such critics, conservatism is always right, but its inability to be proactive also means that it is always wrong. For example, Friedrich Hayek (1899–1992) thought conservatism incapable of offering "an alternative to the direction in which we are moving" because it does not and cannot indicate another direction (p. 398). Since Hayek famously believed that the socialistic path along which society was moving was the road to serfdom, then clearly conservatism, for all its useful maxims, would not do. This attitude helps to distinguish conservatism from that other species of recent politics, the New Right.

What Hayek assumes is the modernist belief in history-as-project, and this makes politics into an engagement between

projects, either a capitalist one or a socialist one. That modernist assumption, at the heart of New Right dogmatics about liberty and choice, finds systematic expression in neoconservatism. Indeed, some of the leading neoconservatives, like Irving Kristol, have radical political backgrounds. Their contribution in the last half of the twentieth century was to provide a systematic critique of "big government" and its policy failures and to show that the market was not only compatible with moral values but also more efficient in the delivery of social goods. Neoconservative arguments helped transform the political climate in the 1970s and 1980s and contributed to the intellectual defeat of socialism. However, there does exist a tension in neoconservatism between market fundamentalism and conservative skepticism. As Michael Oakeshott (1901–1990) once argued, a plan like Hayek's to end all planning is still a species of rationalism and one with which conservatives can only feel uncomfortable. It abstracts the market from the institutional and cultural traditions necessary for its flourishing, and for the skeptic, conservatism does not have a project to realize. That is its strength and not its weakness, for it properly designates the restricted competence in human affairs of such projects like market liberalization. If conservatism has an attitude toward capitalism, it is the endeavor to sustain those conditions that favor the political economy of freedom, a very different notion from the minimal state.

Postmodernism, human rights, and multiculturalism. If in the early twenty-first century revolutionary ideologies like communism no longer threaten, arguments in favor of egalitarianism and the aggrandizing state have taken a new shape. As a result, conservatism has been obliged to engage with new discourses, such as postmodernism, human rights, and multiculturalism. In 1959 Hannah Arendt (1906–1975) wrote that distinction and difference had become private matters of the individual and that simple insight, with its contradictory effects, continues to have profound implications for conservatism. Traditionally, of course, conservatism held distinction and difference not to be private matters at all but to be ones of public significance. According to Robert Nisbet, this is the key to understanding the conservative sociological imagination, where such differences, articulated in social institutions like Burke's "little platoons," mediate the relationship between the state and the individual.

The trend toward privatization has disordered that notion in two ways. First, the contemporary state has come either to absorb many of the functions of these institutions, like the educational responsibilities of churches, or to incorporate them into centrally determined policy networks. Second, it has become attractive for the individual to retire into a private world and to cede public duties to the care of professionals. The consequence of both aspects is an expansion of state influence that many conservatives do believe is inimical to individual freedom and social autonomy. For the conservative, the old radical dynamic that required a straightforward faith in state-fostered egalitarianism to be achieved through the redistribution of wealth between social classes has been replaced by a politics of inclusion that requires a rather contradictory faith not only in cultural "difference" but also in the redistribution of "worth" between social groups. The dynamic in this case is toward the removal of all obstacles in the way of social inclusion, and the motor is a refurbished language of abstract rights.

This new politics is understood to be yet another strategy to achieve the utopian objective of radical democracy, and conservatives believe that the only way it can be realized is by calling on the state to implement an ever-expanding body of entitlements. The influential neoconservative critique of modern liberalism has its roots here, and the concern is that the emphasis on rights will weaken the informal bonds of society and permit the state to become dangerously intrusive in the lives of citizens, destroying the distinction between public and private. Diversity is officially "celebrated," but what is fostered is a culture suspicious of independent thought or behavior or "political incorrectness." This is reminiscent of what George Santayana (1863–1952) once called "vacant liberty." Santayana's problem with the prescriptions of liberalism is its high-minded egalitarianism of respect, which he believes to be at odds with the very pluralism it seeks to promote. For Santayana, unlimited toleration would achieve the "euthanasia of differences," and as a consequence everybody "would be free to be what he liked, and no one would care to be anything but what pleased everybody" (p. 449). This anticipates a common, two-pronged, conservative criticism of contemporary liberalism. First, liberalism defends difference only in theory but cannot really come to terms with it in practice when it discovers that goodwill alone is not enough. Second, it is actually intolerant of dissent from political correctness and seeks to impose a modern version of "rational despotism." Two strands of conservatism, the civil and the cultural, can be identified in response to contemporary political trends.

Conservatism: Civil and Cultural

Civil conservatism draws on a recognizable tradition of limited politics. On the one hand, it proposes that government should not plan the lives of citizens or be an instrument of their collective enlightenment but should uphold a framework of law. On the other hand, it argues that the rights of civil society should not be translated into claims on public expenditure but should be valued as the condition of self-reliance and creativity. Limited but authoritative government remains the proper complement to a society of "difference."

This understanding owes much to the work of Oakeshott, who in turn owes much to Hobbes. Indeed, Oakeshott's celebrated essay "On Being Conservative" draws its inspiration from a distinctive reading of Hobbes's *Leviathan.* Commentators seduced by his poetic description of conservatism as a preference for "the tried to the untried, fact to mystery, the actual to the possible, the limited to the unbounded, the near to the distant, the sufficient to the superabundant, the convenient to the perfect, present laughter to utopian bliss" (Oakeshott, 1991, p. 408) sometimes fail to note that Oakeshott believes this disposition to be inappropriate "in respect of human conduct in general" (p. 415). However, conservatism does remain appropriate in respect of government, all the more so indeed in a modern society that puts so much store by its individualism.

Governing, for Oakeshott, "is recognized as a specific and limited activity; not the management of an enterprise, but the

rule of those engaged in a great diversity of self-chosen enterprises" (1991, p. 429). The philosophic basis of this view of government is explored in *On Human Conduct* (1975). This text has provided fruitful reflection for a diverse range of thinkers seeking a method to secure political legitimacy in contemporary multicultural societies and who identify a common threat to civility in utopian liberalism. Noël O'Sullivan, for example, has attempted to develop a vision of "formal politics" where the bond of association "is neither an agreed end, nor personal approval of the ruler and his actions, but acknowledgement of the procedural considerations which confer authority" (pp. 204–205). He argues that formal politics does not mean a commitment to liberalism but rather a rejection of the sort of "programmatic politics" with which modern liberal politics has become associated. The problem with the formal politics favored by civil conservatives is that it may be (ironically) too abstract and too detached from public sentiment to engage the loyalty of citizens. Certainly, it appears very distant from that sympathy for a traditional way of life normally associated with conservative politics.

Cultural conservatism, by contrast, assumes that a sense of unity rather than diversity is the foundation of political legitimacy. As Roger Scruton argues, the civil vision discounts "prejudices," and for Scruton (as for Burke), prejudices are those prepolitical affections, such as a sense of national belonging, upon which a stable political order depends. As he succinctly expresses it, "Unity is, in the normal instance, social rather than political, and ought also to be national" (1990, p. 54). This sets out a clear skeptical agenda for conservatism on issues—such as immigration, feminism, multiculturalism, and human rights—that are thought to present challenges to the substance of national identity. This cultural conservative agenda can be distinguished from that of the extreme right because of its respect for the conventions of established institutions. The great difficulty with it is that the social unity it assumes is a contentious one and, far from being self-evident, presents an easy target for those who would dismiss conservatism as nostalgic and elegiac. Contemporary conservatism, then, remains an ambiguous identity, a hybrid of civil and cultural elements.

Conclusion

In a century of ideological extremism like the twentieth century, conservatism often appeared something of an affectation and marginal to the march of history in which the advancing forces of modernization were thought certain to rout the retreating forces of conservatism. Insofar as many people have lost faith in the "grand narratives" of the nineteenth and twentieth centuries, like Marxism and other emancipatory ideals, then the conservative disposition may no longer appear so reactionary. Since conservatism never subscribed to the grosser forms of the modernist faith, contemporary skepticism comes as no surprise to it. However, as befits a philosophy of modesty and imperfection, conservatism cannot assume a final victory.

See also **Authoritarianism; Change; Fascism; Liberalism; Monarchy; Radicals/Radicalism; Totalitarianism.**

BIBLIOGRAPHY

Arendt, Hannah. *The Human Condition.* Garden City, N.Y.: Doubleday, 1959.

Aughey, Arthur, Greta Jones, and W. T. M. Riches. *The Conservative Political Tradition in Britain and the United States.* London: Pinter, 1992.

Aveneri, Shlomo. *Hegel's Theory of the Modern State.* London: Cambridge University Press, 1972.

Devigne, Robert. *Recasting Conservatism: Oakeshott, Strauss, and the Response to Postmodernism.* 2nd ed. New Haven, Conn.: Yale University Press, 1994.

Eatwell, Roger, and Noël O'Sullivan, eds. *The Nature of the Right.* London: Pinter, 1989.

Franco, Paul. *The Political Philosophy of Michael Oakeshott.* New Haven, Conn.: Yale University Press, 1990.

Hayek, Friedrich A. *The Constitution of Liberty.* London: Routledge and Kegan Paul, 1976.

Honderich, Ted. *Conservatism.* London: H. Hamilton, 1990.

Kirk, Russell, ed. *The Portable Conservative Reader.* New York: Viking, 1982.

Kristol, Irving. *Confessions of a Neo-Conservative.* New York: Basic Books, 1983.

Mansfield, Harvey C., Jr. "Constitutional Government: The Soul of Modern Democracy." *Public Interest* 86 (1987): 53–64.

Muller, Jerry Z., ed. *Conservatism: An Anthology of Social and Political Thought from David Hume to the Present.* Princeton, N.J.: Princeton University Press, 1997.

Nisbet, Robert. *Conservatism: Dream and Reality.* Milton Keynes, U.K.: Open University Press, 1986.

Oakeshott, Michael. "On Being Conservative." In his *Rationalism in Politics and Other Essays.* New and expanded ed. Indianapolis: Liberty Press, 1991.

———. *On Human Conduct.* Oxford: Clarendon, 1975.

O'Sullivan, Noël. *Conservatism.* London: Dent, 1976.

———. "The Politics of Ideology." In *The Structure of Modern Ideology,* edited by Noël O'Sullivan, 188–212. London: Edward Elgar, 1989.

Santayana, George. *Dominations and Powers.* New York: Charles Scribner's Sons, 1951.

Scruton, Roger. "In Defence of the Nation." In *Ideas and Politics in Modern Britain,* edited by John C. D. Clark, 53–87. London: Macmillan, 1990.

———. *The Meaning of Conservatism.* South Bend, Ind.: St. Augustine's, 2002.

———, ed. *Conservative Texts: An Anthology.* New York: St. Martin's, 1991.

Arthur Aughey

CONSILIENCE.

"Consilience of inductions" is a phrase that was invented by the nineteenth-century English historian and philosopher of science William Whewell (1794–1866; pronounced "Hule"), and introduced in his *Philosophy of the Inductive Sciences* (1840). Whewell was trying to capture the notion of what Isaac Newton (1642–1727) had labeled a "true cause," or *vera causa,* the kind of cause that supposedly lies at the center of the very best kinds of scientific theories. Whewell's friend, the astronomer and philosopher John F. W. Herschel (1792–1871), had argued (in an empiricist fashion) that a true cause is something that we ourselves experience directly or analogically. We know for instance that a force is pulling the moon toward the earth, because we have had direct experience of the tug of a string as we are whirling around with a stone tied to its end.

Whewell, to the contrary, in a rationalist fashion, wanted to characterize a true cause as something that is not necessarily experienced at all, but that is adequate to explain the empirical facts as we know them. He argued therefore that such a cause must be at the center of a scientific explanation, explaining all of the disparate facts and in turn being explained by them. If such a cause can predict and explain new and excitingly unexpected facts, then so much the better. Such a fan-like construction, with the cause at the apex, Whewell labeled a consilience of inductions. He argued also that such a situation is as simple as it is possible for a theory to be, and hence a true cause is also marked by the fact that it is the most economical of explanatory forces, with many parts being reduced to one fundamental mechanism.

For Whewell and Herschel, the paradigmatic example of a true cause was Newtonian mechanics, which used the one force—gravitational attraction—to explain not just the heavenly motions of the planets but also the earth-bound motions of such things as cannonballs. Johannes Kepler's (1571–1630) laws of celestial motion and Galileo Galilei's (1564–1642) laws of terrestrial motion were brought beneath one force. But Whewell and Herschel themselves were arguing over the science of their day, most particularly the nature and causes of light. The beginning of the nineteenth century was the time when the wave theory of Christiaan Huygens (1629–1695) was conquering the particle theory of Isaac Newton. The problem is that no one sees waves. Herschel argued that we have experienced analogous phenomena to light waves, for instance the waves of water in a pond. Hence it is reasonable to suppose that light waves produce such things as interference patterns. Whewell replied that there is no need of analogies—it is enough that the wave theory explains many phenomena that are impossible to explain with the particle theory. The patterns produced by something such as Thomas Young's (1773–1829) double-slit experiment are themselves enough to confirm that light travels in waves and not in particles.

Also dividing Whewell and Herschel was the true nature of geology, with Whewell arguing that it is permissible—even obligatory—to invoke unseen upheavals (catastrophes), and with Herschel agreeing with the uniformitarian geologist Charles Lyell (1797–1875) that unlimited time is enough to produce all changes, given the kinds of causes (rain, sleet, earthquakes, and so forth) that we see around us today. A young scientist who took deep note of Whewell's arguments was Charles Darwin (1809–1882), who, realizing that no one can ever see evolution actually occurring, consciously modeled his *Origin of Species* (1859) on Whewell's thinking. Having introduced his mechanism of natural selection, Darwin then spent the rest of the work showing how selection explains so many different areas—instinct, biogeography, paleontology, embryology, morphology, classification, and more—and how these areas in turn confirm natural selection as a true cause. When challenged, Darwin always referred to this strategy, even though, somewhat paradoxically, Whewell himself never became an evolutionist and supposedly would not allow the book on the shelves of the Cambridge college of which he was principal.

Consilience in Modern Science

The consilience of inductions figures high in modern science. Its broad explanatory power was the main reason that so many geologists were so quickly converted to the theory of plate tectonics. Supposing that the continents move explains so much—the shape of the continents, the position of earthquakes and volcanoes, the trenches in the middle of oceans, the magnetic lines, and much more. In recent years the idea has been extended into philosophy and to thinking about science and knowledge generally. The Harvard student of the ants and of social behavior (sociobiology), Edward O. Wilson, argues that all of human knowledge is heading toward a consilience—a consilience where evolution will be the all-powerful joining and explaining idea. We have a kind of gene-culture coevolution, where culture tries to impose its ways and norms on human behavior and thought, but where the genes always constrain the flights of fancy and make sure that human nature never strays too far from the basic biological.

Wilson argues that morality for instance cannot exist as a disembodied ethereal enterprise, but must be rooted firmly in our evolutionary background—morality exists because and only because it was and is of use to us as creatures struggling to survive and reproduce. Those humans who worked together did better than those who did not. Likewise, religion serves to bind humans together in well-functioning units. It has no correspondence to reality but serves as an adaptation toward the greater success of Homo sapiens. Wilson argues that we must strive to achieve ever-greater consiliences between disparate parts of human knowledge until all is bound together in one big super-picture. Only then will we humans recognize the extent to which we are part of this big picture—a picture that includes all of natural diversity. Only then will we humans be truly motivated to the preservation of the living world around us, something from which we emerged and something without which we can never hope to survive. Consilience has therefore moved from the epistemological norm of William Whewell to the moral imperative of Edward O. Wilson.

See also **Causation; Science, Philosophy of.**

BIBLIOGRAPHY

Ruse, Michael. *The Darwinian Revolution: Science Red in Tooth and Claw.* 2nd ed. Chicago: University of Chicago Press, 1999. Originally published in 1979.
Whewell, William *The Philosophy of the Inductive Sciences.* 2 vols. London: Parker, 1840.
Wilson, Edward O. *Consilience.* New York: Knopf, 1998.

Michael Ruse

CONSTITUTIONALISM. Constitutionalism is commonplace in modern political discourse in the West and beyond, yet it remains an elusive concept. Some have considered it impossible (and unnecessary) to give a definition of it.

Nonetheless, one can discern several common features of the concept: the rule of law, not of men; limitations of political authority; the protection of civic rights and liberties; and rule based on the free consent of the ruled. Placing limitations on the exercise of political power is central to the notion of constitutionalism, and measures for that end include admonition to the deviant ruler; the assertion of the people's right to resist, punish, or depose a tyrant; the division of sovereignty via federalism; and the separation of powers, or other checks and balances.

Paradoxical as it may seem, the presence of a constitution is not necessarily a manifestation of constitutionalism. A constitutionalistic constitution forms a political entity, establishes its fundamental structure, and determines the limits within which power can be exercised politically. But some constitutions in the modern world, like those of the former Soviet Union and the People's Republic of China, do not limit the exercise of political power. A constitution of this sort is designed to constitute and empower the state, but not to control it.

Ancient Conceptions

The idea of controlling political power goes back to ancient Athens, where all state officials were accountable to the citizens who sat on the jury court. This jury-court system is the hallmark of the Athenian constitutionalism based on popular participation, yet it was never conceptualized by the leading Greek philosophers, including Plato (c. 428–348 or 347 B.C.E.) and Aristotle (384–322 B.C.E.). For Plato, democracy—rule by the ignorant masses—was fundamentally flawed. His vision of the ideal state, therefore, allows no space for an assembly or a court: a counterview to the contemporary practice of Athenian politics. Aristotle's tripartite conception of the just political structure—monarchy, aristocracy, and *politeia*—resulted in the idea of the mixed constitution combining the virtues of three. This idea, ill defined by Aristotle, was often confused with the idea of the ideal constitution. The political practice of Republican Rome was described and celebrated by Cicero (106–43 B.C.E.) as the "mixed constitution," which was, however, a pure aristocracy according to his own description. The nature of Republican Rome's political institutions remains elusive: in contrast with Cicero, Polybius (c. 200–c. 118 B.C.E.) depicted them as part of a constitutionalist system, with the popular assembly controlling legislation and the election of magistrates.

Medieval Conceptions

The medieval model of constitutionalism is often associated with Magna Carta (1215); in it, the constitutionalistic idea that personal liberties should be protected from the authority of the prince by established legal procedures was already present. But the medieval contributions to constitutional theory may be found in the sphere of ecclesiology under the label of conciliarism. Conciliarism was the idea that the pope was not an absolute ruler but a constitutional monarch whose authority was ministerial and delegated to him for the common good of the church. The ultimate authority in the church, then, resides in the whole body of the believers or their representatives—namely, the general council. According to twelfth-century canonists, who grappled with the questions surrounding the possible abuse of power by the pope, the pope was an intrinsic part of a general council and the authority of the pope with a general council was greater than without: an argument parallel to the secular idea of the supremacy of the king-in-parliament. The divine nature of papal authority did not necessarily result in theocratic absolutism because of the idea that the power of jurisdiction came from God through the people; the power of the papal office originates from God, but the choice of a person who assumes the office depends on the consent of human cooperation.

The exaltation of papal sovereignty in thirteenth-century mendicant ecclesiology was countered by secular masters' "episcopalist" view: Christ conferred supreme authority not to Peter and his successors alone but equally to the twelve apostles and their successors; thereby ecclesiastical sovereignty was divided. All these elements of thought constituted conciliarism in the later Middle Ages, represented by such thinkers as Pierre d'Ailly (1350–1420) and Jean de Gerson (Jean Charlier; 1363–1429). The historian J. N. Figgis describes early modern constitutionalism as "the last effort of medieval constitutionalism," but the extent to which medieval constitutional thought influenced its modern counterpart remains debatable.

Early Modern Conceptions

Widespread administrative abuses and ecclesiastical corruption in late-sixteenth-century France generated a number of polemical pamphlets, which asserted the rights of the people to depose a tyrant. Huguenot political writers including François Hotman (1524–1590; *Francogallia*), Théodore de Bèze, (Theodorus Beza; 1519–1605; *The Rights of Magistrates*), and Duplessis-Mornay (Philippe de Mornay, Seigneur du Plessis-Marly; 1549–1623; *Vindiciae contra tyrannos; A defense of liberty against tyrants*) made important contributions to early modern constitutionalism by defining the right to resist and depose a tyrannical monarch as the ultimate guarantee of a set of particular controls on political authority. Their works rejected resistance by private individuals but asserted the right of resistance by constituted public power, especially of the Estates and lesser magistrates. Huguenot political thinkers upheld the doctrine of the division of sovereignty between the monarch, representative institutions, and lesser magistrates, whilst their contemporary Jean Bodin (1530–1596), a powerful proponent of the indivisibility of sovereignty, saw anarchy as the alternative to monarchy (just as Thomas Hobbes would do in the following century). Jean Bodin's theory of sovereignty circulated widely in seventeenth-century England, and served to bolster the idea of unlimited monarchical sovereignty manifested by James I (ruled 1603–1625) and Charles I (ruled 1625–1649). Sir Robert Filmer (c. 1588–1653) and Thomas Hobbes (1588–1679) conceptualized the doctrine of monarchical authority. But political authority in England had already been pluralistic, and this reality was crystallized in Sir Edward Coke's (1552–1634) idea that the English judiciary was independent from the crown as well as from Parliament. A more direct reaction to the Bodinian doctrine came from Johannes Althusius (Joachim Althaus; 1557–1638), who attributed indivisible sovereignty, unlike Bodin, to the people as a collective entity.

The people as individuals are under the ruler, and yet the people as a collectivity is superior to the ruler. Althusius's novelty lies in his vision of federalism: he conceived a political community as a hierarchy of corporations, and took care to specify the way in which smaller communities are associated together in larger political entities, which resulted in a system of checks and balances.

Perhaps one of the most important sources for the authors of the American constitution was the epoch-making *L'esprit des lois* (1748; The spirit of the laws) written by Charles-Louis de Secondat, baron de Montesquieu (1689–1755). This eminent lawyer was deeply inspired by the English system of government that, in his view, had effectively secured what he called "political liberty." Montesquieu observed that the highest expression of political liberty was to be found in England. English constitutional practice had protected each citizen from each other, from foreign enemies of the state, and from the state itself. The key to this success, according to Montesquieu, was the functional separation of powers: legislative, executive, and judicial. The institutional separation of powers secured effective control of the coercive authority of the state: a significant departure from the "mixed constitution" model.

The late eighteenth century was the age of constitutions; the first modern written constitution was enacted in the United States of America (1787), followed by the French Declaration of the Rights of Man and the Citizen (1789). *The Federalist,* eighty-five papers written by Alexander Hamilton (1755–1804), James Madison (1751–1836), and John Jay (1745–1829), vindicated the theoretical foundations of the U.S. Constitution that underlined the limits on federal power by means of federalism, separation of powers, and the effective independence of political institutions. These institutional constraints were designed to augment the citizen's exercise of civic virtues to prevent monarchical despotism and to maintain liberty.

What constituted an important intellectual backdrop was republican constitutional ideas. Republicanism, upheld by influential figures such as Montesquieu, Jean-Jacques Rousseau (1712–1778), and Immanuel Kant (1724–1804), distinguished the people as a legislator (constituent power) from the people as a legislative power (constituted power) and envisioned the "good order" of society—that is, the fundamental principles of the working of a political society, or the means by which good laws and good rulers should be made. On the other hand, the U.S. Constitution was initially criticized for the omission of a specific statement concerning basic citizen rights. This was later drawn up as the Bill of Rights, now considered an integral part of the constitution.

Modern Conceptions

The U.S. Constitution generated reaction from British constitutionalists, and at the heart of the debate was the idea of sovereignty. Walter Bagehot (1826–1877), the author of *The English Constitution,* criticized the ambiguity of the locus of sovereignty in it, whereas Albert Venn Dicey (1826–1877) thought highly of the federal system of government that divided legislative powers between national and state authorities. The nightmare of totalitarianism in the first half of the twentieth century, on the other hand, demanded the vindication of constitutionalism, which was quintessentially crystallized in Charles H. McIlwain's *Constitutionalism, Ancient and Modern.*

In the early twenty-first century, issues over constitutionalism became ever more complex. Constitutionalism did not grow out of democratic thought, yet most contemporary states with a constitution are constitutional democracies. This demands that the relationship between constitutionalism and democracy be defined more precisely. The reconciliation between liberal right-based constitutionalism and republican democratic constitutionalism has also been sought. Furthermore, there exists a plurality of constitutions. The British model, for example, manifests parliamentary sovereignty, whereas the American model locates sovereignty in the people. The wide reception of constitutionalism beyond the West has created new varieties of constitutionalism (transformative constitutionalism). The emerging European Union after World War II, followed by the post-1989 developments in Eastern Europe in particular, has brought the debate over constitutionalism to an entirely new phase: constitutionalism beyond the framework of the nation state, and even the possibility of global constitutionalism.

Islamic Conceptions

The idea of limited government was not unknown in early Islamic political thought; the Muslim ruler was more limited than Christian princes in the sense that he had no power to legislate. The Holy Law (*shari'a*) however, was not effective in limiting political power due to the dearth of institutional machinery that imposed the limitations.

In Persia (Iran) in the 1850s, the government reformed the legal system to limit the power of the *'ulama* (scholar-teachers), and introduced the Western notion of constitutionalism. The promoters of constitutionalism, such as Malkom Khan (1833–1908) and Mirza Yusef Khan Mostashar od-Dowle (d. 1895), endeavored to demonstrate that the new idea was anchored in Islamic law and tradition. Mirza Yusef Khan's treatise, *Yek Kalameh* (n.d.; One word), contrasted Western prosperity with Persian stagnation and saw the solution of this problem in *yek kalameh,* a political structure based on law. He highlighted the virtues of the French constitution and demonstrated its compatibility with Islamic ideas. Such endeavors contributed to incorporating the Shiite religious group successfully into the constitutionalist movement, thereby paving the way to the Constitutional Revolution (1905–1911). Similarly, the young Ottomans, including Namik Kemal (1840–1888), who admired the constitution of the French Third Republic, reinterpreted passages in the Koran as arguments for constitutional democracy. Khayr al-Din al-Tunisi (1822/23–1890), who dreamed of the independence of the Islamic world community, was, like the Ottoman and Persian reformers, receptive to the Western constitutional idea that personal liberty and justice should be achieved by the rule of law. But his constitutionalism also echoed the Islamic intellectual tradition, especially the political ideas of Ibn Khaldūn (1332–1406).

Chinese Conception

The term that signifies "constitutional law" is of ancient origin in the Chinese language, and yet it denoted none of the Western ideas associated with modern Western constitutionalism. For the Chinese, constitutionalism was a Western import, dating back to the early nineteenth century. But the idea was not seriously assimilated until Japan established the first constitutional law in East Asia in 1889.

K'ang Yu-wei (1858–1927) was the leader of the Hundred Days of Reform, the movement for constitutional reform. He embraced the evolutionist view that constitutional change from monarchy to democracy was a historical necessity. His 1898 reform program, which included the creation of a parliament and the adoption of a constitution, was welcomed by the Emperor Kuang-hsü, (ruled 1875–1908), but its translation into practice was aborted by the coup d'état under the initiative of the Empress Dowager Tz'u-hsi (1835–1908).

Japan's victory in the war against the Russian Empire in 1905 demonstrated, in the eyes of the Chinese constitutional reformists, the victory of constitutionalism; this gave added momentum to the reception of the idea in China. The Ch'ing government drew up an "Outline of Constitution" modeled on the Japanese constitution, which never took effect, however, due to the 1911 revolution led by Sun Yat-sen (1866–1925) and the downfall of the Ch'ing dynasty. The Republic of China, established in 1912, promulgated a Provisional Constitution, the first modern constitution, modeled on the U.S. Constitution. Sun Yat-sen's *Sanminzhuyi* (1924; The three principles of the people)—the Principle of Nationalism, the Principle of Democracy, and the Principle of People's Livelihood—was inspired by Abraham Lincoln's (1809–1865) Gettysburg Address (1863), and his guiding principle of constitution-making known as the separation of five powers—the powers of administration, legislation, judiciary, examination, and impeachment, the last two being uniquely Chinese—was built upon Montesquieu's notion of the separation of powers.

Japanese Conceptions

The Japanese reception of Western constitutionalism, following the collapse of the Tokugawa Shogunal regime (1603–1867), was motivated by the diplomatic and military needs of national independence. The strengthening of the military needed to be augmented by "the concord of the People's mind (*jinwa* or *jinmin kyôwa*)," which could be achieved through the introduction of Western constitutional government. One of the pressing tasks in domestic politics was to settle the conflict between powers by entrusting supreme authority to parliament. Hence, in his *Tonarigusa* (1861; Grass next door), the first treatise on constitutionalism in Japan, Katō Hiroyuki (1836–1916) proclaimed the establishment of parliamentary politics. The perception of a constitution as the symbol of a modern Western-style state was widely shared by the political leaders of the new Meiji government, which led to the speedy creation of the Meiji Constitution, the first constitutional law in East Asia. Yet, the adoption of a "Westernized" constitution, officially an imperial gift to the Japanese subjects, was not accompanied by wide acceptance of the idea of controlling the power of the state. The prevalent Confucian language that equated the private with the evil and the public (namely, the state, not the civil society) with justice undercut the constitutional idea of the protection of individual liberties.

After Japan's defeat in World War II, constitutionalism, which had experienced a serious setback during the war, was rehabilitated under the new Constitution of Japan. This Constitution, however, was created not by popular demand, but by the initiative of the occupation authority. Ever since, Article 9, which proscribes the use of military means in diplomatic conflict, has been the focal point of post-war constitutional debate.

See also **Democracy; Republicanism; State, The.**

BIBLIOGRAPHY

Beer, Laurence Ward, ed. *Constitutionalism in Asia: Asian Views of the American Influence.* Berkeley: University of California Press, 1979.

Bellamy, Richard, ed. *Constitutionalism, Democracy, and Sovereignty: American and European Perspectives.* Aldershot, U.K.: Avebury, 1996.

Black, Antony. *The History of Islamic Political Thought: From the Prophet to the Present.* Edinburgh: Edinburgh University Press, 2001.

Castiglione, Dario, and Richard Bellamy, eds. *Constitutionalism in Transformation: European and Theoretical Perspectives.* Oxford: Blackwell, 1996.

Figgis, J. N. *Political Thought from Gerson to Grotius, 1414–1625.* 2nd ed. Cambridge, U.K.: Cambridge University Press, 1916.

Franklin, Julian, trans. and ed. *Constitutionalism and Resistance in the Sixteenth Century: Three Treatises by Hotman, Beza, and Mornay.* New York: Pegasus, 1969.

Gordon, Scott. *Controlling the State: Constitutionalism from Ancient Athens to Today.* Cambridge, Mass.: Harvard University Press, 1999.

Lloyd, Howell, A. "Constitutionalism." In *The Cambridge History of Political Thought, 1450–1700,* edited by J. H. Burns and Mark Goldie, 254–297. Cambridge: Cambridge University Press, 1991.

McIlwain, Charles H. *Constitutionalism, Ancient and Modern.* Rev. ed. Ithaca, N.Y.: Cornell University Press, 1947.

Tierney, Brian. *Religion, Law, and the Growth of Constitutional Thought, 1150–1650.* Cambridge, U.K.: Cambridge University Press, 1982.

Takashi Shogimen

CONSUMERISM. Consumerism, the central economic and social policy of contemporary capitalism, is a doctrine of growing the economy through constantly increasing the consumption of commodities and services. The term *consumerism* is also used to describe movements to protect the rights and interests of consumers.

Consumerism and Mass Production

While the consumption of commodities has always been an aspect of human society, consumerism was not possible until after the first and second industrial revolutions (1760–1840 and late nineteenth and early twentieth centuries, respectively). The industrial revolutions, led by Great Britain and the United States, gradually caused the replacement of the artisan system, in which goods were produced locally by skilled workers on a small scale. Technological innovations, like the spinning jenny (1764), allowed fewer and less-skilled workers the ability to produce more goods, while the creation of national transportation networks, such as railroads, allowed for their wide dissemination. The factory system, in which labor was organized by specific tasks, rose into prominence, leading to the growth of cities, rising immigration, and the depletion of natural resources.

As the labor process was divided into separate tasks, laborers became estranged from the products of their labor, destroying the pride in craftsmanship they had experienced in the artisan system. Karl Marx (1818–1883), political economist and theorist of capitalism, described this disconnection as "alienation." Alienation allowed commodities to be seen not as the products of labor, which was hidden from consumers, but as fetishes, things imbued with an almost animate power in the world. A commodity's usefulness, or, in Marx's terms, use-value, became increasingly subordinated to its exchange value, or its social worth (generally its price or monetary value). As commodities lost any connection with objective value, they became fetishized. Advertising has aided and exploited commodity fetishism by suggesting that commodities have magical properties—that is, that buying a product will increase the consumer's social status or attractiveness. As the commodity has become the central aspect of social life, areas that were once outside of the economic sphere, such as the family or religion, are recreated as commodities for sale in the market.

While the industrial revolutions allowed for mass production, it was not until Henry Ford (1863–1947) introduced his assembly-line system for automobile production that goods could be produced in huge quantities cheaply enough to be widely accessible. Using Frederick Taylor's scientific-management principles, Ford assigned workers small, repetitive tasks that by 1913 allowed a car to be produced every ninety-three minutes. While the nature of this work was potentially unfulfilling for workers, Ford paid them well—his legendary five-dollar-per-day minimum wage—as a means of ensuring that he would have a mass of people able to afford the Ford Model T. The success of Ford's venture so changed the American economy and capitalism in general that the Italian Marxist Antonio Gramsci (1891–1937) coined the term *Fordism* to describe it. Fordism is defined by an economy dominated by centralized mass production, state welfare, unionized workers, and consumption of standardized commodities, of which the Model T is the ideal example. This car was designed to appeal to all consumers regardless of class, race, gender, and so on. Under Fordism, yearly or seasonal product changes are minimal or nonexistent.

While advertising had existed previously—from town criers to handbills—advertising as a rationalized, scientific profession began only in the 1850s. In the mid-nineteenth century a variety of products, such as patent medicines, had come to be widely consumed in the national marketplace. Advertising became important as a means of creating desire for new, standardized products and especially of proving to consumers that these products were superior to homemade or local ones. In their search for status as professionals and experts, advertisers

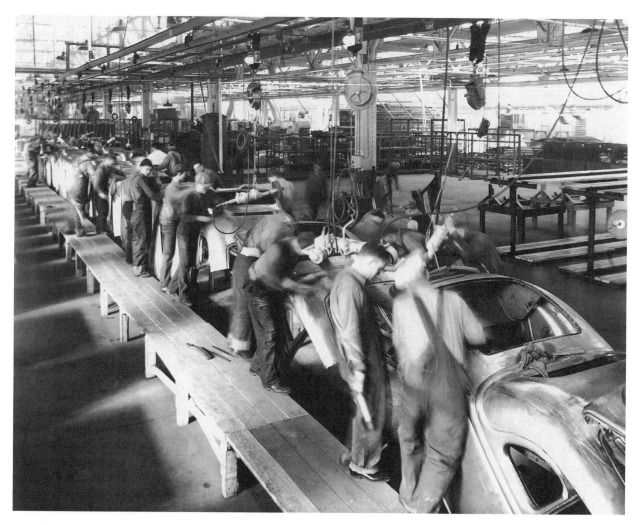

Assembly line at Ford Motor Company factory, Minnesota, 1935. Industrial advancements such as Henry Ford's assembly line, which was instituted in the early twentieth century, allowed products to be available to consumers in mass quantities and at affordable prices. © BETTMANN/CORBIS

sought to distance their practice from the carnivalesque methods of peddlers, snake-oil salesmen, and other hucksters by relying on factual information soberly offered. Yet the carnival tradition never entirely disappeared, and even in this era, pictorial advertisements using magical and sensual imagery continued to appear in mass periodicals, though they were managed by the new national advertising agencies and therefore became increasingly standardized.

By the 1880s and 1890s the modern advertising system was in place. Instead of simply serving as middlemen between businesses and media outlets, advertisers sold their services as designers of campaigns, promoters of products, and experts on the media. Branding, in which products came to be known by a specific brand name, became increasingly important in differentiating essentially similar products from each other in the market. As these brand-name products were distributed across formerly insurmountable barriers of geography by steamships and trains, people in diverse regions could consume the same products, inculcating a sense of nationalism. In this way, the

Fordist era promoted a nation founded on the "democracy of goods" in which everyone used the same consumer products, collapsing consumerism with national identity. Yet this "imagined community" was highly stratified by race, gender, ethnicity, and class. While the Fordist era of mass production shifted the United States, as well as other nations, from a country of artisan production, regional cultures, and individualized commodities to one of national brands, this nationalism came at the expense of many members of the nation itself, particularly people of color, the working class, and women. Blacks, for example, were portrayed in advertisements of this era almost exclusively as happy servants or as icons of slavery, such as Aunt Jemima and Uncle Ben. Working-class people were also rarely seen in advertisements, which presented a relentlessly middle- or upper-class world.

Consumerism and Post-Fordism

The term *post-Fordist* has been used to describe the shift from an economy based on mass production and mass consumption

SOAP

Soap was first sold under a brand name in Great Britain in 1884, placing it indelibly within the history of British imperialism and Victorian notions of gender and race. Soap advertisements portrayed soap as a fetish, imbued with the power to cleanse and bring civilization. As Reverend Henry Ward Beecher (1813–1887) argued in an 1885 testimonial for Pears soap, "If Cleanliness is next to Godliness, then surely SOAP is a means of GRACE." Soap advertisements consistently used magical imagery to hide the intense labor performed by working-class maids employed in middle-class homes. Middle-class women were never shown as laborers, creating a gendered ideology where middle-class women were "angels of the household" whose major role was that of consumer.

Soap advertisements also offered a racial ideology, described as "commodity racism" by Anne McClintock. A Pears soap advertisement of 1899 argued that "The first step toward lightening THE WHITE MAN'S BURDEN is through teaching the virtues of cleanliness. PEARS' SOAP is a potent fact in brightening the dark corners of the earth as civilization advances." The scientific racism that posited evolutionary notions of biology and history came to be projected onto commodities, which would do the work of empire. Soap became the symbolic carrier of whiteness, imperialism, and Victorian gender roles.

of identical goods to one distinguished by "flexible specialization." Production is specialized through the use of technology. The post-Fordist labor force is multiskilled and global, which has eroded the class consciousness of Fordist labor movements. Importantly, consumption has become specialized as well. No longer is there one product designed for the mass of consumers. Instead, products are target marketed to particular niches, using demographics, psychographics, and other marketing techniques. At this point, style becomes the major method of differentiating products. Advertisers encourage consumer desire to become more volatile and individualized. Products are not marketed by extolling their utilitarian value but by proving to the consumer how he or she can use them to display a particular identity to the world. The development of a post-Fordist economy is difficult to pinpoint, though scholars suggest that the 1970s in the industrial West was a turning point. Even within one economy, such as the United States, the development of post-Fordism did not occur unilaterally through all industries. While current Western economies can be described as post-Fordist, Third World economies are not necessarily so, though First World post-Fordism relies on the exploitation of labor, resources, and markets within the Third World.

Scholars agree, however, that one of the most significant aspects of the post-Fordist economy is the reliance on market segmentation as opposed to mass consumption. Market segmentation emphasizes particular aspects of a product or creates a particular product to appeal to specific market segments, which are differentiated by income, gender, race, ethnicity, age, geography, and so on. This marketing paradigm developed out of the baby boom of the post–World War II era and the social and identity movements of the 1960s that became the predominant paradigm by the 1970s and 1980s.

The social and identity movements of the 1960s suggested that people understood their identities as differentiated by a number of characteristics. In response, advertisers and marketers explored the potential for "breaking up America" and the world into an ever-increasing number of segments of people who had "lifestyles" that were defined by the particular commodities they consumed. The development of cable television is an ideal example. Beginning in the late 1970s, cable networks were designed to appeal to particular types of viewers, whether women (Lifetime), African-Americans (Black Entertainment Television [BET]), and youth (Music Television [MTV]), through the content of their programs as well as the flow of shows and commercials. As important as "signaling" or attracting the desired type of viewers, however, was ensuring that unwanted types of viewers were not watching.

Race and ethnicity are becoming increasingly critical market segments. In 1994, according to *Brandweek,* at least half of all Fortune 500 companies were using ethnic or racial marketing techniques. Latinos, for example, are one of the fastest-growing ethnic minorities in the United States, and corporations are searching for ways to appeal to this segment, which is divided into a variety of subsegments (Mexican-American, Puerto Rican–American, Cuban-American).

PSYCHOGRAPHICS

Psychographics is a method of market segmentation based on personality, lifestyle, and geodemographics. These techniques promise to offer marketers the ability to define their target buyers by their beliefs, values, and self-perception. This allows for micromarketing, or marketing tailored to the level of very small segments, such as neighborhoods. For example, a department store that serves a neighborhood of young unmarried people may not carry children's products, while the same department store in a different but nearby neighborhood, with a different geodemographic profile, might do so. Psychographics also allows marketers to appeal to consumers based on their perceived self-perceptions. Does this consumer generally make decisions based on status? Beliefs? The online service "You Are Where You Live" offered by the marketing analysis company Claritas in the early 2000s is an example of the use of psychographics and geodemographics.

An important corollary of these developments is that as style becomes central in product differentiation, it is necessary for styles to change rapidly. What has been described as the essentially postmodern practice of pastiche is an outgrowth of these marketing and economic changes, in which capital recycles old styles in a desperate attempt to create products that seem "new and improved." As the commodity becomes even more divorced from use- or exchange-value, it becomes a sign, able to be given a variety of possible and mutable meanings depending on the particular market segment. Price fluctuates not according to actual production costs but according to how much a particular consumer will pay. Cultural intermediaries, or those members of the professional-managerial class that work in cultural industries such as advertising or public relations, serve as cultural guides for the middle class, helping these consumers navigate the array of potential commodities available for consumption and offering their lifestyles as models of how to live successfully in this new world of constant consumption.

The Politics of Consumerism

As consumerism has become the fundamental doctrine of contemporary capitalism, individuals have been encouraged to consider themselves primarily as *consumers* rather than as citizens, workers, or members of religious denominations. While in many ways this ideological shift has been spurred by capital as a means of ensuring a continual increase in consumer spending as a means of growing the economy, numerous individuals and organizations have used this consumer identity as a way to encourage government control over business and to protest social, racial, political, and economic injustice. For example, during the Great Depression of the 1930s women's organizations such as the General Federation of Women's Clubs and the League of Women Shoppers led consumer protests for food legislation and against rising meat prices. Dr. Kathryn McHale, the general director of the American Association of University Women, summarized the consumer

movement's philosophy in 1935 when she said "there is no interest which is more fundamental than that of consumers. All residents of our nation are consumers in large or limited way. No matter what our other interests, we have in common one function—that of consumption" (Cohen, p. 34).

Even the civil rights movement of the 1950s and 1960s utilized consumer identity to justify its claim for equal rights. The first and most-remembered protests were the Montgomery bus boycott, when African Americans refused to consume public transportation as a protest against their inferior treatment in the transit system, and the lunch-counter sit-ins, when protesters refused to move from whites-only dining areas. These tactics showed the government and the American public the correlation between citizenship and the right to consume—in the consumerist world of post–World War II America, being banned from consumption demonstrated second-class status.

While consumer movements have been successful to a degree in protecting certain rights, they can be faulted for accepting the overwhelming ideology of consumerism and, more widely, capitalism. Instead, other individuals and organizations have sought to protest the ideology of consumerism through a variety of methods and means. While consumerism relies on the creation of desire, anticonsumerist movements focus on "need." Religious sects such as the Amish and the Shakers adapted the Christian idea of voluntary poverty, for example, to create a more godly existence based on need, while the counterculture of the 1960s used voluntary poverty to justify its renunciation of material goods and capitalism. However, even voluntary poverty or its secular corollary, "voluntary simplicity," created by Duane Elgin in the 1980s, have been adapted by the mass media and business. In the 1970s the Stanford Research Institute, a nonprofit corporation that offers corporate clients advice on emerging trends, estimated that almost 75 million Americans had "simple" sympathies that business should utilize (Kleiner, 1996). Still, many people advocate voluntary simplicity as necessary to limit the negative environmental impact of a consumer-driven economy, which produces huge amounts of waste and uses resources at an ever-quickening pace.

Another central critique of consumerism is related to globalization. Multinational corporations are cited for destroying local and indigenous resources and cultures in order to make way for their products. The term *McDonaldization* has been coined to describe the phenomenon of local cultures being stamped out by multinational corporations spreading a homogenous Western (usually American) culture. However, scholars dispute the effects of McDonaldization. While many see local cultures being destroyed by the forces of globalizing popular culture, others assert that local cultures incorporate and adapt these forces, creating a syncretized culture. Still, either side must acknowledge the uneven power relationships that exist between a cultural behemoth like the United States and Third World markets.

See also **Capitalism; Globalization; Marxism.**

BIBLIOGRAPHY

Baudrillard, Jean. *The Consumer Society: Myths and Structures.* Thousand Oaks, Calif.: Sage, 1998.

Campbell, Colin. *The Romantic Ethic and the Spirit of Modern Consumerism.* New York: Blackwell, 1987.

Cohen, Lizabeth. *A Consumers' Republic: The Politics of Mass Consumption in Postwar America.* New York: Knopf, 2003.

Ewen, Stuart. *Captains of Consciousness: Advertising and the Social Roots of the Consumer Culture.* New York: McGraw-Hill, 1976.

———. *All Consuming Images: The Politics of Style in Contemporary Culture.* New York: Basic Books, 1988.

Ewen, Stuart, and Elizabeth Ewen. *Channels of Desire: Mass Images and the Shaping of American Consciousness.* Minneapolis: University of Minnesota Press, 1992.

Frank, Thomas. *The Conquest of Cool: Business Culture, Counterculture, and the Rise of Hip Consumerism.* Chicago: University of Chicago Press, 1997.

Kleiner, Art. *The Age of Heretics: Heroes, Outlaws, and the Forerunners of Corporate Change.* New York: Currency/Doubleday, 1996.

Lears, T. J. Jackson. *Fables of Abundance: A Cultural History of Advertising in America.* New York: Basic Books, 1994.

Lury, Celia. *Consumer Culture.* New Brunswick, N.J.: Rutgers University Press, 1996.

Marchand, Roland. *Advertising the American Dream: Making Way for Modernity, 1920–1940.* Berkeley: University of California Press, 1985.

Marx, Karl. *Capital: A Critique of Political Economy.* New York: Vintage Books, 1977.

McClintock, Anne. *Imperial Leather: Race, Gender, and Sexuality in the Colonial Conquest.* New York: Routledge, 1995.

Ritzer, George. *The McDonaldization of Society: An Investigation into the Changing Character of Contemporary Social Life.* Newbury Park, Calif.: Pine Forge Press, 1993.

Turow, Joseph. *Breaking up America: Advertisers and the New Media World.* Chicago: University of Chicago Press, 1997.

Williams, Raymond. "Advertising: The Magic System." In his *Problems in Materialism and Culture: Selected Essays.* London: Verso, 1980.

Witt, Doris. *Black Hunger: Food and the Politics of U.S. Identity.* New York: Oxford University Press, 1999.

Mary Rizzo

CONTEXT. Like "text," the word "context" is a metaphor derived from the Latin *texere,* "to weave." In the fourth century C.E. the Latin noun *contextio* described the text surrounding a given passage. In the Middle Ages, *contextio* came to mean "literary composition," but an interest in what we call "context," especially in biblical exegesis, was expressed through the term *circumstantiae.* In the ninth century, Sedulius Scotus enunciated the rule of "seven circumstances"—person, fact, cause, time, place, mode, and topic.

Texts in Context

It was in the sixteenth and seventeenth centuries, especially in Italian, French, English, and German, that the term "context" (*contesto, contexture, Kontext*) began to be used with frequency. From the sentences before and after the passage to be interpreted, "context" came to refer to the coherence of a text, the relation of the parts and the whole. The term was also extended to include the intention (*scopus*) of the writer.

"Circumstances" remained a key term. Jurists discussed circumstantial evidence. Moralists studied "cases of conscience," the ethical equivalent of case law. Interpretations of the Bible invoked the need to take circumstances into consideration. The sixteenth-century Florentine historian Francesco Guicciardini offers an example of contextual thinking in early modern style. Guicciardini's *Considerations* on the *Discourses* of his friend Niccolò Machiavelli criticized the generalizations because they were "advanced too absolutely" (*posto troppo assolutamente*), since human affairs "differ according to the times and the other events" (*si varia secondo la condizione de' tempi ed altre occorrenzie*).

The thrust of the movements we call the "scientific revolution" and the "Enlightenment" was anticontextual in the sense that participants were concerned with formulating generalizations that would be valid whatever the circumstances. By the late eighteenth century, however, these "enlightened" attitudes were coming to be viewed as part of an intellectual old regime against which a more "historicist" generation revolted around the year 1800, stressing differences between individuals and cultures at the expense of general laws.

The Rise of Cultural Context

This "Counter-Enlightenment" was associated with a further expansion in the meaning of the term "context," increasingly concerned not only with local circumstances but also with the "historical context" of an entire culture, society, or age. A famous example is Madame de Staël's essay *De la littérature considerée dans ses rapports avec les institutions sociales* (1800; The influence of literature upon society). Within the German tradition of hermeneutics, the classical scholar Friedrich Ast distinguished in 1808 between the literal or grammatical level of interpretation, the historical level (concerned with meaning), and the cultural level, concerned with grasping the "spirit" (*Geist*) of antiquity or other periods.

Karl Marx was a contextualist in another sense, concerned to locate consciousness and its expressions within "life," especially social life. Marxists and non-Marxists alike were increasingly concerned with *Zusammenhang,* the connection between the parts and the whole.

Material context was also taken more seriously in the early nineteenth century than before. In archaeology, the increasing concern with stratigraphy in the early nineteenth century implied a concern with context or location. Antoine Quatremère de Quincy denounced the looting of Italian works of art by Napoleon, Lord Elgin, and others on the grounds that this uprooting or *déplacement* deprived the objects of their cultural value. Later in the century, the German anthropologist Franz Boas caused a sensation in museum circles by arguing that artifacts should be arranged by "culture area" rather than evolutionary sequence because an object could not be understood "outside of its surroundings."

The Discovery of Situation

In a number of disciplines in the 1920s and 1930s, especially sociology, psychology, history, and anthropology, the term "situation" came to play a central role. Karl Mannheim, for instance, one of the pioneers of the sociology of knowledge, treated ideas as socially situated (literally "tied to the situation," *Situationsgebunden*). At much the same time the sociologist William I. Thomas was stressing the importance of what he called "the definition of the situation" for social action. In psychology, Lev Vygotsky and Aleksandr Luria argued that the mentality of illiterates was characterized by "concrete or situational thinking."

In the case of history, we might contrast the French with the British approach. Marc Bloch's famous study *Les rois thaumaturges* (1924) attempted to make the belief in the supernatural power of the royal touch intelligible by presenting it as part of a system of "collective representations," while R. G. Collingwood and Herbert Butterfield concerned themselves with contexts and situations at the individual level. For Butterfield, the historian's task was to place an individual action "in its historical context." For his part, Collingwood declared that "every event . . . is a conscious reaction to a situation, not the effect of a cause."

Anthropology is sometimes perceived as the contextual discipline par excellence. More exactly, it became this kind of discipline in the 1920s, thanks to Bronislaw Malinowski. Meaning, he argued, is dependent on the "context of situation." In a famous example he referred to a stick that might be used for digging, punting, walking, or fighting. "In each of these specific uses," he claimed, "the stick is embedded in a different cultural context." Malinowski's ideas about context were taken further by his pupil Edward Evans-Pritchard in a study of witchcraft, oracles, and magic among the Azande in which the author argued that "an individual in one situation will employ a notion he excludes in a different situation."

The Contextual Turn

In the last generation we have seen what might be called a "contextual turn," on the analogy of so many other turns in intellectual history. One sign of change is the increasing use of terms such as "contextualism," "contextualization," and "de-contextualization." In the case of theology, the "contextual reinterpretation" of religion has been under discussion. In ethics, a movement known as "situationism" has effectively revived casuistry under another name. In philosophy, John Austin's analysis of the "occasion" and "context" of utterances remains influential. In educational sociology and psychology, the work of Basil Bernstein and Jerome Bruner on "context-dependent" and "context-independent" learning illustrates the trend.

In literary criticism the idea of placing a poem "in context," or even "in total context," was defended by the Cambridge critic F. W. Bateson and denounced by F. R. Leavis, who argued that "social context" meant merely "one's personal living."

In the 1950s and 1960s, sociolinguists such as Dell Hymes and William Labov noted that the same people speak differently according to the context or situation. Even in the case of the law, concerned with general rules, the rise of "context sensitivity" has been noted. In sociology, Anthony Giddens described "locale" as essential to what he calls the "contextuality" of social interaction, while feminists such as Donna Haraway revived and revised Mannheim's concept of "situated knowledge."

A concern with situation and performance has become increasingly visible in recent decades in musicology and art history. Thus the phrase "performative context" has come into use to refer to the adaptation of music to suit a certain place, occasion, and audience. In art history, where an artist's style was once taken to be an expression of his or her personality, it is now interpreted as a kind of performance. A movement for a "contextual archaeology" has made its appearance.

In intellectual history the concern with context is even more explicit, above all at Cambridge University. In the 1950s, Peter Laslett argued the case for placing Locke's *Second Treatise of Government* in a "revised historical context." In his *Barbarism and Religion* (1999) J. G. A. Pocock, a student of Butterfield's, set out "to effect a series of contextualizations" of Edward Gibbon's *Decline and Fall of the Roman Empire* (1776–1788). Quentin Skinner's work relies still more on the idea of context, whether linguistic, intellectual, or political. In the philosophy and history of science, the foundation of the journal *Science in Context,* in 1987, offers another example of context-consciousness, at once an attempt to emulate the historians of political thought and a response to a continuing debate over the status of scientific knowledge, universal or local.

See also **Cultural Studies; Historiography.**

BIBLIOGRAPHY

Boas, Franz. "Museums of Ethnology and Their Classification." *Science* 9 (1887): 587–589.

Burke, Peter. "Context in Context." *Common Knowledge* 8, no. 1 (2002): 152–177.

Collingwood, R. G. "Outlines of a Philosophy of History." In *The Idea of History,* edited by Jan van der Dussen, 426–496. Oxford: Clarendon, 1993.

Giglioli, Pier Paolo, comp. *Language and Social Context.* Harmondsworth, U.K.: Penguin, 1972.

Leites, Edmund, ed. *Conscience and Casuistry in Early Modern Europe.* Cambridge, U.K., and New York: Cambridge University Press, 1988.

Mannheim, Karl. *Conservatism: A Contribution to the Sociology of Knowledge.* Edited by David Kettler, Volker Meja, and Nico

Stehr. London and New York: Routledge and Kegan Paul, 1986. Translation of *Das Konservative Denken*.

Thomas, William I. "Situational Analysis" In *W. I. Thomas on Social Organisation and Social Personality,* edited by Morris Janowitz, 154–167. Chicago: University of Chicago Press, 1966.

Toulmin, Stephen. *Cosmopolis: The Hidden Agenda of Modernity.* New York, 1990.

Tully, James, ed. *Meaning and Context: Quentin Skinner and His Critics.* Cambridge, U.K.: Polity Press, 1988.

Peter Burke

CONTINENTAL PHILOSOPHY.

The term *continental philosophy* was coined by English-speaking analytic philosophers in Great Britain and the United States shortly after World War II. Since then, the term has been used primarily by English-speaking philosophers but not by western European philosophers, who see no need to call themselves "continental."

The differences between analytic and continental philosophy are rooted in eighteenth-century European Enlightenment. Generally speaking, analytic philosophers tended to view the Enlightenment positively, while continental philosophers viewed it critically. Taking different stances toward the German philosopher Immanuel Kant (1724–1804), analytic philosophers focused primarily on Kant's epistemological work, *Critique of Pure Reason,* while continental philosophers stressed Kant's ethical and aesthetic works, the *Critique of Practical Reason* and the *Critique of Judgment.* The final divide between analytic and continental philosophy occurred in their respective stances toward post-Kantian German idealism and Romanticism, especially toward the dialectical system of the "Absolute Spirit" posited by Georg Wilhelm Friedrich Hegel (1770–1831). Deeply influenced by Hegel and by the critique of religion devised by Hegel's former student Ludwig Feuerbach (1804–1872), Karl Marx (1818–1883) and Friedrich Engels (1820–1895) transformed Hegel's dialectical idealism into dialectical and historical materialism. In keeping with this post-Kantian philosophy, contemporary continental philosophers are concerned primarily with man's history and culture and with religious, moral, and social issues.

Wittgenstein and Analytic Philosophy

In order to understand continental philosophy, one has to refer indirectly to analytic philosophy, which originated in Germany and Austria through the work of Gottlob Frege (1848–1925) and the Austrian-born British philosopher Ludwig Wittgenstein (1889–1951), its most famous representative. Analytic philosophy was preceded by the logical positivism of the "Vienna Circle" of the 1930s and drew its name from its logical "analysis" of language. Analytic philosophy soon became the mainstream philosophical movement in the English-speaking world, especially after the publication of Wittgenstein's *Tractatus logico-philosophicus* in 1921. With great originality, the later Wittgenstein overshadowed almost all of analytic philosophy with his posthumous book *Philosophische Untersuchungen* (1953; *Philosophical Investigations*), which brought

about a new "linguistic turn," wherein language came to be understood in terms of cultural diversity, or "language games," including ordinary, religious, moral, and aesthetic language. In his later years Wittgenstein criticized his own *Tractatus* and its one-sided, representational "picture theory" of language. The later Wittgenstein reinterpreted language as embedded in the action-oriented, social context of historical "forms of life." In addition, Wittgenstein was deeply concerned with the foundations of religious faith, the nature of religious language, fideism, and ethical and aesthetic issues, which brought him closer to the European, "continental" philosophy of Kant, Arthur Schopenhauer (1788–1860), and even Martin Heidegger (1889–1976).

Wittgenstein opened the way to encounters with continental philosophy. In spite of ongoing differences in subjects and methods, in the late twentieth and early twenty-first centuries continental and analytic philosophers have opened promising new dialogues as exemplified by Richard Rorty, Herbert Dreyfus, Charles Taylor, John McDowell, Hilary Putnam, Stanley Cavell, Alistair McIntyre, Hans-Georg Gadamer, and Jean-François Lyotard, among others. Contemporary philosophy of science, with its historical and sociological sensibility, has also been influenced by continental philosophy as exemplified by Thomas Kuhn, Gaston Bachelard, Jürgen Habermas, Karl-Otto Appel, Ernst Tugendhat, Ian Hacking, Paul Feyerabend, Patrick Heelan, Joseph J. Kockelmans, Ted Kiesel, and Thomas M. Seebohm. Continental philosophy has especially impacted Heidegger-influenced existential psychoanalysis as exemplified by the work of Jean Piaget, Ludwig Binswanger, Medard Boss, Erich Fromm, William J. Richardson, and Jacques Lacan.

With its roots in the Enlightenment, the analytic tradition, for the most part, stresses clarity and precision in thought and language, an ahistorical view of truth, reason, and human nature. It tends to critique traditional religion, morality, and metaphysics. With the exception of the more conservative Wittgenstein, analytic philosophers, for the most part, adhere to a progressive, liberal, and democratic worldview. In contrast, heavily influenced by Hegel's ideas about the intrinsic historicity of human thought and action, continental tradition, for the most part, is concerned with the historical, cultural, and social conditions of human life and tends to be focused on issues of liberation and "emancipation" from individual and social injustice. Some continental philosophers are critical of modernism and liberal democracy, especially Heidegger and some postmodernists. There are many exceptions, including the liberal Western Marxists György Lukács (1885–1971), Ernst Bloch (1885–1977), and Antonio Gramsci (1891–1937), as well as the Frankfurt School. In the twenty-first century, continental philosophy is strongly represented by French philosophers.

Because of the great impact of nineteenth-century German idealism and European Romanticism on continental philosophy, some continental philosophers, in the footsteps of Schopenhauer, Max Weber (1864–1920), Max Scheler (1874–1928), and Oswald Spengler (1880–1936), have been critical of modern, urbanized, and industrialized society. Haunted by the loss of a mostly idealized ancient, medieval world of agricultural and hierarchical life forms, they have sought to recover a holistic view of human life as adumbrated in the "philosophies of life" of Friedrich Nietzsche (1844–1900), Wilhelm Dilthey (1833–1911), and Henri-Louis Bergson (1859–1941). Some continental philosophers, especially feminist philosophers, have emphasized the dimensions of the aesthetic life, the emotional, imaginative, creative, and "unconscious" aspects of human existence.

Freud and the Unconscious

The pioneering work of Sigmund Freud (1856–1939) on the unconscious had a deep influence on modern literature, literary criticism, and on continental philosophy. When continental philosophy rediscovered the unconscious, it inspired a deeper appreciation of the human body and of human sexuality and also supported the rejection of the dualism of René Descartes (1596–1650). Concerned with issues presented by Freud's work, French philosophers such as Jean-Paul Sartre (1905–1980), Simone de Beauvoir (1908–1986), Maurice Merleau-Ponty, Jean Baudrillard, Michel Foucault, Jacques Lacan, and the feminist philosophers Luce Irigaray (b. 1930), Julia Kristeva (b. 1941), Sarah Kofman (1934–1994), Michele Le Doeuff (b. 1948) and Helene Cixous (b. 1937) are now at the forefront of the crossroads between philosophy, linguistic theory, Marxism, psychoanalysis, and literature. For example, Irigaray writes: "Sexual difference is one of the major philosophical issues, if not the issue, of our age" (*Ethique de la difference sexuelle*, 1984; *An Ethics of Sexual Difference*, p. 19).

Phenomenology of Consciousness

In eighteenth-century Germany, Johann Heinrich Lambert (1728–1777), Kant, and Hegel, who wrote *Die Phänomenologie des Geistes* (1807; *Phenomenology of Spirit*), used the term *phenomenology* in different contexts. Edmund Husserl (1859–1938), the founder of contemporary phenomenology, used the term as a pre-suppositionless description of human consciousness in constituting meaning. From his teacher Franz Brentano (1838–1917), Husserl adopted the theory of "intentionality," the notion that every mental act is directed toward something. According to Husserl, phenomenology describes the essential contents (*noema*) of our intentional acts (*noesis*), not objects in the world. The content of consciousness is neutral as to its reality or nonreality.

In his famous *Logische Untersuchungen* (1900–1901; *Logical Investigations*), Husserl sought to go "back to the things themselves" (*Zu den Sachen selbst*) as they appeared to pure consciousness in perceptual and "categorical intuition." Husserl maintained that "being" is given to "categorical intuition" like any other ideal essence. Heidegger critiqued Husserl, maintaining that being is not an "object" of intuition but is understood from the pretheoretical context of man's concrete, factical life. Heidegger transformed Husserl's phenomenology of consciousness into a hermeneutical and existential phenomenology of "being."

Husserl's first work, *Philosophie der Arithmetik* (1891; *Philosophy of Arithmetic*), was written in terms of "psychologism,"

according to which "logical meaning" could be reduced to "psychological acts." When Frege criticized "psychologism," Husserl discarded it and developed a new method, which attempted to gain access to the data of "pure" consciousness by taking a step back ("reduction") from the "natural attitude" of common sense and the sciences. In his new method, Husserl described two different "reductions": (1) *phenomenological reduction,* or *epoché* (suspension), which "brackets" the ordinary, natural world, that is, the "existence" of things, and (2) *eidetic reduction,* which describes the *eidos,* the "essence" of noematic content. Husserl called the intentional activity of consciousness "object-constituting subjectivity" by which all meanings are "constituted," that is, disclosed and made manifest. Although Husserl remained within the Cartesian tradition of subject-object dualism, he consigned this dualism to the noetic-noematic structure of the intentional act. Thus, he undermined the modern "epistemological" problem of an isolated subject and an "external world."

In his early work *Ideen zu einer reinen phänomenologie* (1913; *Ideas: General Introduction to Pure Phenomenology),* Husserl and his students held a "realist" position, focusing on the contents of consciousness, whereas the later Husserl changed to a more "idealist" position, which he called "transcendental," that is, that the world is always "for" a mind. According to Husserl, transcendental consciousness "bestows" meaning upon everything, including its own functioning. In some respects, the later Husserl paralleled Heidegger by turning his phenomenological investigations to questions of "temporality," that is, the temporal flow of transcendental consciousness, and to "intersubjectivity" or social existence. In his later years, Husserl also focused on a "genetic" phenomenology in which the original "genesis" of intentional acts and objects is something passive for consciousness ("passive synthesis"), prior to any voluntary activity of transcendental consciousness. Husserl also became interested in the historical character of science and in the problem of the constitution of the "life-world" (*Lebenswelt*) upon which science is based. Ironically, the later Husserl believed that phenomenology could even constitute the "essence" of the life-world.

Merleau-Ponty was one of the most famous French phenomenologists. Influenced by Husserl and Heidegger, opposed to Cartesian subject-object dualism, he developed an "ontology of the flesh," which centered on the primacy of perceptual experience and the role of the lived and living body as the primary access to a spatio-temporal world (*Phénoménologie de la perception* (1945; *Phenomenology of Perception*). One's perceptions, which are always connected with the flesh of the living body, are historically situated interpretations of the world. Perceptions cannot be reduced to pure "source-data" of intentional consciousness.

Heidegger and the Phenomenology of Being

Heidegger studied Scholastic philosophy and theology at the University of Freiburg, where he became acquainted with Husserl's new phenomenological movement. In 1927 he published his most famous work, *Sein und Zeit (Being and Time)*. In 1933 he served briefly as the rector of the University of Freiburg but was stripped of his professorship in 1945 because of his personal involvement with the national socialist movement and his membership in the Nazi Party. After the war, his stubborn silence about Nazi atrocities and the Holocaust cast a dark shadow over his otherwise brilliant career. He died in 1976, and in accordance with his wishes, he had a Catholic funeral.

In his student days, when he read Brentano's *On the Manifold Meaning of Being since Aristotle* (1862), Heidegger became absorbed with the question of time as experienced by human beings and with the question of the meaning of being (*Seinsfrage*); that is, what it means "to be." He gradually came to the conclusion that all Western philosophy, beginning with Plato's theory of suprasensible Forms, had conceived *being* and *time* as opposites, mutually exclusive of each other. Even Aristotle had interpreted time as constant "presence" and as a "now," without reference to being and past and future horizons. Western metaphysics had described God too as eternal "Now" (*Nunc stans*), beyond all time. Heidegger called attention to this "onto-theological" character of metaphysics and maintained that the actual, unitary relationship between being and time in human existence had been "forgotten" in lieu of dualisms such as time and eternity.

In addition to Heidegger's existential interpretation of such terms as *techne, phronesis,* and *sophia* in Aristotle's *Ethics,* his studies of time in early Christianity, Augustin, Luther, and Kiekegaard had a great influence on *Being and Time.* In turn, Heidegger had a deep impact on contemporary Protestant and Catholic theology.

Reevaluating the relationship between being and time, Heidegger argued that human existence must be understood from three dimensions of "ec-static" (i.e., existential) time: past, present, and future in their intimate, ontological interdependence. He used the German word *Dasein* to describe the human being with his/her implicit understanding of being. The "Da" or "there" of *Dasein* expresses that the human being is not a thing-like "substance" (Aristotle) or an enclosed "subject" (Descartes). Rather, the human being is an open realm, a "clearing" (*Lichtung*) as in a forest, wherein the understanding of being, of other human beings and things, and of man's own self takes place simultaneously. *Dasein* is always already a "being-with-others" in a shared, communal way of life. For Heidegger, *Dasein* is ontologically gender neutral. Because of its temporal character, *Dasein* is not a static entity but a "potentiality-for-being" (*Seinkonnen*), a temporal movement of possible ways of being, which the individual chooses or lets others choose for him. *Dasein* is always a projecting of oneself into the future toward death, its "authentic" acceptance or its "inauthentic" denial.

Another related term for *Dasein* is *existence,* from the Latin *ec-sistence,* meaning "standing out" into the openness of being. Existence applies only to human beings and is characterized by "mineness," which can be "authentic" or "inauthentic." Still another relational word for *Dasein* is "*being-in-the-world,*" which negates the subject-object dualism of Descartes and Husserl, and articulates *Dasein*'s holistic and practical involvement with, and comportment toward, the world. *Dasein* is not disclosed to us through "categories" of things, but rather

through its prescientific characteristics, which Heidegger called "existentials" such as *disposition* (*Befindlichkeit*), existential *understanding* (*Verstehen*), and *speech* (*Rede*).

According to Heidegger, in *Identität und Differenz* (1957; *Identity and Difference*), Western metaphysics erred in its inadequate understanding of time as pure "presence" for a subject. Furthermore, Western metaphysics forgot the primordial "ontological difference" between "being" and "beings" in favor of only "ontical differences" between beings such as God, world, and humanity. Heidegger maintained that metaphysics had to be "destructed" in order to positively unearth and retrieve its forgotten, primordial experience of being as the "unthought" in Western metaphysics. In Derrida's "deconstruction" of texts, which was originally influenced by Heidegger, the term took on a more critical, "disruptive" interpretation of literary texts. Heidegger "deconstructed" Western metaphysics by reinterpreting the texts of numerous Western thinkers from the sixth-century-B.C.E. Greek philosopher Parmenides to Nietzsche.

In his analysis of "being-in-the-world," Heidegger also distinguished between things "ready-to-hand" (*Zuhanden*)—objects of practical concern with a historical and/or social context—and things "present-at-hand" (*Vorhanden*)—things abstracted from their context and made objects of our theoretical, scientific knowledge. Heidegger demonstrated that Western philosophy overlooked the original human context of "ready-to-hand" things in favor of "present-at-hand" things, "objects" in abstract space and time, as exemplified by theoretical, scientific reasoning. In this "metaphysics of presence," being itself was described as a property or essence, constantly present in things as a "substance."

One can only enumerate a few other "existentials" in *Being and Time,* such as the anonymous "they" (*das Man*); temporality in which "care," with its threefold structure of projection, thrownness, and fallenness is rooted; existential "guilt" and "conscience"; anxiety (*Angst*); "*death*" as the ultimate disclosure of "my" finitude and mortality, the impossibility of all my possibilities. A central place in *Being and Time* and other writings is devoted to the distinction between "logical truth" and "ontological truth" as standing in the light of being. According to Heidegger, the Greeks already implicitly distinguished ontological truth as "unconcealment" (*aletheia*) emerging from the background of a deeper "concealment" (*lethe*) prior to any logical, propositional truth.

Heidegger's later philosophy, after his so-called turn (*die Kehre*), was first expressed in the *Brief über den Humanismus* (1947; *Letter on Humanism*), according to which Western "humanism," with its one-sided emphasis on "subject" and "reason," is, nevertheless, rooted in the prior but forgotten relationship of *Dasein* to being. As opposed to traditional "calculative" thinking, as critiqued in *Beiträge zur Philosophie 1936–1938* (1989; *Contributions to Philosophy*), Heidegger's later, "meditative" thinking concerned itself with many new themes, such as art, language, science, and technology. In a highly speculative apocalyptic manner, the later Heidegger considered the present technological stage of the history of being as the abandonment of humankind by being itself. Yet,

Heidegger's later thinking, which he understood as a "thank-ing" response to the call of being, is focused on an "other beginning" for humankind. Humans must "listen" and respond in a new meditative-poetic thinking, which might lead to a transformed way of life after the ages of metaphysics, a "letting-be" (*Gelassenheit*) of beings, a term taken from Johannes Eckehart (c. 1260–?1327) and German, medieval, mystical tradition. In a few German poets (Hölderlin, Trakl, George) Heidegger saw the hidden prophets of the future "destining" (sending) of being itself to humans.

In his growing skepticism even about the use of the word "being," Heidegger looked for new words that would mark the postmetaphysical era. He chose the term "disclosive appropriating Event" (*Ereignis,* from *ereignen,* "appropriate," and *eraeugen,* to see and disclose), a pure subjectless happening, from which the "fourfold" regions of the world, in their interplay between heaven, earth, mortals, and the divinities, emerge into the nearness of humanity. Heidegger's other attempts to say the "unsayable" in expressing the mystery of being (which is not in human control) include the phrases: "dif-ference" (*Unterschied*) of the simultaneous withholding and unfolding of being in beings; and the "fissure" (*Zerklueftung*) of being itself. Finally, he talked about the singular "Event" that gives and approximates being (*es gibt Sein*) and time by a simultaneous self-withdrawal and "expropriation" (*Enteignung*).

Existentialism

Existentialism, as originally presented by Sartre, de Beauvoir, and Albert Camus (1913–1960), emphasized the importance of individual existence, choice, and personal responsibility. It was opposed to impersonal systems of thought and to modern mass society. Partially rooted in the Judeo-Christian tradition of faith, existentialism has also been influenced by Søren Kierkegaard (1813–1855), Fyodor Dostoyevsky (1821–1881), Nietzsche, and by Husserl and Heidegger. Kierkegaard's ethical-religious works impacted many twentieth-century religious existentialists such as Martin Buber, Paul Tillich, Karl Barth, Gabriel-Honoré Marcel, and Emmanuel Lévinas, while Nietzsche's supposed nihilism and atheism ("God is dead') deeply influenced Karl Theodor Jaspers, Heidegger, Sartre, Foucault, Jacques Derrida, Gilles Deleuze, and Luce Irigaray.

Sartre was a philosopher, playwright, social critic, and political activist who became famous with his work *L'existentialism est un humanism* (1946; *Existentialism Is a Humanism*) and his phrase "Existence is prior to essence." In the late 1950s, he supplemented this individualistic, existential humanism with social and critical Marxism as expressed in his book *Critique de la raison dialectique* (1976, 1985; *Critique of Dialectical Reason*). In his early work *L'être et le néant* (1943; *Being and Nothingness*), influenced by Husserl and Heidegger, Sartre described the tension between human consciousness ("being-for-itself," *pour soi*), which is "not a thing" but an activity, and the brute existence of things ("being-in-itself," *en soi*). According to Sartre, man has absolute freedom, even in the most constrained situations as exemplified by Sartre's own experiences in the French resistance movement and his imprisonment in Germany. For Sartre, the self is always an embodied, situated self. Sartre also talked about "bad faith," which he

defined as "inauthentic" flight from the anguished burden of choice and responsibility.

Sartre's lifelong companion Simone de Beauvoir, who had a great influence upon Sartre, especially upon his later socially oriented work, wrote the famous early feminist work *The Second Sex* (1949), which described the historical and existential situation of women. According to de Beauvoir, women continue to be defined within a masculine worldview, which assumes an "eternal feminine," an unchanging biological destiny, and a feminine "essence." Men assume that women are "the other," a designation limiting women's freedom and autonomy. De Beauvoir insisted that femaleness is a social construct: "One is not born but rather becomes a woman." De Beauvoir proposed the way for the first philosophical discussion of "sexual difference" within the context of the structures of powers, and forces of desire in later feminist writers.

Camus, like Sartre, de Beauvoir, and Merleau-Ponty, one of the famous representatives of the post-war existentialist movement in France, is known for his notion of the "absurd" as expressed in his poetic writings such as *The Plague* (1947). According to Camus, the absurdity of existence provokes the question of the meaning of life and the act of suicide as "the only truly serious philosophical problem" (*Le mythe de Sisyphe,* 1942; *The Myth of Sisyphus,* p. 1). The human being must engage in an ongoing "revolt" against absurdity: "I rebel—therefore we exist" (*L'homme révolté,* 1951; *The Rebel,* p. 22).

Jaspers (1883–1969), similar to the early Heidegger, saw the historically situated freedom of the individual within certain "boundary situations" such as guilt, suffering, anxiety, and death. Existence can only be realized in communication. He considered existences a gift of Being, which he called Transcendence, God, or the "Encompassing."

Hannah Arendt (1906–1975), who had studied under Husserl, Heidegger, and Jaspers, emigrated to the United States and became a renowned political philosopher despite her sometimes controversial involvement with the Jewish cause. In her works on totalitarianism, anti-Semitism, and imperialism she took a stance against National Socialism and Heidegger's involvement with it, and against Marxism. She favored political freedom, constitutional democracy, and pluralism in her adopted country, the United States. In addition to Claude Lefort, Cornelius Castoriadis (b. 1932), and Habermas, Arendt is the best known political philosopher in the continental tradition.

Hermeneutics

Hans-Georg Gadamer (1900–2002), Heidegger's student, who taught at many German and American universities after World War II, is the father of contemporary ontological hermeneutics. His great work, *Wahrheit und Methode* (1960; *Truth and Method*), points to the problem underlying all modern philosophy (epistemology) from Descartes to Husserl, namely, the relationship between the original "truth" of human understanding within the "life world" and historical "traditions" on the one hand, and the "methods" of the sciences on the other. Inspired by Heidegger and influenced by Hegel and German Romanticism, Gadamer transformed the method of hermeneutical understanding (*Verstehen*) in the human sciences, history, law, arts, and theology into a "universal" ontological hermeneutics. He went beyond the work of Friedrich Schleiermacher (1768–1834) and Dilthey, who had introduced the "hermeneutical circle" as the relationship of the parts to the whole, and the "implicit" to the "explicit," out of the correspondence of the knower to the known in any interpretation. Gadamer rejected natural sciences' explanations (*Eklaren*) as the *only* way of understanding reality.

Gadamer maintained that as the art of interpretation, hermeneutics is based upon the human, linguistically constituted "life world," the living conversation and dialogue between people that is the horizon of all human experience and knowledge. Hermeneutics aims at mutual understanding between an historically situated "author" of a text and an historically situated "reader" or interpreter. Gadamer called the hermeneutical encounter between an author and a reader the "fusion of horizons." As such, in historical events, literature, or works of art, hermeneutics is always the relationship between two horizons of understanding and interpretation within a tradition, and it has the prospective goal of "consensus."

Criticizing Enlightenment for its ahistorical perspectives and denying that the methods of the natural sciences are the only means to "objective knowledge," Gadamer emphasized the deeper truth in historical understanding, which passes from generation to generation through written texts, which are—contrary to Derrida's primacy of "writing"—always rooted in the living language. As texts are interpreted and reinterpreted throughout history, they produce a "history of effect" (*Wirkungsgeschichte*), which shape and influence our present and future understanding of reality. Since there are hidden presuppositions and cultural "prejudices" in each interpretation, Gadamer sees that hermeneutics does not focus on the isolated "true meaning" of a text or on the author's intention. Rather, universal Hermeneutics focuses on the different suppositions and presuppositions of all interpretations in both the human and natural sciences. After the failed attempt for a fruitful encounter between Gadamer's "phalogical" hermeneuticy and Derrida's "Deconstruction" in the 1980s, which both originated in Heidegger's work, hermeneutics and Deconstruction remain two as yet unreconciled paradigms in contemporary philosophy. The third paradigm is Habermas's "critique of ideology," which rejects Gadamer's positive evaluation of tradition, consensus, authority, and "prejudice," as the continual "distortion of communication" by masked social and political interest. Thus, the special, yet unacknowledged interest of modern bourgeois, capitalist society disrupts and disguises understanding and communication in a worldwide global consumer society.

Paul Ricoeur (b. 1913), the proponent of a phenomenological hermeneutics, is focused on narrative, symbol, metaphor, dreams, and ideologies as the means by which our experience of the world is interpreted. Opposed to postmodernism's abolition of the "subject," he elaborates a notion of "subject" stripped of modern subjectivism. In contrast to Gadamer, Ricoeur does not concede a dualism between "truth" (philosophy) and "method" (science) but bridges them by his interest in the methodological "validation" of interpretation by the methods of the human sciences. He calls the critical point of hermeneutics "the hermeneutics of suspicion" as it reveals the hidden, ideological meaning of texts, events, and social practice. For Ricoeur, the great "masters of suspicion" are Marx, Nietzsche, and Freud.

Postmodernism

Modernism is characterized by Enlightenment values; that is, trust in the autonomous human "subject," scientific reason, and universal principles of law, morality, politics, and economics. In different ways, postmodern philosophers oppose the main ideas of the Enlightenment. Instead, they focus on a "decentered" subject, human knowledge as conditioned by history, and the mistrust of the "grand narratives" of modernity (Kant, Hegel, Marx). The French philosopher and novelist Georges Bataille (1897–1962) initiated the poststructuralist notion regarding the death of the "subject" in order to overcome its isolation in experiences of "excess" (laughter, tears, eroticism, death, sacrifice, and poetry). Similar to Nietzsche's "perspectivism," postmodernism critiques "objective" truth and favors a theory of multiple "interpretations" of texts. Postmodernism was preceded by poststructuralism in literature, the humanities, social sciences, and even architecture in the 1960s and 1970s. Poststructuralism partially opposed the linguistic structuralism of Ferdinand de Saussure (1857–1913). Similar to much of the analytical philosophy, Husserl, and also Derrida, Saussure saw language as a self-contained system of signs rather than as an ongoing, historical process of conversation and dialogue in the Socrates sense. In contrast to "subjective" existentialism, structuralism focused on super-individual structures such as language, kinship, and ritual in order to understand human existence. Saussure influenced the anthropological structuralism of Claude Lévi-Strauss (b. 1908), the Marxist structuralism of Louis Althusser (1918–1990), the social critique of Foucault, the political and cultural critique of Roland Barthes (1915–1980), and the psychoanalytic structuralism of Lacan. Rejecting the scientific pretensions of structuralism, poststructuralism questioned the "objectivity" of knowledge and truth, of the "subject" as a unified self, the oppressive nature of modern institutions, authority, and power. Postmodernism was marked by the abandonment of dogmatic Marxism by French intellectuals, especially after the student-worker revolution of 1968, its critique of Western imperialism, racism, and antifeminism.

Lyotard (1924–1998), through his book *La condition post-moderne* (1979; *The Postmodern Condition*), represents the postmodern movement and its great influence on the literary, political, and cultural milieu beyond professional philosophy. Lyotard pointed out the demise of grand, foundational, totalizing "metanarratives"; that is, grand theories or systems of thought such as liberalism and Marxism, which are being replaced by local narrative or smaller stories of everyday life, which are expressed in limited but pluralistic "language games" (Wittgenstein). Lyotard uses the term "differend" (*differend*) for the incommensurability or heterogeneity of these different language games, literary genres, and idioms, which can never be reduced to logical or ontological "sameness," not even to a political "consensus" in the sense of Gadamer, Habermas, or Rorty. For Lyotard, the knowledge of irreducible differends, that is, disputes and dissensions in politics, is the most important form of resistance to capitalism and its uniformity and injustice. In *Heidegger et "les juifs"* (1988; *Heidegger and "the Jews"*), Lyotard criticized Heidgger's silence on the Shoah (Holocaust). He pointed out the philosopher's duty to stand for the "marginalized" and "the Forgotten."

The Algerian-born French philosopher Jacques Derrida (b. 1930) has had almost as much impact on French continental philosophy as Foucault, but he is hardly criticized by analytic philosophers such as John Learle. Like Heidegger, Derrida attacks the traditional Western "metaphysics of presence" and its reduction of "being" to "substance" (entity). Like Wittgenstein, Derrida asserts that logical meaning is always embedded in the historical, social, and cultural matrix of language. He accuses Western metaphysical tradition of "logocentrism" and "phonocentrism," which favor the immediacy of the "meaning" of the spoken word rather than writing, which is characterized by distance, repeatability, and uncertainty of meaning. According to Derrida, logocentrism utilizes oversimplified, "binary opposites" such as reason-emotion, soul-body, male-female, and so on, which presuppose an unquestioned hierarchy of subordination in classical, philosophical texts and in political discourse.

Derrida's method of "deconstructing" the logocentrism demonstrates that a particular text usually does not have just one clear meaning, understood as what the author intended to convey. Rather, it may have alternative meanings ("alterity"), which do not fit into traditional notions of "binary opposites." The "double meaning" of texts reveals hidden ambiguities and "indeterminacies" of meaning underlying the text. In principle, it is impossible to show what a text "really means." In Derrida's writings, an important neologism is the term *différance,* which is a pun on a French verb meaning both "difference" of meaning and endless "deferral" of a fixed and privileged meaning. Meaning is only possible within a context and within a system where words have a "trace" of other, related words, just as speaking has a "trace" of writing.

Gilles Deleuze (1925–1995) and the psychotherapist Felix Guattari (1930–1992) also opposed the metaphysics of presence ("identity"), the representation of an "object" by a "subject." They favored a metaphysics of difference. In their controversial *L'anti-Oedipe* (1972; *Anti-Oedipus),* they synthesized their neo-Marxist rejection of capitalism with their rejection of Freudian psychoanalysis, which they criticized as a bourgeois repression of instinctual life ("desire") in the name of the bourgeois family (Oedipus complex). Although human nature is controlled socially, it is rooted in the chaotic presence of desire as expressed in its extreme form in schizophrenia. Deleuze also published works on theater, painting, and cinema.

Jean Baudrillard (b. 1929), whose analysis of contemporary culture was influenced by Marx, by structuralism, and by the communications theorist Marshall McLuhan's analysis of electronic media, reversed the Marxian distinction between epiphenominal "superstructure" (culture, the "symbolic") and fundamental "infrastructure" (economy, material production). He pointed out that the "symbolic" is primary for the contemporary media and consumer society, in which the boundary between image and truth, as well as between the virtual and the real, has been transformed into a new symbolic "hyper-reality" in the age of electronic media.

In the tradition of Hegel, Marx, and especially Nietzsche, Michel Foucault (1926–1984) focused on the structures used to create meaning and order in human knowledge and experience. In his early studies in the "archaeology of knowledge," Foucault showed how our present thoughts and social-institutional practices, especially in psychology, psychiatry, and medicine, are the historically contingent outcomes of past, anonymous "epistemes" (paradigms and frameworks of discourse), which can be changed and replaced by new forms of "epistemes." On the "threshold of modernity" at the end of the eighteenth century, the modern episteme brought about the emergence of the modern "subject" and the corresponding "human sciences," which prescribed how the individual (psychology) and society (the state) should act. Foucault attacked modern, universalizing mega-narratives of history as well as the notion of a pre-given "human nature." He saw the self (that is, the "subject") as always historically conditioned within particular situations and contexts. Foucault's antihumanist and anti-Enlightenment critique of the modern notion of "reason" is based upon very detailed historical studies, for instance, his investigations of "mental illness" and "madness" in the age of Enlightenment (*Histoire de la folie á l'âge classique: folie et déraison,* 1961; *Madness and Civilization: A History of Insanity in the Age of Reason*).

In his other works, Foucault discussed the theoretical, "discursive" practices within the larger context of "nondiscursive" practices as manifestations of social control and "power." According to Foucault, these "disciplinary power" systems and their power techniques (as exemplified by Jeremy Bentham's prison "panopticon") have paralleled the development of the human sciences, which have defined what is "natural" or "deviant," especially in sexual behavior. As the human sciences developed, the modern "subject" was defined both as a "self-responsible subject" and as an "object," controllable by disciplinary power. These definitions first appeared in modern psychology and medicine and were then applied in education, hospitals, asylums, factories, and military barracks. Like Nietzsche, Foucault called this later work a "genealogy," which explained the origin of the modern individual as a "subject" within institutional systems of nondiscursive power relations.

In his last work about sexuality, Foucault further developed his analysis of the subject in terms of "practices of the self." He was especially concerned with historical, aesthetic, and repressive practices regarding sexuality. According to Foucault, sexuality is not a category of an unchanging human nature, but is historically conditioned by social "power" practices.

Foucault summarized his work by maintaining that in spite of our involvement in power relations, we are free to struggle against and to resist systems of power by relating to ourselves in new alternative, creative ways, beyond society's system of order and discipline.

Lévinas and the "Other"

Emmanuel Lévinas (1906–1995), the Lithuanian-born, French-Jewish philosopher, introduced France to the work of Husserl and Heidegger, whom he later opposed. He was imprisoned in a German labor camp between 1940–44 and later became a professor at the Sorbonne. Like Buber, Marcel, Simone Weil (1909–1943), and Jaspers, he is usually classified as a philosopher of religion. Lévinas was deeply influenced by Franz Rosenzweig (1886–1929), the German-Jewish philosopher, and his book *The Star of Redemption,* which critiqued Hegel's philosophical totalitarianism in favor of a metaphysics of creation.

In his masterwork *Totalité et Infini* (1961; *Totality and Infinity),* Lévinas accused Western philosophy, from Parmenides to Husserl and Heidegger, of having reduced the "Other" (that is, the other person), to an "object" of consciousness and/or to a neutral, existential relationship. From the vantage point of his Jewish background, he asserted that the ontology of the "same," of being, and of identity leads to the idolatry of power and domination, as for example in Hegel's master-slave dialectic and in Heidegger's "fateful destiny of being." The "face" of the other, its absolute "alterity," cannot be objectified or totally comprehended. The "other" includes the victims of the Holocaust, vulnerable and defenseless, claiming: "Thou shalt not kill!" The face of the "other" reveals the priority of *ethics* over ontology. The infinity of the "other," which defies any objectification, leads to God, to the "Other" beyond the human "other." Human beings do not encounter God through "proofs" for God's existence but rather through their relationship to the human "other," who is a "trace of God."

Habermas and the Frankfurt School

Retrieving some of Marx's early humanistic writings, the original Frankfurt School of the 1920s and 1930s applied critical neo-Marxism to the analysis of the eventual transformation of modern society. The Frankfurt School was also known for its critical neo-Hegelianism, which resembled the phenomenological existentialism of certain neo-Marxist Italian philosophers such as Enzo Paci, the Polish neo-Marxists Adam Schaff and Leszlek Kolakowski, and the Yugoslavian existential-phenomenological Marxists associated with the journal *Praxis.* Max Horkheimer (1895–1973), Theodor Adorno (1903–1969), Walter Benjamin (1892–1940), Erich Fromm (1900–1980), and Herbert Marcuse (1898–1979) expressed the Frankfurt School's critical theory in various ways. Their theory was based on a synthesis between critical theory and social "practice" according to Marx's famous statement that appears as the eleventh of his "Theses on Feuerbach": "Philosophers have always interpreted the world, the point is to change it."

In contrast to orthodox Soviet Marxism and to the literary critic Fredric Jameson's economic interpretation of "late capitalism" and postmodernism, the Frankfurt School increasingly emphasized the importance of the society's "superstructure," including culture and ideology rather than its material "infrastructure." Furthermore, the Frankfurt School combined Marxist theory with Freudian psychoanalysis as important for the emancipation from social domination and from the repression of the individual mind.

Some members of the Frankfurt School, especially Horkheimer and Adorno in their collaborative work *Dialektik der Aufklärung* (1947; *Dialectic of Enlightenment),* stressed the importance of the arts, fantasy, and imagination because of their potential to subvert and emancipate society from its dependence on the one-sided, instrumental rationality of the Enlightenment and on modern science and technology. Yet, because of the failure of Soviet Marxism and the integration of its nonrevolutionary working class into the capitalist system after World War II, some members of the Frankfurt School lost confidence in a future Marxist revolution. Their initial revolutionary fervor gave way to political and cultural pessimism.

Jürgen Habermas (b. 1929), the German philosopher and social theorist, developed a new version of "critical theory" and a partially optimistic view of modernity as an "unfinished project of Enlightenment." Opposed to dogmatic Marxism, to positivist, empirical sociology, to uncritical elements in Gadamer's "universal hermeneutics," and to anti-Enlightenment postmodernism, Habermas attempted to harmonize the best of Kant, Hegel, Marx, and Wittgenstein with the scientific, explanatory systems of modern social science. In his early work *Erkenntnis und Interesse* (1968; *Knowledge and Human Interests),* he argued against the prevailing positivism of the social sciences, distinguishing three basic, human, cognitive interests: (1) *technical;* that is, control of nature; (2) *practical;* that is, communication with the goal of an "ideal speech situation"; and (3) *emancipatory;* that is, the removal of limits to freedom and causes of alienation, oppression, and suffering, with the goal of building an open, liberal-democratic society.

In his book *Theorie des Kommunikativen Handelns* (1981; *The Theory of Communicative Action),* Habermas developed a "critical theory of modernity," which was founded on the difference between "instrumental" and "communicative" rationality. Habermas also critiqued modern society's systems of rationalization, which increasingly "colonize" and destroy the "life world." Habermas's later "discourse ethics," which provided the linguistic background for communicative action, elaborated an intersubjective ethics of practical reason. This ethics too was directed against the modern, one-sided philosophy of the "subject."

Feminist Philosophy

Feminist philosophy examines gender issues and male-oriented "ideological" solutions in Western philosophy and science, while feminist epistemology, which is centered primarily in the analytic tradition, focuses on illegitimate authority and power relationships inherent in modern concepts of the knowing, scientific "subject." In general, feminist philosophers discuss human knowledge, truth, and objectivity in the broader context of gender, class, age, and race, while feminist moral philosophers demonstrate the importance of feminine "caring" in contrast to masculine "justice." Addressing the work of Wittgenstein and Heidegger, feminist philosophers emphasize the contextual, historical, and social aspects of language, while simultaneously critiquing male/female dichotomies, hierarchies, and "power-structures" in traditional "masculine" philosophy and science, which are assumed to be "universal" and "objective."

In her book *The Man of Reason* (1984), Genevieve Lloyd demonstrated that a metaphysical dualism of masculine "reason" and feminine "sense perception" and "emotion" dominates Western philosophy. According to Lloyd, the misogynistic notions of Schopenhauer and of Nietzsche are extreme forms of this antifeminist bias, which has permeated cultural, political, and economic development in the West.

In the late twentieth and early twenty-first centuries, French and North American feminist philosophers have questioned traditional, masculine interpretations of gender issues. Michèle Le Doeuff (b. 1948) has even discussed the inherent tension between being a woman and being a philosopher in the West. The American philosophers Judith Butler, Jean Grimshaw, Sandra Harding, Nancy Hartsock, Helen Longino, Seyla Benhabib, and Susan Bordo have made significant contributions to feminist philosophy, while the French philosophers Luce Irigaray and Julia Kristeva have become the most notable in the field.

Luce Irigaray (b. 1932) critiqued "masculine"-oriented Freudian and Lacanian psychoanalysis and was subsequently expelled from the Paris Psychoanalytic Association and from the University of Paris, after which she became a private psychoanalyst and writer. Best known for "deconstructing" the work of Plato, Kant, Hegel, and Freud, Irigaray demonstrates woman's unique sexual differences; that is, her body and desire (*jouissance*), which contradict masculine-oriented theories of "identity" and "sameness." Women, who have been defined traditionally in terms of "lack," absence," and "default," have been allowed to gain "identity" only by "mimicking" male language and male behavior. Going beyond social "gender roles" in the liberal, feminist fight of legal "equality" with men, Irigaray insisted on the unique "sexual difference" of women, their unique rights, and on the regaining of their own "subjectivity." She often uses Sophocles's *Antigone* and Hagel's interpretation of the play as the example of the masculine bias in Western civilization where Antigone loses her life against the command of king Creon.

The Bulgarian-born French feminist philosopher Julia Kristeva (b. 1941) showed an early interest in the problems of psychoanalysis and linguistics. Influenced by the Russian literary theorist Mikhail Bakhtin (1895–1975) and by Dostoyevsky, Kristeva distinguishes between "semiotic" language (as expressed in the unconscious maternal world of "drives," music, and poetry) and "symbolic" language (the logical world of the "father"). She maintains that "semiotic" language often "erupts" into "symbolic" language and subverts both male and female sexual identity. In contrast to Irigaray, who looks for a specific "female voice," Kristeva questions the very concept of identity, male or female. For Kristeva, the oppression of women is only a portion of contemporary society's more universal social, political, and economic oppression of "marginalized groups." Contrary to Freud and Lacan, Kristeva not only emphasizes the *social* role of the mother in the development of the human subject but also the important role of the child. Yet both are rooted in the mother's contact with the child prior to the "law of the father."

See also **Consciousness; Enlightenment; Existentialism; Identity; Phenomenology; Philosophies: Feminist, Twentieth-Century.**

BIBLIOGRAPHY

PRIMARY SOURCES

Adorno, Theodor, and Max Horkheimer. *Dialectic of Enlightenment.* Translated by John Cumming. London: Verso, 1989.

Askay, Richard, and Jensen Farguhar. *Apprehending the Inaccessible: Freudian Psychoanalysis and Existential Phenomenology.* Evanston, Ill: Northwestern University Press, 2004.

Beauvoir, Simone de. *The Second Sex.* Translated by H. M. Parshley. New York: Vintage, 1974.

Foucault, Michel. *Madness and Civilization: A History of Insanity in the Age of Reason.* London: Routledge, 1989.

Gadamer, Hans-Georg. *Truth and Method.* 2nd rev. ed. Translation revised by Joel Weinsheimer and Donald G. Marshall. New York: Continuum, 1989.

Habermas, Jürgen. *Knowledge and Human Interests.* Translated by Jeremy J. Shapiro. Cambridge, U.K.: Polity, 1987.

———. *Theory of Communicative Action.* 2 vols. Translated by Thomas McCarthy. Cambridge, U.K.: Polity, 1991.

Heidegger, Martin. *Basic Writings.* Edited by David Farrell Krell. Rev. and expanded ed. San Francisco: HarperSanFrancisco, 1993.

———. *Being and Time.* Translated by John Macquarrie and Edward Robinson. New York: Harper and Row, 1962.

———. *Zollikon Seminars: Protocols, Conversations, Letters.* Edited by Medard Boss. Translated from the German and with notes and afterwords by Franz Mayr and Richard Askay. Evanston, Ill.: Northwestern University Press, 2001.

Irigaray, Luce. *An Ethics of Sexual Difference.* Translated by Carolyn Burke and Gillian C. Gill. Ithaca, N.Y.: Cornell University Press, 1993.

Lévinas, Emmanuel. *Totality and Infinity: An Essay on Exteriority.* Translated by Alphonso Lingis. The Hague: Nijhoff, 1979.

Merleau-Ponty, Maurice. *Phenomenology of Perception.* Translated by Colin Smith. New York: Humanities Press, 1962.

Sartre, Jean-Paul. *Being and Nothingness: A Phenomenological Essay on Ontology.* Translated by Hazel E. Barnes. New York: Washington Square Press, 1992.

Wittgenstein, Ludwig. *Philosophical Investigations.* Translated by G. E. M. Anscombe. 2nd ed. Oxford: Blackwell, 1958.

SECONDARY SOURCES

Critchley, Simon. *Continental Philosophy: A Very Short Introduction.* Oxford and New York: Oxford University Press, 2001.

Critchley, Simon, and William Schroeder, eds. *A Companion to Continental Philosophy.* Malden, Mass.: Blackwell, 1998.

Holland, Nancy J., and Patricia Huntington, eds. *Feminist Interpretations of Martin Heidegger.* University Park: Pennsylvania State University, 2001.

Kearney, Richard, ed. *Twentieth-Century Continental Philosophy.* London and New York: Routledge, 1994.

Kearney, Richard, and Mara Rainwater, eds. *The Continental Philosophy Reader.* London: Routledge, 1996.

McNeill, William, and Karen Feldman, eds. *Continental Philosophy: An Anthology.* Oxford: Blackwell, 1997.

Solomon, Robert. *Continental Philosophy Since 1750: The Rise and Fall of the Self.* Oxford and New York: Oxford University Press, 1988.

West, David. *An Introduction to Continental Philosophy.* Cambridge, U.K.: Polity, 1996.

Franz Mayr

CONTRACEPTION. *See* **Family Planning.**

CORE/PERIPHERY. *See* **Geography; World Systems Theory.**

CORRUPTION. Consider the first sentence of Jean-Jacques Rousseau's (1712–1778) *Discours sur les arts et sciences* (Discourse on the arts and sciences, 1750): "Has the restoration of the sciences and arts contributed to the purification of mores, or their corruption?" Corruption denotes deterioration, a qualitative decline from an original (absolutely or relatively) natural or pristine state; related terms include decay, deterioration, disintegration, corrosion, and degeneration. Corruption is sometimes used in a related (but distinct) sense, to denote a state of affairs—a "state of corruption"—often in contrast to one characterized by virtue. In either form (verb or noun) corruption is an intensely historical term, describing either a process of qualitative spoliation or the end result thereof.

The discourse of corruption and virtue offers critics and philosophers a powerful rhetorical tool with which to indict societies' perceived shortcomings vis-à-vis some past standard. When placed into narrative form, corruption accounts generally contain four elements: (1) a description of the symptoms of corruption (social, moral, political); (2) identification of an agent of corruption; (3) a timeline by which critics identify the agent's appearance and trace its corrupting influence; and (4) a call to action to turn back corruption and restore lost virtues.

In the history of ideas and historiography, the discourse of corruption has often, though not exclusively, been associated with the tradition of civic republicanism. More recently, a significant body of research has brought the tools of social science to bear on the identification and measurement of corruption in the political sphere, and offered general theories about conditions under which corruption is fostered or retarded. This entry will point out, in an admittedly abbreviated manner, some of the main lines of research and refer the reader to key texts in the literature on corruption.

Corruption, Civic Republicanism, and Republican Historiography

Perhaps the most rhetorically powerful and historically influential language of corruption appears in the tradition of civic republicanism associated with Italian Renaissance humanists like Niccolò Machiavelli (1469–1527), Francesco Guicciardini (1483–1540), and Leonardo Bruni (c.1370–1444), which emphasizes the civic and social nature of the human good. Drawing on such classical sources as Aristotle (384–322 B.C.E.) and Cicero (106–43 B.C.E.), republicans see the realization of civic virtue as requiring the active involvement of relatively equal citizens in making decisions about their common life. Thus, anything that distracts citizens from the common good—internal factions, luxury, security, foreign influences, great disparities of wealth (even, for some thinkers, Christianity itself)—can be seen as an agent of corruption. Conversely, anything that fosters or rewards citizens' mutual self-regard and

keeps their efforts focused on the good of all promotes civic virtue and helps stave off corruption. Drawing on both classical and Renaissance ideas, Rousseau advances the single most important modern theory of republican virtue.

Republican concerns about virtue and corruption are not limited to Europe: the tradition has also fundamentally affected the historiography of the American experience. Alongside the American obsession with Lockean individualism, a republican school emphasized the Founders' concern for civic virtue in the citizenry. Connecting Italian humanism and the American founding was the contribution of J. G. A. Pocock's monumental *The Machiavellian Moment: Florentine Political Thought and the Atlantic Republican Tradition* (1975). For Pocock, a discernible discourse about corruption, virtue, and the very nature of the political task ran from Renaissance Italy through England's civil wars and across the Atlantic, where it facilitated the development of the American character and the split with England. The ideal of the active citizen, of republican politics as the effort to preserve civic virtue and keep corruption at bay, has exerted a strong pull on the political imagination down to our own time.

Political Corruption
Political scientists have developed sophisticated analyses for the study of political corruption. No single definition of political corruption can avoid controversy since, barring consensus on the proper nature and extent of legitimate politics, we necessarily lack agreement on how to define corrupted politics. Nonetheless, as one would expect, researchers emphasize political, institutional, or bureaucratic locations of corruption; the misuse of public power; or "behavior which deviates from the formal duties of a public role because of private-regarding . . . pecuniary or status gains; or violates rules against the exercise of certain types of private-regarding influence" (Nye, p. 419).

Political corruption presents itself in a host of settings. Susan Rose-Ackerman considers the legislative and bureaucratic arenas, and presents political corruption as an economic, cultural, and political phenomenon with important implications for democratic societies. More broadly, scholars have attempted to analyze political corruption in a variety of global contexts (Heidenheimer, 1970; Heywood, 1997). Nor has this research necessarily involved a turning-away from historical concerns with equality and participation: Patrick Dobel offers a general theory of corruption that draws on classical authors yet speaks to contemporary political life, suggesting practical steps toward staving off corruption in modern states.

Other Contexts
Countless reform movements within the world's major religions have framed their critiques by denouncing the corruption of pure or pristine doctrines. Indeed, on one view, Buddhism itself grew out of a deep dissatisfaction with the corruption and increasingly complex nature of Hinduism, not entirely unlike the early Protestants who attacked the corruption of the Roman Catholic Church and called for a return to simpler ancient doctrines. Often these critiques point to the effects of wealth and luxury on the purity of religious doctrines

Night, **an engraving from the graphic series** ***The Four Times of the Day*** **(1738) by William Hogarth.** Numerous examples of moral corruption and the dissipation of the human spirit are depicted as night falls on a London street. © HISTORICAL PICTURE ARCHIVE/CORBIS

and practices, and moral standards more generally: echoing civic republican themes, the fourteenth-century Islamic scholar Ibn Khaldun bluntly asserted that "luxury corrupts morals" (pp. 131–132).

The biblical account of the Fall is perhaps the paradigmatic corruption metanarrative, with its account of a lost, originally virtuous, condition and the ongoing struggle for redemption. But other religious traditions draw on the images of corruption as well: according to the Buddhist *Milindapañha* "[t]he virtuous and well-conducted man . . . is like a medicine in destroying the poison of human corruption; is like a healing herb in quieting the disease of human corruption; is like water in removing the dirt and defilement of human corruption" (ch. 5, sec. 98). The virtue here described is, of course, not social republican virtue, but rather a specifically religious understanding of what is required to stave off the corruption that can grow from within.

Finally, we should note the classical tradition that utilizes the terms "generation and corruption" in reference to the body and things subject to growth and decay in the physical realm. Plato (c. 428–348 or 347 B.C.E.) describes philosophers as those who love eternal verities "not varying from generation and corruption," and regards gymnastic, given its emphasis on the body, as "having to do with generation and corruption" (*Republic* 485b, 521e). Indeed, Aristotle (384–322 B.C.E.) announces in

the first sentence of his *On Generation and Corruption,* that his task is "to study coming-to-be and passing-away." Later, Augustine (354–430) brought a Christian view of the immortal soul to this classical understanding, describing the "soul pressed down by the corruptible body, and weighed down by earthly thoughts, many and various" (*De Trinitate,* 8.2).

Conclusion

How might we explain the widespread appeal of discourses on corruption? The truth likely remains somewhere deep within the individual and collective dynamics by which people attempt to come to grips with change in their lives, and to construct a meaningful narrative connection between past, present, and future. The power of corruption rhetoric seems to lie in its recognition of the inherent fragility of all human endeavor—indeed, of human bodies. Talking in terms of corruption, for civic republicans, often makes sense of a host of social changes by placing them into a coherent, purposive, and meaningful frame of reference, highlighting past glories, and spurring audiences on to greater things in the future. Corruption accounts, like all political speech, are inherently partial and moralistic, but they are also extremely effective in pointing to the price paid for progress, be it technological, political, or economic. When Adam Smith (1723–1790) boasted, in his *Inquiry into the Nature and Causes of the Wealth of Nations* (1776) that the poorest English laborer lives in material comfort undreamed of by an African king, Rousseau was there to ask about the price paid for this economic "progress," using the language of corruption to frame and reinforce his critique.

But is corruption, however variously defined, always to be lamented? A few scholars have ventured the hypothesis that corruption is necessary, though indeed not sufficient, for such tasks as the smooth operation of an economy. Business practices routinely denounced as "corrupt" may serve a variety of extremely important social and economic functions. Such a view, overtly or not, hearkens back to Bernard Mandeville's (1670–1733) famous dictum that private vices yield public benefits.

See also **Constitutionalism; Humanism; Poverty; Republicanism; Virtue Ethics; Wealth.**

BIBLIOGRAPHY

Dobel, J. Patrick. "Corruption of a State." *American Political Science Review* 72 (1978): 958–973.

Heidenheimer, A. J., ed. *Political Corruption: Readings in Comparative Analysis.* New York: Holt, Reinhart, and Winston, 1970.

Heywood, Paul, ed. *Political Corruption.* Oxford: Blackwell, 1997.

Khaldun, Ibn. *An Arab Philosophy of History: Selections from the Prolegomena of Ibn Khaldun of Tunis.* Translated and arranged by Charles Issawi. London: Murray, 1950.

Nye, Joseph S. "Corruption and Political Development: A Cost-Benefit Analysis." *American Political Science Review* 61 (1967): 417-427.

Pocock, J. G. A. *The Machiavellian Moment: Florentine Political Thought and the Atlantic Republican Tradition.* Princeton, N.J.: Princeton University Press, 1975.

Rose-Ackerman, Susan. *Corruption: A Study in Political Economy.* New York: Academic Press, 1978.

———. *Corruption and Government: Causes, Consequences, and Reform.* Cambridge, U.K.: Cambridge University Press, 1999.

Wood, Gordon S. *The Creation of the American Republic, 1776–1789.* Chapel Hill, NC: University of North Carolina Press, 1969.

Andrew R. Murphy

CORRUPTION IN DEVELOPED AND DEVELOPING COUNTRIES.

While corruption, in one form or another, has perverted virtually all human societies throughout history, it has not had uniform impact on any one of them. Scholars who study corruption in an effort to find ways to minimize it have had to deal with the fact that it is difficult to define and measure, making empirical testing very difficult.

Defining Corruption

Modern social science defines corruption in terms of three basic models: First, corruption is related to the performance of the duties of a public office. According to J. S. Nye, corruption is

> [b]ehavior which deviates from the normal duties of a public role because of private-regarding (family, close private clique), pecuniary or status gains; or violates rules against the exercise of certain types of private-regarding influence. This includes such behavior as bribery (use of reward to pervert the judgment of a person in a position of trust); nepotism (bestowal of patronage by reason of ascriptive relationship rather than merit); and misappropriation (illegal appropriation of public resources for private regarding uses). (p. 419)

Second, corruption is related to the concept of exchange derived from the theory of the market. Jacob Van Klaveren argues that the bureaucrat views his public office as an enterprise from which to extract extra-legal income. As a consequence, the civil servant's compensation package "does not depend on an ethical evaluation of his usefulness for the common good but precisely upon the market situation and his talents for finding the point of maximal gain on the public's demand curve" (p. 26). In an economy pervaded by high levels of government regulations, civil servants may devote most of their time and effort to assisting entrepreneurs in evading state laws and statutes. In exchange the civil servants are paid extra-legal income (Mbaku, 1992).

Finally, the definition of corruption is couched in terms of the public interest, as argued by Carl Friedrich:

> [t]he pattern of corruption may therefore be said to exist whenever a power holder who is charged with doing certain things, that is a responsible functionary or office holder, is by monetary or other rewards, such as the expectation of a job in the future, induced to take actions which favor whoever provides the reward and thereby damage the group or organization to which the functionary belongs, more specifically the government. (p. 15)

Friedrich argues further that the opportunistic activities of corrupt bureaucrats can severely damage the public interest and should be considered important variables in the study and evaluation of corruption.

Public choice theory and corruption. Economists, dissatisfied with these explanations for corruption, have turned to public choice theory, which sees corruption as postconstitutional opportunism designed to generate benefits for individuals or groups at the expense of the rest of society. According to public choice theory, the scope and extent of corruption in a country is determined by that country's institutional arrangements and not necessarily by the character of its civil servants and politicians. Once the constitution has been designed and adopted and a government established, there is an incentive for individuals and groups to subvert the rules in an effort to generate benefits for themselves. Rules subversion, if successful, can allow individuals to secure benefits above and beyond what would have accrued to them otherwise. This kind of behavior can occur in both democratic and nondemocratic societies.

Bureaucrats, whose job it is to design and execute public policies, may attempt to use the process to maximize their private objectives at the expense of serving the general public efficiently and equitably. The desire by civil servants to maximize their private objectives and the effort by organized interest groups to subvert the rules and to extract benefits for themselves create opportunities for corruption. For example, an entrepreneur who wants to secure a lucrative import or production permit may bribe a clerk at the ministry of trade in order to (1) secure the permit and (2) make sure that the bureau protects his new monopoly position by not issuing additional permits to entrepreneurs from the area in which he operates. In exchange for providing the entrepreneur with opportunities to earn supranormal profits, the civil servants at the ministry of trade "earn" extra-legal income, and the importer who receives the permit earns an above normal rate of return on investment, but society loses.

Government regulatory activities usually impose significant transaction costs on enterprise owners and severely affect the profitability of their operations. To minimize these regulation-induced costs, some entrepreneurs may seek help from the civil service, whose job it is to enforce the laws. Usually, the business owner pays a bribe to the government regulator in order to receive preferential treatment and minimize the burden of the regulations on his or her operations. Public choice theorists argue that bureaucratic corruption is directly related to the scope and extent of government intervention in private exchange (i.e., in markets). Effective control of corruption, then, must be based on a modification of existing rules in order to change incentive structures and constrain the ability of the state to intervene in private exchange and create artificial scarcities.

The International Dimension of Corruption

Since the end of the Cold War, policymakers in many countries have recognized the global nature of corruption and are now making efforts to coordinate their control and cleanup efforts. Thus, instead of viewing corruption as a domestic problem caused primarily by the interaction of the bureaucracy with the private sector, many lawmakers, especially those in the developing and transition economies, are now acknowledging the contributions of transnational corporations to the problem.

Many governmental and nongovernmental organizations—including the United Nations (UN), the Organization of American States (OAS), the International Chamber of Commerce, Transparency International (TI), the World Economic Forum (WEF), World Bank, Interpol, and the Organization for Economic Cooperation and Development (OECD)—have developed an interest in dealing with corruption.

Several reasons have been advanced to explain the sudden interest by these organizations. Changes in international political relations during the period from 1989 to 1991 significantly reduced people's tolerance for incompetence, malfeasance, and venality in the public sector. As part of the movement toward improved governance, citizens of many countries demanded the elimination of corrupt practices. Thus, since the late 1980s, the balance of power in many countries has been shifting in favor of more open, transparent, and participatory governance structures.

Scholars have identified three changes that have contributed to the globalization of corruption. First, greater levels of economic integration have increased chances that corruption in one region of the world will have an impact on economic and political activities in other parts of the world. For example, when the corrupt activities of the Bank of Credit and Commerce International (BCCI) forced it into insolvency in 1991, many economies around the world were affected. In fact, several countries in Africa suffered significant financial losses from the BCCI collapse.

Second, developments in communication technology have revolutionized the international financial system and enhanced the ability of traders to engage in corruption. The emergence of electronic networks for the transfer of funds has made it quite difficult for countries to deal effectively with corruption. Many anticorruption organizations have argued that the ease with which funds can be transferred to Europe or the Caribbean from different parts of the world implies that corrupt civil servants can effectively hide their extra-legal income from the public, making it virtually impossible for such funds to be recovered in the event of conviction. Fortunately, policing agencies, especially in the West, continue to innovate and come up with technology that can effectively monitor traffic in these electronic networks. Such technology could prove very helpful in the fight against global corruption.

Third, since the end of the Cold War there has been a significant increase in the number of cooperative alliances between economic units, within countries and across borders. Continued globalization exacerbates the problem of corruption; however, it also offers opportunities for its control.

Pervasive corruption is a major threat to the maintenance of a free, multilateral trading system. In order for a global competitive economy to function properly and efficiently, participants must play by the rules. Opportunism (e.g., corruption) by some market participants can derail the international trading system since it (i.e., corruption) invariably creates an unlevel playing field. For example, corporations or countries that do not tolerate corruption will be placed at a competitive disadvantage. Those countries that encourage their companies to engage in corruption abroad and offer favorable tax treatment for bribes paid to foreign public officials place these firms at a competitive advantage over those from countries in which corruption (including paying bribes to foreign public officials) has been criminalized. In fact, many American firms, which are prohibited by U.S. law from offering bribes to foreign officials, have complained bitterly of the disadvantage that they suffer since, until recently, many of their European counterparts were allowed and often encouraged by favorable tax treatment by their national governments to engage in corrupt practices abroad.

Many policymakers around the world, especially in the developed countries, have come to realize that the long-run social, economic, human, and political costs of global corruption are enormous and that it poses a threat to the rule of law. It can also cause citizens to lose confidence in their leaders and distort market incentives and negatively affect the flow of investment and, hence, wealth creation. Perhaps more important is the fact that corruption can prevent the poor from gaining access to welfare-enhancing and even life-saving public goods and services.

Controlling Corruption

Four strategies have been employed in the past by successive governments to deal with corruption, usually with varying degrees of success. These are societal, legal, market, and political strategies.

In the societal strategy, each society defines a common standard of morality, which can then be employed to determine if a given behavior qualifies as corrupt. Civil society is encouraged to remain vigilant and watch out for individuals who engage in corruption and report them to the police. The government and civil society organizations are expected to educate the general public about corruption and its negative effects on economic growth and development. Through such an educational program, citizens can significantly improve their ability to determine if behavior is corrupt and report perpetuators to the relevant authorities for further action. The private press plays an important role in this approach to corruption cleanup—it investigates and exposes corruption, paving the way for the police to gather the evidence needed for effective prosecution by the judiciary.

In the legal approach, the judiciary, the police, and the mass media are expected to lead the fight against corruption. First, national laws define the responsibilities of civil servants and properly constrain them in the performance of their duties. Second, the law defines corruption and corrupt behavior. Third, citizens are encouraged to be vigilant and report any suspected corrupt activities to the police. Fourth, the police are expected to thoroughly investigate such activities, gather the necessary information, and present the latter to the judiciary. Fifth, the judiciary then prosecutes the accused and imposes the appropriate punishment if found guilty. Special commissions of inquiry or special prosecutors can be constituted and used by the government to investigate incidents that point to large-scale corruption and public malfeasance. Commissions of inquiry are especially important in cases where high-ranking officials have been implicated in corruption.

Police and judiciary officers can only perform their functions properly and efficiently if they are not corrupt—that is, they are effectively constrained by the law. If, on the other hand, these institutions are pervaded by corruption, it would be prudent to first engage in reforms to improve their efficiency before engaging them in the fight against corruption.

In many developing countries, low salaries for public servants have been given as a reason why some of these workers may engage in corruption. As part of the effort to minimize corruption in the civil service, it has been suggested that pay scales in the public sector be made competitive with those in the private sector. One must note, however, that higher pay in the public sector may simply force opportunistic civil servants to demand higher bribes to compensate for the probability of losing what is now a relatively more important and lucrative position. It has also been suggested that any civil-service reforms be supplemented with counteracting agencies such as an independent judiciary or some kind of independent review board, an ombudsman, or other investigative body. One must consider the fact that such bodies can become politicized (as evidence from many developed and developing countries shows) and used by incumbent ruling coalitions to punish the opposition and continue to monopolize political spaces.

The market approach to corruption cleanup is based on the belief that there exists a discernible relationship between market structure and corruption. Government regulation of private exchange creates opportunities for regulators to extort bribes from enterprise owners. The remedy that scholars have usually recommended is decreased government regulation and more reliance on markets for the allocation of resources. Such an approach has at least two problems. First, it is based on the manipulation of outcomes within an existing or given incentive structure (i.e., existing institutional arrangements). Second, the problem here is not with the market but with the incentive structures that traders are facing. Rules define the incentive structure faced by participants in markets and, hence, determine the behavior of these traders and market outcomes. If the government's regulatory activities are reduced and resource allocation made more dependent on the market, there is not likely to be much of a change in outcomes if the incentive structure has not been altered. The most effective way to minimize opportunistic behaviors, including corruption, is to reform or modify existing rules and, by implication, change the incentives faced by traders. Changing or modifying the rules does not imply deregulation, but reconstitution and reconstruction of the state through democratic constitution-making to provide transparent, participatory, and accountable governance and economic structures.

The political strategy emphasizes decentralization of power and argues that the concentration of power in the center enhances the ability of the ruling coalition to engage in corrupt activities. The recommendation is that the public sector be made more transparent. For example, the public budget process should be made more open and participatory and the outcome (i.e., the budget) should be published and made available to the mass media and any other interested individuals and groups. Unfortunately, such reforms can easily be reversed (and power reconcentrated in the center) by subsequent governments in response to lobbying from interest groups.

Traditional approaches to corruption control depend on the effectiveness and professionalism of the country's counteracting institutions (e.g., the police, judiciary, and the mass media). It is assumed that institutions such as the police and judiciary are well constrained by the law and that they are free of corruption. First, a significantly large number of countries around the world do not have fully functioning private media that are free to investigate and expose corruption without fear of censure by the incumbent government.

Second, the judiciary systems of many countries are not independent of the executive branch of government. Instead, the country's chief executive controls the judiciary and retains the power to appoint and dismiss judiciary officers.

Third, many public institutions, especially in the developing countries, are pervaded by high levels of corruption. Hence, a corruption cleanup program developed and implemented by any of these institutions is not likely to be successful. An effective anticorruption program, then, must begin with the selection of appropriate new rules that (1) constrain the exercise of government agency and (2) provide the necessary foundation for the design and adoption of new and more effective counteracting agencies (e.g., an independent judiciary, a well-constrained police force, a professional and neutral military, an independent central bank, a free press, etc.).

Public Choice Theory and Corruption Control

Corruption is a "rules-related" problem. Rules determine the incentives faced by participants in markets. Unless the analyst understands the laws and institutions of the economy being examined, any attempt to study corruption and other forms of opportunism will not yield policy-relevant results.

In a 1985 study, Brennan and Buchanan argue that rules (1) determine the nature of the interaction between individuals within society; (2) provide the means for the peaceful resolution of conflict; (3) provide information to market participants, enhancing the ability of each individual to anticipate the behavior of others; and (4) constrain the behavior of individuals, as well as that of collectivities within the society. To deal effectively with corruption, for example, it is necessary that the police, who investigate and collect evidence to be used in the prosecution of those accused of corruption, be adequately constrained by the law. Since the rules determine the incentive structures faced by market participants, any effort to deal with corruption and other forms of opportunism (e.g., rent seeking) must begin with a negotiated modification of existing rules so that the economy can be provided with a new set of rules that effectively constrains state custodians and makes it quite difficult for them to behave opportunistically.

Rules can be implicit (e.g., tribal custom and tradition) or explicit (e.g., a written constitution). After a country has developed and adopted a constitution, corruption can be seen as post-constitutional opportunism—that is, behavior on the part of individuals or groups designed to generate extra-legal income for themselves, usually through the subversion of rules. One can see corruption then as part of the larger problem of constitutional maintenance or how to enforce compliance to the rules. Here, opportunism is defined as behaviors designed to improve the welfare of an individual or group at the expense of other citizens and includes such behaviors as shirking, corruption, adverse selection, moral hazard, and free riding.

The key to producing a sustainable and effective anticorruption campaign is a thorough and complete examination of the country's existing rules and by implication, its market incentives. This approach to corruption control has many benefits. First, institutional reform, especially if undertaken democratically, can produce rules that (1) reflect the values of the relevant stakeholder groups and hence are most likely to be considered legitimate tools for the regulation of sociopolitical interaction, improving the chance that people would respect and obey them; and (2) effectively constrain the state and make it quite difficult for civil servants and politicians to extort bribes from the private sector.

Second, institutional reform can be used to entrench economic freedom and improve entrepreneurship and wealth creation. Finally, institutional reform can provide each economy with more viable and effective structures for the management of ethnic diversity, resulting in a reduction in communal violence. A more peaceful society should significantly improve the environment for investment and wealth creation.

See also **Civil Society; Constitutionalism; Corruption; Economics; Globalization.**

BIBLIOGRAPHY

Brennan, Geoffrey, and James M. Buchanan. *The Reason of Rules: Constitutional Political Economy.* Cambridge, U.K.: Cambridge University Press, 1985.

Friedrich, Carl J. "Corruption Concepts in Historical Perspective." In *Political Corruption: A Handbook,* edited by Arnold J. Heidenheimer, Michael Johnston, and Victor T. LeVine. New Brunswick, N.J.: Transaction, 1990.

Gillespie, Kate, and Gwenn Okruhlik. "The Political Dimensions of Corruption Cleanups: A Framework for Analysis." *Comparative Politics* 24, no. 1 (1991): 77–95.

Glynn, Patrick, Stephen J. Kobrin, and Moisés Naím. "The Globalization of Corruption." In *Corruption and the Global Economy,* edited by Kimberly A. Elliot. Washington, D.C.: Institute for International Economics, 1997.

Mbaku, John M. "Bureaucratic Corruption as Rent-Seeking Behavior." *Konjunkturpolitik* 38, no. 4 (1992): 247–265.

———. *Bureaucratic and Political Corruption in Africa: The Public Choice Perspective.* Malabar, Fla.: Krieger, 2000.

Nye, J. S. "Corruption and Political Development: A Cost-Benefit Analysis." *American Political Science Review* 61, no. 2 (1967): 417–427.

Ostrom, Elinor, Larry Schroeder, and Susan Wynne, eds. *Institutional Incentives and Sustainable Development: Infrastructure Policies in Perspective.* Boulder, Colo.: Westview, 1993.

Passas, Nikos. "I Cheat Therefore I Exist? The BCCI Scandal in Context." In *Emerging Global Business Ethics,* edited by W. Michael Hoffman, Judith B. Kamm, Robert E. Frederick, and Edward S. Petry Jr. Westport, Conn.: Quorum, 1994.

Rose-Ackerman, Susan. *Corruption: A Study in Political Economy.* New York: Academic Press, 1978.

———. *Corruption and Government: Causes, Consequences, and Reform.* Cambridge, U.K.: Cambridge University Press, 1999.

———. "The Political Economy of Corruption." In *Corruption and the Global Economy,* edited by Kimberly A. Elliot. Washington, D.C.: Institute for International Economics, 1997.

Van Klaveren, Jacob. "The Concept of Corruption." In *Political Corruption: A Handbook,* edited by Arnold J Heidenheimer, Michael Johnston, and Victor T. LeVine. New Brunswick, N.J.: Transaction, 1990.

John Mukum Mbaku

COSMOLOGY.

This entry includes two subentries:

Asia

Cosmology and Astronomy

ASIA

Hindu cosmologies are among the oldest surviving cosmologies in the world, dating back as far as the Vedic writings of the second millennium B.C.E. The oldest sections of the Vedas are the Samhitas (hymns), which express a relatively simple cosmology consisting of either two (earth and sky, representing male and female, respectively) or—more commonly—three parts (earth, atmosphere, and sky or heaven). There seems to be some indication of an underworld, although this is located sometimes in one of the aforementioned parts of the cosmos and at other times simply "beyond" them. Moreover, in these early Vedic works it is unclear if the gods created the cosmos (and if so, which ones) or if they were created within the cosmos. For example, in one famous account *purusha* (the "cosmic man") is sacrificed by the gods and his body divided to form the various aspects of the cosmos and the caste distinctions of Vedic society (*Rig Veda,* book 10, hymn 90). Yet in another prominent cosmogony, the author marvels at how nothing—neither being nor non-being, nor even the gods themselves—existed before the creation of the cosmos, and questions how anyone could know from whence the cosmos arose (*Rig Veda,* book 10, hymn 129). One of the significant contributions to Hindu cosmology in the Vedic hymns, however, is the notion of *rita* (roughly, "cosmic order"). Although it is not the focus of any particular hymn, the concept surfaces explicitly and implicitly in a number of Vedic hymns, and indicates an eternal law, moral standard, and underlying truth that applies to the cosmos generally and to human society in particular. In the hymns, however—and, for the most part, in the subsequent *Brahmanas* and *Aranyakas*—*rita* only suggested a ritual connection of sacrifices, devotion, and observance of a basic caste system with aiding the gods in maintaining cosmic order.

The Upanishads, the concluding sections of the Vedas written in the first millennium B.C.E., provide a more systematic and philosophically sophisticated cosmology. Most significant was the emphasis on the concept of *Brahman* (the ultimate as found in the cosmos as a whole), and its association with *Atman* (the ultimate as discovered through introspection). This shifted the entire focus of the cosmology—indicative of a larger shift in Hindu thought—from maintaining cosmic order (*rita*) to the achievement of liberation (*moksha*) from the cycle of reincarnation through identification with the Ultimate (*Brahman*). Maintaining cosmic order remains important, although it is understood in the Upanishads primarily in terms of *dharma,* which refers not only to the descriptive and normative dimensions of the cosmic order itself (as did *rita*) but also to that order as it applies to the individual's lot in life. Consistent with the identification of *Brahman* with *Atman,* achieving *moksha* is in large part a matter of understanding and observing the dharma of the cosmos as it applies to oneself. Although the Upanishads mark an important shift in Hindu cosmology, this shift was developed—like much of the Upanishads—on the basis of the Vedic hymns. For example, where the hymns distinguished two or three parts to the cosmos, the Upanishads distinguish seven, including a number of higher parts that correspond with achieving *moksha.* Perhaps the best example of this, however, is in the Upanishadic development of the "cosmic egg" cosmology first introduced in the *Brahmana* section of the Vedas: when split in two, the egg—which, significantly, is associated with *Brahman*—formed the earth and sky from its shells, and the mountains, streams, and the like from its insides (*Chandogya Upanishad* III.xix; see also *Shatapatha Brahmana* XI, 1, 6).

While the Upanishads mark the end of the Vedas, the cosmologies introduced there continue to be developed in the subsequent texts (for example, the *Manava Dharmashastra* or *Manusmriti* [Laws of Manu], the *Vishnu Purana,* and sections of the *Mahabharata*). While these texts differ somewhat in content, they mutually inform what has come to be the prevailing cosmology in the Hindu tradition. This cosmology draws on the Vedic account of the "egg of *Brahman*" (*Brahmanda*), although it develops the account with much greater elaboration. The world created from that egg—which, again, is identified with *Brahman*—is centered on a mythical Mount Meru, an inverted mountain that not only stands at the center of the world of the living, but also links it to numerous levels of heaven above and still more numerous hells below. The cosmography of the world includes highly figurative descriptions of geometrically oriented mountain ranges separating different lands, concentric seas of unusual liquids (for example, wine or molasses), and series of ring-shaped islands.

Accompanying this cosmography is an equally detailed account of cosmic time, according to which the world (that is, the world of living beings, as opposed to the cosmos as a whole) passes through four ages (*yuga*): the first is a golden age, and each age degrades further until the world is destroyed after the first. These four *yuga,* however, constitute but one day of Brahma, and—following a night of Brahma, which is a sustained period of cosmic rest—the world is created anew and runs through the four ages once again. This process is often interpreted with respect to the actions of the gods Brahma (the creator, not to be confused with the impersonal *Brahman*), Vishnu (the preserver), and Shiva (the destroyer), which are seen to be three aspects of the world's continual regeneration and renewal. These accounts of time proceed to distinguish periods of time ranging from mere fractions of a second to the span of Brahma's life (numbering in the billions of years).

What is most notable about the development of Hindu cosmology is the extent to which it develops in concert with its social structures. In early Vedic literature, these structures (such as the caste system) are present, but only in their basic contours, just as is the case with Hindu cosmologies. By the time of the Upanishads, however, they have evidently taken on considerably more sophistication—again, as have the cosmologies. Finally, in the post-Vedic literature, caste distinctions and social obligation have been laid out in considerable detail, mirroring the exacting scholasticism present in the accompanying cosmologies. While the precise relation between cosmologies and social structures is a matter of ongoing debate, the development of Hindu cosmologies provides strong evidence that there is at least an important link between the two.

Buddhist Cosmologies

Buddhists are both interested and uninterested in cosmology. They are uninterested, first, because all of the distinctions that are typically taken to characterize the cosmos are seen as expressions of utmost ignorance with respect to the true nature of things. For Buddhists, there are no stable, unchanging things; rather, all things are in perpetual flux, and it is only through one's ignorance and desire that one takes them to be substantive and distinct. As this account of their lack of interest in cosmology should indicate, however, Buddhists are also very interested in cosmology, because it is not only the problem but also the solution that is cosmological. Not only can a cosmology constructed through "skillful means" (*upaya*) illumine the way to overcome ignorance, but overcoming this ignorance is itself adjusting one's understanding of the cosmos.

Thus, Buddhist cosmologies can be, but need not necessarily be, read as objective accounts of the nature of the cosmos; rather, the ultimate aim of these cosmologies is always on the achievement of enlightenment (nirvana), and they must be understood as means to that end. For example, in the *Visuddhimagga* (*Path of Purification*), Buddhaghosha (fifth century C.E.) describes the "world" not in detailed spatial and temporal terms but in terms of possible destinations for rebirth: gods, humans, ghosts, and animals, and hell (strangely, the last is a spatial reference, but primarily indicates a realm for tortured souls). Likewise, in the *Abhidharmakosha,* Vasubandhu (fifth century C.E.) locates a cosmology much like Buddhaghosha's within but one of three spheres (*dhatu*): the sphere of desire (*kamadhatu*); beyond this is a sphere of pure form (*rupadhatu*), and finally a sphere of no-form (*arupadhatu*). Despite their differences, these two prominent early cosmologies serve as a roadmap for the path to enlightenment, complex enough to exemplify the key points of Buddhist doctrine, yet simple enough to serve as an accessible means for traveling along that path.

Buddhist cosmology becomes inordinately more complicated, however, with proliferation of worlds and Buddharealms. The concept of multiple worlds is already evident in Theravadan literature, where one Buddha oversees many worlds at one time; however, this concept becomes much more prominent in Mahayana texts, where most of these worlds are associated with particular Buddha-realms (*buddhakshetra*). Each *buddhakshetra* is overseen by its own fully enlightened Buddha, and is seen as pure, impure, or mixed, depending on the degree of desire and ignorance manifested there. Our own world, Saha, is the *buddhakshetra* of Shakyamuni (the historical Buddha), and is seen alternately as impure or mixed. Significantly, this association of worlds with different Buddhas is what gave rise to Pure Land Buddhism in the Chinese and Japanese contexts: the so-called "Pure Land," Sukhavati, is a pure world overseen by the Buddha Amitayus/Amitabha (Infinite Life/Infinite Light), and all people who are born into this realm—something attained by faith rather than merit—are sure to achieve enlightenment in one lifetime.

It should be noted that, while Buddhist cosmologies are generally intended to embody the Buddhist path to enlightenment, this does not mean that they do not also draw on the cosmologies of other religious traditions—although this is always done with some modification. For example, Buddhist cosmography, like other Indian cosmographies, is traditionally centered on Mt. Meru, although the cosmography is given a distinctively Buddhist slant by placing the entire world of the living under the dominion of *Mara* (death). Likewise, the Buddhist notion of cosmic time borrows from the Hindu account of four *yugas* after which the world is destroyed and formed again; yet this account is again given a Buddhist slant by ridding the process of any creative deities and ensuring that the unenlightened souls are preserved during these recurrent destructions. This process of borrowing and adapting would continue as Buddhism spread into China, Tibet, Korea, and Japan; what would remain constant, however, is the ultimate aim of Buddhist cosmology: namely, enabling those still suffering in ignorance to ultimately achieve nirvana.

Chinese Cosmologies

Chinese cosmologies are, like Indian and Buddhist ones, manifold in their diversity. Some of the oldest originated from the Shang dynasty (c. 1554–1045/1040 B.C.E.), and appear initially to account for the general characteristics of the observed world. For example, the cosmos is often understood as consisting of a dome-shaped heaven (represented as a circle) and a square earth; China, the "Middle Kingdom," is situated at its center, with the surrounding world represented as kingdoms situated at each of the four cardinal points and mountains at each of the corners. Allan notes that this cosmology not only resembles a turtle (as many have observed), but more importantly that it resembles the plastron (breastplate) of a turtle; this association is significant because it points to the mythic overlay that accompanied these cosmologies: the plastron was among the most prominent mediums for divination in early Chinese rituals. In this basic cosmology, two of the most prominent features of Chinese cosmologies are already starting to develop: first, the duality between heaven and earth

anticipates the later and broader duality between *yin* and *yang*; second, there is an assumed correlation between the cosmos in its entirety and the cosmos as found in any one of its parts (such as the turtle plastron). Yet Shang cosmologies remained for the most part very basic, overseen by the supreme Lord, Shang Di, and controlled by various spiritual beings.

The Zhou dynasty (roughly 1100–250 B.C.E.) inaugurated a move from tribal society to feudal society, and the cosmologies of this period reflect that change. For example, the king takes on the title of "Son of heaven," thus situating himself cosmologically as that which links heaven and earth. This move simultaneously afforded him cosmic legitimacy, while also constraining him with the responsibility of ensuring that the order of earth appropriately modeled the order of heaven. This latter responsibility was termed the "Mandate of Heaven," and was taken to be a universal moral law that rulers could either observe (and continue to rule) or neglect (and lose their right to rule). Both duality and correlative thinking remained evident in Zhou cosmology, although the anthropomorphic spiritual powers of the Shang were replaced by moral principle in the Zhou in a way that both validated and restrained rulers even at the highest level, as seen in the *Shijing* (*Classic of Odes*) and the *Shujing* (*Classic of Documents*).

The cosmography of the Zhou also developed that of the Shang in much greater detail. Whereas the Shang understood earth to be square in a broad sense, the Zhou came to see space generally in terms of square units. In order to provide a more detailed description of the earth, squares were divided into nine smaller squares, each of which could be further divided to the desired level of detail; typically, this took the form of a 3 by 3 grid, but there are other variants. The result of such division was that most of Chinese cosmography was understood in terms of nines: nine domains in the Zhou empire, nine branches of the Yellow River, and so on. The most famous example of this division is the well-field system of taxation, whereby eight farmers would each farm one of the peripheral plots on a 3 by 3 grid, with the center square tended by all eight and its yield being given as a tax payment to the government. It is remarkable that even the division of land and labor was taken to be best ordered as a microcosm of the larger cosmic landscape.

What is perhaps most important about Zhou cosmologies, however, is that they set the terms for all subsequent Chinese cosmology. The most prominent features are fourfold: the duality between *yin* and *yang*, the five agents (water, fire, earth, wood, and metal), and the sixty-four hexagrams. First, the duality between *yin* and *yang* is taken to be characteristic of the cosmos as a whole, embodied in the dualities between dark and light, weak and strong, cold and hot, female and male (respectively); the profound message of this duality, however, is that these apparent opposites are actually fundamentally related, balancing, propagating, and flowing out of one another, for example, the *Daodejing* (*Classic of the Way and Virtue*) and the *Yijing* (*Classic of Change*). The theory of the five agents, in turn, represents the perpetual transformation of things as a characteristic and entirely natural feature of the cosmos; Zhou cosmologists correlated these with virtues, feelings, and arrangements of time, and used them to explain changes in

The earliest written accounts of Japanese cosmology are found in the *Kojiki* ("Records of Ancient Matters," 712 C.E.) and the *Nihongi* ("Chronicles of Japan," 720 C.E.). These texts originate in a time in Japanese history when Buddhism was already a significant influence, and thus serve not only as mythico-historical accounts of the origins and history of the Japanese people but also as the founding documents for the Shinto religion (which had hitherto been transmitted in spoken word and ritual practice). The presence of external influences is already apparent in these documents: the *Nihongi*, for instance, compares the initial state of the cosmos to an egg that, as heavy and light parts separate, form the heavens and the earth (as seen in many other Asian cosmogonies). The most significant influences, however, appear to stem from Chinese thought: most notably, *In* and *Yô*, presented in the *Nihongi* as the complementary forces underlying the cosmos, arguably stand as Japanese representations of *yin* and *yang*.

Despite their apparent external influences, Japanese sources also reveal their distinctiveness, as found most clearly in the epic of Izanagi and Izanami as found in *Kojiki*. Izanagi ("male-who-invites") and Izanami ("female-who-invites") represent the last generation of a series of spontaneously generated primordial gods, who develop out of one another in increasing complexity and differentiation. Izanagi and Izanami descend from High Heaven (*Takamahara*) to the unformed world to create the islands of Japan. These islands, as well as a host of smaller gods (*kami*), are brought about primarily as products of the sexual union of Izanagi and Izanami. Ultimately, however, Izanami dies while giving birth to the god of fire—she is scorched to death, producing even more gods in the process—and descends to the land of the dead (*Yomi-no-kuni*). In his rage Izanagi destroys the god of fire for his matricide, and in his grief he enters into the land of the dead to recover his wife. However, when he finds her and sees her decaying corpse, Izanami becomes enraged and pursues him with a host of demons. When he reaches the path between the land of the living and the land of the dead, Izanagi seals the path with a large stone. Following rituals of purification and grief (through which still more gods were created), Izanagi ascends to High Heaven, leaving the land of the living to the gods he has created. These gods continue to propagate and differentiate, eventually giving birth to the Imperial Family, the Japanese people, and the rest of the creatures and features of Japan.

This basic creation myth establishes the basic tripartite cosmology of the Shinto religion, consisting of High Heaven, the world of the living, and the world of the dead. It is also used to account for a wide variety of features of the cosmos, from such mundane features as the prevalence of fire (attributed to the pulverization of the god of fire for his matricide) to the victory of life over death (as embodied by the victory of Izanagi over Izanami at the path to the land of the dead). Although Japanese cosmology would become increasingly influenced by more pan-Asian religious and philosophical traditions—most notably, Buddhism—the Shinto cosmogony and cosmology laid out in the *Kojiki* and the *Nihongi* continue to influence popular belief in Japan. Indeed, insofar as these accounts serve to express the mythical origins of the Japanese people, they have become all the more influential as the Japanese have sought to develop and emphasize their own distinctive national identity.

everything from seasons to dynasties (for example, the *Shujing*, the *Xunzi*, the *Lüshi chunqiu* [*Springs and Autumns of Mr. Lü*]). Finally, the sixty-four hexagrams consist of sets of six lines that are each either broken (associated with *yin*) or unbroken (associated with *yang*); whereas earlier Chinese tradition had used these for the purposes of divination, Zhou cosmologists began to attribute cosmological significance to them by associating them with all of the possible types of change within the cosmos.

Whether explained with respect to *yin* and *yang*, the five agents, or the sixty-four hexagrams (texts often drew on all three), Chinese cosmologies ultimately grounded these differentiations in a common source. This is identified in a number of different ways, but most commonly as the Supreme Ultimate (*tiaji*, which generates *yin* and *yang*), or the Dao itself (which is prior even to the *taiji*). The primary point of Chinese cosmology is that, while the cosmos embodies a wide variety of oppositions, changes, and transformations, these are ultimately the natural expressions of an underlying cosmic balance and harmony. While subsequent Chinese would alter the precise nature of the grounding and differentiation of the cosmos, both the terms laid out in the Zhou and its emphasis on cosmic balance and harmony would remain landmarks of Chinese cosmology.

If the Zhou introduced the main tenets of Chinese cosmology, it was the Han (202 B.C.E.–220 C.E.) who brought these tenets together and systematized them. For example, it was during the Han that the great commentaries on the *Yijing* and the *Chunqiu* (*Spring and Autumn Annals*) were written. Characteristic of this systematization is the heightened role of correlative thinking, which takes on a detailed, precise, and often even numerical character. Perhaps the most prominent example of Han cosmology is that of Dong Zhongshu (c. 195–c. 105 B.C.E.), as found in his *Chunqiu fanlu* (*Luxuriant Gems of the Spring and Autumn Annals*). Whereas the *Yijing* had related all things on a general level, Dong related them in exact detail: every thing or event can be seen as the direct result of other things and events, resulting in a highly complicated but also highly ordered cosmos. More importantly, this order of the cosmos as a whole is replicated at every level of existence, such that the human body, social relations, and imperial governance are all seen to be perfect microcosms of the larger cosmos. Dong's interest in the *Chunqiu fanlu* thus arises from his desire to use past records of interaction to aid present decisions in better modeling the balance and harmony of the cosmos.

Yet for all of their systematization and rigor, Han cosmologies proved too rigid for subsequent dynasties. Scientific advances compromised the perfect order asserted by Han cosmologists, persistent political upheavals rendered many of their political associations irrelevant, and the introduction of Buddhism into China shifted philosophical interest away from cosmology and toward metaphysics. In the Song dynasty (960–1279 C.E.), which witnessed a revival of interest in classical Chinese sources amid the rise of Neo-Confucianism, many of the terms and concepts informing Chinese cosmology were revived—for example, Zhou Dunyi's *Taijitu shuo* (*Explanation of the Diagram of the Supreme Ultimate*) and Shao Yong's *Huangji jingshi shu* (*Book of the Supreme Ultimate Ordering the World*). In both the Song and the Ming (1368–1644 C.E.) dynasties, these concepts were often reworked with remarkable ingenuity—the most prominent example of this is Zhu Xi's (1130–1200 C.E.) reinterpretation of the cosmos in terms of *li* (principle) and *qi* (material form)—although it must be noted that Neo-Confucian interest, following the lead of Neo-Daoism and Buddhism, was decidedly more metaphysical than cosmological. Ultimately, not even this resurgence of interest succeeded in stemming the tide of increasing cosmological skepticism in Chinese thought.

In the Qing dynasty (1644–1912), this skepticism reached its height. Seventeenth-century China experienced a marked increase of interest and renaissance in mathematics, astronomy, and geography, due in part to the introduction of Western science by means of the Jesuits. However, these new studies ran counter to the Chinese traditions of numerology, correlation of the orders of heaven and earth, and geometric cosmogony, thus calling these traditions into serious question. Such critique was far from unprecedented (for example, Wang Chong [c .27–c. 100 C.E.], Ouyang Xiu [1007–1072 C.E.]), but it is only in the late Ming and Qing dynasties that scientific development had enough momentum to seriously call into question such long-standing Chinese traditions (for example, Gu Yenwu [1613–1682 C.E.], Wang Fuzhi [1619–1692 C.E.]). According to John Henderson, this shift was so significant as to inaugurate something of an "anti-cosmology"—a cosmology that, in contrast to the traditional Chinese approach via correlative thinking about an ordered cosmos, took irregularity and nonuniformity to be defining characteristics of the cosmos (for example, Wang Tingxiang [1474–1544 C.E.]). Henderson goes on to argue that it was ultimately this distrust of correlative thinking in cosmology that lead to a similar distrust of scientific models in China, thus effectively cutting it off from the broader scientific revolution and global cosmological conversation.

See also **Calendar; Cosmology: Cosmology and Astronomy; Time: China; Time: India.**

BIBLIOGRAPHY

Allan, Sarah. *The Shape of the Turtle: Myth, Art, and Cosmos in Early China.* Albany: State University of New York Press, 1991.

Aston, William George, trans. *Nihongi: Chronicles of Japan from the Earliest Times to A.D. 697.* Rutland, Vt.: Charles E. Tuttle, 1972.

Black, Alison Harley. *Man and Nature in the Philosophical Thought of Wang Fu-chih.* Seattle: University of Washington Press, 1989.

Chamberlain, Basil Hall. *The Kojiki: Records of Ancient Matters.* Rutland, Vt.: Charles E. Tuttle, 1982.

Chan, Wing-tsit. *A Source Book in Chinese Philosophy.* Princeton, N.J.: Princeton University Press, 1963.

De Bary, William Theodore, and Irene Bloom, comps. *Sources of Chinese Tradition: From Earliest Times to 1600.* 2nd ed. New York: Columbia University Press, 1999.

Flood, Gavin D. *An Introduction to Hinduism.* New York: Cambridge University Press, 1996.

Flood, Gavin D., ed. *The Blackwell Companion to Hinduism.* Malden, Mass.: Blackwell, 2003.

Gombrich, R. F. "Ancient Indian Cosmology." In *Ancient Cosmologies,* edited by Carmen Blacker and Michael Loewe, 110–142. London: Allen and Unwin, 1975.

Henderson, John B. *The Development and Decline of Chinese Cosmology.* Neo-Confucian Studies Series. New York: Columbia University Press, 1984.

Kinsley, David R. *Hinduism: A Cultural Perspective.* 2nd ed. Englewood Cliffs, N.J.: Prentice Hall, 1993.

Kloetzli, Randy. *Buddhist Cosmology: From Single World System to Pure Land—Science and Theology in the Images of Motion and Light.* Delhi: Motilal Banarsidass, 1983.

Klostermaier, Klaus K. *A Survey of Hinduism.* Albany: State University of New York Press, 1994.

Lopez, Donald S. *The Story of Buddhism: A Concise Guide to its History and Teachings.* San Francisco: HarperSanFrancisco, 2001.

Michaels, Axel. *Hinduism: Past and Present.* Translated by Barbara Harshav. Princeton, N.J.: Princeton University Press, 2004.

Miller, Jeanine. *The Vision of Cosmic Order in the Vedas.* Foreword by Raimundo Panikkar. Boston: Routledge and Kegan Paul, 1985.

Picken, Stuart D. B. *Essentials of Shinto: An Analytical Guide to Principle Teachings.* Westport, Conn.: Greenwood Press, 1994.

Radhakrishnan, Sarvepalli, and Charles Alexander Moore. *A Source Book in Indian Philosophy.* Princeton, N.J.: Princeton University Press, 1957.

Rosemont, Henry. *Explorations in Early Chinese Cosmology: Papers Presented at the Workshop on Classical Chinese Thought Held at Harvard University, August 1976.* Chico, Calif.: Scholars Press, 1984.

Sharma, Arvind. *Classical Hindu Thought: An Introduction.* Oxford and New York: Oxford University Press, 2000.

Soifer, Deborah A. *The Myths of Narasimha and Vāmana: Two Avatars in Cosmological Perspective.* Albany: State University of New York Press, 1991.

Walpola, Rāhula. *What the Buddha Taught.* Rev. ed. New York: Grove Press, 1974.

Wang, Aihe. *Cosmology and Political Culture in Early China.* Cambridge, U.K., and New York: Cambridge University Press, 2000.

Robert Smid

COSMOLOGY AND ASTRONOMY

Early cosmologies, or worldviews, envisioned a universe subject to the whims of gods and were anthropocentric: focused on the role and fate of human beings. As such, cosmology and religion were often intertwined.

Babylonian Cosmology

Elimination of everything other than empirical observation and mathematical computation from Babylonian astronomical texts of the Seleucid period has been hailed by some as the first appearance of modern science and cosmology. Ancient Babylonians studied how the celestial motions went, but not why. Nor did they seek causes for physical phenomena or develop comprehensive theories about the universe. Consequently, some scholars dismiss Babylonian cosmology and astronomy as merely a set of mechanical procedures with no more theoretical content than recipes in a cookbook. They look instead to the Greeks for the birth of modern science.

Greek Cosmology

For two millennia, the Aristotelian physical cosmology of rotating spheres carrying the sun, moon, planets, and stars around the central earth permeated Western thought. The natural place for earthy material was at the center of the universe, and earthy material tended to move to its natural place. Planetary spheres rotated because that was their natural motion. Aristotle's teleological explanations, with the world fulfilling a purpose formed by a superhuman mind, would not necessarily be incompatible with Christian philosophy, which also envisioned the world as inherently meaningful and purposive. Concurrent with Aristotle's physical cosmology was Plato's geometrical cosmology, in which astronomers strove "to save

the appearances": to explain apparently irregular planetary motions with combinations of circular motions at constant speeds.

In the context of modern science, saving the appearances with uniform circular motions is an arbitrary and absurd task. The task was, however, widely accepted and pursued for around two thousand years, from the Greeks in the fourth century B.C.E. through Copernicus and the European Renaissance in the sixteenth and seventeenth centuries C.E. The historical importance of a cosmology is not necessarily negated by its absurdity, especially when that label is applied in hindsight by different people in a different age with different standards and values.

Saving the appearances is plausible in the context of Plato's philosophy, which in turn can be understood as his reaction to the moral and political chaos of his age, which left him highly dissatisfied with the physical world. His concept of an ideal reality is simply illustrated. A circle drawn on paper is an imperfect representation in the visible world of experience of a perfect circle, which exists only in the world of thought. In his *Republic,* Plato wrote that the sky was part of the visible world, and the true revolutions of the planets, sun, and moon were to be discerned by reason and thought, not by sight.

Interregnum

Greek geometrical cosmology was systematized and advanced, with rigorous geometrical demonstrations and proofs, by Claudius Ptolemy (second century C.E.). He did for astronomy what Euclid had done for geometry and earned a reputation as the greatest astronomer of the ancient world. Indeed, his *Almagest,* of about 140 C.E., was so comprehensive that its predecessors ceased to be copied and failed to survive.

The match between Ptolemy's reported observations and his theory is too good to be true, and the *Almagest* has been called the greatest fraud in the history of science. It is not a modern scientific research paper, however, but a textbook, and it is in this context that Ptolemy should be judged. He made many observations; errors largely canceled each other out; and he thus obtained an accurate planetary theory. Next he would have selected a few observations in best agreement with the theory to illustrate it, and even fabricated examples to neaten up his pedagogy. The Greek astronomical tradition was far more concerned with general geometrical procedures than with specific numerical results.

Islamic scientists rescued the Aristotelian and Platonic cosmologies when Western civilization crumbled; they transmitted Greek learning back to the West when learning revived there. Initially, Aristotelian cosmology, including the eternity of the world and denial that God could make other worlds, seemingly contradicted dogmas of the Christian faith, and in the thirteenth century the bishop of Paris condemned hundreds of Aristotelian propositions. The condemnations helped free cosmology from Aristotelian dogma and also led to the nominalist, instrumentalist, or positivist thesis. Cosmology was understood as a working hypothesis, the truth of which could not be insisted upon because God could have made the world in a different manner but with the same observational consequences. Imaginative and ingenious discussions, including possible rotation of the earth, subsequently flourished.

Hypothetical cosmologies, however, are not the stuff of revolution. Confidence that the essential structure and operation of the cosmos is knowable would be essential to the achievements of Nicolaus Copernicus (1473–1543), Galileo Galilei (known as Galileo; 1564–1642), Johannes Kepler (1571–1630), and Isaac Newton (1642–1727).

The Copernican Revolution

Ptolemy's planetary theory matched observations, but in Copernicus's opinion, it violated the standard of uniform circular motion. Also, Ptolemy's scheme did not automatically produce phenomena that followed naturally in Copernicus's heliocentric model. An unauthorized foreword to Copernicus's 1543 *De revolutionibus orbium coelestium* presented the heliocentric theory as a convenient mathematical fiction. Copernicus, however, believed that he was describing the real world.

Revolutions in science, as in politics, often exceed the limited changes envisioned by their creators. The sphere carrying the stars was now obsolete, and soon human imagination distributed the stars throughout an infinite space. Furthermore, the earth was no longer unique. Galileo's telescopic observations emphasized that the moon was uneven and rough, like the earth. Also, Jupiter had four satellites similar to the earth's satellite.

Logical consequences of the Copernican system, Galileo's telescopic discoveries, and the principle of plenitude, which interpreted any unrealized potential in nature as a restriction of the Creator's power, all encouraged belief in a plurality of worlds. Also, political and societal critics used the moon as a literary convention, its inhabitants' arrangements being either a model of perfection or a mirror of the earth's vices. Faith in an anthropocentric universe lay shattered, leaving people's relationship with God uncertain. John Donne's 1611 poem *An Anatomy of the World,* its line the "new Philosophy calls all in doubt," and later "all Relation: / Prince, Subject, Father Son, are things forgot," refers to Christian morality as much as to the relative positions of the sun and earth.

The Newtonian Revolution

Tycho Brahe's (1546–1601) observations of comets coursing through the solar system shattered the Aristotelian crystalline spheres, and his observation of a nova, a star flaring up in brightness, pierced Aristotelian belief in an unchangeable heaven. Belief in uniform circular motion died next when Kepler used Brahe's observations to show that planets travel around the sun in elliptical orbits. A new explanation of how the planets retrace the same paths forever around the sun became a central problem of cosmology. Newton showed mathematically how a force of attraction or gravitation toward the sun continually draws planets away from straight-line motion and holds them in Kepler's elliptical orbits.

The Newtonian example of general laws in natural philosophy excited searches for general laws in other realms, including economics. In this branch of philosophy, Adam Smith

(1723–1790) played Newton's role. Also inspired by Newton's achievement, Voltaire (1694–1778) and Montesquieu (1689–1755) searched for natural laws of politics. The French Revolution owed much to Newton.

Newton was convinced that his discoveries demonstrated God's wonders. Yet the revolution in thought following from his new cosmology, particularly the concept of a mechanical, clocklike universe, threatened the historic link between cosmology and religion in Western thought. Writers of the Romantic period sought to breathe divine life back into an overly mechanized and increasingly godless universe. Under the sway of the French Enlightenment's atheistic approach to nature, however, Pierre-Simon Laplace (1749–1827) happily replaced the hypothesis of God's rule with a purely physical theory. According to legend, when Napoléon Bonaparte (1769–1821) asked Laplace whether he had left any place for the Creator, Laplace replied that he had no need of such a hypothesis.

The Newtonian solar system provided Immanuel Kant (1724–1804) a model for the larger stellar system. The same cause that gave the planets their centrifugal force, keeping them in orbits around the sun, could also have given the stars the power of revolving. And whatever made all the planets orbit in roughly the same plane could have done the same to the stars. Nebulous-appearing objects in the heavens became, in Kant's mind, island universes, like colossal solar systems. Late in the eighteenth century, William Herschel's (1738–1822) large telescopes expanded the heavens from a starry sphere to a three-dimensional firmament. He observed that most stars seemed to lie between two parallel planes. This stratum, seen from earth, is the Milky Way.

Twentieth-Century Cosmology

At the beginning of the twentieth century, it was generally thought that the Earth's galaxy was some ten thousand light-years across and that the solar system was near the center of the galaxy. This vision of the universe was soon replaced with a revolutionary new conception. Harlow Shapley at the Mount Wilson Observatory showed that the galaxy is hundreds of thousands of light-years in diameter and the solar system is far from its center. The significance of humans and their particular planet had dwindled still further. Shapley noted a historical progression from belief in a small universe with humankind at its center to a larger universe with the earth farther from the center. The geometry had been transformed from geocentric to heliocentric to acentric. The psychological change was no less, Shapley insisted, from homocentric to acentric. Furthermore, the galaxy containing the Earth is but one of many "island universes," as Edwin Hubble soon proved. Next Hubble found that the universe is expanding. Georges Lemaître, a Belgian priest and astrophysicist, explained the expansion of the universe from an initial "cosmic egg." Einstein confirmed that Lemaître's theoretical investigations fit well into the general theory of relativity.

Advances in nuclear physics fed speculations about an expanding universe resulting from thermonuclear reactions in an early, hot, dense phase. Fred Hoyle at mid-century derisively called it the "big bang," and the term stuck. Hoyle championed instead steady-state creation, in which the universe expands but does not change in density because new matter continuously appears. Pope Pius XII announced in 1951 that big-bang cosmology affirmed the notion of a transcendental creator and was in harmony with Christian dogma. Steady-state theory, denying any beginning or end to time, was associated with atheism, though Hoyle associated it with personal freedom and anticommunism. The debate was resolved observationally with detection of a faint cosmic background radiation, a remnant of the big bang.

In 1979 an American particle physicist, Alan Guth, proposed that important cosmological features can be explained as natural and inevitable consequences of new theories of particle physics. Guth's theory of inflation states that in the first minuscule fraction of a second of the universe's evolution, a huge inflation occurred. After that, the inflationary universe theory merges with the standard big-bang theory.

See also **Astrology; Cosmology: Asia.**

BIBLIOGRAPHY

Berendzen, Richard, Richard Hart, and Daniel Seeley. *Man Discovers the Galaxies.* New York: Science History Publications, 1976.

Crowe, Michael J. *Modern Theories of the Universe: From Herschel to Hubble.* New York: Dover Publications, 1994.

———. *Theories of the World from Antiquity to the Copernican Revolution.* New York: Dover Publications, 1990.

Duhem, Pierre. *To Save the Phenomena, an Essay on the Idea of Physical Theory from Plato to Galileo.* Translated by Edmund Doland and Chaninah Maschler, with an introductory essay by Stanley L. Jaki. Chicago: University of Chicago Press, 1969.

Hetherington, Norriss S. "Cosmic Journey: A History of Scientific Cosmology." Available at http://www.wavian.com/aip/cosmology/index.htm.

Hetherington, Norriss S., ed. *Encyclopedia of Cosmology: Historical, Philosophical, and Scientific Foundations of Modern Cosmology.* New York: Garland, 1993.

Hubble, Edwin. *The Realm of the Nebulae.* New Haven, Conn.: Yale University Press, 1936; repr. New York: Dover Publications, 1958.

Johnson, Francis R. *Astronomical Thought in Renaissance England: A Study of the English Scientific Writings from 1500 to 1645.* Baltimore: Johns Hopkins University Press, 1937; repr. New York: Octagon Books, 1968.

Koyré, Alexandre. *From the Closed World to the Infinite Universe.* Baltimore: Johns Hopkins University Press, 1957.

Kragh, Helge. *Cosmology and Controversy: The Historical Development of Two Theories of the Universe.* Princeton, N.J.: Princeton University Press, 1996.

Kuhn, Thomas S. *The Copernican Revolution: Planetary Astronomy in the Development of Western Thought.* Cambridge, Mass.: Harvard University Press, 1957.

Lovejoy, Arthur O. *The Great Chain of Being: A Study of the History of an Idea. The William James Lectures Delivered at Harvard University, 1933.* Cambridge, Mass.: Harvard University Press, 1936.

Neugebauer, Otto. *The Exact Sciences in Antiquity.* 2nd ed. New York: Dover Publications, 1969.

Nicholson, Marjorie. *A World in the Moon: A Study of the Changing Attitude toward the Moon in the Seventeenth and Eighteenth Centuries.* Northampton, Mass.: Smith College Department of Modern Languages, 1936.

Norriss Hetherington

COSMOPOLITANISM.

Cosmopolitanism refers to both a lifestyle incorporating aspects from all or many parts of the world and an ideology based upon the premise that every human shares, or should share, equal status as a "citizen of the world." The two are not exclusive of one another, but it is certainly possible to encounter either the ideal or the lifestyle without the presence of the other. Though similar to the concept of multiculturalism, cosmopolitanism should be distinguished from this term. Whereas cosmopolitanism entails the "recognition, acceptance, and eager exploration of diversity," multiculturalism includes more concern for boundary maintenance than for empathetic border crossings (Hollinger, p. 84).

The Ideal of Cosmopolitanism

The word *cosmopolitan* can be traced to the Greek Cynic philosophers Antisthenes (c. 445–365 B.C.E.) and his student Diogenes of Sinope (d. c. 320 B.C.E.). In the fourth century B.C.E., Diogenes likely responded to inquiry about his citizenship by boldly asserting, "I am a citizen of the world." His statement, though often used as a humanistic slogan, expressed a rather negative notion. Since he was not a citizen of any particular locale, he was not obligated to serve his particular city-state. He offered his allegiance to no single government. The Stoic philosopher Zeno of Citium (c. 335–c. 263 B.C.E.) articulated a similar sentiment, but with more constructive implications. He imagined citizenship as a series of concentric circles. The self inhabited the innermost ring of this inclusive model, followed by family, city, region, and so on. Thus Zeno understood the individual as a part of all other affiliations.

Early Christianity also offered a unique notion of cosmopolitanism: The disciple obtained a new, spiritual citizenship that transcended the bonds of local government and regional identity through following the teachings of Jesus. St. Paul (c. 66) expressed this in an open letter to devotees in Colossi, proposing that "there is no distinction between Greek and Jew, circumcised and uncircumcised, barbarian, Scythian, slave or free" (Col. 3:11). This deconstruction of status and ethnicity represented a significant development in the cosmopolitanism as a concept, even if the established Christian church has often been a source of division.

Several humanist intellectuals advocated a cosmopolitan ideology during the Enlightenment of the seventeenth and eighteenth centuries. The philosophes imagined themselves as inhabitants in a republic of letters that transcended mere national boundaries. Believing in the preeminence of reason and scientific discovery, these men forged bonds of intellectual discourse throughout the North Atlantic. The ideas of the German philosopher Immanuel Kant (1724–1804) were especially influential through the beginning of the twenty-first century.

His writing advocated perpetual peace between nation-states during a time when nations were still being defined.

Contemporary scholars have implemented the cosmopolitanism of nineteenth- and-early-twentieth-century Indians alongside that of Kant. Swami Vivekananda (1863–1902) united the teachings of the Indian religious leader Sri Ramakrishna (1836–1886) with claims of scientific validity to increase awareness of the physical and spiritual practice of yoga. His contemporary, the poet Rabindranath Tagore (1861–1941), an undoubted anticolonial himself, chided the political and religious leader Mohandas Gandhi (1869–1948) for his penchant toward national self-reliance. Instead, Tagore pleaded for a transnational interdependency. The work of these men still exercises influence upon spiritual and political cosmopolitanism.

In each of these contexts, the ideal of cosmopolitanism sought to eclipse local or regional loyalties with the belief that humans share a bond free from provincial affiliations. Whether predicated on mysticism or reason, cosmopolitanism as an ideal locates the individual within a world community. However, those espousing the ideal have not always turned this admirable belief into a reality. Religious exclusion and ethnic nationalism have continued to flourish despite these recurrent appearances of a cosmopolitan ideal. However, this is not to say that cosmopolitanism has not been practiced in various times and locales.

The Practice of Cosmopolitanism

As a lifestyle, cosmopolitanism embraces, participates in, and combines the customs of several different cultures. The cosmopolitan is not tethered by local or national habits and prejudices. Rather, he or she welcomes encounters with those from different regions and aspires to fluidly navigate from one cultural context to another.

Cosmopolitanism has been achieved in disparate historical and geographical settings. The Ottoman Empire of the fifteenth and sixteenth centuries encouraged the mingling of Northern African, Iberian, and Middle Eastern peoples. In the medieval period, Islamic scholars incorporated the works of ancient Greeks into their learning. Cities such as Istanbul became centers of trade and cosmopolitanism, even housing Freemasonry lodges in the nineteenth century.

At times, people may adapt a cosmopolitan way of life out of necessity as opposed to ideological conviction. Daniel M. Swetschinski's study of Portuguese Jews in the Netherlands of the seventeenth century recounts an historical setting in which members of a displaced ethnic group incorporated the customs of others. These "reluctant cosmopolitans," as Swetschinski calls them, became part of the flourishing Danish mercantilism. Landing in ports all throughout the Atlantic and Mediterranean, they interacted with multiple cultures while maintaining a Jewish identity.

Certain social groups are almost always associated with cosmopolitanism. Intellectuals, diplomats, creative artists, the wealthy, and merchants each to a certain extent maintain a lifestyle that might be described as cosmopolitan. Certainly since the time of the Enlightenment, academia has extended beyond local influence. Intellectual communities, in both the humanities and the sciences, collaborate and compete along disciplinary lines rather than national borders. Diplomats, by the very nature of their profession, must be charming in midst of profound cultural difference. Adaptability to unique settings and a thorough understanding of distinct worldviews qualify political emissaries. Visual, literary, and performing artists, as well as their patrons, have long displayed a fascination with exotic subjects and media. International movements within the arts often indicate the merging of traditionally distinct ideas and people-groups. Historically, though, one need not display any of the aforementioned skills to live a cosmopolitan life. A person might become a world citizen by possessing the means to travel extensively. By journeying to distant climes, speaking foreign languages, and acquiring and displaying exotic goods, the wealthy could be included among the ranks of other cosmopolitans.

However, perhaps more than any other social group, merchants have both exemplified cosmopolitan lifestyles and prompted others to do the same. With the emergence of global capitalism, traders and business people are regularly in contact with multiple cultures and ethnic groups. Transnational enterprise demands its participants be capable of interacting with diverse populations. Moreover, through the commodification of goods produced in foreign lands, merchants encourage consumers to desire nonindigenous wares.

Opposition to Cosmopolitanism

Cosmopolitanism, as both an ideal and a lifestyle, has often been critiqued. Given those who have historically been considered cosmopolitans, it is not surprising that skeptics label it elitist. Cosmopolitanism most often required either remarkable talent or extraordinary financial means, and sometimes both. The vast majority of people simply did not have the option to participate in such a life.

Nationalists and some ethnic leaders have also attacked the concept. Because cosmopolitans lack the "roots" of others, these critics believe they cannot be loyal to the political process of a given geographic region. Ethnic essentialists are similar in that they disdain cosmopolitanism because it involves the internalization of others' cultural beliefs and practices. To the essentialist, people simply are not able to fit into any ethnic group other than their own.

Ironically, global capitalism coupled with national and religious extremism has created a nonelite group of cosmopolitans. Immigrants and refugees now bring a heterogeneous picture of humanity from their respective homelands. Moreover, relatively affordable travel and dazzlingly diverse urban landscapes bring the exotic within reach of many. In the technologically saturated, polyethnic world of the twenty-first century, the ideal and the practice of cosmopolitanism seem much more similar than they have in the past.

See also **Intelligentsia; Migration; Nationalism; Society.**

BIBLIOGRAPHY

Hollinger, David A. *Postethnic America: Beyond Multiculturalism.* New York: Basic Books, 1995.

Nussbaum, Martha Craven. *For Love of Country: Debating the Limits of Patriotism.* Edited by Joshua Cohen. Boston: Beacon Press, 1996.

Schlereth, Thomas J. *The Cosmopolitan Ideal in Enlightenment Thought: Its Form and Function in the Ideas of Franklin, Hume, and Voltaire, 1694–1790.* Notre Dame, Ind.: University of Notre Dame Press, 1977.

Swetschinski, Daniel. *Reluctant Cosmopolitans: The Portuguese Jews of Seventeenth-Century Amsterdam.* London: Littman Library of Jewish Civilization, 2000.

Vertovec, Steven, and Robin Cohen, eds. *Conceiving Cosmopolitanism: Theory, Context, and Practice.* New York: Oxford University Press, 2003. Diverse collection and rich bibliography.

Kevin James Houk

COSTUME. *See* Dress.

CREATIONISM.

Creationism in a general sense refers to the theory that God made the world on his own, by miraculous means, out of nothing. In a more specific sense, the one encountered in America today, creationism is the theory that the Bible, particularly the early chapters of Genesis, is a literally true guide to the history of the universe and to the history of life, including us humans, down here on earth. This encompasses a number of beliefs: a short time since the beginning of everything ("Young Earth Creationists" think that Archbishop Ussher's sixteenth-century calculation of about 6,000 years is a good estimate); six days of creation (there is debate on the meaning of "day" in this context, with some insisting on a literal twenty-four hours, and others more flexible); miraculous creation of all life including Homo sapiens (with scope for debate about whether Adam and Eve came together or if Eve came afterward to keep Adam company); a worldwide flood some time after the initial creation, through which only a limited number of humans and animals survived; and other events such as the Tower of Babel and the turning of Lot's wife into a pillar of salt. Creationists have variously been known as fundamentalists or biblical literalists, and sometimes (especially when they are pushing the scientific grounds for their beliefs) as scientific creationists. Today's creationists are often marked by enthusiasm for so-called intelligent design.

History of Creationism

Creationists present themselves as the true bearers and present-day representatives of authentic traditional Christianity, but historically speaking this is simply not true. The Bible has a major place in the life of any Christian, but it is not the case that the Bible taken literally has always had a major place in the lives or theology of Christians. Tradition, the teachings and authority of the Church, has always had main status for Catholics, and natural religion—approaching God through reason and argument—has long had an honored place for both Catholics and Protestants. Catholics, especially dating back to Saint Augustine (354–430), and even to earlier thinkers like Origen (c. 185–254), have always recognized that at times the Bible needs to be taken metaphorically or allegorically. Augustine was particularly sensitive to this need, because for many years as a young man he was a Manichean and hence denied the authenticity and relevance of the Old Testament for salvation. When he became a Christian he knew full well the problems of Genesis and hence was eager to help his fellow believers avoid the traps of literalism.

It was not until the Protestant Reformation that the Bible started to take on its unique central position, as the great Reformers—especially Martin Luther (1483–1546) and John Calvin (1509–1564)—stressed the need to go by Scripture alone and not by the traditions of the Catholic Church. But even they were doubtful about totally literalistic readings. For Luther, justification by faith was the keystone of his theology, and yet the Epistle of Saint James seems to put greater stress on the need for good works. He referred to it as "right strawy stuff." Calvin likewise spoke of the need for God to accommodate his writings to the untutored public—especially the ancient Jews—and hence of the dangers of taking the Bible too literally in an uncritical sense. The radical branch of the Reformation under Huldrych Zwingli (1484–1531) always put primacy on God's speaking directly to us through the heart, and to this day one finds modern-day representatives like the Quakers uncomfortable with too biblically centered an approach to religion.

Eighteenth- and nineteenth-century revivals. It was really not until the revivals of the eighteenth and early nineteenth century in Britain and America—revivals that led to such sects as the Methodists—that a more full-blooded literalism became a major part of the religious scene. Then, the emphasis was on Christ's dying on the cross for our sins (the Atonement), the priesthood of all believers, and the primacy of the Bible as a guide to the converted heart, although even then there were many opposed, often quite violently. To take but one example, the most significant movement within the Church of England (Anglicanism; Episcopalianism in America) was the High Church movement known as Tractarianism, the Oxford movement of the 1830s, led most significantly by the future Catholic cardinal, John Henry Newman (1801–1890). No one was more vitriolic and sarcastic on the subject of biblical literalism than was Newman. In one of his major writings, Tract 85, he ridiculed those who would use the Bible as a guide to science or religion, and, with the vigor of a hardened humanist, he pointed out inconsistencies in the sacred book.

In America particularly, however, literalism did take hold, and especially after the Civil War (1861–1865), it took root in the evangelical sects—especially Baptists—of the South. It became part of the defining culture of the South, having as much a role in opposing ideas and influences of the North as anything rooted in deeply considered theology. This was the time of Charles Darwin (1809–1882), whose great work, *On the Origin of Species* (1859), provoked much theological opposition. But for the great Christian opponents—Samuel Wilberforce (1805–1873), bishop of Oxford in England, and Charles Hodge (1797–1878), principal of Princeton Theological Seminary in America—simple biblical literalism was far from the front of the objections. They were certainly keen on what became pretty standard arguments against evolution in general and Darwinism in particular. Gaps in the fossil record played a major role, as did the origin of life and the nonexistence of the direct observation of natural selection changing species. But crude reference to the Bible had no place in their scheme of things. Six thousand years of earth history was as far from the thinking of Wilberforce and Hodge as it was from that of Darwin. Problems of natural theology were far more pressing, as were topics that only tangentially have their basis in Genesis, such as the existence of immortal souls.

Early twentieth century. Creationism became more than just a local phenomenon in the early part of the twentieth century, thanks to a number of factors. First, there were the first systematic attempts to work out a position that would take account of modern science as well as a literal reading of Genesis. Particularly important in this respect were the Seventh Day Adventists, especially the Canadian-born George McCready Price (1870–1963), who had theological reasons for preferring literalism, not the least being the belief that the Seventh Day—the day of rest—is literally twenty-four hours in length. (Also important for the Adventists and for other dispensationalists—that is, people who think that Armageddon is on its way—is the balancing and complementary early phenomenon of a worldwide flood.) Second, there was the realized energy of evangelicals as they succeeded in their attempts to prohibit liquor in the United States. Flushed from one victory, they looked for other fields to conquer. Third, there was the spread of public education, which exposed more children to evolutionary ideas, provoking a creationist reaction. Fourth, there were new evangelical currents afloat, especially the *Fundamentals,* tracts that gave the literalist movement its name. And fifth, there was the identification of evolution—Darwinism particularly—with the militaristic aspects of Social Darwinism, especially the Social Darwinism supposedly embraced by the Germans in World War I.

The "Scopes Monkey Trial." This battle between evolutionists and "fundamentalists" came to a head in 1925 in Dayton, Tennessee, when a young schoolteacher, John Thomas Scopes (1900–1970), was prosecuted for teaching evolution in class, in defiance of a state law prohibiting such teaching. There was more at stake than just the facts, evolution versus the Bible. Local businesspeople welcomed the opportunity of a high-profile court case to put their community on the map and to reap financial rewards. The American Civil Liberties Union (ACLU), backing the defense, was eager for such a case to bolster its standing with America's liberals and to highlight its existence (it was founded in 1920). Indeed, the ACLU actively sought out someone who would be willing to stand trial. Prosecuted by the three-time presidential candidate William Jennings Bryan (1860–1925) and defended by the noted agnostic lawyer Clarence Darrow (1857–1938), the "Scopes Monkey Trial" caught the attention of the world, especially thanks to the inflammatory reporting of the *Baltimore Sun* journalist H. L. Mencken (1880–1956). Matters descended to the farcical when, denied the opportunity to introduce his own science witnesses, Darrow put on the stand the prosecutor Bryan. In the end, Scopes was found guilty and fined $100, although this was overturned on a technicality on

appeal. Despite never again being enforced, the Tennessee law remained on the books for another forty years.

Toward the Present

After the *Scopes* trial, the creationism movement declined quite dramatically and quickly. This was not due to Americans losing interest in the science-religion relationship, for now was the time of the foundation of such organizations as the American Scientific Affiliation, which tried seriously to seek a meeting ground between science and various forms of evangelical Christianity. But as is shown well by the trials of this particular organization—forever torn by the quarrels over geology and evolution—full-blooded Creationism no longer captured universal support among biblical Christians. Yet Creationism had its lasting effects, in that textbook manufacturers increasingly took evolution—Darwinism especially—out of their books, so that schoolchildren got less and less exposure to the ideas anyway. Whatever battles the evolutionists may have thought they had won in the court of popular opinion, in the trenches of the classroom they were losing the war badly.

Things started to move again in the late 1950s. A major factor was that, in the years since the *Scopes* trial, evolutionary thinking had not stood still. Indeed, the three decades from 1930 to 1960 were times of great ferment and development, for Mendelian genetics (and after this, molecular genetics) had reached such a point that it could be synthesized with Darwinian selection to make a fully integrated evolutionary theory, known variously as "neo-Darwinism" or the "synthetic theory of evolution." Naturally enough, evolutionists were excited and vocal about their advances, and particularly contemptuous of all who did not follow them down to the last detail. At celebrations in 1959 in Chicago to celebrate the hundredth anniversary of the publication of *On the Origin of Species,* fundamentalist objectors to the new paradigm were objects of particular scorn. This set a general background of unease and determination by biblical literalists, adding to a causal mix that had already started to ferment a year or two earlier when a more specific yeast had been added. It was then that, thanks to Sputnik, the Russians so effectively demonstrated their superiority in rocketry (with its implications for the arms race of the cold war), and America realized how ineffective was the scientific training of its young. In response, the country poured money into the production of new science texts. In this way, with class adoption, the federal government could have a strong impact and yet get around the problem that education tends to be under the tight control of individual states. The new biology texts gave full scope to evolution—to Darwinism—and with this the creationism controversy again flared up.

Fortunately for the literalist, help was at hand. A biblical scholar, John C. Whitcomb Jr., and a hydraulic engineer, Henry M. Morris, together wrote what was to be the new Bible of the movement, *Genesis Flood: The Biblical Record and its Scientific Implications* (1961). Following in the tradition of earlier writers, especially those from Seventh Day Adventism, they argued that every bit of the biblical story of creation given in the early chapters of Genesis is supported fully by the best of modern science. Six days of twenty-four hours, organisms arriving miraculously, humans last, and sometime thereafter a massive worldwide flood that wiped most organisms off the face of the earth—or rather, dumped their carcasses in the mud as the waters receded. At the same time, Whitcomb and Morris argued that the case for evolution fails dismally. The gaps in the fossil record show that there can have been no evolution; the nature of natural selection is such that it allows no genuine check and even if it did, it could not account for the complexity of life; the measures of earth time are dicey; and much, much more.

Genesis Flood enjoyed massive popularity among the faithful, and led to a thriving creation science movement, where Morris particularly and his coworkers and believers—notably Duane T. Gish, author of *Evolution: The Fossils Say No!*—pushed the literalist line. Particularly effective was their challenging of evolutionists to debate, where they would employ every rhetorical trick in the book, reducing the scientists to fury and impotence with their bold statements about the supposed nature of the universe. By the end of the 1970s, creationists were passing around draft bills, intended for state legislatures, that would allow—insist on—the teaching of creationism in state-supported public schools. In the biology classes of such schools, that is. By this time it was realized that, thanks to Supreme Court rulings on the First Amendment to the Constitution (which prohibits the establishment of state religion), it was not possible to exclude the teaching of evolution from such schools. The trick was to get creationism—something that prima facie rides straight through the separation of church and state—into such schools. The idea of creation science is to do this—although the science parallels Genesis, as a matter of scientific fact, it stands alone as good science. Hence, these draft bills proposed what was called "balanced treatment." If one was to teach the "evolution model," then one had also to teach the "creation science model." Sauce for the evolutionist goose is also sauce for the creationist gander. In 1981, these drafts found a taker in Arkansas, where such a bill was passed and signed into law—as it happens, by a legislature and governor that thought little of what they were doing until the consequences were drawn to their attention.

At once the American Civil Liberties Union sprang into action, bringing suit on grounds of the law's unconstitutionality. The judge agreed, ruling firmly that creation science is not science, it is religion, and as such has no place in public classrooms. And that was an end to matters, reinforced by a similar decision (that did not go to trial but that was appealed all the way up to the Supreme Court) in Louisiana.

Phillip Johnson and Naturalism

Nevertheless, by the beginning of the 1990s, creationism had again reared its head. The spark was an antievolutionary tract, *Darwin on Trial* (1991), by a Berkeley law professor, Phillip Johnson. Although smoother in presentation, the work covered familiar ground: gaps in the record, the complexity of DNA, the origin of life, the randomness of mutation. The main difference in Johnson's strategy was to turn the debate in the direction of philosophy. He argued that the creation-evolution debate was not just one of science versus religion or

good science versus bad science, but rather of conflicting philosophical positions—with the implication that one philosophy is much like another, or rather with the implication that one person's philosophy is another person's poison and that it is all a matter of personal opinion. Thus, if it is all a matter of philosophy, there is nothing in the U.S. Constitution that bars the teaching of creationism in schools.

Crucial to Johnson's position are a number of fine distinctions. He distinguishes between what he calls "methodological naturalism" and "metaphysical naturalism," and contrasts them with what he calls "Christian theism" or "theistic realism." A methodological naturalist is one who assumes there is no god when he or she does science. All must be explained through unbroken law. A metaphysical naturalist is one who believes that there is no god. He or she is directly opposed to any kind of theist, who starts with the assumption that there is a god who was and is active in the creation. According to Johnson, although you might think that you can be a methodological naturalist, something which he links with evolutionism, without necessarily being a metaphysical naturalist, in real life the former always slides into the latter. Hence, the evolutionist is the methodological naturalist, is the metaphysical naturalist, is the opponent of the theistic naturalist, which for Johnson is the equivalent of denying God's existence—that is, denying theistic realism. So ultimately, it is all less a matter of science and more a matter of attitude and philosophy. Evolution and creationism are different world pictures, and it is conceptually, socially, pedagogically, and with good luck in the future, legally wrong to treat them differently. More than this, Johnson's argument suggests that creationism (a.k.a. theistic realism) is the only genuine form of Christianity.

Irreducible Complexity

One oft-made criticism of Johnson was that he was too negative. It was obvious that he was against evolution, but he left unsaid whether he was a young-earth creationist like Whitcomb and Morris or whether he believed in something more moderate, perhaps an old earth and some kind of guided, law-bound creation. Later in the decade, with Johnson's encouragement, a number of younger thinkers produced an alternative to Darwinian evolution. This they called "intelligent design theory." There are two parts to this approach, beginning with the empirical. Lehigh University biochemist Michael Behe identifies something that he calls "irreducible complexity." This is "a single system composed of several well-matched, interacting parts that contribute to the basic function, wherein the removal of any one of the parts causes the system to effectively cease functioning." Behe points out that there is no way that something like this could be produced by a slow, gradual evolutionary process, for all of the parts need to be in place in order to get any functioning.

But are there such systems in nature? Behe argues that there are, and he instances the micro-world of the cell and of mechanisms (or "mechanisms") found at that level. Take bacteria, which use a flagellum, driven by a kind of rotary motor, to move around. Every part is incredibly complex, as are the various parts combined. The external filament of the flagellum (called a "flagellin"), for instance, is a single protein that makes a kind of paddle surface contacting the liquid during swimming. Near the surface of the cell, just as necessary is a thickening agent, so that the filament can be connected to the rotor drive. This requires a connector, known as a "hook protein." There is no motor in the filament, so that has to be somewhere else. "Experiments have demonstrated that it is located at the base of the flagellum, where electron microscopy shows several ring structures occur" (p. 70). All are much too complex to have come into being in a gradual fashion. Only a one-step process will do, and this one-step process must involve some sort of designing cause. Behe is careful not to identify this designer with the Christian God, but the implication is that it is a force from without the normal course of nature. Darwinism is ruled out and we must look for another explanation. There is only one possible answer. Irreducible complexity spells design.

The Explanatory Filter

Backing the empirical argument are the conceptual arguments of the philosopher-mathematician William Dembski, who introduced the notion of an "explanatory filter." We have a particular phenomenon. The question is, what caused it? Is it something that might not have happened, given the laws of nature? Is it contingent? Or was it necessitated? The moon goes endlessly round the earth. We know that it does this because of Newton's laws. End of discussion. No design here. However, now we have some rather strange new phenomenon, the causal origin of which is a puzzle. Suppose we have a mutation, where although we can quantify over large numbers we cannot predict at an individual level. There is no immediate subsumption beneath law, and therefore there is no reason to think that at this level it was necessary. Let us say, as supposedly happened in the extended royal family of Europe, there was a mutation to a gene responsible for hemophilia. Is it complex? Obviously not, for it leads to breakdown rather than otherwise. Hence it is appropriate to talk now of chance. There is no design. The hemophilia mutation was just an accident.

Suppose now that we do have complexity. A rather intricate mineral pattern in the rocks might qualify here. Suppose we have veins of precious metals set in other materials, the whole being intricate and varied—certainly not a pattern you could simply deduce from the laws of physics or chemistry or geology or whatever. Nor would one think of it as being a breakdown mess, as one might a malmutation. Is this now design? Almost certainly not, for there is no way that one might prespecify such a pattern. It is all a bit ad hoc, and not something that comes across as the result of conscious intention. And then finally there are phenomena that are complex and specified. One presumes that the microscopical biological apparatuses and processes discussed by Behe would qualify here. They are contingent, for they are irreducibly complex. They are design-like for they do what is needed for the organism in which they are to be found. That is to say they are of pre-specified form. And so, having survived the explanatory filter, they are properly considered the product of real design.

Although his arguments are philosophical, Dembski and his supporters see his work as supportive of the empirical case made by Behe. Most particularly, it speaks to an obvious

theological problem that is raised by irreducible complexity. If indeed such a phenomenon exists and if one has to suppose a designer to explain its origins, then presumably this designer was also involved in the production of the reducibly simple. And this being so, why did he do such a bad job? We have some mutations, like sickle-cell anemia, that have horrendous physical effects causing massive pain, and yet are triggered by the smallest of changes at the molecular level. Surely the designer could have prevented these? Not so, according to Dembski. Malmutations are just chance, and hence no one's fault, especially not that of the designer. Hence he gets credit for the good and is saved from blame for the bad.

Conclusion

Not surprisingly, many Christians (both Protestant and Catholic) as well as scientists object strongly both to traditional creationism and to the more recent intelligent design theory. Both Christians and scientists deny vehemently that being a methodological naturalist at once tips you into being a metaphysical naturalist. In addition, Christians assert, as they always have, that creationism in any form is a distortion of real traditional Christianity. There is absolutely no warrant for literalistic readings of Genesis, whether or not they are dressed up as science. In like fashion, scientists object that traditional creationism (the kind to be found in *Genesis Flood*) is simply wrong in every respect, and that intelligent design is little better. It simply is not true to say that there are examples of irreducible complexity that could never be explained through evolution. Even if all the parts are now necessary for proper functioning, it may well have been the case that the parts were assembled in ways that allowed for incomplete (or completely different) functioning before they reached their present interconnected forms.

Yet, whether or not creationism is good or bad religion, and whether or not creationism is good or bad science, it would be foolish to deny its ongoing appeal. In the early twenty-first century, opinion polls regularly found that 50 percent of Americans supported some form of creationism, and most of the others thought that blind law could never, unaided, have led to the production of the higher animals, especially humans. It would therefore be unwise to pretend that creationism is about to go away or will never raise its political head. It still has the potential to force us back to the 1920s and to attempt to legislate the contents of the science curricula of publicly funded schools.

See also **Evolution; Fundamentalism; Religion; Religion and Science.**

BIBLIOGRAPHY

Behe, Michael. *Darwin's Black Box: The Biochemical Challenge to Evolution.* New York: Free Press, 1996.

Brooks, Deborah J. "Substantial Numbers of Americans Continue to Doubt Evolution as Explanation for Origin of Humans." Poll Analyses, Gallup News Service, 3 May 2001.

Dembski, William A. *The Design Inference: Eliminating Chance through Small Probabilities.* Cambridge, U.K.: Cambridge University Press, 1998.

———, ed. *Mere Creation: Science, Faith, and Intelligent Design.* Downers Grove, Ill.: InterVarsity Press, 1998.

Gilbert, James. *Redeeming Culture in an Age of Science.* Chicago: University of Chicago Press, 1997.

Gish, Duane T. *Evolution: The Fossils Say No!* San Diego: Creation-Life, 1973.

Johnson, Phillip E. *Darwin on Trial.* Washington, D.C.: Regnery Gateway, 1991.

———. *Reason in the Balance: The Case against Naturalism in Science, Law, and Education.* Downers Grove, Ill.: InterVarsity Press, 1995.

Larson, Edward J. *Summer for the Gods: The Scopes Trial and America's Continuing Debate over Science and Religion.* New York: BasicBooks, 1997.

McMullin, Ernan, ed. *Evolution and Creation.* Notre Dame, Ind.: University of Notre Dame Press, 1985.

Miller, Kenneth. *Finding Darwin's God.* New York: Cliff Street Books, 1999.

Numbers, Ronald L. *The Creationists: The Evolution of Scientific Creationism.* New York: Knopf, 1992.

———. *Darwinism Comes to America.* Cambridge, Mass.: Harvard University Press, 1998.

Ruse, Michael, ed. *But Is It Science? The Philosophical Question in the Creation/Evolution Controversy.* Buffalo, N.Y.: Prometheus, 1988.

———. *Can a Darwinian Be a Christian? The Relationship between Science and Religion.* Cambridge, U.K.: Cambridge University Press, 2001.

Turner, Frank M. *John Henry Newman: The Challenge to Evangelical Religion.* New Haven, Conn.: Yale University Press, 2002.

Webb, George E. *The Evolution Controversy in America.* Lexington: University Press of Kentucky, 1994.

Whitcomb, John C., Jr., and Henry M. Morris. *The Genesis Flood: The Biblical Record and Its Scientific Implications.* Philadelphia, Pa.: Presbyterian and Reformed, 1961.

Michael Ruse

CREATIVITY IN THE ARTS AND SCIENCES.

Because creativity is a complex concept, it has multiple definitions. Of the various conceptions, however, three are currently most common. These are the product, person, and process definitions. According to the first, creativity is manifested in an identifiable outcome, such as a poem, painting, invention, or discovery. Moreover, this product must fulfill two essential conditions. First, it must be original or novel, at least with respect to an individual's discipline or culture. Simply repeating what has already been done does not count as bona fide creativity. Second, the product must be useful in some manner. For instance, a scientific discovery will have to satisfy certain theoretical or experimental standards, whereas an artistic creation will have to meet specific aesthetic criteria. This second condition is required to separate creative products from original but psychotic hallucinations and delusions.

The remaining two definitions are closely related to the product definition but shift perspective on the phenomenon. According to the person definition, creativity is whatever attributes individuals must possess to conceive creative products. These attributes may include both cognitive traits, such as intelligence, and personality traits, such as motivation. For the process definition, in contrast, creativity is the process or set of processes by which a person conceives creative products. This definition obliges the investigator to focus on various problem-solving operations, such as insight, intuition, incubation, and even trial and error.

The choice of definition clearly determines how a researcher or scholar studies creativity. Where some assess the attributes of creative products, others examine the characteristics of creative persons, and still others scrutinize the features of the creative process. Nevertheless, despite the diversity of analytical perspectives, it is assumed that all three approaches are looking at the same underlying phenomenon.

Creativity can be manifested in a great variety of situations, from the play activities of young children to industrial research and development teams. However, discussion here will be confined to creativity in the arts and sciences. The discussion begins with historical conceptions of creativity and ends with an overview of contemporary research on the phenomenon.

Historical Conceptions

As a concept, creativity is most strongly associated with European civilization. This is not because other civilizations have not displayed creativity. On the contrary, there is no doubt that other world civilizations—such as the Chinese, Indian, and Islamic—have produced creative geniuses of the highest order. The difference stems largely from how creativity is conceived in various cultures. The basis for the difference is to be found in the very definition of the phenomenon. Although an idea is not creative unless it is both original and useful, the exact proportions of originality and usefulness are not fixed.

At the same time, world civilizations vary greatly in the relative importance they place on individualism versus collectivism. Therefore, more individualistic cultures assign more weight to originality because that feature provides a means to demonstrate personal uniqueness. In contrast, more collectivist cultures tend to stress usefulness. To be "useful" in that case means that an original idea must be compatible with societal values and cultural traditions. If not, then those ideas cannot work insofar as they would prove divisive rather than consensual.

This cultural contrast can be illustrated by looking at philosophical creativity. On the originality-individualistic side is René Descartes (1596–1650), who launches his inquiry by doubting everything he has ever learned and experienced, eventually arriving at a highly egocentric, even autistic first principle—I think, therefore I am (*cogito, ergo sum*)—on which he could base his entire philosophy. On the usefulness-collectivist side is Shankara (c. 700–c. 750), the Indian thinker who communicated his highly influential Vedanta philosophy by writing commentaries on the principal Upanishads and other ancient scriptures. Although great philosophers in other intellectual traditions frequently use the same modus operandi, this tactic is extremely rare in European civilization. Even in the Middle Ages, when Greco-Roman individualism had to yield some ground to the more collectivist values of Christianity, intellectual innovations were seldom embedded in commentaries on traditional texts. For example, Thomas Aquinas's (1225–1274)

Sixteenth-century painting by Qiu Ying depicting Li Bo receiving visitors. Although the concept of genius being linked to madness or unconventional behavior was more prevalent in European societies, one exception was the Chinese poet Li Bo, a reputed drunkard and carefree wanderer. THE ART ARCHIVE / PRIVATE COLLECTION PARIS / DAGLI ORTI

Summa Theologica (1266–1273) synthesized classical philosophy and Christian theology not through commentaries on Aristotle and Augustine but rather by means of a stand-alone treatise. Admittedly, like all generalizations about whole civilizations, many exceptions exist. For instance, the place of poetic creativity in China is not unlike that in Europe.

In any case, although historical conceptions of creativity are quite diverse, three views have been especially prominent: divinity, madness, and craft.

Divinity. In antiquity, creativity was a divine attribute, a capacity narrated in the creation myths that are almost universal in human cultures. Examples include the Creator of the Judeo-Christian-Islamic tradition, Odin of Norse mythology, Ormazd of Zoroastrianism, and Brahma of the Hindu trinity. Even when creativity was attributed to individual human beings, the ultimate source often remained spiritual. This connection is illustrated in the ancient Greek belief in the Muses. According to the myth, Zeus, the reigning god in the pan-

theon, fathered nine daughters with Mnemosyne, the goddess of memory. Each of these nine daughters presided over a different domain of human creativity. In particular, these muses were responsible for epic poetry, lyric poetry, sacred poetry and hymns, tragedy, comedy, music, dance, astronomy, and history. Each muse was thought to provide a guiding spirit or source of inspiration for the mortal creator. This usage underlies several common expressions, such as to say that one has lost one's muse when one has run out of creative ideas. Given this view, human creativity remained subordinate to divine creativity.

The religious or spiritual roots of creativity are also evident in the concept of genius, an idea that would later become intimately identified with creativity. According to Roman mythology, each individual was born with a guardian spirit who watched out for the person's distinctive fate and individuality. With time, the term was taken to indicate the person's special talents or aptitudes. Although in the beginning everybody could be said to "have a genius," at least in the sense of pos-

CORE CONTROVERSIES CONCERNING CREATIVITY

Despite the abundance of scientific research on the subject of creativity, several central issues continue to escape successful resolution. Of these, the following three are probably most critical:

1. Nature versus Nurture—Is creative genius born or made? Or, to phrase the question in less dichotomous terms, what are the relative contributions of genetic endowment and environmental influences, such as family background, education, and training? One special manifestation of this question regards how gender, race, and ethnicity determine individual creativity.

2. Madness versus Mental Health—How much truth is there to the traditional concept of the "mad genius"? Although both psychiatrists and psychologists continue to find provocative connections between creativity and psychopathology, it is also clear that the two phenomena are far from equivalent. Furthermore, humanistic psychologists argue that creativity can actually be considered a sign of supreme mental health.

3. Individual versus Society—To what extent is creativity embodied in the individual and to what extent is creativity a representation of larger sociocultural phenomena? This is often expressed as the debate between genius and zeitgeist theories of creativity. Because psychologists, psychoanalysts, and psychiatrists favor the individual as the unit of analysis, they tend to support some form of the genius theory. In contrast, anthropologists, sociologists, and Marxist philosophers, who prefer cultures and societies as analytical units, are more prone to advocate some version of the zeitgeist theory.

Probably any resolution will be inclusive rather than exclusive. That is, creativity will eventually emerge as a function of nature and nurture, madness and mental health, the individual and society.

---

sessing a unique potential, the term eventually began to be confined to those whose gifts set them well apart from the average, such as the creative genius. Outstanding creativity then became the gift of the gods or spirits, not a human act. Even during the Italian Renaissance rudiments of this ascription persisted. For instance, when Giorgio Vasari (1511–1574) wrote his biography of the "divine Michelangelo," he explicitly asserted that "the great Ruler of Heaven" sent the artist to earth to serve as an exemplar of artistic genius.

Madness. As European civilization became increasingly secularized, especially after the Enlightenment, creativity's spiritual connotations gave way to more naturalistic conceptions. One prominent viewpoint was that creativity, and especially creative genius, was closely linked to madness. This linkage became especially popular during Europe's Romantic period, attaining a peak in the first half of the nineteenth century. It was also during this period that creative genius began to become associated with alcoholism, drug addiction, and other pathological conditions. In the Preface to "Kubla Khan," for example, Samuel Taylor Coleridge (1772–1834) claimed to have conceived this poetic masterpiece in an opium stupor.

Eventually the mad-genius conception of creativity received scientific endorsement from psychologists, psychiatrists, and psychoanalysts. For instance, Cesare Lombroso (1836–1909) attributed exceptional creativity to a genetically based "degenerative psychosis." The only conspicuous disagreements concerned the specific nature of the mental disorder. Unlike Lombroso, Sigmund Freud (1856–1939) saw creativity as a variety of neurotic behavior, whereas William James (1842–1910) viewed creativity as a form of "borderline" personality. Related to this issue was a debate about the extent to which creative genius bears any relation to criminality. Some psychiatrists argued that genius, madness, and criminality were all consequences of the same underlying genetic disorder.

The mad-genius view of creativity is less common in non-European civilizations, but it still appears. An example is the Chinese poet Li Bo (701–762). Popularly known as a "banished Immortal," he was notorious for his undisciplined wanderings and incessant drunkenness. Legend even had him drowning after trying to capture the reflection of the moon while spending an evening intoxicated in a boat.

Craft. In most cultures and civilizations throughout the world, creativity was often inseparable from craft traditions. Rather than artists, there were artisans. The knowledge and skills necessary to make culturally valued objects were passed down from generation to generation through parent-child or master-apprentice relationships. Even in European civilization, the linkage between creativity and crafts persisted in many domains for many centuries. It is telling that not all forms of creativity in ancient Greece had their muses. Evidently, creativity in certain areas required no divine intervention but merely the acquisition of the necessary expertise. Even much later, painters, sculptors, and architects would hold the status of artisans rather than artists. This position held for painters until the time of Giotto (1276–1337). And musical creativity in Europe did not completely emancipate itself from the craft image until the time of Ludwig van Beethoven (1770–1827).

Although creativity came to be separated from craft, many still considered the phenomenon as the outcome of the acquisition of some special expertise. Creativity remained a skill that anyone could acquire if they first mastered the requisite knowledge and skills. The painter Joshua Reynolds (1723–1792) expressed this view in his *Discourses on Art,* which were based on his lectures at the Royal Academy of Art. Unsympathetic to notions that artistic creativity required any special talent or genius, he argued that creativity in the arts demanded only that the student be willing to study and practice. Those who have done so sufficiently, according to Reynolds, would be indistinguishable from the so-called natural genius.

Conceptions of scientific creativity included a variation on this position. Science was defined by a special method—the logic of inference or investigation—by which scientists arrive at their discoveries and inventions. This position was first explicitly stated in Francis Bacon's (1561–1626) *Novum Organum,* which presented his inductive method. A little later Descartes advocated his own method based on deductive reasoning. Eventually, creativity in science became the chief concern of a whole new discipline, the philosophy of science. Notwithstanding the disparate opinions of various philosophers of science, most agreed that scientific creativity consisted of a well-defined method. Like any craft, this method, once mastered, enabled the individual to become a creative scientist. Indeed, some thinkers, such as José Ortega y Gasset (1883–1955), insisted that scientific creativity required no outstanding abilities.

Contemporary Research

In the early part of the twentieth century, distinguished researchers from many different disciplines investigated artistic and scientific creativity. For example, the topic attracted the attention of the anthropologist Alfred Kroeber and the sociologist Pitirim A. Sorokin. However, as the century progressed, the research was increasingly confined to just three fields: psychiatry, psychoanalysis, and psychology. The psychiatrists were primarily interested in the association between creativity and psychopathology, whereas the psychoanalysts were mostly dedicated to psychobiographical studies of eminent creators. Only the psychologists approached the phenomenon from a tremendous diversity of theoretical and methodological perspectives. Perhaps as a result of this breadth, by the end of the twentieth century psychologists came to dominate the study of creativity. Notwithstanding the diversity of approaches, the bulk of the psychological research falls into the following four categories:

1. Cognitive psychology—Cognitive psychologists are interested in the mental processes involved in the creative process. For instance, Howard Gruber has studied Charles Darwin's notebooks to detect the cognitive processes that he used in arriving at the theory of evolution, and Kevin Dunbar has studied the mental operations in scientific laboratories by analyzing recordings of research meetings. Using more experimental techniques, Albert Rothenberg has examined special forms of thinking in artistic creativity, while Tom Ward and his colleagues have studied the cognitive processes involved in invention.

2. Differential psychology—Psychologists from this subdiscipline seek to identify how people vary on various intellectual and personality traits. For example, Robert J. Sternberg has examined the impact of cognitive styles and John Baer has investigated the role of divergent thinking. Gregory Feist has synthesized the accumulated research to indicate how scientific and artistic creators differ on a large number of personality traits.

3. Developmental psychology—Developmental psychologists are interested in two major phases of creative development. The first phase concerns the acquisition of creative potential. Examples include Mark Runco's work on the growth of creativity in children and Mihaly Csikszentmihályi's studies of talent development in teenagers and young adults. The second phase concerns the manifestation of that creative potential in adulthood. An instance is Ravenna Helson's longitudinal investigation designed to determine why some talented women succeed in realizing their potential and others do not.

4. Social psychology—Social psychologists are dedicated to understanding how creativity is influenced by social context, including interpersonal relationships, group dynamics, and sociocultural systems. For example, Teresa Amabile has studied how certain social expectations can either enhance or inhibit creativity, while Paul Paulus has investigated group problem-solving behaviors ("groupthink"). At a more aggregate level of analysis, Colin Martindale has examined the impact of aesthetic traditions on artistic creativity and Dean Keith Simonton has scrutinized ways in which the social, political, and cultural environment shapes creativity in both the arts and sciences.

Even though more researchers than ever before are studying creativity, inquiries still have a long way to go before the phenomenon is completely understood. In particular, some core controversies have yet to be resolved. The field is also in dire need of a theoretical system that will successfully integrate the diverse empirical findings. Although several explanatory accounts have been proposed—including computational, economic, and Darwinian models—no theory has earned sufficient assent to dominate the field.

See also **Analytical Philosophy; Arts; Cartesianism; Cultural Studies; Enlightenment; Europe, Idea of; Imagination; Individualism; Romanticism in Literature and Politics.**

BIBLIOGRAPHY

Amabile, Teresa M. *Creativity in Context.* Boulder, Colo.: Westview, 1996.

Boden, Margaret. *The Creative Mind: Myths and Mechanisms.* New York: BasicBooks, 1991.

Boden, Margaret A., ed. *Dimensions of Creativity.* Cambridge, Mass.: MIT Press, 1994.

Csikszentmihályi, Mihaly. *Creativity: Flow and the Psychology of Discovery and Invention.* New York: HarperCollins, 1997.

Gardner, Howard. *Creating Minds: An Anatomy of Creativity Seen through the Lives of Freud, Einstein, Picasso, Stravinsky, Eliot, Graham, and Gandhi.* New York: BasicBooks, 1993.

Martindale, Colin. *The Clockwork Muse: The Predictability of Artistic Styles.* New York: BasicBooks, 1990.

Murray, Penelope, ed. *Genius: The History of an Idea.* Oxford: Blackwell, 1989.

Runco, Mark A., and Robert S. Albert, eds. *Theories of Creativity.* Newbury Park, Calif.: Sage, 1990.

Runco, Mark A., and Steven R. Pritzker, eds. *Encyclopedia of Creativity.* 2 vols. San Diego: Academic Press, 1999.

Simonton, Dean Keith. *Origins of Genius: Darwinian Perspectives on Creativity.* New York: Oxford University Press, 1999.

Smith, Steven M., Thomas B. Ward, and Ronald A. Finke, eds. *The Creative Cognition Approach.* Cambridge, Mass.: MIT Press, 1995.

Sternberg, Robert J., ed. *Handbook of Creativity.* Cambridge, U.K.: Cambridge University Press, 1999.

Dean Keith Simonton

CREOLIZATION, CARIBBEAN. The concept of creolization lies at the very center of discussions of transculturalism, transnationalism, multiculturalism, diversity, and hybridization. This essay begins by examining the term's roots in the ethnic and cultural complexities of the Caribbean experience. It then goes on to look at the transformation of this experience into a theoretical framework for pluralism that consciously sought to avoid the binary pitfalls of its antecedents. It concludes with a brief look at the work of several key authors and surveys recent critiques of the Caribbean creolization movement.

Despite its currency in literary, cultural, and critical circles, the term *creolization* cannot be fully understood without taking into account its historical background and geographical context. In these terms, creolization must be seen not simply as a synonym for hybridity but as a phenomenon that is indispensable to understanding the New World experience. Although the history of the term dates back several decades earlier, its critical status in the early 2000s is largely the result of a number of publications emanating from the French Caribbean in the 1980s.

Caribbean Context

The origins of creolization for the Caribbean region arguably lie in the contested and interrelated processes of colonization, slavery, and migration that both brought the New World into being and gave it impetus and direction. Once the indigenous New World populations were decimated, the growth and development of plantation economies that arose in the Caribbean in the seventeenth century produced pathbreaking patterns of economic and cultural exchange between Europe, the New World of the Americas—including Central America, the Guianas, Mexico, and Brazil—and the African continent. Catalyzed by the slave trade, which forcibly removed untold numbers of peoples of diverse racial, cultural, and geographical origin from their African homelands and transplanted them onto vast island plantations, these already variegated groups subsequently came into contact with other transplanted peoples from Europe, South Asia, China, and the Middle East. As a result, the Caribbean region quickly became a key nodal point in what would become the creolization of these composite populations.

It was the product of these intersecting influences—the inauguration of a creole society in the Caribbean Sea—that became the subject of the text *Eloge de la créolité/In Praise of Creoleness* (1989). Written by Raphaël Confiant and Patrick Chamoiseau, two Martinican novelists, in conjunction with Jean Bernabé, a Guadeloupean linguist, this manifesto can be seen in one sense as an attempt to come to terms with the paradox of French overseas departmentalization. The fact of these former colonies' incorporation into the French nation in 1946, and the conferral of French citizenship on their citizens, had done nothing to negate the ongoing material differences in history, geography, culture, and ethnicity that continued to separate these territories from the metropole, creating a double trajectory that made their citizens feel both French and West Indian. The "double consciousness" imposed by the duality of their legal and cultural status encouraged these thinkers to come to terms with the dilemma of belonging posed by departmentalization. Their solution was to seek out the origins of this pluralism, and to celebrate it.

Importantly, however, they were certainly not the first to do so. Some twenty years earlier, the Barbadian historian and poet Edward Brathwaite sought to establish patterns of creole interaction as a sort of sociological foundation for Caribbean societies. In his *The Development of Creole Society in Jamaica, 1770–1820* (1971), Brathwaite proposed that the principles of cultural distinction and unitary origin through which societies were typically analyzed and categorized be abandoned in the Caribbean case, recognizing instead the intrinsic ethnic and cultural pluralism of the islands. The cultural intersection, ethnic admixture, and linguistic cross-fertilization that lay at the core of the Caribbean experience would be made to contest the historical discontinuity and geographical and political fragmentation through which the region traditionally had been framed.

From Experience to Theory

On the surface, creolization would appear to be of a piece with *criollo* and *mestizaje* in Spanish, and with *métissage* in French. However, although each of these categories responds to the implicit pluralisms of the colonial encounter, each also reflects specific differences within the colonial experience that are not easily rendered in general terms. What the authors of the *Eloge* sought to convey above all was the abandonment of negative binaries in favor of the creative openness that lies behind any conception of the creole. "Neither Europeans, nor Africans,

---

Patrick Chamoiseau

Patrick Chamoiseau was born in 1953 in Fort-de-France, Martinique. The son of working-class parents, Chamoiseau studied sociology and law in Paris before moving back to Martinique, where he became a social worker. His third novel, *Texaco,* won France's top literary award, the Prix Goncourt, in 1992, making him world-famous. The novel was eventually translated into more than twenty languages. Chamoiseau continues to live in Martinique, where he writes novels as well as short stories, screenplays, autobiography, childhood memoirs, and texts for pictorial histories.

Despite the publication of other novels such as *Solibo le magnifique* and *Biblique des derniers gestes, Texaco* remains by far Chamoiseau's best-known work. The novel traces 150 years of postemancipation Martinican history through the eyes and voice of Marie-Sophie Laborieux, the aging daughter of a freed slave. It is Laborieux's encounter with an urban planner, and her attempt to convince him to abandon his plan to raze, in the name of progress, the shantytown of the title that provides the framework for this episodic story of struggle and resistance. This structure, and its trademark of creole existing alongside and transforming the French language, allows the key nuances of ethnic and cultural exchange and linguistic wordplay to assume pride of place in a portrait of Martinique's creolized society.

---

nor Asians, we proclaim ourselves Creoles" (Bernabé et al., p. 75). Indeed, their aim more specifically was to develop modalities for creative expression in the arts that would reflect and embody the multiplicity and complexity of the creole mosaic. "Our history is a braid of histories . . . We are at once Europe, Africa, and enriched by Asian contributions, we are also Levantine, Indians, as well as pre-Columbian Americans in some respects. Creoleness is '*the world diffracted but recomposed*' . . . a Totality" (p. 88; emphasis original).

Thus the creole language serves as a fundamental metaphor for the key goals and tenets of French Caribbean creolization. As Chamoiseau and Confiant point out in their critical work *Lettres créoles,* this language was the product of the experience of colonization and slavery. Born and nurtured on the plantation, it was brought into being both by the interaction of slaves deliberately separated by ethnic group to forestall the possibility of communication that might lead to resistance and revolt, through the influence of Maroons (runaway slaves) and by the interaction of these groups with the colonial culture. The creole language thus symbolizes cultural continuity, resistance to oppression, and the richness of ethnic admixture; as such, it serves to valorize the region's oral tradition even as it reinforces the qualities of pluralism and transformation that sum up the heterogeneity of the French Caribbean experience in particular.

Antecedents

The arc of this experience explicitly acknowledges the antecedent influence of two other key Martinican writers and thinkers, Aimé Césaire and Edouard Glissant, and the literary movements with which their names are respectively linked: negritude and *antillanité,* or Caribbeanness. The *créolistes,* as the authors of the *Eloge* are called, address the importance of negritude to their thought formation: "To a totally racist world . . . Aimé Césaire restored mother Africa . . . Césaire's Negritude gave Creole society its African dimension" (Bernabé et al., p. 79). Indeed, they make specific reference to the irreplaceable role played here by Césaire himself. "It was Césaire's Negritude that opened to us the path for the actuality of . . . Caribbeanness . . . We are forever Césaire's sons" (p. 80).

At the same time, however, it must be recognized that the *créolistes* simultaneously acknowledge the limitations of the African model of cultural origin for the complex realities of the Caribbean basin. The basic paradox intrinsic to such an approach lay in the fact that adopting the negritude paradigm would simply amount to exchanging one unitary model of culture for another. Neither the European nor the African paradigm could contain the myriad ethnic influences and creative cultural exchange that had given rise to the Caribbean. To adequately account for the region's plural character, another model was necessary. For this, they would turn to the work of Edouard Glissant.

An accomplished novelist and poet as well as an important cultural theorist, Edouard Glissant had produced more than half a dozen creative works by the time he published his groundbreaking *Caribbean Discourse* in 1981. In this work, he

EDOUARD GLISSANT

Edouard Glissant was born in 1928 in the commune of Sainte-Marie in Martinique. A poet, novelist, dramatist, and essayist, Glissant studied philosophy at the Sorbonne and ethnology at the Musée de l'homme. In the 1950s he co-founded the *Front Antillo-Guyanais pour l'indépendance,* and went on to found the Institut martiniquais d'etudes in 1970. In 1982, he went to work as editor of the UNESCO *Courier,* was named Distinguished University Professor at Louisiana State University in 1988, and left there for a position at the City University of New York's Graduate Center in the mid-1990s. He began publishing in the mid-1950s, and his novels, plays, essays, and volumes of poetry have won many outstanding prizes. Perhaps the premier contemporary French West Indian cultural theorist, his influential concepts of *antillanité* (Caribbeanness) and *poétique de la relation* (cross-cultural poetics) promulgated in *Le Discours antillais* (Caribbean Discourse) seek to creatively anchor the Caribbean experience of fragmentation and disjuncture in a framework that gives voice to its central tenets of diversity and hybridity. The interpenetration of languages and cultures that lies at the core of this process of creolization posits contact and chaos, cultural relativity, and exchange and transformation as key tools in a polyvalent system of thought that redefines traditional notions of identity.

also sought to take his vision of Caribbean reality beyond the epistemological boundaries of negritude. Realizing that a response that simply negated the tenets of a colonial discourse did nothing to expunge its essential properties, Glissant sought to specify the terms and conditions of a creole culture that would be inclusive of the wider English, Spanish, and Dutch Caribbean as well as the French overseas departments of Guadeloupe and Martinique, one that would give rein to the region's constant creative flux and its insistent patterns of transformation and exchange. The core of this Caribbean vision, the one on which the *créolistes* would draw, he termed *antillanité,* or Caribbeanness.

Glissant locates the key axes of this concept between uprooting and transformation. Within these patterns of intersection and exchange, he demarcates the terms of Caribbean survival. "I feel that what makes this difference between a people that survives elsewhere . . . and a population that is transformed elsewhere *into another people* . . . and that thus enters the constantly shifting and variable process of creolization . . . is that the latter has not . . . collectively continued the methods of existence and survival, both material and spiritual, which it practiced before being uprooted" (Glissant, p. 15; emphasis original). This generative framework stresses principles of mixture and combination rather than confrontation and rupture; the infinite openness and fluidity of its practice expresses the diversity of the Caribbean collective identity in a way that allowed the architects of *créolité* scope to articulate structurally similar concerns. The productive multiplicity of the Caribbean, one that draws on its peoples and cultures to

continually transform and reinvent themselves, is thus a core principle of both *antillanité* and *créolité.*

Critiques

While the Caribbean focus of these twin discourses was seen as a much-needed corrective to metropolitan visions of the Caribbean as a region mired in fragmentation and loss, an alternative view took a much more critical line, accusing the *créolistes* of having appropriated the issue of creolization and of imbuing it with restrictive, essentialist characteristics that valorized exclusivity over process. From this viewpoint, despite the specific historic context and catalyst of migration, colonialism, slavery, and indentured labor, the concept of creolization was applicable to many cultures and civilizations beyond the Caribbean basin.

By contrast, the creolization of Glissant's *antillanité* sought to subvert universalist notions of pure and impure, positing the world as subject to ceaseless cultural transformation, a joining of braiding and becoming: "Creolization as an idea is not primarily the glorification of the composite nature of a people: indeed, no people has been spared the crosscultural process. . . . To assert peoples are creolized, that creolization has value, is to deconstruct in this way the category of 'creolized' that is considered as halfway between two 'pure' extremes" (Glissant, p. 140).

In their turn, Bernabé, Chamoiseau, and Confiant managed to expand and buttress their own positions in a key interview published some years after their manifesto. Here, they stress the

CRISIS

pluralities of creoleness: "our position is that there are several *créolités*" (Taylor, p. 142); valorize the role of pluralism: "*créolité* is all about understanding mosaic, multiple identities" (p. 153); and suggest that creolization is a process that encompasses more than a simple synthesis, more than *métissage*: "There's metissage in creolization, but creolization is chaos—shock, mixture, combination, alchemy" (p. 136). In these terms, creolization establishes its specific difference from hybridity, reflecting its beginnings in colonialism and slavery as well as the ceaseless redefinition and rebirth that are its primary constituent elements.

See also Africa, Idea of; Black Consciousness; Diasporas: African Diaspora; Identity: Personal and Social Identity; Language and Linguistics; Mestizaje; Negritude; Postcolonial Theory and Literature; Slavery.

BIBLIOGRAPHY

Balutansky, Kathleen M. and Marie-Agnès Sourieau, eds. *Caribbean Creolization: Reflections on the Cultural Dynamics of Language, Literature, and Identity.* Gainesville: University of Florida Press, 1998.

Benítez-Rojo, Antonio. *The Repeating Island: The Caribbean and the Postmodern Perspective.* Translated by James E. Maraniss. Durham, N.C.: Duke University Press, 1992.

Bernabé, Jean, Patrick Chamoiseau, and Raphaël Confiant. "Créolité Bites." *Transition* 7, no. 2 (1998): 124–161. Interview.

———. *Eloge de la créolité.* Paris: Gallimard, 1989.

Bongie, Chris. *Islands and Exiles: The Creole Identities of Post/Colonial Literature.* Stanford, Calif.: Stanford University Press, 1998.

Brathwaite, Kamau. *The Development of Creole Society in Jamaica, 1770–1820.* Oxford: Clarendon, 1971.

Britton, Celia. *Edouard Glissant and Postcolonial Theory.* Charlottesville: University Press of Virginia, 1999.

Burton, Richard D. E. *Afro-Creole: Power, Opposition, and Play in the Caribbean.* Ithaca, N.Y.: Cornell University Press, 1997.

Chamoiseau, Patrick. *Ecrire en pays dominé.* Paris: Gallimard, 1997.

Chamoiseau, Patrick, and Raphaël Confiant. *Lettres créoles: tracées antillaises et continentales de la littérature: Haiti, Guadeloupe, Martinique, Guyana, 1635–1975.* Paris: Gallimard, 1999.

Dash, J. Michael. *Edouard Glissant.* New York: Cambridge University Press, 1995.

Glissant, Edouard. *Caribbean Discourse: Selected Essays.* Translated by J. Michael Dash. Charlottesville: University Press of Virginia, 1989.

———. *Poetics of Relation.* Translated by Betsy Wing. Ann Arbor: University of Michigan Press, 1997.

Lionnet, Françoise. "*Créolité* in the Indian Ocean: Two Models of Cultural Diversity." *Yale French Studies* 82 (1993): 101–112.

Murdoch, H. Adlai. *Creole Identity in the French Caribbean Novel.* Gainesville: University of Florida Press, 2001.

H. Adlai Murdoch

CRISIS. The term *crisis* comes from the Greek noun *krisis* (choice, decision, judgment), deriving from the Greek verb *krinein* (to decide). The word makes an ancient debut in Greek historical writing via the legal, medical, and rhetorical terminology as the turning point in a decision, illness, or argument.

Its definitive reappearance with reference to historical events, periods, or processes dates from the late eighteenth century, its classic formulation from the second half of the nineteenth century, and its proliferation as a catchall term for a crucial or decisive stage or state of affairs from the last half of the twentieth century. The history of the notion of crisis veers between failed attempts at precise definition and its inflation and devaluation as a tool of analysis.

Focus and flexibility inhere in the concept of crisis and account for much of its appeal. Crises, to be regarded as such, must occur in the course of specific events, but they can be characterized in organic, mechanistic, or revolutionary terms as critical episodes in a life cycle, indices of structural dysfunction, or corollaries of revolution. In the ideological reckoning with the great upheavals of modern history since the revolutions of the late eighteenth century, historical crises have often been cast as liberating by the Left and as proof of human fallibility by the Right. The language of crisis can be charged with drama, plotted as narrative, objectified as analysis, and pinned to empirical data.

Modern Concepts of Crisis

Karl Marx and Jacob Burckhardt brought out alternative emphases in their benchmark reflections on crisis. Marx (*Das Kapital*) developed a theory of economic crisis centered on the economics of overproduction, specifically on the chronic disequilibrium between production and consumption under capitalism; each crisis, he believed, would be more severe than the last until a "general crisis" occurred wherein the working class would rise against their exploiters. Burckhardt took politics and culture as a starting point for his pronouncements on crisis in one of his lectures on world history, first delivered in the 1860s. Historical crises typically begin with a "negative, accusing aspect," then peak in utopian visions before giving way to reactions and restorations; the permanent results are "astonishingly meagre in comparison with the great efforts and passions which rise to the surface during the crisis." The typology, based on the French Revolution and the European revolutions of 1848, is clear enough, but it dissolves in a rush of historical examples underwritten by the patrician conservative's anxieties over modernization and not a little *Schadenfreude* in praise of crisis (Burckhardt, pp. 289–290).

More specialized—if less demanding—usage was widespread by the later nineteenth century and is still current, for example in political or diplomatic crisis, financial or commercial crisis, or *crise de conscience*. However, until as late as 1960, the fields of economics and economic history produced the only relatively systematic theories of crisis. Marx's views were developed, debated, and projected back in time for a crisis of European feudalism variously dated between the fourteenth and the seventeenth centuries. Non-Marxist versions concentrated on cyclical fluctuations in price data or on the "checks" of famine, disease, and war to surplus population in Malthusian demographic cycles of preindustrial society. The thesis of a general crisis of the seventeenth century (as the transition from feudalism to capitalism) was advanced in 1954 by the British Marxist historian Eric Hobsbawm (Aston, pp. 5–58) and became a debating point in a long-running controversy over the timing and extra-economic dimensions of what was alleged to be the formative crisis of the modern world.

By the 1960s, crisis had become a broad and expanding catchword—an alternative to the more potent idea of revolution—for practically any challenge-and-response situation or scenario. The tumultuous events of midcentury, from World War II, the collapse of colonial empires, and the Cold War to the traumas of the 1960s, were cast as symptomatic of the crisis not only of Western civilization but of established orders everywhere.

Field-specific crisis literature depended on the discourse or discipline but shared a preoccupation with breakdown or breakthrough in an established system of behavior or belief. A neoorthodox Protestant theology of crisis, a psychology of identity crisis following Erik Erikson (1902–1994), and an epistemology of crisis in "paradigm shifts" during scientific revolutions as analyzed by Thomas Kuhn (1922-1996), had their own extensive literatures. The crises of the Italian Renaissance, the Protestant Reformation, and the seventeenth-century English aristocracy were major topics for historians of early modern Europe, and a U.S. textbook series on major crises in history, including the crisis of August 1914 and the Great Depression of 1929, appeared in 1962. The Cuban missile crisis of that year became the exemplary real-world case of international diplomatic crisis at a time when crisis management, based on game theory, had become a political science specialty recognized by U.S. government research contracts.

Contemporary Definition and Usage

Two comprehensive entries on crisis in the *International Encyclopedia of the Social Sciences* (1968) and the first *Dictionary of the History of Ideas* (1968) cited, respectively, "unrestricted usage" and continuing "uncertainty." Any number of studies had accumulated on crises of moments, decades, even eras; on political, social, economic, mental, and moral crises; on minor, major, and mid-level crises. The most exacting definitions were abstract and redundant, as in the decision-planners' twelve "generic dimensions" of crisis (*International Encyclopedia of the Social Sciences,* v. 2, s.v. "crisis"). While suggestive connections were being made across fields, they came at the expense of clarity and coherence and sometimes recycled arguments that had already been discounted by experts in their own disciplines. Both articles placed hope in more precise future work.

In fact, the widespread interest in and development of crisis studies had already peaked by the early 1970s. Toward the end of the twentieth century, the language of crisis was worn out by overuse even as it was being eclipsed by the triumphalism of post–Cold War ideologies that prophesied, however credulously, the end of history and the containment of the upheavals and confrontations that had fueled it. The big crisis debates among historians mostly receded before the emphasis on long-term structural trends, the dismantling of so-called grand narratives, the deconstruction of the rhetoric of history, and the unfazed appreciation that conflict and confrontation were not the exception but the rule in history. The most concerted theoretical attention to crisis came from political scientists who continued to model schematic strategies for "crisis management," especially in international affairs.

They salvaged analytical precision only by abstract model building and academic distinctions such as a sequence of phases of international crises from onset and escalation to de-escalation and impact.

The most conspicuous use of crisis terminology in the early twenty-first century is activist and political. Social movements, nongovernmental organizations, and government institutions, including the United Nations, have appropriated the term on occasion as a watchword to promote intervention in "crises" of genocide, women's rights, HIV-AIDS, environmental degradation, or economic globalization. A "crisis of liberal values" has become a target of both radical supporters of multi-cultural politics and self-styled traditionalists who feel called upon to defend their ideals of family, patriotism, and religion. These developments, together with the leveling effects of everyday usage, have furthered the depletion of the term as an all-purpose slogan or a banal cliché.

See also **Continental Philosophy; Cycles; Feudalism, European; Game Theory; Marxism.**

BIBLIOGRAPHY

Aston, Trevor, ed. *Crisis in Europe, 1560–1660.* London: Routledge, 1965.

Brecher, Michael. *Crisis in World Politics: Theory and Reality.* New York and London: Pergamon, 1993.

Burckhardt, Jacob. *Force and Freedom: Reflections on World History.* Translated by James Hastings Nichols. Boston: Beacon Press, 1964.

Eisenstein, Zillah R. *Feminism and Sexual Equality: Crisis in Liberal America.* New York: Monthly Review Press, 1984.

Erikson, Erik H. *Identity, Youth, and Crisis.* New York: Norton, 1968.

Fowler, Richard A., and H. Wayne House. *Civilization in Crisis: A Christian Response to Homosexuality, Feminism, Euthanasia, and Abortion.* Grand Rapids, Mich.: Baker Book House, 1988.

Koselleck, Reinhart. "Krise." In *Geschichtliche Grundbegriffe: Historisches Lexikon zur Politisch-Sozialen Sprache in Deutschland,* Vol. 3, edited by Otto Brunner and Werner Conze, 617–650. Stuttgart: Klett-Cotta, 1978.

Kuhn, Thomas S. *The Structure of Scientific Revolutions.* 3rd ed. Chicago: University of Chicago Press, 1996.

Masur, Gerhart. "Crisis in History." In *Dictionary of the History of Ideas,* Vol. 1, edited by Philip P. Wiener, 589–595. New York: Scribner, 1973.

Médecins Sans Frontières, eds. *World in Crisis: The Politics of Survival at the End of the Twentieth Century.* New York: Routledge, 1997.

Parker, Geoffrey. *Europe in Crisis, 1598–1648.* London: Fontana, 1979.

Starn, Randolph. "Historians and Crisis." *Past & Present,* no. 52 (August 1971): 3–22.

Randolph Starn

CRITICAL RACE THEORY.
One of a family of related progressive movements in the law—others include critical legal studies, Latino critical legal studies ("Lat/Crit"), and feminist legal theory—critical race theory sprang up in the late

1970s in response to a widespread perception that the powerful civil rights coalition of the 1960s and early 1970s had stalled. Conservative administrations and an American public that seemed increasingly weary of hearing about race required new strategies and theories to deal with subtle, institutional, or color-blind forms of racism and a judiciary that no longer seemed eager to champion civil rights.

Derrick Bell, an African-American professor of law at Harvard Law School (later at New York University) and Alan Freeman, a white scholar teaching at SUNY-Buffalo Law School, laid the foundations of the movement that came to be called critical race theory and that would go on to transform our understanding of the relationship among race, racism, and official power. For his part, Bell contributed groundbreaking analyses of conflict of interest in civil rights litigation and of the role of white elite self-interest in explaining the twists and turns of blacks' racial fortunes. In an impressive article in *Yale Law Journal*, Bell pointed out that lawyers for elite civil rights organizations like the NAACP (National Association for the Advancement of Colored People), where he himself worked before entering law teaching, often were eager to pursue one agenda—law reform and innovation—while the client community wanted something else—say, better schools. The NAACP Legal Defense Fund, for example, relentlessly and courageously pursued school desegregation, while black parents often wanted something different—better funding for black schools.

If the first essay produced consternation and soul-searching among his colleagues in the civil rights movement, a second piece, on the role of interest convergence in determining the course of racial reform and retrenchment, raised eyebrows even higher. In "*Brown v. Board of Education* and the Interest Convergence Dilemma," Bell posited that the breathtaking advances of the early civil rights years came about not so much because of moral breakthroughs by the American public or liberal judges. Rather, they were needed in order to burnish America's tarnished image in the eyes of the rest of the world and also to avert the possibility of racial unrest at home. At the time, the United States had just concluded a world war of mammoth proportions and was in the early stages of a Cold War against the forces of godless, soulless communism. In this campaign for the loyalties of the uncommitted Third World (much of which was black, brown, or Asian), it ill served this nation for the world to see front page stories and photographs of lynchings, the Emmett Till murder, and southern sheriffs turning vicious police dogs loose on peaceful civil rights leaders such as Martin Luther King Jr.

At the same time, wartime service in the U.S. military had exposed black and brown servicemen and -women to environments comparatively free of racism, in which diligent service brought rewards, promotions, and even battlefield commissions. These black and brown soldiers, having fought and exposed their lives in defense of American democracy and freedom, were unlikely to return to the former regime of menial jobs and servile relations with white society. Unrest loomed.

This convergence of black and white self-interest—rather than altruism or advancing morality—brought about *Brown v. Board of Education* (1954), the 1964 Civil Rights Act, and other reforms of that era. And when black advances no longer served the interests of elite whites, they were quietly withdrawn or limited by narrow judicial interpretation, administrative foot-dragging, or delay. Although his skeptical hypothesis was met at first with cries of outrage, Bell subsequently applied his interest-convergence hypothesis to explain the full sweep of black civil rights history, showing how the material interests of elite whites explain practically every major advance or retreat. And Mary Dudziak, a white professor teaching at the University of Southern California Law Center, verified Bell's hypothesis by examining a host of documents, memos, and archival material related to *Brown v. Board of Education.*

Around the same time Bell was writing, Alan Freeman was carrying out an extraordinary reinterpretation of the role of the U.S. Supreme Court in guiding the course of civil rights progress. Freeman showed how our usual interpretation of the role of the liberal Warren court was both right and wrong. The Court did indeed champion civil rights causes. But in doing so, it also served as a powerful legitimating tool by confining change to manageable dimensions and denying relief for any but the most clear-cut violation.

An Organization Forms

Others (including Richard Delgado, one of the authors of this essay) soon joined Bell and Freeman, and in the summer of 1989 about thirty law scholars of color from around the United States met at a convent outside Madison, Wisconsin, to forge a new movement in the law. Settling on a name (critical race theory) and a general program, the group resolved to coordinate their scholarship and hold future meetings aimed at developing a new, radical approach to race, racism, and American law. Since then, the group has held a series of public conferences and periodic smaller workshops aimed at the development of particular themes. The group's scholarship grew rapidly to include a few dozen books and hundreds of law-review articles and essays. Many law schools around the country include critical race theorists among their ranks; perhaps two-thirds of all law schools offer one or more courses on it or a related subject.

The movement's ideas also spread to other fields. Educators use its approaches and theories to help understand hierarchy in schools, tracking, school discipline, and battles over the Western canon. Political scientists are intrigued by its studies of the role of courts in law reform; sociologists, by its analyses of racial power and authority; American Studies scholars and rhetoricians, by its use of storytelling, counterstorytelling, and revisionist history. What are some of the movement's dominant ideas? Critical race theory is a very loose collection of scholars, not all of whom would agree on this or any other platform or set of defining tenets. But most "race-crits" would acknowledge some of the following as the movement's defining themes:

Interest convergence and material determinism. Just as the movement began with Derrick Bell's impressive analysis of the role of white institutional self-interest and its relation to racial reform, critical race theorists have continued to explore this dimension of American society. Scholars such as Lani Guinier examine how voting behavior and laws affect the quality of the representation that the minority community receives in national and state legislatures. Guinier and others study the idea of merit, standardized testing, and occupational qualifications in order to see how seemingly neutral measuring instruments and criteria incorporate bias. Writers such as Spencer Overton examine the role of property, wealth, and ownership in inhibiting black advances. A host of scholars examines affirmative action and job-hiring patterns in higher education.

Racism as ordinary and normal.

Most Americans believe that their society is fair and just, and the legal system frames antidiscrimination law and doctrine with this presupposition in mind. Most critical race theorists believe the opposite is true, however; racism for them is ordinary, normal, and deeply embedded in everyday life and institutions. From songs, rhymes, and nursery stories such as Snow White, to movie roles and stereotypes, job and school criteria, and old-boy informal networks, favoritism for white, European ways exerts a subtle, ever-present force. If racism and race-themed ideas and preferences are everywhere, this makes them invisible and difficult to confront. They seem ordinary and natural; the person seeking to challenge them strikes others as impossible, nitpicky, or lacking in a sense of proportion. Litigants suing for discrimination confront the same obstacle. Unless what the defendant did was outrageous, intentional, and outside the pale, courts are unlikely to award relief.

Critique of color blindness.

Currently, one of society's—and the legal system's—dominant approaches to race is color blindness. This perspective insists that race does not matter. The law should not take account of race either for the purpose of helping or handicapping any group. By the same token, advocates of color blindness assert that in ordinary life one should behave the same way—simply refusing to take note of the race of people with whom one comes into contact.

Some critical race theorists have mounted a powerful and sustained attack on the idea of color blindness, pointing out, for example, that to disregard another person's race, one first has to notice it, and that many color-blind institutions—such as an alumni preference at private colleges—strengthen white privilege and disadvantage blacks and other minorities.

The social construction of race.

Most race-crits hold that race is not real and objective but that ideas of race nevertheless exert great social power. Supported by scientific findings that individuals of different races share a huge majority of their genes (perhaps as much as 99.9 percent) and the scientific community's agreement that the few genes that do account for minor differences such as hair texture and skin color cannot possibly influence distinctively human traits such as intelligence, personality, or propensity for moral or immoral behavior, critical race theorists examine how we nevertheless come to believe in the reality of race. If race is a social construction—something we choose to believe in the face of scientific evidence to the contrary—what are the mechanisms of that social construction and what keeps them in place? Social constructionists examine how scripts, narratives, stories, and habits enable society to continue to believe that something important distinguishes blacks and whites, for example, and hold to those beliefs even in the face of evidence that people everywhere are pretty much alike (some good, some bad). They also examine the role of law in maintaining racial lines and classifications through such measures as immigration categories, rules forbidding intermarriage, and state statutes defining blackness, such as the "one-drop rule," according to which any individual with a detectable trace of black blood is black.

Differential racialization.

A recently developed theme within critical race theory discourse is differential racialization. This theory holds that the various racial groups in the United States—blacks, Latinos, Asian-Americans, and Native Americans, for example—have been racialized in different ways in response to different needs of the majority group. Moreover, the laws and legal structures society devises for each group—such as English-only laws for Latinos, alien land laws for Asians, and Jim Crow laws for blacks—operate differently in the case of the various groups. The groups feature different histories and struggles. They had to contend with different sets of discriminatory laws and practices. With Indians, for example, society wanted their land; with blacks, labor; with Latinos, first land, then labor; and so on. Social stereotypes of the various groups changed accordingly over time to facilitate society's obtaining what it wanted from the group in question. For example, during slavery, when southern whites had matters well in hand, the dominant narratives, songs, and stories about blacks were reassuring: Blacks were happy with their lives and pleased to serve whites. Later, when blacks received their freedom and were perceived as a threat, social images of them changed. Writers, cartoonists, and filmmakers depicted blacks as frightening, larger-than-life figures with (in the case of men, at least) designs on white women. These figures, of course, justified cruel repression. They would not have served well during the slave period because they would have suggested that blacks were unhappy with their lot.

The black/white binary of race.

Related to the above is the notion that American concepts—and laws—related to race incorporate a black/white binary paradigm, in which two, and only two, races define the study, and system, of race. Those two races are, of course, the white and the black. Other groups, such as Latinos, Asian-Americans, Indians, and Filipinos enter into the equation only insofar as their treatment and experiences can be analogized to those of African-Americans. Sometimes the analogy holds. If antidiscrimination law would afford redress for an African-American worker whose supervisor calls him a "lazy n——" and assigns him to the least desirable tasks, it would also provide relief for an Asian worker called a "damn chink" and sent off to do unpleasant work.

But suppose the basis for discrimination is that a Latino or Asian worker speaks with an accent, or because the employer fears, wrongly, that such a worker may be an undocumented alien. Neither accent nor national-origin discrimination affects most blacks; therefore, remedial law coined with them in mind may afford no redress for these other kinds of discrimination. By the same token, Asians may be discriminated against because of a radically different set of stereotypes—the super-achiever or humorless drone who steals jobs from more well-balanced American workers, while Latinos may suffer because of the opposite stereotype—the happy-go-lucky lover of song, dance, and women. Again, none of these stereotypes affects blacks generally, with the result that courts and other decision makers are apt to be unschooled in the need to be on guard against them.

Intersectionality and antiessentialism.

A further critical theme that, like differential racialization and the black/white binary, has to do with categories and power is intersectionality and antiessentialism. Opposite sides of the same coin, these two themes draw attention to the evils of overgeneralization. Both have to do with identity. Intersectionality names a phenomenon in which individuals are often found to exhibit identities that are complex. A Latino may also be black, or gay. An African-American may be female and a single parent. An Asian-American may have a parent who is Filipino or a grandparent who is Latino, and so on.

Complex identities may turn out to have legal consequences. For example, imagine an African-American woman worker who suffers discrimination on the job site because of her black womanhood. Her supervisor may dislike black women, believing them lazy or haughty. The supervisor may harbor no such dislike for black men or white women, and may treat them fairly. His discrimination runs only to black women.

Suppose that our hypothetical worker sues for workplace discrimination. How would she frame her case? She could invoke one existing body of case and statutory law that redresses discrimination on the grounds of sex. She is, after all, a woman, and her boss does discriminate against her because she is a woman—a black woman. Alternatively, she could file suit on the grounds of racial discrimination. Her supervisor treats her badly, in part, because she is an African-American. Regardless of the avenue she chooses, however, her suit will confront serious obstacles. Her boss can maintain, truthfully, that he does not discriminate against all women. In particular, he treats white women well, promoting them when they deserve it and otherwise treating them fairly.

He can also prove that he does not discriminate against African-Americans across the board. In particular, he likes black men and treats them well at work. The black woman's claim, then, could fail because her discrimination is intersectional—aimed at her because of her status as a black woman, someone with an intersectional identity. All individuals with complex identities run the risk that a system of power and authority that hinges on prefabricated categories, none of which perfectly fit the individual's situation, fails to do them justice.

Antiessentialism points to the mirror image problem. An organization, such as a woman's group, whose dominant membership is, let us say, white, may give short shrift to the needs and priorities of nonwhite members because it thinks in terms of an "essential" woman, who is, of course, white. The organization then devises strategies to advance the objectives of this member, whose aims and needs are considered to be representative of the group. The needs of nonstandard members—say,

white lesbians, or black single mothers—are deemed of secondary importance. The group will deal with them as soon as the needs of women, as women, are dealt with. And this paradigmatic woman is apt to turn out to be white and middle class.

Legal storytelling and narrative analysis.

Out of the concern that conventional legal discourse—and perhaps discourse of any kind—will fail to do justice to the needs, experiences, and histories of minorities, critical race theorists have been experimenting with new modes of presenting their ideas. These new vehicles include legal storytelling and narrative analysis. Legal storytelling received a large boost when Derrick Bell, at the height of his career, received a prestigious invitation to write the foreword to *Harvard Law Review*'s 1985 Supreme Court issue, devoted to the analysis of recent opinions. Disdaining the usual heavily footnoted, ponderous prose in which most of the forewords are written, Bell instead published a series of conversations—"The Civil Rights Chronicles"—with an imaginary superheroine lawyer named Geneva Crenshaw. His alter ego is young and brash; his own voice is tempered and moderate. The two discuss the current racial scene and developments in the law. Bell tries to defend the system and its steady, incremental progress. Geneva destroys every illusion with devastating wit and analysis.

Others followed Bell's lead, using fable, myth, and close observation to unmask items of the liberal faith, such as that blacks are making constant progress, color blindness is capable of redressing most racial ills, and most social institutions are prepared to grant minorities full access so long as they meet the institution's standards. Storytelling aims at increasing empathy and allowing the reader a glimpse into what life is like for the author of color. Counterstorytelling aims to debunk the many myths and generalizations that white people believe and that enable them to be comfortable in a system in which they enjoy a disproportionate share of the benefits and privileges. Both types of writing aim at a broad, multiracial audience. Storytellers such as Patricia Williams, Robert Williams, and Richard Delgado have won wide audiences and national acclaim for their work.

Attorneys and legal scholars have also applied the lessons of legal storytelling and narrative analysis to judicial proceedings and the dynamics of the courtroom. A trial is, in some respects, a battle of narratives. And the relationship between an attorney and a client may be seen as an effort to impose a narrative, or understanding, on their mutual journey. Writers such as Lucie White and Anthony Alfieri show how attention to the narrative side of lawyering allows lawyers to understand their function and provide a better brand of justice.

Hate speech.

Along with the above-mentioned emphasis on language, discourse, and narrative comes a focus on an especially problematic form of expression—hate speech. Some of the earliest critical race theory work, which continues today, examines the law's treatment of racial epithets, slurs, and name-calling. Speech is a highly protected value in our legal system, yet vicious put-downs based on a person's unchangeable characteristics endanger another set of values, including health, psychological well-being, and equality. Critical theorists such as Mari Matsuda, Charles Lawrence, and Richard Delgado analyze this conflict between free expression and equal dignity in an effort to provide greater protection for the latter value. Some have participated in the drafting of campus hate-speech codes aimed at assuring an atmosphere conducive to equal participation. They also address issues such as the Confederate flag, teams that sport demeaning Indian logos, and public monuments that memorialize slavery and a segregated past.

Spin-Off Movements

Critical race theory has spawned a number of successor movements that, while continuing to maintain relations with the original movement, pursue courses and directions of their own. Concerned about an unduly Afrocentric emphasis in critical race theory and inattention to groups falling outside the black/white binary of race, Latino scholars in the mid-1990s began caucusing separately during critical race theory meetings, then broke off to form their own multiracial organization, the conference on Latino/Critical studies. The group focuses on a number of issues—such as immigration law and policy, language and accent discrimination, and discrimination based on conquest or territorial status—to which the parent organization gives short shrift.

In similar fashion, a national organization of radical Asian-American scholars meets separately to develop a body of knowledge related specifically to the needs and problems of that population, including many of the above-named issues and, in addition, such issues as Orientalism and the notion of Asians as a model minority. For their part, gay and lesbians of color have been developing a sophisticated set of ideas and a body of scholarship devoted to sexual minorities. Critical race feminism examines issues pertaining to women within the various communities of color, including sweatshop labor, sexual abuse in minority communities, and global human rights, including resistance to genital mutilation and other practices directed against women.

A final spin-off movement is critical white studies, in which scholars apply the techniques and approaches of critical race theory—including social constructionism, historical revisionism, and close attention to myth and narrative—to whites. Scholars such as Ian Haney-López examine Supreme Court cases dealing with the legal definition of whiteness and the requirement—which endured until recently—that an applicant seeking to naturalize (acquire American citizenship) establish that he or she is white. Others examine the abovementioned "one-drop" rule and laws governing interracial marriage and adoption in an effort to learn how white preference figures in. Still others examine seemingly race-neutral laws, such as the income tax code, in search for provisions that favor whites and tacitly enact a system of white privilege, while a final group examines white-collar crime and leniency afforded sympathetic white defendants who have erred over ones who are less sympathetic, nonwhite, but who committed the same offense.

Criticism

As the reader might imagine, audacious movements championing sweeping insights into American society and employ-

ing nontraditional forms of scholarship have come in for their share of criticism. At first, criticism was relatively muted. Book reviewers and tenure committees welcomed the new scholarship and gave it a warm reception. However, critics have taken the movement to task for making undocumented assertions and substituting personal experience and anecdote for provable fact. Other critics have focused on the movement's critique of merit and other Eurocentric mainstays. With merit, for example, Daniel Farber and Suzanna Sherry ask, what will replace it as a basis for distributing jobs, places in a law school class, and other scarce social goods? And, what are we to make of the current distribution of wealth and influence? If it was improperly gained, as the critics suggest, through a series of rigged competitions, what of minority groups such as Asians and Jews who have done well under the current regime? Perhaps the critique of merit is implicitly anti-Semitic.

Critics from the left level a different type of criticism. Interest convergence, a Supreme Court that subtly discourages racial reform even in the act of advancing it, and other bleak scenarios are too depressing to serve as rallying cries for liberal reformers. Moreover, they are poor tools for students and young attorneys, who require more action-oriented, inspiring fare. Derrick Bell and his colleagues reply that happy myths about progress and faith in the law that, in the end, turn out to be untrue discourage the activist even more and lead to disillusion and dropout. The solution for the reformer is to learn to derive meaning from the act of struggle itself—whether or not it brings immediate victory.

Other mainstream critics take the movement to task for departing from a conception of law as a system of exact, predictable, formal rules and teaching, instead, that it is full of indeterminacy and veiled, clashing interests. Some of these critics charge that critical race theory's focus on narrative and subjectivity, instead of objectivity and uniform rules, is dangerous. Jeffrey Rosen, legal affairs editor for the *New Republic,* for example, rebuked several critical race authors for providing the basis for the O. J. Simpson acquittal. When Simpson's lawyer, Johnny Cochrane, successfully appealed to the jury to imagine a different story from the one the state prosecutor advanced—a story in which the Simpson prosecution was infected at every stage with racial prejudice—Cochrane was simply using applied critical race theory. This strategy—"playing the race card," in Rosen's view—amounted to a dangerous departure from what should have been the main objective of a trial: finding the truth.

Methodology

As the above description suggests, critical race theorists address a broad span of issues having to do with race, and from a variety of perspectives. Most pay close attention to context and historical situation, valuing the individual over the universal in social and legal analysis. They also credit multiplicity, for example of narratives and identities, over broad generalization. They emphasize how legal rules and regimes look from the perspective of the disempowered and outsider groups—in Matsuda's memorable phrase, "looking to the bottom." And a significant faction places primary importance on material factors—labor demand, immigration needs, conquest,

DERRICK BELL

Raised in Pittsburgh, Pennsylvania, the son of working-class parents, Derrick Bell graduated from Duquesne University and the University of Pittsburgh law school, where he was the first African-American to gain membership to its prestigious law review. After graduating from law school, he worked for a number of law reform agencies, including the NAACP, then entered teaching at Harvard Law School in 1969, the first of his race to teach in a tenure-track capacity there. At the end of 1980, he left Harvard to assume the position of dean at University of Oregon Law School, the first black to lead a major, white-dominated law school in the United States. After leaving Oregon in protest over the faculty's refusal to hire a well-qualified Asian-American female professor, he returned to Harvard Law School, where he mentored students and young scholars across the country, helped found the critical race theory movement, and constantly pressed for liberalization of racial policies at his school. His persistent, heroic, sometimes quixotic struggles are recounted in two books and countless newspaper stories. An inspiration to two generations of lawyers and scholars, Bell taught as a permanent visiting professor at New York University law school in the early 2000s.

RELATED LEGAL MOVEMENTS

One of a group of progressive movements in the law, critical race theory bears close relations with a forerunner movement—critical legal studies—that flourished in the 1960s and 1970s and was still alive in the early 2000s. Building on the insights of the early-twentieth-century legal realists, critical legal studies scholars attacked the ideas of legal determinacy—that every legal problem has exactly one correct solution—and autonomy, the notion that law exists in a realm by itself. Instead, the critical legal studies scholars urged, law bears a close relation to economics, politics, social science, and even art and aesthetics. Critical race theorists build on all these ideas, as well as on the Continental school of philosophy from which many critical legal studies scholars draw inspiration.

Critical race theory also builds on some of the key ideas of radical feminism, including hierarchy, patriarchy, and the notion that everyday terms, categories, and roles advance implicit agendas and encode power relations in a way that benefits those in charge. The movement also learned from revisionist historians, such as Charles Beard and Patricia Limerick, who examined history from hitherto unexplored perspectives, such as those of women, workers, and members of outsider groups. Finally, critical race theory scholars such as Derrick Bell and Richard Delgado draw from neo-Marxist theory in exploring how race relations in the United States reflect economic struggles, shifting labor needs, and the clash of interest groups.

international tensions—in understanding the ebb and flow of U.S. racial politics. Critical of both liberal incrementalism and conservative color-blind philosophies, critical race theorists carve out new ground that places central importance on power, economics, narrative, and social construction in coming to grips with America's social problems.

The next wave of critical race theorists will likely consider the relationship between race and class, the role of minorities in a two-party political system, and the implications of globalization for domestic minorities. The United States' population of color is rapidly growing and was expected to exceed 50 percent sometime in the mid-twenty-first century. Latinos were expected to surpass blacks as the nation's largest group of color. The implications for race relations and civil rights of all these developments are sure to be on critical race theory's agenda well into the future.

The movement is sure to remain controversial—but, of course, many social movements were in their early years. Yet in some respects, it has become the new orthodoxy. Some judges now apply its insights in understanding the racial dynamics of particular cases. Mainstream presses publish its authors; undergraduates study its teachings on hate speech, narrative, and race coding. Two critical race theorists were nominated for high positions within the Clinton administration, but proved too controversial to be confirmed. As the United States struggles to come to terms with a multiracial world and a domestic population that is increasingly black, brown, and Asian, the insights of these progressive, divergent thinkers are apt to become more and more relevant.

See also **Identity, Multiple; Identity: Personal and Social Identity; Race and Racism.**

BIBLIOGRAPHY
Bell, Derrick A. *And We Are Not Saved: The Elusive Quest for Racial Justice.* New York: Basic Books, 1987. Expansion of the "Civil Rights Chronicles."
———. "*Brown v. Board of Education* and the Interest Convergence Dilemma." *Harvard Law Review* 93 (1980): 518ff. Classic statement of materialist interpretation of race.
———. "Serving Two Masters: Integration Ideals and Client Interests in School Desegregation Litigation." *Yale Law Journal* 85 (1976): 470ff. Convincing demonstration of tensions inherent in civil rights advocacy.
Calmore, John O. "Critical Race Theory, Archie Shepp, and Fire Music: Securing an Authentic Intellectual Life in a Multicultural World." *Southern California Law Review* 65 (1992): 2129ff. Classic work on the minority condition.
Crenshaw, Kimberlé, et al., eds. *Critical Race Theory: The Key Writings That Formed the Movement.* New York: New Press, 1995.
———. "Race, Reform, and Retrenchment: Transformation and Legitimation in Antidiscrimination Law." *Harvard Law Review* 101 (1988): 1331ff. Early statement of antiliberal critique.
Delgado, Richard. *The Rodrigo Chronicles: Conversations about America and Race.* New York: New York University Press, 1995. Renowned example of legal storytelling.
Delgado, Richard, and Jean Stefancic, eds. *Critical Race Theory: The Cutting Edge.* 2nd ed. Philadelphia: Temple University Press, 2000. Widely used reader on critical race theory.
———, eds. *Critical White Studies: Looking behind the Mirror.* Philadelphia: Temple University Press, 1997. Broad collection of writings about whiteness.
———, eds. *The Latino/a Condition: A Critical Reader.* New York: New York University Press, 1998. Collection of Lat/Crit writings.
Dudziak, Mary L. *Cold War Civil Rights: Race and the Image of American Democracy.* Princeton, N.J.: Princeton University Press, 2000. Extended treatment of forces leading to *Brown v. Board of Education.*
Farber, Daniel, and Suzanna Sherry. *Beyond All Reason: The Radical Assault on Truth in American Law.* New York: Oxford University Press, 1997. Searching criticism of the critical race theory movement.
Freeman, Alan D. "Legitimizing Racial Discrimination through Antidiscrimination Law: A Critical Review of Supreme Court Doctrine." *Minnesota Law Review* 62 (1978): 1049ff. Illuminating examination of role of Supreme Court in achieving social justice.
Guinier, Lani. *The Tyranny of the Majority: Fundamental Fairness in Representative Democracy.* New York: Free Press, 1994. Innovative study of voting mechanisms.
Haney-López, Ian F. *White by Law: The Legal Construction of Race.* New York: New York University Press, 1996. Groundbreaking study of role of law in drawing boundaries of the white race.
Harris, Angela P. "Race and Essentialism in Feminist Legal Theory." *Stanford Law Review* 42 (1990): 581ff. Powerful treatment of white bias in mainstream feminism.
Lawrence, Charles R., III. "The Id, the Ego, and Equal Protection: Reckoning with Unconscious Racism." *Stanford Law Review* 39 (1987): 317ff. Demonstrates the prevalence of unconscious racism and proposes ways the law may take account of it.
Matsuda, Mari J. "Public Response to Racist Speech: Considering the Victim's Story." *Michigan Law Review* 87 (1989): 2320ff. Classic exposition of critical methodology.
Perea, Juan F. "Demography and Distrust: An Essay on American Languages, Cultural Pluralism, and Official English." *Minnesota Law Review* 77 (1992): 269ff. Famed treatment of language rights.
Ross, Thomas. "Innocence and Affirmative Action." *Vanderbilt Law Review* 43 (1990): 297ff. Study of the role of the power of white innocence.
"Symposium: Critical Race Theory." *California Law Review* 82 (1994): 741ff. First and defining symposium on critical race theory.
Williams, Patricia J. *The Alchemy of Race and Rights.* Cambridge, Mass.: Harvard University Press, 1991. Illustrious example of legal storytelling.
Wing, Adrien K., ed. *Critical Race Feminism: A Reader.* New York: New York University Press, 2003. Classic collection of critical race feminist writings.

Richard Delgado
Jean Stefancic

CRITICAL THEORY. In the humanities, the term *critical theory* has had many meanings in different historical contexts. From the end of World War II through the 1960s, the term signified the use of critical and theoretical approaches within major disciplines of the humanities such as art history, literary studies, and more broadly, cultural studies. From the 1970s, the term entered into the rapidly evolving area of film and media studies. Critical theory took on at the same time a more specialized sense describing the work of the Frankfurt School that itself spread steadily through many disciplines of the humanities and social sciences in the English-speaking world from the 1970s on.

While critical theories were entering the humanities throughout the world, a proliferation of new theoretical approaches from France, often associated with structuralism and then poststructuralism and postmodern theory, generated new discourses that were also assimilated to the cover concept of critical theory. Moreover, different groups such as women, gays and lesbians, and people of color also developed specific critical theories within a wide range of disciplines from the 1970s into the early twenty-first century. The situation was further complicated when many of the theoretical discourses (such as deconstruction) were associated with philosophy, which in turn gave rise in the humanities to a tendency to speak of Theory with a capital *T* when describing the proliferation of critical theories and methods and to privilege them as a necessary instrument of criticism.

To sort out this complex trajectory, it is useful to first broadly sketch the role of critical theory in the various fields of the humanities, then present the Frankfurt School version of critical theory, and finally engage the mutations of critical theory from the theory proliferation of the 1960s and 1970s, the rise of the "posts," the interconnection of critical theory with groups associated with new social movements, its connection with philosophy, and the emergence of Theory as a privileged discourse. While this narrative is partly historical, it is mainly analytical, for in the contemporary context, different people use the term *critical theory* in diverse and contested ways following the various models and stages of the discourse. Thus there is not one single or dominant understanding of critical theory in the university of the early twenty-first century.

Critical Theory in the Disciplines

As Jürgen Habermas has documented, during the Enlightenment of the eighteenth century various modes of political, literary, and cultural criticism emerged from the salons, public houses, and other sites of the bourgeois public sphere, leading to the production of journals and books that discussed the latest cultural fashions and political trends. Major eighteenth- and nineteenth-century writers such as Jonathan Swift, Alexander Pope, Charles-Pierre Baudelaire, and Edgar Allan Poe practiced forms of criticism, as did nineteenth-century novelists such as Jane Austen, Charlotte Brontë, Charles Dickens, and George Eliot.

Critical discourse in a broad range of cultural criticism developed from philosophical and critical responses to genres of art and evaluative responses to specific art works. From Aristotle's *Poetics* through Matthew Arnold and F. R. Leavis in the literary arts, critical aesthetic theories attempted to define the key features of genres and to distinguish what constituted artistic excellence and experience.

Critical approaches in literature, art, music, dance, and the arts began emerging as a specific discipline in the nineteenth century throughout the Western world. In the first decades of the twentieth century, critics such as György Lukács, Ernst Bloch, and Walter Benjamin began applying Marxist theory to a broad range of the arts. Freudians such as Ernest Jones began using psychoanalytic theory to study culture, while Herbert Read deployed Jungian theory. By the 1950s, a variety of schools of critical theory started using major theoretical discourses of the period to discuss, analyze, interpret, and critique

the arts. There was a reaction against this theory turn, however, both from those who wanted a more scientific approach to the aesthetic work, such as I. A. Richards, and from those who wanted a more empathetic immersion in cultural artifacts, such as some members of North American New Criticism, who advocated close readings of literary texts without what they saw as the blinders of theory.

Some critical theories and methods such as Marxism, feminism, psychoanalysis, and semiotics were taken up in the 1960s in the new disciplines of film and media theory, which also developed their own autonomous discourses and methods. Critical approaches to mass communication and culture, however, were first developed by the Frankfurt School, which generated its own concept of critical theory.

The Frankfurt School and Critical Theory

"Critical theory" stood as a code for the quasi-Marxist theory of society developed by a group of interdisciplinary social theorists collectively known as the Frankfurt School. The term *Frankfurt School* refers to the work of members of the Institut für Sozialforschung (Institute for Social Research) that was established in Frankfurt, Germany, in 1923 as the first Marxist-oriented research center affiliated with a major German university. Max Horkheimer became director of the institute in 1930, gathering around himself many talented theorists, including Erich Fromm, Franz Neumann, Herbert Marcuse, and Theodor W. Adorno. Under Horkheimer, the institute sought to develop an interdisciplinary social theory that could serve as an instrument of social transformation. The work of this era was a synthesis of philosophy and social theory, combining sociology, psychology, cultural studies, and political economy, among other disciplines.

In a series of studies carried out in the 1930s, the Institute for Social Research developed theories of monopoly capitalism, the new industrial state, the role of technology and giant corporations in monopoly capitalism, the key roles of mass culture and communication in reproducing contemporary societies, and the decline of democracy and of the individual. Critical theory drew alike on Hegelian dialectics, Marxian theory, Friedrich Nietzsche, Sigmund Freud, Max Weber, and other trends of contemporary thought. It articulated theories that were to occupy the center of social theory for the next several decades. Rarely, if ever, has such a talented group of interdisciplinary intellectuals come together under the auspices of one institute. They managed to keep alive radical social theory during a difficult historical era and provided aspects of a neo-Marxian theory of the changed social reality and new historical situation in the transition from competitive capitalism to monopoly capitalism.

During World War II, the institute split up because of pressures from the war. Leo Lowenthal, Marcuse, Neumann, and others worked for the U.S. government as their contribution to the fight against fascism. Adorno and Horkheimer, meanwhile, moved to California, where they worked on their collective book, *Dialectic of Enlightenment,* which discussed how reason and enlightenment in the contemporary era turned into their opposites, transforming what promised to be instruments of truth and liberation into tools of domination. In their scenario, science and technology had created horrific tools of destruction and death, culture was commodified into products of a mass-produced culture industry, and democracy terminated into fascism, in which masses chose despotic and demagogic rulers. Moreover, in their extremely pessimistic vision, individuals were oppressing their own bodies and renouncing their own desires as they assimilated and created their own repressive beliefs and allowed themselves to be instruments of labor and war.

After World War II, Adorno, Horkheimer, and Friedrich Pollock returned to Frankfurt to reestablish the institute in Germany, while Lowenthal, Marcuse, and others remained in the United States. In Germany, Adorno, Horkheimer, and their associates published a series of books and became a dominant intellectual current. At this time, the term *Frankfurt School* became widespread as a characterization of this group's version of interdisciplinary social research and of the particular critical theory developed by them. They engaged in frequent methodological and substantive debates with other social theories, most notably "the positivism dispute" in which they criticized more empirical and quantitative approaches to theory and defended their own more speculative and critical brand of theory.

The Frankfurt School eventually became best known for their critical theories of "the totally administered society," or "one-dimensional society," which analyzed the increasing power of capitalism over all aspects of social life and the development of new forms of social control. During the 1950s, however, there were divergences between the work of the reestablished institute and the developing theories of Fromm, Lowenthal, Marcuse, and others who did not return to Germany, which were often at odds with both the current and earlier work of Adorno and Horkheimer. Thus it is misleading to consider the work of various critical theorists during the postwar period as members of a monolithic Frankfurt School. Whereas there was both a shared sense of purpose and collective work on interdisciplinary critical theory from 1930 to the early 1940s, thereafter critical theorists frequently diverged, and during the 1950s and 1960s *Frankfurt School* as a term can really be applied only to the work of the institute in Germany under Horkheimer and Adorno.

From Structuralism to Poststructuralism and Beyond

The development of structuralism and poststructuralism in France in the 1950s and 1960s and rapid global transmission of books and ideas contributed to the development of an interdisciplinary mode of theory that became prevalent in the humanities. Structuralism is often associated with the French anthropologist Claude Lévi-Strauss, whose studies of myth, culture, and language discerned a binary structure in myth, for example, between nature and culture or the raw and the cooked. For Lévi-Strauss, culture was articulated into systems that could be described with the precision and force of a science.

Structuralism spread through the human sciences in the 1960s and 1970s, moving from Lévi-Strauss's anthropology and study of myth, to structuralist theories of language (often combined with semiotics), to structuralist Marxism that produced structuralist accounts of the capitalist economy (Louis Althusser) and state (Nicos Poulantzas).

The human sciences were conceptualized by structuralists as self-contained systems with their own grammar, rules, and structuring binary oppositions. Texts were seen as structured networks of signs determined not by what they referred to so much as through their differential relation to other signs. Structuralist critical theory thus focused on detecting the system of binary oppositions through which textual systems were structured, and it delineated oppositions between synchronic and diachronic arrangements, or langue/parole, with the former referring to the synchronic social system of language and the latter referring to specific speech at a particular time.

Whereas structuralism had ambitions of attaining the status of a super science, which could arbitrate among competing truth claims and provide a foundational discipline, poststructuralism challenged any single discipline's claim to primary status and promoted more interdisciplinary modes of theory. Poststructuralism turned to history, politics, and an active and creative human subject, away from the more ahistorical, scientific, and objectivist modes of thought in structuralism.

The poststructuralist moment was a particularly fertile one as important theorists such as Roland Barthes, Jean-François Lyotard, and Michel Foucault wrote new poststructuralist works and younger theorists such as Jacques Derrida, Jean Baudrillard, Paul Virilio, and others entered into productive periods. The poststructuralist turn was evident in the famous 1966 conference on "Critical Languages and the Sciences of Man" at Johns Hopkins University, which featured an important intervention by Derrida, "Structure, Sign, and Play in the Discourse of the Human Sciences." Rejecting structuralist theories of language, Derrida stressed the instability and excess of meaning in language, as well as the ways in which heterogeneity and difference were generated. Derrida also questioned the binary opposition between nature and culture upon which Lévi-Strauss had erected his system, thus undermining a certain glorification of the human sciences in the humanities and opening the discipline for a greater appreciation of philosophy, literature, and less-scientific modes of discourse.

Derrida became one of the most prolific writers of his generation and generated great interest in philosophy throughout the humanities, but he also crossed boundaries between disciplines and contributed to both a proliferation of critical theories and more interdisciplinary humanities. Derrida's deconstruction took apart philosophical and closed scientific systems, showing that their foundational beliefs affirmed one side or another of the binary oppositions, for example, nature, with Jean-Jacques Rousseau; or culture, with cultural anthropologists who described the constructed nature of society and culture (a theme that would move into poststructuralism and many of the humanities).

Poststructuralism stressed the openness and heterogeneity of the text, how it is embedded in history and desire, its political and ideological dimensions, and its excess of meaning.

This led critical theory to more multilevel interpretive methods and more radical political readings and critiques. Foucault described how texts and discourses are embedded in power; Edward W. Said articulated the "Orientalism" of Western-centric ideology and the construction of non-Western cultures in both colonial and postcolonial discourses; and feminists described how patriarchy and the concepts of totalitarianism and subordination are inscribed in texts.

Following the poststructuralist moment of the late 1960s and 1970s, there was a proliferation of new theoretical moments of critical theory that connected with new social movements, producing a proliferation of "posts" and theory wars from the 1970s into the early twenty-first century. Baudrillard, a French theorist, took up poststructuralism and deconstruction in idiosyncratic ways. His early work analyzed the "system of objects" and "political economy of the sign" in the media and consumer society, showing how the system of commodities and consumer values were organized in a hierarchal system. Yet by the mid-1970s, Baudrillard entered a deconstructive and poststructuralist phase, taking apart in sequence the claims of Marxism and political economy, Freud and psychoanalysis, Foucault, and other forms of theory. For Baudrillard, the consumer and media society was generating novel forms of sign and signification, technology, and cultural spaces, which produced a break with modernity itself. While modern societies, he argued, were organized around production and political economy, postmodern societies were organized around technology and generated new forms of culture, experience, and subjectivities.

In *Le différend,* Lyotard valorized those voices that had been suppressed or muted in social and academic spheres. He advocated "the end of grand narratives" in the humanities and politics, and the production of small, "minor narratives" and microanalysis. This theme was also taken up by Gilles Deleuze and Félix Guattari who proliferated a dazzling range of critical theories to engage salient cultural, social, economic, and political phenomena of the day.

French poststructuralist critical theory is extremely hard to categorize as it combines social theory, cultural and political commentary, philosophy, literary stylistics, and many social and human sciences in its work, crossing boundaries between academic disciplines and fields. This interdisciplinary focus links French critical theory to Frankfurt School critical theory and to certain types of feminism and other cultural theories that practice "border crossing" (that is, they cross the borders between disciplines and the traditional division of topics and academic labor).

The proliferation of theories also produced a tendency to use the term *Theory* (with a capital *T*) to describe the wealth of conflicting critical theories. In this sense, Theory replaces philosophy as the most abstract and general mode of theoretical discourse. Theory has emerged as an autonomous enterprise in many academic disciplines, giving rise to a tendency to do work in Theory, which engages various critical theories, problems, and concepts, or explores the nature and function of theory itself in the academic disciplines.

Critical theory turned to a "politics of representation" during the 1960s and 1970s. This enterprise involved analysis of the ways in which images, discourses, and narratives of a wide range of cultural forms—from philosophy and the sciences to the advertising and entertainment of the media culture—were embedded in texts and reproduced social domination and subordination. British cultural studies, for instance, showed how problematic representations of gender, race, class, sexuality, and other identity markers were found throughout cultural forms. Cultural studies developed different critical theories and methods to analyze the production of texts, their multiple meanings, and their complex uses and effects.

Critical theories were also developed within feminism, critical race theory, gay and lesbian theory, and other groupings associated with new political movements, making critical theory part of political struggle inside and outside the university. Feminists, for instance, demonstrated how gender bias infected disciplines from philosophy to literary study and was embedded in texts ranging from the classics of the canon to the mundane artifacts of popular culture. In similar ways, critical race theorists demonstrated how racist images and discourses permeated cultural artifacts, while gay and lesbian theorists demonstrated how their sexual orientation was negatively represented and marginalized.

These critical theories also stressed giving voice to groups and individuals marginalized in the dominant forms of Western and then global culture. Critical theory began going global in the post-1960s disseminations of critical discourses. Postcolonial theory in various parts of the world developed particular critical theories as a response to colonial oppression and to the hopes of national liberation. Frantz Fanon in Algeria, Wole Soyinka in Nigeria, Gabriel García Márquez in Latin America, Arundhati Roy in India, and others all gave voice to specific experiences and articulated critical theories that expanded the global and multicultural reach of critical theory.

The past decades have thus witnessed a proliferation of critical theory to the extent that the very concept is a contested area. In the early twenty-first century, conflicting models of critical theory are used by different individuals and groups in various fields of inquiry in different parts of the world. There is also a tendency to combine critical theories in one's work, following a recommendation by Foucault in the 1970s that many have taken up. Others who took up the anti-theory discourse of Richard Rorty and various critics of Theory have called for rigorous empirical and contextual engagement with topics and subject matter. *Critical theory* is thus a multidimensional term that continues to take on differing connotations and uses and is embedded in many different disciplines and debates.

See also **Literary Criticism; Literary History; Literature; Postcolonial Literature; Structuralism and Poststructuralism.**

BIBLIOGRAPHY
Althusser, Louis, and Étienne Balibar. *Reading "Capital."* Translated by Ben Brewster. London: Verso, 1997.

Baudrillard, Jean. *The System of Objects.* Translated by James Benedict. London: Verso, 1996.

Bhavnani, Kum-Kum, ed. *Feminism and "Race."* Oxford: Oxford University Press, 2001.

Corber, Robert J., and Stephen Valocchi, eds. *Queer Studies: An Interdisciplinary Reader.* Malden, Mass.: Blackwell, 2003.

Deleuze, Gilles, and Félix Guattari. *A Thousand Plateaus: Capitalism and Schizophrenia.* Translated by Brian Massumi. Minneapolis: University of Minnesota Press, 1987.

Derrida, Jacques. *Writing and Difference.* Translated by Alan Bass. Chicago: University of Chicago Press, 1978.

Foucault, Michel. *Power/Knowledge: Selected Interviews and Other Writings, 1972–1977.* Edited and translated by Colin Gordon. New York: Pantheon, 1980.

Habermas, Jürgen. *The Structural Transformation of the Public Sphere.* Translated by Thomas Burger with the assistance of Frederick Lawrence. Cambridge, Mass.: MIT Press, 1989.

Horkheimer, Max. *Critical Theory.* Translated by Matthew J. O'Connell et al. New York: Herder and Herder, 1972.

Horkheimer, Max, and Theodor W. Adorno. *Dialectic of Enlightenment.* Translated by John Cumming. New York: Herder and Herder, 1972.

Lévi-Strauss, Claude. *The Raw and the Cooked.* Translated by John and Doreen Weightman. New York: Harper and Row, 1969.

Lewis, Reina, and Sara Mills, eds. *Feminist Postcolonial Theory: A Reader.* Edinburgh: Edinburgh University Press, 2003.

Lyotard, Jean-François. *The Differend: Phrases in Dispute.* Translated by Georges Van Den Abbeele. Minneapolis: University of Minnesota Press, 1988.

Rorty, Richard. *Contingency, Irony, and Solidarity.* Cambridge, U.K.: Cambridge University Press, 1989.

Said, Edward W. *Orientalism.* New York: Pantheon, 1978.

Tong, Rosemarie Putnam. *Feminist Thought: A More Comprehensive Introduction.* 2nd ed. Boulder, Colo.: Westview, 1998.

Douglas Kellner

CULTURAL CAPITAL. The concept of cultural capital originated in the work of Pierre Bourdieu (1979, pp. 10, 12), who defined it as high cultural knowledge that ultimately redounds to the owner's financial and social advantage. An example would be knowing how to "dress for success." This cultural knowledge can pay off. Although they naturally seek competent personnel, employers also prefer executives who dress, talk, and comport themselves in accordance with their elite status. As a result, a job-seeker's sartorial knowledge commands a salary beyond what his or her productivity alone would have commanded. In effect, the well-dressed candidate gets a salary bonus. Most people do not know how to dress for success, do not even know the importance of doing so, and do not, in fact, do so. For this reason, the acquisition of high cultural knowledge and style, including stylish dress, table manners, golf, knowledge of wine, the right neighborhood, and arty chit-chat, represents a capital resource of the owner, vested in the owner, but it is not human capital. Usually human capital and cultural capital go together because people who have one usually have the other as well, but the two capitals are in principle distinct. Anyone may have human capital without cultural capital, or cultural capital without human

capital. In principle, adults might acquire cultural capital by hiring a tutor (Eliza Doolittle benefited from one in *My Fair Lady*). However, cultural capital is prohibitively inconvenient and expensive to acquire that way. In reality, people normally acquire cultural capital informally when they grow to maturity in advantaged socioeconomic households.

Forms of Capital

Capital: A store of value that facilitates action.

Financial capital: Money available for investment.

Physical capital: Real estate, equipment, and infrastructure of production.

Human capital: Education or training that increases productivity on the job.

Cultural capital: High cultural knowledge convertible into social and economic advantage.

Social capital: Relationships of trust embedded in social networks.

Examples of Cultural Capital

Bourdieu defines cultural capital narrowly as fluency in a society's elite culture. Fluency in low- or middle-status culture does not represent cultural capital because these cultural fluencies do not transmute into elite status; they transmute into middle or low status. Bourdieu was interested in how elites reproduced themselves from one generation to the next. High-status culture emphasizes classical art, music, dance, and literature, but it also includes furniture, architecture, cuisine, vacation resorts, and clothing. Knowledge of these arts represents capital because and to the extent that this knowledge can be turned to the owner's financial and social advantage at multiple points in the owner's life span. For example, when Josephine Smith wears the right suit, handbag, and shoes to a job interview on Wall Street, she makes a favorable impression and lands the job. Josephine's mother and peers taught her how to dress, a culturally monitored skill that paid off when Josephine landed a lucrative job. When Josephine subsequently marries a millionaire and obtains a share of his fortune, her cultural capital has produced additional financial capital.

Upper-class people acquire cultural capital in the family and in formal schooling. When the school curriculum reinforces the home curriculum, as it routinely does for children of the affluent, students obtain additional access to their own culture in school. Conversely, when the school curriculum contradicts or subverts the home culture, as it does for poor, immigrant, or ethnic minority children, students have to master a foreign culture at school while mastering their own at home. Even if they accomplish this difficult task, poor, immigrant, and minority children still do not learn everything they need to know in order to access the upper class later in life. Schools do not teach all the cultural knowledge needed for that access. For example, they do not teach dress, table manners, and demeanor. The parallel curriculum of the upper-status home teaches children much class-linked knowledge that schools ignore. Since poor or minority children cannot acquire many forms of class-linked cultural knowledge at school or at home, this cultural knowledge is virtually impossible for them to acquire at all.

The parallel curriculum gives children of the affluent a superior endowment in cultural capital. However acquired, at home or in school or both, cultural capital is converted to social and economic advantage in several ways of which the principal is prestige diplomas. Although formal education culminates in diplomas, degrees, and certificates, cultural capital is quite different from human capital, which also emerges from formal education. The difference between human capital and cultural capital resides in how the capital benefits its owner. Human capital increases its owner's productivity, a competence employers reward with high wages. In contrast, cultural capital conveys social recognition and acceptability on the strength of which people get desirable jobs, marriages, and business contacts. Therefore, the same diploma has value as human capital and as cultural capital; and the difference depends on whether we emphasize the real vocational competencies that diploma represents or the prestige recognition it commands. When a person's education has bestowed both enhanced productivity and prestige recognition, that person has two forms of capital (human and cultural), both of which transmute into money and social networks.

Occupational Culture and Competence

Although Bourdieu analyzed the high culture of the bourgeoisie, calling this cultural capital, he neglected the occupational culture of the bourgeoisie. This disjuncture led George Farkas to complain that cultural capital ignored competence. Sociologists understand culture as a tool kit, not a veneer. Crafted for a special purpose, Bourdieu's narrow concept of cultural capital stresses aesthetic judgment as if entrepreneurs and chief executive officers (CEOs) had only to attend art openings and poetry readings. In actuality, entrepreneurs and CEOs discharge real responsibility, which requires real vocational competence. Granted, some well-connected people obtain lucrative jobs on snob appeal alone, but an economy cannot run on snob appeal. What Brigitte Berger has called "the culture of entrepreneurship" is an occupational culture, not an aesthetic culture. The occupational culture of the business class is the skills, knowledge, attitudes and values needed to run a market economy. Like its aesthetic culture, the occupational culture of the business class is transmitted from one generation to the next at home as well as in schools. Bourgeois occupational culture means cultural traits (values, skills, attitudes, knowledge) characteristic of business owners and executives around the world. A business class equips its youth with class-appropriate cultural capital, both aesthetic and vocational.

Immigrant Experience

Oddly, immigration studies have provided a favorable context for the application of cultural capital theory as well as for its criticism and improvement. This advantage arises from often-remarked disparities in socioeconomic mobility of immigrant groups. Some groups move up the social ladder more quickly than others (consider Jews, Koreans, and Cubans). Often this disparity arises because immigrants bring quite different financial resources with them. Some are wealthy on arrival, others impoverished. These cases are easy to explain. The most perplexing cases have been those in which equally impoverished immigrant groups obtain unequal socioeconomic results after one or two generations. Such cases compel attention to intergroup disparities in cultural capital. For instance, in 1900, Jewish, Polish, and Italian immigrants arrived in the United States. All were equally and wretchedly poor, but two decades later, the Jews were well ahead of the others in business ownership. Similarly, in the 1920s, southern-born black Americans and Caribbean-born black immigrants arrived in New York City. Both groups were impoverished, but the Caribbean blacks soon owned more businesses than did the American-born blacks. Again, in the 1960s, Cubans and Haitians arrived in Miami as impoverished immigrants, but a generation later, Cubans had built a flourishing and lucrative enclave economy whereas Haitians still worked in the informal sector.

In all these cases, socioeconomically mobile immigrant groups had more access than less mobile counterparts to vocationally relevant cultural capital. In two cases, this capital belonged to ethnic rather than class cultures, but it served nonetheless as a functional equivalent to the vocational culture of the business class. Among the Jews and the Caribbean blacks, entrepreneurship had been honed and built into the ethnic culture by centuries of harsh necessity. Although poor on arrival, they knew how to run businesses. Expropriated by the communists, Cuban business owners left their money and property in their island homeland, but they took with them their cultural capital. Thanks to this cultural knowledge, they recouped their money and property within two generations through entrepreneurship. Knowing how to run a business is an obvious advantage for socioeconomic mobility. Cultural capital's vocational component conveys exactly this know-how. Like the aesthetic knowledge that Bourdieu emphasized, this vocational capital is transmitted intergenerationally in households. Normally, we do not expect poor people to understand entrepreneurship, but infrequently they do, and, when they do, they obtain socioeconomic advantages from the knowledge.

See also **Class; Education; Human Capital.**

BIBLIOGRAPHY

Berger, Brigitte. "The Culture of Modern Entrepreneurship." Chap. 1 in *The Culture of Entrepreneurship,* edited by Brigitte Berger. San Francisco: ICS Press, 1991.

Böröcz, József, and Caleb Southworth. "Decomposing the Intellectuals' Class Power: Conversion of Cultural Capital to Income, Hungary, 1986." *Social Forces* 74 (1996): 797–821.

Bourdieu, Pierre. *La distinction: critique sociale du jugement.* Paris: Editions de Minuit, 1979.

———. "Les trois etats du capital culturel." *Actes de la Recherche en Sciences Sociales* 30 (1979): 3–5.

DiMaggio, Paul. "Social Structure, Institutions, and Cultural Good." In *Social Theory for a Changing Society,* edited by Pierre Bourdieu and James S. Coleman. Boulder, Colo.: Westview Press, 1991.

Farkas, George. *Human Capital or Cultural Capital? Ethnicity and Poverty Groups in an Urban School District.* New York: Aldine de Gruyter, 1996.

Huuskonen, Visa. "The Process of Becoming an Entrepreneur: A Theoretical Framework of Factors Influencing Entrepreneurs' Start-Up Decisions (Preliminary Results)." In *Entrepreneurship and Business Development,* edited by Heinz Klandt. Aldershot, U.K.: Avebury, 1993.

Lamont, Michele, and Annette Lareau. "Cultural Capital: Allusions, Gaps, and Glissandos in Recent Theoretical Developments." *Sociological Theory* 6 (1988): 153–168.

Lee, Jennifer. *Civility in the City: Blacks, Jews, and Koreans in Urban America.* Cambridge, Mass.: Harvard University Press, 2002.

Light, Ivan H. *Ethnic Enterprise in America: Business and Welfare among Chinese, Japanese, and Blacks.* Los Angeles: University of California, 1972.

Light, Ivan, and Steven J. Gold. *Ethnic Economies.* San Diego: Academic Press, 2000.

Sowell, Thomas. *Migrations and Cultures: A World View.* New York: Basic, 1996.

Szelényi, Iván. *Socialist Entrepreneurs: Embourgeoisement in Rural Hungary.* Madison: University of Wisconsin, 1988.

Ivan Light

CULTURAL HISTORY. As a discipline, cultural history is a bit over two centuries old, but it has an extensive prehistory going back to Renaissance scholarship, especially in areas of the history of literature and the history of philosophy. In the Renaissance, *cultus* or *cultura* was commonly associated with the cultivation of literature, philosophy, eloquence, law, arts, and sciences, whose fruits were the human virtues necessary for civil society. In the seventeenth century the form "culture" (*cultura*) was employed by Francis Bacon, Thomas Hobbes, Samuel Pufendorf, Gottfried Wilhelm von Leibniz, Johannes F. Buddeus, Christian Thomasius, and others, who spoke of the cultivation of the soul, mind, intellect, or reason (*cultura animi, mentis, intellectus, rationis*); and Leibniz, for one, rendered it into the vernacular as "Cultur," or "Kultur."

The terminology was shifted from an individual to a social level as a way of indicating levels of civilization and judging "which peoples may be judged to be barbaric and which cultivated," in the words of Pufendorf in 1663. "True culture" (*vera cultura*), according to Buddeus, was an indication of morality, sociability, and emergence from an animal state; and the first question centered on the "origin of human culture and civility" and their emergence from a "primeval condition." In 1774 Jean–Bernard Mérian wrote of primitive savages as "a people of hunters, navigators, without culture, without laws, without arts." Thus "culture," together with its companion, "barbarism," represents the judgments passed by Europeans on their own and other societies, past and present.

"Cultural history" (*Kulturgeschichte*) arose as a term and a concept in the later eighteenth century, as "culture" replaced earlier equivalents, including "spirit" (*mens, esprit, Geist,* etc.), which was extended from individual psychology to collective mentality (e.g., *Volksgeist* or *Zeitgeist*), and literature, referring to all the written remains of human cultural achievement. The "history of the human spirit" (*historia intellectus humani; histoire de l'esprit humain; Geschichte des menschlichen Geistes*) was a phrase often used by eighteenth–century historians of particular disciplines. "Literary history" (*historia literaria*), was a major genre, treating (as the seventeenth–century polyhistor Gerhard Joannes Vossius wrote) "the lives and writings of learned men and the invention and progress of the arts." As Nicholas Wickenden has put it, "What Vossius called 'literary history' was really what would now be called cultural history."

Culture and Language

In 1781, the year when Immanuel Kant's *Critique of Pure Reason* marked a revolution in philosophy, Johann Adelung, in his *Versuch einer Geschichte der Cultur des menschlichen Geschlechts,* identified "the first beginnings of culture" with the origins of language, adding that thereafter, through the development of agriculture and private property, "language follows culture," and furthermore, "Since the language of every nation has the closest relationship with its culture, its history can never be understood without continual reference to the conditions and progress of culture." For Adelung "culture is the transition from a more instinctive and animal–like condition to the more complex relations of social life" so that "When culture ceases, so does true history." Deliberately or not, Adelung set a terminological and conceptual fashion that has figured prominently in modern historiography and the human sciences for two centuries.

The best–known convert to the new terminology was Johann Gottfried von Herder, whose *Another Philosophy of History* (1784) told the story of the development of the "human spirit" from its appearance in the state of nature to the emergence of the *Volksgeist*; but a decade later, in his *Ideas for the Philosophy of History of Mankind,* he referred to the process or "chain of culture" in the sense of the cultivation of intellectual and linguistic attributes. To Kant's "critique of pure reason" he opposed a "metacritique," arguing that the object of criticism must be not pure but human reason, not transcendent and ahistorical spirit but concrete, temporal manifestations, beginning with language, without which "reason" could not express itself. For Herder, cultural history aspired not only to criticize but even to replace philosophy as the foundational discipline of human understanding. And other scholars followed Herder in associating cultural history with critical philosophy, including Christoph Meiners, Karl Franz von Irwing, K. H. L. Pölitz, Dietrich Hermann Hegewisch, and Johann Gottfried Eichhorn.

"Cultural history" had an extraordinary *fortuna* in the generations after Adelung and Herder. The quantity of published works was striking, and their topics were global and local, ancient and modern, general and special (including cultural histories of literature, medicine, commerce, etc.), and they were often designed for a general rather than merely a learned readership. The heyday of cultural history in this tradition was reached in the Victorian period with the voluminous publications of Wilhelm Wachsmuth, Gustav Klemm, Georg Friedrich Kolb, Gustav Freitag, Wilhelm Riehl, Friedrich

Anton Heller von Hellwald, Otto Henne am Rhyn, Karl Grün, J. J. Honegger, and Julius Lippert. Klemm, who was the founder of an extraordinary ethnographic museum in Dresden, an early model for the Smithsonian Institution, asked such questions as "What were the oldest tools of the human race? and How did early man eat, drink, shelter and cloth himself?" His *Allgemeine Cultur–Geschichte der Menschheit* (1843), while paying homage to the old Herderian tradition, presented its subject from an entirely "new standpoint," according to which human thought and action were seen not primarily in a Biblical framework but in a prehistorical, evolutionary continuum that denied supernatural privilege to humanity and emphasized what, long before Fernand Braudel, was called "material culture" (*materielle Kultur*).

Material and Spiritual Culture

In the nineteenth century as today, the most important interdisciplinary connection of cultural history was the new field of anthropology. In the famous formula of Edward Tylor, father of modern anthropology, in his *Primitive Culture* (1881): "Culture or Civilization taken in its wide ethnographic sense is that complex whole which includes knowledge, belief, art, morals, law, custom, and any other capabilities and habits acquired by man as a member of society." Tylor referred in particular to Klemm's conception of "Culture–History," which he preferred to the more conventional terminology of "civilization." And the influence was mutual, reflecting back on German scholarship: "What is Culture?" asked the cultural historian J. J. Honegger in 1882 and, by way of answer, gave a paraphrase of the very definition given by Tylor in 1865.

Victorian scholars were poised, or torn, between two conceptions of culture. One was the material culture rooted in primitive life and the other the spiritual culture reflected in such human creations as art, literature, philosophy, and religion. "Culture and anarchy" was the famous formula of Matthew Arnold, who sought, in an idealized and progressivist culture, "the study of perfection" and perhaps "a great help out of our present difficulties." Opposed to the focus of scholars such as Klemm were the cultivated students of spiritual culture (*geistige Kultur*), of whom Jacob Burckhardt was the most notable representative. While the first took the low road, the latter took the high road to the study of culture, although Burckhardt did not ignore popular culture, as shown by in the pages of his *Civilization of the Renaissance in Italy* (*Kulturgeschichte* was his term) devoted to costume, etiquette, domestic life, festivals, and other topics rediscovered recently by the "new cultural history." Like Klemm, Burckhardt was a collector, drawn especially to art and literature, and he defined culture "as the sum total of those mental developments which take place spontaneously and lay no claim to universal of compulsive authority." Suspicious of modern power politics, he was also critical of the material progress of his age, which he regarded as a principal threat to his cultivated world. "We may all perish," he wrote, "but at least I want to discover the interest for which I am to perish, namely, the culture of old Europe" (*Letters*, p. 197).

By the end of the century, cultural history had achieved high public visibility and a significant academic base, with a large bibliography, several journals, and historiography of its own; and it became a subject of contention among historians. The battle of methods (*Methodenstreit*) began in 1888 when Dietrich Schäfer gave a lecture denouncing the trivialities of cultural history and reasserting the primacy of politics. This manifesto was answered the next year by Eberhard Gothein, who defended cultural history against the charges of materialism and urged the value of other cultural forms—religion, art, law, and economics—in the effort to understand historical change. This was the view also taken by Karl Lamprecht, who for a generation occupied the storm center of the historical *Methodenstreit* heralded by this exchange and who became the leading figure in the theory and practice of cultural history before World War I.

In 1886 Lamprecht turned to his lifework, *Deutsche Geschichte,* which was a survey of the whole cultural history of Germany; he established at the University of Leipzig a "historical seminar" and then a more ambitious Institute for Cultural and Universal History. In his late years Lamprecht's public life was torn by controversy about the status, role, and value of cultural history in scholarship and teaching. Lamprecht's "new history," as it was pejoratively called, was based on advances in linguistics, archeology, art history, economics, and especially recent psychology (i.e., *Völkerpsychologie,* social psychology). Although few of his professional colleagues, aside from students, accepted his eccentric and aggressively argued views, and he died in some disrepute, the popularity of his work testified to the appeal of his arguments.

Lamprecht's "new history" had counterparts elsewhere in the West, especially France and the United States, which also emphasized the central role of culture. Henri Berr was already working out the agenda expressed in his concept of "synthetic history," which underlay the efforts of his younger colleagues leading to the formation of the *Annales* school of history. It was in the wake of such discussions that James Harvey Robinson of Columbia University, in 1912, proclaimed his own version of the "new history," which was likewise opposed to conventional political history. These views were echoed by other scholars, including Johann Huizinga, who delivered his manifesto on "the task of cultural history" in 1926. After World War I a kind of cultural history was continued in Germany in a debased form in the racialist *Volksgeschichte,* which reinforced the ideology and imperialist policies of the Third Reich.

In the French and Anglophone world the semantic rival of "culture" was "civilization" (replacing "civility"), which was also a neologism of the eighteenth century, associated with Voltaire and what Carl Becker called the "new history" of the Enlightenment and which was also contrasted with "barbarism" and intended to designate the highest stage of human development. The classic history of the rise of "civilization" in the West was that of François Guizot, for whom "civilization is a fact like any other," and indeed "the fact par excellence," which in his famous lectures, given before the Revolution of 1830 drew him into politics, he traced from classical antiquity down to the French monarchy, which was the highest expression of this fact. Guizot set the line of argument for several generations of cultural history in France. In England Henry Thomas Buckle's *History of Civilization in England* was hardly less influential, although its doctrinaire scientism and materialism eventually rendered it unfashionable and indeed obsolete.

Twentieth–Century Developments

The writing of cultural history expanded further in the twentieth century as textbooks and popular works presented the results of generations of research and interpretation. Notable examples were the one hundred volumes of Henri Berr's series *Evolution of Humanity* (begun in 1920); Egon Friedell's *A Cultural History of the Modern Age* (1931), which, dedicated to Bernard Shaw and glorying in its journalistic style, carried the story from the Renaissance to psychoanalysis and the "collapse of reality"; Preserved Smith's *History of Modern Culture* (1934), which, in the spirit of Robinson's new history, surveyed early modern sciences, humanities, social control, and "spirit of the times"; and *European Civilization: Its Origin and Development,* edited by Edward Eyre (7 vols., 1934–1939), which included also global frontiers beyond the West. In such works the whole world, private and public, real and imagined, natural and social, becomes a field of anthropological inquiry, interpretation, and speculation.

From the beginning the defining feature of cultural history, shared with anthropology, has been an inclination to holism—the effort to grasp "the history of everything," in Berr's famous phrase, or as Harry Elmer Barnes wrote of the new history, "the recording of everything which has happened in the past"—but of course "in the light of twentieth–century knowledge and methods." Yet cultural history was turned to analysis as well as synthesis, and so in 1940 in the United States, for example, there appeared a volume, *The Cultural Approach to History* ("edited for the American Historical Association"), which explored a wide range of techniques of cultural analysis, means of analyzing social groups, nationality, institutions, and ideas as sources of cultural history.

In this generation little has changed save the rhetorical claims in the "new cultural history," so–called since the publication of the volume by the same name by Lynn Hunt in 1989, supplemented also by the "new historicism," which has made its own contributions to cultural history, and by the study of mentalities and cultural practices carried on from the *Annales* school by Roger Chartier. In general, recent cultural history has come to embrace a wide and miscellaneous range of topics, such as crime, madness, childhood, old age, gesture, humor, smells, space, and other items (appearing on the world wide web) from addiction to unbelief. In terms of theory this self–proclaimed "new cultural history" has arisen out of the wreckage of scientific and Marxist history, which sought the concealed mechanisms of social change beneath the surface of collective behavior. This is true in the sense not only that many new cultural historians such as Natalie Davis and Lynn Hunt have emerged from the materialist assumptions of socioeconomic historical practice and/or Marxist theory, but also that cultural history has always contained a powerful critique of such methods.

In general, cultural history rejects economic and political reductionism, gives up the noble dream of objectivity, recognizes the role of imagination in historical reconstruction, and, no longer aspiring to rigorous explanation, turns instead to what has been called "interpretive social science." As represented by Clifford Geertz and Charles Taylor, interpretive social science places understanding (*Verstehen*) above explanation and so hermeneutics above causal analysis as the principal access to a knowledge of the human condition, past and present. Explanation requires some sort of reduction of experience, or evidence, to crucial factors at the expense of excluding other experience, or evidence, which not only lends color or, as Geertz says, thickness to description but also qualifies simplistic and naturalistic notions of causation.

The new cultural history may entail a sort of relativism distasteful to historians of the older schools, but the positive aspect is a more critical awareness of the meaning of the historian's craft. Not only the objects of history but the works of historians are themselves subject to the conditions of their cultural environment, and so (in contemporary parlance) "culturally constructed." Yet the premise of the new cultural history that, as Hunt writes, "the representations of the social world themselves are the constituents of social reality," is an insight not unfamiliar to earlier cultural historians; for as Huizinga reminded us, "The historical discipline is a cultural process." And like culture it is still changing and renewing itself, though not always with much appreciation for its own history.

See also **Cultural Studies; Historiography; Ideas, History of.**

BIBLIOGRAPHY

PRIMARY SOURCES

Breysig, Kurt. *Kulturgeschichte des Neuzeit.* Berlin: G. Bondi, 1900.

Burckhardt, Jacob. *Die Cultur der Renaissance in Italien.* Basel: Schweighauser, 1860.

Dean, Amos. *The History of Civilization.* 7 vols. Albany, N.Y.: J. Munsell, 1868–1869.

Eichhorn, J. G. *Allgemeine Geschichte der Cultur und Litteratur des neueren Europas.* 2 vols. Göttingen, 1796.

Guizot, François Pierre Guillaume *History of Civilization in Europe: From the Fall of the Roman Empire to the French Revolution.* 3 vols. 1846.

Henne am Rhyn, Otto. *Kulturgeschichte der neueren Zeit.* Leipzig: O. Wigand, 1870–1872.

Honegger, Johann Jakob. *Allgemeine Kulturgeschichte.* 1882.

Klemm, Gustav Friedrich. *Allgemeine Cultur–geschichte der Menschheit.* 1843.

Kolb, Georg Friedrich. *Culturgeschichte der Menschheit.* 2 vols. Leipzig: A. Felix, 1872–1873.

Lamprecht, Karl. *Die kulturhistorische Methode.* Berlin: H. Heyfelder, 1900.

———. *What is History? Five Lectures on the Modern Science of History.* Translated by E. A. Andrews. New York and London: Macmillan, 1905.

Lippert, Julius. *The Evolution of Culture.* Translated by George Peter Murdoch. New York: Macmillan, 1931.

Steinhausen, George. *Geschichte der Deutschen Kultur.* Leipzig and Vienna: Bibliographisches Institute, 1904.

Weber, Alfred. *Kulturgeschichte als Kultursoziologie.* Munich: R. Piper, 1951.

SECONDARY SOURCES

Burke, Peter. *Varieties of Cultural History.* Ithaca, N.Y.: Cornell University Press, 1997.

Chartier, Roger. *Cultural History: Between Practices and Representations.* Translated by Lydia G. Cochrane. Ithaca, N.Y.: Cornell University Press, 1988.

Febvre, Lucien. *A New Kind of History: From the Writings of Febvre.* Edited by Peter Burke. Translated by K. Folca. London: Routledge and Kegan Paul, 1973.

Haas, Stefan. *Historische Kulturforschung in Deutschland 1880-1930.* Cologne: Böhlau, 1994.

Hunt, Lynn, ed. *The New Cultural History: Essays.* Berkeley: University of California Press, 1989.

Kelley, D. R. "The Old Cultural History." *History and the Human Sciences* (1996): 101–126.

Weintraub, Karl J. *Visions of Culture: Voltaire, Guizot, Burckhardt, Lamprecht, Huizinga, Ortega y Gasset.* Chicago: University of Chicago Press, 1966.

Wickenden, Nicholas. *G. H. Vossius and the Humanist Conception of History.* Assen: Van Gorcum, 1993.

Donald R. Kelley

CULTURAL REVIVALS. The term *cultural revival* refers to the formation of group identity around a common culture, where a claim is forwarded that the aspects of culture with which the group identifies have been recovered after losses due to colonization, forced or voluntary relocation, oppression, or modernization. Cultural revival is predominantly associated with minority populations and frequently underwrites demands for rights, restitutions, and political or legal recognition as an ethnic group. Much scholarship on the subject has taken examples of cultural revival at face value, undertaking to document the strategies such groups employ and analyze the cultural practices and materials they recover. Work by historians, anthropologists, and sociologists in the 1980s and 1990s, however, theorized the phenomenon as a hallmark of social formations under capitalist modernity.

According to these scholars, cultural revival is a tactic pursued—consciously or unconsciously—by minority communities to consolidate political identity and gain recognition through an appeal to foundationalist cultural logic—that is, the belief that "authentic" traditions are unchanging and ancient, unique to and defining of a given community, and properly transmitted only to members of that group through heredity and ancestry.

Critical Approaches

Scholarship on cultural revivals has been shaped by theoretical developments in three major areas: ethnicity, nationalism, and modernity. Since the work in the 1960s of Nathan Glazer and Daniel Patrick Moynihan, theories of ethnicity have regarded ethnic groups as "interest groups": ethnic identity is

proposed, maintained, or solidified when political or economic gains accrue to the group through doing so, rather than because primordial ties, distinctive customs, and cultural heritage cannot be relinquished. While early scholars were interested in the persistence of ethnic identification among migrants in an assimilationist United States, subsequent Marxist anthropologists have focused on cultural revivals and ethnic nationalisms. They link them to competition between subnational communities over access to material resources and suggest that the uneven nature of capitalist expansion creates spaces in which marginalized groups bid for access to the benefits of development with culture operating as their symbolic legitimation and means of solidifying group loyalty.

Moving beyond this "instrumentalist" position, but also remaining skeptical of the "primordialist" claims of revivalists themselves, the insights of historians of nationalism have shed light on the crucial role of cultural practices, understandings, and performances in the formation and functioning of cultural revivals, and the affective experience of those involved in them. Like cultural revival, cultural nationalism is predicated on a supposed shared language, tradition, and culture, and an appeal to foundational history, which, no matter how artificially constructed (through the suppression of minority dialects, for example), is experienced as profoundly real and binding. The work of Benedict Anderson illuminated the cultural means through which the abstraction of nation produced for its members a sense of deep loyalty and belonging—an "imagined community"—otherwise absent in a secular, atomized, competitive, and individualist modernity. An influential collection by Eric Hobsbawm and Terence Ranger similarly troubles the primordialist claims of cultural revivalism while pointing to its cultural and historical significance and the power of its appeal. The essayists in *The Invention of Tradition* argued that significant bodies of what we regard as "tradition" are, in fact, of comparatively modern origin, "responses to novel situations which take the form of reference to old situations, or which establish their own past by quasi-obligatory repetition" (p. 2). The editors proposed that the rapid changes and violent discontinuities of modernity (including the dislocations of diaspora, colonization, and forcible "modernization" that frequently occasion later attempts at cultural revival) called for the formalizations of tradition that "established and symbolized social cohesion or the membership of groups, real or artificial communities" through ritual performance (p. 9).

Postmodernist interpretations of cultural revival are premised on the axiom that "culture" is a text, which, like all texts, is an assemblage of signifiers from the sign systems of cultural discourse at large. While specific signifiers become attached to specific groups by social convention (a doughnut is associated with the United States, the attribution of heightened aesthetic sensibility attaches to the French), these relations are essentially arbitrary (doughnuts, for example, originated in Germany, and heightened aesthetic sensibility is a rhetorical proposition rather than an empirical claim). Arguments that specific signifiers authentically, naturally, or historically belong to a given group—the central claim of cultural revival—operate as "truth claims," attempts to secure and authorize a particular version of reality against possible competing versions. The irony of this analysis for cultural revivalists is that the cultural elements reclaimed by reviving groups can, more frequently than not, be proved to be integral aspects of the sign system of the dominant culture against which the revivalists stake their claim. The idea that an indigenous people lives in harmony with nature, for example, is a recurrent theme of cultural revivals and can be argued to have much more to do with postindustrial Western romantic structures of belief than with the historical lifeways of specific indigenous populations. (See Hanson for a concise, and later controversial, application of postmodernist analysis to Maori cultural revival). Theorists such as Dean MacCannell have gone further in suggesting that contemporary cultural revivals are not only semiotic constructions (like other cultural and ethnic identities), but that they are a uniquely postmodern phenomenon that he calls "reconstructed ethnicity," in which authenticity itself has taken on a commodity value. This fetishization of authenticity, he argues, stunts cultural agency and evacuates the particularity of local cultural expression, as groups come to project and identify with a generalized and interchangeable image of "traditional" values.

While some thinkers in the postmodernist or poststructuralist camp believe the essentialist logic of cultural revivalism—the idea that members of the group are distinguished by their unique possession of an inherent, authentic, and unchanging essence expressed through culture—to be an inherently unsound basis for a resistant politics, and devote their critical energies to discrediting such claims, others (among them, Gayatri Spivak) understand it to be a strategic necessity that can authorize beleaguered minorities (with "scrupulously conscientious" aims) to speak as political subjects within a dominant system.

Fourth World Revivals

Perhaps the most dramatic and effective cultural revivals have been those of "Fourth World" populations, defined as indigenous peoples who hold the status of political and/or numerical minorities within the nation-states that encompass their ancestral territories. These groups include North American Indians, New Zealand Maori, Australian Aboriginal, Norwegian Sami, and many others. In these contexts, cultural revival appears as a logical response to histories of state-supported genocide, assimilation, and the disruption or prohibition of cultural practices. Where such state strategies attempted, usually deliberately, to erode ethnic allegiances that opposed state hegemony, cultural revival seeks to reconstruct these communities and networks as the first step in resistance to domination. It thus indirectly addresses the conditions of socioeconomic deprivation, prejudice, and lack of opportunity that have for these groups been the corollaries of colonization, by validating cultural identities devalued by dominant or colonial culture, and providing the basis for collective pride, unity, and action. The long-term sustainability of such initiatives, however, is frequently determined by existing institutional and governance structures, both within and outside the community in question.

An example of a successful Fourth World cultural revival is the case of New Zealand Maori. After the devastating losses of a century and a half of colonization, cultural assimilation, and urbanization, a "Maori renaissance," beginning in the

1970s, was centered around the fight for rights to land illegally taken during colonization and was inspired by independence movements in still-colonized territories and civil rights struggles in the United States. Early goals of this revival were the promotion of Maori language learning (spoken by less than one percentage point of the population in the 1970s) and the rehabilitation of knowledge of *Maoritanga* (Maori culture, custom, and identity), particularly among the youth of the community. In both of these matters, the Maori revival has been extremely effective, fostering Maori language use throughout the population and training a whole generation of Maori political leaders whose primary commitments are to their ethnic community and who understand themselves as acting in consonance with Maori priorities and customary protocol. Aided by the resilience and strength of tribal networks that survived the ravages of colonization, the united front presented by early protests forced a reconsideration of land-rights policy by the state, and subsequent restitution processes have led to the recognition of Maori cultural considerations as an integral element in national governance. While claims to authenticity were strategically important in legitimating the revival during its early stages, primordial arguments have given way with the securing of state recognition to a broad understanding that Maori culture is a living, inventive, and syncretic set of practices that provides a flexible basis for collective identity and action in changing conditions.

In contrast to these Fourth World examples, the rhetoric of cultural revival is rarely observed in postcolonial states where previously colonized ethnic groups have gained the power of self-governance, giving further credence to the theory that cultural revival is a tactic pursued predominantly by the politically marginal. In postcolonial states, culture-based claims are more likely to be suppressed in favor of the liberal individualist humanism that legitimates Western-style government, or alternatively, to be branded as divisive and backward.

Ethnic Nationalisms and Race-centered Solidarities

Similar processes of politically motivated cultural revival can be seen at work even in cases where cultural continuity has been violently severed, and collective heritage has been erased by historical traumas such as occupation or slavery. An example of this kind of revival is the race-based solidarity forged by black nationalists in the United States. Recognizing the failure of strategies of racial accommodation and integration in the face of continued structural oppression, black nationalism offered not only a framework for analysis—the black nation was colonized by white America—but a strategy for resistance: collective, anticolonial struggle. Advocates such as Harold Cruse argued in the language of cultural nationalism, claiming that championing an autonomous cultural heritage would not only create unity in a vastly diverse population, but it would also foreground and counter the colonial exploitation and derogation of black culture by whites within the United States, with all its destructive psychological effects, and suggest radical alternatives to liberal accommodationism of civil rights. Movements such as the Harlem Renaissance, Negritude, and pan-Africanism were cultural revivals in that they recognized, celebrated, and discovered cultural continuities with a shared African heritage, fostered invented traditions (such as Kwanzaa), and authorized their ideological claims through reference to this resurgent culture.

Theoretical Trajectories and Contemporary Contexts

While it may seem at first glance that cultural revivals work to undermine the political hegemony of the nation-state, and oppose themselves to dominant cultural and economic interests, these relationships are complex and frequently ambivalent. A new generation of research on cultural revivals parses their role in the sociopolitical formations, economies, and belief systems of nations.

Antimodernism, revival, and the tourism and heritage industry.
Scholars have noted the constitutive place that appeals to lost heritage have in the rhetoric of modernity. If to be "modern" is to be severed from one's ethnic past and the holistic sense of community it represents, critiques of industrial modernity tend to be expressed through the idealization of heritage and the cultural integrity of "primitives" or "exotics." This yearning for a lost wholeness and authenticity results in support for salvage and preservation efforts that in turn present the "lost" or "recovered" cultural materials for the consumption of the dominant, modern culture, frequently as tourist or heritage attractions. The ironic structure of belief underpinning this process has been called "imperialist nostalgia"—where imperialist or capitalist expansion causes the ongoing damage and erasure of traditional lifeways, and is "nostalgically" lamented by its agents even as they continue to perpetuate it, or "ethnological antimodernism," expressing one's commitment to the superiority and normativity of modernity through a romantic, consumerist overvaluation of "premodern" peoples and their cultures.

In material practice, this can lead to an uncomfortable symbiosis as the group in the process of cultural revival becomes a symbolic resource and economic asset for the very state that is responsible for their oppression as an ethnic minority. The power to articulate cultural identity, meanwhile, remains clearly in the hands of the state, the market, or the dominant ethnic interest: cultural identities are validated insofar as they conform to hegemonic agendas, and particular forms of cultural expression (a ritual, distinctive costume, or festival, for example) are selected for preservation and display while others are neglected or actively repressed. At best, cultural revival under these conditions can offer some minimal form of recognition, representation, or leverage that can be capitalized on by a minority group.

Theorists such as Barbara Kirschenblatt-Gimblett have elaborated these observations, suggesting that the action of naming and presenting a set of cultural practices as heritage constitutes in itself an ironic form of cultural revival. The culture that becomes "heritage" is both given a second life (endowed with cultural and economic value by its prospective consumers) and declared dead in the same gesture, as it enters the domain of cultures deemed to belong to "history." An instance of this is the preservation of closed Welsh coalmines by local governments with the aim of reconstituting them as tourist attractions that feature the lifeways and work of the colliers of a past age. This development strategy obviously has mixed implications for those for whom this way of life is a living concern and whose political energies are devoted to encouraging reinvestment in coal production by the British government.

Liberal multiculturalism.
Some scholars have examined the paradoxical codependence of cultural revivals and the states against which they articulate themselves through the lens of political discourse and juridical practice. Anthropologists such as Elizabeth Povinelli, drawing on work in radical political theory, have noted that liberal multiculturalism demands the demonstration of cultural difference to validate its prevailing ethic as a "rational, non-violent form of association based on competing knowledges and moral values" (p. 6). Yet the national recognition of difference is always conditional, disqualifying differences that prevailing morality finds repugnant, however irrationally, or that are incompatible with Western constructions of "tradition" (preferring, for example, continuity over revival, spiritual over economic or material orientation). This logic is particularly conspicuous in cases where revival is accompanied by legal procedures for restitution. As in the Aboriginal land hearings that Povinelli discusses, court proceedings function as public revival rituals, occasions for the collective demonstration of national repentance and the celebration of majority tolerance, which center paradoxically around the state's legislation of what constitutes "traditional custom," and its demand that aboriginals not only identify with but perform this version of culture as a prerequisite of their recognition as political subjects.

Globalization and revival.
The phenomenon of cultural revival is entering a new phase with the changes in social and political formation that accompany globalization, giving rise to cultural revivals that operate above the level of the nation-state, linking members of an ethnic group residing in geographically distant locations, and appealing for recognition not just to national governments but to transnational publics. Scholars of contemporary cultural revival are beginning to focus on the new strategies and discourses that emerge as revivals are shaped by their challenge to transnational rather than national relations of ethnicity and race, and operate predominantly through the dissemination of images and discourse in communications media, rather than through the immediacy of cultural performance and territorial sentiment. What new forms of affinity and belonging do global revivals draw on? What new ideas about culture do they produce, and which old ones do they perpetuate? These may well be the questions asked of cultural revival in the future.

See also **Ethnicity and Race; Ethnohistory, U.S.; Modernity; Nationalism; Practices; Tradition.**

BIBLIOGRAPHY

Anderson, Benedict. *Imagined Communities: Reflections on the Origin and Spread of Nationalism.* London: Verso, 1983.
Hanson, Allan. "The Making of the Maori: Culture Invention and Its Logic." *American Anthropologist* 91, no. 4 (1989): 890–902.

Hobsbawm, Eric, and Terence Ranger, eds. *The Invention of Tradition.* Cambridge, U.K.: Cambridge University Press, 1983.

Kirschenblatt-Gimblett, Barbara. *Destination Culture: Tourism, Museums, and Heritage.* Berkeley: University of California Press, 1998.

MacCannell, Dean. *Empty Meeting Grounds: The Tourist Papers.* London and New York: Routledge, 1992.

Omi, Michael, and Howard Winant. *Racial Formation in the United States: From the 1960s to the 1980s.* New York and London: Routledge and Kegan Paul, 1986.

Povinelli, Elizabeth A. *The Cunning of Recognition: Indigenous Alterities and the Making of Australian Multiculturalism.* Durham, N.C.: Duke University Press, 2002.

Spivak, Gayatri Chakravorty. *The Post-Colonial Critic: Interviews, Strategies, Dialogues.* Edited by Sarah Harasym. New York: Routledge, 1990.

Wilmsen, Edwin. "Introduction: Premises of Power in Ethnic Politics." In *The Politics of Difference: Ethnic Premises in a World of Power,* edited by Edwin N. Wilmsen and Patrick McAllister. Chicago: University of Chicago Press, 1996.

Wood, Robert. "Touristic Ethnicity: A Brief Itinerary." *Ethnic and Racial Studies* 21, no. 2 (1998): 218–241.

Margaret Werry

CULTURAL STUDIES. Cultural studies is one of the more controversial intellectual formations of the 1990s and the first decade of the third millennium. It has experienced a period of rapid growth in the academy, appearing at many universities in a variety of forms and locations (although rarely as degree-granting departments). At the same time, it has been broadly attacked both from inside the university and outside academia.

Definitions

There are at least five distinct uses of cultural studies, making it difficult to know exactly what people are attacking or defending. It has been used to describe, alone or in various combinations:

1. Any progressive cultural criticism and theory (replacing "critical theory," which served as the umbrella term of the 1980s);

2. The study of popular culture, especially in conjunction with the political problematic of identity and difference;

3. So-called "postmodern" theories that advocate a cultural or discursive constructionism (and, thus, supposedly embrace relativism);

4. Research on the politics of textuality applied broadly to include social life, especially based in poststructuralist theories of ideology, discourse, and subjectivity;

5. A particular intellectual formation that is directly or indirectly linked to the project of British cultural studies, as embodied in the work of Raymond Williams, Stuart Hall, and the Centre for Contemporary Cultural Studies (CCCS).

This entry discusses only the last of these referents even though it is especially difficult to define this intellectual formation. Even the simple claim of British origin is, in the end, probably unacceptable. Still, it provides a reasonable starting point for this discussion. The English origins of cultural studies can be linked to at least four elements of the post–World War II context. First, one of the major issues organizing political debate was framed as the challenge of Americanization, which was perceived in largely cultural terms, both in the growing presence of U.S. popular culture and in the apparent disappearance of many aspects of traditional, working-class culture.

Second, the New Left emerged as a small but influential discussion group, and included many immigrants from the "colonies." It was sympathetic to (but not aligned with) the growing Campaign for Nuclear Disarmament. The New Left had a specific and ambivalent relation to Marxism, engaging Marxist theory and politics even as it criticized it for its failure (and inability?) to account for and respond to the challenges posed by the importance of ideology, colonialism and imperialism, race, and the failures of existing socialism. This work was enabled by the translation and publication of the early writings of Marx and a wide range of European Marxist thinkers.

Third, the British university system was, to put it mildly, elitist and classist, in terms of its student population and in its isolation, aestheticization, and limitation of culture to the field of the arts. Many of the influential early figures in cultural studies were working-class or immigrant students attending university on scholarship, who were driven to look for other accounts of culture that both expanded its referent and took it more seriously.

Finally, many of these figures were deeply influenced by their experience as teachers in various institutions of adult education outside the university. If nothing else, this experience played a role in convincing them, first, of the importance of culture (and intellectual work on culture) to both political struggle and people's everyday lives, and second, of the fact that the important questions do not usually respect the disciplinary boundaries of academic competence and expertise.

Culture and Context

In this context, a number of writers—especially Raymond Williams and Richard Hoggart—began to explore the political and theoretical significance of the concept of culture in relationship to the broader contexts of social life. Trained as literary critics, they argued that cultural texts provided insights into social reality unavailable through the traditional social sciences and enabled one to understand what it felt like to be alive at a particular time and place—to grasp what Williams called "the structure of feeling." They sought to describe culture's concrete effects on people's lives. Hoggart's *The Uses of Literacy* (1957), for example, entered into the debate over Americanization, using close textual analyses to ask whether the new forms of popular culture were unsettling the established relations between working-class cultural practices and the patterns of everyday life of the working classes. Williams—in *Culture and Society* (1958) and *The Long Revolution* (1965), and in other works throughout his career—sought the theoretical and methodological tools that would allow for description of the concrete relations among cultural practices, social relations, and organizations of power.

In 1964 Richard Hoggart set up the CCCS to continue these efforts when he was hired as professor of English literature at the University of Birmingham. This was done with the permission of both his department and the university, but with only their minimal support. He funded the Centre himself from monies he received for testifying in defense of D. H. Lawrence at an obscenity trial, and he hired Stuart Hall, who had already published *The Popular Arts* (1964) with Paddy Whannel. Hall became director in 1969 when Hoggart left to become assistant director of UNESCO. When Hall took a position as professor of sociology at the Open University in 1980, he was replaced by Richard Johnson. In the following years, the Centre was transformed and combined in a number of administrative incarnations until 2002, when the University of Birmingham dismantled the Department of Sociology and Cultural Studies.

The Centre undertook, both individually and collectively, a wide range of sometimes evolving and sometimes discontinuous researches, both theoretical and empirical, into culture and society, and was characterized internally by a wide range of positions and practices. Externally, it came to represent a more limited body of work as it engaged over the years in a number of highly visible public debates with other groups interested in the politics of culture. The Centre is most widely known for having offered a number of models of cultural studies from the mid-1970s to the mid-1980s, including models of: ideological analysis; studies of working-class cultures and subcultures, and of media audiences (all of which, taken together, constituted a particular understanding of culture as a site of resistance); feminist cultural research; hegemonic struggles in state politics; and the place of race in social and cultural processes. The Centre was primarily associated, quite commonly, with the work of the Italian Marxist Antonio Gramsci.

The work of the Centre was not known widely outside of England, and only marginally known in the United States—primarily in departments of education and communication—until the mid-1980s. In the summer of 1983, a series of events organized around the theme "Marxism and the Interpretation of Culture" at the University of Illinois brought Hall and other key figures from the Centre to the United States. In the mid-1980s, the *Australian Journal of Cultural Studies* was founded, and when it followed its editor John Fiske (a student of Raymond Williams who had emigrated to Australia) to the United States, it became the first international journal explicitly devoted to the field.

In 1992 the University of Illinois hosted a second major conference, "Cultural Studies Now and in the Future." During and after this conference, the validity of assuming British cultural studies to be the origin of cultural studies on a larger scale was increasingly challenged. It became clear that the

British tradition was less an origin than a term around which a set of similar projects from all over the world could gather and work. People from Latin America, Asia and the Pacific Rim, Europe, and Africa offered their own indigenous traditions of cultural studies, many of which had developed without any knowledge of the British work, and often had no agreed-upon common label. During the 1990s cultural studies became visible—as something both claimed and contested—in many of the major disciplines of the humanities and social sciences (especially literary studies and anthropology) in the United States and in other parts of the world. In 2002 the first international Association for Cultural Studies was launched.

The founding insight of the British tradition was that what had been traditionally approached as an external relationship between two objects of study—the relation of culture and society—was somehow inscribed in the very complexity of culture itself: culture as a set of privileged activities (inevitably raising questions of value); culture as the uniquely human, mediating activities of symbolic life (for example, textuality, sense-making, signification, and representation); and culture as a whole way of life (linking culture to the totality of social life, including conduct, relations, and institutions). Cultural studies is about the relationship of anthropological, hermeneutic, and aesthetic discourses and practices of culture. It treats culture, then, as more than either a text or a commodity. It looks at culture as the site of the production of (and struggle over) power.

Formations of Cultural Studies

Cultural studies is concerned with describing (and intervening in) the ways cultural forms and practices are produced within, inserted into, and operate in and affect the everyday life of human beings and social formations, so as to reproduce, struggle against, and perhaps transform the existing structures of power. That is, if people make history—but within conditions not of their own devising—cultural studies explores the ways this process is enacted with and through cultural practices, and studies the place of such practices within specific historical formations. Cultural studies explores the historical possibilities of transforming people's lives by trying to understand the relationships of power within which individual realities are constructed. That is, it seeks to understand not only the organizations of power but also the possibilities of survival, struggle, resistance, and change. It takes contestation for granted, not as a reality in every instance, but as an assumption necessary for the existence of critical work, political opposition, and even historical change. Cultural studies is not simply about texts or ideologies, but about the relationships that are historically forged among cultural practices and the contexts in which they operate.

Any further attempt to define cultural studies poses rather unique problems. It cannot be equated with any particular political agenda or with any particular theoretical position. Thus, on the one hand, while British cultural studies is often thought to have investigated class politics, it includes many examples of both feminist cultural studies and cultural studies invested in the politics of race, ethnicity, or postcoloniality. Unlike post-1960s academic formations associated with a particular political agenda (and a pre-constituted constituency outside the academy), cultural studies has no such guaranteed agenda or constituency. On the other hand, cultural studies is not a school of thought that can be linked irrevocably with a particular theory. Again, the British school is assumed to be grounded in Marxism (and especially in the work of Gramsci), but this is only because the diversity of that tradition has been reduced to a single, small set of representatives and examples. In fact, in England as well as elsewhere, cultural studies has drawn upon, and embodied, an enormously wide range of theoretical positions, from humanism to poststructuralism, from Marx to Foucault, from pragmatism to psychoanalysis.

Raymond Williams's distinction between the common project of cultural studies, and its many different formations, recognizes that practicing cultural studies involves redefining it in response to its changing context (its geographical, historical, political and institutional conditions).

The Project of Cultural Studies

The most basic—and most radical—assumption of cultural studies is that the basic unit of investigation is always relationships, and that anything can only truly be understood relationally; thus, studying culture means studying the relationships between configurations of cultural texts and practices on the one hand, and everything that is not in the first instance cultural—including economics, social relations and differences, national issues, social institutions, and so forth—on the other. It involves mapping connections, to see how those connections are being made and where they can be remade. As a result, cultural studies always involves the study of contexts—sets of relations located and circumscribed in time and space, and defined by questions. And cultural studies is always interdisciplinary because understanding culture requires looking at culture's relationship to everything that is not culture.

Moreover, cultural studies is committed to a radical contextualism; it is a rigorous attempt to contextualize intellectual (and political) work. This contextualism shapes the project of cultural studies profoundly, and involves a commitment to complexity, contingency, and constructionism.

Contexts are not random and chaotic collections of bits and pieces on which people attempt to impose order or meaning; they are already ordered or configured when the scholar embraces them in their complexity rather than reducing them to a simplicity defined ahead of time by a theoretical or political agenda. Cultural studies refuses to reduce the complex to the simple, the specific to the exemplary, and the singular to the typical. It refuses to see this complexity as an inconvenience to be acknowledged only after the analysis. It employs a conjunctive logic—where one thing is true, another may also be true—and thereby refuses the illusion of a total, all-encompassing answer. It avoids confusing projects with accomplishments (as if intentions guaranteed effects); and it refuses to put off until later the resistances, the interruptions, and the fractures and contradictions of the context.

Cultural studies believes in contingency; it denies that the shape and structure of any context is inevitable. But cultural

studies does not simply reject essentialism, for anti-essentialism is, in its own way, another version of a logic of necessity: in this case, the necessity that there are never any real relations. Cultural studies is committed to what we might call an anti-anti-essentialism, to the view that there are relationships in history and reality, but they are not necessary. They did not have to be that way, but given that they are that way, they have real effects. Above all, there are no guarantees in history (or in reality) that things will form in some particular way, or work out in some particular way. Reality and history are, so to speak, up for grabs, never guaranteed. Cultural studies operates in the space between, on the one hand, absolute containment, closure, complete and final understanding, total domination, and, on the other hand, absolute freedom and possibility, and openness.

Finally, cultural studies assumes that relationships are produced or constructed, and not simply always the result of chance. The relations that make up a context are real through the various activities of different agents and agencies, including (but not limited to) people and institutions. Insofar as we are talking about the human world—and even when we are describing the physical world, we are within the human world as well—cultural practices and forms matter because they constitute a key dimension of the ongoing transformation or construction of reality. However, the effects of cultural practices are always limited by the existence of a material or nondiscursive reality. Cultural studies, then, does not make everything into culture, nor does it deny the existence of material reality. It does not assume that culture, by itself, constructs reality. To say that culture is constitutive—that it produces the world, along with other kinds of practices—does not mean that real material practices are not being enacted, or that real material conditions do not both enable and constrain the ways in which reality functions and can be interpreted. Cultural studies is, in the first instance, concerned with cultural practices. To put it simply, the culture we live in, the cultural practices we use, and the cultural forms we place upon and insert into reality, have consequences for the way reality is organized and lived.

The commitment to a radical contextualism affects every dimension of cultural studies, including its theory and politics, its questions and answers, and its analytic vocabulary—which includes concepts of culture (text, technology, media), power, and social identity (race, gender, sex, class, ethnicity, and generation). Cultural studies derives its questions, not from a theoretical tradition or a disciplinary paradigm but from a recognition that the context is always already structured, not only by relations of force and power, but also by voices of political anger, despair, and hope. Cultural studies attempts to engage the existing articulations of hope and disappointment in everyday life and to bring the messy and painful reality of power—as it operates both outside and inside the academy—into the practice of scholarship.

Cultural Studies, Theory, and Power

While cultural studies is committed to the absolute necessity of theoretical work, it sees theory as a resource to be used to respond strategically to a particular project, to specific questions and specific contexts. The measure of a theory's truth is its ability to enable a better understanding of a particular context and to open up new—or at least imagined—possibilities for changing that context. In this sense, cultural studies desacralizes theory in order to take it up as a contingent strategic resource. Thus, cultural studies cannot be identified with any single theoretical paradigm or tradition; it continues to wrestle with various modern and postmodern philosophies, including Marxism, phenomenology, hermeneutics, pragmatism, poststructuralism, and postmodernism.

Cultural studies does not begin with a general theory of culture but rather views cultural practices as the intersection of many possible effects. It does not start by defining culture or its effects, or by assembling, in advance, a set of relevant dimensions within which to describe particular practices. Instead, cultural practices are places where different things can and do happen. Nor can one assume, in advance, how to describe the relation of specific cultural formations to particular organizations of power. Consequently, the common assumption that cultural studies is, necessarily, a theory of ideology and representation, or of identity and subjectivity, or of the circulation of communication (production-text-consumption), or of hegemony, is mistaken. Cultural studies often addresses such issues, but that is the result of analytic work on the context rather than an assumption that overwhelms the context.

Like a number of other often overlapping bodies of intellectual and academic work that have emerged since World War II (feminism, critical race theory, postcolonial theory, and queer theory, among others), cultural studies is politically driven; it is committed to understanding power—or more accurately, the relationships of culture, power, and context—and to producing knowledge that might help people understand what is going on in the world (or in particular contexts) and the possibilities that exist for changing it.

The project of cultural studies, then, is a way of politicizing theory and theorizing politics. Cultural studies is always interested in how power infiltrates, contaminates, limits, and empowers the possibilities that people possess to live their lives in dignified and secure ways. For if one wants to change the relations of power—if one wants to move people, even a little bit—one must begin from where people are, from where and how they actually live their lives. Cultural studies attempts to strategically deploy theory (and empirical research) to gain the knowledge necessary to redescribe the context in ways that will enable the articulation of new or better political strategies. Cultural studies also approaches power and politics as complex, contingent, and contextual phenomena and refuses to reduce power to a single dimension or axis, or to assume in advance what the relevant sites, goals, and forms of power and struggle might be. Consequently, it advocates a flexible, somewhat pragmatic or strategic, and often modest approach to political programs and possibilities.

Two of the most important political assumptions of cultural studies are also among its most controversial. Cultural studies refuses to assume that people are dupes, constantly manipulated by the producers of culture and ignorant of their

own subordination. On the other hand, it does not assume that people are always in control, always resisting, or operating with an informed understanding of the context. That does not mean that cultural studies doesn't recognize that people are often duped by contemporary culture, that they are lied to, and that at times—and for a variety of reasons—either don't know it or refuse to admit it. But it does mean that cultural studies is opposed to the vanguardism of so much of contemporary political and intellectual discourse.

Cultural studies is committed to contestation, sometimes as a fact of reality, but always as a possibility that must be sought out. Contestation can also serve as a description of cultural studies' own strategic practice, which sees the world as a field of struggle and a balance of forces. Intellectual work is required to understand the balance and find ways of challenging and changing it. Of course, cultural studies recognizes that the relations among survival, change, struggle, resistance, and opposition are not predictable in advance, and that there are many forms and sites that each can take and has taken; these range from everyday life and social relations to economic and political institutions. Cultural studies, then, is an effort to produce knowledge about the context that will help to strengthen, existing struggles and constituencies, helping to relocate and redirect them, or to organize new struggles and constituencies. It seeks knowledge that will make the contingency of the present visible and open up possibilities that will help to make the world a better, more humane, place.

While it attempts to put knowledge in the service of politics, cultural studies also attempts to make politics listen to the authority of knowledge. It believes that its political commitment (and its desire for intervention) demands that it maintain a justifiable claim to authority in the face of the threat of a relativism often linked to contextualist and constructivist projects. Cultural studies, like many of its political allies in the academy, rejects foundationalism. It does believe that knowledge is dependent on its context, and hence, that all knowledge is limited and partial. There is no knowledge that is not always marked by the possibilities and the limits of the position and perspective from which it is constructed and offered.

Yet cultural studies also rejects relativism, for like foundationalism, relativism assumes that knowledge and culture exist on a different plane from the context they purport to represent. But if the knower is a constituent part of the very context he or she is trying to know, the description plays an active part in the construction of the very context it describes. The question of better or worse knowledge is, then, no longer a matter of comparing two things (the description and the reality) as if there were some place outside the reality that we could stand in order to compare them. The question is rather a matter of the possible effects of the knowledge on the context—what possibilities for change does it enable? The better the knowledge, the more (new) possibilities it will offer for transforming the present. That is what cultural studies means when it talks about knowledge without truth, and about useful knowledge. Cultural studies does demand a kind of self-reflection on its own limitations, but this is not, as in some other projects, a requirement that one define one's identity as if it were determining, but rather that one offer a rigorous analysis of institutional conditions and a reflection of one's own contextual existence.

The question of what cultural studies will (or should) look like is only answerable within the particular context that calls cultural studies into existence. Cultural studies is not alone in privileging the questions of power or in its commitment to relationality and constructionism; it is not alone in its embrace of contingency and contextuality or in recognizing the importance of culture. But the practice that is defined by the intersection of all these commitments—*that* is the project of cultural studies. Cultural studies is an intellectually grounded practice for intervening into the "becoming" of contexts and power. It attempts, temporarily and locally, to place theory in-between in order to enable people to act more strategically in ways that may change their context for the better.

Diversity in Cultural Studies

The diversity of cultural studies is as important as its unity; yet there is no obvious single best way to organize or describe that diversity. One could display the range of objects and discourses that cultural studies has explored—including art, popular culture, media culture, news, political discourses, economies, development practices, everyday practices, organizations, cultural institutions, and subcultures. One could display the different theoretical paradigms (including pragmatism, phenomenology, poststructuralism, Marxism, and so forth) or theoretical influences (Harold Innis, Michel de Certeau, Gramsci, and Michel Foucault, among others). One could display the different political agendas—feminist, Marxist, antiracist, anti-homophobic, anti-postcolonial, anti-ageist—or the more positive political agendas of socialism, radical democracy, and global justice, that have driven the work. One could consider the different ways the major concepts of culture, power, articulation, and context have been used. One could describe the implications of disciplinary diversity—literary studies, anthropology, sociology, communication, history, education, and geography, among others—and methodological diversity—forms of textual analysis, ethnography, interviewing, archival research, statistical analysis, and so forth. Finally, one could speculate about the significance of geographical diversity, which has become increasingly visible and important. A more useful way might be to describe some exemplary instances of cultural studies.

A first model, found in the work of Raymond Williams, reads texts as ideologies in context. That is, it uses texts to try to locate and define the common structure (e.g., homology, structure of feeling) that unites the disparate elements of social formation into a unified social totality. But this common structure of unity is available only by thinking of ideology contextually—that is, by looking at the relations among texts, and between texts and other discursive and nondiscursive practices.

A second model, found in the work of communication scholar James Carey, looks at particular cultural practices as rituals that reenact the unity—shared meanings, structures, and identities—of a community.

A third model locates cultural texts and practices within a dialectic of domination and resistance and was closely associated with the CCCS in the 1970s, especially in the early work of David Morley, Dick Hebdige, and Angela McRobbie. The politics of culture are determined by the relations among a number of relatively autonomous moments—primarily of production and consumption—but later work added distribution, exchange, and regulation. It provided an alternative model of media communication (encoding-decoding) with an emphasis on the audience as an active interpreter of messages and of subcultures in which subcultural styles were seen to be expressions of, and symbolic responses to, lived contradictions—defined by class and generation—of the social experiences of the members of the subculture.

A fourth model explores cultural and social identities as complex sets of relations. It involves the production of differences (or structures of otherness such as race and gender) within a population, the effort to naturalize such identities as biological, the distribution of people into those categories, and the assignment of particular meanings to each identity. These differences provide the basis, along with the inequalities of power and resources, that are defined within a particular society. But they are not natural, inevitable, or fixed; instead, identities are the site of constant work and struggle over the practices by which people come to be represented and to represent themselves. This work studies the dialectical production of identity and difference, often in a kind of Hegelian dialectic of recognition. This is a logic in which the formation (identity) of one term (the self) can only be constructed through, or on top of, the assimilation and exclusion of the other. There are various tropes for this process circulating throughout the cultural studies literature (and beyond), including difference, border-crossing, hybridity, third space, and most recently, diaspora (although the last often attempts to escape the Hegelian negativity of difference). Obviously, such work in cultural studies overlaps here with many other bodies of related work, but its influence—through the work of people like Stuart Hall, Paul Gilroy, Angela McRobbie, Gayatri Spivak, and Judith Butler—has been profound.

A fifth model is concerned with the relationship between culture and the state. Influenced in part by Gramsci, such work was best illustrated by the important work of Stuart Hall and John Clarke on hegemony as an alternative to notions of civil politics as ideological consensus. Hegemony, as a struggle for the gain and consolidation of state power, involves the attempt by a particular coalition of social factions to win popular consent to its leadership. Hegemony is not a battle to the death between two camps, but a constant attempt to negotiate with various factions to put together temporary agreements for the leadership of the ruling bloc at different sites. It therefore works on (and through) the popular languages and logics of the society, and reconfigures the national common sense in order to reconstitute "a balance in the field of forces."

A sixth model of "governmentality" emphasizes the variety of ways in which culture is used by state and other institutions to produce particular kinds of subjects and to regulate their conduct. This work focuses on the material effects of bureaucratic cultural apparatuses; it looks at how institutional discourses produce a particular structure of the subject itself as an historical effect of power. For example, Tony Bennett looks at cultural institutions such as museums in terms of the way they discipline people, organizing their behavior and teaching them, as it were, to behave properly in public as citizens. Similarly, Bennett has also argued that the pedagogy of cultural criticism functioned to render students always inadequate and incomplete, not only in terms of the classroom but as human beings in need of constant self-improvement. In his view, it is only the teacher who can recognize the politically problematic claims of any text, while the students are always guaranteed to fail. Another example involves the work of Nikolas Rose and his colleagues, who attempt to analyze the contemporary forms of neoliberal state power by looking at the micropractices of institutions and everyday life.

Finally, the seventh model looks at culture as formations or organizations of both cultural and noncultural practices, often related to, or even identified with, particular institutions. Such cultural apparatuses function in complicated ways to produce and organize social reality itself. That is to say, they are "technologies of power" that are connected on the one hand to the lived realities of everyday life (itself understood to be an organization of power) and, on the other hand to the larger structures of political and economic power. Cultural or discursive practices are integral pieces of the institutional formations of power that organize the very lived reality and structures of power in space and time. Examples of such work can be seen in the anthropological critiques of development offered by Akhil Gupta and Arturo Escobar, and in Meaghan Morris's studies of the place of history as a cultural formation in Australian social life.

See also **Critical Theory; Hermeneutics; Marxism; Phenomenology; Structuralism and Poststructuralism; Text/ Textuality.**

BIBLIOGRAPHY

Bennett, Tony. *The Birth of the Museum: History, Theory, Politics.* London: Routledge, 1995.

———. *Outside Literature.* London: Routledge, 1990.

Butler, Judith. *Gender Trouble: Feminism and the Subversion of Identity.* New York: Routledge, 1990.

Carey, James W. *Communication as Culture: Essays on Media and Society.* Boston: Unwin Hyman, 1989.

Clarke, John. *New Times and Old Enemies: Essays on Cultural Studies and America.* London: Routledge, 1992.

Gilroy, Paul. *Against Race: Imagining Political Culture beyond the Color Line.* Cambridge, Mass.: Harvard University Press, 2000.

Grossberg, Lawrence. *Bringing It All Back Home: Essays on Cultural Studies.* Durham, N.C.: Duke University Press, 1997.

Grossberg, Lawrence, Cary Nelson, and Paula Treichler, eds. *Cultural Studies.* New York: Routledge, 1992.

Hall, Stuart. *The Hard Road to Renewal: Thatcherism and the Crisis of the Left.* London: Verso, 1988.

Hall, Stuart, and Paddy Whannel. *The Popular Arts.* Boston: Beacon, 1964.

Hebdige, Dick. *Subculture: The Meaning of Style.* London: Methuen, 1979.

Hoggart, Richard. *The Uses of Literacy: Aspects of Working-class Life.* London: Chatto and Windus, 1957.

McRobbie, Angela. *Feminism and Youth Culture.* London: Macmillan, 1991.

Morley, David. *Television, Audiences and Cultural Studies.* London: Routledge, 1992.

Morley, David, and Kuan-Hsing Chen, eds. *Stuart Hall: Critical Dialogues in Cultural Studies.* London: Routledge, 1996.

Morris, Meaghan. *Too Soon Too Late: History in Popular Culture.* Bloomington: Indiana University Press, 1998.

Nelson, Cary, and Lawrence Grossberg. *Marxism and the Interpretation of Culture.* Urbana: University of Illinois Press, 1988.

Rose, Nikolas. *Powers of Freedom: Reframing Political Thought.* Cambridge, U.K.: Cambridge University Press, 1999.

Spivak, Gayatri. *In Other Worlds: Essays in Cultural Politics.* New York: Methuen, 1987.

Williams, Raymond. *The Country and the City.* New York: Oxford University Press, 1973.

———. *Culture and Society, 1780–1950.* New York: Harper & Row, 1958.

———. *The Long Revolution.* Middlesex: Penguin, 1965.

———. *Television: Technology and Cultural Form.* London: Fontana, 1974.

Lawrence Grossberg

CYCLES.

The idea that history is composed of cycles is ancient. Many peoples (including the Egyptians, Chinese, Babylonians, Hindus, Maya, and Greeks) observed recurrences in astronomical phenomena. These early observations were often related to calendar systems and were the foundation for later written schemes of cosmic and historical cycles in various parts of the world.

The Ancient World

One of the oldest written systems of historical cycles originated in India among the Hindus. Hindu cosmology operates within vast cycles of time, or world ages: the universe exists for the life span of the creator god Brahma (quadrillions of solar years), disappears at his death, and is reborn when a new Brahma arises. A brahmic day and night (*kalpa*) consists of one thousand *maha yugas* (great ages). A *maha yuga* is comprised of four cyclic *yugas* (ages) of 4,000, 3,000, 2,000, and 1,000 divine years (one divine year being nearly 130,000 solar years) with intervals of latency between the ages. The advancement through the *yugas* is characterized by spiritual and moral decline. The present time is considered a dark age and falls near the beginning of the fourth *yuga,* which began at Krishna's death in 3002 B.C.E.

Greek philosophers postulated the existence of cosmic cycles. Some of them (such as Empedocles, c. 495–c. 435 B.C.E.) proposed that the events within a given cosmic cycle were identical (or very similar) to the events in earlier cycles. The Stoics held a clear conception of historical cycles. Largely based on the physics of the pre-Socratic philosopher Heraclitus (c. 535–475 B.C.E.), the Stoics theorized that the sun would periodically heat the world and cause a great conflagration (*ekpyrosis*). Unlike Heraclitus, the Stoics identified this purgative fire with God, who would subsequently recreate the world from the condensation of the elements (air, water, earth, and fire). The process of creation and destruction would then begin again.

Plato (427?–347 B.C.E.) understood cosmic and human history to be cyclical. He included statements about the cyclic nature of the world and accounts of natural disasters from which human civilization had reemerged in his *Statesman, Timaeus, Critias,* and *Laws.* Aristotle (384–322 B.C.E.) also presented history as cyclical. He mentioned the possibility of periodic cataclysms in the *Politics* and the *Meteorologica.* He stated in the *Politics* and *De caelo* (On the Heavens) that human knowledge had repeatedly been lost and rediscovered. In addition, Aristotle advanced the notion of the degeneration of governmental forms. He proposed that governments devolve in a specific order: monarchies fall into oligarchies, followed by tyrannies, and then democracies. This idea was adopted and further developed by the Greek historian Polybius (c. 203–c. 120 B.C.E.). In the *History,* he postulated a theory of constitutional cycles (*anacyclosis*). According to Polybius, six forms of government devolve in succession: monarchical governments, tyrannies, aristocracies, oligarchies, democracies, and finally rule by the mob. The cycle would then repeat.

The Early Modern Period

Polybius's ideas were revived in the Renaissance and especially influenced Niccolò Machiavelli (1469–1527), who argued for the superiority of mixed governments in his *Discourses* (1512–1517). However, notions of cyclicality were evident before the revival of Polybius. For example, a system of cyclic historical development is apparent in the *Chronicle of Florence* by Giovanni Villani (c. 1275–1348). A later example is Giorgio Vasari's (1511–1574) theory of cycles in the history of art in his *Lives of the Artists* (1550 and 1568). Vasari viewed the history of art as a long series of advances and declines. However, he believed that art had reached a peak of perfection in his own age in the works of Michelangelo; having been perfected, art could not rise further but would either be maintained or decline.

In the eighteenth century, Giambattista Vico (1668–1744) divided history into three ages in his *New Science* (1725): the age of gods, the age of heroes, and the age of humans. He saw history as the occurrence (*corsi*) and recurrence (*ricorsi*) of these ages. According to Vico, every nation follows a similar pattern of development. During the first age, nations invoke imagination in order to comprehend the world as the creation of the gods. The age of gods then gives way to the second age, wherein humans use imagination to establish moral values and institutions following heroic models. The age of heroes declines into the third age, a time when social order is created through reason. Vico's vision of history was the infinite repetition of these three ages.

The Twentieth Century

In the twentieth century, Oswald Spengler (1880–1936) and Arnold Toynbee (1889–1975) presented important theories of historical cycles. In *The Decline of the West* (1918–1922), Spengler proposed that individual societies have a life cycle similar to living organisms: they experience periods of growth, maturity, and decline. According to him, these cycles repeat themselves as new societies develop. Toynbee was influenced by his reading of Spengler's work. In *A Study of History* (1934–1961), he argued that civilizations emerge when faced with physical or social challenges. He believed that the history of a civilization was largely the record of its response to a unique challenge. On a larger scale, he saw that history moved through periods governed by universal states followed by shorter periods of religious rule. In Toynbee's view, societies decline when they fail to surmount a challenge and thereafter lose social cohesiveness. However, he acknowledged the possibility that a civilization could repeatedly meet its challenges.

Another prominent twentieth-century historian who proposed a theory of historical cycles was Fernand Braudel (1902–1985). Associated with the Annales school of historians, Braudel developed a system that encompassed short-term (individual), medium-term (social), and long-term (geographical) time periods. While acknowledging the significance of short-term events, he emphasized their integration with larger historical cycles. He incorporated an interdisciplinary approach that examined the complex interactions between history, economics, geography, politics, and culture. His major works include *The Mediterranean and the Mediterranean World in the Age of Philip II* (1949) and *Civilization and Capitalism: 15th–18th Century* (1967–1979).

See also **Historiography; History, Idea of; Life Cycle; Periodization.**

BIBLIOGRAPHY

Braudel, Fernand. *Civilization and Capitalism, 15th–18th Century.* Translated by Siân Reynolds. 3 vols. New York: Harper, 1982–1984.

Polybius. *The Histories of Polybius.* Translated from the text of Friedrich Hultsch by Evelyn S. Shuckburgh. 2 vols. London and New York: Macmillan, 1889.

Spengler, Oswald. *The Decline of the West.* Authorized translation with notes by Charles Francis Atkinson. London: Allen and Unwin, 1980.

Toynbee, Arnold. *A Study of History.* 12 vols. London and New York: Oxford University Press, 1934–1961.

Vico, Giambattista. *The New Science of Giambattista Vico.* Translated by Thomas Goddard Bergin and Max Harold Fisch. Ithaca, N.Y.: Cornell University Press, 1984.

Frederick Liers

CYNICISM. The word *cynic* generally conveys negative ideas in modern languages. It describes someone who is unduly critical and suspicious, apathetic about certain issues and rebellious in response to others, selfish, and indifferent toward traditions and accepted beliefs, and unconcerned with the public welfare. The cynic is often viewed as a person who has severed all ties with his social context. To be cynical in the midst of political issues and events is equivalent to being aloof from such things—the cynic does not participate because he has lost his faith in others.

Cynicism, however, has an ancient meaning, the roots of which are traceable to the classical Greeks, specifically to Socrates and his associates in the late fifth century B.C.E. A review of the history of Cynicism reveals that its meaning is significantly different from what modern cynicism has come to mean, and it is not unreasonable to agree with what Bertrand Russell said—namely, that modern cynics have hardly anything in common with the classical Cynics. As a result of a curious perversion of language, the meaning of modern cynicism appears to have been transformed into the opposite of what it once meant, despite undeniable external similarities between the old and the new cynics.

The word *cynic* is etymologically related to the Greek word *kynikos,* which literally means "like a dog." When Aristotle, for instance, refers to Diogenes of Sinope (d. c. 320 B.C.E.), he calls him "the Dog" because that is how Diogenes was known. Likewise, when Lucian speaks of the crowds of Cynics found in every Roman town in the second century C.E., he calls them "the Army of the Dog." The association between the Cynics and dogs seems to have originated not among the Cynics themselves, but among outsiders who discerned in them behavioral traits reminiscent of dog behavior. Beginning with Diogenes, however, the Cynics accepted the uncomplimentary appellation with enthusiasm and were happy to call themselves "the dog philosophers."

The question as to who the first dog philosopher was has been often raised. Some argue that it was Antisthenes (c. 445–365 B.C.E.), an associate of Socrates, and others opt for Diogenes, a disciple of Antisthenes, and see Diogenes as the "founder" of Cynicism. It must be borne in mind, however, that Cynicism was not a school of philosophy comparable to Plato's Academy or Zeno's Stoa. Accordingly, it had neither a founder nor an identifiable place of origin nor a set of principles or beliefs. For this reason, the classical Cynics constitute an assortment of different types of individuals (men and women) who exhibited diverse styles of life and held a variety of beliefs. What allows us to distinguish them from other philosophers is a certain attitude toward their cultural and political world, as well as a distinctive way of expressing their rejection of that world.

The history of Cynicism begins in the early fourth century B.C.E. and ends in the fifth century C.E. We can define Cynicism as a practical philosophy that exhibits a permeating and inflexible commitment to saying no to the values, norms, beliefs, practices, traditions, and all other forms of living which, in the light of what the Cynics called clarity of mind, appear to be senseless or misguided. The Cynics persisted in the conviction that most people live as if immersed in a cloud of smoke (*typhos*) that prevents them from seeing clearly and does not allow them to use that which distinguishes humans

from animals—namely, the capacity to reason. In abandoning this capacity, people forsake their true nature. Diogenes often said that the human world is an enormous madhouse in which every sort of madness is found everywhere: cruelty, greed, deception, mendacity, brutality, uncontrolled hedonism, and the rest of the all-too-common diseases that afflict humanity and have become endemic in the form of things such as religion, patriotism, tradition, and other manifestations of irrationality. It was against such a condition that the Cynics declared war.

Cynicism can be understood, accordingly, as a philosophy of revolt. Although certain principles can be identified in it, the scarcity of primary sources makes this task difficult. Cynic writings are mostly nonextant, and we suspect that even if they were available they would not be helpful because the Cynics expressed their convictions not so much through writings, but through actions and speech. It is, for example, difficult to understand precisely the sense in which the Cynics understood the concept of reason except by literally looking at what they did. A good idea of Cynicism can be gathered by reviewing the countless anecdotes found in secondary Greek, Latin, and Arabic sources, in which we encounter the Cynics in action and in many of which there is probably some element of historical truth. From such sources we can compile a list of Cynic virtues—that is, modes of behavior through which the Cynics sought to combat the world: they opposed avarice and greed with poverty, servility and submissiveness with independence and self-sufficiency, patriotism and factionalism with cosmopolitanism, addiction to pleasure with abstinence and asceticism, deceptiveness and fraud with truth-telling, social distinctions and prejudices with egalitarianism, faith in religion and superstition with skepticism and agnosticism, chatter and gossip with silence, prudishness with impudence, and irrationalism and brutality with an undeviating attachment to reason.

Although Cynicism eventually came to an end, it is undeniable that its influence has persisted until our time. After all, the Cynics exemplified a human tendency found among a small number of people of every culture and time to stand in opposition to what is unnatural and irrational. Stoicism, for instance, owed its inception and development to the ideas of the Cynics. Indeed, as long as the world remains the madhouse recognized by Diogenes, there are bound to be cynics—both in the modern sense of this word and in its ancient sense. In the former, cynicism takes the form of rebelliousness born out of selfishness and irrationality, and in the latter, it assumes a stance of defiance rooted in a desire to return humanity to its true nature, which entails a return to reason.

See also **Dialogue and Dialectics: Socratic; Stoicism.**

BIBLIOGRAPHY

Bracht, Branham R., and Marie-Odile Goulet-Gazé. *The Cynic Movement in Antiquity and Its Legacy.* Berkeley: University of California Press, 1966.

Navia, Luis E. *Antisthenes of Athens: Setting the World Aright.* Westport, Conn.: Greenwood Press, 2001.

———. *Classical Cynicism: A Critical Study.* Westport, Conn.: Greenwood Press, 1996.

———. *Diogenes of Sinope: The Man in the Tub.* Westport, Conn.: Greenwood Press, 1998.

———. *The Philosophy of Cynicism: An Annotated Bibliography.* Westport, Conn.: Greenwood Press, 1995.

Sloterdijk, Peter. *Critique of Cynical Reason.* Translated by Michael Eldred. Minneapolis: University of Minnesota Press, 1987.

L. E. Navia

D

DADA. Presided over by the poet and essayist Tristan Tzara (1896–1963), who served as its principal spokesman, dada was the first truly international avant-garde movement. Although the term *dada* was invented in Zurich, the movement's origins were by no means limited to Switzerland. The dada spirit existed previously in several other countries, where it expressed itself in outrageous avant-garde activity. Dada's chief concern was the achievement of total liberty: social, moral, and intellectual. Its members questioned, through their art, poetry, and performance, the basic postulates of rationalism and humanism as few had done before.

The period 1912–1914 witnessed the emergence of two of the movement's influential figures in Paris: Francis Picabia (1879–1953) and Marcel Duchamp (1887–1968). After World War I erupted, the two men moved to New York, where they proved to be important catalysts. The first dada journal had already appeared in print a few months earlier. Entitled *291,* it was edited by a group centered around Alfred Stieglitz (1864–1946) and his review *Camera Work.* Another contingent met at Walter Conrad Arensberg's apartment at 33 West 67th Street. The two groups welcomed the French artists, who were soon joined by friends and family, and emulated their latest experiments.

Emerging independently in 1916, the Zurich dadaists published an eclectic journal entitled *Cabaret Voltaire.* Named after the artistic cabaret founded by Hugo Ball, which was notorious for its outrageous productions, the journal was replaced by *Dada* in 1917. Ball himself was soon eclipsed by the flamboyant Tzara, who became the movement's chief theorist and publicist. Consisting of Romanian expatriates and former German Expressionists, the Zurich group included several accomplished poets and artists but specialized in theatrical performances. A third dada faction was situated in Barcelona during the war. Revolving about the Dalmau Gallery, it included several French expatriates in addition to Catalan artists and writers such as Joan Miró and Josep Maria Junoy. The Barcelona movement gained momentum in 1917 with the arrival of Francis Picabia, who founded the iconoclastic journal *391.*

After the War

Following the end of World War I, the dada movement underwent a significant transformation. While the original three groups continued to exist, the balance of power shifted from countries situated at the war's edge to Germany and France. Beginning in 1919, the German branch was composed of three separate factions. Dominated by Richard Huelsenbeck and

Marcel Duchamp (1887–1968). The French-born Duchamp moved to the United States in the early twentieth century and helped introduce the concept of dada to his new country. Duchamp dabbled in many different art forms, among them sculpture, painting, and even short film. © CORBIS-BETTMANN

Raoul Hausmann, Berlin dada was preoccupied with a series of political issues. In addition to satirizing politics in their art, its members sought to create a new social order. Centered around Jean Arp (also known as Hans Arp) and Max Ernst on the one hand and Kurt Schwitters on the other, Cologne dada and Hanover dada were more concerned with aesthetic issues. Despite the three groups' relatively brief lives, they were a potent force for social and artistic change. In Paris, the dada movement coalesced around four future surrealists: André Breton, Louis Aragon, Paul Eluard, and Philippe Soupault. Other participants included Francis Picabia, Marcel Duchamp, and Tristan Tzara, who arrived in 1920. In spite of dada's impressive vitality, the international movement ceased to exist a few years later. Some members, such as Picabia and Schwitters, continued to incarnate the dada spirit in their work, but most became surrealists or developed new interests.

Montage satirizing contemporary images of men and women, 1919, by Hannah Hoch. After World War I, the dada movement in Germany was partly centered on politics and political satire. Photocollages of newspaper and magazine clippings by artists such as Hannah Hoch and Raoul Hausmann denigrated German government and society. © JORG P. ANDERS, BERLIN/BILDARCHIV PREUSSIS-CHER KULTURBESITZ/ART RESOURCE

Monogram **(1955–1959) by Robert Rauschenberg. Mixed media.** A neo-dadaist revival in the mid-twentieth century was led by pop artists such as Rauschenberg, whose unusual combinations of objects and media had a profound impact on modern art. ROBERT RAUSCHENBERG, "MONOGRAM" (WOOD)/PRIVATE COLLECTION/ WWW.BRIDGEMAN.CO.UK. ART © ROBERT RAUSCHENBERG/ LICENSED BY VAGA, NEW YORK, NY

Despite its geographical distribution and diversity, the dada movement was amazingly cohesive. Although there was no central committee to regulate what transpired, there was widespread agreement about dada's methods and goals. Interestingly, André Breton's efforts to organize such a committee in 1922 spelled the death of Paris dada. Paradoxically, as Tristan Tzara explained to the Spanish critic Guillermo de Torre, dada's surprising unity stemmed from its lack of direction. Despite the absence of rules and regulations, the dadaists were united in their opposition to any form of authority. Dada was not an artistic credo, in any case, but a common set of values. Its adherents shared an adventurous lifestyle and a rebellious joie de vivre.

Reconstructing Reality
Outraged at the carnage of World War I, which they attributed to the stupidity of bourgeois politicians, the dadaists strove to wipe the slate clean so that they could begin all over. Reducing aesthetic expression to its fundamental elements— sound and typography in poetry; sound, gesture, and action in theater; color and line in art—they experimented with new, uncorrupted genres. Besides reconstructing reality to more accurately reflect modern experience, they adopted an anti-art stance that revolutionized artistic expression. Adopting as their

motto Tzara's declaration "Thought is made in your mouth," they strove to liberate language in particular.

Like their artist colleagues, the dada poets wished to stimulate thought and to achieve new states of consciousness by exploring their medium. While the dadaists valued scandal above all else, they also prized spontaneity. Both tenets derived from the fanatical devotion to freedom that characterized the dada adventure. Just as the dadaists were interested in the activity of the mind, so their preoccupation with spontaneity and the gratuitous reflected their fascination with prelogical experience and thought. In attempting to grasp our being in its primitive coherence (or incoherence), they strove to discover absolute psychological reality. In particular, the dadaists believed that the playful dimension of art offered a path to liberation. Although their poetry was necessarily verbal, it communicated on a primal level by means of images, emotions, and rhythms. Combining discursive and nondiscursive strategies, the dadaists discovered that words could be used to convey information situated outside the linguistic arena.

Critical Revaluation
At first glance, many dada works seem impervious to critical analysis. For one thing, they contain an irrational streak that was intensified by the war and by the accompanying decay of social values. For another, their aesthetic strategies exploit the calculated misuse of convention. Employing the techniques of subversion, distortion, and disruption, dada compositions are fervently antilogical. Rejecting bourgeois values in life and in art, the dadaists considered logic to be a correlative of traditional authority. Like the latter, it was reviled for confining and debasing mankind. Because the dadaists deliberately cultivated scandalous behavior, their readers and viewers tended to react to them with hostility. Like the hapless members of the audience, contemporary critics assumed that the dada movement was a hoax. Dada was a purely destructive phenomenon, they declared, whose sole virtue was to have prepared the way for surrealism.

By contrast, the 1960s witnessed an enthusiastic neo-dadaist revival that permeated art, literature, music, and the theater. Inspired by the *Cabaret Voltaire* and similar ventures, performance artists invented a new postmodern genre: the happening. The latest in a long series of dada derivatives, including the Theater of the Absurd and abstract expressionism, the neo-dada movement shows no signs of abating. While current audiences have grown used to pop, op, and kinetic art, they continue to be scandalized by sound poets like Henri Chopin, visual poets like Fabio Doctorovich, junkyard sculptors like Robert Rauschenberg, aleatory composers like John Cage, and experimental choreographers like Alwin Nikolais. With the rediscovery of dada in a sympathetic light, the movement's positive aspects have become more apparent. The end of the twentieth century and the beginning of the twenty-first have witnessed a steadily increasing interest in dada and a series of benchmark studies by scholars such as Mary Ann Caws, J. H. Matthews, Michel Sanouillet, and Henri Béhar. Although the movement is as resistant to logical analysis as ever, it has acquired a certain respectability that threatens, ironically, to undermine its basic premises.

See also **Arts; Avant-Garde; Language, Linguistics, and Literacy; Poetry and Poetics; Theater and Performance.**

BIBLIOGRAPHY

Caws, Mary Ann. *The Poetry of Dada and Surrealism: Aragon, Breton, Tzara, Éluard and Desnos.* Princeton: Princeton University Press, 1970.

Dachy, Marc. *The Dada Movement, 1915–1923.* New York: Rizzoli, 1990.

Foster, Stephen, and Rudolf Kuenzli, eds. *Dada Spectrum: The Dialectics of Revolt.* Iowa City: University of Iowa, 1978. Incisive and wide-ranging study.

Gale, Matthew. *Dada and Surrealism.* London: Phaidon, 1997. Primarily devoted to art.

Matthews, J. H. *Theatre in Dada and Surrealism.* Syracuse: Syracuse University Press, 1974.

Motherwell, Robert, ed. *The Dada Painters and Poets: An Anthology.* 2nd ed. Cambridge, Mass.: Belknap, 1989. A valuable collection of essays, manifestos, and illustrations.

Richter, Hans. *Dada: Art and Anti-Art.* London: Thames and Hudson, 1965. A classic study by a former participant.

Willard Bohn

DANCE. Dance is broadly conceived as physical movement organized into patterns in time and space. Writings on dance grounded in the European intellectual tradition have tended to distinguish dance from other systems of organized movement (such as sport, military drills, synchronized labor, festival processions, and sometimes ritual) by identifying a dimension of conscious craft or artistry. The discipline of anthropology has shown that this distinction is not universal by investigating how organized human movement functions in different cultures, as well as how it relates to music, theater, pantomime, storytelling, and other kinds of performative behavior.

Dance in Intellectual Traditions

The idea of dance varies within intellectual traditions. Two ancient treatises serve as examples. Where ideas are treated as a function of language, and knowledge is derived from analysis of phenomena, the body is often written out of epistemological projects. Aristotle's *Poetics* (fourth century B.C.E.), for example, analyzes the plot structure, poetry, and ethical issues presented by fifth-century Athenian tragedies. The *Poetics* mentions only briefly the physical movement of the tragic chorus as a contributor to the effect (emotional or intellectual) of a theatrical experience or as a component in knowledge. In contrast, where cognitive processes, observation, and abstract thinking include bodily experience, physical movement is thought to generate and represent abstract concepts. The body and corporeal experience have a more prominent place in the formation of ideas. The Indian treatise *Natyasastra* (c. second century B.C.E. to second century C.E.), describes in meticulous detail how correct performance of hand gestures, eye movements, posture, steps, coordination with music, and posture will affect an audience's comprehension of the narrative and its meaning.

The *Poetics* and *Natyasastra* both assume dance to be inseparable from the performance of music, theater, poetry, and dress (including masks and makeup). Both treatises also assume that performance takes place in a ritual context, where form and content are already dictated by established conventions.

Even so, the relationship between movement, emotion, and cognition is conceptualized differently in each treatise, which suggests the need for continued attention to the intellectual formulations that define the interpretation of human movement.

Until relatively recently, dance has been on the margins of the modern Western intellectual tradition. Dance appears as an object of study in two particular domains of modern Western thought: aesthetic criticism and anthropology. Aesthetic criticism, emerging in eighteenth-century dictionary projects and then taking root in nineteenth-century philosophy parallel with the development of the romantic ballet, considers dance to be an artistic practice. As performance, dance is distinguished from folk, social, or ceremonial dancing (though it may represent them) and requires formal training. The idea of dance as a formalized performance tradition is usually associated with industrial economies, urban societies, and a culture's economically secure or educated classes. Appreciation of technical mastery and performance conventions is considered evidence of cultural sophistication or artistic sensibility; meaning is communicated primarily in the visual realm of symbolic representation, mimesis, and technique. Dance criticism is an intellectual project involving analysis of choreography, performers' skill, aesthetic conventions, historical developments in dance styles, innovations in genre, and the success of performances.

Aesthetic Criticism and Analysis of Culture

In dance practice, at the beginning of the twentieth century Sergey Diaghilev's (1872–1929) experimental productions with the Ballets Russes famously challenged the aesthetic sensibilities of classical ballet by introducing parallel feet, ambiguous story lines, a lowered center of gravity, and representation of "primitive" cultures. The creation of new forms of art dance, such as expressionistic modern dance in Europe after World War I and Butoh in Japan after World War II, deliberately defied ballet's conventions of beauty but stayed within the domain of artistic performance. Aesthetic criticism accounted for and dealt with the creation of new dance genres. The purpose of aesthetic criticism remains a greater understanding of established and new dance styles, choreography (recorded in notation systems such as Labanotation), individual performances, and criteria on which stage performances can be evaluated.

The emergence of anthropology as a scientific discipline in the mid-nineteenth century, parallel with aesthetic criticism's elevation of dance as an art form and tensions in experimentation with the form, expanded a Western idea of dance to non-Western cultures and societies, often treating dance practices as folk traditions. Franz Boas (1858–1942), A. R. Radcliffe-Brown (1881–1955), and E. E. Evans-Pritchard (1902–1973) included social dancing, ceremonies, and rituals in their field studies. Curt Sachs's *World History of the Dance* (English translation, 1937) offered an evolutionary and universalizing theory of world dance forms and was followed by Franziska Boas's collection, *The Function of Dance in Human Society* (1944). Though guided by the scientific commitment to objectivity and evaluation of empirical data, early anthropological studies interpreted dances from non-Western cultures as less aesthetically developed than those on the European stages and presented the dance traditions of North Africa, the Middle East, India, Asia, and the Americas as more primitive forms of dance. The images provided by early anthropologists were reproduced as artifacts of exotic cultures in World's Fair exhibits and romanticized in exoticized, popular stage performances such as those of Ruth St. Denis (1879–1968) and Ted Shawn (1891–1972).

Since the 1960s and 1970s, this early anthropological work on dance has been significantly revised. The idea of dance, expanded to the broader notion of movement practices, allows for greater attention to the categories that define movement systems within individual cultures, nations, or societies, as well as for comparative studies. For anthropology and its related disciplines (folklore, ethnomusicology, ethnology, and ethnography), aspects of culture are revealed in dance practices. These disciplines also look at dancing itself as a culturally constructed activity that offers information about human behavior and, by extension, culture. These interrelated disciplines, along with methods drawn from sociology, kinesthetics, and linguistics, operate with a heightened sensitivity to the imposition of Western values and desires on non-Western, indigenous, or nonindustrial cultures.

Awareness of Western ethnocentric tendencies in dance research generated different categories of analysis and new questions. Researchers began to work toward a deeper understanding of the language, customs, social structures, and modes of thinking governing localized "dance events" before attempting to interpret them. Adrienne L. Kaeppler's work on Tongan dance in the late 1970s did much to advance the study of structured human movement in a specific cultural context. In the late 1980s Paul Stoller advocated the importance of a sensual dimension in ethnographic work. Major contributors to the assessment and development of anthropological approaches to human movement in the 1960s, 1970s, 1980s, and into the 1990s include Gertrude Prokosch Kurath, Anya Peterson Royce, Helen Thomas, and Judith Lynne Hanna.

The treatment of dance as a social practice and a form of expressive culture goes beyond descriptions of local customs, ceremonies, and movement idioms. Through proscribed methods of observation, data collection, documentation, interviewing, participant observation, and interpretation of data, these methods analyze how human movement relates to culture. Many studies analyze the function and meanings of dances or dancing in situated contexts. Others track changes in the performance and interpretation of dance styles such as the tango, rumba, samba, flamenco, and hula as they are transmitted across cultures, including in the inquiry of the mechanisms of transmission. Still other studies are concerned with visual and kinesthetic communication, or how dance communicates as a kind of language. Behaviors surrounding a dance performance, such as audience participation and dancers' preparation, may be as important as the performance itself. Religious beliefs, political restrictions, integration of dance with other performance forms, and vocabularies used by practitioners to describe movement are all significant to interpreting data gathered in fieldwork.

Theory and Praxis

In the 1990s and into the twenty-first century, the critical concerns of feminism, postmodernism, poststructuralism, new historiography, cultural studies, semiotics, race and ethnic studies, and queer theory have brought to light a wide range of issues that remain crucial in studies of dance and human movement systems, namely, how dance constructs or challenges gender and sexuality, how dance practices negotiate power relations, the effects of colonialism and cultural imperialism on dance practices, exoticization of cultural "others," institutionalization of dance practices, how dance is used to demonstrate cultural or ethnic difference, cultural ownership and authenticity of dance idioms, dance as a display of national identity, dance in marketing and tourism, the effects of stylistic hybridity on individual or group identities, performers' agency, multiple meanings in complex symbol systems, how dance practices link to social class, dance as a means of building ideological consensus, and dance as a medium of resistance and social change.

The work of scholars such as Jane Cowan, Cynthia J. Novack, Ann Daly, Sally Ann Ness, Jane C. Desmond, and Susan Leigh Foster has opened interdisciplinary territory in the effort to address these and other issues in the study of human movement in culture and as a means of cultural production. Their theoretical work has broken down the notion that Western art forms are a model of aesthetic progress. Studies of female dancers in Egypt and Morocco in the 1990s, for example, have used methods from sociology to examine performance in social conditions that define both dance and dancer. More recent attention to these concerns through ethnographic methods has shown how social control was exercised in the costuming, movements, songs, and visual spectacle in women's dances at rallies for political candidates in Malawi.

Methods of inquiry rooted in anthropology take aesthetic conventions as culturally determined rather than as marks of progress or as by-products of modernity. Aesthetics can thus serve as an entry point, whether the project is to understand culture through human movement, or human movement through culture. Applying anthropological methods to the aesthetics of classical ballet reveals, for example, that control of the body and individuality against uniformity are Western values. Cross-cultural comparisons of ballet's reception as scandalous in non-Western cultures, in contrast, show how ballet performs a desire to expose and transcend the body in contrast to local movement practices that value a body's individuality and are grounded in everyday activities. Joann Kealiinohomoku's (1983) work on ballet as ethnic dance has been followed by studies of ballet's adaptation in non-Western cultures and of how ballet choreography structures desire in its narratives.

Information made available through anthropological approaches has also led to popular appropriations of local dance forms within new cultural or social contexts. National dance troupes, such as Ballet Folklórico de México, present indigenous social dances as commercial art with aesthetic aims, often with an educational mission. Ceremonial, ritual, and communal dances may be taken out of context, adapted for the stage, and performed as a recuperation or preservation of "traditional" cultures. Scholars have interrogated the affected aesthetics, claims to national identity, and cross-cultural misinterpretations at work in such performances. While dance forms identified with specific cultures are staged for international audiences, the same dance forms might be reinterpreted and invested with new meaning within the home culture. Kathak and Bharata Natyam as popular dance practices in India, for example, have been analyzed as resistance to the colonial legacy and as recuperation of the precolonial past. Such analyses show how adaptations of traditional dances within a culture can be used to define national, cultural, or class identity.

Reciprocity between theory and practice is evident in other areas as well. By the mid-twentieth century, ethnic fusion forms such as Afro-Cuban-jazz combined Western dance styles with those of other cultures, sometimes raising issues of cultural authenticity and appropriation. Dance forms identified with ethnicity within a dominant culture, for example African-American dance, have been analyzed as distinct and unique and, conversely, as in the process of adapting or challenging movement idioms from the dominant culture. Contemporary Western "belly dance" has been shown to remain deeply bound to nineteenth-century European Orientalist fantasies.

Dance as Experience

Though their methods, goals, and objects of inquiry differ, both aesthetic criticism and anthropology deal at some level with the fundamental question: What is being communicated, to whom, and how? This disciplinary imperative takes the human body as an agent of communication in an interpretive community or as an embodied subject acted upon by social forces. The psychological experience of dancing is generally irrelevant to aesthetic criticism's analysis of dance as a visible medium and tangential to research grounded in kinesthetics or linguistics (though audience response can be analyzed). Beyond Romanticism and notions of the sublime in art in the Western philosophical tradition, phenomenology has offered the most appropriate frame for the ephemeral qualities of human movement, as Maxine Sheets-Johnstone demonstrated in 1966. First-person descriptions of movement as a conduit for spiritual or metaphysical experience are, however, not easily adapted to Western modes of thinking and analysis, even in studies of mainstream liturgical dance.

Paranormal experiences, dissociational states, expressions of deep inner feelings, mystical experiences, and intense emotion generated by participating in a dance are usually associated with non-Western, nonindustrial, or indigenous cultures. Movement practices that produce such experiences are identified by terms such as shamanic dancing, trance dancing, exorcism, healing dance, voodoo, spirit possession, and ritual dance. In the Western stage dance tradition, such states may be represented in artistic performance, as with the expressionist choreography of Mary Wigman (1886–1973). Numerous dance forms in Western popular culture, for example Gabrielle Roth's "Ecstatic Dance," the appropriation of African dances as "healing dance," and so-called "spiritual belly dance" do emphasize altered states of consciousness and/or physical healing. Such practices—especially those that identify with practices of nonindustrial or non-Western cultures in their costuming, symbols, stories, and idioms—offer rich sources for cultural analyses. Though some work has been done to integrate experiences of altered states of consciousness into scholarly discourse, this area requires attention.

As suggested by the example of how the ancient Greek *Poetics* and Sanskrit *Natyasastra* frame dance, understandings of human movement are not uniform across cultures. In the early twenty-first century, collaboration among researchers from different intellectual traditions reveals differences in research methods, modes of interpretation, analytical vocabularies, descriptive categories, and goals in dance research. International conferences such as the Congress on Research in Dance (CORD) and the World Dance Association (WDA) insure that ongoing research will reflect a diversity of intellectual as well as movement systems.

See also **Anthropology; Cultural Studies; Ethnography; Theater and Performance.**

BIBLIOGRAPHY

Buckland, Theresa J., ed. *Dance in the Field: Theory, Methods, and Issues in Dance Ethnography.* New York: St. Martin's Press, 1999.

Cowan, Jane K. *Dance and the Body Politic in Northern Greece.* Princeton, N.J.: Princeton University Press, 1990.

Daly, Ann. *Critical Gestures: Writings on Dance and Culture.* Middletown, Conn.: Wesleyan University Press, 2002.

Desmond, Jane C, ed. *Meaning in Motion: New Cultural Studies of Dance.* Durham, N.C.: Duke University Press 1997.

Dils, Ann, and Ann Cooper Albright, eds. *Moving History/ Dancing Cultures: A Dance History Reader.* Middletown, Conn.: Wesleyan University Press, 2001.

Foster, Susan Leigh, ed. *Choreographing History.* Bloomington: Indiana University Press, 1995.

Fraleigh, Sondra Horton, and Penelope Hanstein, eds. *Researching Dance: Evolving Methods of Inquiry.* Pittsburgh: University of Pittsburgh Press, 1999.

Hanna, Judith Lynne. *Dance, Sex and Gender: Signs of Identity, Dominance, Defiance, and Desire.* Chicago: University of Chicago Press, 1988.

Kaeppler, Adrienne L. "Dance in Anthropological Perspective." *Annual Review of Anthropology* 7 (1978): 31–49.

Kealiinohomoku, Joann. "An Anthropologist Looks at Ballet as a Form of Ethnic Dance." In *What Is Dance? Readings in Theory and Criticism,* edited by Roger Copeland and Marshall Cohen, 533–549. Oxford: Oxford University Press, 1983.

Kurath, Gertrude Prokosch. "Panorama of Dance Ethnology." *Current Anthropology* 1 (1960): 233–254.

Ness, Sally Ann. *Body, Movement and Culture: Kinesthetic and Visual Symbolism in a Philippine Community.* Philadelphia: University of Pennsylvania Press, 1992.

Novack, Cynthia Jean. *Sharing the Dance: Contact Improvisation and American Culture.* Madison: University of Wisconsin Press, 1990.

Royce, Anya Peterson. *The Anthropology of Dance.* Bloomington: Indiana University Press, 1977.

Sheets-Johnstone, Maxine. *The Phenomenology of Dance.* Madison: University of Wisconsin Press, 1966.

Spencer, Paul, ed. *Society and the Dance: The Social Anthropology of Process and Performance.* Cambridge, U.K.: Cambridge University Press, 1985.

Thomas, Helen. *Dance, Modernity, and Culture: Explorations in the Sociology of Dance.* New York: Routledge, 1995.

Donnalee Dox

DAOISM. Defining the features of Daoism (or Taoism) as one of the predominant trends in the history of Chinese thought involves accounting for its religious traits. As often happens outside the Western hemisphere—Buddhism may be the best-known example, but the same is true of Islam—the boundary between thought and religion in China is tenuous, unstable, and sometimes simply impossible to identify. Daoism, Buddhism, Confucianism, and other legacies have defined themselves as "teachings" (*jiao*) or "lineages" (*jia,* a word that primarily means "house" or "family"). The terms for "philosophy" and "religion" (*zhexue* and *zongjiao*) have become part of the standard Chinese vocabulary through late-nineteenth- and early-twentieth-century translations of Western books.

In the most general way, Daoism may be defined as a traditional form of thought and religion, based on some central notions, cults, and practices but never subject to systematization as a whole, and syncretic but at the same time self-contained—in the sense that it integrates many elements from other traditions, but frequently emphasizes its distinction from them. These basic features underlie different formulations of doctrinal notions and a large variety of practices, ranging from self-cultivation to communal rituals.

Daoism and Chinese Thought and Religion

Historically, the Daoist tradition has consisted of several schools, or rather lineages, usually based on one or more primary texts and associated with one or more divine or semi-divine beings. As a whole, these lineages and corpora have represented the higher but "unofficial" form of native religion in China. This definition points to the complexity of questions that surround the status of Daoism and its relation to Chinese religion; it is also relevant to its relation to Chinese thought, for the status of Daoism as a religion was often defined with reference to ideas and notions formulated in its early doctrinal texts.

In relation to the different forms of common religion in China, the stated purpose of Daoism is "transforming" (*hua*) people, in the sense of educating them to venerate pure deities that impersonate the Dao, instead of joining other cults—those defined as "vulgar" (*su*) or "illicit" (*yin*), which often included sacrifice and involved the assistance of spirit-mediums. The continuous incorporation of new deities and ritual forms, resulting from the interaction of Daoism with local communities and cults, upgraded these deities by admitting them into the "correct" (*zheng*) hierarchy of gods and of amending them by integrating them into the proper way of communicating with the divine world. As has often been noted, the spirit-medium, and not the Confucian officer or the Buddhist monk, was the first competitor of the Daoist priest within local communities.

The relation between Daoism and Buddhism has been fertile, with reciprocal borrowings of doctrinal formulations, theological elements, technical terminology, and forms of practice. Even though Buddhist polemical authors have often accused Daoists of appropriating Buddhist notions and topoi and even of plagiarizing their scriptures, these disputes have usually occurred in the surroundings of the imperial court. In that milieu, providing evidence of doctrinal preeminence in order to obtain official patronage was more important than highlighting any shared ground. Daoism provided Chinese Buddhism with some of that ground in the early stages of its development and, in turn, drew from it in later times. For the average faithful, anyway, subtle doctrinal distinctions surely were not the main concern, and Daoist or Buddhist deities could equally be addressed as suitable and practicable.

Daoism's relation to Confucianism—the dominating influence behind the system of social norms, upheld by the central government, maintained by the local officers, supported by the literati, and transmitted through education—has been complex. Classical Confucianism focuses on the social aspects of human life. Daoism is by no means uninterested in these issues, but its views are based on different doctrinal grounds. Despite this, and with exceptions with respect to Neo-Confucianism, the contrast between Daoism and Confucianism has not primarily involved their philosophical views (the respective claims in this respect were known and quietly acknowledged by both), but their religious aspects. As Anna Seidel has noted (1997, pp. 39–41), although Daoism is the higher form of Chinese native religion, it has always occupied a position subordinate to the imperial—that is, official—cults. For the Confucian officers, the Daoist priests represented spiritual powers over which they had no control. Replacing the state ceremonies to Heaven and Earth, or to paragons of Confucian virtue, with rituals performed by Daoist priests and addressed to the divine personifications of the Dao, would be equivalent to granting Daoism an official role in the administration of the empire. For this reason, the Confucian officer and literatus did not hesitate to acknowledge Daoism only in its philosophical, mystical, or literary aspects, and even to regard it as equal to common religion.

The Roots of Daoism

The main early Daoist text is the *Daode jing* (Scripture of the way and its virtue), a short work consisting of aphorisms attributed to Laozi (the Old Master, or Old Child). Although some scholars have suggested that other sources might be slightly earlier, virtually all movements and lineages within Daoism consider this as the founding scripture of the entire tradition, even though they may venerate their own texts and their own founders. Another early work, the *Zhuangzi* (Book of Master Zhuang), has provided Daoism with doctrines, notions, and technical vocabulary throughout its history.

The present general consensus among scholars is that the *Daode jing* was not written by a single author, and that Laozi is the appellation of the symbolic Daoist sage whose doctrines are reflected there. The text appears to have existed in a form close to the present one between 350 and 300 B.C.E., but many of its statements likely derive from oral traditions whose dates are impossible to determine. The *Zhuangzi,* which is deemed to be one of the masterpieces of Chinese literature, is different from the *Daode jing* from the point of view of its formal features and consists mainly of stories, anecdotes, and reflections. Zhuangzi himself probably authored the seven so-called Inner Chapters in the late fourth century B.C.E., with the other portions dating from one or two centuries later. Despite differences in emphasis, the two texts present the same view of the Dao and its relation to the world, outlined below on the basis of the *Daode jing* (references in parentheses are to the number of sections in this text).

The Dao. The word *dao* has two main meanings, "way" and "method." These two meanings refer, respectively, to the way in which something is or the way it functions, and to the way of doing something (including the extended meaning of "practice" in a religious sense). The early Daoist texts are the first ones to use this word to mean the Absolute (Robinet, p. 26). For the *Daode jing,* the Dao has no name and is beyond any description or definition; the word *dao* itself is used only because one "is forced" to refer to it (25). The Dao is unknowable, has no form, and therefore does not undergo change (41), is "constant" (1), and is "invisible, inaudible, and imperceptible" (14). The two principles of Non-being (*wu*) and Being (*you*) are contained within it. Yet the Dao, in spite of its being "indistinct and vague" (*huanghu*), contains an "essence" (*jing*) that is the seed of the world of multiplicity (21). Under this second aspect—which can be distinguished from the previous one only within the domain of relativity—the Dao is the "origin" of the world and its "mother" (1).

The faculty that the Dao has to give life to the particular objects is its *de,* or "virtue," and is described as "a mystery within a mystery" (1). The *Daode jing* outlines this process, which happens spontaneously and has no cause or purpose, in a famous statement: "The Dao generates the One, the One generates the Two, the Two generate the Three, the Three generate the ten thousand things" (42). According to this formulation, which like all similar outlines found in Daoist texts is meaningful only from a relative point of view, the Dao first generates the One (*yi*), the principle of the unity of existence in which the individual entities defined by forms and names are included, but have not yet emerged. The One differentiates itself into the two polar and complementary principles, Yin and Yang. The Three is the product of the joining of Yin and Yang; it represents the One reestablished at the level of each individual entity. The "ten thousand things" (*wanwu*) are the sum of entities generated by the joining of Yin and Yang. The sentence of the *Daode jing* quoted above therefore formulates both a metaphysics, by arranging the single items in a hierarchical sequence designed to show their ultimate origin in the Dao, and a cosmogony, which does not take place once and for all *in illo tempore* but is continuously reiterated within each of the cosmic cycles that the Dao brings into existence.

Both the Dao and the manifested world model themselves on *ziran* (25), a term that literally means "to be so of its own." In reference to the Dao, the principle of *ziran* means that the Dao only regulates itself upon itself; in reference to the world generated by the Dao, *ziran* means that there is no ultimate reason for things being as they are: the Dao generates the "ten

thousand things," but while for the relative the Absolute is its "mother," for the Absolute the relative does not even exist. Aside from generating the world, therefore, the Dao does nothing else: it does not act in it, it is not affected by the transformation, decay, and disappearance of the forms it generates, and it neither rejoices in nor is hurt by what is, in a relative sense, good or bad.

The saintly person. Just as the Dao does nothing, so is "non-doing" or "non-action" (*wuwei*) the way to attain to it. Non-action is the practice of *ziran* in the human world: one fully responds to circumstances and events, doing no more and no less than what is required, without taking the initiative unless there is an immediate need to do so, and without being moved by personal desire, interest, or advantage (3, 19, 34, 37, 57). In particular, there is no need of striving to perform what is "good," and even less so of attempting to impose it on others, for "when everyone knows the good as good, evil is already there" (2).

The person who has "returned to the Dao" (28, 40, 52) is called in the *Daode jing* the *shengren,* a term that in a Daoist context may be translated as "saint" to distinguish him from the Confucian "sage." As the highest realized human being who has achieved liberation in life, the Daoist saint has transcended the limitations of individuality and form; he continues to remain in the world of multiplicity until he has completely fulfilled his function in it, but from an absolute point of view, which is the one in which he constantly dwells, his self-identity is already null, for he is identified with absolute principle. Death for him, therefore, is not even a change of state, for he has attained the state in which no change can occur. In the human world, he "practices the teaching without words" and "makes it possible for the ten thousand things to function, but does not start them" (2). He does not take an active leading role in society but benefits his fellow human beings by his mere presence. This is so even when the saint is the ruler, a figure to whom the *Daode jing* devotes much attention. In that position, the saint governs according to the principle of non-action, and that is how he ensures the well-being of his country and his subjects. In the ideal description given by the *Daode jing,* no one even needs to know who the ruler is. "Therefore the saint in his government empties their heart [i.e., their mind], fills their belly, weakens their will, and strengthens their bones. He always wants people to be without knowledge and without desires." He does so because "not exalting the worthy prevents people from competing, not valuing goods hard to obtain prevents people from becoming thieves, and not seeing desirable things prevents the people's heart from becoming confused" (3).

Revelations and Textual Corpora

To a significant extent, the history of Daoism may be seen as a continuous restatement of the principles enunciated in the early founding texts. To an equally significant extent, its development has been marked by the adaptation to varying historical circumstances, the response to the needs and demands of different social groups, and the incorporation of notions, beliefs, cults, and practices derived from other trends of thought and religion. These multiple factors gave rise to the idea, apparently unknown to the early Daoist thinkers, that the Dao may appear under the guise of gods or other divine beings, and may through them take an active role in the world, in particular by granting revelations to some adepts.

The first Daoist revelation.

The process that led, in the second half of the second century C.E., to the formation of the first major Daoist religious movement can only be understood in the light of the politico-religious ideals of ancient China, synthesized in the notion of Great Peace (*taiping*) and shared by different traditions including Confucianism. At the center of that process was the deification of Laozi, now represented not only as the sage who expounds the metaphysical doctrines of the *Daode jing,* but also as a messiah who embodies the Dao and reappears at different times either as a sage counselor of political rulers, or as the inspirer of religious leaders (Seidel, 1969). Scholars have pointed out the association among the spread of beliefs concerning Lord Lao (Laojun, i.e., Laozi in his divine aspect), the cults offered to him outside and even within the imperial court in the second century, and the political decline of the Han dynasty (202 B.C.E.–220 C.E.). Based on the notion that the emperor symbolized and guaranteed the balance between Heaven and Earth, the weakening of political power at the end of the Han, and the concurrent natural disasters and social unrest were deemed to reflect a rupture between the supernatural and the human world. Hence the millenarian beliefs and the messianic wait for a Savior—a new incarnation of Lord Lao who would restore Great Peace and confer the Celestial Mandate (*tianming*) to a new ruler.

In one of his transformations, Lord Lao appeared (in 142 C.E., according to the traditional date) to a healer, Zhang Daoling, in the southwestern region of Sichuan. Lord Lao established a covenant (*meng*) with Zhang Daoling, revealing to him the teaching of Orthodox Unity (*zhengyi*) and bestowing upon him the title of Celestial Master (*tianshi*). This revelation, which has been dubbed "the New Testament of the Dao" to distinguish it from the teaching of the *Daode jing,* is at the origin of the Way of the Celestial Masters (*Tianshi dao*), a priestly lineage that continues to exist in the present day (the current Celestial Master resides in Taiwan). The early Celestial Masters established a theocratically based enclave in Sichuan that maintained its political semi-independence for several decades, until the end of the Han period. Its purpose was not to terminate and replace the imperial power; rather, the intent of Zhang Daoling and his successors was to realize the kingdom of the Great Peace on earth until a new sovereign would receive the mandate to rule from Heaven.

The administrative structure of the early Way of the Celestial Masters was based on that of the Han empire; both in turn reproduced on earth the bureaucratic ordering of Heaven. Since that time, Daoist texts have often represented Heaven as an administration divided into ministries and offices, with a hierarchical classification of primary deities (often called "emperor," *di*) and a host of ancillary gods. The same bureaucratic features are displayed in Daoist ritual, which is based in part on the forms established by the early Way of the Celestial Masters: requests of audiences in the courtly halls of celestial palaces, arrangement of the deities on seats arrayed according to their rank, and written petitions delivered to the gods.

The Three Caverns.

The diaspora of the Celestial Masters' communities after the end of the Han resulted in the expansion of the new religion to other parts of China. Its spread in Jiangnan, the region south of the lower Yangzi River, was one of the prerequisites for the formation of two other major corpora of Daoist doctrines, texts, and practices in the second half of the fourth century. The representatives of the religious legacies of Jiangnan responded to the newly imported cults by reformulating and codifying some aspects of their own traditions in ways that admitted elements of the practices of the Celestial Masters, but were mainly based on the local traditions, which included meditation, alchemy, self-cultivation practices, and various methods for communicating with the gods and expelling demons. The first corpus, known as Shangqing (Highest Clarity), derived from revelations that occurred from 364 to 370 C.E. and was centered on meditation practices; the second, known and Lingbao (Numinous Treasure), derived from revelations that occurred between circa 395 and 405 C.E. and was based on communal ritual. These two codifications clearly define, for the first time, the two main poles of the Daoist religious experience, namely inner, individual practices on the one hand, and collective practices for the community of the faithful on the other.

The relations among these traditions were formally codified in the early fifth century in the system of the Three Caverns (*sandong*). Its main purpose was to hierarchically arrange the different legacies of Jiangnan, assigning the higher rank to Shangqing, the intermediate one to Lingbao, and the lower one to other earlier and contemporary traditions. Around 500 C.E., the corpora associated with the *Daode jing,* the *Taiping jing* (Scripture of Great Peace), alchemy, and the Way of the Celestial Masters were assigned to the so-called Four Supplements (*sifu*). The Three Caverns also provided the formal schema for other important aspects of Daoist doctrine and practice, including the ordination stages of the Daoist priest (*daoshi*) and the arrangement of scriptural and other writings in the collections of Daoist texts (*Daozang*) that began to take shape from the early fifth century.

This model continued to perform this function even after the contours of Daoist religion were reshaped by various new revelations and codifications during the Song period (960–1279) and later, and by the creation in the early thirteenth century of Quanzhen (Complete Reality, or Complete Perfection), a monastic order that is, along with the Way of the Celestial Masters, the main branch of present-day Daoism.

Cosmos and Gods

The cosmos generated by the Dao and the heavens inhabited by deities that personify the Dao are intermediaries between the Absolute and the human world. These two domains overlap to a significant extent, for certain deities and certain features of the cosmos correspond to each other. Both of them play an essential role in the various ways that Daoism provides for "returning to the Dao" (*fandao*), which are addressed either to the single individual or to the community as a whole.

Correlative cosmology. The features and workings of the cosmic domain are explicated in Daoism largely by means of the language and images of the standard Chinese cosmological system. This system, often referred to as "correlative cosmology" by scholars, is based on several patterns of emblems (*xiang*) such as Yin and Yang, the five agents (*wuxing*), and the eight trigrams and sixty-four hexagrams of the *Book of Changes* (*Yijing*). These emblems function as categories to which the single entities or phenomena can be assigned. The five agents, for instance, emblematize the modes or states in which the one Original Pneuma (*yuanqi*) appears in the cosmos, represented by Wood, Fire, Soil, Metal, and Water. Directions of space, segments of time cycles, numbers, colors, planets, viscera of the human body, musical notes, and so forth can be assigned to one of these emblematic categories in order to define not only the relations that occur among the elements of a series, but also those that occur among the different domains. Wood, for instance, is associated with the east, spring, the numbers 3 and 8, the color green (or blue), Jupiter, the liver, and the note *jiao*. The purpose of correlative cosmology, therefore, is not so much to explain what causes an entity to exist or a phenomenon to occur as it is to define its relation to other entities and phenomena. An important corollary to this view is that an event or action happening or performed in one domain may affect the corresponding components in another domain according to the principle of "stimulus and response" (*ganying*), by which things of the same "category" (*lei*) influence each other.

Correlative cosmology, which took shape as a comprehensive system between the third and the second centuries B.C.E., is not tied to any specific intellectual or religious legacy and is the result of an effort to create a comprehensive analytic and synthetic system with contributions both by thinkers and by specialists of various traditional sciences, including diviners, astronomers, and physicians. Daoism is one of several traditions that have drawn upon correlative cosmology to formulate its views and to frame its techniques or practices. In Daoism, correlative cosmology serves not only to explicate the functioning of the cosmos, but also to illustrate the notion that single entities and phenomena ultimately originate from the Dao and that the different forms in the world of multiplicity are governed by the One, the principle of the unity of the cosmos. At the same time, the emblems of correlative cosmology serve to regulate the process of "returning to the Dao" through the support of a microcosmic framework—the ritual area, the alchemical laboratory, or the human being itself. The ritual area, for instance, is arranged so as to correspond to the cosmos and its temporal and spatial configurations (Lagerwey, 1987, pp. 3–48). In alchemy, the stages of the compounding of the elixir reproduces in a reverse sequence the cosmological configurations that intervene between the absolute Dao and the domain of relativity.

Communicating with the gods. The supreme Daoist deities are the Three Clarities (*sanqing*), each of whom rules over one of the many heavens distinguished in Daoist cosmography. They are associated with different precosmic eras and are at the origin of the textual corpora associated with the Three Caverns. Above them some traditions place the Celestial Worthy of Original Commencement (*Yuanshi tianzun*), who dwells in the supreme Great Canopy Heaven (*Daluo tian*). The unity of the cosmos is represented in a deified form by the Great One (or Great Unity, *Taiyi*); he resides at the symbolic center of the cosmos in the Northern Dipper (*beidou*), whose apparent rotation distributes Original Pneuma to the regions of space and sustains the cycles of time. Several other gods, such as the "emperors" of the five directions (north, south, east, west, and center), also represent cosmological principles. In addition, a multitude of deities, most of whom are the expression of local cults, contribute to form a pantheon with indefinite boundaries that takes different forms according to place and time.

The highest gods, or their representatives, reveal texts, teachings, and practices. The scriptures belonging to the Shangqing and Lingbao corpora are deemed to have taken shape from graphs coagulated from Original Pneuma, or from sounds generated by its vibration, in the early stages of the formation of the cosmos. Those graphs constitute the prototypes of the revealed scriptures, which at first are transmitted from one god to another, undergoing various stages of materialization until they are delivered to humans by a divine being. Just as the gods grant revelations mostly in the form of scriptures, and consistently with the bureaucratic metaphor mentioned above, the typically Daoist form of communicating with the gods is by writing. In Daoist ritual, the priest delivers a "memorial" (or "statement," *shu*) to the deities to announce that a ceremony will be performed in their honor, declare its purpose, specify its program, and list the names of those who sponsor it. The so-called talismans (*fu*, a word that corresponds almost exactly to Greek *symbolon*) are traced on paper or other supports, including air, in graphs intelligible to the gods. Like the revealed scriptures—some of which, in fact, are deemed to have evolved from them—the talismans have a counterpart in Heaven, and thus serve to identify and authenticate their possessor. Talismans confer power to summon certain deities and to control demons, but they also protect space and heal illnesses; they are worn on one's body, affixed at the four directions, placed along the path that leads to one's dwelling, or made into ashes and drunk with water. Another important ritual object that has a written form is the "register" (*lu*), a formal document of investiture that the Daoist priest receives at various stages of his ordination and that defines his rank, the rites that he may perform, and the deities and spirits over which he has control.

The Human Being

Despite significant variations among the different traditions, the basic view of the human being and its potentialities in Daoism reflects its doctrinal principles. Many texts devoted to this subject state that full comprehension of their teachings grants the status of Real Man, or Perfected (*zhenren*). The related practices do not consist in a process of "increase" or "becoming perfect" but vice versa in reducing what obstructs one's potential for realization, according to the principle of the *Daode jing* that "practising the Dao is called reducing; reduce and then again reduce and thereby attain to non-doing" (sec. 48). Some authors of texts of inner alchemy were aware of the ambiguity involved in the very notion of "doing" a practice in order to attain the state of "non-doing" and emphasized that the practice operates within the domain that the adept is called to transcend; its final purpose is to reveal the limitations of that domain.

The heart (*xin*) is the symbolic center of the human being. It is the residence of spirit (*shen*) and corresponds to the Northern Dipper in heaven. Just as Oneness takes multiple forms in the cosmos, so the center of the human being reappears in multiple locations. The most important are the three Cinnabar Fields (*dantian,* immaterial loci in the regions of the brain, the heart, and the abdomen) and the five viscera (*wuzang,* namely liver, heart, spleen, lungs, and kidneys). The three Cinnabar Fields and the five viscera represent, respectively, the vertical and horizontal dimensions of the cosmos within the human being.

According to some traditions within Daoism, these and many other loci of the body are also residences of an inner pantheon of major and minor gods. The most important among them correspond to those that dwell in Heaven and perform multiple related roles: they personify the formless Dao or impersonal notions such as Yin and Yang, allow the human being to communicate with the gods of the outer pantheon, and administer the body and its functions. Several texts describe meditation practices in which the visualization of inner deities is combined with channeling essences and pneumas to the residences of the inner gods in order to provide them with nourishment. From the Tang period, these practices were largely replaced by other methods of contemplation and introspection influenced by Buddhism, but the inner gods have continued to perform an important function in ritual when they are summoned forth by the priest in order to submit the memorial to the gods in Heaven.

Alchemy, in its "inner" form (*neidan*), framed its practices in part by drawing from meditation methods and from techniques for "nourishing life" (*yangsheng*). The latter term refers to a large variety of methods that share a physiological foundation, including *daoyin* (a form of gymnastics that is one of the precursors of modern *taiji quan*), breathing, and sexual practices. Using the same word that other sources apply to the cults of common religion, several alchemical texts qualify those techniques as "secular" or "vulgar" (*su*); as other traditions within Daoism do with deities and rites, alchemy incorporates elements of those techniques but grafts them onto its own doctrinal background.

In alchemy and several other traditions, the purpose of the practice is to acquire transcendence or "immortality." In religious imagery, in both its mystical and popular aspects, "immortality" is a state attained by superior beings, often entirely legendary, through their practices. For others, "immortality" consists in undergoing transformation, in the literal sense of "going beyond the form" and returning to the unconditioned state.

See also **Buddhism; Chinese Thought; Confucianism; Humanism: Chinese Conception of; Legalism, Ancient China; Religion: East and Southeast Asia.**

BIBLIOGRAPHY

Barrett, T. H. *Taoism under the T'ang: Religion and Empire during the Golden Age of Chinese History.* London: Wellsweep, 1996.

Bokenkamp, Stephen R. *Early Daoist Scriptures.* Berkeley: University of California Press, 1997.

Boltz, Judith M. *A Survey of Taoist Literature: Tenth to Seventeenth Centuries.* Berkeley: Institute of East Asian Studies, University of California, 1987.

Despeux, Catherine. *Taoïsme et corps humain: Le Xiuzhen tu.* Paris: Guy Trédaniel Editeur, 1994.

Kohn, Livia, ed. *Daoism Handbook.* Leiden, Netherlands, and Boston: Brill, 2000.

Lagerwey, John. "Écriture et corps divin en Chine." In *Corps des dieux,* edited by Charles Malamoud and Jean-Pierre Vernant. Paris: Gallimard, 1986.

———. *Taoist Ritual in Chinese Society and History.* New York: Macmillan, 1987.

Lau, D. C., trans. *Tao Te Ching.* Hong Kong: Hong Kong University Press, 1982.

Little, Stephen, with Shawn Eichman. *Taoism and the Arts of China.* Chicago: The Art Institute of Chicago, 2000.

Pregadio, Fabrizio, ed. *The Encyclopedia of Taoism.* London: Routledge, 2004.

Robinet, Isabelle. *Taoism: Growth of a Religion.* Translated by Phyllis Brooks. Stanford, Calif.: Stanford University Press, 1997.

Schipper, Kristofer. *The Taoist Body.* Translated by Karen C. Duval. Berkeley: University of California Press, 1993.

Schipper, Kristofer, and Franciscus Verellen, eds. *The Taoist Canon: A Historical Companion to the Daozang.* 3 vols. Chicago: University of Chicago Press, 2004.

Seidel, Anna. "Chronicle of Taoist Studies in the West 1950–1990." *Cahiers d'Extrême-Asie* 5 (1989–1990): 223–347.

———. *La divinisation de Lao tseu dans le Taoïsme des Han.* Paris: École Française d'Extrême-Orient, 1969.

———. "Taoism: The Unofficial High Religion of China." *Taoist Resources* 7, no. 2 (1997): 39–72.

Stein, Rolf A. "Religious Taoism and Popular Religion from the Second to Seventh Centuries." In *Facets of Taoism: Essays in Chinese Religion,* edited by Holmes Welch and Anna Seidel. New Haven, Conn., and London: Yale University Press, 1979.

Watson, Burton, trans. *The Complete Works of Chuang tzu.* New York: Columbia University Press, 1968.

Fabrizio Pregadio

DARWINISM *See* **Evolution**

DEATH.

The idea of death—the irreversible end to life—has preoccupied, fascinated, and struck fear into human beings through the millennia. In the early twenty-first century, artists continue to sing about death, write about death, and depict it in paintings and photographs. Religious leaders are still talking about how to live a meaningful life in the face of death's inevitability. Governments go to war in the name of peace and the defense of the living, causing death on a massive scale. Ethicists and activists argue over the right to die, the right to live, the right to kill. Medical personnel strive to prevent it, are often present at the bedside of the dying, and pronounce when death has occurred. Biologists and physiologists puzzle over when it occurs and how it can be measured. Counselors, therapists, relatives, and dear friends help those

The Sorrow of Andromache (1781) by Jacques-Louis David. Oil on canvas. The concepts of death, grief, and mourning have been represented by innumerable artists throughout the centuries. During the Enlightenment, themes in art were frequently linked to human mortality. ERICH LESSING/ART RESOURCE, NY who are dying make peace with their death, and help those left behind to live on. Young children wonder what has happened to their loved ones, and families struggle with their grief.

Defining Death

Death is clearly a part of life—every day. And yet, the word defies simple definition, because there are so many aspects to death and so many perspectives. A 1913 edition of *Webster's Dictionary* defined death as "the cessation of all vital phenomena without capability of resuscitation, either in animals or plants." The current *Concise Oxford Dictionary* defines death both as "dying" (a process) and as "being dead" (a state). As intoned in the Old Testament of the Bible, "All flesh is as grass" (Isaiah 40:6–8). The body dies but in the religious and philosophical traditions of many observers, the soul or spirit lives on.

The Roman Catholic Church, for example, advances the thought that death is the "complete and final separation of the soul from the body." The church, however, concedes that diagnosing death is a subject for medicine, not the church. In the Zen Buddhist and Shintō religious traditions, mind and body are integrated, and followers have difficulty accepting the brain-death criteria that are now common in Western medical and legal circles. For some Orthodox Jews, Native Americans, Muslims, and fundamentalist Christians, as long as the heart is beating—even artificially—a person is still alive.

Advances in life-supporting technologies in the 1960s spawned the growth of medical ethics as a distinct field, and a new definition for physiological death was needed. For centuries death was indicated by the absence of a pulse or signs of breathing, but new technologies, including the respirator and heart–lung machine, made it possible for physicians to artificially maintain heart and lung function, blurring clear signs of an individual's death. In the United States many states have adopted legislation recognizing brain death—the loss of brain function, which controls breathing and heartbeat—as the certification of death. Canada, Australia, and most of the nations of Europe and Central and South America have broader definitions for death: either loss of all independent lung and heart function, or the permanent, irreversible loss of all brain function.

From a physiological standpoint, somatic death—the death of the organism as a whole—usually precedes the death of individual organs, cells, and parts of cells. The precise time of somatic death is sometimes difficult to determine because transient states, such as coma, fainting, and trance, can closely resemble the signs of death. Several changes in the body that occur after somatic death are used to determine the time of death and circumstances surrounding it. The cooling of the body, called *algor mortis,* is mainly influenced by the air temperature of the surrounding environment of the body. The stiffening of the skeletal muscles, called *rigor mortis,* begins from five to ten hours after death and ends in three or four days. The reddish-blue discoloration that occurs on the underside of the body, called *livor mortis,* is the result of blood settling in the body cavity. Shortly after death, blood clotting begins, along with autolysis, which is the death of the cells. The

decomposition of the body that follows, called putrefaction, is the result of the action of enzymes and bacteria.

Bereavement, Grief, and Mourning

The word *bereavement* comes from a root word meaning "shorn off" or "torn up." It suggests that one has been deprived or robbed, dispossessed, left in a sad and lonely state. Bereavement is the state of being in which a person has suffered the death of a relative or friend.

Grief refers to the total range of emotions humans feel in response to a loss. The word suggests negative responses, including heartbreak, anguish, distress, guilt, shame, and thoughts of suicide. Grief also encompasses feelings of relief, anger, disgust, and self-pity.

Mourning is the expression of grief over someone's death. It is the process by which people incorporate the experience of loss into their ongoing lives. In mourning, a person searches for answers: How do I carry on in life? How do I survive this? Approaches to mourning are culturally prescribed: Each world culture has certain cultural "rules" for mourning in an appropriate manner. Mourning today is less formal than it was in the past, and so-called modern cultures are less formal in their rituals for mourning than traditional cultures.

Why Must People Die?

A number of answers to this question have been proposed by philosophically oriented biologists such as Sherwin B. Nuland and Basiro Davey and colleagues. The results of tissue cultures indicate that cells are "preprogrammed" by their genetic code to cease the dividing processes after a certain number of divisions have occurred, and then die. A further argument proposes that death is adaptive at the population level, ensuring that individuals do not compete with their offspring for scarce resources and instead channel precious energy into reproduction. Research accounts of the biochemical changes that occur in cells as they age support both these theories and a more straightforward "wear and tear" argument, indicating that death on a biological level can be understood as a combination of a number of factors.

These biological explanations for the occurrence of death focus on the process of aging. The death of younger people, especially one's own child, opens up broader philosophical questions that may be even more difficult to answer: "Why did my baby die, God?" is one of the ways human beings ask this type of question. If God truly is in his heaven and all is right with the world, why do babies die? Human beings have struggled with this type of question through the millennia, and there do not appear to be any definitive, widely accepted answers. Individuals seem to come to grips with such questions in an extraordinarily varied range of ways.

Historical Perspectives

In 1900 the average life expectancy at birth in the United States was 47 years, and this figure increased to a record high of 77.2 years a century later. The gap between female and male life expectancy peaked in 1979 when women outlived men an average of 7.8 years. By 2001 the gap was down to 5.4 years.

That year, women lived an average of 79.8 years and men an average of 74.4 years. White males averaged 75.0 years and black males 68.6 years; white females averaged 80.2 years and black females 75.5 years (Arias and Smith).

In 1900 more than half of the deaths involved young people, age fourteen and younger. By 2001, only 1.6 percent of the total reported deaths occur among young people. Heart disease and cancer are the leading causes of death in the early twenty-first century, together accounting for more than half of all deaths in the United States each year. In order, the top fifteen leading causes of death, comprising fully 83.4 percent of all U.S. deaths in 2001, were: heart disease, cancer, stroke, chronic lower respiratory diseases, accidents (unintentional injuries), diabetes, influenza and pneumonia, Alzheimer's disease, kidney disease, septicemia (infection from microorganisms), intentional self-harm (suicide), chronic liver disease and cirrhosis, assault (homicide), hypertension, and pneumonitis (inflammation of the lungs) due to solids and liquids.

In the past century the experience of death has changed from a time when the typical death was rapid and sudden, often caused by acute infectious diseases such as tuberculosis, typhoid fever, syphilis, diphtheria, streptococcal septicemia, and pneumonia, to a time when the typical death is a slow, progressive process. In 1900 microbial diseases, often striking rapidly, accounted for about 40 percent of all deaths; in the early 2000s accounted for only about 3 percent. In sum, in the past century U.S. society has evolved from one in which many children and young people died to a society in which death has become increasingly associated with older-aged people. The U.S. infant mortality rate reached a record low level in 2001: 6.8 deaths per 1,000 live births.

Observers of this phenomenon have proposed a theory of epidemiologic transition, a three-stage model that describes the decline in mortality levels and the accompanying changes in the causes of death that have been experienced in Western populations. The first stage, called the Age of Pestilence and Famine, is characterized by high death rates that vacillate in response to epidemics, famines, and war. Epidemics and famines often go hand in hand, because malnourished people are susceptible to infectious diseases. The second stage, the Age of Receding Pandemics, describes a time in which death rates decline as a result of the improved nutrition, sanitation, and medical advances that go along with socioeconomic development. The third stage, labeled the Age of Degenerative and (Hu)man-Made Diseases, describes the period in which death rates are low (life expectancy at birth exceeds seventy years) and the main causes of death are diseases related to the process of aging. The biggest challenge to this theory comes from the emergence of new diseases (such as AIDS/HIV, Legionnaires' disease, and Lyme disease) and reemergence of old infectious diseases (such as smallpox and malaria) in the latter part of the twentieth century. HIV/AIDS, for example, took the lives of between 1.9 million and 3.6 million people worldwide in 1999.

According to the Population Reference Bureau, life expectancy at birth for the world's population at the turn of the twenty-first century was 67 years—69 years for females, 65 years for males. In more developed countries life expectancy averaged 76 years—79 years for females, 72 years for males. In less-developed countries, life expectancy averaged 65 years—66 years for females, and 63 years for males.

Death throughout Art History

Death, an emotionally wrenching idea, has been both a subject for artists and an incentive for artistic production throughout history. Perhaps as much as, perhaps more than, any other subject, artists have dealt with death, dying, the threat of death, escape from death, thoughts of death, and preparation for death through the centuries.

The importance of death as a concept in ancient Egyptian culture is clearly seen in the creation of the pyramids and other burial artifacts. Ancient art in Greece focused on materialistic representations of life in an ideal state, including the physical perfection of its mythological heroes. This can be interpreted as art affirming life as the Greeks experienced it or desired life to be, and the cultural rejection of the finality of death. Looking at art in the Christian tradition with its focus on the death of its central figure, some art historians have described Christianity as a highly developed death cult; the idea of death, mediated through works of Christian art over the centuries, is ultimately affirming of life. Many artists in the period of the Enlightenment of the eighteenth century were commissioned to work in service to the lay aristocracy and eventually the merchant class. The social hierarchy in this time was reinforced through highly developed techniques in portrait painting. Portraiture, seen as self-constructed identity through painting, constitutes a large segment of traditional Western art. Thus, art during the Enlightenment was closely linked to the idea of personal mortality. Major themes in modern art include the importance of self-expression in the face of the forces of mass conformity and antihumanist ideas. The universal theme of mortality is seen in many modern works, and death remains firmly established as a central theme in contemporary art, though the themes surrounding the concept of death are not as likely to reflect religious, romantic, or metaphysical concerns as they were in earlier historical periods.

No one can predict future directions in artists' responses to death, but it is most likely that humankind will continue to look to these visionaries to both document and inform our thinking. Mourners in Greece during the early fifth century were depicted striking their heads, tearing out their hair, beating their breasts, and scratching their cheeks until they bled. Today, many find solace from the largest ongoing community arts project in the world, the AIDS Memorial Quilt. In both instances, artists helped society commemorate the lives of deceased loved ones, and they supported the living in their efforts to find meaning and the strength to endure their tragic feelings of loss.

The Psychology of Dying

The American psychiatrist Elisabeth Kübler-Ross developed a five-stage model of the psychology of dying and grief. In her book titled *On Death and Dying* (1969), she proposed that in response to the awareness of their impending death, individuals move through stages of denial, anger, bargaining, depression, and acceptance. Other authorities note that these stages do not occur in any predictable order, and feelings of hope, anguish, and terror may also be included in the range of emotions experienced.

Bereaved families and friends also go through stages from denial to acceptance. Grief can begin before a loved one has died, and this anticipatory grief helps lessen later distress. During the next stage of grief, after the death of the loved one, mourners are likely to cry, have trouble sleeping, and lose their appetite. Some feel alarmed, angry, or wounded by being left behind. After formal services for the deceased are over and conventional forms of social support end, depression and loneliness often occur.

Feelings of guilt are quite common, and in some cases individuals think seriously about taking their own life for somehow failing the loved one. This is especially true in response to the loss of a child. Though people often talk about healthy and unhealthy grief, it is very difficult to measure emotional pain in any precise way or advise how long one's grief should last. Many clinicians believe that those who abandon their grief prematurely are living in denial and make healing more difficult; but, on the other hand, it is also possible to become mired in despair. The death of a loved one, thus, threatens to take all the life out of the person who feels left behind.

Research on attitudes toward death and anxiety about death has been conducted mostly by social scientists around the world. There are more than one thousand published studies in this area, and four broad themes emerge from the findings:

1. Most people think about death to some extent and report some fear of death, but only a small percentage exhibit a strong preoccupation with death or fear of death.

2. Women consistently report more fear of death than men, but the difference in levels of fear is typically minor to moderate from study to study.

3. Fear of death does not increase with age among most people.

4. When considering their own death, people are more concerned about potential pain, helplessness, dependency, and the well-being of loved ones than with their own demise.

Death Education

The death-related experiences of most Americans and people in other Western and industrialized societies in the early twenty-first century are markedly different from how people experienced death a century ago. At present, death is much more likely to take place in a medical facility under the control of well-trained strangers. In the past, death more commonly was an intimate family event and usually took place at home with family members caring for the dying person. Loved ones were most likely present when the individual passed, and young children witnessed the events surrounding the death. The loved one's body was washed by the family and prepared for burial. A local carpenter or perhaps even family members themselves constructed a coffin, and the body lay in state for viewing by family and friends in the parlor of the home. Children kept vigil with adults and sometimes slept in the room with the body. The body was later carried to the gravesite, which might be on the family's land or at a nearby cemetery. The local minister would be present to read Bible verses and say goodbye, and the coffin would be lowered and the grave covered, perhaps by relatives.

In the early 2000s, death has been sanitized and separated from everyday lives. It is likely to happen in a high-tech, multilayered bureaucratic hospital. The body is soon whisked away from view. It is carefully prepared for viewing and subsequent burial by professionals with an artistic flair, and placed in an elaborate and expensive casket. The body is then carried via a dazzling motor coach to the cemetery for internment in a carefully draped burial plot giving little hint that the loved one will actually end up in the earth.

The choreography of the modern death and burial process has become so elaborate that many people react in frustration and dismay and seek more simple, emotionally connected experiences of death. At the same time, the field of death education has grown as colleges and universities create courses on death and dying. These courses include both formal instruction dealing with dying, death, and grief, plus considerable time invested in talking about the participants' personal experiences with death. These developments can all be interpreted as parts of a movement toward bringing death back into people's lives, as a painful and puzzling event to be explored, experienced, and embraced rather than denied and avoided.

See also **Death and Afterlife, Islamic Understanding of; Heaven and Hell; Heaven and Hell (Asian Focus); Immortality and the Afterlife; Suicide.**

BIBLIOGRAPHY

Arias, Elizabeth, and Betty L. Smith. "Deaths: Preliminary Data for 2001." *National Vital Statistics Reports* 51, no. 5 (2003): 1.

Arias, Elizabeth, et al. "Deaths: Final Data for 2001." *National Vital Statistics Reports* 52, no. 3 (2003): 21.

Carroll, Nöel. *Philosophy of Art.* London: Routledge, 1999.

Davey, Basiro, Tim Halliday, and Mark Hirst, eds. *Human Biology and Health: An Evolutionary Approach.* 3rd ed. Buckingham, U.K.: Open University Press, 2001.

DeFrain, John, Linda Ernst, and Jan Nealer. "The Family Counselor and Loss." In *Loss during Pregnancy or in the Newborn Period: Principles of Care with Clinical Cases and Analyses,* edited by James R. Woods Jr. and Jenifer L. Esposito Woods, 499–520. Pitman, N.J.: Jannetti Publications, 1997.

DeSpelder, Lynne Ann, and Albert Lee Strickland. *The Last Dance: Encountering Death and Dying.* 7th ed. Boston: McGraw-Hill, 2005.

Kastenbaum, Robert. *The Psychology of Death.* 3rd ed. New York: Springer, 2000.

Kastenbaum, Robert, ed. *Macmillan Encyclopedia of Death and Dying.* New York: Macmillan Reference, 2003. See especially the entries on "Art History," "Causes of Death," and "Psychology."

New Dictionary of the History of Ideas

Kübler-Ross, Elisabeth. *On Death and Dying.* London: Macmillan, 1969.

Nuland, Sherwin B. *How We Die.* London: Chatto and Windus, 1994.

Olshansky, Stuart Jay, and A. B. Ault. "The Fourth Stage of Epidemiologic Transition: The Age of Delayed Degenerative Diseases." *Milbank Memorial Fund Quarterly* 64 (1986): 355–391.

Omran, Abdel R. "The Theory of Epidemiological Transition." *Milbank Memorial Fund Quarterly* 49 (1971): 509–538.

Population Reference Bureau. "Life Expectancy at Birth by World Region, 2001." In *2003 World Population Data Sheet.* Washington, D.C.: Population Reference Bureau, 2003.

Seale, Clive. *Constructing Death: The Sociology of Dying and Bereavement.* Cambridge, U.K.: Cambridge University Press, 1998.

Wollheim, Richard. *Painting as an Art.* Princeton, N.J.: Princeton University Press, 1987.

Wyatt, R. "Art History." In *Encyclopedia of Death and Dying,* edited by Glennys Howarth and Oliver Leaman, 34–36. London: Routledge, 2001.

John DeFrain
Alyssa DeFrain
Joanne Cacciatore-Garard

DEATH AND AFTERLIFE, ISLAMIC UNDERSTANDING OF.

Islamic views of death and the afterlife encompass two broad streams: the individual and the collective or cosmological. The existence of an afterlife for individuals and final judgment of all creation are both central tenets of the faith. The Koran provides the foundation for Muslim views of death, with eschatological imagery leaping out from nearly every page. The Koran is supplemented by hadith, reports of the words and deeds of the prophet Muhammad (c. 570–632), as well as by numerous commentaries and treatises. While the specific beliefs and practices surrounding death and the afterlife display significant sectarian and cultural variety, the following account will focus on the most widely shared views.

Overview

Death is built into God's plan for his creation. God alone determines and knows the time and manner of each person's death and of Judgment Day. Tradition holds that an angel implants in the womb of each expectant mother a speck of soil from the place where that child is eventually fated to die. While God retains authority over death, he delegates oversight of individual deaths to an angel named Izra'il. Orthodox Sunni theology recognizes God's total omniscience and omnipotence. Thus God appoints not only each person's day of death but also the individual actions for which one is judged. This view is balanced by a recognition of God's infinite justice, a sense that humans choose and deserve their ultimate fate. The apparent paradox is addressed in the complex theological formula of "acquisition" (*iktisab*), which holds that while God authors human acts, people "acquire" them as products of free will. This doctrine is buttressed with an appeal to divine mystery, a belief that God's ways are beyond human comprehension.

In the end, most Muslims display a firm commitment to both predestination and free will, holding themselves accountable for their deeds while acquiescing to God's power. If intellectually untidy, such a view is emotionally rich and satisfying for many.

Rather than "fear," Muslim sources prefer to counsel the "remembrance" of death, the awareness that it may come at any time, and the need to be always prepared. Al-Muhasibi (c. 781–857) advises that

> You need only know that death has no hour known to the servant that he might fear that particular time but be secure at other times. . . . If it does not come down at any particular period of life, one cannot be secure from it in childhood or maturity, in youth or in old age. Since it has no particular cause, one cannot be secure from it in health or in illness, in city or in desert, on land or on sea. . . . When he is watchful for death, he hastens to be prepared for it and races to complete good works before the angel of death can reach his spirit. (Sells, pp. 181–182)

Death of the Body

A tree is said to stand beneath God's heavenly throne, each leaf bearing the name of an individual, and forty days before death that person's leaf falls from the tree as a signal to the angel of death. As death nears, one should prepare by repenting from sin and reading generally from the Koran, especially sura 36, "Ya sin," and others considered notable for their reflections on death. One should face toward Mecca, as in prayer, and repeat the *Shahada* (profession of faith): "There is no god but God, and Muhammad is the Messenger of God." This serves as preparation for the questioning of the soul in the grave, and it is auspicious to die with these words on one's lips. For the incapacitated, family or other fellow Muslims should whisper pious invocations in the dying person's ears. The dying are considered particularly susceptible to Satan's temptations, and their faith must be reinforced with pious reminders.

Burial should proceed without delay. No embalming or cremation is allowed; aside from being cleaned, the body is left minimally altered. Muslims do not present the dead for viewing, as has become customary in the West. The washing of the corpse is ritualized, echoing purification for worship; it begins with the face, head, hands, and feet, as in ritual ablution, then extends to the rest of the body, proceeding from the right side to the left and accompanied by the appropriate prayers. (The body of a martyr is considered pure and is not washed.) The private parts are to be covered from sight, with the washing proceeding under the covering. The washing is preferably done by a family member of the same sex or a spouse or parent. Soap and scent may be used, and the washing is repeated three times. The body may be perfumed, and orifices covered with scented cloth. A simple white, seamless cloth shroud (preferably in three sections for men and five for women) is wrapped around the corpse, and at this point it may be laid out at home or in a mosque for the special *salat al-janaza* (prayer for a funeral). Though the Prophet urged restraint in mourning, wailing for the dead is common, and professional mourners

> After being created by God, the Angel of Death cried out: "I am death who separates all loved ones! I am death who separates man and woman, husband and wife! I am death who separates daughters from mothers! I am death who separates sons from fathers . . . [and] brother from his brother! I am death who subdues the power of the sons of Adam. I am death who inhabits the graves. . . . Not a creature will remain who does not taste me."
>
> SOURCE: Quoted in Jane Idleman Smith and Yvonne Yazbeck Haddad. *The Islamic Understanding of Death and Resurrection,* p. 35.

> When the sun shall be darkened, when the stars shall be thrown down, when the mountains shall be set moving, when the pregnant camels shall be neglected [something no Bedouin would allow], when the savage beasts shall be mustered, when the seas shall be set boiling, . . . when heaven shall be stripped off, when Hell shall be set blazing, when Paradise shall be brought nigh, then shall a soul know what it has produced.
>
> SOURCE: Koran 81:1–14, Arberry's translation.

may even be hired. Mourning traditionally consists of three days of ascetic behavior (longer for widows), and may include special observances of grief and remembrance on the fortieth day after the funeral, as well as periodic visits to the grave. The spirits of the dead are said to remain close to the grave between death and Judgment Day, and to gain comfort when they are visited by the living, who themselves benefit from the reminder of death.

After prayers, the body is borne to the burial site, accompanied by a procession of loved ones and other Muslims. A coffin is not required, and if one is used, it should not be ostentatious. A traditional grave is several feet deep with a niche to one side for the body. The body is placed in the grave on its right side, with its head facing Mecca, the niche is sealed with bricks, and the grave is filled with earth. Often the surface of the grave is built up with earth or bricks slightly above ground level. Conservative Muslims hold that graves should be minimally adorned, though many employ a marker bearing the deceased's name and some religious text. Some go much further, the Taj Mahal being an extreme example of the elaborate tombs of the wealthy and powerful. Exceptionally pious individuals or "saints" may be buried in special shrines, typically with a domed roof and a space for gathering near the grave. Such saints are popularly credited with miraculous powers and the ability to mediate between believers and God, powers that only increase upon death and draw pilgrims to saints' tombs seeking aid and blessings. Such practices are historically widespread, yet they have inspired equally widespread criticism. Orthodox Sunni theology recognizes only the prophet Muhammad as a potential intercessor between individuals and God, and conservative Muslims decry the impression of idolatry left by the veneration of saints. Still, such practices persist in many areas as a supplement or alternative to orthodox ritual observances.

Individual Resurrection, Judgment, and Afterlife

After death each individual faces initial testing and preliminary judgment (except the martyr, one who dies "in the path of God," who goes straight to heaven [see Koran 2:154]). The Koran says relatively little regarding this time in the grave, called the *barzakh* (interval), but other genres give much, if not always consistent, detail. Most accounts treat the time in the grave as a foretaste of one's final fate on Judgment Day, and perhaps as a time of purgation of sins so that the deceased is purified and made fit for heaven. Though the exact order of events varies among the sources, the typical account begins with angels visiting the dead and drawing the soul out of the body. Abu al-Layth al-Samarqandi (d. 983) describes the worthy soul coming forth "as easily as a drop from a waterskin," whereas for the soul of an unbeliever, "the angel drags it forth like the dragging of an iron spit through moist wool, tearing the veins and sinews" (Peters, pp. 403–404). The soul is borne up to the gates of heaven; the faithful soul is carried in perfumed shrouds and admitted into heaven to be greeted by the blessed inhabitants of the seven heavens, perhaps even by God himself, while the unbeliever, carried in rough and reeking rags, is turned away at the gate. Each soul is then returned to the body, whereupon angels interrogate it, asking who is its Lord, *din* ("religion"), and prophet. The faithful answer correctly, while unbelievers falter and misspeak. Next the dead may be visited by the person's deeds personified in the appropriately pleasant or foul form, while the grave is either cooled by a fragrant comforting breeze or blasted with tormenting smoke and fire. Some hold that these conditions endure until resurrection, others that the dead slip into a form of sleep so that the ages pass in an instant.

Resurrection and Judgment Day

At a time known only to God, all creation will be undone and all people, living and dead, will face final judgment. The Koran vividly describes the apocalyptic physical and social chaos of the end time. As these frightening events unfold, al-Dajjal, the Antichrist, will emerge, promising riches, working miracles, and gathering followers. However, as one hadith relates, "he will have with him what will appear like paradise and fire. But that which he will call paradise will be the Fire" (al-Nawawi, p. 308). This is a time of testing, and those of good faith will see through the deceits of al-Dajjal. Al-Nawawi (1233–1278) relates that at this time God

> will raise the Messiah, [Jesus] the son of Mary, . . . his hands resting on the wings of two angels. . . . He will pursue the Anti-Christ and will encounter him at the gate of Lud [said to be in Palestine, but compare Gen. 10:13] and will slaughter him. The Messiah will then come to people whom God has shielded from the Anti-Christ. He will wipe away the dust from their faces and will inform them about their grades in Paradise. (al-Nawawi, p. 305)

In some accounts Jesus is preceded or accompanied by the Mahdi ("guided one"), a messianic figure who will revive Islam from decline during the end times.

These events will culminate in the sounding of a great horn (Koran 39:68, 69:13), signaling the final extinction (*fana*) of all creation as God alone remains, completing the full reversal of original creation. God then restores the earth, resurrects all human bodies, reunites them with their souls, and presides over their final judgment. Two interwoven sets of images characterize this "reckoning" (*hisab*): a written record of each person's deeds—handed to the wicked in their left hand, to the righteous in their right hand—and the balance (*mizan*) in which an individual's deeds are weighed, the good against the bad. The Koran attests to both means of accounting, though the exact relation of the two is not clear. Many accounts then proceed to yet another test, in the form of a bridge (*sirat*) over the fires of hell (see Koran 36:66 and 37:23–24); for the faithful this is wide, while for the wicked it narrows to a knife-edge from which they tumble into perdition. While God's judgment is final, he is depicted as profoundly merciful, permitting Muhammad to intercede on behalf of some sinners, and rescuing from the fires even those with the merest trace of goodness. Some even hold that God will ultimately redeem all the inhabitants of hell, thus treating punishment as purgation rather than eternal fate.

Heaven and Hell

Heaven, sometimes said to have seven levels, is generally described as a lush garden where the faithful reap the rewards of obedience and morality. Its inhabitants revel in "gardens underneath which rivers flow" (Koran 4:57, 22:23, etc.), peaceful serenity, cool shade and breezes, rivers of water, milk, and honey, luscious foods and drink (including nonintoxicating wine), luxurious furnishings and clothing, and so forth. While some interpret these images as metaphorical, envisioning a purely spiritual bliss in the presence of God, most tend toward literalistic and corporeal interpretations, while recognizing that the true reality of heaven is beyond earthly comprehension.

Although the afterlife is generally the same for both men and women, one aspect of heaven appears to have distinctly gendered overtones. The *hur*, virginal "companions, with beautiful, big and lustrous eyes" (Koran 56:22), are mentioned four times in the Koran (44:54, 52:20, 55:72, and 56:22), though without much detail; post-Koranic sources extrapolate on these accounts. The *hur* are understood to be rewards for males in heaven, and differ from earthly women in their delicate beauty, purity, and lack of illness, menstruation, and pregnancy. Ordinary Muslim women may also go to heaven, where each is said to have just one husband, usually her earthly husband. Thus the *hur* appear to join earthly wives as additional heavenly companions for men. However, some commentators see the *hur* as companions and servants of female believers as well: "Just as the gardens, rivers, milk, honey, fruits, and numerous other things of Paradise are both for men and women, even so are the *hur*" (Smith and Haddad, p. 167).

Hell, often called simply "the fire" (*al-nur*), is depicted in the Koran as a place of unending torment, filled with flame, acrid smoke, boiling waters, and the wails of its unfortunate inhabitants. The damned can gain no comfort: "he is given to drink of oozing pus, the which he gulps, and can scarce swallow, and death comes upon him from every side, yet he cannot die; and still beyond him is a harsh chastisement" (Koran 14:16–17, Arberry's translation). Further, "as often as their skins are wholly burned, we shall give them in exchange other skins, that they may taste the chastisement" (Koran 4:56). As noted, however, some Muslims ascribe to God such profound mercy that he ultimately rescues even the most undeserving sinner from these torments.

The vivid imagery of heaven and hell in Muslim sources adds weight to the call to "remember" death. As a late-twentieth-century Muslim author observed,

> This clear reality of the future Life is always before the mind and consciousness of the devout Muslim. It is this awareness which keeps the present life, in the midst of the most intense happiness and the deepest pain alike, in perspective: the perspective of a passing, temporary abode in which one has been placed as a test in order to qualify and prepare himself for his future Home. . . . Therefore the Muslim, knowing that God alone controls life and death, and that death may come to him at any time, tries to send on ahead for his future existence such deeds as will merit the pleasure of his Lord, so that he can look forward to it with hope for His mercy and grace. (Haneef, p. 37)

See also **Death; Free Will, Determinism, and Predestination; Heaven and Hell; Islam; Paradise on Earth; Philosophies: Islamic.**

BIBLIOGRAPHY

Arberry, Arthur J. *The Koran Interpreted.* 2 vols. New York: Macmillan, 1955.

Averroës. *The Distinguished Jurist's Primer: A Translation of Bidayat al-Mujtahid.* Translated by Imran Ahsan Khan Nyazee. 2 vols. Reading, U.K.: Garnet, 1994. A good English-language source for death-related ritual law.

Denny, Frederick Mathewson. *An Introduction to Islam.* 2nd ed. New York: Macmillan, 1993. Useful treatment of death rituals.

Haneef, Suzanne. *What Everyone Should Know about Islam and Muslims.* 2nd ed. Chicago: Library of Islam, 1996.

Ibn al-Naqib, Ahmad al-Misri. *Reliance of the Traveler: A Classic Manual of Islamic Sacred Law: "Umat al salik."* Edited and translated by Nuh Ha Mim Keller. Rev. ed. Beltsville, Md.: Ammana, 1999. Another good English-language source for death-related ritual law.

al-Nawawi. *Gardens of the Righteous: Riyadh as-Salihin of Imam Nawawi.* Translated by Muhammad Zafrulla Khan. London: Curson, 1975.

Peters, F. E. *A Reader on Classical Islam.* Princeton, N.J.: Princeton University Press, 1994.

Sells, Michael A., trans. and ed. *Early Islamic Mysticism.* New York: Paulist Press, 1996.

Smith, Jane Idleman, and Yvonne Yazbeck Haddad. *The Islamic Understanding of Death and Resurrection.* Albany: State University of New York Press, 1981. The definitive scholarly study of the topic.

Paul R. Powers

DECADENCE. *See* **Cycles.**

DECONSTRUCTION. *See* **Structuralism and Poststructuralism: Overview.**

DEISM. *Deism* holds more meanings than one word should be asked to bear. Generally, to the point of almost being meaningless, it refers to the notion that reason plays an important role in determining religious knowledge. By this definition the pre-Socratic philosophers, Plato, Aristotle, Epicurus, the Stoics, Cicero, Lucretius, Buddha, Moses, Jesus, and Muhammad all qualify to varying degrees as Deists. With more historical precision the term embraces the religious philosophy of the Enlightenment. But there is a wide range of meanings here too. To religious traditionalists, Deists were effectively atheists. To atheists and materialists, Deism represented a half-realized understanding of the universe. For those who would not have balked had the word been applied to them—hardly anyone in the eighteenth century self-identifies as a "Deist"—it signified belief in a God who could be known by naturally given reason rather than solely by revelation.

But even among this last group the word contained many antinomies. Some Deists upheld the authority of the church; others aggressively criticized customary religious thought and practice. Some used reason to develop more rigorous methods of biblical criticism; others argued that rather than texts, reason in nature offers the proper route to religious truth. Almost all Deists denied God's providence; but a few retained the vestiges of providentialism by virtue of their reasoned belief that God maintained an active, judging presence in the universe. Deism held positive meaning both for moderate Enlightenment figures and those who belong more properly in what the historian Margaret Jacob twenty years ago called the "Radical Enlightenment"; it held negative meanings for traditionalists as well as nonbelievers. The object of this entry will therefore be to explain this word's various meanings more fully by looking closely at how and in whose hands those meanings changed over time.

Early History

The word *déiste* carried a negative valence in its first appearance in the Lausanne reformer Pierre Viret's (1511–1571) *Instruction chrestienne* (1564). Viret recognized a difference between Deism and atheism, if only in seeing the latter as the superlative of the former, but by *déiste* he was likely referring to a group of Lyonnaise anti-Trinitarians rather than those who would later be identified by their rejection of Christian revelation. The word's emergence in the mid-sixteenth century was, whatever its precise referent, not accidental. Much like early modern skepticism, Deistic ideas were fueled by four major changes associated with the late fifteenth and sixteenth centuries: the ongoing recovery of works from antiquity; European encounters with non-European cultures; the confessional conflicts, both conceptual and material, that followed the Protestant and Catholic Reformations; and the spread of experimental science. All had the effect of destabilizing certainties and encouraging some men and women to recover fundamental truths from doubt. And all contributed to the context in which cultural conservatives hurled "Deist" as a term of abuse in their various attempts to confute heterodox ideas and restore unsettled epistemological foundations.

The effects of these four destabilizing changes shaped the earliest expression of arguments that prefigure Enlightenment Deism, which were published in *De veritate* (1624) by the English ambassador to France, Edward, Lord Herbert of Cherbury (1583–1648). Herbert argued that "common notions" would ultimately lead men and women of any religious upbringing to worship God piously, avoid sin, and intuit divine justice. Reason given to us by nature, in other words, could rescue belief from skepticism. The argument seemed flimsy to René Descartes (1596–1650) and Pierre Gassendi (1592–1655), much as in a later form it would strike Hume as entirely empty. But the notion that we all have the capacity to understand religious truth regardless of culture and tradition became a compelling central assumption of later Deists.

British Deism

The high point of Deism began in Britain in the wake of the civil wars of the mid-seventeenth century. The conflicts of the 1640s and the republican experiment of the 1650s opened up a social and cultural space in which the nature of government, God, gender, and virtually every other worthwhile topic under the sun were called into question. Countless tracts printed after church and state censorship collapsed in the early 1640s assailed religious authority and gave primacy over religion to reason. When this period of kingless rule ended in 1660 with the return of Charles II (1630–1685), the religious experimentalism and enthusiasm of the 1640s and 1650s came to be associated by many with social and political instability. But Deistic ideas were nevertheless out of the bag. The splintering that would later be evident within the ranks of Deistic thinkers reflects this ambivalence about the midcentury crisis and its larger meaning. On the one hand, moderate Deists, who borrowed conservatively from the various radicalisms of the 1640s and 1650s, sought to maintain a balance between reason and religion in order to make religion less intense, more sociable, and more conducive to social and political stability. On the other hand, radical Deists with more undiluted intellectual links to the midcentury's most extreme ideas—atheism and materialism—were less bothered by the religious consequences of the rigorous application of reason to revelation.

The paragons of moderate Deistic arguments were the Enlightenment's two discursive founders: Isaac Newton (1642–1727), born the year civil war broke out, and John Locke (1632–1704), the intellectual product of the nexus of puritan selfhood, parliamentary government, and experimental science. Newton ascribed supreme importance to his investigations into natural phenomena because they brought him closer to the God who set the universe in motion; how active God was in his creation would continue to be a divisive issue for Newtonians. Locke captured in the title of his *The Reasonableness of Christianity, as Delivered in the Scriptures* (1695) his basic idea that rational interpretations of our perceptions can lead to the fundamental truths expressed in the Bible. Those same changes we noted with respect to skepticism were also at work here. Both men embraced experimental science and had a stake in securing the stability of the nation after the revolutions of 1688 to 1691, which, like the conflict four decades earlier, also stemmed from religious divisions. And if the influence of ancient ideas was showing early signs of waning, Locke was intensely interested in cultural variation, which led him to seek basic truths about the human mind that held in varied cultural conditions.

Almost as soon as Newton and Locke defined their moderate brand of Deism, radicals began to apply reason to religion more strenuously. A "Deist controversy" in printed tracts and sermonic literature erupted with the publication of *Christianity Not Mysterious* (1696) by the Irish-born Protestant convert and likely son of a Catholic priest, John Toland (1670–1722). His work appeared not accidentally a year after censorship became a nonissue after the lapsing of the Licensing Act of 1695. Toland drew from radical thinkers such as Spinoza, Gerrard Winstanley, Epicurus, and Giordano Bruno (none of whom should be classified as a Deist), but he was also the logically extreme product of Newton and Locke. Newton and Locke had argued that by reason we come to a closer understanding of the fundamental truths of Christianity; Toland deduced that if a religion's reasonableness could not be established, one had license to explore better—more reasonable—religious or even nonreligious options.

More than anyone, Toland gave Deism a deconstructive edge. He questioned the authenticity of the New Testament and argued that the Jews were originally Egyptians, while also controverting Britain's legally institutionalized anti-Semitism. Toland himself became, by his own neologism, a "pantheist," but his ideas were picked up by others who shared his Whig politics, animosity for priestcraft, and gifts for persuasive writing. Another son of a cleric, Matthew Tindal, undercut biblical authority when he wrote that "it's an odd jumble to prove the truth of a book by the truth of the doctrines it contains, and at the same time conclude those doctrines to be true because contained in that book" (p. 49). William Wollaston used Lockean logic to solve the conundrum of whether or not God can create a mountain he cannot destroy—"God cannot be unjust or unreasonable in any one instance"—while another Lockean, Anthony Collins (1676–1729), reasoned that Christianity was a mere sect, a self-fulfilling Old Testament prophecy that the passage of time gave global prominence (Wollaston, p. 205). Even the pious skeptic Thomas Woolston claimed in the spirit of radical Deism that the supposed miracles of Jesus were, if actually anything other than pure fiction, the products of wizardry rather than divinity.

These authors and utterances did not go unchecked or unchallenged. The moderate Deists who more closely followed Newton's and Locke's intentions, particularly the late-Stuart "latitudinarians" Richard Bentley (1662–1742), Benjamin Hoadly (1676-1761), John Tillotson (1630–1694), and Samuel Clarke (1675–1729), upheld religious belief through a combination of rationality (directed against religious enthusiasm more than the Bible), faith, and reliance on textual authority. High- and low-church traditionalists alike more critically saw Deism as one of many heterodox ideas that threatened the fundamental meaning of the church, if not religion itself, while from a very different point of view the diehard skeptic David Hume (1711–1776) viewed it as a "license of fancy and hypothesis" in a realm of philosophical thinking he thought should be devoid of religious belief (1779, 94).

Around the time the minister John Leland (1691–1766) published his four-volume *Principal Deistical Writers that Have Appeared in England in the Last and Present Century* (1754–1756), an antagonistic work that nevertheless largely determined the canon of Deists, the controversy had cooled—but not before Deism "cross-examined religion naturalistically, socially and psychologically" (Porter, p. 122). "If Mankind had never Sinn'd, Reason would always have been obeyed, there would have been no Struggle for Dominion, and Brutal Power would not have prevail'd," wrote the protofeminist Mary Astell (1666–1731), longing for the world's return to a more reasonable state (Astell, p. 97). Edmund Burke may have rhetorically asked, Who reads Toland, Tindal, Collins, and so on? But William Wollaston's *Religion of Nature Delineated* (1724) sold 10,000 copies while radicalizing the already Deistic religious outlook of the printer who set the type for its third edition, Benjamin Franklin. Equally important, Deism became, via Newton, Locke, and their followers, the de facto religion of science, which encouraged the rationalization of religion among scientific practitioners in the British Isles, North America, and Europe's learned academies.

Deism in Europe

British Deists widely and intensively read European authors such as Spinoza, Balthasar Bekker, Descartes, Gassendi, Pierre Bayle, Faustus Socinius, and Bruno. European Deists of the next generation in turn bought clandestine French translations of British Deistic works that circulated among European texts in the underground book trade. Many of those trade networks originated in the liberal and tolerant Dutch Republic, a refuge for freethinkers that, along with Britain, forged the early Enlightenment. Journals like *De Haegse Mercurius* (1697–1698) defended Toland's Deism in the late seventeenth century; French-language presses, safe from the French censors, spread Newtonian science and theology to readers all over Europe; and later in the century Masonic lodges and other voluntary organizations disseminated Deistic thinking throughout civil society. The epitome of Dutch (radical) Deism was the *Traité des trois imposteurs* (1719; The Treatise of the Three Impostors), authored, in the international language of the time, most likely by the lawyer Jan Vroese. On the basis of textual criticism, inquiry into first causes inspired by scientific thinking, and attention to cultural variety across the globe, the *Traité* made the case that Moses, Jesus, and Muhammad were ordinary men who exploited common ignorance in order to legitimate their prophecies: "Christianity like all other Religions is no more than a crudely woven imposture, whose success & progress would astonish even its inventors if they came back to the world" (quoted in Jacob, 2001, p. 109).

Less iconoclastically, Voltaire (François-Marie Arouet, 1694–1778), the agent and nonpareil of the Anglomania that swept Europe in the 1730s and 1740s, virtually propagandized moderate British Deism as he strove to find the laws governing nature as well as God, the unity behind cultural variety, the right balance between enthusiasm and unbelief, and the compelling evidence that a God existed who could terrify the high and mighty. Deism via Voltaire in turn spread as far as Poland by way of the poetry of the satirist Bishop Ignacy Krasicki and the libertine Stanislaw Trembecki. Denis Diderot (1713–1784) and Jean Le Rond d'Alembert (1717–1783) assimilated British Deism in their *Encyclopédie* (1751–1772) and made an impression—about more than just Deism—on Russia's Catherine II. Even Rousseau's idiosyncratic and deeply influential deification of nature is unthinkable without Lockean Deism, notwithstanding Rousseau's cynicism about what society does to nature in the long term.

More radical French Deism also had influences more diverse than Newton and Locke. Henri de Boulainvilliers (1658–1722) came slowly to a Deistic position mainly by way of Baruch Spinoza (1632–1677). The Marquis d'Argens (1703–1771) drew from Spinoza, as did the Huguenot champion of religious toleration, Pierre Bayle (1647–1706). The shadowy, anti-Voltairean Themisuel de Saint-Hyacinthe (1684–1746) read Spinoza but lived in religious exile in the Dutch Republic amid Anglophiles such as Albert-Henri de Sallengre, a Dutch citizen of Huguenot origins with English connections through whom Saint-Hyacinthe would have come to know both British Deism and science. It is inaccurate to label the idiosyncratic Spinoza a "Deist" according to contemporary conceptions of the word. The same holds true for the atheist-atomists

Epicurus and his Roman mouthpiece Lucretius. But Spinozist and Epicurean writings nevertheless simmered along with British Deism in a stew of heterodox ideas that European freethinkers consumed with various appetites that were themselves determined by a complex mix of personality, cultural dispositions, and social and political conditions.

Deistic ideas also pervaded the German Enlightenment. The Prussian "philosopher-king" Frederick II may have ultimately been a disappointment to Voltaire, but he nonetheless facilitated the spread of heterodox religious thinking by making the Berlin Academy of Sciences an entrepôt for French, British, and Dutch thought as well as the homegrown Deistic ideas of Gottfried Wilhelm Leibniz (1646–1716) and Christian Wolff (1679–1754). What Kant would later call onto-, cosmo-, and physicotheology were all indebted to the writings of Deists, even if later "neologians"—rational theologians who upheld the possibility of truth in revelation—deliberately distanced themselves from radical Deism. But that should not obscure the fact that later eighteenth-century theologians such as Johann Salomo Semler (1725–1791) were as unrelenting in their textual criticism of the Bible as Woolston and others had been decades earlier.

In the more radical tradition, Hermann Samuel Reimarus's posthumously published *Apologie oder Schutzschrift für die vernünftigen Verehrer Gottes* (1774–1777; Apology or Defense of the Rational Worshipers of God) dispelled revelation as unreliable, miracles and mystery as fictional, and the New Testament as fraudulent. But like the British Deists by whom he was influenced, he also made as strong a case against atheism. Gotthold Lessing (1729–1781), who among other things published Reimarus's *Apologie*, took the small step from Deism to religious toleration in his dramatic poem *Nathan der Weise* (1779; Nathan the Wise), which gave equal treatment to Judaism, Christianity, and Islam. But the case was made more forcefully by the inspiration for Lessing's Nathan, the German-Jewish freethinker Moses Mendelssohn (1729–1786), who, instead of arguing for the dissolution of the distinctions among the Mosaic religions, made the case that all were equal but still meaningful and should be accommodated by an enlightened state. Meanwhile, the primacy of reason over revelation was underscored by Immanuel Kant (1724–1804). Kant started out maintaining the neologian position on revelation, but in later life he argued that the Bible should be judged rather than judge, that churches had value only insofar as their ends accorded with a rationally derived course for human progress, and that claims to have experienced divine revelation could never be admitted by reasonable people.

The Legacy of Deism

What also makes Deism the unofficial religious philosophy of the Enlightenment is its expiration at the close of the eighteenth century as the French Revolution turned from the apparent culmination of Deism to reaction against heterodoxy. In fact the word and concept were already showing signs of waning among British and European elites by the time the century had reached its fourth quarter. Hume wrote unsparingly in his posthumous *Dialogues Concerning Natural Religion* (1779) that belief cannot in any way be rationally defended. Even that stark judgment of the French materialists that matter in motion in a godless universe was a sufficient foundational principle for both science and morality became less repulsive to many philosophers and scientists.

We know less about Deism as a popularly held belief. Bookstore inventories and detailed wills reveal that Deistic ideas could penetrate all levels of European and North American society. There were no Deists churches—although Deism was briefly institutionalized in revolutionary France—and therefore we have no attendance sheets on which we can count rank-and-file adherents; but many of the ideas associated with Deism also made their way into popular forms of religious thought and practice. Eighteenth-century British dissenters academies—schools for non-Anglicans—encouraged the spread of heterodox ideas alongside critical thinking and prominently featured Newton and Locke in their curricula. John Jebb's church in late-eighteenth-century London was Deist in all but name. Some religious denominations, such as Presbyterianism, became Unitarian under the pressures of, among other things, the biblical criticism pioneered by Deists. But Deism in Britain, North America, and Germany was also targeted as early as the mid-1700s on the popular level alongside other forms of intellectualized religion by much more numerous Methodists, traditionalist Anglicans, and Pietists, who stressed God's active role in our earthly lives.

In America a prominent handful of elites in the later 1700s identified themselves as Deists. Benjamin Franklin proudly and publicly recollected reading the Boyle lectures as a youth, in which "the arguments of the Deists which were quoted to be refuted, appeared to me much stronger than the refutation" (p. 63). Thomas Jefferson put Deism into practice when he took a cue from Tindal and wrote the separation of church and state into the Virginia Statute for Religious Liberty (1786), which sounded an echo the next year in the First Amendment to the United States Constitution. If the final lines of the Declaration of Independence invoke an un-Deistic "firm reliance on the protection of divine Providence," "the laws of nature and of nature's God" in that document's more memorable opening paragraph get to the core—in a telling sequence—of a definition of Deism. But the late embrace of these ideas in America did not forestall their antagonistic reception. The British-born American patriot Thomas Paine was the target of deep animosity when in *The Age of Reason* (1794–1795) he trivialized the personal experience of divine revelation. As early nineteenth-century America witnessed a return to traditional Christianity, even onetime Deists like George Tucker of Virginia, in contrast to Jefferson, came to view religion as a form of social control that the state should subsidize.

Since Deism has no defining textual or customary point of reference, its legacy is as difficult to follow with precision as its meaning. Its most direct descendent in the nineteenth and early twentieth centuries may be the scholarly study of religion, but here the parentage is mixed. F. Max Mueller (1823–1900) and E. B. Tylor (1832–1917), for example, both owe their scientization of religious studies to the rationalism of the atheistic Hume and Spinoza as much as to Newton and Locke. Its legacy is more widely dispersed in modern variants of all three Mosaic religions—Reformed Judaism, Unitarianism, and the Baha'i faith, for example—as well as in hybrid forms of

intellectualized religiosity that borrow more consciously from Buddha and Confucius than from Tindal and Toland. One recent study has even connected Deism to the rise of Philippine nationalism by way of José Protasio Rizal's Enlightenment education at the University of Madrid in the 1880s and later attacks on the Catholic Church.

Deism's greatest legacy may be the principle of religious toleration written into the constitutions of the world's democracies. A survey of the early-twenty-first-century political landscape might suggest a disjunction between constitutional theory and practice. But that makes these ideas and their legacy more interesting than they have been since before the beginning of the nineteenth century, as religious conflict and toleration have become as culturally significant as they were during the destructive confessional struggles that defined early modern Europe.

See also **Agnosticism; Atheism; Enlightenment; Religion.**

BIBLIOGRAPHY

PRIMARY SOURCES

Astell, Mary. *Reflections upon Marriage: . . . To Which Is Added a Preface in Answer to Some Objections.* London: Wilkin, 1706. Originally published in 1700, with an appendix added to this later edition.

Bentley, Richard. *Remarks upon a Late Discourse of Free Thinking.* Cambridge, U.K.: Printed for C. Crownfield, 1725.

Blount, Charles. *The Oracles of Reason . . . In Several Letters to Mr. Hobbs and Other Persons of Eminent Quality and Learning.* London, 1693.

Chubb, Thomas. *A Discourse concerning Reason with Regard to Religion and Divine Reason.* London, 1731.

Clarke, Samuel. *A Demonstration of the Being and Attributes of God.* London: James Knapton, 1705.

Collins, Anthony. *A Discourse of Free Thinking.* London, 1713.

———. *A Discourse of the Grounds and Reasons of the Christian Religion.* London, 1724.

Diderot, Denis, and d'Alembert, Jean Le Rond. *The Encyclopedia: Selections.* Edited and translated by Stephen J. Gendzier. New York: Harper and Row, 1967.

Franklin, Benjamin. *The Autobiography and Other Writings.* Edited and with an introduction by Kenneth Silverman. Harmondsworth, U.K., and New York: Penguin Books, 1986.

Hume, David. *Dialogues concerning Natural Religion.* London, 1779.

Leland, John. *A View of the Principal Deistical Writers that Have Appeared in England in the Last and Present Century.* London: B. Dod, 1754–1756.

Lessing, Gotthold Ephraim. *Nathan the Wise.* Translated by Edward Kemp. London: Nick Hern, 2003.

Locke, John. *The Reasonableness of Christianity, as Delivered in the Scriptures.* London, 1695.

Paine, Thomas. *The Complete Writings of Thomas Paine.* Collected and edited by Philip S. Foner, 2 vols. New York: Citadel Press, 1945.

Reimarus, Hermann Samuel. *Reimarus, Fragments.* Edited by Charles H. Talbert, translated by Ralph S. Fraser. Chico, Calif.: Scholars Press, 1985.

Samuel, Moses. *Moses Mendelssohn: The First English Biography and Translations.* Introduction by James Schmidt. Bristol, U.K.: Thoemmes Press, 2002.

Spinoza, Benedictus de. *The Collected Works of Spinoza.* Edited and translated by Edwin M. Curley. Princeton, N.J.: Princeton University Press, 1985.

Tindal, Matthew. *Christianity as Old as the Creation; or The Gospel a Republication of the Religion of Nature.* London, 1732.

Toland, John. *Christianity Not Mysterious; or, A Treatise Showing, That There Is Nothing in the Gospel Contrary to Reason, Nor Above It, and That No Christian Doctrine Can Be Properly Call'd a Mystery.* London, 1696.

———. *Letters to Serena.* London: Bernard Lintot, 1704.

———. *Reasons for Naturalising the Jews in Great Britain and Ireland.* London, 1714.

Voltaire, F. M. *Letters concerning the English Nation.* Translated by John Lockman. Dublin: George Faulkner, 1733.

Wollaston, William. *The Religion of Nature Delineated.* London, 1724.

Woolston, Thomas. *Six Discourses on the Miracles of our Savior and Defences of His Discourses.* New York: Garland, 1979.

SECONDARY SOURCES

Bedford, R. D. *The Defence of Truth: Herbert of Cherbury and the Seventeenth Century.* Manchester, U.K.: Manchester University Press, 1979. Comprehensive work on the "first English Deist."

Betts, C. J. *Early Deism in France: From the So-called "Déistes" of Lyon (1564) to Voltaire's "Lettres philosophiques" (1734).* Boston: Martinus Nijhoff, 1984. The most detailed English study of French Deism; deals well with the complexities of the word's definition.

Bonoan, Raul. "The Enlightenment, Deism, and Rizal." *Philippine Studies* 40 (1992): 53–67.

Byrne, Peter. *Natural Religion and the Nature of Religion: The Legacy of Deism.* London and New York: Routledge, 1989. Maintains that Deistic ideas about natural religion laid the groundwork for modern religious studies.

Champion, J. A. I. *The Pillars of Priestcraft Shaken: The Church of England and Its Enemies, 1660–1730.* Cambridge, U.K.: Cambridge University Press, 1992. Deals mainly with anticlericalism but shows, among other things, that even the most radical Deists had a religious impulse, which was filtered through notions of civil society.

Clark, William. "The Death of Metaphysics in Enlightened Prussia." In *The Sciences in Enlightened Europe.* Edited by William Clark, Jan Golinski, and Simon Schaffer. Chicago: University of Chicago Press, 1999.

Dzwigala, Wanda. "Voltaire and the Polish Enlightenment: Religious Responses." *Slavonic and East European Review* 81 (2003): 70–87.

Hazard, Paul. *The European Mind, 1680–1715.* Translated by J. Lewis May. London: Hollis and Carter, 1953. A still-essential study of European intellectual history, with a chapter dedicated to Deism.

Israel, Jonathan. *Radical Enlightenment: Philosophy and the Making of Modernity, 1650–1750.* Oxford: Oxford University Press, 2001. Should be called "Spinoza's Enlightenment." But in following Spinoza's influence of major and minor European freethinkers, this work is important.

Jacob, Margaret C. *The Enlightenment: A Brief History with Documents.* Boston: Bedford Books, 2001. Excellent collection of documents on Enlightenment religion, prefaced by a clear and concise introduction.

———. *The Newtonians and the English Revolution, 1689–1720.* New York: Gordon and Breach, 1990. Puts forward an important and compelling argument about Newton's as well as Locke's concerns with social and political instability and therefore deals at length with rational religion.

———. *The Radical Enlightenment: Pantheists, Freemasons, and Republicans.* London and Boston: Allen and Unwin, 1981. The original and still essential work that situates Deism among the ideas of the "radical Enlightenment"; excellent coverage of Toland and Freemasonry.

Lund, Roger D., ed. *The Margins of Orthodoxy: Heterodox Writing and Cultural Response, 1660–1750.* Cambridge, U.K.: Cambridge University Press, 1995. Important collection of essays related to Deism.

Marshall, John. *John Locke: Resistance, Religion and Responsibility.* Cambridge, U.K.: Cambridge University Press, 1994. The most engaging and rigorously contextualized recent work on Locke's politics and religion.

May, Henry Farnham. *The Enlightenment in America.* New York: Oxford University Press, 1976. Still the standard work on this subject and good for further exploration of Deism in America.

Page, Anthony. *John Jeeb and the Enlightenment Origins of British Radicalism.* Westport, Conn.: Praeger, 2003. Interesting study of the Cambridge cleric and London reformer.

Popkin, Richard H. *The History of Scepticism from Erasmus to Spinoza.* Berkeley: University of California Press, 1979. Continues to be the standard work on Skepticism; frames well the causes of the skeptical crisis and contains a useful section on Herbert.

Porter, Roy. *The Creation of the Modern World: The Untold Story of the British Enlightenment.* New York and London: W. W. Norton, 2000. Will be the unrivaled synthetic study of the British Enlightenment for years to come; brilliantly written with an excellent chapter on rational religion.

Roche, Daniel. *France in the Enlightenment.* Translated by Arthur Goldhammer. Cambridge, Mass.: Harvard University Press, 1998. Provides essential background for understanding Deism in France.

Sullivan, Robert. *John Toland and the Deist Controversy: A Study in Adaptations.* Cambridge, Mass.: Harvard University Press, 1982. Good on the slipperiness of the definition of "Deism."

Sullivan, Roger J. *Immanuel Kant's Moral Theory.* Cambridge, U.K.: Cambridge University Press, 1989. A lucid interpretive guide through Kant's theories of religion.

Matthew Kadane

DEMOCRACY. Democracy, a direct translation of the Greek *dēmokratia,* means rule (*kratos*) by the people (*dēmos*). Both as a political idea, and as a political institution, democracy originated in the thought and practice of the ancient Greeks. They understood democracy literally: the people, deliberating and acting together in an assembly, was both sovereign and legislator. The people was not only the source of legitimate authority, but also the wielder of political power. In modern times the role of the people is limited to the legitimation of political authority, and power is wielded by elected representative assemblies.

Greek Origins

In the history of Western political thought the Greeks were the first to think and reflect about their political and social organization. The polis, with its multiple forms and varied institutions, was the center of Greek life and culture. This plurality of political associations engendered intense philosophical speculation and lively intellectual debate regarding the relative merits of different types of government. In the process the Greeks elaborated a language and a vocabulary adequate to the analysis of the political world they had constructed.

Herodotus (484–420 B.C.E.), in his constitutional debate, weighed the value of the three governmental forms of a polis: monarchy, oligarchy, and democracy. Democracy promotes equality before the law, yet it brings to power the many who are ignorant, incompetent, unstable, and violent. Oligarchy is equally unstable and violent, and both forms eventually lead to tyranny. Only a law-abiding monarchy can inhibit the few and the many from succumbing to tyranny.

The "Old Oligarch," a short pamphlet from the fifth century B.C.E., presents a similar picture of the many and their democracy: feckless, unreliable, and irrational. Only the best and cleverest, that is, the few, are capable of rule. At the same time the argument adds a novel element to the analysis of democracy: class conflict and factional strife. The problem is whether the demos is capable of understanding and recognizing their own particular good, a question that permeates classical political thought.

In his *History of the Peloponnesian War,* Thucydides (d. c. 401 B.C.E.) describes the moderate democracy under Pericles (c. 495–429 B.C.E.), and praises his prudence and wisdom in leading the people. The distinction he makes between Pericles and Cleon (d. 422 B.C.E.) underlines his dislike of the many and his preference for a democracy guided by the wise and the best. He attributes the fall of Athens to the rise of demagogic leaders who flattered the masses and catered to their appetites and desires. Athens was defeated by Sparta because the war generated among Athenians factionalism, greed, violence, and lust for power and for acquisition. He introduces a theme later amplified by Plato and Aristotle: external expansion and imperialism are directly related to the rise of democracy in Athens. Democracy whets the many's appetite for power, which only expansion can satisfy and secure. For Thucydides the desire for power and the appetite for expansion are inherent to the nature of the people such that their rule is always accompanied by violent disturbances, expropriation, and instability. The rise of the many to power liberates the passions and the appetites to such an extent that the democracy is inexorably led to imperial conquest, overextension, and finally violent collapse.

Plato (c. 428–348 or 347 B.C.E.), in such works as *Gorgias, The Statesman,* and *The Republic,* translated Thucydides' historical narrative of the Athenian decline and fall into a thoroughgoing critique of contemporary practices and institutions within the polis. He found all politics wanting, because those who possess knowledge are powerless, and those who have power are ignorant and thus do not know how to rule. The problem was to discover ways in which power and knowledge, politics and philosophy may be so wedded as to ensure a just and stable sociopolitical order. Statesmanship requires within the individual the rule of reason over appetite, and within the polis the rule of those who know over those who do not know.

As such, it means the exercise of self-discipline and self-restraint by both the rulers and the ruled.

To Plato, all states are divided into the few who are rich and the many who are poor, and therefore class struggle and class strife are endemic to all states. Both democrats and oligarchs pursue their particular self-interest, and thus both are motivated not by rational thought but by appetite, desire, and lust for power. Each faction when in power pursues its interest to the exclusion of the other's, such that the polis is subjected to unstable and violent cycles of revolution and counterrevolution. The conflict between the two factions leads to the destruction of both and to the rise of tyranny. Thus no just society is possible unless the passions and appetites are subordinated to rational control, and unless the conflicts they engender are resolved and harmonized by wise and just leadership.

Aristotle (384–322 B.C.E.), following Plato, presents in his *Politics* a six-fold classification of constitutions or governments: the rule of one is monarchy or tyranny, the rule of the few is oligarchy or aristocracy, and the rule of many is either law-abiding or lawless democracy. Three are just and legitimate, three are unjust and illegitimate. The first of each set is lawful and rule is for the good of all, the second is lawless and rule is in the rulers' particular interest. Each in its pure form is inherently unstable because its foundation is narrow and exclusive. Democracy rests on mere number and thus excludes ability and property. Similarly, because oligarchy is based on property and birth, it excludes the propertyless many. Thus each type tends toward faction, strife, and instability. The problem is to construct a type that would combine stability, legitimacy, and competent rule. This type is the polity, a constitutional government that includes the best elements of democracy, oligarchy, and monarchy. It combines number, ability, and property, and so guarantees that the class base of polity avoids the opposing poles of overly rich and overly poor. The welding of the best elements of democracy and oligarchy enables the polity to escape the cycle of violence and instability endemic to many Greek cities.

The polis, whether oligarchic or democratic, was class based, and most writers, especially Aristotle, recognized the close relationship between property, power, and stability. They also recognized, and never questioned, the centrality of slavery to the polis. Even in democratic Athens the slavery and subjection that prevailed within the private sphere of the household made possible the liberty and equality of the male citizens as they came together in public to deliberate in the assembly.

After the Polis

Greek political theory is a reaction to the decline of the polis, which was superseded first by the territorial Hellenistic monarchies and later by the Roman republic. Polybius (c. 200–c. 118 B.C.E.), who wrote his history to show how Rome came to dominate the Mediterranean, ascribes its success to its republican institutions. He superimposes Greek categories onto Roman political experience, and using the six-fold classification of governments, sees Rome as having a mixed constitution.

The consuls represent the monarchical element, the senate the aristocratic, and the popular assemblies the democratic. Wealth, ability, birth, and number were each given a role in the constitution. When the people became too violent and tumultuous, or the senate too arrogant and selfish, the republic nevertheless survived. The mixed constitution established a self-regulating system in which each element checked and balanced the other.

Cicero (106–43 B.C.E.) repeated the now-standard Greek classification of governments (monarchy, aristocracy, democracy) as well as the traditional critiques of each. Although he preferred monarchy, he understood that practical prudence required a mixed form that combined the best of all three. The state is a res publica, or "public affair," and is therefore also a *res populi*, or "people's affair." It exists to provide justice, security, and peace. Although legitimacy and power emanate from the people, competent administration and stable authority require the wisdom and ability of the senate.

The fall of the republic and the rise of monarchy signaled the death of republican and democratic politics. The growth of quietistic philosophies such as Stoicism, the advent of Christianity, and the barbarian invasions together combined to destroy the classical world and to create a feudal and medieval civilization in which democracy and republic had no meaning.

Democratic and republican thought and practice regained their vitality and importance with the rise of the Italian communes and the concomitant rebirth of classical thought. Such an interest, when added to the historical experience of the Italian—especially Florentine and Venetian—city-states culminated in Niccolò Machiavelli's (1469–1527) rediscovery of the people (and of the "opinion of the many") as the foundation and ground for a new type of politics, both republican and democratic.

The passing of medieval society was a long process of religious, social, political, and economic transformation. It culminated in profound social, cultural, and political change: the disintegration of traditional ties, the Protestant Reformation and the resulting fragmentation of European Christianity, the spread of commerce and trade, the proliferation and dissemination of knowledge and wealth, literacy and printing.

The English Civil War (1642–1649), the Dutch rebellion (1621–1648) against Spain and the Holy Roman Empire, and the Glorious Revolution (1688–1689) heralded the rise and growing importance of these new developments. The execution and deposition of kings exploded traditional beliefs in the passive acceptance of governmental authority, and revealed its basis in human will and action. Major political theorists such as Thomas Hobbes (1588–1679); Hugo Grotius (Huigh de Groot; 1583–1645); Samuel von Pufendorf (1632–1694); Charles-Louis de Secondat, baron de Monstesquieu (1689–1755); and John Locke (1632–1704) reflected these far-reaching changes by reevaluating and retranslating traditional ideas of natural law, human nature, and government. Dutch republicans such as Benedict de Spinoza (1632–1677) and the de la Court brothers, Jan (Johan; 1622–1670) and Pieter (c. 1618–1685), distilled ancient Roman writers, Florentine

and Venetian republicans, and the work of Thomas Hobbes, and envisioned a democratic politics whereby the state is the expression of the people's will. Hobbes, with his absolute individualism and radical skepticism, expressed the breakdown of traditional forms of community and legitimate government and their reconstitution by human reason and will. Locke tried to wed natural law with emerging individualism and used them to domesticate and limit the power of the newly centralized state. His theory of government as a trust located authority with the representative of the people, who always retained their right to withhold consent to the government. Montesquieu, reacting to the growing absolutism of the French monarchy, translated the classical theory of mixed government into his concept of separation of powers. His theory of despotism and the balanced constitution was a major source for liberal constitutionalism and for the theory of limited government. Natural right, political obligation, social contract, and natural law were ideas used to explain and to justify radical and revolutionary change. Yet, at the time, their range and application was circumscribed, and the notion of the people to which they referred was interpreted narrowly.

Age of Enlightenment and Revolution

The Enlightenment, by underlining the human capacity for rational and critical thought, for scientific and intellectual inquiry, and generally for the future growth and "perfectibility" of humanity, slowly subverted the cultural, religious, and traditional foundations of state and society. Thinkers such as Voltaire (1694–1778) and Denis Diderot (1713–1784) in France, and David Hume (1711–1776) and Jeremy Bentham (1748–1832) in Britain, inquired into the natural and historical sources of political and social power. They produced a body of work that linked political and civil liberty and freedom of thought and speech with cultural, moral-intellectual, and scientific progress. Jean-Jacques Rousseau's (1712–1778) critique of the Enlightenment paradoxically affirmed the movement's belief in the centrality of human will and liberty. For Rousseau, liberty and equality define the human, such that the people assembling together as sovereign generate the general will that looks to the public, as opposed to the private, good. The general will as the embodiment of popular sovereignty was a radical critique of the inequality and the competition within civil society.

The spirit of opposition to established forms of authority (whether secular or religious), the distrust of any government not derived from rational consent, culminated in the American Revolution and its penchant for constitution building. American revolutionaries proclaimed the sovereignty of the people while simultaneously constructing a political structure that would limit and channel the power of popular majorities. They preached a new secular order while buttressing it with arguments that reached back to the English Civil War and the Glorious Revolution. The political literature of the Revolution adumbrated and summarized the arguments for and against democracy since Plato. From Thomas Paine (1737–1809), who explicitly defended democracy, to John Adams (1735–1826), who feared direct popular rule, Americans during the two decades of revolution and constitutional experimentation attempted to find a balance between the few and the many, the rich and the poor. The compromise presented by the federalists asserted the legitimating and authorizing role of the people while establishing a self-regulating system of checks and balances at both the state and national levels. Legitimate power would issue from popular majorities, but institutional mechanisms such as separation of powers, federalism, bicameral legislatures, and indirect election would channel, control, and check the power of the people.

The American Revolution began the slow process that changed the meaning of democracy as it was understood from the Greeks to Rousseau (direct rule of the people meeting together in their assembly). As James Madison (1751–1836) noted, direct democracy, which is feasible (according to Rousseau and Claude-Adrien Helvétius) only in small states, is prone to violence and class strife; what is needed is a republic where representation refines and filters the opinion of the people. Representation both controls popular passions and makes popular government possible over a large territory and a numerous population.

The French Revolution, in terms more radical and clear than the American, proclaimed the rights of man and the citizen. It contrasted these with the privileges and aristocratic inequalities of the old order. In Jacobin ideology, the people were increasingly identified with the nation. Jacobin terror and the supremacy of Maximilien de Robespierre (1758–1794) reinforced the traditional historical unease and distaste with popular rule. Republican and democratic ideas—popular sovereignty, government as guarantor and custodian of natural rights, the idea of citizenship, and the right to liberty and equality under law—spread throughout Europe. Lively and sometimes bitter polemics emerged, some like Edmund Burke (1729–1797) attacking the Revolution, others like Tom Paine and Mary Wollstonecraft (1759–1797) defending it. The novelty was that for the first time democracy and popular government were defended by elements of the educated and wealthy classes.

Threat and Promise of Mass Democracy

Both the American and French Revolutions signaled the emergence of the popular masses as a force in history. Henceforth the people became a factor in the power equation. Whether for ill or good, whether democratic or antidemocratic, rulers must address the people to attain or to maintain power. This profound realignment of the relation between ruler and ruled produced three responses during the nineteenth century: liberal, conservative, and revolutionary.

The liberal response is embodied in the thought of John Stuart Mill (1806–1873) and Alexis de Tocqueville (1805–1859). Tocqueville believed that the European future could be foreseen in the American present. And Mill's thought was heavily influenced by Tocquevillian concerns with the safeguarding of ability, virtue, and liberty. Tocqueville analyzed the social and cultural conditions of American democracy and found in them the germs of a future tyranny. Democracy is founded on a belief in individual rights, equality, and self-government, yet the public opinion it spawns is more tyrannical than any monarch. The passion for equality generates a

uniform mass of self-centered individuals whose opinions will dominate those of the minority. This passion is antithetical to ability and strives to level all forms of excellence and skill. Mill elaborates on Tocqueville's antithesis between equality and liberty and tries to find a solution that incorporates both the people's desire for equality and the need for competence and ability. Though democracy means the rule of the many, government and administration presuppose the rule of the few over the many. Mill sees representative government based on an educated and responsible electorate as best able to link the egalitarian aspirations of the many with the competence and ability of the few.

Political participation (voting and office holding) in the West was at first circumscribed within a narrow social, ethnic-racial and economic base: property holders and white males. During the nineteenth century and the first half of the twentieth century, various political and social groups arose calling for the extension of full civil and legal rights to all. Elite competition for power combined with popular social movements gradually to expand the electorate. In the United States, the property qualification was eliminated with the rise of Andrew Jackson, in Britain with the various reform bills of the middle-to late-nineteenth century. The expansion of male suffrage in continental Europe was a complex and contradictory process. In France it was hostage to successive revolutions and changes in governmental systems, in imperial Germany it was achieved under the auspices of Bismarck as a means of bolstering the power of the ruling elites, and in Italy it facilitated elite manipulation of the parliamentary elections. Suffrage expansion in pre-World War II Italy and Germany ultimately led to the breakdown of liberal democratic institutions, while in Britain and the United States it promoted the integration of the lower classes into the pre-existing liberal structures.

In the United States, the Civil War (1861–1865) abolished slavery, and the fourteenth and fifteenth amendments to the Constitution gave the emancipated slaves full political rights. Yet through such devices as the poll tax, the white-only primary, literacy requirements, as well as the use of legal and extra-legal force, African Americans were effectively denied these rights until the advent of the Civil Rights movement and the passage of the 1965 Voting Rights Act.

The struggle over the vote was intimately linked with the struggle for the emancipation of women. Women's suffrage movements, whose prominent figures included Elizabeth Cady Stanton (1815–1902), Susan B. Anthony (1820–1906), and Emmeline Pankhurst (1858–1928), were particularly powerful in the United States and Britain. Women were granted the vote in 1920 and in 1928 respectively, though not until 1945 in Italy and France. Even today, in many countries women are excluded from public and political life. Ethnic-racial and gender equality and the integration of excluded groups into the prevailing system are considered crucial to the contemporary understanding of democracy. The right to vote is fundamental to democracy. Yet the struggle for universal suffrage underlines the importance of establishing a widely accepted culture of civil liberties and civil rights, without which the suffrage would become meaningless.

Industrialization and urbanization, as well as painful social and economic dislocations, intensified mass mobilization and mass participation in politics, which in turn created new demands partly addressed by the liberalization of social welfare measures and by the expansion of the franchise. The expansion of the electorate in turn made the system more democratic and thus more responsive to mass politics. Revolutionaries such as Karl Marx (1818–1883) and his followers argued that the equality and liberty guaranteed by liberals and democrats were merely political and formal. They did not address the material basis of rule, which is social and economic. The rights of the citizen are spurious given the underlying inequality of bourgeois capitalism, where the few wealthy dominate the many poor. What Marxism and socialism desired was a democracy both social and economic, where the unequal relations of power established by private property are eliminated. Such a concern underlay most critiques of liberal democracy, whether social democratic, syndicalist, or communist. They differed, however, in both their methods and their goals. The socialists accepted the rules of the game and worked within the system, while the latter two worked for a revolutionary overthrow. Lenin (Vladimir Ilich Ulyanov; 1870–1924) and the Bolsheviks represented a shift in the location of revolution, from the center of the bourgeois world to its periphery.

The conservative reaction to democratic politics ranged from the reactionary ideas of Joseph-Marie de Maistre (1753–1821) and Louis de Bonald (1754–1840) to the elitism of Vilfredo Pareto (1848–1923), Gaetano Mosca (1858–1941), and Roberto Michels (1876–1936). While the former wanted to return to prerevolutionary and aristocratic Europe, the latter accepted modernity and the political consequences of the American and French Revolutions. Pareto and Mosca argued that in all societies the rulers are always the few, that wealth and ability will always prevail over numbers. Michels formulated an iron law of oligarchy, which asserted that in modern society where bureaucracies and organizations are constantly proliferating only minorities can rule. Democracy—with its representative systems, electoral mechanisms, referenda, initiatives, and recall—is an illusion, a mere political formula devised to veil oligarchic power. What these writers attempted to show was the empirical and sociological impossibility of democracy. Whatever the claims of democratic ideals, government and administration must inevitably rely on organized minorities to function well and effectively.

Recent Concepts

In the first half of the twentieth century democratic theory was devoted to addressing the claims of elitists such as Mosca and Michels. First Joseph Schumpeter (1883–1950) and later Robert Dahl (b. 1915) tried to devise a theory that would account for the empirical reality of democracy (the necessity for elites) and simultaneously retain its ideals. Schumpeter saw democracy as an institutional arrangement of elite competition for the electorate's favor guaranteed by legal and procedural mechanisms. Twenty years later Dahl saw democracy as a polyarchy of social groups whose competition was also guaranteed by procedural arrangements, while Samuel Lipset and Barrington Moore Jr. distinguished between the empirical and

normative criteria of democracy. They too discerned a contradiction between the claims of majority rule and the empirical reality of mass electoral politics. The attack on the classical democratic theory produced a fundamental reinterpretation of democracy itself. Democracy no longer means rule by the people, or rule by the many. The majority legitimate power and consent to it, but organized elites rule. Whether the many rule is not as important as whether the system provides free and open elections guaranteed by civil liberties and civil rights.

Democracy as a political form and as an ideal arose from the conflict in society between the few and the many, between the wealthy and the poor. The cycle of violence and instability produced by this conflict led to attempts to establish political structures that would address the egalitarian and just demands of the many while simultaneously maintaining the rule of law. It is from the struggle to resolve the opposing interests and values of these two antagonists that the social and political ideals associated with modern democracy emerged and developed.

Today democratic theory centers on critiques of liberal democracy and on devising alternatives to it. Critics such as Hannah Arendt (1906–1975), Jürgen Habermas (b. 1929), and John Rawls (1921–2002) identified an elitist, inegalitarian, and antiparticipatory core in liberal theories of democracy. They questioned the validity and desirability of liberal democracy's major principles: interest aggregation, economic utility, rational choice and game theory, methodological individualism. Most important, they objected to the reduction of political activity to economic categories and lamented the use of the market as the model for democratic politics. While retaining the procedural and constitutional guarantees so important to liberal theory, its critics aspire to a democracy where the people may come together as citizens and participate in public deliberations and discussions.

The criticism of liberal and elite democratic theory has produced two major schools of thought: civic republicanism and deliberative democracy. Both share a classical Aristotelian belief in the possibility of achieving a common good by means of an egalitarian politics of participation. They believe that political activity is crucial to developing a well-rounded and educated citizen. Civic values, civic engagement, and open discussion help create a public space in which the business common to all citizens may be conducted. Civic republicanism and deliberative democracy, by emphasizing such ideas as the common good, virtue, common action, and political education, delve into the ways that a public-political space may emerge and grow. They also recall the ideals of political virtue and political participation first enunciated by classical thinkers, and later reclaimed by Machiavelli and Rousseau.

See also **Constitutionalism; Equality; Liberty; Public Sphere; Republicanism.**

BIBLIOGRAPHY

Ball, Terrence, and Richard Bellamy, eds. *The Cambridge History of Twentieth-Century Political Thought.* New York: Cambridge University Press, 2003.

Bohman, James, and William Rehg, eds. *Deliberative Democracy: Essays on Reason and Politics.* Cambridge, Mass.: MIT Press, 1997.

Burns, James Henderson, ed. *The Cambridge History of Political Thought, 1450–1700.* Cambridge, U.K.: Cambridge University Press, 1991.

Cnuddle, Charles F. and Deane E. Neubauer, eds. *Empirical Democratic Theory.* Chicago: Markham, 1969.

Dahl, Robert A. *Democracy and Its Critics.* New Haven, Conn.: Yale University Press, 1989.

Dunn, John, ed. *Democracy: The Unfinished Journey, 508 B.C. to A.D. 1993.* Oxford: Oxford University Press, 1992.

Finley, Moses I. *Democracy Ancient and Modern.* New Brunswick, N.J.: Rutgers University Press, 1973.

Fontana, Biancamaria, ed. *The Invention of the Modern Republic.* Cambridge, U.K.: Cambridge University Press, 1994.

Hazard, Paul. *European Thought in the Eighteenth Century.* Translated by J. Lewis May. New Haven, Conn.: Yale University Press, 1954. Translation of *Pensée européenne au XVIIIème siècle.*

Held, David. *Models of Democracy.* 2nd ed. Stanford, Calif.: Stanford University Press, 1996.

Lijphardt, Arend. *Democracies.* New Haven, Conn.: Yale University Press, 1984.

Palmer, Robert R. *The Age of the Democratic Revolution.* 2 vols. Princeton, N.J.: Princeton University Press, 1959–1964.

Pateman, Carole. *Participation and Democratic Theory.* Cambridge, U.K.: Cambridge University Press, 1970.

Rahe, Paul A. *Republics Ancient and Modern.* 3 vols. Chapel Hill: University of North Carolina Press, 1994.

Rowe, Christopher, and Malcolm Schofield, eds. *The Cambridge History of Greek and Roman Political Thought.* Cambridge, U.K.: Cambridge University Press, 2000.

Sartori, Giovanni. *The Theory of Democracy Revisited.* Chatham, N.J.: Chatham House, 1987.

Skinner, Quentin. *Foundations of Modern Political Thought.* 2 vols. Cambridge, U.K.: Cambridge University Press, 1978.

Benedetto Fontana

DEMOCRACY, AFRICA. In the mid-1980s, democratic theory and politics in Africa entered a new phase as struggles for democratization spread across the continent and scholars began to vigorously debate the processes, prospects, and problems of Africa's democratic projects. This process was captured in an important collection edited by Peter Anyang Nyong'o, *Popular Struggles for Democracy in Africa* (1987), and in debates conducted in the influential newsletter of the Council for the Development of Social Science Research in Africa, *Codesria Bulletin* (1989). In 1990, all but five of Africa's fifty-four countries were dictatorships, either civilian or military. By 2000, the majority of these countries had introduced political reforms and had become either democratic or were in the process of becoming so. In the meantime, the literature on African democracy exploded. Initially, analyses centered on the forces behind the democratic transitions and their modalities; later they focused on the challenges of democratic consolidation. There were also vigorous debates on the meaning and content of democracy in which instrumental, institutional, cultural, and historical approaches vied for definitional, analytical, and ideological preeminence.

Before the mid-1980s, African political systems were dominated by authoritarian regimes and African political thought was preoccupied with developmentalism: how to overcome the challenges of development through socialist- or capitalist-oriented strategies. In the 1960s, many leading political scientists even applauded the one-party state as a vehicle for nation-building and economic development; it supposedly minimized societal conflicts and conformed to African cultural traditions and a preference for consensus politics. Several prominent African political leaders and thinkers—Julius Nyerere of Tanzania (1922–1999), Leopold Senghor of Senegal (1906–2001), Sekou Touré of Guinea (1922–1984), and Kwame Nkrumah of Ghana (1909–1972)—argued passionately that African socialism not only represented a creative and viable fusion between the "communal" values and practices of precolonial African societies and Western socialist ideas, but that it embodied and ensured democracy. In the self-proclaimed Marxist–Leninist regimes, such as those of Ethiopia, Mozambique, and Angola, "democratic centralism" of the ruling party was upheld as the basis of "communist democracy" and contrasted to Western "bourgeois democracy" (Zeleza, 1997, part VI; Idahosa).

Modalities of Africa's Democratic Transition

The African transitions to democracy from the late 1980s were quite varied and characterized by progress, blockages, and reversals. In many countries, the transitions occurred quite rapidly following the onset of internal protests and external pressures on the incumbent autocratic regimes. At first, the protests and pressures were not taken seriously by many of these regimes, which responded with both repression and reform, depending on the relative strengths of the prodemocracy forces and the regimes themselves. The latter always sought to manipulate differences within the opposition; indeed, by the mid-1990s many African leaders had learned to play the new democratic game of multiparty electoral politics to their advantage.

The actual mechanisms and modalities of transition from dictatorship to democracy took three broad paths. First, there were countries in which opposition parties were legalized and multiparty elections authorized through amendments to the existing constitutions by the incumbent regime. This pattern was followed mainly in one-party states in which the opposition forces were too weak or fragmented to force national regime capitulation and the regimes still enjoyed considerable repressive resources and hegemonic capacities, for example, Zambia, Malawi, Kenya, and Tanzania. Zambia was the first country in southern Africa to undergo democratization when President Kenneth Kaunda's (b. 1924) United National Independence Party, which had ruled the country since independence in 1964, lost the elections in 1991. Three years later, President Banda's (1898–1997) Malawi Congress Party lost the elections in Malawi. In Tanzania, however, the ruling party won several multiparty elections, while in Kenya the ruling party prevailed over a fractured opposition in two elections in the 1990s, finally losing in 2002.

Second, there were countries where the transition to democracy was effected through national conferences in which members of the political class and the elites of civil society came together to forge a new political and constitutional order. These conferences were largely confined to Francophone countries and South Africa. They succeeded in countries where they were held early, before incumbent regimes had learned how to manipulate them, and where the opposition was strong and united and the regime weakened and factionalized, as was the case in Benin, Congo, and Niger. Benin held the first national conference in 1989, which succeeded in toppling the regime of Mathew Kérékou. The opposite was true in countries such as Gabon, Togo, Côte d'Ivoire, and the Congo Democratic Republic (then called Zaire), where incumbent regimes managed to retain power for a while. In South Africa, the Convention for a Democratic South Africa, held between 1991 and 1993, was prompted by the strategic stalemate between the nationalist forces and the apartheid white minority regime and paved the way for the transition to democratic rule in 1994.

Finally, there was the path of managed transition pursued by military regimes, which tried to oversee and tightly control the process and pace of political reform. For example, in Ghana, the military ruler, Jerry Rawlings (b. 1947), turned himself into a civilian and won the multiparty elections of 1992 and 1996, but his party lost the elections of 2000, while in Nigeria the military refused to accept the results of the multiparty elections of 1992 and proceeded to entrench a repressive regime that ended only after the death of the military dictator Sani Abacha (1943–1999), when multiparty democracy was reinstalled. In Uganda, the government of Yoweri Museveni (b. 1941) clung to power while claiming to pursue "no party politics," a rehashed doctrine of the one-party state. In Algeria, the military-backed government annulled the elections in 1992 when the Islamic Salvation Front won the first round and looked poised to win the final round. Instead of democracy, the country became involved in a vicious civil war that lasted many years.

Explanations of Africa's Democratization

By the turn of the new century, then, much had changed on Africa's political map. Democratic regimes, at least in terms of electoral politics and constitutional changes of government, had become quite common. Indeed, many countries were into their second or third round of multiparty elections, but several countries were still in the grip of authoritarian rule and autocratic tendencies persisted in many of the new democracies. Also, some elected governments were overthrown and several intrastate and interstate wars raged across the continent, all of which raised serious questions about the content and direction of the continent's democracies. Clearly, the trajectories of this wave of democracy in Africa have been quite complex and uneven.

Debate on Africa's democratization processes and prospects has centered on four interrelated issues: the relative roles of (1) internal and external factors; (2) historical and contemporary dynamics; (3) structural and contingent factors; and (4) economic and political dimensions. Those who stress the primacy of internal factors behind the democratic transitions tend to underscore the strength of domestic political protests and prodemocracy movements engendered or energized by the failures of development, the economic crises of the 1980s and 1990s, and the disintegration of the postcolonial state's legitimacy and capacity. They also highlight the demonstration effects of regional transitions, such as Benin in Francophone West Africa, Zambia in southern Africa, the Palestinian Intifadah for North Africa, and South Africa, across the continent. Those who emphasize external forces point to the decisive impact of the end of the Cold War, the demonstration effects of the collapse of communism in Eastern Europe, and the imposition of structural adjustment programs and political conditionalities by Western bilateral and multilateral financial institutions. But some have questioned the West's commitment to the promotion of democracy in Africa, arguing that it is more rhetorical than real and is motivated by donor interests rather than recipient needs.

Proponents of the two approaches tend to place Africa's transitions to democracy in different historical contexts, either in terms of global waves of democracy or in African histories of struggles for freedom. Advocates of the first approach tend to see Africa's democratization as part of what Samuel Huntington calls the third wave of democracy, which apparently began in the 1970s in southern and eastern Europe. While each democracy wave is propelled by a different constellation of factors, it is said to be a process driven by the victorious democratic hegemonic powers. Others argue that, while Africa's democratization was influenced by developments elsewhere in the world, it was primarily rooted in the continent's long history of struggle against slavery, colonialism, and postcolonial misrule. Mohamed Salih talks of Africa's own "'waves of democratization' (colonial, early independence, postindependence, and the 1990s)" (p. 19). At the very least, the 1980s and 1990s—the era of democratization—represented a period of struggles for the "second independence"; the "first independence" was fought for in the 1950s and 1960s—the era of decolonization. Thus, African democratic struggles are linked to, structurally and symbolically, the rich reservoirs of earlier struggles against exploitation and oppression.

Observers also do not agree on the extent to which democratization is a product of structural factors as opposed to individual actions and events. Proponents of the latter approach stress the role of specific leaders, closely following the ebb and flow of events and tailoring their interpretations accordingly. Their focus tends to be on contingent factors, the unpredictability of developments, and human agency. Structuralist analyses, on the other hand, dwell on the structural conditions that have forestalled and facilitated and might sustain or frustrate democratization. These include colonial legacies, levels of economic development and education, size of the middle classes, the nature and vibrancy of civil society, and impediments imposed by the global system. Predictions of the prospects for the democratic project in different countries and across the continent—whether positive or negative—are often based on how these "democratic preconditions" are evaluated. To many commentators, from Western cynics and beleaguered African leaders to pessimistic intellectuals, the prospects of democracy in Africa are undermined by the enduring realities or legacies of underdevelopment.

Finally, there is considerable debate as to whether Africa's democratization is attributable to economic or political factors. The first approach examines the role played by postcolonial development failures and, particularly, the economic crises during the "lost decade" of the 1980s, which were exacerbated by structural adjustment programs imposed by the World Bank and International Monetary Fund and generated widespread opposition from various social groups, especially the pauperized middle and working classes, who spearheaded the democratic reform movements. The second approach concentrates on the political crisis of the postcolonial state, particularly its inability to forge nationhood and manage the centrifugal forces of postcolonial society, specifically ethnicity. As Dickson Eyoh has argued, scholarly disenchantment with the performance of the postcolonial state was not only expressed in the accretion of demeaning epithets to describe the African state, it spawned the rapid growth of "civil society" as the master concept around which the dynamics of politics were increasingly debated and the possibilities of African renewal invested.

A comprehensive understanding of democratization in Africa would have to transcend these dichotomous analyses. Clearly, the struggles for democracy in the 1980s and 1990s represented the latest moment of accelerated change in a long history of struggles for freedom, an exceptionally complex moment often driven by unpredictable events and new social movements and visions, anchored in the specific histories, social structures, and conditions of each country, in which national, regional, and international forces converged unevenly and inconsistently, and economic and political crises reinforced each other, altering the terrain of state–civil society relationships, the structures of governance, and the claims of citizenship.

Visions of African Democracy

Fundamental to the question of democracy in Africa have been different conceptions and visions of what democracy means and entails. The views range from minimalist conceptions of liberal democracy, emphasizing competitive electoral processes and respect for civil and political rights, to maximalist notions of social democracy embracing material development, equality and upliftment, and respect for the so-called three generations of rights, civil and political, social and economic, and development or solidarity rights. Five prescriptive models can be identified in the writings of African political thinkers and leaders: nativist, liberal, popular democratic, theocratic, and transnational.

Nativist model. To the proponents of the nativist model, democracy in Africa can be consolidated only if it is articulated with the "consensus" or "consultative" model of democracy found in "traditional" institutions. Maxwell Owusu believes mobilizing the language, rituals, and working assumptions of traditional chieftaincy that are easily understood by local communities is essential to what he calls the "domestication of democracy." This vision is shared on the ideological right by George Ayittey, who urges a return to indigenous practices and

values in political and economic management if Africa is to recover from its debilitating crises of poor governance and development, and on the ideological left by Claude Ake, who believes it is imperative to ground democratic movements and practice in the "communal ethos" that defines many Africans' perception of self-interest, their freedom, and their location in the social whole.

Liberal model. To the pragmatic defenders of the liberal model, such as Jibrin Ibrahim and Peter Anyang' Nyong'o (1995), democracy rests solidly on a multiparty system and periodic electoral contests to promote the trinity of good governance: efficiency, accountability, and transparency. Their critics have charged that this model offers a mechanism of elite competition, recruitment, circulation, and control but presents limited benefits to the often atomized and powerless citizenry. A modified version incorporates the development imperative, the need for Africa's emerging democracies to "bring development back in." Thandika Mkandawire argues that a developmentalism will emerge out of the early-twenty-first-century context, democratic because of the continuing popular struggles against authoritarianism, and capitalist because capitalism constitutes the political program of the key actors in the struggles for democracy and of the dominant forces at the global level, following the collapse of "actually existing" Soviet socialism. Adebayo Olukoshi contends that the struggles for democracy ultimately entail struggles for material existence, although they are not purely economic, and that the possibilities of democratic consolidation are firmly tied to democracy's ability to deliver development.

Popular democratic model. Many of the critics of liberal democracy advocate the popular democratic model in which both the political and economic domains are based on democratic principles. For Samir Amin, a democracy restricted to the political sphere, as in Western democratic regimes, while economic organization is held captive to nondemocratic principles of privatization, is an incomplete one. Besides the incorporation of economic rights, the defenders of popular democracy emphasize the rights of subnational communities as a necessary part of the process of reconciling the colonial bifurcation of power between a racially exclusive urban civil society for immigrant settler citizens and a decentralized rural despotism for the "native" subjects. According to Mahmood Mamdani, African states are confronted with the challenges of democratizing the state, particularly customary power, removing state control of citizenship rights, deracializing civil society, and restructuring the unequal external relations of dependency. Feminist scholars such as Amina Mama and Ifi Amadiume have called attention to the gendered dimensions of state formation and power and the fact that democratization without women's empowerment and gender equality is clearly inadequate.

Theocratic model. All these debates and visions are secular in orientation. There are also theocratic visions and discourses about political transformation and democracy in Africa. The debate has been particularly contentious in Muslim communities undergoing revivalism due to contemporary religious, political, and cultural imperatives and pressures facing them.

Ali Mazrui has argued that different forces in different countries have fostered Islamic revivalism. For example, in Somalia and Sudan

> it grew out of desolation; in the case of Libya and Iran revivalism grew out of the hazards of newly acquired oil wealth. . . . Muslims were rediscovering their faith either in dependence or in renewed self-confidence. (p. 516)

On the one hand, there are militant clerics and intellectuals, such as Hassan El-Tourabi (b. 1932) in the Sudan, who propose sweeping political changes to enshrine Islamic law (shari'a), ostensibly to strengthen the Islamic community and eradicate the corrupt Western influences of modern society. On the other hand, there are reformist scholars, such as Abdullahi An-Na'im, also from the Sudan, who offer a radical reinterpretation of the Koran in an effort to develop a modern version of Islamic law that conforms to international standards of human rights. Feminist scholars, such as Ayesha Imam, have also sought to reinterpret women's rights under Muslim laws to advance women's empowerment.

Transnational model.   Finally, in response to the perceived pressures of globalization, which seem poised to erode the already diminished powers of the postcolonial state, a transnational model of democratization has emerged as embodied in new visions of regional and continental integration. Some scholars argue that none of the models above, all focused, more or less, on the nation-state, hold the key to lasting change for Africa. The economic and diplomatic justifications of regional integration for Africa's global competitiveness are as old as independence; the cultural and racial rationales go back to colonization and the origins of Pan-Africanism. What was new by the 1990s were the arguments centering on the democratic possibilities of regional integration: that it might curtail the authoritarian reflexes of the postcolonial state, thwart coups or raise the costs for the perpetrators, and facilitate the decentralization and dispersal of power, thereby dissolving incendiary clashes in conflict-prone countries.

The African Union, launched in 2002 as the successor to the Organization of African Unity, embodied the new hopes of African integration, development, and democratization. It envisioned the creation of an African parliament, a court of justice, a peace and security council, and an economic, social, and cultural council, some of whose members would come from civil society organizations, including some from the diaspora. Various economic instruments were also created, most importantly, the New Economic Partnership for African Development and a peer review mechanism for African states to evaluate each other's adherence to the principles of democratic governance and human rights.

Challenges of Democratic Consolidation

Most African scholars recognize that consolidating democracy on the continent will remain a difficult and daunting task. Available evidence indicates that, in the first fifteen years, many of the new democratic regimes were still fragile and some of

the euphoria of the early 1990s had evaporated. Some scholars and observers, such as Michael Bratton and Nicholas de Walle, even argue that democratization in Africa has been more illusory than fundamental, marking a transition from patrimonialism to neopatrimonialism. This is debatable, however. By the beginning of the twenty-first century, the authoritarianism and statism of the early postindependence years was in retreat, and, where it persisted, was vigorously contested in a context in which democratic aspirations were firmly implanted in popular consciousness and the pluralization of associational life was an integral part of the political landscape. It was indeed a mark of the changed times that, whereas previously development had been regarded as a prerequisite of democracy, now democracy was seen as indispensable for development.

The challenges facing Africa's democratic experiments are many and complex. Julius Ihnovbere and John Mbaku provide a useful summary. They include entrenching constitutionalism and the reconstruction of the postcolonial state, preventing military intervention in politics, instituting structures for the effective management of ethnic diversity, promoting sustainable development and well-enforced property rights regimes, nurturing effective leadership, combating the HIV/AIDS pandemic, empowering women, managing globalization, protecting the youth, and safeguarding human rights and the rule of law.

See also **Apartheid; Capitalism: Africa; Civil Society: Responses in Africa and the Middle East; Colonialism: Africa; Corruption in Developed and Developing Countries; Development; Globalization: Africa; Modernization Theory; Multiculturalism, Africa; Nationalism: Africa; Neocolonialism; Pan-Africanism; Socialisms, African; Westernization: Africa.**

BIBLIOGRAPHY

Abrahamsen, Rita. *Disciplining Democracy: Development Discourse and Good Governance in Africa.* London: Zed, 2000.

Ake, Claude. *The Feasibility of Democracy in Africa.* Dakar, Senegal: Codesria, 2000.

Amadiume, Ifi. *Daughters of the Goddess, Daughters of Imperialism: African Women Struggle for Culture, Power, and Democracy.* London: Zed, 2000.

Amin, Samir. "The Issue of Democracy in the Third World." In *Academic Freedom in Africa,* edited by Mahmood Mamdani and Mamadou Diouf. Dakar, Senegal: Codesria, 1994.

An-Na'im, Abdullahi Ahmed. *Indigenous African Institutions.* New York: Ardsley-on-Hudson, 1991.

———. *Toward an Islamic Reformation: Civil Liberties, Human Rights, and International Law.* New York: Syracuse University Press, 1990.

Ayittey, George B. N. *Africa in Chaos.* New York: St. Martin's Press, 1998.

Bielefeldt, Heiner. "'Western' versus 'Islamic' Human Rights Conceptions? A Critique of Cultural Essentialism in the Discussion on Human Rights." *Political Theory* 28, no. 1 (2000): 90–121.

Bratton, Michael, and Nicolas van de Walle. *Democratic Experiments in Africa: Regime Transitions in Comparative Perspective.* Cambridge, U.K.: Cambridge University Press, 1997.

Chabal, Patrick. "A Few Considerations on Democracy in Africa." *International Affairs* 74, no. 2 (1998): 289–303.

Cowen, Michael, and Liisa Laakso, eds. *Multi-Party Elections in Africa.* Oxford: James Currey, 2002.

Eyoh, Dickson. "From Economic Crisis to Political Liberalization: Pitfalls of the New Political Sociology for Africa." *African Studies Review* 39, no. 3 (1999): 43–80.

Ibrahim, Jibrin. "Democratic Transition in Africa: The Challenge of a New Agenda—Concluding Remarks." In *Democratization Processes in Africa,* edited by Eshetu Chole and Jibrin Ibrahim. Dakar, Senegal: Codesria, 1995.

Idahosa, P. L. E. *The Populist Dimension to African Political Thought: Critical Essays in Reconstruction and Retrieval.* Trenton, N.J.: Africa World, 2004.

Ihonvbere, Julius O., and John M. Mbaku, eds. *Political Liberalization and Democratization in Africa: Lessons from Country Experiences.* Westport, Conn.: Praeger, 2003.

Imam, Ayesha. "The Muslim Religious Right (Fundamentalists) and Sexuality: Women Living under Muslim Laws." *Dossier* 17 (1997): 7–25.

———. "The Place of Women under Sharia." *CRP/FNS Lagos* (2000): 16–31.

Joseph, Richard. "Democratization in Africa after 1989: Comparative and Theoretical Perspectives." *Comparative Politics* 29, no. 3 (1997): 363–382.

Makinda, Samuel M. "Democracy and Multi-Party Politics in Africa." *Journal of Modern African Studies* 34, no. 4 (1996): 555–573.

Mama, Amina. "Challenging Subjects: Gender, Power, and Identity in African Contexts." *Research and Action Report* 23, no. 2 (2002): 6–15.

———. "Feminism or Femocracy? State Feminism and Democratization in Nigeria." In *Expanding Democratic Space in Nigeria,* edited by Jibrin Ibrahim, 63–80. Dakar, Senegal: Codesria, 1997.

Mamdani, Mahmood. "Africa: Democratic Theory and Democratic Struggles." *Dissent* 39 (1992): 312–318.

———. *Citizen and Subject: Contemporary Africa and the Legacy of Late Colonialism.* Princeton, N.J.: Princeton University Press, 1996.

Mazrui, Ali A. "African Islam and Competitive Religion: Between Revivalism and Expansion." *Third World Quarterly* 10, no. 2 (1988): 499–518.

Mbaku, John M., and Julius O. Ihonvbere, eds. *The Transition to Democratic Governance in Africa: The Continuing Struggle.* Westport, Conn.: Praeger, 2003.

Mengisteab, Kidane, and Cyril Daddieh, eds. *State-Building and Democratization in Africa: Faith, Hope, and Realities.* Westport, Conn.: Praeger, 1999.

Mkandawire, P. Thandika. *Thinking about Developmental States in Africa.* Geneva: United Nations Conference on Trade and Development, United Nations, 1998.

Nyong'o, Peter Anyang'. "Discourses on Democracy in Africa." In *Democratization Processes in Africa: Problems and Prospects,* edited by Eshetu Chole and Jibrin Ibrahim. Dakar, Senegal: Codesria, 1995.

———. *Popular Struggles for Democracy in Africa.* London: Zed, 1987.

Olsen, Girm Rye. "Europe and the Promotion of Democracy in Post Cold War Africa: How Serious Is Europe and for What Reason?" *African Affairs* 97, no. 388 (1998): 343–367.

Olukoshi, Adebayo O. "Africa: Democratizing under Conditions of Economic Stagnation." Paper presented at Codesria Eighth General Assembly, Dakar, Senegal, June 26–July 2, 1995.

———. "Democratization, Globalization, and Effective Policy-making in Africa." In *The Politics of Trade and Industrial Policy in Africa: Forced Consensus?,* edited by Charles C. Soludo, Osita Ogbu, and Ha-Joon Chang. Trenton, N.J.: Africa World; Ottawa, Canada: International Development Research Centre, 2004.

Owusu, Maxwell. "Democracy and Africa: A View from the Village." *Journal of Modern African Studies* 30 (1992): 369–396.

———. "Domesticating Democracy: Culture, Civil Society, and Constitutionalism in Africa." *Comparative Studies in Society and History* 39, no. 1 (1997): 120–152.

Salih, Mohamed. *African Democracies and African Politics.* London and Sterling, Va.: Pluto, 2001.

Sandbrook, Richard. "Economic Liberalization versus Political Democratization: A Social-Democratic Resolution." *Canadian Journal of African Studies* 31, no. 3 (1997): 482–516.

Zeleza, Paul Tiyambe. *Manufacturing African Studies and Crises.* Dakar, Senegal: Codesria, 1997.

———. "The Struggle for Human Rights in Africa." In *Human Rights, the Rule of Law and Development in Africa,* edited by Paul T. Zeleza and Philip J. McConnaughay, 1–18. Philadelphia: University of Pennsylvania Press, 2004.

Paul Tiyambe Zeleza

DEMOGRAPHY.

Demography is the study of human population and its changes due to deaths, births, marriages and divorces, and migration. The term *demos* denotes people in Greek—the term *demography* literally means the systematic study of people. In the early twenty-first century the discipline encompasses a broad array of subject matters, covering, among others, economic, social, public health, and political issues. This entry will provide a brief overview of the uses of demographic data and key trends.

Contemporary demographers focus on two broad areas. The first is the size, composition, and characteristics of populations. The second focus is on processes that influence population change. Demographers need data to conduct analyses: censuses, surveys, and civil and vital registrations are sources of population-related information. Censuses collect data or information at the household level and are conducted at regular intervals. Surveys based on scientific sampling principles are conducted as needed for a variety of purposes, but participation by individuals is voluntary. The registration of births, deaths, marriages, and divorces, along with mandatory reporting requirements for communicable diseases or for residence changes, serve as excellent sources of data on fertility, mortality, nuptiality, and migration. An additional source of population data includes estimations, which are increasingly sophisticated calculations based on information not directly related to the sources listed here.

In addition to the size and spatial aspects of settlement, demographers examine and analyze factors related to the composition of populations, namely age groupings and race/ethnic and gender distributions. Characteristics of populations, such as education and economic status, are also studied. Generally these factors are examined from a single point in time or cross-sectional perspective as well as in reference to dynamic changing processes (longitudinal).

Data on the size, composition, and characteristics of populations are used for a variety of public and private purposes. Drawing political boundaries for elections, determining commercial investment decisions, and assessing the prevalence of health problems are three examples of uses of demographic data. For example, the number of congressional districts in the United States has remained constant at 435 for nearly a century, despite a tripling of the nation's population. The allocation of congressional districts is based on a state's share of the national population.

Another example of the use of demographic analyses occurs when states, counties, and cities make decisions about infrastructure investments, such as the location of new fire stations, schools, and public libraries. Furthermore, private firms use population information such as education level and incomes to target households for marketing purposes or to estimate the need for commercial services. Demographic data are also used to calculate rates of prevalence of disease in order to assess the magnitude and the need for intervention. The incidence of communicable disease—for example, tuberculosis—is standardized (e.g., per 10,000 population), facilitating comparisons across administrative boundaries and helping to focus attention on health disparities between areas and population subgroups.

Demography addresses the processes that change populations. Three related factors affect population change:

• Fertility, which measures the average number of children born to a woman (or populations) during child-bearing ages;

• Mortality, which is the process by which deaths occur in populations; and

• Migration, which is the movement of individuals or groups that involves a permanent or semipermanent change of residence across administrative and political boundaries, that is, across county, state, and national boundaries.

The twentieth century was characterized by what has been termed a *demographic transition,* in which mortality rates dropped dramatically due to advances in sanitation, access to health care, rapid socioeconomic changes, including a change in the status of women and altered attitudes toward contraception. The reduction in mortality was followed by declines in fertility rates. The fertility decline was evident in Europe, North America, and Oceania throughout the latter part of the twentieth century, with fertility rates at or below the replacement level of 2.1 children per women. By the year 2000, most Asian and Latin American countries had entered a transition toward lower fertility, and by the start of the twenty-first century, some low-fertility countries had adopted policies to reverse the declines. Many of the countries that had not shown

fertility declines were located in sub-Saharan Africa. In addition to high infant mortality rates, mortality among the working-age population in Africa was also high as a result of the Acquired Immune Deficiency Syndrome (AIDS) epidemic, which was having a profound and detrimental impact.

By the early twenty-first century, the population aged sixty-five and above in low-fertility countries was increasing at a much faster rate than those of lower age ranges because of increased life expectancy combined with low birth rates. Since older populations typically need more health care along with support during retirement, increases in elderly populations put a strain on health care, social security, and pension systems. The aging population had a significant impact on health care systems and workforce recruitment and training and initiated a debate on how to support an aging population through publicly funded social security schemes. These debates occurred at a time when the size of the younger working population was shrinking.

In low-fertility countries, immigration mediated the impact of fertility declines. In North America and Oceania, large-scale immigration began in the nineteenth century, and net migration became a significant and increasing component of the population increase by the early twenty-first century. Other Western countries have had a history of emigration, that is, an outflow of people rather than immigration. But from the 1960s onward, an influx of African and Asian immigrants to Europe, both legal and illegal, gave rise to social and political pressures.

While fertility levels are declining in Asia, Latin America, and the Middle East, population size will continue to grow for the foreseeable future because large proportions of the population are in the younger reproductive ages. Emigration plays only a small role in reducing population growth in these regions. The challenge for many of these countries is to provide education, workforce training, and employment to their predominantly young populations, and failure to meet these needs may lead to political instability and sometimes acts of violence. Most spheres of human activity—political, social, and economic—now involve consideration of the size, composition, and characteristics of the population. This is unlikely to change as nations confront the issues discussed here.

See also **Family Planning; Migration; Population.**

BIBLIOGRAPHY

Nam, Charles B. *Understanding Population Change.* Itasca, IL: F. E. Peacock, 1994.

Namboodiri, Krishnan. *A Primer of Population Dynamics.* New York: Plenum, 1996.

Saunders, John. *Basic Demographic Measures: A Practical Guide for Users.* Lanham, Md.: University Press of America, 1988.

United Nations. *World Population Prospects: The 2000 Revision.* Vol. 3, *Analytical Report.* New York: United Nations, 2002.

Ramdas Menon

DEMONOLOGY. Some years ago, Richard Cavendish, an eminent demonologist and student of the so-called black

The Devil from the Earth (c. 1255–1260). **Illustration on parchment.** In his original historical incarnation, Satan was merely an angel who defied God and was banished from Heaven. The introduction of Zoroastrian concepts of evil to Judaism resulted in Satan's transformation into the ultimate antagonist. COURTESY OF THE J. PAUL GETTY MUSEUM

arts, observed that "[b]elief in the existence of evil supernatural beings" is so widespread that it "seems to be instinctive" (p. 8). Whether, as Cavendish suggests, these beliefs are in fact instinctive is still very much an open question. However, human beings do indeed appear to have a deep-seated penchant for explaining misfortune by attributing it to evil and malicious spirits and deities—that is, to demons. Such beliefs can be documented in virtually every known human society for which adequate information exists. This essay explores some of the more salient manifestations, modern as well as ancient, of this well-nigh universal component of several belief systems.

In the great majority of cases, demonic figures occur in conjunction with their opposites, that is, beneficent deities to whom worshipers turn for succor when misfortune strikes or when in need of assurance that crops will grow, illness will be avoided, and prosperity will continue. One of the earliest documented examples of such a pair can be found in ancient Egypt in Osiris and his demonic brother Seth.

Osiris and Seth
Dating from Old Kingdom times (2700–2200 B.C.E.), this pair of opposites was defined in the Pyramid Texts and other ancient Egyptian mythological texts as brothers. While Osiris—

together with his sister/wife Isis—was the incarnation of fertility and, eventually, life everlasting, Seth was evil personified. He was also a reflection of the arid desert that presses in on either side of Osiris's domain: the fertile Nile Valley. Seth was jealous of his brother and, through trickery, caused his death. However, with the help of Isis and their son Horus, who was iconographically represented as a falcon-headed man, Osiris was resurrected and ascended to heaven to become the judge of the dead. Meanwhile, Horus and Seth struggled mightily. It was one of the first examples of a supernatural conflict between good and evil, between a demon and his diametric opposite (Horus later became identified with the pharaoh, who was worshiped as a god incarnate). The falcon-headed god finally prevailed, and Seth was killed and dismembered. But the latter remained a quintessential demon, the template, as it were, for a great many later Western demonic figures.

Ahura Mazda and Angra Mainyu
Another extremely important ancient demon can be found in the Iranian figure Angra Mainyu, or "Evil Spirit," later known as Ahriman, who was paired in early Iranian mythology, especially as shaped by the prophet Zarathustra (or Zoroaster, as he was known to the ancient Greeks), with the beneficent deity Ahura Mazda, the "Wise Lord," called Ormazd in Middle Persian. Although they were not held to be siblings, Angra Mainyu and Ahura Mazda were believed to be engaged in an ongoing cosmic struggle, both for world hegemony and for each individual soul. Angra Mainyu/Ahriman was a true "Prince of Darkness," the diametric opposite—and eternal opponent—of the light-filled Ahura Mazda/Ormazd. The most extreme variant of this good-evil dichotomy was promulgated during the third-century C.E. by the Iranian religious reformer Mani (ca. 216–276 or 277 C.E.), founder of the Manichean sect, which, for a time, was a serious rival to nascent Christianity. According to the Manicheans, who emphasized free will, one could choose to follow the evil Ahriman, who might ultimately defeat Ormazd in their final, apocalyptic confrontation.

Satanism
The origins of Satan and related figures are complex. The word *satan* itself simply means "adversary" in Hebrew; in his earlier manifestations as Lucifer, the "Light-Bearer," who rebelled against God and was cast out of heaven (cf. Isaiah 14: 12–15), he is not unlike the Greek figure Prometheus, albeit negatively valued. However, as the Zoroastrian theology of evil incarnate came to permeate post-exile Judaism, the Rebel evolved into a full-fledged evil adversary, in effect a malevolent twin of Yahweh who presided over the corrupt world of the senses.

Several centuries later, this evolution was greatly facilitated by the emergence of Gnosticism (from Greek *gnosis*, "knowledge"), a heretical movement that emerged in Alexandria and elsewhere in the early years of the common era. Gnosticism held that the mortal realm was created by a fool called the Demiurge, a corrupt if not totally malevolent pseudo-deity the Gnostics identified with the God of the Old Testament. This rejection of God linked Manichaeism to Gnosticism, but for the Gnostics the "real" world, that is, the world of the senses, was evil, and their goal in life was to escape it and return to the Pleroma, or "Fullness," a light-filled spiritual realm that was the antithesis of corrupt mortality. These ideas, although roundly condemned by the early church fathers, from Athanasius to Augustine, lingered on and reappeared in the twelfth century in southern France in the Cathay heresy, which was brutally suppressed during the infamous Albigensian Crusade (1208). It was out of this heretical crucible, which also came to include the "pagan" witchcraft beliefs that incited such intense persecutions between the mid-thirteenth century and the end of the seventeenth century, that Satanism as we know it today emerged. Indeed, the idea that a divine adversary who governs the sensate world is the "true" god still persists in cults such as the late Anton Szandor LaVey's (1930–1997) Church of Satan, founded in San Francisco in 1966, and the Temple of Set, founded in 1975 by Michael Acquino (b. 1946). The idea that people are susceptible to possession by demons persists in the Roman Catholic ritual of exorcism, so graphically depicted in the film *The Exorcist* (1973).

Non-Western Demonology

Such beliefs are, of course, by no means limited to the West. Islam conceives of the demon Iblis as Allah's prime adversary, aided by a host of malevolent spirits called jinn (the English word "genie" derives from this Arabic word), who are capable of all manner of mischief. Moreover, a great many non-Western cultures also share a belief in demonic figures. In Japan, demonic figures that have the ability to possess human beings and cause them great harm are called *oni*. There are a great many varieties of *oni*, not all of whom are really evil; however, most of them are at least mischievous. Among the more dangerous *oni* are animal spirits, including fox spirits, who are believed to be especially malevolent and are held responsible for a wide variety of personal misfortunes. Moreover, they are extremely difficult to exorcise. Similar folk beliefs can be found throughout East Asia, Southeast Asia, the Indian subcontinent, Africa, the Caribbean, and Oceania, as well as the Americas.

Hindu mythology is replete with demonic figures, the most famous of whom is the evil *raksha*, or demon, Ravanna, king of Sri Lanka, and abductor of Sita, the devoted wife of the demigod Rama. Indeed, the plot of the ancient Indian epic known as the *Ramayana*, which spread throughout much of Southeast Asia during the early centuries of the common era, turns on Rama's conflict with Ravanna and Sita's eventual rescue—once again, an account of an epic struggle between good and evil, although Ravanna and Rama are not conceived as siblings.

In the high Andean plateau, or *altiplano*, of Bolivia, as June Nash reports, the local miners believe that the mountains are haunted by a demon called Huari, whom they refer to as Tio, or "Uncle," and who must be propitiated to avoid cave-ins and other calamities. This reflects another important dimension of demonology: the propitiation of evil forces and beings so as to preclude disaster and misfortune.

A further example of this ambiguous attitude toward evil figures can be found in Afro-Caribbean religions such as Santeria and Voodoo, where the *orishas*, or deities, are considered both evil and beneficent, depending on the context.

Both good and evil manifestations of the gods are found in the pantheon and are regularly the recipients of sacrifices. Although for the most part absent in fully evolved Judeo-Christian demonology, this ambiguous attitude toward evil and the propitiation of what we might consider demons is an integral element of folk religious beliefs in a great many parts of the non-Western world—as well as in classical antiquity, where, for example, the ancient Greek god Pan was both benevolent and capable of creating havoc, whence the English word *panic*.

She-Devils and Female Demons

Although the majority of demons in most cultures tend to be male, female demons, she-devils, and the like are also common. One of the oldest examples of such a figure can be found in the Sumero-Babylonian demon Tiamat, wife of the primordial being Apsu. The supreme Babylonian god Marduk engaged in an epic struggle with Tiamat and, after finally defeating her, created the world from her corpse. Ancient Greek mythology abounds with evil female creatures, from the Gorgons, the most famous of whom was snaky-locked Medusa, whose glance could turn a mortal into stone, to the monster Python, whom Apollo killed at the site of Delphi, to the equally bloodthirsty female Sphinx, whose riddle Oedipus managed to solve, causing her to drop dead.

In Shinto mythology, Izanami-no-Mikoto, the wife of the primeval male figure Izanagi-no-Mikoto, changed into a raging demon after she died giving birth to the Fire-god, Kagu-Tsuchi, and descended into Yomi, the land of the dead. When Izanagi visited Yomi in order to bring her back to life, she led a band of female demons, the so-called Hags of Yomi, against him and almost succeeded in killing him. More recently, medieval European folklore knew the succubus, a demon or evil spirit who seduced unwitting mortal men and produced demonic offspring.

Space Aliens as Demons

In recent years, since accounts of UFOs and space aliens have become widespread in Europe and especially the United States, some fundamentalist Christians have asserted that these presumed extraterrestrial visitors are in fact manifestations of Satan and his demonic horde. Indeed, according to this contemporary "school" of demonology, those persons who claim to have been abducted by aliens and forced to have sex with them are believed to be victims of the same demonic possession that was reported in premodern times, which also frequently had a strong sexual component. In sum, demonology continues to persist in this otherwise secular age, just as it has since the dawn of human culture.

See also **Evil; Syncretism; Witchcraft.**

BIBLIOGRAPHY
Cavendish, Richard. *The Black Arts.* New York: Berkeley Publishing Group, 1967.
Duchesne-Guillemin, J. *The Western Response to Zoroaster.* Westport, Conn.: Greenwood Press, 1959.
Fairman, H. W., ed. and trans. *The Triumph of Horus: An Ancient Egyptian Sacred Drama.* Berkeley: University of California Press, 1974.

Gettings, Fred. *Dictionary of Demons: A Guide to Demons and Demonologists in Occult Lore.* North Pomfret, Vt.: Trafalgar Square Publishers, 1988.

Littleton, C. Scott. "Japanese Religions." In *Religion and Culture: An Anthropological Focus,* edited by Raymond Scupin. Upper Saddle River, N.J.: Prentice Hall, 2000.

Marrs, Jim. *Alien Agenda: Investigating the Extraterrestrial Presence among Us.* New York: Harper Paperbacks, 1997. See pp. 548–555.

Murphy, Joseph M. *Santeria: An African Religion in America.* Boston: Beacon Press, 1988.

Nash, June. "Devils, Witches, and Sudden Death." In *Magic, Witchcraft, and Religion: An Anthropological Study of the Supernatural,* edited by Arthur C. Lehmann and James E. Myers. 3rd ed. Mountain View, Calif.: Mayfield, 1993.

O'Flaherty, Wendy Doniger. *The Origins of Evil in Hindu Mythology.* Berkeley: University of California Press, 1976.

The Ramayana of Valmiki. Translated by Hari Prasad Shastri. London: Shanti Sadan, 1962.

Russell, Jeffrey Burton. *The Devil: Perceptions of Evil from Antiquity to Primitive Christianity.* Ithaca, N.Y.: Cornell University Press, 1977.

———. *Witchcraft in the Middle Ages.* Ithaca, N.Y.: Cornell University Press, 1972.

Wilson, Colin. *The Occult: A History.* New York: Vintage, 1973.

C. Scott Littleton

DEPENDENCY. During the 1960s and 1970s, Latin American dependency theorists produced an important challenge to modernization and growth theories of development. Associated with a number of key intellectuals from Latin America—Andre Gunder Frank, Fernando Henrique Cardoso, and Peter Evans in Latin America, Samir Amin and Walter Rodney in Africa—the *dependentistas* turned modernization theory upside down by arguing that contact with Western capitalism created (rather than solved) underdevelopment in the Third World. They challenged the Eurocentric notion that development was a "catch-up game" in which a "backward" Third World, mired in "tradition" (and thus outside modern history), could only become developed (like the West) with the help of Western capitalism.

While significant variations within this perspective would emerge, certain central tenets can be identified. Most notably, the *dependentistas* rejected the dual approach to development, arguing for a more global approach that examined unequal terms of trade and the role of Western capital in the perpetuation of these inequalities. At the same time, dependency theorists were unable to break completely from the Eurocentric discourse they were challenging. While critiquing the nation-state focus of modernization theory, their policy prescriptions tended to assert the centrality of the nation-state, with particular attention to state structures, technology, and national economic planning, thereby appropriating many of the key elements in mainstream development's toolkit. This limitation has inspired critiques of dependency writings from many different perspectives.

The Intellectual Roots of Dependency Thinking

The dependency challenge grew out of historical and economic analyses grounded in Latin America's colonial and postcolonial experiences. The historical work of Latin American scholars such as Eric Williams highlighted the links between the colonial plantations and Western economic development, particularly the use of plantation profits to bankroll European industrial development. The plantations were not precapitalist remnants of indigenous economies, they argued, but the result of capitalist penetration. This historical work undermined modernization theory's dual conception of Third World economies, arguing instead for a more integrated approach, one that paid attention to global inequalities and their link to uneven development. This argument greatly influenced the thinking of key dependency theorists, most notably Andre Gunder Frank.

The dependency approach was also influenced by a group of Latin American economists working for the Economic Commission for Latin America (ECLA), a United Nations agency established in Santiago, Chile, in 1948. Led by Raul Prebisch, these economists sought to understand why, after years of applying modernization and growth "solutions" to Latin American economies, so little progress had been made. They began to see the world as divided into an industrial core and an agrarian periphery. Rather than accepting modernization theory's premise that "backward" economies would gradually move through stages to mass consumption and industrial development, with help from northern capital and development experts (Rostow), the ECLA economists insisted that the core–periphery gap was produced (and reproduced) through patterns of unequal world trade. The very system that was supposed to develop the Third World was leading to its underdevelopment.

Prebisch and the ECLA economists thus challenged neoclassical theories of international trade, called for attention to distribution, and warned that the gap between the core/metropole and the periphery would continue unless there were explicit interventions to challenge structures of international capitalism. Yet, they still believed Latin America's development depended on industrialization and that the domestic capitalist class was the natural leader for that development. Hence, they argued for policies that would nurture this class, encourage import substitution industrialization, and put up protective tariffs until local manufacturers were ready to compete in the global economy.

Radical Dependency Theorists

Andre Gunder Frank and other radical dependency theorists drew on some of these ideas as well as the work of the neo-Marxist Paul Baran. Frank's influential English-language publications adopted the global perspective of the *latifundia* ("large landed estates," "plantations") historians (Williams), as well as Prebisch's focus on unequal terms of trade and his core/periphery model of the world economy. However, Frank rejected the ECLA economists' optimistic assessment of Third World elites. Influenced by Baran, Frank and other radical *dependentistas* argued that collusion between Third World elites and monopoly capital in the industrialized countries was one of the leading factors causing underdevelopment in the periphery. They also rejected the dual economy assumptions of modernization theory, arguing that capitalism had penetrated all corners of the globe since its emergence in the sixteenth century. The Third World periphery was not a "backward" region that would catch up with the industrialized world; its underdevelopment was necessary for metropole's prosperity. As Frank argued, the core and periphery were not separate entities, but, rather, the logical consequence of an integrated global capitalist system. According to Frank:

A mounting body of evidence suggests . . . that the expansion of the capitalist system over the past centuries effectively and entirely penetrated even the apparently most isolated sectors of the underdeveloped world. Therefore, the economic, political, social, and cultural institutions and relations we now observe there are the products of the historical development of the capitalist system no less than are the seemingly more modern or capitalist features of the national metropoles of these underdeveloped countries. (p. 18)

Frank and his *dependentista* colleagues challenged the assumption that decolonization had truly liberated the newly independent nations in the Third World. They argued that, in fact, exploitation had intensified, both between nations and within Third World countries, and concluded that Third World elites and their Western capitalist allies could bring nothing but underdevelopment and despair to the periphery. They called for revolutionary action to remove local political elites from power and to establish governments based on socialist ideals and structures. Only then would Third World nations be able to break their bonds of dependency, challenge global capitalist patterns of inequality, and develop as autonomous, self-reliant nations.

Radical dependency theory influenced thinkers outside Latin America as well, particularly in Africa, where it found a welcome audience among intellectuals and many policymakers. The Guyanese historian Walter Rodney wrote a widely acclaimed analysis blaming Africa's historical underdevelopment on the systemic inequalities resulting from capitalism, colonialism, and imperialism, and Samir Amin, an Egyptian political economist, concluded that Europe had underdeveloped large parts of Africa during the colonial period. This had led to the creation of dependent peripheral economies characterized by weak capitalist sectors focused on a small elite luxury market, with little attention to manufacturing for mass consumption or to promoting links between agriculture and industry. Deeply suspicious of Eurocentric explanations of the world and believing Western capitalist structures inevitably and inherently caused underdevelopment in the periphery, Samir Amin has been an ardent advocate of delinking from the West. Whether this is to be a regional or national project is unclear, but the imperative of delinking is never questioned.

In a similar vein, although skeptical of delinking, Immanuel Wallerstein has drawn on Frank and other radical *dependentistas* for his own project, analyzing commercial relations since the sixteenth century. His World Systems Theory (WST)

expands and complements Frank's ideas, providing a broad global analysis of the way successive emerging cores, their peripheries, and semiperipheries have experienced capitalism over the last few centuries. While seeing capitalism as a zero-sum game, in which winners bring inevitable losers, by advancing the notion of a semiperiphery (rather than a binary world of metropole/periphery) and emphasizing its skepticism toward the benefits of delinking in a global world, World Systems Theory acknowledges the dynamics and dialectics within capitalist development. While many critics find this approach too sweeping, WST continues to have passionate advocates (as well as opponents) around the world.

Reformist Dependency Theory

During the 1970s, the emergence of vibrant economies in some parts of the Third World, especially in countries like South Korea and Taiwan, challenged the radical *dependentistas'* argument for the inevitability of underdevelopment within the capitalist system. Reformist dependency thinking emerged to deal with these contradictions. In particular, the Brazilian social scientist Fernando Cardoso and his colleague, the sociologist Enzo Faletto, while sympathetic to much of radical dependency thinking, rejected the assertion that peripheral underdevelopment was completely determined by the logic of capital accumulation, and argued that Latin America economies were better understood by looking at "forms of local societies, reactions against imperialism, the political dynamics of local societies, and attempts at alternatives" (pp. xv–xvi). Dependency, for them, depended more on local dynamics and the maneuvers of politicians, particularly their willingness to be co-opted by foreign capital, than on the inevitable workings of the world capitalist system. Indeed, they rejected the notion of a world economy, positing instead a world of multiple capitalist systems, with each nation having its own specific social formation and style of capitalism.

Cardoso and Faletto also rejected the radical *dependentistas'* blanket hostility to the national bourgeoisie. Their focus on internal factors highlighted the importance of discovering which groups and classes were willing and able to push for national development. This could include the national bourgeoisie as well as labor, peasants, ethnic groups, and civil society. No class or group was inevitably seen as inclined to help or hinder national development. Cardoso (1972) posited three ways that nations in the Global South could attain development: (1) gaining political autonomy and using that power to industrialize; (2) developing an export-oriented economy capable of accumulating enough capital to industrialize; and (3) being assisted by multinational capital investments that would foster technology transfer and eventual industrialization (a dependent form of development, however). While accepting the tendency toward dependent development rather than the achievement of economic and political autonomy in the Global South, the reformist dependency theorists stake out a very different position than their radical colleagues. For Cardoso and other reformists, genuine autonomous development can occur in the South if the correct alignment of internal forces, both structural and cultural/ideological, can be set in place.

Critiques of Dependency

Both radical and reformist dependency thinking soon encountered strong opposition. While openly hostile to the radical *dependentistas,* mainstream development policy-makers and practitioners increasingly recognized the validity of some of their arguments about the failures of modernization "solutions" to Third World underdevelopment. Organizations such as the World Bank, the International Monetary Fund, and some large government aid agencies responded to this challenge by emphasizing the need to pay more attention to basic human needs and poverty. Reassured by the reformist arguments, some mainstream agencies sought to collaborate with more "reasonable" scholars, such as Cardoso and others who were opposed to delinking and believed in the possibility of working for change within the status quo.

Interestingly, the reformists' focus on the national bourgeoisie and class relations resonated with some of the Marxist critics of the radical *dependentistas.* For example, Ernesto Laclau condemned Frank for focusing on the market rather than class relations, despite his call for a class-based socialist revolution. Bill Warren, in a trenchant, well-researched challenge, questioned the assumption that Third World nations are inevitably caught in a cycle of underdevelopment. Citing various Third World success stories, he argued for a more specific, historical, and class-based analysis of global capitalist relations. Moreover, rather than automatically condemn the national bourgeoisie, he suggested that they could, under the right circumstances, play a crucial role in Third World development. In Africa, some *dependentistas,* such as Colin Leys, retracted their earlier positions and resurrected the national bourgeoisie as a potential instrument for escape from underdevelopment (see also Kitching).

Some feminists concerned with development issues have applauded dependency theorists for criticizing modernization theory and for grounding their analysis in Southern experiences and problems. However, dependency thinking has paid little attention to gender in general, preferring the broad sweep of global forces. Gender and development analysts have been particularly disturbed by dependency theorists' failure to pay attention to cultural dimensions of domination. This is particularly problematic for those concerned with gender equality issues because cultural attitudes and practices clearly play a crucial role both in reinforcing and strengthening patriarchal power structures. The focus on structures rather than agency and culture are, thus, serious problems for feminists interested in utilizing the insights of dependency theory, whether radical or reformist.

Scholars and practitioners concerned with gender, alternative approaches to development, and postcolonial writings argue that in crucial ways dependency thinking has not freed itself from many of the categories of modernization theory. Development is still conceived largely in terms of economic growth, industrialization, and liberal democracy, as an evolutionary process to be led by the correct elites, whether socialist leaders or committed national bourgeoisies. The ecological implications of this growth-oriented model have been ignored, along with the voices and concerns of marginalized peoples.

Agency and difference disappear in a world dominated by powerful global forces. The possibility that hegemony is never complete, that the marginal may influence development practice and thinking, is never considered. Moreover, both the discourse and assumptions of dependency theorists focus on national economic plans, with well-developed national targets. Thus, at the level of discourse and practice, dependency perspectives are based on top-down models of development familiar to the most ardent advocates of modernization.

While there are lessons to be discovered in the writings of dependency theorists, most notably those that pay attention to specific historical forces and their relation to global structures and patterns, the shortcomings of dependency theorists, particularly their inability to move beyond the confines of modernization theory, remain serious impediments for many who are concerned with development questions in an increasingly global/local world. At the same time, the early twenty-first-century conjuncture inevitably raises questions about global forces and the potential of dependency theory's global perspective for understanding the present. Creative, but critical, analysis, drawing on dependency thinking as well as other strands of development thought, may well be possible. Certainly the global focus of the *dependentistas* has much to say to us as we grapple with financial flows and communication systems of an intensity and speed never envisioned in the past. Perhaps useful syntheses will emerge, and, with them, the possibility of reevaluating and using much of the rich scholarship of the dependency perspective.

See also **Capitalism; Class; Colonialism; Corruption in Developed and Developing Countries; Development; Globalization; Human Capital; Marxism; Modernization Theory; Neocolonialism; Scarcity and Abundance, Latin America; State, The: The Postcolonial State; Third World; World Systems Theory, Latin America.**

BIBLIOGRAPHY

Amin, Samir. *Accumulation on a World Scale: A Critique of the Theory of Underdevelopment.* 2 vols. New York: Monthly Review Press, 1974.

———. *Delinking: Towards a Polycentric World.* London: Zed, 1980.

———. *Unequal Development: An Essay on the Social Formation of Peripheral Capitalism.* New York: Monthly Review Press, 1977.

Baran, Paul A. *The Political Economy of Growth.* New York: Monthly Review Press, 1957.

Bergeron, Suzanne. *Fragments of Development: Nation, Gender, and the Space of Modernity.* Ann Arbor: University of Michigan Press, 2004.

Cardoso, Fernando H. "Dependency and Development in Latin America." *New Left Review* 74 (1972): 83–95.

Cardoso, Fernando H., and Enzo Faletto. *Dependency and Development in Latin America.* Berkeley: University of California Press, 1979.

Chilcote, Ronald H. *Theories of Development and Underdevelopment.* Boulder, Colo.: Westview, 1984.

Evans, Peter. *Dependent Development: The Alliance of Multinationals, the State, and Local Capital in Brazil.* Princeton, N.J.: Princeton University Press, 1979.

Frank, Andre G. *Capitalism and Underdevelopment in Latin America: Historical Studies of Chile and Brazil.* New York: Monthly Review Press, 1967.

———. "The Development of Underdevelopment." *Monthly Review* 18 (1966): 17–31.

———. *Latin America: Underdevelopment or Revolution.* New York: Monthly Review Press, 1969.

———. *Lumpen-Bourgeoisie: Lumpen-Development, Dependency, Class, and Politics in Latin America.* New York: Monthly Review Press, 1970.

Kitching, G. N. *Development and Underdevelopment in Historical Perspective: Populism, Nationalism, and Industrialization.* London: Methuen, 1982.

Laclau, E. "Feudalism and Capitalism in Latin America." *New Left Review* (May–June 1971): 19–38.

Leys, Colin. "Kenya: What Does 'Dependency' Explain?" *Review of African Political Economy* 17 (1980): 108–113.

Marchand, Marianne, and Jane Parpart, eds. *Feminism/Postmodernism/Development.* London: Routledge, 1995.

Pieterse, Jan N. *Development Theory: Deconstructions/Reconstructions.* London: Sage, 2001.

Rodney, Walter. *How Europe Underdeveloped Africa.* London: Bogle-L'Ouverture, 1972.

Rostow, W. W. *The Stages of Economic Growth: A Non-Communist Manifesto.* Cambridge, U.K.: Cambridge University Press, 1960.

Tucker, Vincent. "The Myth of Development: A Critique of a Eurocentric Discourse." In *Critical Development Theory,* edited by R. Munck and D. O'Hearn, 1–26. London: Zed, 1999.

Wallerstein, Immanuel M. *The Capitalist World Economy: Essays.* New York: Cambridge University Press, 1979.

———. *The Modern World System.* Vol. 1: *Capitalist Agriculture and the Origins of the European World-Economy in the Sixteenth Century.* New York: Academic, 1974.

———. *The Modern World System.* Vol. 2: *Mercantilism and Consolidation of the European World-Economy, 1600–1750.* New York: Academic, 1980.

Warren, Bill. *Imperialism, Pioneer of Capitalism.* London: New Left Books, 1980.

Williams, Eric E. *Capitalism and Slavery.* Chapel Hill: University of North Carolina Press, 1944.

Jane L. Parpart

DETERMINISM.

The most general idea is that all events without exception are just effects. This idea has been associated with science since the seventeenth century, but it was put in some doubt by an interpretation of quantum theory in physics at the beginning of the twentieth century.

Events are things that happen. Roughly speaking, they are such occurrences as a chair having such a property as a particular location for a time. So determinism is not the idea that everything is an effect. There is a reasonable doubt, by the way, about the items that quantum theory is often interpreted as saying are not effects. Are these items actually events? Are they like numbers instead, say three? If so, then the interpretation of quantum theory is actually irrelevant to determinism.

As for effects, they are not just probable. They are events that had to happen or could not have been otherwise. They were settled in advance. They were, as philosophers sometimes

say, necessitated. There have been different thoughts about what all this comes to.

One thought is that an effect is something that would still have happened just as it did, given certain things that preceded it, whatever else had also preceded it. That match would still have lit, since it was struck the moment before and there was oxygen present and so on, whatever else had also been true.

There is a less-general idea of determinism, of greater interest to most people and to philosophers. It is an idea of human determinism, the main subject of this article. It is that human choices and decisions and the like, and also actions that flow from them, are just effects. Deciding to move one's little finger now is just an effect—as is moving it. So with buying something, getting divorced, or killing somebody. The word *just* in either idea of determinism is only a reminder that whatever else is true of them, the events had to happen, could not have been otherwise, and so on.

The reader may want to say at this point, reasonably enough, that there is a third idea of determinism. It is that people's choices, and so their actions, are not free. Certainly that idea exists. But it is probably better to begin with the second one, about human activities being effects. This is so for the reason that for centuries philosophers and others have disagreed about what follows logically from the second idea, about choices and actions being effects—if that is the case.

Many philosophers have of course said that if determinism in this sense is true, then people are not free. The two things seem to them obviously incompatible. Also, people are not morally responsible for their choices and actions. However, about as many philosophers have said that if this determinism is true, many of one's choices and actions are still perfectly free.

The present article will focus on the second idea of determinism. What is really important of course is not to confuse it with the third sense, the no-freedom sense, or with the first sense, or any other sense.

One large question is whether people really are subject to this determinism. Is this determinism true? A prior question, just as important, is whether this determinism is really clear. For a start, is it clear what choices and decisions and other episodes or facts of consciousness come to? One could call this the question of clarity as against the question of truth. A third question of course is the one this discussion has been noticing. What follows about one's freedom and responsibility if determinism is true?

One way of getting rid of the clarity question is by declaring that the mind is no more than the brain. Conscious events like deciding something are just events of the brain, neural events, nothing more. Deciding something is an event that has only electrochemical properties.

Certainly that makes determinism pretty clear. This old materialism from the seventeenth century can be dressed up, and it certainly is. But no matter how it is dressed up, it is impossible for anyone who gets it straight to believe it. People know, or think they know, that there is a big difference between consciousness or being conscious and any other thing or event—say a neuron or nerve cell composed of protein and so on or a little chemical substance passing between this neuron and the next neuron.

Maybe the reader will say at this point that while consciousness is mysterious, people do have a grip on it. One may say people have a better grip on it than on anything else. One may say, a little obscurely, that it is what people actually live in. People know what it is to decide something. This subjectivity as it is called, as against the objectivity of the world, is what people know immediately and best, whatever the difficulty of analyzing it.

Let us take this line about the subject matter of human determinism, which is very common philosophically and pretty respectable. It leads to the question of whether this determinism is true.

Is Determinism True?

For about a century, this question has been tied up with what is now called neuroscience—the science of the brain and the central nervous system. If nobody or hardly anybody really believes conscious deciding and so on is just neural activity and nothing else, almost everybody who looks into the question thinks there is a close connection between brains and minds, between neural activity and conscious or mental activity.

Neuroscience has been much concerned to relate particular kinds of conscious events to particular kinds of neural events. It assigns kinds of conscious events to certain locales of the brain, if not in the simple way of early neurophysiologists. But the main point is that neuroscience has taken the brain to be subject to causation. It has taken neural events to be effects. That is, it has assumed that the most general idea of determinism, the one with which this discussion started, is true of all the events in the brain. It still does, despite thoughts brought to bear on it by a few enthusiasts for the interpretation of quantum theory also mentioned at the start.

The argument that comes out of this, in short, is that if the brain is just effects, and the mind is closely connected with the brain, intimately bound up with it, then the mind has to be just effects too. If all neural events have to happen as they do, without any other possibility, then the same is true of the conscious events that go with them—different events but events that cannot possibly be separated from the brain events. If the brain is a machine, then what is bound up with it must also be a sequence of cause and effect.

The argument going the other way is about all of reality, not just brains, and it is owed to taking physics as somehow the fundamental science. In particular it is owed to the interpretation of quantum theory mentioned already. Reality is divided into two levels, the very small particles and the like of what can be called the microworld, and then the larger things in the macroworld, say from ordinary neural events that go with decisions and the like up to explosions and tides. The main proposition is that in the microworld there are events—they really are events—that are not effects.

Therefore they are chance or random events. That is not to say that one is unable to find the explanations of why they finally happen—as distinct from finding out that they are probable or what makes them probable. To say an event is a real chance or random event is to say there is no explanation in reality of why it finally happens. God, if he tried to explain this, could not, since there is no explanation to be found. There is no such thing in the world.

The present author does not go along with this argument. One reason is that although quantum theory is very useful indeed, the interpretation of it has never been proved in the ordinary sense of the word.

A second reason has to do with the two worlds and in particular with the two worlds in so far as they have brains in them. Conscious events like decisions, as one knows, are bound up with macroworld events in the brain, the ordinary events studied in neuroscience. And to add something left implicit so far, these larger events are of course related to or somehow consist in small microworld events in the brain.

The next thing to be said is that the ordinary events investigated by neuroscientists are like all the rest of the events in the macroworld: they certainly do not seem to be and certainly are not taken to be chance or random events. Whether a transmitter substance is released by a neuron, for example, is taken to be a matter of cause and effect. It is definitely not taken as something absolutely without an explanation. This is a reason, as one has heard, for thinking that the related conscious event is also a matter of cause and effect, but that is not the present concern.

How does the ordinary neural event relate to the microevents down below, microevents that at least enter into the ordinary event? If the microevents are chance or random events, as people ask, does this translate upward into the ordinary events? Does it make the ordinary events indeterministic? For anyone who wants to deny determinism with respect to the ordinary events, there seems to be a certain dilemma here.

Either there is a kind of tight relation between the microevents and the ordinary events or there is not. Either there is translation upward or there is not. Well then, since the ordinary events are plainly a matter of cause and effect, there are two possibilities, both of them bad news for the antideterminist. (1) Since ordinary events are effects and there is translation up from below, then the microevents must also be effects—despite exactly what is said of them. (2) Or given that the ordinary events are effects, it could be that the microevents are not effects but there is no translation upward. But then the fact about microevents not being effects does not matter. It is irrelevant.

But this article has to leave that and come to the main question considered by philosophers. It is not the truth of determinism but the question of what follows if it is true. What are the consequences of determinism—consequences for people's lives, for their freedom and responsibility?

Compatibilists and Incompatibilists

As indicated earlier, the history of philosophy up to the present moment has in it compatibilists, philosophers who say determinism is compatible with freedom and hence that determinism does not matter much. But the history also has in it incompatibilists, those who say determinism is incompatible with freedom and hence determinism matters a lot. Both of these regiments of philosophers can make a case.

Who do you yourself think is not free?

One good answer, or a start on a good answer, is a man in handcuffs. Another is a man in jail. There is also the woman facing a man with a gun or a knife who has to do what he says. There is also a whole people or nation who cannot run their own affairs because a foreign army has invaded and is in control. Then there is somebody who is not subject to actual physical constraints—handcuffs or prison bars or to threats or coercion by other people—but is the victim of an inner psychological compulsion. It is very natural to include as unfree at least some drug addicts and also a woman who has to wash her hands about forty times a day. Probably you will also say someone is unfree who is argued into some conclusion or into doing something that goes against his or her whole personality.

The central thought is that freedom is an absence of coercion or constraints. Or to put it positively, freedom is an ability to decide and do what one wants. Freedom is being able to decide and act in accordance with one's own desires, not something conflicting with them. Maybe this idea of freedom as voluntariness, as one can call it, can be enlarged in various ways. Thinking of the drug addict, can one allow that he or she wants the heroin, but he or she is unfree in that he or she does not want to be the victim of that desire for heroin?

This voluntariness, if one thinks about it, is perfectly consistent with determinism. This kind of freedom can certainly exist—lots of it—even if determinism is absolutely true. What this amounts to is that this kind of freedom is not an absence of cause and effect but rather is a matter of a certain kind of effects. One is free in this sense, so to speak, when one's decisions and actions are owed to one, come from causes that are one's own desires or certain of one's desires, not from causes that are against one's desires.

One can also see that this kind of freedom goes with a kind of moral responsibility for what one does. If the cause of the disaster is in me, so to speak, then I am responsible for the disaster. Furthermore, if you want to reduce future disasters, I am the one to disapprove of or blame or put in jail.

So that is compatibilism, the idea that determinism is no threat at all to freedom. But it is certainly not the only way of thinking about these things. Ask that question again.

Who do you think is not free?

The best general answer, probably, is that it is somebody who does not have to do what he or she does. But does not that obviously mean that he or she is left room for choice, that he or she has different possibilities in front of him or her, that he or she can do otherwise than he or she does? And to come to the crucial bit, the crunch, does that not mean that he or she is not caused or necessitated to do what he or she does?

If that is not completely obvious, think of somebody who is really subject to determinism when he or she is unfaithful to his or her partner—say when he or she decides to dial a telephone number. If determinism is true, the dialing had to happen because of certain causes, and those causes had to happen because of still earlier ones, and so on back—say to before the person was born. The dialing could only be up to the person in question if those causes before he or she was born were up to him or her, which is impossible.

So, very differently, if somebody is free and responsible in dialing a telephone number, that must be something that is just inconsistent with determinism. It must be that the dialing is not just an effect or rather that it is owed to something that is not just an effect. It must be owed to an act of will. It must come from what philosophers call origination—very roughly, causing something without being caused to do it and thus being responsible for it in a special way.

Recent Thinking

The main philosophical dispute about determinism has been presented. It began at least as early as the seventeenth century, when the great Thomas Hobbes propounded the compatibilist case and was roundly attacked by Bishop John Bramhall. In the twentieth century the Cambridge philosopher G. E. Moore said that if one says "he could have decided otherwise," one roughly means "he would have decided otherwise if he had seen the other reasons," which is perfectly consistent with determinism. The Oxford philosopher J. L. Austin said in reply, as a cautious incompatibilist, that *if* is a tricky word and to say X if Y is not always to say that Y is a cause or a different cause or anything like that. Think of "there's a beer in the fridge if you want one."

One will find new arguments, or anyway new versions of old arguments, in good new textbooks on determinism and freedom. Most philosophers and others who write about the subject are either compatibilists or incompatibilists. It may seem a person has to be one or the other. Either determinism is compatible with freedom or it is not. Many compatibilists are of a scientific outlook, many incompatibilists more traditional and maybe inclined to religious belief or an elevated kind of humanism.

Still, one does not actually have to join either of those regiments. A few philosophers think the idea of freedom as origination is so vague or confused that determinism can be true without there being any consequence that a serious person has to worry about. This can be distinguished, maybe, from compatibilism.

Go back to that question that was asked twice, "Who do you think is not free?" The reader may have liked both answers, the compatibilist one and the incompatibilist one. In fact if one spent some time thinking, one might have come up with both answers oneself. After all, they are not surprising or novel answers, are they? People in jail are not free, and people who do not really have two choices are not free.

Now think of what compatibilism and incompatibilism have in common. They have in common the proposition that people have one idea of freedom or maybe one important idea. Compatibilists say it is voluntariness, and incompatibilists say it is origination. But surely it is just a mistake that people—the reader and the present author and the rest of the human race, or anyway those in Western culture—have only the one idea.

The truth of the matter is that people have both and that both are important. So compatibilism and incompatibilism are both mistaken. One does not have to be either a compatibilist or an incompatibilist if it just is not true that a person has only one idea of freedom.

That gets rid of one problem but certainly not all the problems about determinism and freedom. It does not get rid of what seems the real problem. It is a kind of practical problem. If one thinks determinism is true, how is he or she to deal with the fact that he or she also wants one of his or her ideas of freedom to be true—and it can not be if determinism is true?

There is something else too, not the same. A person can believe, and not just want, that his or her life has been up to him or her in some important sense even if that person is convinced of determinism, even if he or she believes his or her life was all just effects. One can still blame himself or herself for things in something like the way that involves what he or she does not accept, freedom as origination.

Could it be that what people need to do is really go back to the beginning and think about the nature of a conscious life, think about consciousness itself? Subjectivity? Was your life up to you, and do you have to have certain feelings about it, because it involves a kind of unique world in a way dependent on you?

See also **Causation; Consciousness; Free Will, Determinism, and Predestination; Subjectivism.**

BIBLIOGRAPHY

Berofsky, Bernard, ed. *Free Will and Determinism.* New York: Harper and Row, 1966. A strong selection of papers representing mainly twentieth-century thinking.

Dennett, Daniel. *Freedom Evolves.* New York and London: Penguin, 2003. A robust and individual defense of compatibilism by a well-known philosopher.

Double, Richard. *The Non-Reality of Free Will.* Oxford and New York: Oxford University Press, 1991. A radical dissolution of the whole problem.

Honderich, Ted. *How Free Are You? The Determinism Problem.* 2nd ed. New York and Oxford: Oxford University Press, 2002. A fuller expression of the views in the entry above. Like all the books above, it contains a full bibliography on determinism and freedom.

Honderich, Ted, ed. *Essays on Freedom of Action.* London and New York: Routledge and Kegan Paul, 1973. Papers by good analytic philosophers on compatibilism and incompatibilism.

Hook, Sidney, ed. *Determinism and Freedom in the Age of Modern Science: A Philosophical Symposium.* New York: New York University Press, 1958. Another good selection of twentieth-century papers with more attention to the question of the truth of determinism.

Kane, Robert. *The Significance of Free Will.* Oxford and New York: Oxford University Press, 1996. A realistic discussion of both incompatibilism and freedom of origination.

Kane, Robert, ed. *The Oxford Handbook of Free Will.* New York and Oxford: Oxford University Press, 2001. A large, excellent, and up-to-date survey of the problem through the writings of contemporary philosophers.

Magill, Kevin. *Freedom and Experience: Self-Determination without Illusions.* New York: St. Martin's Press, 1997. Excellent and novel arguments for compatibilism.

Mele, Alfred R. *Autonomous Agents: From Self-Control to Autonomy.* New York: Oxford University Press, 1995. Neither compatibilist or incompatibilist.

Morgenbesser, Sidney, and James Walsh, eds. *Free Will.* Englewood Cliffs, N.J.: Prentice-Hall, 1962. Historical introduction to the problem. Twelve selections from across the centuries.

Pereboom, Derk. *Living without Free Will.* Cambridge, U.K., and New York: Cambridge University Press, 2001. Strong nonstandard rejection of origination.

Strawson, Galen. *Freedom and Belief.* Oxford: Clarendon, 1986. The argument that the idea of origination is so confused that there is no opposition to determinism.

Van Inwagen, Peter. *An Essay on Free Will.* Oxford: Clarendon, 1983. A much discussed defense of incompatibilism, including the argument about past causes not being up to us.

Ted Honderich

DEVELOPMENT.

Development in biology refers to the process of growth and differentiation that is characteristic of living organisms. It describes the continuous changes during the life cycle of individual organisms from the early stage of a single cell until death. *Development* also refers to what is today known as the process of evolution, the transformation of species through time. Other meanings of *development* are connected to economic and psychological processes. The German term *Entwicklung* has the same connotations, especially with respect to the two temporal processes of ontogeny (individual development) and phylogeny (evolutionary development), and its meaning also extends into artistic and literary domains (*Entwicklungsroman*).

Due to the gradual nature of developmental processes and the wide-ranging diversity of organisms (animals, plants, microbes) and modes of reproduction (sexual, asexual), it is not possible to clearly define a unique starting point of development that applies universally to all organisms. Nevertheless, development is a fundamental property of all organisms and one that sets them apart from other physical and chemical systems. In the language of molecular biology, development is the process that translates the sum of the genetic characteristics of an organism (its genotype) into the morphological, physiological, and behavioral features of an individual (its phenotype). Since the 1970s the prevailing interpretation of this process had become increasingly preformistic—the idea that the genotype largely determines the phenotype. With the twenty-first century, however, this view has gradually been replaced by a more interactive, or epigenetic, interpretation of development that sees the individual phenotype as the product of a dynamic interaction between the genotype and the various environments of an organism (cellular, organismal, physical, cultural). These recent positions in developmental biology also reflect the long-standing dichotomy of interpretations of development—preformistic and epigenetic—that characterized the scientific and philosophical discussion of the last 2,500 years.

Aristotle on Development

The (human) life cycle and several aspects of development, such as the fertilization of plants, the grafting of fruit trees, and the principle of generation, were already known in antiquity. As with so many other areas of knowledge, it was Aristotle who summarized existing knowledge and by adding his own observations created the first inclusive theory of development. Aristotle expressed his conception of development in *De generatione animalium* (The generation of animals) and in his whole corpus of zoological writings, and development played an integral part in his overall science and philosophy. Aristotle's view of the world was intrinsically dynamic, based on matter and change. Matter is always structured. Form is the realized potential of matter, its entelechy, which is already present within it. In organisms, according to Aristotle, the potential form (entelechy) is gradually realized in the course of development. This dynamic process of development, as well as the resulting organism, requires all four causes of the Aristotelian physics: the material, formal, efficient, and final causes. In embryological development, the female fluid, the menstrual blood, contributes the material cause on which the semen acts, providing the initial stimulus for the dynamic sequence of development. In the course of development the combination of male and female fluids allows the formal and efficient causes to shape the emerging potential of the organism, its telos. This entelechy of the organism, however, has been present from the very beginning as the potential of this particular form of matter (the combination of male and female fluids). In later periods the Aristotelian entelechy has often been identified with the notion of a "soul," but for Aristotle entelechy is not something separate that directs development from the outside, but rather is always already present within the emerging organism as its potential to be realized gradually.

Ideas of Development in the Seventeenth and Eighteenth Centuries: Preformism and Epigenesis

Aristotle's conception of development was shaped by what he could observe—fluids and semen at conception and the gradual emergence of form in the course of development. It is therefore only logical that the next major changes in the philosophical and scientific analysis of development are connected with emerging possibilities of observation during the seventeenth century. One instrument, in particular, played a central role in discussions about development—the microscope. The microscope allowed for the first time analysis of the constitution of those observable fluids at the beginning of development. Looking at semen with his single-lens microscope, Anton van Leeuwenhoek could see structures in the head of the spermatozoa. But what did those structures represent? In the wake of the scientific revolution, a mechanical approach dominated the sciences and medicine. William Harvey had found a mechanical solution to the circulation of blood, and generations of anatomists had analyzed the form and function of the human body in similar terms. In this context of mechanical ideas, Leeuwenhoek's observations took on a specific meaning. For some of his contemporaries, the structures inside the sperm thus represented a smaller, already preformed version of the adult organism, called an "homonculus" by some. Development then was simply a mechanical unfolding and subsequent growth of structures already present at the very beginning in either the sperm or the egg. Others, such as Harvey, continued to advocate the epigenetic position of Aristotle. These epigenesists also claimed that their views only described what they could observe.

Clearly, observations were ambiguous and often fit theory-driven expectations. Preformists were committed to a mechanical and materialistic explanation. They did not want to rely on any form of entelechy or vital force in order to account for development and were also opposed to ideas and reports of spontaneous generation. Epigenesists, on the other hand, were committed to the action of a vital force in nature. They also emphasized the role of observation and pointed out that several facts, such as the existence of hybrids or "monsters," could not easily be explained within the preformist framework. The influence of metaphysical commitments in shaping the interpretation of observations can best be seen in the mid-eighteenth-century debate between Caspar Friedrich Wolf and Charles Bonnet. Both looked at chick embryos at the same stage (twenty-eight hours after fertilization). Both described in detail what they saw—no clearly defined beating heart, for instance. And both arrived at radically different conclusions. For Wolf it was obvious that the heart would only form later due to the agency of a vital force (vis essentialis); Bonnet, on the other hand, concluded that even though he could not see it, the heart must nevertheless already be there.

Metamorphosis and Recapitulation

The eighteenth-century debates about preformism and epigenesis brought development into the spotlight of biological investigations. Ordering the known diversity of life, increasing by the day as a result of European voyages of exploration, was another major concern. For many, especially the Romantic scientists at the turn of the nineteenth century, these two areas of natural history were connected. Did the diversity of nature not arise in the course of development from similar structures? Are the creative principles in nature not the same as in the arts? Pondering these questions on a trip to Italy, the poet-philosopher-scientist Johann Wolfgang von Goethe discovered the principle of metamorphosis and established the foundations of morphology. Specifically, Goethe realized that all the diverse structures of flowering plants are transformations of one basic morphological form, the leaf. Understanding these principles of transformation, or metamorphosis, then allows the scientist or the artist to recreate all existing organic forms, as well as those that could exist but have not yet been realized. This morphological building plan (*Bauplan*) is intrinsically dynamic and developmental; it is a principle that unfolds itself in nature small and large, in the individual and the cosmos. Morphogenesis focused, for Goethe and others, on the emergence of form within a context of change.

Ideas about transformation were soon applied to species as well as individuals. In 1809 Jean-Baptiste de Lamarck published his theory of evolution, which gave development the additional meaning of the transmutation of species. For Lamarck the transmutation of species was driven by an intrinsic drive toward perfection. In this "escalator theory" of evolution, primitive forms, created spontaneously, pass through increasingly complex stages in the course of subsequent generations. The essence of nature is thus transformation, both in the course of individual development and in the generation of the diversity of life. Lamarck's theory was readily attacked, especially by his colleague George Cuvier, the founder of comparative anatomy. Cuvier had established the most sophisticated classification system of animals of his time, based on the recognition of four distinct types of animals and a strict hierarchy of systematic categories within each of these embranchements. Within this system species were considered immutable, and their relationships were defined by the degree of similarity between them.

Development was one way of explaining this similarity among species. All organisms begin their life as fertilized eggs—Karl Ernst von Baer would discover the mammalian egg in 1827—and the early stages of development also resemble each other more closely than later stages. Summarizing these observations, Johann Friedrich Meckel proposed in 1811 that the embryological stages of advanced organisms represent the adult stages of more primitive organisms. This was the first formulation of the principle of recapitulation, in which development became the causal explanation for the similarity as well as the differences between species. The evolutionary implications were obvious. Defending the clear separation of different systematic groups, Karl Ernst von Baer summarized his opposition to the principle of recapitulation in his developmental laws. He stated that no adult organism is like any embryo of another organism, that each developmental trajectory is unique, but that in each developmental sequence the more general features of the organismal structure appear earlier in development, which explains the close similarities between the early embryos of different species.

Von Baer's authority carried the day, but only briefly. In his theory of evolution as descent with modification, Charles Darwin also relied on embryological evidence, especially when he needed a mechanism that would explain the origin of new variations. Another consequence of the Darwinian theory was that the historical connections between species, their genealogy, immediately suggested an explanation for the similarity between them. The more closely two species are related to each other, the more similar they will be. Homologies, those structures that were considered the same in different organisms, could now be explained as being derived from a common ancestor. The only practical problem was that the genealogical relations between species were not obvious and needed to be inferred based on the similarity between them.

Studying the development of different species offered a way to escape this circularity of reasoning. Ernst Haeckel postulated that ontogeny recapitulates phylogeny, that the developmental sequence of an individual parallels the historical sequence of evolution. For Haeckel development was simultaneously a record of history and an explanation of diversity, as new structures would occur as terminal additions in the developmental process. Development also provided a way to establish ho-

mologies; those structures that were derived from the same embryological precursors (anlagen) could be considered to be homologies and used for the reconstruction of phylogenies. Haeckel's ideas, largely discredited today, were extremely influential in the second half of the nineteenth century and led to many proposals about the shape of the "tree of life."

Entwicklungsmechanik and Developmental Genetics

The Haeckel program in evolutionary morphology, with its descriptive outlook and its tendency to speculate about phylogenetic relationships, left many younger scientists dissatisfied. They sought a mechanistic understanding of development, more in tune with the emphasis on experimentation and causal interpretation that characterized sciences like physiology or chemistry. Championed by Wilhelm Roux, this new approach to the study of development dominated late-nineteenth-century biology in Germany and the United States. In detailed and technically demanding experiments, biologists tested the influence of physical and chemical conditions such as gravitation, pressure, temperature, and varying chemical concentrations in the environment on development of select model organisms (mostly amphibians and marine invertebrates) whose free-living embryos were easy to manipulate. This new experimental program in embryology also benefited from the newly founded marine research stations. Many of these experiments were only possible in well-equipped laboratories in close proximity to the diverse biological material of the sea.

The canonical experimental styles in *Entwicklungsmechanik* were the destruction of certain parts of the embryo and the transplantation of specific tissues between and within embryos. Both kinds of experiments disrupted normal development and allowed researchers to discover the effects of certain parts of the embryo. Puncturing one of the two cells in a two-cell-stage frog embryo, Roux found in 1888 that only half an embryo developed. In his mosaic theory of development he then argued that during differentiation the determining factors, which are all present in the fertilized egg, are gradually distributed among the daughter cells. In a similar vein, August Weismann argued in 1892 for the separation of the germ line, which he saw as retaining the full developmental potential and being passed on through the generations, and the soma, those elements of an organism that undergo differentiation. Weismann, too, thought that an unequal distribution of hereditary material accounts for the differentiation of cells during development.

When Hans Driesch repeated Roux's experiment, shaking sea urchin embryos apart during the two- and four-cell stages, he observed the formation of complete, albeit smaller, pluteus larvae. Driesch began to think that development could not be interpreted in strictly mechanical terms. The embryos' demonstrated ability to regulate their own developmental sequence led him to argue that organisms are harmonious equipotential systems and not just complex physico-chemical machines. Organisms as individuals are instead characterized by an irreducible telos, their entelechy, that shows itself in their regulatory abilities. Driesch subsequently embraced a form of neovitalism.

The vast majority of biologists, however, did not accept Driesch's philosophizing but remained committed to experimental study of development, mapping cell lineages and investigating fates of transplanted tissues. It was in this context that Hans Spemann and Hilde Mangold found in 1924 that a small region near the dorsal lip transplanted into the ventral side (belly) of a newt embryo could organize a second set of body axes, thus resulting in a "Siamese-twin-like" embryo. They called this specific region of the embryo the organizer, as it was capable of organizing the basic form of the full organism. In addition, researchers demonstrated that interactions between certain tissues such as mesoderm and ectoderm led to the differentiation of phenotypic structures such as the lens of a vertebrate eye, in a phenomenon called induction. The search began for the specific chemical properties of what was assumed to be the material organizer.

It was also clear that ultimately these developmentally active substances would have to be the products of heredity, since the inherited nuclear chromosomes and the genes they presumably carried, together with the material inside the egg, are what is passed on to the next generation. Research programs in developmental and physiological genetics investigated these questions and, after long and painstaking research, could identify specific causal chains, from a gene product to a phenotypic effect. Mutants, such as eye-color mutants of moths and flies, were the preferred experimental systems for this line of research. In 1940 a group headed by the biochemist Adolf Butenandt and the biologist Alfred Kühn were the first to identify and chemically characterize the substance that induced the red-eye phenotype in the moth *Epestia kühniella*.

After World War II, developmental biology gradually transformed itself into developmental genetics, especially after the techniques of molecular biology allowed researchers to study genes in their cellular context. One of the first genetic systems studied molecularly was the so-called lac-operon system, which regulates the expression of a lactose-digesting enzyme inside a bacterial cell. This focus on regulation continued as more and more regulatory networks of genes were found. In the context of molecular biology, development—the growth and differentiation of an organism—had been redefined as a problem of the regulation of gene expression. Aristotle's epigenesis had given way to the mechanistic preformationism of the seventeenth and eighteenth centuries and had come around again to a more sophisticated blend of preformism through heredity and epigenesis through development.

Evolutionary Developmental Biology

During the last decades of the twentieth century, evolutionary developmental biology emerged to reintegrate the two temporal processes within biology, development and evolution. Evolutionary developmental biology (Evo-Devo) is based on the recognition that all genetic changes must be expressed during development in order to produce a phenotype and thus amount to observable evolutionary changes. Development is thus the mechanism that produces the raw material of phenotypic evolution. Phenotypic evolution, in contrast, appears to be highly constrained. Of all the possible forms (the total morphospace), only a small number are actually realized. Furthermore, the diversity of life is organized in a nested hierarchy, whereby millions of species can be subsumed within a few dozen phyla, each characterized by a basic body plan (*Bauplan*). In other words, the many mutational changes of genotypes are translated into a much smaller number of phenotypic variants.

In addition, discoveries since the 1980s have lent further support to the idea that the number of developmental modules (transcription factors, such as Homeobox genes and regulatory networks) is relatively small. Furthermore, these developmental modules have been conserved through millions of years during evolution, in that flatworms, insects, and mammals share a number of regulatory genes. Thus, a limited "genetic toolkit of development" produces the astonishing diversity of life. These findings have serious consequences for the age-old discussions of preformism versus epigenesis. The fact that a small number of genetic elements is responsible for the enormous diversity of life indicates that development is essentially a problem of regulation and the interaction of genetic and environmental factors. In other words, the effects of genes in development are largely context dependent. Whether a specific transcription factor turns on a gene that triggers a cascade leading to the formation of an eye or whether it establishes the gradient for differentiation of the arm, for example, depends on the specific cellular and organismal context. In addition, environmental factors, which can affect developmental plasticity, are increasingly recognized as important. The current conception of development is thus largely epigenetic, within the context of inherited material genes.

Human and Social Dimensions of Development

Interpretations of individual development have also had powerful social impacts, especially as we have learned more about human embryology and reproductive biology. For those who hold the strongest versions of the view that each individual organism begins from unformed material, the emphasis on epigenetic emergence of form suggests that investing in "nurture" will pay off. It is worth investing in parenting that requires time and energy because this can shape the developmental process. In contrast, those who accept the view that the organism has some clear defining point at which it begins as an individual, and that its form or individuality is in some important sense already set, see much less value in investing in trying to shape what develops. Development in these cases is largely a matter of playing out the intrinsic causes. The dominant version of this interpretation maintains, of course, that heredity sets the individual's differentiation and that development is really just a matter of growth.

Though no respectable scientist today would hold either of these extreme interpretations, there are strong preferences depending on whether the researcher is a genetic determinist or a proponent of developmental regulation. Historically, we can find some supporters for almost any interpretation along the range of possibilities. The public's very deeply held views about individual as well as species development make it all the more important that we have a clear understanding of the historical, philosophical, and biological contexts for developmental ideas and that we understand the social implications.

See also **Biology; Evolution; Life; Life Cycle; Science, History of; Scientific Revolution.**

BIBLIOGRAPHY

Bowler, Peter J. *The Eclipse of Darwinism: Anti-Darwinian Evolution Theories in the Decades around 1900.* Baltimore: Johns Hopkins University Press, 1989.

Carroll, Sean B., Jennifer K. Grenier, and Scott D. Weatherbee. *From DNA to Diversity: Molecular Genetics and the Evolution of Animal Design.* Oxford, U.K.: Blackwell Science, 2001.

Correia, Clara Pinto. *The Ovary of Eve: Egg and Sperm and Preformation.* Chicago: University of Chicago Press, 1997.

Gilbert, Scott F., ed. *A Conceptual History of Modern Embryology.* Baltimore: Johns Hopkins University Press, 1994.

Hamburger, Viktor. *The Heritage of Experimental Embryology: Hans Spemann and the Organizer.* New York: Oxford University Press, 1993.

Horder, T. J., J. A. Witkowski, and C. C. Wylie, eds. *A History of Embryology.* Cambridge, U.K.: Cambridge University Press, 1986.

Jahn, Ilse. *Geschichte der Biologie.* Heidelberg and Berlin: Gustav Fischer Verlag, 2000.

Krauße, Erika. *Ernst Haeckel.* Leipzig, Germany: Teubner, 1984.

Maienschein, Jane. "Competing Epistemologies and Developmental Biology." In *Biology and Epistemology,* edited by Richard Creath and Jane Maienschein, 122–137. Cambridge, U.K.: Cambridge University Press, 2000.

———. *Whose View of Life?* Cambridge, Mass.: Harvard University Press, 2003.

Richards, Robert J. *The Meaning of Evolution: The Morphological Construction and Ideological Reconstruction of Darwin's Theory.* Chicago: University of Chicago Press, 1992.

Roe, Shirley A. *Matter, Life, and Generation: Eighteenth-Century Embryology and the Haller-Wolff Debate.* New York: Cambridge University Press, 1981.

Manfred D. Laubichler
Jane Maienschein

DIALOGUE AND DIALECTICS.

This entry includes two subentries:

Socratic
Talmudic

SOCRATIC

Socrates (c. 470–399 B.C.E.) developed a method of inquiry and instruction that involved question and answer, or the "Socratic method." Although Socrates professed to be ignorant of the answers to his questions, his questioning and testing of the answers given were designed to expose the weakness of the opinions held by his interlocutors and to refine those opinions. While Socrates left no writings of his own, the Socratic method is demonstrated in the writings of several of his pupils, especially his most famous pupil, Plato (c. 428–348 or 347 B.C.E.). The Socratic dialogues of Plato present Socrates in conversation with known contemporaries. These early dialogues involve question and answer, but most of these arrive at no definite conclusion or firm agreement.

The Greek noun *dialogos* derives from the verb *dialegesthai,* meaning "to enter into a conversation." The term *dialectic,* or the art of argumentation (*dialectike techne*), is derived from

> If, after this conversation, you try to become pregnant with other conceptions, and if, Theaetetus, you succeed, you will become great with better conceptions. And, if you are empty, you will prove less irksome to your companions and a gentler person, since in your new wisdom you will not think that you know what you do not know. These are the limits of my art.
>
> SOURCE: Socrates in *Theaetetus* 210B–C.

this verb as well, but in the case of Socratic dialectic the relevant Greek term is *elegkhos* (*elenchus*). Elenchus means a testing, and, since those tested by Socratic questioning are often shown inadequate in their responses, it comes to mean refutation.

The Literature of Socratic Conversations

In Greek literature, dialogue, or argument, is as old as Homer and the exchange between Achilles and Agamemnon in *Iliad* 1; it is a salient feature of both Attic comedy and tragedy. Philosophical dialogue began with the conversations Aristotle (384–322 B.C.E.) knew as the *Sokratikoi logoi,* a form of imitation (*mimesis*) that captured the conversations of Socrates. Although some of the dialogues of Plato and Xenophon (c. 431–c. 352 B.C.E.) claim to record a conversation of the historical Socrates and an interlocutor (or interlocutors), all the Socratic dialogues are literary fictions based on a reality we shall never recover.

The literary presentation of philosophical conversation had antecedents in the prose comedies of the Sicilian, Epicharmus (c. 530–c. 440 B.C.E.). Our first example of a Socratic conversation comes from Aristophanes's *Clouds* (423 B.C.E.), in which a fictional Socrates tests the intelligence and character of an older pupil. It is clear from their exchange that Socratic questioning was designed to test not only the intelligence but also the character of an interlocutor.

The "invention" of the dialogue form.

In antiquity there was a dispute over who was the "inventor" of the dialogue form as a vehicle for philosophy. Our knowledge of the rival claims to this honor goes back to Aristotle, who in his dialogue *On Poets* mentions Zeno of Elea (c. 495–c. 430 B.C.E.) as the founder of what he calls dialectic and an unknown Alexamenós as the "inventor" of the mimetic dialogue. According to Diogenes Laertius, a 3rd century B.C.E. Greek writer and source of information about the Greek philosophers, an Athenian cobbler called Simon was the first to represent the conversations of Socrates in "dialectic" form. Like Xenophon, Simon was regarded as a stenographer of conversations he merely overheard.

We know something too of the Socratic dialogues of Antisthenes (c. 445–c. 365 B.C.E.) and Aeschines Socraticus (4th cent. B.C.E.). Antisthenes certainly wrote before Plato. We have several citations from Aeschines' *Alcibiades,* which gives an example of the kind of characterization we find so brilliantly displayed in the Socratic dialogues of Plato. Xenophon's dialogues probably came after Plato's, during the long period of Xenophon's exile from Athens (a city he left in 401). These include his *Apology, Symposium, Oeconomicus,* the conversations of Books 2 through 4 of the *Memorabilia* (Memoirs of Socrates's conversations), and a brief passage from his *Cyropaedia* where we meet an Armenian Socrates (3.31.10–14; 38). Both Antisthenes and Xenophon wrote quasi–philosophical dialogues in which Socrates was not a speaker; Antisthenes's *Cyrus* and Xenophon's *Hiero* are examples.

Thus, by the time he began to write his dialogues, Plato was one of many Socratics and writers of Socratic dialogues, but it was he who transformed the dialogue into a powerful instrument of philosophical inquiry. In his works, there is a distinction between the "Socratic" dialogues, in which Socrates figures as the principal speaker, and the late dialogues, in which he is either present but mainly silent (*Sophist, Statesman,* and the *Timaeus/Critias*) or from which he is absent (the *Laws*). Symptomatic of his disappearance in the Platonic dialogues are the long unbroken speeches of a dominant character that take up most of the *Timaeus/Critias* and the *Laws,* where we encounter Timaeus, Critias, and a stranger from Athens.

Alternatives to dialogue. To appreciate the radical character of the Platonic dialogue, it is necessary to consider the alternatives to philosophical discourse available to Plato as he began to write his first Socratic dialogues, beginning perhaps with the *Apology of Socrates,* written just after the execution of his "older friend" in 399 B.C.E. In the context of the democratic culture of fifth–century Athens, alternatives included the long display speeches the sophists delivered before large audiences. Plato's *Protagoras* is a good example of this form of exposition given by a skilled speaker who brooks no interruption or interrogation. Another alternative was the philosophical treatise or poem. Anaxagoras (c. 500–c. 428 B.C.E.), a contemporary of Socrates, reveals no evidence of dialogue in his *On Nature.* The rhetoric of early philosophical poetry tends to unbroken hierophantic pronouncements by a philosopher poet who claims divine authority for what he says, as in the case of Parmenides (b. c. 515 B.C.E.) and Empedocles (c. 490–430 B.C.E.), who actually claims that he is a god. Heraclitus (c. 540–c. 480 B.C.E.) claims his *logos* (discourse) is an expression of the higher *Logos* (principle of intelligibility).

As for "dialectic," the short anonymous treatise entitled *Dissoi Logoi* (Arguments for and against) is contemporary with the young Plato; but here, as in Protagoras's (c. 485–410 B.C.E.) more famous *Antilogiai,* dialectic or the art of argument serves as a primer for developing the ability to argue pro and con on any question. Some of the arguments of the *Dissoi Logoi* are important to the Platonic dialogues: for example, the question of whether virtue (*aretē*) can be taught is addressed in Plato's *Meno.* This handbook is an example of the training in logic given

in the Academy and recorded in the eight books of Aristotle's *Topics and Sophistical Refutations.* All these works exercise the young in debate. They treat rules and types of argument (known as *topoi*), but these arguments are disembodied and lack the characterization that is so important a feature of the Platonic dialogues.

The Socratic Dialogues of Plato

Because of their success, the originality of Plato's Socratic dialogues is easily forgotten. More than any other Socratic, Plato invested most of his Socratic dialogues in a historical context that grounds the questions they pursue in a historical reality. Likewise, his dramatic genius in characterization of Socrates and his interlocutors is sometimes overlooked. The opening of the *Charmides* gives a good example of Plato's early style. Socrates has just returned from Boeotia and the Athenian retreat of 425. He engages in a long conversation on the nature of prudent self–restraint (*sophrosyne*) with two young men whose courage was yet to be tried, Charmides and Critias, both of whom were to be tested as they emerged as two of the "Thirty Tyrants" in 404. Here historical context, characterization, and Plato's philosophical art of dramatic irony are all in evidence. Unlike the dialogues of the other Socratics, Plato's are polyphonic in that they often involve a large cast of characters.

It has long been thought that Plato's *Apology* represents what Socrates actually said in court, but it is more likely the posthumous vindication of Socrates' life. There is now a growing commitment among interpreters of Plato to understand the "literary" qualities of the Platonic dialogues in terms of Plato's philosophical intentions. And there is now less of a tendency to see Socrates (or the Eleatic Stranger of the *Sophist* and *Statesman* or the Athenian Stranger of the *Laws*) as a "spokesman" for Plato or, in the case of the earlier "Socratic" dialogues, to take Plato at Socrates' word.

The case of the *Republic* is an example of the interpretative dangers of mistaking Socrates, who has a great deal to say about the ideal state and the ideal "state" of the individual soul, for Plato, who remains silent and anonymous in all his dialogues. The assent of Plato's brothers, Glaukon and Adeimantus, to the long series of propositions Socrates advances, are easily reversed (as the opening of book 5 of the *Republic* makes clear). Here and earlier, assent to the odd proposal that the women and children of the guardian class of Socrates' state should be held in common (*Republic* 4.423B) is called into question and the dialogue is opened suddenly to the prospect of women guardians and a philosopher king (the questions of books 5–7). Like Socratic questioning, the dialogues of Plato are all open ended.

The Socratic method. The "Socratic method" is often held up as a model for education by educators, but perhaps with insufficient awareness of how complex it is. In Plato's Socratic dialogues, there is no evidence of an interlocutor being moved by Socrates to abandon a vitiated point of view in search for a view that is philosophically superior. In the case of the early series of dialogues that question four Greek virtues, there is no way out of perplexity. The Socratic *elenchus* or cross examination usually ends up by showing that a general claim made by an interlocutor has exceptions or conceals hidden assumptions that the interlocutor cannot accept. For this reason the examination of self–restraint in the *Charmides,* virtue in the *Meno,* courage in the *Laches,* and the unity of the virtues in the *Protagoras,* is termed "aporetic." That is, they provide no way (*poros*) to a solution; yet they provide the stimulus of frustration. These early dialogues test Plato's "audience of second intent" more than they test Socrates' interlocutors. In the dialogues that lead to the *Republic,* in the *Theaetetus* (On knowledge), *Sophist,* and *Statesmen,* and, indeed, in all his dialogues, Plato seems to be offering a philosophical challenge and training to his readers to come to their own solutions to the problems he raises.

Socrates' maieutic art. Plato clearly felt that it was impossible in one–on–one conversation or in a conversation with a great variety of possible readers to inculcate philosophical understanding. The most vigorous of Socrates' opponents (Thrasymachos in the *Republic,* Kallikles in the *Gorgias,* and Zeno in the *Parmenides*) refuse to agree with Socrates after a long give–and–take. The genius of the "Socratic method" is that it involves frustration, not inculcation. It prompts in the interlocutor a dissatisfaction with his settled convictions.

At the end of the *Theaetetus* Socrates represents himself as the son of a midwife who is himself a midwife to the mental offspring of his interlocutors. He can either help deliver a superior conception or induce a kind of modesty in the recognition of one's barrenness. This is his maieutic art (Gk. *maieutikos,* of midwifery). Socrates recognizes the claims to a knowledge of inspired men of the past and present. They possess a knowledge they can transmit; Socrates can only deliver knowledge already present in the individual. Thus, in the *Republic* he compares his method to a protreptic turning a companion to the light rather than cramming vision into his eyes. Such are Plato's descriptions of the "Socratic method."

See also **Philosophy, History of; Philosophy, Moral: Ancient; Philosophy of Mind: Ancient and Medieval; Platonism.**

BIBLIOGRAPHY

Bakhtin, Mikhail M. *The Dialogic Imagination: Four Essays.* Edited by Michael Holquist. Translated by Caryl Emerson. Austin: University of Texas Press, 1981.

Blondell, Ruby. *The Play of Character in Plato's Dialogues.* New York: Cambridge University Press, 2002.

Clay, Diskin. "The Origins of the Platonic Dialogue." In *The Socratic Movement,* edited by Paul A. Vander Waerdt. Ithaca and New York: Cornell University Press, 1994.

Friedländer, Paul. *Plato: An Introduction.* Translated by Hans Meyerhoff. New York: Pantheon, 1958. Translation of *Platon: Seinswahrheit und Lebenswirklichkeit.*

Giannantoni, Gabriele, ed. *Socratis et Socraticorum Reliquiae.* 4 vols. Naples: Bibliopolis, 1990.

Griswold, Charles H., Jr. Introduction to *Platonic Writings/ Platonic Readings.* University Park: Pennsylvania State University Press, 2002. Originally published 1988.

Kahn, Charles H. *Plato and the Socratic Dialogue: The Philosophical Use of a Literary Form.* Cambridge, U.K.: Cambridge University Press, 1996.

Nightingale, Andrea. *Genres in Dialogue: Plato and the Construct of Philosophy.* Cambridge, U.K.: Cambridge University Press, 1995.

Vlastos, Gregory. *Socratic Studies,* edited by Myles Burnyeat. Cambridge: Cambridge University Press, 1994. See "The Socratic Elenchus: Method Is All."

Diskin Clay

TALMUDIC

The Talmuds are compendia of commentaries, legal opinions, and sayings by and about rabbis of the first six centuries C.E. There are two: the Palestinian (or Jerusalem) Talmud (c. 400) and the Babylonian Talmud, or Bavli (c. 600). Both are arranged as commentaries, tractate by tractate, of the Mishnah—the compendium of the law of Judaism—itself a collection of legal sayings of rabbis and sages from up to the third century B.C.E.

Dialectical argument is a tool of systematic analysis. In the Talmudic framework, everything is in the moving, or dialectical, argument, the give–and–take of unsparing rationality, which, through their own capacity to reason, later generations are expected to reconstitute. Following the argument as set forth in the Talmud affords access to the issues, the argument, and the prevailing rationality. The Bavli sets forth not so much a record of what was said as a set of notes that permit the engaged reader to reconstruct thought and recapitulate reason and criticism.

A dialectical argument sets forth give–and–take in which parties to the argument counter one another's arguments in a progression of exchanges, often in what seems like an infinite progress to an indeterminate conclusion. A dialectical argument does not merely address the problem and a single solution; it takes up the problem and the various ways by which a solution may be reached. It involves not merely questions and answers or exchanges of opinion, a set–piece of two positions, with an analysis of each, such as formal dialogue exposes with elegance. Moving in an unfolding analytical argument, it explains why this and not that, then why not that but rather the other thing; and onward from the other thing to the thing beyond that—a linear argument in constant forward motion. A dialectical argument is not static and merely expository, but dynamic and always contentious. It is not an endless argument, an argument for the sake of arguing, but a way to cover a variety of cases in testing a principle common to them all.

The Role of Dialectics in the Bavli

The Bavli translates Pentateuchal narratives and laws into a systematic account of Israel's entire social order. In its topical presentations of thirty–seven of the Mishnah's sixty–three topical tractates, the Bavli portrays not so much how people are supposed to live—this the Mishnah does—as how they ought to think, the right way of analyzing circumstance and tradition alike. The Bavli shows a way of thinking and talking and rationally arguing about reform. When we follow not only what the sages of the Bavli say, but also how they express themselves, their modes of critical thought and—above all—their examples of uncompromising, rigorous ar-

AN EXAMPLE OF A DIALECTICAL ARGUMENT

The Mishnah is a law code organized by topics, and Baba Mesia—the Middle Gate—concerns civil law, in the present case, torts and damages and contradictory claims.

Mishnah Baba Mesia 1:1

A. Two lay hold of a cloak—

B. this one says, "I found it!—

C. and that one says, "I found it!"—

D. this one says, "It's all mine!"—

E. and that one says, "It's all mine!"—

F. this one takes an oath that he possesses no less a share of it than half,

G. and that one takes an oath that he possesses no less a share of it than half,

H. and they divide it up.

Bavli Baba Mesia 5B–6A

[5b] IV.1. A. This one takes an oath that he possesses no less a share of it than half, [and that one takes an oath that he possesses no less a share of it than half, and they divide it up]

B. Is it concerning the portion that he claims he possesses that he takes the oath, or concerning the portion that he does not claim to possess? [Samuel Daiches, *Baba Mesia* (London, 1948), ad loc.: "The implication is that the terms of the oath are ambiguous. By swearing that his share in it is not 'less than half,' the claimant might mean that it is not even a third or a fourth (which is 'less

than half'), and the negative way of putting it would justify such an interpretation. He could therefore take this oath even if he knew that he had no share in the garment at all, while he would be swearing falsely if he really had a share in the garment that is less than half, however small that share might be]."

C. Said R. Huna, "It is that he says, 'By an oath! I possess in it a portion, and I possess in it a portion that is no more than half a share of it.'" [The claimant swears that his share is at least half (Daiches, *Baba Mesia,* ad loc.)].

D. Then let him say, "By an oath! The whole of it is mine!"

E. But are we going to give him the whole of it? [Obviously not, there is another claimant, also taking an oath.]

F. Then let him say, "By an oath! Half of it is mine!"

G. That would damage his own claim [which was that he owned the whole of the cloak, not only half of it].

H. But here too is it not the fact that, in the oath that he is taking, he impairs his own claim? [After all, he here makes explicit the fact that he owns at least half of it. What happened to the other half?]

I. [Not at all.] For he has said, "The whole of it is mine!" [And, he further proceeds,] "And as to your contrary view, By an oath, I do have a share in it, and that share is no less than half!"

SOURCE: Jacob Neusner, *Tractate Baba Mesia.*

gument, we encounter a massive, concrete instance of the power of intellect to purify and refine. For the sages of the Bavli, alongside the great masters of Greek philosophy and their Christian and Muslim continuators, exercise the power of rational and systematic inquiry, tenacious criticism, the exchange not only of opinion but also of reason for opinion, argument, and evidence. They provide a model of how intellectuals take up the tasks of social criticism and pursue the disciplines of the mind in the service of the social order. This explains the widespread interest in the Bavli as shown by repeated translations of, and introductions to, that protean document. Not an antiquarian interest in a long–ago society, nor an ethnic concern with heritage and tradition, but

a vivid and contemporary search for plausible examples of the rational world order, animate the unprecedented interest of the world of culture in the character (and also the contents) of the Bavli.

The Bavli embodies applied reason and practical logic in quest of the holy society. That model of criticism and reason in the encounter with social reform is unique. The kind of writing that the Bavli represents has serviceable analogues but no known counterpart in the literature of world history and philosophy, theology, religion, and law. That is because the Bavli sets forth not only decisions and other wise and valuable information, but the choices that face reasonable persons and the bases for deciding matters in one way rather than in some other. And the Bavli records the argument, the constant, contentious, uncompromising argument, that endows with vitality the otherwise merely informative corpus of useful insight. "Let logic pierce the mountain"—that is what sages say.

Talmudic Dialectics and Philosophical Dialectics

In that aspect, the Bavli recalls the great philosophical dialogues of ancient and medieval times. Those familiar with the dialogues of Socrates as set forth by Plato—those wonderful exchanges concerning abstractions such as truth and beauty, goodness and justice—will find familiar the notion of dialectical argument, with its unfolding, ongoing give–and–take. But Talmudic dialectics differ in two ways. First, they deal with concrete cases and laws, not abstract concepts. Second, the meandering and open–ended character of Talmudic dialectics contrasts with the formal elegance, the perfection of exposition, that characterizes Plato's writings. While the Talmud's presentation of contrary positions and exposition of the strengths and weaknesses of each will hardly surprise philosophers, the inclusion of the model of extensive exposition of debate is sometimes puzzling.

The Bavli's texts of dialectical arguments are in effect notes, which we are expected to know how to use in the reconstruction of the issues under discussion, the arguments under exposition. That means we must make ourselves active partners in the thought–processes that they document. Not only is the argument open–ended, so too the bounds of participation know no limits. Indeed, the Bavli declines to tell us everything we need to know. It exhibits the remarkable confidence of its compilers that generations over time will join in the argument they precipitate, grasp the principles they embody in concrete cases, and find compelling the issues they deem urgent. It is that remarkable faith in the human intellect of age succeeding age that lifts the document above time and circumstance and renders it immortal. In transcending circumstance of time, place, and condition, the Bavli attains a place in the philosophical, not merely historical, curriculum of culture. That is why the Bavli makes every generation of its heirs and continuators into a partner in the ongoing reconstruction of reasoned thought, each generation adding its commentary to the ever welcoming text.

See also **Dialogue and Dialectics: Socratic; Judaism; Philosophy; Sacred Texts.**

BIBLIOGRAPHY
Neusner, Jacob. *The Divisions of Damages and Holy Things and Tractate Niddah.* Vol. 2 of *Talmudic Dialectics: Types and Forms.* Atlanta: Scholars Press for South Florida Studies in the History of Judaism, 1995.
———. *Introduction. Tractate Berakhot and the Divisions of Appointed Times and Women.* Vol. 1 of *Talmudic Dialectics: Types and Forms.* Atlanta: Scholars Press for South Florida Studies in the History of Judaism, 1995.
———. *Tractate Baba Mesia.* Vol. 21 of *The Talmud of Babylonia: An Academic Commentary.* Atlanta: Scholars Press for USF Academic Commentary Series, 1990.

Jacob Neusner

DIASPORAS.

This entry includes two subentries:

African Diaspora
Jewish Diaspora

AFRICAN DIASPORA

The African diaspora, together with the Jewish diaspora—the etymological and epistemological source of the term *diaspora*—enjoys pride of place in the increasingly crowded pantheon of diaspora studies. Studies of African diasporas can be divided into two broad categories. First, there are those that discuss the patterns of dispersal of African peoples around the world and the kinds of diasporic identities these populations developed in their new locations. Distinctions are increasingly drawn between the "historic" and "contemporary" or "new" African diasporas, referring respectively to diasporas formed before and during the twentieth century. Second, some studies are concerned with analyzing the various linkages that the diasporas have maintained with Africa. Here emphasis is on the demographic, cultural, economic, political, ideological, and iconographic flows.

The term *African diaspora* gained currency from the 1950s and 1960s in the English-speaking world, especially the United States. As pointed out by George Shepperson, none of the major intellectual forerunners of African diaspora studies, from Edward Blyden (1832–1912), the influential nineteenth-century Caribbean-born Liberian thinker, to W. E. B. Du Bois (1868–1963), the renowned African-American scholar-activist, used the term *African diaspora.* The Negritude writers from Francophone Africa and the Caribbean also did not use it. Instead, the term used to define and mobilize African populations globally was *Pan-Africanism.* One of the challenges in African diaspora studies, then, has been to overcome an American and English language-centered model of identity for African diasporas globally.

Defining Diasporas

There are several conceptual difficulties in defining the African diaspora—indeed, in defining the term *diaspora.* Contemporary theorizations of the term *diaspora* tend to be preoccupied with problematizing the relationship between diaspora and nation and the dualities or multiplicities of diasporic identity or subjectivity; they are inclined to be condemnatory or celebratory of transnational mobility and hybridity. In many cases, the term *diaspora* is used in a fuzzy, ahistorical, and uncritical manner in which all manner of movements and migrations between countries and even within countries are included and no adequate attention is paid to the historical conditions and experiences that produce diasporic communities and consciousness—how dispersed populations become self-conscious diaspora communities.

Various analytical schemas have been suggested for diaspora studies in general and African diaspora studies in particular. Based on what he regards as the nine common features of a diaspora, Robin Cohen distinguishes between the "victim diasporas" (Africans and Armenians), "labor diasporas" (Indi-

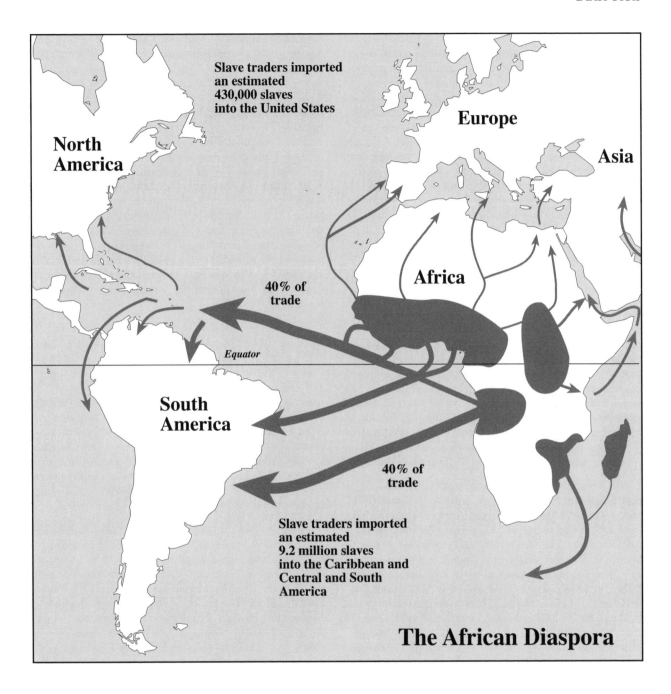

Slave traders imported
an estimated
430,000 slaves
into the United States

North
America

Europe

Asia

Africa

40% of
trade

Equator

South
America

40% of
trade

Slave traders imported
an estimated
9.2 million slaves
into the Caribbean and
Central and South
America

The African Diaspora

ans), "imperial diasporas" (British), "trade diasporas" (Chinese and Lebanese), and "cultural diasporas" (the Caribbean). Kim Butler, a historian of the African diaspora in Brazil, suggests another schema for diasporan study divided into five dimensions: first, reasons for and conditions of the dispersal; second, relationship with homeland; third, relationship with host lands; fourth, interrelationships within diasporan groups; and finally, comparative study of different diasporas.

Diaspora refers simultaneously to a process, a condition, a space, and a discourse: the continuous processes by which a diaspora is made, unmade, and remade; the changing conditions in which it lives and expresses itself; the places where it is molded and imagined; and the contentious ways in which

it is studied and discussed. In short, diaspora is a state of being and a process of becoming, a condition and consciousness located in the shifting interstices of "here" and "there," a voyage of negotiation between multiple spatial and social identities. Created out of movement—dispersal from a homeland—the diaspora is sometimes affirmed through another movement—engagement with the homeland. Movement, it could be argued, then, in its literal and metaphorical senses is at the heart the diasporic condition, beginning with the dispersal itself and culminating with reunification. The spaces in between are marked by multiple forms of engagement between the diaspora and the homeland—of movement, of travel between a "here" and a "there" both in terms of time and space.

New Dictionary of the History of Ideas

African Dispersals

It is quite common in academic and popular discourses to homogenize and racialize the African diaspora and see it in terms of the Atlantic experience of forced migration and in terms of "black" identity. The first ignores African dispersals and diasporas in Asia and Europe, some of which predated the formation of the Atlantic diasporas and which emerged out of both forced and free migrations. The second is largely a legacy of Eurocentric constructions of the continent whereby sub-Saharan Africa, from which North Africa is excised, is seen as "Africa proper," in the words of Georg Wilhelm Friedrich Hegel (1770–1831). Early-twenty-first-century research has tried to go beyond these limitations.

There are numerous dispersals associated with African peoples over time. Colin Palmer has identified at least six: three in prehistoric and ancient times (beginning with the great exodus that began about 100,000 years ago from the continent to other continents) and three in modern times, including those associated with the Indian Ocean trade to Asia, the Atlantic slave trade to the Americas, and the contemporary movement of Africans and peoples of African descent to various parts of the globe. While such a broad historical conception of diaspora might be a useful reminder of common origins and humanity, it stretches the notion of diaspora too far beyond analytical recognition to be terribly useful. So most scholars tend to focus on the "modern" historical streams of the global African diasporas. Studies of African diasporas focus disproportionately on the Atlantic world, but literature is growing on the Indian Ocean and Mediterranean diasporas.

The historic African diasporas can be divided into four categories in terms of their places of dispersal: the intra-Africa, Indian Ocean, Mediterranean, and Atlantic diasporas. The challenges of studying intra-Africa diasporas meaningfully are quite daunting, given the extraordinary movements of people across the continent over time. Clearly it will not do to see every migration across the continent as a prelude to the formation of some diaspora. More fruitful is to focus on communities that have constituted themselves or are constituted by their host societies as diasporas within historical memory. And here may be distinguished five types based on the primary reason of dispersal: the trading diasporas (the Hausa and Doula in western Africa); the slave diasporas (West Africans in North Africa and East Africans on the Indian Ocean islands); the conquest diasporas (the Nguni in southern Africa); the refugee diasporas (e.g., from the Yoruba wars of the early nineteenth century); and the pastoral diasporas (the Fulani and Somali in the Sahelian zones of western and eastern Africa).

These intra-Africa diasporas have been studied in their own right, often without using the term *diaspora* except for the trading diasporas and the slave diasporas. But it should not be forgotten that the other diasporas, insofar as they existed, filtered into the historic diasporas or served as historical switching stations for the emergence of the new African diasporas in the twentieth century. At the same time, the formation of colonial borders and new national identities reinforced their diasporic identities and sometimes pushed them into the circuits of international migration.

African Diasporas in Asia and Europe

Recent studies clearly demonstrate that the African diaspora has very old roots in Asia, to which Africans traveled as traders, sailors, soldiers, bureaucrats, clerics, bodyguards, concubines, servants, and slaves. Hence unlike the historic Atlantic diasporas, the Indian Ocean diasporas were composed of both forced and free migrants. In India, for example, according to Richard Pankhurst, there were numerous African diasporan rulers and dynasties established between the thirteenth and eighteenth centuries by the Habshi (corruption of *Habash,* the Arabic name for Abyssinia), Sidi (corruption of the Arabic *Saiyid,* or "master"), and Kaffir (from the Arabic *Kafir,* or "unbeliever"), as the Africans were known, throughout India from the north and west (Delhi, Gujarat, the Gulf of Khambhat, Malabar, Alapur, and Jaunpur) to the northeast (Bengal), the south (Deccan), and the west coast. Besides the Indian subcontinent, significant African communities also existed in the Persian Gulf from present-day Iran and Iraq to Oman and Saudi Arabia.

Exploration of the African diasporas in the Mediterranean worlds of western Asia and southern Europe has been fraught with considerable difficulties, not least the fact that until modern times this was the most intensive zone of cultural traffic and communication, in which communities straddled multiple spaces in complex networks of affiliation. The case of the Arabs from the Arabian peninsula, who swept through northern Africa following the rise of Islam in the seventh century, is a case in point. They traversed northern Africa and western Asia, the so-called Middle East, although with the rise of the modern nation-state and national identities, notwithstanding the enduring dreams of the Arab nation, it is possible to talk of, say, the Egyptian diaspora in the Gulf.

Before the Atlantic slave trade, the most significant African presence in southern Europe was the Moors from northwestern Africa, who occupied and ruled much of Spain between the early eighth century and the late fifteenth century. As is well known, the Moors made enormous contributions to Spanish culture and society and to the modernization of Europe more generally during those seven centuries, but they are rarely discussed in diasporic terms—as an *African diaspora.* Discussions of African diasporas in the Mediterranean world, which are still relatively scanty, tend to focus on "blacks," that is, Negroid peoples, in ancient Rome or in the Mediterranean lands of Islam, where African diasporas were absorbed into the host communities thanks to the integrative principles and capacities of Islam.

Beyond the Mediterranean littoral in Europe, there are ancient African communities from Russia to Britain. The origins of the scattered African communities on the Black Sea coast of the Caucasus mountains are in dispute. Some argue that they were brought there between the sixteenth and nineteenth centuries as slaves for the Turkish and Abkhazian rulers, while others trace their origins many centuries earlier as remnants of an Egyptian army that invaded the region in antiquity. Allison Blakely believes the two explanations may not necessarily be contradictory, in that there were probably different waves of Africans. Modern Russia did not develop a significant practice of African slavery, but some Africans did come as slaves; others came as servants for the wealthy nobility or as immigrants, usually seamen, including some who came from the Americas. One of these Africans was Abram Hannibal from Ethiopia, who arrived as a boy around 1700 and was raised as a favorite of Peter the Great, became a general and an engineer, and was the great-grandfather of Alexander Pushkin (1799–1837), the great Russian poet.

The history of Africans in Britain can be traced back two thousand years, but the African presence became more evident following the rise of the Atlantic slave trade. Many of the Africans worked as domestic servants, tradesmen, soldiers, and sailors. A growing stream of Africans coming for education—a tradition that began in the eighteenth century and accelerated in the nineteenth and twentieth centuries—later joined them. In the nineteenth century they included some of West Africa's most illustrious intellectuals and nationalists. Out of these waves emerged a "black" British culture with its own associational life, expressive cultural practices, literature, and political idioms, all forged in the crucible of unrelenting racial violence and oppression.

The Atlantic Diasporas

The Atlantic diasporas are the most recent of the global diasporas and are far better known and researched than the others. The diaspora in the United States often stands at the pedestal, the one against which to judge the identities of the other diasporas. The fact that Brazil has the largest African diaspora in the Americas, indeed in the world, is often forgotten, and so is the fact that in the Caribbean the African diaspora is the majority, rather than a minority population as in the United States. Debates about African diasporan identities have tended to be framed in terms of African cultural retentions or erasure on the one hand and diasporan adaptations and inventions on the other. Paul Gilroy's influential text, *The Black Atlantic,* is essentially a celebration of the supposedly new and distinctive Anglophone diaspora culture in which Africa is an irrelevant reality.

In effect, the two were not mutually exclusive, insofar as diasporic communities and consciousness were forged out of complex and sometimes contradictory encounters and negotiations between what Sheila Walker, in *African Roots/American Cultures* (2001), calls the three puzzles and Stuart Hall calls the presences in the Americas—the African, European, and Native American puzzles or presences. It is also important to note that there were continuous movements of people from Africa and the diaspora and back that kept connections alive.

On the whole, studies of African diasporas in the Americas continue to be heavily focused on national histories. In situations where the African puzzle or presence is marginalized, as is often the case in the United States, excavating the dynamic import of the African cultural, religious, artistic, social, economic, and political imprint on mainstream American society has produced some exciting scholarship. In societies that have tried to "whiten" themselves, such as Argentina, the object has been to demonstrate the African demographic presence. Similar attempts have been made to demystify Africa's "absence" in the histories of other countries in America's Southern cone:

Bolivia, Paraguay, Uruguay, and Venezuela, and in the histories of the United States' immediate neighbors, Mexico and Canada, and to chronicle the contributions of African diasporas beyond picturesque folklore.

For Brazil, great store has been placed on explaining the remarkable survival and transformation of the Africans and their cultures as well as exposing the brutal realities behind the mystifications of race mixture and cultural syncretism. With their large African populations, the Caribbean islands reflect Brazil in terms of the evident demographic and cultural visibility of the African presence. Also as in Brazil, this presence, ubiquitous though it may be, has not always been valorized—at least not until the black consciousness movement of the 1970s. Perched in the Atlantic in the middle of the Middle Passage, as it were, the African diaspora in the Caribbean in fact embodies all the complex connections, crisscrossings, and cultural compositions of the African diasporas of the Atlantic. Not surprisingly, Caribbean activists and intellectuals played a crucial role in all the transatlantic Pan-African ideologies and movements, from Garveyism to Negritude to socialism.

The New African Diasporas

In the twentieth century there were several new dispersals from Africa, a continent divided into colonial territories and later into independent nation-states. Unlike their predecessors, whose communities of identity, either as imagined by themselves or as imposed by others, were either ethnic or racial (not to mention sometimes religious), the new African diasporas had to contend with the added imperative of the modern nation-state, which often frames the political and cultural itineraries of their travel and transnational networks. The "new" or "contemporary" African diasporas, as they are sometimes called, can be divided into three main waves: the diasporas of colonization, of decolonization, and of structural adjustment that emerged out of, respectively, the disruptions of colonial conquest, the struggles for independence, and structural adjustment programs imposed on African countries by the international financial institutions from the late 1970s and early 1980s.

As with the historic diasporas, the challenge has been to map out the development of these diasporas and their identities and relations with the host societies. Needless to say, and also in common with the historic diasporas, the contemporary diasporas are differentiated and their internal and external relations are mediated by the inscriptions of gender, generation, class, political ideology, and sometimes religion. Where they differ from the historic diaspora, complicating analysis, is that they have to negotiate relations with the historic diasporas themselves and also not just with "Africa" but with their particular countries of origin and the countries of transmigration. The revolution in telecommunications and travel, which has compressed the spatial and temporal distances between home and abroad, offers the contemporary diasporas, unlike the historic diasporas from the earlier dispersals, unprecedented opportunities to be transnational and transcultural, to be people of multiple worlds and focalities. They are able to retain ties to Africa in ways that were not possible for earlier generations of the African diasporas. The diasporas of the late twentieth century were even more globalized than those earlier in the century in terms of the multiplicity of their destinations and networks.

Particularly rapid in the closing decades of the twentieth century was African migration to Europe, which was characterized by increasing diversification in the number of countries both sending and receiving the immigrants. The African diaspora from the continent and the diaspora itself grew in Britain and France, the old colonial superpowers. Quite remarkable was the emergence as immigration countries of southern European countries such as Italy, Portugal, and Spain, which were themselves emigration countries. This development was as much a product of the improving economic fortunes in these countries and their integration into the prosperity and political sphere of western Europe as it was of mounting immigration pressures on their borders to the east and the south. New African immigrant communities also formed in central and eastern Europe, especially following the end of the Cold War.

Equally rapid was the growth of African migration to North America, especially the United States. By 2000 there were 700,000 African-born residents in the United States, up from 363,819 in 1990. This new African diaspora constituted only 2.5 percent of the total U.S. foreign-born population, up from 1.9 percent in 1990. The African migrants in the United States tended to be exceedingly well educated, in fact they enjoyed the highest levels of education of any group in the United States, foreign-born or native-born. According to the 2000 U.S. Census, among the African-born residents aged twenty-five and above, 49.3 percent had a bachelor's degree or more, as compared to 25.6 percent for the native-born population and 25.8 percent for the foreign-born population as a whole (U.S. Census Bureau, 2001).

Diaspora Linkages

The continuous formation of African diasporas through migration is one way in which the diaspora and Africa have maintained linkages. There have also been numerous movements among the diasporas themselves, for example, of Caribbean communities to Central, South, and North America and Europe, so that the entire Atlantic world, including the United States, is constituted by Earl Lewis's "overlapping diasporas."

One critical measure of the diaspora condition as a self-conscious identity lies in remembering, imagining, and engaging the original homeland, whose own identity is in part constituted by and in turn helps constitute the diaspora. This dialectic in the inscriptions and representations of the homeland in the diaspora and of the diaspora in the homeland is the thread that weaves the histories of the diaspora and the homeland together. Two critical questions can be raised. First, how do the different African diasporas remember, imagine, and engage Africa, and which Africa—in temporal and spatial terms? Second, how does Africa, or rather the different Africas—in their temporal and spatial framings—remember, imagine, and engage their diasporas? Given the complex ebbs and flows of history for Africa itself and for the various regional host lands of the African diasporas, it stands to reason that the engagements between Africa and its diasporas have been built with and shaped by continuities, changes, and ruptures.

The fluidity of these engagements is best captured by the notion of flow: that flows of several kinds and levels of intensity characterize the linkages between the homeland and the diaspora. The diaspora-homeland flows are often simultaneously covert and overt, abstract and concrete, symbolic and real, and their effects may be sometimes disjunctive or conjunctive. The diaspora or the homeland can also serve as a signifier for the other, subject to strategic manipulation. The flows include people, cultural practices, productive resources, organizations and movements, ideologies and ideas, and images and representations. In short, six major flows can be isolated: demographic flows, cultural flows, economic flows, political flows, ideological flows, and iconographic flows.

Clearly, engagements between Africa and its diasporas have been produced by many flows that have been carried on by a variety of agents; but not all flows and agents are equal, nor have they been treated equally. Much scholarly attention has gone toward the political and ideological flows across the Atlantic, as manifested, for example, in the role that the transatlantic Pan-Africanist movement played in engendering territorial nationalisms across Africa and how continental nationalism and the civil rights movement in the United States reinforced each other. Only recently has the discussion of cultural flows begun to transcend the question of African cultural retentions and survivals in the Americas to examine not only the traffic of cultural practices from the Atlantic diasporas to various parts of Africa but also the complex patterns and processes of current cultural exchanges through the media of contemporary globalization, from television and cinema to video and the Internet.

The historiography of these other forms of engagement is still relatively underdeveloped. Indeed, as with the history of the dispersals analyzed above, far less is known about the engagements between Africa and its diasporas in Asia and Europe than is the case with the Atlantic diasporas. The challenge in African diaspora studies, then, is twofold: to map out more accurately the dispersals of African peoples globally, and to map out the various engagements between Africa and its diasporas for each of the major world regions.

See also **Black Atlantic; Black Consciousness; Creolization, Caribbean; Pan-Africanism; Religion: African Diaspora; Slavery.**

BIBLIOGRAPHY

Blakely, Allison. *Russia and the Negro: Blacks in Russian History and Thought.* Washington, D.C.: Howard University Press, 1986.

Butler, Kim D. "Brazilian Abolition in Afro-Atlantic Context." *African Studies Review* 43, no. 1 (2000): 125–139.

Cohen, Robin. *Global Diasporas: An Introduction.* Seattle: University of Washington Press, 1997.

Fryer, Peter. *Staying Power: The History of Black People in Britain.* London: Pluto, 1984.

Gilroy, Paul. *The Black Atlantic.* Cambridge, Mass.: Cambridge University Press.

Hall, Stuart. "Cultural Identity and Diaspora." In *Theorizing Diaspora: A Reader,* edited by Jana Evans Braziel and Anita Mannur, 233–246. Malden, Mass.: Blackwell, 2003.

Harris, Joseph E., ed. *Global Dimensions of the African Diaspora,* 2nd ed. Washington, D.C.: Howard University Press, 1993.

Hine, Darlene Clark, and Jacqueline McLeod, eds. *Crossing Boundaries: Comparative History of Black People in Diaspora.* Bloomington and Indianapolis: Indiana University Press, 1999.

Hunwick, John, and Eve Trout Powell, eds. *The African Diaspora in the Mediterranean Lands of Islam.* Princeton, N.J.: Markus Wiener, 2002.

Koser, Khalid, ed. *New African Diasporas.* London and New York: Routledge, 2003.

Lewis, Earl. "To Turn as on a Pivot: Writing African Americans into a History of Overlapping Diasporas." *American Historical Review* 100, no. 3 (1995): 765–787.

Okpewho, Isidore, Carole Boyce Davies, and Ali A. Mazrui, eds. *African Diaspora: African Origins and New World Identities.* Bloomington: Indiana University Press, 1999.

Palmer, Colin. "The African Diaspora." *Black Scholar* 30, nos. 3/4 (2000): 56–59.

Pankhurst, Richard. "The Ethiopian Diaspora in India: The Role of Habshis and Sidis from Medieval Times to the End of the Eighteenth Century." In *The African Diaspora in the Indian Ocean,* edited by Shihan de Silva Jayasuriya and Richard Pankhurst, 189–221. Trenton, N.J.: Africa World Press, 2001.

Shepperson, George. "African Diaspora: Concept and Context." In *Global Dimensions of the African Diaspora,* 2nd ed., edited by Joseph E. Harris, 41–49. Washington, D.C.: Howard University Press, 1993.

Thompson, Lloyd A. *Romans and Blacks.* Norman: University of Oklahoma Press, 1989.

U.S. Census Bureau. *Profile of the Foreign Born Population in the United States.* Washington, D.C.: U.S. Census Bureau, 2001.

Walker, Sheila S. "Introduction: Are You Hip to the Jive? (Re) Writing/Righting the Pan-American Discourse." In *African Roots/American Cultures: Africa in the Creation of the Americas,* edited by Sheila S. Walker, 1–44. New York: Rowan and Littlefield, 2001.

Paul Tiyambe Zeleza

JEWISH DIASPORA

The Greek term *diaspora,* meaning "dispersion," has been used since ancient times as a means of describing the Jewish experience as well as the fact of Jewish settlement outside of the Jewish homeland to the present day. Originally, the term *diaspora* was used with respect to only three groups whose populations were dispersed in classical times: the Greeks, the Jews, and the Armenians. More recently, the term *diaspora* has been applied to a variety of other groups throughout the world who have endured dispersion from their original homelands. To the extent recent usage has changed the term's original connotation, its continued use to characterize the Jewish historical experience in its entirety can be misleading.

Classical scholars distinguish the forced exile of the Jews following the destruction of the First and Second Temples at Jerusalem (586 B.C.E. and 70 C.E., respectively) from the voluntary emigration out of the Jewish state that first occurred on a large scale under Persian rule after 538 B.C.E. and lasted through the escalating Roman occupation and administration

of Judea after 6 C.E. Only voluntary emigration, by their analysis, truly falls under the heading of "diaspora." Forcible expulsion is more appropriately characterized by the Hebrew terms *galut* or *golah,* both referring to the state of living in exile. Part of the confusion between "diaspora" and "exile" arose after the destruction of the Second Temple in 70 C.E., when the two kinds of dispersion became inextricably intertwined and the terminology merged. The terms were not again seen to be separate and distinct until the creation of the modern State of Israel in 1948, when the creation of a central Jewish polity ended the enforced exile of Jews while many Jews elected to remain in diaspora—that is, living in areas outside the new Jewish state. After 1948, Israeli scholars began to apply the Hebrew term *tefutsoth,* which does not carry the connotation of forcible expatriation, to refer to the Jewish diaspora.

The Jewish diaspora is said by classical scholars to have begun during the First Temple period, with the establishment of a community of Jewish mercenaries within the military outpost of Elephantine (Southern Egypt) and with the removal of Jewish captives from the conquered Hebrew kingdom of Israel by the Assyrians in 722 B.C.E. However, the notion of diaspora as "exile" is theologically tied to the destruction of the First Temple and the sacking of Jerusalem by the Babylonians under Nebuchadnezzar in 586 B.C.E. As part of their conquest of the Hebrew kingdom of Judah, the Babylonians exiled the Jewish elite to Babylon, where they were said to have remained for three generations. Although the Assyrian captives had also been exiled by force, it was only during the Babylonian captivity that Jews developed the institutional structures that would later allow Judaism to survive without a homeland in the nineteen centuries following the destruction of the Second Temple and the complete suppression of a Jewish polity in Judea. In Babylon, exiled Jewish scholars completed the compilation of the written Torah, to which they added some prophetic writings and chronicles. The innovation of the synagogue for small group devotions changed the practice of public worship significantly by putting scholars at the forefront in place of the High Priest of the Temple at Jerusalem. It was during the Babylonian exile that scholarly debates over the meaning of scripture began to evolve into the study networks of rabbinic Judaism that would sustain Jewish life and traditions without access to the Temple, the central focus of all Jewish religious life where the holy Ark of the Covenant was housed.

The Babylonian exile ended in 538 B.C.E. when the Persian king Cyrus conquered Babylon and issued an edict that permitted the Jewish captives to return to their homeland. Although the exiles then had the freedom to return to Judah and re-establish the Temple under Persian rule, most chose to remain in Babylon where they had adapted to life in exile. This represented the beginning of a pronounced shift within Jewish culture with respect to the relationship between individual Jews and the Jewish state. The structures developed by the exiles in Babylon to maintain their commitment to Judaism while absent from the Jewish polity meant that it was now possible, for the first time, to sustain Jewish life without having to live in the Jewish homeland. Following the example of the former Babylonian captives, a growing number of Jews began to embrace the capacity created by the new and portable forms of Jewish ritual life to reside in places were there were better opportunities. In the years after the completion of the Second Temple in 515 B.C.E., a growing proportion of the Jewish population lived outside the Jewish polity, some through forcible exile, and some voluntarily in pursuit of economic ventures outside the Jewish state. By the first century B.C.E., the Greek geographer Strabo noted that the Jewish diaspora had penetrated nearly every part of the known world.

Hellenism and the Jewish Diaspora

Voluntary dispersion from the Jewish homeland in the kingdom of Judah, and later Judea, was sparked by the development of a plastic Hellenistic culture, of which Judea itself would become a part, which formed following the conquests of Alexander the Great in 333 B.C.E. As Hellenistic political rule expanded throughout the Mediterranean world, the colonies, institutions, and commerce it created attracted Jews in search of trade to venture out into far-flung areas of Greek settlement, where they came into closer contact with Hellenistic ideology. It was during this period that Jews began to disperse throughout the Mediterranean basin in substantial numbers. As the philosopher Philo Judaeus noted in the first century C.E., the area of Jewish settlement within the Hellenistic world spread from Libya to Ethiopia. Important and influential diaspora communities formed at Alexandria (Egypt), Cyrene (Libya), Antioch (Syria), Pergamon (Turkey/ Asia Minor) and other large Hellenistic port cities. In these places, Jews were exposed to Hellenistic teachings in philosophy and science. Some important Jewish individuals, such as Philo Judaeus of Alexandria, flourished in this bicultural environment, but the impact of Hellenistic thought on rabbinic Judaism was slight overall. This was because of a revival of Jewish nationalism and violent resistance to Greek influence within Judea, under the leadership of Judah Maccabbee, as well as the emergence of Babylon, which remained outside the sphere of Hellenistic culture, as the main center for Jewish theological development and scholasticism.

The migration of Jews out of Judea continued under the Romans, but under different conditions and therefore with different motivations. The economic and social environment of the Hellenistic empire had drawn Jews out of Judea of their own volition without substantially disrupting Jewish theocratic traditions. Roman rule, however, aimed at conquest and subjugation of the Jewish state apparatus. This created a fundamental tension between Judea's inhabitants and Roman administrators that frequently erupted into violence. Jewish migration into the Roman Empire therefore, while still voluntary, was driven in large part by the desire to escape violence and oppression in Judea. Growing conflict led to two revolts by the people of Judea and the employment of ever more brutal tactics by the Romans. Roman military occupation of Judea in 63 C.E. and ongoing violence (including the destruction of the Second Temple in 70 C.E.) through the crushing of the Bar Kochba Revolt, made Judea less desirable as a place for Jews to live and encouraged further dispersion of Judea's Jews throughout the Roman world. Judea's role as the center for Jewish life declined rapidly after 138 C.E. By the

seventh century C.E., the vast majority of Jews resided in communities outside of biblical Judah and Israel, and by 1600 only one percent of the Jewish people could be found in the traditional Jewish homelands of the Hebrew scriptures.

Interpretations of the Jewish Diaspora

Rome's imperial aims involved the destruction of Jewish political independence. Once that had been achieved and Judea no longer represented a threat to Rome's territorial advances, Jews were as readily absorbed into the empire as other conquered peoples. In 212 C.E., an edict extended Roman citizenship to all free inhabitants, including Jews. Judaism was officially recognized, and Jews were free to pursue an autonomous communal life without interference from the Roman state. Although they were banned from Jerusalem, they could move and settle freely throughout the rest of the empire. This situation began to change with the spread of Christianity, as the church fathers found it imperative that they distinguish the new faith from its predecessor. In 313, the emperor Constantine issued an edict granting freedom of worship to all religious sects. For the first time, the Christian religion was no longer suppressed and it quickly came to predominate within the empire. This had negative consequences for Jews, as the Christian Church began to call for the official separation of Jews from Christians.

Initially, the Jewish diaspora throughout the Mediterranean had helped to advance the diffusion of Judaism into regions where it had previously been unknown. By the fall of the Roman Empire in the fifth century C.E, Jewish communities were well-established in sites throughout the Roman world, from Asia Minor to Spain. Rome itself had at least thirteen synagogues. A wider Jewish presence led to better knowledge of Judaism, and upon occasion to conversion of local populations. About 700 C.E, for example, Bulan, leader of the nomadic Khazar people of Central Asia, decided to convert his nation to Judaism, creating an autonomous Jewish state that lasted for some five hundred years. However, after 500, Judaism faced growing threats from the spread of Christianity and (after 632) Islam, both of which found the continuing evolution of Jewish thought threatening to their respective theological postures as successors to Judaism.

Jewish leaders of medieval Europe such as Rabbi Moses ben Nachman (otherwise Nachmanides) saw the Roman conquest of Israel as the beginning of a permanent Jewish diaspora within the Christian world. This understanding of the Jewish diaspora was grounded in personal experience with the Holy Roman Church and its dictates. By 1215, the Roman Catholic Church's Fourth Lateran Council advocated the wearing of special insignia by Jews living in Christian lands, to identify them for an uneducated Christian populace as people to be avoided and as a "badge of shame" to highlight the inferiority of their religious beliefs. Moreover, Jews living in diaspora in Europe faced successive waves of expulsion, forced conversion, and segregation into ghettos as Christians attempted different tactics to control and constrain the development of a Jewish communal presence in their midst. From the Jewish perspective, the sense of diaspora as exile was also acutely heightened (particularly during the Crusades) by the inability of Jews to return to the Holy Land to rebuild the Temple and gather in Jewish exiles—that is, to reestablish a Jewish state as an independent political and theological entity. Exile became the dominant understanding of the diaspora in subsequent generations of both Jews and Christians. Jewish and Christian thinkers put a different spin on the notion of "exile" however. For Jews, the exile, although painful, was part of God's plan for the Jews as a test of their faith and commitment to the Torah. Christians saw the diaspora as God's just punishment of the Jews for their role in the death of Christ. While Islamic rulers treated Jews less harshly than did their Christian counterparts. Muslims similarly distinguished themselves from Jews and Judaism and there were scattered instances of persecution, including forced conversions, in Muslim lands.

By the late eighteenth century many Jews had come to believe that their exile from the Jewish state was permanent. For some, accepting that the diaspora was inescapable meant developing the means for resolving persistent questions about the place of Jews in the various societies within which they resided. Influenced by the developing Enlightenment, Jewish intellectuals in Europe believed that the contemporary mission of the Jewish people was to adapt to their surroundings and find ways to participate in the nation state on equal terms with other citizens. The most important of these advocates was Moses Mendelssohn in Berlin. Following Mendelssohn's call for civil integration of the Jews, later generations of Reformers suggested a series of modifications to Jewish ritual practice that were intended to harmonize Judaism with modern life and make it possible for Jews to present their community as well disposed for social and political participation. The Reformers had great success and influence in Germany and the United States during the nineteenth and twentieth centuries. In other places, the idea of Jewish integration and acculturation was not as readily embraced. The outbreak of violence after the death of Tsar Alexander II in 1881 pushed the Jews of Russia and Poland in the opposite direction, toward Jewish nationalism, and awakened interest in reestablishing a Jewish state at the site of the original Jewish homeland. After the anti-Semitic debacle of the Dreyfus Affair in France, a broad range of European and American Jewish intellectuals were forced to the conclusion that the kind of complete civil integration imagined by the Reformers would never be possible. Accordingly, the first Zionist Congress was held at Basel, Switzerland, in 1897, to organize the push for the Jewish return to Palestine. Zionism, in effect, called for an end to the demeaning conditions in which diaspora Jews were generally forced to live through the creation of a new, modern Jewish state in Palestine.

Diaspora in the Twenty-First Century

In the early 2000s, the diaspora is commonly understood to comprise all Jews living outside modern Israel, regardless of their nation of birth. The establishment of the state of Israel following the United Nations partition plan created the opportunity to end the Jewish diaspora. The new nation attempted an ingathering of Jewish exiles from around the world, in part by establishing the Law of Return (1950), which permitted any Jew to immigrate to Israel, and the Citizenship Law (1952), which

permitted Jews to claim Israeli citizenship upon touching Israeli soil. In the first year of its independence, Israel took in and absorbed 203,000 Jews from forty-two different countries, comprising not only the survivors of European Jewry (largely Ashkenazim), but also large numbers of "Oriental" Jews from Arab lands who had become the victims of escalating violence and persecution as international pressure mounted to sanction the creation of a Jewish state in the British mandate. Some Jewish refugees arrived via special convoys organized by the Jewish Agency to move large numbers of Jewish refugees living in exigent circumstances, including Jews from Yemen (Operation Magic Carpet, 1949), Iraq (Operation Ezra and Operation Nehemiah, 1950), and later from Ethiopia (Operations Solomon, 1974, and Moses, 1984–1985). Due to extensive immigration from Europe and Arab lands where anti-Semitism surged, the Jewish population of Israel increased from 657,000 in 1948 to 1,810,000 by 1958.

There remain, in the early twenty-first century, multiple interpretations of the diaspora and its significance to Jewish history and to the modern state of Israel. Many Jews, for a variety of complex reasons, continue to reside outside the Jewish state, not only in the affluent nations of Europe and North America, but in countries around the world.

See also **Exile; Ghetto; Identity, Multiple: Jewish Multiple Identity; Judaism.**

BIBLIOGRAPHY

Baer, Yitzhak F. *Galut.* Translated by Robert Warshow. Reprint. Lanham, Md.: University Press of America, 1988.

Barnavi, Eli, ed.. *A Historical Atlas of the Jewish People: From the Time of the Patriarchs to the Present.* New York: Knopf, 1992.

Baron, Salo Wittmayer. *The Jewish Community: Its History and Structure to the American Revolution.* 3 vols. Westport, Conn.: Greenwood Press, 1972. Originally published in 1942.

Comay, Joan, with Beth Hatefutsoth. *The Diaspora Story: The Epic of the Jewish People among the Nations.* New York: Random House, 1980.

Eisenstadt, Shmuel Noah. *Jewish Civilization: The Jewish Historical Experience in a Comparative Perspective.* Albany: SUNY Press, 1992.

Gilbert, Martin. *The Atlas of Jewish History.* 3rd ed. New York: Dorset Press, 1984.

Rawidowicz, Simon. *Israel: The Ever-Dying People and Other Essays.* Edited by C. I. Ravid. Rutherford, N.J.: Fairleigh Dickinson University Press, 1986.

Rubinstein, Hilary L., et al. *The Jews in the Modern World: A History since 1750.* New York: Oxford University Press, 2002.

Holly Snyder

DICTATORSHIP IN LATIN AMERICA. It is a somewhat common refrain in Latin America that countries need the *mano dura* (strong hand) of a military dictatorship in order to get things done. Surveys in the early twenty-first century reveal a growing disenchantment with civilian governments, with a surprisingly large minority of Latin Americans stating a preference for a dictatorial form of government over democracy. Such sentiments date back to the founding of the Latin American republics in the early nineteenth century. After the removal of the Iberian crowns, conservatives argued that the new states were like children who needed parental guidance. These conservatives favored a centralist form of government in which a small group of elites would hold power and rule paternalistically on behalf of the rest of the country. Positivism, with its emphasis on order and progress, often provided a philosophical basis for such regimes in Latin America.

Military rule has been a feature of Latin America dating back to the colonial period. Rather than interpreting this as a cultural phenomenon, many observers have pointed to a failure of civilian institutions to address persistent problems of poverty and corruption. Some twentieth-century military dictatorships follow the pattern of nineteenth-century caudillo leaders who often ruled more through a use of personal charisma than brute military force. In fact, the only remaining nonelected executive in Latin America at the end of the twentieth century was Fidel Castro in Cuba, and his personalist style was more in line with the leadership of classic caudillos than what many would understand as the defining characteristics of a military dictatorship. However, while caudillos could be civilians and presented a variety of ideological stripes, "dictatorship" in Latin America normally refers to right-wing rulers who maintain themselves in power through overwhelming military force. For example, the Somoza and Pinochet dictatorships in Nicaragua and Chile maintained power more through repressive means than through personalist, caudillo styles of government. Particularly in South America in the 1960s and 1970s, bureaucratic-authoritarian regimes like those in Chile and Argentina attempted to use the power of state institutions to enact a fundamental reordering of society.

In Nicaragua, a series of three Somozas established a family dynasty that ruled the country from 1936 to 1979. The United States placed the first Somoza, Anastasio Somoza García, at the head of a national guard in order to continue a fight against the nationalist hero Augusto César Sandino after the United States withdrew its military forces from the country. Somoza, as well as his two successors, his sons Luis Somoza Debayle and Anastasio Somoza Debayle, spoke English fluently and remained submissive to United States foreign policy objectives. As Franklin Roosevelt allegedly said of the elder Somoza, "He may be a son-of-a-bitch, but he is our son-of-a-bitch" (Schmitz, p. 4). Over time, the Somoza family dynasty became increasingly brutal as it extended complete control over the country. A growing disparity in land distribution and gaps between the rich and the poor led to increasing discontent. Mounting repression and corruption finally led to alienation of the middle class and evaporation of business support for the regime. On 19 July 1979 Sandinista guerrillas overthrew the dictatorship and implemented a leftist revolutionary government.

In Chile, General Augusto Pinochet overthrew the democratically elected government of Salvador Allende in a bloody 11 September 1973 coup. Allende was the first Marxist elected to the chief executive office in Latin America in freely contested elections. His goals of agrarian reform, nationalization of industry, and a shift in production from luxury to consumer goods alienated the United States, which helped engineer Pinochet's coup. In power, Pinochet proved to be vicious, destroying the existing political system, engaging in extensive human rights abuses, and privatizing industry while taking services away from the lower classes. Although supported by the United States, Pinochet's military dictatorship dealt a staggering blow to democracy, freedom, and reform. Until handing partial power back to civilian leaders in 1990, Pinochet provided a classic example of a military dictatorship.

The Revolutionary Government of the Armed Forces, which came to power in Peru in 1968 under the leadership of General Juan Velasco Alvarado, provides an interesting counterpoint to these conservative military dictatorships. At first, Velasco's rise to power appeared to be just another military coup, but he soon announced plans for deep changes in government, including the nationalization of industries, worker participation in the ownership and management of these industries, and a sweeping agrarian reform law designed to end unjust social and economic structures. In implementing these reforms, Velasco challenged the incompetence and corruption of civilian politicians who were unable to implement badly needed reforms. He announced a "third way" of national development between capitalism and socialism. As a result of his reforms, food production increased, and peasants' wages and quality of life improved. Much as nineteenth-century caudillos sometimes brought positive changes to their countries, supporters viewed Velasco's military government as what Peru needed to improve and advance the country.

While progressive military governments in Peru and, to a lesser extent, Ecuador and Panama ruled in favor of the lower classes, implementing agrarian, labor, and other reforms, their ultimate aim was to undercut leftist organizing strategies. Providing agrarian reforms, even though they were partial, limited, and served to support the existing class structures, drew strength away from peasant and guerrilla demands. Ultimately, however, these reforms failed to address fundamental structural problems in society. These failures reveal how difficult it was to escape from dependent development without radical structural changes in class, property relations, and income distribution. At the same time, this history reveals that military governments are not always as reactionary as one might think. Furthermore, various branches of the military also tend to have different ideological orientations. Specifically, the army is sometimes seen as progressive because of its development work in rural communities, whereas the navy is usually affiliated with the elite and the police are often accused of committing the bulk of human rights abuses. This reveals the need for a more careful and complex interpretation of the role of the military, to break away from simplistic and unidimensional perspectives on the history of dictatorships in Latin America.

See also **Authoritarianism: Latin America.**

BIBLIOGRAPHY
Hamill, Hugh M., ed. *Caudillos: Dictators in Spanish America.* Norman: University of Oklahoma Press, 1992.
Kornbluh, Peter. *The Pinochet File: A Declassified Dossier on Atrocity and Accountability.* New York: New Press, 2003.

McClintock, Cynthia, and Abraham F. Lowenthal, eds. *The Peruvian Experiment Reconsidered.* Princeton, N.J.: Princeton University Press, 1983.

Schmitz, David F. *Thank God They're on Our Side: The United States and Right-Wing Dictatorships, 1921–1965.* Chapel Hill: University of North Carolina Press, 1999.

Zimmermann, Matilde. *Sandinista: Carlos Fonseca and the Nicaraguan Revolution.* Durham, N.C.: Duke University Press, 2000.

Marc Becker

DIFFERENCE. *See* **Diversity; Identity.**

DIFFUSION, CULTURAL. The concept of diffusion was born to controversy. The initial debate over this issue took place during the late nineteenth and early twentieth centuries.

Contention

On one side were British thinkers such as G. Elliot Smith (with William J. Perry), who strove to trace all myths, rituals, and social institutions (except for those of hunters and gatherers) back to a single, seminal civilization—in Smith's case, that was Egypt (hence its characterization as pan-Egyptian and heliolithic). Pitted against the diffusionists were the evolutionists, such as E. B. Tylor (1832–1917) in England and the American Lewis Henry Morgan (1818–1881), who held that significant inventions are independently created in many societies because of the common mental and psychological characteristics of our species. Influenced by the biological evolutionism of Charles Darwin (1809–1882) and evolutionary paradigms of the French philosopher Henri Bergson (1859–1941), they ascribed to an essentially unilinear theory of the development of culture and may be referred to as independent inventionists and isolationists. A more moderate form of diffusionism, which absorbed certain aspects of evolutionary thought, was maintained by German-Austrian anthropologists such as Fritz Gräbner (1877–1934) and Father Wilhelm Schmidt (1868–1954), who claimed that culture originated in several areas of the world that they called *Kulturkreise* ("culture circles"). They were referred to as the culture-historical (*kulturgeschichtliche*) school.

Bronislaw Malinowski (1884–1942) and A. R. Radcliffe-Brown (1881–1955) vigorously contested the more extreme forms of diffusionism and evolutionism through what is known as functionalism. The functionalists held that biological models should not be applied to sociological inquiries and stressed that cultural traits, even when it is possible to prove that they have been imported, are frequently radically reinterpreted in the societies to which they are introduced.

In the 1920s, with Franz Boas (1858–1942) at the helm, American anthropology clung to an essentially atheoretical position that rejected the polarizing assumptions of both diffusionists and evolutionists and considered functionalism to be overly schematic and insufficiently historical. While accepting the fact that cultural traits were manifestly transmissible, they emphasized the distinctiveness of cultures and the contingent,

selective nature of borrowing. Among Boas's students was Alfred L. Kroeber (1876–1960), who put forward the modified notion of stimulus diffusion, according to which the general idea or principle of a cultural trait is thought to be adopted from one culture by another culture, but not its specific signification and purpose. Such concerns led to the examination of the mechanisms of adoption and adaptation.

Elaboration

After more than half a century of dissension over the opposition between cultural diffusionism and independent invention, many scholars began to search for means to circumvent the counterproductive impasse. A landmark event in diffusionist thinking took place at the 1948 International Congress of Americanists in New York when a Mesoamericanist archaeologist, Gordon F. Ekholm, and an art historian of South and Southeast Asia, Robert Heine-Geldern, presented an exhibition of Old World and New World artifacts that revealed startling similarities. In a subsequent series of publications, they suggested possible Hindu-Buddhist influences on the Maya and the Toltec. The methodology of new diffusionists such as Ekholm and Heine-Geldern differed markedly from that of their predecessors in that it downplayed unicentric theory and emphasized the accumulation of overwhelming amounts of juxtaposed, concrete evidence. Their work was carried on with the utmost attention to detail by researchers such as Paul Tolstoy, who pointed out striking cultural parallels between the manufacture of bark cloth in Southeast Asia and in Mesoamerica. On the theoretical plane, Tolstoy drew an important distinction between diffusion as explanation (arguable) and diffusion as event (demonstrable). Empirically grounded studies were also continued in the investigations of Stuart Piggott, who plotted the path of wheeled vehicles across large swaths of Eurasia, displaying a good example of a finely worked case study of technological diffusion.

By the beginning of the twenty-first century and the age of globalization, the discussion had been entirely recast (whether conceived of as a quantitative or qualitative difference in how cultural ideas have moved around since the dawn of humanity). A leading figure of this approach to macro- and micro-analysis of cultural contagion is Arjun Appadurai. One of Appadurai's most frequently cited texts is the essay entitled "Global Ethnoscapes: Notes and Queries for a Transnational Anthropology" (now Chapter 3 in his *Modernity at Large*), where he talks about the role of "imagination" in the transnational flow of culture that is associated with globalization. In the pathbreaking book entitled *The Social Life of Things*, edited by Appadurai, ethnohistorians look at the problem of how the objects of material culture change as they migrate, lending subtlety to the treatment of an unspoken diffusionism. It should, however, be pointed out that none of the anthropologists who are fascinated with such global phenomena claim any influence from the older schools of diffusionist thought and would undoubtedly disown it.

Resolution

While diffusionism remains unfashionable (indeed, virtually unmentionable) within anthropology, studies of diffusion in other fields are commonplace and fruitful. Investigations of the diffusion of innovations are regularly undertaken by researchers in agricultural economics, communication, education, sociology (especially early sociology and rural sociology), food processing and preservation, geography (particularly economic geography), general economics, industrial engineering, manufacturing, marketing and management, packaging, public health and medical sociology, psychology, public administration and political science, statistics, and other areas.

Prominent among scholars who undertake this relatively uncontested kind of pragmatic diffusionism, often employing sophisticated mathematical models, are Torsten Hägerstrand, Lawrence A. Brown, and Peter J. Hugill. These researchers have made fundamental contributions to the understanding of the diffusion of innovations in global communications, the analysis of world trade patterns, and the relationship between geopolitics (including its manifestations in war and espionage) and the transfer of technology. It is odd that the mere mention of diffusion among anthropologists is still capable of evoking paroxysms of indignation, whereas in most other disciplines it is considered a perfectly normal topic for discussion. One can only conclude that issues pertaining to diffusion in anthropology carry potent politico-ideological overtones and are borne on sensitive ethnological undercurrents that are wholly lacking in more utilitarian, less value-laden research fields.

The discipline of history has finally managed to extricate itself from the more acrimonious aspects of the debate over diffusionism. This is above all true of scholars aligned with William McNeill, who has for more than four decades identified intercivilizational contact as the main motor of human history. World history is now a vibrant subfield with its own lively journal (*Journal of World History,* edited by Jerry H. Bentley) in which researchers routinely write about world systems, interaction spheres, interregional contact and exchange, and other highly productive topics in noncircumlocutory terms. It is intriguing to observe that world historians increasingly resort to reticular imagery to show that the transmission of goods and ideas is multidirectional and totally interwoven. A parallel, but not always congruent, line of intellectual history is that of world systems theory, which flourished in the 1970s and 1980s, particularly as advocated by the economic historian Immanuel Wallerstein. A major concern of world systems theorists was the movement of precious metals among polities, some of which were separated by enormous distances. The Marxian aspects of this theory, together with the postmodern reaction against it, undoubtedly is one source of contemporary anthropology's lingering unease with diffusionism.

See also **Communication of Ideas; Ideas, History of; Oral Traditions.**

BIBLIOGRAPHY

Appadurai, Arjun. *Modernity at Large: Cultural Dimensions of Globalization.* Minneapolis: University of Minnesota Press, 1996.

———. ed. *The Social Life of Things: Commodities in Cultural Perspective.* Cambridge, U.K.: Cambridge University Press, 1986.

Cavalli-Sforza, Luigi Luca, and Marcus W. Feldman. *Cultural Transmission and Evolution: A Quantitative Approach.* Princeton, N.J.: Princeton University Press, 1981.

Christian, David. *Maps of Time: An Introduction to Big History.* Berkeley: University of California Press, 2004.

McNeill, J. R., and William H. McNeill. *The Human Web: A Bird's-Eye View of World History.* New York: W. W. Norton, 2003.

Rogers, Everett M. *Diffusion of Innovations.* 5th ed. New York: Free Press, 2003. The second edition, by Rogers with F. Floyd Shoemaker, was published as *Communication of Innovations: A Cross-Cultural Approach,* New York: Free Press, 1971.

Victor H. Mair

DISCIPLINE. *See* **Asceticism.**

DISCRIMINATION. Discrimination should be understood as action and therefore distinguished from prejudice, which is a matter of thought, attitude, or belief. Racial discrimination then would consist of social action that produces unjust allocation of valued resources, based on racial categorizations of individuals or groups (Banton; Kairys, 1996). This is the standard definition and still serves in many cases: where race is concerned, it provides basic standards for distributional justice, and it permits one to disaggregate prejudice and discrimination (Merton). What the standard definition does not provide, however, is a link between unjust action and social structure, and this presents serious difficulties both for social thought and for social justice.

Patterns and understandings of racial discrimination have undergone significant change during the years since World War II. Such long-established practices of racial favoritism as the South African apartheid system and the system of state-enforced racial segregation in the U.S. South (that is, "Jim Crow") have been overturned in a complex sociopolitical process that combined sustained social movement activity with state-based racial reform. As a result, the formal (de jure) rules and agencies of racial preference have been largely if not entirely jettisoned, and explicit practices of discrimination on the part of resource holders and gatekeepers, such as employers, landlords, service providers, and schools to name but a few, have been stigmatized, though these practices often persist in more concealed and publicly deniable fashions.

It is undoubtedly a significant issue that an individual, group, or agency unfairly withholds resources (say, mortgages, university admissions, or trade union membership cards), denying access on an equal basis to persons of a negatively valued racial identity or, conversely, granting privileged access to persons of a favored racial group. But action of this type is identifiable and sanctionable, precisely because it is action: that is, transitive and predicated in the material present. Of course, such action often is not identified and very often is not sanctioned; it remains widely accepted or at least tolerated. But it is at least recognizable and comprehensible as the work of particular subjects, whether individual or collective.

Past racial discrimination, though, is much more difficult to address directly. Because discriminatory action is accretive and cumulative over time, especially over long durations, its effects can be felt without the presence of any active agent. Prolonged, transgenerational access to socially valued resources, such as elite university degrees, high-status jobs and professions, political power, and culturally afforded honor of various kinds (not to mention wealth), is facilitated by belonging to the "right" racial group (Harris; Feagin). Conversely, impeded opportunities, low status, culturally attributed dishonor (e.g., stereotypes of laziness, ugliness, or low intelligence), and frequently impoverishment are all outcomes of prolonged, transgenerational denial of access to resources and opportunities (Oliver and Shapiro; Brown et al.).

Thus racial discrimination is more than social action; in its repeated and reiterated forms it develops into a social structure. It becomes habitual and is taken for granted in all sorts of invisible ways: in the design of neighborhoods, the making of foreign policy or tax policy, or the writing of television news; in the way one is addressed by a policeman, treated by a doctor, or expected to speak the language.

This invisible structural discrimination evades attempts to regulate it, for example, through the law. After the 1960s civil rights reforms of state racial policy in the United States, for example, and after the 1994 dismantling of the apartheid regime in South Africa as well, the social structure of discrimination still exhibited a great deal of resilience (Winant; Zegeye). Some of this persistence may be attributable to the weakness of reform policy and the reluctance of courts to intervene strongly in sanctioning discriminatory practices (Kairys, 1993; Ezorsky), but a great deal of discrimination escapes public attention (sometimes even from those it damages) because it has little or no active agent, is hardly or not at all the work of intention, and is regarded as normal practice. This "transparent" discrimination in effect has no living perpetrators; it is the legacy of such past practices as slavery and colonial rule.

The presence of structural racial discrimination also has the effect of legitimating much intentional discrimination, which can be rendered agentless simply by the refusal to intervene on behalf of principles of fairness or equality as resources of social value are allocated. In large-scale terms (such as determining housing or wage policies), in medium-scale terms (such as carrying out university admissions), and in small-scale terms (such as hailing a cab, or "driving while black"), present-tense, active racial discrimination is supported and camouflaged by structural discrimination.

Thus state regulation alone is insufficient to effectively eliminate discrimination. Of course, discrimination can be maintained by state regulation: notably in the United States but elsewhere as well, courts have demonstrated how effectively they can sustain discrimination at socially acceptable levels. For example, U.S. courts have established legal standards that turn on the demonstration of explicit intent to discriminate as the prerequisite for enforcement of civil rights laws. In response to this, explicit profession of an intention to discriminate has become quite rare, and active discriminators have learned to dissemble and mask their practices under such code words as "colorblindness" and "merit" (Brown et al.).

Far more intensive measures have been proposed to eliminate or at least seriously reduce structural discrimination. These measures would be based on a policy of redistribution of resources according to a compensatory formula, sometimes viewed as reparations for past discrimination, and would also contemplate large-scale social therapy and healing projects, such as have occurred after the fall of dictatorships and after the military defeat of repressive regimes. Examples of such intensive projects include the Reconstruction period after the U.S. Civil War (Du Bois), the promulgation of a new South African constitution after the end of apartheid in 1994, and the "denazification" and supervised democratization processes that followed the defeat of the Axis powers in 1945.

While juridical processes, such as trials of human rights abusers and state-sponsored commissions like the South African Truth and Reconciliation Commission (TRC) or the Argentine National Commission on the Disappeared (CONADEP), might be expected to play a role in these transformations (Weschler), important work also would have to be undertaken at the level of civil society, of everyday life. Such activity would require an advanced commitment to democracy. Some of the TRC's innovations, such as provision of guarantees of nonretribution to those who acknowledged their own abusive practices, may serve as an initial model. While developing the large-scale dedication needed for such intensive antidiscrimination measures would be very difficult, preliminary work done by movement activists and scholars on the implementation of reparations suggests future directions (Bittker; Brooks; Dawson and Popoff).

See also **Apartheid; Prejudice; Race and Racism; Segregation.**

BIBLIOGRAPHY
Banton, Michael P. *Discrimination.* Philadelphia: Open University Press, 1994.
Bittker, Boris I. *The Case for Black Reparations.* New York: Random House, 1973.
Brooks, Roy L., ed. *When Sorry Isn't Enough: The Controversy over Apologies and Reparations for Human Injustice.* New York: New York University Press, 1999.
Brown, Michael K., et al. *Whitewashing Race: The Myth of a Color-Blind Society.* Berkeley: University of California Press, 2003.
Dawson, Michael C., and Ravana Popoff. "Reparations: Justice and Greed in Black and White." *Du Bois Review: Social Science Research on Race* 1, no. 1 (spring 2004): 47–91.
Du Bois, W. E. B. *Black Reconstruction: An Essay toward a History of the Part Which Black Folk Played in the Attempt to Reconstruct Democracy in America, 1860–1880.* New York: Harcourt, Brace, 1935. Reprint, New York: Atheneum, 1977.
Ezorsky, Gertrude. *Racism and Justice: The Case for Affirmative Action.* Ithaca: Cornell University Press, 1991.
Feagin, Joe R. *Racist America: Roots, Current Realities, and Future Reparations.* New York: Routledge, 2000.
Harris, Cheryl. "Whiteness as Property." *Harvard Law Review* 106, no. 8 (1993): 1709–1791.
Kairys, David. "Unexplainable on Grounds Other Than Race." *American University Law Review* 45 (February 1996): 729–749.

———. *With Liberty and Justice for Some: A Critique of the Conservative Supreme Court.* New York: New Press, 1993.

Massey, Douglas S., and Nancy A. Denton. *American Apartheid: Segregation and the Making of the Underclass.* Cambridge, Mass.: Harvard University Press, 1993.

Merton, Robert K. "Discrimination and the American Creed." In *Discrimination and National Welfare,* edited by Robert W. MacIver. New York: Harper, 1949.

Oliver, Melvin L., and Thomas M. Shapiro. *Black Wealth/White Wealth: A New Perspective on Racial Inequality.* New York: Routledge, 1995.

Weschler, Lawrence. *A Miracle, a Universe: Settling Accounts with Torturers.* New York: Pantheon Books, 1990.

Winant, Howard. *The World Is a Ghetto: Race and Democracy since World War II.* New York: Basic, 2001.

Zegeye, Abebe, ed. *Social Identities in the New South Africa.* Colorado Springs: International Academic Publishers, 2001.

Howard Winant

DIVERSITY. *Diversity,* as a word or concept, can apply to rocks, plants, animals, people, systems of law, and much else. In the United States, since the 1970s, its immediate reference, if the word is presented with nothing more to specify it, is to the diversity of races, ethnic groups, and language groups that make the United States possibly the most diverse country in the world. But its import extends far beyond its use as a neutral descriptor of this variety: It rather refers to an ideology in which this diversity is prized, considered a benefit to the society, and is to be responded to positively in public policy and by major nongovernmental interests.

Of course the differences among people can be described in many ways aside from race or ethnicity: One can refer to their opinions, their character, their height and weight, the degree of their health, and so on. But "diversity," as it is has come to be used in public and scholarly discourse since the 1970s, refers specifically to those differences, primarily in race and ethnicity, that have been the basis of exclusion or segregation or differential treatment in public action and private social interaction. Its use and import is intimately linked to the great divide of race that has shaped so much of American history, society, and culture. This specific current meaning of *diversity* grows out of the great effort in the 1950s and 1960s to overcome the inferior position, in law and social treatment, of American blacks. The civil rights revolution of the 1950s and 1960s, marked by major constitutional legal decisions, major legislation, insurgent social movements, violence, and changing ideologies and political demands, shaped the emergence of diversity as a central concept used to justify policies to favor excluded groups, primarily American blacks.

Very rapidly groups whose disabilities could be, with more or less justice, considered equivalent to those that blacks had suffered were included among those who contributed to the diversity of American society, a diversity that was now to be seen not as a problem but a benefit and a virtue, a pillar of American society. Most directly parallel to blacks in making up the roster of groups that were part of this diversity were the nonwhite races—American Indians ("Native Americans," in one increasingly popular formulation) and Asians (Chinese, Japanese, and many other groups, all of which are considered separate "races" in the U.S. census). A fourth group, "Hispanic Americans," as the census came to call them in 1980 (after trying "Spanish surnamed" in earlier censuses as a means of identifying a group considered "different" but clearly not a "race"), became part of the roster of the diverse, because they too suffered from disabilities—discrimination on the basis of physical differences from whites that approximate differences of race, and difference in language. These four groups emerged in the 1960s as those among the diversity of American groups that deserved some redress because of the discrimination they suffered. Asian Americans then consisted almost entirely of Chinese and Japanese, while Hispanics consisted almost entirely of Puerto Ricans and Mexicans. But very rapidly, as a result of major immigration reforms in 1965, the Asians expanded to include Indians, Koreans, Vietnamese, and many other Asian groups; and the Hispanics expanded to include Cubans, Nicaraguans, Salvadorans, Dominicans, and many other peoples from Central and Latin America and the Caribbean who left their native lands because of civil war and economic hardship.

In the wake of the civil rights legislation of the 1960s, and the institution of federal requirements for affirmative action by employers and federal contractors, employers and educational institutions were required to provide counts of their employees and students according to these ethnoracial groups and by gender. Women were part of the roster of the recognized diverse that deserved some public acknowledgment from the beginning. The disabled were soon included, under legislation parallel to civil rights legislation prohibiting discrimination against them. Those different because of sexual orientation—gays and lesbians—are also considered part of American diversity, but they receive as yet no public recognition parallel to that of the four ethnoracial groups and women. But in the world of higher education in particular, their distinctiveness and contribution to a valued diversity is broadly recognized, in ways parallel to those that recognize and respond to ethnoracial and gender diversity: through recognized student groups, courses of study devoted to the group, and the like.

Before Diversity

One kind of diversity, ethnic diversity among white Americans, is not much recognized in the current discourse on diversity, or in policies that recognize or respond to diversity. Yet before diversity became a prevailing concept to recognize and appreciate significant differences among Americans, other concepts—such as the "melting pot" and "cultural pluralism"—emerged to respond to and recognize ethnic differences among white Europeans (though they were then not all necessarily considered "white"). These concepts emerged because the large new immigrant groups of the late nineteenth and early twentieth centuries—Jews, Italians, Poles, Slavic groups, Greeks, and others from eastern and southern Europe and the Near East—were seen as different from and inferior to previous immigrants from Great Britain and northern and western Europe, and were subject to various degrees of discrimination.

The concept of the melting pot was given wide circulation by the popular play of that name, written by the English Jewish writer Israel Zangwill in 1908. But there are earlier parallels to the melting pot in the works of the nineteenth-century American writers Ralph Waldo Emerson, Herman Melville, and Walt Whitman. The melting pot concept disputes the assumption of inferiority of the newer immigrants that was so widespread among scholars and political leaders in the early twentieth century. It implies the equality of all European groups and their equal qualifications and right to form part of and merge into the common American people. While it has on the whole a positive and benign import, the melting pot gives no acknowledgment to the idea that these groups to be merged into Anglo-America might resist assimilation, might want to cling to differences in culture and language and religion. Associated with the prevailing melting pot ideology of the early twentieth century were programs of "Americanization," the teaching of English and American history and political practice. These became particularly intense and intrusive during World War I, when it was widely feared that immigrant and ethnic groups would respond to this crisis by taking the part of their native countries, rather than as assimilated Americans.

The melting pot was then countered by a new ideology of "cultural pluralism," formulated in World War I by the philosopher Horace Kallen, who argued that America could be a symphony of diverse cultural strands that resisted forceful assimilation and Americanization. The condition of American blacks played no role in the philosophy of cultural pluralism—it referred only to European immigrants. But cultural pluralism was a rather isolated concept, advocated by few and overwhelmed by the rush to assimilation. It emerged under other names and forms in World War II—for example, "intercultural education"—because in that war the buried identifications with European homeland were seen as aiding the American war effort rather than countering American loyalty; German dictator Adolf Hitler had oppressed so many people who could be energized to oppose him. The appreciation of difference that emerged in World War II and the postwar world now began to include blacks. Hitler's racism was the enemy. Could American racism be unaffected? As American racism became for the first time since Reconstruction part of the national American political agenda, the stage was set for the civil rights revolution, civil rights legislation, and the canonization of diversity.

From Affirmative Action to Diversity

Affirmative action—federal policies and court decisions requiring employers and federal contractors and local and state governments to try to employ persons from the four ethno-racial groups and women in numbers proportionate to their presence in the labor force—was instituted in the late 1960s. It has been controversial ever since. Alongside of affirmative action in employment, colleges and universities instituted programs to increase the number of black and Hispanic students, though blacks comprised the main group of interest. These programs were not (for the most part) legally required but were instituted voluntarily, or in response to black student protest. Taking account of race required reducing the weight

of academic achievement in admissions decisions. Both in the case of affirmative action in employment and in admissions to colleges and universities, greater diversity as such was initially neither the objective nor the justification: Getting higher numbers of black students than could be admitted on the basis of academic grades was the objective, and making up for past discrimination was the justification. But in a key U.S. Supreme Court case from 1978, *Regents of University of California v. Bakke* (438 U.S. 265), diversity as a value in education became the sole legitimate legal basis for special consideration in admissions on the basis of race. Institutions—primarily in the South—that had once discriminated against blacks were already required by federal intervention and court order to institute quotas and preference for blacks. Most institutions in the North and West, however, had no such history.

The University of California, Davis, medical school, which was sued for impermissible discrimination against whites on the basis of race in the *Bakke* case, could not claim that its quota for underrepresented minorities was making up for past discrimination; as a young medical school, it had never discriminated. Nevertheless it had a quota for underrepresented minorities. Four justices asserted that race could not be taken into account, four asserted it could because of societal discrimination against blacks, and one justice, Lewis Powell, joined the latter four with his own justification for preference for underrepresented minorities: Student diversity would improve the educational environment by introducing the views of underrepresented groups into the educational process. This was the argument made in an amicus brief filed in the case by Columbia, Harvard, and Stanford Universities, and the University of Pennsylvania. The brief described Harvard's admissions process as giving a plus for race to help create this diverse environment.

Various weaknesses in this argument for consideration of race have been pointed out, such as that there is no necessary connection between race and ethnicity and the views students bring to the classroom, but student diversity has since became the sole legal basis for preference. Educational institutions—undergraduate, graduate, and professional—began to lean heavily on diversity as their justification for a preference to which they are uniformly committed, for a range of reasons that would not pass constitutional muster. Important and large-scale research has been conducted to demonstrate the benefits of racial and ethnic diversity in higher education.

In 2003 the Supreme Court was forced to return to the issue of racial and ethnic preference in higher education because federal circuit courts were divided on the issue. In *Grutter v. Bollinger* (539 U.S. 306), which challenged race preference in admissions to the University of Michigan Law School, the centrality of diversity as *the* justification for affirmative action was enshrined in a new decision. The Court was very much in the same divided posture as in 1978: for four justices, to take race into account was unconstitutional; in opposition, four liberal justices defended this policy on wide grounds; and a single justice, Sandra Day O'Connor, joined the four liberal justices for the single reason, spelled out at length, that diversity aided the educational process:

The Law School's educational judgment that such diversity is essential to its educational mission is one to which we defer. The Law School's assessment that diversity, will, in fact, yield educational benefits is substantiated by respondents and their *amici*. . . . These benefits are not theoretical but real, as major American businesses have made clear that the skills necessary in today's increasingly global marketplace can only be developed through exposure to widely diverse people, cultures, ideas, and viewpoints. [Here Justice O'Connor refers to briefs by 3M Company, General Motors Corporation, and other corporations.]. . . What is more, high-ranking retired officers and civilian leaders of the United States military assert that, "[b]ased on [their] decades of experience," a "highly qualified, racially diverse officer corps . . . is essential to the military's ability to fulfill its principle [*sic*] mission to provide national security." (*Grutter v. Bollinger,* pp. 330–331)

When the military-industrial complex, as well as the leaders of major U.S. universities, embrace diversity as a valued objective, it is clear that a great deal happened in the twenty-five years between Justice Powell's somewhat surprising choice of this single justification of affirmative action and Justice O'Connor's wide-ranging argument in its favor. America had changed. Affirmative action might still be opposed by a majority of Americans (state referenda in California and Washington had rejected it). Diversity, however, had been embraced by all.

The Diverse Society
This change cannot be ascribed only to these Supreme Court decisions, important as they are for the behavior of colleges, universities, and professional schools; it also reflects a large cultural change, and an evaluation of diversity's pragmatic benefits by key interests in American society. In the 1980s, under the administration of President Ronald Reagan, high officials hoped to limit government's affirmative action requirements by modifying the executive order that had instituted it. They discovered to their surprise, however, that big business no longer wanted to change what they had once seen as a burden. To have employees from a wide range of groups was now seen as a benefit in dealing with increasingly diverse customers and suppliers. Appreciation of diversity was widely taught in the business world, and business was perhaps more energetic in training its employees in the proper consideration of diversity than higher education itself. Affirmative action had been launched when minorities consisted overwhelmingly of blacks alone. With the opening of immigration in 1965, and the beginning of a large and unceasing flood of immigrants from Latin America, Asia, the Caribbean, and increasingly Africa, the groups considered "minority" swelled, diversity expanded, and responding to it became ever more important to businesses, the military, and politicians.

Education, however, remains in the forefront of the response to and embrace of diversity. In the 1960s, multicultural education—the inclusion in curricula of material on the four minority groups, and furthermore, the reflection of their grievances and interests everywhere in the curriculum—

became a key demand of minority groups, leading to fierce controversies. Very rapidly these demands were widely recognized as legitimate. (*Multiculturalism* was the term under which these battles were fought, but it raised the same issues as *diversity:* The only difference was that *multiculturalism* had a more muscular and aggressive tone, whereas *diversity* seemed a more accommodating concept.) The content of major parts of elementary and secondary education was transformed, particularly history, English, and social studies; sometimes even mathematics and science were affected. Textbooks were transformed under new state requirements to recognize diversity. Diversity also called for increasing efforts to recruit minorities as teachers and administrators, and many minority educational leaders became superintendents of major school systems.

The impact on higher education was as great but somewhat more restricted. The demands of diversity were reflected in new programs of black studies; Hispanic, Asian, and Native American studies; women's studies; and gay and lesbian studies. Furthermore, on many campuses special living quarters and social centers were created for minority groups, and there was a heightened emphasis on the recruitment of faculty from each group. The philosophy of diversity became the common linking outlook of university presidents—all embraced it, and there were no dissidents.

The military was possibly the most successful institution in responding to and reflecting the new appreciation of diversity. The military academies—like all institutions of higher education—instituted programs to recruit larger numbers of minority officers, and it was particularly essential that they succeed because so many of those enrolled in the voluntary military forces were from minority groups. In America's wars in the 1990s against Iraq, black and Hispanic officers held the highest positions.

Governing a Diverse Society
The United States is of course not the only diverse society. Other immigrant and liberal democratic societies—such as Canada, Australia, and New Zealand—have been as active or more active in the recognition of diversity. The liberal democracies of western Europe have become more diverse under the impact of immigration, first fostered because of labor shortages, then continuing because their liberal traditions accept such reasons for immigration as the unification of families and the seeking of refuge from persecution. In this way, the ideology of diversity has spread throughout the liberal democratic world.

In each country one may see variations in the response to diversity. Thus, Canada became a leader in promoting multiculturalism in its efforts to accommodate the demands and interests of francophone Quebec. This has made it particularly sensitive to claims of other groups, and it offered opportunities to maintain cultural distinctiveness to immigrant groups that cannot lay claim to a specific territory. It would go too far afield to describe all the various responses to diversity, but in general the kind of forceful assimilation that was common in the past—as in the case of "Russification" in the Russian empire—is everywhere in the liberal democratic world in retreat. Turkey, for example, which had long suppressed the language and autonomy claims of its large Kurdish minority, has had to acknowledge these claims as it aims to enter the European Union.

But liberal democratic political theory, which is oriented to the individual and the individual's rights, does not sit easily with the range of issues raised by diversity. What are the rights of the group, or the rights of an individual as part of a group? The classic work of twentieth-century liberalism, John Rawls's *A Theory of Justice* (1971), takes no account of this issue—the individual confronts the state or society with no intermediate formation, and this is true of classic liberal political theory generally. If a group is concentrated in a territory, one can accommodate its interests through some degree of autonomy, but when, as in the United States and in other immigrant societies, a group is spread through the population, the recognition of diversity raises difficult questions, as was particularly evident in the battles over multiculturalism in the 1980s and 1990s in the United States. Similar conflicts are ever more evident in western Europe. What becomes of the historic national identity when a range of diverse groups is given recognition, appreciation, and places at the tables of education, culture, and government? These issues will be part of the agenda of the liberal democratic world for many years to come.

See also **Americanization, U.S.; Assimilation; Ethnicity and Race; Nation.**

BIBLIOGRAPHY

Bowen, William G., and Derek Bok. *The Shape of the River: Long-Term Consequences of Considering Race in College and University Admissions.* Princeton, N.J.: Princeton University Press, 1998.

Glazer, Nathan. *We Are All Multiculturalists Now.* Cambridge, Mass.: Harvard University Press, 1997.

Kallen, Horace M. *Culture and Democracy in the United States.* New York: Boni and Liveright, 1924. Reprint, with a new introduction by Stephen J. Whitfield, New Brunswick, N.J.: Transaction, 1998.

Kymlicka, Will, ed. *The Rights of Minority Cultures.* Oxford: Oxford University Press, 1995.

Lynch, Frederic R. *The Diversity Machine: The Drive to Change the "White Male Workplace."* New York: Free Press, 1997.

Schuck, Peter H. *Diversity in America: Keeping Government at a Safe Distance.* Cambridge, Mass.: Harvard University Press, Belknap Press, 2003.

Wood, Peter. *Diversity: The Invention of a Concept.* San Francisco: Encounter Books, 2003.

Nathan Glazer

DRAMA. *See* **Theater and Performance; Tragedy and Comedy.**

DREAM. It is midnight in the desert, and the full moon has just passed its apex. On the sandy ground, staff in hand, guitar and jug by his side, a dark-skinned man is nuzzled by a tawny-maned lion. Is the man dreaming? Are we? Or is this

the dream of the artist, Henri Rousseau (1844–1910)? If, as some traditions have it, the Universe was dreamed into existence by its Creator, then it makes perfect sense that all of art—the microcosm created by human beings in emulation of the Creator's macrocosm—is a dream of sorts. And art is a dream, in a way—a projection of the deepest subconscious and unconscious desires upon canvas and stone, the etching plate and the loom. But when artists depict dreams and dreaming, whether explicitly, with the dreamer in the picture, or implicitly, with the picture illustrating the dream, ambiguities flourish, and polyvalency abounds.

There are many loci classici of the dream in art, in many times, places, and cultures. Some are explicit, yet ambiguous, like Rousseau's *Sleeping Gypsy* of 1897. Some are explicit and distinctly unambiguous, such as Francisco Goya's (1746–1826) *Capricho 43: El Sueno de la Razon Produce Monstruos* (1797–1798, "The Sleep/Dream of Reason Begets Monsters") or Henry Fuseli's (1741–1825) *The Nightmare* (1781) where dreams are made manifest in oil on canvas. Even those depictions in which the intention to depict a dream is overt are fraught with a multiplicity of interpretive possibilities—Maurice Sendak's (b. 1928) nightmare creatures in *Where the Wild Things Are* (1963) are both the products of the dreams of Max, the young protagonist, and of Sendak's own family history, wherein those things that go bump in the night are stand-ins for his loud, invasive, cheek-pinching aunts and uncles.

Antiquity

Just as Max creates a world in his dream, Krishna acts out the role of Vishnu in his sleep, and the universe is created out of the navel of the dreaming god. The individual adept, like the artist, assumes the role of conscious creator. Dreams have been represented in art for thousands of years. The Talmud describes sleep as "one-sixtieth part of death," one part in sixty being the threshold of perception for Jewish legal purposes— a taste, in other words, of what death is like. Likewise did the ancient Egyptians consider sleep a sort of preliminary glimpse of death, and in dreams, certain aspects of what one would call the soul encountered the upper and lower realms. The lessons thus learned were transmitted by the forces of the other world to the priests of the cult of the dead, who could then advise the dead about the pitfalls and pratfalls of the journey before them. The Ba, the spiritual entity that was believed to leave the body both in dreams and in death, is represented as a jabiru bird in art, whether in reliefs or in papyri. It is depicted hovering over the inert body as it is in the famous *Scroll of Ani* of the *Theban Book of the Dead* (c. 1250 B.C.E.).

The Egyptians also evoked the topos of the dream in art in the representation of Bes, god of crossroads and transitions, on the headrests they used as pillows. And the great Sphinx of Giza is among the earliest artworks attributable to a dream, that of Pharaoh Tutmosis IV, who either constructed or— some sources say—uncovered or rediscovered the colossus around 2620 B.C.E. on the basis of a night vision.

Some of the loveliest depictions of sleep and dreams come out of the Hellenistic-Roman world. In Greek mythology, Nyx (Night) gives birth to Hypnos (Sleep) and Thanatos (Death).

The god of dreams is Morpheus, whose symbols are a smoking horn and a staff, symbols respectively of false and true dreams. Morpheus is not often represented in art, but Hypnos is, quite often and quite beautifully. He receives a melancholically sensitive treatment in a Roman copy of a lost Bronze statue of the fourth century B.C.E., which simply depicts a winged, sleeping, boyish head. And on the famous and controversial Euphronius (flourished c. 520–470 B.C.E.) krater (Greece, 520–510 B.C.E.), a winged Hypnos is paired with his twin brother Thanatos, gently bearing Sarpedon to his eternal sleep.

The Bible in the Middle Ages

In the biblical tradition, sleep is rarely personified, but dreams bear great significance as prophetic moments, or as the means of connection between the divine and the earthly realms. Thus, occasions arise in art not to depict images that are "dreamlike," or that one may imagine represent the artists' dreams, but that, rather, explicitly represent dreams as described in the text of the bible. Most often, these depictions include the dreamer, with the dream itself in a realm slightly above and beyond. In both Jewish and Christian art from late antiquity through the Renaissance, the biblical dreams of the Patriarchs Jacob and Joseph, the Egyptian Pharoah, and of King Nebuchadnezzar are favorite subjects for depiction. The New Testament and, particularly, its apochrypha introduce the subjects of the dreams of Joseph the husband of Mary, those of Three Magi, and that of Pilate's wife. The dreams are depicted sometimes simply, sometimes with elaboration, but the fact that the viewer recognizes that these are crucial prophetic turning points in the story make them ever powerful.

While many of the illustrations, illuminations, and carvings depicting these subjects are anonymous, biblical and apocryphal dreams were treated by artists known to history, such as Simone dei Crocifissi (1330–1399), whose "Dream of the Virgin" heralded an interest in this topos in Italian painting of the fourteenth century, and Piero Della Francesca's (1415–1492) quiet and lyrical depiction of *Constantine's Dream* as part of the fresco cycle of the *Legend of the True Cross* in the Church of San Francesco in Arezzo, Italy (c. 1457–1458). Night scenes are notoriously difficult to depict, yet the artists, through the simple devices of positioning and composition, manage to convey a supernal and pervasive sense of quietness, calm, and sacred anticipation.

Saints and Holy People, East and West

Depictions of prophetic dreams or dreams that advance the narrative of a sacred tale or myth are not limited to the biblical realm—saints and holy people of all religious traditions are depicted in art. Vittore Carpaccio's (c. 1455–c. 1525) lyrical *Dream of St. Ursula* (Italy, early sixteenth century) is devoted mostly to a depiction of the saint asleep in bed, with a rather self-effacing angel as the only evidence that we are witnessing a dream. Again, a modesty, a sense of calm permeates the composition. In Asian art, one can view depictions of the dream of Maya, the Buddah's future mother, in which, wakeful, she sees the white elephant that symbolizes her son's birth. The Indian *Bhagavata Purana* of the nineteenth century describes a spontaneous out-of-body experience, a dream flight by a woman named Usha, from which she returned with verifiable information. Her flight is depicted in illuminated manuscripts with a jewel-like clarity that parallels the clarity of her vision. And in Muslim iconography, Muhammad's nighttime conversations with the angel Gabriel show the prophet awake but in his bed, engaged in a rather static conversation (Iran, fifteenth century). By way of contrast, the beautiful iconography of the famous *Night Journey* tends to show Muhammad in action—on his mount al-Buraq, speeding through the clouds and accompanied by angels and celestial beings.

While we like to think of dreams as spontaneous, it has long been known that they can be incubated or induced, and from antiquity through the modern period, sacred sites were used as loci of incubation. In the East and in the West, temples and churches dedicated to various deities and saints were places whose architecture and geographical disposition were believed to be conducive to dream incubation, and where believers retreated, prepared themselves, and received their visionary experiences. The total environment of these places—as enhanced by art, among other factors—was key in terms of the potential success of the visionary process.

And when dreams do come, they could advocate reconsideration of even those aspects of the culture most taken for granted—the appearance of the gods. Like the dream that gave birth to the sphinx, dreams can often be the cause of the creation of new iconography or the alteration of existing iconographic conventions, as they represent the direct intervention of the higher powers through the realm of vision. Although part of a strictly aniconic culture when it came to the depiction of the deity, the visions of the prophets Isaiah and Ezekiel, though both glimpses of the God of Israel, presented radically different "images" of that imageless deity that influenced the way those in the West envision God. Likewise, Kan Hiu, a Chinese Buddhist monk who was also a painter and a poet in the late ninth and early tenth century, was able to radically change conventional portrayals of the Buddhist saints through the inspiration of dreams. The way in which he envisioned these people was sometimes at odds with historical tradition as transmitted by the mainstream, but his vision was so compelling that the tradition changed to accommodate it. And in the same way, the visions of St. Bridget of Sweden (c. 1303–1373) completely altered the view of the Nativity for Christianity. The snowy landscape, the broken manger, the many details of the story as it is commonly depicted are responses to her dream.

Finally, inspiration and even instruction in art is attributed to dreams. William Blake (1757–1827) claimed he was instructed in painting by a spirit who appeared in his dreams in the form of a man, and whom he depicted in a lost sketch (copied, fortunately, by a friend around 1819).

Native and Tribal Societies

The dream as a time out of time, depicted from the perspective of a soul out of body, is an important topos in native and tribal cultures. The native peoples of what is now Australia imagined the Dreamtime—an era in which humans and nature came to be as they are now. They created *churinga*, magical depictions, tracings, or maps of Dreamtime events seen from the point of view of the spiritual essence of the individual, that part of the self that exists outside of time. These are similar to maps made by shamans in a number of cultures—both in the northern and southern hemispheres and over the historical *longue durée*—depicting their dream journeys.

In native and tribal society, the active dream—the one that the dreamer calls down upon him or herself and in which he or she is a conscious participant—is an important factor in religious and spiritual life, and art and adornment help create the atmosphere in which such dreams may be invoked. An Arapaho dress, made in Oklahoma around 1890, situates the dreamer at the conjunction of various symbols that make it clear that she is on the threshold between light and darkness, between the spirit and the material worlds.

Iroquois people danced in cornhusk masks in order to help recall forgotten dreams, since these were believed to be windows on the soul. The masks, with their hungry, haunted, and longing looks, were meant to symbolize the psychological state of the dreamers seeking to remember their dream-desires and enact them in order to fulfill the hunger of their souls.

Dreams as Symbolic and Spiritual

Sleep and dreams in art can also take on symbolic and what one would term psychological valences, what would have been called at the times and places of the creation of the art stages or stations in the spiritual journey. The story of the *Seven Sleepers of Ephesus* was current in the sixth century and remained popular in both East and West throughout the Middle Ages. Paintings of this theme based in the Sufi tradition depict the seven sleepers as seven stages of human personality and its awakening into full development. Likewise, in some Arab and Muslim traditions, five sleeping, dreaming, and waking figures may represent the five organs of spiritual perception into the care of which one is delivered after regaining consciousness in sleep. The dream as a nexus for the quest for love and knowledge is vividly illustrated in the *Hypnerotomachia Poliphili* (1499), an erudite, enigmatic, and beautifully illustrated example of the book arts of the Renaissance that depicts the dream of the protagonist Poliphilo in his quest for his beloved Polia (Greek for "many things"). And the waking of the self from the dream is drawn in parallel with the alchemical process of the refinement of metals in the woodcuts of Giovanni Battista Nazari's (1533–1599) *Della Transmutatione Metallica, sogni tre* (Brescia, 1599).

Dreams and the Visionary: Fifteenth to Eighteenth Centuries

The late medieval and early modern periods saw the triumph of the visionary in art. While not illustrations of dreams or dreamers per se, the work of this period, including the phantasms of Hieronymous Bosch (c. 1450–1516), Pieter Bruegel the Elder (c. 1525–1569), and others, first in large-scale commissions and later in more popular prints, brought the realm of the dream-like and highly imaginative to a growing audience, taking the visionary beyond the confines of the physical building of the church, and into the street. Popular series, some anonymous, some attributable to artists like Jean Duvet

(1485–1561), include prints illustrating visions of heaven and hell and of the apocalypse.

The rise of popular interest in the natural world—particularly in alchemy—gave rise to a host of fantastic images in alchemical works of the seventeenth century illustrated by Theodor de Bry (1528–1598) and others. Baroque art transformed the quotidian into the phantasmagoric, and as such, can also be viewed as dreamlike in its elaboration and imaginative ornamentation. But however dreamlike the imagery, less emphasis is ultimately placed in this period on dreams and the dreamer—on imaginative phenomena occurring outside the range of perceivable reality and nature—and more attention is devoted to the overriding interest in the ingenious exposition of the natural in fanciful ways.

Psychoanalysis, the Dream, and Art in the Nineteenth and Twentieth Centuries

The nineteenth century heralded a revolution in the understanding of the dream, with Sigmund Freud (1836–1939) and Carl Jung (1875–1961) engaging very different interpretations of what both agreed was a phenomenon highly significant for the understanding of the farthest reaches of the human subconscious. Freud argued that dreams revealed the most occluded aspects of the individual unconscious, particularly the realm of sublimated sexual desire, the universal constant of the human condition. Jung saw the dream as tapping into the universal consciousness of humankind, and containing symbols that permeate all human cultures, ultimately uniting humans in what he argued was a more elevated universal and common bond than Freud's lowest common denominator. Art since the nineteenth century has blended these two currents, with most manifestations depicting the dream experience from the perspective of the individual (one sees the dream but not the dreamer), displaying a pervasive sexuality (whether implicit or explicit), and drawing upon the rich symbolic treasury of the entire history of world art. Consciousness of the importance of the dream experience for and in art has resulted in the creation of dream realms that are awe-inspiring, fascinating, and quite often frightening. Salvador Dali (1904–1989) and René Magritte (1898–1967) both play with the idea of the elasticity of time and perspective in the dream, while Giorgio De Chirico's (1888–1978) dreamscapes have to do with the bending of space. Paul Delvaux's (1897–1994) dreamlike scenes are simultaneously sexual and menacing, whereas Marc Chagall's (1887–1985) work is playful, blending the quotidian and the bizarre in a lush, colorful, and romantic synthesis that is instantly recognizable as "dreamlike." Max Ernst's (1891–1976) overlapping and repeated images—recognizable, yet juxtaposed incongruously, Paul Klee's (1879–1940) often extremely playful and "light" images that yet conceal a highly intellectual subtext, Rousseau's lush forests and spare deserts of the imagination, and the elemental power of Constantin Brancusi's (1876–1957) visions of flight (a common element in dreams) are but a few manifestations of the dream in twentieth century art.

The dream is a particularly widespread theme in film and photography. From Edwin Porter's (1969–1941) early short films, notably *An Artist's Dream* (1900) and *Dream of a Rarebit*

Fiend (1906), to the dream sequence in Alfred Hitchcock's (1899–1980) *Vertigo* (1958), Akira Kurosawa's (1910–1998) *Dreams* (1990), and the vivid dream landscapes of Ingmar Bergman's (b. 1918) *Wild Strawberries* (1957) and Federico Fellini's (1920–1993) *8 1/2* (1963), the very nature of film has proved fertile ground for the exposition of dreams through the varying lenses of each director. The deceptive realism of film provides an excellent foil for the recounting of dreams through the eyes of the dreamer.

Contemporary Art

Contemporary art is so much enamored of the idea of the dream that one would be hard-pressed to name an artist in the postwar era who did not engage the subject on some level. The work or stages in the work of some artists revolves around dreams. African and African-American artists such as Olu Amoda (b. 1959), in his *Window of Dreams* (1991), and Jacob Lawrence (1917–2000), with his *Dreams #2* (1965), have engaged the dream as a metaphor in particularly poignant and affecting ways.

Though photography is a static medium, it is like film in that it is self-conscious about giving the appearance of replicating reality while never actually and completely doing so. Jerry Uelsman's (b. 1934) untitled images with dream themes owe their sensibility to the painted dreamscapes of the nineteenth century, while works like Ralph Gibson's (b. 1939) *Sonambulist Series* (1968), with its creepy hand reaching out of a doorway, draw on the fearful depths of human consciousness, known to the ancients, filtered through Freud and Jung, and always lurking under the surface.

Yet the dark and menacing vision, as eternal and pervasive as it is, is matched by an equally pervasive transcendent mythic consciousness. Contemporary photographers Suzanne Scherer (b. 1964) and Pavel Ouporov (b. 1966), in their preoccupation with the dream, draw on such mythic archetypes as a dream maze replete with minotaur, and an Icarus-like flying dreamer, a topos they share with contemporary artists, notably Jonathan Borofsky (b. 1942) in his series titled *I dreamed I could fly. . . .* These works articulate and draw upon common dream themes in all times and places, from Muhammad's flight to Usha's, to the launching of the very universe from Krishna's dream.

See also **Consciousness; Mind; Psychoanalysis; Surrealism.**

BIBLIOGRAPHY

Bergson, Henri. *Dreams.* Translated with an introduction by Edwin E. Slosson. London: Unwin, 1914.

Campbell, Joseph, ed. *Myths, Dreams, and Religion.* New York: Dutton, 1970.

Coxhead, David, and Susan Hiller. *Dreams: Visions of the Night.* London: Thames and Hudson, 1976.

Devereux, George, ed. *Psychoanalysis and the Occult.* New York: International Universities Press, 1973.

Freud, Sigmund. *On Dreams.* Vols. 4 and 5. Translated from the German under the general editorship of James Strachey. London: Hogarth Press, 1953. The standard edition of the complete psychological works of Sigmund Freud.

Gamwell, Lynn, ed. *Dreams 1900–2000: Science, Art, and the Unconscious Mind.* Ithaca, N.Y.: Cornell University Press, 2000.

Jung, Carl Gustav. *Dreams.* Translated by R. F. C. Hull. Princeton, N.J.: Princeton University Press, 1974.

Marc Michael Epstein

DRESS.   Since the 1980s new generations of academics, collectors, curators, and enthusiasts have discovered the value of the study of dress as an analytical research tool through which to examine aspects of social and economic history, material culture, cultural and gender studies, art history, anthropology, and sociology. As a consequence, the study of the history of dress has been transformed from its marginalized place of professional connoisseurship and amateur enthusiasms to become a firmly established academic and museum-based subject.

In the world of ethnography, a reconsideration of the cultural significance of clothing coupled with a rejection of old imperial approaches to ethnographical artifacts has revolutionized the field. In the early twenty-first century ethnographical museums have reconfigured their collections and displays, creating "living culture" exhibitions. These, as Michael Ross and Reg Crowshoe insist, must "see the world through another's eyes" and must ensure that "respect [is] given to another world view" (p. 240). Many ethnographical museums are also faced with serious questioning about their right to hold on to artifacts that are specifically sacred to their communities of origin, who now demand their return.

The study of dress, especially European-American fashionable dress, has long had to deal with accusations, usually from male academics, that the entire subject is a frivolous, female, trivial interest. However, the use of material culture and history of consumption debates have finally overwhelmed these prejudices. Material culture approaches stem from the premise that all goods carry a weight of cultural meanings that can be specifically "read" through object-based and consumption analysis. Anne Smart Martin states that "material objects matter because they are complex, symbolic bundles of social, cultural and individual meanings fused onto something we can touch, see and own" (p. 142).

Even when the clothes themselves have gone, their shadows survive through archives such as diaries and family accounts. Amanda Vickery studied the dress of Mrs. Elizabeth Shackleton, a well-off textile merchant's widow from the north of England, through a set of surviving personal papers dating from 1762 to 1781. Vickery concludes that Mrs. Shackleton used her clothing to identify her exact place in her gentry/ merchant-class community. She did this by simplifying aristocratic style, consuming fashion with care and consideration, and altering her favorite clothes. Vickery shows that some clothes became so important to Shackleton in terms of family memory that they acquired talismanic characteristics. Vickery declares finally that her study of Mrs. Shackleton indicates significantly that women were highly responsible managers of "daily household consumption" (1993, p. 274) and far from frivolous spenders.

In 1998, Christopher Breward usefully outlined dress research developed from cultural and media studies. He noted a new interest in dress within social anthropology and semiotics, for example, citing approaches by Ferdinand de Saussure and Roland Barthes as offering "cultural signifying systems, allowing the scholar to examine the social specificity of representations and their meaning across different cultural practices" (p. 306). Such dress-related representations include issues of behavior, the construction of appearance, the political question of identities (race, gender, and sexuality), subcultures, and semiotic interpretations of dress in films, literature, and magazines.

Caroline Evans discusses punk dress (with its patched-together use of schoolgirl uniform, bondage dress, and aggressive hair styling) as epitomizing a set of signs whose meaning is changed "through being jumbled up, re-ordered and re-contextualised next to other signs" (1997, p. 107). Fred Davis, in *Fashion, Culture, and Identity* (1992), also examined clothing as a nonverbal means of communicating social identity, "as this is framed by cultural values bearing on gender, sexuality, social status, age, etc." (p. 191). In refuting the trickle-down style-diffusion theory, he concludes that there are two fashion systems at play at the turn of the millennium, the globalized world of mass, commodified, international fashion and the "veritable cacophony of local, sometimes exceedingly transient, dress tendencies and styles each attached, however loosely, to its own particularity, be it a subculture, an age grade, a political persuasion an ethnic identity" (p. 206).

Feminist approaches. Vickery, Jane Gaines, and Elizabeth Wilson have argued that feminist consumption analysis of the 1970s all too easily accepted a male view that women's interest in dress was frivolous and that women had indeed allowed themselves to become "the gilding of the patriarchal cage," on display for male pleasure (Vickery, 1998, p. 274). Wilson comments how strange it is that "when so much else has changed there still exists such a strong hostility to fashion amongst so many radicals" (p. 28). She proposes that feminists should accept "fashion as a legitimate and highly aesthetic pleasure," (p. 33), a view shared by Caroline Evans and Minna Thornton, who wrote in 1989 that fashion "is a field in which women have found pleasure in the elaboration of meaning—meaning which is there to be taken and used" (p. xv).

Analysis of male dress. A new development in the 1990s, building on Farid Chenoune's innovative *History of Men's Fashions* (1993), has been the emergence of new critical examinations of menswear. This differs from the subcultural focus of Dick Hebdige in that it looks at a far wider social range of male clothing. Christopher Breward, Frank Mort, and John Tosh focus on the late nineteenth and twentieth centuries rather than on earlier periods. Their studies investigate not only the style, retailing, and consumption of men's clothing, but also the cultural processes surrounding the construction of masculinity and they provide, for the first time, an analysis of gay culture and its impact on mainstream dressing.

Thus, the whole field of dress history and dress studies has undergone a dynamic transformation since the 1980s, though it is useful to remember Patricia Cunningham's warning of 1988 that dress historians should not "follow other approaches

blindly, but rather let our own questions and materials lead us to new approaches" (p. 79).

Constructions of Beauty: Sexuality and Issues of Gendered Dress

Classical Greek art, including dress, has formed the basis of constructions of ideals of male and female bodily and facial beauty in the Western world, as witnessed by the continuing rereferencing of images such as the charioteer of Delphi, a bronze, life-size, votive statue from the Apollo Sanctuary, Delphi, dating from 475 B.C.E., at the end of the early classical period. In her study *Fabrics of Vision: Dress and Drapery in Painting* (2002) Anne Hollander notes that the cutting and shaping of cloth was unknown in ancient Greece. Rather "the beauty of clothing dwelt in the distinction of its woven fabric and the elegance or aptness with which it was draped around the individual body" (pp. 13–14). Typically, the charioteer of Delphi wears a long, simple, Ionic tunic held in place with cords over the shoulders that tie at the front waist. This system frees the arms and allows drapery to fall over the waist and then straight down to the ankles. Hollander notes that "the life likeness in carved Greek clothes and bodies has often produced perfection—a stylization of natural appearances so subtle as to seem absent" (pp. 13–14).

This classical draped perfection has been continually reworked within European-American dress design, nearly always in white fabric, and usually with a high waist. It was most famously appropriated as the symbol of freedom and equality during the French Revolution. Originating in the 1770s antiestablishment, neoclassical paintings of Jacques-Louis David, the style was adopted for use by women in French revolutionary festivals in the period from 1790 to 1795 and became, in modified fashion form, the fashionable attire of European and American women from 1800 until about 1825, when the high waist was abandoned. The next revivals came out of the English arts and crafts and aesthetic movements in the period from 1878 to 1910, favored by progressive, antifashion dressers. This reflected the very same search for natural feminine perfection at a time when the shape of fashionable women was distorted and restricted by corsets and bustles. The search was repeated again by Mariano Fortuny, who famously created his own "Delphos" dresses in finely pleated, plain-colored silk, modeled exactly on the tunic of the charioteer of Delphi. Fortuny produced these from his Venetian palazzo from 1910 until his death in 1949. They were worn by a group of progressive women, in defiance of the fashion of their time. Paris couturiers too, however, have famously reworked classical Greek drapery into the height of seasonal fashion, including Madeleine Vionnet, from about 1918 into the 1930s; Alix, also known as Madame Grés, through the 1930s and 1950s; and since the 1980s, John Galliano.

Maori culture. The ethnographer Dorota Starzecka confirms that among the Maori of New Zealand, ideals of beauty, fashion, and glamour, and concern over creating a strong "visual impact" were traditionally embedded in the cultural practices of both men and women. "Even the most mundane dress or humble ornament was aesthetically pleasing or tasteful; the most successful fashion statement implied

Maori warrior in traditional dress, c. 1840–1940. In Maori culture, great emphasis is placed on appearance, and garments for all purposes—ceremonial or everyday—are chosen to make the most pleasing visual impact. © SEAN SEXTON COLLECTION/ CORBIS

harmony of function, texture and design as well as glamour" (p. 45).

Starzecka, quoting Margaret Mead, notes that a Maori man "anxious to follow the fashion to its highest level would need to dress his hair into a top knot have greenstone pendants and white feathers hanging from his ears; have the rei puta [pendants carved from the teeth of sperm whales] suspended from his neck, have a dogskin cloak around his body" as well as "elaborate indelible tattoo designs over his face and forehead, and over his buttocks and thighs." (p. 39).

Starzecka describes the *moko*, or tattoo, as a fashion, albeit with mythic origins, a sacred practice, which came to New Zealand "as part of the cultural template from Eastern Polynesia. . . . With this elaborate and tastefully designed array of jewelry and other ornaments, including the permanently inscribed indigo-black patterning of the *moko*, the Maori were acutely conscious of personal appearance" (pp. 39–40).

China. In Europe and America trousers were gendered as masculine until women very gradually, through progressive dress movements, encroached on this ownership little by little from the mid-nineteenth century. In China, however, trousers were

worn by both sexes, especially among the rural peasantry. Made in blue cotton dyed with indigo and worn with simple matching jackets, this style can be seen in eighteenth- and nineteenth-century travelers' drawings of the Chinese peasantry.

When Chairman Mao sought to represent sartorially a uniformed image of his evolution from the late 1940s, he selected the same indigo-dyed trousers and jackets for civilian use and the entire population had to wear versions of this work uniform (*zhifu*). Women's patriotic trousered suits (*aiguo ni*), however, had "different styles of shirt and jacket to choose from, primarily distinguished by the detailing of the collar" and the shortness of the jackets (Roberts, p. 23). However, Claire Roberts notes that these differences were so slight that they "may have appeared the same to Western eyes" (p. 22). Despite the shift in political ideology and lifting of harsh dress regulations after Mao's death in 1976, similar styles continued into the new millennium; in the early twenty-first century many ordinary women in China still wear plain trousers and jackets, though Chinese-made jeans often replace Communist-style trousers.

Clothing as a Powerful Container of National and Community Identity

Studies in clothing, as shown in Eileen Hooper-Greenhill's discussion of the return of a Ghost Dance shirt from Glasgow to

Two young Chinese women wearing silk tunics and pants, c. 1900, southern China. While in the cultures of many countries trousers are regarded as a distinctly masculine form of attire, in China they have been part of women's wardrobe for centuries. © MICHAEL MASLAN HISTORIC PHOTOGRAPHS/CORBIS

Lakota Sioux Ghost Dance shirt, c. 1890. In some cultures, certain garments possess great sacred or spiritual importance, such as the Ghost Dance shirt, which the Sioux believed would protect the wearer from harm. MUSEUM OF THE SOUTH DAKOTA STATE HISTORICAL SOCIETY, PIERRE, SOUTH DAKOTA

A designer of Kente cloth holds the textile stamp used to make the design in the fabric hanging behind him. Bonwire, Ghana, c. 2000. Although it originated as the traditional national dress of Ghana, Kente cloth has become popular in the United States as well, where it serves as a symbol of African-American identity and of pride in the wearer's African heritage. © PENNY TWEEDIE/CORBIS

the Lakota Sioux, confirm that dress can carry a profound talismanic weight of sacred meaning, related to the specific religious practices of their community of origin. In the late twentieth and early twenty-first centuries, museums that contained such examples, either looted by conquering and occupying forces or collected by missionaries, anthropologists, or traders, found themselves at the center of demands for their return.

The clash here lies between old imperialist museum approaches and the determination of communities to be respected as living cultures on their own terms. Many such communities see their sacred artifacts as defiled through storage and display in museums. In 1993 the Wounded Knee Survivors Association started a campaign for the repatriation of a Ghost Dance shirt to the Cultural Heritage Center in Pierre, South Dakota. George Crager had collected this shirt after the massacre at Wounded Knee in 1890, when nearly three hundred Lakota Sioux were killed by the Seventh U.S. Cavalry. Crager sold the shirt to Kelvingrove Museum in Glasgow, Scotland, in 1892. By then he was the Lakota interpreter

on Cody's Wild West Show, which visited the city that year. In an awful irony, among the cast were Short Bull and Kicking Bear, both survivors of the massacre.

In the 1880s, Ghost Dance shirts were the center of Sioux ceremonies and were seen as so deeply imbued with protective qualities that they offered protection to wearers against the white man's bullets. As Eileen Hooper-Greenhill explains in her study *Museums and the Interpretation of Visual Culture,* the Glasgow shirt, displayed since the 1950s, had been exposed in a large case with little explanation alongside mixed "Indian" items. Museum curators in Glasgow refused to return the shirt, suggesting that it was a fake. The Wounded Knee Survivors Association petitioned the city, arguing that, as a sacred symbol of their cultural heritage, the shirt's return home would bring healing and dignity to a community plagued with despair, alcoholism, suicide, and loss of identity. The City Council voted in favor of the shirt's return, and it was taken back to Pierre in 1999. Hooper-Greenhill comments that even if doubts over provenance remain, the sacred cultural weight of the shirt to the Lakota Sioux in the 1990s "merited serious consideration" (p. 156).

Kente cloth. Dress exhibitions and debates also question the role of dress within concepts of national identity. National dress, as Lou Taylor confirms, "bears the weight of representation of an entire nation . . . stemming from an urban, knowing, intellectualised awareness of the concept of nationhood" (p. 213). The UCLA Fowler Museum of Cultural History exhibition and book, *Wrapped in Pride: Ghanaian Kente Cloth and African American Identity* (1998), edited by the museum's director, Doran H. Ross, tracks the meanings placed on kente cloth from its "traditional" design, manufacture, and ritualized use in Ghana, including its use as national identity dress, to its consumption in the United States, where it has become a symbol of African-American identity. Ross explains that "the strength of kente [is] in the ideas that bind it to African American life and tie it to the Motherland" (p. 194). Research shows kente-inspired design has been used to mark out specific African-American identity through use in women's fashions, by children to mark Dr. Martin Luther King Jr.'s birthday, for kente ornaments for the African-American Kwanza holiday, and to trim academic and church robes. Ross confirms that all of this anchors this cloth specifically within African-American culture, "enabling" increasing numbers of African-Americans to relate to and buy into their African heritage.

European peasant dress. Dress in rural communities historically carries highly specific visual forms of ethnic identity because it is deeply embedded in local sociocultural tradition and practice. The design of dress is specific to each community, and clothes are worn with pride, uniting the village into one cohesive social and spiritual identity.

Peasant dress was worn in the more isolated rural communities of Europe until World War II. In Hungary, for exam-

ple, over 50 percent of the population lived in the countryside until 1940. In Poland the number was 80 percent. European peasant communities led a parallel existence alongside urban cities (Hofer and Fél, p. 56). Their land was usually owned by wealthy urban families, and their art was informed by urban style, though always on their own terms.

As well as identifying a community, the use of artifacts and festive clothing in seasonal, religious, and life-cycle ceremonies was so central to community belief systems that Tamás Hofer and Edit Fél state that they "represent intentions, emotions and they solemenize human relationships and sanctify them" (Csillery, Fél, and Hofer, p. 3). Every step of a villager's life cycle (birth, courtship, marriage, and death) was celebrated by the entire community, following long-established rules that involved specific use of clothing, which represented their social and spiritual strength and unity.

Among the Matyó people of Mezokövesd, for example, if "a woman died young, her best clothes—followed her into the grave," while "a man's shroud was made from the loose sleeves of the shirt he had worn as a bridegroom" (Csillery, Fél, and Hofer, p. 23). Even though Mezokövesd was poor, interest in

Hungarian peasants in native dress, Mezokövesd, c. 1950. In many rural societies, clothing reflects the historical traditions and ethnic identity of the members. These garments may be worn primarily for special occasions or on an everyday basis. © Hulton-Deutsch Collection/Corbis

Madame de Pompadour (1763–1764) by François-Hubert Drouais. **Oil on canvas.** During the eighteenth century, France was the fashion center of the world. Louis XV's mistress, Madame de Pompadour, introduced many new style innovations to the court. © NATIONAL GALLERY COLLECTION; BY KIND PERMISSION OF THE TRUSTEES OF THE NATIONAL GALLERY, LONDON/CORBIS

Young girl wearing mourning dress consisting of corseted dress with pleated skirt and ruffled neckline and cuffs, c. 1875. British mourning dresses helped usher in a ready-to-wear fashion market to the middle class. Prior to this most clothing was individually ordered and tailored to meet the specific needs of the purchaser, rather than mass-marketed to retail stores. © HULTON-DEUTSCH COLLECTION/CORBIS

clothing was so strong that it was a "leading inspiration of peasant taste and style for surrounded area from the 1870s" (p. 50) because both men's and women's clothes were a riot of proudly flaunted decoration and color. Such clothes were central expressions of ethnic identity and reflected a community's "struggle, sacrifice and joy" (p. 60).

Issues of European-American Fashion Development and Consumption

Paris became the provider of modern, elegant, and costly fashions for royal and aristocratic wear across Europe beginning in the late seventeenth century. Louis XIV established his personal image as *le Roi Soleil* (Sun King) by creating at his palace of Versailles a luxury world entirely devoted to his glorification. Key to this was the appearance of his court and especially the clothing of his courtiers. All encouragement was given to the development of a new silk-weaving industry in the city of Lyon to provide luxury fashion fabrics for the court. Thus, from the early eighteenth century Lyon became the center for the design and manufacture of the most desired fashion silks, which were worn at every European royal court. Paris itself be-

came the center for the retailing of dress and fashion accessories. This successful Paris/Lyon commercial twinning led to the development of the Paris haute couture industry by the late nineteenth century. Through this, Paris held its place as the creator and arbiter of European-American fashion right through to the 1960s, a period of over 350 years. Paris remains the most famous center for the display of fashion, though its designers come from all over the world and are rivaled by those in New London, Milan, Tokyo, and London.

In the eighteenth century, court dressmakers and their urban and aristocratic clients were the orginators of new styles. Aileen Ribeiro emphasizes the centrality of the creative fashion role of the *marchands des modes* in Paris, who "supplied and arranged" all the fancy trimmings on women's dress (p. 68). In 1745, Madame de Pompadour became mistress to Louis XV and, as Ribeiro shows in her study *Dress in Eighteenth-Century Europe,* "her fashion sense was dominant for the next decade; she summed up the elegance of the Rococo" (p. 136). Interestingly, Colin Jones (2002) confirms that Paris, rather than Versailles, set the fashions; Madame de Pompadour "shopped on the Rue St. Honoré and spurred the court to follow the city fashions, rather than rely on the city aping the court" (p. 153).

Britain. In Britain, nineteenth-century mourning dress can be seen as an example of the social control of women through etiquette, but also as an example of the development of a middle-class fashion market, through ready-to-wear manufacture, department store retailing, and advertising. Social pressures to enact every last detail of the three stages of mourning dress were so intense that between 1850 and 1900, no woman who sought any kind of public respectability and community approbation for her family dared defy the rules. Thus sales in dull black silk mourning crape, white widows' caps, black woolen bombazine, and ready-made widows' weeds flourished until the ghastly death toll of World War I eroded the pressures and etiquette regulations.

Globalization of Fashion

Since the 1980s and the growth of the global economy, there has been massive growth in what Joanne Eicher has termed "world fashion" (p. 300). At the start of the twenty-first century, the preferred garments of young people of both sexes from around the world tend to be jeans, sweatshirts, T-shirts, and sneakers. These clothes are also international icons of American culture. The global young wear the same clothing, a phenomenon made possible by the exploitative mechanisms of the globalization of clothing manufacture, distribution, and retailing and by new technologies, global commodity advertising of branded leisure clothing, and the cultural and political domination of the United States. The reasons for wearing such clothing vary, but these clothes signify youth, modernity, and an eagerness to belong to the newly globalized capitalist world.

Dress as the Image of the Cutting Edge

In the period from 1964 to 1970, styles of dress worn by young women in Britain were the most famous visible representation of the "teenage revolution" and of the cutting edge of cultural modernity. Miniskirts exposed thighs to public view for the first time in European-American fashion history. These changes were rooted in the major social and cultural upheavals of the late 1950s, generated, as Tony Bennett explains, by "a watershed around which a series of significant "before" and "after" contrasts can be drawn" (p. 7). Young, radical filmmakers, painters, writers, photographers, and designers then successfully challenged the British establishment's hold on cultural power. Many who came from working-class backgrounds were helped into university and art-school education by postwar state grants to cover fees and living costs.

The London couture trade ignored these developments, maintaining their prewar function of creating elegant clothing for the annual high society calendar. The fashionable age in 1955 was around thirty-five but could easily be fifty-five if a woman kept a slim figure. By 1965 the fashionable age was sixteen, a near twenty-year drop in ten years.

Countercultural groups and their dress. This fashion shift was created by the young on their own terms. Angela Carter, a radical feminist writer and anti–Vietnam War ac-

tivist, felt that "one was living on the edge of the unimaginable; there was a constant sense of fear and excitement" (p. 211). Young countercultural dressers from the late 1950s wore clothing appropriated from workers' clothing and army-surplus store outlets. "Ban the Bomb" campaigners and art students (the women often with long loose hair and the men with beards) wore fishermen's pullovers, road-menders' jackets, and ex-Naval duffel coats, in an effort to defy existing barriers of gender, class, and occupation. At about the same time, the subcultural, androgynous Mods focused their attention on modern jazz and on acquiring motor scooters, drugs, and neat expensive suits and short smart hair cuts. It was a tidy "look," originally male, but one that belied an "alternative" fascination with drugs and hard partying after the end of the working day.

It was a fusion of these styles and interests that by 1964–1965 evolved into the hard-edged bright "look" of London fashion and propelled the bold, colorful geometrics of Pop and Op art. By the late 1960s however a far more exotic, ethnic, and historical revival of styles, largely drawn from the hippie culture of the West Coast of the United States became commonplace in both alternative and mainstream fashion circles.

In Britain, state art colleges were the central catalyst for the blossoming of radical fashion, producing key designers such as

Twiggy models a dress in London, 1966. During the 1960s, British fashion began to showcase youthful, eye-catching designs that featured short skirts and bold colors. Also popular was the hippie look, imported from the United States. © BETTMANN/ CORBIS

Mary Quant, Ossie Clarke, and Barbara Hulanicki of Biba. As the most directional British style creator of the mid-1960s, Mary Quant's work cannot be underestimated. Always more interested in creating a whole "look," her innovative, simple clothes (with colored stockings and flat shoes appropriated from art-college, countercultural dress) were retailed at mid-market price levels. These designers threw out centuries of British upper-class clothing etiquette and nearly destroyed the London couture industry in the process.

The contrast with Paris could not be greater. There, the couture houses themselves produced a new generation of dynamic designers, such as Paco Rabanne, whose metal/plastic disc minidresses were not only more radical than London designs but also, crucially, helped keep Paris couture alive because of their direct appeal to the young.

Yoruba fashion, Nigeria. Through the 1990s the academic study of fashionable dress began to reject its Eurocentric focus and a long-held view, as Joanne Eicher comments, that "dress outside the boundaries of western civilization has experienced little change and is therefore traditional" (p. 4). Acknowledgement has finally been made that the term *fashion* applies as equally to dress designed, manufactured, and consumed, for example, in Lagos, Dakar, Rajasthan, and Chiang Mai as in Paris, London, and Milan.

One of the most useful texts is *Cloth, Dress, and Art Patronage in Africa* (1999), by Judith Perani and Norma H. Wolff. This details the design, manufacture, and consumption of contemporary Yoruba strip-weave *aso-oke* cloth, which forms the basis of fashionable women's Yoruba dress in Nigeria. Made up into wrapper, blouse, and head tie, a competitive fashion in the late twentieth century was "shine-shine" lace cloth woven from specially imported Japanese, synthetic, gold, filament yarn.

Perani and Wolff explain that "shine-shine" cloth, made on narrow, traditional Yoruba strip-weave looms by male weavers, "has been adopted by wealthy urbanites as a visible symbol of prosperity, status and pride in ethnic heritage." They show that the weavers "have their fingers on the pulse of fashion through on-going interaction with their elite consumer-patrons" (pp. 171–172). Because of the flexibility of these craft processes, the weavers can alter the design of these fabrics rapidly, in keeping with fashion shifts. As Perani and Wolff make clear, none of this bears any relationship whatsoever to elite levels of European-American "designer" dress, except through the same constant search for design modernity and newness.

Designer fashion in the twenty-first century. The world of couture has always responded to the zeitgeist of its times, as much in the twenty-first century as in Madame de Pompadour's day. In the twenty-first century's fascination with brand labels as symbols of modernity and "cool," the top designer fashion trade now serves as the glamorous front for the billion-dollar global marketing of designer-branded products of every kind. This mass retailing of branded fashion accessories, cosmetics, and perfume is built on near-mystical, magical designer images of beauty and celebrity, seen in glossy advertisements, on catwalks at the Academy Awards, and in

Japanese youth wearing American T-shirt, Tokyo, 1991. The global mass-marketing of fashion has frequently resulted in a demand for popular designer brands that is not limited to any certain culture, race, or gender. © CATHERINE KARNOW/ CORBIS

much-reported fashion shows. With only a few thousand clients personally buying couture, designers are given free reign to create. All involved—particularly the two major fashion conglomerates, of Moët Hennessy Louis Vuitton (also known as the LVMH group, which owns the salons of Givenchy, Christian Dior, Louis Vuitton, Marc Jacobs International, Kenzo, Christian Lacroix) and Pierre Bergé, owner of Yves St. Laurent, and of Gucci (which in the early 2000s owned majority holdings in the companies of Alexander McQueen and Stella McCartney)—recognize the central need for brand images to be "individual," seductive, and at the cutting edge of modernity. John Galliano's London sense of extreme, romantic, youthful modernity has, for example, been successfully appropriated in Paris, transforming the international image and bank balance of the house of Dior.

Weaving in and around this world are the conceptual designers, such as Martin Margiela, Rei Kawakubo of Comme des Garçons, and Hussein Chalayan. Defined as designers who are more interested in the ideas behind their designs than in commercial viability, all of these produce both commercial and conceptual collections. Some, such as Alexander McQueen, fuse both approaches successfully into one. Caroline Evans in

Alexander McQueen's "What a Merry-Go-Round" fashion show. By the twenty-first century, much of the emphasis of fashion began to center on spectacle and image, as seen in McQueen's 2001–2002 collection. AP/WIDE WORLD PHOTOS

her seminal study *Fashion at the Edge* (2003), argues that from the 1990s avant-garde fashion design has reflected "the dark and deathly side" of consumer capitalism (p. 37). She notes the deliberate creation of "spoiled work that reflects a spoiled world" (p. 307), spoiled by deconstruction, remaking, cutting, slashing, damaging, even despoiling with mould and bacteria as in Margeila's exhibition work in the Netherlands in 1997. She describes these clothes as "apocalyptic visions" typified by notions of trauma, deathliness and haunting (p. 4). Evans sees these clothes as contemporary representations of cutting edge modernity, through their sartorial articulation of the political, cultural, social, and technological instabilities of the turn of the twenty-first century.

Evans shows how the work of Alexander McQueen illustrates many of these themes. She highlights his "What a Merry-Go-Round," autumn-winter 2001–2002 collection, based on a circus theme, with models made up as white clowns "to produce a mournful and alienated image—rather than celebrating circus performance" (p. 102). Evans notes that this show stressed "the frightening and strange elements of the circus—and thus the darker side of modernity" (p. 102).

Conclusion

The wide range of past and present approaches to the study of clothing and fashion outlined here were well established by the early 2000s, as confirmed by their use within museum exhibitions and a full range of dress publications dealing with

historical, ethnographical, and fashion analysis. As Ann Smart Martin clearly states, all of this reflects, finally, "the shifts in intellectual feelings about the core relationships between humans, goods and society" (p. 143).

See also **Body, The; Cultural Revivals; Cultural Studies; Masks; Textiles and Fiber Arts as Catalysts for Ideas.**

BIBLIOGRAPHY

Bennett, Tony, et al. *Politics, Ideology, and Popular Culture.* Milton Keynes, U.K.: Open University Press, 1982.

Breward, Christopher. "Cultures, Identities: Fashioning a Cultural Approach to Dress." *Fashion Theory* 2, no. 4 (December 1998): 301–313.

Carter, Angela. "Truly It Felt Like Year One." In *Very Heaven: Looking Back at the Sixties,* edited by Sara Maitland, 209–216. London: Virago, 1988.

Csillery, Klára, Edit Fél, and Tamás Hofer. *Hungarian Peasant Art.* Budapest: Corvina, 1969.

Cunningham, Patricia. "Beyond Artifact and Object Chronology." *Dress* 14 (1988): 76–79.

Davis, Fred. *Fashion, Culture, and Identity.* Chicago: University of Chicago Press, 1992.

Eicher, Joanne B. *Dress and Ethnicity.* Oxford: Berg, 1995.

Evans, Caroline. *Fashon at the Edge: Spectacle, Modernity, and Deathliness.* New Haven, Conn.: Yale University Press, 2003.

———. "Street Style: Subcultures and Subversion." *Costume* 31 (1997): 105–110.

Evans, Caroline, and Minna Thornton. *Women and Fashion: A New Look.* London: Quartet, 1989.

Hitchcock, Tim, and Michèle Cohen. *English Masculinities, 1660–1800.* New York: Addison Wesley, 1999.

Hofer, Tamás, and Edit Fél. *Hungarian Folk Art.* Translated by Mária Kresz and Bertha Gaster. New York: Oxford University Press, 1979.

Hollander, Anne. *Fabrics of Vision: Dress and Drapery in Painting.* London: National Gallery, 2002.

Hooper-Greenhill, Eileen. *Museums and the Interpretation of Visual Culture.* London: Routledge, 2000.

Jones, Colin. *Madame de Pompadour: Images of a Mistress.* London: National Gallery, 2002.

Martin, Ann Smart. "Makers, Buyers, and Users: Consumerism as a Material Culture Framework." *Winterthur Portfolio* 28, nos. 2/4 (summer/autumn 1993): 141–157.

Mort, Frank. *Cultures and Consumption: Masculinities and Social Space in Late Twentieth-Century Britain.* London: Routledge, 1996.

Perani, Judith, and Norma H. Wolff. *Cloth, Dress, and Art Patronage in Africa.* New York: Berg, 1999.

Ribeiro, Aileen. *Dress in Eighteenth-Century Europe, 1715–1789.* New Haven, Conn.: Yale University Press, 2002.

Roberts, Claire. *Evolution and Revolution: Chinese Dress, 1700s–1990s.* Sydney, Australia: Powerhouse, 1997.

Ross, Doran H., ed. *Wrapped in Pride: Ghanaian Kente Cloth and African American Identity.* Los Angeles: UCLA Fowler Museum of Cultural History, 1998.

Ross, Michael, and Reg Crowshoe. "Shadows and Sacred Geography: First Nations History-Making from an Alberta Perspective." In *Making Histories in Museums,* edited by G. Kavanagh, 240–256. Leicester, U.K.: Leicester University Press, 1996.

Starzecka, Dorota. *Maori: Art and Culture.* Auckland, New Zealand: British Museum, 1996.

Taylor, Lou. *The Study of Dress History.* London: Manchester University Press, 2002.

Vickery, Amanda. "Women and the World of Goods: A Lancashire Consumer and Her Possessions, 1751–1781." In *Consumption and the World of Goods,* edited by John Brewer and Roy Porter, 274–301. London: Routledge, 1993.

———. *The Gentleman's Daughter: Women's Lives in Georgian England.* New Haven, Conn.: Yale University Press, 1998.

Wilson, Elizabeth. "All the Rage." In *Fabrication: Costume and the Female Body,* edited by Jane Gaines and Charlotte Herzog. London: Routledge, 1990.

Lou Taylor

DUALISM.

DUALISM. Dualism is a doctrine positing two equally powerful and antagonistic metaphysical principles, which are constitutive of the world and must explain our experience of the world. They are often conceived as dichotomies, such as good and evil, light and darkness, attraction and repulsion, or love and strife.

In religion, perhaps the most important early doctrine was Zoroastrianism (Persia, today's Iran, sixth century B.C.E.). Zoroaster (c. 628–c. 551 B.C.E.) himself is thought to have only authored the *Gathas,* the earliest part of the Avesta, the sacred texts of Zoroastrianism. In Zoroastrianism, the world is the outcome of the struggle between Ormuzd, the author of good, and Ahriman, the principle of darkness and evil. For Zoroaster, the divinities of the Persian pantheon were servants of Ahriman. Man is a creation of Ormuzd, who created him to be free in his actions, and so open to the influences of evil. Man will be rewarded or punished in the afterlife for his choices. Ultimately, a final battle will be won by Ormuzd against evil.

Manes (Mani; 216–276 or 277 C.E.) developed a form of Gnosticism, subsequently called Manichaeism, which sought to fuse elements from Christianity with the dualism of Zoroastrianism. Manichaeism spread east as far as northern India and western China and west as far as France and Spain. In Manes's system, the Father of Light and his aeons, the good, are opposed by the King of Darkness, who tried to invade the former's kingdom. From this strife both the world and humans were born. Humans have seeds of light in their soul, and Jesus was sent to bring the knowledge necessary to free the light from darkness. Ultimately, darkness will be conquered. Although Manichaeism sought to include Christianity, or because it did, it was actively fought by the Christian establishment, especially St. Augustine of Hippo (354–430), who was a Manichaean in his youth. Later Christian dualistic heresies, thought to be derived from Manichaeism, include the Paulicians (Armenia, Albania, seventh–eighth century), the Bogomils (Bulgaria, tenth century) and the Cathars (Albigensians; southern France, twelfth and thirteenth centuries).

The Sankhya school is the most consistent example of Indian dualism. Founded by the legendary Kapila around the seventh century B.C.E., its earliest known text is Isvarakrsna's *Samkhya-karikas* (Stanzas of Samkhya, presumably written in the third century C.E.). The Samkhya school proffered a dualism of matter (prakriti) and soul or self (purushas). The two are originally separate; however, purusha, from being pure unqualified consciousness comes close to, and identifies itself with, aspects of matter as its object. Individualized, ego-based ahankara divides itself into the five senses, thus immersing purusha in the world of matter. Right knowledge consists of the ability of soul to rise above the ego and individuation and regain its distinction from matter. Samkhya ideas are mentioned in the earlier *Mahabharata* (one of the most famous Sanskrit texts, composed in a number of years; it reached its present version by 400 C.E.).

Earlier forms of dualism can be traced in ancient Egyptian religion, with the contest between Seth, disorder and sterility, and Osiris, fertility and life, that manifests itself in a cycle of murder and resurrection. Forms of dualism can be found in mythologies around the world, such as Native American myths (Chippewa, Navajo, Blackfeet), or Australian tribes. In such mythologies, ambivalent figures (such as the Native American coyote myths, the Bamapana of the Australian Murnging tribe, and the Melanesian spider-god Marawa) can be present such as a demiurge or "trickster," who can either cooperate or rival the main deity and is often conceived as independent of him.

Metaphysical dualism is a philosophical system positing two basic nonreducible substances, typically matter (or body) and spirit (or soul). Among the early Greeks, (the pre-Socratics) Anaximander (610–c. 647 B.C.E.) and, later, Heracleitus (c. 540–c. 480 B.C.E.), Empedocles (c. 490–c. 430 B.C.E.), and Anaxagoras (c. 500–c. 428 B.C.E.) all held doctrines of opposed natural substances, where the interplay of opposites is part of the developed world. Pythagoreanism, believed to have been founded by Pythagoras of Samos (c. 580–c. 500 B.C.E.), focused on opposing dyads such as one/two, male/female, and so forth. Plato's (c. 428–348 or 347 B.C.E.) metaphysics divides the world into two realms: the unchanging intelligible world of "forms" and the perceptual world of change. Human sense experience is of material things that are imperfect copies or likenesses that "participate" in the unchangeable and perfect forms (Ideas). Plato's *Republic* and *Timeus* give mythical accounts of the relationship between things and forms.

There is no true dualism in the Judeo-Christian tradition, though a subordinate metaphysical distinction is posed between God and created substances, and, derivatively, between soul and matter. God is uncreated, all-powerful, all-good, and infinite. Everything else is created and utterly dependent. Among created substances, soul or mind is not reducible to matter. Satan or the devil, while not as powerful as God, seems to have a power that God cannot control. Herein lie theological worries such as the problem of evil. This framework characterizes the Christian philosophy, especially high medieval Scholastic tradition such as St. Thomas Aquinas (c. 1224–1274), who attempted to reconcile Christianity with Aristotelian and neo-Platonic theories. With a very few exceptions (such as the thirteenth-century philosopher David of Dinant), dualism of created substances remained unchallenged until the revival of atomism, and the successes of the new science and mechanical philosophy in the seventeenth century (Galileo Galilei, Robert Boyle).

Most often, *dualism* is used to refer to Cartesian mind/body dualism. René Descartes (1596–1650), in his *Meditations on First Philosophy* (1641) and *Discourse on Method* (1637) developed a method, based on clear and distinct ideas, that he thought proved that thinking things were distinct from extended, inert material things. The exemplar of a clear and distinct idea was his "I think, therefore I am." Descartes struggled with the problem of how matter and mind, being different substances, could causally interact Reactions to Cartesian dualism, in the eighteenth and nineteenth centuries, stressed the incoherence of causal connections between two different kinds of substance, and took the forms of idealism (George Berkeley, 1685–1753) or materialism (Julien Offroy de La Mettrie, 1709–1751) wherein dualism was eschewed in favor or a world composed only of ideas (spirit) or matter.

During the late nineteenth century an epistemological form of dualism arose, from Descartes's influence, that distinguished knowledge of the human sciences from the natural sciences. Wilhelm Dilthey (1833–1911) argued for a noncausal human science that would use a method of *verstehen* or interpretation of particular events as distinct from the causal inquiry of the natural sciences, and Edmund Husserl (1859–1938) began the school of phenomenology, wherein human science was based on introspections of one's own consciousness, made while bracketing the physical world.

Challenges to Dualism

In postmodern times (after 1968), Jacques Derrida (b. 1930) developed deconstruction. Derrida believes that Western thought was centered on binary hierarchical oppositions (dualisms). Examples were male and female, mind and body, nature and culture, object and subject, and so forth. Critical analysis should expose the dualistic assumptions that are taken as "given," and show the polarity itself to be a "construct," rather than something existing independently. To Derrida and his postmodern followers must be added the challenge from feminist epistemology and philosophy of science. Interestingly the male/female polarity had been "deconstructed" well before Derrida, in Simone de Beauvoir's (1908–1986) *The Second Sex,* where she wrote, "Thus humanity is male and man defines woman not in herself but as relative to him; she is not regarded as an autonomous being . . . She is defined and differentiated with reference to man and not he with reference to her; she is the incidental, the inessential as opposed to the essential. He is the Subject, he is the Absolute—she is the Other."

See also **Heresy and Apostasy; Manichaeism; Monism; Other, The, European Views of.**

BIBLIOGRAPHY

Block, Ned, Güven Güzeldere, and Owen Flanagan, eds. *The Nature of Consciousness: Philosophical Debates.* Cambridge, Mass.: MIT Press, 1997.

de Beauvoir, Simone. *The Second Sex.* Translated and edited by H. M. Parshley. New York: Knopf, 1953.

Guttenplan, Samuel, ed. *A Companion to the Philosophy of Mind.* Oxford: Blackwell, 1994.

Hamilton, Janet, and Bernard Hamilton, trans. and ann. *Christian Dualist Heresies in the Byzantine World, c. 650 – c. 1450: Selected Sources.* Assistance with the translation of Old Slavonic texts by Yuri Stoyanov. Manchester, U.K.: Manchester University Press, 1998.

Lycan, William G., ed. *Mind and Cognition: An Anthology.* Malden, Mass.: Blackwell, 1999.

Peter Machamer
Francesca di Poppa

DYSTOPIA. Dystopia is utopia's polarized mirror image. While utilizing many of the same concepts as utopia—for example, social stability created by authoritarian regimentation—dystopia reads these ideas pessimistically. Dystopia angrily challenges utopia's fundamental assumption of human perfectibility, arguing that humanity's inherent flaws negate the possibility of constructing perfect societies, except for those that are perfectly hellish. Dystopias are solely fictional, presenting grim, oppressive societies—with the moralistic goal of preventing the horrors they illustrate.

A single literary work serves as the origin for both utopia and dystopia, the latter by critical examination of the social structures it presents as desirable and good. Thomas More's *Utopia* (1516) depicts a fictitious country named for Utopus, its first conqueror. Having reshaped a savage land into an ideal society through planning and reason, King Utopus's benevolent reign fulfills Plato's ideal of the philosopher-king expressed in *The Republic* (c. 400 B.C.E.). Derived from the Greek *ou* ("not" or "no") and *topos* (place), a utopia is "no place," a land that does not exist. In addition to its social structure, utopia's pronunciation irresistibly suggests "eutopia" (*eu topos*), a "good place" free from civil conflict and social inequality—so a utopia is a good place that does not exist, but which is shown to be possible through social engineering.

By contrast, a dystopia (*dis topos*) is a "bad place," deliberately written to frighten the reader; the fact that it, too, is fictitious offers scant comfort, because it is equally possible. More's fictive land has eliminated most class distinctions, but with a concomitant loss of individual freedom and artistic creativity. John Stuart Mill used the term "dystopia" as early as 1868 (*Hansard Commons,* 12 March) but critics struggled for much of the twentieth century with such unwieldy terminology as "anti-utopia," "utopian satire," "reverse utopias, negative utopias, inverted utopias, regressive utopias, cacoutopias . . . non-utopias, satiric utopias, and . . . nasty utopias" (Lewis, p. 27), to say nothing of "George Knox's 'sour utopias in the apocalyptic mode' and George Woodcock's 'negative quasi-Utopias'" (Aldridge, p. 5). Given this confusing proliferation of generic labels, J. Max Patrick may be forgiven for believing that he created the term *dystopia* in 1952 as the appropriate categorization for Joseph Hall's 1605 *Mundus Alter et Idem* (Negley and Patrick, p. 298). Patrick unquestionably picked the winner, and *dystopia* has eclipsed these other labels as the term of choice for a burgeoning literary genre. As dystopian fiction has become more widespread and popular since the end of World War II, critics have grown comfortable in classifying dystopias based on their own generic qualities, rather than explicitly by contrasting them against utopias. The term *dystopia* has also grown more familiar and is commonly used to refer to any dark or unpleasant future. Finally, by the end of the twentieth century, critics seemed to have abandoned the effort to segregate dystopia from science fiction, the larger literary genre to which dystopia belongs.

Goals of Dystopian Fiction

Dystopia walks a fine line between evoking the sensations of fear and inducing a sense of futility. A dystopia must arouse fear, but fails if it completely overwhelms the reader, leaving no room whatsoever for hope of amelioration. Finding crumbs of hope within powerful dystopias can be difficult, but they are present: for example, both the Afterword of Margaret Atwood's *The Handmaid's Tale* (1985) and the Appendix on Newspeak in George Orwell's *Nineteen Eighty-four* (1949) are written in the past tense, obliquely informing the reader that the totalitarian regimes of Gilead and Oceania were not invincible and ultimately fell. Depictions of grim futures mask dystopia's basic optimism. Dystopia is a fundamentally didactic genre, of which the old saw "the best is the enemy of the good" is truly spoken. By proving that a completely perfect society is not possible—showing the awful results of what happens if the goal is social perfection rather than incremental social improvement—dystopia shocks the reader into accepting humanity's flaws as ineradicable and thereby working toward a better society rather than an ideal one.

Film still from *1984* (1956), directed by Michael Anderson. George Orwell's 1949 novel—later transferred to film—tells the story of a totalitarian regime that controls its population through constant governmental surveillance. Adhering to the rules of the dystopia, however, the appendix to Orwell's work suggests that the oligarchy was not sustained. COLUMBIA/THE KOBAL COLLECTION

Nineteenth-century Dystopias

The utopia reached its greatest popularity in the nineteenth century. As the proud confidence of the nineteenth century crumbled when faced with the horrors of the twentieth, the utopian impulse has faltered, and dystopia has grown to be the more vital and relevant of the two genres. Dystopia began to evolve as a separate literary genre late in the nineteenth century as writers published anti-utopian "answers" and "replies" attacking utopian works. Edward Bellamy's highly popular socialistic utopia *Looking Backward* (1888) incited such direct refutations as Richard Michaelis's *Looking Further Forward* (1890) and Conrad Wilbrandt's *Mr. East's Experiences in Mr. Bellamy's World* (1891). Other writers attacked Bellamy's utopian ideals without targeting *Looking Backward* directly, and in so doing produced much more absorbing fiction. Ignatius Donnelly's *Caesar's Column* (1890) and Jack London's *The Iron Heel* (1907) reverse the utopian dream of ideal society by creating repressive totalitarian oligarchies determined to hold power at any cost. H. G. Wells wrote on both sides of the divide. Like Bellamy, Wells attracted direct "replies" with such utopian fictions as *When the Sleeper Wakes* (1899) (revised and reprinted in 1910 as *The Sleeper Awakes*) and *A Modern Utopia* (1905), but unlike Bellamy, Wells also wrote anti-utopian fiction, including *The First Men in the Moon*

Film still from *Things to Come* (1936), directed by William Cameron Menzies. Based on H. G. Wells's novel *The Shape of Things to Come, the Ultimate Revolution* (1933), this film adaptation was one of the first to depict a dystopian society. THE KOBAL COLLECTION

(1901), *The War in the Air* (1908) and *The Shape of Things to Come, the Ultimate Revolution* (1933). Wells's influence on dystopian fiction has been more substantial than Bellamy's. Writers wishing to deconstruct Wells's assumptions of human social perfectibility aided by technological innovation (such as E. M. Forster, Yevgeny Zamyatin, Aldous Huxley, and Orwell) found it impossible to fully do so in mere parodies or refutations, so instead they wrote standalone fictions that depict the horrid, repressive societies that they believed would arise if Wells's ideas were carried to their ultimate conclusions.

Twentieth-Century Dystopias

The twentieth century itself lent strength and scope to the development of dystopian fiction, as horrific events and movements rendered the utopian ideal increasingly absurd and made it possible for dystopias to posit terrible fictive societies. The most powerful dystopias from this period firmly cemented the genre as independent from utopia and remain relevant to the present day: Yevgeny Zamyatin's *We* (1920), Aldous Huxley's *Brave New World* (1932) and George Orwell's *Nineteen Eighty-four* (1949). All three of these novels present totalitarian oligarchies (*Brave New World, Nineteen Eighty-four*) or dictatorships (*We*). Other dystopias appearing at this time include Wells's *The Shape of Things to Come*, one of the first dystopias

to be filmed, as *Things to Come* (1936). Writing as Murray Constantine, Katharine Burdekin published *Swastika Night*, which was based on the premise of the Nazis taking over the world, in 1937. Cyril Connolly's dystopian short story "Year Nine" appeared in 1938 and seems to prefigure some of the same approaches Orwell explored at greater length in *Nineteen Eighty-four* (although Connolly's story, unlike Orwell's novel, is mordantly funny).

At midcentury, dystopia crossed the Atlantic—or rather, reemerged in the United States nearly fifty years after Jack London's *The Iron Heel* (1907). Kurt Vonnegut's *Player Piano* (1952), Ray Bradbury's *Fahrenheit 451* (1953), David Karp's *One* (1953), and Walter Miller's *A Canticle for Leibowitz* (1959) all took the dystopia in different directions, primarily away from the focus on repressive totalitarian societies that dominates the earlier British dystopias. Bradbury's and Vonnegut's dystopias focus on the impact of the repressive culture on the individual protagonists (Montag the Fireman in *Fahrenheit 451*, Paul Proteus in *Player Piano*) rather than on the horrific sweep of the entire society; both also foreground human dependence on machines as contributing factors in the creation of repressive societies. Britain did not abandon the dystopia. While Erika Gottlieb opens her recent study with the assertion that "[d]ystopian fiction is a post-Christian genre" (p. 3), Anthony Burgess recasts an explicitly Christian conflict in *A Clockwork Orange* (1962, filmed by Stanley Kubrick in 1971): in Alex's struggle against state-imposed behavioral conditioning, Burgess recasts the opposing views of mankind argued in the fifth century between St. Augustine of Hippo (who held that humanity is permanently stained by original sin) and the heretical British monk Pelagius (who denied original sin and argued that humans can create perfect societies). Writ large, the utopist's perspective is Pelagian, while the dystopist's is Augustinian (Kumar, p. 100). Burgess went on to publish a second dystopia, which grew out of an appreciation of Orwell's *Nineteen Eighty-four* published in that year—the first half of *1985* comments on Orwell's fiction, while the second shows a dystopian society in which trade unions have become the rulers of England (now TUCland, after the Trade Union Council that holds all real power).

Recent Directions

Although usually set in the future, typically the near future, dystopian fictions invariably reflect the concerns and fears of the writer's contemporaneous culture. As a given fear fades over time, dystopias founded upon it lose their ability to disturb (e.g., Burdekin's *Swastika Night*: the possibility of a world dominated and controlled by the Nazis, powerfully affective in 1937, has lost its force since the end of World War II). The reverse is also true, in cases where reality has caught up with ideas that were once utterly fantastic. Arguably, Huxley's *Brave New World* is a more powerful dystopia now than when published in 1932, given that genetic engineering, use of designer drugs, and relentless vapid entertainment media have evolved from fictions to facts. The shifting foci of dystopias display the changing philosophical preoccupations of the late twentieth century, revealing through grim fictions what their creators feared and wished to prevent.

Three interrelated trends have dominated dystopian fiction since the 1970s, although prefigurations of all three emerged before that time. The first is a concern over technological advances progressing beyond human ability to manage them effectively, if at all. As with the eponymous Machine in E. M. Forster's "The Machine Stops" (1909) and the computer EPICAC in Kurt Vonnegut's *Player Piano* (1952), several dystopias have shown societies turned horrific as people cede responsibilities to machines, or in which repressive regimes seize and hold power through deployment of advanced technologies. Harry Harrison's *Make Room! Make Room!* (1966, filmed in 1973 as *Soylent Green*) shows an overpopulated Earth dependent on government-sanctioned cannibalism, while Philip Dick's 1968 *Do Androids Dream of Electric Sheep?* (filmed as *Blade Runner* by Ridley Scott in 1982) questions whether an individual's humanity inheres in biology or in behavior. In Andrew Niccol's *Gattaca* (1997), deliberate genetic manipulation (including discrimination based on DNA) produces a population in which undesirable characteristics cannot emerge. The *Terminator* trilogy (*The Terminator*, 1984; *Terminator 2: Judgment Day*, 1991; *Terminator 3: Rise of the Machines*, 2003) shows a terrifying world in which a self-aware computer works to eliminate the human race. The *Matrix* trilogy (*The Matrix*, 1999; *The Matrix Reloaded*, 2003; *The Matrix Revolutions*, 2003) envisions a postapocalyptic society in which humans have been spared solely to provide energy for the dominant machines—and are kept ignorant through a collective hallucination, the Matrix.

The postapocalyptic dystopia allows the writer to sweep away the complexities of civilization and concentrate instead on small groups of survivors—often showing them struggling to re-create the very circumstances that originally brought on apocalypse. Because these fictions tend to take place far in the future, they sometimes fail to be understood as dystopias. Miller's *A Canticle for Leibowitz* (1959) broke this ground early. Other examples of postapocalyptic dystopias include Harlan Ellison's *A Boy and His Dog* (published 1969, filmed by L. Q. Jones in 1975), Russell Hoban's *Riddley Walker* (1980), Terry Gilliam's *Twelve Monkeys* (1995) and Danny Boyle's *28 Days Later* (2002). Though the first of George Miller's *Mad Max* movies was little more than a series of chase scenes, the second and third installments (*Mad Max II: The Road Warrior*, 1981; *Mad Max Beyond Thunderdome*, 1985) are clearly dystopian: chaos reigns, the strong dominate the weak, and scarce commodities like gasoline are prized far more than human life. Alan Moore's and David Lloyd's collaboration on *V for Vendetta* (1998) presents an Orwellian postapocalyptic England in graphic novel format.

The most intriguing development since the 1970s has been the proliferation of dystopian fictions exploring gender issues. Early examples include Thomas Berger's *Regiment of Women* (1973) and Ursula Le Guin's *The Dispossessed: An Ambiguous Utopia* (1974). Suzy McKee Charnas's four-volume *Holdfast Chronicles* began with the publication of *Walk to the End of the World* in 1974, continued with *Motherlines* in 1978 and *The Furies* (1994), and concluded in *The Conqueror's Child* (1999). Set long after a global environmental catastrophe that has destroyed civilization, Charnas's fiction presents an oppressive patriarchal village (the Holdfast), a nomadic culture of women who can reproduce without men (the Riding Women) and a group of ex-slave women who have escaped the Holdfast (the Free Fems). All of these groups are presented as morally defective: in the changing relationships between them, Charnas suggests that oppression and using power for its own sake are intrinsic human flaws, irrespective of gender. Octavia Butler's *Parable of the Sower* (1993) largely agrees, but acknowledges that women, children, and ethnic minorities suffer most during social upheaval. Butler's dystopia revolves around Lauren Olamina, a young black woman who suffers from hyperempathy. As American civilization decays, Lauren leads a small group of refugees to safety while instructing them in her self-created religion, "Earthseed." But the sequel, *Parable of the Talents* (1998), shows the Acorn community destroyed and its people killed or enslaved by fundamentalist Christians. Lauren is forced to choose between rescuing her followers (including her daughter) and saving Earthseed from destruction.

Margaret Atwood's *The Handmaid's Tale* (a film version appeared in 1990) is much more narrowly focused on a patriarchal dystopia in which fertile women are reduced to breeder-slaves. Offred, Atwood's first-person narrator, only dimly understands how the ultra-fundamentalist Republic of Gilead has come to be, but she gives a firsthand look into the horribly repressive techniques necessary to keep the oligarchs (Commanders) in power. The first two of Suzette Haden Elgin's *Native Tongue* novels (*Native Tongue,* 1985; *Native Tongue II: The Judas Rose,* 1987) create a patriarchal but not overtly religious dystopia, one in which a few hundred Linguists are responsible for all communication between humanity and dozens of alien races; while all of humanity hates the Linguists, it is the Linguist women who are even more thoroughly oppressed. Elgin foregrounds the feminist concern with language as a tool of patriarchal repression, and she shows her Linguist women building a "women's language," Láadan, intended to be the tool of their liberation.

See also **Genre; Technology; Utopia.**

BIBLIOGRAPHY

PRIMARY SOURCES

Atwood, Margaret. *The Handmaid's Tale.* Boston: Houghton Mifflin, 1986.

Burgess, Anthony. *A Clockwork Orange.* 1st American ed. New York: W.W. Norton, 1963.

Huxley, Aldous. *Brave New World.* New York: Harper and Row, 1947.

Orwell, George. *Nineteen Eighty-four.* London: Secker and Warburg, 1949.

Zamyatin, Yevgeny. *We.* Translated by Gregory Zilboorg. Boston: Gregg Press, 1975.

SECONDARY SOURCES

Aldridge, Alexandra. *The Scientific World View in Dystopia.* Ann Arbor: UMI Research Press, 1984.

Booker, M. Keith. *Dystopian Literature: A Theory and Research Guide.* Westport, Connecticut: Greenwood Press, 1994.

———. *The Dystopian Impulse in Modern Literature: Fiction as Social Criticism.* Westport, Connecticut: Greenwood Press, 1994.

Gottlieb, Erika. *Dystopian Fiction East and West: Universe of Terror and Trial.* Montreal and Ithaca, N.Y.: McGill-Queen's University Press, 2001.

Kumar, Krishan. *Utopia and Anti-Utopia in Modern Times.* Oxford, UK: Basil Blackwell, 1987.

Lewis, Arthur O., Jr. "The Anti-Utopian Novel: Preliminary Notes and Checklist." *Extrapolation: A Science-Fiction Newsletter* 2, no. 2 (May 1961): 27–32.

Negley, Glenn, and J. Max Patrick, eds. *The Quest for Utopia: An Anthology of Imaginary Societies.* New York: Henry Schuman, 1952.

Sargent, Lyman Tower. *British and American Utopian Literature, 1516–1985: An Annotated, Chronological Bibliography.* Garland Reference Library of the Humanities, vol. 831. New York: Garland, 1988.

David W. Sisk

E

ECLECTICISM. Ancient eclecticism, according to the second century C.E. doxographer Diogenes Laertius, began with Potamon of Alexandria, who broke with traditions of discipleship and doctrinal loyalty by making a selection from the tenets of all the existing sects, including Platonists, Aristotelians, Stoics, Epicureans, and Cynics. The Roman adaptation of eclectic attitudes was given legitimacy by the famous, often repeated motto of Horace (65–8 B.C.E.), "I am not bound over to swear as any master dictates." Eclecticism included women philosophers, especially (whatever her religion) the beautiful, intellectually peerless, and ill-fated Hypatia (c. 370–415), whose death, according to Denis Diderot (1713–1784), marked also the end of ancient eclecticism. The Christian fathers also inclined to this view in their search for pagan anticipations of their wisdom, so that for example St. Clement of Alexandria (c. 150–between 211 and 215) celebrated the value of Greek and even "barbarian" philosophy according to this method, which he also called "eclectic" (*eklektikon*). This approach, which was inadvertently comparative and necessarily historical, was a prototype of the more self-conscious ideas of eclecticism, German and then French, which emerged in modern times, especially in the search for a "new philosophy." Thus Petrus Ramus (Pierre de La Ramée; 1515–1572) claimed membership in the *secta veritatis,* "the sect not of Aristotle, of Plato, or of any man, but only of truth" (*Aristotelicae Animadversiones,* 1543; Aristotelian criticisms).

Modern Era

If the locus classicus of eclecticism was Diogenes Laertius' *Lives of the Eminent Philosophers,* the *locus modernus* was the *Introduction to Stoic Philosophy* (1604) of Justus Lipsius (1547–1606), who argued that the method of critical choosing or "election" was superior to the dogmas of particular schools and represented the true road to truth. From the second quarter of the seventeenth century the term and concept of *eclectic philosophy* gained currency, as did the associated idea of the *liberty of philosophizing* (*libertas philosophandi*)—that is, the freedom to choose between philosophical schools, or indeed a philosophy beyond the schools. Gerardus Johannes Vossius (Gerrit Jansz Vos; 1577–1649) served philosophical apprenticeships in various schools—Aristotelians, Platonists, Stoics, and Epicureans—and concluded, "Clearly, I have become an eclectic." Later he defended eclecticism (*secta electiva . . . sive electrix*) as a permanent condition of philosophizing and urged, "How would it be in the future if we should be not Ionic philosophers, or Italians, Eleatics, Platonists, or Peripatetics, not Stoics, Epicureans, Skeptics, or any other such sects, but all of these?" (*De philosophia et philosophorum sectis,* 1658; Philosophy and the schools of philosophy).

The recognized founder of the eclectic school (*eclectica philosophia; Wahl-Philosophie* [Selective philosophy]) in Germany was Christian Thomasius (1655–1728), for whom, as for Vossius, philosophy was a collective enterprise not reducible to the teaching of one author or separable from learned tradition and succession of teachers. "I call eclectic philosophy," Thomasius wrote in his *Introductio ad philosophiam aulicam* (*Einleitung zur Hof-Philosophie* [Introduction to court philosophy]) in 1688, "not what depends on the teaching of an individual or on the acceptance of the words of a master, but whatever can be known from the teaching and writing of any person on the basis not of authority but of convincing arguments." For Thomasius the key to understanding was the alliance between history and philosophy. "History and philosophy are the two eyes of wisdom," he argued. "If one is missing, then one has only half vision" (*einäugy*).

Other adherents to eclecticism included J. C. Sturm, J. F. Buddeus, C. A. Heumann, Nicolas Gundling, J. G. Heineccius, Ephraim Gerhard, Arnold Wesenfeld, J. J. Brucker, and their students in many dissertations written in the late seventeenth and early eighteenth centuries in theology, mathematics, and medicine as well as philosophy. Eclecticism was a method of separating truth from opinion and falsehood, science from superstition, and so a process of intellectual enlightenment and human progress. As Heineccius concludes in his *Elementa philosophiae rationalis et moralis* (1756; Elements of rational and moral philosophy), "one should not seek truth by oneself, nor accept or reject everything written by ancients and moderns, and so no other method of philosophizing is more reasonable than the Eclectic Method."

Eclecticism was thus given new life in early modern times, appearing at the confluence of several intellectual movements: the revival of ancient and patristic learning, evangelical religious reform, the "liberty of philosophizing," and the adoption of critical history as the basis for understanding.

The most lasting consequence of eclectic philosophy was the emergence of a new discipline, the history of philosophy, beginning with Georg Horn and Thomas Stanley (*History of Philosophy,* 1655) and culminating in the first journal dedicated to the history of philosophy, the *Acta Philosophorum* by C. A. Heumann and the survey of J. J. Brucker (*Historia critica philosophiae,* 1742–1744; Critical history of philosophy), which set the canon for the modern history of philosophy and which was the basis for Diderot's entry in the French *Encyclopédie.*

Nineteenth Century

It was in the nineteenth century, however, that eclecticism achieved its greatest notoriety, especially under the leadership of Victor Cousin (1792–1867), who proposed "to select in all systems what appears to be true and good, and consequently everlasting,—this, in a single word, is ECLECTICISM." And Cousin added, "If this philosophy is to be Eclectic, it must also be sustained by the history of philosophy." In post-Revolutionary France philosophy was in great disarray, and Cousin looked back to the great schools of the earlier generation—French, Scottish, and German, represented respectively by Étienne Bonnot de Condillac (1715–1780), Thomas Reid (1710–1796), and Immanuel Kant (1724–1804). "It would be an interesting and instructive study," he proposed, "to examine the weaknesses of these schools by engaging one with another and by selecting their various merits in the context of a great eclecticism which would contain and surpass all three" (*Lectures on the True, the Good, and the Beautiful*, 1858).

Over the next three decades this doctrine was publicized and extended by Cousin's many scholarly publications, by his lectures, by his many international contacts and disciples, by translations of his works, and by his public career as minister of education and as virtually the "official philosopher" of the July Monarchy. Historian though he was, he attached little importance to German precedents in the belief that "eclecticism is a French doctrine and peculiar to us" (*Premiers essais de philosophie*, 1862, p. 280).

Among philosophers, in fact, eclecticism lost much of its credit in the nineteenth century, and indeed Cousin's major significance was as a scholar and a founder of the "history of ideas," which had been pioneered by Brucker, whom he honored as "the father of the history of philosophy," and Giambattista Vico (1668–1744), whose work he was instrumental in introducing to nineteenth-century readers. In the long term, indeed, the principal contribution of Cousin and his school, as of the earlier German eclectics, was not the establishment of a viable philosophical doctrine but the exploration of the modern field of intellectual history.

See also **Aristotelianism; Epicureanism; Ideas, History of; Platonism; Stoicism.**

BIBLIOGRAPHY

Hochstrasser, T. J. *Natural Law Theories in the Early Enlightenment.* Cambridge, U.K.: Cambridge University Press, 2000.
Kelley, Donald R. *The Descent of Ideas: The History of Intellectual History.* London: Ashgate, 2002.
———. "Eclecticism and the History of Ideas." *Journal of the History of Ideas* 62 (2001): 577–592.
Kelley, Donald R., ed. *History and the Disciplines: The Reclassification of Knowledge in Early Modern Europe.* Rochester, N.Y.: University of Rochester Press, 1997. See especially Martin Mulsow, "Gundling and Buddeus: Competing Models of the History of Philosophy," 103–126, and Ulrich Johannes Schneider, "Eclecticism and the History of Philosophy," 83–102.

Donald R. Kelley

ECOLOGY. Ecology is commonly seen as a lineal descendant of traditional natural history extending back to such classical figures as Aristotle, Theophrastus, and Pliny. Notable persons in this tradition include the Swedish botanist, Carl von Linné (Carolus Linnaeus; 1707–1778), who coined the phrase "economy of nature" in 1749. Gilbert White (1720–1793), a British cleric, made astute ecological observations of his parish in *The Natural History and Antiquities of Selborne* (1789). Charles Darwin's (1809–1882) work on evolution, published in 1859, was acknowledged as the stimulus for coinage, in 1866, of the term *ecology.* Henry David Thoreau (1817–1862), poet and naturalist, in 1860 anticipated a key phenomenon of ecology, and its name, in an article, "The Succession of Forest Trees." In 1864 George Perkins Marsh (1801–1882), an American diplomat, anticipated the environmental crisis that was widely recognized a century later, in his book *Man and Nature in America,* which described the deleterious impact of humans on the earth.

The ubiquity of such observations was explicit in the observations of the historian Clarence Glacken (1967), who said that ecological theory originated in the design argument of nature and that every thinker from the fifth century B.C.E. to the end of the eighteenth century had something to say about one or more of the ideas about environments. Even this extended attribution omits consideration of the detailed, and commonly insightful, traditional natural history knowledge of nonliterate aboriginal cultures the world around. The premier British ecologist Charles Elton dubbed ecology as scientific natural history in 1927. Increasing recognition of the extended history of ecological insights, anticipating a formal science of ecology, called up the apt term *protoecologist* (protoecology) in 1983.

Origins

The undisputed source of the term *ecology* is the eminent German zoologist, Ernst Haeckel (1834–1919), who coined it in 1866. It is well to revert to Haeckel's expanded definition in 1869 as translated by Allee and others:

> By ecology we mean the body of knowledge concerning the economy of nature—the investigation of the total relations of the animal both to its inorganic and to its organic environment; including above all, its friendly and inimical relations with those animals and plants with which it comes directly or indirectly into contact—in a word ecology is the study of all those complex interrelations referred to by Darwin as the conditions of the struggle for existence. (Allee, 1949)

Haeckel's definition illustrates the continuing tendency to distinguish animal and plant ecology. His emphasis on Darwinian evolution was echoed by numerous early ecologists, and later historians, and persists as evolutionary ecology.

The term *ecology* appeared sparingly in the scientific literature until the 1890s. In 1893 the president of the British Association for the Advancement of Science described ecology as a branch of biology coequal with morphology and physiology and by far the most attractive. Also in 1893, the Madison

Botanical Congress, a large meeting of professional botanists, formally adopted the term *ecology*. A chair of ecological botany was established at Uppsala University in Sweden in 1897, and in 1904 Oscar Drude, a German plant geographer, described the sudden recognition of ecology in a talk at a Congress of Arts and Sciences at the Universal Exposition in St. Louis. Charles E. Bessey, a prominent American botanist, commented in 1902 that ecology had become a fad—a slight exaggeration, as the "fad" was largely confined in America to a few Midwestern universities and state agencies. The first named textbook of ecology was published in Danish by a Danish botanist, Johannes Eugenius Bülow Warming, in 1895; and the first doctorate in ecology in the United States was granted to Henry Chandler Cowles in 1898 by the University of Chicago for his work on the dunes of Lake Michigan.

Institutionalization

In Great Britain, plant ecology was initiated by botanical surveys done by members of hundreds of local natural history societies. Arthur S. Tansley, a pioneer British plant ecologist, suggested formation of the British Vegetation Committee, which brought the scientific leadership of the natural history societies together to study British vegetation.

Continental ecology was stimulated by the experience of European biologists in tropical colonies. Several of these, notably Drude, Andreas Franz Wilhelm Schimper, and Warming produced significant works of plant ecology that influenced British and American ecology.

Ecology in America was much influenced by early state-run natural history agencies, notably in the Midwest. Stephen A. Forbes was director of the Illinois State Laboratory of Natural History for many years, influencing numerous ecologists employed there as well as producing many of the most insightful ecological articles published before 1900. Edward A. Birge was director of the natural history division of the Wisconsin Geological and Natural History Survey and a pioneer in ecological studies of lakes. Bessey organized the Botanical Survey of Nebraska, which produced the major theorist of American plant ecology, Frederic E. Clements (1874–1945). American ecologists were influenced by federal surveys of the trans-Mississippi West. Ronald Tobey traced the development of plant ecology in the Midwestern grasslands, influenced by the developments of prairie agriculture and the Clements school of ecology.

Formal ecological societies were established in Britain in 1913 and in the United States in 1915. Academic ecology developed notably in Midwestern universities. In its century as a recognizable science, ecology acquired new and expanded significance. This is evident in the proliferation of journals of ecology. English language journals numbered four in 1940, increasing to twelve by 1980. The Institute for Scientific Information (ISI) included 102 journals under ecology in 2000, fifty of which had a clear reference to ecology in the title. The journal *Ecology* went from quarterly to monthly and the number of pages per year increased from approximately 750 in 1940 to about 2,250 in 2000. This proliferation of journals is a mixed blessing, making keeping up with the literature well nigh impossible at a time that ecologists are becoming involved in increasingly diverse enterprises.

Paradigms

Thomas Kuhn's concept of paradigm, introduced in *The Structure of Scientific Revolutions* (1962), changed the common view of how science progresses. A paradigm is a set of overarching principles and methods shared by a scientific community within which its adherents conduct "normal science." Science advances by changing its paradigms in revolutions.

The earliest putative ecological paradigm, the Clementsian organismic paradigm was a descendant of the traditional design or balance-of-nature concept, presuming a stable or equilibrium state as a norm. It is associated with Nebraska botanist Frederic E. Clements, who developed a concept of community or "association" as an organism or superorganism (1916). Clements envisioned the community as developing to converge on a "climax" or a stable endpoint determined by climate. This paradigm dominated early-twentieth-century ecology in America and was evident in major animal ecology references and general textbooks.

Some scholars describe a "revolution," or paradigm change, in ecology in the 1950s, with the revival and widespread acceptance of the "individualistic concept" of H. A. Gleason (1939). The shift from Clementsian ideas of equilibrium, homogeneity, and determinism to Gleasonian ideas of nonequilibrium, heterogeneity, and stochasticity greatly increased the difficulty of ecology and has dominated its recent development.

Another paradigm in ecology, population regulation, has a long natural-history tradition and was introduced into ecology in the 1920s, described by some as the "Golden Age" of theoretical mathematical ecology. Raymond Pearl resurrected the earlier "logistic curve" $dN = rN(K - N)$ and introduced it as a "law" of population growth. The equation includes r as the rate of population growth, K as the limiting maximum population, N as the number of individuals, and d signifying change. Subsequently the physicist Alfred J. Lotka, who joined Pearl's laboratory, and Vito Volterra, a mathematician, expanded the logistic to two species cases, especially competition. Mathematical population ecology persisted in the face of extended criticism and subsequent concerns about the basic equation. It remains to the present in much-elaborated forms with the assurance that populations at some scale are regulated but the mechanisms remain elusive.

Ecosystem

Early ecology recognized living (biotic) and nonliving (abiotic) aspects of nature but conventionally treated them separately. Environment acted on organisms, and organisms reacted on environment, according to Clements's familiar usage. The term *ecosystem* was coined by the British ecologist Arthur S. Tansley in 1935 to treat organisms and environment as a unit system. Tansley defined ecosystem as the whole system (in the sense of physics) including not only the organism complex, but also the whole complex of physical factors forming what we call the environment of the biome—the habitat factors in the widest sense.

Tansley's concept was particularly useful in aquatic ecology. It was used by Raymond Lindeman (1942) in a pioneer study of a lake ecosystem. Lindeman adapted the familiar food-chain, or trophic-structure concept of ecology and emphasized the energy and nutrient relations in a pyramid of production diminishing at higher levels and relating it to a succession of lakes. A major stimulus to ecosystem ecology was the influential textbook by Eugene Odum, *Fundamentals of Ecology* (1953).

The ecosystem concept was widely hailed as a new ecology in the 1970s, particularly when designated as "systems" ecology, which changed the emphasis in ecology from organisms to "ecoenergetics," the flux of energy in the ecosystem, along with the flow of chemicals through the ecosystem. Systems ecology flourished as ecology was turned into "big biology" by its first venture into heavily funded research in an International Biological Program (IBP) principally directed to formulating mathematical models of large-scale ecosystems. Another approach to ecosystems was the Hubbard Brook Program, begun in 1963, an intensive program of studies of a forested watershed, which examined nutrient flow and biomass accumulation. The program used computer simulations to model the complexity of natural ecosystems.

Opinions as to the merits of systems ecology in its philosophical and mathematical format vary, but the ecosystem persists as a major aspect of ecology and is frequently cited in the conservation, environmental, and even economic and political arenas. It is widely considered as producing ecosystem services, the valuable consequences of the multitudinous activities performed by biological systems to the great advantage of humans and often in spite of them. In 1988 "ecosystem" was designated "most important ecological concept" in a survey of members of the British Ecological Society, and it remains significant today.

Transecology

Ecology as a science developed largely in academia and in state, federal, and private conservation agencies until it came to the consciousness of the general public in the context of the environmental crisis of the 1970s in the guise of environmentalism. This is clearly evidenced in Mohan Wali's "Ecology Today: Beyond the Bounds of Science." Wali collected terms using "eco," "ecological," and "ecology" by professional ecologists and by nonecologists, and found that nonecologists use the term *ecology* as ideology, metaphor, allegory, myth, or gospel. Furthermore, while terms coined by professional ecologists numbered 276, those coined by nonecologists numbered over a thousand. Wali categorized the latter as General Ecologies (e.g., metaphysical ecology), Eco-business (e.g., eco-pornography), Eco-Health (e.g., gyn-eco-logical), Eco-types (e.g., eco-freak), Ecosport (e.g., ecogolf), Ecophilosopy (e.g., deep ecology), and Eco-religion (e.g., ecological sin). The problem for the unwary reader is that environmentalism is exceedingly diverse and for most of the users of these terms ecological science does not exist.

Another concern is the growth since around 1980 of environmental history, which takes a more encompassing view of environmental and ecological science and sometimes confounds it with ecologism, a loose construction of philosophy and ecology. Environmental history includes many works attending to the human environment with due cognizance of ecology and history. Other works, claiming to be histories of ecology, completely ignore the science and attribute diverse human and political foibles to ecology. One such cites no ecological science journals, but asserts that ecologists call for complete social and economic change. It links ecological ideas to Marxism, anarchism, Boy Scouts, anti-Semitism, fascism, and the German disease—Nazism.

The gross extension of the term ecology by nonscientists prompted the director of the public affairs office of the Ecological Society of America (ESA) to draft a letter to disclaim equating ecology and environmentalism, which, the letter said, diminished the credibility of ecology, and to urge members of the ESA to send it to offending publications such as the *Wall Street Journal*.

Complexity

Ecology has long been recognized as complex. One discouraged ecologist suggested, "ecology is not only more complex than we think, it is more complex than we can think." Ecology has assembled an extended body of information about the earth's ecosystems, but consensus on a general theoretical foundation remains elusive and some question its likelihood.

A notable effort to provide a theory of ecology was G. E. Hutchinson's formalization of the niche concept. A species niche is its response to all variables, biological and physical. Hutchinson influenced Robert MacArthur (1969), who pursued a theory of ecology predicated on competition that was widely accepted but subsequently questioned, as other factors such as predation and disturbance were shown to influence species relations.

An early consensus on "dynamic" ecology, focusing on the ubiquitous process of succession or change in ecosystems, regarded succession as "primary" if beginning on a previously unoccupied area, or "secondary" if following disturbance. This remains a factor in complex ecology. Disturbance by biotic or abiotic factors at varied intervals, intensities, or different area sizes is common and some disturbances (e.g., fire) are integrated into the development of an ecosystem, adding to its complexity.

One of the difficulties of assessing regularities in ecology is that ecological entities exist, and functions occur, at different scales of size, time, and rate, and the perspective of history is essential. Consideration of scale is widely evident in recent ecology, increasing its inherent complexity. The traditional ecological entities, population and community, are now expanded to metapopulations, populations of a species connected by migrations among them, and landscape ecology, an extended area including diverse communities. Taxonomic populations are also considered as guilds, species with similar functions apart from their systematic relations. At an extreme the biosphere, the whole-earth system, may be considered, and has been transformed into the GAIA hypothesis, treating the earth as an integrated superorganism transcending conventional ecology.

Another approach to ecological complexity is offered in hierarchy, an effort to deal with the scale problem in ecology.

Ecological systems are considered as hierarchies in which processes at higher levels are predictable in some degree based on processes at lower levels. Some properties of the whole are said to be emergent and must be considered at the appropriate hierarchical level.

Evolutionary Ecology and Conservation Biology

Ecology was initially linked with Darwinian evolution. These ideas persist in evolutionary ecology, which explores the distribution and abundance of organisms and the control of their numbers, as in the interest in invasive species. Conservation biology is a following, overlapping discipline which focuses on the preservation of species incorporating genetic diversity. No feature of the earth is more striking than its enormous number of species. In ecological parlance number of species is called richness, number of species weighted by their proportionate abundance (number of individuals) is called diversity, and an amalgamation of all biological qualities is called biodiversity. In much ecological and common usage, however, biodiversity is simple number of species. Biodiversity has long charmed naturalists but in recent decades it has been considered a key ecological concept or paradigm and entered into environmental and political discourse as concerns grow about declining biodiversity. The emerging concern about loss of biodiversity has created urgency about its putative relation to stability and functioning of ecosystems.

Increasing recognition of the complexity of ecological systems called forth new mathematical considerations of fractals, chaos, and complexity. It led to the formation of a National Center for Ecological Analysis and Synthesis (NCEAS) on the West Coast of the United States. The NCEAS funds studies of large areas using meta-analysis of existing data and has had substantial impact on recent ecology.

Human Ecology

Early ecology had links with sociology. Patrick Geddes, British botanist-turned-sociologist, provided a classification of science in 1880 that included ecology in sociology. Much early plant ecology was called phytosociology, and a pioneer animal ecologist, Warder Clyde Allee, published *Animal Aggregations: A Study in General Sociology* in 1931. Early sociology at the University of Chicago was influenced by the ideas of the plant ecologist, Frederic E. Clements. An early animal ecologist, C. E. Adams, boldly anticipated convergence of animal and human ecology.

Both the British and American ecological societies were reluctant to engage in advocacy, and a president of the British Ecological Society said the society cannot have a corporate opinion on practical affairs lest its credibility over scientific aspects be damaged. Although many ecologists, notably Paul Sears in the United States and Arthur S. Tansley in Britain, were active proponents of environmental concerns and conservation, there was a common reluctance among ecologists and their societies to become involved in political affairs and public policy. Widespread recognition of the environmental crisis in the 1970s and the popularity of Earth Day emboldened many ecologists, their societies, and their journals to substantially change their

position in respect to advocacy. In spite of reservations, ecologists and their organizations are increasingly becoming involved in matters of public policy if not politics.

One indication of increasing involvement of ecologists in public affairs is the Millennium Ecosystem Assessment, in which ecologists join with other scientists and social scientists from sixty-six countries to address the relations between ecosystems and human well-being on a global scale. These assessments (1) address the current and future capacity of ecosystems to provide services to humans, (2) determine human responses to changes in ecosystems, and (3) consider how assessments can be conducted at scales from villages, to river basins, countries, regions, and globally. It is clear that ecological science is becoming increasingly involved in the realm of public policy. Some ecologists have noted the failure of our educational system to train students to participate in science-policy discussions. Ecologists and economists, in order to change the status quo, are attempting to provide innovative courses.

An extremely difficult problem for contemporary ecologists is to respond to the suggestions that ecology extends beyond the bounds of science. This grandiose view of ecology is a contradiction of Ralph Waldo Emerson's assertion in "Nature" of an essence unchanged by human beings: "But his operations taken together are so insignificant, a little chipping, baking, patching, and washing, that in an impression so grand as that of the world on the human mind, they do not vary the result." Ecology confirms the fear that humans vary the result decisively.

See also **Biology; Environmental Ethics; Environmental History; Evolution; Natural History; Nature; Wildlife.**

BIBLIOGRAPHY

Allee, Warder C., et al. *Principles of Animal Ecology.* Philadelphia: Saunders, 1949.

Bocking, Stephen. *Ecologists and Environmental Politics: A History of Contemporary Ecology.* New Haven, Conn.: Yale University Press, 1997.

Cherrett, J. M. "Key Concepts: The Results of a Survey of Our Member's Opinions." *Journal of Ecology* 76 (1989): 1–16.

Glacken, C. J. *Traces on the Rhodian Shore.* Berkeley: University of California Press, 1967.

Golley, Frank B. *A History of the Ecosystem Concept in Ecology: More Than the Sum of the Parts.* New Haven, Conn.: Yale University Press, 1993.

Graham, Michael H., and Paul K. Dayton. "On the Evolution of Ecological Ideas: Paradigms and Scientific Progress." *Ecology* 83 (2002): 1481–1489.

Graham, Michael H., Paul K. Dayton, and Mark A. Hixon, eds. "Special Feature: Paradigms in Ecology: Past, Present, and Future." *Ecology* 83 (2002): 1479–1559.

Kingsland, S. E. *Modeling Nature: Episodes in the History of Population Ecology.* Chicago: University of Chicago Press, 1985.

Lawton, J. H. "Are There General Laws in Ecology?" *Oikos* 84 (1999): 177–192.

Lindeman, R. L. "The Trophic-dynamic Aspect of Ecology." *Ecology* 23 (1942): 399–418.

MacArthur, R. H. "Species Packing and Competitive Equilibrium for Many Species." *Theoretical Population Biology* 1 (1969): 1–11.

McIntosh, R. P. *The Background of Ecology: Concept and Theory.* Cambridge, U.K.: Cambridge University Press, 1985.

Mitman, Gregg. *The State of Nature: Ecology, Community, and American Social Thought.* Chicago: University of Chicago Press, 1992.

Shrader-Frechette, K. S., and E. D. McCoy. *Method in Ecology and the Logic of Case Studies.* Cambridge, U.K.: Cambridge University Press, 1993.

Wali, Mohan. "Ecology Today: Beyond the Bounds of Science." *Nature and Resources* 35 (1999): 38–50.

Robert P. McIntosh

ECONOMICS. The term *economics,* from the Greek *oikonomika,* means a science or art of managing the household. In modern usage, it refers to the efficient allocation of scarce resources in the production, distribution, and consumption of goods and services to satisfy various desires. As a branch of knowledge, economics or economic science is the study of how to efficiently use limited resources—natural resources (land), capital, labor, entrepreneurship, and information—to achieve maximum satisfaction of human material wants. Like other social sciences, economics studies human behavior but focuses on maximizing satisfaction or benefit as efficiently as possible or at minimum cost in the production, distribution, and consumption of goods and services. Hence, economics deals with decision making, theory, and management of the economy or economic systems. The decision makers or economic units of the economic system are households, businesses, and government.

Microeconomics is the branch of economics that deals with individual or specific economic units such as an individual industry, firm, or household and their interactions. In 1817, David Ricardo (1772–1823) wrote on the forces that determine the functional distribution of income and the theories of value and price, and it was from these theories that microeconomic theory originated. Microeconomics in the early twenty-first century includes the theory of consumer behavior, theory of production, and the theory of markets. It deals with such topics as prices of a specific product, the number of workers employed in a specific firm, the revenue or income of a particular firm or household, and the expenditures of a specific firm, government entity, or family. Microeconomic analysis focuses mostly on optimization and equilibrium analysis.

Macroeconomics deals with the aggregate economy and the behavior of its major units—households, businesses, government, and the foreign sector. Developed in the 1930s, macroeconomics was practically invented by the English economist John Maynard Keynes (1883–1946) in his attempt to develop an answer to the Great Depression. Keynes argued that the Great Depression was a problem of insufficient aggregate demand and that if the private economy could not generate sufficient demand, it was the government's responsibility to do so. Macroeconomics focuses on such issues as growth, recessions, inflation, unemployment, and government policy and deals with such topics as total output or gross domestic product (GDP), total employment, total income, aggregate expenditure, and general level of prices.

Historical Development

Although economics originally referred to the management of the affairs of the household (*oikonomia* in Greek), its meaning evolved into political economy—"[t]he financial branch of the art or business of government" (Milgate et al., eds., vol. 2, p. 58)—then into how to make a country wealthy, and finally into a social science that studies the production, distribution, and consumption of commodities.

The economic problem or the objective of the economic arrangement, be it in a primitive hunting and gathering society or in the most sophisticated modern industrial society, is that of provision—how to use scarce resources to produce goods and services and how to appropriately distribute the product. This problem has remained basically unchanged in human history. Over time, what has differed or changed are the modes of economic organization that correspond to the cultural arrangements in human societies. But the existence of the economic problem is different from an analysis of the economic problem. Organized economic systems existed in ancient Egypt, the great African empires of Western Sudan, the Aztec and Incan civilizations of the Americas, and the Assyrian and Babylonian theocracies. But according to Joseph Schumpeter, there is no trace of analytic effort until Greece. Even the beginning of the analytic effort did not become systematic until the eighteenth century. Hence, as a field of study, economics is relatively young, and only emerged as a full-fledged separate discipline following the publication of Adam Smith's *The Wealth of Nations* in 1776.

In Western civilization wealth was the primary and original concern of economics, and in economics the questions about wealth concerned the means of acquiring, maintaining, and increasing it. Wealth was seen by Aristotle not as an end, but as a means of achieving ethical and political ends. Whereas the treatment of wealth in the noneconomic fields of religion, history, politics, and the like focused mostly on its distribution and its effect on affluence, poverty, and the state, the approach of the economists was to focus on the means to wealth.

In addition to the attempts to understand the sources of wealth, pioneer economists sought to understand human nature and the sources of value. Human nature has been viewed both in the traditional conservative view as natural and preordained and in the critical liberal view as socially determined. The traditional conservative view from the Middle Ages through slavery in the Americas and the industrial revolution sees ideas, drives, and practices as natural, inherent, God-given, or innate. Hence, the classical and neoclassical economists believed that capitalism was natural and eternal and consumer preferences were given, since individuals were born with them in the same manner that the conservative religious leaders believed that serfdom was natural and the American conservative southerners believed that slavery was ordained by God. Critical economists or the liberal view originating from Karl Marx (1818–1883), Thorstein Veblen (1857–1929), and John Maynard Keynes focused more on the evolution and transformation of economic systems and their impact on people's ideas and preferences. This premise was based on the belief that ideas and preferences are shaped by the society in which people live (Hunt and Sherman).

With all its accomplishments, economics is plagued with a crisis of identity and dissension and disagreements on how it should be taught, how it should be practiced, and how it should be used. Furthermore, the field of economics has been slow in reintegrating itself into the social sciences to become, once again, more problem-driven and more eclectic. Indeed the shift to abstraction and quantification that was started by David Ricardo continued until relatively recently and is at the source of the dispute about the usefulness of economics in modern society. Many economists complain about an undue attention paid to esoteric models, and the tendency by some economists, mostly of the orthodox school, to provide a uniquely economic answer to such social questions as the causes of growth and why some countries are underdeveloped.

Undeniably, as the twentieth century drew to a close, there was a greater recognition of the importance of noneconomic factors in explaining major economic questions and problems. For instance, mainstream economics has come to acknowledge the importance of history, political conditions, sociocultural factors, the environment, geography, and international variables in explaining such economic problems as lack of growth, underdevelopment, inequality, and poverty. This recognition notwithstanding, the field of economics has still not seriously focused on the critical and endemic problems that plague the world. For instance, despite being the least developed continent in the world representing arguably the most daunting economic challenge in modern history, Africa has been all but ignored by economics. This is amazing in light of the fact that the field's supposedly central preoccupation is the problems of income, growth, distribution, and human welfare.

Notable contributions to the field of economics include Richard Cantillon's *Essay on the Nature of Commerce* (1755), Adam Smith's *Wealth of Nations* (1776), Karl Marx's *Das Capital* (1867), Thorstein Veblen's *The Theory of the Leisure Class* (1899), and John Maynard Keynes's *General Theory of Employment, Interest, and Money* (1936). Before the publication of the *Wealth of Nations,* there were other schools of thought whose main preoccupation was wealth creation and the organization of the economy, most prominently, mercantilism and physiocracy.

Mercantilism or bullionism.
Mercantilism or bullionism is a loose economic school of thought whose basic belief is that a nation's wealth originated from gold and silver bullion and other forms of treasure. The mercantilist ideas were spread in an uncoordinated three-hundred-year effort, mostly through the English pamphlet writers of the seventeenth and eighteenth centuries, a period marked by significant shortages of gold and silver bullion in Europe. Mercantilism believed in trade regulation, industrial promotion, imposition of protective duties on imports of manufactures, encouragement of exports, population growth, and low wages. This belief in regulating wealth was grounded in the conviction that favorable balance of trade leads to national prosperity.

Mercantilists assumed that the total wealth of the world was fixed and reasoned that trade would lead to a zero-sum game. Consequently, they surmised that any increase in the wealth and economic power of one nation was necessarily at the expense of other nations. Hence, they emphasized balance of trade as a means of increasing the wealth and power of a nation.

Physiocracy.
The term *Physiocracy* (the order or rule of nature) developed for less than two decades as a reaction against the doctrines and restrictive policies of mercantilism. Founded on a doctrine of noninterference, the physiocratic ideas were first enunciated by the Frenchman François Quesnay (1694–1774). Quesnay argued that only agriculture can produce net output (*produit net*). According to Physiocracy, the farmers and landowners were considered to be the productive classes whereas the merchants and industrialists were not. The Physiocrats believed in natural laws, the free enterprise system, and the free operation of the natural order of things. Quesnay also developed the famous *Tableau Economique* (economic table) in an attempt to establish a general equilibrium through a basic input-output model. The main ideas of Physiocracy that were promoted by the intellectual disciples of Quesnay—a group of French social reformers—came directly or indirectly from his *Tableau Economique.* Another important contributor to Physiocracy is Anne-Robert-Jacques Turgot (1727–1781), whose *Reflections on the Formation and the Distribution of Wealth* (1769–1770) was one of the most important general treatises on political economy written before Smith's *Wealth of Nations.*

Major Theories
The study of economics is driven by theories of economic behavior and economic performance, which have developed along the lines of the classical ideas, the Marxist idea, or a combination of both. In the process, various models were developed, each trying to explain such economic phenomena as wealth creation, value, prices, and growth from a separate intellectual and cultural setting, each considering certain variables and relationships more important than others. Within the aforementioned historical framework, economics has followed a trajectory that is characterized by a multiplicity of doctrines and schools of thought, usually identifiable with a thinker or thinkers whose ideas and theories form the foundation of the doctrine.

Classical economics.
Classical economic doctrine descended from Adam Smith and developed in the nineteenth century. It asserts that the power of the market system, if left alone, will ensure full employment of economic resources. Classical economists believed that although occasional deviations from full employment result from economic and political events, automatic adjustments in market prices, wages, and interest rates will restore the economy to full employment. The philosophical foundation of classical economics was provided by John Locke's (1632–1704) conception of the natural order, while the economic foundation was based on Adam Smith's theory of self-interest and Jean-Baptiste Say's (1767–1832) law of the equality of market demand and supply.

Classical economic theory is founded on two maxims. First, it presupposes that each individual maximizes his or her preference function under some constraints, where preferences and constraints are considered as given. Second, it presupposes the existence of interdependencies—expressed in the markets—between the actions of all individuals. Under the assumption of perfect and pure competition, these two features will determine resource allocation and income distribution. That is, they will regulate demand and supply, allocation of production, and the optimization of social organization.

Led by Adam Smith and David Ricardo with the support of Jean-Baptiste Say and Thomas Robert Malthus (1766–1834), the classical economists believed in Smith's invisible hand, self-interest, and a self-regulating economic system, as well as in the development of monetary institutions, capital accumulation based on surplus production, and free trade. They also believed in division of labor, the law of diminishing returns, and the ability of the economy to self-adjust in a laissez-faire system devoid of government intervention. The circular flow of the classical model indicates that wages may deviate, but will eventually return to their natural rate of subsistence.

Marxist economics. Because of the social cost of capitalism as proposed by classical economics and the industrial revolution, socialist thought emerged within the classical liberal thought. To address the problems of classical capitalist economics, especially what he perceived as the neglect of history, Karl Marx (1818–1883), a German economic, social, and political philosopher, in his famous book titled *Das Kapital* or *Capital* (1867–1894) advanced his doctrine of dialectical materialism. Marx's dialectics was a dynamic system in which societies would evolve from primitive society to feudalism to capitalism to socialism and to communism. The basis of Marx's dialectical materialism was the application of history derived from Georg Wilhelm Friedrich Hegel (1770–1831), which maintained that history proceeds linearly by the triad of forces or dialectics called thesis, antithesis, and synthesis. This transition, in Marx's view, will result from changes in the ruling and the oppressed classes and their relationship with each other. He then envisaged conflict between forces of production, organization of production, relations of production, and societal thinking and ideology.

Marx predicts capitalist cycles that will ultimately lead to the collapse of capitalism. According to him, these cycles will be characterized by a reserve army of the unemployed, falling rate of profits, business crises, increasing concentration of industry into a few hands, and mounting misery and alienation of the proletariat. Whereas Adam Smith and David Ricardo had argued that the rational and calculating capitalists in following their self-interest promote social good, Marx argued that in rationally and purposefully pursuing their economic advantage, the capitalists will sow the seeds of their own destruction.

The economic thinking or school of economic thought that originated from Marx became known as Marxism. As the chief theorist of modern socialism and communism, Marx advocated fundamental revolution in society because of what he saw as the inherent exploitation of labor and economic injustice in the capitalist system. Marxist ideas were adopted as the political and economic systems in the former Soviet Union, China, Cuba, North Korea, and other parts of the world.

The neo-Marxist doctrines apply both the Marxist historical dimension and dialectics in their explanation of economic relationships, behavior, and outcome. For instance, the dependency theory articulates the need for the developing regions in Africa, Latin America, and Asia to rid themselves of their endemic dependence on more advanced countries. The dependency school believes that international links between developing (periphery) and industrialized (center) countries constitute a barrier to development through trade and investment.

Neoclassical economics. The period that followed Ricardo, especially from 1870 to 1900, was full of criticism of classical economic theory and the capitalist system by humanists and socialists. The period was also characterized by the questioning of the classical assumption that laissez-faire was an ideal government policy and the eventual demise of classical economic theory and the transition to neoclassical economics. This transition was neither spontaneous nor automatic, but it was critical for the professionalization of economics.

Neoclassical economics is attributed with integrating the original classical cost of production theory with utility in a bid to explain commodity and factor prices and the allocation of resources using marginal analysis. Although David Ricardo provided the methodological rudiments of neoclassical economics through his move away from contextual analysis to more abstract deductive analysis, Alfred Marshall (1842–1924) was regarded as the father of neoclassicism and was credited with introducing such concepts as supply and demand, price-elasticity of demand, marginal utility, and costs of production.

Neoclassical or marginalist economic theories emphasized use value and demand and supply as determinants of exchange value. Likewise neoclassicals, William Stanley Jevons (1835–1882) in England; Karl Menger (1840–1925) in Austria; and Léon Walras (1834–1910) in Switzerland, independently developed and highlighted the role of marginal utility (and individual utility maximization), as opposed to cost of production, as the key to the problem of exchange valuation. Neoclassical models assume that everyone has free access to information they require for decision making. This assumption made it possible to reduce decision making to a mechanical application of mathematical rules for optimization. Hence, in the neoclassical view, people's initial ability to maximize the value of output will, in turn, affect productivity and determine allocation of resources and income distribution. Neoclassical economics is grounded in the rejection of Marxist economics and on the belief that the market system will ensure a fair and just allocation of resources and income distribution.

Since its emergence, neoclassical economics has become the dominant economic doctrine in the study and teaching of economics in the West, especially in the United States. A host of economic theories have emerged from neoclassical economics: neoclassical growth theory, neoclassical trade theory, neoclassical theory of production, and so on. In the neoclassical growth theory, the determinants of output growth are technology, labor, and capital. The neoclassical growth theory stresses the importance of savings and capital accumulation together with exogenously determined technical progress as the sources of economic growth. If savings are larger, then capital per worker will grow, leading to rising income per capita and vice versa.

The neoclassical thinking can be expressed as the Solow-Swan model of the production function type $Y = F(N,K)$ which is expanded to

$$\Delta Y / Y = \Delta A / A + \Delta N / N + \Delta K / K$$

where Y represents total output, N and K represent the inputs of labor and capital, and A represents the productivity of capital and labor, and $\Delta Y / Y$, $\Delta A / A$, $\Delta N / N$, and $\Delta K / K$ represent changes in these variables, respectively.

The Solow-Swan model asserts that because of the diminishing marginal product of inputs, sustained growth is possible only through technological change. The notion of diminishing marginal product is rooted in the belief that as more inputs are used to produce additional output under a fixed technology and fixed resource base, additional output per unit of input will decline (diminishing marginal product). This belief in the stationary state and diminishing marginal product led neoclassical economics to believe in the possibility of worldwide convergence of growth.

Known also as the neoliberal theory, neoclassical economics asserts that free movement of goods (free trade), services, and capital unimpeded by government regulation will lead to rapid economic growth. This, in the neoclassical view, will increase global output and international efficiency because the gains from division of labor according to comparative advantage and specialization will improve overall welfare. Even modern trade models (such as the Heckscher-Ohlin) are based on the neoclassical trade theory, which assumes perfect competition and concludes that trade generally improves welfare by improving the allocation of factors of production across sectors of the economy.

Rational expectation. Rational expectation is the economic doctrine that emerged in the 1970s that asserts that people collect relevant information about the economy and behave rationally—that is, they weigh costs and benefits of actions and decisions. Rational expectation economics believes that because people act in response to their expectations, public policy will be offset by their action. Also known as the "new classical economics," the rational expectation doctrine believes that markets are highly competitive and prices adjust to changes in aggregate demand. The extent to which people are actually well informed is questionable and prices tend to be sticky or inflexible in a downward direction because once they go up, prices rarely come down. In the rational expectation doctrine, expansionary policies will increase inflation without increasing employment because economic actors—households and businesses—acting in a rational manner will anticipate inflation and act in a manner that will cause prices and wages to rise.

Monetarism. Like rational expectations theory, monetarism represents a modern form of classical theory that believes in laissez-faire and in the flexibility of wages and prices. Like the classical theorists before them, they believe that government should stay out of economic stabilization since, in their view, markets are competitive with a high degree of macroeconomic stability. Such policies as expansionary monetary policy will, in their view, only lead to price instability. The U.S. economist Milton Friedman, who received the Nobel Prize in 1976,

is widely regarded as the leader of the Chicago school of monetary economics.

Institutionalism. Institutional economics focuses mainly on how institutions evolve and change and how these changes affect economic systems, economic performance, or outcomes. Both Frederick Hayek and Ronald Coase, major contributors to the Institutionalist School in the tradition of Karl Marx and Joseph Schumpeter, look at how institutions emerge. Hayek examines the temporal evolution and transformation of economic institutions and concludes that institutions result from human action. Hence, he suggests the existence of a spontaneous order in which workable institutions survive while nonworkable ones disappear. Coase believes that institutions are created according to rational economic logic when transaction costs are too high. Other notable contributors to institutionalism include Thorstein Veblen, Clarence Ayers, Gunnar Myrdal, John R. Commons, Wesley Cair Mitchell, and John Kenneth Galbraith.

The New Institutionalism, represented mostly by Douglas North, Gordon Tullock, and Mancur Olson, uses the classical notions of rationality and self-interest to explain the evolution and economic impact of institutions. It considers such issues as property rights, rent-seeking, and distributional coalitions and argues that institutional transformation can be explained in terms of changes in property rights, transaction costs, and information asymmetries.

Themes

As an academic discipline, economics encompasses a wide variety of themes that represent its historical and contemporary intellectual development. Some of the discipline's major themes include economic methodology, development economics, Endogenous Growth theory, feminist economics, environmental economics, monetarist economics, and econometrics.

Economic methodology. Economic methodology refers to the method of economic investigation. It mirrors and derives from economic theory and has come to be known as the formulation and testing of hypotheses of cause-and-effect relationship. Like the field itself, which is very much in dispute, economic methodology has evolved and transformed in time from a more formal scientific approach in which methodology was emphasized to a period of lesser emphasis on scientific methodology. Before the formalization of economic theory, economists employed discourse to state and test theories and hypotheses. This heuristic approach did not permit hypothesis to be tested in a manner acceptable as scientific.

In time, economics adopted the use of the scientific method to either formulate economic laws, theories, or principles or to ascertain their validity. The process involves observing facts, making assumptions and hypothesizing about facts, testing hypotheses (to compare outcomes with predictions), accepting or rejecting hypotheses, systematically arranging and interpreting facts to draw generalizations and establish laws, theories, or principles, and often formulating policies, addressing economic problems, or achieving specific economic goals.

At the two levels of microeconomics and macroeconomics, economic methodology can either be inductive or deductive, quantitative or qualitative, positive or normative. Economists express economic theory in terms of equations and relationships between economic variables in algebraic form and make inferences using mathematical operations. Over time, the economics discipline has witnessed an intensified mathematization of economic methodology and an increased role of abstraction and esoteric modeling that has, in effect, made it inaccessible to the untrained.

In this regard, econometrics, especially linear regression analysis, mathematical economics, game theory, and the like have played a great role. There has also been a move away from the scientific methodology involving data collection, hypothesis, analysis, and theory to an emphasis on modeling.

The 1960s and 1970s saw enormous advances in formal statistical testing and logical positivism and Popperian falsification, mostly in an attempt to establish one correct method of economics. Karl Raimund Popper (1902–1994) is one of the most influential philosophers of the twentieth century who produced influential works and political philosophy, particularly *The Logic of Scientific Discovery* (1959). Falsification is "a methodological standpoint that regards theories and hypotheses as scientific if and only if their prediction are at least in principle falsifiable, that is, if they forbid certain acts/states/ events from occurring" (Blaug, 1992, p. xiii).

Development economics. Development economics or the economics of development is the application of economic analysis to the understanding of the economies of developing countries in Africa, Asia, and Latin America. It is the subdiscipline of economics that deals with the study of the processes that create or prevent economic development or that result in the improvement of incomes, human welfare, and structural transformation from a predominantly agricultural to a more advanced industrial economy. The subfield of development economics was born in the 1940s and 1950s but only became firmly entrenched following the awarding of the Nobel Prize to W. Arthur Lewis and Theodore W. Schultz in 1979. Lewis provided the impetus for and was a prime mover in creating the subdiscipline of development economics.

As a subfield concerned with "how standards of living in the population are determined and how they change over time" (Stern), and how policy can or should be used to influence these processes, development economics cannot be considered independently of the historical, political, environmental, and sociocultural dimensions of the human experience. Hence development economics is a study of the multidimensional process involving acceleration of economic growth, the reduction of inequality, the eradication of poverty, as well as major changes in economic and social structures, popular attitudes, and national institutions.

Development economics covers a variety of issues, ranging from peasant agriculture to international finance, and touches on virtually every branch in economics: micro and macro, labor, industrial organization, public finance, resource economics, money and banking, economic growth, international trade, etc., as well as branches in history, sociology, and political science. It deals with the economic, social, political, and institutional framework in which economic development takes place.

The study of economic development has been driven by theories of economic development, which have developed along the lines of the classical ideas, the Marxist idea, or a combination of both. Some approaches have focused on the internal causes of development or underdevelopment, while others have focused on external causes. Economic growth— increase in output and income—has been used as a substitute for development and, in some cases, has been treated as synonymous with development. Economic growth and economic development have been mostly studied by means of cross-country econometric analysis.

Development economics has an assortment of theories and models to inform its teaching and research—neoclassical, Marxist, demand-driven, balanced growth, unbalanced growth, stages of growth, structuralist, dependency, neoclassical, and endogenous—each trying to explain development from a separate intellectual and cultural setting, each considering certain variables and relationships more important than others. Kaushik Basu identifies three major surges in economic growth theory in this century: the Harrod Domar model and the responses it orchestrated, the neoclassical response to Harrod Domar led by Solow (1956), and the works of Lucas (1986) and Romer (1988) that gave rise to the theory of endogenous growth.

Endogenous growth theory. Proponents of the endogenous growth theory focus on technological progress and innovation and believe that technological change is endogenous, not exogenous, as neoclassical economics claims. Originally developed by Frankel, and then Lucas and Romer, endogenous growth theory argues that in addition to the accumulation of capital, technical progress is not exogenous but is planned and produced through research and development efforts. It recognizes the role of private sector and free market enterprise as the engine of growth, but suggests an active role of public policy in promoting economic development. In sum, in endogenous growth economics, several factors come together to determine the level of output in a country: government policy, economic behavior, and technology, which are determined by the expenditure on research and development, the rate of accumulation of factors of production—land, labor, capital, entrepreneurship, and savings. One could summarize the entire focus as being to explain the existence of increasing returns to scale and divergent long-term growth patterns among countries.

Feminist economics. Feminist economics is the branch of economics that advances a theory of economic equality of the sexes and deals with gender equality or the elimination of gender subordination. Feminist economics originated from the organized feminist activities and movement whose influence became more visible in the 1970s and 1990s on behalf of women's rights and interest. It continues to exert an increasing influence on the field of economics by questioning the existing paradigms, approaches, and assumptions.

Through journals and feminist publications, feminist economists criticize what they refer to as the social construction of economics as a discipline, in particular neoclassical orthodoxy. They highlight what they consider to be the androcentric (male-centered) nature of conventional economic thinking, question its wisdom, and reveal biases in conventional microeconomic models. Feminist economists question the nature and functioning of the markets and the classical market society, especially with regard to economic rationality and maximizing behavior. They also highlight the absence of power relations and unequal exchanges, gender, and race in mainstream economic analysis. They question the focus on choices in mainstream analysis and advocate focusing, instead, on provisioning, which, in their view, would account for such social issues as poverty and income inequality. Feminist economics also indicts the lack of emphasis on women's economic role and the noninclusion of domestic and other unpaid work in national income accounts and statistics.

Environmental economics. Environmental economics is the branch of economics that deals with the application of economic tools and principles to the understanding and analysis of environmental issues and to solving environmental problems. Environmental economics draws from both microeconomics and macroeconomics, focusing on individual decisions that have environmental consequences and changes in institutions and policies to achieve desirable environmental goals.

A major preoccupation of environmental economics is the question of externalities or spillovers, especially negative externalities or spillover costs of human action. The cost of and responses to pollution, emissions, and other negative externalities as well as population, natural resources, energy, water, agriculture, forests, and wildlife are issues considered in environmental economics. Likewise, environmental economics deals with economic dimensions of problems of both regional and global pollutants, including acid rain, ozone depletion, and global warming.

Environmental economics involves the valuation of the environment and natural resources as well as the assessment of environmental damage, management, and regulation of environmental risk, and the markets for the environment. Environmental economics takes account of sustainable development and the impact on the environment of trade, transport, deforestation, water pollution, and climatic change. It also involves analysis of the costs and benefits of the environment.

Mathematics and economics. Mathematical economics involves the use of formal and abstract analysis to develop hypotheses and analyze economic relationships. It refers to the application of mathematical techniques to the formulation of hypotheses and building economic models. The introduction of mathematics into economics by the Frenchman Antoine Augustin Cournot (1801–1877) in 1838 marked the beginning of a steady course that led to the emergence of mathematical economics. The antecedents of Léon Walras in 1874–1877 and Vilfredo Pareto in 1896–1897 were also essential in advancing mathematical economics. Henceforth, geometrical figures became conventional in economic literature and so did differential calculus and linear algebra. Game theory—the application of mathematics to the analysis of competitive situations and actions—has become a popular aspect of mathematical economics following the publication of *The Theory of Games and Economic Behavior* in 1944 by John von Neumann and Oskar Morgenstern.

Econometrics. Econometrics is the application of mathematical and statistical techniques to the testing of hypotheses and quantifying of economic theories and the solution of economic problems. Econometrics combines mathematical economics as it is applied to model-building and the hypothesis-formulation and statistical analysis involving data collection, analysis, and hypothesis-testing. The emergence of econometrics has provided economists with a tool for analyzing macroeconomic models for forecasting, simulation, and economic policy.

As the most widely used tool for empirical analysis and for constructing theories, econometrics provides a method that allows the expression of economic theory using statistical data or using statistical data to estimate economic theory. Estimation methods range from Ordinary Least Squares to panel data and time series analysis.

New methodological approaches have been developed to address some of the weaknesses of the traditional methodology. For instance, there is more emphasis on rigorous diagnostic testing, including coefficient, residual, and stability tests as well as Unit Root and Johansen tests for cointegration and Granger Causality test. Cointegration analysis of time series to determine whether a group of nonstationary series are cointegrated is an important development in empirical modeling. Improvements in multiple regression analysis often involving tests of correlation and causality as well as linear and nonlinear regression methods have proved to be important for the development of econometrics.

Global Organization and Orientation

Between the two world wars, two important phenomena affected the organization and orientation of economics in the world. The first was the Bolshevik Revolution of 1917 and the exceptionally rapid industrialization of the Soviet Union. The second was the Great Depression of the 1930s. The former led to the development of the Marxist-Stalinist economic system and state-directed development, collectivization, and the establishment of a command economy. The Great Depression led to a declining faith in the classical (laissez-faire) self-regulating free market capitalism, and the emergence of government interventionism, following the publication, by John Maynard Keynes in 1936, of *The General Theory of Money, Interest, and Employment.*

The new field of development economics was born in the 1940s and 1950s with W. Arthur Lewis providing the impetus for and being a prime mover in creating the subdiscipline. The new Keynesian macroeconomics and development economics advocated widespread government intervention in the economic process. Likewise, the powerful and far-reaching movements of the developing countries in Africa, Asia, and Latin America in the 1940s gave rise to the rejection of free-market capitalism in those regions. In the 1940s and 1950s, economists advocated for a dominant role of the state and comprehensive national development planning was recommended as a way to eliminate the "vicious circle of poverty" and underdevelopment. The advocacy for dirigisme was founded on the notion of market segmentation and failures as well as on information asymmetries and resource constraints. Disappointing results after World

War II forced a serious questioning and tempering of this development dirigisme.

As a social science, economics is subject to ideological manipulation. Aside from the orthodox (mainstream) and heterodox spheres, in the neoclassical intellectual tradition, there has been a split since the late nineteenth century as can be seen in the case of its liberal and conservative wings. Led by Paul Samuelson, liberal thinking is associated with advocacy for government intervention to correct market imperfections and market failures while conservatism or neoclassicism led by Milton Friedman is associated with a more pronounced advocacy for laissez-faire.

Impact of Influential Economic Ideas

Throughout the history of nations, economic ideas, notably those of Adam Smith, Karl Marx, and John Maynard Keynes, have had a profound influence on politics and society. Economics has influenced the emergence of political systems, political ideology, and the societal organization of production and distribution. The political and economic systems of democratic capitalism and socialism owe their existence to the ideas of Adam Smith and his followers and Karl Marx, respectively. Recognizing this fact, Keynes, in a famous passage from chapter 24 of *General Theory of Employment, Interest, and Money,* states: "The ideas of economists and political philosophers, both when they are right and when they are wrong, are more powerful than is commonly understood. Indeed the world is ruled by little else. Practical men, who believe themselves to be quite exempt from any intellectual influences, are usually the slaves of some defunct economist."

Adam Smith's invisible hand of competitive markets, self-interest, and division of labor gave rise to the American style of individualistic market capitalism. Smith's notion of the natural tendency of an economic system to establish equilibrium through the pursuit of self-interest and competitive markets became the foundation of liberal economics in the nineteenth century. Likewise, Marx's analysis of capitalism, his prediction of its ultimate demise, and the triumph of socialism and communism became the foundation for the socialist economic systems of the former Soviet Union and other Eastern European, African, and Asian countries. His idea of the inevitability of the historical evolution of societies from primitive society to feudalism to capitalism to socialism, and ultimately to communism due to the internal conflicts resulting from the exploitation of workers, led to socialist ideas of centralization, planning, and public ownership of resources.

The commitment by governments to macroeconomic policies that ensure full employment and economic growth; the establishment of social security systems; and even deposit insurance guarantees in the banking system are all by-products of influential economic ideas of Keynes. Keynes argued that the answer to the existence of the Great Depression was insufficient aggregate demand and recommended increase in public demand by the government as a means of increasing total demand and output. Since then, discretionary macroeconomic stabilization has become a policy goal of many countries.

Much of the distinction between political conservatism and liberalism is based on economics and in this regard, the differentiation lies on the belief of the role of government versus the market and what type of government intervention, if any, will bring about the most optimum outcomes. In the United States, for instance, liberal politicians tend to favor government spending over lower taxes, while conservative politicians tend to favor tax reductions over government spending as fiscal policy measures against economic recessions.

See also **Capitalism; Communism; Conservatism; Liberalism; Marxism; Socialism.**

BIBLIOGRAPHY

Aghion, Philippe, and Peter Howitt. *Endogenous Growth Theory.* Cambridge Mass.: MIT Press, 1998.

Baran, Paul A. *The Political Economy of Growth.* New York: Modern Reader Paperbacks, 1975.

Basu, Kaushik. *Analytical Development Economics: The Less Developed Economy Revisited,* Cambridge, Mass.: MIT Press, 1997.

Benería, Lourdes. *Gender, Development, and Globalization: Economics as if All People Mattered.* New York and London: Routledge, 2003.

Blaug, Mark. *Economic Theory in Retrospect.* 5th ed. Cambridge, U.K., and New York: Cambridge University Press, 1997.

———. *The Methodology of Economics, or, How Economists Explain.* 2nd ed. Cambridge, U.K., and New York: Cambridge University Press, 1992.

Brewers. Anthony. *Marxist Theories of Imperialism: A Critical Survey.* London and Boston: Routledge and Kegan Paul, 1980

Frank, Andre Gunder. *Latin America: Underdevelopment or Revolution.* New York: Monthly Review Press, 1969.

Frankel, M. "The Production Function in Allocation and Growth: A Synthesis." *American Economic Review* 52 (1962): 995–1022.

Hunt, E. K. *History of Economic Thought: A Critical Perspective.* 2nd ed. New York: HarperCollins, 1992.

Hunt, E. K., and Howard J. Sherman. *Economics: An Introduction to Traditional and Radical Views.* 6th ed. New York: Harper and Row, 1990.

Lucas, Robert E. "On the Mechanics of Economic Development." *Journal of Monetary Economics* 22, no. 1 (January 1988): 3–42.

McGrew, Anthony G., and Paul G Lewis. *Global Politics: Globalization and the Nation-State.* Cambridge, Mass.: Blackwell, 1992.

Milgate, Murray, John Eatwell, and Peter Newman, eds. *The New Palgrave: A Dictionary of Economics.* 4 vols. New York: Palgrave 1998. Reprint, 2002.

Nelson, Judy A. *Feminism, Objectivity and Economics.* London and New York: Routledge, 1996.

Nnadozie, Emmanuel, ed. *African Economic Development.* San Diego, Calif.: Academic Press, 2003.

Romer, Paul M. "Endogenous Technological Change." *Journal of Political Economy* 98, no. 5 (1990): 71–102.

Schumpeter, Joseph A. *History of Economic Analysis.* Edited by Elizabeth Boody Schumpeter. New York: Oxford University Press, 1954.

Sen, Amartya. "The Concept of Development." In *Handbook of Development Economics,* edited by Hollis Chenery and T. N. Srinivasan. 3 vols. Amsterdam: Elsevier Science, 1988–1995.

Solow, Robert. M. "A Contribution to the Theory of Economic Growth." *Quarterly Journal of Economics* 70 (February 1956): 65–94.

Stern, Nicholas. "The Economics of Development: A Survey." *The Economic Journal* 99 (1989): 597–685.

Swan, T. W. "Economic Growth and Capital Accumulation." *Economic Record* 32 (1956): 334–361.

Tietenberg, Tom. *Environmental Economics and Policy.* New York: HarperCollins, 1994.

Emmanuel Nnadozie

ECOSYSTEM. *See* **Ecology.**

ECUMENISM.
Ecumenism derives from the Greek adjective *oikoumenikos* (ecumenical) and the noun *oikoumenē,* the latter term employed since the time of Herodotus (5th century B.C.E.) to mean "the inhabited earth" or "the whole world." *Oikoumenē* then came to refer specifically to the realm of the Greco-Roman empire and its culture as distinguished from so-called barbarian lands and cultures. During the fourth century C.E., *oikoumenē* took on the combined political-religious meanings of "the one Christian empire" or "the unified Christian world."

Christianity
The word *ecumenism* itself became prevalent after the 1910 World Missionary Conference in Edinburgh, Scotland. Delegates from missionary organizations met to address the incongruity—and scandal, no less—of historically divided and competing Christian denominations preaching a message of peace and harmony among non-Christian peoples. The World Council of Churches, the primary organizational outgrowth of the Edinburgh Conference that currently comprises more than 330 communions in over 120 countries, applies "ecumenical" to all that relates to the whole task of the whole unifying church to bring the message of Christ to the whole world.

This inhabited earth that was the point of departure for what it is to be ecumenically minded is becoming ever more interconnected and "smaller" as a result of dramatic technological advances in communications and mobilization. Whatever threatens or is of advantage to some carries embedded repercussions for all. The past half-century also witnesses to a slowly evolving consensus on what constitutes authentic human life. (The United Nations' 1948 Universal Declaration of Human Rights was a significant moment at the beginning of this process.) With the emergence of these phenomena collectively known as "globalization," there is a growing awareness in all religions that to be religious is to be interreligious; also, that each religion bears the responsibility to contribute to human security, justice, peace, planetary well being, and the development of a global ethic. Attenuation of the role that religions play as an intensifying factor in regional social conflicts and the increasing incidence of interreligious marriages further accent the need for improved interreligious relations.

Globalization "opens out" the concept of ecumenism beyond its original identity as an intra-Christian concern for unity to include the sense of mutual understanding and reconciliation among all the world's religions. The World Council of Churches stipulated dialogue as the most appropriate method to foster improved interreligious relationships at its 1967 consultation in Kandy, Sri Lanka. Stephen J. Duffy elucidates the dimensions of interreligious dialogue:

1. Dialogue of life and hospitality, in which people living in open neighborliness share joys and sorrows, problems and concerns.

2. Dialogue of concerned service that promotes collaboration for the integral development of all persons and a more humane world.

3. Dialogue of religious experience, in which persons firmly grounded in their own traditions share their spiritual riches, prayer life, contemplation, and ways of searching for the absolute.

4. Dialogue of doctrinal exchange, in which specialists seek deeper understanding of the doctrines and practices of other heritages as well as their own to establish a communion of horizons arrived at through critical evaluations, correctives, and above all, through the openness of all to change in a shared quest for truth and identity.

These dialogues are intended to assist in breaking down prejudices and misconceptions accumulated over centuries. They enrich, enlarge, challenge, and correct the way some religions have understood and approached religious life in other traditions.

The World Council of Churches' interreligious subunit lists the following as being among its foci: multireligious reflection on secularization; the role of religion in public life and the challenges of religious plurality; Christian-Jewish-Muslim dialogue on the issue of Jerusalem; Hindu-Christian dialogue on issues such as proselytization, religious extremism, and caste; and Christian-Muslim forums on human rights.

The Roman Catholic Church, though not a member of the World Council of Churches, committed to the ecumenical enterprise unreservedly two years before the Second Vatican Council (1962–1965) was called into session. In 1960 Pope John XXIII established the Secretariat for Promoting Christian Unity, renamed the Pontifical Council for Promoting Christian Unity by Pope John Paul II in 1988. Pope Paul VI established the Secretariat for Non-Christians in 1964, renamed the Pontifical Council for Interreligious Dialogue by Pope John Paul II in 1988.

The following catalog illustrates the fact that impetus for improved interreligious relations is not derived from solely Christian initiatives and responses.

Buddhism. His Holiness the Fourteenth Dalai Lama, Tenzin Gyatso, 1989 Nobel Peace Prize winner, freely offers direction on Buddhism's spiritual path to enlightenment that entails the three higher trainings of wisdom, meditation, and moral living. The majority of the path's foundational precepts are monastic in nature; thus it is that believers that identify with religions possessing monastic traditions find a ready dialogue partner in Buddhism with regard to this particular religious aspect. Establishments that serve the dialogues of life, religious experience, and academic exchange that involve Buddhist participation include the following: The Ecumenical Institute for Study and Dialogue in Sri Lanka; Inter-Religio, a network of institutions in eight East Asian countries; the Nanzan Institute for Religion and Culture in Japan; the bulletin published by Monastic Interreligious Dialogue. The "dialogue of concerned service" is an emerging new frontier as witnessed by the success of a 1996 conference, "Socially Engaged Buddhism and Christianity," sponsored by the Society for Buddhist-Christian Studies. This fifth international conference of the society included such noted Asian Buddhist leaders as the Dalai Lama, Maha Ghosananda from Cambodia, Sulak Sivaraksa from Thailand, and A. T. Ariyaratne from Sri Lanka, as well as leaders from the Japanese Rissho Kosei-kai and Soka Gakkai movements, and the Korean Chogye Buddhist Order.

Issues between the two main types of Buddhism, Theravada Buddhism of South and Southeast Asia and Mahayana Buddhism of Tibet and East Asia, reflect a universal human tendency to advocate either a literalist-conservative regard for tradition (Theravada Buddhism) or a more open-ended, experimental and expansive handling of tradition (Mahayana Buddhism).

Hinduism. Philosopher-statesman Sarvepalli Radhakrishnan (1888–1975) was a particularly powerful advocate for a "dialogue of religions" while at Oxford in the early 1930s. Presently, Seshagiri Rao, general editor of the forthcoming *Encyclopedia on Hinduism,* is an active promoter of interreligious dialogue. Foundations that embody religious intercourse between Hinduism and Christianity include The North American Board for East-West Dialogue and the European Dialogue Interreligieux Monastique (same as the Monastic Interreligious Dialogue, mentioned above), both founded in 1978, and the Society for Hindu-Christian Studies, founded in 1994.

Hindus and Muslims have lived together in the subcontinent of India, Pakistan, and Bangladesh for over a millennium. The story of their coexistence is one of frequent and violent bloodletting. Here the main ecumenical challenge is to convince that dialogue is even possible. Hinduism initially encountered Islam as the religion of conquerors, and this fact continues to condition the reflexive reaction that some individual Hindus have toward Muslims in general. Yet the "dialogue of life" continues by the very fact of their juxtaposed and intermingled lives. Courageous visionaries who espy possibilities for the full range of dialogical types issue the call to fellow Hindus, Muslims, and Sikhs alike to acknowledge and celebrate their commonalities (for example, their love of intellectual pursuits, the arts, and literature) while forging a common effort to raise the quality of life in that part of the world.

The three principle Hindu branches of Vaishnavism, Saivism, and Shaktism have at times each splintered into sectarianism at their outermost reaches; at those points, Hindus who embody their religion's renowned characteristics of toleration, inclusiveness, and ease amidst conditions of plurality are challenged to come to the fore.

> In Dialogue we affirm hope. In the midst of the many divisions, conflicts and violence there is hope that it is possible to create a human community that lives in justice and peace. Dialogue is not an end in itself. It is a means of building bridges of respect and understanding. It is a joyful affirmation of life for all.
>
> SOURCE: Article 20, the World Council of Churches' 2002 document, "Ecumenical Considerations for Dialogue and Relations with People of Other Religions."

Islam. "Historically, Muslims have had little or no interest in interreligious dialogue even with other believers in God, including the 'Ahl-al kitab' ('People of the Book'—Jews and Christians) . . . [Muslims] have, in general, taken the truth of Islam to be self-evident and have not expressed any great interest in having an open-ended philosophical and theological dialogue with people of other faiths," writes Riffat Hassan. Hassan then registers the point that the universal quality of the Islamic truth as affirmed in the Koran should condition reception of non-Muslims for the purpose of constructive dialogue (in Swidler, 415–416). Indeed, representatives of the Muslim World Congress, the World Muslim League, and the World Islamic Call Society have met regularly with representatives of the Vatican and the World Council of Churches. The Royal Institute for Inter-Faith Studies, established in 1994 in Amman, Jordan, provides a venue for interdisciplinary study and rational discussion of religion and religious issues, with particular reference to Christianity in Arab and Islamic societies.

Trust building with Jews is a crucial issue. In the early 1990's Dr. Gutbi Ahmed, the former North American director of the Muslim World League, called for cooperation between Muslim and Jewish communities for the good of society. Joint efforts leading to trust building that can affect the world at large are rightly promoted, not as a luxury, but as an immediate necessity.

As with other religions, Islam itself exhibits diversity in interpretations and expressions, and is an incubator for both dynamic growth and internal conflict. The distinctions between Sunni and Shiite Muslims are subtle but very real. They have hurled the charge "Worse than the infidels" against one another. When and where they can peacefully coexist is primarily a matter of political rather than religious exigency; this reality places in relief the value of emphasizing their common religiosity whenever the traditional alarm-cry "Islam in Danger!" is sounded. Behind the bold headlines, a quieter revolution in discourse and activism is transpiring as Muslims, like Christians and Jews, struggle with the challenges of secularism and materialism.

Judaism. Spokespersons from Judaism in ecumenical forums attest to a sense of speaking in Galuth, that is, in exile. A primary task of these representatives is to stress that Judaism is a living, complexifying religion not to be simply equated with the religion of the Hebrew Scriptures. Judaism must be defined by Jews themselves rather than by others who speak from a majority position and who have little or no sense of exile. For this reason Jewish ecumenical initiatives are numerous, and a high degree of presence is maintained in multilateral dialogues worldwide.

Relations with Christians vastly improve wherever there is real and perceivable growth in awareness of the horrors of the Shoah (Holocaust) of the World War II period, and in detection and condemnation of anti-Semitic attitudes among church members. Bilateral Bible studies also contribute to enhanced relations. This writer's personal experience with meeting Jewish initiative was in assisting Catholic-based Villanova University to join Jewish-based Gratz College in establishing the "I Am Joseph, Your Brother" partnership program in Jewish studies for Christian educators (1996–1999). Another fine, and continuing, example of academic cooperation is the Center for Christian-Jewish Learning at Boston College.

Of course, there are diverse ways of being Jewish: Reformed, Orthodox, Conservative, Reconstructed, secular, Yiddish ethnic, and Zionist among them. The image of Jacob wrestling with the stranger (Genesis 32: 23–32) has been employed to portray the dynamic of Jewish internal and external relations. The stranger blesses and changes Jacob's name to Israel, meaning "he who has wrestled with God and human beings and prevails." Adherence to Judaism continues in internal dialogues on the meaning of being a Jew and in interfaith dialogue on improved human relations. (*World Religions Today,* p. 178.)

Conclusion

The ecumenical movement does not proceed without opposition. One source of rejection stems from the fact that the contemporary globalization process is not celebrated by all. Religious fundamentalists tend to be suspicious of dialogue and cooperation across boundaries; their preference is to live within closed sets of codes and beliefs. In some eastern religions contact with the "other" continues to be regarded as an occasion of defilement. For many, ecumenism represents a temptation to religious syncretism. For such as these, truth is not served but sacrificed in dialogue, and obedience to the mission imperative dictates that conversion should be the only goal of conversation. There can also be detected among "grassroots" members of highly institutionalized religions the conviction that ecumenism is the work of elite, self-justifying cadres of ecclesiastical bureaucrats. Yet, despite determined pockets of resistance, the ecumenical spirit has created numerous college and university interfaith centers and continues to energize an ever increasing number of religious adherents and imbue them with a worldwide sense of accountability for that which lies beyond the realm of privatized concern.

See also **Deism; Religion; Toleration.**

BIBLIOGRAPHY
Bretton-Granatoor, Gary M., and Andrea L. Weiss, eds. *Shalom/Salaam: A Resource for Jewish-Muslim Dialogue.* New York: Union of American Hebrew Congregations, 1993.
Duffy, Stephen J. "Mission and Dialogue in a Pluralistic Global City." *Ecumenical Trends* 25 (April 1996): 10–12.
Esposito, John L., Darrell J. Fasching, and Todd Lewis. *World Religions Today.* New York: Oxford University Press, 2002. Distinguished among the myriad of survey-type works for its ecumenical perspective.
Gros, Jeffrey, Harding Meyer, and William G. Rusch, eds. *Growth in Agreement II: Reports and Agreed Statements of Ecumenical Conversations on a World Level, 1982–1998.* Geneva and Grand Rapids: WCC and Eerdmans, 2000.
Hassan, Riffat. "The Basis for a Hindu-Muslim Dialogue and Steps in that Direction from a Muslim Perspective." In *Muslims in Dialogue: The Evolution of a Dialogue,* edited by Leonard Swidler, Lewiston, N.Y.: Mellen, 1992.
Kinnamon, Michael, and Brian E. Cope, eds. *The Ecumenical Movement: An Anthology of Key Texts and Voices.* Geneva: WCC, 1997.
Lossky, Nicholas, et al, eds. *A Dictionary of the Ecumenical Movement.* 2nd ed. Geneva: WCC, 2002. Seven hundred entries by 370 leaders in the ecumenical movement—a cornerstone for any ecumenical library.
Rusch, William G. "The State and Future of the Ecumenical Movement." *Pro Ecclesia* 9, no. 1 (2000): 8–18.

Joseph A. Loya

EDUCATION.

This entry includes eight subentries:

Asia, Traditional and Modern
China
Europe
Global Education
India
Islamic Education
Japan
North America

ASIA, TRADITIONAL AND MODERN

The history of education in Asia reflected and extended the influence and teachings of three major philosophical, religious traditions: Hinduism (including Buddhism), Islam, and Confucianism (including Neo-Confucianism). Over time, these traditions interacted with one another, although the interaction was not entirely mutual, nor did it blunt the cultural distinctions of the various regions of South Asia, Southeast Asia, and East Asia. Indeed, while Buddhism exerted its widespread influence across East Asia from the third century B.C.E on, it never replaced the primacy of Confucianism. Similarly, although Islam infiltrated India from the eighth century C.E. on, the foundation of Hindu cultural traditions remained unshaken.

A middle region, Southeast Asia, was influenced by Buddhism and Confucianism, resulting in a unique blended educational experience. From the eighteenth century on, as Western culture came into the region, Asia's educational practices in general underwent a sea change that resulted in a previously unknown level of uniformity. Regional diversity, however, remains visible, reflecting the differences in political settings, cultural values, and economic development, making a comprehensive overview of education in Asia impossible. For this reason, the following discussion will deal primarily with educational practices in South and East Asia with a focus on exploring the ideological dynamics embedded within those regions and the impact of historical change from without.

South Asia

South Asia is known particularly for its cultural and linguistic heterogeneity, a feature influenced by both its topography and its history. Although the Deccan Plateau divided the subcontinent into north and south, two invasions, first by the Aryans (c. 1500 B.C.E.), then by the Turkish-speaking Muslims (from the eighth century C.E. on), deepened this division, causing social and political tensions among various ethnic groups for centuries. These invasions also, albeit temporarily, fostered a degree of political unity that makes it possible to identify some characteristics of educational practices in traditional India.

In North India, for example, where the Aryans dominated, cultural and linguistic unity was evident. Classical Hindu culture, as reflected in Vedic learning and other literary works in Sanskrit, flourished during the Gupta period (300–c. 500 C.E.) Given the religious nature of Vedic learning, the form higher learning took in Hindu culture, it was only taught exclusively among the Brahmans, the Hindu priest class. This situation remained unchanged for centuries, even under Muslim rule. The two classes just below the Brahmans, the Kishatriyas (which means "protector of gentle people"; they were the rulers and warriors) and Vaisyas (traders, businesspeople, and farmers), were allowed to enter a different type of school where they learned basic skills in writing, arithmetic, and reading, using texts written in the vernacular. Although some members of these castes pursued knowledge beyond the elementary level, they were usually allowed to excel only in areas outside of Vedic learning, such as medicine. The bottom class, the Sudras, and women were prohibited from receiving any formal schooling, although exceptions always existed.

Strict social hierarchy and diverse cultural traditions prevented India from developing a centralized educational system prior to the arrival of the British. Educational initiatives for establishing a school and selecting its teacher thus often came from a specific class or community. Most schools hired only one teacher, but though most teachers came from the Brahman class, their qualifications varied greatly. Wealthy aristocratic communities supported their schools and the teachers' salaries with land endowments, whereas less wealthy communities paid their teachers with student fees. Whatever the case, teachers, or gurus, usually received considerable respect from their students and the community, partially because the teacher-student relationship replicated the social hierarchy of Hindu society and partially because of the way knowledge was imparted in the schools. Perhaps because the Vedas were transmitted orally for many generations before they were written

down, oral learning figured centrally in the methods of teaching. In fact the term *Veda* is called *Sruti* in Sanskrit, which means "heard from the guru," and Vedic teachers demanded that their pupils repeat aloud what they heard for better retention. The emphasis on oral instruction also served a religious and social purpose. Since written texts were not easily accessible to students, it allowed the Brahmans to mystify and monopolize Brahmanic education and maintain and safeguard their social privilege.

The subjects of teaching varied in different historical periods, even among schools in the Brahmanic tradition. Because of the Buddhist challenge, for example, the study of *nyaya,* or logic, flourished. Buddhism exerted its influence in Indian education in other areas as well. Its egalitarianism, for instance, opened the door for members of the non-Brahman classes to become teachers. The Buddhist emphasis on writing was also reflected in the school curricula at various levels. Likewise, the Indian educational system absorbed influences from Islam. Muslim education, which centered on recitation and memorization of the Koran, suited the Hindu emphasis on oral instruction. Like the Hindus, the Muslims also valued person-to-person transmission of knowledge, which reinforced the traditional guru-disciple relationship in Hindu culture.

East Asia

In contrast to the diverse development of education in South Asia, the history of education in East Asia related primarily to the development of Confucianism, but variations and vicissitudes were also present. Indeed, while Confucius (c. 551–479 B.C.E.) was commonly regarded as the first teacher in ancient China, he had many competitors both during and after his time. As in India, oral instruction was the main means of education in China, as shown in the *Analects,* which record the conversations between Confucius and his disciples. However, Confucius was also credited with compiling the *Six Classics.* During the Han period (206 B.C.E.–220 C.E.), when Confucianism was established as the official ideology in China, these *Classics* and their commentaries became the principal texts in the school system, which included a state university. These texts became the means by which the dynastic ruler hoped to centralize the educational system. Indeed, while each village funded its schools and hired its teachers, there was discernible unity in the educational system of imperial China. By using these texts and their derivatives, teachers imparted both knowledge and moral values to their students in an effort to prepare at least some of them for government positions. This interest intensified during the Sui (581–618 C.E.) and Tang periods (618–907 C.E.), following the establishment of the civil service examination system, for the system legally permitted any successful students, regardless of their social origin, to enter officialdom.

The cultural atmosphere in the Tang period was distinctly cosmopolitan in that the dynasty patronized, though not always concomitantly, Confucianism, Buddhism, and Daoism (an indigenous reaction to the challenge of Buddhism) while at the same time absorbing many Buddhist elements into its practices. The Buddhist influence was also present in Confucianism. Inspired by the Buddhist emphasis on lineage in knowledge transmission, Tang scholars, in their attempt to combat the intrusion of Buddhism and Daoism and restore the Confucian orthodoxy, also identified key figures in Confucian genealogy. This restorationist project was continued and expanded in the Song period (960–1279 C.E.), marked by the rise of Neo-Confucianism. The Neo-Confucians, such as Zhu Xi (1130–1200), set out to reform education not only by supplying a new set of texts, namely the *Four Books,* but also by establishing a new type of school, the academy. Zhu's compilation of the *Four Books* extended the restorationist project of reshaping the Confucian genealogy, whereby Mengzi (c. 371–289 B.C.E.; romanized as Mencius) was canonized, as were some excerpts from the original Confucian canons, which Zhu identified as the essence of Confucian teaching. The proliferation of the academies from this period onward also provided a new venue for students, supplementing the one-teacher village schools and state-run colleges and universities.

This change had little effect on women's education, however. As in India, Chinese women usually received only a rudimentary education at home that prepared them to be good wives and mothers. Outstanding women scholars and poets, however, appeared in every historical period, for example, Ban Zhao (c. 41–120 C.E.) often argued for the necessity of women's education.

During the Ming (1368–1644) and Qing (1644–1911) periods, Neo-Confucianism consolidated its position as the ideological orthodoxy, thanks to the entrenchment of civil service examinations. As Neo-Confucianism exerted its influence beyond China and became the orthodox ideology of Korea and Japan, it also faced many challengers and critics. By the eighteenth century, a new intellectual trend arose simultaneously across East Asia that, while sharing the restorationist sentiment of the Neo-Confucians, attempted to transcend the Neo-Confucian discursive system and revive the teachings of classical Confucianism. This trend emphasized practical knowledge and scholarship; the latter was characterized by the endeavor to ascertain the authenticity of Confucian texts and the veracity of their contents by the methods of history and philology. All of this had a noticeable impact on the goals and methods of Confucian education.

South Asia

Toward the end of the eighteenth century, as education in East Asia underwent important changes associated with the ebb and flow of Neo-Confucianism, a more drastic transformation was introduced by the British in South Asia. Having undermined the native educational system via both economic and cultural means, the British introduced modern schools, initially for the purpose of training interpreters and future government officials. In so doing, it weakened the tie between students and their communities, changing the traditional goal of education in South Asia. By teaching English in those schools, the British created an additional barrier between the educated elite and the common people.

Slowly, by the mid-nineteenth century, the British had established, for the first time in history, a centralized educational system in South Asia. It consisted of three tiers of schools—elementary, secondary, and college levels—that purported to transcend the religious and ethnic division of the populace.

This system was, by and large, continued after countries in the region had gained independence from the mid-twentieth century on. In fact it is the educational norm throughout Asia in the early twenty-first century.

Modernization

In East Asia, Japan was the first country to embark on modern educational reform. In the wake of the Meiji Restoration of 1868, the government sent out a group of distinguished officials to tour many countries in Europe and America, hoping to gain firsthand knowledge about social, political, and educational systems in the modern West. The educational measures introduced by the Meiji government included creation of the ministry of education, compulsory elementary education (extended also to women), and establishment of a national university—Tokyo University—started in a renovated state school formerly devoted to Confucian learning.

By comparison, as the first country that confronted the Western powers in East Asia, China lagged behind Japan in initiating educational reform. In its struggle against the Western challenge, the reigning Qing dynasty established a few translation schools and sent out a few groups of students abroad, but throughout most of the nineteenth century China apparently lacked the desire to adopt more comprehensive educational reforms. It was not until 1895, after its shattering defeat by Japan in the Sino-Japanese War (1894–1895), that the dynasty, as well as Chinese educators, began to realize the importance of modern education. In the aftermath of the war, China witnessed a short-lived political reform, which resulted, among other things, in the founding of a modern university in 1898—the Metropolitan University—now Beijing University. As a large number of its students went abroad, most to Japan because of its proximity, to receive a modern education, the country also embarked on a rapid course of educational reform. In 1905 the thousand-year-old civil service examination was abolished, paving the way for the establishment of a modern educational system. Accompanying this change was an unprecedented opportunity for Chinese women to receive formal schooling.

All in all, the structure of modern education took root in most of Asia from the late nineteenth century on. Over time, it evolved into a uniform system across the continent and bore a striking resemblance to that of the modern West. Meanwhile, it demonstrates in its ideals and practices the diverse influences of the religious and cultural traditions and political ideologies of the region.

See also **Confucianism; Daoism; Education: China; Education: India; Education: Islamic Education; Education: Japan; Hinduism; Islam: Southeast Asia; Religion: East and Southeast Asia; Westernization: Southeast Asia.**

BIBLIOGRAPHY

Crook, Nigel, ed. *The Transmission of Knowledge in South Asia: Essays on Education, Religion, History, and Politics.* Delhi and New York: Oxford University Press, 1996.

De Bary, W. Theodore, and John W. Chaffee, eds. *Neo-Confucian Education: The Formative Stage.* Berkeley: University of California Press, 1989.

Dore, Ronald P. *Education in Tokugawa Japan.* Berkeley: University of California Press, 1965.

Elman, Benjamin A., and Alexander Woodside, eds. *Education and Society in Late Imperial China, 1600–1900.* Berkeley: University of California Press, 1994.

Hayhoe, Ruth, and Marianne Bastid, eds. *China's Education and the Industrialized World: Studies in Cultural Transfer.* Armonk, N.Y.: M. E. Sharpe, 1987.

Ko, Dorothy. *Teachers of the Inner Chambers: Women and Culture in Seventeenth-Century China.* Stanford, Calif.: Stanford University Press, 1994.

Lee, Thomas H. C. *Education in Traditional China: A History.* Leiden, Netherlands: Brill, 2000.

Q. *Edward Wang*

CHINA

Since antiquity Chinese placed an inordinately high value on education. During the classical era (600–250 B.C.E.), the Chinese advanced the notion that merit and ability measured by training should take precedence over race or birth in state appointments. Since the early empire (200 B.C.E.–200 C.E.), clans and families mobilized financial and cultural resources to provide boys (and sometimes girls) with the tools of classical literacy. However, a society based on merit remained only an ideal. Through the middle empire (600–900 C.E.) education remained the privilege of landed aristocrats and prosperous merchants.

The imperial state increased its expenditures on education during the Tang (618–906) and Song (960–1280) dynasties, when it created the first examination system for selecting officials. In addition, the rise of Buddhism in medieval China created charitable institutions for the common people, which included temple schools and monasteries, where many commoners—male and female—were educated. Building on such precedents, late imperial (1400–1900) statesmen and local leaders, except for the occasional Daoist eccentric, agreed that education, particularly a classical, moral education, was one of the foundations of public order and civilized life.

Educational Ideals in Late Traditional China

Teachers in late imperial times aimed at training a highly literate elite and socializing the far less literate, or even illiterate, common people by means of exhortations and rituals. This concept never hardened into a tidy formula, given the dissatisfactions with the educational status quo that have characterized Chinese history. Wang Yangming (1472–1529) and his followers, for example, opened schools for commoners on a wider scale than ever before. The line between elites and commoners could also be blurred by political turmoil. When emperors feared that heterodox popular religions were spreading, they often conflated learning with indoctrination from above. Many literati accused Wang Yangming and his followers of heterodoxy and deceiving the people.

Separate from official studies, schools of learning among literati included poetry societies, private academies, or lineages of teachings associated with local classical, medical, or statecraft traditions. Medical and statecraft traditions were tied to

the teachings of a master, who bequeathed his teachings to his immediate disciples. In the absence of public schools in Ming China (1368–1644), education in lineage schools, charity and temple schools, or at home transmitted the classical or technical training needed by young men to pass local civil or military examinations or practice their local trades.

In Ming times, the "Learning of the Way" (Neo-Confucianism) tradition became an empirewide orthodoxy. Its followers created an imperial curriculum that was strengthened by the civil examinations. Although moralistic predispositions were favored in civil examinations, alternative and dissenting learning proliferated. Natural studies, particularly medical learning, was also a legitimate focus of private study when literati sought alternatives to official careers. The wider scope of civil policy questions dating from the early fifteenth century often reflected the dynasty's interest in astrology, calendrical precision, mathematical harmonics, and natural anomalies.

Learning was guided by examples of past worthies and sages and encouraged by good companions and teachers. In traditional schools, the prestige of learning led to more regimentation than many literati might have wished, but this was tempered by numerous local traditions of learning outside the state. Members of literary schools held that because literature and governing were not separate, writers should avoid religious vocabulary, colloquial phrases, or popular novels. Knowledge of numbers using the abacus in tax-related economic transactions, debates about "hot" and "cold" medical therapies to deal with epidemics, and the astronomical expertise for reform of the calendar were also widespread.

Education, Society, and Examinations

After 1000, Chinese appealed to meritocratic ideals in which social prestige and political appointment depended on written examinations to establish public credentials. Elite status was corroborated by examination, which in turn produced new literati social groups that endured from 1400 to the twentieth century. Classical learning became the empirewide examination curriculum, which reached into counties and villages for the first time.

After the Ming fell, civil examinations were reinstituted by the succeeding Manchu Qing dynasty (1644–1911). As before, examinations were regularly held in 140 prefectures and about 1,300 counties. Medieval examinations had been held only in the capital, while from 1000 to 1350, regular examinations only occurred in the provincial and imperial capitals. Qing emperors granted the examination system a central educational position in Chinese government and society until 1905, when the civil examinations were abolished.

Education restructured the complex relations between social status, political power, and cultural prestige. A classical education based on nontechnical moral and political theory was as suitable for selection of elites in China as humanism and a classical education were for elites in early modern Europe. The examination life, like death and taxes, became a fixture of elite education and popular culture.

Examinations represented the focal point through which imperial interests, family strategies, and individual hopes and aspirations were directed. In the absence of alternative careers of comparable social status and political prestige, the goal of becoming an official took priority. Once set in place, the civil service recruitment system achieved for education a degree of empirewide standardization and local importance unprecedented in the premodern world. Moreover, the education ethos carried over into the domains of medicine, law, fiscal policy, and military affairs.

Several centuries before Europe, the imperial Chinese state committed itself financially to supporting an empirewide school network. Despite their initial success, dynastic schools were eventually absorbed into the examination system and remained schools in name only. Because the classical curriculum was routinized, dynastic schools became way stations, or "testing centers," for students to prepare for civil examinations.

Training in both vernacular and classical literacy was left to families. Dynastic schools in China never entertained goals of mass education that the Maoists would later call for. Rulers recognized elite education based on the classics as an essential task of government to recruit talent. Chinese elites perceived a classical education as the correct measure of their moral and social worth. Both believed that ancient wisdom, properly generalized and inculcated, tempered men as leaders and prepared them for wielding political power.

Rulers and elites equated social and political order with moral and political indoctrination through education. High-minded officials also appealed for the autonomy of education as an antidote to the warping of classical goals by the cutthroat examination process. Private academies frequently became centers for dissenting views. Such academies also served as important educational venues for literati who preferred teaching and lecturing to pass on their classical learning. Compared to some five hundred Song and four hundred Yuan dynasty private academies, the Ming overall had in place from one to two thousand academies by its end. The Qing had upwards of four thousand empirewide.

Political Uses of Education

Imperial support of education was contingent on the examinations to supply talented and loyal men for the bureaucracy to employ. Political legitimacy was an assumed by-product of preparation for the civil and military service. In a convoluted ideological canvas of loyalties encompassing state and society, even emperors became educated in the orthodox rationale for their imperial legitimacy—by special tutors selected from the civil examinations.

Imperial support of literati-inspired cultural symbols, which were defined in terms of classical learning, painting, literature, and calligraphy, enabled the dynasty in concert with its elites to maintain the institutional conditions necessary for its own survival. The examination hierarchy stabilized existing social hierarchies by redirecting wealth and power derived from commerce or military success into education to prepare for civil and military service. A by-product was the creation of a large number of classically literate elites who produced essays, poetry, stories, novels, medical treatises, and scholarly works.

Social Consequences of Education

Education was premised on social distinctions between literati, peasants, artisans, and merchants in descending order of rank. Under the Ming, sons of merchants for the first time were legally permitted to take the civil examinations. However, occupational prohibitions, which extended from so-called mean peoples to all Daoist and Buddhist clergy, kept many others out of the civil service competition, not to mention an unstated gender bias against all women.

Because the dynastic school system was limited to candidates already literate in classical Chinese, initial stages in training and preparing a son for the civil service became the responsibility of families seeking to attain or maintain elite status. Careerism usually won out over idealism among talented young men who occasionally were forced to choose between their social obligations to their parents and relatives and their personal aspirations. Failures could, however, because of their classical literacy, choose teaching and medicine as alternate careers.

Unlike contemporary Europe and Japan, where absolute social barriers between nobility and commoners prevented the translation of commercial wealth into elite status, landed affluence and commercial wealth during the Ming dynasty were intertwined with high educational status. Because of the literary requirements, artisans, peasants, and clerks were poorly equipped to take advantage of the openness of the civil service. Clear boundaries were also erected to demarcate male education from female upbringing, which remained intact until the seventeenth century, when education of women in elite families became more common.

Nevertheless, when compared with the fatalistic ideologies common among Buddhist or Hindu peasants in South and Southeast Asia, for example, the Chinese ideology of teaching and learning did promote beliefs in the usefulness of education and created a climate of rising expectations for those who dreamed of glory but sometimes rebelled when their hopes were repeatedly dashed.

Culture and Education

Classical literacy—the ability to write elegant essays and poetry—was the crowning achievement for educated men and increasingly for elite women in the seventeenth century. This learning process began with rote memorization during childhood, continued with youthful reading, and concluded with mature writing. Literati believed that the memory was strongest at an early age, while mature understanding was a gradual achievement that derived from mastering the literary language and its moral and historical content.

Educated men, and some women, became members of a "writing elite" whose essays would mark them as classically trained. The educated man was able to write his way to fame, fortune, and power, and even if unsuccessful in his quest for an official career, he could still publish essays, poetry, novels, medical handbooks, and other works. The limitation, control, and selection of the "writing elite," not the enlargement of the "reading public," was the dynasty's goal in selecting officials.

Local lineages translated their social and economic strength into educational success, which in turn correlated with their control of local cultural resources. Lineages required classically literate and highly placed leaders who moved easily in elite circles and could mediate on behalf of the kin group with officials. Economic surpluses produced by wealthy lineages, particularly in prosperous areas, enabled members of rich segments to receive a better classical education, which via success on state examinations allowed access to political and economic prestige outside the lineage.

Dominant lineages and merchant families maintained their local status through their schools, medical traditions, and academies. Elite education stressed classical erudition, historical knowledge, medical expertise, literary style, and poetry. The well-publicized rituals for properly writing classical Chinese included cultural paraphernalia long associated with literati culture: the writing brush, ink stick, inkstone, stone monuments, fine silk, and special paper.

Although muted in practice, elites achieved a degree of cultural and linguistic uniformity through a classical education. The classical curriculum represented a cultural repertoire of linguistic signs and conceptual categories that ensured elite political power and social status. Education in dynastic schools and private academies was a fundamental factor in determining cultural consensus and conditioning the forms of reasoning and rhetoric that prevailed in elite written texts of the period.

Reform and Revolution

During the twentieth century, classical literati values, dynastic imperial power, and elite gentry status unraveled. Manchu rulers gave up civil examinations as one of their major weapons of cultural control that had for centuries successfully induced literati acceptance of the imperial system. Traditionalists who reformed classical learning after 1898 paid a form of "symbolic compensation" to classical thought by declaring its moral superiority as a reward for its historical failure. The modern Chinese intellectual irrevocably replaced the late imperial literatus in the early republic.

Increasingly, traditional education was dissolved within a westernizing reformist project. Shu Xincheng (1893–1960), an early republican educator and historian, recalled the pressure of the times to change: "The changeover to a new system of education at the end of the Ch'ing appeared on the surface to be a voluntary move by educational circles, but in reality what happened was that foreign relations and domestic pressures were everywhere running up against dead ends. Unless reforms were undertaken, China would have no basis for survival. Education simply happened to be caught up in a situation in which there was no choice" (Borthwick, p. 38).

The floodgates broke wide open after the 1904–1905 Russo-Japanese War, which was largely fought on Chinese soil. Given the frantic climate of the time, the classical educational system was a convenient scapegoat. Court and provincial officials submitted a common memorial calling for the immediate abolition of the civil examinations at all levels. The civil examinations in particular were perceived as an obstacle to new schools because a classical degree still outweighed new school degrees and prevented realizing the ideal of universal education.

A separate Education Board was established in December 1905 to administer the new schools and oversee the many semiofficial educational associations that emerged at the local and regional levels. The board reflected the increasing influence of Han Chinese officials and served the interests of the modernists in undoing the schooling mechanisms under which classical literacy and essay writing had been achieved.

Still missing, however, was the need to address the role of classical versus vernacular language in school instruction and in written examinations. Full-scale educational reform still required champions of a "literary revolution," who became vocal during the May Fourth period after 1919. Not until the republican Ministry of Education began to move on the vernacular language of education could popular education move from ideal to practical reality.

Many unofficial organizations and groups entered the fray of school reform, which eroded the Manchu court's control over education policy. Through the portal of local education, local official and unofficial elites took over the educational domains of the central bureaucracy. As the imperial court grew weaker, regional and local tiers of power began to create the educational institutions that would accelerate the demise of the dynasty and form the educational pillars of the republic after 1911.

The Education Board established in 1905 was renamed as a "ministry" in the republican period and remained on the side of new schools. The educational institutions of the Republic of China after 1911 were the direct legacy of the late imperial reforms. Sun Yat-sen (1866–1925) created the examination bureau as part of the republic's 1920s "five-power constitution," which echoed traditional institutions. The twentieth-century examination life, which was associated with university and public school entrance examinations in China and later in Taiwan, is the cultural heir of the imperial examination regime.

Despite important continuities, the affinity between long-standing expectations of traditional Chinese families and the dynasty's objective political institutions was ripped apart. Increasingly reformed on Western and Japanese models, new schools in China precipitated a generalized down-classing of traditional education and the classical curriculum. Many conservative families failed to convert their inherited educational and literary cultural resources into new academic degrees for their children. A revolutionary transformation in student dispositions accompanied the radical change in the conditions of recruitment of public officials after 1905.

Reform of education and examinations in China after 1900 was tied to newly defined goals of Western-style change that superseded conservative imperial goals for reproducing dynastic power, granting gentry prestige, and affirming classical orthodoxy. The ideal of national unity replaced dynastic solidarity. The sprawling, multiethnic Manchu empire became a struggling Han Chinese republican state that was later refashioned as a multiethnic communist nation.

*See also **Chinese Thought; Confucianism; Examination Systems, China.***

BIBLIOGRAPHY

Bastid, Marianne. *Educational Reform in Early Twentieth-Century China.* Translated by Paul J. Bailey. Ann Arbor: University of Michigan China Center, 1988.

Borthwick, Sally. *Education and Social Change in China: The Beginnings of the Modern Era.* Stanford, Calif.: Hoover Institution Press, 1983.

De Bary, William Theodore, and John W. Chaffee, eds. *Neo-Confucian Education: The Formative Stage.* Berkeley: University of California Press, 1989.

Elman, Benjamin A., and Alexander Woodside, eds. *Education and Society in Late Imperial China, 1600–1900.* Berkeley: University of California Press, 1994.

Keenan, Barry. *Imperial China's Last Classical Academies: Social Change in the Lower Yangzi, 1864–1911.* Berkeley: University of California Press, 1994.

Ko, Dorothy. *Teachers of the Inner Chambers: Women and Culture in Seventeenth-Century China.* Stanford, Calif.: Stanford University Press, 1994.

Lee, Thomas H. C. *Education in Traditional China: A History.* Leiden, Netherlands: Brill, 1999.

Meskill, John. *Academies in Ming China: A Historical Essay.* Tucson: University of Arizona Press, 1982.

Rawski, Evelyn Sakakida. *Education and Popular Literacy in Ch'ing China.* Ann Arbor: University of Michigan Press, 1979.

Walton, Linda. *Academies and Society in Southern Sung China.* Honolulu: University of Hawai'i Press, 1999.

Benjamin A. Elman

EUROPE

European pre-university education began its long odyssey with Homer. The social and literary values expressed in his poetry informed Greek education, which became the basis of Roman education. The Renaissance revived ancient literary texts and educational programs, which were modified and adapted in subsequent centuries. European humanities education still embraces in part ancient Greco-Roman educational ideals and goals.

Greek Education

The great poems the *Iliad* and the *Odyssey* believed by the ancient Greeks to have been composed by Homer during the eighth century B.C.E. contained the fundamental idea of Greek education, that the ideal warrior must also be eloquent. He won battles of words as well as arms. Homer made the point by inserting many formal speeches into his poems. And Greek children later memorized long sections of the *Iliad* and the *Odyssey.*

In the seventh and sixth centuries B.C.E. an educational program for aristocratic males of gymnastics, music, and letters developed. Then the Sophists, the first professional educators, appeared in the second half of the fifth century B.C.E. to teach well-born Athenian youths between the ages of thirteen and seventeen. Learning how to be an effective orator became the most important goal of education for Athenian males destined to rule. Simultaneously, a series of directives and principles that could be taught and learned replaced observation and imitation as the means to the goal. Then Isocrates (436–338 B.C.E.) added the view that the study of Greek literature and history

would inculcate the right moral and civic virtues in upper-class Greek males.

Greek education reached full development in the fourth century B.C.E. The Greeks passed this form of education to the rest of the known world during the Hellenistic period, which began with the conquests of Alexander the Great (r. 336–323) and lasted through the fourth century C.E. A Greek boy attended a primary school from about age seven to fourteen and learned to read, write, do a little arithmetic, and participate in music and gymnastics. In the secondary school the student read the classics of Greek literature, especially the poet Homer and the tragic dramatist Euripides (c. 484–406 B.C.E.). He also read in whole or part other authors in the Greek literary tradition, such as the epic poets Hesiod (fl. c. 700 B.C.E.) and Apollonius of Rhodes (3rd century B.C.E.), the lyric poet Callimachus (c. 305–240 B.C.E.), the tragedians Aeschylus (525–456 B.C.E.) and Sophocles (c. 496–406 B.C.E.), and the comedians Menander (342–292 B.C.E.) and Aristophanes (c. 450–c. 388 B.C.E.). He also read the histories of Herodotus (c. 484–c. 420 B.C.E.), Xenophon (428–354 B.C.E.), and Thucydides (c. 460–c. 400 B.C.E.). But which texts received most attention is difficult to determine. The most important part of the secondary school curriculum was rhetoric, learning how to write and speak well. The program consisted of practice, followed by writing various kinds of works, and then constructing formal speeches according to rules. The goal was to produce the educated upper-class Greek male who could express himself well and persuade others.

The Greeks also had higher schools for those who wished to learn more in specialized branches of knowledge. Plato's Academy, founded about 380 B.C.E. and lasting until 529 C.E. albeit undergoing many changes, had no fixed curriculum. It probably emphasized extended philosophical discussions on a variety of topics, including rhetoric. The Lyceum or Peripatetic School founded in 335 by Aristotle (384–322 B.C.E.) began with the purpose of collecting and studying scientific research and had a strong philosophical and scientific orientation. Theophrastus (c. 370–c. 288 B.C.E.) led the Lyceum after Aristotle's death, and it endured until the third century C.E. Alexandria in Egypt became famous for its museum and library (founded c. 280 B.C.E., destroyed in or about 651 C.E.) and as a center for higher scientific learning. None of the above schools offered organized formal education. Rather, they were centers of learned men who attracted followers.

Roman Education

Education in the early centuries of the Roman Republic consisted primarily of fathers passing on family traditions and skills to their sons. After reaching adulthood at the age of sixteen, the young man came under the guidance of an older man who groomed him in public speaking and other useful skills for a career as a member of a republic. He also served in the army because he would in time be expected to command troops. By the middle of the second century B.C.E., when Rome ruled a far-flung empire, formal education had developed. Greek educational ideas and practices influenced Rome, as they did the rest of the Mediterranean world. The education of upper-class Romans was Greek schooling that later became Latin. The conquest of Greece aided this process by producing Greek slaves, some much better educated than their Roman masters. A Greek slave tutored the child in simple reading until he went to elementary school at six or seven to be taught reading, writing, and arithmetic. At twelve or thirteen the boy went to a secondary school, where he studied mostly Greek literature until the middle of the first century B.C.E. Upper-class Romans were bilingual at this time. Then, after the lifetime of Marcus Tullius Cicero (106–43 B.C.E.), who had popularized Greek pedagogical and philosophical ideas in his many works, Roman schools became Latin. Students read the great Roman poets Virgil (70–19 B.C.E.) and Horace (65–8 B.C.E.), the historians Livy (59 B.C.E.–17 C.E.) and Sallust (86–35 or 34 B.C.E.), the comic dramatist Terence (186 or 185–?159 B.C.E.) and, of course, Cicero, whose treatises systematized Greek rhetorical instruction. While Greek remained part of the curriculum, bilingualism declined.

The highest level of Roman education began at about the age of sixteen and focused on rhetoric. As in Greek education, the goal was to learn to speak and write effectively as needed in public life and the law courts. If anything, the emphasis on oratory in Roman schools was stronger than in Greek schools because other parts of the Greek curriculum, such as music and athletics, were eliminated, and the Romans had little interest in science and philosophy. Roman schools used rhetoric manuals that systematized Greek rhetorical instruction.

Greco-Roman education prepared upper-class males for leadership roles. Educators hoped to give their students the proper civic and moral values based on the traditions and literature of the Greek city or Roman state. They tried to educate the person rather than impart knowledge. Above all, Greco-Roman education taught rhetoric, a practical skill for future leaders of self-governing societies in which the spoken word meant a great deal. The emphasis on rhetoric continued even after Rome had become a dictatorship ruled by the will and whims of emperors. Despite the great mathematical, medical, philosophical, and scientific accomplishments of ancient Greece, Greco-Roman education did not stress these.

Education of Women in Greece and Rome

Little is known about the education of girls and women in Greece and Rome. It is likely that educational opportunity for girls was limited in Greece, but a little more available in Rome. During the Roman republican period ending in 27 B.C.E., it is likely that upper-class mothers who were able to do so taught their sons and daughters reading and writing in Latin and Greek. During the Empire at least a few girls studied alongside boys in primary and secondary schools outside the home. The poet Martial (c. 40–c. 104 C.E.) mentioned boys and girls studying together in what must have been secondary-level schools. For most girls formal education probably ended with marriage in the early to mid-teens. Nevertheless, the fact that many Roman wives and mothers played roles in Roman imperial politics suggests that they were reasonably well educated, and that more schooling was available for upper-class girls than can be documented. The rest of the population, male and female, below the elite in both Greece and Rome probably received no education or learned only rudimentary skills.

Medieval Education

The Roman educational system disintegrated as the empire declined in the fifth and sixth centuries. Church institutions of the early Middle Ages (c. 400–c. 1000) were forced to establish schools to train future churchmen. Bishops established schools attached to their cathedrals to train priests for their dioceses. Religious orders organized schools in their monasteries to educate young members of the order. An unknown number of parish priests taught boys from the parish or town. In each case the primary purpose was to train future clergymen, although church schools often enrolled boys who would not become clergymen. The curriculum was limited to learning medieval Latin, which differed from classical Latin, the Bible and other religious works, a little bit of arithmetic, and skills such as chanting needed to perform church rituals.

After 1100, many more Latin grammar schools appeared. Supported by towns as in Italy or endowments in England, they educated both future clergymen and lay boys. These schools developed a more sophisticated Latin curriculum that included reading manufactured verse texts of pious sentiments, grammar manuals and glossaries, and a little bit of ancient poetry, especially passages from Virgil's *Aeneid*. At the secondary level they taught *ars dictaminis,* the theory and practice of writing prose letters by following the principles found in medieval manuals. The latter offered rules for prose composition derived from Cicero's *De inventione* and the pseudo-Ciceronian *Rhetorica ad Herennium,* both written in the first century B.C.E. Upper-level students, especially those beginning university study, might also study introductory logic or dialectic, a key part of Scholastic method.

A new kind of school teaching vernacular literature and commercial mathematics and bookkeeping skills appeared in Italy in the second half of the thirteenth century. These schools taught little or no Latin, but did teach popular vernacular texts, often stories illustrating the benefits of Christian virtues and the terrible consequences of vices. The commercial mathematics (called *abbaco*) and bookkeeping skills were quite complex. The vernacular schools educated boys who would become merchants or otherwise enter the commercial world. Other parts of Europe, especially Germany, had vernacular schools in the sixteenth century, which probably means that they began in the Middle Ages, but little is known about them. Outside Italy vernacular schools did not teach the sophisticated commercial mathematics and bookkeeping skills of Italian vernacular schools until much later. These modest vernacular schools marked a new departure in European education because they educated boys for secular nonprofessional and nonuniversity careers. They marked the beginning of a separation between Latin humanistic education for the elite, university-bound student and a practically oriented education for the rest who would enter the world of work. This division lasted through World War II (1939–1945) and is still found in Europe in some measure.

From the Renaissance to the Enlightenment

The Renaissance created an educational revolution by adopting a classical curriculum for its Latin schools. This happened in Italy in the fifteenth century and in the rest of Europe in

perceptualize the mind and its operations, while rationalists tend to intellectualize it. With its down-to-earth emphasis on concrete experience and clarity, empiricism has flourished in Anglophone countries, whereas the more speculative rationalist and Kantian ideas have flourished on the Continent. This is one aspect of the divide between Continental philosophy and Anglo-American, "analytic," and "linguistic" philosophies.

In the twenty-first century nearly everyone is an empiricist in the everyday sense of taking experience seriously as a basis for knowledge claims about the natural world and human behavior, but most philosophers reject traditional, doctrinaire empiricism—the view that human sense experience provides a special connection of the knowing mind to the world and thus provides a foundation on which knowledge can build, step by step.

A Thumbnail History

In ancient times Aristotle was an empiricist relative to Plato's other-worldly rationalism. Modern empiricism began around 1600 with Francis Bacon (1561–1626), who promoted a new, experimental philosophy combining experience and reason, and with Galileo Galilei (1564–1642), who united experimental observation with a Platonic mathematical framework. Thomas Hobbes (1588–1679) further enriched early empiricist thinking, but the "big three" British empiricists were John Locke (1632–1704), George Berkeley (1685–1753), and David Hume (1711–1776). Locke first systematically expounded modern empiricism (see below). He was followed in the eighteenth century by Berkeley, notorious for his subjective idealism, the radical empiricist view that there are no material objects, that everything can be analyzed into minds and their ideas. Hume then took the further step of denying that there is even a substantial mind or ego. We introspect only a bundle of passing impressions. The mind is governed by natural laws of association, analogous to Isaac Newton's (1642–1727) law of gravitation, without needing an executive overseer. Hume also denied that inductive inference can be justified by logical argument, but he defended a wider conception of rationality (or at least sensible action) based on our natural impulses to believe and act. As he wrote in *A Treatise of Human Nature* (1739–1740) and its popularization, *An Enquiry Concerning Human Understanding* (1748), passion or custom, not reason, is "the great guide of human life."

The leading nineteenth-century empiricist was John Stuart Mill (1806–1873), who developed a full-fledged phenomenalism. Mill held that simple induction by enumeration (ravens 1, 2, 3, . . . n are black; therefore all ravens are black) is sufficient to support both science and mathematics: even the principles of logic and mathematics are very general empirical laws. Twentieth-century empiricists such as Bertrand Russell (1872–1970), George Edward Moore (1873–1958), and Alfred Jules Ayer (1910–1989) denied this, as did the logical empiricists of the Vienna Circle, who contended that the laws of logic and mathematics are both a priori and analytically true, that is, true by virtue of logical form and our linguistic conventions, hence completely empty of empirical content. By contrast, many twentieth-century thinkers, following Willard Van Orman Quine (1908–2000), have returned to a more naturalistic pragmatism.

The most damaging criticisms of British empiricism were leveled first by Immanuel Kant (1724–1804) and by the German and British idealists who followed him, then by Ludwig Wittgenstein (1899–1969), Gilbert Ryle (1900–1976), Quine, Wilfrid Sellars (1912–1989), Thomas Kuhn (1922–1996), and other twentieth-century figures, who attacked the entire Cartesian-Lockean conception of mind, experience, and language. Shocked by Hume's apparent skepticism about causality and Newtonian science, Kant synthesized rationalism and empiricism, while critically transcending both. The human mind itself furnishes the conceptual and rational apparatus necessary to organize our experience, as he argued in his *Critique of Pure Reason* (1781). "Concepts without percepts are empty; percepts without concepts are blind." Kant retained a vestige of the rationalist idea that we possess a special sort of intuition that enables us to make substantive, "synthetic" claims about the world that are nonetheless known a priori. He held that Euclidean geometry and the basic principles of Newtonian mechanics are such "synthetic a priori" truths. Post-Kantian empiricists deny this.

Foundational Empiricism

The traditional empiricists and rationalists were foundationists in epistemology. Foundationism postulates a base set of propositions that play a distinctive epistemic role plus a superstructure (comprising the bulk of our knowledge) appropriately related to the base. The empiricists and rationalists added the constraints that the basic statements must be certain and self-justifying (self-evident to reason for the rationalists and evident to the senses for the empiricists) and that the relation of base to superstructure be one of logical inference: deductive and perhaps inductive logic must suffice to generate the superstructure from the base. The justification is one-way or "linear" in the sense that the various layers of superstructure depend only on lower layers and, hence, ultimately on the base for their justification. Euclidean geometry provides the intellectual model. In this case the inferences are strictly deductive.

Given such a Euclidean geometry–inspired model, one wants the largest possible superstructure from the narrowest and most certain possible base. Two main problems stand in the way: the base problem (whether the base itself can be adequately justified) and the superstructure problem (whether the inferential resources are sufficient to support the desired superstructure on the base). From the beginning, empiricists have addressed the second problem by restricting the superstructure to claims within reach of observation and experiment and by developing the resources of logic, probability theory, and statistical inference. The British empiricists did not fully recognize the seriousness of the first problem.

Within this foundationist framework, Locke established the overall structure of a specifically empiricist theory in *An Essay Concerning Human Understanding* (1690), one of the founding works of the Enlightenment:

1. All simple ideas come from experience. There are no innate ideas. Contrary to nativists such as

René Descartes (1596–1650), the mind is a tabula rasa—that is, a blank slate—at birth.

2. Ideas of solidity, movement, number, and so forth, resemble features of the real world (primary qualities), whereas sensations of color, sound, taste, and so forth, do not resemble the physical powers (secondary qualities) in objects that produce these sensations in the mind. They are mind-dependent.

3. Complex ideas are compounds of simple, atomic ideas, and, so, are image-like.

4. Thus knowledge, which is the intellectual recognition of the agreement or disagreement of ideas, cannot go beyond the limits of experience. (Locke's is an "idea empiricism," but knowledge requires an operation of mind in addition to the presence of ideas.)

5. Neither can meaningful language transcend experience, since the meaning of a word is an idea in the mind. Having the appropriate idea in mind is what distinguishes a person's from a parrot's uttering, "I want a cracker."

6. We each learn our native language by attaching public noises or marks (words) to ideas. We can then communicate our ideas to others by making the appropriate noises or marks.

7. Thought is a connected sequence of ideas.

8. The immediate objects of perception and thought are ideas in the mind, which in turn represent external things and situations (doctrine of representative perception, two-object theory of cognition).

9. All existing things are concrete and particular.

Empiricists immediately encountered the superstructure problem. Locke recognized that most meaningful words are general and many are abstract (rather than proper names of concrete objects, e.g., *canine* versus *Lassie*), so how do we get the corresponding ideas (meanings) from experience, which furnishes only particular ideas? From an image of a particular triangle, said Locke, we can *abstract* from its being equilateral, isosceles, or scalene, and thus construct a general idea of a triangle that is "all of these and none of these at once." Berkeley and Hume improved on this unsatisfactory solution, but to this day empiricist abstraction accounts face serious difficulties. Hume added to the superstructure problem by denying the adequacy of reason alone to produce, from particular experiences, either (a) moral judgments, about what one ought to do, or (b) inductive conclusions, such as "All ravens are black" and Newton's laws. The former is his point that one cannot deduce "ought" from "is" or value judgments from objective facts, and the latter is the aforementioned problem of induction. Meanwhile, Berkeley had challenged Locke's empirical base by rejecting his distinction between primary and secondary qualities.

The Appearance-Reality Distinction

The two problems resurrect the old difficulty of bridging the gap between appearance and reality. Seventeenth-century advocates of the new science joined Plato in sharply distinguishing the world of everyday experience from underlying reality. Empiricists, with their limited resources, have tended to stick close to the experiential surface of the world by either narrowing the gap between appearance and reality, denying the existence of an underlying reality altogether, adopting the skeptical position that we simply cannot know it, or rejecting all talk of a reality beyond experience as "metaphysical" and hence meaningless. In short, they have wavered over commitment to the reality of unobservable entities and processes.

Locke denied that we can know the real essences of things. Our classifications are not natural but artificial—conventions made for human convenience. Hume and the later positivists, with their verifiability theory of meaning, ruled out metaphysics as meaningless. Ernst Mach (1838–1916), the Viennese physicist and positivist, denied the existence of atoms and developed a phenomenalistic account of the world. Berkeley had denied the existence of matter with his principle, "To be is to be perceived or to perceive" (*Principles of Human Knowledge,* 1710). Only minds and ideas exist. Does the cat then go out of existence when it disappears beyond the sofa? No, because God (the biggest mind) still perceives it, replied Berkeley. Mill later used a logico-linguistic device to remove the need for God and thus obtain a full-fledged phenomenalism. In *An Examination of Sir William Hamilton's Philosophy* (1865), he attempted to reduce physical objects to "permanent possibilities of sensation," expressible by (impossibly) long series of statements about what a person *would* experience or *would have* experienced in such-and-such a situation. Russell, using the new symbolic logic to the same end, attempted to reduce mind itself to a logical construction out of experiences. He took the same line for the postulated theoretical entities of physics: "Wherever possible, logical constructions out of known objects are to be substituted for inferred entities" ("The Relation of Sense Data to Physics," in *Mysticism and Logic,* 1917). This was a halfway house between realism and instrumentalism or fictionalism. If electrons are logical constructions out of actual and possible laboratory operations and the resulting observations, then they are not real entities of underlying reality; but neither are they complete fictions. Rather, electron talk is a convenient, economical *façon de parler.*

The Twentieth Century and Beyond

Twentieth-century thinkers abandoned or at least transformed British empiricism for its failure to solve the base and superstructure problems. These developments include: (1) The linguistic turn. Linguistic philosophers speak about terms in a language rather than, vaguely, about ideas in the mind. They also employ the full power of symbolic logic or the subtle devices of ordinary language to address the twin problems of relating subjective experience to basic statements and basic statements to superstructure. (2) The holistic turn. This is a further shift from the atomism of individual ideas or terms to

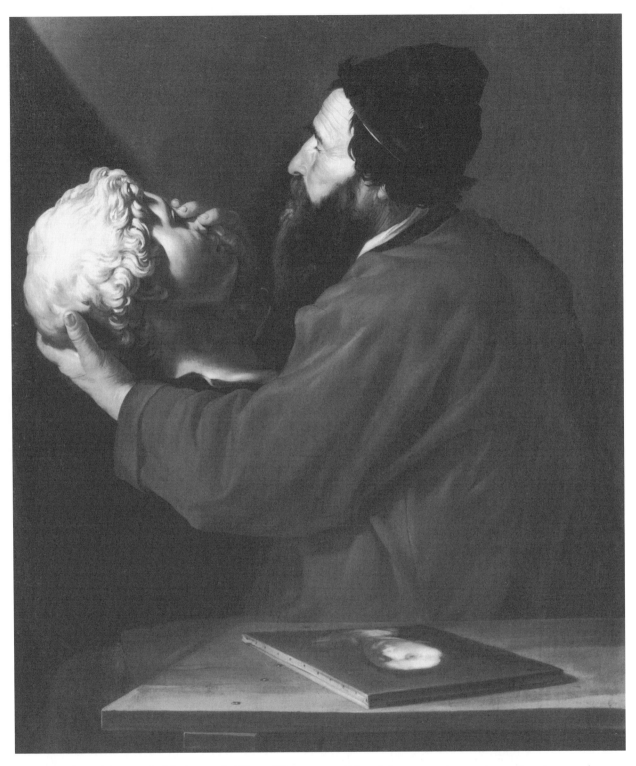

The Sense of Touch (1615–1616) **by Jusepe de Ribera. Oil on canvas.** Although its roots can be traced to ancient times, modern empiricism began in the early seventeenth century. Empiricists believe that knowledge comes from experience, such as that which can be gained through the senses. THE NORTON SIMON MUSEUM whole statements, representing completed thoughts, and even to entire languages and conceptual frameworks. In "Two Dogmas of Empiricism" (1951), Quine argued that neither individual terms nor even full statements (not even basic observation statements) can be directly correlated with experience. Moreover, the data of experience logically underdetermine our theoretical claims. (3) Rejection of the analytic-synthetic distinction, also by Quine. We cannot factor theories into purely empirical and purely analytic components, only the first of which is vulnerable. "No statement is immune to revision," come what may, not even the statements of mathematics—for example, it is now known that Euclidean geometry is not the only conceivable geometry and that it is not even true. Quine's work called into question not only the concept of analytic statement but also that of analysis as a philosophical method, for no one has provided an adequate analysis of analysis! (4) Rejection of the scheme versus content distinction by Donald Davidson, who proclaimed this the third and last dogma of empiricism. (5) Rejection of the correspondence theory of truth and of (6) the linear-foundational model of justification. These doctrines give way either to a weaker, nonlinear and fallibilist foundationism or to a coherence theory of justification based on the idea of a mutually supporting network of claims and practices. For some, pragmatic problem-solving supplants truth as a goal of research. (7) Anti-Kantian Kantianism. Despite the rejection of Kantian intuition and synthetic a priori claims, logical empiricists Hans Reichenbach (1891–1953) and Rudolf Carnap (1891–1970) and historian Kuhn in different ways defended the need for larger structures, at least temporarily immune to serious revision, in order to make sense of the history of science as well as individual cognition. These structures are not mere hypotheses up for testing, alongside the others, for they are *constitutive* of experience and of normal scientific practice, in a quasi-Kantian way. To reject them would be to throw out the baby with the bath water. (8) Rejection by Karl Popper (1902–1994) and the positivists of the traditional identification of empiricism with inductivism, the view that we must gather and classify facts prior to theorizing. They developed a sophisticated, hypothetico-deductive model of scientific research, which was in turn subjected to severe criticism.

(9) Rejection of the imagist tradition that treats cognitive states or contents as little pictures before consciousness, and of (10) "the myth of the given," by Sellars and others, the idea that subjective experience provides a special, direct, infallible, nonnatural connection of knowing mind to known world. These difficulties highlight the problem of the empirical base. Insofar as our experiential claims are certain they are not about physical reality (because we have had to retreat into the certainty of our subjective sense data of the moment), and insofar as they are about reality, they are not certain (because they are now subject to override by other observers or even by widely accepted theories). The price of relevance is fallibility. Thus accepting a basic statement is a social decision. All conceptual thinking, including perception, is mediated by language (a further phase of the linguistic turn). There is no prelinguistic cognitive (conceptual) awareness. There is no thought, no fully human perception or scientific observation, prior to language. Roughly, "language games" (Wittgenstein's term) take over the

role played by Kant's categories. All inquiry is thus fallible and mediated by language and by participation in an appropriate community of inquirers. The isolated Cartesian inquirer is a myth. The result is (11) the failure of phenomenalism and sense datum theories of perception and, more generally, (12) rejection of the whole Cartesian-Lockean conception of cognition and language. This conception is based on a Cartesian dualism of mind and body and, specifically, upon the privacy, immediacy, and alleged epistemological privilege of one's current mental contents. Philosophical and psychological behaviorism provided strong arguments against the Cartesian conception even for those thinkers, such as Sellars, who went beyond behaviorism.

(13) The failure of attempts to define knowledge precisely as justified true belief, which inspired (14) externalism versus internalism in epistemology. Internalism is the Cartesian-Lockean view that a person's knowledge claims must be justified in terms of the beliefs to which that person has access. The most popular form of externalism is reliabilism. According to process reliabilists, knowledge or justification consists of true beliefs formed by a reliable process whether or not the believer has sufficient Cartesian access to that process to justify it internally. Virtue epistemology, analogous to virtue ethics, is a variant of this idea: reliable beliefs are those formed by an intellectually virtuous process. (15) Recognition of the importance of tacit versus explicit knowledge (knowledge-how vs. knowledge-that) and of embodied knowledge, for example, skilled practices that we cannot fully articulate. (16) The feminist introduction of gender variables into epistemology. (17) Competing attempts to naturalize and socialize epistemology. Increasingly, empiricist philosophers work in the cognitive sciences, although few share Quine's view that epistemology will simply become a branch of psychology. Meanwhile, sociologists of knowledge regard their sociological approach as more fundamental than psychological studies of cognition. (18) The postmodern critique of empiricism. Postmodernists, including Richard Rorty and radical feminists and sociologists, regard empiricism, epistemology in general, and, indeed, the entire Enlightenment project to replace a tradition-bound life with modern life based on empirical science as a "modern" enterprise whose time is past. It is a mistake, they say, to abstract from sociohistorical contexts with their specific power and gender relations to seek the "one true account" of the world, as if there were a determinate world out there waiting for us to provide a correct description in its own language. Rather, say the critics, the world and our modes of inquiry are all socially constructed, as is empiricism itself. It is now time to deconstruct it. These controversial oppositions have generated "the science wars."

Although philosophical thinkers have abandoned both traditional rationalism and empiricism and although Quine, Davidson, and others have rejected the "dogmas" of empiricism and hence empiricism itself as a technical philosophical doctrine, there is a wider sense in which empiricism wins. For everyone is an empiricist in regarding observation and experience as crucial to justifying claims about the world, while almost no one believes that such claims can be defended purely a priori or on the basis of some kind of nonempirical intuition.

However, this is no longer an empiricist *epistemology* in the old sense, for gone is the idea that epistemology commands special resources that can provide external or transcendental justification for any enterprise. The sciences, for example, can only justify their claims internally, by applying further scientific tests and by their own fruits.

See also **Knowledge; Positivism; Rationalism; Realism.**

BIBLIOGRAPHY

Alston, William P. *Epistemic Justification: Essays in the Theory of Knowledge.* Ithaca, N.Y.: Cornell University Press, 1989.

Barnes, Barry, David Bloor, and John Henry. *Scientific Knowledge: A Sociological Analysis.* Chicago: University of Chicago Press, 1996.

BonJour, Laurence. *The Structure of Empirical Knowledge.* Cambridge, Mass.: Harvard University Press, 1985.

Dancy, Jonathan, and Ernest Sosa, eds. *A Companion to Epistemology.* Oxford: Blackwell, 1992.

Goldman, Alvin I. *Epistemology and Cognition.* Cambridge, Mass.: Harvard University Press, 1986.

Kornblith, Hilary, ed. *Naturalizing Epistemology.* 2nd ed. Cambridge, Mass.: MIT Press, 1994.

Longino, Helen E.. *The Fate of Knowledge.* Princeton, N.J.: Princeton University Press, 2002.

Quine, Willard Van Orman. "Two Dogmas of Empiricism." Reprinted in his *From a Logical Point of View: Logico-Philosophical Essays.* Cambridge, Mass.: Harvard University Press, 1953.

Rorty, Richard. *Philosophy and the Mirror of Nature.* Princeton, N.J.: Princeton University Press, 1979.

Schmitt, Frederick F., ed. *Socializing Epistemology: The Social Dimensions of Knowledge.* Lanham, Md.: Rowman and Littlefield, 1994.

Van Fraassen, Bas C. *The Empirical Stance.* New Haven, Conn.: Yale University Press, 2002.

Woolhouse, R. S. *The Empiricists.* Oxford: Oxford University Press, 1988.

Thomas Nickles

ENCYCLOPEDISM.

Encyclopedism is not restricted to the history of encyclopedias as we now know them. Certainly, since the eighteenth century, this identification has been the dominant one; however, the term *encyclopedism* is best seen as a heuristic device that can legitimately be applied to other intellectual projects. Three main forms of encyclopedism can be discerned: first, the classical Greek and Roman notion of a circle of learning that an educated person should pursue; second, various schemes aimed at comprehensive collection and classification of an intellectual field or an aspect of the world; and third, the aim of condensing and summarizing knowledge from a wide range of subjects in a set of volumes, variously called compendium, dictionary, or encyclopedia.

The Circle of Learning

We owe the word *encyclopaedia* to Quintilian's (first century C.E.) Latinized version of the Greek term denoting a circle of learning. Works such as Marcus Terentius Varro's *Disciplines*

(c. 50 B.C.E., now lost) defined this circle as the "seven liberal arts," which later formed the trivium and quadrivium of the medieval university curriculum. Varro also included medicine and architecture. However, the circle of learning, comprising selected subjects, must be distinguished from the circle of all knowledge. A similar outlook is found in authors of the Middle Ages who placed the classical learning within a Christian framework, seeking to document the knowledge required by man for salvation. Important examples of such works are Flavius Magnus Cassiodorus's *Institutiones* (c. 560 C.E.), Isidore of Seville's *Etymologiae* (636), and Hugh of St. Victor's *Didascalicon* (c. 1130). Including both sacred and secular learning, these works expanded the original Greek concept; indeed, in Isidore there are hints of encyclopedism as near-comprehensive coverage of knowledge, including topics outside the liberal arts.

The most famous of the medieval works was the *Speculum maius* (The greater mirror), compiled between 1245 and 1260 from a range of authorities by the Dominican friar Vincent of Beauvais; it was reprinted as late as 1624. It comprised three books, or mirrors—of nature, of history, and of doctrine. The last book, the *Speculum doctrinale* (Mirror of doctrine), covered the liberal and mechanical arts, mathematics, and natural philosophy. Gregor Reisch's *Margarita philosophica* (The philosophic pearl), first published in Freiburg in 1496, is one of the most successful examples of an encyclopedic compendium. Reisch summarized arts and sciences in the university curriculum of his day and implied a sequence of disciplines, sometimes by matching subjects to particular stages of life. This work went through ten editions between 1503 and 1599. At the other end of the Renaissance period Johann Heinrich Alsted's (1588–1638) *Encyclopaedia* (4 vols, 1630), considered the last and best of the neo-Scholastic encyclopedias, treated thirty disciplines in separate treatises arranged in accordance with a philosophical schema; in addition, an index to each treatise allowed access to a specific discipline. Yet even such a large work was conceived as a summary of subjects that in principle outlined an educational path. Alsted described his work as presenting a "methodological understanding of everything than man must learn in this life" (book 1).

Who could truly encompass this circle of knowledge? Indeed there were already doubts, especially given Francis Bacon's (1561–1626) stress on new knowledge, steadily accumulating over time. Nevertheless, the idea of "encyclopaedia" revived by Renaissance humanists was still selective, conceived as a circle of learning, not a summary of all knowledge in a single work. A version of this ideal supported the notion of general learning in the arts curriculum of the early modern European universities. In the English case, for example, this included rhetoric, logic, mathematics, and moral and natural philosophy. This curriculum was predicated on the interdependence of various branches of knowledge, a conviction elaborated by the Cambridge mathematician and divine, Isaac Barrow (1630–1677), who advised that "one Part of Learning doth confer Light to another, . . . that he will be a lame Scholar, who hath not an insight into many kinds of knowledge, that he can hardly be a good Scholar, who is not a general one" (Barrow, vol. 1, p. 184). In his *Glossographia* of 1656 Thomas Blount (1618–1679) reflected this position by defining the "encyclopedy" as "that learning which comprehends all Liberal Sciences; an Art that comprehends all others, the perfection of all knowledge."

Encyclopedic Collections

Pliny the Elder's *Naturalis historia* (77 C.E.) is often cited as an early encyclopedic work. His thirty-seven books and 2,493 chapters collated information from over four hundred authors, offering (in his estimate) some twenty thousand facts about the natural history of animals, objects, and techniques. However, Pliny was not concerned with the unity of knowledge or the relations between disciplines. Instead, he managed to give "encyclopedia" a wider denotation by announcing in his opening epistle that the Greeks meant by this a complete body of arts and sciences. Pliny thereby forged a link between natural history and the notion of encyclopedism imagined as comprehensiveness. During the Renaissance the *Natural History* came to be seen as a museum catalog, a shopping list for assembling a cabinet of curiosities. Moreover, the activity of collecting was informed by the ideal of encyclopedic learning. By possessing rare or otherwise valuable objects, an individual collector displayed his knowledge of them, their classical literary associations, and their place in a larger schema, such as the Great Chain of Being. The polymath Athanasius Kircher (1601–1680) established a museum in the Jesuit College in Rome and regarded it as his "enciclopedia concreta" (actual or tangible encyclopedia). Gabriel Naudé, in his *Advis pour dresser une bibliothèque* (1627; Instruction concerning establishing a library), declared that a library should represent the encyclopedic circle of learning. The architecture of the buildings (museums and libraries) that held such treasures was often seen as a physical expression of the encyclopedia, now increasingly regarded as a model or microcosm of divine creation.

Eventually, however, large collections began to tell against the notion of the individual collector as knowing his possessions as one might be said to know the seven liberal arts. Sir Hans Sloane's (1660–1753) private collection (the founding collection of the British Museum) comprised some forty thousand books, three thousand manuscripts, and two hundred thousand objects, such as coins and medals, natural history, anthropological specimens, and other curious items. Such collections were often called "encyclopedic," but this now indicated that they were so extensive as to be beyond the capacities of a single mind, or memory. By at least the early 1700s critics were saying that once a collection reached a certain size, its value must be found in the various uses different people might make of it. Encyclopedism, in this guise, severed its link with the notion of the "encyclopedia" as a path of individual learning.

It is also possible to consider encyclopedism as supporting the notion of virtual collections. Conrad Gesner's (1516–1565) *Bibliotheca universalis* (1545; Universal library) was a bibliography of all known books—eighteen hundred authors and ten thousand titles—rather than a catalog of any existing library. During the eighteenth century, attempts to classify books, objects, or aspects of nature—even if not held in any collection—were regarded as encyclopedic because they allowed a large number of things to be comprehended by a single person, independent of being actually seen or touched. This is how the taxonomies of the plant and animal worlds, such as those of Carolus Linnaeus (1707–1778), were understood and promoted.

In German universities from the eighteenth century, particular disciplines were given "encyclopedic" arrangements, so that encyclopedias of philology, law, and medicine were offered as introductory and summary courses within particular departments. As Henri Abrams wrote in his *Encyclopédie juridique* (1855; Juridical encyclopedia), "An encyclopedia may be regarded in general as a synthetic plan embracing a science in all its parts."

Alphabetical Encyclopedias

By the early 1700s, a new expression of encyclopedism was the publication of encyclopedias in the form of alphabetical dictionaries of terms and subjects. These were regarded as summaries of accumulated information in various fields of knowledge, produced in a form accessible to a wide readership. Such works acknowledged the medieval and Renaissance legacy of encyclopedism, but the scope of these new works extended beyond the subjects of the university and also explicitly confronted the problem of keeping pace with the incessant progress of knowledge in all fields.

Distinctions must be made within the set of alphabetical dictionaries that emerged toward the end of the seventeenth century. By 1700 there were specialist lexicons for anatomy, chemistry, and other subjects; the predecessors of the modern language dictionary; the historical (and biographical) dictionary; and the dictionary of arts and sciences. The last two kinds are most relevant here because for a time the distinction between them had a bearing on the contemporary definition of an encyclopedia. Louis Moréri's *Grand Dictionnaire Historique* (Great historical dictionary), first published in Lyon in 1674 and then issued in an expanded second edition in 1681, is usually regarded as the first work (other than bibliographies) to summarize a range of subjects in strictly alphabetical order. Pierre Bayle's *Dictionnaire historique et critique* (2 vols., 1697; enlarged 2nd ed., 1702; Critical and historical dictionary,) began as an attempt to remedy Moréri's errors. Although large works for their time, neither pretended to the title of "encyclopaedia" because they were conceived as historical dictionaries covering major aspects of sacred and secular history by means of biographical entries on key figures.

The new genre of the dictionary of arts and sciences was the more direct predecessor of the modern encyclopedia. Three significant examples are Antoine Furetière's (1619–1688) *Dictionnaire universel,* published in three volumes at the Hague in 1690, two years after his death; John Harris's *Lexicon technicum* (2 vols., 1704, 1710); and Ephraim Chambers's (1680–1740) *Cyclopaedia* (2 vols., 1728). These works consisted of entries on terms (mainly from the arts and sciences) in alphabetical order, but they professed to be more than definitions of words by also being descriptions of things. The category of "arts and sciences" was flexible enough to embrace apparently disparate subjects such as law, music, and architecture, as well as the disciplines of the physico-mathematical disciplines and the new experimental sciences. The *Lexicon technicum* was strong on the latter but far less comprehensive than

Chambers's *Cyclopaedia,* which justified its use of that title by covering systematic disciplines belonging to the category *"scientia"*—such as grammar, theology, logic, music, astronomy, mechanics, optics, and other parts of natural philosophy, as well as of subjects capable of being brought into scientific order, such as anatomy, medicine, natural history, and the practical and mechanical arts and trades. It did not include biography or history. Thus early-eighteenth-century encyclopedism tolerated a division of labor—between historical/biographical dictionaries and those dealing with the arts and sciences (and assuming the title of encyclopedia). The *Grosses vollständiges Universal-Lexicon aller Wissenschaften und Künste . . .* (Great, complete universal lexicon of all sciences and arts . . .), begun in 1732 by the Leipzig publisher Johann Zedler, is an example of an historical dictionary that included entries on scientific topics in addition to those on history, theology, philosophy, and biography; it reached sixty-four folio volumes by 1750. By at least the early 1800s, encyclopedic coverage meant a comprehensive survey of all knowledge of the kind attempted by the *Encyclopaedia Britannica,* especially in its ninth edition (25 vols, 1875–1889).

Chambers compiled his *Cyclopaedia* single-handedly, drawing from various sources and presenting the information under key terms. With the famous *Encyclopédie* (1751–1780), edited by Denis Diderot (1713–1784) and Jean Le Rond d'Alembert (1717–1783), encyclopedism became collaborative. While acknowledging their debt to Chambers, the French editors declared that a complete survey of knowledge required the efforts of many hands and so recruited contributions from leading members of the Republic of Letters. When completed, the *Encyclopédie* consisted of seventeen folio volumes of text and eleven volumes of plates, incorporating an extensive documentation of the arts, crafts, and trades, and illustrated by some twenty-five hundred engravings. Whereas Chambers's sought to condense "the vast bulk of universal knowledge into a lesser compass" (Chambers, 1738, vol. 1, xxiv), the French editors welcomed long essays covering the history and current views on a particular subject. This set the pattern for subsequent encyclopedias. The *Encyclopaedia Britannica* (3 vols., 1771) departed from Chambers's format of relatively short entries on terms, instead presenting major disciplines as "systems" in separate treatises of at least twenty-five pages each. From its third edition (10 vols., 1788–1797) experts were invited to write these treatises. Similarly, the *Encyclopédie methodique* (166 vols., 1782–1832), the successor to the *Encyclopédie,* was organized by disciplines, so that, for example, there were at least nine volumes on natural history. Each subject was under the control of a leading expert with a license (almost without a word limit) to describe and codify a field. Previously a concept that assumed the value of general learning, encyclopedism now depended on specialists.

This shift had implications for the rationale of Enlightenment encyclopedias. Both Chambers and Diderot claimed that the integrity of particular sciences and the relations between them could still be perceived, in spite of alphabetical arrangement. This is why they provided maps or charts of knowledge in their prefaces, albeit recognizing that such classification was to some degree arbitrary. Given the expansion of knowledge, especially in the natural sciences, they admitted that there was no longer a

Woodcut from Gregor Reisch's *Margarita philosophica* (1496). Reisch's popular compendium, published during the early Renaissance period, sought to summarize and compartmentalize the disciplines of art and science. ANNENBERG RARE BOOK & MANUSCRIPT LIBRARY, UNIVERSITY OF PENNSYLVANIA

single circle of learning (such as the seven liberal arts) but insisted that their works were informed by an awareness of the links between subjects and that cross references allowed the reader to follow these in a methodical fashion. By the late 1700s, however, most encyclopedias had abdicated responsibility for any systematic classification of the subjects they covered. The *Britannica* never included a map of knowledge. One exception was the *Encyclopaedia metropolitana* (26 vols, 1827–1845), organized on a plan devised by the English poet Samuel Taylor Coleridge. This was a return to the systematic, or at least thematic, format of earlier encyclopedic works. Rejecting alphabetical arrangement, Coleridge recommended an order of subjects that reflected the hierarchy of the disciplines in the classification he supplied, beginning with the abstract, formal subjects of logic, grammar, and geometry (all in the first two volumes), then the mixed-mathematical disciplines such as astronomy, optics, and music; then the various parts of natural history, and so on. This sequence of subjects was intended to prescribe a proper order of study. But this format had limited appeal, and the work was a commercial failure. Encyclopedism had finally lost touch with the original sense of the Greek concept of a circle of learning that an individual could, and should, pursue.

Nevertheless, understood as comprehensive coverage of either a single subject or the totality of knowledge, encyclopedism

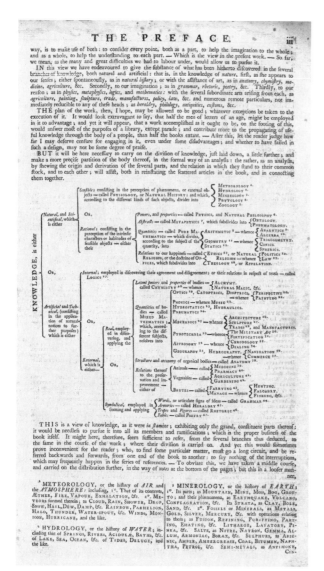

Diagram showing the "View of Knowledge" from *Cyclopaedia* **(1728) by Ephraim Chambers.** Chamber's two-volume work featured descriptions of subjects from a range of topics, mostly drawn from the fields of arts and science. ANNENBERG RARE BOOK & MANUSCRIPT LIBRARY, UNIVERSITY OF PENNSYLVANIA

still flourished into the twentieth century. The nationalist emphasis of the nineteenth century (replacing the cosmopolitanism of the Enlightenment) continued to inspire encyclopedias. In various European countries, and in the Soviet Union, encyclopedias were emblems of national culture—for example, the *Enciclopedia Italiana* (1929–1939) in thirty-six large volumes, directed, in part, by the philosopher Giovanni Gentile. Other manifestations include H. G. Wells's call for a new encyclopedia to function as the "World Brain," and the *International Encyclopedia of Unified Science*—a collection of monographs planned by members of the Vienna Circle, notably by Otto Neurath (1892–1945) and Rudolf Carnap (1891–1970). In the late twentieth and early twenty-first centuries, the electronic storage and retrieval of information has allowed vast collection

projects, larger than anything earlier versions of encyclopedism had contemplated.

By the late twentieth century, the role of encyclopedias in textual form was being questioned. The *Encyclopaedia Britannica* was issued on CD-ROM and then online; but with the increasing power of search engines on the Internet, the reference function of encyclopedias has been challenged. The tradition of encyclopedism in the West has emphasized the importance of categories of knowledge, relations between subjects, and the authority and credibility of the selections and summaries contained in catalogs, taxonomies, museums, and encyclopedias. Regardless of the medium in which information is stored in the twenty-first century, these issues remain.

See also **Classification of Arts and Sciences, Early Modern; Knowledge; Museums; Scholasticism; University.**

BIBLIOGRAPHY

PRIMARY SOURCES

Barrow, Isaac "Of Industry in Our Particular Calling, as Scholars." In *The Works of the Learned Isaac Barrow, published by his Grace Dr. Tillotson.* 3rd ed., 3 vols in 2. London: J. Round, J. Tonson, and W. Taylor, 1716.

Blount, Thomas. *Glossographia; or, a Dictionary, Interpreting All Such Hard Words . . . Now Used in Our Refined English Tongue.* Menston: Scolar Press, 1969. First published in 1656.

Chambers, Ephraim. *Cyclopaedia; or, an Universal Dictionary of Arts and Sciences.* 2 vols. London: J. and J. Knapton, J. Darby, D. Midwinter et al., 1728. 2nd ed. 1738.

Coleridge, Samuel. "General Introduction or Preliminary Treatise on Method." *Encyclopaedia Metropolitana; or, Universal Dictionary of knowledge, on an original plan: comprising the twofold advantage of a philosophical and an alphabetical arrangement,* edited by Edward Smedley, Hugh James Rose, and Henry Rose, 26 vols., London: B. Fellowes, F. and J. Rivington et al., 1827-45, vol. 1, 1–43. Reprinted in Robert Collison, *Encyclopaedias: their History through the Ages,* New York: Hafner Publishing, 1964, 243–299.

d'Alembert, Jean Le Rond. *Preliminary Discourse to the Encyclopedia of Diderot.* Translated by Richard N. Schwab, with the collaboration of Walter E. Rex. Chicago: University of Chicago Press, 1995. First published in 1751.

Diderot, Denis, and Jean Le Rond d'Alembert, eds. *Encyclopédie, ou dictionnaire raisonné des sciences, des arts et des métiers.* 17 vols. of text (1751–1765), 11 vols. of plates (1762–1777), 4 supplemental vols. of text, 1 supplemental vol. of plates, and 2 supplemental vols. of index. Paris: Briasson, 1751–1765; 1776–1780. Reprinted in 34 vols., Stuttgart-Bad, Cannstatt: Frommann, 1966–1967.

Pliny the Elder. *Natural History Ten Vols.* Translated by H. Rackham. New ed. London: W. Heinemann, 1974.

Reisch, Gregor. *Margarita Philosophica.* Freiburg: Joanne Schottu Argen, 1503.

Zedler, Johann Heinrich, *Grosses vollständiges Universal-Lexicon aller Wissenschaften und Künste.* 64 vols. Halle and Leipzig: J. H. Zedler, 1732–1750.

SECONDARY SOURCES

Arnar, Anna S., ed. *Encyclopedism from Pliny to Borges.* Chicago: University of Chicago Library, 1990.

Collison, Robert. *Encyclopaedias: Their History through the Ages.* New York: Hafner, 1964.

Chartier, Roger. *The Order of Books: Readers, Authors, and Libraries in Europe between the Fourteenth and Eighteenth Centuries.* Translated by Lydia G. Cochrane. Cambridge, U.K.: Polity Press, 1994.

Darnton, Robert. "Philosophers Trim the Tree of Knowledge." In his *The Great Cat Massacre and Other Episodes in French Cultural History.* London: Penguin, 1985.

Findlen, Paula. *Possessing Nature: Museums, Collecting, and Scientific Culture in Early Modern Italy.* Berkeley: University of California Press, 1994.

Kafker, Frank A., ed. *Notable Encyclopedias of the Seventeenth and Eighteenth Centuries: Nine Predecessors of the Encyclopédie.* Studies on Voltaire and the Eighteenth Century, vol. 194. Oxford: Voltaire Foundation, 1981.

Kafker, Frank A., ed. *Notable Encyclopedias of the Late Eighteenth Century: Eleven Successors of the Encyclopédie.* Studies on Voltaire and the Eighteenth Century, vol. 315. Oxford: Voltaire Foundation, 1994.

Yeo, Richard. *Encyclopaedic Visions: Scientific Dictionaries and Enlightenment Culture.* Cambridge, U.K., and New York: Cambridge University Press, 2001.

Richard Yeo

ENLIGHTENMENT.

In the years since the publication of the first *Dictionary of the History of Ideas,* the Enlightenment has become an increasingly fragmented and decreasingly coherent historical rubric. In fact that fragmentation began in the *Dictionary of the History of Ideas* itself, in an article titled "Counter-Enlightenment," written by Isaiah Berlin and categorized out of alphabetical order, appearing as an appendix to the main entry on "Enlightenment," written by H. O. Pappe.

Pappe defined the Enlightenment as a historical period extending from the late seventeenth century (the Glorious Revolution, the era of John Locke [1632–1704] or Pierre Bayle [1647–1706]) to the late eighteenth or early nineteenth century (American Revolution, French Revolution, or the defeat of Napoleon and the Romantic reaction against the Enlightenment). The Enlightenment was also a mood emphasizing individualism, toleration, and cosmopolitanism. The Enlightenment was a social philosophy with common basic conceptions about humanity and society and a common methodological approach involving the search for laws that govern nature and society and commonly held values directed toward social reform. By this definition the Enlightenment was monolithic, but it was not all-encompassing. It was an avant-garde "movement" involving a relatively small number of thinkers. The movement began in England and reached its climax in mid-eighteenth-century Paris and Scotland, while the "Italian and German Enlightenment, though distinguished by outstanding contributors, was derivative."

Counter-Enlightenment

Berlin's counterargument focused specifically on those "derivative" countries, offering Giambattista Vico (1668–1744), Johann Georg Hamann (1730–1788), Johann Gottfried von Herder (1744–1803), and Immanuel Kant (1724–1804) as the bearers of a genuine, indigenous, and innovative agenda alternative to the mainstream Enlightenment of France and Britain. Vico rejected the existence of a timeless, universal natural law that could be explained by mathematics or logic. Mathematics was certain only because it was a human invention; it did not correspond to an objective structure of reality. Mathematics was a method only, not a body of truth, and while it could explain *what* happened in the world, it could not explain *why* or to what end. Human beings had no access to the final causes or purposes of nature. What they could know were human truths, human behavior, and human motives. These human truths were particular, not universal—that is, each nation developed its own standards of beauty, truth, and goodness. Because different nations asked different questions of the universe, they came up with different answers.

Hamann represented the distinctly antirational strain of Berlin's Counter-Enlightenment. For Hamann too truth was particular, never general. As a human invention, reason was a tool for the arrangement and classification of data to which nothing in reality corresponded. The true language was divine: Nature, plants, animals, and society were the symbols by which God communicated with his creatures. To understand was to be communicated with, either by people or by God. True knowledge was direct perception—experience—not logical proof. Only love, the most intimate form of direct experience, could demonstrate anything. Through the medium of Herder, Berlin placed a hermeneutic of empathy at the center of his Counter-Enlightenment. To understand something was to understand its individuality and unique development. Only by entering into the experience of another, through the imagination and rigorous scholarship, could one understand the organic structure of society. Berlin emphasized what he (not Herder) called the "incommensurability of cultures" that "should flourish side by side like so many flowers in the great human garden."

Kant's autonomy of the will represented the fourth aspect of Berlin's antirational Counter-Enlightenment. Figures of the Counter-Enlightenment recognized that the model of the universe espoused by Cartesianism, rationalism, and natural law was inherently deterministic (in that all motion was caused by previous action and conformed to specific natural laws) and fatalistic (no action could violate those natural laws). Applied to society, such a view divested human actors of their moral responsibility. If all action was regulated by nature, then an individual could blame the system of the universe for any evil perpetrated by himself. In response, Kant held that only as independent actors—not acted upon by previous or external forces—could human beings be considered moral agents.

All of this amounted to a tacit apology for hermeneutics: the emphasis on language as the defining characteristic of a nation; cultural particularism and the uniqueness of each; the attempt to understand by entering the experience of another in an act of empathy. Even if the methods and assumptions of the Counter-Enlightenment differed from the mainstream rationalists, the goals and values described by Berlin nevertheless sound distinctly similar to those described by Pappe: cosmopolitanism, pluralism, tolerance, and social reform. Indeed to those who championed the Enlightenment from the end of World War II to the 1970s, eighteenth-century social thought was a convenient platform from which to display their own liberal sensibilities.

Fractured Enlightenment

In 1973, then, we see the Enlightenment divided in two parts: a western European rationalist Enlightenment and a negatively defined central European antirational Counter-Enlightenment. In fact defining the Enlightenment, even in 1973, was not as easy as creating a binary opposition. Beginning in the 1960s Franco Venturi also divided Continental Europe into two distinct political traditions, with multiethnic empires in central and eastern Europe and "great states" in western Europe. He emphasized concurrent developments in republican Mediterranean Europe (Italy, Iberia, France) and monarchical eastern Europe, but he excluded England from the equation, saying that "in England the rhythm was different." Venturi defined the Enlightenment by the presence or absence of philosophes, self-appointed secular intellectuals who critiqued society and presented themselves as its guides toward modernity and reform. Although they were present in Scotland in the mid-eighteenth century, intellectuals of the stature of Voltaire, Jean Le Rond d'Alembert, Denis Diderot, and so on did not emerge in England until the 1780s and 1790s with Thomas Paine, Richard Price, William Godwin, and Jeremy Bentham. Venturi acknowledged a problem in his definition given the Englishness of Edward Gibbon (1737–1794), whom he considered "a giant of the Enlightenment": either Gibbon was no philosophe or he was a lonely figure in England in the 1760s and 1770s.

In fact the French philosophes were great admirers of the English in the 1760s, wrote Roy Porter in *The Enlightenment in National Context* (1981): "Certainly England produced no *Critique of Pure Reason*. But why should systematic theorizing be the touchstone of Enlightenment?" Voltaire noted that the English were "the only people upon the earth who have been able to prescribe limits to the power of Kings by resisting them." That resistance was galvanized in institutions of sociability—gentlemen's clubs, Masonic lodges, colleges, coffee houses—where private individuals might gather in public discourse to discuss and debate matters of law, politics, religion, and culture. Gibbon might have been a lonely giant among enlightened Lilliputians, but E. P. Thompson pointed to scores of minor "intellectual enclaves" throughout the United Kingdom where individuals exercised their rational and critical faculties.

The very title of Porter and Teich's volume, *The Enlightenment in National Context,* indicates the direction of Enlightenment historiography in the late 1970s and 1980s. That volume still took the Enlightenment to be monolithic ("a cultural movement," p. xi) and headed in a specific direction, although the constituent parts of that movement expressed enlightened values in terms of their indigenous and traditional concerns. Thirteen separate national expressions of the Enlightenment were identified by the contributors, and the editors acknowledged that even that number was not adequate.

Should the Swiss Enlightenment have been considered a unit, or were there distinct traditions in the French and German cantons? Contemporaries of the eighteenth century expressly believed the latter. Germany was divided into two Enlightenments, Catholic and Protestant, but among the Protestant at least three distinct movements can be identified based on divisions within German Lutheranism: an Orthodox Lutheran Enlightenment centered at Leipzig and Dresden in Saxony; a Pietist Enlightenment centered at Berlin and Halle, where a university was founded in 1690 specifically as a platform for an intellectual movement that saw itself as separate from the Orthodox; and a post-Pietist Enlightenment centered at Göttingen, which defined itself in opposition to both Saxony and the Brandenburg of Frederick the Great. Were the Württemberg Protestants allied with the Hanoverians? Can the Danish and Swedish Lutherans be taken as a unit, and how should their relationships with the Germans be defined? The possibilities for a rigorous classification of cultural movements in the eighteenth century boggle the mind.

The attempt to rescue the Gulliverian Gibbon continues into the twenty-first century. In the first installment of a study of Gibbon that is well on its way toward rivaling the length of Gibbon's own *Decline and Fall of the Roman Empire,* J. G. A. Pocock invented an Enlightenment in which Gibbon did participate. Pocock started by pluralizing Enlightenments, declaring it "a premise of this book that we can no longer write satisfactorily of 'The Enlightenment' as a unified and universal intellectual movement" (*The Enlightenments of Edward Gibbon,* 1999, p. 12; notice the plural in the title). Pocock accepted Venturi's thesis that there was no Enlightenment in England, and he showed that Gibbon did not participate in a separate French Enlightenment either. Instead he placed Gibbon in an "Arminian Enlightenment," referring to the heretical movement within Calvinism and defining an area that extended from Lake Geneva down the Rhine to the Netherlands and across the Channel to Oxford. Pocock presented the Arminian Enlightenment as a unit that unified intellectuals from a variety of backgrounds, and by his participation in the movement, Gibbon could move easily across national, linguistic, and regional boundaries and still find intellectual continuity.

For Pocock this solution had the advantage of retaining "the philosophes and their enterprises, Venturi's *settecento riformatore* and perhaps even 'the Enlightenment Project,' as cosmopolitan and Europe-wide phenomena, while denying them the privilege of defining 'Enlightenment,' or 'Europe,' by formulae from which either Gibbon or England must be excluded" (p. 295). On the other hand, one wonders whether a series of regional Enlightenments that do not even conform to national or linguistic boundaries, each presented as more or less autonomous from the others, dooms the Enlightenment to an increasingly fractured existence and perhaps renders the rubric altogether useless.

The New Cultural History

One result of Enlightenment historiography in the past thirty years, then, has been to carve the movement into different geographic, confessional, and linguistic groupings. And even within these groupings, further fragmentation has taken place.

In the original "Enlightenment" article in the *Dictionary of the History of Ideas,* Pappe explicitly declared the Enlightenment to be an elite movement. In a parenthetical digression he acknowledged that:

> Side-by-side with these productions, the period witnessed the growth of a new cheap entertainment literature as well as a greater diffusion of writings in the old tradition, which aimed at the new enlarged reading public. Although popular reading habits and crowd behavior have come to fascinate some modern historians, such publications are ignored here, as they hardly contributed to the march of ideas, that is to the *incivilimento* due to man's creative liberty.

Indeed it is precisely the study of reading habits and crowd behavior that have fueled the redefinition of the Enlightenment in the past thirty years. In the mid-1970s Peter Burke pointed out the rediscovery of "the People," by which he meant a renewed interest in folklore, festivals, and the early Germanic and Celtic oral tradition that swept across Europe beginning in about the 1760s, spurring the Romantic movement. Working initially in the *Kulturgeschichte* mode of Jacob Grimm, Jacob Burckhardt, Aby Warburg, and Johan Huizinga but augmenting that totalizing method with anthropological and literary techniques, scholars such as Natalie Davis, Carlo Ginzburg, and Keith Thomas began to study the social function of myth, ritual, and behavior in early modern Europe itself.

Robert Darnton examined not just the ideas of the Enlightenment but the "business" of it as well in a publishing history of the *Encyclopédie* in the last quarter of the eighteenth century. In *The Literary Underground of the Old Regime* he looked beyond the successes of Voltaire, d'Alembert, Étienne Bonnot de Condillac, and Jean-Jacques Rousseau to the failure of a host of would-be philosophes who lacked the patronage, money, and access to presses enjoyed by the Encyclopedists and members of learned academies. This too in effect split the Enlightenment into two parts, high and low—or those who got published by presses on Fleet Street and the Strand versus hacks living on Grub Street who were lucky if they got published at all. Darnton showed how the world of those lesser authors functioned—their pirating of copyrighted texts, sale of pornographic and censored books and serials, and the fortune of their original satires and social critiques that never acquired the reputation of Voltaire's.

Darnton called his method the "social history of ideas" (as Peter Gay had done years before). While it lacked a grand narrative of social and intellectual development, the microhistorical approach of scholars such as Darnton was important because if the Enlightenment and French Revolution were the products of new ideas (or of old ideas newly interpreted), then the logistical process of how those ideas were conveyed to the public sphere was just as important as the content of the ideas in themselves. Which texts were circulated? What were the motives of the authors, publishers, and booksellers? Which texts were intended to be circulated but never reached the market due to silly logistical failures? To what extent were authors,

The Triumph of Virtue and Nobility Over Ignorance (c. 1740–1750) by Giovanni Battista Tiepolo. Oil on canvas. The Age of Enlightenment began in England in the late seventeenth century and reached its pinnacle in the mid-eighteenth century. The period was characterized by a desire for reason, toleration, and social reform. NORTON SIMON COLLECTION, PASADENA, CALIFORNIA/THE BRIDGEMAN ART LIBRARY, WWW.BRIDGEMAN.CO.UK

publishers, and booksellers motivated by their economic and social circumstances? That is, how business was conducted influenced what kinds of ideas were circulated in the public sphere.

Rather than taking "popular culture" to be monolithic, Roger Chartier emphasized the different uses of print by different segments of society. These segments frequently overlapped, and a single member might perform several roles depending on the context in which he or she acted. Chartier worked to abolish some of the presumptive categories such as high and low Enlightenment, philosophe and Grub Street hack, even printed text and oral tradition. Whereas the historiography of popular culture of the 1960s and 1970s used techniques of historical anthropology appropriate to understanding forms of expression and communication in preliterate societies, Chartier's cultural history focused on the production, circulation, and function of printed texts. Early modern society was thoroughly dependent on writing, even those who could not read or who grasped a text only when it was read aloud to them. In reconstructing social practice, Chartier found that advice manuals, mandates, and slogans were *appropriated* by the audience (or, better, plural "audiences," because he emphasized that different overlapping groups read, understood, and acted upon a given text in their own ways). A text might be creatively interpreted, its message adjusted or diverted to purposes not intended by the author or even resisted. Chartier was interested chiefly in action: the act of reading; followed by behavior inspired by the text. He was less interested in the creation of ideas than the reception of ideas once those ideas left the author's desk, or how ideas walked, as it were, around in society.

The most glaring example of how ideas walked around in eighteenth-century society was the French Revolution. Were ideas responsible for the collapse of the Old Regime? Was there a necessary and causal connection between the Enlightenment and the French Revolution? Were ideas really that effective in producing constitutional change and touching off events like the Terror? Assuming that Daniel Mornet was at least partially correct in *Les origines intellectual de la Révolution Française* (1933) that ideas bore at least some responsibility for the Revolution, Chartier wanted to know: How, exactly? "Is it certain that the Enlightenment must be characterized exclusively or principally as a corpus of self-contained, transparent ideas or as a set of clear and distinct propositions?" Chartier asked. "Should not the century's novelty be read elsewhere—in the multiple *practices* guided by an interest in utility and service that aimed at the management of spaces and populations and whose mechanisms (intellectual or institutional) imposed a profound reorganization of the systems of perception and of the order of the social world?"

In the 1990s, then, the connection between ideas and practice moved to center stage in eighteenth-century historiography. The inquiry into practices of "sociability" was assisted by the translation into English of Jürgen Habermas's *Structural Transformation of the Public Sphere* (1989, originally 1956). Dena Goodman, Daniel Gordon, and others explored institutions and practices of sociability in prerevolutionary France and the movement of ideas from the closed intellectual circles of salons to the active realm of political reform. Margaret Jacob explored the Enlightenment's direct relationship to "lived political experience," particularly through the window of Freemasonry, emphasizing international trends such as the republicanism described by Franco Venturi. And Daniel Gordon has edited a volume on "Postmodernism and the Enlightenment."

Given the many directions of Enlightenment research, it is no wonder James Schmidt reopened the question of the 1780s: "What is Enlightenment?" Yet even that question was limited to Protestant Germany, taken for granted (or, rather, not formulated at all) in the rest of Europe. If the 1780s had answers, the 1990s had only questions, and it is unlikely that any time soon there will be an answer as definitive as the one offered in the first *Dictionary of the History of Ideas.*

See also **Deism; Historiography; Renaissance; Revolution; Romanticism in Literature and Politics.**

BIBLIOGRAPHY

Burke, Peter. *Popular Culture in Early Modern Europe.* New York: Harper and Row, 1978.

Chartier, Roger. *The Cultural Origins of the French Revolution.* Translated by Lydia G. Cochrane. Durham, N.C.: Duke University Press, 1991.

———. *The Cultural Uses of Print in Early Modern France.* Translated by Lydia G. Cochrane. Princeton, N.J.: Princeton University Press, 1987.

Darnton, Robert. *The Business of Enlightenment: A Publishing History of the Encyclopédie, 1775–1800.* Cambridge, Mass.: Belknap Press, 1979.

———. *The Literary Underground of the Old Regime.* Cambridge, Mass.: Harvard University Press, 1982.

Goodman, Dena. *The Republic of Letters: A Cultural History of the French Enlightenment.* Ithaca, N.Y.: Cornell University Press, 1994.

Gordon, Daniel. *Citizens without Sovereignty: Equality and Sociability in French Thought, 1670–1789.* Princeton, N.J.: Princeton University Press, 1994.

Habermas, Jürgen. *Structural Transformation of the Public Sphere: An Inquiry into a Category of Bourgeois Society.* Translated by Thomas Burger with the assistance of Frederick Lawrence. Cambridge, Mass.: MIT Press, 1989.

Jacob, Margaret C. *Living the Enlightenment: Freemasonry and Politics in Eighteenth-Century Europe.* New York: Oxford University Press, 1991.

Pocock, J. G. A. *Barbarism and Religion.* Vols. 1–3. Cambridge, U.K., 1999–2003.

Porter, Roy, and Mikulás Teich. *The Enlightenment in National Context.* Cambridge, U.K.: Cambridge University Press, 1981.

Schmidt, James, ed. *What Is Enlightenment? Eighteenth-Century Answers and Twentieth-Century Questions.* Berkeley: University of California Press, 1996.

Venturi, Franco. *Settecento Riformatore.* 4 vols. Turin: Einaudi, 1969–1984. Vols. 3 and 4 have been translated into English by R. Burr Litchfield as *The End of the Old Regime in Europe (1768–1776)* and *The End of the Old Regime in Europe (1776–1789).* Princeton, N.J.: Princeton University Press, 1989, 1991.

———. *Utopia and Reform in the Enlightenment.* Cambridge, U.K.: Cambridge University Press, 1971.

Michael C. Carhart

ENTELECHY. *See* **Development.**

ENVIRONMENT. The term *environment* became specialized beginning in about the 1960s to designate the context of human and animal groups, with a special emphasis on the natural world and its physical and vegetal components. Within this framework, the word took on an even more limited meaning and in the early twenty-first century refers primarily to the interaction between human and animal activity on the one hand and to humans and the natural world on the other, principally the impact of the former on the latter. In this context, "environment" is often linked with notions of habitat deterioration and species endangerment, and with appropriate responses to these threats, such as species recording and protection and natural-resource and habitat conservation. In a broader sense, however, *environment* refers to all elements (physical, biological, psychological, social, and cultural) that constitute the context in which life (vegetal, animal, and human) has evolved and continues to evolve. Four major components of this complex notion are taken into consideration here for their particular historical relevance and importance in Western culture: the notion of animism; materialist conceptualizations of environment (including diseases, medicines, and astrology); theological understandings; and contemporary approaches to the environment and environmental issues.

Early Environment and Animism

In addition to sustaining life, the environment has been a major factor in the shaping of life (vegetal, animal, and human) from its origins. For example, some plants produce chemical substances called alkaloids, known for their therapeutic properties; in some cases alkaloids have a toxic effect, interpreted as an adaptive response of the plant to a stress from the environment, specifically predation. Through their negative action on animal physiology (producing intestinal disturbance or even death), such substances aim at provoking an adaptive reaction in predators (avoidance of grazing), defending the plant species against animal aggressions and reducing the risk of or avoiding extinction.

Human beings are so deeply shaped by environment that not only their behavior but their individual physical characteristics have been interpreted as adaptive responses to environmental parameters. A science of the impact of external factors (including but not limited to the social environment) on individual physical features developed as early as the fourth century B.C.E. in ancient Greece; physiognomy dealt with the description and interpretation of individual physical characteristics. In its original form, it consisted in comparing human and animal characteristics, and in interpreting the former with respect to a resemblance to the latter. Although this science did not explicitly appear before the fourth century B.C.E., it certainly predates that time: already in Homer's *Iliad*, which related historical happenings dating back to the twelfth century B.C.E. and was probably written during the eighth century B.C.E., warriors are frequently compared to animals. In one of its most evolved forms, such theory aimed, principally with the Italian physician Cesare Lombroso (1836–1909), at predicting the behavior (especially deviant) of individuals on the basis of the observation, measurement, and type of their physical characteristics, as they were considered to be almost totally determined by environmental factors, particularly but not exclusively of a social and economic nature.

Although the earliest history of the conceptualization of environment cannot be reconstituted, anthropology throws some light on the subject by means of a comparison with contemporary Aboriginal societies. Australian Aborigines, for instance, believe that the environment was created by ancestor beings who are still living in the physico-geographical peculiarities they created (mountains, rivers, deserts, and so on). As a consequence, the environment cannot be modified, for it is charged with totemic value. Similarly, humans belong to and are shaped by their environment (not vice versa). This is so ingrained in Aboriginal thought that individuals consider that they cannot be separated from their territory.

Another approach is provided by analytic ethnobotany and ethnopharmacology—that is, the analysis of the constitution of botanical and pharmacological knowledge in the so-called traditional culture (in fact, non-Western ones). Discovery on the part of human beings of the properties of environmental constituents (for example, the nutritive and therapeutic value of plants) is interpreted as having occurred in two different and opposite ways in the general context of a learning theory by trial and error: (1) by biological transmission from animal to human (namely genetic vertical transmission in the tree of life);

or (2) by cultural acquisition through at least two possible procedures (neither of which is exclusive): human imitation of animal behavior (for example, that of bees gathering pollen), and human assessment of heads of poppy as remarkable influenced human cultivation of poppies for medicinal use.

Aboriginal thinking was not absent in the Western tradition. In the cultures of the Near East (Mesopotamia), human diseases were understood to be caused by spirits living in specific areas. Ponds, for instance, were supposedly inhabited by bad spirits generating illness, perhaps what a later age would determine to be malaria. Animistic conceptions of the environment lasted until the classical period, as the treatise *On Sacred Disease,* attributed by tradition to Hippocrates (c. 460–after 377 B.C.E.), shows: the author, probably a physician of the second half of the fifth century B.C.E., argued that epilepsy resulted not from spirit possession but from an internal physical malady.

Materialist Conceptualization and Pharmaceuticals

Within Western culture, materialist conceptions of the environment do not seem to take shape until the sixth century B.C.E. by the philosophers of the school of Miletus (in Asia Minor). From Thales (625?–?547 B.C.E.) to Anaximander (610–c. 547 B.C.E.) to Anaximenes (fl. c. 545 B.C.E.), these thinkers proposed to reduce the multiplicity of the world to its primary substance or *archê* (principle): water (in the case of Thales), air (Anaximenes), and an undetermined, eternal substance (*apeiron*) containing all contraries (Anaximander). It was Aristotle (384–322 B.C.E.) who fully transformed the environment into an object of study by introducing the concept of matter (*ulê*), which made it possible to conceptualize physical processes (from generation to transformation and movement). Significantly, the period from the sixth to the fourth centuries B.C.E. saw the first systematic inventories of all components of the world: physical geography with Anaximander and Hecataeus (sixth–fifth century B.C.E.) also from Miletus; human geography with Herodotus (c. 484–c. 420 B.C.E.); astronomy with Thales and Eudoxus of Cnidus (c. 400–c. 350 B.C.E.); zoology with Aristotle and his *Historia animalium* (Research on animals); botany and geology with Theophrastus (c. 372–c. 287 B.C.E.) in the *Historia plantarum* (Research on plants) and *De lapidibus* (On stones), respectively.

A fundamental question was the interaction between environment and humans, particularly health issues. The Hippocratic treatise *Airs, Waters, Places,* probably by the same author as *On Sacred Disease* (second half of the fifth century B.C.E.), is a study of the implications of environment on human health. The wealth of data provided in the work suggests that the idea was not new at the time, and indeed probably had a long history. The discussion centers on diseases and medicines (especially those made from plants). Diseases were attributed to two different, but possibly complementary, causes: internal disturbances (imbalance of the bodily components) and external effects of the environment. The latter was especially implicated in cases of contagious disease—epidemics, in the current meaning of the word—provoked by some corruption of the air, specifically material particles (the *miasmata*). As for medicines, their action was explained according to two systems, which perhaps developed chronologically: first, a physical immaterial property (heat or cold, for instance) was understood to be transmitted from the medicinal matter to the body. This system implicitly underpins the most important treatise on medicines of antiquity, *De materia medica* by the Greek Dioscorides (first century C.E.). Whatever its nature, such a property was conceived as a material element transmitted from the medicinal plant—for example, to the body—in a way that recalls an archaic conceptualization wherein an immaterial element is transmitted from environment to humans. The nature of the property to be introduced into the body was determined by the nature of the disease, and was intended to compensate for a deficiency according to the principle of allotherapy (*contraria contrariis*). In this way, the environment allowed a return to the natural state of the body.

In a more abstract and probably successive phase, the action of medicines (including plants) was conceived as an exchange of atoms (considered as small indivisible particles, not the atoms of contemporary science). Such a system, which was rooted in atomistic thinking and its medical application, so-called methodism (first century B.C.E.), was best represented by the Greek physician Galen (129–after 216 C.E.). Although more elaborated (since it could account for a wider range of properties), such explanation relied at the end on the same idea as the previous—that is, an exchange between environment and human physiology—with the idea of reestablishing the natural equilibrium of the body. Dioscorides's system, which was most probably not devised by him but utilized anterior knowledge, included a classification of environmental materials ranked so as to form a hierarchy from positively connoted elements to their opposite, with a gradual loss of qualities according to the principle of entropy. Such a classification reflected the history of the world as narrated in the account of the four ages of humankind. According to ancient tales, humankind passed through four ages (from gold to silver, bronze, and eventually iron), each of which corresponded to a degradation of humans' environment and living conditions. Iron era, the present one, is characterized by work, sufferance, and death. Evolution was seen as regressive, not dynamic as in nineteenth-century Darwinian theory, where evolution proceeds by adaptation to changing circumstances and, consecutively, by selection.

Environment and Theology

Astrology presented a special case of the relationship between the environment and health. According to the archaic theory of the symbiosis of environment and humans, planets were among the elements that exerted an influence on individuals, particularly one's health and the course of one's life. Such a system, already attested in Babylonia at the end of the sixth century B.C.E., was transformed in the Greek world from the fourth century B.C.E. onward, with the development of scientific (observational and explanatory) astronomy: as the passage of planets across the sky was predictable, so was their action on the human body. At the end of the fourth century B.C.E., astronomic astrology encountered Eastern and Egyptian religions (where celestial bodies were personalized and venerated as divinities), particularly with the expedition of Alexander the

Great (356–323 B.C.E.) to Persia and India, the conquest and occupation of Egypt, and the creation of Alexandria (332 B.C.E.). Astrology had a new meaning: from its abstract mathematical form, it was personalized and transformed into a religion-like practice, in which the action of divinities—that is, of elements of the world—could be solicited and guided to a determined target, provided that ritual forms were duly followed.

Such para-religious practices, which were not incompatible with the official forms of religion of the Hellenistic and Roman world, collided with Christianity. Following the Jewish tradition, indeed, the new religion conceived the world as God's creation. A new literary genre appeared as early as the fourth century C.E., the *Hexaemeron* (The account of the six days [of creation]), which narrated the whole process of Creation, from the universe to humankind, including the paradisiacal environment. Similarly, a new anthropology developed, first represented by Nemesius of Emesa (fourth/fifth centuries C.E.). Creation included a hierarchy at the top of which was human beings, who had been created in God's image. In this context, there was no place for evolution: Creation was perfect, all the more because the negative forces of the world had been defeated. Humans were entrusted with the mission of governing and preserving the world, because humans were a reflection of God's wisdom. This theological concept had an impact on such scientific questions as the causes of disease and the origin of the therapeutic properties of plants and other natural substances. Neither resulted from natural causes: diseases were inflicted by God as punishment of sins, and plants were curative owing to the grace of God. The materialistic system was abandoned in favor of that proposed by Galen, which was much more compatible with the Christian understanding of the environment, due to its immaterial nature. As a result of this new vision of the world, human beings' relationship with the environment was no longer direct, but mediated through God. Such a triangular understanding, which lasted until the seventeenth century at least, did not prevent, however, humans from studying and knowing the world: such an undertaking reflected human beings' nature as God's creation. The study and contemplation of the environment, and the exploitation of its resources, became occasions for individuals to discover and adhere to the plan of God.

Contemporary Approaches

From the Renaissance onward, the idea of the environment underwent several successive and rapid transformations. The natural world became a sphere of aesthetic feeling and theist religiosity; it could restore well-being and reflect as well as be imbued with human emotion. It became an object of positivist study and exploitation for human economic activity during the industrial revolution and afterward. In the twentieth century, understanding of the environment was shaped by a broad range of factors such as extensive farming and overexploitation of natural resources; the systematic screening of floras in search of new molecules with previously unknown therapeutic activity; global transportation favoring the transfer of plants and animals into nonnative habitats, where they become invasive, threatening native biota; and the escalation in the size of industrial plants and commercial vectors. The latter concern is related to such major environmental catastrophes as the oil spill of the supertanker *Torrey Canyon* off the coast of England in 1967, and of a spill by the *Amoco Cadiz* almost ten years later (1978) affecting the beaches of France and England; the emission of a vapor cloud containing toxic dioxin after a chemical facility explosion in Seveso, Italy, in 1976; the partial meltdown of an atomic reactor at Three Mile Island in the United States in 1979; and the explosion of a similar reactor at Chernobyl, in Ukraine, in 1986.

The absence of preventive regulations and of policies to compensate for damages to persons and the environment after such disasters, in addition to advances in genetic engineering enabling modifications in nature, and globalization, creating a feeling of ubiquity and a common model of thought, contributed during the last decades of the twentieth century to initiatives addressing uncontrolled technological development and the dangers posed to the environment. The modern ideology of continuous and cumulative advances in technological civilization and hence of social well-being came into question, with lingering concerns that history does not necessarily lead to a better future. This was accompanied by the notion that social and technological progress had led to humans being cut off from their environment. Perhaps in reaction to this feeling, an avid search for connection began, for a recovery of a direct and personal contact with nature, a reengagement with traditional environmental values. Such a return took several different forms and affected many if not all areas of contemporary societies in developed countries, from scientific research in traditional (natural) medicines, for instance, to repatriation programs, to protection of the intellectual property of local, namely traditional, communities on the uses of natural substances, to large-scale international agreements such as the Convention on Biological Diversity (1992). "Ecotourism," environmental management, and sustainable development were all concepts aimed at leaving to future generations a healthy and viable world.

See also **Animism; Bioethics; Evolution; Materialism in Eighteenth-Century European Thought; Nature; Religion; Science: Overview; Technology.**

BIBLIOGRAPHY

Black, Jeremy, and Anthony Green. *Gods, Demons, and Symbols of Ancient Mesopotamia: An Illustrated Dictionary.* Austin: University of Texas Press, 1992.

Chadwick, Derek J., and Joan Marsh, eds. *Ethnobotany and the Search for New Drugs.* Chichester, U.K.: Wiley, 1994. An overview of current research methods and approaches.

Convention on Biological Diversity. Available at http://www.biodiv.org/convention/articles.asp.

Dubos, René. "Environment." In *Dictionary of the History of Ideas: Studies of Selected Pivotal Ideas.* Edited by Philip P. Wiener. Vol. 2. New York: Scribners, 1973.

Fritz, Robert S., and Ellen L. Simms, eds. *Plant Resistance to Herbivores and Pathogens: Ecology, Evolution, and Genetics.* Chicago and London: University of Chicago Press, 1992.

Johns, Timothy. *The Origins of Human Diet and Medicine: Chemical Ecology.* Tucson: University of Arizona Press, 1996. On the adaptive responses of plants to stresses from the environment, including the process of domestication.

Larchet, Jean-Claude. *Théologie de la maladie.* Paris: Editions du Cerf, 1991.

Robic, Marie-Claire et al., eds. *Du milieu à l'environnement: Pratiques et représentations du rapport homme/nature depuis la Renaissance.* Paris: Economica, 1992.

Rumsey, Alan, and James Weiner, eds. *Emplaced Myth: Space, Narrative, and Knowledge in Aboriginal Australia and Papua New Guinea.* Honolulu: University of Hawaii Press, 2001.

Schultes, Richard Evans, and Siri von Reis, eds. *Ethnobotany: Evolution of a Discipline.* Portland, Ore.: Dioscorides, 1995. A selection of readings.

Touwaide, Alain. "Therapeutic Strategies: Drugs." In *Western Medical Thought from Antiquity to the Middle Ages,* edited by Mirko D. Grmek. Cambridge, Mass., and London: Harvard University Press, 1998.

Whorton, James C. *Nature Cures: The History of Alternative Medicine in America.* Oxford and New York: Oxford University Press, 2002.

Alain Touwaide

ENVIRONMENTAL ETHICS. Environmental ethics emerged as a subdiscipline of philosophical ethics in the early 1970s, following the first Earth Day in 1970 and a sharply increased awareness of environmental problems at that time. Courses began appearing in university curricula, and books, articles, and journals proliferated to meet the growing interest. To judge by student demand and university courses and programs, environmental ethics is today a mature and robust subject. To judge by intellectual content, however, it is still in the early stages of development.

Antecedents

The intellectual sources of environmental ethics go back at least to God's first injunction in Genesis 1:28: "Be fruitful, and multiply, and replenish the earth, and subdue it: and have dominion over the fish of the sea, and over the fowl of the air, and over every living thing that moveth upon the earth." Literary discussions of the value of nature in the West, having been stimulated by global exploration and the European discovery of the Americas, go back at least to the sixteenth century. Wilderness began to appear as an allegorical theme in European and American painting in the eighteenth century. The awesome forces of nature remind us that the human condition demands the virtues of faith, hard work, and steadfastness as we negotiate the path of our lives on earth. These writings and images of course helped shape the themes of contemporary environmental ethics, and today's writers also pay homage to Ralph Waldo Emerson (1803–1882), Henry David Thoreau (1817–1862), and the views of early-twentieth-century writers like Gifford Pinchot (1865–1946) and John Muir (1838–1914).

Of these early sources for environmental ethics, none is more significant than Aldo Leopold (1887–1948), an ecologist and wildlife manager who in his essays argued the need to reconsider our attitude toward nature. Writing in *A Sand County Almanac* (1949), his frequently cited classic of American nature writing, Leopold bemoaned the fact that, as it appeared to him, "there is as yet no ethic dealing with man's relation to land and to the animals and plants which grow upon it," and called for an evolutionary shift in what he viewed as the traditional perspective in ethics. "All ethics so far evolved rest upon a single premise: that the individual is a member of a community of interdependent parts. His instincts prompt him to compete for his place in that community, but his ethics prompt him also to cooperate" (pp. 203–204). Arguments for cooperation in ethics, however, had been limited in scope to other humans. Leopold urged his readers to think about co-operation in a more expansive sense, which would include the environment. This land ethic, as he called it, "simply enlarges the boundaries of the community to include soils, waters, plants, and animals, or collectively: the land." Without much defense or argument, Leopold went on to formulate some basic principles of a land ethic, but his influence on later writers comes mainly from his vision that enlarging the scope of ethical concern is a mark of intellectual progress.

The Debate over Anthropocentrism

Following Leopold's suggestion, the central issue in the first quarter century of environmental ethics has been a debate about anthropocentrism and the idea of intrinsic ethical value. Traditional ethical theories are characterized as anthropocentric because they regard only humans or human experience (or reason) as having intrinsic ethical worth. Everything else is valuable only as a means to promoting or enhancing human interests. For Aristotle, this much is obvious. "Clearly, then, we must suppose . . . that plants are for the sake of animals, and that other animals are for the sake of human beings. . . . If then nature makes nothing incomplete or pointless, it must have made all of them for the sake of human beings" (*Politics*, 1256b15–22) John Locke, writing in the seventeenth century, reflected the consensus view when he spoke of the distinction between man and nature. Mankind is "the workmanship of one omnipotent, and infinitely wise maker," and thus the law of nature teaches us that man "has not the liberty to destroy himself," and that "no one ought to harm another in his life, health, liberty, or possessions" (*Second Treatise of Government*, chap. 2, par. 6). But reason also tells us that, "land that is left wholly to nature, that hath no improvement of pasturage, tillage, or planting, is called, as indeed it is, *waste*; and we shall find the benefit of it amount to little more than nothing" (chap. 5, par. 42). For land to have value, it must be made to serve human needs and ends.

The classical utilitarians were the first to move explicitly beyond anthropocentrism. They argued that sentience was the locus of intrinsic value, and thus the ultimate ethical end was an existence "exempt as far as possible from pain, and as rich as possible in enjoyments." Morality consists of "rules and precepts," as John Stuart Mill (1806–1873) put it in his *Utilitarianism* (1861). Its aim is to secure such an existence "to all mankind; and not to them only, but, so far as the nature of things admits, to the whole sentient creation" (chap. 2). Although utilitarianism may provide a basis for rejecting an-

thropocentrism, it will not get us to anything resembling a land ethic. Even if sentience is a sufficient basis for gaining intrinsic worth or value, it gives us no reason for regarding endangered species, forests, wilderness, or ecosystems as worth preserving in their own right. Thus, philosophers who follow Leopold have rejected utilitarianism along with anthropocentric conceptions of ethics.

The problem with extending the scope of morality beyond sentience is to explain the basis for attributing intrinsic value to entities that have no inner lives and are not subjects of experience. Two ways of attempting this extension figure most prominently in the literature. The first is to identify intrinsic value with having an interest, which is interpreted in turn as having an end or a natural good. If it makes sense to say of any thing that it has an end, then we can make sense of talking about what is good or bad for that thing. And just as sentient beings have an interest in not suffering, all living things, sentient and nonsentient alike, have an interest in realizing their natural ends. It is in this sense good for any such thing to thrive (Goodpaster).

One objection to extending the scope of intrinsic ethical value in this way is that the idea of having an end or a natural good applies to more than living organisms. This might appear to be a good thing for the purposes of developing environmental ethics in the direction of a land ethic, because it would allow us to include entities like species and ecosystems within the community of intrinsically valuable beings. An ecosystem is not a living organism, but it has a good (however difficult it may be to determine it), which it is in its interest to realize. The problem is that this analysis does not allow us to discriminate among living things to exclude deadly viruses or invasive species from having intrinsic moral worth, nor does it allow us to discriminate among other nonliving entities with ends, such as gangs, terrorist cells, or corrupt political regimes. Each of these has ends and an interest in thriving, but surely they do not all have intrinsic moral worth.

A second objection to this proposal is that it equivocates on the morally relevant concept of an interest. Utilitarians extend the idea of intrinsic moral worth to sentient creatures because nonhuman animals not only have an interest in avoiding suffering, they can act in ways that show that they take an interest in seeking enjoyment and avoiding pain. If human suffering is morally relevant not merely because we are capable of suffering but because as conscious agents we care about or take an interest in avoiding suffering, then nonhuman suffering should be morally relevant for the same reason. But when we talk about the interests of nonsentient entities (and perhaps the interests of many species of lower animals, such as sponges or clams), we do so in a different sense. They may *have* interests, but they cannot *take* an interest in anything. It begs the question to suppose that having an interest in any sense that does not presuppose subjectivity or consciousness has any moral relevance of its own.

A second way to reject anthropocentrism and extend the scope of intrinsic ethical value beyond sentience is associated with deep ecology, a political movement that emerged in the

1980s in response to disillusionment with large, well-funded environmental groups that some critics saw as having been co-opted by prevailing political powers. The "shallow ecology" of these large environmental organizations, in the eyes of their critics, was associated exclusively with the fight against pollution and resource depletion, which were seen as elitist and anthropocentric goals of affluent classes living in developed countries. Deep ecology defends the idea of ecocentric identification, a form of self-realization, which calls on us humans to see ourselves not at the top of creation but as merely one part of the "web of life," on an equal footing with every other part. The deep ecology manifesto claims that nonhuman life has value in itself that is "independent of the usefulness of the nonhuman world for human purposes" (Devall and Sessions, p. 70) If a living, free-flowing river is a good thing to have on this planet, then it is good independently of human existence and interests, and it would equally be a good thing on a planet that never hosted conscious life.

Leaving political agendas aside, many people who have sympathy for Leopold's land ethic find deep ecology an unsatisfying way to develop the idea. It is one thing to believe that traditional conceptions of ethics have perhaps wrongly viewed nature as having no value except as resources for human satisfaction. It is quite a different matter to think that the only alternative to such a conception of ethics is ecocentric identification in the sense demanded by deep ecology.

Value as a Feature of Actions and Attitudes

Early in the twentieth century, G. E. Moore (1873–1958) argued that goodness was a nonnatural property that good things possessed, and although his arguments for this view have had a profound influence on the course of ethical theory, the view itself is not widely accepted (chaps. 1–3). There seems no satisfactory way to resolve disagreements over what things have this property or how to act and make tradeoffs when necessary. Should we preserve the redwood trees, or clear them to make room for the weeds that will thrive in their place? It will not do to identify ethical value with the products of evolution or natural processes, for humans are natural creatures and our creations are in some sense as much a part of nature as fossils and spider webs. What makes the forest more valuable in its own right than the strip malls along the highway? The idea that value is a nonnatural intrinsic property of things is mysterious, and many philosophers simply reject Moore's intuitions about what has it and what does not. Nor could the existence of such value in itself tell us much about what to do or how to act and choose. These same issues arise for deep ecology and for any attempt to move beyond anthropocentrism in locating intrinsic ethical value.

If we think about value as something we express in our actions and attitudes, rather than as an intrinsic property of objects, then the difference between anthropocentrism and its opposite seems smaller and less significant. For even those who insist that value originates in reasons and attitudes are quick to acknowledge that we value different parts of the world in different ways and for a multitude of reasons. This includes valuing things other than humans, human experiences, and reason as ends. We can realize Leopold's vision of

a land ethic without rejecting anthropocentrism, by concentrating instead on the reasons we have for attitudes toward nature that see it as worth preserving in its own right. Thinking of nature as a resource for our use in promoting human enjoyment is of course one attitude we may have, and thinking about the effects of environmental change on human health is another. But we also find it reasonable to adopt attitudes of appreciation, reverence, awe, love, and fear toward different parts of the world around us, and the appropriateness of these attitudes moreover seems to be connected intimately to other aspects of morality, such as the virtues of humility and gratitude (Hill).

Ethics and Environmental Policies

The appropriateness and implications of these attitudes give rise to other substantive issues in environmental ethics because they imply that it is reasonable to value different parts of nature in ways that go beyond the distinction between valuing something instrumentally and valuing it as an end. Thus, one topic in environmental ethics concerns the appropriateness of using decision-making techniques developed by economists for determining environmental policies. These techniques are enormously flexible, and they include regarding aspects of the environment as having existence value as well as use value. But these techniques in the end measure values in terms of a willingness to pay for different levels and kinds of protection. They assume that environmental values are commensurable, but it remains an open question in environmental ethics whether this is true. Distinguishing between use value, existence value, and the addition of other values that can be measured by these techniques may also fail to address the appropriate ways to express reverence or respect, and these are the kinds of attitudes that some people believe a reasonable land ethic demands.

A related topic in environmental ethics concerns the way we interpret the value of ecosystems. An endangered ecosystem, or an endangered species within an ecosystem, may be valued differently according to whether we think of an ecosystem only as providing useful services or also as worth preserving in its own right. Debates on this issue go to the meaning of environmental protection and to the reasonableness of some statutes like the Endangered Species Act.

At least three other kinds of substantive issues have emerged recently as major topics in environmental ethics. One has to do with the nature of environmental risk of the kind one finds in issues surrounding possible climate change and global warming. What are rational decision procedures in areas involving great uncertainties but also possibilities of very large consequences and irreversible changes? Should we be aiming to maximize expected values, or should we be trying instead to develop and apply more precautionary principles? A second issue has to do with depleting nonrenewable environmental resources. What are our obligations as stewards of the environment to future generations, and what do we regard as appropriate substitutions for the resources we deplete, so that we can protect the environment in a sustainable way? A third issue concerns environmental justice. Do we need special principles of distributive justice to ensure that economically disadvantaged or politically vulnerable populations do not bear unfair environmental burdens?

These issues are often addressed by writers who express little concern with the philosophically more basic questions about the nature of environmental values, but as discussion of these substantive issues proceeds, it usually leads back to basic questions in ethical theory. For these reasons, environmental ethics is not only a popular and apparently permanent part of university curricula, it is also a subject that increasingly draws the attention of philosophers who are concerned with the more basic and theoretical parts of their subject.

See also **Ecology; Nature; Wildlife.**

BIBLIOGRAPHY

Crocker, David A., and Toby Linden, eds. *Ethics of Consumption: The Good Life, Justice, and Global Stewardship.* Lanham, Md.: Rowman and Littlefield, 1998.

Devall, Bill, and George Sessions. *Deep Ecology.* Salt Lake City: G. M. Smith, 1985.

Feinberg, Joel. "The Rights of Animals and Unborn Generations." In *Philosophy and Environmental Crisis,* edited by William T. Blackstone, 43–68. Athens: University of Georgia Press, 1974.

Goodpaster, Kenneth. "On Being Morally Considerable." *Journal of Philosophy,* 75, no. 6 (1978): 308–325.

Hill, Thomas E., Jr., "Ideals of Human Excellence and Preserving Natural Environments." *Environmental Ethics* 5 (1983): 211–224.

Leopold, Aldo. *A Sand County Almanac, and Sketches Here and There.* New York: Oxford University Press, 1949. Reprint, 1987.

Naess, Arne. "The Shallow and the Deep, Long-Range Ecology Movement. A Summary." *Inquiry* 16 (1973): 95–100.

Nash, Roderick, *Wilderness and the American Mind.* 3rd ed. New Haven, Conn.: Yale University Press, 1982.

Plumwood, Val. *Feminism and the Mastery of Nature.* London and New York: Routledge, 1993.

Rolston, Holmes, III. "Values in and Duties to the Natural World." In *Ecology, Economics, Ethics: The Broken Circle,* edited by F. Herbert Bormann and Stephen R. Kellert, 73–96. New Haven, Conn.: Yale University Press, 1991.

Singer, Peter. "The Environment" In his *Practical Ethics,* 264–288. 2nd ed. Cambridge, U.K., and New York: Cambridge University Press, 1993.

Sober, Elliott. "Philosophical Problems for Environmentalism." In *The Preservation of Species: The Value of Biological Diversity,* edited by Bryan Norton, 173–194. Princeton, N.J.: Princeton University Press, 1986.

Douglas Maclean

ENVIRONMENTAL HISTORY. Environmental history is the study of the changing affairs of humans within the natural world. This definition, in contrast to other useful phrasings, such as the study of "interactions between humans and nature" (Merchant, 2002, p. xv), embodies a fundamental, not merely semantic, point of emphasis. First, and obviously, humans are part of nature, biological organisms subject to the laws of physics and biology. More importantly, hu-

mankind must be situated within natural processes because, not only do they affect human societies and economies, but human actions increasingly influence natural processes. In the past one hundred years and more, human transformation and degradation of the environment has grown to such proportions that humanity fondly imagines it is liberated from physical limitations and controls nature. It does not. What people need, instead, is an accurate view of their place in nature. Environmental history is a powerful tool for gaining knowledge that can secure humanity's future.

Certain key characteristics of the relatively new field of environmental history, especially its parameters and achievements, can be apprehended in a number of ways: by describing its emergence since the 1970s as a coherent subfield of historical inquiry; identifying the range of interests pursued by environmental historians; assessing the crucial importance of interdisciplinary methods in its practice; considering how environment intersects with gender as an analytical category; and discussing the interplay of different genres and narrative strategies, and the progressive expansion of scale in individual studies.

Development of the Field
Environmental history seemingly burst into view in the scholarly world in the 1970s. Intellectual and political trends, such as the controversy over Rachel Carson's *Silent Spring* (1962) and the first Earth Day (1970), motivated many historians to explore historical aspects of environmental problems. But there were important precursors to the developments of the 1970s, even though this research derived from other specialties and was not explicitly conceived as environmental history. Samuel P. Hays's *Conservation and the Gospel of Efficiency* (1959) was a landmark work on environmental politics, and Roderick Nash's *Wilderness and the American Mind* (1967) carefully documented evolving perceptions of nature as embodied in wilderness in the United States. Walter Prescott Webb and James Malin produced even earlier work on the Great Plains, which are now acknowledged as pioneering environmental histories, though their primary impact only came later. Influential work by Marc Bloch, Fernand Braudel, and other French historians of the Annales school (founded 1929) inspired others to look anew at agricultural landscapes and the broader role of geography in human affairs.

From the 1940s, the Berkeley school of historical demographers (including historians Woodrow Borah and Lesley Simpson, physiologist Sherburne Cook, and geographer Carl Sauer) initiated the study of Indian population decline in colonial Mexico and the related topics of economic stagnation, land exploitation, and soil erosion. But among the most important contributors to this "prehistory" of environmental historiography were historically minded researchers who were not professional historians, such as geographers Sauer and Clarence Glacken and scientists such as Carson and Aldo Leopold, as well as unclassifiable intellectuals such as Lewis Mumford. By the mid-1970s, with the founding of the American Society for Environmental History and its journal, *Environmental Review* (now *Environmental History*), a distinct field of inquiry had emerged, making it almost impossible to discuss the environment without referring often to the substantial contributions of history.

What Is Environmental History?

A coherent definition helps one understand environmental history. The field emerges still more clearly when considering its range and subject matter, including the prominent issues raised in public discourse on the environment—land degradation, air and water pollution and waste disposal, wildlife conservation and wilderness preservation—but its importance goes beyond simply adding time-depth to current political debates. Environmental history encompasses a holistic view of history through the human–nature nexus, and, while not all history is environmental, the field has quite broad parameters. A recent list of topics in U.S. environmental history applies well, with modifications, to global concerns:

  modes of living and patterns of natural resource use of indigenous peoples in the Eastern and Western hemispheres;

  ideas, plants, animals, diseases, people, and production systems transplanted or encountered by European colonizers and entrepreneurs;

  interactions between genders and racial and ethnic groups vying for control of resources;

  practices, regulations, and laws used to manage the land;

  effects of industrialization and urbanization in creating environmental problems;

  ideas about nature and humans' place in it; and

  struggles to direct or moderate the impacts of economic development (Merchant, 2002, p. xiv).

Environmental historians also address issues specific to particular places and times, and in this endeavor they are strongly influenced both by historic and current events. The African droughts and famines of 1968 to 1974 and 1984 to 1985 drew attention to the history of famine and food supply, and highlighted the importance of fluctuations in global climate related to El Niño episodes (the periodic warming of ocean currents in the South Pacific), which helped account for still earlier droughts. The post-Columbian collapse of Native American populations brought on by European-introduced diseases inspired fierce debates and research on this unprecedented catastrophe, and on the history of disease in general. Asia's densely populated agrarian landscapes and ancient cities shaped historians' interest in agricultural ecology, irrigation systems, and patterns of urban production and consumption. Few of these issues are exclusive to one area: they point to the necessity of addressing variations in the historical experience of different regions and indicate the broad scope of environmental history.

Richard White's overview of environmental history shows how the field has expanded. While early studies often focused on ideas about nature or political struggles over conservation, partly because of abundant data in the written sources tradi-

tionally available to historians, White speculated on future developments in environmental history. After twenty years, one major trend is clear: the proliferation of studies that document and analyze the actual processes of ecological change occurring around the world. Environmental historians have not abandoned their interest in politics and philosophy; they increasingly link them in suggestive ways to interpret observable transformations. Carolyn Merchant formulates a promising synthesis with her theory of ecological revolutions, which are

  major transformations in human relations with nonhuman nature. They arise from changes, tensions, and contradictions that develop between a society's mode of production and ecology, and between its modes of production and reproduction. These dynamics, in turn, support the acceptance of new forms of consciousness, ideas, images, and worldviews. (1989, pp. 2–3)

Her New England study identified colonial and capitalist ecological revolutions, and posited a coming global ecological revolution, offering hope for a sustainable world. Searching everywhere for the same sequence of revolutions would be problematic; in much of Africa and Asia, for instance, capitalism arrived before formal colonialism. But the general concept of ecological revolutions is a valuable one, and has been applied elsewhere (see Jacobs, p. 75).

Interdisciplinary Methods

As the preceding discussion indicates, environmental history draws on an array of disciplines for data, research methods, analytical frameworks, and theoretical insight. Like other historians, environmental historians still rely on written evidence for primary source material. But their subject matter, emphasizing the role of nonhuman nature in human history, requires them to look beyond written records, which contribute so much to history, because for many times and places the physical environment is sparsely documented. Those conventional sources that do exist may not readily yield answers to the questions asked of them, compelling researchers to turn to other disciplines for interpretive assistance. Anthropology, ecology, economics, epidemiology, geography, philosophy, political science, religion, sociology, the history of technology, and women's studies all make vital contributions to understanding the history of humans within nature. Environmental history developed out of necessity as a kind of "interdisciplinary discipline," and it remains so at the start of the twenty-first century, albeit with most practitioners identifying themselves as historians.

Some environmental historians initially drew on ecology, in particular, to enhance their work, attracted by its holistic conception of the earth as a web of organic relationships. In practice it has proven difficult to apply concepts derived from the sciences to human history directly, with all its messy indeterminacy, contingency, and unpredictability. Geography probably did more to shape the field by documenting changing patterns of settlement, land use, and alterations in landscape itself. Field scientists, geographers, and anthropologists inspired the strong commitment to field research that distinguishes environmental history from other kinds of history. As

R. H. Tawney famously observed, "What historians need is not more documents but stronger boots" (quoted in Hancock, p. 95). His point was more about engaging with the wider world, but some historians responded literally by pulling on boots and exploring the great outdoors.

Anthropology's fieldwork methods, particularly participant observation, increasingly influenced environmental historians, who took up extended residence in the communities and environments they studied and learned how people actually utilized and interacted with nonhuman nature. Such fieldwork, including data from oral interviews with informants, opened new avenues of inquiry, especially in regions like Africa, the Americas, and other places where literacy either developed relatively recently or reflected the experiences of dominant political and economic actors (Jacobs; Moore and Vaughan). The most fruitful approaches combine written sources with the results of community-based fieldwork.

Environment and Gender

One sign that environmental history is still an evolving field is an awareness of gaps in coverage of its subject matter. As William Cronon notes, environmental historians need to do more "to probe below the level of the group to explore the implications of social division. . . . In the face of social history's classic categories of gender, race, class, and ethnicity, environmental history stands much more silent than it should" (cited in Jacobs, p. 17). It is not enough to document the role of irrigated rice production in South Asian economies, Americans' changing perceptions of nature, or the benefits to Argentina of commercial wheat and beef production. One must always ask who dug or maintained irrigation works and who appropriated the harvest; who wrote and read books on wilderness; and which Argentines owned or worked the fields and factories.

Analyzing class and race or ethnic relations in these and other settings clearly strengthens environmental history, as recent studies show. Perhaps the most crucial analytical category for environmental history is gender, and not only because this "minority" actually comprises a majority of humankind. Past discussions of gender and environment mythologized men as hunters or exploiters of nature and females as mothers, nurturers, and protectors of nature, with the latter an especially problematic class- and race-based notion. Merchant provides much data on women's work in New England agriculture and industry, but this issue emerges still more clearly when examining the lives of women beyond modern Europe and America. For the vast majority of non-Western women, living with nature involves hard, unrelenting work: fetching water and wood for fuel, growing and preparing food, craft and commodity production to generate income, in addition to the demands of childcare. Enjoying nature's beauty is an unaffordable luxury in such circumstances. One recent study does much to bridge the gap in understanding by revealing the history of women in U.S. national parks, with a strong oral history component linking their activities as tourists and conservation advocates to professional careers as National Park Service employees. As Kaufman shows, accurately reconstructing past lives requires using sophisticated and multilayered levels of analysis.

Genre, Scale, and Narrative

In what form does environmental history scholarship reach its audience? The choice of unit of study influences research and writing. This is often geographical, such as a national park, river valley, dam, region, or individual city, but can be an idea like environmentalism or an occupation such as hunting; detailed case studies presented in research monographs and articles comprise the most common publications. Despite occasional misgivings among practitioners, the case study is the essential building block for knowledge in environmental history. The need for in-depth research, using archives, field exploration, oral history, and expertise in related disciplines helps keep projects within manageable size. Singling out any particular book discriminates against numerous other fine case studies, but Nancy Jacobs's *Environment, Power, and Injustice* (2003), on the Kuruman region in South Africa, realizes much of environmental history's potential in exploring the connections between nature, race, class, gender, state power, and economic development.

Some of the most exciting environmental histories synthesize primary data and case studies to expose crucial connections between regions or events previously examined in isolation. Alfred Crosby's excellent *The Columbian Exchange* (1972) shows how exchanges of people, plants, animals, and germs between Eastern and Western hemispheres shaped their history. His *Ecological Imperialism* (1986) extended that analysis with the concepts of "demographic takeover" of Neo-Europes (including North America, Australia, New Zealand, Argentina, and Uruguay), though his earlier emphasis on mutual exchanges between colonizers and colonized is missing. Richard Grove's many publications on the history of environmentalism break new ground by showing the development of environmental thinking in Europe's island colonies such as Mauritius, St. Helena, and the Caribbean, and also India and South Africa. His work extends the search for environmentalism's roots beyond U.S. intellectual history, though the issue of whose influence was first and greatest is best viewed in terms of multilinear intellectual evolution. Such works conceived on a global scale seem well suited to making connections between human activity and nonhuman nature over time.

Environmental histories often have a characteristic structure, a declension narrative, or story of decline and degradation. The facts of ecological change and nature's devastation by humans provide ample evidence of destruction, but historians increasingly recognize the need for more conscious choice in telling such stories. Describing the replacement of indigenous species by exotic invaders, for instance, as a process of decline, let alone in terms of good or bad, reveals an implicit value system. Do people destroy nature or improve on it? Cronon's analysis of soil erosion in 1930s America shows how the same events can be variously interpreted, depending on how one perceives change. Part of the burden originates in assumptions that major historical processes, such as the spread of capitalism or colonialism, are inherently wrong, yet even Karl Marx viewed capitalism as a progressive force, creating as much as it destroyed. In Cronon's words, "At its best, historical storytelling keeps us morally engaged with the world by showing us how to care about it and its origins in ways we had not done before" (p. 1375; also see McCann). The challenge is to avoid unknowingly smuggling one's moral values into a narrative under the guise of objectivity.

Present and Future Prospects

An accurate conclusion requires a dose of realism. In spite of its numerous contributions and the respect accorded to individual practitioners, environmental history has not taken over the historical profession. Some other historians continue to view it as marginal, even trendy, though an endeavor that flourishes for decades surely constitutes more than a "trend." The finite influence of intellectuals in public discourse, notably in the United States, amplifies this marginalization, as does any public perception that environmental regulation entails job losses or lower standards of living. Unlike disciplines such as economics or public health, history is more suited to reflection, not solving practical problems, so a presentist quest for utility or "relevance" remains a lesser priority.

Despite these caveats, environmental history helps to educate an informed citizenry. Contemporary environmental challenges are not going away, and will likely worsen in the twenty-first century: a global capitalist economy that neglects environmental and social costs of maximizing profits; a growing and aging human population that everywhere aspires to higher material standards of living; sharper conflicts over access to increasingly depleted critical resources such as water, land, food, and sources of energy. These and other potential crises must be confronted if humans are to sustain life on the planet. One is left hoping, as Merchant suggests, that a global ecological revolution in thought and behavior is on the horizon, and environmental history has a part to play in this transformation.

See also **Development; Ecology; Environment; Environmental Ethics; Nature; Science; Wildlife.**

BIBLIOGRAPHY

Arnold, David, and Ramachandra Guha, eds. *Nature, Culture, Imperialism: Essays on the Environmental History of South Asia.* Delhi, India: Oxford University Press, 1995.

Cronon, William. "A Place for Stories: Nature, History, and Narrative." *Journal of American History* 78 (1992): 1347–1376.

Crosby, Alfred W. *The Columbian Exchange: Biological and Cultural Consequences of 1492.* Westport, Conn.: Greenwood, 1972.

———. *Ecological Imperialism: The Biological Expansion of Europe, 900–1900 A.D.* Cambridge, U.K., and New York: Cambridge University Press, 1986.

Grove, Richard H. *Green Imperialism: Colonial Expansion, Tropical Island Edens, and the Origins of Environmentalism, 1600–1860.* Cambridge, U.K., and New York: Cambridge University Press, 1995.

Hancock, W. K. *Country and Calling.* London: Faber and Faber, 1954.

Jacobs, Nancy J. *Environment, Power, and Injustice: A South African History.* Cambridge, U.K., and New York: Cambridge University Press, 2003.

Kaufman, Polly Welts. *National Parks and the Woman's Voice: A History.* Albuquerque: University of New Mexico Press, 1996.

McCann, James C. *Green Land, Brown Land, Black Land: An Environmental History of Africa, 1800–1990.* Portsmouth, N.H.: Heinemann, 1999.

Merchant, Carolyn. *The Columbia Guide to American Environmental History.* New York: Columbia University Press, 2002.

———. *Ecological Revolutions: Nature, Gender and Science in New England.* Chapel Hill and London: University of North Carolina Press, 1989.

Moore, Henrietta L., and Megan Vaughan. *Cutting Down Trees: Gender, Nutrition, and Agricultural Change in the Northern Province of Zambia, 1890–1990.* Portsmouth, N.H.: Heinemann, 1994.

White, Richard. "American Environmental History: The Development of a New Historical Field." *Pacific Historical Review* 54 (1985): 297–335.

Thomas Pyke Johnson

EPICUREANISM. Epicureanism gets its name from Epicurus (341–270 B.C.E.), who founded his philosophical school (The Garden) in 306 B.C.E. at Athens. Epicureanism emerged at roughly the same time as Stoicism, which was founded by Zeno of Citium (c. 335–c. 263 B.C.E.) and developed by Chrysippus of Soli (c. 280–206 B.C.E.). Epicureanism was introduced into Rome in the early second century B.C.E. where it caught the attention of Cicero (106–43 B.C.E.) and also the poet Lucretius (c. 96–c. 55 B.C.E.), who wrote *De rerum natura* in an effort to explain Epicureanism. Horace (65–8 B.C.E.) and Virgil (70–19 B.C.E.) were also notably associated with Epicureanism.

Epicureanism, as an acceptable metaphysical viewpoint, was suppressed once Christianity began to experience some success by the second century C.E. Christians were critical of the apparently selfish nature of Epicurean teachings on pleasure. Epicureanism essentially disappeared for about one thousand years until it was revived by Lorenzo Valla (1405–1457), who criticized Scholasticism in *Disputazioni dialettiche* and supported Epicureanism in *De Voluptate.* Pierre Gassendi (1592–1655), the critic of Scholasticism and of Descartes, often gets the credit for rediscovering Epicureanism, however, with his *De vita et Moribus Epicuri.* The influence of Gassendi's work on John Locke (1632–1704) has been credited with providing the impetus for Locke's social contract theory and, by extension, for the American Revolution. Indeed, Thomas Jefferson (1743–1826) himself claimed, in a letter to William Short (dated 31 October 1819), to be an Epicurean. Finally, Epicureanism must be distinguished from utilitarianism, which arose during the nineteenth century. Utilitarianism retains the Epicurean view that humans naturally seek pleasure and avoid pain, but while Epicureans laud pleasure seeking and pain avoidance for their effects on the psychological state of the actor, utilitarians use it to express the consequentialist view that a good action maximizes pleasure and minimizes pain.

Epicurus on Pleasure

While Epicureanism is not strictly an ethical theory, it has been most influential in the field of ethics. Epicurus emphasized empiricism, and his theories were foundationalist in the sense that he believed all sense perceptions were true (Inwood and Gerson, A53.63). In keeping with this, he denied that a theory of meaning was possible. Rather, we come to a "basic grasp" (prolepsis) of what people say based on our memories of "what has often appeared in the external world" (Inwood and Gerson, A7.33). As such, the Epicurean notion of *areté* (human excellence) involves pleasure, and we do have some sensible experience with pleasure. It should be very easy to attain human excellence in this sense, but Epicurus believed that many people were not excellent. To address this problem, Epicurus developed a psychological theory, which argued that most people suffer from neurotic beliefs that inhibit the pursuit of the pleasant life. He identified the neurotic beliefs as a fear of death and a misunderstanding of the gods. He claimed that neither death nor the gods concerned humans and thus they should not fear them. We must overcome these fears in order to live a pleasant life.

Epicurus conceived of pleasure in two ways. "Kinetic" pleasure is that pleasure felt while performing an activity, such as eating or drinking. "Katastematic" pleasure is that pleasure felt while being in a state. This is the pleasure of not being disturbed, of being free from pain. Both types of pleasure occur in the body and the soul. The absence of pain (katastematic pleasure) in the soul (*ataraxia*), though, is the highest good for Epicurus.

Epicurus has often been misunderstood as a "sensualist." Cicero, an avowed Stoic, seemed to think that kinetic pleasure was also an end for Epicurus (*De Finibus* II.31–32). But this does not seem to be correct. While kinetic pleasures are desirable for Epicurus, they are not always to be pursued. In fact, it seems that they should be pursued only when they contribute to *ataraxia* (untroubledness). In some cases it might even be necessary to endure pain in order to preserve or contribute to *ataraxia*.

Epicurus on Human Excellence

According to Stephen Rosenbaum, most scholars now recognize that Epicureanism did not advocate a life of sensual delights. Rather, the Epicurean pursues "sober reasoning" to achieve the "pleasures" of *aponia* (absence of pain in the body) and *ataraxia* (p. 21). Nonetheless, this does not entail the elimination of desires. When one is in the state of *ataraxia,* one does not avoid opportunities to enjoy kinetic pleasures, but at the same time one is not bothered by the absence of these opportunities. If one has developed a taste for caviar, for example, one enjoys it when it is available and is not disturbed by its absence.

Epicurus has also been criticized for his notion of excellence. Excellence and pleasure are inseparable for Epicurus. But we do everything for the sake of pleasure (*ataraxia* in particular) not excellence. *Ataraxia,* then, is the highest human good. Cicero argues that occasions might arise where pleasure-seeking conflicts with acting virtuously (i.e., for the right reason) (*De Finibus* II.68–73, 111ff.). He claims that it is not possible to do something for the right reason and at the same time to get pleasure from the act in the way Epicurus claims. Rather, because the Epicurean always seeks what is pleasurable, what is right can always be redefined. In other words, excellence is never stable in the Epicurean scheme because whatever leads to pleasure in a specific instance is always right. So in one instance one may benefit (in terms of pleasure) from acting unjustly while in some other instance one may benefit

from acting justly. On Cicero's account, then, both actions would be right actions for the Epicurean because both lead to pleasure. But this understanding rests on a faulty assumption. It assumes that the Epicurean feels no remorse. Thus, he need not act justly if acting unjustly leads to pleasure. However, for the Epicurean the "greatest fruit of justice is freedom from disturbance," or *ataraxia* (Inwood and Gerson, A120). As such, it seems that, for the Epicureans, the fruits of injustice would be disturbance and not *ataraxia*. Pleasure, then, can align with justice, and thus with excellent activity.

Epicureans and Stoics Compared

While both the Epicureans and the Stoics emphasize *ataraxia,* the Epicurean view of the highest human good, or *eudaimonia* (happiness), differs from the Stoic view. Epicurus believed that excellence is natural in the sense that we naturally seek pleasure and avoid pain. This contrasts with the Stoic view of nature and thus of excellence. The process leading to *eudaimonia,* then, is fundamentally different for the Stoics.

Stoic ethics differ from Epicurean ethics in at least three ways. First, their views of nature differ. For the Stoics, self-preservation is the first natural instinct while pleasure plays this role for the Epicureans. This difference affects their views of human excellence (*areté*). Epicurus saw pleasure and excellence as inseparable while for the Stoics, self-preservation leads to valuing reason for itself, which leads to the accordance of a special value to excellence.

The second difference between Stoics and Epicureans involves their views of the emotions. For the Epicureans, it was not necessary to eliminate pathos. As Gisela Striker notes, the Epicurean realizes that only a few desires are needed for a pleasant life and they can be easily satisfied (p. 100). In the Epicurean state of *ataraxia* one does not avoid desires, but one is not bothered by the inability to satisfy one's desires either. As such, the Epicurean is "unperturbed" (p. 100.). The Stoic, on the other hand, is "unperturbable" because he or she has completely eliminated pathos (p. 100).

Finally, the Epicureans and Stoics differ on the role of excellence. For the Stoics, excellence alone is sufficient for *eudaimonia,* and it results directly from reason. The Epicureans attach pleasure to excellence, but this does not lead to *eudaimonia.* Rather, the rational person recognizes that the highest form of pleasure (*areté*) is *ataraxia.* And actions performed from the state of *ataraxia* are the actions of the *eudaimon* (happy) individual. This individual is tranquil, and she or he has good reasons for feeling tranquil.

Other Aspects of Epicureanism

The Epicureans were noted for their emphasis on physics. They were materialists and, in particular, followers of Democritean atomism. Sextus reports that "Epicurus said that all sensibles are true and that every presentation comes from something existing and is of the same sort as that which stimulates sense-perception" (Inwood and Gerson, A53.63). This belief drove his empiricism, which depended upon the existence of void (or space) and bodies. The bodies, in turn, were compounds of atoms, which were not "subject to dissolution in any way or fashion. Consequently, the principles of bodies must be atomic natures" (Inwood and Gerson, A2.40–41).

Epicureanism is not known for its politics. Epicurus showed very little interest in politics and, as a result, had very little to say about it. In fact, Plutarch reports that Epicurus urged his "adherents to avoid public life and express disgust for those who participate in it . . . providing there is no fear of beatings and punishments" (Inwood and Gerson, A35). Epicurus does, however, appear to have hewed to the idea of a harm principle. The thirty-first of his "principal doctrines," as reported by Diogenes Laertius, claims that the "justice of nature is a pledge of reciprocal usefulness, [i.e.,] neither to harm one another nor be harmed" (Inwood and Gerson, A5.XXXI). This view lends itself well to a liberal social contract theory, though no such theory seems to have ever been proposed by Epicurus or his immediate followers.

See also **Emotions; Foundationalism; Happiness and Pleasure in European Thought; Social Contract; Stoicism; Utilitarianism.**

BIBLIOGRAPHY

Cicero, Marcus Tullius. *De Finibus Bonorum et Malorum.* Translated by H. Rackham. Cambridge, Mass.: Harvard University Press, 1983.

Inwood, Brad. *Ethics and Human Action in Early Stoicism.* New York: Oxford University Press, 1985.

Inwood, Brad, and L. P. Gerson, trans. *Hellenistic Philosophy: Introductory Readings.* Indianapolis: Hackett, 1988.

Irwin, Terence. "Virtue, Praise and Success: Stoic Responses to Aristotle." *The Monist* 73 (1990): 59–79.

Jones, Howard. *The Epicurean Tradition.* London and New York: Routledge, 1989.

Mitsis, Phillip. *Epicurus' Ethical Theory: The Pleasures of Invulnerability.* Ithaca, N.Y.: Cornell University Press, 1988.

Osler, Margaret J., ed. *Atoms, Pneuma, and Tranquillity: Epicurean and Stoic Themes in European Thought.* Cambridge, U.K., and New York: Cambridge University Press, 1991.

Osler, Margaret J., and Letizia A. Panizza. "Introduction." In *Atoms, Pneuma, and Tranquillity: Epicurean and Stoic Themes in European Thought.* Edited by Margaret J. Osler. Ithaca, N.Y.: Cornell University Press, 1991.

Reesor, Margaret E. *The Nature of Man in Early Stoic Philosophy.* London: Duckworth, 1989.

Rosenbaum, Stephen E. "Epicurus on Pleasure and the Complete Life." *The Monist* 73 (1990): 21–41.

Striker, Gisela. "Ataraxia: Happiness as Tranquillity." *The Monist* 73 (1990): 97–110.

Tim Duvall

EPIGENESIS. *See* Development.

EPISTEMOLOGY.

This entry includes three subentries:

Ancient

Early Modern

Modern

ANCIENT

Many ancient cultures had sophisticated methods for organizing knowledge. However, systematic, self-conscious reflection on the nature of knowledge itself appears to have originated in Greek philosophy.

Pre-Socratic Philosophy

Greek philosophy began, around 600 B.C.E., with a series of attempts to specify the fundamental constituents of the universe. Questions soon began to be raised about the prospects for success in this enterprise. The poet-philosopher Xenophanes (c. 560–c. 478 B.C.E.) denied that knowledge—as opposed to belief or opinion—was possible, at least about the gods and the nature of the universe. However, since Xenophanes himself had much to say about gods, he must have considered some opinions more reliable than others; and other evidence seems to support this. Similarly, Democritus (c. 460–c. 370 B.C.E.) expressed very serious doubts about our ability to know the real nature of things. But he too was the proponent of an ambitious cosmological theory—the original atomic theory—so he must have found room for some types of reasonable beliefs. He does speak of reason as superior to the senses, and able to go further than the senses alone. Yet he recognizes the need to rely on the senses as a starting point for inquiry, and this sets limits to how far anyone can repudiate the evidence they provide. How exactly he resolved this tension is debatable.

A sharp distinction between the senses and reason had earlier been drawn by Parmenides (born c. 515 B.C.E.), again to the detriment of the senses. But Parmenides also criticized those who relied on their senses as out of touch with true being, to which only pure reason can give access; the division between cognitive faculties is thus paralleled by a division

---

XENOPHANES

And as for what is clear, no man has seen it, nor will there be anyone

Who knows about the gods and what I say about all things;

For even if one should happen to say what has absolutely come to pass

Nonetheless one does not oneself know; but opinion has been constructed in all cases.

SOURCE: Xenophanes, fragment DK B34 (translation author's).

> ## ARISTOTLE
>
> We think we know a thing without qualification . . . whenever we think we know the explanation because of which the thing is so, know that it is the explanation of that thing, and know that it does not admit of being otherwise.
>
> SOURCE: Aristotle, *Posterior Analytics,* 71b9–12. In *Aristotle: Selections,* trans. Terence Irwin and Gail Fine.

between levels of reality—the ordinary world around us being stigmatized as less than fully real. This division is a prototype for Plato's distinction between purely intelligible Forms and the world perceived by the senses.

Socrates and Plato

Socrates (c. 470–399 B.C.E.), as portrayed in numerous dialogues of Plato (c. 428–348/347 B.C.E.), is famous for professing his ignorance. He does not say, as often claimed, that he knows he knows nothing, but that he knows he knows nothing truly valuable. How, then, does Socrates conceive the truly valuable knowledge that he lacks? A plausible answer is that it is knowledge of the nature of the human virtues—knowledge that, if one possessed it comprehensively, would amount to a quite general grasp of how to live our lives. In some of the same dialogues, Socrates also proposes a principle that has been called the Priority of Definition: unless one can provide a definition of a thing—unless one can specify what it is—one is in no position to say anything authoritative about that thing. It is difficult to see how inquiry can proceed if this principle is fully adopted, a problem that Plato has Socrates face in the *Meno.* Socrates' answer is the Pythagorean-influenced doctrine that "learning is recollection." We all have lived many past lives, and have knowledge buried within us; the trick is to reactivate this knowledge or bring it to the surface. The same dialogue also includes an account of the difference between knowledge and opinion; knowledge involves an ability to explain why things are as they are. Knowledge (or *epistêmê,* one of the words regularly translated "knowledge") thus seems to be a kind of systematic understanding of some subject-matter, as opposed to the mere awareness of isolated facts designated by the term "opinion."

The idea that learning is recollection recurs in other works of Plato, but in conjunction with the notion of separate, purely intelligible Forms. How exactly Plato conceives of Forms, and the motivations he has for postulating them, are controversial. But it is clear that each Form is thought of as encapsulating the being, or the essence, of the quality of which it is the Form; the Form of Beauty, for example, is the true nature of beauty,

which particular beautiful objects in the world around us exemplify only in a limited or partial way. It is emphasized in the *Republic* that genuine knowledge is restricted to those who have a grasp of the Forms; anyone whose experience is limited to the everyday sensory world is only capable of opinion. To grasp Forms requires lengthy training, focused on minimizing one's reliance on the senses; a central tool in this process is pure mathematics.

The one dialogue of Plato devoted specifically to the question "What is knowledge?" is the *Theaetetus;* but this, though probably a mature work, surprisingly contains no mention of Forms whatever. The three definitions of knowledge considered are "Knowledge is perception," "Knowledge is true judgment," and "Knowledge is true judgment plus an account." While all three definitions are rejected, the third seems to come closest to success; and this interestingly resembles the picture of knowledge as appropriately justified true belief, favored by many contemporary epistemologists.

Aristotle

Aristotle (384–322 B.C.E.) has comparatively little to say directly about knowledge. But it is clear that he too conceives of knowledge as involving systematic understanding. The findings of a properly developed science, he thinks, can ideally be laid out in connected sequences of explanations. The starting points are the natures or essences of the objects being studied—say, the essence of a cow; these natures or essences explain why the objects have certain features, which in turn explain why they have certain other features, and so on. Aristotle's remarks on how we come to know the starting points are somewhat baffling. What is clear is that sense perception is a crucial ingredient in the process of coming to know, but that sense perception by itself does not constitute knowledge. This is because sense perception shows us only particular objects; genuine knowledge is by definition about universal characteristics of things. One thus needs to be able to grasp the universal characteristics present in a body of related sensory information. Aristotle shows no lack of confidence in the ability of human beings to do this reliably. But this is no surprise; it is clear that he conceives of the world as ordered in such a way as to be understandable, and of human beings as having the capacities necessary to achieve that understanding—most notably, rationality. However, he stresses, particularly in his ethical works, that one cannot expect complete precision in all subjects; the study of ethics, no matter how expertly conducted, is bound to yield conclusions less exact and more subject to exceptions than the study of mathematics.

Hellenistic Theories

Neither Plato nor Aristotle was particularly concerned with how knowledge is possible, or with warding off doubts on that score. In the Hellenistic period (roughly, the last three centuries B.C.E.) this topic became much more prominent; this was also the period of the organized skeptical movements. The Stoics shared Aristotle's conception of *epistêmê* as involving a systematic understanding of a body of truths. But they were also much concerned with the notion of an "apprehensive appearance," which is an impression, sensory or otherwise, that somehow guarantees its own correctness. It is not entirely clear how this was supposed to work. Some evidence suggests that the Stoics considered such impressions to have an inherent clarity or distinctness that left no room for error; but the guarantee of truth may instead have been regarded as due to their having been appropriately caused by their objects. The leading members of the Academy (the school founded by Plato) in this period relentlessly attacked the idea of "apprehensive appearances"; they also argued that nothing of the sort was necessary for living a reasonable human life.

The Epicureans, in the same period, also seem to have been concerned with minimizing error. They strikingly claimed that "all perceptions are true," and that error occurs only in our interpretations of them. However, this seems to be bound up with the atomist theory of sense perception, in which objects give off constant streams of atoms that enter our eyes (or other sense organs). "All perceptions are true" in the sense that there is no possibility of error concerning the configuration of atoms that strikes the sense organ. But that configuration need not accurately represent the shape of the original object; the film of atoms given off by a square tower, for example, may be eroded in transit, so that it is round when it reaches one's eye. There is therefore no guarantee that we perceive the world as it really is. Nonetheless, this theory does have the resources to explain how we manage to be mostly correct about the world around us, while also explaining why we sometimes make mistakes.

The Academics were not the only skeptical movement in Greek philosophy. There was also the Pyrrhonist movement (claiming inspiration from Pyrrho (c. 365–c. 275 B.C.E.), which began in the first century B.C.E. but is best known through the writings of Sextus Empiricus (probably 2nd century C.E.). According to Sextus, the skeptic suspends judgment on all questions about the nature of things, because of the "equal strength" of the opposing arguments and impressions available on any given topic. Sextus also claims that this posture results in *ataraxia*, "freedom from disturbance"; the stakes, for a skeptic, are simply much lower than for everyone else.

See also **Empiricism; Rationalism; Skepticism.**

BIBLIOGRAPHY

PRIMARY SOURCES
Aristotle. *Aristotle: Selections.* Translated, with introduction, notes, and glossary, by Terence Irwin and Gail Fine. Indianapolis: Hackett, 1995.
———. *Posterior Analytics.* 2nd ed. Translated with a commentary by Jonathan Barnes. Oxford: Clarendon Press, 1993.
Inwood, Brad, and L. P. Gerson, eds. *Hellenistic Philosophy: Introductory Readings.* 2nd ed. Indianapolis: Hackett, 1997.
McKirahan, Richard D., Jr. *Philosophy before Socrates: An Introduction with Texts and Commentary.* Indianapolis: Hackett, 1994.
Plato. *Complete Works.* Edited, with introduction and notes, by John M. Cooper. Indianapolis: Hackett, 1997.

SECONDARY SOURCES
Burnyeat, Myles, and Michael Frede. *The Original Sceptics: A Controversy.* Indianapolis: Hackett, 1997.
Everson, Stephen, ed. *Epistemology.* Cambridge, U.K., and New York: Cambridge University Press, 1990. White, Nicholas. *Plato on Knowledge and Reality.* Indianapolis: Hackett, 1976.

Richard Bett

EARLY MODERN

Modern philosophy is generally thought to be distinguished by an "epistemological turn." Prior philosophical tradition accorded special status to metaphysics, or "first philosophy" (the general philosophical investigation into the nature of reality). The modern tradition, by contrast, holds that it is necessary to determine the nature and bounds of human knowledge before any sure advance into metaphysics can be achieved.

Modern epistemologies are traditionally sorted out as "rationalist" or "empiricist." According to the rationalist position, the intellect is the foundation of all human knowledge, including knowledge of the material world; the classic expression of rationalism in the modern era is found in the philosophy of René Descartes (1596–1650), who took a cue from Plato and held that the senses are detrimental to true knowledge. But according to the empiricist position, sense experience is the foundation of knowledge. Much of the development of empiricism in the early modern era involved the purification of its principles through the removal of vestigial traces of Cartesian rationalism; this purification reached its pinnacle in the philosophy of David Hume (1711–1776). The "critical philosophy" of Immanuel Kant (1724–1804) is generally regarded as the culmination of the modern tradition, since it arose out of an assessment of the shortcomings of both empiricism and rationalism, and a synthesis of their insights.

Defining the Modern Tradition: Cartesian Beginnings
It is convenient to point to Descartes's *Meditationes de prima philosophiae* (1641; Meditations on first philosophy) as the inauguration of modern philosophy, since it advertises its project as making a radical break with the Aristotelian-scholastic tradition. "Some years ago," its narrator begins, "I was struck by the large number of falsehoods that I had accepted as true in my childhood, and by the highly doubtful nature of the whole edifice that I had subsequently based upon them" (*Philosophical Writings*, vol. 2, p. 12). The meditator's first task is the "general demolition" of all of his "opinions"; this is necessary, he claims, in order to establish the foundations of scientific knowledge.

Since a central tenet of the rejected Aristotelian-scholastic tradition is the empiricist thesis that "nothing is in the intellect that was not first in the senses," the work of mediation is conceived as a radical withdrawal from the senses. Through it, the mind is supposed to find itself "in its own freedom" and to "distinguish without difficulty what belongs to itself, i.e., to an intellectual nature, from what belongs to the body" (p. 9). Mind and physical body, according to Descartes, are the two kinds of reality or "substance." The essence of mind is thinking; it is fundamentally active and self-determining. The essence of body is to be extended, or to take up space; it is fundamentally passive, and the state of one body is determined solely through its relation to other bodies. The *Meditationes* are supposed to demonstrate that humans have better knowledge of the mind than of any material body: the first certainty established after the "general demolition" of the meditator's former opinions is the certainty of his own existence as a "thinking thing."

According to Descartes, whatever can be known through the intellect alone—including the nature of the intellect itself—is known "clearly and distinctly." The famous experiment with a piece of wax in the Second Meditation is supposed to show that humans know the nature of body by means of the intellect as well. On the basis of sense experience, one can appreciate the color, texture, smell, and size of the piece of wax; but these determinations are known only in an "imperfect and confused" manner, since they all undergo alteration as the wax is brought nearer the fire. One can have "clear and distinct" knowledge only of the material substance that underlies these changes—that is, "merely something extended, flexible and changeable" (p. 20).

Although Descartes's conception of mind and its essential distinctness from body is not itself a universally shared theory of modern philosophy, it nevertheless sets out a problem with which the entire ensuing tradition must deal. To understand how that unfolds, it will be helpful to consider three central concerns of early modern philosophy in general: its "mechanistic" conception of nature, the theory of sense perception that is tied to that conception of nature, and skepticism.

Nature as Mechanism

The root of the modern conception of nature lies in Descartes's idea that there are but two kinds of substance: spiritual substance (mind) and material substance (body). Since the essence of body is extension, and extension can be determined quantitatively, mathematics is the language of nature. The modern conception of nature departs from the Aristotelian-scholastic conception, which placed heavy emphasis on teleological explanation. According to this view, distinct principles determine the character or essence of different kinds of things in nature (or "natural kinds"); each kind of thing is driven, as it were, to express its "nature" according to its principle. In contrast, the modern mechanistic view deemphasizes the importance of determining natural kinds, focusing instead on universal laws of the motion of matter.

The natural philosopher Robert Boyle (1627–1691) and others charged that the Aristotelian framework was unable to yield satisfying explanations of natural phenomena. As Boyle developed his account, he advanced a hypothesis about minute particles of matter called "corpuscles": according to the "corpuscular philosophy," particular phenomena—including the appearance of qualities like color—can, in theory, be explained in terms of the arrangement and motion of these atoms. The theory of corpuscles was merely a hypothesis advanced on the recommendation of its explanatory power: "corpuscles" were theoretical entities, which had not been perceived even with the aid of instruments.

Theory of Sense Perception

The early modern theory of sense perception combined aspects of the mechanistic conception of nature with the Cartesian dualism of mind and body. Sense representations are "ideas," things proper to the immaterial mind; they are caused by qualities that are attributed to material bodies. It was thought to be possible, at least in principle, to give a mechanistic account of how a particular arrangement of the corpuscular microstructure brings about—through the motion of bodies—a certain "impression" on our sensory organs. But without overcoming the problematic of Cartesian dualism, no satisfying explanation of how some such physical impact (an "impression") could yield something mental (an "idea"). John Locke (1632–1704), an empiricist philosopher who ambivalently accepted aspects of Cartesian dualism, claimed in his *Essay concerning Human Understanding* (1690) that one must "take notice" of impressions in order to enjoy ideas of sense or have any sense perception at all (book 2, chapter 5). This capacity of the mind to "take notice" of impressions thus figures as an unexplained explainer in Locke's philosophy.

Descartes and Locke both thought that unnoticed judgments play an important role in sense perception. This again has to do with the Cartesian conception of the mind: the mind is transparent to itself, having infallible awareness of its own contents, or "ideas." People err only when they make judgments about the world on the basis of these ideas. To account for this, Descartes distinguishes between the understanding, which is simply an active capacity to be conscious of the mind's ideas, and the will, which affirms or denies that certain relations of ideas represent states of affairs in the world. For Descartes, judgment involves an act of the will. Although Locke denies Descartes's view about the role that the will plays in judgment, he agrees that unnoticed and habitual judgments play an important role in perception. When looking at a sphere of a uniform color, Locke claims, "the *Idea* thereby imprinted on our Mind, is of a flat Circle variously shadow'd"; but a habitual judgment "alters the Appearances into their Causes" so that what is perceived is "a convex Figure, and an uniform Colour" (p. 145).

Skepticism and the Cartesian Framework

The Cartesian meditative project invites a skeptical worry about the existence of the external world, for when the mind withdraws from the senses, it cuts itself off from the material world altogether. Indeed, in order for the narrator of the *Meditationes* to achieve his goal of razing the edifice of all of his former opinions, he must deliberately cultivate a radical form of skepticism, accepting the possibility that his ideas do not represent any independent material reality but may instead be the work of a "malicious demon." By the end of the *Meditationes,* the existence of the external world is supposed to have been established through a proof of the existence of God, which is in turn supposed to yield results about the reliability of the meditator's cognitive faculties (on the testimony of which the meditator supposes that there is a world independent of his mind).

Philosophers after Descartes continued to struggle with the fact that the Cartesian framework compels one to conclude that perception does not put us in direct contact with the outside world. One has contact with the world only through a "veil of ideas," and it seems one can only infer the presence of an external, independent, material world.

George Berkeley (1685–1753) tried to defend common sense against this skeptical worry by advancing an idealist account of perception in *Three Dialogues between Hylas and Philonous* (1713). His account is "idealist" because it argues that there is no mind-independent reality. At bottom Berkeley disputes the coherence of the Cartesian conception of material substance. Building on the premise that one cannot represent any physical object without having "ideas" of its qualities, he argues that objects are identified by the constant conjunction of certain ideas: "Take away the sensations of softness, moisture, redness, tartness, and you take away the cherry. Since it is not a being distinct from sensations; a *cherry*, I say, is nothing but a congeries of sensible impressions" (p. 130). The cause of these ideas cannot be material substance, Berkeley argues, but only the mind of God. Berkeley's curious defense of common sense comes down to a denial that there is any reality independent of "mind" at all.

The Scottish philosopher Thomas Reid (1710–1796) saw more clearly than any of his predecessors that skepticism about the "veil of ideas" is the unavoidable result of any adherence to the dominant modern theory of perception. He argues so at length in *An Inquiry into the Human Mind, on the Principles of Common Sense* (1764) and *Essays on the Intellectual Powers of Man* (1785) and offers a new account of perception that is not based on the modern "way of ideas." Although Reid was largely neglected by historians of philosophy for most of the twentieth century, his account of perception has received greater attention since the mid-1990s as a source of philosophical insight in its own right.

Humean Skepticism

Hume's epistemology is quite unencumbered by skeptical worries about the existence of the physical world. However, Hume's philosophical preoccupations are shaped by a new kind of skepticism, which is most clearly expressed in the *Enquiry concerning Human Understanding* (1748).

For Hume, the problem of epistemology is justificatory: it must be established how people take themselves to have knowledge of the causal order of nature. For "nature," Hume remarks, "has kept us at a great distance from all of her secrets, and has afforded us only the knowledge of a few superficial qualities of objects; while she conceals from us those powers and principles, on which the influence of these objects entirely depends" (*Enquiry*, §4, p. 21).

The problem Hume identifies can be traced back to Locke, who noted that people do not have knowledge of the corpuscular microstructure of things (see *Essay*, book 4, chapter 3). They have knowledge only of the "nominal essence" of things; in other words, humans identify natural kinds on the basis of observable qualities that are constantly conjoined in experience, but since they cannot give an account of the corpuscular microstructure that allows them to observe these qualities, they

do not have knowledge of the "real essence" of things. Hume generates a skeptical worry out of this: given that one has no cognitive access to the "secret nature" of things, then for all one knows this "secret nature" could change without any alteration in the observable properties of things. Hume recognizes that ordinary human cognitive practices carry on without people becoming encumbered by this skeptical worry. Yet "as a philosopher," he wonders: On what basis do we infer that the regular course of our experience should be a guide to determining a necessary connection of events observed in nature?

Hume responds to his "skeptical doubts" with a "skeptical solution" (*Enquiry*, §§4–5). People are able to make causal determinations only in a "subjective" fashion. In the course of experience, human minds are shaped by repetitions in circumstances. The result is the formation of tacit expectations, or anticipatory dispositions, which Hume calls "customs." These anticipatory dispositions are formed mechanically through associations of the imagination. The necessary connection thought in the concept of cause is merely something that "we *feel* in the mind, this customary transition of the imagination from one object to its usual attendant" (*Enquiry*, §7, p. 50). This "sentiment," Hume argues, is the source of the concept of causality. Thus Hume ends up with the following view. It cannot be said that one thing (A) brings about an effect in another thing (B); it may be said that representations of A are customarily conjoined with representations of B. Thus the necessity thought in the concept of cause is merely subjective: when faced with an event of type A, a subject cannot help but to anticipate an event of type B.

Kant's Critical Philosophy

Philosophy in Germany in the late seventeenth and early eighteenth centuries was largely dominated by the legacy of the rationalist philosopher G. W. Leibniz (1646–1716), but by the middle of the eighteenth century German philosophers were increasingly well read in the empiricist philosophy of Locke and Hume. Kant's mature philosophy, advanced in his *Kritik der reinen Vernunft* (1781, rev. 1787; Critique of pure reason) and presented in a "popular" form in his *Prolegomena* (1783), is generally thought to be a critical synthesis of these two traditions.

Hume's skeptical worries focused Kant's attention on the nature of scientific knowledge. For Kant, the very idea of such knowledge rests on a presupposition that humans can have cognitive access to laws (as opposed to mere regularities) of nature. Given the viability of scientific knowledge, Kant supposes, one must be in the possession of certain concepts on the basis of which one can combine representations independently of experience. One such concept is "cause and effect." But Hume's attempt to account for the concept of causality within a skeptical, empiricist framework required that he hold that genuine laws of nature are cognitively inaccessible. Hume's skeptical worries, Kant famously remarked, "first interrupted my dogmatic slumber" (*Schriften*, vol. 4, p. 260); but Hume's skeptical solution was not a happy one for Kant, who never doubted human capacity for genuine scientific knowledge.

In the *Critique*, Kant is particularly interested in the questionable status of metaphysics as a science. The first words of the book attest to the "peculiar fate" of human reason—namely, that it is compelled to ask questions that are beyond its capacity to answer. Kant principally has in mind the classic questions of metaphysics: for example, whether the soul is simple or composite or whether the world is finite or infinite. Reconceiving of what the proper task of metaphysics should be, Kant takes a cue from the flourishing science of Newtonian physics. But while the goal of physics is to explain some particular array of phenomena, the goal of metaphysics is to give an account of nature as such. For Kant, metaphysics begins with an exhaustive account of human cognitive capacity as the source of the fundamental principles that determine what it is to figure in the domain of nature at all. The main argument of the *Critique* is a demonstration of the relevant principles, which Kant takes to be the basis of the laws of nature.

See also **Epistemology: Ancient; Epistemology: Modern; Idealism; Kantianism; Skepticism.**

BIBLIOGRAPHY

Berkeley, George. *Three Dialogues between Hylas and Philonous.* Edited by Jonathan Dancy. Oxford and New York: Oxford University Press, 1998.

Boyle, Robert. *Selected Philosophical Papers of Robert Boyle.* Edited by M. A. Stewart. Manchester, U.K.: Manchester University Press, 1979.

Descartes, René. *Oeuvres de Descartes.* Edited by Charles Adam and Paul Tannery. New ed. 11 vols. Paris: CNRS/Vrin, 1974–1986. The standard edition of Descartes's works, in the original Latin and French.

———. *The Philosophical Writings of Descartes.* Translated by John Cottingham, Robert Stoothoff, and Dugald Murdoch. 3 vols. Cambridge, U.K.: Cambridge University Press, 1984–1991. The standard edition of Descartes's works in English translation.

Hume, David. *An Enquiry concerning Human Understanding.* Edited by Eric Steinberg. Indianapolis and Cambridge, U.K.: Hackett 1977.

———. *Treatise of Human Nature.* Edited by L. A. Selby-Bigge and P. H. Nidditch. 2nd ed. Oxford: Clarendon 1978. Although the *Enquiry concerning Human Understanding* is largely a restatement of book 1 of the *Treatise,* it is generally thought to contain the more emphatic expression of Hume's skeptical position.

Kant, Immanuel. *Critique of Pure Reason.* Translated by Paul Guyer and Allen W. Wood. Cambridge, U.K.: Cambridge University Press, 1997.

———. *Gesammelte Schriften.* Edited by the Königlich Preussischen Akademie der Wissenschaften, later the Deutschen Akademie der Wissenschaften zu Berlin. 29 vols. Berlin: Walter de Gruyter, 1900– . The standard edition of Kant's works, in the original German and Latin.

———. *Prolegomena to Any Future Metaphysics That Will Be Able to Come Forward as Science.* New ed. Translated by Paul Carus and revised by James W. Ellington. Indianapolis and Cambridge, U.K.: Hackett, 1977.

Locke, John. *An Essay concerning Human Understanding.* Edited by Peter H. Nidditch. Oxford: Clarendon, 1975.

Reid, Thomas. *Essays on the Intellectual Powers of Man.* Edited by Derek R. Brookes. Edinburgh: Edinburgh University Press, 2002.

———. *An Inquiry into the Human Mind on the Principles of Common Sense.* Edited by Derek R. Brookes. Edinburgh: Edinburgh University Press, 1997.

Melissa McBay Merritt

MODERN

The understanding of knowledge at work, implicitly or explicitly, in much of ancient and modern epistemology is that of knowledge as *justified true belief.* According to this traditional account (TAK), a subject, S, knows that *p* if and only if the following three conditions are met: (i) *p* is true; (ii) S believes that *p*; (iii) S is justified in, or has adequate evidence for, believing that *p*. While (i) and (ii) are almost entirely uncontroversial, (iii) lies at the heart of intense controversy. It is generally agreed that (i) and (ii) are not sufficient; knowledge cannot be analyzed as true belief. Suppose S took a medication that causes paranoid delusions. As a result, S believes he is being followed. Suppose further that S's belief happens to be true. There is broad agreement that accidentally true beliefs like that do not count as knowledge. However, what knowledge requires in addition to truth and belief is highly controversial. According to TAK, it is justification.

The Gettier Problem

If TAK were correct, conditions (i)–(iii) would be sufficient for knowledge. Using a couple of clever examples, Edmund Gettier showed that they are not. Ever since, it has become common practice to refer to cases that demonstrate the insufficiency of (i)–(iii) as "Gettier cases." Here is a simple example. Suppose S believes that there is a sheep in the field. But what S takes to be a sheep is merely a rock that, bizarrely, looks exactly like a sheep. Since S has no reason to assume that he is misled in that way, he is justified in believing that there is a sheep in the field. Thus far, S's belief is justified and false. But suppose further that, behind a bush that blocks S's view, there really happens to be a sheep in the field. Given this further assumption, S's belief turns out to be a justified true belief that clearly fails to be an instance of knowledge. What condition must be added to (i), (ii), and (iii) to rule out Gettier cases? Even today, about three decades after the publication of Gettier's 1963 article, this puzzle, commonly referred to as the "Gettier problem," remains unresolved.

According to philosophers who favor traditional epistemology, the existence of the Gettier problem does not establish that TAK is without merit. It merely shows that TAK is an approximation that needs further refinement. From this point of view, if S is to know that *p*, S must indeed have justification, or a good reason, for believing that *p*. But if the justification requirement is understood as a demand for the possession of good reasons, then the following problem—known as the regress problem—arises. Suppose S's reason for believing *p* is *q*. Now, if *q* is to justify S's belief that *p*, S must have justification for accepting that *q*. Given that justification requires the possession of a good reason, it follows that S must have a further reason, *r*, for *q*, and that S must have a still further reason, *s*, for *r*, and so forth. Regarding the structure of this regress, there are the following possibilities: (i) it continues ad infinitum; (ii) it terminates in basic belief: a belief that is justified without receiving its justification from any other beliefs; (iii) it circles back to its origin, the belief that *p*. These possibilities allow for the following positions, characterized in rough outline: Skeptics endorse (i) and conclude that justification is impossible. Infinitists agree with skeptics that the regress cannot be stopped, but hold that a chain of reasons can justify even it is infinite. Foundationalists advocate (ii), and coherentists favor (iii). Neither infinitism nor skepticism enjoys broad appeal. Foundationalism and coherentism, therefore, may be considered the main contenders.

Foundationalists claim the following: (i) in addition to mediately justified beliefs—beliefs that receive their justification from other beliefs—there are immediately justified, or basic, beliefs: beliefs that are somehow justified without depending for support on any other beliefs; (ii) ultimately, all mediately justified beliefs have their justification conferred upon them by immediately justified beliefs. Accordingly, foundationalists face two main challenges. They must give a plausible and detailed account of how it is possible for a belief to be justified without receiving its justification from any other beliefs, and they need to explain precisely how basic beliefs provide justification for mediately justified beliefs. According to classical foundationalism, basic beliefs are infallible and entail the mediately justified beliefs that are inferred from them. According to more recent, modest versions of foundationalism, basic beliefs need not enjoy any epistemic privilege as strong as infallibility, and can support nonbasic beliefs without entailing them.

Coherentists claim that there are no basic beliefs. All justified beliefs receive their justification from other beliefs. The chief idea coherentists invoke is that justification is holistic. For a given belief, *B*, to be justified, the subject must have justification for an entire set of other beliefs that, together with *B*, form a coherent whole. Coherentist theories are typically defended by highlighting the difficulties involved in the idea of immediate justification. For example, Sellars points out that, when it comes to explaining how basic beliefs are justified, foundationalists face the dilemma of having to conceive of a basic belief's justification as being either propositional or nonpropositional. In the former case, the regress problem returns, for if what justifies an allegedly basic belief that *p* is a proposition *q*, the question immediately arises of what reason there is for believing that *q* is true. In the latter case, the problem is how we are to conceive of nonpropositional justification. Presumably, such justification arises from what is "given" in perceptual experience: some kind of nonpropositional content. But, according to Sellars, if what is experientially given is nonpropositional, it simply is not the kind of thing that has the capacity to justify anything. Coherentism, then, derives its main defense from the apparent impossibility of immediate justification. Unfortunately, the alternative coherentists offer is no less problematic. Versions of coherentism that are developed in detail either suffer from circularity or regress problems, or else threaten to collapse back into foundationalism. The regress problem may, therefore, be viewed as one of the persistent and seemingly unsolvable puzzles of epistemology.

A straightforward, though certainly not uncontroversial, response to the regress problem becomes available when the traditional conception is rejected on behalf of a radical epistemological reorientation, according to which justification is a matter of, not possessing evidence or good reasons, but instead originating in causes of the right kind. Obviously, if justification does not require reasons, placing a justification condition on knowledge will not generate a regress of reasons. The key idea of the reoriented approach is that beliefs are caused by cognitive processes that are either reliable or unreliable. Perception, memory, and introspection are reliable processes. Biased thinking, wishful thinking, and making hunches are unreliable processes. According to reliabilism, this distinction is crucial for developing a successful theory of justification. The basic idea is roughly that a belief is justified (or, according to other versions, an instance of knowledge) if and only if it is caused by a reliable cognitive process—that is, a process that would produce mostly true beliefs in a wide range of different circumstances. Related theories assert, roughly, that S's belief that p qualifies as knowledge if S would not believe that *p* if *p* were false, or that S's true belief that *p*, on the basis of a reason *r*, qualifies as knowledge if S would not have *r* if *r* were false.

Advocates of TAK reject such theories on the following grounds. First, for a belief to be justified, it need not have its origin in a reliable cognitive process. Consider the victim of an evil demon. Such a subject has a belief system and evidence analogous to that of a normal person. But unlike the beliefs of a normal person, those of an evil demon victim are massively false. Reliabilism implies, implausibly, that the victim's beliefs are unjustified. Second, origination in reliable cognitive processes is not sufficient for making a belief justified, or, if true, an instance of knowledge. Advocates of TAK would argue that, for S to be justified in believing that *p*, or to know that *p*, it is necessary for S to have a good reason for *p*. (For a *locus classicus* of that kind of criticism, see BonJour, chapter 3.)

Theories that favor the traditional conception of knowledge are typically labeled "internalist." In contrast, causal theories that make de facto reliability the key notion of epistemic assessment are referred to as "externalist." Traditional theories, which identify justification with the possession of a good reason, are claimed to be internalist on the following ground: whether a subject, S, has a good reason for believing that *p* is something that S can determine merely by reflecting on the matter. Advocates of reliabilism and related theories are considered externalists because they deny that what determines a belief's justificational status must be something that is recognizable upon reflection.

In recent years, an approach closely related to causal theories and reliabilism—virtue epistemology—has received much attention (Sosa; Zagzebski). Virtue epistemologists advocate that justification and knowledge must be understood as arising from the employment of virtuous—that is, reliably working—cognitive faculties. Plantinga developed in detail a widely discussed theory of this kind. Its basic claim is that warrant—the property that a true belief into knowledge—must be identified with the proper functioning of faculties that are well designed, either by God or natural selection.

A central concern of contemporary epistemology, connecting back to such seminal figures as René Descartes, David Hume, Thomas Reid, George Edward Moore, and Bertrand Russell, is skepticism. The modern version of Descartes's evil demon is the mad scientist who controls the thoughts and beliefs of a brain in a vat (BIV). A BIV's evidence is, *ex hypothesi,* the same as yours or mine. For example, you have experiences of your hands—you see and feel them—on the basis of which you claim to know that you have hands. A BIV has hand-like experiences just as you do, but of course is mistaken in her belief that she has hands. On what grounds, then, can you claim to know that you have hands? The skeptical problem arises because the skeptical hypothesis in question—I am BIV—is incompatible with many of the ordinary propositions you take yourself to know. For example, if you are a BIV, then your current beliefs about your location, and the objects in your immediate environment, are all false. A skeptic, then, could argue as follows: You don't know that (say) you have hands unless you know that the BIV hypothesis is false. But you don't know that that hypothesis is false. Consequently, you don't know that you have hands.

In response to such skepticism, the following responses have been advocated: (i) evidentialism: I actually have evidence for believing that I am not a BIV; (ii) the relevant alternatives theory: the skeptical hypothesis fails to undermine ordinary knowledge claims since it is not a relevant alternative; (iii) inference to the best explanation: the skeptical hypothesis fails to defeat ordinary knowledge claims because it explains our beliefs and experiences less well than the hypothesis that the world is pretty much what we take it to be. A relatively new and influential response to skepticism is (iv) contextualism, according to which knowledge attributions are true or false depending on the attributor's standards of knowledge. When skeptical hypotheses are entertained, the standards of knowledge rise and become extremely stringent. As a result, a subject in such a context would be incorrect in saying she knows that she is not BIV, or that she has hands. However, in contexts in which skeptical hypotheses are ignored, the standards of knowledge remain low. It will then be correct to say that one has knowledge of one's hands. According to contextualists, what recommends this approach is that it preserves the truth of our ordinary knowledge claims and, at the same time, gives skepticism its due. For the gist of the contextualist solution is that our typical knowledge attributions, such as "I know I have hands," are in ordinary situations correct, and incorrect only in those contexts in which we concern ourselves with skeptical hypotheses. (For a collection of important essays on the problem of skepticism, see De Rose and Warfield. For a collection of essays debating a wide range of contemporary epistemological issues of the kind mentioned above, see Sosa and Steup.)

See also **Epistemology: Ancient; Foundationalism; Hermeneutics; Skepticism.**

BIBLIOGRAPHY

BonJour, Laurence. *The Structure of Empirical Knowledge.* Cambridge, Mass.: Harvard University Press, 1985.

Chisholm, Roderick M. *The Theory of Knowledge.* 3rd ed. Englewood Cliffs, N.J.: Prentice Hall, 1989.

De Rose, Keith, and Ted A. Warfield, eds. *Skepticism. A Contemporary Reader.* New York: Oxford University Press, 1999.

Dretske, Fred I. *Knowledge and the Flow of Information.* Cambridge, Mass.: MIT Press, 1981.

Gettier, Edmund. "Is Knowledge Justified True Belief?" *Analysis* 23 (1963): 121–123.

Goldman, Alvin I. *Epistemology and Cognition.* Cambridge, Mass.: Harvard University Press, 1986.

Lehrer, Keith. *Theory of Knowledge.* Boulder, Colo.: Westview, 1990.

Nozick, Robert. *Philosophical Explanations.* Cambridge, Mass.: Harvard University Press, 1981.

Plantinga, Alvin. *Warrant and Proper Function.* New York: Oxford University Press, 1993.

Sellars, Wilfrid. "Empiricism and the Philosophy of Mind." In his *Science, Perception and Reality.* London: Routledge and Kegan Paul, 1963.

Sosa, Ernest. *Knowledge in Perspective: Selected Essays in Epistemology.* Cambridge, U.K.: Cambridge University Press, 1991.

Sosa, Ernest, and Matthias Steup. *Contemporary Debates in Epistemology.* Oxford and Cambridge, Mass.: Blackwell, 2004.

Zagzebski, Linda Trinkhaus. *Virtues of the Mind: An Inquiry Into the Nature of Virtue and the Ethical Foundations of Knowledge.* Cambridge, U.K., and New York: Cambridge University Press, 1996.

Matthias Steup

EQUALITY.

This entry includes three subentries:

Overview
Gender Equality
Racial Equality

OVERVIEW

Though simple as a mathematical concept, equality is complex and contested as a political goal and philosophical concept. Many political struggles, both historical and ongoing, have engaged in the contests over the nature of equality. This contestation revolves around the basic question, What kinds of equality matter? The answer to this in part depends on whether the topic is approached from a predominantly political, economic, ethical/philosophical, or social perspective. Discussing the history of ideas on the concept of equality poses two further challenges. First, equality is so intimately related to the concept of justice that it is impossible to fully untangle the two. Second, there are so many voices and movements to consider on the subject that any concise discussion requires difficult choices on who to include and who to neglect. This overview thus will (1) touch on many (but not all) the important thinkers and developments in the history of ideas in the Western tradition, and (2) introduce some of the major debates and conflicts in that tradition over the concept of equality.

Ancient Views of Equality

For the purposes of understanding the concept of equality within the Western tradition, one has to look back to the two most influential strands of thought that inform the modern West: the Hebrew (and later Judeo-Christian) tradition and the Greek. While the Hebrews did not undertake an analysis of the concept of equality, the worldview and subsequent laws were steeped with a sense of equality unusual in the Western tradition at or before their time. The distance between a supremely powerful single God and humanity was most likely fundamental to this worldview, in which God's creations seemed relatively equal in comparison. Unlike other well-known law codes of the age (e.g., the code of Hammurabi), Jewish law applied to all Hebrews equally, regardless of their sex or class (see especially Exodus 19–35 and Deuteronomy 12–26). At the founding of the second temple in Jerusalem, Jewish law became a kind of first social contract—quite literally in the public reading of the Torah and the people signing that they will live by these laws—establishing a direct relationship between all the Hebrew people and their God (see Ezra-Nehmiah). There was not one secret teaching for the elites and another for the people; rather, all the teachings were available to all the people, and the covenant required the understanding and consent of all.

The first systematic analyses of equality as a concept comes from the Greeks of the classical age, which is perhaps not surprising given their intense interest in mathematics. One of the most thorough of these early systematic explorations of equality was undertaken by Aristotle (384–322 B.C.E.) in several of his works. In his investigation into the virtue of justice in the *Nicomachean Ethics,* Aristotle uses the Greek word for "equal" (*isos*) but gives it a meaning that is more akin to "fairness." Equality is a state to be striven for, intermediate between giving someone more or less than he or she is due, relative to a specific activity or social realm. In disputes over contracts, for instance, a judge must determine the differences in harms inflicted by the breaking of a contract and restore the position of equality by subtracting the profit the offender has reaped from the infraction (*Ethics,* 1132a1–19).

It is in Aristotle's discussion of political justice that he examines equality in a way that more closely resembles the usual meaning of the term today. Political justice is a matter for citizens, whom he defines as "those who share in common a life aiming at self-sufficiency, who are free and either proportionally or numerically equal" (*Ethics,* 1134a27–29). Justice, in the political sense, can occur only among those who are free and fundamentally equal in their capacity as citizens, most importantly, in their equality in ruling and being ruled *(Ethics,* 1134b14–16). In the *Politics,* Aristotle further refines the concept of political equality in his discussions of justice in a political association. He tells us that the virtue of justice is agreed by all to be a proportionality based on desert or merit, but he adds that "some consider themselves to be equal generally if they are equal in some respect, while others claim to merit all things unequally if they are unequal in some respect" (*Politics,* 1301b35–39). As neither view is wholly right or wrong, and since reason alone cannot resolve the fundamental conflict, a good regime will attempt to see the legitimacy and limitations

of both and attempt to arrange politics and political institutions so that the factions that normally form around these competing views enter into constructive negotiation rather than risk intense civil conflict or rule by superior power alone (*Politics,* 1301b39–1302a15, 1318a27–b1).

While Aristotle believes in some natural inequalities among humans that today we reject—between men and women, between "natural slaves" and free men—he does lay a foundation for a political critique of economic inequalities. The best regime will be one without extremes of wealth or poverty, not because these inequalities are inherently unjustifiable but because they undermine good politics. The wealthy, because they are unequal (i.e., superior) in wealth to their fellow citizens, believe they should be superior in political power as well—a false and dangerous belief. As a solution to the potential of class rule by either the wealthy or the poor, Aristotle encourages regimes to nurture the growth of the middle classes, whom he sees as better able to grasp the merits and limitations of the two extremes and thereby be a moderating political force (*Politics,* 1295a33–1296a21; for a brief general introduction to the topic, see Terchek and Moore).

Athenian political practice is just as important as Athenian philosophy to understanding the Greek contribution to ideas of equality. Through the centuries of reforms that would lead to the rise of full-fledged democratic government, three stand out. The first, *isonomia,* means literally equality of law, embodying both the concept that all citizens be treated equally with regard to the laws and that they participate equally in their making. The second reform, *isēgoria,* or equality of speech, allows all citizens, regardless of class, to rise in the assembly and attempt to convince their fellow citizens on the best policies and laws. The final reform allows all citizens to participate equally in the agenda-setting aspect of politics rather than just expressing preference on the agenda given to them. While political equality in contemporary democracies has been restricted for most citizens to the voicing of preference rather than the ability to effectively participate in setting or influencing the political agenda, the Athenian reforms highlight that this is only one aspect of true political equality (see Ober, 1989, 1996).

Like the Athenians, Rome came to base its laws on the notion that they should apply to all citizens equally. And as with the Athenians, it was the result of a struggle between the many and the few. During the republic, the plebian class, angered that the laws were applied differently to them and to the elites of the patrician class, pushed for reforms that resulted in the adoption of the Twelve Tables. Stating basic laws in a clear way helped to eliminate their ad hoc alteration in legal proceedings, where they could be made to say one thing for the elite and another for the many.

Equality in the Church
and the Protestant Reformation

During the Middle Ages, there were two important developments that affect the modern conception of equality. First, a natural law tradition developed around the notion that all humans, as God's creations, are owed certain rights and protections and that these natural laws cannot be altered by political associations or rulers. Thus we see in thinkers like St. Thomas Aquinas (c. 1224–1274) a rigorous defense of the principle that all people are due a certain minimal set of legal protections based solely on the fact of their humanity.

The second role the church played is more subtle, serving as a force for the gradual and irresistible movement toward a society organized around the fundamental fact of equality. The church took in members of the lower classes, gave them an education, allowed them to rise through the church hierarchy, and, given the important role church officials played in European state affairs, made it possible for individuals of humble origins to join the royal state's inner circle of advisers. It thus provided a clear counterexample to the notion that one is born to one's station, contributing to the decline of the view that society should be based on fundamental inequality in accordance with one's birth (Tocqueville, pp. 9–10).

As the Protestant Reformation approached, Christian humanists set out to understand the precise meaning of the founding texts (the Bible and doctrines of the early church fathers). This, combined with the advent of the printing press and the widespread publication of the Bible and other writings in the common tongues of the people, created an atmosphere in which intense scrutiny of and debate over the meaning of Christian doctrine was considered appropriate, and individuals came to see themselves as capable of judging doctrine for themselves based on their knowledge and skills. This culminated in Martin Luther's (1483–1546) statement, in a debate with Johann Eck, that the Bible, not the pope or church councils, is the sole guide for human conscience. It is a short leap from these views to the modern liberal notion that individuals, with no need of an intermediary or authority to tell them what to think, can best determine their own beliefs and interests. In the Reformation era, individuals became radically equal in their capacities to judge matters for themselves.

Liberalism, Civic Republicanism, and the Age of Revolution

Modern conceptions of equality are deeply rooted in both the liberal and civic republican traditions of thought as well as in the age of revolution. Here we will look at each of these as well as at the socialist challenge to liberalism in particular. As we will see, in addition to natural, legal, and political forms of equality, economic equality (or inequality) also concerns many modern thinkers.

At its core, liberalism grew out of the social contract theories espoused by Thomas Hobbes (1588–1679) and John Locke (1632–1704). For Hobbes (a proto-liberal), the individual is naturally equal because in a hypothetical state of nature he or she is equally at the mercy of other people, as even the weakest can kill the strongest through guile or collected effort. Escaping this environment of all against all is the reason for and basis of our entering into a social contract whereby we agree to give over most of our natural rights to a sovereign who will protect us, thereby allowing us to pursue our own interests. The focus in Hobbes is on abstract and radically equal individuals, and in his solution he does not worry much about

the individual carrying his or her equal natural rights into the civil society that results from the social contract.

As the first true liberal, Locke emphasizes natural equal rights, roughly equal reason, and the need for a social contract to protect equal rights to pursue one's interests and realize the benefits of one's labor and property. However, Locke deemphasizes the salience of economic inequalities for politics. As we shall see, unlike the civic republicans, Locke does not emphasize that property is a means to an end and therefore should not be pursued without limit. In the commons-based economy of Locke's state of nature, and in the absence of money, it would be unjust to hoard forms of property that would "spoil," but in a private-property-based, money economy there is no natural limit to accumulation and therefore no natural limit to inequalities of property. In fact Locke argues that since money only has value through the "tacit and voluntary consent" of human beings, "men have agreed to a disproportionate and unequal possession of the earth" (*Second Treatise*, p. 29). Material inequalities are not only inevitable, humans have chosen them. Moreover Locke emphasizes that privatization of the commons—and the inequalities that entails—will allow a more productive use of resources. While Locke repeatedly reminds readers that God "hath given the world to men in common," he offers no admonition—on the basis of natural law, reason, or religious teaching—that we limit our accumulation of wealth, and he does not offer warnings about the effects of inequalities of property on politics (*Second Treatise*, p. 18).

For Adam Smith (1723–1790), the key economic inequality of his time that needed to be eliminated was mercantilist monarchy's awarding economic opportunities not to all alike but to a few well-connected subjects. Out of Smith's critique of mercantilism comes the notion of equality of economic opportunity. Given equal economic opportunities, individuals will pursue their own interests on the basis of their abilities, and the fact that inequality of outcome will result is not a problem for Smith as long as political equality is protected. Smith is fundamentally worried, however, about an economic system in which the players have unequal market power. His ideal market comprises many small producers and consumers, none of whom have the power to significantly influence prices and thereby infringe on the liberty of others by extracting benefits beyond what they would as equally powerless players. Furthermore, while Smith does not worry overly much about economic inequality per se, he is troubled both by the dangers of pursuing wealth too avidly and by the deprivations of having too little, especially when they force one into dependence on a work environment that dulls one's reasoning faculties.

A slightly different strand within the liberal tradition follows Immanuel Kant (1724–1804). Kant's important contribution to the notion of equality has to do with his contention that from a moral or ethical point of view there is an obligation (categorical imperative) to treat individuals as ends in themselves and not merely as means for some other end. This rises from the human capacity to reason and therefore the will to be self-determining (see *Practical Philosophy*, pp. 77–82). This notion will deeply influence modern ethical thought, especially thinking about human rights as it informs the Universal Declaration of Human Rights adopted by the General Assembly of the United Nations in 1948.

Civic Republicanism

The civic republican tradition—including thinkers such as Aristotle, Niccoló Machiavelli (1469–1527), Jean-Jacques Rousseau (1712–1778), and Thomas Jefferson (1743–1826)—differs from that of the early liberals by emphasizing economic inequality as a threat to liberty and democratic government. For Rousseau, liberal social contract theory undermines itself in that it does not resolve the fundamental conflict over the unequal private property that lies at the very heart of the social contract. For thinkers such as Locke, individuals form a social contract in order to escape the conflicts that develop over property so that they may enjoy their property and the fruits of their labor. Rousseau, however, contends that by leaving property unequally distributed, Locke failed to resolve the conflict that stands in the way of civil peace and individual liberty. For Rousseau, the logical missing step necessary to solve Locke's error is for all individuals to give up their private property as a condition of entering the social contract. This property is then distributed equally as a private holding of all citizens under the contract. This arrangement allows all individuals equal capacity to tend to their interests and needs and to participate in their collective self-governance. Rousseau's ideas will inform the French Revolution and its Declaration of the Rights of Man and of the Citizen, which calls for liberty, equality, and fraternity and attempts to eliminate the privileges of the old aristocratic order.

For Jefferson and for other early U.S. thinkers such as J. Hector St. John de Crèvecoeur (1735–1813), one of the great characteristics of the United States was its egalitarian distribution of property compared to Europe's. Americans, according to Crèvecoeur, work for themselves, not lords. He boasts that in America, even the "meanest of our log-houses is a dry and comfortable habitation. Lawyer and merchant are the fairest titles our towns afford" (*Letters*, p. 46). We see here an American expression of the civic republican aspiration of working for oneself, with no master or overseer. This aspiration is also egalitarian in its societal outcomes: the poorest live in dry and comfortable homes, and the richest are merely lawyers or merchants.

Clearly the reality in the colonies and the United States was never this egalitarian. However, Crèvecoeur's vision is an exemplar of mainstream American views on equality in that it does not require anything other than equality of opportunity. The redistribution from the rich and aristocracy necessary to achieve some kind of equality in Europe is rendered invisible through the myth of a frontier of largely empty land that can be settled by Americans of European descent. The equality of opportunity that is the basis of the American consensus has never been the sole cause for the realization of the ideal of a citizen free from overt dependence (Bercovitch; Appleby).

Jefferson was similarly egalitarian in his attitudes toward work and property (and perhaps similar in his tendency to neglect the realities of inequality in early America). In 1785 he wrote to James Madison that

I am conscious that an equal division of property is impracticable. But the consequences of this enormous inequality producing so much misery to the bulk of mankind, legislators cannot invent too many devices for subdividing property. . . . Whenever there is in any country, uncultivated lands and unemployed poor, it is clear that the laws of property have been so far extended as to violate natural right.

He goes on to argue that where persons are excluded by the privatization or enclosure of land, governments must "take care that other employment be furnished to those excluded from the appropriation" (*Jefferson*, p. 396).

For Jefferson, as for other thinkers in the civic republican tradition, a relatively egalitarian distribution of property and the ensurance of all households' livelihoods are not merely ends in themselves but are important means to good democratic citizenship.

Here [in America] every one may have land to labor for himself. . . . Every one, by his property, or by his satisfactory situation, is interested in the support of law and order. And such men may safely and advantageously reserve to themselves a wholesome control over their public affairs, and a degree of freedom, which, in the hands of the *canaille* of the cities of Europe, would be instantly perverted and to the demolition and destruction of everything public and private. (*Jefferson*, p. 538)

Ordinary Americans have something to lose; they have something at stake in the political economic regime. (On stakes in civic republican thought, see Terchek, 1997.) They will not threaten property relations since they are neither impoverished nor exploited. Therefore, from the perspective of elites, ordinary Americans can be trusted as democratic citizens. Extremes of economic inequality—in which some citizens have much more than they need and others have no livelihood with which to sustain themselves and their families—are not just violations of natural law; they threaten democracy by undermining the respect for law and moderation that allows democracy to function well.

We need also notice the important role equality plays in the founding of the United States. Jefferson inserts at the heart of the preamble of the Declaration of Independence the phrase "We hold these truths to be self-evident, that all men are created equal, that they are endowed by their Creator with certain unalienable Rights, that among these are Life, Liberty and the pursuit of Happiness." However, while espousing a basic equality at the very core of the American political experiment, the 1787 Constitution also institutionalized a great deal of inequality. First is the compromise that protects the practice of slavery and determines that slaves count as three-fifths of a person for the purpose of determining representation, even though they cannot participate in selecting those representatives. The Constitution excluded those who do not own property from full citizenship until the reforms of the Jacksonian era, and women were excluded from full citizen status until the beginning of the twentieth century. Furthermore, even once the United States adopted universal adult suffrage, it maintained one of the most unequal instances of representation in any of the stable, advanced democracies: the U.S. Senate. The Senate is based on the principle of equality for states, not for citizens. Thus a citizen of the least populous state has about sixty times as much voting power as a citizen of the most populous state in determining Senate representation.

Socialism

Although the socialist tradition is much more diverse than this choice suggests, we will focus on the ideas of Karl Marx (1818–1883) as exemplary of the socialist critique of liberal capitalism. The political economic philosophy of Marx approaches economic inequalities with a concern for freedom, rejecting the liberal assumption that economic inequalities do not affect political equalities and breaking with both the republican and liberal traditions by focusing on the inequalities of neither individuals nor citizens but entire classes. For Marx, the most fundamentally problematic inequality is that between those who own the means of economic production and those who do not. That some are rich and others poor is of concern, but this is only symptomatic of the former, deeper inequality. Moreover, from a Marxist perspective, inequalities that seem not to be economic in nature—inequalities between the sexes, for instance—are outgrowths of the fundamental economic inequality that forms the basis of a capitalist political economic system.

In a capitalist political economy it is not just the economy that is driven and controlled by the capitalist class. All the institutions of society, or superstructure of society, rest on an economic base and serve to legitimate but also disguise that base. The ideologies of liberal democracy only serve to legitimate what is in fact a system of freedom and democracy only for some. The political equality emphasized by liberals is but a veil for the economic inequality that is so fundamental to a capitalist society and so detrimental to human freedom.

For Marx, the central normative problem with capitalism is not simply the poverty or powerlessness of the proletariat or the inequality between the classes in and of itself. The central problem is that no one is truly free in a capitalist regime. According to Marx the fundamental nature of our species is to produce—ideas and art as well as the material objects necessary for survival. By appropriating the workers' product, capitalism denies them, or alienates them from, their fundamental nature. In this alienation workers are unfree, because they are unable to become their fully human selves. Even members of the bourgeoisie are unfree, because in using others to produce for them they are also alienated from their nature as producers. Freedom, then, would be the end of alienation and the realization of humanity's species being as producers. A classless society, in which all own the means of production and all are producers in the deepest sense, is the only means of achieving the end of alienation and therefore freedom (*Economic and Philosophic Manuscripts of 1844*). As for other thinkers, equality is not an end in itself for Marx. Instead, equality in ownership and control of the means of production is a necessary prerequisite for freedom.

There are several important developments in contemporary thought about what equality means and which equalities matter. In contemporary capitalist democracies, political theorists and philosophers still debate whether or not the economic inequalities generated by a capitalist economy are consistent with political equality. Defenders of the theories and practices of capitalism, such as F. A. Hayek and Milton Friedman, argue that if a political economic system provides all persons with an equal opportunity to succeed, then inequality of outcome or result is acceptable. That some are rich and others poor fairly reflects individuals' differing aptitudes, work ethics, and even luck. Free markets, according to such thinkers, justly distribute the economic products of a society among its members because they reward economic contributions on the basis of existing demand for those contributions. Efforts to equalize the living standards of rich and poor would rely on coercive governmental power that would sacrifice individual freedom and rights to a kind of equality that may not even be politically important. For such thinkers, then, economic inequality is not problem as long as political equality—equal rights and capacities to participate in political processes—exists.

Capitalism and Its Critics

Critics of free-market capitalism attack these claims on philosophical, historical, and practical bases. Many question whether indeed the market is a just distributor of the economic products and economic burdens of a society—and therefore whether economic inequalities are just in and of themselves. More generally, non-Marxist critics such as Michael Walzer want a society in which no social good "serves or can serve as a means of domination" (*Spheres of Justice,* p. xiv; see also Lindblom, 1977, 1982). Other thinkers approach concerns over economic inequalities from a more ethical perspective that incorporates the Kantian and social contract approaches to liberalism. Most notable among these is John Rawls, who contends that to correct the inequalities that arise in society we should begin with a thought game in which we imagine ourselves behind a "veil of ignorance," not knowing what circumstances we will be born into, what attributes and handicaps we will be born with, or what fortune will bring us in life. If we did not know what our situation was, how would we arrange society and what programs to remedy inequality would we propose? He contends that as rational beings we would favor an initial position in the social contract that is basically equal and maintains some meaningful degree of fairness. According to Rawl's difference principle, inequalities are justified only to the extent that they are designed to bring (and actually bring) the greatest possible benefit to the least advantaged among us.

Generally, political thinkers today also debate whether equality of opportunity—assuming it truly exists in advanced capitalist regimes—is indeed enough to ensure political equality, which all in liberal democratic regimes agree is necessary for a polity to be just. Many observers of U.S. politics today, including some who support a free-market capitalist economy, worry that the wall separating political from economic inequalities is regularly breached. One of the most obvious ways in which the wall is breached is through the financing of political campaigns by private, independent economic actors. Such contributions amount to a powerful form of political influence with which it is difficult for ordinary citizens to compete and which undermines the political equality on which democracy rests.

A less obvious way in which the wall between economic inequalities and political equality is breached is described by Charles Lindblom. For Lindblom, even when corporations do not gain unequal political influence through campaign contributions, they enjoy a "privileged position" in policy-making because of their very real ability to shape economic outcomes. For example, polluting industries have special leverage in lobbying Congress not to enact stricter air-quality standards because they can convincingly claim that the effects of such standards would cause them to lay off workers.

The concentration of economic power in the hands of a few, then, may translate quite directly into a concentration of political power in the hands of the same few. Even if economic inequalities are tolerable in and of themselves, most agree that political equality is sacrosanct and that the translation of economic inequality into political inequality is a serious problem when or if it occurs. These problems with economic inequality exist alongside any threats to good democratic citizenship discussed by civic republican thinkers, such as the tendency of rule by one class in its own interest, which worried Aristotle, and the threat to democratic stability posed by a class with nothing to lose, as Jefferson discussed.

Another, more recent set of questions has been raised by those concerned with global inequalities—especially those inequalities between the economically advanced countries and the less wealthy nations of the world—who point out that limiting discussions of equality and remedies to address perceived inequalities within the nation-state are not appropriate to a highly economically interconnected world. The international political economic environment has inherited inequalities of the colonial era, to which are added the unequal outcomes of international goods and capital markets and the privileging of economically advanced countries by the major international political economic institutions, principally the International Monetary Fund (IMF), World Bank, and World Trade Organization (WTO). Yet most of the mechanisms by which we address socioeconomic inequalities within a nation-state are inappropriate or impractical for use in addressing global inequalities.

Related to these concerns are challenges raised by the rise of international governance institutions—the above-mentioned political economic institutions, the United Nations, regional international organizations, bodies set up to address specific issues, and so on. If the notion of equal representation is fundamental to liberal democratic politics, how ought it be applied to international governance bodies? Generally today such bodies give representation either to each nation-state equally (as with the United Nations) or in some proportion to financial contribution (as with the IMF). The former approach is a holdover from the early days of the modern nation-state, when the state was identified with a monarch who was being represented in the international realm. However, liberal democracy is based on representation being roughly proportional to population of districts or regions—but this could privilege the elites of populous but nondemocratic states. Basing representation on IMF contributions, many argue, simply reinforces the global economic and political advantages already possessed by the advanced capitalist regimes.

Movements for Equality—Equal to Whom?

Since the mid-1800s, equality has been the rallying cry in the United States for abolitionists, suffragists, the civil rights movement, the feminist movement, gay and lesbian movements, and even some sectors of the environmental movement. One striking aspect of many such movements is their persistence in appropriating the language of the Declaration of Independence that "all men are created equal" or, more broadly, in returning to what Martin Luther King Jr. called the "great wells of democracy . . . dug deep by the Founding Fathers" ("Letter from the Birmingham Jail," pp. 33–34). Frederick Douglass's abolitionism, the Declaration of Sentiments of the early U.S. women's movement, King's rhetoric, and some voices in the gay and lesbian movement have generally called not for changing the fundamental institutions or political values of the United States but for fully and equally including particular groups in American political life. Equality for these movements has to a large extent meant equal rights, including equal voting rights for women, equal civil rights for African-Americans, and equal marriage rights for same-sex partners (although the latter is debated within gay and lesbian communities).

Members of such movements have debated whether this emphasis on inclusion—in place of a broad critique of the system that has excluded certain groups—is a strength or a weakness. More moderate activists have argued that American ideals and institutions are fundamentally sound and that the problem lies in the unequal inclusion in practice of certain groups into political life. Radical voices in all these movements have suggested that it is not enough to assert a right to the privileges enjoyed by heterosexual white men. The political theorist Wendy Brown has built on this critique. She argues that to the extent that feminists as well as racial and ethnic minority movements operate within the framework of the liberal individualist tradition, they privilege their particular identity as the basis for equality claims. Such thinking "overburdens" their particular identity with the harms they perceive. It also overburdens with blame members of the group defined as dominant in the unequal relationship between identity groups (for women, men; for African Americans, whites; for gays and lesbians, heterosexuals). A larger analysis of the political economic system and inequalities that come from their other social relationships (particularly class) tends to be absent. This, in Brown's words, "wounds" equality claims by failing to notice the power of the capitalist political economic system to unequally distribute harms and goods. This overburdening also can produce a backlash by placing too much blame for one group's perceived harms on members of the dominant identity groups. In a sense the dominant group is "wounded" beyond the harm they may have caused when a critique of the political economic system is missing. Such thinking also fails to notice that many harms are also suffered by members of the dominant group who are in inferior social relationships themselves along some axes of domination—especially class.

Questions such as what kinds of equality are important, as well as equality to whom and for whom, are still contested, even within movements for equality. Multiple identities—ethnic, racial, class, sexual, religious, and so on—create multiple sites for inequalities to emerge, and movements often choose to focus on one site of inequality, sometimes at the expense of another. Moreover, with the globalization of economic production and consumption and the emergence of institutions such as the European Union, questions about the equal treatment and equal rights of migrant and minority groups remain unresolved (see Kymlicka).

Concerns about Equality

Many political thinkers have worried that applications of an ideal of equality may undermine freedom. For Alexis de Tocqueville (1805–1859), equality can easily come to dominate people's political aspirations. As he puts it, citizens (Americans in particular) "want equality in freedom, and if they cannot have that, they still want equality in slavery" (p. 506). Worse, people may tolerate not being free as long as everyone is equally unfree. Equality also isolates individuals, according to Tocqueville. It ends any sense of mutual responsibility that may have previously existed; there is no longer any sense of duty either to one's "superiors" or one's "inferiors" because there are no real superiors or inferiors. Hannah Arendt echoes Tocqueville in her distinction between liberation and freedom. Liberation of the poor from crushing material necessity and dependence on others is a prerequisite to freedom, but it is not freedom because it does not entail participation in self-governance. However, there is a tendency for revolutionary movements to settle for liberation—for relative material equality—rather than seeking complete freedom. Finally, the liberal John Stuart Mill (1806–1873) is concerned that with the undermining of "differences of position" in society, and with "the ascendancy of public opinion in the State," groups and individuals are increasingly the same and find less and less room for dissent and nonconformity (p. 70). All these thinkers share a general sense that while some forms of equality are key prerequisites of a good politics, equality must not be mistaken for the ultimate political ideal, which for these thinkers is freedom.

Conclusion

For political thinkers concerned with what constitutes good democratic politics, concentrations of power are sources of concern wherever they are found. This is especially the case when these concentrations of power threaten the basic democratic notion that citizens should have a meaningful capacity to govern themselves and participate on a roughly equal basis with other citizens in their collective self-governance. In thinking about what constitutes a good democratic politics we need to recognize the inherent contestability of the very concept of equality and that equality is one value among many (albeit a very important value to democracy). Democracy, by its very nature, requires that no conception of the nature of equality can be taken off the table of political discourse and debate.

Furthermore, no single conception should always prevail in democratic deliberations or it risks the commitment of citizens who do not share the dominant conception of the democratic project. It is in fact the rich contestation over equality and its relation to other political values that helps ensure that new forms of domination cannot creep unnoticed into democratic polities.

See also **Democracy; Liberalism; Marxism.**

BIBLIOGRAPHY

Appleby, Joyce. *Capitalism and a New Social Order: The Republican Vision of the 1790s.* New York: New York University Press, 1984.

———. *Liberalism and Republicanism in the Historical Imagination.* Cambridge, Mass.: Harvard University Press, 1992.

Aquinas, Thomas. *Summa Theologiae.* 3 vols. Translated by the Fathers of the English Dominican Province. New York: Benzinger Bros., 1948.

Arendt, Hannah. *On Revolution.* New York: Viking, 1963.

Aristotle. *Nicomachean Ethics.* Indianapolis, Ind.: Hackett, 1999.

———. *Politics.* Chicago: University of Chicago Press, 1984.

Bercovitch, Sacvan. "The Rites of Assent: Rhetoric, Ritual, and the Ideology of American Consensus." In *The American Self: Myth, Ideology, and Popular Culture,* edited by Sam B. Girgus, 5–42. Albuquerque: University of New Mexico Press, 1981.

Brown, Wendy. *States of Injury: Power and Freedom in Late Modernity.* Princeton, N.J.: Princeton University Press, 1995.

hooks, bell. *Feminist Theory: From Margin to Center.* Boston: South End Press, 1984.

Jefferson, Thomas. *The Portable Thomas Jefferson.* Edited by Merrill D. Peterson. New York: Viking, 1977.

Kant, Immanuel. "Groundwork of the Metaphysics of Morals." In his *Practical Philosophy,* translated and edited by Mary J. Gregor, 37–60. Cambridge, U.K.: Cambridge University Press, 1996.

Kymlicka, Will. *Multicultural Citizenship: A Liberal Theory of Minority Rights.* New York: Oxford University Press, 1995.

Lindblom, Charles. "The Market as Prison." *Journal of Politics* 44 (1982).

———. *Politics and Markets.* New York: Basic Books, 1977.

Locke, John. *Second Treatise on Government.* Edited by C. B. Macpherson. Indianapolis: Hackett, 1980.

Marx, Karl, and Friedrich Engels. *The Marx-Engels Reader.* 2nd ed. Edited by Robert C. Tucker. New York: Norton, 1978.

Mill, John Stuart. *On Liberty.* Edited by Elizabeth Rapaport. Indianapolis: Hackett, 1978.

———. *The Subjection of Women.* Mineola, N.Y.: Dover, 1997.

Ober, Josiah. *The Athenian Revolution.* Princeton, N.J.: Princeton University Press, 1996.

———. *Mass and Elite in Democratic Athens.* Princeton, N.J.: Princeton University Press, 1989.

Rae, Douglas, et al. *Equalities.* Cambridge, Mass.: Harvard University Press, 1981.

Rawls, John. *A Theory of Justice.* Rev. ed. Cambridge, Mass.: Harvard University Press, 1999.

Rousseau, Jean-Jacques. "A Discourse on the Origin of Inequality." In his *The Social Contract and Discourses,* translated by G. D. H. Cole. New ed. London: Dent, 1993.

Schneir, Miriam, ed. *Feminism: The Essential Historical Writings.* New York: Vintage, 1994.

St. John de Crèvecoeur, J. Hector. *Letters from an American Farmer.* Garden City, N.Y.: Doubleday, n.d.

Terchek, Ronald J. *Republican Paradoxes and Liberal Anxieties.* Lanham, Md.: Rowman and Littlefield, 1997.

Terchek, Ronald J., and David K. Moore. "Recovering the Political Aristotle: A Critical Response to Smith." *American Political Science Review* 94, no. 4 (December 2000): 905–911.

Tocqueville, Alexis de. *Democracy in America.* Translated by George Lawrence. New York: Harper and Row, 1969.

Walzer, Michael. *Spheres of Justice: A Defense of Pluralism and Equality.* New York: Basic Books, 1983.

Alexandra Kogl
David K. Moore

GENDER EQUALITY

The coupling of equality and gender may indicate a paradox, if not an oxymoron. If equality were to exist, would gender? Does the persistent salience of the idea of gender with regard to equality provide evidence of fundamental flaws or contradictions in theories and practices of equality? Can the pursuit of equality reproduce rather than undermine gender dominance? While these questions are central to contemporary discourses on equality and gender, consensus on answers or even means to address them is absent.

Equality is a relational term. It entails establishing a relation between two or more things. Logically, differences between the objects of comparison must exist, for otherwise the question of their equivalence would not occur. However, establishing equality requires specifying a characteristic potentially shared by each thing. Furthermore, it demands identifying a class of objects among which the characteristic might be found. For example, if one declares, "all men are born equal," then one must specify the criterion that warrants this statement. In so doing, the boundary marking equality's terrain is simultaneously established. In this case, equality is significant, or meaningful, only in relations among men, not men and other beings; within this formulation the question "Are men and animals equal?" is unintelligible. Establishing equality thus requires identifying the common criterion and commensurable objects. Having done so, it is then possible to evaluate the relation of each relevant thing to the common measure—if each partakes of the common quality to the same degree, then equality exists.

Thus establishing equality does not require that the objects within its specified class be in all respects identical. However, while discourses of equality do not deny that differences exist, they do claim that in regard to some practices or claims, existing differences are irrelevant. In these practices or claims, what matters is partaking of the common quality. Those who share the quality equally ought to count identically or have equal access to the practice or claim. For example, if one claims that natural rights are innate to each human, then each human's rights are entitled to the same treatment and regard as every other human's. So equality requires a commitment to disregard some characteristics when distributing certain goods or treatment in favor of a presumption of equivalence.

Equality, Liberalism, and Feminism

The idea that public life ought to be organized on the basis of this presumption of a formal equivalence and its ensuing entitlements emerged relatively recently. It is a distinguishing characteristic of modern liberalism, modes of thought and practices that emerged in seventeenth- and eighteenth-century Western Europe. Thomas Hobbes (1588–1679), John Locke (1632–1704), and Jean-Jacques Rousseau (1712–1778) are among the most important early liberal theorists. Their writings reflect and refine the new bourgeoisie's claims of equality arising in the political struggles in early modern Europe against older feudal hierarchal orders. These new movements rejected the ideas of a natural basis for authority or the relevance of certain ascribed characteristics, such as one's family of origin, to the legitimacy of claims to rule or to the distribution of public power.

In the apparent rejection of the significance of at least some ascribed characteristics to the distribution of power, discourses of equality would appear to have the potential to dissolve the basis of many asymmetrical relationships. Indeed, one can argue that modern feminisms emerged simultaneously with and within theories and practices of liberal equality. However, while perhaps siblings, feminisms and their related liberal discourses are not identical. From the first, feminisms exposed the contradictions and limits of liberal equality. Feminist movements fought (and in some countries, continue to fight) sustained and difficult battles to attain suffrage and equal rights to education, reproductive freedom, employment, and protection under the law. Such rights are called formal equality. As more countries extend formal equality to previously excluded groups and declare their commitment to gender neutrality, however, the contradictions and limits of formal equality become more evident. Consequently the meanings of and relationships between equality and gender are increasingly complex and contested.

Equality and Sexual Difference

Tensions between equality and gender exist partially as the result of each term's traditional construction. While equality is understood as equivalence and entails stipulating a common quality or uniform measure, gender has been constituted through difference, specifically "sexual difference." Until recent feminist discourses, *gender* and *sexual difference* have been interchangeable and identical terms. As traditionally conceived, gender is constituted in and through "naturally occurring" sexual (anatomical) differences. Male and female are dichotomous natural kinds; gender categories simply reflect a biologically determined order. All humans are one and only one of gender's constituent binary pair: man/woman. Conventionally, gender is not only a binary, but an asymmetrical, hierarchical one. The male is the norm and superior, the female deviant and lacking.

Given this ranking, when theorists began to evaluate the significance of equality discourses to women's situations, certain questions inevitably arose. These included whether sexual difference was a kind of difference relevant to theories and practices of equality and, if so, if women's difference was misconceived. In other words, despite women's difference, were they in the relevant sense equal to men? The relevant sense would be that they sufficiently partake of the common quality the possession of which warrants claims to equality. Thus eighteenth-century writers such as Mary Wollstonecraft (1759–1797) argue that reason is the common quality that renders humans equal. Women are as capable of reasoning as men; hence, they deserve equal enjoyment of all public rights. Later John Stuart Mill (1806–1873) argues that given the existing subordination of women, it is impossible to know what their true nature might be. Therefore, one ought to assume that they are as able and desiring as men to exercise the innate capacities of self-development and reason that define humanness.

Gender Asymmetries and the Limits of Formal Equality

Coupled with strenuous political activity, such claims of women's sameness—in regard to being "like men" in their possession of the essential quality grounding equality—eventually produced formal legal equality for women in most states. In most countries in the early twenty-first century, according to law, women can vote, own property, enter professions, receive an education, hold public office, and so forth. However, despite this formal equality, few would argue that gender asymmetries have disappeared. Women worldwide are far more likely than men who are otherwise similarly situated in race, ethnic, and class positions to be poor or illiterate; to perform the most dangerous, low-paying work; to suffer sexual violence; and to be absent from positions of public, economic, and cultural power.

The persistence of such gender asymmetries generates vigorous feminist debate. Some argue discourses of equality replicate rather than undermine male dominance. The male side of the gender binary remains the norm, hence female difference is devalued. Equality simply means the integration of women within "male-ordered" states. Insofar as individual women seek to emulate male-dominant values, they may attain equal access to political, cultural, and economic institutions. Such individual access will do nothing to transform the devaluation of the feminine or undermine patriarchal ways of life. True equality would require a revaluation of female difference and its incorporation, not erasure, within revised norms and social practices. Alternatively, some argue that the persistence of gender asymmetry is a symptom of pervasive, systemic domination. Equality is insufficient or inappropriate to overturn such social relations. Instead, theorists recommend a variety of alternate approaches, for example, ones rooted in theories and practices of justice, radical democracy, or sex or class revolution.

Beyond Gender Neutrality

Other feminists deconstruct the apparently gender-neutral qualities said to ground human equality and question the putative neutrality of the liberal state. They examine abstract notions of reason and the individual posited by philosophers such as Immanuel Kant (1724–1804) or John Rawls (1921–2002) to warrant formal equality. Abstract reason and individualism require a split between the particular, phenomenal, material, embodied person and the universal, noumenal, unsituated mind. The identification of body with error and mind with capacity to grasp truth maps too neatly with the gendered split of female (body)/male (mind). In particular, some argue, it replicates the devaluation or denial of the unique, generative power of women—only they can give birth to children. Excluding female difference from the public world enables the actual constitution of its modal citizens, male heads of households, to remain obscured. Incorporating sexually differentiated embodiment within reason would undermine its universalistic appearance and hence its capacity to ground equality. If females were no longer the only markers of embodied difference, the gender specificity of all citizens could no longer be denied. Once this were to occur, the patriarchally ordered nature of existing public worlds would be evident. Unless transformed, a patriarchal state cannot institute true gender equality.

Some deconstructive approaches raise the further question of whether there are any universalizable (gender-neutral) qualities that could ground equality, and if so what they might be. Equality would have to be radically rethought without recourse to the presumption that such qualities exist. Such questions intersect with the concerns of gender activists in "postcolonial" states. Here, as in the West, states may use gender as the basis for differential social control and distribution of resources, but such practices may also be justified in the name of a "tradition" that resists contemporary forms of cultural and political-economic Western imperialism. For example, in contemporary Iran and Saudi Arabia, state-sanctioned constraints on women's mobility, public activities, and employment are justified as protecting women's modesty. This modesty is said to be required by the Koran, and in turn Islam is represented as a barrier to postcolonialist Western domination. Given the effects of globalization and transnational politics on the postcolonial states, whether discourses of equality are intrinsically "Western" and colonizing remains an important concern for feminists of these countries.

Inequality or Domination?

Rather than a reflection of biologically given sexual difference, feminists argue, gender is socially constructed or an effect of power. Male/female is constituted so as to sustain male dominance. So are all other aspects of human existence—work, culture, family, politics, knowledge, sexuality, and subjectivity. Writers point, for example, to the structure of work in capitalist economies. Working hours and responsibilities are often inflexible and do not easily fit with caretaking or other household responsibilities. Hence, work replicates and reproduces a gendered public/private split and the sexual division of labor. The modal worker is a heterosexual, married male. His wife takes care of children and all other domestic responsibilities. Due to their reproductive capacities and existing gender expectations, women are disadvantaged within these structures. Formal equality cannot resolve or even recognize such systematic disadvantage, for it only comes into play when women are already equally situated relative to men. Equality stipulates equal pay for equal work, but it does not transform the workplace to take equally into account the multiple demands of wage labor and caretaking. Thus structural disadvantage persists.

Indeed some writers argue that it is in precisely those areas where sexual difference most disadvantages women that formal equality is most ineffective or even counterproductive. Three areas of particular concern are reproduction, the sexual division of labor, and sexual violence. Women are not similarly situated to men in any of these areas. Currently only women can be pregnant; moreover, public policies regarding matters such as abortion or forced sterilization, maternity leave, and exclusion from certain jobs on "health" grounds will necessarily impact women differently than men. Similarly, women are far more likely to suffer sexual violence and harassment than are men. The power of cultural norms and pressures of socialization and unconscious subjective desires and identity formation sustain gendered norms of caretaking so that most responsibility for domestic labor, child care, tending to the elderly, and so forth, continues to fall on women. Differential effects of public policies (or the lack of them)—concerning social welfare provision, divorce law, and health care—on women and men result from this sexual division of labor. Insistence that women are "like men" or that there is a gender-neutral norm in such areas is likely to sustain women's current disadvantages.

Politics of Inequality and Difference

Writers differ, however, on policies to remedy such problems. Some emphasize the need to reorganize the sexual division of labor within the family so as to render males and females equally situated there. Others envision a radical reorganization of all spheres so that caretaking is treated as a public matter and civic responsibility, not simply a private duty. Some extend this argument to support a more extensive breakdown of the gendered split between nurturance and public action and a revaluation of stereotypically female values. They argue that the "female virtues" of care and attention to particulars ought to inform practices of citizenship and all other aspects of political-economic life.

Attention to disadvantages arising from women's difference has generated many social movements. Some activist groups have pushed for reproductive rights for women (both for legal abortion and for women's ability to shape "population" policy and eliminate forced sterilization). Other groups have successfully generated pressure to recognize sexual harassment as a form of sexual discrimination, actionable under law. Reproductive-rights activists in some countries have succeeded in ensuring that women now have increased access to legal and safe abortions and more control over decisions affecting their own bodies. Still other groups focus on the social provision of resources in areas typically seen as women's responsibility; such resources range from child care to clean water, care of the old and sick, and "microloans" to fund small-scale economic enterprises so that women can support themselves and their children.

Gender, Sexuality, and Sexual Difference

While respecting the practical achievements resulting from attention to gender/equality, whether in the form of formal equality or sexual difference/disadvantage, some writers and activists claim neither approach goes far enough in identifying and combating the fatal flaws intrinsic to current construc-

tions of gender and equality. Of central importance are the constructions of gender itself. Some writers argue that gender, sexual difference, and sexuality must be delinked and reconceived. Others stress the internal complexity of gender and its simultaneous constitution through social relations such as race, sexuality, class, and geographic location. Attention to these concerns raises further questions about the relevant measure by which equality ought to be gauged and also in whose name "equality" is claimed.

Judith Butler and others argue that sex difference should not be understood as a "natural" kind. Rather, gender relations produce sexual difference by organizing the body in particular ways and attributing social significance and meaning to certain of its features. There is no necessary relation between anatomy and gender; rather, each subject is engendered through mandatory social practices. These social practices, rather than biology, demand that individuals locate themselves and others on one or the other side of the binary male/female. Absent gender domination, there might be many genders, or none at all, and embodiment would not be read as and through "sexual difference." Similarly, there is no necessary relationship between anatomy and sexuality. Sexuality is about desire and pleasure, and practices expressing and gratifying these affects are highly variable. Hetero- and homosexuality are equally social constructs, ones that reinforce and naturalize gender and sexual difference. Appropriate objects of desire are specified and gender identities are stabilized by linking desire and "sexual difference"; I am a man because I desire a woman; I desire a woman because my penis makes it "natural" to do so.

In this view the goal is not equality between men and women, but an end to compulsory gender and heterosexuality. This would both produce and necessitate radically different notions and practices of subjectivity, family, and kinship. Rather than distribute labor more evenly among men and women within heterosexual families, the emphasis should be on multiplying the possibilities of affective ties and seeking their legal-social recognition and support. These ideas both undergird and reflect a move toward "queer" politics, in which the goal is to resist gender and to undermine male/female as mandatory subject positions. In pursuit of such goals, queer politics advocates policies including recognition of legal rights of homosexual partners and alternate kinship relations, nontraditional adoption, treating homophobic or violent acts toward those who resist traditional gendering as legally actionable wrongs, and extending the right of privacy beyond heterosexual practices.

Race, Gender, Class, and Geographic Location

Another area of sharp contention is whether gender can be understood best as the subordination of women by men. What then defines women is their shared inequality. While some writers such as Catharine A. MacKinnon and Susan Moller Okin claim that gender subordination is universal (all women are oppressed by male domination), others argue for a more differentiated view. First, the question remains, what is the valid standard or norm serving as the unit of measurement? Is it the social, political, economic, and cultural positions of the most privileged men in the world? In relation to this group, many men, due to their race, ethnicity, geographic location, sexuality, or other social relations, are extremely disadvantaged. Are women to be situated in relation to men who share their other social locations? In this case, a poor woman might in many dimensions be equal to her male peer, yet highly disadvantaged in relation to other women.

Second, the binary approach to gender cannot do justice to the multiple ways it is enacted. Binary conceptions occlude the particular, complex qualities of women's and men's locations. The doing of gender is shaped by many factors. Gender is always inflected by other social relations, just as those relations are inflected by gender. Global patterns of the distribution of resources have an enormous impact on women's (and men's) lives, and not all these patterns are solely a function of male dominance. Relative to some marked female, others constituted differently enjoy many privileges. The privilege of some women, due to constituting constellations of race, sexuality, class, or location, and so forth, often rests on the continuing disadvantage of others. For example, the sustained economic deterioration of some areas leads to the immigration of poor women into more prosperous countries. The low-wage labor of these women enables other women to purchase domestic services and compete more effectively for access to higher-paid professions. Conversely, the shared oppressions of many women and men along race, location, ethnic, class, or other lines produces forms of solidarity and common interest among some women and men. In the United States, for example, the intersections of race and gender have produced complex patterns of deep loyalty among many women and men of color as well as oppression of these women both by men of color and by white men and women. Similarly, the horrific forms of colonialist and racist domination of men by other men and some women's complicity in it cannot be ignored. Thus struggles for meaningful transformations of women's condition and gender relations must take local and diverse forms. Unable any longer to speak in the name of a singular subject or to generate a consensus on a universalizable equivalent, discourses of equality may be poorly suited to address such complexities.

See also **Feminism; Gender; Human Rights: Women's Rights; Identity, Multiple.**

BIBLIOGRAPHY

Butler, Judith. *Gender Trouble: Feminism and the Subversion of Identity.* New York: Routledge, 1990.

Butler, Judith, and Joan W. Scott, eds. *Feminists Theorize the Political.* New York: Routledge, 1992.

Collins, Patricia Hill. *Black Feminist Thought: Knowledge, Consciousness, and the Politics of Empowerment.* New York: Routledge, 2000.

Davis, Angela Y. *Women, Race, and Class.* New York: Vintage, 1983.

Flax, Jane. "Beyond Equality and Difference." In *Beyond Equality and Difference: Citizenship, Feminist Politics, and Female Subjectivity,* edited by Gisela Bock and Susan James. New York: Routledge, 1992.

———. "On Encountering Incommensurability: Martha Nussbaum's Aristotelian Practice." In *Controversies in Feminism,* edited by James P. Sterba. Lanham, Md.: Rowman and Littlefield, 2001.

MacKinnon, Catharine A. *Feminism Unmodified: Discourses on Life and Law.* Cambridge, Mass.: Harvard University Press, 1987.

Mill, John Stuart. "The Subjection of Women." In *John Stuart Mill: Three Essays.* New York: Oxford University Press, 1975.

Mohanty, Chandra Talpade, Ann Russo, and Lourdes Torres. *Third World Women and the Politics of Feminism.* Bloomington: Indiana University Press, 1991.

Nussbaum, Martha. "In Defense of Universal Values." In *Controversies in Feminism,* edited by James P. Sterba. Lanham, Md.: Rowman and Littlefield, 2001.

Okin, Susan Moller. *Justice, Gender, and the Family.* New York: Basic Books, 1989.

Scott, Joan W. "Deconstruction Equality-Versus-Difference: Or, the Uses of Poststructuralist Theory for Feminism." In *Conflicts in Feminism,* edited by Marianne Hirsch and Evelyn Fox Keller. New York: Routledge, 1990.

Wollstonecraft, Mary. *A Vindication of the Rights of Woman.* Edited by Charles W. Hagelman, Jr. New York: Norton, 1967.

Jane Flax

RACIAL EQUALITY

Racial equality is the belief that individuals, regardless of their racial characteristics, are morally, politically, and legally equal and should be treated as such. Furthermore, it is the belief that different racial groups, as groups, are equal, with none being inherently superior or inferior in intelligence, virtue, or beauty. In the United States the term is commonly linked to the belief in equal treatment under the law as well as equal opportunity as a principle to ensure individuals, regardless of their race, an equal opportunity in education, employment, and politics.

In reality, the ideal of racial equality, however defined, has not always been practiced, nor has it been fully achieved anywhere in the world. This is because the belief in racial equality has historically had to counter both deeply rooted beliefs in racial inequality as well as the concrete political, legal, and customary practices of racial discrimination and oppression. Hence racial equality is expressed in antiracist philosophy and in antiracist political mobilization.

Racism as Ideology

The idea of racial equality has disputed long-standing beliefs in racial inequality that can be traced back several hundred years. Centuries ago, the colonization or enslavement of a people was often justified on grounds of cultural superiority (as in the case of British colonial control over India) and even on religious grounds (for example, slavery was rationalized as biblically ordained by Noah's curse of Ham or as a process of bringing Christianity to heathens). In the 1700s, however, racial inequality was increasingly given a scientific justification.

Contemporary categories of race ("white," "black," etc.) were given a scientific status by Carolus Linnaeus and Johann Friedrich Blumenbach. Typical of the era, each explained race with reference to climate and geography. In 1758, Linnaeus classified humans as "Americanus" (currently Native American), whom he described as red, upright, choleric, and ruled by habit; "Europaeus" (currently European), whom he described as white, sanguine, muscular, and ruled by custom; "Asiaticus" (currently Asian), whom he described as pale yellow, melancholy, stiff, and ruled by belief; and "Africanus" (currently African), whom he described as black, phlegmatic, relaxed, and ruled by caprice. Later, in 1795, Blumenbach asserted the moral equality of races but still categorized and ranked them according to his conception of beauty: Caucasians were his ideal, with Malays and Ethiopians representing one line of "degeneration" and Americans and Mongolians representing a second line. These typologies had the inevitable result of not only reifying race as a scientific category, but also solidifying the alleged link between race, beauty, intelligence, and the capability of exercising self-government.

In the nineteenth and early twentieth centuries, racial inequality was justified by several different scientific approaches. First, polygenism attempted to explain that each race is genetically distinct, with Europeans seen as superior to blacks, Asians, and Native Americans. Indeed, in his *Essay on the Inequality of Human Races,* Joseph Arthur de Gobineau asserted that whites were superior to other races and advised great nations to preserve their racial purity, since racial mixture, he claimed, led to cultural degeneration and political decline. Then craniometry was used in an attempt to explain intelligence according to brain size. Similarly, criminal anthropology attempted to explain criminality with reference to facial features such as the slope of one's forehead. Also, World War I–era intelligence quotient tests were originally used to link intelligence to heredity, ranking whites above European immigrants and African-Americans. By reducing race to biology, these approaches, as Ashley Montagu observed:

alleged that something called "race" is the prime determiner of all the important traits of body and soul, of character and personality, of human beings and nations. And it is further alleged that this something called "race" is a fixed and unchangeable part of the germ plasm, which, transmitted from generation to generation, unfolds in each people as a typical expression of personality and culture. (p. 14)

Because biological determinism alleges that race is fixed, unchangeable, and hierarchical, these approaches lend favor to discriminatory, reactionary, or do-nothing policy approaches (Gould, pp. 51–61).

These approaches, however, were flawed both because they were tainted by the prejudices of the researchers and because they lacked scientific rigor. For example, Montagu's reanalysis of early intelligence quotient tests found that the average score for blacks from the North was higher than the average score for whites from the South. If these results reveal anything, it is *not* that intelligence is innately connected to race but that the quality of and funding levels for public education are strongly correlated with results (Gould, pp. 249–250). This lends support not to heredity and biology as inherently connected to intelligence but to an approach that stresses the social and educational environment in which a person grows up. Since racial inequality in practice provides some groups with access to good educational opportunities and denies them to

others, it is no surprise if test scores differ across these groups. If racial inequality is affected by unequal social factors, this environmental approach suggests that improving those social factors will promote racial equality.

In the twentieth century, scholars such as Franz Boas and Montagu have argued that attempts to reduce race to biology should be rejected because they prop up ideologies and practices of inequality. Going one step further, Montagu suggested, "[b]ased as it is on unexamined facts and unjustifiable generalizations, it were better that the term 'race,' being so weighed down with false meaning, be dropped altogether from the vocabulary" (p. 62). Many scientists continue to point out that race does not exist in any scientific sense. For example, human beings are genetically 99.988 percent identical, with more genetic variation existing within racial categories than between them. Despite this, social scientists have not dropped "race" from their vocabulary. Instead, while they agree that race is indeed a useless scientific category, it is nevertheless real because race has very real social consequences that affect an individual's or group's opportunities, rights, and resources, or lack thereof, in a particular society.

In this sense, race is socially and legally constructed, and its meaning varies across time and place. F. James Davis, for example, illustrates how different legal definitions of "black" were codified during slavery and segregation to maintain the racial hierarchy on which each was based. Furthermore, Howard Winant illustrates how race is defined differently according to historical, cultural, economic, and legal contexts when one compares the United States, South Africa, Brazil, and other countries. Scholarship such as this rejects the biological or scientific notion of race as a myth but accepts the notion that race is socially, politically, and economically "real" because of the ways in which people are privileged or disadvantaged by its meanings and practices.

The Politics of Racial Inequality

This discussion will now look at how racial inequality manifests itself in a variety of constitutional, legal, policy, and cultural practices.

In the United States, the Constitution accommodated the interests of the slaveholding states in three areas: first, the famous "3/5ths clause" that counted five enslaved blacks as three free persons for purposes of taxation and representation; second, the new Congress was prohibited from even considering abolishing the importation of slaves until 1809; and third, the Constitution (Article IV, section 2) required states to assist in returning any person escaped from bondage back to the state from which they had escaped. Indeed, citing the intent of the framers of the Constitution, the Supreme Court ruled in the *Dred Scott* decision of 1857 that enslaved Africans and their descendants in the United States were never intended to be citizens. The Court ruled that black people "had no rights that the white man was bound to respect."

Racial equality was constitutionally established through three amendments during the Reconstruction Era. The Thirteenth Amendment barred slavery or involuntary servitude, the

Wedgwood medallion bearing the inscription "Am I not a man and a brother?" (1787). Jasper ware. The knowledge that all humans are almost completely identical on the genetic level has led many social scientists to consider the use of the term *race* as more of a social concept than a biological term. WILBERFORCE HOUSE, HULL CITY MUSEUMS AND ART GALLERIES, UK / THE BRIDGEMAN ART LIBRARY, WWW.BRIDGEMAN.CO.UK

Fourteenth Amendment established standards of due process and equal treatment under the law for all citizens, and the Fifteenth Amendment guaranteed that the right to vote could not be denied due to race, color, or previous condition of servitude. However, by the end of the nineteenth century blacks were effectively disenfranchised as a result of violence, intimidation, and a range of tricks adopted by states (e.g., the Grandfather Clause, white primaries, poll taxes, and literacy tests) to avoid compliance with the Fifteenth Amendment. Furthermore, the Supreme Court issued decisions that limited the effectiveness of the civil rights acts passed by Congress during Reconstruction. Finally, in the *Plessy v. Ferguson* decision of 1896, the Supreme Court ruled that "separate but equal" accommodations in public transportation were not a violation of the Fourteenth Amendment's equal protection clause. This phrase, "separate but equal," was then applied to all spheres of life and epitomized the era of "Jim Crow" segregation. Facilities were separate but they were anything but equal. For example, white schools in some states received ten times the financial support compared to black schools (Fairclough).

In Germany, the biological determinism of nineteenth-century writers such as Gobineau was influential in the emergence of nationalism, fascism, and Nazism. For instance, Jewish people were seen as a biologically inferior race that represented a cultural and political threat to the superiority and purity of the Aryan race idolized by Adolf Hitler. As a result,

they were subjected to economic and political ghettoization, used as forced labor, and targeted for genocide. Also, in South Africa, a gradual process of racial separateness, or apartheid, began with the Native Land Act of 1913 that divided land to promote white ownership and domination as well as limited face-to-face interaction between blacks and whites. With the victory of the Nationalist Party in 1948, apartheid was fully institutionalized as a complete set of policies whereby the white minority completely segregated and dominated the black majority (Frederickson, 1981, pp. 239–249).

Countries have also used immigration policy as a discriminatory device, often basing immigration law on notions that certain racial groups were inferior and represented cultural or economic threats. In the mid-1800s in the United States, Chinese laborers were relied on to help build the transcontinental railroad. However, a nativist movement emerged, with white working-class men viewing Chinese laborers as an economic threat. As a result, the U.S. Congress passed the Chinese Exclusion Act in 1882, which prohibited Chinese immigration as well as the naturalization of Chinese laborers already in the United States. By 1917, U.S. immigration law prohibited immigration of labor from all of Asia except for Japan, as well as placing a tax on Mexican employees. Also in the early twentieth century, Australia adopted immigration laws designed to limit the number of Indian, Pacific Islander, and Asian immigrants. Such laws were adopted on the biological-determinist argument that these immigrants were racially inferior and a cultural threat to the superior "white Australia" (Miles, pp. 90–98).

Institutionalized racial inequality is also intertwined with economic inequality. In the United States, enslaved blacks provided a labor source for the Southern agrarian economy. Even after slavery was abolished, Southern blacks were still treated as a source of tenant farmers and laborers. In the twentieth century, blacks have typically faced twice the unemployment rate of whites and have struggled against discrimination in hiring, promotion, and pay. In 1942, due to labor shortages caused by World War II, the U.S. government established the Bracero program, under which Mexico sent to the United States workers who were given some legal status but exploited as cheap labor. Also during World War II, Japanese-Americans, but not Italian- or German-Americans, were subject to relocation and internment because of President Roosevelt's Executive Order 9066 in 1942, resulting in a gross violation of civil rights as well as a loss of property and businesses.

The Struggle for Racial Equality
To combat and dismantle racial inequality, a variety of groups and tactics emerged throughout the twentieth century in the United States and other countries. The predominant strategy has been nonviolent disobedience, the political mobilization of resources, and moral suasion to mobilize public opinion. However, some groups have advocated armed self-defense or violence as a strategy for revolutionary change.

By the dawn of the twentieth century, several strategies emerged to oppose Jim Crow and challenge the United States to live up to its professed ideals. Some reformers, such as Booker T. Washington, urged blacks to not push for civil and

political rights but instead to work hard, acquire a trade, and eventually hope for white acceptance. Others, such as W. E. B. Du Bois, argued that black people had every right to mobilize for equal civil and political rights that were now constitutionally guaranteed and that to do anything less was to accept a permanent second-class status. Du Bois and other reformers formed what turned into the preeminent civil rights organization of the twentieth century, the National Association for the Advancement of Colored People (NAACP), in 1909. The NAACP marched, protested, and, under the guidance of Charles Hamilton Houston, created a legal defense fund to pursue a strategy of social change through litigation.

This strategy came to fruition with the landmark *Brown v. Board of Education, Topeka* decision of 1954, in which the Supreme Court overturned the *Plessy* standard of "separate but equal" and declared that separate educational facilities are inherently unconstitutional. In the 1960s and 1970s, the litigation strategy and the NAACP Legal Defense Fund itself were used as models for other groups: the Mexican American Legal Defense and Education Fund (MALDEF), formed in 1968; the Puerto Rican Legal Defense and Education Fund (PRLDF), formed in 1972; and the Native American Rights Fund (NARF), formed in 1970.

The economics of racial inequality were also opposed and changed with a range of tactics. In the United States there have been several campaigns organized under the "don't shop where you can't work" strategy. Furthermore, in the 1950s and 1960s, economic boycotts were used to withdraw financial support from businesses and public transportation systems that engaged in segregation. Many of these were successful, the most famous one being the Montgomery bus boycott of 1955, which made Rosa Parks a civil rights icon and helped Martin Luther King, Jr., become a national civil rights leader. In 1962, Cesar Chavez helped form the National Farmworkers Association (NFWA) to defend the rights of Mexican-American and Asian-American agricultural workers. The NFWA helped negotiate contracts with corporate growers and was supported by consumer boycotts of targeted products, such as grapes. Also, in the 1980s, a global antiapartheid movement used economic and cultural boycotts, as well as pressuring companies and governments to divest from South Africa, to force the National Party to negotiate the dismantling of apartheid.

Nonviolent marches, sit-ins, and freedom rides were tactics used both to pressure private companies to end segregation but also to pressure the federal government to enforce civil rights laws in Southern states. The Southern Christian Leadership Conference (SCLC) was formed in 1957 with King as its leader. The SCLC drew on the organizational support of black churches and ministers to organize marches and protests across the South as well as the March on Washington for Jobs and Freedom in 1963, at which King gave his famous "I have a dream" speech. Other groups and tactics also emerged. The Student Nonviolent Coordinating Committee (SNCC) was led by college-aged black youth and eventually included white college-aged members. SNCC was active in sit-ins to integrate segregated lunch counters in Greenville, North Carolina. Together with members of the interracial Congress

of Racial Equality (CORE), SNCC members were active in "freedom rides" to desegregate bus terminals in the South, and members of both organizations were active in voter-registration efforts in Mississippi in 1963 and 1964 (Dittmer).

Such efforts finally pressured Congress and the president to act. The Civil Rights Act of 1964 guaranteed equal access and equal treatment under the law, banned segregated public accommodations, and prohibited discrimination in hiring on the basis of race, gender, or national origin. A year later, the Voting Rights Act of 1965 banned all discriminatory voter-registration laws and gave the Justice Department power to ensure that voting and election laws were not discriminatory. Indeed, with this act the promise of the Fifteenth Amendment was finally fulfilled. Also in 1965, immigration policies were reformed finally to dismantle any legacies of racial preference and discrimination. In 1968, the final major civil rights act of the era banned discrimination in the sale or rental of property and housing.

With these victories in the courts and in Congress, many Americans thought the nation's principles of equality were finally matched by its practices. In one way, this is true. For example, black voter-registration rates in Mississippi went from about 6 percent of eligible voters in 1965 to about 63 percent in 1971 and 1972 (Lawson). On the other hand, while legislation and litigation helped establish the principles of equality under the law, voting rights, and equal access to public accommodations, there still exists a legacy of economic inequity and social injustice.

Occasionally, groups pursued a strategy of armed self-defense or violence as a means to combat entrenched racial inequality. Contrary to the nonviolent philosophy of the civil rights movement in the 1950s and 1960s, individuals such as Robert F. Williams in North Carolina and groups such as the Deacons for Defense and Justice in Louisiana advocated civil and political rights but also reserved the right to self-defense when facing violent opposition (Tyson). In South Africa, the African National Congress (ANC) was formed to resist apartheid and originally set out on a course of nonviolent disobedience. However, some within the ANC eventually adopted a strategy of limited armed resistance that used selective acts of force for purposes of economic sabotage (Fredrickson, 1995). For this, Nelson Mandela was imprisoned until 1990, when he was released as part of South Africa's dismantling of apartheid.

The Continuing Struggle

Historically speaking, it is only recently that the belief in racial equality has refuted biological arguments that support racial hierarchies. In the early twenty-first century it has been commonplace for scholars to refer to race not as a biological concept but as a social construction. It is also only recently that the belief in racial equality has helped mobilize social change through a variety of tactics that resulted in the dismantling of legalized segregation in the United States and apartheid in South Africa. Despite these gains, however, racial equality remains elusive. As King and others had already observed in the late 1960s, changes in the attitudes of whites as well as legal and legislative changes to promote equal treatment, voting rights, and equal opportunity are all necessary steps in the effort to establish racial equality. The next set of steps includes a strong enforcement of civil rights as well as a major restructuring of economic resources, economic opportunities, educational opportunities, and political influence (King).

In the United States, several issues since the early 1970s serve as reminders that racial equality remains elusive. Fifty years after the *Brown* decision, there are increasing levels of segregation in the public schools of large, Northern cities, indicating that residential segregation also exists. College attendance rates for Latinos and blacks continue to lag behind those of whites and Asian-Americans. Indeed, gaps in educational achievement measured by standardized test scores have spurred the reemergence of biological explanations of race and intelligence (Gould). Incidents of police brutality and the harassment of black motorists (referred to as "racial profiling" or "driving while black") are signs that civil rights enforcement is still needed. And despite an emerging black middle class, there is controversy surrounding "affirmative action," a range of policies to ensure equal educational and employment opportunity.

On affirmative action and other issues, large differences of opinion between white and black Americans are emerging—so large that some scholars have labeled them "chasms" (Smith and Seltzer). Ironically, some invoke Dr. King's notion that individuals should be judged by the content of their character, not the color of their skin, to oppose policies intended to promote racial equality. Some find the goal of "color blindness" laudable; others believe diversity should be respected through pursuance of a "multiracial" set of policies that are conscious of race and targeted at ameliorating racial inequalities as a better path toward racial equality in the United States.

In global terms, several issues continue to demand attention and controversy. The legacies of past injustices, such as the Holocaust, slavery, segregation, and apartheid, have led to debates surrounding apologies, compensation, and reparations. South Africa has established a Truth and Reconciliation Commission to document the injustices of apartheid as well as to promote national reconciliation as it builds a multiracial democracy. The U.S. Congress passed the Civil Liberties Act of 1988, which issued an apology and offered a small monetary compensation to Japanese Americans interned during World War II. However, calls for an apology or compensation to black Americans for the legacies of slavery and segregation remain controversial (Brooks).

Additionally, the rights of economic and political refugees and migrants continue to be a focal point of the struggle for racial equality in Europe and the United States. Indeed, migrants and refugees constitute a cheap and exploitable source of labor but also spark xenophobic and nationalist reaction. Right-wing movements and leaders have emerged in France, Germany, Austria, and the United States to oppose the immigration of people they see as culturally, linguistically, or racially inferior. These and other concerns were the focus of the United Nations Conference against Racism, Racial Discrimination, Xenophobia, and Related Intolerance, held in Durban, South Africa, in August and September of 2001.

However, due to concerns that the conference would take strong stands against Israeli treatment of Palestinians as well as potentially open the door to reparations for slavery, the United States did not participate.

It is clear from these and other issues that the goal of racial equality remains in a constant and ongoing struggle against racism, both its current manifestations and its legacies, within the United States and around the world.

See also **Apartheid; Justice; Prejudice; Race and Racism.**

BIBLIOGRAPHY

Brooks, Roy L., ed. *When Sorry Isn't Enough: The Controversy over Apologies and Reparations for Human Injustice.* New York: New York University Press, 1999.

Davis, F. James. *Who Is Black? One Nation's Definition.* University Park: Pennsylvania State University Press, 1991.

Dittmer, John. *Local People: The Struggle for Civil Rights in Mississippi.* Urbana: University of Illinois, 1994.

Fairclough, Adam. *Better Day Coming: Blacks and Equality, 1890–2000.* New York: Viking, 2001.

Fredrickson, George M. *Black Liberation: A Comparative History of Black Ideologies in the United States and South Africa.* New York: Oxford University Press, 1995.

———. *White Supremacy: A Comparative Study in American and South African History.* New York: Oxford University Press, 1981.

Goldhagen, Daniel Jonah. *Hitler's Willing Executioners: Ordinary Germans and the Holocaust.* New York: Knopf, 1996.

Gould, Stephen Jay. *The Mismeasure of Man.* Rev. ed. New York: W.W. Norton, 1996.

King, Martin Luther, Jr. *Where Do We Go from Here: Chaos or Community?* Boston: Beacon Press, 1968.

Lawson, Steven. F. *Running for Freedom: Civil Rights and Black Politics in America Since 1941.* New York: McGraw-Hill, 1991.

Miles, Robert. *Racism.* London: Routledge, 1989.

Montagu, Ashley. *Man's Most Dangerous Myth: The Fallacy of Race.* 5th ed. New York: Oxford University Press, 1974.

Smith, Robert C., and Richard Seltzer. *Contemporary Controversies and the American Racial Divide.* Lanham, Md.: Rowman and Littlefield, 2000.

Tyson, Timothy B. *Radio Free Dixie: Robert F. Williams and the Roots of Black Power.* Chapel Hill: University of North Carolina Press, 1999.

Winant, Howard. *The World Is a Ghetto: Race and Democracy since World War II.* New York: Basic Books, 2001.

Gregory W. Streich

ESCHATOLOGY. The concept of eschatology was created by the Lutheran theologian Abraham Calov (1612–1686) and became popular through the works of the Prussian Reformed theologian F. D. E. Schleiermacher (1768–1834). It is derived from a sentence in *Jesus Sirach:* "In whatever you do, remember your last days [Greek: *ta eschata*], and you will never sin" (Sir. 7:36). Calov's concept is nothing but a new name for the traditional genre of Christian dogmatic treatises about "the last things" (Latin: *De novissimis* or *De extremis*). Generally, it can be said that eschatology deals with death and the things that, according to Christian doctrine, happen after death: the resurrection, the last judgment, and the eternal life in the Beyond. Relatively recently scholars in religious studies have begun to apply the concept of eschatology to the teachings about death and immortality in virtually all religions. But a continuous tradition of eschatological doctrine exists only in Christian theology.

Jewish Roots
Christian eschatology emerges from Jewish apocalypticism. The early Jewish apocalypses, such as those in the biblical book of Daniel, were written in the Hellenist period, when the Ptolemaic, the Seleucid, and later the Roman empires ruled Palestine. A growing number of Jews no longer believed in the coming of a messiah who would renew the glorious kingdom of David. Having seen one empire follow another, they believed the Jewish people had successively lost the ability to establish an independent kingdom. The gap between their consciousness of being God's elected people and political reality led to a deep crisis of the Jewish self-understanding (best described in the apocryphal Fourth Book of Ezra). The crisis was solved by the discovery of the Beyond. Modern historians of religion emphasize that Persian, Egyptian, Greek, and other historical influences played a role in this intellectual process, but the apocalyptic authors themselves describe the paradigm shift as a revelation (apokalypsis), gained in visionary experiences. They often give detailed accounts about the journeys they made into the Beyond.

The basic ideas of Jewish apocalypticism live on in Christian eschatology, in orthodox doctrine as well as in the preaching of sects and heretical groups. Mankind and the world are in a pathological state, for they are corrupted by original sin—a hereditary disease that cannot be cured. Therefore God will destroy this world and create a new one. But he will save the just believers and transfer them into the perfect order of the Beyond. Since the apocalyptics had lost all faith in national messianism, the decisive question is no longer whether a believer belongs to the elected people of Israel. The Jews might have a certain prerogative, but no guarantee of salvation. God is no longer the God of Israel but the ruler of the universe; the structure of world history is predetermined by his unchangeable plan. All the empires and political orders, the tyrants and the warlords are tools in the hand of God used to test the believers. The just ones must not partake in the political and military struggles of the corrupted world but must stay strong in their faith and wait for the annihilation of all evil and the beginning of God's kingdom.

All features of Christian eschatology that differ from Jewish apocalypticism are related to the experience of Christ. Although there is a variety of sometimes contradictory meanings of the word "Christ" already to be found in the New Testament, they all agree on one point: the presence of Christ among sinful mankind moderates the sharp distinction between this world and the Beyond. Christ answers the Pharisees, a Jewish group of apocalyptic intellectuals, who were waiting for dawn of the new eon: "The kingdom of God is not coming with

signs to be observed; nor will they say, 'Lo, here it is!' or 'There!' for behold, the kingdom of God is in the midst of you" (Luke 17:20–21).

According to Christian experience, the presence of the Savior introduces an anticipation of the Beyond; it signifies a breakthrough of the future into the present. The eschata, the resurrection of the dead, the last judgment, and the creation of the new world, are therefore the completion of a process already started by Christ in this world.

Pauline and Augustinian Contributions
The most influential interpretation of the experience of Christ was given by the Apostle Paul. He preached that Christ's incarnation, passion, and crucifixion redeem from sin anyone who becomes a member of the church (ekklesia), the mystical body of Christ. Paul's concept of the church points to two specific features of Christian eschatology. First, collectivity: The eschaton is not a personal event. Salvation from death is available only for the members of Christ's mystical body. On judgment day, the dead members of the church will be resurrected and unite with the living to form a single community of salvation (1 Thess. 4:13–17). Throughout Christian history, Hellenist-influenced theologians challenged Paul's collective eschatology by emphasizing the individual ascent of the immortal soul. They could justify their view with some quotations from the Gospels. Paul, however, clearly rejects the idea of the soul's solitary ascent and insists on the resurrection of the spiritually transformed body. Second, processuality: in this world the church already collects all the citizens who will establish the heavenly citizenship (politeuma) of the Beyond (Phil. 3:20). Therefore the creation of a new world is not a single event at the end of history but can be observed now in the church (2 Cor. 5:17). The establishment and growth of the church already belongs to the eschata. Christian existence is an eschatological existence between "already now" and "not yet." The Holy Spirit transforms the "inward man" of the members of the church, but a purely spiritual existence will be achieved only in the Beyond, after the "outward man," the carnal and mortal body, has died (2 Cor. 4:16, 5:6; Phil. 3:21).

The Gospels and the letters of Paul show that the early Christians awaited the final events in the imminent future. Yet the church became a historical reality and, after the Roman emperors turned to Christianity, a powerful institution in this world. This new experience led to two different variations of Christian eschatology. First, theologians such as Eusebius of Caesarea (c. 263–c. 339) worked out an imperial eschatology. The basic dogma was that God chose the Roman Empire to spread Christianity all over the world. Church and empire seemed to melt together under the rulership of the Constantinian dynasty. According to Eusebius, the Roman emperors succeeded Christ to fulfill the divine plan on earth; and at the end of history, Christ would return and succeed the emperors. The eschaton, the kingdom of God, appears as the perfection of the Roman Empire. Second, other Christians returned to apocalypticism and insisted that only the just ones who did not collaborate with the worldly powers would be saved. The chiliasts, who also appeared in later epochs of Christian history, believed

New Dictionary of the History of Ideas   709

that Christ would return in the near future and, after the destruction of all worldly empires, would establish a kingdom lasting a thousand (Greek: *chilia*) years. The Revelation of John, which was incorporated into the canon of the New Testament, seemed to confirm their view (cf. Rev. 20:4).

In the early fifth century, when the decline of the Western empire became obvious, empirical reality seemed to speak in favor of the apocalyptics. But the church father Augustine (354–430) rejected the imperial theology as well as apocalypticism by reformulating the Pauline eschatology as a theology of history. In his view, all of the elected—those who had received the grace of God—form the true body of Christ, the City of God (*civitas Dei*). And all wicked ones form the body of the devil, the earthly city (*civitas terrena*). Sacred history is nothing but the struggle between these two cities. Augustine calls the two cities mystical communities, since they are not identical with any empirical society. Even the Catholic Church is not identical with the City of God, but a *corpus permixtum*, a mixed body, composed of just and wicked human beings. The elect are only pilgrims in this world and its political orders. Only after the final judgment, after the separation of the just and the wicked, will the mystical societies become visible. The citizens of the City of God will be seen going to heaven and the others, to hell.

The Joachimite Turn

Augustinian eschatology governed the self-understanding of the Catholic Church until it was heavily shaken by the theology of an Italian abbot, Joachim of Fiore (c. 1135?–1202) and the numberless movements that referred to him. Joachim was convinced that God had revealed to him a new understanding of the Bible. He predicted the beginning of a third age (*tertius status*) of the Holy Spirit that would follow the first age of the Father, as described in the Old Testament, and the second age, which ran from the incarnation of Christ to Joachim's present. The abbot taught that the Trinity reveals itself in three progressive stages. The revelation of the Father had formed the patriarchal society of Israel; the revelation of the Son had formed the church of the clerics. And soon the revelation of the Holy Ghost would create the new spiritual church (*ecclesia spiritualis*), a church dominated by monks. In Joachim's view, the third age appears as an anticipated realization of the perfect order of the Beyond.

Several scholars of the twentieth century, such as Karl Löwith (1897–1973), Eric Voegelin (1901–1985), Norman Cohn (1915–), and Jacob Taubes (1923–1987), claimed that Joachim of Fiore started a process in which Christian eschatology was "immanentized" (Voegelin) or "secularized" (Löwith). The four authors recognized the transformation of Christian eschatology into ideologies of inner-worldly progress as the decisive formative power of modernity. The third stadium of Auguste Comte's positivism was to be seen as a modern transformation of Joachim's third age, as well as the Third Reich of the National Socialists and the Marxist realm of freedom.

See also **Christianity; Judaism; Millenarianism; Mysticism.**

BIBLIOGRAPHY

PRIMARY SOURCES

Augustine. *The City of God against the Pagans.* Ed. and trans. R. W. Dyson. Cambridge Texts in the History of Political Thought. Cambridge, U.K., and New York: Cambridge University Press, 1998.

Charlesworth, James H., ed. *The Old Testament Pseudepigrapha. Vol 1. Apocalyptic Literature and Testaments.* New York: Doubleday, 1983.

McGinn, Bernard, trans. *Apocalyptic Spirituality: Treatises and Letters of Lactantius, Adso of Montier-en-Der, Joachim of Fiore, the Franciscan Spirituals, Savonarola.* Classics of Western Spirituality. New York: Paulist Press, 1979.

SECONDARY SOURCES

Bultmann, Rudolf Karl. *History and Eschatology.* Edinburgh: University Press, 1957.

Cohn, Norman. *Cosmos, Chaos, and the World to Come: The Ancient Roots of Apocalyptic Faith.* New Haven, Conn.: Yale University Press, 1993.

———. *The Pursuit of the Millennium: Revolutionary Millenarians and Mystical Anarchists of the Middle Ages.* Rev. and expanded ed. New York: Oxford University Press, 1970.

Löwith, Karl. *Meaning in History: The Theological Implications of the Philosophy of History.* Chicago: University of Chicago Press, 1949.

Reventlow, Henning Graf, ed. *Eschatology in the Bible and in Jewish and Christian Tradition.* Sheffield, U.K.: Sheffield Academic Press, 1997.

Taubes, Jacob. *Abendländische Eschatologie.* Munich, Germany: Matthes and Seitz, 1991.

Voegelin, Eric. *Modernity without Restraint,* edited by Manfred Henningsen. Columbia: University of Missouri Press, 2000.

Matthias Riedl

ESSENTIALISM. Essentialists believe true essences exist. In the *Metaphysics,* Aristotle (384–322 B.C.E.) specifies the classic definition: an essence of a thing is that which it is said to be per se. It is that which is most irreducible, unchanging, and therefore constitutive of a thing. A thing's essence is that property without which the thing would cease to exist as itself. Each individual thing is one and the same as its essence, necessarily and not accidentally. Objects derive their coherence and intelligibility from the unchangeability and homogeneity of their underlying essences. Essence belongs primarily and simply to substance. The substance of things is their primary cause of being. Essences are anterior to and causative of ideas or practices. All things that have the same substance or essence are identical. Only a species or genus can have an essence. An essence is true of the thing in general, it does not derive from the manifold particulars of a thing. To define an essence is to give an account of a primary real—one that does not imply the assertion of something about something else. A distinctive set of ontological postulates thus appears intrinsic to essentialism. A realm of being outside time and culture or historical change exists. This realm is the real, the stable, the structured and eternal underlying the flux and chaos of the infinite variety of transitory appearances. The real world is made up of homogeneous, clear, and distinct essences. Innate or given essences sort objects naturally into species or kinds (natural kinds). The resulting categories are eternal, unchanging, stable, and universal.

Essences and Knowledge

Philosophers differ on whether humans can apprehend such constituting essences. While Plato (c. 428–348 or 347 B.C.E.) and Aristotle argue they can, others such as Immanuel Kant (1724–1804) deny the possibility of directly grasping the noumenal world (how things are in themselves). Thus, a belief in the intelligibility of essences requires supplementary assumptions concerning the nature of mind and language. The mind itself must have an essence, some essential faculty empowering it to directly and accurately register the essences of things. For Plato and Aristotle, this faculty is reason. The intelligibility of essences also requires positing language as a neutral, transparent medium. Language is a reporting device; it can neither enter into the constitution of the recorded essence nor distort it, for then our knowledge of essences could never attain eidetic accuracy.

Essentialism is a response to problems of recognition and meaning. Amid all the variety of empirical experience and the multiple forms that objects assume, how do we recognize many differently appearing things as instances of the same phenomenon? Where do the categories in and through which we organize empirical experience come from? As the Scottish philosopher David Hume (1711–1776) and others argue, we do not have direct empirical experience of abstract, general categories. Unmediated empirical experience is a transitory flux of fleeting sense impressions and sensations. Chairs, for example, come in many colors, sizes, and shapes. Yet, we recognize many variations as instances of one species. How is this possible? Plato argues that such recognition is contingent on the prior existence of a form or an essence, chairness, or the idea of a chair. Such an idea is pure form, and all empirical chairs are simply approximations of this idea. While approximations are changeable and all empirical objects will eventually decay or disappear, the idea or pure form of a chair is eternal.

Essences and Ethics

For both Plato and Aristotle, essence is intertwined with another notion, telos. Telos connotes purpose, end, and good. Its essence is what a thing is meant to be. Matter is merely full potential, unactualized. Only by realizing its essence, can the thing fully exist. However, Plato and Aristotle differ on how fully an essence can be realized in the empirical world. For Plato, a pure essence can be at best imperfectly realized as long as it is mixed with any empirical matter. Aristotle does not think all such mixtures are intrinsically flawed. Nonetheless, for both, this necessity has ethical as well as existential connotations. Understanding humans' essence simultaneously and necessarily stipulates what we are and what (or how) it is good for us to be. Humans must actualize and conform to this true essence. Only then can we live a fully human life. However for the good, the real, and the true to coincide, supplementary metaphysical assumptions are necessary. For example, both Plato and Aristotle postulate that an eternal and universal natural law governs the real world. Natural law endows each thing, person, and human association or practice with its particular telos. It guarantees that the purpose, end, and good of each thing are identical. In realizing its purpose, the thing also attains its natural completion and its good. Natural law is knowable, but not created, by human reason. Intrinsic to reason is the obligation and capacity to discover this law and adjust our souls and social arrangements accordingly.

Empiricist Objections to Essentialism

Many philosophers object to essentialism. Empiricists like the English philosopher John Locke (1632–1704) reject its a priori postulation of innate ideas or universal truths. They claim that the only preexisting real is the human capacity for sense experience and reflection upon it. Unlike Aristotle, Locke claims that all knowledge originates in sense experience, and the simple ideas derived from our sensations and unmediated thoughts represent the limits of the knowable. Real essences can only be discovered by close empirical observation; all else is idle and potentially dangerous speculation. Every truth claim, including essentialist ones, must be subject to any individual's empirical investigation and verification. Otherwise, objective evaluation of whether such claims actually reflect nothing but the weight of tradition or the power of authority masquerading as truth is impossible.

Modern philosophers, including Karl Popper, extend Locke's rejection of unverifiable claims regarding essences. Rationality demands a skepticism regarding the self-evident existence of anything. For a claim to have truth value, it must be possible to specify conditions under which it can be falsified. These conditions must be translatable into empirical tests that at least conditionally rule out the falsity of the statement. What intersubjectively verifiable tests could we possibly devise for claims like "humans have a soul," much less that it is our essence?

Kripke: Essentialism Recast

Some philosophers such as Saul Kripke attempt to rescue essentialism by situating its claims within semantics. Kripke asserts that "rigid designators" exist. A rigid designator is an expression that designates the same object in all the possible worlds in which it designates at all. It is determined by an essential property of its referent. Modern semantics can devise meaningful tests for propositions about essences. Properties must be physical and their correlated mental states incorrigibly knowable. For example, Kripke claims the term *pain* is a rigid designator. Pain is necessarily a physical state. It is identical to this physical state. If any phenomenon is picked out in exactly the same way we pick out pain, it must be correlated with that physical state, and hence the phenomenon must be pain.

However, this and other forms of essentialism are vulnerable to objections posed by pragmatists and social constructionists. Pragmatists argue that coherence, meaning, and intelligibility arise out of our immersion in a common way of life, from practical agreement, or a shared understanding for some purpose or activity. Meaning arises from use; use is enabled through sharing a common set of practices. Over time, practices generate a tacit, usually background network of meanings that appear to always have been there, existing independently outside the practices that create and sustain them. These ordered patterns reflect neither metaphysical reality nor ontological necessity, but rather the effects of social expectations, chance, shared language games, convention, or force.

Pragmatist and Social Constructionist Objections to Essentialism

Twentieth-century philosophers have supplemented such criticism by critiquing essentialist philosophies of language. For example, Richard Rorty advocates permanently abandoning essence. Essentialism necessarily requires a value-free vocabulary that can report facts and render sets of factual statements commensurable. However, language is not a neutral medium through which truth or fact is reported; it is also neither an arbitrary nor a necessary system of signs connecting words and things. Language cannot be understood as composed of words or sentences in any nominalist way. Words are saturated with social meanings. They incorporate accounts of experience and ways of recognizing it as a case of x as opposed to y. Even what feels like empirical experience is already linguistically organized. Language is best apprehended in terms of language games, complex sets of practices that constitute ways of life. Furthermore, these games are not grounded in anything outside or beyond themselves. Relationships of reference, for example, are not objectively necessary but simply further parts of the world of the present day.

Social constructionists typically emphasize the constituting effect of human practices. However, some, for example Michel Foucault (1926–1984), extend the domain of relevant practices and propose novel approaches to questions of meaning and truth. Unlike many pragmatists and constructionists, Foucault pays close attention to relations of power and how these both enable and constrain modes of subjectivity, meaning, knowledge and truth. Foucault relocates problems of identity, truth, knowledge, reality, and meaning outside their traditional domains of ontology, epistemology, and metaphysics into discourse analysis. Discourses are complex, dynamic systems of practices, knowledge, and multiple kinds of power. Such discourses generate disciplinary norms that simultaneously produce and constrain subjects and question formation; they enable participants to recognize and evaluate truth claims. Foucault suggests displacing "what/who is it?" as central questions about any of these topics with a different one—"how is it?" How is it requires a genealogy that unpacks multiple kinds of practices. Among the practices some subjects are expected to enact are the discovery or enunciation of the essences of things, including themselves. Genealogies of historically specific discourses indicate that questions about essences could arise and remain salient or even intelligible only within certain ways of life.

Feminist Disputes

Essentialism is a contested topic within feminist discourses. Feminist theorists critique traditional, essentialist accounts of woman. One could argue that contemporary Western feminism began with the publication of Simone de Beauvoir's (1908–1986) *The Second Sex* (1949). De Beauvoir asserts that woman is made, not born, and proceeds to delineate recurrent attempts within Western culture to reduce woman to her putative, biological essence. Since at least Aristotle, philosophers have claimed that woman has an essence and that this essence is a material one. Woman is matter; she is defined by her unique physical property (reproduction). The identity of each individual, actually existing woman is ultimately and necessarily determined by this essence.

Feminist discourse extends this critique into an investigation of the interdependence of gender arrangements, gender-based asymmetries, heterosexism, and the "essential" or natural, factual meanings of body, matter, nature, and sex. Judith Butler's work is especially influential. Butler argues that "sex" is an effect of gender and heterosexism. How we understand bodies and matter and what is assigned to categories of "natural" and "social" fact, indeed these very categories, must be deconstructed into the social and linguistic practices and power relations that generate them. An adequate response to essentialist constructs of woman requires a strategy different from disconnecting the social (gender) and the biological (sex) and claiming that the biological does not determine the social. To claim that woman is made is still to assume that "woman" exists. Furthermore, it leaves sex undisturbed as a natural kind, inaccessible to genealogical investigation.

Subaltern Objections to Essentialism

Feminists also question "feminist" essentialism. Angela Harris defines essentialism as the belief that a monolithic race or gender experience exists that can be described independently of other social relations. To be antiessentialist means to understand that the lives of women of color and all people generate and enact multiple forms of subjectivity. It is erroneous to posit heterosexuality as the norm or that black male experience is the exemplar for black women and all minorities. The authors of the influential collection *Home Girls* (1983) and Elizabeth Spelman label essentialist any claim that an essential woman exists beneath differences among women. Any assertion of a universal property or position shared by all women is suspect. Such claims obscure the many important differences among women. Belief in a common identity requires conflating one group of women with the whole and erasing differences, especially those of race, class, and sexuality. Differences among women can be safely ignored or relegated to footnotes. However, this approach simply obfuscates the effects of whiteness and other dominant social relations on and as particular modes of womanhood. It obscures the ways race is constituted in contemporary practices such that only people of color are marked by race and white remains the unmarked, unraced. Within such practices, any woman leached of all color is actually white. Removing race only results in removing black women. Black women then become white women only more so. White women can then represent all women. Paradoxically, this then redounds more so to warrant assertions of the common oppression of all women, including white ones. All women, from the most impoverished "third world woman" to the wealthiest white one, are equally instances of women's universal condition.

New Dictionary of the History of Ideas

Paul Gilroy and others within cultural and subaltern studies also critique essentialism. In their view, it enables, expresses, and reproduces global systems of domination. Colonialist discourses postulate essential human traits that non-Western others lack or could only imperfectly possess. The homogeneity of such essences existed only through contrast with heterogeneous others. Projecting all impurity, materiality, and instability on these others enabled certain subjects to imagine themselves as instances of the pure and eternal—reason, the soul, the fully human, etc. Such ideas then underwrote Western claims of the right to rule and civilize (to the extent possible) these inferior others.

Feminist Essentialism

These antiessentialist arguments are controversial. Some insist that social movements require a deep notion of shared position and condition. Writers such as Diana Fuss and Gayatri Spivak argue that essentialism itself has no essence; the problem is how it is used. Oppressed groups can deploy essentialism strategically. Essentialist concepts enable the oppressed to organize resistant forms of identity and sustain a powerful sense of solidarity.

Other theorists such as Luce Irigaray, Catharine MacKinnon, and Martha Nussbaum also deploy a feminist essentialism. Irigaray argues that the problem is not that woman has been conceived in essentialist terms but rather the content of those terms. Woman's essence has been defined by men, as not-man or lesser man. Women have never articulated their own difference, among themselves and for themselves. For Irigaray, this essence can never be one; it does not conform to the unitary logic of homo-centric discourse. Irigaray employs the metaphor of the labia; two lips, always two, not divisible into one; neither one nor two. Two lips provide the basis for a speaking (as) woman, to articulate a feminine imaginary. MacKinnon insists that gender difference is a socially constructed concept invented to sustain male dominance. Under patriarchy, all women share a common essence—sexuality. Sexuality is a social process that creates and directs desire. Woman is produced through this process as an object whose only purpose is to gratify men. While Nussbaum situates herself within the language of rights and human capacities, she too insists that male dominance is universal and universally experienced by all women. Their liberation requires stipulating universal norms. Justice cannot exist without a binding consensus on a universalist account of human functioning and its regulative force. Those most deprived of support for the essential human capacities (often women outside the West) are most in need of such norms.

Despite ingenious attempts to rescue it, modern essentialism has yet to provide satisfactory responses to skeptical inquiries regarding how we know if we have grasped a true essence. While problems of meaning, representation, intelligibility, and identity remain, essentialists have yet to persuade skeptics to abandon their doubts.

See also **Feminism; Form, Metaphysical, in Ancient and Medieval Thought; Humanity; Metaphysics; Natural Law.**

BIBLIOGRAPHY

Butler, Judith. *Bodies That Matter: On the Discursive Limits of 'Sex.'* New York: Routledge, 1993.

De Beauvoir, Simone. *The Second Sex.* Translated by H. M. Parshley. New York: Bantam, 1961.

Foucault, Michel. *Ethics: Subjectivity and Truth.* Edited by Paul Rabinow. Translated by Robert Hurley and others. New York: New Press, 1997.

Fuss, Diana. *Essentially Speaking: Feminism, Nature, and Difference.* New York: Routledge, 1989.

Gilroy, Paul. *Against Race: Imagining Political Culture beyond the Color Line.* Cambridge, Mass.: Harvard University Press, 2000.

Harris, Angela. "Race and Essentialism in Feminist Legal Theory." In *Critical Race Feminism: A Reader,* edited by Adrien Katherine Wing. New York: New York University Press, 1997.

Irigaray, Luce. *This Sex Which Is Not One.* Translated by Catherine Porter with Carolyn Burke. Ithaca, N.Y.: Cornell University Press, 1985.

Kripke, Saul. "Identity and Necessity." In *Philosophy As It Is,* edited by Ted Honderich and Myles Burnyeat. New York: Penguin, 1979.

MacKinnon, Catharine A. *Feminism Unmodified: Discourses on Life and Law.* Cambridge, Mass.: Harvard University Press, 1987.

Nussbaum, Martha. *Sex and Social Justice.* New York: Oxford University Press, 1999.

Popper, Karl R. *Conjectures and Refutations: The Growth of Scientific Knowledge.* New York: Basic Books, 1962.

Rorty, Richard. *Philosophy and the Mirror of Nature.* Princeton, N.J.: Princeton University Press, 1979.

Smith, Barbara, ed. *Home Girls: A Black Feminist Anthology.* New York: Kitchen Table: Women of Color Press, 1983.

Spelman, Elizabeth V. *Inessential Woman: Problems of Exclusion in Feminist Thought.* Boston: Beacon Press, 1988.

Spivak, Gayatri Chakravorty. *A Critique of Postcolonial Reason: Toward a History of the Vanishing Present.* Cambridge, Mass.: Harvard University Press, 1999.

Jane Flax

ETHICS. *See* **Bioethics; Environmental Ethics; Philosophy, Moral; Virtue Ethics.**

ETHNICITY AND RACE.

This entry includes three subentries:

Africa
Anthropology
Islamic Views

AFRICA

There is an abiding paradox in the concept of race. It is a biological fiction but a social reality. Biologically it is now established beyond doubt that there are no distinct races among human beings and that the genetic variation within particular groups of people is much higher than between groups. The view that people possess inherent personality characteristics attached to particular irreducible phenotypes has been systematically discredited, yet the outward appearance of people still plays a profound social role in the manner in which different people relate to each other. These readily perceived phenotypical differences are often the bases upon which people construct social differences between themselves. Skin color is the most obvious of these differences. The apartheid (translates as "separateness") regime in South Africa represented the clearest possible expression of the political use of skin color to discriminate against blacks, by disenfranchising them, excluding them from the central institutions of the state, and by ensuring that they would be available as cheap labor in the mines, on the farms, and in the factories.

The instrumental use of race as a convenient means to attain political and economic goals was forcefully articulated by Oliver Cox when he insisted that race should be defined socially, not biologically, since it connotes social relations of exploitation between people and not biological differences. There is an ongoing debate about the origin of the concept of race and its adjuncts, racism and racialism. While some argue that these are concepts that are as old as humanity itself, others argue that they arose as a direct result of the modern era and are intimately connected to colonial conquest and the slave trade. Anthony Appiah has drawn an interesting distinction between racialism and racism. *Racism* refers to negative varieties of discrimination on the basis of an ideology that orders society into a hierarchy of supremacy and domination, where some people may see others as inherently inferior on the basis of an undefined racial essence. It has both an institutionalized form (for example, apartheid) and an interpersonal presence. Racism thus consists of the view that this unspecified racial essence translates into certain inherent, usually objectionable properties (such as laziness, filth, lack of punctuality, and so on) that justify treating people differently, usually unequally. On the other hand, *racialism* refers to the recognition of physical difference between people as being socially and psychologically significant in the sense that they share certain traits and characteristics, but without attaching any inherently inferior or superior characteristics to different people. Many argue that this position is debatable, suggesting that perceiving such differences almost invariably implies the acceptance of inequality between people.

Race in Africa

Frantz Fanon offered a trenchant critique of colonialism as a form of racism at both the institutional and interpersonal levels. Being a psychiatrist, he was particularly interested in the manner in which colonial racism created problems of self-identification for blacks since it conveyed the brutal message that might was right and might was almost invariably white. By simple deduction, therefore, white was almost always right. Fanon argued very forcefully that the colonizers had successfully imposed their image of the colonized on Africans and that it was incumbent on Africans to rid themselves of this image of inferiority, often through violence. Colonial subjugation had a devastating effect on black subjects that the postcolonial regimes have not overcome, because in many ways the new black elites have simply mimicked their past rulers in the most grotesque fashion.

The Senegalese poet and president Léopold Sédar Senghor, in developing the concept of negritude, provided an eloquent negation of French culture and the colonial policies of assimilation and acculturation that produced black Frenchmen and -women as "photographic negatives of the colonizers." While their knowledge of French culture, their French accents, and their appreciation of the finer qualities of French wine may have been impeccable, a racial line prevented blacks from becoming fully fledged Frenchmen and -women. Thus, Senghor and a host of others reacted in various ways to this racial exclusion that Paul Gilroy captured so eloquently for England in his captivating title *There Ain't No Black in the Union Jack.*

Amilcar Cabral, for example, articulated a theory of liberation based on the retained collective cultural identity of blacks as distinct from that of the Portuguese colonialists, in his clarion call to "return to the source." His theory was rooted in the material conditions of Guinea that he regarded as a reservoir of local experiences ripe for anticolonial mobilization. Under these conditions liberation was necessarily an act of asserting and affirming African culture.

The Francophone and Lusophone (Portuguese-speaking) African experiences were very different from the Anglophone, where, for example, racial exclusion led Steve Biko to a departure from the white liberal student organization as part of the Black Consciousness movement. The move was couched in political as well as psychological terms. Having seen blacks oppressed to such an extent that they started to actively despise themselves, Biko preached a counterideology of psychological liberation as a precondition for true emancipation, using slogans such as "Black man you are on your own" and "Black is beautiful." The apartheid regime defined *black* in the narrow sense to mean only those Africans who spoke indigenous languages, excluding the so-called coloreds and Indians. The black consciousness movement responded with a generic definition of blackness to encompass all those who suffered a common political disability, having been disenfranchised. *Black* was thus defined politically to mean all those who would readily support the struggle against apartheid, while those who worked the machinery of their own oppression were termed sellouts, just as similar people were called Negroes in the United States.

Given the extreme, official, and institutionalized form of racism of apartheid, it was appropriate that the third United Nations World Conference against Racism, Racial Discrimination, Xenophobia and Related Intolerance (Durban, 2001) should be held in South Africa. One of the debates of relevance to the definition of racism concerned whether Zionism should be included as a form of racism in terms of the manner in which the Israeli state treated the Palestinians. Both the Israeli and United States governments withdrew from the conference on account of this and other issues, while Yasser Arafat was adamant in describing the Israeli occupation of Palestinian land as "a racial discrimination policy in their ugliest forms and image" and "a new and advanced type of apartheid."

The Concept of Ethnicity

While *race* thus refers to the social construction of difference on the basis of perceived physical or morphological differences, *ethnicity* is supposed to refer to cultural differences between people. The two obviously intersect in many ways since racists readily use the concept of ethnicity to mask their racism. The apartheid regime, for example, changed its official nomenclature from *race* and *tribe* to *ethnic group* and then to *nation* in an effort to legitimize its policy of territorial segregation. The term closest to *ethnicity* and in fact still in use after being systematically discredited for many years is *tribalism*.

In broad terms there are two main approaches to the study of ethnicity. On the one hand, the primordialist approach sees ethnicity and ethnic diversity as relatively permanent features that are deeply rooted in the essential and particularistic experiences of groups of people. People are thus divided on an enduring basis and in an unchanging manner. In this view ethnic groups are seen as distinctive units usually based on the idea of a common descent, where the commonality of culture is inherited and thus given from the past and people are born into particular ethnic groups. On the other hand, the social constructionist approach sees ethnicity as a modern instrumentalist symbol in advancing the material interests of groups whose composition may change in response to competitive opportunities. In this sense ethnicities are created or "invented" by elites as they seek to manipulate ideas about ethnicity in order to secure their own interests. The primordialist/constructionist divide has had a profound impact on the debate about the significance of ethnicity in Africa. The main terms of this debate concern whether ethnic groups connote real categories of people or whether cultural differences are manipulated by pernicious political leaders for their own reasons of personal aggrandizement and petty ambitions of power. The position of the primordialists on ethnicity comes close to the concept of race as a historical given, and the distinctions between these are quite blurred. However, the constructionists reject these essentialisms and instead allow room for choice and individual agency in the formation of ethnicities.

Ethnicity Debates in Africa

The tensions in these approaches have polarized studies on ethnicity in Africa. Okwudiba Nnoli, for example, takes up the primordialist position, accepting that ethnic groups do exist, are real with clearly defined interests, and play a pervasive role in African politics. Arguing along the same lines that ethnic conflict needs to be taken seriously, Ibbo Mandaza ends with an entirely different conclusion, suggesting that the persistent danger of ethnic conflict imposes a necessary reconciliation of the elites of the various groups (he includes tribes) in the nation-building project of postcolonial Africa. In response to this widespread position among African leaders and scholars, Mohamed Salih advances the opinion that recognizing rather than denying ethnicity may be the key to the democratization project in Africa. Taking the ethnic basis of political mobilization at face value, Salih argues that this reality rests awkwardly next to the public denial of ethnicity manifested in the banning (across Africa, except in Ethiopia) of political parties that are explicitly ethnically based with an unambiguous ethnic constituency. On the basis of an impressive array of empirical evidence, Salih makes the point that most African political parties are ethnically based in any case, and it is time to simply recognize this reality to allow for it to play a positive legitimizing force in contemporary African politics. While it is clear that ethnicity is endemic in Africa, Salih does not elaborate on how to overcome the inevitable problems of exclusion and inclusion in a political process that is ethnically based. Put bluntly, if ethnically based political parties win an election, then they would have to deliver to an ethnic constituency that would obviously define the winners and losers in ethnic terms. It is extremely difficult to imagine how this could translate into a legitimate polity.

Archie Mafeje scolds Nnoli and others for not providing an analysis of ethnicity and for treating ethnic groups as things in themselves, following the empiricism rife in American political science. Instead he dispels the idea that there are discrete, naturally occurring entities of belonging that may be called ethnic groups in Africa. He draws a distinction between social groups and social categories, where the former are characterized by inevitable patterns of social interaction such as lineages or associations, and the latter does not imply such regular interaction at all but is rather defined by common identity, such as members of the same religion. Mafeje's argument is that ethnicity is related to the national competition for scarce resources in response to the centralization of power rather than to local particularistic conflicts. In this sense, ethnicity has a recent derivation since it refers to an ideological ploy used by political elites to yield the benefits of power and wealth. In this view, ethnicity does not represent some preexisting African cultural essence but a convenient means of political mobilization for elites.

In a paper delivered at the Networking with a View to Promoting Peace conference in 1999, Dan Nabudere attempts to reconcile these two perspectives by drawing a distinction between positive and negative aspects to ethnicity, where the former refers to the notion of self-identification, self-expression, and enjoyment in membership of a stable entity in a "posttraditional" manner capable of coping with the demands of modernity. The negative aspect of ethnicity accommodates Mafeje's concern with elite manipulation of ethnic sentiment for narrow political ends of positions in the state.

In the postcolonial period, there was a flurry of scholarly activity as the new elites tried to redefine their pasts in ways that placed the ambivalent significance of the colonial period in its proper perspective. The question of race and ethnicity was crucial, especially in the southern African settler societies. History was being rewritten just as history was being made. New myths were invented in an effort to construct united national cultures since separate ethnicities were regarded as threatening to the nation-building project.

According to Mahmood Mamdani, one of the key challenges of the process of independence from colonial rule was to break down the barriers between ethnically defined rural subjects and racially defined urban citizens. However, Mamdani argues that decolonization did not have "an agenda for democratising customary power." Michael Chege provides a very critical review of Mamdani's thesis, arguing that it is simplistic in its dualism and does not appreciate the nuances of rural African society. Chege is particularly scathing about Mamdani's use of *tribe, tribespeople, tribalism,* and *customary law* "as concrete categories of political behaviour."

South African historiography, especially during the 1970s and 1980s, was dominated by endless debates on the relation between race and class in attempts at explaining the nature of the apartheid regime. For some there was a contingent relation between the two; for others the relation was an instrumental one, with race being used as a convenient tool for the class exploitation of blacks; for still others race had an independent existence. The race/class debate in South Africa provides a useful historiographical glimpse of an important era in the evolution of social science thought.

Ethnic Experiments in Africa

Ethiopia and South Africa represent two opposite poles in dealing with ethnicity. The two countries are on entirely separate constitutional journeys. South Africa has emerged from the ethnic balkanization of apartheid and moved toward the constitutional establishment of a unitary state with the idea of a single nation. Ethiopia, on the other hand, has emerged from an imposed imperial unity via a centralist, militarized distortion of socialism to a dispensation of ethnic federalism. Ethiopia is the only country in Africa that explicitly recognizes ethnicity in its constitution, enshrined in the construction of ethnically based regional states and the official acknowledgment that there are many nations. In the case of Ethiopia, the nature of feudal autocracy determined the invariably ethnic-based form of opposition. For example, virtually all the liberation movements involved in the overthrow of the military regime had secession from Ethiopia as an integral part of their programs. This aim was obviously influenced by the slogan of the rights of nations to self-determination. Imperial oppression was structured along the lines of imposing a policy of Amharization (officially promoting the language and culture of the Amhara) in an effort to construct a unitary national culture in Ethiopia. It is not surprising, therefore, that opposition was founded on the affirmation of separate peoples, nations, and nationalities and that virtually all multiethnic or nonethnic political parties have failed dismally in Ethiopia. It is instructive that the form of rule is termed ethnic federalism, but the groups that occupy these positions are referred to as peoples, nations, or nationalities.

If South Africa and Ethiopia represent two poles on a continuum, then Nigeria exists somewhere between these two in the manner in which it has chosen to deal with ethnicity. The Nigerian constitution does not explicitly recognize ethnicity, but it recognizes the federal character of the country, or the regional (read ethnic) differences between people. Here sharing of the national cake is very explicitly seen in ethnic terms, even if ethnically based parties are banned. The federal character principle adopted in the First Republic was supposed to be reflective of the wide diversity of the Nigerian population, but it has not prevented Northern domination of the federal government. It was in response to this tendency toward Northern control that a system of rotating presidencies was proposed by parties in the running for the presidential elections.

People obviously have different cultural practices. These mark the distinctive ways in which identity and consciousness are formed in different communities. Whether these ethnic identities should be politicized is an ongoing debate in African social thought. All African societies are diverse, and how to accommodate and even celebrate that diversity without the endless civil strife and ethnically inspired violence remains an abiding challenge.

See also **Africa, Idea of; Anticolonialism: Africa; Apartheid; Black Consciousness; Colonialism: Africa; Humanity: African Thought; Multiculturalism, Africa; Nationalism: Africa; Pan-Africanism; Race and Racism.**

BIBLIOGRAPHY

Chege, Michael. Book review of Mahmood Mamdani's *Citizen and Subject. African Studies Quarterly: The Online Journal for African Studies* 1 (1997). Available at http://web.africa.ufl.edu/asq.

Cox, Oliver. *Cast, Class, and Race.* Garden City, N.Y.: Doubleday, 1948.

Fanon, Frantz. *Toward the African Revolution.* Translated by Haakon Chevalier. New York: Grove Books, 1967.

Hymans, Jacques Louis. *Léopold Sédar Senghor: An Intellectual History.* Edinburgh: Edinburgh University Press, 1971.

Mafeje, Archie. "Multi-party Democracy and Ethnic Divisions in African Societies: Are They Compatible?" In *Breaking Barriers, Creating New Hopes: Democracy, Civil Society, and Good Governance in Africa,* edited by Abdalla Bujra and Said Adejumobi. Trenton, N.J.: Africa World Press, 2002.

Mamdani, Mahmood. *Citizen and Subject: Contemporary Africa and the Legacy of Late Colonialism.* Princeton, N.J.: Princeton University Press, 1996.

Mandaza, Ibbo. *Southern Africa in the Year 2000: An Overview and Research Agenda.* Harare, Zimbabwe: SAPES, 1993.

Nnoli, Okwudiba, ed. *Ethnic Conflicts in Africa.* Dakar: CODESRIA Book Series, 1998.

Salih, M. A. Mohamed. *African Democracies and African Politics.* London: Pluto Press, 2001.

Fred Hendricks

ANTHROPOLOGY

Ethnicity, as defined in the public domain, is "the cultural characteristics that connect a particular group or groups of people to each other" (http://en.wikipedia.org/wiki/Ethnicity). Twenty-first-century anthropologists, however, are likely to complicate simple notions of ethnicity, or they might refuse to accept a general definition of the concept without first demanding accounts of the particular formation of an ethnic identity in a unique place and time. Citizens of the United States, for example, are enculturated to associate ethnicity with a mapping of cultural or national origin to language, religious practices, styles of adornment, types of non (or un-) American foods, and oftentimes, physical looks. Anthropologists, however, are much more interested in ethnicity as a historically and politically situated set of identity practices, rather than as a state of natural or expected correspondence between physicality, behaviors, and attitudes. Such a nuanced view of ethnicity has not always been the norm in anthropology or in

Franz Boas, Ethnicity, and Contemporary Physical Anthropology: Continuing Tensions

Franz Boas (1858–1942), widely considered to be the father of American anthropology, spent much of his career arguing vigorously against racism and theories of the fixed physiological nature of ethnicity. Though fondly remembered by most anthropologists as a rigorous ethnographer and mentor to such famous names as Margaret Mead and Zora Neale Hurston, he remains a contradictory and complicated figure for two disparate groups: Native Americans and physical anthropologists. First, for some Native American people, his participation—along with many of his museum curator and academic contemporaries—in the looting and desecration of Native graves for the collection of "specimens" for comparative anatomical research has forever tarnished his reputation. Likewise, some of the research methods of the time, considered controversial both when they were practiced and into the twenty-first century, included a simple anthropometry, or the measurement and comparison of certain continuous human characteristics. Native Americans and other nonwhite people are often and rightly suspicious of such techniques, since anthropologists used them to substantiate racist hierarchies.

Boas, however, employing the same anthropometric methodology, stringently critiqued the assumed fixity of human cranial dimensions, arguing that even slight changes in developmental and environmental conditions could make the simple measurements meaningless for human classification. For example, a ratio of the length to the width of the skull—the cranial index—was considered by early anthropologists to be a reliable measurement for distinguishing people of different ethnicities from each other, such as Hungarians, Poles, and European Jews. Boas disagreed.

Concerned about the rise of anti-immigrant prejudice in the United States, Boas, a German Jewish immigrant himself, secured funding from Congress in 1908 to undertake a massive cranial measurement study of immigrants in New York City, ostensibly to substantiate his views on human cranial plasticity and to prove the uselessness of the cranial index (see Boas). His conclusions, that the children of immigrants are different physically from their "ethnic" parents and therefore successfully integrating into American society, were embraced by sociocultural anthropologists (but not politicians, to Boas's dismay) as undeniable proof of the intergenerational flexibility of bodies. Cranial morphology was proven to neither be a direct function of ethnicity, culture, or language group. Anthropologists, then, could no longer pin ethnicity reliably and regularly to physical type, at least in the anthropological literature. Boas also argued, given his analysis, that anthropologists could not use cranial size and shape to link past skeletal populations with living human groups.

Boas's historical place among the physical anthropologists in the twenty-first century, though, especially given the methodological similarities between them, is growing even more complicated. Physical anthropologists, while no longer participating in the construction of racial taxonomies, often use detailed anthropometric techniques to track morphological changes and microevolution in human populations through time. Many physical anthropologists claim that new and detailed cranial metric techniques can distinguish different past groups from each other by culture or ethnicity, directly contradicting Boas's earlier findings. Some of these comparisons, ironically, are used to assign cultural labels to Native American skeletal remains for repatriation and reburial under the Native American Graves Protection and Repatriation Act (NAGPRA, P.L. 101–601).

In the early 2000s Boas's landmark study of cranial plasticity was the subject of a debate between two teams of physical anthropologists. Both teams reevaluated some of Boas's data using updated statistical methods. Sparks and Jantz conclude: "[O]ur analysis reveals high heritability . . . and variation among the ethnic groups, which

(continued on the next page)

FRANZ BOAS, ETHNICITY, AND CONTEMPORARY PHYSICAL ANTHROPOLOGY: CONTINUING TENSIONS

(continued from previous page)

persists in the American environment" (p. 14637). Gravlee and his colleagues, however, contradicted the first team, affirming Boas's conclusions that statistically significant differences exist between U.S.-born children and their foreign-born parents.

However this debate is resolved, most anthropologists still have Franz Boas to thank for his early critiques of the former assumption that race or ethnicity should correspond with language and culture. Furthermore, *sociocultural* anthropologists have little interest in quantifying morphological difference between people. Physical or biological anthropologists, however, are still struggling to define the meaning of some of the differences they find, especially when comparisons between different past skeletal populations have policy implications in the present.

---

social science. A central story of ethnicity in anthropology is its labored disentanglement from now discredited biological and evolutionary notions of "race," ideas that continue to contribute to the general public's conceptualization of the "ethnic" as a physically distinct type of person.

In the mid-nineteenth century the terms *ethnic* and *racial* first came into common use, employed by pre- and post-Darwinian scientists, and later anthropologists, to construct human racial and cultural taxonomies. As the social corollary of race, "ethnic" (*ethnicity* as a unique term does not emerge in the United States until the 1950s) initially served to reinscribe physical notions of racial, and in some cases national, identity onto groups of people often naively assumed to have a shared cultural, historical, or even evolutionary past.

Throughout the nineteenth and into the twentieth century, race, was the dominant concept for the scientific, social, and political classification of human groups in the Western world. Though scientific and popular ideas of what makes a race, who embodies race, and what being of a certain race means have changed drastically through time, the eighteenth-century Enlightenment ushered in a very specific scientific classification of human beings, particularly the ordering of non-European and colonized peoples. Before the scientific community accepted the theory of evolution by natural selection in the nineteenth century, human races were thought to be the product of divine creation. Following the Adam and Eve story closely, monogenists believed in a single creation from which all people and consequently all races arose. Polygenists, though, believed that there was a separate creation for each major race. Furthermore, proponents of both of these pre-evolutionary models used continental labels for creating physical races as bounded groups. Anthropologists assumed that all Europeans, Asians, Africans, and Native Americans were naturally distinct from each other—even on the level of the species—through differentiation over time (monogeny) or through natural, created difference (polygeny). Cultural-historical notions of identity as essentially unchanging and the delineation of fixed anatomical categories also served to determine a certain people's "racial type."

The adoption of an evolutionary framework for understanding human difference, however, did little to transform early anthropologists' fixed ideas of race and racial connections to ethnic identity. Instead, scientists quantified human variation through morphology, mostly using erroneous comparisons of skull size and shape. These practices became the basis for the development of methodology in physical (or biological) anthropology in the United States and Europe. Based on misinterpreted and even falsified anthropometric data, physical anthropologists wrongly assigned labels of either "less evolved" or "degenerated" to nonwhite peoples. Evolutionary ideas initially applied to global racial taxonomies were also used to classify people on other physical, behavioral, or cultural scales. Anthropologists also considered white women, European and European-American people of lower socioeconomic classes, convicted criminals, disabled people, and people who practiced homosexual or other seemingly scandalous sexual practices (such as adulterers and prostitutes) lower on natural scales of evolution and development. Similarly, nonwhite people were wrongly thought to be more naturally susceptible to various behavioral and cultural vices, damaging stereotypes that persist among racists and cultural isolationists in the United States in the early twenty-first century.

Likewise, until ethnicity's emergence in the 1960s and 1970s as a term describing more fluid social processes of identity formation, social scientists used *ethnic* to describe a natural or fixed category of person. In the United States, especially during the intense debate over Eastern European and Mediterranean immigration in the early portion of the twentieth century, an "ethnic" was a person of a marked, lower, category, opposed to a bourgeois white identity. Ethnics, in this context, became lower-class whites, Jews, and nonwhite, colonized, or indigenous peoples.

Ideas of ethnicity have, therefore, consistently been relational; that is, one's ethnic identity, either physical or cultural, is defined through both assumed similarities within a group and assumed differences between groups. Franz Boas's 1912 study of cranial plasticity in American immigrants, however,

ARCHAEOLOGIES OF ETHNICITY

Traditional archaeologists, whose field developed in the same racialized and colonial context as the rest of anthropology, were typically concerned with tracking the material remains of contemporary groups into the past. This cultural historical approach and the search for ethnicity in the archaeological record often led archaeologists to uncritically project modern and national identities into the past. Prominent examples include French claims to Roman and Gallic identities, Nazi projections of past "Aryan" peoples onto much of Northern and Western Europe, and general European continental claims to the material heritage of ancient Greece and classical Egypt (see Jones).

New approaches to identity in archaeology, though, are leading to more accurate and complex reconstructions of past peoples. Moreover, archaeologies of gender, sexuality, and ethnicity are encouraging researchers to include different and historically marginalized voices, such as African resistance to slavery in Kenya and African-American cultural expressions in the colonial archaeology of the United States. Researchers in these areas generally resist drawing simplistic conclusions between desires to trace "ethnic origins" in the past for mobilization and political use in the present.

was the first and arguably most influential anthropometric contestation of the fixed physical nature of ethnicity and racial identity. Among some anthropologists, though, fear of the negative or racially degrading influence of a large ethnic presence in America was used to argue against Boas's conclusions, and for increasingly strict immigration policies and the establishment of eugenics programs across the nation.

Moreover, after the devastating results of such "Aryan" hysteria in Europe during World War II, greater anthropological use of the term *ethnic group* coincided with a general repudiation of biological determinism and racism within the social sciences as a whole, as well as with a particularly anthropological recognition of the emergence of anticolonial nationalism outside the First World. Specifically, anthropologists replaced *tribe* or *tribalism* with *ethnic group,* especially when describing African migrants to colonial urban centers. Still, all these early uses of the term *ethnic* in anthropology imply a bounded set of cultural traits, historical commonalities, or mental similarities between people of the same ethnic group, even if they later became delinked from physical or racial characteristics.

Cultural Fundamentalism and Instrumental Ethnicities

Disengaging race and ethnicity from biology, though, does not automatically imply equality under the law or in all aspects of political, economic, and social life. As theorists rejected race biology in the mid-twentieth century, a new "cultural fundamentalism" emerged in many places in the world. Anthropologist Marisol de la Cadena eloquently describes this shift: "The academic repudiation of biological notions of race

was significant for anthropology, as it meant the emergence of the concept of 'ethnic groups' to explain human differences . . . it implied the reification of culture, which thus potentially prolonged the naturalization of sociohistorical differences earlier contained in the European notion of biological race" (p. 28). In the twentieth century, ethnicities were just as stable and unchanging whether they were formed out of biology or culture.

As well, the initial glosses of ethnic described above were also etic in nature. That is, most ideas of ethnicity in anthropology before the late twentieth century served as theoretical or methodological techniques of classification from outside the group being classified. Anthropologists and other social scientists were not alone, though, in reifying or naturalizing ethnic groups and ethnicity. From approximately the end of World War II to the 1970s, "ethnics," nonwhite and other marginalized or oppressed people across the world fought for and won greater sovereignty, more influential voices on regional or national political stages, and generally more civil and political rights to self-representation.

This new agency, though patently different in different areas of the world, empowered previously colonized or oppressed people to create and affirm ethnic identities for use in varied political spheres. These uses, though, often included the drawing of fixed boundaries around ethnicities or cultures and the exclusion of individuals who were not perceived to be ethnic enough. For example, most federally recognized Native American nations or tribes use blood quantum, or the proportion of "Indian blood" within a person calculated by the percent within their parents or grandparents, to determine who makes the official membership rolls. Widespread implementation of blood quantum rules have effectively excluded Indian people of African descent from official membership in communities they and their families have lived in for centuries (see Brooks).

Ethnicity and Difference

In early-twenty-first-century sociocultural anthropology, ethnicity is envisioned as a complicated, fluid, politically charged, perhaps even ephemeral quality or qualities of individual or group identity that map differently to various social categories depending on people's particular histories. The formation or maintenance of an ethnicity, then, is not a necessary by-product of predictable biological, cultural, or social forces. Anthropological thinking on ethnicity is also informed by newer theories of race as a political category, differently expressed and marked within particular political and cultural struggles.

Anthropologists are also adapting frameworks from fields theorists in cultural studies, who focus on difference not to the exclusion of others, but toward the multiplication of meanings and the highlighting of marginal identities. As Stuart Hall cautions: "We are all . . . ethnically located and our ethnic identities are crucial to our subjective sense of who we are. But this is also a recognition that this is not an ethnicity which is doomed to survive . . . only by marginalizing, dispossessing, displacing, and forgetting other ethnicities" (p. 447).

Further, acceptance of the social construction of race in the humanities and social sciences, and lately by progressives in the U.S. public at large, has spurred anthropologists to more widely publicize disciplinary views on race and ethnicity as both educational and policy recommendations. In particular the American Anthropological Association's "Statement on Race" deconstructs the dangers of relying on fixed notions of identity in social and cultural research and interactions, saying that "racial myths bear no relationship to the reality of human capabilities or behavior." Likewise, myths of ahistorical, unchanging ethnicities are also falling by the wayside in anthropological thought.

See also **Anthropology; Other, The, European Views of; Race and Racism.**

BIBLIOGRAPHY

American Anthropological Association. *Statement on Race.* 1998. Available at http://www.aaanet.org/stmts/racepp.htm

Banks, Marcus. *Ethnicity: Anthropological Constructions.* New York: Routledge, 1996.

Boas, Franz. "Changes in Bodily Form of Descendants of Immigrants." *American Anthropologist* 14 (1912): 530–563.

Brooks, James F, ed. *Confounding the Color Line: The Indian-Black Experience in North America.* Lincoln: University of Nebraska Press, 2002.

Cadena, Marisol de la. *Indigenous Mestizos: The Politics of Race and Culture in Cuzco, Peru, 1919–1991.* Durham, N.C.: Duke University Press, 2000.

Gould, Stephen Jay. *The Mismeasure of Man.* New York: W.W. Norton, 1981.

Grant, Madison. *The Passing of the Great Race; or the Racial Basis of European History.* New ed., rev. and amplified, with a new preface, by Henry Fairfield Osborn. New York: C. Scribner's Sons, 1918.

Gravlee, Clarence C., H. Russell Bernard, and William R. Leonard. "Heredity, Environment, and Cranial Form: A Reanalysis of Boas's Immigrant Data." *American Anthropologist* 105 (2003): 125–138.

Hall, Stuart. "The New Ethnicities." In *Ethnicity,* edited by John Hutchinson and Anthony D. Smith. New York: Oxford University Press, 1996.

Jones, Siân. *The Archaeology of Ethnicity.* London: Routledge, 1997.

Morley, David, and Kuan-Hsing Chen, eds. *Stuart Hall: Critical Dialogues in Cultural Studies.* New York: Routledge, 1996.

Omi, Michael, and Howard Winant. *Racial Formation in the United States: From the 1960s to the 1980s.* New York: Routledge, 1986.

Pierpont, Claudia R. "The Measure of America: How a Rebel Anthropologist Waged War on Racism." *New Yorker* 8 March 2004.

Sparks, Corey, and Richard Jantz. "A Reassessment of Human Cranial Plasticity: Boas Revisited." *Proceedings of the National Academy of Sciences* 99 (2002): 14636–14639.

Stocking, George W. *Race, Culture and Evolution: Essays in the History of Anthropology.* London: Collier-Macmillan, 1968.

Williams, Raymond. *Keywords: A Vocabulary of Culture and Society.* Rev. ed. New York: Oxford University Press, 1985.

Ann M. Kakaliouras

ISLAMIC VIEWS

The Koran makes only passing reference to racial or ethnic categories. One verse refers to "the variety of your tongues and hues" as one of the many signs of God's divine power (30:22). Another proclaims the primacy of piety over racial or tribal distinction: "O mankind, we have created you male and female, and appointed you races and tribes, so that you may know one another. Surely the noblest among you in the sight of God is the most godfearing of you" (49:13). Revealed to a largely homogeneous Arab ethnic community, explicit ethnic or racial stratification and prejudice are absent from the Koran. The most fundamental category of differentiation and identification in Islam's sacred scripture is that of religion, of the new community of Muslims as "the best community [*umma*] ever brought forth to men" (3:106), and hence as the central focus of loyalty and affiliation for a believer.

As the Muslim community expanded beyond the confines of the Arabian peninsula and over time incorporated numerous ethnic and racial groups, both an awareness of ethnic distinctions and a sense of racial hierarchies developed. The sunna, the voluminous body of normative sayings and practices (hadith) collected by pious Muslims in the early Islamic centuries and attributed (sometimes erroneously) to the Prophet Muhammad, contain sayings both asserting Arab ethnic supremacy within Islam ("If the Arabs are humbled, Islam is humbled") and challenging Arab precedence within the *umma* ("The people with the greatest share in Islam are the Persians"). Other hadith of the early centuries alternatively give voice to a sentiment of the superiority of white over black ("beware of the *Zanji* [black], for he is a distorted creature"), and declare the irrelevance of color in the eyes of God ("in Paradise the whiteness of the Ethiopian will be seen over a stretch of a thousand years"). Still others insist on the universality of Islam, as in the Prophet's saying "I was sent to the red and the black," a hadith interpreted to mean that the message of Islam was intended to encompass all humanity.

The heterogeneity of the sunna notwithstanding, in religious writings the dominant normative view echoed the Koran's insistence that religiosity took precedence over ethnic or racial background. As the thirteenth-century commentator Abd Allah Baydawi (d. 1292 or 1293) stated the prevailing theological position, "we have created every one of you by means of a father and mother. All are equal in this and there is no reason therefore for boasting of one's lineage. . . . [L]et him who desires honour seek it in piety" (Levy, p. 55). The most important practical implication of this assertion of the primacy of religious affiliation lay in the central discipline of Islamic law, which made no legal distinctions based on ethnicity or race. This was particularly relevant in regard to slavery, where the law made no presumption of slavery being linked to race and forbade the enslavement of free Muslims regardless of ethnic origin. Slavery was never indelibly associated with color in the Muslim world, as came to be the case in the Western world.

If Islamic theology and law were color-blind, Muslims were not. There is a considerable body of what can be termed ethnographic literature written by Muslims, in which Muslim geographers and others describe the physical characteristics and the moral qualities of different ethnic and racial populations. Reflecting the increasing diversity of Muslim society as time progressed, ethnic and racial hierarchies were a contested issue in this literature. Where one author would assert the supremacy of Arab over Persian or black over white, another would defend the virtues of the group in question. A common ethnographic schema was one privileging neither black nor white, but the "brown" people of the Middle East. For the tenth-century author Abu Bakr Ahmad ibn Ibrahim al-Hamadhani ibn al-Faqih (writing in 902/903), the "pale brown color" of the people of Iraq was "the most apt and proper color." Unlike the Slavs of the north, with their "blond, buff, blanched and leprous coloring," or the *Zanj* and Ethiopians of the south, "black, murky, malodorous, stinking, and crinkly-haired," "the Iraqis are neither half-baked dough nor burned crust, but between the two" (Lewis, 1974, vol. 2, p. 209). For many medieval Muslims, brown was beautiful.

Within the *umma* itself, ethnic stereotyping, ranking, and snobbery sometimes undercut the theoretical equality of all believers. The fact that Islam had originally been revealed to the Arabs and the preeminence of Arabs in the early centuries of Muslim history initially fostered a sense of Arab superiority to other ethnic groups that expressed itself in literature, in an initial reluctance to accept non-Arab converts as the equals of Arab Muslims, and in a lingering prejudice against Arab marriage with non-Arabs justified on the basis of the saying "marry like with like."

Arab ethnocentrism in time produced a backlash. A social and literary movement of importance in the ninth and tenth centuries was the Shu'ubiyya, a school of Iranian Muslim writers who challenged the presumption of Arab superiority over other Muslims by extolling the more refined and civilized social customs practiced by Iranians, emphasizing the rich historical heritage of pre-Islamic Iran, and asserting the richness and beauty of the Persian language in comparison to Arabic. A similar if more muted sense of ethnic distinctiveness has been identified in medieval Egypt, where Egyptian Muslim authors praised the legendary fertility of Egypt, the country's historical role as a source of science and wisdom, and later Egypt's prominence in serving as a bulwark of Islam against the Crusader and Mongol onslaughts.

The biblical story of the curse of Ham made its way into Muslim legend, and formed part of the basis for the negative stereotypes of black Africans as physically unattractive and morally deficient that comprise a sinister undercurrent in medieval Muslim literature. The images attached to particular ethnic groups could also evolve as social and political conditions shifted. Thus the Turkic peoples, originally outside the Muslim world and known primarily as military slaves, were initially stereotyped as uncouth barbarians. As Turkic groups converted to Sunni Islam, entered the Muslim world en masse, and eventually became politically dominant, the prevailing image shifted first to the Turks as opponents of Shii heresy, later as champions of Islam against the pagan Mongols, and eventually as ruthless alien overlords tyrannizing other Muslims.

The increasing salience of ethnic identity and the corresponding growth of nationalist movements based on language across much of the Muslim world in the nineteenth and twentieth centuries was by and large a new phenomenon only tangentially connected to preexisting attitudes regarding ethnicity and race. It was specific social and political conjunctures of the modern era, as well as the impact of nationalist concepts from the West, that produced Arab, Turkish, Iranian, and other modern nationalisms among Muslim peoples. Arab pride in their historical role as the founders of Islam; Turkish awareness of their political prominence as the ruling elite of a later period; Iranian glorification of the achievements of ancient Iran: these echoes of previously expressed attitudes regarding ethnic groups reinforced and served as ammunition for modern ethnic nationalism, but were not the fundamental cause of the same.

Similarly, modern ethnic nationalism has been only incidentally influenced by the racist theory that developed in and disseminated outwards from Europe in the nineteenth and early twentieth centuries. Most modern nationalisms among Muslim peoples antedate Muslim awareness of modern racist theory and were produced by other causes. The one Middle Eastern area where racist thought had a temporary impact was Iran (that is, Aryan), where the world prominence of the fellow-Aryans of Germany in the early twentieth century influenced both Iranian constructs of self and more briefly the foreign policy of the Iranian state. Modern Arab animosity toward Jews ("Arab anti-Semitism" in its literal sense is an oxymoron, since Arabic is a Semitic language) originated in the political circumstances of the national conflict over Israel/Palestine rather than in racist theory. It has found convenient fodder in the occasional negative references to Jews found in the Koran as well as in a growing familiarity with European anti-Semitic tracts such as the

Protocols of the Elders of Zion, but at base is rooted in and driven by national conflict.

In the later decades of the twentieth century and beyond, the ethnic nationalisms so prominent earlier in the century began to be superseded by a religiously-based sense of identity and by activism defined in terms of religion rather than of ethnicity. Islamism—the reassertion of the primacy of the religious bond over that of language, "race," or territory, and the emergence of transnational movements of Muslims working to cleanse the entire *umma* of foreign influence—was an old/new phenomenon of increasing prominence at the start of the twenty-first century. Its ultimate trajectory, as well as that of the ethnic nationalisms that it denounces as alien to Islam, is yet to be determined.

See also **Anti-Semitism: Islamic Anti-Semitism; Nationalism: Middle East.**

BIBLIOGRAPHY

Goldziher, Ignaz. *Muslim Studies.* Edited by S. M. Stern, translated by C. R. Barber and S. M. Stern. London: Allen and Unwin, 1967. An English translation of the classic study of tribal and ethnic sentiment in medieval Islam.

Haarmann, Ulrich W. "Ideology and History, Identity and Alterity: The Arab Image of the Turk from the 'Abbasids to Modern Egypt." *International Journal of Middle East Studies* 20, no. 2 (May 1988): 175–196.

———. "Regional Sentiment in Medieval Islamic Egypt." *Bulletin of the School of Oriental and African Studies* 43, no. 1 (1980): 55–66.

Levy, Reuben. *The Social Structure of Islam.* Cambridge, U.K.: Cambridge University Press, 1962. Contains a chapter on "The Grades of Society in Islam."

Lewis, Bernard. *Islam: From the Prophet Muhammad to the Conquest of Constantinople.* 2 vol. New York: Harper and Row, 1974.

———. *Race and Slavery in the Middle East.* New York: Oxford University Press, 1990. A survey of the issues of race and slavery, mostly in the premodern period.

James Jankowski

ETHNOCENTRISM. Ethnocentrism is a notion not widely used in the early twenty-first century. Coined by William Graham Sumner in the early twentieth century, the term owes what conceptual life it has to the likes of anthropology and intercultural communication. Dominant strains of these disciplines, especially anthropology, have examined the lives and cultural expressions of ethnically defined or identified groups and the misinterpretations resulting from Western perspectives.

Nevertheless, a survey of contemporary critical works on ethnicity and race, including those in critical anthropology, reveal an almost complete lack of engagement with the concept. In Anglo-American studies, the term *ethnocentrism* carries a largely descriptive and fleeting connotation, its meaning more or less taken for granted. It has been overshadowed perhaps by more readily invoked characterizations or charges of racism, racialization, and ethnoracial determination. This is perhaps less the case in mainstream European social analysis, where race remains a largely taboo category and ethnic configurations and characterizations are far more readily and uncritically invoked. It is unsurprising, then, that the thickest critical engagement to be found with the notion of ethnocentrism is in French works from the late 1980s (Taguieff; Todorov).

Definition

Ethnocentrism can be understood as the disposition to read the rest of the world, those of different cultural traditions, from inside the conceptual scheme of one's own ethnocultural group. The ethnocentric attitude assumes that one's own ethnic *Weltanschauung* (worldview) is the only one from which other customs, practices, and habits can be understood and judged. Ethnocentrism thus is conceived critically as involving overgeneralizations about cultures and their inhabitants, others' or one's own, on the basis of limited or skewed, if any, evidence. So the notion of ethnocentrism is conceived as a profound failure to understand other conceptual schemes, and, by extension, practices, habits, expressions, and articulations of others on their own terms. Standing inside our own conceptual schemes, we are blinded even to the possibilities of other ways of thinking, seeing, understanding, and interpreting the world, of being and belonging—in short, other ways of worldmaking.

It would seem to follow, as many definitions in fact insist, that ethnocentrism is a claim about the superiority of one's own culture or ethnic standing. While this is perhaps a strong presumption in many ethnocentric claims, we should be careful not to make it definitionally so. One can imagine claims of inherent and inescapably culture-bound judgments about ethnically ascribed others, about inherent differences, without assumption or assertion of cultural superiority. If there is any coherence to the concept, "differentialist ethnocentrism" must factor into any working definition of the term as well.

As an analytic concept, ethnocentrism took hold only in the late 1960s and 1970s, and the word did not appear in authoritative dictionaries until the mid-1970s. The reasons are not unrelated to the conceptual history of the term *racism.* While invocation of the notion of "race" in regard to human beings (and by extension, discussion of racism) became a taboo subject in Europe in the wake of the Holocaust, concerns around racism, socially and analytically, emerged forcefully in the United States. The anthropological concern with culture turned increasingly to the language of ethnicity, reinforced by the emergent hold of area studies and liberal distribution of development aid as an arm of geostrategic politics in the face of colonial liberation and the Cold War. The romance with ethnicity seemed more respectful than the legacy of race, its faux universalism enabling an easy evasiveness. At the same time, the concept of ethnocentrism—largely descriptive and individualist in analytic disposition—could offer a liberal contrast to the more critically pressing concept of "institutional racism," with its sociostructural connotations, emergent in the late 1960s (Carmichael and Hamilton). Indeed, proponents of ethnocentrism today will often claim both racism and colonialism as subspecies of ethnocentrisms. But this would seem to undercut the sociohistorical specificities of both racisms and colonialisms.

Billboard erected on California's Highway 99 during the Depression. Practitioners of ethnocentrism assume that their own ethnic worldview is the only one from which other customs, practices, and habits can be understood and judged. HULTON ARCHIVE/GETTY IMAGES

Universalizing Ethnocentrism

There is a widespread insistence among those who readily invoke the notion that ethnocentrism is a universal condition. All cultures, the argument goes, express enthnocentric attitudes toward others. This might be called the "universality of ethnocentrism" claim. It is the supposition that everyone necessarily stands inside one—and perhaps only one—culture. It would follow that we must (cannot but? always?) express inherently partial judgments about others from inside the inescapable frame, whether or not we thereby assume our own cultural commitments to be preferable or better.

This claim suggests that there is a spectrum of ethnocentrisms. They supposedly range from the less to the more pernicious, from judgments about others inescapably expressed from, and expressive of, a cultural stance not theirs to a dismissal of cultural differentiation as inferior, as lesser. Analysts or commentators usually define ethnocentrism in the latter sense, that is, as belief in or claim to the superiority of one's own culture, as this article suggests earlier. For example, mainstream Japanese society is deemed ethnocentric for its sense of discriminatory superiority over "Burakumin," or social outcasts, those deemed barely human and good only for menial employment (Weiner). Defined as such, ethnocentrism is seen as deeply linked, or leading to, the scapegoating of those deemed inferior or difficult, demanding, or incapable. Consider the enmity between Hutu and Tutsi in Rwanda during the 1990s Those deemed "incapable" are often identified as the cause of things gone wrong in society, of dangers threatening, of social conditions gone sour, of frustrations with socioeconomic concerns turning to ethno-tensions and fast exploding into violence. "They" are the cause of "our" difficulties. If "we" have "failed" it must be "their" fault. But it also reveals that the socially produced responses to such ethnocentrisms vary widely from avoidance or dismissal to outright rejection or, worse still, to outright attack, purging, or ultimately to genocide.

The universality claim thus expressed, however, undercuts critical judgments against ethnocentric commitment. If we are all party to such narrowness, if we are inescapably of and judge from (inside) our culture, then it cannot be that bad. After all, those so judged have their own culture not only from which to render their inescapably ethnocentric judgments but also as a form of defense. Ethnocentrism as a claim to universal inevitability conceptually reduces to a case of culture war.

The universalizability claim is considered by self-satisfied critics as revealing the poverty of extreme forms of relativism. Value universalists cannot be so smug, however. The "universality of ethnocentrism" claim on the more extreme relativistic side has its characteristic correlate among bigoted universalists too. Call this by contrast the "ethnocentrism of universality" claim. Tzvetan Todorov revealingly defines ethnocentrism to capture just this characterization. Ethnocentrism, he writes, takes the values of one's own society without warrant as universal, as applying to all anytime, everywhere.

Consider Keith Windschuttle's characteristic assumptions in attacking what he questionably deems the "ethnocentrism of [the anthropologist] Clifford Geertz," who Windschuttle reads as the quintessential relativist.

> From its origins in classical thought and Christianity, Western culture has always had a strong tendency towards universalism. This principle has long been expressed in the idea of the unity of human kind and the belief that all human beings had a common origin and were equal before God. During the European Enlightenment, these Christian concepts were secularized to produce the notions of a common human nature and universal human rights. . . . In other words, the universalizing principle has been one of the great strengths of Western culture and has been central to the self-assurance and development of Western civilization.

Here the universalizing project of "Western Enlightenment," precisely in the name of criticizing relativistic ethnocentrism, is the project to universalize its values. This is to insist that, because these are universal values, they ought to be universally recognized. Blaise Pascal writes that "We have to admit that there is something astonishing about Christian religion . . . though I was born in it, I soon found it astonishing" (p. 23). So astonishing, it turns out, that its values—the only religion whose values are rationally produced, Pascal says—should hold for all, absolutely, everywhere, always. The assertion of the universality of one's society's or religion's values fails to acknowledge that even such general values as liberty and equality are open to interpretation and inflection. Liberty and equality may be general values aspired to very widely. But value universalists all too often generalize the specific interpretation or meanings of those commitments from within their own sociocultural boundaries, insisting that they should apply universally, thereby denying interpretations to these terms diverging from dominant, usually Western conceptions (though proselytizing Islamic universalists, for example, might be guilty of this too).

These presumptively universal values and interpretations, which proponents such as Windschuttle seek to generalize and have rule the world, turn out invariably to be those of a relatively small group of people. They are a distinct minority actually in the global scheme of things, with a particular history of domination and subjugation. Critics of ethnocentrism often contrast ethnocentric disposition to that of tolerance, which is promoted as the proper response to ethnic distinction and differentiation. It is curious consequently to note accordingly how critics of value universalism are dismissed by proponents such as Windschuttle as incorrigible relativists, or even worse as relativistic multiculturalists. These are charges that themselves reveal the ethnocentric reification of such universalistic claims, not to mention the

distinct horizons of application and scope when it comes to tolerance, which after all is always expressed from a position of power (Goldberg). But as Todorov points out, regarding what he calls the "ethnocentric spirit" exhibited by Pascal, having absolutized local values or interpretations ethnocentrists then judge their own values and practices as universally ordained. The "ethnocentrism of universality" becomes at once the rationalization of local values imposed universalistically.

The "ethnocentrism of universalism" and the "universalism of ethnocentrism" thus converge in the end. The ethnocentrism of universalism ends up flattening out all distinction. If I universalize the values of "my" culture (given that I can identify a coherent universalizable set) to apply to all cultural and social arrangements, I effectively deny or belie what makes those cultures unique. And if I insist, seemingly by contrast, that all societies, universally, are ethnocentric, and so their members do and perhaps can only exercise value judgments from within their cultural horizons, then effectively I must be claiming that the universalism of ethnocentrism amounts to no more than the ethnocentrism of universalism: my judgment from within a culture is, from my point of view, all there can be, and so must perversely be the grounds of universal judgment. The ethnocentric disposition at least implicitly denies historical relations connecting the ethnically dominated to the ethnically dominant. Whether taken substantively as a standpoint from which judgments are expressed about others or as an analytic framework for understanding historical circumstances, ethnocentrism implodes on the common claim to social homogeneity.

Conclusion

The social dynamics of ethnocentric charge and countercharge are confined almost exclusively to the cultural wars over values and their scope. Social power and the relative positionings of those charging and charged remain largely unaddressed. And yet power is at the heart of the ethnocentric concern, in both its universalistic versions, to maintain and refine social homogeneity. The most extreme form of ethnically predicated and produced homogenization is reflected in the phenomenon of "ethnocratic states." These are states in which a single ethnically defined or self-ascribed group seeks, and seeks to maintain, power on just those terms (Yiftachel, 2002, 2004). In the self-defining extreme, ethnocratic states are keen to remove all those identified within as "minorities" who refuse or (more likely) are refused to join or affirm the dominant conception of social value and belonging, the common "nation-state." The ethnocratic state takes itself to be born out of a single, common history, cultural legacy, language, religious tradition, and racial kinship. Consider, for example, the radical Romanian nationalist Radu Sorescu who first defined the "ethnocratic state" as an aspiring commitment, in his case for Romania in the 1930s (Dreapta). The ethnocratic state thus conceived fashions a peculiar sort of state personality, mixing the perceived need to defend society against or "clean" it of threatening heterogeneities with the related concern to claim power by asserting it over those deemed inferior or immature, distinct or detrimental.

Ethnocentrism as a concept fails in its self-assured lack of relational analysis. It refuses, by extension, any engagement with relations of social power and differentiated social positionings that has been the mark, by contrast, of race critical theory (Essed and Goldberg).

See also **Colonialism; Critical Race Theory; Ethnicity and Race; Race and Racism.**

BIBLIOGRAPHY

Barger, Ken. "Ethnocentrism: What Is It? Why Are People Ethnocentric? What Is the Problem? What Can We Do about It?" 2003. Available at http://www.iupui.edu/~anthkb/ethnocen.htm

Carmichael, Stokely, and Charles Hamilton. *Black Power: The Politics of Liberation in America.* New York: Random House, 1967.

Dreapta, Noua. "The Romanian Ethnocratic State." In *Fascism,* edited by Roger Griffin, 207–209. Oxford and New York: Oxford University Press, 1995.

Essed, Philomena, and David Theo Goldberg, eds. *Race Critical Theories: Text and Context.* Oxford: Blackwell, 2001.

Goldberg, David Theo. *The Death of Race.* Oxford: Blackwell, 2005.

———. *The Racial State.* Oxford: Blackwell, 2002.

Mamdani, Mahmood. *When Victims become Killers: Colonialism, Nativism, and the Genocide in Rwanda.* Princeton, N.J.: Princeton University Press, 2001.

Pascal, Blaise. *Pascal's Pensees.* Translated by Martin Turnell. London: Harvill, 1962.

Taguieff, Pierre-Andre. *The Force of Prejudice: Racism and its Doubles.* Translated and edited by Hassan Melehy. Minneapolis: University of Minnesota Press, 2001.

Todorov, Tzvetan. *On Human Diversity: Nationalism, Racism, and Exoticism in French Thought.* Translated by Catherine Porter. Cambridge, Mass.: Harvard University Press, 1993.

Weinter, Michael, ed. *Japan's Minorities: The Illusion of Homogeneity.* London and New York: Routledge, 1997.

Windschuttle, Keith. "The Ethnocentrism of Clifford Geertz." October 2002. Available at http://www.newcriterion.com/archive/21/oct02/geertz.htm

Yiftachel, Oren. " 'Ethnocracy': Land, Settlement, and the Politics of Judaising Israel/Palestine." 2002. Available at http://www.palisad.org/papers/yiftachel1.htm

———. "Ethnocratic States and Spaces." 2004. Available at http://www.usip.org/fellows/reports/2004/0121_yiftachel.html

David Theo Goldberg

ETHNOGRAPHY. Ethnography, often paraphrased as "participant observation," is a mode of deriving knowledge about particular, local worlds through direct engagement with their peoples and ways of life. As a mode of inquiry, it is primarily associated with the discipline of anthropology, the comparative study of human societies and cultures that took definitive shape as a scholarly field in the early years of the twentieth century. But the implications of the approach are more complex than suggested by this definition; for while ethnography is empirical in spirit, in practice it flouts many of the assumptions underlying positivist investigation, and has long enjoyed something of a maverick status within the social sciences.

Tracing its mythic origins to the celebrated research of Bronislaw Malinowski in the Trobriand Islands in Melanesia in the teens of the last century, anthropological ethnographers have classically worked in non-European contexts, relying less on written records or formal techniques than on qualitative perceptions gleaned from interpersonal encounters in the field. In this enterprise, writes Claude Lévi-Strauss, "[t]he observer apprehends himself as his own instrument of observation" (p. 35). Such frank reliance on the role of subjective experience in empirical investigation sits somewhat uneasily with the value-free ideals of mainstream social science methodology. In fact, while it is in many ways a product of the Enlightenment impetus to bring the universe under the Western gaze, ethnographic observation, and the cultural relativism with which it has long been associated, has always been controversial. While hailed by many as a uniquely sensitive means of unsettling European hegemonies and revealing the cogency of other orders of meaning and value, it has also been accused of biases, ranging from insurmountable ethnocentrism to a fetishism of difference. Ironically, as critique of the method has mounted *within* anthropology in recent years, ethnography has been ever more enthusiastically embraced in several fields *outside* itself, among them cultural and legal studies, musicology, education, sociology, and political science. True, it is often hard to gauge, once the method is separated from the anthropological perspective that spawned it, just what it implies (besides "talking to people"). But even in watered-down form, its current popularity is surprising: How are we to explain its appeal in these postcolonial, global times, when many scholars have come to question the capacity of small-scale qualitative methods to grasp the ever more intensive translocal forces spanning the planet?

The Paradox

In fact, such ironies are not new. Ethnography was founded on a paradox that has rendered it both unusually useful and vulnerable to critique. This conundrum is also integral to modern anthropology, which is simultaneously universalizing in its key assumptions (about the intrinsic nature of humans as social, signifying beings, for example) and relativizing (about the fact that societies and cultures vary fundamentally with context). As a critic once quipped, anthropologists believe that "people everywhere are the same, except where they are different." Put in more generous terms, the discipline seeks to subvert modern universalist assumptions by making Westerners aware of other viable forms of reasoning and rectitude, kinship and sexuality, religion and representation, politics and politesse. But this procedure also raises thorny epistemological problems. To what degree can one assume that cultural categories are translatable across lines of difference? Is it not the case that the platonic referents of the whole enterprise—not to mention the politics of its practice—remain indisputably Eurocentric? What violence do we do to African assumptions that people can harm each other by powerful, superhuman means when we refer to these etiologies as "witchcraft"? How does such a term, which Europeans associate with dark ages past, color our rendering of African existential realities in the present? How does one establish the qualities and currency of such a "belief" in the first place?

These questions of method rest on a host of interpretive presumptions: What constitutes a field for analytical purposes? How systematic is culture, and how much is it the stuff of conscious reflection? How much does one impose order on action through one's very observation and description? Such things clearly are also matters of theoretical assumption, and here again ethnography can never simply be distinguished from the presuppositions and interests of those who practice it. What is more, scholarly values have varied across time and place: the accounts of the early ethnographers Edward Evans-Pritchard (1902–1973) and Margaret Mead (1901–1978) were hailed in their time as relativist correctives to unquestioned Western orthodoxies. But in a later, postcolonial climate, their texts have quite often been criticized for offering timeless, essentialist, exoticized depictions of "others" (Said, and Clifford and Marcus).

Intrinsic Features

In what ways are these vulnerabilities inherent in the way ethnography has been harnessed to the project of anthropology? As a method, ethnography seems quaintly anachronistic. It puts its primary trust in evidence generated by the human senses, being vested in the direct empirical gaze—the naked eye, as it were. This way of seeing characterized the early-nineteenth-century biological sciences (Foucault), which served as a model for early anthropology, described by one of its founders as the "natural science of society" (Radcliffe-Brown). Yet despite occasional scientific pretensions, anthropology has remained at base a resolutely humanistic art (Evans-Pritchard, 1950) vested in insights generated by a "long conversation" between ethnographer and subject(s) (Bloch). Mastering this somewhat underspecified art is still a crucial component of recruitment to the anthropological profession. And certain canons of practice did become standard, at least as ideals: fluency in the primary field language, for example; minimal reliance on formal interviews and artificial situations; sufficient time in situ to distinguish patterns of repetition from random events; and sensitivity to the ethical implications of one's presence and one's representations of local life. The qualitative nature of such observation, coupled with the anthropological concern with demonstrating the salience and complexity of meaning and value in human action, makes writing a crucial aspect of the ethnographic enterprise: the observer must communicate his or her insights in language that conveys the expressive richness and texture of local experience, yet retains the authority of objective reportage. In the late twentieth century, a heightened sensitivity in the human sciences to the independent life—and political mediation—of texts brought the conventions of ethnographic prose under new scrutiny. More than one observer has noted that ethnography preserves features from an era of travel writing and adventure and that it is still dependent in large part on the legitimacy of first-hand experience and interpretation (Pratt).

Yet it could be argued that what some see as the greatest weaknesses of ethnography are also its major strengths. Most significantly, its practitioners refuse to put their trust in techniques that grant scientific (and above all, quantifying) methods an exaggerated sense of objectivity. They distrust instruments that rely on a priori questions and units of analysis, for instance,

preferring to derive their categories of inquiry from a direct engagement with the phenomena at issue; and they are critical of investigative means that reify human action by divorcing it from its social context or claim to eliminate subjective bias. The very concept of participant observation—an oxymoron to some—implies that knowledge is inseparable from its knower. Thus, while ethnographers do seek to objectify social facts in the world, and also to make viable generalizations about them, their assertions remain clearly identified as the fruit of interaction between reporters and their subjects. But in this, ethnography is merely a marked instance of the inescapable interplay of fact and value that renders all human observation partial, imperfect, and a product of its time and place.

The Native's Point of View?

If ethnographers are unusually aware of the dangers of vulgar empiricism, why have they themselves frequently been accused of essentializing others? To what extent has such critique actually been aimed at the wider anthropological project? How much does it reflect a growing discomfort, in a postcolonial world, with experts—still largely of Western origin—who claim a privileged ability to interpret other cultures, or to represent those threatened by a dominant world order? The claim that anthropology was directly complicit with colonial rule, and that it remains irredeemably orientalist in perspective, is clearly overdrawn: much early ethnography was liberal, even critical in intent, and the discipline has long been subversive of establishments of most kinds, at home and abroad. At the same time, the discipline's enduring investment in cultural difference and local particularity—and in the independent existence of the powerless peoples within the world order—has laid it open to the charge that it fails realistically to come to terms with the oppressive, large-scale forces ravaging these local contexts (Graeber, and Comaroff and Comaroff, 2003). The taint of European paternalism lingers—although this does not necessarily attach itself to ethnography per se, which some see as having the potential to empower its former subjects. Thus Archie Mafeje, a respected African scholar, has declared that ethnography, to be true to itself, needs to be liberated entirely from anthropology so that it can become a source of "social texts authored [solely] by the people themselves" (Mafeje).

There is also a history of efforts to deploy participant observation beyond the orbit of anthropology in Western contexts. From the classic "Chicago School" of urban sociology in the 1920s, to those of the late-twentieth-century Birmingham Centre for Contemporary Cultural Studies, investigators have seized on what Graeme Turner has called "the democratic impulse" of ethnography—its promise to give expression to human worlds that exist beyond established cultural discourses, elite institutions, and highbrow media (Turner, p. 178). The approach has yielded resonant accounts of European and American phenomena like youth cultures and urban underclasses (Park, Whyte, Willis, Duneier) and the everyday life of formal institutions and the professions (Goffman, Becker). The impetus to understand forms of ordinary activity that lie in the shadow of grand institutions is closely related to the methods of social history, the kind that aim to recuperate the texts and traces from other times to uncover "hidden" chronicles, written "from below" (Samuel, Davis). It has often been noted that, to the degree that they treat the past as "another country," historians work very much like participant observers, practicing what amounts to an "ethnography of the archives" (Comaroff and Comaroff, 1992; Hobsbawm; Cohn). But nonanthropological ethnographers have not entirely escaped the accusation of paternalism, or of exoticizing "local" worlds. Speaking of British cultural studies, an approach that shares anthropology's concern with culture (but more as a function of class differences within societies than totalizing differences between them) Turner suggests that "the democratic impulse and the inevitable effect of ethnographic practice . . . contradict each other" (p. 178). Here one might do well to recall that there are non-Western critics who believe that the method might serve as a means of empowerment. It might also be argued that the tendency to fetishize "marginal" cultures is not altogether absent from the paradigm of cultural studies itself.

Ethnography and Globalization

While rooted in phenomena that pass directly before the observer's eye, ethnographic description also involves selection and interpretation. Its practitioners usually aim to produce generalizations about the nature of relations and significations, about reproduction, rupture, or change in specific kinds of contexts. Classically, participant observation has been deployed within tightly bounded analytic fields, within which a certain coherence was presumed to exist (whether it resided in kin ties, productive forces, norms, signs, networks, subcultures, or nations). While holism of this sort has often lent itself to bold theory-making, ethnography-generated insights tend to be of human scale and humanist by implication. Ethnographers have tended to mount strong arguments against formalist models of economy and society that divorce phenomena like markets or international relations from actual social contexts, or that reduce human motivation to formulae like "rational choice."

The small-scale compass of ethnography, and the relatively bounded fields within which it has been effective, have raised new questions at a time of heightened global awareness, when most social phenomena seem so obviously to extend beyond local situations. At a moment when many domestic groups count transnational migrants among their close kin, and consume goods and images from across the planet, it becomes less and less possible to divorce intimate contexts from larger social forces, such as worldwide movements of capital.

The challenge of practicing ethnography "in the modern world system" (Marcus) should not be underestimated. It has produced creative efforts intended to extend the range of existing methods to accommodate the intensified circulation of persons and things in the world, and to comprehend these expanded flows. In part, this has involved combining ethnographic observation with other ways of generating social knowledge—those of political economy and literary theory, for example. But the most significant response has been to insist that now, more than ever, as people everywhere seem captured by material processes of planetary scale, it is necessary to demonstrate that no world-transforming force exists without the engagement of tangible human agents and interests. As the

ideologies of the powerful seek to make their policies seem like technical necessities, operating beyond the realm of politics and value, the perspectives of ethnography insist on the opposite: that all activities, large and small, can be shown to have social and cultural determinations and, hence, are susceptible to debate, contestation, and intervention. Therein lies appeal of participant observation in an unpromising age.

See also **Anthropology; Borders, Borderlands, and Frontiers, Global; Cultural Studies; Ethnocentrism; Ethnohistory, U.S.; Globalization; Identity, Personal and Social Identity; Interdisciplinarity.**

BIBLIOGRAPHY

Asad, Talal. "Two European Images of Non-European Rule." In *Anthropology and the Colonial Encounter,* edited by Talal Asad, 103–118. London: Ithaca, 1973.

Becker, Howard, et al. *Boys in White: Student Culture in Medical School.* Chicago: University of Chicago Press, 1961.

Bloch, Maurice. "The Past and the Present in the Present." *Man* 12 (1977): 278–292.

Clifford, James, and George E. Marcus, eds. *Writing Culture: The Poetics and Politics of Ethnography.* Berkeley: University of California Press, 1986.

Cohn, Bernard. *An Anthropologist Among the Historians and Other Essays.* Delhi: Oxford University Press, 1987.

Comaroff, Jean, and John Comaroff. "Ethnography on an Awkward Scale: Postcolonial Anthropology and the Violence of Abstraction." *Ethnography* 4, no. 2: 291–324.

Comaroff, John, and Jean Comaroff. *Ethnography and the Historical Imagination.* Boulder, Colo.: Westview, 1992.

Davis, Natalie Zemon. *Women on the Margins: Three Seventeenth-Century Lives.* Cambridge, Mass.: Harvard University Press, 1995.

Duneier, Mitchell. *Slim's Table: Race, Respectability, and Masculinity in America.* Chicago: University of Chicago Press, 1992.

Evans-Pritchard, Edward E. "Social Anthropology: Past and Present." *Man* no. 198 (1950): 118–124.

———. *Witchcraft, Oracles and Magic among the Azande.* Oxford: Clarendon, 1937.

Foucault, Michel. *The Birth of the Clinic: An Archaeology of Medical Perception.* Translated by A. Sheridan Smith. London: Tavistock, 1973.

Goffman, Erving. *Asylums: Essays on the Social Situation of Mental Patients and Other Inmates.* Garden City, N.Y.: Doubleday, 1961.

Graeber, David. "The Anthropology of Globalization (with Notes on Neomedievalism, and the End of the Chinese Model of the Nation-State)." *American Anthropologist* 104, no. 4 (2002): 1222–1227.

Hobsbawm, Eric J. "Escaped Slaves of the Forest." *The New York Review of Books* 37, no. 19 (6 December 1990): 46–48. A review of *Alabi's World.*

Lévi-Strauss, Claude. *Structural Anthropology,* vol. 2. Translated by Monique Layton. New York: Basic, 1976.

Mafeje, Archie. "Anthropology and Independent Africans: Suicide or End of an Era?" *African Sociological Review* 2, no. 1 (1998): 1–43.

Marcus, George E. "Contemporary Problems of Ethnography in the Modern World System." In *Writing Culture: The Poetics and Politics of Ethnography,* edited by James Clifford and George Marcus. Berkeley: University of California Press, 1986.

Mead, Margaret. *Coming of Age in Samoa: A Psychological Study of Primitive Youth for Western Civilisation.* New York: New American Library, 1949.

Park, Robert E., Ernest W. Burgess, and Roderick D. McKenzie. *The City.* Chicago: University of Chicago Press, 1925.

Pratt, Mary Louise. "Fieldwork in Common Places." In *Writing Culture: The Poetics and Politics of Ethnography,* edited by James Clifford and George Marcus. Berkeley: University of California Press, 1986.

Radcliffe-Brown, Alfred R. *A Natural Science of Society.* Glencoe, Ill.: Free Press, 1957.

Said, Edward. "Representing the Colonized: Anthropology's Interlocutors." *Critical Inquiry* 15 (winter 1989): 205–225.

Samuel, Raphael. "Heroes Below the Hooves of History." *The Independent* no. 902 (31 August 1989): 23.

Turner, Graeme. *British Cultural Studies: An Introduction.* Media and Popular Culture series, 7. Boston: Unwin Hyman, 1990.

Whyte, William F. *Street Corner Society: The Social Structure of an Italian Slum.* Chicago: University of Chicago Press, 1993.

Willis, Paul E. *Learning to Labour: How Working Class Kids Get Working Class Jobs.* Farnborough, U.K.: Saxon, 1977.

Jean Comaroff

ETHNOHISTORY, U.S.

Ethnohistory, first used in Vienna in the 1930s by ethnologist Fritz Roack and the Viennese Study Group for African Cultural History, and a subfield of anthropology, is the use of ethnological and historical methods and materials to gain knowledge of the nature and causes of change in a culture defined by ethnological concepts and categories. This definition, as the ethnohistorian Robert C. Euler explained in 1972, is the basic premise upon which American ethnohistorians can base their studies, formulate their methodologies, and construct their hypotheses. The concept and practice of ethnothistory is largely confined to the United States. Usually dealing with small groups that do not have written histories, ethnohistory offers a way of utilizing the rich record of historical experience in the search for processes. It is defined by ethnological concepts and categories gained through field observations and combines cross-disciplinary methods of historical document research and ethnographic studies such as linguistics, archaeology, and ecology to provide as complete a picture as possible of a whole culture.

Ideally, according to most American ethnohistorians, the discipline of anthropology should provide a natural meeting ground for ethnology and history. The supposed harmonious connection between the ethnological and historical fields has allowed for a more complete historical understanding of the materials and their uses and of the various approaches to the practice of ethnohistory, and offers suggestions and direction for the growth of the ethnohistorical field. Yet, as the ethnohistorian Bruce C. Trigger noted in 1982, significant social and ideological implications are inherent in the distinction between ethnohistory and history. Not the least of these dis-

tinctions appears in the argument put forward by the anthropologist Shepard Krech III, who suggested in 1991 that if one restricts the application of ethnohistory to particular groups or extends it to certain ethnic groups (minorities?) but not others (majorities?), then one may be charged with applying a special name to the history of the culturally distant Other.

Introduced in the United States during the 1950s, ethnohistory was virtually synonymous with the study of North American Indian societies. Ethnologists studied North American Indians, particularly their kinship and religion, because their societies were accessible, diverse, and perhaps most significant, safe subjects for scrutiny because the cultural artifacts were confined to specific areas and for the most part were not contaminated by previous study. But before the early 1950s ethnologists concerned themselves with the study of ethnic entities without a historical focus. This means that the identities, locations, contacts, and movements of various Indian tribes were studied—but not the history of how these variables come to be. As such, the understanding of ethnohistory, federal legislation, and ethnologists' focus on ethnic entities, combined with their lack of historical training, presented a number of problems in relation to the study and development of ethnohistory in the post-1970 period.

The first problem was that ethnohistory, as it came to be understood in the early 1950s, too long delayed in achieving a realistic position in American historical anthropological research because, in the first half of twentieth-century America, anthropology was dominated by the followers of Franz Boas (1858–1942). The anthropologist Robert Carmack indicated in 1972 that the Boasian school represented the field of "specific history" or the writing of histories of specific societies in terms of their past events or culture traits as manifested in time, space, and concrete act. Within this context, the main task of the Boasians was to infer historical reconstructions of aboriginal American Indian cultures with data obtained primarily from oral tradition. This type of research discounted the necessity for a "history in the round," in which a more narrative history—or ethnohistory—of the American Indians would be written in order to counterbalance the Boasian accounts.

Thus, as the ethnohistorian Karl Schwerin noted in 1976, "ethnohistoric research," and its influence on the post-1970s period, goes back at least to the time of Lewis H. Morgan who in 1877 drew on a variety of historical records in writing *Ancient Society: or, Researches in the Line of Human Progress from Savagery through Barbarism to Civilization.* Chief among the early-twentieth-century ethnohistories are John Swanton's 1931 *Source Material for the Social and Ceremonial Life of the Choctaw Indians,* Alfred Goldsworthy Bailey's 1937 study *The Conflict of European and Eastern Algonkian Cultures, 1504–1700: A Study in Canadian Civilization,* William Duncan Strong's 1940 *From History to Prehistory in the Northern Great Plains,* Thomas Dale Stewart's 1939 *Anthropomeric Observations on the Eskimos and Indians of Labrador,* and Bronislaw Malinowski's 1945 *The Dynamics of Culture Change: An Inquiry into Race Relations in Africa.* Philip Dark and John Crosskey's 1958 *Mixtec Ethnohistory: A Method of Analysis of* the *Codical Art,* which also needs to be included, provided one of the earlier studies of ethnohistoric methodology. The totality of these studies suggests that they influenced American anthropologists to attempt to weld data from ethnography, history, and archaeology (ethnohistory) in the reconstruction of culture history. Yet, not every anthropologist agreed with this assessment.

Robert Carmack, offering a position on ethnohistoric theory and methodology, suggested in 1972 that it would be unwise to label the theoretical use of history by such a wide variety of anthropologists as ethnohistory because any exclusive definition of ethnohistory depends primarily on methodological considerations. Carmack argued this point because anthropologists' inclusion of a historical dimension is basically recognition of the dynamic nature of social living and the need to build change into their explanatory models. Yet, Carmack's focus on anthropology in general was a type of disciplinary chauvinism, insisting that ethnohistorical theory is drawn from anthropology simply because anthropologists have been more explicit in stating their assumptions than have historians. Up till 1972, this was not the only theory to alter the direction of ethnohistory.

Federal legislation, the Indian Claims Commission Act of 1946, greatly influenced the course of ethnohistory. In the course of doing research, ethnologists examined realistically the reliability and validity of historical documentary sources, oral tradition, and ethnographic studies in the attempt to verify the extent of past control over territories claimed by particular Indian groups.

Although oral tradition and ethnographic studies are also valuable, documentary sources were used by ethnologists partly as a way of moving the field of ethnohistory from the once-promising use of "upstreaming" (working back from the present functioning society through the minds of individual informants to release cultural memories of which the informants themselves were but dimly aware) and partly because, as Eleanor Leacock and Nancy Lurie suggested in 1971, ethnographic reconstruction rather than "specific history" had become the overriding interest in the field. Still, there are anthropological theories that argue for the combination of the documentary sources with the oral tradition as a major part of ethnohistory. This is because the most common genre in ethnohistoric work is without question the historical narrative, which chronicles (part of) the past of a tribe or nation.

This anthropological involvement in the Indian Claims Commission Act led to the founding in the same year of the American Indian Ethnohistoric Conference. Two years earlier, the journal *Ethnohistory* had been founded under the chairpersonship of Erminie Wheeler Voegelin, of the Ohio Valley Historical Indian Conference. From the beginning, as Henry Dobyns noted in *Ethnohistory* in 1972, "many of the publications" in this journal were directly relevant to the serious problem of fair dealing with Native Americans by the central government.

Some twenty years later (1966), following an open invitation to students in the fields of Oceanic, Asian, African, and Latin American ethnohistory to join and contribute research papers to *Ethnohistory,* the American Indian Conference changed its name to the American Society for Ethnohistory. The anthropologist Francis Jennings suggested in 1980 that the name change reflected "in microcosm the movement of interest [in ethnohistory] among collaborating historians and anthropologists in the United States, starting from a subject matter base in American Indians and broadening their sights to encompass tribal and peasant societies everywhere" (p. 90). This call for participation and contribution in the field of ethnohistory led to studies appearing in *Ethnohistory* on Peru, Bolivia, Chile, Argentina, and other countries not typically associated with this field of study.

Consequently, in relation to the ethnologist's focus on ethnic entities, or what could be labeled the study of folk culture (which could be a literal meaning of the word *ethnohistory*), ethnohistoric research began to include much of North American and Latin American history. Reasons for including Latin American history vary, but research based on documents that ethnologists used to study the North American Indian before the early 1950s has a long and honorable history in Latin America. Indeed, it can be argued that one of the fertile fields for future ethnohistoric research is to be found in Latin America. Two pre-1970s essays—Richard Adams's 1962 essay *Ethnohistoric Research Methods: Some Latin American Features* and William Sturtevant's 1966 essay *Anthropology, History, and Ethnohistory*—made clear that as the 1970s approached there were strong suggestions that the progression of the ethnohistoric field depended on scholars and students of ethnohistory (with a increasing connection to the physical sciences) studying Indian societies outside the United States.

Indeed, there is a link between ethnohistory and physical science and biology (natural history). In a most basic form, the ethnologist, who deals with affairs of the mind through observation, classification, and interpretation, viewed himself as a natural scientist and as much a humanist as the historian. And since the humanist focus is the ethnologist's stock in trade and its analysis and description in time and space is the business of ethnology, ethnohistory has the virtue of neither reducing anthropology to history nor excluding a scientific viewpoint.

Directly related to this point was the organization of one of the first U.S. symposia on the concept of ethnohistory. Held in 1961, the symposium's theme, outside of historical aspects of folklore and the relationship of archaeology to ethnohistory, was providing a definition for ethnohistory. From the standpoint of the ethnohistorians and others who attended, ethnohistory came to be defined as original research in the documentary history of the culture of primitive peoples.

One year later (1962), Fenton argued that he was struck by the fact that the field collecting and laboratory work of the natural scientists and the arrangement of collections had influenced anthropological research in natural history, particularly in archaeology and material culture. Thus, one of the legacies of the natural sciences is that ethnologists and natural historians share a sense of problem and a sense of design. This sense of connection provides a lead-in to several points and suggestions to improve the state, outlook, and direction of ethnohistory in the twenty-first century.

Perhaps the most realistic argument to be made is that a stronger position for ethnohistory in the curricula of academic departments of both history and anthropology, with a focus on seminar classes, would improve the ethnohistorical approach to research. Fellowships and professorships would allow scholars and students to work at centers of materials and to examine the languages and cultures of the New World in light of their contribution to Western thought as reflected in the literatures of linguistics, anthropology, and social theory.

There should also be a continuation of a cultural historic approach to folk history, including studies of North American Indian tales and pre-Hispanic Mesoamerican folk history. In relation to demography and the close attention it has recently received in ethnohistory, there is still a need to focus on the causes of population growth and the factors that influence the stabilization of populations. And, although once considered a rare field for ethnohistoric study, a comprehensive ecological examination of human impact upon the land can lead to the change over time of the connections between humans and their culture. And finally, ethnohistoric study can have a profound impact on the study of ideology that could lead to electrifying growth within this field.

Whereas it has been noted that most of the interest in ethnohistory results from native people creating a new awareness of themselves among European-Americans, the growing interest and research in ethnohistory finds support in a number of journals outside of *Ethnohistory*. These include the *Journal of African History,* the *Journal of Pacific History,* the *Journal of Comparative Society and History,* and the *Proceedings of the American Philosophical Society.* These journals provide a broad view of important ethnohistoric work on African cultures, cultures of the Pacific islands, and Judeo-Christian cultural development in the West.

See also **Anthropology; Cultural Studies; Ethnography.**

BIBLIOGRAPHY

Adams, Richard N. "Ethnohistoric Research Methods: Some Latin American Features." *Ethnohistory* 9, no. 2 (1962): 179–205.

Axtell, James. "Ethnohistory: An Historian's Viewpoint." *Ethnohistory* 26, no. 1 (1979): 1–13.

Berkhofer, Robert F. Jr. "Faith and Factionalism among the Senecas: Theory and Ethnohistory." *Ethnohistory* 12, no. 2 (1965): 99–112.

Carmack, Robert M. "Ethnohistory: A Review of Its Development, Definitions, Methods, and Aims." *Annual Review of Anthropology* 1 (1972): 227–246.

Dobyns, Henry F. "Ethnohistory and Contemporary United States Social Problems." *Ethnohistory* 19, no. 1 (1972): 1–12.

Euler, Robert C. "Ethnohistory in the United States." *Ethnohistory* 19, no. 3 (1972): 201–207.

Fenton, William N. "Ethnohistory and Its Problems." *Ethnohistory* 9, no. 1 (1962): 1–23.

Fixico, Donald L., ed. *Rethinking American Indian History.* Albuquerque: University of New Mexico Press, 1997.

Jennings, Francis. "A Growing Partnership: Historians, Anthropologists, and American Indian History." *The History Teacher* 14, no. 1 (1980): 87–104.

Krech, Shepard III. "The State of Ethnohistory." *Annual Review of Anthropology* 20 (1991): 345–375.

Leacock, Eleanor Burke, and Nancy Oestreich Lurie, eds. *North American Indians in Historical Perspective.* New York: Random House, 1971.

Schwerin, Karl H. "The Future of Ethnohistory," *Ethnohistory* 23, no. 4 (1976): 323–341.

Sturtevant, William C. "Anthropology, History, and Ethnohistory." *Ethnohistory* 13, no. 1–2 (1966): 1–51.

Trigger, Bruce G. "Ethnohistory: Problems and Prospects." *Ethnohistory* 29, no. 2 (1982): 1–19.

Glen Anthony Harris

ETIQUETTE. The practice of etiquette has been central to all cultures and civilizations because it functions to establish boundaries of proper comportment in the realm of social relations and hierarchies. The Bible contained imperatives to regulate indecorous behavior, with the Book of Ecclesiastes advising one to "Eat as it becometh a man . . . and devour not, lest thou be hated," while in the Talmud, the importance of controlling the self's more primal urges is asserted in enjoinments against licking fingers, belching, drinking wine in one gulp, or giving off "an offensive odor." Even more important was the manner in which etiquette prescribed deference toward teachers, elders, social superiors, and those at the center of power; according to an Egyptian conduct book dating from 2000 B.C.E., not only is it "worthy" when a "son hearkens to his father," but so should one practice flattery towards a superior, for example, by "laugh[ing] when he laughs."

A Civilizing Process

Though the Middle Ages in Europe witnessed the harnessing of knights to a code of chivalry and the flourishing of a romance troubadour culture demanding particular rules of conduct, it was the Renaissance that brought social codes and conventions to new heights of importance. Courts now served elites and sycophants as thriving centers of power, requiring the ability to fashion one's identity and climb the social ladder in a frequently precarious, if not treacherous, milieu. With the development of the printing press, courtesy books such as Giovanni della Casa's *Il Galateo* (1560) flourished to meet a growing demand, but it was Baldassare Castiglione's *Book of the Courtier* (1528) that most brilliantly epitomized the rules by which the perfect courtier—urbane, witty, sporty, educated, and discrete—should live. In a world dependent upon networks of patronage and the dispensing of favors, right manners at the table or on the playing field were an essential aspect of self-projection along the trajectory of personal and professional advancement.

Manners preoccupied early modern intellectuals as well, most notably Desiderius Erasmus (1466?–1536), whose *De civilitate morum puerilium* (1530; On civility in boys) was one of the most influential and best-selling treatises of the sixteenth century. Underneath Erasmus' injunctions that boys not eat with their mouths open or cast sidelong glances at others were deeper issues concerning self-regulation and emerging notions of shame that centered upon the body. It was the sociologist and social historian Norbert Elias who most seminally examined this shift from the Middle Ages in individual self-restraint and bodily control and labeled it a "civilizing process"; according to Elias, the emergence in the early modern period of the state, with its monopoly over physical force and its growing social interdependencies, resulted in a transformation of human relationships and with it "corresponding changes in men's manners [and] in their personality structure, the provisional result of which is our form of 'civilized' conduct and sentiment." The theory, while not without its critics—who declared it Eurocentric, misrepresentative of history, or overly teleological—nevertheless witnessed from the 1970s onward a resurgence of interest among anthropologists and historians, who found in it a guiding framework in understanding the history of the body, power relations, social and gender relations, the history of private life, and the larger connection between historical currents and social and psychological processes.

Elias paid particular attention to the relationship between manners and the rise of the absolutist state, and certainly Louis XIV's seventeenth-century court at Versailles constituted another defining moment in the history of etiquette and the French notion of *civilité*. According to the court observer Saint-Simon, the king cast a watchful eye over his realm of co-opted noblemen, projecting his royal aura through material ostentation, expecting flattery even from his preachers, and spending equal time on cookery as on politics. Knowing "how to make the most of a word, a smile, even . . . a glance," Louis, by addressing another with some trifling remark, could cause "all eyes [to turn] on the person so honored," just as he could with equal frivolity "ruin . . . many men in all ranks of life." The emphasis on protocol and display and on competing for the king's favor also served to reinforce a larger centralization of power, since, as Saint-Simon puts it, the king "compelled his courtiers to live beyond their income, and gradually reduced them to depend on his bounty for means of subsistence."

As notable figures at court, women could also play a significant role in determining the tone of conduct that would prevail; the highly educated and needlepointing (though occasionally crude) Elizabeth I (1533–1603), for example, oversaw such well-bred, neochivalric luminaries as Sir Philip Sidney and Sir Walter Raleigh. Women, however, were more frequently the intended audience for courtesy book writers, who sought to instill values of proper wifeliness, including compliance, modesty, and, according to one seventeenth-century English guidebook, protectiveness (or "extreme . . . tender[ness]") toward the husband's reputation. Civility in this respect represented the confluence of manners with morals as well as the assertion of social control and structures of domination—all of which would continue through the proliferating etiquette and domestic-life books of the nineteenth century.

Manners in Modern Times

The eighteenth century continued to advance a program of proper court behavior, with the influential Lord Chesterfield (1694–1773) coining the term *etiquette* in letters to his son that spoke of the "art of pleasing" at court and the necessity of cultivating "that easy good breeding, that engaging manner, and those graces, which seduce and prepossess people in your favour at first sight." It was this kind of naked and cynical self-aggrandizement that caused the backlash by Dr. Samuel Johnson (1709–1784), who claimed that the letters instilled in readers "the morals of a strumpet with the manners of a dancing master." Rather than simply reflecting the privileged if arbitrary codes of the aristocratic class, however, manners were also seen in the eighteenth century as reinforcing stability in society, with Edmund Burke (1729–1797) stating famously that "Manners are more important than laws. Upon them . . . the laws depend," and John Locke (1632–1704) similarly connecting good conduct with the stability and health of a democratic polity.

The art of social decorum nevertheless suffered further reputational damage with the Romantic movement and its more rough-hewn ideals of authenticity. Not only was society itself perceived by Jean-Jacques Rousseau and (1712–1778) others as a realm of corrupt artifice opposed to more truthful nature, but they considered that the manners on which that society depends expedite the process of self-alienation. At the same time, the nineteenth century gave rise in England and America to a surging middle class and a new ethic of the sentimental and domestic that allowed ideals of behavior to take on new forms and vibrancy. Where before etiquette had been associated with the aristocratic class, it now became diffused among a broader, albeit still privileged, middle class. To know the rules—that coffee was not to be served at the dinner table, that introductions were to be handled in a particular way, that one took one's place in a quadrille at the front rather than the back of the ballroom—marked one's place in the world as being on the inside of social privilege; to be otherwise was to be "vulgar" or "common" and coldly cast out.

In the New World, Americans' manners, such as hastily eating (or "devouring") their food, particularly galled the English, with Charles Dickens (1812–1870) describing Washington, D.C., as the "headquarters of tobacco-tinctured saliva" shooting forth from the mouths of "not always good marksmen." Nevertheless, Americans, and particularly women, proliferated as authors of etiquette manuals, which counseled on housework, child-raising, personal grooming, and marriage as well as entering polite society. In this regard America undertook its own "civilizing process," trafficking in lifestyle aspirations under the stern but gentle injunctions of an Emily Post, a Miss Manners, or, in its postmodern incarnation, a Martha Stewart.

See also **Class; Everyday Life; Tradition.**

BIBLIOGRAPHY

Arditi, Jorge. *A Genealogy of Manners: Transformations of Social Relations in France and England from the Fourteenth to the Eighteenth Century.* Chicago: Chicago University Press, 1998.

Aresty, Esther. *The Best Behavior: The Course of Good Manners—from Antiquity to the Present—As Seen through Courtesy and Etiquette Books.* New York: Simon and Schuster, 1970.

Ariès, Philippe, and Georges Duby, eds. *A History of Private Life.* 5 vols. Cambridge, Mass.: Belknap Press, 1987–1991.

Bryson, Anna. *From Courtesy to Civility: Changing Codes of Conduct in Early Modern England.* Oxford: Clarendon, 1998.

Elias, Norbert. *The Civilizing Process.* Translated by Edmund Jephcott. Oxford and Cambridge, Mass.: Blackwell, 1994.

Sarah Covington

EUGENICS. The term *eugenics,* derived from the Greek *eugenes,* was first coined by the English mathematician and geographer Francis Galton (1822–1911) in his *Inquiries into Human Faculty and Its Development* (1883) to refer to one born "good in stock, hereditarily endowed with noble qualities." As an intellectual and social movement in the early twentieth century, eugenics came to mean, in the words of one of its strongest American supporters, Charles B. Davenport (1866–1944), "the improvement of the human race by better breeding." For both Galton and Davenport, better breeding involved using the known scientific principles of heredity. Eugenics was the human counterpart of scientific animal and plant husbandry. It seemed ironic to eugenicists that human beings paid such careful attention to the pedigrees of their farm and domestic stock while ignoring the pedigrees of their children. The ideology of eugenics was characterized by a strong belief in the power of heredity in determining physical, physiological, and mental traits; an inherent ethnocentrism and racism that included belief in the inferiority of some races and superiority of others (a view extended to ethnic groups and social classes as well); and a belief in the power of science, rationally employed, to solve social problems, including ones so seemingly intractable as pauperism, crime, violence, urban decay, prostitution, alcoholism, and various forms of mental disease, including manic depression and "feeblemindedness" (retardation).

Eugenics movements did not begin to arise in Europe or the United States until the first decade of the twentieth century, and they did not become generally effective in promoting social and political programs nationally or internationally until after 1910. The earliest eugenics movements were founded in Germany in 1904, in Britain in 1907, and in the United States in 1908–1910. Other eugenics movements appeared subsequently around the world: in Western Europe (France, Norway, Sweden, Denmark), Russia, Latin America (Cuba, Brazil, Mexico), Canada, and Asia (Japan). However, it was in the United States, Britain, and Germany that eugenics as an intellectual and social movement made its greatest strides and, from eugenicists' point of view, achieved its greatest ideological and political effects.

Because eugenics developed in a variety of national contexts with a wide range of ideological and political programs, its content and style varied from one country to another and over time, from the early 1900s until just before the onset of World War II. For example, British eugenicists were particularly concerned with the high fecundity and inherited mental degeneracy of the urban working class, particularly those labeled as "paupers." By contrast, American eugenicists were more concerned with the number of feebleminded who filled the prisons and insane asylums and, after World War I, with the supposed genetic deficiencies of immigrants. In Germany mentally ill, psychotic, psychopathic, and psychiatric patients along with the congenitally deaf, blind, and feebleminded were of greatest concern. German eugenicists were also particularly interested in increasing the number of "fitter" elements in society (positive eugenics)—where prior to the National Socialist takeover in 1933, "fitness" was understood more in terms of class than of race. Certain core principles and beliefs did link various eugenics movements together, however, and the three major international eugenics congresses, held in 1912, 1921, and 1932, emphasized the similarities among the various movements while also revealing the differences.

The core principles of eugenics as they came to be understood by the mid-1930s were summarized in a report, *Eugenical Sterilization: A Reorientation of the Problem,* published in 1936 by the Committee for the Investigation of Eugenical Sterilization of the American Neurological Association. The report articulates four major principles: first, that a number of social and behavioral problems, such as "insanity, feeblemindedness, epilepsy, pauperism, alcoholism and certain forms of criminality are on the increase"; second, that people bearing these various defective traits "propagate at a greater rate than the normal population"; third, that such defects in mental function and behavior are "fundamentally and mainly hereditary"; and fourth, that the environment in which a person was raised was of much less importance than the germ plasm inherited from his or her parents as the cause of "adverse social status," criminality, or general "social maladjustment." Significantly improving the cognitive ability of the feebleminded or making the criminal into a model citizen was deemed virtually impossible. Biology was destiny.

The Historical Development of Eugenics, 1904–1950

In most countries eugenics movements combined theory with various forms of social and political programs, from education committees to lobbying political leaders. Before 1925 most eugenicists were well-respected members of the scientific community, and the eugenic ideas they espoused were not considered eccentric or bizarre. The acknowledged leader of American eugenics, Charles Davenport, received his Ph.D. from Harvard, taught at the University of Chicago, and then established his own research laboratory to promote the study of heredity and its relationship to selection and evolution. In Britain, Davenport's equivalent was Karl Pearson (1857–1936), director of the Eugenics Record Office and Galton Professor of Eugenics at University College, London. In Germany, Eugen Fischer (1874–1967), the academic leader of *Rassenhygiene* (racial hygiene), was the director of the newly founded Kaiser-Wilhelm Institute for Anthropology, Human Genetics, and Eugenics (KWIA) in Berlin-Dahlem. Along with other colleagues, these investigators contributed solid work on aspects of human inheritance as well as more tenuous studies on inheritance of feeblemindedness, mental capacity, and social traits.

In addition to such conspicuous national leaders, many well-known, rank-and-file biologists, especially in the period 1910–1925, enthusiastically endorsed the aims of eugenics. The attraction for these biologists was that the new science of genetics appeared to offer a solution to recurrent social problems that had eluded social workers and charitable organizations. Eugenics was seen as the efficient, rational, and scientific way to solve these problems by eliminating the cause rather than treating the symptoms. These supporters all contributed in some way to spreading the eugenics message to a broader public.

Financial support for eugenics research and propaganda came from the economic, political, and social elite and clearly served several special interests. First was economic efficiency: it was expensive to let defective people be born and then spend taxpayers' money to keep them in institutions for much of their lives. Second, the eugenic argument that social problems originated in "bad genes" deflected criticism of social policies and conditions and placed the blame for social problems on individuals.

Research Methods

Eugenicists were faced with the problem of defining and measuring the traits whose patterns of inheritance they wanted to determine. Definition posed a considerable problem when the traits were complex behaviors that were often defined in different ways in different cultures or different historical periods. What counted as an alcoholic or a criminal? How was "feeblemindedness" defined? Recognizing that such conditions are culturally defined, Davenport, for example, lumped all such individuals into the category of "social defectives" or "socially inadequate persons." For most of the behavioral and mental traits in which eugenicists were interested, no objective and quantitative definitions or measurements existed. For the most part, they had to rely on highly qualitative, subjective methods of defining traits and categorizing individual behavior.

One trait that could be expressed quantitatively was intelligence, tests for which were developed, particularly in the United States. In 1912 Davenport arranged for Henry H. Goddard (1856–1962) to administer versions of the French Binet-Simon test to immigrants arriving at Ellis Island. Although the Binet-Simon test was intended to measure only an individual's mental functioning at a given point in time, Goddard and a host of American psychometricians considered that it also measured innate, genetically determined intelligence. Goddard coined the term "feeblemindedness" to refer to those who scored below seventy on his tests. He claimed, "Feeblemindedness is hereditary and transmitted as surely as any other character. We cannot successfully cope with these conditions until we recognize feeblemindedness and its hereditary nature, recognize it early, and take care of it" (p. 117).

Psychometricians and eugenicists maintained their belief that their tests measured innate capacity rather than merely accumulated knowledge despite the abundance of culturally specific material and terminology in the tests. Even when results from the U.S. Army tests during World War I showed that the longer recruits from immigrant families had lived in the United States, the better they did on the tests, Carl C. Brigham (1890–1943), a Princeton psychologist who analyzed the data, argued that the trends showed a decline in the quality of immigrants over time, not their degree of familiarity with the cultural content of the tests.

The family pedigree chart was one of the main means for displaying and analyzing data on the heredity of a behavioral trait. The data were often anecdotal and subjective and many times were obtained from second- and thirdhand sources. Typical examples are the family studies carried out through the auspices of the Eugenics Record Office at Cold Spring Harbor. Starting with an individual, usually incarcerated in a mental or penal institution, field-workers would interview not only that individual but as many members of the family as possible. Where possible, medical records would be obtained. The data were then organized into pedigree charts to suggest how heredity influenced many behavioral, personality, and mental traits. For example, in a study published in 1919, Davenport claimed that thalassophilia, or "love of the sea," was due to a sex-linked Mendelian recessive appearing in the families of prominent U.S. naval officers. That the condition must be sex-linked was clear to Davenport, since in pedigree after pedigree only males showed the trait. Similar simplistic arguments were extended to explain the differences between racial, ethnic, and national groups, such as the claim that blacks showed genetic tendencies toward "shiftlessness" and the Irish toward "alcoholism."

Eugenics in the Public Arena

Eugenics ideology was spread not only through scientific but also through popular channels, including the press, exhibits, the eugenicists' own popular journals such as *Eugenical News,* various movies, "fitter family" contests at state fairs, and even a eugenical sermon contest. The number of articles on eugenics in popular magazines rose precipitously between 1910 and 1914 and again in the 1920s, especially when the immigration restriction issue was being debated in Congress between 1921 and 1924. Most high school biology textbooks included some discussion of eugenics. By the early to mid-1920s many segments of the American, British, and wider European public were at least aware of a claim, made in the name of modern science, that many social, especially mental, traits were genetically determined, that many segments of society were genetically unfit for anything but the most menial work, and that in these respects blacks, Native Americans, and many non-Nordic or non-Anglo-Saxon groups were genetically inferior.

From the start most eugenicists were anxious to play a role in the public arena. A good deal of eugenicists' efforts focused on lobbying for compulsory sterilization laws for the "genetically unfit" and, especially in the United States, for eugenically informed immigration restriction.

The United States pioneered in the passage of eugenical sterilization laws. The majority of such laws were passed by state legislatures during the interwar period. Eugenical sterilization was aimed specifically at those individuals in mental or penal institutions who, from family pedigree analysis, were considered likely to give birth to socially defective children. Eugenical sterilization reached astounding proportions worldwide in the first half of the century. In the United States over sixty thousand eugenical sterilizations were performed between 1907 and 1963. A similar number was estimated for Sweden, while the Germans ultimately sterilized over 400,000.

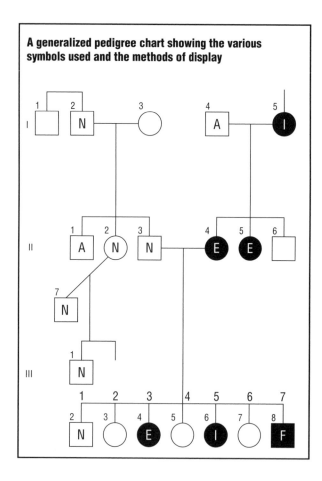

A generalized pedigree chart showing the various symbols used and the methods of display

In the United States eugenicists were instrumental in the passage of the 1924 Immigration Restriction Act. Immigration from Europe, especially from eastern and southern Europe, had increased significantly since the 1880s, replacing the traditional immigrant groups from northern Europe and the British Isles. IQ test scores and data on institutionalization of various immigrant groups for feeblemindedness, insanity, criminality, blindness, and so on were used to support the claim that recent immigrants were less genetically fit than the older, northern European stock. Eugenics provided an air of scientific objectivity for what various nativist groups wanted to accomplish for reasons of economics or prejudice.

Because racial policy and eugenics formed one of the cornerstones of National Socialism, eugenics research and policy found considerable support in Germany after 1933. When Fischer retired as director of the KWIA in 1942, he was succeeded by his protégé Otmar von Verschuer, one of the pioneers in the use of identical twins in genetic and eugenic research. Verschuer eventually took the institute's research into extermination and slave-labor camps, where his assistant and former doctoral student, Josef Mengele, made pairs of twins available, especially for research on pathological conditions. For example, twins (with non-twins as controls) were infected with disease agents to study the effects of the same and different hereditary constitutions on the course of disease. After they died or were killed, twins' body organs were sent back to

the KWIA for analysis. Such procedures, when brought to light at the Nuremberg trials, not only shocked the world but indicated the extent to which eugenic work could so easily transgress the bounds of acceptable scientific practice.

Criticisms of Eugenics

Almost from the beginning, many of the basic premises of eugenics received critical scrutiny by biologists, medical doctors, social workers, and laypersons from all walks of life. Criticisms emerged in most countries by the mid-1920s, though the reasons differed widely.

In Catholic countries criticism of eugenics was made official by the papal encyclical *Casti connubi* of 1930. Prior to the encyclical, however, in countries like France eugenic claims were tempered by the prevailing theory of inheritance of acquired characters, sometimes referred to as "neo-Lamarckism" after the French zoologist Jean-Baptiste de Lamarck (1744–1829), who had emphasized the influence of the environment as a cause of adaptations acquired by organisms during their lifetime and passed on to their offspring. If such adaptations could be inherited, then the environment had a much larger role to play in changing human behavior than eugenicists thought. Consequently in France prior to 1930 and in the countries whose scientific culture it influenced (particularly in Latin America), eugenics was always coupled with programs for public health reforms and attention to improving environmental conditions.

Russia had a small but flourishing eugenics movement before the Bolshevik Revolution of 1917. With the advent of the Communist regime, some biologists hoped that the application of scientific principles to reproductive policies, as to agriculture, would receive official support. But many Soviet biologists, recognizing that complex human behaviors and social values cannot be ascribed to genes in any clear way, found the claims of Western eugenicists naive and class-based. Moreover the "hard" hereditarian line promoted by most Western eugenicists was at odds with the Communist views of the malleability of human nature and thus appeared to provide no role for the environment in shaping human destiny. The Central Committee of the Communist Party outlawed work on eugenics in 1930, making the Soviet Union the only country where eugenics was officially denounced by governmental legislation.

In Western countries like the United States and Britain, criticisms began to arise over the sloppiness of many eugenicists' research methods. Among the first and most important critics in the United States was Thomas Hunt Morgan (1866–1945), a geneticist at Columbia University and prior to 1915 a moderate supporter of eugenics. Morgan felt that the movement had become more propagandistic than scientific and criticized eugenical claims in print, starting with his book *Evolution and Genetics* (1925). He chastised eugenicists for lumping many mental and behavioral conditions together under a rubric like "feeblemindedness" and treating it as if it had a single underlying cause in a single gene. He argued that because environmental influences on mental and nervous development are so strong and since it is impossible to raise humans

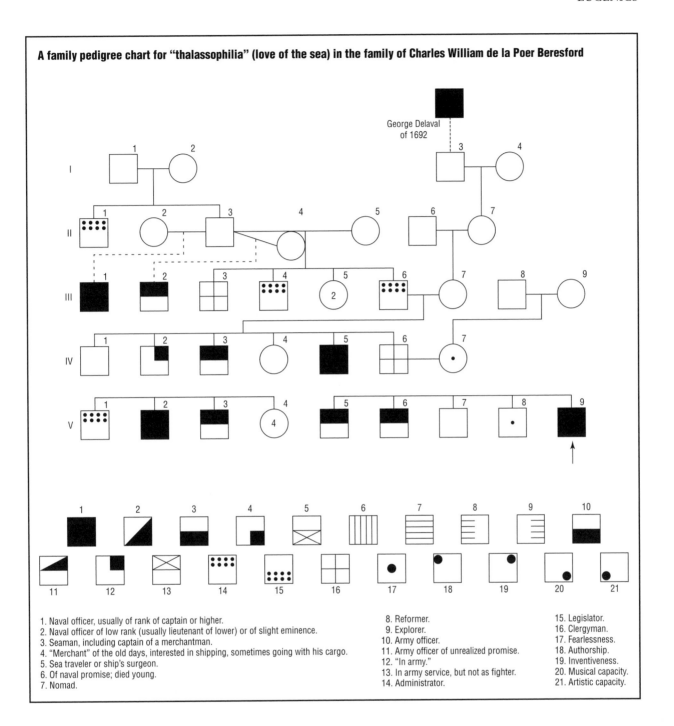

A family pedigree chart for "thalassophilia" (love of the sea) in the family of Charles William de la Poer Beresford

George Delaval
of 1692

1. Naval officer, usually of rank of captain or higher.
2. Naval officer of low rank (usually lieutenant of lower) or of slight eminence.
3. Seaman, including captain of a merchantman.
4. "Merchant" of the old days, interested in shipping, sometimes going with his cargo.
5. Sea traveler or ship's surgeon.
6. Of naval promise; died young.
7. Nomad.
8. Reformer.
9. Explorer.
10. Army officer.
11. Army officer of unrealized promise.
12. "In army."
13. In army service, but not as fighter.
14. Administrator.
15. Legislator.
16. Clergyman.
17. Fearlessness.
18. Authorship.
19. Inventiveness.
20. Musical capacity.
21. Artistic capacity.

under controlled conditions like fruit flies, no rigorous claims could be made about a genetic basis for such traits.

Echoing similar concerns, the English mathematician and geneticist and sometime eugenicist Lancelot Hogben (1895–1975) made one of the clearest statements at the time about the oversimplified concept of genetics that informed much of the eugenics movement: "No statement about a genetic difference has any scientific meaning unless it includes or implies a specification of the environment in which it manifests itself in a particular manner" (Ward, p. 305). Furthermore, as Reginal C. Punnett (1875–1967) noted, even if a trait were

found to be controlled by a single Mendelian gene, unless it was a dominant, it would take hundreds of generations of rigorous selection to eliminate it from the population.

A more public attack on eugenics came from Raymond Pearl (1879–1940) at Johns Hopkins University, himself a onetime eugenics supporter. Pearl and his Hopkins colleague Herbert Spencer Jennings (1868–1947) both agreed with the basic principles and aims of eugenics but felt that propagandists like Harry Laughlin and others made claims that went far beyond any reasonable biological evidence. Jennings wrote a series of rebuttals of Laughlin's claims and a small book

(*Prometheus, or Biology and the Advancement of Man*, 1925) condemning the vulgarization and racism of some eugenic writers. H. J. Muller (1890–1967), a student of Morgan, delivered a searing attack on "old style" eugenics at the Third International Eugenics Congress in New York City in 1932. Muller, who harbored strong eugenical beliefs as well as socialist leanings, argued that until the economic and social environment could be equalized, it would be impossible to know how much of any individual's "social inadequacy" was due to heredity and how much to environment.

Except for Germany and the countries it influenced or occupied, by the mid-1930s eugenics began to decline in general popularity and political effectiveness. Scholars have suggested several possible reasons for this change of fortune. Clearly both the depression of 1929–1933 and reports of Nazi eugenics activity played some part in a general disaffection with eugenical principles. In the depression people without jobs became "paupers" and "social inadequates" overnight with no change in their genetic makeup, while in Germany the sterilization and infamous Nuremberg Laws (1935) showed the extent to which eugenical legislation under a powerful central government could erode personal liberties. An additional factor may have been the recognition that eugenicists were increasingly out of touch with the most recent findings of laboratory genetics. Davenport's and Laughlin's simple unit-character concept did not square with recent experimental data suggesting that most traits were produced by the interaction of many genes and that evidence for a clear-cut genetic basis of complex human social behaviors was almost nonexistent.

Eugenics in the Twenty-First Century

The history of the eugenics movement raises many issues relevant to the expanding work in genomics at the beginning of the twenty-first century, especially the Human Genome Project (HGP). Since the advent of new technologies associated with test-tube babies, sequencing the human genome, cloning new organisms from adult cells, stem cell research, genetic testing, and the prospects of gene therapy, the term *eugenics* has once again come into popular culture. Since it is possible, through in utero testing, to determine if a fetus is male or female or has Down syndrome or a mutation for Huntingon's disease, cystic fibrosis, thalassemia, or Tay-Sachs disease, should these tests be required for all pregnant women? And if so, who should have access to the results? Can medical insurance companies refuse to cover families or their children if the mother does not undergo genetic testing of the fetus? Some medical ethicists argue that the outcome—controlling births in order to reduce the number of "defective" people in society—is identical to that issuing from the old eugenics movement. According to this view, it makes little difference whether state legislation or social and economic pressures force people to make reproductive decisions they might not otherwise make. Other ethicists, however, argue that state coercion, as in the old eugenics movement, is qualitatively different from various forms of social pressure, since the latter still gives the individual some range of choice. In addition it can be argued that modern genetic decisions are made on a case-by-case ba-

sis and do not involve application of policies to whole groups defined racially, ethnically, or nationally.

Clearly it is in the interests of insurance companies to reduce as much as possible the medical costs incurred by their clients. And some would argue that it is also in the interest of individual families to avoid bringing a seriously disabled child into the world. But ethicists raise the question of what is "disabled" and who should be the judge. These issues have become more pressing the more costly medical care has become and the more ancillary social services are cut back. Ironically, as a result of sequencing the human genome, a project that carried with it funds for ethical considerations, geneticists now know that there is no one-to-one correspondence between genotype and phenotype and that the reading out of the genetic code is far more plastic than previously believed. Individuals with the same mutation in the cystic fibrosis gene, for example, can have quite different phenotypes (some are seriously affected and others are not or the effects manifest themselves in different organs and at different stages in development). Thus in utero genetic testing may reveal a mutant gene but will provide little information on how the child will turn out phenotypically.

While these various ethical issues are problematical, with well-defined clinical conditions, they are infinitely more so when mental, behavioral, and personality traits are the center of discussion. From the last quarter of the twentieth century many claims have been made for identifying genes that affect human behavior or personality (alcoholism, manic depression, criminality, homosexuality, shyness, aggression). No gene or group of genes has ever been isolated or shown clearly to affect any of these conditions, yet the belief that the conditions are to a significant degree genetically determined has become widespread throughout the media and in the public. Reproductive decisions based on circumstantial or nonexistent data add another level of ethical considerations in the growing debate about reproductive technologies. Recognizing the consequences of policies put forward under the guise of the old eugenics movement can help avoid some of the more obvious errors of the past.

See also **Biology; Class; Development; Evolution; Family Planning; Genetics; Health and Disease; Hygiene; Lysenkoism; Medicine: Europe and the United States; Race and Racism; Social Darwinism.**

BIBLIOGRAPHY

Adams, Mark B., ed. *The Wellborn Science: Eugenics in Germany, France, Brazil, and Russia*. New York: Oxford University Press, 1990.

Allen, Garland E. "The Eugenics Record Office at Cold Spring Harbor, 1910–1940: An Essay in Institutional History." *Osiris*, 2nd ser., 2 (1986): 225–264.

———. "Mendel and Modern Genetics: The Legacy for Today." *Endeavour* 27, no. 2 (2003): 63–68.

American Neurological Association, Committee for the Investigation of Eugenical Sterilization. *Eugenical Sterilization: A Reorientation of the Problem*. New York: Macmillan, 1936.

Barkan, Elazar. *The Retreat of Scientific Racism: Changing Concepts of Race in Britain and the United States between the World Wars.* Cambridge, U.K.: Cambridge University Press, 1992.

Broberg, Gunnar, and Nils Roll-Hansen, eds. *Eugenics and the Welfare State: Sterilization Policy in Denmark, Sweden, Norway, and Finland.* East Lansing: Michigan State University Press, 1996.

Carlson, Elof Axel. *The Unfit: A History of a Bad Idea.* Cold Spring Harbor, N.Y.: Cold Spring Harbor Laboratory Press, 2001.

Chase, Allan. *The Legacy of Malthus.* New York: Knopf, 1977.

Davenport, Charles B. *Naval Officers, Their Heredity and Development.* Washington, D.C.: Carnegie Institution of Washington, 1919.

Davenport, Charles B., et al. *The Study of Human Heredity.* Eugenics Record Office Bulletin no. 2. Cold Spring Harbor, N.Y.: Eugenics Record Office, 1911.

Galton, Francis. *Inquiries into Human Faculty and Its Development.* New York: Macmillan, 1883.

Goddard. Henry Herbert. *The Kallikak Family: A Study in the Heredity of Feeble-Mindedness.* New York: Macmillan, 1913.

Kevles, Daniel J. *In the Name of Eugenics.* New York: Knopf, 1985.

Kühl, Stephan. *The Nazi Connection: Eugenics, American Racism, and German National Socialism.* New York: Oxford University Press, 1993.

Lombardo, Paul A. "Three Generations of Imbeciles: New Light on *Buck v. Bell.*" *New York University Law Review* 60 (1985): 30–62.

Mazumdar, Pauline M. H. *Eugenics, Human Genetics, and Human Failings: The Eugenics Society, Its Sources, and Its Critics in Britain.* London: Routledge, 1992.

Müller-Hill, Benno. *Murderous Science: Elimination by Scientific Selection of Jews, Gypsies, and Others, Germany 1933–1945.* Oxford: Oxford University Press, 1988.

Paul, Diane B. *Controlling Heredity.* Montclair, N.J.: Humanities Press, 1995.

Proctor, Robert. *Racial Hygiene: Medicine under the Nazis.* Cambridge, Mass.: Harvard University Press, 1988.

Selden, Steven. *Inheriting Shame: The Story of Eugenics and Racism in America.* New York: Teachers College Press, 1999.

Tucker, William H. *The Funding of Scientific Racism: Wickliffe Draper and the Pioneer Fund.* Urbana: University of Illinois Press, 2002.

Ward, Harold. "The Dilemma of Eugenics." *New Republic,* 24 (April 1925): 305.

Garland E. Allen

EUROCENTRISM. *Eurocentrism* refers to a discursive tendency to interpret the histories and cultures of non-European societies from a European (or Western) perspective. Common features of Eurocentric thought include:

- Ignoring or undervaluing non-European societies as inferior to Western;

- Ignoring or undervaluing what Asians or Africans do within their own society or seeing the histories of non-European societies simply in European terms,

or as part of "the expansion of Europe" and its civilizing influence.

Eurocentrism is very old indeed. Already in the fifth century B.C.E. the Greek historian Herodotus mentions "barbaric" Asian hordes who, despite splendid architecture, lack European individuality.

Although Eurocentrism has been common through the ages, it has not been constant, nor has it affected the way Europeans have viewed all non-European societies equally. Moreover, Europeans have not always been in full agreement with each other over the merits or failings of particular non-European societies. In some writers and periods we find a tendency to romanticize Asia and Africa. In general, Eurocentrism has been more pronounced during periods of greatest European assertiveness or self-confidence, the most outstanding example being the age of imperialism and colonialism in the nineteenth and early twentieth centuries.

There are certain beliefs, valid or otherwise, that have led Eurocentric thinkers toward ignoring, undervaluing, or condemning non-European societies. There is a wide range of these, some applying more broadly in chronological terms than others. They include the following:

- Non-European societies tend to be despotic and servile, as against the West's freedom and individualism.

- Non-European societies are Islamic, or pagan, or believe in strange religions, which are inferior to Christianity, or lack its truth.

- Non-European societies are cruel and lack concern for human life. They practice barbaric customs toward women, such as female genital mutilation (north Africa), widow-burning (*sati,* India) or footbinding (China).

- Non-European societies are inflexible and unchanging. Some European thinkers have attributed this lack of change to topography or climate, for instance extreme dependence on a major river, such as the Nile or the Yellow River, or extreme heat or dryness.

- Non-European societies are poor, backward, and underdeveloped, as opposed to the industrialized, progressive, and rich West.

- Non-European societies lack rational modes of thinking and scientific approaches.

Examples

There are innumerable European or Western observers who can be categorized as Eurocentric or otherwise. Between extreme Eurocentrism and its antithesis is a whole spectrum of attitudes toward non-European cultures and peoples, some thinkers being quite Eurocentric in general, but still showing remarkable sympathy toward non-Europeans in some respects, and vice versa. To some extent, the history of Western Asian

England, it is true, in causing a social revolution in Hindostan, was actuated only by the vilest interests, and was stupid in her manner of enforcing them. But that is not the question. The question is, can mankind fulfil its destiny without a fundamental revolution in the social state of Asia? If not, whatever may have been the crimes of England she was the unconscious tool of history in bringing about that revolution.

SOURCE: Karl Marx, "The British Rule in India," p. 493.

and African studies shows a spectrum from extreme Eurocentrism to opposition to Eurocentrism, though in most periods the mean tends toward the Eurocentric end. A few examples of major Western thinkers or ideas on Asian and/or African peoples and cultures are selected as illustrations.

Aristotle (384–322 B.C.E.) regarded Africa and Asia as monolithic and influenced by their hot climates, contrasting with temperate or cold Europe. He saw their governments as despotic and peoples as servile and lacking in spirit. On the other hand, he regarded Asians as intelligent and was impressed with Egypt because leisure among the priestly caste had allowed them to found the mathematical arts.

Medieval Europe's main impression of North Africa and Asia was distrust, then fear of, and hostility to, Islam. And in 1242, the Mongols came very close to Vienna and could have captured it but for news reaching them of their khan's death. Yet the thirteenth century also produced Marco Polo, who traveled through much of Asia and left a detailed account of life in China, which is remarkably positive and even romanticized.

The missionaries of the Catholic Society of Jesus (Jesuits) worked in many parts of Asia and Africa. In that they preached a religion that was strongest in their own (European) countries, they were Eurocentric. However, their policy was to try to understand the people they were converting and to adapt to local conditions, practices, and rites as far as they could. Moreover, they were pioneers in scholarship about several Asian countries, especially China. Jesuit missionaries sent back to Europe a flood of information from various parts of Asia, including, from 1703 to 1776, the "Lettres édifiantes et curieuses" (Edifying and curious letters), about one-third of which dealt with China.

Enlightenment. The Enlightenment philosophers also discussed Asia and Africa. Although most of their ideas were Eurocentric, some were remarkably inclusive thinkers. Non-European civilizations became part of major philosophical debates in Europe about government, economy, and religion.

Among his three kinds of government, republic, monarchy, and despotism, Charles-Louis de Secondat, baron de Montesquieu (1689–1755) puts Asian societies unequivocally in the last. Being of the view that climate and topography influence government system, Montesquieu saw despotism in Asia, especially in China and India, as the result of vastness and heat. Although he does see some merits in Asia, such as lenient laws in India, the general picture he presents of Asia is grim and Eurocentric. To be fair, his *Lettres persanes* (1721; Persian letters) is in a style new to his time and explicitly non-Eurocentric in showing Persian visitors to Europe criticizing what they found.

Montesquieu's most vigorous opponent was François Quesnay (1694–1774), the leader of the philosophical school called the Physiocrats. His primary interest was in the economy, and specifically agriculture, and the model he chose was China. His main work, *Le despotisme de la Chine* (1767; Despotism in China), shows that he regarded that country as an example of despotism. However, it was an enlightened despotism, with the emperor governing according to natural laws both he and all his subjects must obey.

The most famous of the Enlightenment thinkers was Voltaire (1694–1778). His great *Essai sur les mœurs et l'esprit des nations et sur les principaux faits de l'histoire depuis Charlemagne jusqu'à Louis XIII* (1756; Essay on the customs and spirit of the nations and the principal facts of history from Charlemagne to Louis XIII) is a world or "universal" history, and the first ever written to treat the growth of civilization as a whole. It has two chapters on China, two on India, one on Persia, and two on the Arabs. In that sense it is the very antithesis of Eurocentrism, even though it does give much more space to European than to other cultures.

Voltaire's picture of China and India was very positive, especially China, which drew his praise for its secular government. However, he regarded both civilizations as having made their greatest contributions many centuries before, at a time when Europe was still at the stage of barbarism, and having since become static.

Marx. Karl Marx (1818–1883) belongs in the tradition of Eurocentric thinkers. He developed the idea of "oriental despotism" into his theory of the "Asiatic mode of production," the most important plank of which was an absence of private property in land—the commune, state, or monarch being the owner of all land. Marx's main exemplars for his theory were India and China, but also included Egypt and the countries of the Sahara, as well as Arabia and Persia. Ironically he exempted Japan from the "Asiatic mode of production," being thus one of a number of Western thinkers for whom Japan was in many respects more like a Western than an Asian society.

The basis of "Asiatic mode" societies was villages and communities, which Marx regarded as backward, miserable, and lacking in historical spirit. He believed the government of such societies was despotic, because communal agriculture necessitates large-scale hydraulic works and irrigation, itself requiring large-scale bureaucracy. Marx was thus in a long line of environmental determinists.

Because of Marx's environmental determinism, he castigated "Asiatic mode" societies as unchanging. It required outside force to impose change and, while that may have been painful, it was necessary. In an article entitled "The British Rule in India," published in the *New-York Daily Tribune* on 25 June 1853, he condemns British activity in India, but still believes that British colonialism there was historically progressive.

The chief follower of Marx's environmental determinism in the twentieth century was Karl A. Wittfogel (1896–1988), whose main work concerned China. Wittfogel was initially an activist in the German Communist Party but migrated to the United States and became naturalized in 1939, turning strongly against communism. He continued his work on Asia there, especially in *Oriental Despotism* (1957), where he argues strongly that the need for large-scale waterworks spawns despotic bureaucracies that impact on the whole nature of societies.

Weber. Max Weber (1864–1920) is most famous for attributing the growth of the capitalist spirit to the Puritan Protestant work ethic, especially John Calvin's (1509–1564) belief in predestination. Yet he also deserves a mention here for his attempts to develop a comparative methodology of sociology through his studies of the religious cultures of Asia, notably India and China.

In order to determine *why* Asian societies had failed to develop the "spirit of capitalism," Weber examined in great detail the impact on society and "personality" of great religions such as Confucianism, Buddhism, Hinduism, and, though to a slighter extent, Islam. His conclusion: that none of the Asian religions engaged with the world in such a way as to seek salvation through exertion in a calling and through profitable work in the way that ascetic Protestantism did. Confucianism he characterized as the ethic of officials, which adapted to the world, while Buddhism divorced itself from the world and Islam sought to rule it. Weber believed that the religions of Asia all accepted the world just as it was, the implication of this being that there was no incentive to transform it. He also saw the family systems in societies such as China and India as major inhibitors of modernization.

Weber's views, including those on Asia, remain controversial. In the late twentieth century many argued that Confucianism, including the Confucian emphasis on family, was responsible not for economic backwardness, but for capitalist progress. Despite his attempts to compare cultures dispassionately, Weber's basic conclusions point to commendation for the accomplishments of peoples following ascetic Protestantism, and criticism for other cultures, including Asian and African.

Twentieth-Century Critics of Eurocentrism

Frantz Fanon (1925–1961) was born in Martinique but trained mostly in France, serving in the French army during World War II. A strongly anticolonial theorist, he became involved in the Algerian war against the French and was the most articulate spokesperson for its cause. He did not live to see peace restored, dying of leukemia in Washington, D.C. in 1961. His most famous work is *Les damnés de la terre* (1961;

So, my brothers, how is it that we do not understand that we have better things to do than to follow that same Europe?

That same Europe where they were never done talking of Man, and where they never stopped proclaiming that they were only anxious for the welfare of Man: today we know with what sufferings humanity has paid for every one of their triumphs of the mind.

Come, then, comrades, the European game has finally ended; we must find something different. We today can do everything, so long as we do not imitate Europe, so long as we are not obsessed by the desire to catch up with Europe.

SOURCE: Frantz Fanon, *The Wretched of the Earth*, pp. 251–252.

The wretched of the earth), which is a passionate indictment of colonialism, especially that in Africa.

A major point of criticism of Eurocentrism in Fanon's work is his attacks on those Africans who internalize European culture at the expense of their own. He calls on Africans to promote their own culture as the symbol of their national consciousness. And that involves rejecting Europe and its sense of superiority, in other words Eurocentrism.

Edward Said (1935–2003) was a Palestinian Arab, who was born in Jerusalem but was trained in Cairo and the United States. He spent most of his professional career working at Columbia University in New York. Famous as a public intellectual and thinker generally, Said became a passionate critic of Eurocentrism.

Said's best known work is *Orientalism* (1978), a strong attack on Western scholarship on Islamic West Asia and North Africa, which he regarded as deeply ethnocentric or "Orientalist." By its nature, the theory of "Orientalism" applies to all non-Western societies, even though its focus is West Asia. He claims that in colonizing West Asia and North Africa, European states also "colonized" knowledge about these regions, meaning that there is a power factor of superior/inferior in Western scholarship concerning them, which is deeply "hegemonic." The result is that Western scholarship is generally simply an abstraction or invention shot through with various kinds of racism or imperialism. Certainly, it is incapable of examining Asian or African cultures and societies in their own terms. It is in line with a Western political agenda and suits Western interests generally.

Despite what many critics have claimed as an extreme view, Said does acknowledge the possibility that Western scholarship can be "decolonialized." His belief was that allegiance to a discipline, not to area studies, can lead to scholarship "that is not as corrupt, or at least as blind to human reality" as the Orientalist type (p. 326). Naturally, it is essential that all links between scholar and state be very specifically ruptured.

Said's work has attracted both support and criticism. Among the supporters is Ronald Inden, who has written works with similar thrust concerning India, especially *Imagining India* (1990). It has also sparked an opposite theory of "Occidentalism," which lies outside the scope of this entry.

The twentieth century saw numerous other critics of Eurocentrism closely involved in antiracist and anticolonial movements. A particularly distinguished American example was W. E. B. Du Bois (1868–1963), a leader of the American civil rights movement as well as an advocate of black rights worldwide. A distinguished academic as well as a political activist, he wrote many books attacking Eurocentric and racist thinking, as well as defending black integrity, identities, and traditions. Du Bois was also notable in his understanding of the relationship between racism and sexism and in his high evaluation of the contributions of black women. He was born and lived most of his life in the United States, but emigrated to Africa in 1961, dying in Ghana.

Eurocentrism, Anticolonialism, Modernity, Postcolonialism

The tendency to examine the histories of Asia and Africa through the prism of "European expansion" was very common, even prevalent, in Western scholarship on these two continents in the nineteenth and twentieth centuries. The rise of nationalism, anticolonialism, and independence movements brought greater realization of the importance Asians and Africans had played in their own country, and hence a trend away from Eurocentrism. Scholars from Africa and Asia went to live in the West in increasing numbers for training. They brought understandings from their own countries as well as taking back ideas from the West. At the same time, the rise in influence of many former colonies brought about a shift in attitude in the West itself toward Asia's and Africa's histories and cultures.

One illustrative example is the literary movement *negritude* of the 1930s to the 1950s. Led by Léopold Sédar Senghor, who was elected first president of the previously French-colonized West African Republic of Senegal in 1960, this movement arose in Paris, where several major literary figures from French African colonies lived. It attacked the humiliation and contempt European colonialism had inflicted on Africa and black people. Above all, it opposed colonialism and Eurocentrism by seeking to reassert the value and dignity of African traditions.

Modernity. Modernity and the question of when the modern age began are important in Eurocentrism. Until World War II, most scholars studying Asian and African peoples were content to attach modernity to European colonialism or imperialism. But this attitude came under attack in the postwar West, and even more with the Vietnam War of 1965–1973, because it ignores or underplays processes that might have been taking place in the country of concern.

Taking China as an example of a major civilization that never actually became a colony despite major attacks from imperialist powers ranging from Britain to Japan, we find that prewar Western historians of the "modern" period tended to see the beginnings of modernity in the middle of the nineteenth century, which was when the Western impact began in earnest. For example, the great American sinologist John King Fairbank (1907–1991) developed a theory of "change within tradition" before the Western impact, but "transformation" brought about by the West in the nineteenth century. Since the 1970s, more and more historians see internal dynamics within the long range of Chinese history, in which the Western impact of the nineteenth century was an important factor, but certainly not one so fundamental as to define the boundaries of "modern" China. They challenge the notion of a stagnant China awaiting deliverance from a dynamic West as Eurocentric, and either see no point in assigning the boundary of a "modern" China or choose times other than the mid-nineteenth century.

Postmodern and postcolonial studies. Since the 1980s Eurocentrism has been more closely associated in the humanities and social sciences with ideologies such as sexism and racism. "Subaltern studies," which attack all forms of scholarship and ideology that give space to any kind of dominationism or inequality have become increasingly influential in the humanities and social sciences.

One highly significant example is the rise of gender and feminist scholarship that associates Eurocentrism, imperialism, and racism with sexism. These theories argue against the possibility of fully understanding imperialism without reference to gendered power. Colonialism was male in its interests and violent in its methods. Europe was essentially male, the colonies female.

An interesting case study of the way anti-Eurocentrism has merged with antiracism in the field of ancient history is the argument that Ancient Greek civilization derived from Asia and Africa, especially Egypt. Ancient Greece is generally regarded as one of the most important sources, or even "the cradle," of European civilization. But Martin Bernal (1987) suggests that it was nineteenth-century racism that exalted the Ancient Greeks as racially pure Aryans, even though the roots of their civilization were Semitic, Phoenician, and Egyptian.

Together with the existence of a thinker like Edward Said, these examples of alternative paradigms suggest that Eurocentrism is on the decline in the postcolonial era. But it is very far from dead.

See also ***Anticolonialism; Colonialism; Cultural Revivals; Internal Colonialism; Negritude; Occidentalism; Orientalism; Other, The, European Views of.***

BIBLIOGRAPHY

Amin, Samir. *Eurocentrism.* Translated by Russell Moore. New York: Monthly Review, 1989. Major attack on Eurocentrism.

Bernal, Martin. *The Fabrication of Ancient Greece, 1785–1985.* Vol. 1 of *Black Athena: The Afroasiatic Roots of Classical Civilization.* London: Free Association Books, 1987. Argues that Ancient Greek civilization had its roots in Africa and Asia.

Blaut, James M. *The Colonizer's Model of the World: Geographical Diffusionism and Eurocentric History.* New York: Guilford, 1993.

Fanon, Frantz. *The Wretched of the Earth.* Preface by Jean-Paul Sartre. Translated by Constance Farrington. Harmondsworth, U.K.: Penguin, 1967. Classic text condemning colonialism, including its influence on the mind.

Goody, Jack. *The East in the West.* Cambridge, U.K.: Cambridge University Press, 1996. Major anti-Eurocentrist theory of world history.

Inden, Ronald B. *Imagining India.* Oxford: Blackwell, 1990.

Lach, Donald F. *Asia in the Making of Europe,* 3 vols. Chicago: University of Chicago Press, 1965–1993. In three volumes and nine books covers South Asian, East Asian, and Southeast Asian impact on Europe over three centuries.

Mackerras, Colin. *Western Images of China.* Oxford: Oxford University Press, 1989. Covers all periods.

Marx, Karl. "The British Rule in India." In *Karl Marx and Frederick Engels: Selected Works, in Three Volumes.* Vol. 1. Moscow: Progress Publishers, 1969. Classic text summing up Marx's views on environmental determinism and colonialism.

McClintock, Anne. *Imperial Leather: Race, Gender, and Sexuality in the Colonial Contest.* New York and London: Routledge, 1995. Using mainly African examples, argues interconnections among imperialism, sexism, racism, and class.

Said, Edward W. *Orientalism.* New York: Pantheon, 1978. Major twentieth-century theory attacking Eurocentrism.

Wittfogel, Karl A. *Oriental Despotism, A Comparative Study of Total Power.* New Haven, Conn.: Yale University Press, 1957. Summation of Wittfogel's ideas on the "hydraulic society."

Colin Mackerras

The Rape of Europa **by Maerten de Vos (1531–1603).** According to myth, the Greek god Zeus changed into a beautiful white bull to lure the princess Europa onto his back. He then swam with her to Crete, where he seduced her. Europa's name was given to the continent as recompense for her ill treatment. © Archivo Iconografico, S.A./Corbis

EUROPE, IDEA OF. In classical times *Europe* was above all a geographical and mythological notion, the word referring to one of the three known continents—Asia and Africa (or Libya) being the other two. In the famous story of "the rape of Europa," the daughter of Phoenix, king of Phoenicians, was kidnapped and abducted by the Greek god Zeus, who in the guise of a white bull brought her to the island of Crete. In the Middle Ages, Europe was identified with Western Christianity or the commonwealth of Christians. This commonwealth, however, was considered to include only the western part of the Continent, thereby excluding the Eastern Church. The term *Europe* was commonly replaced by *Christianity,* although as early as the ninth century Charlemagne, the king of the Franks, was honored as "the king, father of Europe" (*rex, pater Europae*).

In the early modern period Europe was increasingly compared with the other continents and considered the most civilized part of the world. After the "discovery" of America, world maps usually depicted Europe as an empress surrounded with various symbols of power. The idea of Europe had been secularized by the Enlightenment, and the term was used without its former religious connotations. This was the first time in history when the urban elites thought of themselves as Europeans and proclaimed in Parisian salons that, in the words of the conservative Englishman Edmund Burke, "no European can think himself as a foreigner in any part of the continent."

The American Revolution and the new U.S. Constitution were models for many Europeans wanting to establish "the United States of Europe." In the nineteenth century, however, when waves of nationalism swept across Europe, the idea of a federal European state was not powerful enough to seize the people of the Continent. Having shed his illusions in World War I, an inhabitant of the lost Austro-Hungarian Empire, Count Richard Coudenhove-Kalergi, sought in the 1920s to raise a Pan-European movement based on the Continental superpowers, excluding Britain as "an Atlantic empire." In Coudenhove-Kalergi's view, Europe had to unite because the East (that is, Russia) wanted to conquer it, and the West (the United States) aimed to buy it. It was only the two world wars of the twentieth century, though, that finally forced the nations of Europe to pursue more peaceful cooperation.

European Identity

The feeling of togetherness and solidarity among European nations and peoples has tended to increase in periods of perceived external threat. As early as the classical period, the Greeks regarded the inhabitants of Asia Minor as *barbars* or "mumblers," people who could not speak clearly and were therefore considered irrational. Later the term *barbarians* also referred to non-Christian people. At various times Persians, Muslims, Mongols, Turks, and Russians have all been treated as barbarians and enemies of Europe; the dichotomy between "Us" and "the Other" has been very persistent in European history. There is little wonder that the question has sometimes been raised whether European identity and solidarity among European people in fact depends on a picture of an enemy.

At the beginning of the twenty-first century the European Union (EU) has eagerly pursued more peaceful definitions of a common European identity. The discussion of the idea of Europe and European identity started at the very time that European integration was finally beginning to move forward. In the 1940s Federico Chabod, an Italian historian, wrote the first book on the idea of Europe, rooting it in classical Greece but also emphasizing the Enlightenment as the cornerstone of a common European identity. Since the middle of the twentieth century, European identity has usually been seen as built on three pillars dating from the classical period: Greek reason and rational thinking, Roman law and order, and Christian faith and religion. Other factors have since been added to the list, among them the scientific revolution and the idea of progress typical in the Enlightenment period.

Some critical voices, however, have increasingly considered these kinds of factors too abstract to animate the Europeans. Thus Anthony D. Smith, a British professor of political science, has repeatedly asked whether the attempts to build such an identity are actually efforts to impose western European values and ideas on the eastern and northern peripheries of the Continent. It is a moot point whether Europe really has a common history and memories to be shared; such sharing is crucial if one is to engage emotionally with an identity.

European Regions

It is obvious that the different regions of Europe have different histories and therefore also different memories. The idea of a German-ruled central Europe (*Mitteleuropa*) had been elaborated already by the beginning of the twentieth century. After the collapse of the Third Reich, eastern central Europe came under Soviet hegemony and was referred to as Eastern Europe. In the 1970s and 1980s the idea of a culturally constructed *Mitteleuropa* was revived by dissidents, such as the Czechs Milan Kundera and Vaclav Havel, who were living under Soviet-dominated socialist rule. After the reunification of Germany and the collapse of the Soviet Union, however, the idea of a "third way" between consumer capitalism and socialist planned economy lost much of its former meaning.

Besides the division between East and West, there are also other demarcation lines in Europe. When the European Economic Community (EEC), the predecessor of the European Union, was founded in 1957, the six founding states (Belgium, France, Italy, Luxembourg, the Netherlands, and West Germany) were mostly Christian countries of central Europe. Later many southern and northern states with different historical traditions, religions, and political and social systems joined what became the European Union (EU). The Nordic countries, for example, have emphasized "the northern dimension" in the politics of the EU, while one of the organization's fundamental and ongoing issues has been the question of Britain's role in the "common European family."

In accordance with its famous slogan "Unity in Diversity," the European Union has sought to accommodate various value systems. Moreover, since the enlargement it will undertake further enlargement, when the Mediterranean islands of Malta and Cyprus as well as a number of former Eastern European (socialist) countries will join the EU. The question of European identity and the legitimization of the union will probably become even more crucial for the EU in the near future. However, the idea of Europe has in fact always been contested and in a state of transition.

Political Integration and European Citizenship

Since the 1990s there has been growing discussion of whether European integration should be above all political and cultural and not just an economic matter. In 1992 the Maastricht Treaty established a formal European citizenship, but this has had few practical consequences in the politics of the union. Some European thinkers, including the British-based Gerard Delanty and the German Jürgen Habermas, have emphasized the need to build a common political forum, a European demos, where all the inhabitants of the Continent could take part in decision-making processes. In the present situation many minority groups, such as immigrants, have only a few political rights in the EU. In addition to the issues of ethnicity and religion, many European women have felt that European society has developed in accordance with patriarchal cultural roots and thus marginalized women's roles in society.

Habermas and Delanty have sought a new political identity for all the inhabitants of the Continent. Instead of a mythic common European history and common traditions that can never be shared by all inhabitants of the Continent, this identity could be a genuine force in building up a truly democratic European Union. It remains to be seen whether the bureaucrats in the salons of Brussels will take up this challenge. By giving European citizenship real political value, the EU could perhaps create a union—in the Enlightenment vision—where "no European could think himself a foreigner" any more.

See also **Africa, Idea of; America; Barbarism and Civilization; Colonialism; Cultural History; Education: Europe; Empire and Imperialism: Europe; Eurocentrism; Migration: Migration in World History; Nationalism; Other, The, European Views of.**

BIBLIOGRAPHY

Delanty, Gerard. *Inventing Europe: Idea, Identity, Reality.* New York: St. Martin's, 1995.
Guerrina, Roberta. *Europe: History, Ideas, and Ideologies.* London: Arnold, 2002.
Habermas, Jürgen. *The Inclusion of the Other: Studies in Political Theory.* Cambridge, Mass.: MIT Press, 1998.
Mikkeli, Heikki. *Europe as an Idea and an Identity.* New York: St. Martin's, 1998.
Pagden, Anthony, ed. *The Idea of Europe: From Antiquity to the European Union.* Washington, D.C.: Woodrow Wilson Center Press; New York: Cambridge University Press, 2002.
Shore, Cris. *Building Europe: The Cultural Politics of European Integration.* London and New York: Routledge, 2000.

Smith, Anthony D. *Nations and Nationalism in a Global Era.* Cambridge, U.K.: Polity Press, 1995.

Heikki Mikkeli

EVERYDAY LIFE. When everyday life was first considered a proper subject for reflection it is obviously impossible to say, but an increasing interest in the subject can be traced over the last few centuries, at least in the West. Mystics have long regarded everyday things and everyday routines as a way to become closer to God. From the fifteenth century onward, painters in the Netherlands in particular paid more attention to everyday objects and to the everyday lives of ordinary people, creating new genres such as the still-life and the genre painting. Whether painters or their patrons were becoming more interested in daily life for its own sake, or whether their aim was to look beneath the everyday surface for moral or mystical meanings, remains controversial. For example, Louis Le Nain's painting of peasants having a meal (*Le repas des paysans,* 1642), now in the Louvre, has been variously interpreted as an example of realism and as an attempt to sanctify the everyday in the manner recommended by the religious writer Jean-Jacques Olier a few years later in his *La journée chrétienne* (1657).

Everyday Antiquities

The antiquarians of the Renaissance were another group who were taking an interest in everyday life in the fifteenth century as part of their attempt to revive the culture of ancient Rome. Writing about "antiquities" exempted them from respecting the principle of the "dignity of history," a principle that ruled out references to ordinary people or things. Antiquarians wrote about practices such as burying the dead, reclining at table, gladiatorial shows, and religious and secular festivals, as well as about everyday objects such as clothes, rings, shoes, beards, lamps, and vehicles.

Out of the work of the antiquarians there developed in the eighteenth century what was known in English as the "history of society" and in French as *histoire de la vie privée.* One French scholar, Jean-Baptiste Couture, studying ancient Rome in this way, drew attention to "what an individual living an ordinary life did in the course of a day" (*ce qu'un particulier menant une vie commune, faisoit dans le cours d'une journée*) in an article in the *Memoires de l'Academie des Inscriptions.* In the nineteenth century, the new disciplines of folklore, archaeology, anthropology, and sociology all focused on everyday life, for somewhat different reasons, while some historians continued to study the subject, from Jacob Burckhardt in his famous essay on the Renaissance to the Dane T. H. Troels-Lund in his great work *Dagligt Liv i Norden* (Daily life in the north), published in fourteen volumes from 1879 onward.

The Everyday in Academic Discourse

It was only in the first half of the twentieth century, however, that the everyday became academically respectable across a whole range of disciplines. Freud was well aware of the value of studying everyday events such as lapses of memory or slips of the tongue as evidence of an individual's psychological

The Peasant's Meal (1642) by Louis Le Nain. Oil on canvas. Works of art depicting everyday habits are often open to interpretation, as some critics see in them a deeper moral or mysterious subtext, while other simply see an attempt at realism. LOUVRE, PARIS, FRANCE. LAUROS/GIRAUDON/THE BRIDGEMAN ART LIBRARY, WWW.BRIDGEMAN.CO.UK

states. Franz Boas, one of the founders of the discipline of anthropology in the United States, argued in *Race, Language and Culture* that "To the ethnologist, the most trifling details of social life are important."

In sociology Max Weber launched the idea of *Veralltäglichung,* a term normally translated as "routinization," though "quotidianization" might be nearer the mark. Norbert Elias followed the lead of Max Weber in his historical sociology, famously describing the details of changes in table manners, for instance, as a means to arrive at a grand interpretation of what he called "the civilizing process." Forty years later, Elias would offer one of the most incisive critiques of the ambiguities of the concept "everyday," noting the confusion between everyday life and ordinary people and between working days and festivals. Aimed at a more general public was the successful series on the history of everyday life launched by the French publisher Hachette in 1938 (*Histoire de la vie quotidienne*). The volume on the everyday life of ancient Rome by Jérôme Carcopino became a classic and the series eventually included nearly 250 volumes.

The phenomenologist Edmund Husserl has been described as giving the everyday world, the *Lebenswelt,* "philosophical dignity," and a similar comment might be made about the British philosophers who saw their task as unravelling the implications of ordinary language. As a means of underlining the traditional division between art and life, artists such as Marcel Duchamp became interested in ordinary objects (*objets trouvés*), while composers like John Gage introduced ordinary sounds into their music.

The Discovery of the Everyday

From the 1950s onward, the everyday or the "ordinary" was discovered in the sense of becoming a focus of interest as a way of inserting human experience into an increasingly abstract social theory and social history. Alfred Schutz, in studies of "the world of everyday life," bridged the gap between the philosophy of Husserl and the practice of sociologists, like the Hungarian Agnes Heller, who combined ideas from Marx, Weber, and Husserl in her work. Phrases such as "everyday culture," "everyday knowledge," and "everyday thought" became commonplace.

In France, the sociologist Henri Lefebvre offered a critique of recent changes in everyday life from a Marxist point of view. The philosopher Michel Foucault drew attention to the importance of power relations at an everyday level. The polymath Michel de Certeau's study of French society in the late 1970s, which emphasized the freedom of ordinary people to construct or "invent" their daily life as workers, consumers, or viewers, helped bring the concept of the everyday into common currency (a historian of mysticism as well as a sociologist, Certeau may have been inspired by treatises like that of Olier mentioned above).

In Russia, the semiologist Yuri Lotman studied what he called the "poetics of everyday behavior," for example the influence of literature on life or the theatralization of the behavior of Russian nobles in the late eighteenth century. In the English-speaking world, Erving Goffman's vision of everyday life as a series of dramas has attracted much attention, while feminist sociologists such as Dorothy Smith have used the everyday as a point of entry into the social world of women.

The idea of "practices" has become central to the study of the everyday, especially the "rules" or conventions underlying everyday life, what Lotman called "poetics" and the anthropologist-sociologist Pierre Bourdieu the "theory of practice." Thus the history of science is being rewritten as the history of practices such as experiment. A linked concept is that of "tactics," in other words attempts to obtain what one wants within the framework of the rules or by finding ways round them. Thus the American anthropologist James Scott has drawn attention to the importance of what he called the "everyday resistance" of agricultural laborers, viewed as a middle way between obedience and open revolt.

The History of the Everyday

The history of everyday life, once the preserve of amateurs, was taken up by academic historians after World War II. In the 1960s, Fernand Braudel produced an ambitious comparative study of material life in the early modern world, viewed as the sphere of routine, as opposed to economic life, the sphere of change. In Germany a little later, there was a movement of social historians such as Hans Medick and Alf Lüdtke under the banner of "the history of the everyday" (*Alltagsgeschichte*), defining themselves against the scholars interested in the more abstract history of social structures. To join the two approaches, linking the micro level with the macro level, remains an unrealized ambition of historians and social scientists to this day.

See also **Anthropology; Historiography; Practices.**

BIBLIOGRAPHY

Boas, Franz. *Race, Language and Culture.* New York: Macmillan, 1940.

Braudel, Fernand. *The Structures of Everyday Life.* London: Collins, 1981. Translation of *Les structures du quotidien.* A pioneering study of material culture in early modern Europe, first published in 1967.

Certeau, Michel de. *The Practice of Everyday Life.* Translated by Stephen Rendall. Berkeley and Los Angeles: University of California Press, 1984. Translation of *L'invention du quotidien.* A classic that put the sociological study of everyday life on the intellectual map.

Elias, Norbert. "The Concept of Everyday Life." In *The Norbert Elias Reader: A Biographical Selection,* edited by Jan Goudsblom and Stephen Mennell, 166–174. Oxford, U.K., and Malden, Mass.: Blackwell Publishers, 1998. An incisive reminder of the ambiguities of the concept. Translation of "Zum Begriff des Alltags."

Freud, Sigmund. *Psychopathology of Everyday Life.* New York: Macmillan, 1914. Translation of *Zur Psychopathologie des Alltagslebens,* 1904.

Goffman, Erving. *The Presentation of Self in Everyday Life.* Garden City, N.Y.: Doubleday, 1959. An influential study, viewing the everyday in terms of drama.

Heller, Agnes. *Everyday Life.* Translated by G. L. Campbell. London and Boston: Routledge and Kegan Paul, 1984. A philosophy of everyday life drawing on Marx, Husserl, and Weber, originally published in Hungarian in 1970.

Lefebvre, Henri. *Critique of Everyday Life.* London and New York: Verso, 1991. Translation of *Critique de la vie quotidienne.* A pioneering sociological study, insufficiently appreciated when it was first published in 1947.

Lotman, Juri. "The Poetics of Everyday Behaviour in Russian Eighteenth-Century Culture." In *The Semiotics of Russian Culture.* Edited by Ann Shukman. Ann Arbor: University of Michigan Press, 1984.

Lüdtke, Alf. "The Historiography of Everyday Life." In *Culture, Ideology and Politics,* edited by Raphael Samuel and Gareth Stedman Jones, 38–54. London: Routledge, 1982.

Schutz, Alfred. "On Multiple Realities." In his *Collected Papers.* Vol. 1. Edited by Maurice Natanson. 3 vols. The Hague: M. Nijhoff, 1962–1966. Originally published in 1945.

Scott, James C. *Weapons of the Weak. Everyday Forms of Peasant Resistance.* New Haven, Conn.: Yale University Press, 1985.

Peter Burke

EVIL. The descriptive-normative term *evil* is a significant anomaly in our relativistic and noncognitivist age. Otherwise careful thinkers deploy it as if its extension were obvious and indisputable. And yet it is used in widely differing ways even in our own time. A narrow meaning confines it to the deliberate infliction of harm. This corresponds to only part of the so-called problem of evil, and it is different again from what is feared by those who pray, "deliver us from evil."

Aspects of the problems of wickedness, of suffering, of finitude, and indeed of meaning come together in reflection on evil. But it is not obvious that these problems form a larger whole. Paul Ricoeur (1985) suggests that it is distinctive to western thought to see "sin, suffering and death" as aspects of a single enigma.

Evil's enigmatic character seems to demand narrative treatment. How did evil come into the world? Why and how are human beings sucked into it? And no less important: what can be done to escape it? Given the variety and extent of evils, we should perhaps not be surprised to find every tradition replete with stories and theories. As Wendy Doniger O'Flaherty has suggested, a welter of often incompatible stories may be the most psychologically satisfying response to an insoluble problem.

Yet evil is not just an intellectual challenge. Some of the worst forms of suffering human beings endure are caused by human agents. Our capacity for inflicting such suffering challenges our very understanding of human agency. Can a will capable of evil ever be fully trusted—or even understood?

The challenge goes deeper yet. Because vulnerability to evil and a capacity to inflict it are parts of human nature, evil is not something we can hope to consider in a disinterested way. The very desire to generate a disinterested account of it has often been seen as itself a manifestation of evil, whether as hubris, *curiositas,* or disregard for the humanity of one's fellows. Religious ritual is turned to because we are out of our depth, our capacities for understanding and reform so weak it is a danger to take comfort in them.

It is sometimes thought a specifically modern condition to be suspicious of philosophical theodicies, but the truth seems closer to the opposite. What is specifically modern, rather, may be supposing that we can peer into the abyss without being overwhelmed by it.

The following discussion will first survey understandings of evil as a problem so broad that it defies conventional intellectual or ethical response. An account of the changing fortunes of philosophical accounts of "the problem of evil" will show the distinctiveness of modern discussions. Reference to other traditions will be made, but the discussion will focus on Western materials.

Evil

Modern understandings of religion make accounting for evil one of the fundamental tasks of religion. It is widely believed, for instance, that Buddhism is primarily a response to a universal "problem of evil." But *dukkha,* "suffering, unsatisfactoriness" is not evil. Different traditions define different things as evils (as they do goods), and prescribe different kinds of responses. Thinking about evil is usually accompanied by ritual.

Myth. Ricoeur has argued that an "enigmatic element" makes evil the realm of human experience most profoundly ruled by myth.

Cosmogony. Myth narrates the creation or emergence of the world, often out of chaos. Suffering and death are often presented as the consequences of poor choices made by the first humans. But the miserable lot of humanity is also sometimes seen as the result of the carelessness, malice, or envy of the

gods. Not all gods are good. The orderly world we know may be the result of the destruction and dismemberment of a primordial evil power. In many traditions the world remains evil, a place of exile or punishment.

The creation or imposition of meaning and order is precarious. Jon Levenson has shown that the fear that chaos will return permeates the Hebrew Bible. The force of evil, associated with the seas and often represented as a sea monster (Leviathan), continually threatens order and is continually reconquered by God. That God will prevail is never in question. He may need reminding, however.

Dualism. The world may be the site of a struggle between good and evil forces. True dualism, such as that of the Manichaeans, is rare; even in Zoroastrianism, the eventual victory of good and light over evil and darkness is assured. But dualism haunts monotheism, as the near-omnipresence of the devil in Christian tradition shows. While defeated by Christ, Satan is still the prince of this world. His power and indeed his very existence are a serious problem for monotheism. What kind of God permits the devil such power—or is God too weak to control him?

Beyond good and evil. One response is to assert that evil happens when God turns his back on creation or is silent. The hidden God is beyond our understanding. But perhaps evil is no less an expression of the divine nature than is good. "I form the light, and create darkness," says the God of Second Isaiah, "I make peace, and create evil" (45:7). It has even been suggested, as the Jewish mystical *Book of Bahir* puts it, that "God has an attribute called 'evil'."

Metaphysical accounts. Metaphysical views of the nature of evils arose in response to tensions within and among mythical views.

Fate. Many traditions speak of a fate or order to which even the gods are subject. This fate can be just, as in Buddhism's karmic "law of cause and effect." It can also be meaningless. "Vanity of vanities," says Qoheleth, "all is vanity and vexation of spirit" (Eccles. 1:2).

Among the most widespread of these views is the view that time itself leads to decay and returns creation to chaos. Rituals like the human sacrifices of the Aztecs sought to erase time. In most ancient traditions, time moves in greater and smaller cycles. Even if all rituals are correctly performed, the world will one day succumb to chaos, but from its ashes a new world will emerge. Only in noncyclical traditions are the depredations of evil seen as final.

The philosophical correlate of cosmological dualism is the view that evil is an inescapable part of creation: the stuff of which the world is made is inert or even resistant to order. In his *Timaeus* Plato argues that the demiurge brought the best possible order to unruly matter. Aligned with other dualities inherited from Pythagoras, the dualism of reason and matter was soon connected with mind/body dualism. While opposed to each other, Gnosticism and Neoplatonism both offered dualisms of matter and spirit.

Saturn Devouring One of His Sons (1820–1823) by Francisco José de Goya y Lucientes. Mural transferred to canvas. Due to its amorphous nature, evil is said by some to be the concept of human experience most profoundly influenced by mythology. © Archivo Iconografico, S.A./Corbis

Privation. In response to dualisms, evil was reconceptualized. It is not a substance or a force at all, but just an absence, a privation. God created ex nihilo, nothing constraining him. "Whatever is, is good, and evil . . . is not a substance, because if it were a substance it would be good" (St. Augustine, *Confessions* 7.12). This was the official view of medieval theologians, but it is difficult to maintain in practice. Reproducing a similar move in Plotinus, Augustine conflated it with a dualism of body and soul to arrive at the view that it is because we are made of nothing that we are prone to error and sin.

Contrast. A different kind of view claims that it is impossible or undesirable to create a world without evil, either because there cannot be evil without good, or because good cannot be recognized without evil with which to contrast it. These often conflated views are sometimes described as examples of "aesthetic theodicy." The place of evils in a good cre-

ation is justified by reference to the value of beauty or variety. A mosaic is not only more beautiful with dark as well as light pieces but impossible without them.

Human evil. As the pawn or the prize of the forces that made and govern the world, the human being has always been seen as a source of evil.

Ignorance. Humanity may be seen as essentially limited because its understanding is finite. Justifications of evil almost always appeal to a bigger picture the questioner does not or can not see. Incomplete understanding of things not only leads to error but is also a reason human beings should not expect to be able accurately to judge God's work. Finite reason may be seen as essentially incompetent to understand reality or divinity at all. "My thoughts are not your thoughts, neither are your ways my ways, saith the LORD. For as the heavens are higher than the earth, so are my ways higher than your ways, and my thoughts than your thoughts" (Isa. 55:8–9).

Negative theology starts from this premise, as do those views that insist on the centrality of paradox to a proper human understanding of God. God may operate by different standards than ours. He may indeed make the rules. The moral and even the logical laws that rightly bind us come from God but in neither case do they give us access to his nature. Human evil can thus arise from resentment at creaturely dependence—but also from misplaced efforts of *imitatio Dei.*

Freedom. Free will is the centerpiece of reflection on human evil. This view goes beyond the evil that humans do out of ignorance to assert that free will is the ability to choose between good and evil. Evil can be deliberately willed, not just under the view that it is good. It undermines freedom to invoke a tempter here. (It also makes the creator of the irresistible temptation the true author of evil!) A free act has no cause beyond itself. As St. Anselm of Canterbury put it when asked why Satan willed evil: "Only because he wills . . . this will has no other cause by which it is forced or attracted, but it was its own efficient cause, so to speak, as well as its own effect" (*De casu diaboli* 27).

But an understanding of freedom as "liberty of indifference" does not yet explain why human agents might choose evil, and indeed has a hard time doing so. Augustine insisted that trying to understand an evil will "is like trying to see darkness or to hear silence (*City of God* 12.7). Immanuel Kant thought evil "radical"—it is not grafted onto a human will predisposed to the good but is a tendency at its very "root." Friedrich Wilhelm Joseph von Schelling took the next step and insisted that freedom is abyssal in good no less than in evil acts, opening the way for postmodern explorations.

Not all human beings were thought to be similarly able to use their free will for good. It was Eve who succumbed to the serpent's wiles and submitted to Adam's authority in punishment. Throughout history groups denied (and so demonstrated) their own capacity for evil by projecting this onto outsiders.

Original sin. Not all explanations of evil as the consequence of poor or perverted human choices think human will is free.

Woodcut of a witch, a demon, and a warlock, c. 1400. Throughout the centuries, humans have sought to understand evil by ascribing it to certain supernatural beings or even to other humans who they perceived to be "different" from the accepted norm of society. HULTON GETTY/LIAISON AGENCY

On some accounts, the wills of fallen humanity are no longer free to do good at all; only humanity's original parents had complete freedom. The idea that we are responsible for the sins of our ancestors and for evil acts of our own that we could not avoid seems incoherent and masochistic. It does, however, give human agency a cosmic significance. It was a human act that brought death into the world.

Original sin can be understood in less dramatic ways as a humility that expects human failure and so is not thrown into despair by it. It may also provide a framework for conceptualizing the ways in which our societies and characters are shaped by the ignorance and injustice our ancestors left us.

The Problem of Evil

The experiences of wickedness, suffering, and death are presumably universal, but they do not come to pose intellectual problems—let alone a single problem—until there are philosophical expectations with which they clash. For most of Western history, the problem of evil has been dismissed as beyond our ken. Philosophical engagement with it is the historical exception.

Antiquity. Discussions of various kinds of evil appear in some of the oldest texts from antiquity.

Job. The biblical Book of Job is often seen as an early response to the problem of evil, but it is both less and more than this. The Book of Job recounts the vindication of the innocence of a human sufferer by the very God who permitted the infliction of the suffering and—despite Job's pleas and accusations—never explains why. Appearing in a whirlwind, God rails at Job for the effrontery of his demand to understand what was going on. "Where wast thou when I laid the foundations of the earth?" (38:4) But it is Job's friends, who interpreted Job's suffering as punishment,

MORAL AND NATURAL EVIL

A distinction is commonly made between evils that are caused by free human acts (moral evil) and those that are part of nature (natural or physical evil). Moral evils alone seem our responsibility, and so natural evil has largely fallen away in secular discussion. (It lives on in a different form as the problem of suffering.) And yet in experience the two seem entangled.

Moral evil causes suffering in its victims, and suffering seems to be the only way to atone for it. But evil seems deeper than the distinction between agent and victim. Paul Ricoeur (1985) describes a "strange experience of passivity at the very heart of evil-doing." And the extremest forms of suffering, as Simone Weil argued, can feel deserved.

Caution about these categories is in order. Historically, they are the remains of the closed system of *culpa* (fault) and *poena* (penalty), which from Saint Augustine of Hippo on claimed to justify all evils at once. All natural suffering, including death and even the carnivorousness of animals, was understood to be just punishment for the crimes of men (or angels), crimes defined not in terms of the harm they do to other creatures but of disobedience or rebellion. Ignoring victims, this system elides the central problematic of modern discussions, innocent suffering.

Conceptually, most discussions of moral evil subscribe to a philosophically embattled understanding of human freedom, which is threatened also by developments in the sciences. By restricting discussion to intentional individual acts, these theories also obscure (and quite literally naturalize) social or cultural evils.

whom God condemns: "ye have not spoken of me the thing that is right, as my servant Job hath" (42:7).

Is the Book of Job itself an answer to the problem of evil? Job's example shows that the faithful can live without knowing the reason for their suffering, but his story's power comes from its insistence that the problem of the suffering of the just is at once inescapable and insoluble.

Hellenistic debates. In its philosophical form, the problem of evil seems to be one we inherit from Hellenistic philosophy. Stoics asserted the existence and intelligibility of providence. Epicureans argued that the way to achieve happiness was to accept that there is in fact no providence, to avoid such pains as can be avoided and stop thinking of the rest (like death) as evil. Skeptics argued that it was best to avoid strong views for or against providence, and poked holes in the arguments of both sides.

What made this the first real debate on the problem of evil was the overall agreement of the parties concerned on means—philosophical analysis of human experience—and ends—*eudaimonia,* happiness in this life. Both of these would be called in question by Christianity, leading to an eclipsing of this problem until the revival of the Hellenistic philosophies in the changed world of early modernity.

Religious views. Religious traditions are important sources for thinking about evils.

Jewish views. Jewish tradition does not offer systematic accounts of evil before the medieval period. Apparent injustices are either consequences of past or foreign sins or tests that will be redressed in the world to come, but the point is that God, who has bound himself to Israel despite its flaws, is perfect and perfectly in charge. "The Lord has made all things for Himself: yea, even the wicked for the day of evil" (Prov. 16:4).

While there may or may not be evil powers, there is an evil inclination in human nature itself, which the human individual is free to resist. This evil inclination, too, is part of a creation that the God of Genesis deemed "very good," however, so it is not to be rejected as alien but assimilated. In a widely quoted early rabbinic view, "had it not been for the Evil Inclination, no man would build a house or marry a woman or procreate children." Even when kabbalistic authors argued that evil came from the godhead or was a consequence of the flawed design of the Creation, the emphasis was always on the power of free human good deeds to repair the world.

Christian views. An understanding of a God mercifully active in history shaped the way Christians, too, approached (or avoided) the problem of evil. Christian views were various, but John Hick has argued that Augustine was the father of all the most important elements. Alongside aesthetic views and the claim that God brings a greater good out of every evil, the central claims were the privative nature of evil and the Fall. The last were not explanations for woes of the world so much as reasons for the questioner not to get stuck in the question, however. The answer lies not in philosophy but in conversion and repentance.

This is not to say that philosophical reflection has no part to play. No less a figure than Thomas Aquinas mentioned the problem of evil as the first objection to the existence of God.

> ## EPICURUS' OLD QUESTIONS
>
> The monotheistic problem of evil is often summarized as a trilemma cited in David Hume's *Dialogues Concerning Natural Religion* (book 10): "Epicurus' old questions are yet unanswered. Is he [God] willing to prevent evil, but not able? then is he impotent. Is he able, but not willing? then is he malevolent. Is he both able and willing? whence then is evil?"
>
> While it seems to force the question, "God or evil?" the trilemma can be approached in other ways. Ancient skeptics and dualists found it congenial to their ends. Theological reflection has taken the "aporetic" path of accepting all of the three claims as valid. So understood, the trilemma challenges us to deepen our understanding of the nature of the divine attributes and of evil.

Aquinas discussed evil in many places and even devoted a separate work to it, but his final view was that it was the special kind of nonproblem that *privatio* implies, pointing toward the good, and so toward God. The point was that philosophical reflection conducted without the acknowledgement of the differences between ourselves and God leads nowhere.

The problem of evil remained a challenge to natural theology. Theodicy became harder to avoid as physico-theology came to seem more and more important. Reformation theologians insisted the issue be faced head-on, albeit for a different reason. Martin Luther thought it necessary for philosophy to experience shipwreck over evil. And John Calvin insisted that while it was importunate to claim to be able to understand the fallen world, a view of God without providence was tantamount to atheism.

Theodicy and modernity. The problem of evil as a philosophical challenge to the intelligibility of the world, with or without God, became a central concern of Western thinkers with the rise of the modern age.

The invention of theodicy. The goodness and intelligibility of creation became a battlefield in the fight for religion as the world became increasingly disenchanted, as religious authority fractured, and as confidence in the capacity of human beings to make objective moral judgments grew. The problem of evil was presented as proof for the incompatibility of reason and faith by the skeptic Pierre Bayle in the 1690s. Gottfried Wilhelm Leibniz responded with the claim that this is "the best of all possible worlds," a view he traced back to Plato. His argument is entirely a priori, however, and designed precisely to prevent anyone's drawing conclusions like those of Pangloss in Voltaire's *Candide* (1759). Sounding more Stoic than he knew, Leibniz argued that if we knew all that God does, we would see why this was the world he chose.

The challenge of new Skeptics and Epicureans made this position seem weak, and a half century of nervous teleologizing ensued. Arguing that human beings can and should see the optimality of everything in the world, from bedbugs to avarice, these arguments were quickly conflated with arguments like Bernard Mandeville's linkage of "private vice" with "public virtue," and seemed to many to undermine not only religion but morality too. If the world, with all its horrors, cannot be improved upon, and for reasons we cannot hope (and perhaps do not need) to understand, why do anything at all?

Theodicy overturned. Immanuel Kant presented theodicy as the enemy of piety and ethics. In a manner Luther would have appreciated, he argued that the experienced "failure of all philosophical efforts in theodicy" ensures the continued importance of moral struggle and makes religious faith both permissable and necessary. Kant commended the figure of Job for basing his religion on his morality and not his morality on his religion: both do better when the pretension to theodicy is abandoned. Georg Wilhelm Friedrich Hegel and Arthur Schopenhauer in their very different ways found this view premature, insisting that one needed either to find the meaning of suffering in history or to accept that there is and never will be one.

Friedrich Nietzsche dealt the decisive blows to theodicy. In the *Genealogy of Morals* (1887) he argues that "evil" is not merely a human category, but a bad one, developed by creatures of ressentiment chagrined by the excellence of other human beings. Arguing that the others must be evil because they themselves were good, "slaves" and their priests succeeded in upsetting an earlier and more noble set of values. The noble "free spirit" does not ask whether the world is good or meaningful (this question defines nihilism) but affirms it in all its joys and pains. Value is not found in the world but generated by the overflowing vitality of creative spirits. Nietzsche's historical relativization of value categories and his call for a transvaluation of contemporary values spelled the end of theodicy, at least in continental European thought.

Contemporary developments. But the philosophical problem of evil has not gone away, in part because the twentieth century brought with it new and unprecedented horrors. Some religious thinkers have responded to the "logical problem of evil" (Is the existence of evil compatible with divine omnipotence and goodness?) by proposing views of a divinity in some way limited in power; the growing, suffering God of process thought is an example. Hick's "Irenaean" view of theodicy argues that God is doing as well as anyone could at the time-consuming task of getting human beings freely to love him.

Analytic philosophers of religion have largely moved beyond the logical to the "evidential problem of evil" supposedly inaugurated by Hume in his *Dialogues.* The question is no longer whether evil in the abstract is compatible with theism—that may even be true—but whether the quantity and variety of evils we find do not constitute an argument for the irrationality of theism. While still far from concrete, discussion now hangs on the existence of "horrendous" or "irredeemable" forms of evil.

But there are also strong religious movements rejecting the very enterprise of theodicy, in Christian thinkers like Karl Barth (building on the Lutheran Søren Kierkegaard) and Jewish thinkers like Emmanuel Levinas (building on the Neokantian Hermann Cohen). Especially in response to the Holocaust, thinkers have argued for the obsolescence of all traditional views and have urged reconceptualizations of God and his relation to human history and suffering.

Conclusion

After decades of neglect, the language of evil has been reintroduced to public life in the rhetoric used by political leaders in the early twenty-first century. Some political theorists, too, have argued that a revival of the language of evil is required to maintain a sufficient outrage at genocide, nuclear weapons, terrorism, and threats to the ecological stability of the planet.

Shared indignation at the worst things people do seems to be all that remains of a shared normative view of the world. But does this justify reviving the language of evil? Feminist scholars are not the only ones to caution against so quintessentially dualistic a concept. Evil allows no compromise. But the history of human societies shows that it is almost always the other who is demonized. Perhaps what Carl Gustav Jung called a "morality of evil"—an integration through honest recognition of the capacity for evil in human nature—is safer.

The modern problematic of theodicy, with its confidence in reason and shared conceptions of the good, may not survive our postmodern age. As long as we try to make moral sense of the world and of human life, however, "evil" will remain a challenge and a temptation.

See also **Christianity; Free Will, Determinism, and Predestination; Natural Theology; Religion; Theodicy.**

BIBLIOGRAPHY

Adams, Marilyn McCord. *Horrendous Evils and the Goodness of God.* Ithaca, N.Y.: Cornell University Press, 1999.

Bernstein, Richard J. *Radical Evil: A Philosophical Interrogation.* Cambridge, U.K.: Polity Press, 2002.

Copjec, Joan, ed. *Radical Evil.* London: Verso, 1996.

Hick, John. *Evil and the God of Love.* 2nd ed., with a new preface. Basingstoke: Macmillan, 1985.

Howard-Snyder, Daniel, ed. *The Evidential Argument from Evil.* Bloomington: Indiana University Press, 1996.

Larrimore, Mark. *The Problem of Evil: A Reader.* Oxford: Blackwell, 2001.

Leaman, Oliver. *Evil and Suffering in Jewish Philosophy.* Cambridge, U.K.: Cambridge University Press, 1995.

Levenson, Jon. *Creation and the Persistence of Evil: The Jewish Drama of Divine Omnipotence.* Princeton, N.J.: Princeton University Press, 1994.

Marquard, Odo. "Unburdenings: Theodicy Motives in Modern Philosophy." In *In Defense of the Accidental: Philosophical Studies.* Translated by Robert M. Wallace, pp. 8–28. New York and Oxford: Oxford University Press, 1991.

Noddings, Nel. *Women and Evil.* Berkeley: University of California Press, 1989.

O'Flaherty, Wendy Doniger. *The Origins of Evil in Hindu Mythology.* Berkeley: University of California Press, 1976.

Ormsby, Eric L. *Theodicy in Islamic Thought: The Dispute over al-Ghazālī's "Best of All Possible Worlds."* Princeton: Princeton University Press, 1984.

Ricoeur, Paul. "Evil: A Challenge to Philosophy and Theology." *Journal of the American Academy of Religion* 53, no. 3 (1985): 635–648.

———. *The Symbolism of Evil.* Translated by Emerson Buchanan. New York: Harper and Row, 1967.

Russell, Jeffrey Burton. *The Prince of Darkness: Radical Evil and the Power of Good in History.* Ithaca, N.Y.: Cornell University Press, 1988.

Schreiner, Susan. *Where Shall Wisdom Be Found: Calvin's Exegesis of Job from Medieval and Modern Perspectives.* Chicago: University of Chicago Press, 1994.

Schwarz, Hans. *Evil: A Historical and Theological Perspective.* Translated by Mark. W. Worthing. Lima, Ohio: Academic Renewal Press, 2001.

Surin, Kenneth. *Theology and the Problem of Evil.* Oxford: Blackwell, 1986.

Weil, Simone. "The Love of God and Affliction." In *Waiting for God,* pp. 117–136. Translated by Emma Craufurd. New York: Harper and Row, 1951.

Whitney, Barry L. *Theodicy: An Annotated Bibliography on the Problem of Evil, 1960–1990.* New York: Garland, 1993.

Williams, Rowan. "Insubstantial Evil." In *Augustine and His Critics: Essays in Honour of Gerald Bonner.* Edited by Robert Dodaro and George Lawless, pp. 105–123. London and New York: Routledge, 2000.

Mark Larrimore

EVOLUTION. Although it can encompass cosmic and cultural change, *evolution* is a term usually associated with the modern scientific theory of species change and is most closely associated with the work of Charles Darwin (1809–1882) and, to a lesser extent, Alfred Russel Wallace (1823–1913). Darwin himself did not refer to his specific theory as "evolution" but instead used the phrase "descent with modification." Only the very last word of his famous work laying out the argument for his theory, *On the Origin of Species,* which appeared in 1859, was "evolved." The term gained widespread currency especially in the English language and came to be virtually synonymous with Darwin and Darwinism because of its use by contemporaries like the social theorist Herbert Spencer (1820–1903) and by the numerous commentators, advocates, and translators, such as Thomas Henry Huxley (1825–1895) and Ernst Haeckel (1834–1919), who were carrying meanings into the theory of species change from areas of biology concerned with developmental processes like embryology.

Before then, the term *evolution* had been used in a number of contexts. Stemming from the Latin verb *evolvere,* the term generally refers to an unrolling or unfolding. The substantive form *evolutio* refers to the unrolling of a scroll. Implied in these meanings is the fact that something is there to unfold, develop, or unroll. Its scientific use was first noted in mathematics in the sixteenth century, but it was soon applied to the development or unfolding of ideas or principles. In the seventeenth century the term began to take on a biological cast when it was first used by an anonymous English reviewer to characterize the embryological theories set forth by Jan Swammerdam (1637–1680). A preformationist, Swammerdam postulated a theory of insect development that relied on preexisting or preformed parts that expanded and grew in the embryonic larva. The semen of the male was required in this process, but only as a stimulus to realize the development of the adult form already encased in the semen of the female. The term *evolution* was thus coined initially to describe a developmental or embryological process of unfolding resulting in the reproduction of an adult form. Its application to the process of species change took place gradually in fits and starts over the next 150 years or so by a broad range of thinkers who increasingly carried over meanings of developmental or embryological unfolding in reproduction to theories of species change within historical, temporal, or geographical frame of references.

The extent to which the German *Naturphilosophen* ("nature philosophers") or German Romantic thinkers like Friedrich Wilhelm Joseph von Schelling (1775–1854) may have held evolutionary theories and the extent to which such views of *dynamische Evolution* ("dynamic evolution") shaped or even resembled subsequent evolutionary theories leading eventually to Darwinian evolution is the subject of lively discussion and controversy among historians of evolution of the eighteenth and early nineteenth centuries. The received view of the history of evolutionary thought does not usually locate the origins of Darwinian evolution in the German philosophical context, or in movements like Romanticism, but has instead located its intellectual origins in the context of Enlightenment views that included belief in progress, in theological movements like natural theology, and in the shifting views and practices of traditional natural history that led to reforms in taxonomic practices and in emerging related "sciences" like geology. Its social origins are generally linked to late-eighteenth-century economic theories that articulated laissez-faire policies, to the rise of industrial capitalist societies and states, and to the increasing linkage between natural history (and indeed science as whole) to colonialism and to imperialist ambitions, especially in Great Britain. In the received view, the history of

evolution long predates Darwinian developments, though Darwin and his theory are given exceptional emphasis.

Evolution as a Theory of Species Change

The belief in a changing or dynamic universe can be first seen in ancient Greek philosophy. Heracleitis (c. 540–c. 480 B.C.E.), also known as the "flux philosopher," believed that change was a fundamental property of the universe. His successor, Empedocles (c. 490–430 B.C.E.), first articulated a crude but dynamic theory that postulated that the origin of life had taken place in a manner that suggested evolution. With the philosophical worldview established by Aristotle (384–322 B.C.E.), the belief in a changing universe fell into disfavor. Aristotle and his numerous medieval and Renaissance translators, commentators, and supporters instead believed in a static universe which held that living organisms were created initially by a designer (the Demiurge of Plato's *Timaeus* or the biblical Creator) and then remained essentially unchanged. These ideal types or species were arranged hierarchically in what came to be known as the *scala naturae,* or the ladder of creation. Like the rungs of a ladder, each species was arranged hierarchically, with lower forms of life on the bottom and higher forms of life on the top. During the Renaissance, the ladder of creation gave way to the popular metaphor of the "great chain of being," which referred to a progression of living forms linked in an orderly chainlike arrangement. Extinction, the sudden disappearance of a species, in such a scheme was unthinkable since it meant that the chain would lose a vital link. Belief in the fixity of species and in the species characterized by an ideal type therefore dominated thinking about living entities and was most clearly demonstrated in the modern classification scheme that originated with Carolus Linnaeus (1707–1778).

Belief in species change, or more precisely what was termed "transmutationism," slowly began to emerge during the Enlightenment. One reason for this was the recognition that the earth was of greater antiquity than previously thought and that fossils, long held to be curiosities of nature that adorned the shelves of Renaissance collectors were in fact the remnants of once living organisms. The organic origin of fossils had been suggested earlier by Nicholas Steno (1638–1686) and others who were concerned with them.

Another reason was that the Enlightenment also saw the emergence of the belief in a progressive world, both scientific and social, at the same time that it was slowly realized that the earth itself had a long and tumultuous history of its own. The closing of the eighteenth century saw the beginnings of attempts to understand the history of the earth in terms of natural causes and processes. These geological theories suggested that fossils were of organic origin and that uniform or constant processes rather than catastrophic or one-time events had shaped the Earth's history. In the eighteenth century two rival schools of thought existed: the first, known as the catastrophists, upheld the belief in the uniqueness of geological events, while the second upheld the belief that geological processes were not unique or catastrophic but instead were part of a uniform and largely gradual process of natural change.

The latter school was associated with a "uniformitarian" theory of geological change and its advocates known as uniformitarians.

The French naturalist Georges-Louis Leclerc, comte de Buffon (1707–1788), was one of the first to embrace a uniformitarian philosophy, to question the fixity of species, and to suggest a transmutationist theory for species change. Although he was a respected naturalist, writing a forty-four-volume treatise on the natural history of the world known as *L'historie naturelle* (Natural history), his theoretical explanations for the origin of life and of species change were not accepted during his time; he provided no cogent mechanism for such changes. Buffon's transmutationist ideas were also not accepted because they were undermined by the philosophical teachings of his successor, Georges Cuvier (1769–1832), an anti-uniformitarian who thought successive "revolutions" or catastrophes had shaped the pattern of diversity of life on earth. Cuvier was a pioneer of comparative anatomy and is generally regarded as the father of modern vertebrate paleontology. He upheld the fixity of species despite fossil evidence of species change. Ironically, although he opposed transmutationism strongly, Cuvier was the first to recognize the phenomenon of extinction, or the view that species had disappeared from the biological record. His system of classification placed living organisms into four distinct groupings or what he termed *embranchements:* the Vertebrata, Articulata (arthropods and segmented worms), Mollusca, and Radiata (echinoderms and cnidarians). The four "branches" were distinct from one another and could not share any evolutionary transformation. If any similarities existed, this was due to shared functional circumstances and not to any common ancestry. Cuvier's influence in zoology in particular and in French science generally was enormous and played a role in discrediting efforts to formulate transmutationist theories.

The first to suggest a viable theory of transmutation was the Frenchman Jean-Baptiste de Lamarck (1744–1829), a contemporary of Cuvier's who faced notable opposition from him. First an expert on botany, Lamarck was given the lowly task of organizing the invertebrate collections at the Musée National d'Histoire Naturelle (National Museum of Natural History). In the process of working with the little-known group (Lamarck coined the term *invertebrate*), he began to note progressive trends in the group. He became particularly interested in adaptation, or the manner and process by which organisms are able to adapt physiologically and morphologically to their environment, and he was especially interested in how well-adapted organs originated. His most celebrated example was the modification of the neck of the giraffe, which became elongated in response to stretching during feeding on the leaves of trees on the African plains. This and other examples were explored in works such as *Philosophie zoologique* (Zoological philosophy), published in 1809. According to Lamarck, the use, or in many cases the disuse, of such vital organs could lead to the origin of novel but well-adapted traits; the cumulative effect of these adaptations could eventually lead to new species. Lamarck never provided a cogent mechanism by which this physical transformation took place, however, though he did draw on contemporary theories from animal physiology to suggest that the body heat generated by physical exercise could lead to such structural transformation. Sometimes called "the

inheritance of acquired characters," Lamarckian transmutationism, also later called Lamarckian evolution or "Lamarckism," was subsequently shown to be erroneous because changes acquired as a result of use and disuse were shown to be not heritable. The German experimental biologist Auguste Weismann (1834–1914) is generally credited with disproving Lamarckian inheritance through a number of experiments that included cutting off the tails of hundreds of mice, and through his famous theory that first made the distinction between germ-plasm (cells that passed on hereditary information) and somatic or bodily cells. The "Weismann Barrier," which eventually became one of the central dogmas of modern biology, postulated that hereditary information moves only from the genes to the somatic cells and not vice versa.

Lamarck's ideas were, however, very popular throughout much of the nineteenth century, especially among naturalists interested in adaptation, and continued to gain support in some communities well into the twentieth century, sometimes being associated with "neo-Lamarckian" theories of species change. Darwin himself relied heavily on the inheritance of acquired characters to explain many adaptations that he later outlined in laying out his own transmutationist theory as it finally appeared in 1859.

Transmutationism itself became increasingly acceptable in the early decades of the nineteenth century. It captured the interest of Darwin's own grandfather, Erasmus Darwin (1731–1802), who suggested that life had originated from "one living filament" in his two-volume work *Zoonomia* (1794–1796). Other transmutationists included the French anatomist Étienne Geoffroy Sainte Hilaire (1805–1861), who studied teratology, or the science of birth defects. He suggested that through such "monstrous births" new species might arise in a sudden or rapid process, a theory later challenged by modern genetics.

In the nineteenth century a series of scholars began to uphold not just transmutationist doctrines but theories suggestive of what eventually would become known as Darwinian natural selection. In 1813 William Wells delivered a paper to the Royal Society with the title "An Account of a Female in the White Race of Mankind." Wells suggested that new human races originated when groups moved into new territories where they encountered new conditions of life. In the process of adaptation to these new conditions, newer improved races of humans would emerge. In 1831 Patrick Matthew came even closer to formulating a view of natural selection in the appendix to an obscure treatise, *On Naval Timber and Arboriculture.* In this account Matthew invoked the extinction of species by catastrophic events, after which the survivors would diversify into new, better-adapted species that would remain stable for long periods of time. In 1835 yet another scholar, Edward Blyth (1810–1873), in a paper titled "An Attempt to Classify the Varieties of Animals," suggested a competitive process echoing natural selection whereby the elimination of the unfit groups would take place.

In 1844 the work of one transmutationist in particular drew the attention of wide Victorian audiences. Writing anonymously at first, Robert Chambers (1802–1871) outlined a transmutationist theory under the title *Vestiges of the Natural*

History of Creation. The book became an instant sensation for its many readers, who were greatly entertained by the provocative—and indeed some thought scandalous—account of the origins of the solar system and of the origins of humanity, which postulated evolution from the apes. Though it was widely read and discussed, it received devastating criticism from scientists; this was so much the case that Charles Darwin, witnessing the controversy precipitated by *Vestiges,* is thought to have been dissuaded from publishing his own transmutationist views for nearly fifteen years.

Charles Darwin and Descent with Modification by Means of Natural Selection

Charles Darwin was the leading transmutationist of the nineteenth century. The grandson of Erasmus Darwin, and the son of a fairly successful country physician, Robert Waring Darwin, Charles was born into an educated and affluent English family that fostered his interest in natural history. His mother, Susanna Wedgwood, was the daughter of the famed industrialist and potter Josiah Wedgwood (1730–1795) and heir to a family fortune. Charles was the youngest of two sons and had three sisters, who doted on him after the premature death of his mother when Charles was only eight. His scholastic achievements were less than stellar, though he early on developed a passion for natural history. He first made an attempt to study medicine at Edinburgh University but gave up after witnessing an operation on a young child without the aid of anesthesia. Although his formal medical studies disappointed him, Darwin did enjoy interactions with local experts in natural history. In particular he fell under the influence of an ardent transmutationist, Robert E. Grant (1793–1874), a keen student of marine invertebrates who encouraged Darwin's interest in natural history and also encouraged him to consider the leading transmutationist theories of the day. Under Grant's tutelage at Edinburgh, Darwin was exposed seriously to the scientific theories of Lamarck and to the insights of his own grandfather Erasmus, which he entertained but did not enthusiastically accept, at least at that time. He also made some of his first scientific observations using a microscope on the mode of fertilization of the marine polyp *Flustra.*

His second attempt at formal education shortly thereafter in theology at Cambridge University exposed him to the popular views of natural theology, with its focus on adaptation and design, especially the work of William Paley (1735–1805) and his *Natural Theology* (1802). Darwin's only formal scientific training had been in geology under the tutelage of Adam Sedgwick (1785–1873) when John Stevens Henslow (1796–1861), the professor of botany and his mentor, recommended him to the Admiralty for a geographic expedition to chart the coast of South America. Under the command of Captain Robert FitzRoy (1805–1865), the HMS *Beagle* set sail in 1831, with Darwin on board serving as gentleman-companion to the captain and increasingly playing the role of ship's naturalist. The five-year voyage, which charted the coastline of South America and then continued to the Galapagos Islands, Tahiti, New Zealand, and Australia, exposed Darwin to the variation and distribution of living organisms in both continental and island environments. Darwin collected extensive specimens of flora and fauna and made notable observations of the geological history of the locales he visited. Frequently referring to Charles Lyell's (1797–1875) recently published *Principles of Geology* (1830–1833), which was part of the personal library that he had taken with him, Darwin sought to understand the geographic distribution of plants and animals in terms of a uniformitarian geology. He was especially struck by the manner in which related forms appeared to replace each other as one traveled up and down the coast of eastern South America, by the resemblance of extinct fossil forms to extant life, by the similarity between island species in the Galapagos to nearby continental areas like western South America, and by the differences displayed between those island species on the Galapagos. All of these patterns suggested that some natural and gradual process that involved migration and adaptation to local environments had taken effect, rather than some act of unique or special creation.

Darwin increasingly sought a general explanation for his observations of the natural world during the five-year voyage, and after returning to England he devoted himself to this end by revising his journals, reexamining his specimens, consulting with noted experts, and reading extensively in the scientific literature available to him. Between 1837 and 1838—generally regarded as the crucial years in the formulation of his famous theory—Darwin read the *Essay on the Principle of Population* by Thomas Robert Malthus (1766–1834). More than any other work, the essay provided Darwin with the intellectual backdrop for his theory by suggesting that competition for natural resources was a fact of life and that populations remained stable as a result of processes that included checks and balances. In this competitive world where there was a struggle for existence, those organisms with the most favorable characteristics would be favored to survive and reproduce themselves. Given enough time, those with favorable traits and characters would diverge from the ancestral forms to give rise to new species. The new elements to transmutationism that Darwin introduced thus included the struggle for existence, but also the fact that heritable variation that was favorable and that conferred an advantage would be likely preserved in the process of reproduction.

Darwin recorded the development of his ideas at this time in a series of notebooks that reveal his attempts to understand the branching process for the origin of species, which had "descended" from some common ancestor. Although he had the major features of his theory at this time, Darwin did not make his work public until much later. There is much speculation in the scholarly literature about the delay in publishing his theory, but there is general agreement that Darwin spent the next interval of his life collecting evidence in support of what he knew would be a contentious theory. He wrote to experts collecting information that might be useful in support of his theory, he engaged in detailed taxonomic work on some little-known species of barnacles to familiarize himself with general problems in the taxonomy of a particular group, and most importantly he closely followed the practices of domestic breeders, especially by frequenting exhibitions and shows on popular or fancy breeds of pigeons. In 1842 he wrote a historical sketch outlining his theory and extended it into a longer historical essay in 1844, neither of which was made public, while all the while compiling the data he was amassing from experts all over the world and from his own research and reading. He was finally forced into joint publication of an abbreviated version of his theory in 1858 shortly after the English naturalist Alfred Russel Wallace independently formulated his own parallel theory. Up to that point, Darwin had been laboring for some twenty years to complete a comprehensive work he planned to title "Natural Selection."

Under pressure to complete a manuscript, Darwin took less than a year to outline his theory of species change, which he ultimately called "descent with modification" by means of natural selection. The full title of his famous book was *On the Origin of Species by Means of Natural Selection; or, The Preservation of Favoured Races in the Struggle for Life.* It appeared in bookstores on 24 November 1859 and sold out on the first day. It went through six editions as Darwin modified his theory in response to his many critics. Historians generally cite the first edition of this book for their scholarly attempts to understand Darwin's theory, since subsequent editions included such prolonged attempts to accommodate his critics that the text and scientific explication is considered unclear, if not actually inaccurate.

In addition to natural selection, Darwin included some four or five other ways that species change could take place, including the inheritance of acquired characters. Though he did not address human evolution in this book (only one sentence alludes to human evolution), Darwin's readers quickly made the connection between humans and primates thanks in part to the efforts of earlier transmutationists like Robert Chambers. Darwin turned to human evolution only later, in 1871, when he wrote the two-volume *Descent of Man and Selection in Relation to Sex.* In this book Darwin corrected earlier misconceptions of his work and made it clear that humans had not evolved from apes or monkeys but that both had shared a common ancestor. The book also included pronounced reflections on Darwin's views of human societies and the evolution of civilizations, some of which supports the present-day idea that Darwin himself was indeed a "Social Darwinist." The second part of this book, sexual selection, was an explication of Darwin's theory of sexual selection that was first articulated in 1859. Sexual selection was the process by which Darwin thought fanciful characters like male plumage had evolved, largely through the process of female mate choice. It was one point that led to a disagreement with Wallace, who did not support sexual selection because he thought it acted against natural selection.

Darwin's theory did face notable criticism in his day. One problem had to do with the absence of any viable theory of heredity in it. This led to the criticism—most closely ascribed to Fleeming Jenkin (1833–1885) in a famous review of 1867—that new or novel characters would be diluted or "swamped" out with subsequent generations. Darwin was aware of this criticism, and in his 1868 book *The Variation of Animals and Plants under Domestication,* he attempted to formulate his "provisional hypothesis of pangenesis," a theory postulating that organs of the body generate hereditary information in the form of gemmules which become combined in the gonads during reproduction. The hypothesis remained largely just an unproven hypothesis. This problem was eventually addressed,

during the "rediscovery of Mendel" in 1900, by the discovery that heredity is particulate in nature.

Another problem was the age of the Earth, which, according to estimates made by William Thomson, later Lord Kelvin (1824–1907), was about one hundred million years old. This was an insufficient amount of time to account for the slow, gradual process that Darwin envisioned. The problem was solved after the late-nineteenth-century discovery of radioactivity, which, when accounted for in estimates of the age of the earth, increased it to nearly five billion years, an estimate of time long enough to account for evolution. Yet another problem came from objections to the randomness of the process and the apparent lack of rigor in Darwin's methodology. Leading this charge against Darwin's theory, the astronomer J. F. W. Herschel (1792–1871) described Darwinian natural selection as the "law of higgledy-piggledy." Perhaps most problematic of all was the fact that Darwin had no direct proof for a process that took place over such a long stretch of time and that had not been easily detected in the fossil record (most of his evidence was indirect, based on evidence from biogeography, from analogies to artificial selection, or from "imaginary illustrations"). Darwin knew this, and he predicted that it would take some fifty years for evidence to support this theory. The first direct proof of evolution by means of natural selection in natural populations was finally provided beginning in the 1920s with the example of industrial melanism in the peppered moth, *Biston betularia.* Though the peppered moth example was later challenged by some who thought that the shift to the melanic form did not constitute a true speciation event, it remains a famous example of evolution in action since it demonstrates the rapid shift in allele frequencies following strong selection pressure. Since the case of industrial melanism became known, numerous studies in the wild or under laboratory conditions have provided definitive evidence in support of Darwinian natural selection. Some of the best examples are the morphological responses in beak shape and size to drought conditions on some of the Darwin finches in the Galapagos, and the evolution of antibiotic resistance in pathogenic strains of microorganisms that cause diseases like tuberculosis.

More difficult to resolve were the theological and philosophical questions that followed from the mechanistic theory of natural selection. Even though Darwin had only one line in his 1859 book on human evolution, the theory implied that humans were subject to the same mechanistic process as plants and animals. Natural selection challenged the argument for God's existence from design and led to a nonpurposive view of the world. To some, this echoed the fears raised earlier by the poet Alfred, Lord Tennyson (1809–1892), that such a competitive and nonpurposive view of nature implied that it was "red in tooth and claw." Darwin's own views of "nature," as embodied in works such as *On the Origin of Species,* appeared to be much more subtle. Nature, to Darwin, appeared to be benignly passive or indifferent to the drama playing itself out in the struggle for existence. Darwin's religious views became increasingly secular; there was no "death-bed conversion" to religious belief.

Despite considerable controversy over the mechanism, the fact of evolution was rapidly accepted by scientists and by pop-

In Darwin's Shadow: Alfred Russel Wallace and the "Darwin-Wallace Theory of Evolution."

Though Darwin's name is virtually synonymous with the theory of evolution, the name of his codiscoverer Alfred Russel Wallace (1823–1913) is very often forgotten or relegated to the role of minor player. Yet Wallace himself was a gifted naturalist who distinguished himself for his scientific insights, especially in understanding island biogeography, and for his literary talents, especially excelling in the genre of the travel narrative.

Unlike Darwin, Wallace was born to a family of modest means in Usk, Monmouthshire, England. Lacking an extensive formal education, Wallace was an autodidact, frequenting lending libraries and attending public lectures on science. His first formal job at the age of fourteen was assisting his older brother at surveying counties in England, which gave him technical skills at observation and measurement, and he was later appointed as drawing master at the Collegiate School in Lancaster, where he fell in with Henry Walter Bates (1825–1892), a fellow teacher who shared a passion for the natural world.

In 1848 the two friends decided to embark on joint careers as commercial collectors of precious natural history specimens by traveling to the Amazon. They eventually took separate routes, collecting in increasingly unexplored regions, with Wallace traveling extensively up the Rio Negro, a tributary of the Amazon River. In 1852 Wallace returned to England, but nearly all of his magnificent collection was lost when his ship caught fire and sank. Wallace recovered from his setback rapidly, writing his account of the expedition in 1853, mostly from memory, as *A Narrative of Travels on the Amazon and Rio Negro*.

One year later he was once again in search of commercial specimens, this time setting off to the Malay Archipelago, where he traveled for nearly eight years. During this time he made one of the most notable observations in the history of island biogeography now associated with "Wallace's Line," an imaginary line that separated the two islands of Bali and Lombock; entirely different flora and fauna existed on either side of this geographic line. This disjuncture was only understood in the later twentieth century as the product of continental drift (the two areas are on separate plates).

Wallace's acute observations also led to his formulation, independently of Darwin, of a general theory of evolution that included a process closely resembling natural selection. In 1858, while suffering from malarial fever, Wallace connected the ideas of Malthus with his observations of the distribution of plants and animals and quickly drafted his celebrated paper "On the Tendency of Varieties to Depart Indefinitely from the Original Type." He proceeded to send the completed paper to Darwin, with whom he had had some previous correspondence. Darwin received the letter and immediately recognized the parallel views that Wallace had independently formulated. To avoid an unseemly priority dispute, Darwin turned over Wallace's paper along with his own historical sketch, essay, and correspondence with Asa Gray documenting the independence of the two efforts to Charles Lyell and Joseph Hooker and relied on them to negotiate the awkward situation. Both these men communicated these documents and a joint paper written by Darwin and Wallace to the Linnaean Society on 1 July 1858. Later that year the joint paper titled "On the Tendency of Species to form Varieties; and on the Perpetuation of Varieties and Species by Natural Means of Selection," by Charles Darwin and Alfred Wallace, was published in the *Journal of the Proceedings of the Linnaean Society*. Strangely enough, the paper failed to garner much negative attention or controversy. A year later, Darwin completed the famous "abstract" of his theory, published as *On the Origin of Species*, and from that point on Wallace's original contribution played at best only a supporting role.

(continued on the next page)

IN DARWIN'S SHADOW: ALFRED RUSSEL WALLACE AND THE "DARWIN-WALLACE THEORY OF EVOLUTION."

(continued from previous page)

Wallace himself was generally pleased to play this lesser part. He was a lifelong friend and supporter of Darwin, serving finally as pallbearer at Darwin's funeral with Huxley and Hooker. Darwin in turn supported Wallace through some especially difficult times, helping him secure a government pension. Wallace never properly attained financial security, and he also continued to uphold some radical ideas for his day that included land nationalization and an extreme opposition to vaccination campaigns in addition to more popular causes such as women's suffrage, labor reform, and universal education. Most disturbing to many establishment Victorian scientists generally, and Darwin in particular, was Wallace's growing support of spiritualist movements: Wallace's own support of the materialistic and mechanistic natural selection made an exception of the evolution of the human mind; he believed the "human spirit" could continue to progress even after the process of death.

His scientific work continued, earning him a permanent place in the history of science. Especially noteworthy were his contributions to island biogeography, which included the publication of *The Geographical Distribution of Animals* in 1876 and *Island Life* in 1880. In the late twentieth century Wallace's initial insights on the ecological dynamics of smaller island populations provided the intellectual backdrop to sciences such as conservation biology and to biodiversity studies.

---

ular audiences. Some of the greatest advocates and promoters of Darwin and his theory in fact disagreed with some rather major aspects of the theory. In the United States, the leading advocate of Darwin's theory was the botanist Asa Gray (1810–1888) at Harvard University. Though Gray found Darwin's theory useful to biogeography, he found the mechanistic implications of natural selection distasteful. It was Gray who brought Darwinian evolution to the attention of many American scientists and who defended Darwin against critical assaults by figures like his Harvard colleague in zoology Louis Agassiz (1807–1873). In Germany, Darwin and evolution found especially fertile ground in one of his greatest advocates, Ernst Haeckel. Beginning in 1866 with his *Generelle Morphologie der Organismen* (General morphology of organisms), Haeckel promoted Darwin and his evolutionary theory because of its materialistic flavor yet either misunderstood or disagreed with Darwinian natural selection. Rather than upholding an intricately branching and nonprogressivist view of evolution as Darwin had described in *Origin,* Haeckel retained a linear, progressive model only with some lateral branching. Haeckel continued to draw on embryological or developmental models for the evolutionary process and believed that evolution was guided by historical evolutionary forms that could still be seen in the process of individual development. In the process of development, the ontogeny (or developmental pattern of the organism) recapitulated the phylogeny (or the evolutionary history of the organism). Though German embryologists like Karl Ernst von Baer (1792–1876) argued against such a crude linear progressivist model of evolutionary development in favor of more complex branching models, the view that "ontogeny recapitulated phylogeny," also known as "the biogenetic law," continued to have mass appeal especially in Germany.

Haeckel was a prolific and popular writer whose numerous attempts to reconstruct "phylogenetic trees" with the main trunk running upward to the human "race" as the pinnacle of development shaped popular understanding of evolution in the late nineteenth century. Haeckel's influence also had the unfortunate effect of linking Darwinian evolution with what he thought were materialist progressivist leanings toward the struggle for national development. His *Generelle Morphologie* and subsequent writings, which gained currency in the late nineteenth century, eventually provided pseudo-scientific justifications for nationalism and racism.

Darwin's most famous, indeed notorious, advocate was his close friend, the anatomist Thomas Henry Huxley. It was Huxley, along with the Kew Gardens botanist Joseph Dalton Hooker (1817–1879) and Charles Lyell, who formed the "inner circle" of friends and supporters who promoted and defended Darwin's name and his theory. Though Huxley earned himself the title of "Darwin's Bulldog" while supporting Darwin's theory—which stressed slow, gradual evolution—he preferred instead the view that evolution could take place more suddenly and rapidly. Like others of his time, Huxley closely linked views of evolutionary progress with social progress; he used the principles of evolution to support his reformist views of English society.

By the turn of the twentieth century, a staggering number of evolutionary theories—that added to, amended, or outright disagreed with Darwin's selection theory—were being actively entertained. These included a revitalization of the inheritance of acquired characters into movements associated with neo-Lamarckism; directed evolution, aristogenesis, and orthogenesis, all of which upheld the view that evolution was guided by an internal driving force; and "creative evolution," a quasi-mystical evolutionary theory endorsed by the French philosopher Henri Bergson (1859–1941), who postulated that living organisms were guided by an *élan vital,* or special living force.

One of the most popular alternatives to Darwinian selection theory was the "mutation theory" of the Dutch botanist Hugo de Vries (1848–1935). One of the "rediscoverers of Mendel," de Vries upheld a particulate theory of heredity that stressed the importance of what he termed "mutation pressure" in generating evolutionary novelty. Much of his theory was based on observations he made on the evening primrose plant, *Oenothera lamarckiana,* which appeared to throw off new varieties or species suddenly. De Vries erroneously interpreted these new forms as being entirely new species that had been generated by strong mutation pressure (these new forms of the primrose were subsequently shown to be regularly occurring varieties that resulted from its genetic structure). Natural selection was not ruled out, but it came into play only in selecting the most advantageous of these forms; it therefore played an eliminative role in evolution, while mutation pressure played the more active or creative role. Because it drew on the newer science of genetics, which appeared to be more rigorous because it was experimental, mutation theory was widely adopted by younger scientists at the turn of the century, who did not favor the natural-history-oriented approach associated with Darwin or his naturalist followers. The interval of time between approximately the rediscovery of Mendel and the late 1920s thus saw a period of dissonance between younger geneticists and older naturalists, all of whom sought a viable evolutionary theory that could be a rigorous experimental science that could also explain patterns of adaptation in natural populations. Others, who were strict followers of Darwinian selectionism and stressed the fact that Darwin endorsed a slow, gradual process that operated at the level of small, individual differences, turned to the newer science of statistics to create a new school known as "biometry." Francis Galton (1822–1911), Darwin's famous first cousin, was an exponent of the biometrical school, which tried to understand evolution in statistical terms. He was also the individual who coined the term *eugenics* in this attempt to formulate a viable theory of heredity and evolution that could then provide social reformers with the tools to "improve society" through selective breeding.

The turn of the century as a whole saw a series of proposed evolutionary theories that some have claimed were in fact "non-Darwinian" evolutionary theories. This was so much the case that Julian Huxley (1887–1975) the famous grandson of Thomas Henry Huxley, designated this interval of time "the eclipse of Darwin," a period of confusion and disagreement over the mechanism and mode of evolution. Only after the mechanism of heredity was understood and only after the science of genetics was integrated with natural history was the debate over the mechanism of natural selection extinguished. This did not take place until the interval of time between 1920 and 1950 and was part of the event called the "evolutionary synthesis." The synthesis brought together Darwinian selection theory with Mendelian genetics in a populational view of evolution to account for the origin of biological diversity. It first drew primarily

on the work of three mathematical population geneticists, R. A. Fisher (1890–1962) and J. B. S. Haldane (1892–1964) in England and Sewall Wright (1889–1988) in the United States, all of whom offered models demonstrating the efficacy of natural selection under a range of different parameters. The theoretical work of these modelers was tested in field conditions with natural populations of organisms in the mid-1930s. This then led to the writing of a series of synthetic accounts that integrated Darwinian selection theory with Mendelian genetics.

The new science called evolutionary genetics was most closely associated with Theodosius Dobzhansky (1900–1975) and his synthetic book *Genetics and the Origin of Species* (1937). In addition to genetics, the "evolutionary synthesis" drew on systematics, botany, paleontology, cytology, and morphology to create what is now called the "synthetic theory of evolution" or the "neo-Darwinian theory of evolution." In addition to drawing on the work of Dobzhansky, it drew on the work of twentieth-century biologists like Ernst Mayr (b. 1904), George Ledyard Stebbins (1906–2000), George Gaylord Simpson (1902–1984), and Julian Huxley. It endorses the view that natural selection is the dominant mechanism that drives evolutionary change. Within such a modern, populational frame of reference, evolution itself became redefined as "any relative change in gene frequencies." This definition has been debated extensively, especially by naturalists-systematists who prefer a more inclusive consideration of the process of speciation.

Accompanying the emergence of the "modern synthesis" (Julian Huxley's exact phrase for the new science of evolution), the first international Society for the Study of Evolution (SSE) was formed in 1946 and sponsored the journal *Evolution,* the first international journal for the dissemination of scientific knowledge of evolution. With the "evolutionary synthesis," the varied sciences that informed evolution thus became reorganized into the new science of evolutionary biology. Because it drew on so many scientific disciplines, encompassing the breadth of the biological sciences and many of the social sciences, like psychology and anthropology, evolutionary biology began increasingly to play a central, integrative role in the biological sciences, especially beginning in the late 1950s and early 1960s. In 1975 Dobzhansky stated the important fact that "nothing in biology makes sense except in the light of evolution." In stating this, he was stressing the fact that evolution by means of natural selection serves as the central, unifying principle of the modern science of biology.

Though there have been varied attempts to amend or alter the synthetic theory as it was formulated during the "evolutionary synthesis" in the latter half of the twentieth century, the theory remains fundamentally intact. Among the varied points of agreement are included the primacy of natural selection, the continuation between microevolutionary and macroevolutionary processes, and the fact that evolution takes place at the level of small individual differences—all pretty much formulated in the 1930s–1950s. New techniques and methods from molecular biology have led to a virtual revolution in understanding evolution at the molecular level, while more traditional evolutionary biologists continue to mine the fossil record and to explore developmental biology, areas such as behavior and functional morphology as well as biochemistry to give a more detailed account of the evolutionary history of life on earth.

See also **Biology; Creationism; Development; Eugenics; Genetics; Lysenkoism; Natural History; Natural Theology; Nature; Naturphilosophie; Progress, Idea of; Social Darwinism.**

BIBLIOGRAPHY

Appleman, Philip. *Darwin.* New York: Norton, 1970.

Bowler, Peter J. "The Changing Meaning of 'Evolution.'" *Journal of the History of Ideas* 36 (1975): 95–114.

———. *The Eclipse of Darwinism: Anti-Darwinian Evolution Theories in the Decades around 1900.* Baltimore: Johns Hopkins University Press, 1983.

———. *Evolution: The History of an Idea.* 3rd ed. Berkeley: University of California Press, 2003.

———. *The Non-Darwinian Revolution. Reinterpreting a Historical Myth.* Baltimore: Johns Hopkins University Press, 1988.

Browne, Janet. *Charles Darwin: A Biography.* 2 vols. New York: Knopf, 1995–2002.

Burkhardt, Richard W., Jr. *The Spirit of System: Lamarck and Evolutionary Biology.* Cambridge, Mass: Harvard University Press, 1977.

Darwin, Charles. *On the Origin of the Species by Means of Natural Selection: or, The Preservation of Favoured Races in the Struggle for Life.* London: J. Murray, 1859.

Desmond, Adrian J. *The Politics of Evolution: Morphology, Medicine, and Reform in Radical London.* Chicago: University of Chicago Press, 1989.

Desmond, Adrian J., and James R. Moore. *Darwin.* London: Michael Joseph, 1991.

Dobzhansky, Theodosius Grigorievich. *Genetics and the Origin of Species.* New York: Columbia University Press, 1937.

Fichman, Martin. *An Elusive Victorian: The Evolution of Alfred Russel Wallace.* Chicago: University of Chicago Press, 2004.

Gould, Stephen Jay. *The Structure of Evolutionary Theory.* Cambridge, Mass: Belknap Press, 2002.

Greene, John C. *The Death of Adam: Evolution and Its Impact on Western Thought.* Rev. ed. Ames: Iowa State University Press, 1996.

Huxley, Julian. *Evolution: The Modern Synthesis.* London: Allen and Unwin, 1963.

Kohn, David, ed. *The Darwinian Heritage.* Princeton, N.J.: Princeton University Press, 1985.

Mayr, Ernst. *The Growth of Biological Thought: Diversity, Evolution, and Inheritance.* Cambridge, Mass: Belknap Press, 1982.

———. *What Evolution Is.* New York: Basic Books, 2001.

Mayr, Ernst, and William B. Provine, eds. *The Evolutionary Synthesis: Perspectives on the Unification of Biology.* Cambridge, Mass: Harvard University Press, 1980; rev. ed., 2000.

Raby, Peter. *Alfred Russel Wallace: A Life.* Princeton, N.J.: Princeton University Press, 2001.

Richards, Robert J. "Evolution." In *Keywords in Evolutionary Biology,* edited by Evelyn Fox Keller and Elizabeth Lloyd, 95–105. Cambridge, Mass: Harvard University Press, 1992.

———. *The Meaning of Evolution: The Morphological Construction and Ideological Reconstruction of Darwin's Theory.* Chicago: University of Chicago Press, 1992.

———. *The Romantic Conception of Life: Science and Philosophy in the Age of Goethe.* Chicago: University of Chicago Press, 2002.

Ruse, Michael. *The Darwinian Revolution: Science Red in Tooth and Claw.* 2nd ed. Chicago: University of Chicago Press, 1979.

———. *Monad to Man. The Concept of Progress in Evolutionary Biology.* Cambridge, Mass.: Harvard University Press, 1996.

Secord, James A. *Victorian Sensation: The Extraordinary Publication, Reception, and Secret Authorship of* Vestiges of the Natural History of Creation. Chicago: University of Chicago Press, 2000.

Shermer, Michael. *In Darwin's Shadow: The Life and Science of Alfred Russel Wallace. A Biographical Study on the Psychology of History.* Oxford and New York: Oxford University Press, 2002.

Smocovitis, Vassiliki Betty. *Unifying Biology: The Evolutionary Synthesis and Evolutionary Biology.* Princeton, N.J.: Princeton University Press, 1996.

Wallace, Alfred Russel. *Island Life.* Amherst, N.Y.: Prometheus Books, 1998. Originally published in 1881.

Young, Robert M. *Darwin's Metaphor: Nature's Place in Victorian Culture.* Cambridge, U.K., and New York: Cambridge University Press, 1985.

Vassiliki Betty Smocovitis

EXAMINATION SYSTEMS, CHINA. Civil examinations in late imperial China (1400–1900) intersected with politics, society, economy, and Chinese intellectual life. Both local elites and the imperial court influenced the dynastic government to reexamine and adjust the classical curriculum and to entertain new ways to improve the system for selecting officials. As a result, civil examinations represented a test of educational merit that served to tie the dynasty and literati culture together bureaucratically.

Civil examinations were not an obstacle to modern state building. Classical examinations were an effective cultural, social, political, and educational construction that met the needs of the dynastic bureaucracy while simultaneously supporting late imperial social structure. Gentry and merchant status groups were defined in part by examination degree credentials. Although civil examinations themselves were not an avenue for widespread social mobility, nevertheless a social by-product was the limited circulation of elites in the government from gentry, military, and merchant backgrounds.

In addition, the large pool of examination failures created a source of literary talent that flowed easily into ancillary roles as novelists, playwrights, pettifoggers, ritual specialists, and lineage agents. The unforeseen consequences when the civil examinations were summarily eliminated by modern reformers in 1905 reveals that late imperial civil examinations represented a partnership between the dynasty in power and its gentry-merchant elites. Imperial interests and literati values were equally served. They fell together in the twentieth-century Chinese revolution.

Late imperial examinations broke with medieval (650–1250) poetic and literary traditions and successfully made "Learning of the Way" (Neo-Confucianism) the state orthodoxy. The intersections between elite social life, popular culture, religion, and the mantic arts reveal the full cultural scope and magnitude of the examination in 1,300 counties, 140 prefectures, and 17 provinces. These testing sites elicited the voluntary participation of millions of men—women were excluded—and attracted the attention of elites and commoners.

Its demise brought with it consequences that the last rulers of imperial China and reformist gentry underestimated. The Manchu Qing dynasty was complicit in its own dismantling after the forces of delegitimation and decanonization were unleashed by reformist Chinese gentry, who prevailed in late-nineteenth-century education circles and convinced the imperial court to eliminate the entire examination institution in 1904.

Reform of education and the elimination of examinations in China after 1905 was tied to newly defined national goals of Western-style change that superseded conservative imperial goals of maintaining dynastic power, granting gentry prestige, and affirming classical orthodoxy. Since the Song-Yuan-Ming transition (1250–1450), the struggle between insiders and outsiders to unite the empire had resulted in over four hundred years of so-called barbarian rule over the Han Chinese. With the Republican Revolution of 1911, that historical narrative ended.

Power, Politics, and Examinations

Classical philosophy and imperial politics became partners during the Mongol Yuan dynasty, when Song dynasty (960–1279) classical interpretations were made the orthodox guidelines for the imperial examination system. Ming (1368–1644) and Qing (1644–1911) appropriations of that orthodoxy affected how literati learning would be interpreted and used in later dynasties as a political ideology.

The late imperial civil system elaborated the Song-Yuan civil examination model under the impact of commercialization and demographic growth, which allowed the process to expand to all 1,300 counties. In addition, the upsurge in candidates meant that officialdom became the prerogative of a very slim minority. As the door to a fixed number of official appointments, civil examinations also conferred social and cultural status on families seeking to become or maintain their status as local elites.

Competitive tensions also explain the policelike rigor of the civil service examinations that Han Chinese insiders and Manchu warrior outsiders both supported. Political forces and cultural fears forced Han Chinese and their non-Han rulers to agree publicly how imperial and bureaucratic authority was conveyed through the accredited cultural institutions of the civil examinations. Political legitimation transmitted through education succeeded because enhanced social status and legal privileges were an important by-product of the examination competition.

Quotas based on the ratio between successful and failed candidates further demonstrated that the state saw access to the civil service as a means to regulate the power of elites. Government control of selection quotas was most keenly felt at the initial, licensing stages of the examination competition. By 1400, for example, there were about 30,000 classical literate licentiates out of an approximate population of 65 million, a ratio of almost one licentiate per 2,200 persons. In 1600 there were perhaps 500,000 licentiates in a total population of some 150 million, or a ratio of one licentiate per 300 persons.

Because of economic advantages in South China (especially the Yangzi Delta but also Fujian and Guangdong), candidates from the south performed the best on the civil examinations. To keep the south's domination of the examinations within acceptable bounds, Ming education officials settled in 1425 on an official ratio of 60 to 40 for allocations of the highest degrees to candidates from the south versus the north, which was slightly modified to 55 to 10 to 35 a year later by adding a central region.

The examination hall became a contested site, where the political interests of the dynasty, the social interests of its elites, and the cultural ideals of classical learning were compromised. Examination halls were supervised by literati officials, who were in charge of the military and police apparatus to control the thousands of men brought together to be tested at a single place. Forms of resistance to imperial prerogative emerged among examiners, and widespread dissatisfaction and corruption among the candidates at times triumphed over the high-minded goals of some of the examiners.

Literacy and Social Dimensions

The monopolization of cultural resources by literati and merchant elites depended on their linguistic mastery of nonvernacular classical texts. Imperial examinations thus created a written linguistic barrier between those who were allowed into the empire's examinations compounds and classical illiterates who were kept out. Because there were no public schools, the partnership between the court and the bureaucracy was monopolized by gentry-merchant literati who organized into lineages and clans to provide superior classical educations.

Language and classical literacy played a central role in culturally defining high and low social status in late imperial Chinese society. The selection process permitted some circulation of elites in and out of the total pool, but the educational curriculum and its formidable linguistic requirements eliminated the lower classes from the selection process. In addition, an unstated gender ideology forbade all women from entry into the examination compounds.

Literati regularly turned to religion in their efforts to understand and rationalize their emotional responses to the competitive examinations. Examination dreams and popular lore spawned a remarkable literature about the temples candidates visited, the dreams that they or members of their family had, and the magical events in their early lives that were premonitions of later success. Popular notions of fate influenced the examination marketplace and were encoded as cultural glosses with unconscious ties to a common culture and religion.

Anxiety produced by examinations was a historical phenomenon, experienced personally and deeply by boys and men.

Fathers and mothers, sisters and extended relatives, shared in the experience and offered comfort, solace, and encouragement, but the direct, personal experience of examination success or failure belonged to the millions of male examination candidates who competed with each other against difficult odds.

The civil service competition created a dynastic curriculum that consolidated gentry, military, and merchant families into a culturally defined status group of degree holders that shared a common classical language, memorization of a shared canon of classics, and a literary style of writing known as the "eight-legged essay." Internalization of elite literary culture was in part defined by the civil examination curriculum, but that curriculum also showed the impact of literati opinion on imperial interests.

In addition to helping define literary culture, the examination curriculum also influenced the literatus's public and private definition of his moral character and social conscience. A view of government, society, and the individual's role as a servant of the dynasty was continually reinforced in the memorization process leading up to the examinations themselves. For the literatus, it was important that the dynasty conformed to classical ideals and upheld the classical orthodoxy that literati themselves had formulated.

The bureaucracy made a financial commitment to staffing and operating the empirewide examination regime. Ironically, the chief consequence was that examiners could not take the time to read each individual essay carefully. Final rankings, even for the eight-legged essay, were haphazard. We should guard against overinterpreting the classical standards of weary examiners as a consistent or coherent attempt to impose orthodoxy.

An interpretive community, canonical standards, and institutional control of formal knowledge were key features of the civil examination system. The continuities and changes in linguistic structures and syllogistic chains of moral argument in the examination system reveal an explicit logic for the formulation of questions and answers and an implicit logic for building semantic and thematic categories of learning. These enabled examiners and students to mark and divide their cognitive world according to the moral attitudes, social dispositions, and political compulsions of their day.

Fields of Learning

Literati fields of learning, such as natural studies and history, were also represented in late imperial examinations. Such inclusion showed the influence of the court, which for political reasons widened or limited the scope of policy questions on examinations, and of the assigned examiners, whose classical knowledge echoed the intellectual trends of their time. In the eighteenth century new guidelines were also applied to the civil examination curriculum. As a result, the Song rejection of medieval belles lettres in civil examinations was revoked.

In the late eighteenth century the examination curriculum started to conform with philological currents popular among literati. The scope and content of the policy questions increasingly reflected the academic inroads of newer classical

scholarship among examiners. Beginning in the 1740s, high officials debated new initiatives that challenged the classical curriculum in place. They restored earlier aspects of the civil examinations that had been eliminated in the Yuan and Ming dynasties, such as classical poetry.

In the mid-eighteenth century, because of the increasing numbers of candidates, Qing officials emphasized "ancient learning" to make the examinations more difficult by requiring all the Five Classics. In addition, the formalistic requirements of poetry gave examiners an additional tool, along with the eight-legged essay grid, to grade papers more efficiently. Later rulers failed to recognize that an important aspect of the civil examinations was the periodic questioning of the system from within that gave it credibility from without.

Delegitimation and Decanonization

After 1860 radical reforms were initiated to meet the challenges of the Taiping Rebellion (1850–1864) and Western imperialism. The Taipings instituted their own Christian-based civil examinations. In the last years of the Qing dynasty, the civil examinations lost their cultural luster and became the object of ridicule by literati officials as an unnatural educational regime that should be discarded. During the transition to the Republic of China, new political, institutional, and cultural forms emerged that challenged the creedal system of the late empire.

The emperor, his bureaucracy, and literati cultural forms quickly became symbols of backwardness. Traditional forms of knowledge were uncritically labeled as superstition, while modern science was championed by new intellectuals as the path to knowledge, enlightenment, and national power. Most representative of the changes was the dismantling of the civil examination regime that had lasted from 1370 to 1905.

By dismantling imperial institutions such as the civil examination system so rapidly, Chinese reformers and early republican revolutionaries underestimated the public reach of historical institutions that had taken two dynasties and five hundred years to build. When they delegitimated the institutions all within the space of two decades starting in 1890, Han Chinese literati helped bring down both the Manchu dynasty and the imperial system of governance. Its fall concluded a millennium of elite belief in literati values and five hundred years of an empirewide imperial orthodoxy.

See also **Chinese Thought; Confucianism; Education: Asia, Traditional and Modern; Education: China.**

BIBLIOGRAPHY

Chaffee, John W. *The Thorny Gates of Learning in Sung China.* New ed. Albany: State University of New York Press, 1995.

Des Rotours, Robert. *Le traité des examens, traduit de la Nouvelle histoire des T'ang.* Paris: Leroux, 1932.

Elman, Benjamin. *A Cultural History of Civil Examinations in Late Imperial China.* Berkeley: University of California Press, 2000.

Herbert, P. A. *Examine the Honest, Appraise the Able: Contemporary Assessments of Civil Service Selection in Early T'ang China.* Canberra: Australian National University, 1988.

Ho, Ping-ti. *The Ladder of Success in Imperial China.* New York: Wiley, 1962.

Kracke, E. A. *Civil Service in Early Sung China.* Cambridge, Mass.: Harvard University Press, 1968.

Lo, Winston W. *An Introduction to the Civil Service of Sung China.* Honolulu: University of Hawaii Press, 1987.

Miyazaki, Ichisada. *China's Examination Hell.* Translated by Conrad Schirokauer. New Haven, Conn.: Yale University Press, 1981.

Twitchett, Denis. *The Birth of the Chinese Meritocracy: Bureaucrats and Examinations in T'ang China.* London: China Society, 1976.

Wittfogel, Karl. "Public Office in the Liao Dynasty and the Chinese Examination System." *Harvard Journal of Asiatic Studies* 10 (1947): 13–40.

Zi, Etienne. *Pratique des examens litteraires en Chine.* Shanghai: Mission Catholique, 1894. Reprint, Nendeln, Liechtenstein: Kraus, 1975.

Benjamin A. Elman

EXISTENTIALISM.

Existentialism is a philosophical movement that became associated with the philosophy of Jean-Paul Sartre (who rejected the name as too confining) and whose roots extend to the works of Søren Kierkegaard and Martin Heidegger. Sartre, like most of his existentialist colleagues, was too much the individualist to accept the idea of being part of a movement, no matter how exclusive. Both Heidegger and the writer Albert Camus rejected the label, offended by being so linked to Sartre. But the name stuck, and Sartre, at least, accepted it with reservations. And so existentialism came to name one of the most powerful intellectual and literary movements of the last century and a half.

Sartre's philosophy is generally taken as the paradigm of existentialist philosophy, and other figures are usually considered existentialists insofar as they resonate with certain Sartrean themes—extreme individualism, an emphasis on freedom and responsibility, and the insistence that we and not the world give meaning to our lives. Thus some key figures who might be considered existentialist, Camus and Friedrich Nietzsche, for example, are sometimes excluded because they are not sufficiently Sartrean. Existentialism can be defined as a philosophy that puts special emphasis on personal existence, on the problems and peculiarities that face individual human beings. It tends to distrust abstractions and overgeneralized formulations of "human nature," on the grounds that each of us, in some important sense, makes his or her own nature. Søren Kierkegaard emphasized the "existence" of the individual and the importance of individual choice. The first conception of a movement should be credited to Karl Jaspers (1883–1969), a German philosopher-psychiatrist who noted the similarities between Kierkegaard and Nietzsche and identified them as early practitioners of what he called "existence-philosophy" (*Existenzphilosophie*).

Kierkegaard and Nietzsche differed radically, most famously in their approach to religion (Christianity in particular).

Kierkegaard was devout while Nietzsche was a blasphemous atheist. But so, too, twentieth-century existentialism would include both religious and atheistic philosophers. The religious existentialists include, among others, Karl Barth (1886–1968), Martin Buber (1878–1965), Gabriel Marcel (1887–1973), Jacques Maritain (1882–1973), and Paul Tillich (1886–1965). Among those labeled atheistic existentialists, Jean-Paul Sartre, Simone de Beauvoir (1908–1986), Albert Camus, and Maurice Merleau-Ponty (1908–1961) are prominent. But existentialism also includes a number of more ambiguous figures, notably Martin Heidegger, who was certainly no orthodox Christian thinker but nevertheless bemoaned modernity's abandonment of religion and insisted that "only a new god can save us." So, too, existentialism usually embraces such tormented literary figures as Fyodor Dostoyevsky (1821–1881), André Gide (1869–1951), and Franz Kafka (1883–1924), writers like Norman Mailer (b. 1923), and sympathetic international figures like Miguel de Unamuno (1864–1936) and Keiji Nishitani (1900–1990).

Twentieth-century existentialism was greatly influenced by phenomenology, originated by Edmund Husserl (1859–1938) and pursued into the existential realm by his student Heidegger. The "ontological" problem for Heidegger, "the problem of being," was to find out who one is and what to do with oneself or, as Nietzsche had asked earlier, how one is to become what one is. Phenomenology, for Heidegger, becomes a method for "disclosing [one's] being." Following both Husserl and Heidegger, Sartre used the phenomenological method to defend his central thesis that humans are essentially free, and Merleau-Ponty further refined both that method and the resulting notion of freedom to incorporate a more bodily conception of human existence, pointing to the complexities of freedom in a politically conflicted and ambiguous world.

Oddly enough, the existentialists, perhaps the most moralistic or in any case moralizing philosophers of modern times, often seem to avoid ethics. Kierkegaard noted that ethics was one choice among several. Nietzsche insisted that Western morality is slave morality, and he wrote with delight (in *Die fröhliche Wissenschaft*, 1882, 1887; English trans. *The Gay Science*) about dancing on morality's grave. Heidegger emphatically insisted that he was not offering any ethics, and he continued to speak with disdain about those who confusedly worry about values. Even Sartre, moralist par excellence, followed Heidegger in insisting that his existentialism was not an ethical philosophy, although he did promise that the "phenomenological ontology" of his great tome *L'être et le néant* (1943; English trans. *Being and Nothingness*, 1956) would be followed up by an ethics, which never came.

The existentialists were rejecting a certain "bourgeois" conception of morality, the kind of ethics that worries about keeping one's promises, paying one's debts, and avoiding scandal. Instead, they were after an ethic of a larger kind, an ethics of "authenticity" or what we would call personal integrity. They called for responsibility, even heroism, in the face of the bourgeois modern world. They rejected traditional philosophical and scientific rationality and typically resorted to literature, prophecy, pamphleteering, and ponderous obfuscation, any means necessary to wake up the world from its boring bourgeois and at the same time brutal and irresponsible behavior.

Jaspers's special word, *existence,* which he took from Kierkegaard to summarize the centrality of self-doubt and painful freedom that defined the human condition, focused a new kind of attention on the individual. Thus existentialism tends to be a solitary philosophy. Kierkegaard, in particular, wrote at length about "subjective truth" and saving "The Individual" from the crowd, the "public," the Hegelian collective "Spirit." Nietzsche encouraged a muscular individualism in which the "higher man" should reject "the herd" and follow his own noble instincts. Heidegger calls mass-man (*Das Man*) "inauthentic" and urges us to discover our own unique "authentic" self. Camus exploded onto the literary and philosophical scene with his novel *The Stranger,* whose protagonist had only the most tenuous connections with other people, lost as he was in his own sensuous experience. Sartre focused on individual consciousness as "being-for itself" and treated "being-for-others" as a continuous threat. In his play *Huis clos* (1944; English trans. *No Exit,* 1947), he even tells us "Hell is other people."

One might generalize that existentialism represents a certain attitude particularly appropriate for modern (and postmodern) mass society. The existentialists share a concern for the individual and personal responsibility (whether or not they embrace "free will"). They tend to resist the submersion of the individual in larger public groups or forces. Thus Kierkegaard and Nietzsche both attacked "the herd," and Heidegger distinguished "authentic existence" from mere social existence. Sartre, in particular, emphasizes the importance of free individual choice, regardless of the power of other people to influence and coerce our desires, beliefs, and decisions. Here he follows Kierkegaard, especially, for whom passionate, personal choice and commitment are essential for true "existence."

Søren Kierkegaard (1813–1855)

Kierkegaard was born and raised in Copenhagen, where he spent virtually his entire life. He was a pious Lutheran who once defined his task in philosophy as "a Socratic task," to define (or redefine) what it is to be a Christian. At the time, the rationalist influence of Immanuel Kant (1724–1804) and Georg Wilhelm Friedrich Hegel (1770–1831) dominated the Lutheran church, but Kierkegaard insisted that faith was by its very nature irrational, a passion and not a provable belief. Against Hegelian Holism, Kierkegaard insisted on the primacy of the individual and the profound "Otherness" of God. And against the worldly Lutherans, Kierkegaard preached a stark, passionate, solitudinous, and unworldly religion that, in temperament, at least, would go back to the monastery. To properly and passionately choose to be a Christian—as opposed to merely being born into the church and mindlessly reciting its dogmas—was to enjoy true existence. To be or become a Christian, according to Kierkegaard, it is necessary to passionately commit oneself, to make a "leap of faith" in the face of the "objective uncertainty" of religious claims. One cannot know or prove that there is a God; one must passionately choose to believe.

Kierkegaard formulated the seemingly self-contradictory notion of "subjective truth" in opposition to the idea that all life choices have a rational or "objective" resolution. In choosing the religious life, for example, Kierkegaard insists that there are no ultimately rational reasons for doing so, only subjective motives, a sense of personal necessity and a desire for passionate commitment. Similarly, choosing to be ethical, which is to say, choosing to act according to the principles of practical reason, is itself a choice, which is not rational. The notion of subjective truth does not mean, as it may seem to mean, a truth that is true "for me." It means resolution in the face of the objectively unknown. More important than what is believed is how it is believed. Against the calm deliberations of so much of the history of philosophy, in opposition to the celebration of reason and rationality, Kierkegaard celebrates angst and the passions, the "leap" into the unknown, and the irrationality of life.

Friedrich Nietzsche (1844–1900)

Nietzsche was a German philosopher whose writing was flamboyant and deliberately provocative, repudiating the whole Judeo-Christian tradition and liberal ethics. Nietzsche saw a conflict between the West's heroic Greek heritage and its Judeo-Christian history. He was struck, for example, by the difference between the two traditions' approaches to human suffering. While the Judeo-Christian tradition sought the explanation of misfortune in sin, the ancient Greeks took profound suffering to be an indication of the fundamentally tragic nature of human life. His first book, *Die Geburt der Tragödie* (1872; English trans. *The Birth of Tragedy,* 1909), analyzed the art of Athenian tragedy as the product of the Greeks' deep and nonevasive thinking about the meaning of life in the face of extreme vulnerability.

Nietzsche applauded the ancient Greeks for their ethical outlook, which stressed the development of excellence and nobility in contrast with what he saw as the Judeo-Christian obsession with sin and guilt. In short, he defended an ancient ethics of virtue and excellence in opposition to the modern morality of equality and "the good will" that he found, for example, in Kant's formalization of Judeo-Christian moral philosophy.

In contrast with the morality of the Homeric Greeks, a morality of heroism and mastery, Christian morality made the mediocre person of no great enthusiasm or accomplishments the moral exemplar. A good person, on this view, is someone who does no harm, breaks no rules or laws, and "means well." Nietzsche complains that the Christian moral worldview has urged people to treat the afterlife as more important than this one. Instead of urging self-improvement in earthly terms, the Christian moral vision emphasizes abstaining from "selfish" action. The person who does essentially nothing with his or her life but has avoided "sin" might merit heaven, in the Christian view, while a creative person will probably be deemed "immoral" because he or she refuses to follow "the herd." Thus the prohibitions of Judeo-Christian and Kantian ethics are in fact "leveling" devices that the weak and mediocre resentfully use to put more talented and stronger spirits at a disadvantage. Accordingly, Nietzsche suggests that we go "beyond good and evil," beyond our tendencies to pass moralistic judgment and toward a more creative and naturalistic perspective.

Nietzsche denied the very idea of the "otherworldly" and the idea of an all-powerful benign deity. As an antidote to the Christian worldview, which treats human life as a mere path to the afterlife, Nietzsche advocates a revival of the ancient view of "eternal recurrence," the view that time repeats itself cyclically. If one were to take this image of eternal recurrence seriously and imagine that one's life must be lived over and over again, suddenly there is enormous weight on what otherwise might seem like the mere "lightness" of being. But it is life, this existence, that alone counts for anything.

Martin Heidegger (1889–1971)

Heidegger was a theology student before he became a phenomenologist, and his concerns were existentialist concerns, questions about how to live and how to live "authentically," that is, with integrity, in a politically and technologically seductive and dangerous world. His philosophy falls into two parts. His early work as a phenomenologist, culminating in his great tome, *Sein und Zeit* (1927; English trans. *Being and Time,* 1962), suggests that he deserves to be counted among the existentialists. Like Kierkegaard, he investigates the meaning of authentic existence, the significance of our mortality, our place in the world and among other people as an individual. Heidegger's later work takes a different turn as he comes to see how his early work is still mired in the suppositions of traditional metaphysics. His philosophy seeks a new openness, a new receptivity toward the world, one that turns out to be very much in line with the program of many radical or "deep" ecologists and, as Heidegger himself later discovered, with several non-Western cultures, which had never been distracted by humanistic arrogance of his own philosophical tradition.

Heidegger's "existentialist" philosophy begins with a profound anti-Cartesianism, an uncompromising holism that rejects any dualism regarding mind and body, the distinction between subject and object, and the very language of "consciousness," "experience," and "mind." Thus he begins with an analysis of *Dasein* (literally, "being-there"). But the question emerges, because we are the "ontological" (self-questioning) creatures we are, just who this *Dasein* is. Thus Heidegger's philosophy becomes a search for authenticity or "own-ness" (*Eigentlichkeit*), or personal integrity. This search for authenticity will carry us into the now familiar but ever-renewed questions about the nature of the self, and the meaning of life, as well as Heidegger's somewhat morbid central conception of "Being-unto-Death." It will also lead to Heidegger's celebration of tradition and "heritage," the importance of resolutely committing oneself to one's given culture.

In contrast to the Cartesian view of the primacy and importance of knowledge, Heidegger suggests that what attaches or "tunes" us to the world is not knowledge but moods. It is in our moods, not the detached observational standpoint of knowledge, that we are "tuned in" to our world. Mood is the starting point for understanding the nature of the self and who we are, and much of Heidegger's analysis of *Dasein* is in terms of its moods, angst and boredom, for example.

What *Dasein* cannot be is what Descartes called "a thinking thing." But, then, who is *Dasein,* what is the self? It is, at first, merely the roles that other people cast for me, as their son, their daughter, their student, their sullen playmate, their clever friend. That self, the *Das Man* self, is a social construction. Their is nothing authentic, nothing that is my own, about it. The authentic self, by contrast, is discovered in profound moments of unique self-recognition, notably, when one faces one's own death. It is not enough to acknowledge that "we are all going to die." That, according to Heidegger, is merely an objective truth and inauthentic. It is one's own death that matters here, and one's "own-ness" thus becomes "Being-unto-Death," facing up in full to one's own mortality.

Jean-Paul Sartre (1905–1980)

Sartre developed his existentialist philosophy during the difficult years of World War II and the Nazi occupation of Paris, where he lived and spent virtually his entire life. At the center of his philosophy was an all-embracing notion of freedom and an uncompromising sense of personal responsibility. In the oppressive conditions of the Nazi occupation and during the embattled years following the war, Sartre insisted that everyone is responsible for what he or she does and for what he or she becomes or "makes of oneself," no matter what the conditions, even in war and in the face of death. Sartre later insisted that he never ceased to believe that "in the end one is always responsible for what is made of one" (*New Left Review,* 1971) an only slight revision of his earlier, brasher slogan, "man makes himself." To be sure, as a student of Hegel and Marx—and as one afflicted by physical frailty and the tragedies of the war—Sartre had to be well aware of the many constraints and obstacles to human freedom. But as a Cartesian, he never deviated from Descartes's classical portrait of human consciousness as free and sharply distinct from the physical universe it inhabited. One is never free of one's "situation," Sartre tells us, but one is always free to "negate" that situation and to try to change it.

In his early work, Sartre follows Edmund Husserl's phenomenology, but he distinguishes between consciousness and the self. The self, Sartre suggests, is out there "in the world, like the self of another" (*Transcendence of the Ego*). It is an ongoing project in the world, and Sartre's existentialism is very much bound to the question of how we create that self and how we try to evade that responsibility. This preliminary defense of freedom and the separation of self and consciousness provide the framework for Sartre's great philosophical treatise, *Being and Nothingness.*

Sartre defines his existentialist ontology of freedom in terms of the opposition of "being-in-itself" and "being-for-itself," which in us as individuals is manifested in the tension between the fact that we always find ourselves in a particular situation defined by a body of facts that we may not have chosen—our "facticity"—and our ability to transcend that facticity, imagine, and choose—our transcendence. We may find ourselves confronting certain facts—poor health, a war, advancing age, or being Jewish in an anti-Semitic society—but it is always up to us what to make of these and how to respond to them. We may occupy a distinctive social role as a policeman or a waiter, but we are always something more; we always transcend such positions. When we try to pretend that we are identical to our roles or the captive of our situations, however, we are in "bad faith." It is bad faith to see ourselves as something fixed and settled, defined by a job or by "human nature." It is also bad faith to ignore the always restrictive facts and circumstances within which all choices must be made. We are always trying to define ourselves, but we are always an "open question," a self not yet made. Thus, Sartre tells us, we have a frustrated desire to "be God," to be both in-itself and for-itself, defined and free.

Sartre also defines a third ontological category, which he calls "being-for-others." Our knowledge of others is not inferred, for example, by some argument by analogy, from the behavior of others. Our experience of other people is first of all the experience of being looked at, not spectatorship or curiosity. Someone "catches us in the act," and we define ourselves in their terms, identifying ourselves with the way we appear "for others." We "pin down" one another in the judgments we make, and these judgments become an inescapable ingredient in our sense of ourselves.

In his *Critique of Dialectical Reason* (1958–1959), Sartre turned increasingly to politics and to a defense of Marxism in accordance with existentialist principles. He rejected the materialist determinism of Marxism, but he contended that political solidarity was the condition most conducive to authenticity. Not surprisingly, Sartre found the possibility of such solidarity in revolutionary engagement.

Simone de Beauvoir (1908–1986)

Simone de Beauvoir deserves special mention as a philosophical novelist who shared with Sartre this emphasis on freedom and responsibility for what one is and "what one makes of what is made of one." In her *Pour une morale de l'ambiguité* (1947; English trans. *Ethics of Ambiguity,* 1948) she spelled out the ethical implications of Sartre's philosophy. Beauvoir advanced the important thesis (shared with Merleau-Ponty) that the "ambiguity" of situations always undermines the wishful thinking that demands "right" and "wrong" answers. Beauvoir was always fascinated by her society's resistance to sensitive topics and consequently became one of the most controversial authors of the age. Beauvoir was appalled that her society, and virtually all societies, gave very little attention to the problems and inequities afflicting women. Later in life, she attacked the unsympathetic insensitivity to the inevitability of aging.

Beauvoir's most lasting contribution to philosophy and social thought was her revolutionary discussion of what it meant to be a woman. In *Le deuxième sexe* (1949; English trans. *The Second Sex,* 1953) Beauvoir initiates a discussion on the significance of gender. Hers is a powerful existentialist perspective in which gender becomes a matter of choice and imposition (being-for-others) and not a matter of mere biological facticity.

Albert Camus (1913–1960)

Camus borrowed from Heidegger the sense of being "abandoned" in the world, and he shared with Sartre the sense that the world does not give meaning to individuals. But whereas Sartre joined Heidegger in insisting that one must make meaning for oneself, Camus concluded that the world is "absurd," a term that has (wrongly) come to represent the whole of existentialist thinking. Indeed, one of the persistent errors in the popular understanding of existentialism is to confuse its emphasis on the "meaninglessness" of the universe with an advocacy of despair or "existential angst." Camus insists that the absurd is not license for despair.

At the outset of World War II, Camus published a novel entitled *L'étranger* (1942; first trans. in English as *The Outsider,* 1955; best known by the title *The Stranger*) and an essay called *Le Mythe de Sisyphe* (1942; English trans. *The Myth of Sisyphus,* 1955). With those two books, he became a spokesman for the new modern morality, the ability to face life in the face of "the Absurd," a metaphysical a sense of confrontation between ourselves and an "indifferent universe." *The Myth of Sisyphus* is ostensibly a re-telling of the story of Sisyphus, who was condemned to spend all of eternity pushing a rock up a mountain, where it would then roll back down of its own weight. This is the fate of all of us, Camus suggested. We expend all of our energy pushing our weight against futility and frustration. Camus presents the question of whether life is worth living, or, put differently, whether we ought to commit suicide. Camus's Sisyphus throws himself into his meaningless project, and thereby makes it meaningful. "One must consider Sisyphus happy," concludes Camus, and so, too, by acknowledging and throwing ourselves into the absurdity of our own lives, might we be.

The protagonist of *The Stranger,* by way of contrast, accepts the absurdity of life without much thinking about it. Is our acceptance of the absurd therefore tinged with bitterness and resentment? Camus seems torn between acceptance and defiance. Similar themes motivate *La Peste* (1947; English trans. *The Plague,* 1948) and *L'Homme révolté* (1951; English trans. *The Rebel,* 1954). In Camus's final novel, *La Chute* (1956; English trans. *The Fall,* 1957), a perverse character named Jean-Baptiste Clamence exemplifies the culmination of all of the bitterness and despair for the most part rejected by his previous characters and in his earlier essays. Clamence, like Meursault in *The Stranger,* refuses to judge people, but Clamence makes the refusal to judge a matter of philosophical principle, "for who among us is innocent?" Indeed, how can one be innocent in a world that is absurd?

Existentialism today has weathered thirty years of postmodernism and a shift of the center of philosophy from Europe to America. Enthusiasm for Kierkegaard, Nietzsche, Heidegger, and Sartre is as great as ever, and the philosophy of choice and responsibility remains the cornerstone of a great deal of American philosophy, even among those who would not recognize their debt to the existentialists.

See also **Marxism; Phenomenology; Rationalism; Religion; Romanticism in Literature and Politics.**

BIBLIOGRAPHY

de Beauvoir, Simone. *The Second Sex.* Translated and edited by H. M. Parshley. New York: Knopf, 1953.

Camus, Albert. *The Fall, and Exile and the Kingdom.* Translated by Justin O'Brien. New York: Random House, 1957.

———. *The Myth of Sisyphus and Other Essays.* Translated by Justin O'Brien. New York: Random House, 1955.

———. *The Plague.* Translated by Stuart Gilbert. New York: Knopf/Random House, 1948.

———. *The Stranger.* Translated by Matthew Ward. New York: Knopf, 1993.

Heidegger, Martin. *Being and Time.* Translated by John Macquarrie and Edward Robinson. New York: Harper, 1962.

Kierkegaard, Søren. *Concluding Unscientific Postscript to Philosophical Fragments.* Edited and translated by Howard V. Hong and Edna H. Hong. Princeton, N.J.: Princeton University Press, 1992.

———. *Either/Or.* Edited and translated by Howard V. Hong and Edna H. Hong. Princeton, N.J.: Princeton University Press, 1987.

Nietzsche, Friedrich. *The Birth of Tragedy.* Translated by Douglas Smith. Oxford, England, and New York: Oxford University Press, 2000.

———. *The Gay Science: With a Prelude in Rhymes and an Appendix of Songs.* Translated by Walter Kaufmann. New York: Random House, 1974.

———. *Twilight of the Idols, or, How to Philosophize with a Hammer.* Translated by Duncan Large. Oxford, England, and New York: Oxford University Press, 1998.

Sartre, Jean-Paul. *Being and Nothingness: an Essay on Phenomenological Ontology.* Translated by Hazel E. Barnes. New York: Philosophical Library, 1956.

———. *No Exit, and Three Other Plays.* Translated by S. Gilbert and L. Abel. New York: Vintage Books, 1956.

Solomon, Robert C. *From Hegel to Existentialism.* New York: Oxford University Press, 1987.

Robert C. Solomon

EXPERIMENT. This entry traces the life of experiment from its emergence in the early seventeenth century to its transformation to a collective activity after World War II. The topics discussed include the rise of experimental philosophy and its institutional expression in the new scientific societies of the seventeenth century; the spread and character of experimentation in the eighteenth century; the quest for precision and the rise of laboratories in the nineteenth century; and the emergence of a new form a collective experimental life after World War II.

The Emergence of Experiment

The birth of experiment has been the subject of considerable debate among historians of early modern science. The received view is that experimentation emerged in the seventeenth century as part of an era of radical discontinuity in the methods and practices of investigating nature. Among the natural philosophers who developed and practiced experimentation, some of the most eminent were Francis Bacon (1561–1626), Galileo Galilei (1564–1642), Robert Boyle (1627–1691), and Isaac Newton (1642–1727). There have been challenges to this

view, most notably by A. C. Crombie, who suggested in the early 1950s that the experimental method originated in the late medieval period. In the thirteenth and fourteenth centuries medieval scholars reflected in a systematic fashion on experiment as a method for the acquisition of natural knowledge. Furthermore, experiments had been performed, mostly in the context of mathematical sciences such as optics, well before the seventeenth century. Other historians have pointed out that experimentation had a prehistory in craft traditions and in occult practices, such as alchemy and natural magic. The practical skills of craftsmen and artisans and the experimental practices of alchemists contributed significantly to the emergence of experimental science in the seventeenth century.

It remains the case, however, that *systematic* and *extensive* attempts to understand and manipulate nature by means of experiment did not take place before the seventeenth century. Before the scientific revolution, the dominant means of acquiring information about the natural world was unaided observation. That was in line with Aristotelian natural philosophy, which attributed a prominent epistemological role to quotidian (common, everyday) experience. In the seventeenth century that role was gradually taken over by experiment—the active "interrogation" of nature—which was carried out by intervening in nature's workings and by manipulating its forces. In the process, unaided observation gave way to observation by means of instruments (such as the barometer, thermometer, air pump, and microscope), which enabled natural philosophers to measure and explore nature under controlled and, sometimes, artificial conditions. Those instruments considerably extended the range of phenomena that was accessible to the senses.

Two Experimental Traditions: Classical and Baconian

To understand the rise of experiment, it would be helpful to recall a significant distinction, drawn by Thomas S. Kuhn, between two different traditions in the development of the sciences. The first tradition, the classical sciences (mathematics, astronomy, harmonics, optics, and statics), had been well developed since antiquity. Those sciences were radically transformed in the sixteenth and seventeenth centuries. In that transformation, however, experimentation played a minor role. The second tradition, the Baconian sciences that emerged in the seventeenth century, investigated electric, magnetic, chemical, and heat phenomena. Experimentation was instrumental in the emergence and development of this tradition.

Furthermore, the mode of experimentation was different in the two traditions. In the classical tradition experiments were guided by theory, involved idealization, and were, often, not clearly distinguished from thought experiments. Their outcomes were presented in the form of universal, lawlike generalizations. In the Baconian tradition, on the other hand, experiments had an exploratory character and were carried out with an eye to the local, contingent conditions that gave rise to the observed phenomena. Detailed circumstantial information about those phenomena was included in the written reports of the experiments, whose aim was to establish particular "matters of fact." Those phenomena were created or measured by some of the new instruments that were invented in the seventeenth century (such as thermometers, air pumps, and electrostatic generators).

These two traditions started to merge only toward the end of the eighteenth century in France, where Pierre-Simon Laplace (1749–1827) and his followers attempted to develop mathematical theories of the phenomena investigated by the Baconian tradition.

Galileo Galilei

The extent to which Galileo did experiments has been a controversial issue. The dominant view well into the twentieth century was that Galileo was among the first "scientists" who experimented extensively and developed his theories on the basis of his experiments. In the 1930s Alexandre Koyré disputed that view and argued strenuously that Galileo's engagement with experiment was minimal. Galileo, according to Koyré, was a Platonist philosopher, who, for the most part, did not perform real experiments and reached his theoretical conclusions relying on a priori (deductive) reasoning and thought experiments. A significant reason for Koyré's claim was the excessive accuracy of many of the experimental results that Galileo reported in his published work.

Subsequent scholars have disputed some of Koyré's claims. Starting in the early 1960s, Thomas B. Settle and Stillman Drake, among others, drawing on a wider range of Galileo's manuscripts than was available to Koyré, managed to replicate several of Galileo's experiments on motion and obtained results that were close to the ones that he reported. In the wake of these studies, a consensus has developed among Galileo scholars that he was an ingenious experimenter, who designed and carried out a variety of experiments. Furthermore, experimentation and measurement were essential to Galileo's widely known discoveries, the law of free fall and the parabolic trajectories of projectiles. Galileo's image as the preeminent experimental philosopher has been reinstated.

One of the problems faced by experimental philosophers was how to legitimize experimentation as a means of acquiring knowledge of nature. Common experience could function as an unproblematic foundation for natural philosophy because of its familiarity and accessibility to everyone. The novel phenomena discovered by means of experiment, on the other hand, were neither familiar nor accessible to all. Two issues had to be tackled: first, the veracity of experimental results had to be attested. Second, particular results obtained under local, contingent circumstances had to acquire the status of general truths about nature.

An instance of how Galileo attempted to address these issues is provided by his investigations of free fall, which were carried out in the early years of the seventeenth century and published many years later in his *Two New Sciences* (1638). In that work he did not provide any circumstantial information about the particular experiments he had performed with rolling balls on incline planes. Furthermore, he did not report the specific results he had obtained. Rather he gave a generic description of the experimental setup and pointed out that the

results conformed repeatedly ("a full hundred times") to what he had anticipated.

Experimental philosophers in the Baconian tradition also faced the problem of legitimizing experiment, but they confronted it differently. This tradition is the topic of the next two sections.

The Baconian Program and Its Institutional Expression

Francis Bacon was one of the most eloquent advocates of the new experimental method. In *The New Organon* (1620), a logical treatise that was meant to supersede Aristotle's *Organon,* he stressed the importance of inductive reasoning for the investigation of nature. Bacon argued, however, that the starting point of inductive reasoning should not be the information obtained by the unaided senses, because it is limited or even deceptive. Rather, the senses should be assisted by "instances and experiments fit and apposite" (p. 53). The knowledge thus acquired about natural phenomena would then be codified in natural or experimental "histories." Furthermore, the point of natural knowledge was to give humans the power to intervene in natural processes for their own benefit. The understanding of nature and its manipulation were inextricably tied: "Nature to be commanded must be obeyed" (p. 39).

Another important aspect of Bacon's program was his emphasis on the social nature of the knowledge-seeking enterprise. In his utopian *New Atlantis* (1627) he suggested that investigation of the natural world should be a collaborative pursuit, carried out in special institutions. Bacon's vision inspired the founding of the Royal Society of London (1660) and the Académie Royale des Sciences in Paris (1666). Christiaan Huygens (1629–1695), a prominent member of the Paris Academy, contended that "the principal occupation of the Assembly and the most useful must be, in my opinion, to work in natural history somewhat in the manner suggested by" Bacon (Dear, p. 116). The primary aim of the Royal Society was also Baconian, namely the advancement of experimental knowledge. As one of its statutes reads, "The business of the Society in their Ordinary Meetings shall be to order, take account, consider, and discourse of philosophical experiments and observations" (Hall, p. 1).

Yet, the experiments that were carried out and discussed under the auspices of the Royal Society had a different aim than that envisaged by Bacon. Bacon viewed experiment as a means for discovering general truths about nature. Experimental outcomes were not just particular events, but instances of universal generalizations. The kind of experimentation practiced in the Royal Society, on the other hand, aimed at establishing particular facts. The presentations of experiments that were published in *The Philosophical Transactions of the Royal Society* were written in a specific manner, containing detailed and circumstantial information about the experiments in question. The point of this rhetorical strategy was to create the illusion of "virtual witnessing" and thereby persuade the intended audience of the veracity of the results obtained. This fascination with particular "matters of fact" is evident in the work of Robert Boyle.

The Boyle–Hobbes Dispute

Boyle was among the more eminent followers of the Baconian program. Many of the issues and difficulties faced by that program can be seen in his controversy with the philosopher Thomas Hobbes (1588–1679) over the character of knowledge in natural philosophy. For Boyle knowledge of nature should be descriptive and based on consensus. The aim of experimental inquiry had to be the establishment of matters of fact and not the discovery of their underlying causes. Hobbes, on the other hand, argued that knowledge should be demonstrative, causal, and necessary. Thus, the experimental production of artificial effects could not lead to true knowledge, because the inference from effect to cause is always hypothetical.

In the course of their controversy Hobbes and Boyle debated the implications of the latter's experiments with the air pump. By means of that instrument, Boyle had managed to create a vacuum. In defending his results, he claimed that his experiments were publicly performed and could be replicated at will. Hobbes disputed those claims and emphasized the artificiality of Boyle's results. Hobbes's critique was an instance of a more general skepticism toward scientific instruments, some of which created phenomena that did not exist in nature. For that reason, their legitimacy was contested. At issue was whether they revealed natural processes or produced artifacts and, thereby, distorted nature.

According to Steven Shapin and Simon Schaffer, the significance of the Boyle–Hobbes debate extended far beyond natural philosophy. Shapin and Schaffer made a fascinating case that the eventual establishment of the experimental "form of life" implicated wider social and religious issues. In particular, they argued that Boyle's experimental program was in tune with the need for order and consensus in Restoration England. The general validity of this thesis, however, is questionable. By the end of the seventeenth century the "experimental philosophy" had spread throughout continental Europe, where the social and religious conditions differed significantly from those in England.

The rise of experimental philosophy gradually undermined the identification of science with demonstratively certain knowledge. Experimental results came to be seen as only "morally" certain—that is, certain for all practical purposes. Explanatory hypotheses, on the other hand, came to be regarded as merely probable. The quest for certainty, though, was never entirely abandoned, as is testified to by Isaac Newton's work.

Newton as an Experimental Philosopher

Newton famously claimed that hypotheses are not admissible in natural philosophy. The proper method of inference was deduction from the phenomena:

> whatever is not deduced from the phenomena is to be called an hypothesis; and hypotheses, whether metaphysical or physical, whether of occult qualities or mechanical, have no place in experimental philosophy. In this philosophy, particular propositions are inferred from the phenomena, and afterwards rendered general by induction. (p. 547)

As several historians and philosophers of science have pointed out, however, there was a gap between Newton's methodological pronouncements and his actual scientific work. Newton himself frequently made use of hypotheses. His various deductions from the phenomena relied on various theoretical assumptions, and thus the "deduced" propositions were not, strictly speaking, deduced from the phenomena.

Newton was a prominent member of the Royal Society, and its president from 1703 until his death. His main experimental contributions concerned the mathematical science of optics. In his experimental work Newton attempted to come up with "crucial experiments" that would enable him to choose among competing hypotheses of the phenomena under investigation. Robert Hooke (1635–1703), in his *Micrographia* (1665), coined the term *experimentum crucis*.

During the 1660s Newton carried out a series of experiments on light, using a familiar instrument, the prism. Based on those experiments, he concluded that light was a composite entity, consisting of distinct rays, whose refractive properties depended on their color. Newton reported the experiments he had carried out in a paper that was published in the *Philosophical Transactions of the Royal Society* in 1672, where he adopted the customary presentation style of the Royal Society. That paper got him involved in a prolonged controversy with Hooke, who was then the curator of experiments in the Royal Society, a controversy that lasted until 1678. Hooke did not dispute the results of Newton's experiments, which he managed to reproduce. Rather he challenged Newton's inferences from those results and, in particular, Newton's conclusions on the composition of light.

After that controversy Newton remained silent on optics until Hooke's death. He then published his experimental and theoretical investigations on light in *Opticks* (1704), a book that was written in the vernacular without the use of mathematics. In that book Newton developed a corpuscular theory of light, which encountered opposition in continental Europe. Newton took advantage of his presidency of the Royal Society and his ever-growing power to face that opposition. He directed the work of the official experimentalists of the Royal Society, Francis Hauksbee (c. 1666–1713) and John Desaguliers (1683–1744), who effectively promoted the Newtonian worldview through their experimental researches, public lecturing, and textbook writing.

The Spread of Experimental Philosophy in the Eighteenth Century

The fortunes of experimentation in the eighteenth century were closely linked with the spread of Newtonianism. *Opticks* functioned as a model of a developing experimental tradition. Prominent representatives of that tradition were the Dutch Newtonians Willem Jacob 's Gravesande (1688–1742) and Petrus van Musschenbroek (1692–1761), who wrote very influential books, whose main function was educational.

In the first half of the eighteenth century there was still no clear distinction between professional and amateur experimental philosophers. It was customary for experimentalists to obtain part of their income by performing striking electrical or optical experiments in public. This aspect of experimentation enlarged the audience for natural philosophy. However, it annoyed some university professors, who observed with dismay that the popularity of experiments was based on their potential for entertainment.

Experimentation for most of the eighteenth century was predominantly empirical and qualitative, without systematic guidance by mathematically formulated theories. Various phenomena (electrical, thermal, and chemical) were explored experimentally, on the assumption that they were manifestations of hidden imponderable entities (electric fluids, caloric, and phlogiston, respectively). The invention of new instruments (for example, the Leyden jar), and the improvement of existing ones (such as the thermometer), played a seminal role in investigating these phenomena. Earlier in the century the acquisition of instruments was the responsibility of well-off professors of experimental physics, who collected and stored them in "physical cabinets." In the second half of the century the task of establishing and maintaining collections of instruments was gradually taken over by universities and scientific academies.

Toward the end of the century, and especially in France, there was a shift toward the quantification of experimental physics. New quantifiable concepts were introduced, such as charge and heat capacity, which facilitated this shift and led to the construction of mathematical theories of static electricity and heat. Furthermore, precise measurements were systematically carried out and meticulously reported in numerical tables. Precision measurement gradually became a central preoccupation of experimental physics.

The Nineteenth Century

Experiment continued to be a significant driving force in the development of the physical sciences in the first half of the nineteenth century. The experimental discovery of novel phenomena (for example, electromagnetism) and the precise measurement of physical parameters (such as the mechanical equivalent of heat) were instrumental in the development of electromagnetic theory and thermodynamics. The articulation of these theories in the second half of the nineteenth century guided, in turn, the further experimental exploration of thermal and electromagnetic phenomena. In the process the mathematical and the experimental traditions of physical science merged.

By the end of the nineteenth century, precision in measurement had become almost an obsession among physicists, who believed that it held the key to the further development and eventual closure of their discipline. In the words of James Clerk Maxwell (1831–1879),

This characteristic of modern experiments—that they consist principally of measurements, —is so prominent, that the opinion seems to have got abroad, that in a few years all the great physical constants will have been approximately estimated, and that the only occupation which will then be left to men of science will be to carry on these measurements to another place of decimals. (Badash, p. 50)

Several experimental developments (such as X rays, radioactivity, the photoelectric effect, and blackbody radiation) at the end of the nineteenth century put off the end of physics. Under the weight of these and other experimentally probed phenomena, the edifice of classical physics would crumble.

The nineteenth century was also an important period for the establishment of a new physical and institutional space devoted to experimentation, the academic laboratory. With some exceptions, laboratories had previously been private places, usually located in the houses of wealthy experimentalists. In the 1870s and 1880s the founding of new university laboratories (including the Cavendish Laboratory at Cambridge, the Clarendon Laboratory at Oxford, the Jefferson Laboratory at Harvard) and new institutes (for example, the Physikalisch-Technische Reichsanstalt near Berlin) devoted to experimental research marked a new era for experimentation, which became an essential element of both research and teaching in the physical sciences.

Coda: Experimentation in the Twentieth Century

In the twentieth century perhaps the most significant break with respect to the character of experimentation came via World War II. The Manhattan Project for the development of the atomic bomb marked the beginning of experimentation on an enormous industrial scale. After the war a new form of experimental life, so-called big science, developed. Laboratories in certain areas of physics came to resemble huge factories, where hundreds, or even thousands, of scientists collaborated to design and carry out extremely expensive and time-consuming experimental projects. In these fields, tabletop experiments by a few experimentalists became a thing of the past.

See also **Empiricism; Science; Science, History of.**

BIBLIOGRAPHY

Bacon, Francis. *The New Organon and Related Writings.* Edited by Fulton H. Anderson. New York: Macmillan, 1985.

Badash, Lawrence. "The Completeness of Nineteenth-Century Science." *Isis* 63 (1972): 48–58.

Buchwald, Jed Z., and Sungook Hong. "Physics." In *From Natural Philosophy to the Sciences: Writing the History of Nineteenth-Century Science,* edited by David Cahan, 163–195. Chicago: University of Chicago Press, 2003.

Cohen, H. Floris. *The Scientific Revolution: A Historiographical Inquiry.* Chicago: University of Chicago Press, 1994.

Crombie, A. C. *Robert Grosseteste and the Origins of Experimental Science, 1100–1700.* Oxford: Clarendon, 1953.

Dear, Peter. *Revolutionizing the Sciences: European Knowledge and Its Ambitions, 1500–1700.* Princeton, N.J.: Princeton University Press, 2001.

Galison, Peter. *How Experiments End.* Chicago: University of Chicago Press, 1987.

———. *Image and Logic: A Material Culture of Microphysics.* Chicago: University of Chicago Press, 1997.

Gooding, David, Trevor Pinch, and Simon Schaffer, eds. *The Uses of Experiment: Studies in the Natural Sciences.* Cambridge, U.K.: Cambridge University Press, 1989.

Hall, Marie Boas. *Promoting Experimental Learning: Experiment and the Royal Society, 1660–1727*. Cambridge, U.K.: Cambridge University Press, 1991.

Heilbron, J. L. *Electricity in the Seventeenth and Eighteenth Centuries: A Study of Early Modern Physics*. Mineola, N.Y.: Dover, 1999.

James, Frank A. J. L., ed. *The Development of the Laboratory: Essays on the Place of Experiment in Industrial Civilisation*. New York: American Institute of Physics, 1989.

Kuhn, Thomas S. *The Essential Tension: Selected Studies in Scientific Tradition and Change*. Chicago: University of Chicago Press, 1977.

Newton, Isaac. *Sir Isaac Newton's Mathematical Principles of Natural Philosophy and His System of the World*. Translated by Andrew Motte in 1729. Reprint, with translations revised by Florian Cajori, Berkeley: University of California Press, 1934.

Peltonen, Markku, ed. *The Cambridge Companion to Bacon*. Cambridge, U.K.: Cambridge University Press, 1996.

Price, Derek J. de Solla. *Little Science, Big Science*. New York: Columbia University Press, 1963.

Sargent, Rose-Mary. *The Diffident Naturalist: Robert Boyle and the Philosophy of Experiment*. Chicago: University of Chicago Press, 1995.

Shapin, Steven, and Simon Schaffer. *Leviathan and the Air-Pump: Hobbes, Boyle, and the Experimental Life*. Princeton, N.J.: Princeton University Press, 1985.

Wise, Norton M, ed. *The Values of Precision*. Princeton, N.J.: Princeton University Press, 1995.

Theodore Arabatzis

EXPRESSIONISM. Of all the "isms" in the early twentieth century, Expressionism is one of the most elusive and difficult to define. Whereas, on the one hand, Expressionism has been said to reveal its "universal character," abandoning all theories that imply a narrow, exclusive nationalistic attitude, on the other, it has been considered a "specific and familiar constant in German art for hundreds of years" (Vogt, p. 16). Scholarship has attempted to address the problematic range of the term and the contradictory emphases in its historiography. Although Expressionism did not constitute a cohesive movement or homogenous style, attention has been directed to the origins of the word and its meanings in critical discourse as well as to the contingent issues of art, society, and politics framing Expressionist avant-garde culture. Spurred on by an increasing overlap of the humanities with social, cultural, and gender studies, recent investigations reject notions of a transcendent *Zeitgeist* in focusing on Expressionism's interface with the public sphere.

Expressionism in Germany flourished initially in the visual arts, encompassing the formation of Künstlergruppe Brücke (Artists' Group Bridge) in Dresden in 1905 and the Blaue Reiter in Munich in 1911. The notion of the *Doppelbegabung*, or double talent, characterized many artists' experimentation in the different art forms, whether lyric poetry, prose, or drama. The notable precedent for this was the music-dramas of Richard Wagner and the attendant concept of the *Gesamtkunstwerk*, which excited artists' and writers' interests in the union of the arts into a theatrical whole. Performed at the Wiener

Kunstschau in 1909, Oskar Kokoschka's (1886–1980) *Mörder, Hoffnung der Frauen* (Murderer, hope of women) is considered one of the first Expressionist plays to involve a high degree of abstraction in the text, *mise en scène*, sound effects, and costume. Comparatively speaking, Reinhard Sorge's (1892–1916) play *Der Bettler* (The beggar), written in 1910, is more discursive, though no less abstracted in relaying the metaphysical stages (*Stationen*) achieved by the chief protagonist, "the Poet" himself (Furness, in Behr and Fanning, p. 163). Hence, by 1914, the concept of Expressionism permeated German metropolitan culture at many levels, gaining momentum during World War I and in the wake of the November Revolution in 1918. However, any attempt to define Expressionism chronologically is as problematic as doing so in terms of style, since its influence was still felt in film after the holding of the first *Neue Sachlichkeit* (New Objectivity) exhibition in Mannheim in 1925.

It is telling that the kernel concept of the "expressive"—the primacy of the creative process at the expense of verisimilitude—became significant in Germany at the height of the Second Empire, corresponding to the reign of the Hohenzollern king of Prussia, Wilhelm II. The period between 1890 and 1914 was characterized by colonial expansion abroad, an unprecedented degree of urbanization and technical transformation at home, and promotion of a hide-bound national public art. Generally speaking, Expressionism grew out of late-nineteenth-century dissatisfaction with academic training and the mass spectacle of state-funded salons, the Munich (1892) and Berlin secessions (1898) withdrawing from such official or professional affiliation. In their exhibitions, the secessions fostered a sense of pluralism and internationalism, maintaining links with the art market and Paris-based Impressionism and Postimpressionism.

Within this shifting ambience between tradition and the modern, the term *Expressionisten* (Expressionists) was initially applied to a selection of French Fauvist and not German artists in the foreword to the catalog of a Berlin Secession exhibition, held in April 1911. Given the largely Impressionist leanings of the Secession, the collective term was a convenient way of signifying the "newest directions" in French art. Here the art of self-expression, or *Ausdruckskunst* as it was articulated in German, involved a degree of expressive intensification and distortion that differed from the mimetic impulse of naturalism and the Impressionist mode of capturing the fleeting nuances of the external world. This aesthetic revolt found theoretical justification in the writing of the art historian Wilhelm Worringer (1881–1965), whose published doctoral thesis *Abstraktion und Einfühlung* (1908, Abstraction and empathy) proposed that stylization, typical of Egyptian, Gothic, or Primitive art, was not the result of lack of skill (*Können*) but was propelled by an insecure psychic relationship with the external world. An impelling "will to form," or *Kunstwollen*, underscored art historical methodology at the time (Jennings, in Donahue, p. 89).

Evidently, the label *Expressionism* was not invented by the artists themselves but abounded in the promotional literature and reviews of current exhibitions. The proliferation of specialist journals and technological invention in publishing at the turn of the twentieth century was integral to the avant-garde's dissemination of their ideas in Expressionist literary and artistic journals, such as *Der Sturm* (Riot) and *Die Aktion*. Although the milieu encompassed a diverse political and disciplinary spectrum, commentators were united by the historical concept of *Neuzeit,* or modernity, "embodying a particular experiential pattern, in which it was the future that was the bearer of growing expectations" (Koselleck, p. 243). In their manifesto, members of the Brücke declared their independence from older established forces and called on all youth to look toward the future in searching for authentic expression. Similarly, in Wassily Kandinsky's (1866–1944) theoretical treatise *Über das Geistige in der Kunst* (1912, On the spiritual in art), he invoked the principle of "inner necessity" in postulating the evolution of art toward a utopian, transcendent form of creative expression.

Yet Expressionism was marked by a profound ambivalence toward modernity, and subject matter frequently operated between the antimonies of metropolitan alienation and the rural idyll. Both literary and artistic groups who frequented the Café des Westens in Berlin drew on the Nietzschean concept of "pathos" to convey their embrace of the dynamism of contemporary life. In emulation of the Neopathetisches Cabaret that attracted well-known poets, the painter Ludwig Meidner (1884–1966) adopted the title *Die Pathetiker* for his major group exhibition that was held in November 1912 at the Sturm Gallery. The city landscape was invested with elements of primal and cosmic destruction, comparable to the *Bild,* the word picture, which marks the Expressionist poetry of Georg Heym's (1887–1912) *Umbra vitae* (1912) or Jacob van Hoddis's (1887–1942) *Weltende* (1911, End of the world). Clearly, their utopian assumptions were compromised by a modernizing world, which was perceived as fallen and chaotic.

Kulturkritik (cultural criticism) aimed to heal this tired civilization through the reference to untainted, preindustrialized and autochthonous communal traditions. Viewed through the lens of modern French painting, the Brücke artists—Ernst Ludwig Kirchner, Karl Schmidt-Rottluff, Erich Heckel, Max Pechstein—located authenticity in old German woodcuts, African and Oceanic tribal art, which informed their carved sculpture, graphic techniques, studio interiors, and figural landscapes. In the *Blaue Reiter Almanac* (1912), the editors, Kandinsky and Franz Marc (1880–1916), interspersed essays on art, music, poetry, and theater with photographs of Russian and Bavarian folk art, African and Oceanic masks, and child art, seeking to legitimize the technical radicalism of modern painting through resonances with so-called primitive examples. As has been argued, primitivism was a permutation of agrarian romanticism. By the end of the nineteenth century the image of the European peasantry and nature had exhausted itself. "Nostalgia had now to cast its net wider and beyond rural Europe" (Lübbren, pp. 57–58).

On the eve of war, in his book *Der Expressionismus,* the art critic and newspaper feuilletonist Paul Fechter (1880–1958) invested Expressionism with the connotations of the anti-intellectual, the emotional, and the spiritual—

the "metaphysical necessity of the German people" (Fechter, p. 29). Here he drew heavily on Worringer's professorial thesis *Formprobleme der Gotik* (1911, Form in gothic), which constructed a genealogy for German artistic identity based on the anticlassical features of the Gothic past. By this time, the engendering of Impressionism as feminine, as celebrating sensory, passive experience, was well established in critical debates, and Fechter strove to inculcate a more masculine *Ausdrucksgefühl* (expressive feeling) in contemporary German art. However, the Teutonic nationalization of Expressionism was inconsistent.

Internationalism was advanced through the agencies of dealership and dispersal. The musician, writer, and dealer Herwarth Walden (1878–1941), whose Sturm Gallery was established in Berlin in 1912, displayed the works of Expressionists as well as those of Futurists and Cubists. Before and after the outbreak of war, he sent traveling exhibitions to Scandinavia, Holland, Finland, and Tokyo. As a founding member of Zurich dada, the German Poet Hugo Ball (1886–1927) provided a link between Expressionism and Dada. Ball's preoccupation with mysticism and anarchism led him to Switzerland during the war, and in a key lecture he delivered on Kandinsky (1917), he proclaimed the value of abstraction in painting, poetry, and drama to cultural regeneration.

Even in 1916, in his book *Expressionismus,* the art critic, novelist, and playwright Hermann Bahr (1863–1934) remained warmly disposed toward Picasso and French art since Manet. Bahr was writing at a time when Germany had suffered staggering reversals on the battlefield and disillusionment had set in with mechanized warfare of a kind that no one had imagined. Fiercely antitechnological and antibourgeois, he characterized the era as a "battle of the soul with the machine," articulating the desire for a prelapsarian state of innocence (p. 110). In 1917 literary Expressionism came of age with Kasimir Edschmid's (1890–1966) manifesto *Über den Expressionismus in der Literatur und die neue Dichtung,* strengthening the emphasis on *Schauen,* or "visionary experiences," rather than on *Sehen* ("observation of visual details") (Weisstein, p. 207). Given its emphasis on spiritual values, the literary critic Wolfgang Paulsen would have labeled this genuine Expressionism so as to distinguish it from Activist Expressionism, deriving from the lineage of Karl Marx. However, not all socialism ran counter to the notion of "spiritual revolution" and, according to Rhys Williams, Georg Kaiser's (1878–1945) play *Von morgens bis mitternachts* (1916, From morn to midnight) can be read as a "dramatization of [Gustav] Landauer's indictment of capitalism" and the search for the *verbindender Geist* (unifying spirit) that he advocated (Behr and Fanning, pp. 201–207).

With the Revolution of November 1918 and the collapse of the Second Reich, such intellectuals saw the opportunity for the initiation of a new society, and the link between Expressionism and revolutionary theory became more emphatic. A second generation of Expressionists emerged that, although widespread in regional centers throughout Germany, was more cohesively defined by its members' antiwar sentiments. As the son of a working-class family, the artist Conrad Felixmüller (1897–1977) spearheaded the formation of the Dresden Secession Group in 1919 and was committed to an agenda of proletarian culture.

In Berlin, the organization Novembergruppe was founded. It called on all Expressionists, Futurists, and Cubists to unite under the banner of cultural reform and reconstruction. Although initially attracting dadaists to its ranks, the equation between Expressionism and radicalism became more difficult to sustain within the stabilization of order brought about by the Weimar government. Due to democratization and to pressure exerted by various artists' councils, Expressionism made inroads into the public sphere and was avidly collected by major museums throughout Germany. Moreover, well-known Expressionists such as Kandinsky and Paul Klee (1879–1940) were approached to teach at the Bauhaus in Weimar, founded in 1919 by the architect Walter Gropius (1883–1969). This school was based on socialist and utopian principles that placed artists at the center of a new kind of design that served modern society. Though Kandinsky sustained his belief in the expressive and mystical values of art, he abandoned the expressive abstraction of the Munich years and explored geometric formal elements in a more systematic manner.

However, the death knell of Expressionism, according to many commentators, lay in its commercialization and consequent loss of authenticity. It was considered debased in losing its soul to mass culture. In the early twenty-first century, scholars tend to regard the ability of Expressionism to adapt to the demands of technological advancement as a measure of its success. The silent film *The Cabinet of Dr. Caligari*, directed by Robert Wiene (1881–1938), was released in Berlin in 1920 and achieved resounding international acclaim. Fritz Lang's (1890–1976) *Metropolis* (1927) and Josef von Sternberg's (1894–1969) *The Blue Angel* (1930) appeared after Expressionism's demise and Georg Wilhelm Pabst's (1885–1967) *Pandora's Box* in 1928.

During the 1930s, the polarization in German politics and society led views on the left and the right to target Expressionism. From a position of exile in Moscow, the Marxist theoretician Georg Lukács (1885–1971) launched an attack in his essay "'Größe und verfall' des Expressionismus" (1934; Expressionism: its significance and decline, Washton-Long, pp. 313-317). Favoring a form of typified realism that was deduced from nineteenth-century literary sources, Lukács considered Expressionism the product of capitalist imperialism. According to this model, its subjectivity and irrationalism would inevitably lead to fascism. Debates ensued in the émigré literary journal *Das Wort,* the Marxist philosopher Ernst Bloch (1885–1977) vigorously defending the role of autonomous experimentation in the visual arts in his essay "Diskyssion über Expressionismus" (1938; Discussing Expressionism, Washton-Long, pp. 323-327). In post-1945 historiography, critics tended to lose sight of Bloch's salvaging of the utopian and communal aspirations of Expressionism.

Interestingly, even after the Nazis assumed power in 1933, there was rivalry between the antimodernist Alfred Rosenberg (1893–1946) and the Minister of Public Enlightenment and Propaganda Joseph Goebbels (1897–1945), who considered Expressionism and the works of Emil Nolde (1867–1956) to be uniquely German. Indeed, Goebbels's novel *Michael* adopted the declamatory style and format of the Expressionist *stationendrama* in tracing the journey of the eponymous hero from soldier to Nazi superman (1929). In 1934, Rosenberg's appointment as spiritual overseer of the National Socialist Party sealed the fate of the avant-garde. Official confiscation of works from public collections accompanied the dismissal of Expressionists, left-wing intellectuals, and Jews from prominent positions in the arts.

In 1937, moreover, the infamous exhibition *"Entartete Kunst"* (Degenerate art) was inaugurated in Munich, signaling the Third Reich's devastating efforts to expunge Expressionism's claim to cultural status. Expressionism underwent transformation in exile as refugee artists, writers, and filmmakers reexamined their cultural identity in light of the demands of their adoptive countries. Others were not as fortunate. Kirchner resided in Switzerland since 1917, and his frail psychological state was exacerbated by the pillaging of 639 of his works from museums and by the inclusion of thirty-two in the *"Entartete Kunst"* exhibition. He committed suicide in 1938. The poet Van Hoddis, who was of Jewish origin and suffered mental disorders for many years, was transported to the Sobibor concentration camp in 1942, the exact date of his murder being unrecorded.

See also **Avant-Garde; Dada.**

BIBLIOGRAPHY

PRIMARY SOURCES

Bahr, Hermann. *Expressionism.* Munich: Delphin, 1916. Translated by R. T. Gribble. London: Frank Henderson, 1925.

Edschmid, Kasimir. *Über den Expressionismus in der Literatur und die neue Dichtung.* Berlin: Reiß, 1919.

Fechter, Paul. *Der Expressionismus.* Munich: Piper, 1914.

Goebbels, Joseph. *Michael: Ein Deutsches Schiksal in Tagebuchblätten.* Munich: Franz Eber, 1929.

Kandinsky, Wassily, and Franz Marc, eds. *Blaue Reiter Almanac.* Munich: Piper, 1912.

———. *Complete Writings on Art.* Edited by Kenneth Lindsay and Peter Vergo. London: Faber, 1982.

———. *Über das Geistige in der Kunst.* Munich: Piper, 1912.

Miesel, Victor, ed. *Voices of German Expressionism.* Englewood Cliffs, N.J.: Prentice-Hall, 1970.

Paulsen, Wolfgang. *Aktivismus und Expressionismus: Eine typologische Untersuchung.* Berne and Leipzig: Gotthelf, 1935.

Raabe, Paul, ed. *The Era of German Expressionism.* London: Calder and Boyer, 1974.

Washton-Long, Rose-Carol, ed. *German Expressionism: Documents from the End of the Wilhelmine Empire to the Rise of National Socialism.* Berkeley: University of California Press, 1995.

Worringer, Wilhelm. *Abstraktion und Einfühlung.* Munich: Piper, 1908. Translated by Michael Bullock. New York: International Universities Press, 1953.

———. *Formprobleme der Gotik.* Munich: Piper, 1911. Translated by Herbert Read. London: Putnams, 1927.

SECONDARY SOURCES

Barron, Stephanie, ed. *Degenerate Art: The Fate of the Avant-garde in Nazi Germany.* Los Angeles: Los Angeles County Museum of Art, 1991.

———. *German Expressionism, 1915–1925: The Second Generation*. Los Angeles: Los Angeles County Museum of Art, 1988.

Barron, Stephanie, and Wolf-Dieter Dube, eds. *German Expressionism: Art and Society*. Milan: Bompiani, 1997.

Behr, Shulamith. *Expressionism*. New York: Cambridge University Press, 1999.

———. *Women Expressionists*. New York: Rizzoli, 1988.

Behr, Shulamith, David Fanning, and Douglas Jarman, eds. *Expressionism Reassessed*. Manchester, U.K.: Manchester University Press, 1993.

Bridgwater, Patrick. *Poet of Expressionist Berlin: The Life and Work of Georg Heym*. London: Libris, 1991.

Bushart, Magdalena. "Changing Times, Changing Styles: Wilhelm Worringer and the Art of His Epoch." In *Invisible Cathedrals: The Expressionist Art History of Wilhelm Worringer*, edited by Neil H. Donahue, 69–85. University Park: Pennsylvania State University Press, 1995.

Furness, Raymond. "The Religious Element in Expressionist Theatre." In *Expressionism Reassessed*, edited by Shulamith Behr and David Fanning, 163–173.

Gordon, Donald E. "On the Origin of the Word 'Expressionism.'" *Journal of the Warburg and Courtauld Institute* 29 (1966): 368–385.

Jennings, Michael. "Against Expressionism: Materialism and Social Theory in Worringer's *Abstraction and Empathy*." In *Invisible Cathedrals: The Expressionist Art History of Wilhelm Worringer*, edited by Neil H. Donahue, 87–104. University Park: Pennsylvania State University Press, 1995.

Koselleck, Reinhart. *Futures Past: On the Semantics of Historical Time*. Translated by Keith Tribe. Cambridge, Mass.: MIT Press, 1985.

Lloyd, Jill. *German Expressionism: Primitivism and Modernity*. New Haven, Conn.: Yale University Press, 1991.

Lübbren, Nina. *Rural Artists' Colonies in Europe, 1870–1910*. Manchester, U.K.: Manchester University Press, 2001.

Manheim, Ron. "Expressionismus—Zur Enstehung eines Kunsthistorischen Stil—und Periodenbegriffes." *Zeitschrift für Kunstgeschichte* 49, no. 1 (1986): 73–91.

Perkins, Geoffrey. *Contemporary Theory of Expressionism*. Frankfurt am Main: Peter Lang, 1974.

Rumold, Rainer, and O. K. Werckmeister, eds. *The Ideological Crisis of Expressionism: The Literary and Artistic War Colony in Belgium, 1914–1918*. Columbia, S.C.: Camden House, 1990.

Vogt, Paul. "Introduction." *Expressionism: A German Intuition, 1905–1920*. New York: Solomon R. Guggenheim Museum, 1980.

Weinstein, Joan. *The End of Expressionism (Art and the November Revolution in Germany, 1918–19)*. Chicago: University of Chicago Press, 1990.

Weisstein, Ulrich. "Expressionism in Literature." In *Dictionary of the History of Ideas*, edited by Philip P. Wiener. Vol. 2. New York: Charles Scribner's Sons, 1973.

Werenskiold, Marit. *The Concept of Expressionism: Origin and Metamorphoses*. Oslo: Universitetsforlaget, 1984.

Williams, Rhys. "Culture and Anarchy in Expressionist Drama." In *Expressionism Reassessed*, edited by Shulamith Behr, David Fanning, and Douglas Jarman, 201–212. New York: Manchester University Press.

Shulamith Behr

EXTINCTION. *See* **Environment; Evolution; Nature.**

EXTIRPATION.   The term *extirpation* is most commonly associated with the Catholic Church's project to eradicate traditional religious practices in the Americas after the Spanish conquest. The Andean highlands, Mesoamerica, and other areas of high indigenous cultural development have rich religious traditions that predate the Spanish conquest by millennia. Ending these practices became an early and determined goal of European missionary efforts in the Americas and in a sense was an extension of the wars of conquest. In 1571, Philip II decided to exclude Indians from the Spanish Inquisition because of their poor understanding of the Catholic faith. Although never as institutionalized as the Holy Office of the Inquisition, which sought to wipe out heretical thought from the Iberian population in both Europe and the New World, campaigns for the "extirpation of idolatries" emerged out of the same context of religious intolerance and visited similar consequences of pain and suffering on the target populations. In a sense, as some scholars have observed, these extirpation campaigns were a bastard child of the Inquisition. "The systematic visitations, interrogations, torture, punishments, and exiles," Mills notes, "represent perhaps the most sustained religious persecution of indigenous peoples in the history of colonial Latin America" (p. 170). Organized legal campaigns that recorded native beliefs and traditions with the goal of exterminating "diabolical deceptions" took place primarily in the viceroyalty of Peru, but similar attitudes influenced Spanish actions toward native religions throughout the Americas. These attempts were never completely successful, and indigenous and African religious practices continue to thrive in the Americas in the early twenty-first century.

Francisco de Avila was one of the earliest and most noted leaders in attempts to suppress indigenous religions. Avila oversaw the drafting of a document known as the *Huarochirí Manuscript* to use as a tool in his prosecution of religious practices that he considered to be diabolical. Avila pursued his extirpation of native idolatries with an usual religious zeal, probably as a revenge against local villagers who had accused him of economic exploitation and violations of moral standards of behavior. In 1609 Avila began to grandstand his cause, engaging in show trials designed to procure public confessions of idolatry while undermining his enemies. His success led to even more aggressive and repressive campaigns to destroy Andean religions, similar to what would happen later in North America with the Salem witch trials in the 1600s and the McCarthy hearings in the 1950s. Ideological deviance alone cannot explain the fury with which such campaigns are carried out. The extirpations advanced the reputation and career of Avila along with the colleagues who joined him, as well as economically benefitting the campaigners because Spanish law rewarded them with the confiscated wealth from these pagan deities. While the veracity of charges in the extirpation campaigns is questionable, they clearly built on existing ideological constructions and played off local social conflicts.

Written in the Andean Quechua language, the *Huarochirí Manuscript* records traditional practices with the goal of exterminating them while at the same time, ironically, preserving a historical memory of these beliefs. Trial records provide rich ethnographic data that document indigenous cultures. In the Andes, traditional religious practices revolved around a reverence for deities known as *huacas*. Rooted in the practice of ancestor worship, *huacas* were often local physical markers such as a tree, stone, or cave from which inhabitants believed their ancestors emerged. In general, *huacas* were material objects or sometimes even humans that were assigned supernatural attributes. Particularly objectionable to the Spanish was the tradition of preserving the bodies of dead family members and parading these mummies during religious ceremonies. Worshipping these objects provided a mechanism for mediating societal controls.

Avila's extirpation campaigns illustrate the similarities and differences between Spanish crusades against native religions and the function of the Inquisition. Both used judicial tools and a repressive apparatus to root out native religious deviance. Trials typically culminated in an auto-da-fé, with the destruction of offending objects and the punishment of the convicted. Unlike the Inquisition, however, extirpation campaigns never became institutionalized. Attempts to root out idolatries came and went according to the interests of local church leaders, and a lack of support from central authorities would lead to the collapse of an extirpation campaign. Furthermore, charges of idolatry often became a cover for local conflicts. While the Inquisition provided checks against the testimony of personal enemies that might undermine the legitimacy of a conviction, extirpation trials thrived on local conflicts in order to extract compromising information.

Extirpation campaigns did not end with Avila's persecutions but, rather, continued sporadically throughout the colonial period, occasionally reaching points of extreme repression in attempts to reform the lives and practices of indigenous peoples. These campaigns, which are sometimes referred to as an "Inquisition for Indians" (Mills, p. 171), have been divided into three periods: 1609 to 1621, 1625 to 1626, and 1646 to 1670. The irregular appearance of these campaigns leads Griffiths to conclude that they were aberrations, not a commonplace phenomenon in colonial Latin America. In the final period, which Griffiths considers to be the zenith of the campaigns, Archbishop Pedro de Villagómez sent prosecutors to extract origin stories from native provincial elites outside Lima. These campaigns often targeted the most vulnerable subjects and were not above using torture and blackmail to extract confessions. Native priests in particular were targeted. Victims were whipped, exiled, or even executed, and ancestor-cult mummies and other religious artifacts were burned.

Villagómez declared his efforts successful, and the extirpation campaigns slowed and became less vicious. In their final stages, the Catholic Church considered *huaca* worship to be simple acts of superstition that could be more easily tolerated than idolatry. The Spanish and native worlds appeared to be finally coming to an accommodation with each other. Mills challenges standard interpretations that contend that this development represents a victory of extirpation campaigns and a passive acceptance on the part of indigenous peoples of the European religion. It represented more of a change in terminology than attitude. Traditional practices persisted, and as a result, occasional prosecutions continued to the mid-1700s. By the end of the colonial period, extirpation campaigns had finally sputtered out without the ideological drive and passion of earlier efforts.

In New Spain, these campaigns became even more localized and less rooted in institutional structures. Without active leadership, the viceroyalty never experienced the waves of religious repression that swept through Peru. Rather than large-scale extirpation campaigns, anti-idolatry programs became "an ongoing struggle, engaged in on a day-to-day basis by individual missionaries, with the support of the military garrison" (Warner, p. 171). Idolatry became a very vague and shifting concept that served different purposes at various times. "No systematic test for idolatry ever existed," Tavárez notes and because of this, "an act of idolatry could only be committed by native subjects who were *willing* to confess to someone" (pp. 135, 136). Intent became a key part of the extirpation campaigns. As Chuchiak observes, "the term idolatry can be understood as expressing the shared realities of a religiously bifurcated region of the colonial world" (p. 167). Practitioners tended to hide their activities by camouflaging them as Catholic rituals. As a result, indigenous conversion to European religious practices was superficial at best. Often the two religions coexisted in a syncretic mixture.

The story of the Virgin of Guadalupe in Mexico is the most noted example of a syncretic religion, and reflects the failure and even co-optation of attempts at religious extirpation. In this event, the Virgin Mary allegedly appeared to Juan Diego in 1531 at the Tepeyac Hill just north of the recently conquered Aztec capital of Tenochtitlan. The local bishop finally believed the Indian shepherd when the virgin's image was miraculously imprinted on his cloak. Scholars have noted how anachronisms, inconsistencies, internal difficulties, and the European structure of the story cast doubt on its veracity. Not only does the Indian have a Spanish name, but "Guadalupe," a dark-skinned virgin from Spain, is an Arabic word that would be difficult for a Nahua-speaker to pronounce. The cult appears to be a Spanish fabrication to redirect Indian "idolatry" from a "pagan" to a Christian focus. In fact, during the Spanish conquest it had become a common practice to construct Spanish temples on top of Indian pilgrimage sites. Although the intent of these efforts was the extirpation of idolatrous practices, the result was somewhat different, as the Virgin of Guadalupe became a symbol of cultural pride in Mexico. She has also been seen as a defender of the Indians and was successfully used as a symbol of liberation during campaigns for Mexican independence, during the Mexican Revolution, and among Hispanic civil rights struggles in the United States.

As the Virgin of Guadalupe indicates, there is some question as to the lasting impact and legacy of extirpation campaigns. "Andean beliefs and practices survived because they changed and were adapted to colonial realities," Mills argues, "and because people assimilated Christian terms, ideas, rituals, and explanations into an expanding religious framework" (p. 4). In attempting to eradicate "demonic" religious practices, the Spanish forced adaptations that allowed indigenous religious to survive and also led to modifications of the Spanish religion. Even the structure and approach of the Inquisition had to be adapted to the native world in the form of the extirpation campaigns. What theologically should have been a stark opposition instead became a space for negotiated adaptations. Catholicism continued to be the dominant religion in Latin America, but it assumed a flavor strongly influenced by native and even African religious practices. The failure of the extirpation campaigns highlights the partial, contradictory, and incomplete nature of the Spanish conquest of the Americas.

See also **Colonialism; Genocide; Syncretism.**

BIBLIOGRAPHY
Chuchiak, John F., IV. "Toward a Regional Definition of Idolatry: Reexamining Idolatry Trials in the *'Relaciónes de Méritos'* and Their Role in Defining the Concept of *'Idolatria'* in Colonial Yucatán, 1570–1780." *Journal of Early Modern History* 6, no. 2 (May 2002): 140–167.

Griffiths, Nicholas. *The Cross and the Serpent: Religious Repression and Resurgence in Colonial Peru.* Norman: University of Oklahoma Press, 1996.

Mills, Kenneth. *Idolatry and Its Enemies: Colonial Andean Religion and Extirpation, 1640–1750.* Princeton, N.J.: Princeton University Press, 1997.

Poole, Stafford. *Our Lady of Guadalupe: The Origins and Sources of a Mexican National Symbol, 1531–1797.* Tucson: University of Arizona Press, 1995.

Salomon, Frank, and George L. Urioste, eds. *The Huarochirí Manuscript: A Testament of Ancient and Colonial Andean Religion.* Austin: University of Texas Press, 1991.

Tavárez, David E. "Idolatry as an Ontological Question: Native Consciousness and Juridical Proof in Colonial Mexico." *Journal of Early Modern History* 6, no. 2 (May 2002): 114–139.

Warner, Rick. "'Ambivalent Conversions' in Nayarit: Shifting Views of Idolatry." *Journal of Early Modern History* 6, no. 2 (May 2002): 168–184.

Marc Becker

F

FALLACY, LOGICAL. A logical fallacy is a mistake in reasoning. The premises of good arguments support the conclusion, so that in the case of deductive arguments, if the premises are true, the conclusion must also be true. In the case of inductive arguments, true premises make the conclusion more likely. Deductively valid argument forms can be defined as those in which true premises never lead to a false conclusion, no matter what content is presented in that form. In logic, arguments and argument forms are studied and a system of rules is created to systematically distinguish between valid and invalid arguments. Invalid argument types that appear frequently and that seem to be especially deceptive have been categorized and given names. The study of logic and the naming of logical fallacies began with Aristotle (384–322 B.C.E.), and standard Latin names of fallacies have been inherited from the Middle Ages, so "logical fallacy" is not a concept that has changed much with time. However, the teaching of logical fallacies has been revived with the popularity of courses entitled "critical thinking" rather than "logic'" in order to highlight their emphasis on natural language and informal fallacies, rather than on formal logical systems.

Formal Fallacies

It is standard practice to distinguish formal and informal fallacies. Formal fallacies break one or more of the rules of a system of logic and can be seen when an argument is presented in either schematic form or in a natural language. Informal fallacies, by contrast, can often only be seen when the argument is presented in natural language, since they depend often on ambiguity or some other misuse of language. Other common fallacies that do not clearly break a rule of logic are also classified as informal, even when they do not depend on misuse of language.

In traditional Aristotelian logic, a set of rules can be established for the formation of valid arguments. Because breaking any one of the rules results in an invalid argument, there is a logical fallacy corresponding to each rule. Examples of such fallacies include excluded middle, illicit major, illicit minor, etc. One important formal logical fallacy is affirming the consequent, which can be given schematically as an argument of the form "If P, then Q. Q. Therefore, P." The logic of conditional statements has been thought to be essential to the testing of scientific theories, since predictions are written in conditional form. A fact such as "Water freezes at 32° F" can be written as the conditional "If (pure) water is below 32° F, then it will freeze." However, as Karl Popper (1902–1994) emphasized, one cannot claim to prove anything if one obtains a positive result, and indeed would be committing the formal logical fallacy of affirming the consequent if this reasoning is used to support one's claim. Suppose someone had claimed that they have a magic box that freezes water, and that water always freezes when it is put into the box. One should not be impressed if this prediction comes true, not even if this experiment is repeated multiple times. What is needed is a way of isolating the different factors that may be relevant to the change of state that water undergoes—is it being in the box, or being in the dark, or being in the cold that is the crucial factor? This problem of scientific reasoning is highlighted by the fallacy of affirming the consequent. A conditional statement can properly be rejected if a negative result is obtained, but nothing can be concluded deductively from a positive result.

Informal Fallacies

The multitude of names given to informal fallacies can be more confusing than helpful, but nevertheless, the names of logical fallacies are important terms of art in any kind of argumentative writing or speech. Informal logical fallacies can be classified in different ways, but it is common to put them into groups such as fallacies of relevance, weak induction, ambiguity, and presumption.

Fallacies of relevance. Slippery slope, red herring, and straw person are fallacies that change the issue under discussion to something that is easier to attack. An ad hominem argument attacks the person, rather than the issue. The fact that someone is untrustworthy, for example, does not guarantee that the conclusion of their argument is wrong or that their argument is invalid. The question of whether or not such information is relevant can, however, be rather subtle, because a person's trustworthiness would legitimately lead to questioning what they say. "Tu quoque" means "you too" and is a fallacious argument used in a debating situation to try to undermine the criticism of an opponent, but without actually presenting evidence in one's own defense. Appeal to the popularity of an idea (*ad populum*), to force, and to pity are further examples of arguments that present irrelevant evidence and draw attention away from the issue being debated.

Fallacies of weak induction. Premises may present relevant information without justifying the claim made in the conclusion. A hasty generalization, for example, makes use of either too few cases or unrepresentative cases to make a broad claim. An appeal to ignorance attempts to justify a positive claim by rejecting the evidence on the other side as insufficient. To say, for example, that there is no intelligent life except on Earth, because there is no evidence of such life, is too strong a claim. However, the burden of proof is generally on those who make a positive claim, so it would be legitimate to say that there is no reason to believe in extraterrestrial intelligence. Appeal to authority is also a fallacy of weak induction. Although people constantly rely on information given to them by others, the opinions of experts alone are insufficient to justify a controversial opinion. Experts must have some reasons by which they were convinced of their beliefs and these should be communicated to others.

Fallacies of ambiguity. The fallacy of equivocation describes an argument in which a word is used in two different senses. Such an argument can be thought of as formally invalid, but since only subtle changes of meaning are misleading, this fallacy is considered to be informal. Amphiboly is the name given to an argument that relies on ambiguity, but involving the grammar of the sentence rather than the meaning of an individual word. Composition and division are a pair of fallacies, in which an illicit inference is made from the properties of individuals in a class to the class itself, or from the class to the individuals. No one would be taken in by an argument that the concept "mammal" must be hairy because all mammals are hairy, but arguments that have seemed very compelling to many people may be of the same form. For example, some versions of the argument from design argue that the order and purpose found in every object in the universe implies that the universe as a whole has a purpose and a designer.

Fallacies of presumption. Using the conclusion of the argument as a premise or otherwise assuming what is being claimed in the conclusion is called "begging the question." Circular reasoning appears to be formally valid, since the conclusion really does follow from the premises (*P*, therefore *P*). However, if it is assumed that *P* is controversial and therefore requires some kind of justification, it is clear that a circular argument will not advance the discussion. "That begs the question" is a phrase that is changing its meaning, at least in colloquial usage, to simply mean "that raises the question." This dubious usage loses any connection to the idea of logical fallacy, since the phrase is no longer being used to evaluate an argument. Begging the question is usually classified as an informal fallacy because it relies on tricking the reader into not noticing that the subject of controversy is being assumed.

See also **Logic; Rhetoric.**

BIBLIOGRAPHY

Aristotle. *Aristotle on Fallacies; or, the Sophistici Elenchi.* Translated by Edward Poste. New York: Garland, 1987.

Copi, Irving M. *Introduction to Logic.* New York: Macmillan, 1994.

Fearnside, W. Ward. *Fallacy: The Counterfeit of Argument.* Englewood Cliffs, N.J.: Prentice-Hall, 1959.

Hurley, Patrick J. *A Concise Introduction to Logic.* Belmont, Calif.: Wadsworth, 1997.

David J. Stump

FALSIFIABILITY. Karl Popper (1902–1994) made falsifiability the key to his philosophy of science. It became the most commonly invoked "criterion of demarcation" of science from nonscience.

According to the simple, hypothetico-deductive (H-D) model of scientific inquiry, a law claim, theory, or hypothesis H is falsifiable when a potentially checkable prediction O can be logically deduced from it, that is, when H→O. If O is observed to be true, then H passes this predictive test (although it may fail other tests). If O tests false, then H must also be false, since no true statement can logicaly imply a falsehood. For example, Isaac Newton's (1642–1727) theory of gravitation predicts a slow rotation of the orbit of the planet Mercury different from what astronomers observe. Thus Newton's theory is not only falsifiable (empirically vulnerable) but also actually falsified (shown to be false). Albert Einstein's (1879–1955) general theory of relativity is subject to the same test, so it, too, is falsifiable; but it passes the test. "All life in the universe employs the same genetic coding found on Earth" is falsifiable in principle but not in current practice, since to date (2004) we have identified no examples of extraterrestrial life. By contrast, "The universe is recreated at each instant by a divine being" yields no predictive tests at all, so it is not falsifiable even in principle.

Note that *falsifiable* does not mean "falsified" or "false" any more than *breakable* means "broken." On the simple model, even if, *per impossibile,* an empirical law could be known to be absolutely true in our universe, it would still be falsifiable in the sense that it would be empirically testable and would test false were the world relevantly different. A falsifiable claim rules out some potentially observable situations; and the more it excludes, the greater is its empirical content, that is, the more it claims about the structure of our universe.

Popper's Emphasis on Falsifiability

Falsifiable contrasts with *verifiable*. A claim is empirically verifiable if possible observation statements logically imply the truth of the claim. If actual observation statements do imply the claim, then it is verified. "This raven is black" verifies "There are black ravens." During the 1930s the logical empiricists of the Vienna Circle proposed verifiability both as a criterion of demarcation of science from nonscience and a criterion of meaning. Their idea was that a statement is meaningful if and only if verifiable in principle, and its meaning is given by its method of verification. For the logical empiricists, only empirically verifiable claims make genuine assertions about the world and are, in this broad sense, scientific. All other claims (metaphysical, religious, ethical, etc.) are cognitively meaningless. In his *Logik der Forschung* (1934; *Logic of Scientific Discovery*), Popper replied by rejecting the logical empiricists' concern with language and meaning and by noting that verifiability as a criterion of demarcation excludes scientific law claims and thus the core of science itself. For since a law claim is universal in scope (in simplest form, "All As everywhere and everywhen are Bs"), it cannot possibly be verified: there are always actual or potential instances beyond those so far observed. Yet a universal claim can be falsified by a single negative instance. The first observed black swan refuted the claim "All swans are white." (Law claims of statistical-probabilistic forms are more problematic.) Based on this logical asymmetry of verification and falsification, Popper proposed falsifiability as a criterion of demarcation of science from nonscience, although not as a criterion of meaning. According to Popper, nonscience includes pseudoscience (e.g., Freudian psychology and Marxism) and metaphysics, the one fraudulent, the other sometimes providing a valuable heuristic for science. Many deep scientific problems have their roots in metaphysics, but to be scientific, a claim must take an empirical risk. Moreover, falsifiability, as the ongoing risk of falsification in *our* world, is a permanent status for Popper. No amount of successful testing can establish a hypothesis as absolutely true or even probable: it forever remains conjectural. That all scientific theories remain falsifiable entails fallibilism, the view that our best epistemic efforts remain open to future revision. There can be no certain foundations to knowledge.

Popper's falsifiability doctrine lies at the heart of his empiricist epistemology and scientific methodology of "conjectures and refutations." The latter, he claims, shows how it is possible to learn from experience without induction from the facts. Previously, empiricism had been equated with inductivism. Popper attacked as question-begging the view that we must arrive at our ideas by induction, that is, by first gathering masses of facts and then gradually detecting regular patterns in them—letting nature speak for herself. Rather, said Popper, we first propose a conjecture to solve a problem, then test the conjecture by trying to falsify it. It is the conjecture that tells us which observations are even relevant. Contrary to the inductivists, it does not matter where our ideas come from, only how we test them. There is no logic of discovery, only a logic of testing.

Since law claims can be falsified but not verified, Popper concluded that the way to truth is indirect, by elimination of falsehood. Hence, error, in the sense of faulty hypotheses, is not a bad thing. On the contrary, it is necessary to scientific progress. "We learn from our mistakes." This is Popper's more extreme form of the nineteenth-century idea that science is a fallible but self-correcting enterprise. Since bold hypotheses that yield novel predictions are risky and hence easier to test, Popper urged boldness. He explicitly forbade, as a form of intellectual dishonesty, ad hoc tinkering to save a hypothesis from falsification. Popper spoke of degrees of falsifiability and attempted, with limited success, to measure both simplicity and the empirical content of a claim (how much it says about the world) in terms of its degree of falsifiability.

Complications of the Simple Model

Many scientists, administrators, and the legal community take falsifiability seriously as a criterion of demarcation of science from nonscience. But other scientists and science-studies experts consider falsifiability a heuristic rule of thumb at best, not a rigid requirement. Among the difficulties facing Popper's conception are these: In most scientific research, a hypothesis is tested against a competitor (often the "null hypothesis") rather than in isolation. The test typically discloses the comparative fit of the two hypotheses to the data rather than the outright falsity of one of them. The history of science discloses

many cases in which a claim is not immediately falsifiable by known methods, yet the claim remained important to scientific investigation and later became testable. In the nineteenth century, August Comte (1798–1857) notoriously announced that we could never know which chemical elements were present in the Sun, yet only a few years later new spectrographic techniques revealed this information, including the existence of a hitherto unknown element, dubbed helium. In 1931 Wolfgang Pauli (1900–1958) postulated the existence of the neutrino, a chargeless and presumably massless particle that scarcely interacted with ordinary matter and was hence undetectable by any known means. Yet this turned out to be one of the more fruitful ideas of twentieth-century physics, and various kinds of neutrino are now detectable. By the end of the twentieth century, science-studies disciplines were characterizing science in terms of its practices rather than simply in terms of the logical status of its claims.

Furthermore, Popper himself admitted that absolute logical falsification, and hence absolute falsifiability, are impossible in scientific practice, since the allegedly refuting observations can never be known with certainty. Since observations themselves are not statements and can have no logical relations to statements, Popper held that observation statements (roughly, data) are accepted by convention. Moreover, they are theory-laden; there is no such thing as pure observation. Although Popper never employed falsifiability as a criterion of meaningfulness, attempting to formulate the falsifiability requirement with logical precision runs afoul of the same sorts of difficulties faced by the logical empiricists with their verifiability theory of meaning.

A specific difficulty, raised already by Pierre Duhem (1861–1916) and extended by Willard Van Orman Quine (1908–2000), is that, in isolation, universal claims yield no specific predictions. By itself, the hypothesis H, "All As are Bs," implies no testable prediction, not only because of its logical form but also because A and B will be typically abstract, theoretical terms. To generate predictions from hypothesis H, we must conjoin H with one or more auxiliary premises, $A_1, \ldots, A_n$. So the simple H-D model of the testing situation must be replaced by a more complex logical model: $(H \& A_1 \& \ldots \& A_n) \rightarrow O$, where "&" means the logical "and." If prediction O is false, logic now tells us that at least one of the conjoined premises was mistaken, but not which one(s). Logic permits us to blame the failure on an auxiliary assumption rather than on H. In his influential article "Two Dogmas of Empiricism," Quine parlayed the Duhem problem into a controversial argument for holism: "our statements about the external world face the tribunal of sense experience not individually but only as a corporate body." We do not test scientific claims individually against nature but instead adjust our entire "web of belief" to fit our experience. Critics reply that deductive logic does not exhaust the distinctions licensed by scientific practice. Quineans forget that experiments are *designed* to test specific components of a theory or model, that an experiment designed to test H will rarely test the auxiliary assumptions as well (Sober). Furthermore, the relation of observation to theory is typically more complex than even the Duhem model, which remains deductive rather than probabilistic. Typically, several levels of data processing and theoretical modeling occur between theory and observation.

Thomas Kuhn (1922–1996), a leading opponent of H-D models of science, famously argued that Popper's falsificationist methodology fails to fit the history of physical science. In *The Structure of Scientific Revolutions* (1962), Kuhn advanced an alternative conception of physical science, according to which normal scientific work is highly constrained by "paradigms," the central tenets of which are immune from serious criticism and competition and hence unfalsifiable in practice. Only when a paradigm breaks down do we find the kind of critical and revolutionary ferment that Popper advocated for all scientific work. Moreover, much of normal science consists of tinkering of just the sort that the Popperians considered ad hoc. Subsequently, Popper's former student Imre Lakatos distinguished several kinds of falsificationist methodology, from simple to sophisticated. Attempting a compromise between Popper and Kuhn, he analyzed science in terms of competing research programs involving entire series of not-always-successful theories rather than individual theories in isolation. Predictive failure does not directly and immediately falsify a research program.

Finally, Larry Laudan deplores the ritual invocation of Popper's "toothless" falsifiability criterion in legal proceedings (such as the 1981–1982 creationism trial, *McLean v. Arkansas*) to distinguish good science from pseudoscience. Traditionally, the term *science* demarcated a body of established truths or scientifically warranted assertions, whereas falsifiability requires only empirical testability. For example, so-called Creation Science is false and hence falsifiable. By Popper's standard it is scientific—and so is the statement that the Earth is flat! A useful concept for certain purposes, falsifiability, by itself, fails as the hallmark of good science sought by the legal and political community.

See also **Empiricism; Paradigm; Positivism; Science; Science, History of.**

BIBLIOGRAPHY

Cartwright, Nancy. *The Dappled World: A Study of the Boundaries of Science.* Cambridge, U.K.: Cambridge University Press, 1999.

Lakatos, Imre, and Alan Musgrave, eds. *Criticism and the Growth of Knowledge.* Cambridge, U.K.: Cambridge University Press, 1970.

Laudan, Larry. *Beyond Positivism and Relativism: Theory, Method, and Evidence.* Boulder, Colo.: Westview, 1996.

Popper, Karl. *Conjectures and Refutations: The Growth of Scientific Knowledge.* New York: Basic Books, 1962.

———. *The Logic of Scientific Discovery.* New York: Basic Books, 1959. Popper's expanded translation of his *Logik der Forschung,* 1934.

Quine, Willard Van Orman. "Two Dogmas of Empiricism." Reprinted in his *From a Logical Point of View: Logico-Philosophical Essays.* Cambridge, Mass.: Harvard University Press, 1953, pp. 20–46.

Sober, Elliott. "Testability." *Proceedings and Addresses of the American Philosophical Association* 73 (1999): 47–76.

Worrall, John. "Falsification, Rationality, and the Duhem Problem." In *Philosophical Problems of the Internal and External Worlds,* edited by John Earman et al., 329–370. Pittsburgh: University of Pittsburgh Press, 1993.

Thomas Nickles

FAMILY.

This entry includes two subentries:

Modernist Anthropological Theory
Family in Anthropology since 1980

MODERNIST ANTHROPOLOGICAL THEORY

Although anthropology has devoted a great deal of attention to families, anthropologists do not generally speak of studying the *family,* a word whose meaning varies so much throughout history and around the world that it may be said to have no objective or transcultural meaning whatsoever. Many of the families that anthropologists and historians study bear little resemblance to the nuclear family portrayed in American mass culture. There are the enormous, rigidly hierarchicalized patrilineal families of pre-revolutionary China, which bound together ranked sets of wives, sons, and servants under the control of a senior male; the gender-segregated villages of twentieth-century Amazonian South America, where men might well consider "home" to be the central men's house where they live for years at a time, rather than the smaller residences occupied by their wives, children, and dogs; the "bands" of foraging societies like the Ju/'hoansi (ZHUN-twasi) of southern Africa, with their flexible membership and fluid boundaries; or the "houses" of some gay prostitutes in the urban United States, where senior transvestites rename themselves "Mother" and take in younger boys off the streets, offering them a new kind of family to replace the biological kin who disowned them. Furthermore, this confounding word, *family,* is made even more slippery by the great burden of quite specific emotional, symbolic, and pragmatic meanings with which people invest it: it is the opposite of a value-neutral descriptive term.

In their efforts to bring some analytical rigor to the study of this confusing but important concept, anthropologists have come to speak not of "the family" but of "kinship," a larger, more inclusive category that can refer to any and all of the ways in which we find or forge relationships between ourselves and others, although it is usually confined to those relationships that are at least metaphorically connected to coresidence and/or reproduction. The study of kinship was long a mainstay of anthropology, and dominated the field during the heyday of modernist anthropology; indeed, so central is it to the discipline's identity that the decline of interest in kinship studies during the latter decades of the twentieth century was seen by many as an indication that anthropology itself was about to disappear. By the same token, the emergence of a revitalized but vastly changed form of kinship studies at century's end seemed to indicate that anthropology, too, would continue to reinvent itself to fit the changing circumstances of the twenty-first century.

The history of kinship studies is a contentious one, filled with lively debates and sudden changes in direction that make distinguishing three clearly distinguishable phases relatively easy, although some underlying intellectual trends do not conform to these neat temporal divisions. Broadly speaking, there was an early phase dominated by evolutionary theories; an early-to mid-twentieth-century period of modernist anthropology—the true heyday of kinship studies; and a final, heterogeneous period of change and reformulation, spurred first by feminist and later by gay and lesbian anthropology, as well as by intellectual movements that refocused attention away from underlying structures and toward the practices of everyday life, and the interplay of biology, technology, and society. The focus here is primarily on the first two of these phases, but the emphasis is on those aspects of early kinship studies that are most relevant to contemporary anthropological thought about the family.

The Family in Early Social Evolutionary Theory

The origins of the academic discipline of anthropology—and of the study of kinship—can be found in the writings of nineteenth-century European and European-American intellectuals, men who constructed grand comparative schemes designed to clarify the relationship between their own societies and those of the colonized peoples of Africa, Asia, and the Americas, a relationship that most of these scholars understood as intrinsically hierarchical, with Western Europe representing the pinnacle of human cultural achievement and racial superiority. A countervailing strain of romantic primitivism within this same intellectual tradition found in simpler societies a purity later contaminated by modernity, but even these more favorable interpretations of what were imagined to be our "primitive" forebears did not challenge the notion that all human societies, and all of human history, could be placed within a single evolutionary framework. These writers too often melded an entirely hypothetical history of early human life—and of the family—with anecdotal evidence from contemporary societies deemed to be primitive, or not yet fully "evolved," creating a matrix in which geographical distance from Western metropolitan life was equated with temporal distance from modernity.

Twentieth-century social scientists would reject such speculative histories, and later anticolonialist writers would excoriate the scientific racism that undergirded their construction. Nevertheless, the quest for a single human history, and for an overarching theory that explained the coexistence at a single moment in time of societies that differed enormously in their scale and organization, inspired much of the foundational thinking of twentieth-century social science, including that of Karl Marx (1818–1883), Sigmund Freud (1856–1939), Émile Durkheim (1858–1917), and Max Weber (1864–1920). And while most of the social sciences and humanities have rejected these evolutionary schemas, they retain a fascination outside of academia, where notions of primitive matriarchies and shamanic tribal religions continue to have romantic appeal. Within academia, too, hypothetical early histories of the family continue to find a place among evolutionary psychologists, who find evidence of long-vanished primitive sexual and reproductive customs in the foibles of contemporary urban-dwellers.

In the nineteenth century, along with the evolution of religious thought from animism to polytheism to monotheism, the purported evolution of the family was a central theme for intellectuals interested in social history, who typically proposed a tripartite development of family life from an earliest phase, that of the promiscuous horde, through matriarchy to patriarchy. Perhaps best exemplified in the Swiss scholar J. J. Bachofen's

(1815–1887) *Das Mutterrecht* (1861; Mother Right), this narrative imagines humans beginning their social existence with a sexual life barely distinct from bestiality, in which an undifferentiated group mated indiscriminately, producing children without distinct social identities. Women, finding this form of life abhorrent, then initiated a social revolution, in which they introduced religious worship and the family, the latter centered on the bond between a mother and her children. This was, however, an incomplete revolution, with human potential still to be finally realized by a second transformation, led by men, in which matriarchy was converted to patriarchy, primitive earth religions to monotheism, and the role of motherhood and of the family confined to an interior, domestic life, while the larger social sphere became the world of politics and, ultimately, of the state, understood to be the domain of men.

Bachofen's writings were very influential at the time, but the writer whose work would endure into the twentieth century was the American lawyer Lewis Henry Morgan (1818–1881); the sharply bifurcated history of Morgan's influence on later scholars exemplifies a fundamental conflict in kinship studies between historical materialism and structural functionalism. Morgan's master narrative of social evolution, *Ancient Society* (1877), with its detailed framework of evolutionary stages extending from "savagery" through "barbarism" to "civilization," was clearly his most significant contribution to nineteenth-century intellectual life. Two significant attributes of this work are its materialist orientation, in which basic technological and economic developments such as fishing or farming were seen as causal factors that determined the shape of social life, and an underlying moral interpretation of human history that was far more ambivalent about progress and civilization than most of his social-evolutionary peers.

This combination of a materialist slant and a critical stance toward contemporary capitalist society made Morgan's work an inspiration to two German intellectuals, Karl Marx and Friedrich Engels (1820–1895). After Marx's death, Engels found among his papers detailed notes on *Ancient Society,* and used them to write his own tome on world history, *The Origin of the Family, Private Property and the State* (1884). This book, although it follows the same sort of evolutionary scheme as many others, and despite its clear debt to Morgan, differs radically from its sources in its insistence that the evolution of the family can best be seen as the development of an institution dedicated to the oppression of women. Its other enduring contribution is its clear articulation of an idea also found in Bachofen and Morgan: that far from being a universal, unchanging institution that predates the development of complex social structures such as capitalism or the state, the family is a structure that takes radically different forms within different political economies or modes of production. Recapitulating the stages of evolution described by Morgan, Engels emphasizes the fundamental differences between "barbaric" social forms such as the ancient Roman family—a structure of domination rooted in a slave-holding economy, in which the paterfamilias exerted absolute control over slaves, wives, and children—and "civilized" nineteenth-century forms of marriage as found among the bourgeoisie, for whom the management of assets mattered intensely, and among the proletariat, whose lack of inheritable property freed women and men to marry for love. In each case, the fundamental economic organization of the class or society in question determined not only the shape of the family itself, but individual access to such fundamental human rights as control over sexual access or the right to have children.

Although Engels's evolutionary scheme would remain central to the development of anthropology within the Soviet Union and would, in turn, influence Third World scholars within the Soviet sphere, intellectual history in Western Europe and the United States soon took a new turn that sidelined Engels's insights, and evolutionary social theory in general, for several decades. Within the newly emergent paradigm of what would later be called modernist anthropology, Morgan would still have an important role to play as a founding figure in the study of kinship, but only through a sharply limited and partial reading of his work designed to excise all that Marx had found most stimulating about it.

The Modernist Study of Kinship

Twentieth-century anthropology was founded on a total rejection of what had come before. Instead of pseudohistory and pseudoscience, this new social science would be based on a rigorous empiricism that would examine social groups as they are, in the present, with an emphasis on the functionality of existing social structures and institutions. Taking as a basic premise that all living humans share the same intellectual and moral capacities, scholars such as Franz Boas (1858–1942) in America, or E. E. Evans-Pritchard (1902–1973) in England, regarded all human cultural laws as based on rational principles, regardless of the race of a society's members, the alien nature of their customs, or the simplicity of their material culture. The evolutionary thinking of the past was declared anathema, but an exception was made for Lewis Henry Morgan because in his work was to be found the germ of the new scientific study of kinship. Morgan, an American, differed from his European contemporaries in one important respect: as a young man in upstate New York, he had done actual empirical research among the Seneca, one of the Iroquois nations, with the assistance of an astute Iroquois intellectual named Ely Parker (1828–1895). If Morgan's *Ancient Society* was now to be consigned to the dustbin, his publications on Iroquois kinship terminology—the first to accurately record the kinship nomenclature found within a unilineal descent system—became the subject of exhaustive study. This new approach to reading Morgan, with its emphasis on the elucidation of principles of descent through a close analysis of the language of kinship terms and relations, exemplified the modernist theory of culture, which envisioned the latter as a complex system of rules and rites. Although field-workers would collect a great deal of evidence about everyday work practices in the ensuing decades, this evidence would be valued primarily for what it could reveal about underlying structures and principles, which were taken to be the real focus and goal of ethnographic research. And for all its liberal championing of human equality and of non-European cultures, a fundamental conservatism would drive this new anthropology. Engels's emphasis on the family as an institution that could support multiple inequities, from the oppression of women to the sexual abuse of slaves, would completely vanish, replaced by a Durkheimian emphasis on social cohesiveness and the stability of institutions. The study of everyday practice, of social inequality, and of the deployment of power would have to wait for a different era.

These new structural-functionalist anthropologists, as they came to be called, were still deeply interested in comparative ethnology, but now, instead of an evolutionary paradigm, unprejudiced comparisons would be made based on the discovery of similar structural patterns between different societies. In the small-scale, non-Western, and premodern societies that were the focus of much anthropological work, economic, political, and religious life was organized among kin, so that these underlying structural principles were especially to be found through study of the rules of kinship.

Reading the work of the structural-functionalists in the early twenty-first century, a curious dichotomy emerges. On the one hand, this intellectual paradigm freed scholars to study non-Western societies with as few presuppositions as possible, and stimulated an enormous amount of excellent research on native peoples throughout the world. Once-obscure places and peoples—the Andaman Islands, the Trobriands, the Nuer, the Azande—were made famous in anthropological circles. The rules of non-Western kinship became ever clearer, as did the fact that, while other peoples did not share Western assumptions about family and society, every society had social rules that provided systems of etiquette, standards of morality, and a way to ensure continuity over time. Anthropologists elucidated three key structural elements that constituted any given kinship system: descent, residence, and marriage. Descent systems included unilineal structures, such as patriliny and matriliny, and bilateral systems like those in most of the United States. Residence might be uxorilocal (meaning that the new family lives in the wife's family's home), virilocal (the family lives in the husband's family's home), or neolocal (the couple moves to their own home). Marriage might be monogamous or polygamous. Some of the findings challenged Western ideas more than others. E. E. Evans-Pritchard, in his study of the North African Nuer, found that a vast network of segmentary lineages could take the place of the state, allowing thousands of people to live together without an overarching centralized political authority. Bronislaw Malinowski (1884–1942), like Morgan before him, studied a matrilineal people, for whom the role of the father was far different, and much less important, than in European society. Instead, it was the mother's brother, the adult male who came from the mother's lineage, who represented authority, discipline, and an ideal of adulthood for young males, a fact that led Malinowski to challenge Freud's ideas about the Oedipus complex. Pointing out that young men within matrilineal societies channel their hostility toward their mother's brothers, rather than their own fathers, he posited that competition over the right to claim political authority, rather than sexual tension, underlies the resentment that growing boys feel toward adult men within their family circle. This use of the cross-cultural record to challenge assumptions about human universals would become the hallmark of twentieth-century anthropology, as seen in the later arguments of Margaret Mead (1901–1978) about adolescence.

But if structural-functionalists were engaged in documenting the diversity of forms of family to be found in global societies, at the same time they oddly insisted on the supposed universality of a certain basic family form, hidden within the apparent diversity of polygyny and polyandry, lineage and clan, band and tribe. Whether these (mostly) male scholars were motivated to insist on the universality of women's status as wife and mother by a desire to oppose feminist movements within their own society would later become the subject of some debate, as would, more recently, the question of whether they also suppressed or downplayed evidence of homosexuality in other societies. What is clear is that the claim of a biologically determined basic family structure was critically important for the modernist anthropologists as a refutation of the evolutionists' claim that the human family had not always been the same, and it is difficult, given the intellectual climate of the Cold War, not to see a certain political utility in this hostility toward a body of theory so closely associated with Marxist intellectual history.

A. R. Radcliffe-Brown (1881–1955), a founding father of functionalist kinship studies, saw an unchanging natural "substratum" beneath the whole edifice of social structure, which he called the "elementary family." In 1969 Meyer Fortes began an important lecture in honor of Morgan with an oblique reminder that the "momentous importance" of the scientific study of kinship lies in its special insight into the basis of human social life. The implication was made explicit in 1973 when John Barnes in turn introduced a tribute to Meyer Fortes by flatly stating that kinship is the aspect of human culture with the closest links to the natural world. All of these statements spring from an underlying assumption that the structures of kinship and culture are built on a natural foundation: the biological link of physiological reproduction that connects mother and child. As Malinowski stated, in the domain of kinship, above all others, physiology creates purely cultural institutions.

Malinowski placed greater emphasis on the biological underpinnings of culture than his peers, for whom the elementary or natural family, because of its ahistorical, essential nature, was unimportant. What really mattered, because it was the locus of cultural creativity, was what Meyer Fortes called the "jural dimension" (1969): the social edifice constructed on this natural base. Underlying this distinction is a theory of procreation—and of gender—succinctly summarized in John Barnes's (1973) equation "'genetrix:genitor::nature:culture.'" Roger Keesing elaborates:

> Humans everywhere observe the same processes of sex and reproduction. A female has sexual intercourse. . . . Once she is pregnant, it is ultimately obvious that she is, and that the infant is connected to her by the most physical of bonds—by the umbilical cord, by childbirth, by the milk of her breasts. But the connection of the one or several men who had intercourse with the mother . . . to the process of pregnancy and childbirth is far from obvious . . . [creating] a gulf between 'social' and 'physical' kinship, or between pater [the legitimate social father] and genitor [the presumed physical begetter of the child]. (1975, pp. 11–12)

The diversity of kinship forms that anthropology celebrated, then, with the implication that humans are free to invent their own societies as they will, is here invested with a strict gender segregation: while creativity and historicity are granted to males, females remain rooted in a biological reality that precludes them from becoming fully cultural actors or agents of history. Men may invent many forms of social fatherhood, as Malinowski had documented, but women must always be simply mothers. That the actual data gathered by these anthropologists contained ample evidence to contradict this assertion, such as the multiple cases in which people insisted on calling other women "mother" within their kinship network, such as their mother's sisters or father's or brother's wives, and the prevalence of socially constructed forms of motherhood completely divorced from biological reproduction, such as the "Mother Superior" of a convent, did not seem to matter.

With the rise of feminist anthropology in the 1970s, these assumptions would come under rigorous scrutiny and produce vigorous debates. A precursor to these events was the turn that kinship studies took toward a still greater emphasis on the symbolic realm, and even further away from Malinowski's emphasis on the family's role in fulfilling basic physiological needs. The two figures most prominently associated with this move are the great French philosopher–anthropologist Claude Lévi-Strauss (b. 1908), and the American cultural anthropologist David Schneider (1918–1995). While their work did not directly address questions of gender—and Lévi-Strauss, in particular, was seen by many later anthropologists to be antifeminist—it is in their writings that feminist scholars would find the inspiration for a new form of kinship studies in which the agency of women, both as mothers and on their own terms, would be front and center.

Lévi-Strauss's *Les structures élémentaires de la parenté* (1967; *The Elementary Structures of Kinship,* 1969), the great masterpiece of modernist kinship studies, rests on the insights of previous scholars from Durkheim to Radcliffe-Brown. Durkheim had early recognized the significance of the incest taboo as a foundational law that created the social fabric by forcing people out of their natal families and into alliances with other groups. Radcliffe-Brown had emphasized the social-structural and juridical aspects of marriage, such as the exchanges of gifts between kinspeople in Africa, which served to sever women from their natal kin and bind them to their husband's family, and he had insisted that kinship "results from the recognition of a social relationship between parents and children, which is not the same thing as the physical relation, and may or may not coincide with it" (1967, p. 4), and that the primary purpose of the institution of marriage was as a "social arrangement by which a child is given a legitimate position in the society" (p. 5). In other words, it organized descent more than it facilitated union. Lévi-Strauss took these themes and built from them a single Hegelian (Georg Wilhelm Friedrich Hegel [1770–1831]) principle of social organization in which the opposition between descent and alliance is continually forced, through the operation of the incest taboo, to create new, synthetic social units. Consanguinity (social relationships based in the parent–child link) and affinity (social relationships based in marriage, such as between husband and wife, or son-in-law and father-in-law) thus joins the set of great, foundational oppositions out of which each human society then constructs its own unique cultural pattern, along with life and death, youth and age, masculinity and femininity. Like Radcliffe-Brown, he saw marriage, not from the point of view of the actual spouses, but as a system of exchange between descent groups compelled by the incest taboo to give away some of their kin to other groups in order to gain spouses and, thereby, children. This emphasis on exchange—of persons, and of the flow of gifts that surrounds this central transfer—is a direct outgrowth of the Durkheimian tradition, and especially of Marcel Mauss's (1872–1950) *The Gift.* And, like Radcliffe-Brown, Lévi-Strauss envisioned this exchange not in gender-neutral terms, but specifically as an exchange of women by men.

Where Lévi-Strauss departs from previous authors is in his more direct engagement with the question of what is natural and what is cultural, and his insistence that this contrast is itself part of culture: the very idea of nature, he argued, is itself "an artificial creation of culture" (1969, p. xxix). Similarly, he states in the book's conclusions that, while kinship reshapes "biological relationships and natural sentiments," it is ultimately a completely social product; it is, in fact, "the social state itself" (1969, p. 490). The text is contradictory on this point: he is sometimes even more explicit than previous modernist anthropologists in defining consanguinity and descent as produced by, and symbolic of, physical reproduction and, thus, as something that appears to be part of the natural sphere, in contrast to the purely social structure of alliances between kin groups created through the exchange of women. Unlike his predecessors, however, he insists that the incest taboo does not derive from natural law, but is a purely cultural invention, and is, in fact, the prototypical form of all cultural rules. Similarly, his understanding of the position of women within the system is more nuanced than that of his predecessors: while he assumes the existence of an apparently universal patriarchal ideology, implicit in symbol and language, that posits women as objects rather than subjects, he nevertheless famously asserted that, whatever meaning may be given to "women in general" within a particular symbolic system, each woman is always, in actual fact, "a person . . . a generator of signs . . . never purely what is spoken about," but also one who speaks (1969, p. xx).

In the twenty-first century, it is difficult to remember how deeply and widely influential Lévi-Strauss was in Europe and the United States, both inside anthropology and beyond. His work on kinship spurred a wide range of new research, and his compelling, but ambiguous, arguments about nature, culture, and gender stimulated tremendous debate within the emerging field of feminist anthropology. The path-breaking text, *Woman, Culture, and Society* (1974, Rosaldo and Lamphere), contained two influential articles that, in very different ways, engaged his arguments. One was Sherry Ortner's "Is Female to Male as Nature is to Culture?," in which she used Simone de Beauvoir's reading of Lévi-Strauss to assert that women's reproductive lives condemned them to be seen forever as closer to nature than men. In response, Carol P. MacCormack and Marilyn Strathern produced an edited volume of their own, *Nature, Gender, and Culture* (1980), in which each

author used Lévi-Straussian analysis to demonstrate the quite distinct workings of the nature:culture and female:male oppositions within various cultural settings. Their goal was both to disprove Ortner and to reclaim structural analysis for feminist ends. Strathern would go on to produce a dazzling series of influential analyses of kinship and gender in which traditional modernist anthropology and feminist theory are brought to bear on one another, culminating in a series of publications about postmodern Britain in which she uses the example of new reproductive technologies and their rearrangement of conventional categories of kinship to argue that the nature:culture dichotomy has finally disappeared, and with it the modernist era in which Lévi-Strauss was so dominant a figure.

David Schneider, while couching his argument in less lofty philosophical terms than Lévi-Strauss, would eventually take an even stronger position against biologistic interpretations of kinship. More so than other authors, he would provide inspiration to an entire generation of feminist anthropologists, many of them his students, to reinvent kinship studies yet again. Schneider attacked the biological assumptions that underlay conventional kinship studies directly, arguing forcefully that they derived from the folk beliefs of European-American kinship itself, rather than from any scientific basis, and that the rules of kinship, like those of culture itself, should be seen as a purely symbolic system in which any aspect of the natural world or physiological processes could become centrally meaningful. The great importance that kinship theorists had placed on the biological links between a birth mother and her child, and their insistence that these were of a different order than other kinds of relationships, had more to do with the culturally specific beliefs from the anthropologists' own culture, such as "blood being thicker than water," than with the structures of meaning they found within other societies.

One trajectory in kinship studies in the modernist period, then, was away from biologistic and toward increasingly symbolic analyses of the underlying rules that govern descent and alliance. In these discussions, the dichotomy between nature and culture, and debates about gender, became ever more salient. Feminists saw—and were quick to condemn—clear continuities between the assumptions about the opposition between the "elementary" family and the larger social world, and Bachofen's earlier notion that progress was achieved when women were confined to the domestic sphere, safely under men's control. Discussion of the opposition between public and private spheres, and whether this existed within all societies, thus also became part of the debate over the nature of the family, and the role of women within it. This particular argument, like early feminist social science in general, was also influenced by another important trend in American academia during the latter part of the twentieth century: the reemergence of Marx and Engels.

Marxism reentered American anthropology from a number of directions outside of kinship studies: the growing politicization of American society in the wake of the Vietnam war, and a renewed interest in evolutionary theory, now linked to the newly emerging field of ecological anthropology and to intellectual developments within archaeology. Once the door was open, younger, mostly women anthropologists began reading Engels, and found there the focus on inequality and the oppression of women that they found missing in twentieth-century anthropology. Eleanor Leacock, Karen Sacks, and Richard Lee are among the many American scholars who reintroduced Engels's assumption that the form of the family, even at its most fundamental level, differs radically from society to society. An especially lively debate arose over whether, or to what degree, women had greater equality within the small-scale, egalitarian societies of foragers where "family" and "society" were coterminous, rather than separated into public and private domains. Another productive area of research was whether, as Engels had posited, the rise of the state coincided with a loss in female autonomy and power. A third, more theoretical question dealt with the relationship between production and reproduction.

One of the most stimulating sets of ideas was introduced by Gayle Rubin in her essay on "The Traffic in Women," which also appeared in *Woman, Culture, and Society,* and which brought together Lévi-Strauss and Marx in a single, breathtaking argument. Bringing Marxian questions about inequality and feminist interests in gender and sexuality to bear on conventional kinship studies, she extended the notion of the incest taboo into the very creation of gender itself, which she named "the taboo against sameness." As Lévi-Strauss had done with the incest taboo and with the idea of nature itself, Rubin assumed that the difference between women and men was itself a product of culture, rather than nature, despite its apparent naturalness. This argument presaged the later development of gay and lesbian anthropology and of queer theory, fields in which Rubin would continue to play an important role.

As the end of the twentieth century approached, modernist anthropology began to lose its appeal, and with it the study of kinship as conventionally defined. Marx and Lévi-Strauss, key intellectual figures in the 1970s and 1980s, began to fade from view, replaced in the 1990s by Pierre-Félix Bourdieu (1930–2002), Michel Foucault (1926–1984), and Judith Butler (b. 1956), as structuralism was replaced by a poststructuralist and postmodernist emphasis on the practices of everyday life, and analyses of inequality by a diffuse notion of power. With the publication of his private diaries, with their controversial racial language, Malinowski would become the object of scornful critique by writers who wished to "decolonize" anthropology, just as the modernist anthropologists had rejected nineteenth-century evolutionism. In general, many of the classics of British and American structural-functionalism would cease to be much read by younger anthropologists. Conventional kinship studies, with their emphasis on rules, structures, and terminology, their avoidance of questions about power relations within the family, and their insistence on an "elementary" set of essential, biologically determined relations at the heart of every kinship system, would become a thing of the past. But new questions—about the reshaping of kinship by new reproductive technologies; about the relationship between biological and social reproduction; and above all, about gender and sexuality—would bring younger anthropologists back to the study of the family, and would also find them bringing to

bear some of the same techniques and theoretical insights utilized by the modernist and even the evolutionary anthropologists of the past.

See also **Anthropology; Equality: Gender Equality; Gender; Gender Studies: Anthropology; Kinship; Marriage and Fertility, European Views; Matriarchy; Motherhood and Maternity; Property; Sexuality; Society; Work.**

BIBLIOGRAPHY

Carsten, Janet. *Cultures of Relatedness.* New York: Cambridge University Press, 2000.

Goody, Jack. *The Development of the Family and Marriage in Europe.* Cambridge, U.K.: Cambridge University Press, 1983.

Fortes, Meyer. *The Web of Kinship among the Tallensi.* London: Oxford University Press, 1949.

———, ed. *Marriage in Tribal Societies.* Cambridge, U.K.: Cambridge University Press, 1962.

Fortes, Meyer, and E. E. Evans-Pritchard, eds. *African Political Systems.* London: Oxford University Press, 1940.

Keesing, Roger M. *Kin Groups and Social Structure.* New York: Holt, Rinehart and Winston, 1975.

Lévi-Strauss, Claude. *The Elementary Structures of Kinship.* Translated from the French by James Harle Bell, John Richard von Sturmer, and Rodney Needham, editor. Boston: Beacon Press, 1969.

MacCormack, Carol, and Marilyn Strathern, eds. *Nature, Culture, and Gender.* Cambridge, U.K.: Cambridge University Press, 1980.

Morgan, Lewis Henry. *Systems of Consanguinity and Affinity of the Human Family.* Washington, D.C.: Smithsonian Institution, 1870.

Parkin, Robert, and Linda Stone. *Kinship and Family: An Anthropological Reader.* Malden, Mass.: Blackwell, 2004.

Rosaldo, Michelle, and Louise Lamphere, eds. *Woman, Culture, and Society.* Stanford, CA: Stanford University Press, 1974.

Schneider, David. *American Kinship: A Cultural Account.* Englewood Cliffs, N.J.: Prentice-Hall, 1968.

———. *A Critique of the Study of Kinship.* Ann Arbor: University of Michigan Press, 1984.

Weston, Kath. *Families We Choose: Lesbians, Gays, Kinship.* New York: Columbia University Press, 1991.

Mary J. Weismantel

FAMILY IN ANTHROPOLOGY SINCE 1980

Until the last decades of the twentieth century, anthropological definitions of the family were heavily influenced by largely unexamined Western cultural assumptions about biology and its relationship to kinship. Indeed, disentangling the history of family studies from kinship studies in anthropology is very difficult because, among researchers, kinship early on became the basis for understanding family. In an effort to make cross-cultural comparisons meaningful, anthropologists concerned themselves with attempting to find a universal definition of the "family"—one that could be used across time and place. Family was distinguished from household, with "family" most often defined as a group composed of individuals who share some genetic connection—expressed most obviously in the nurturing of children—and having jural rights to property, especially land. In practice, the first part of this definition resulted in a tendency for researchers to place women at the emotional and reproductive centers of the family, while the second part served to place men, through whom inheritance usually occurred, in the jural and productive center. "Household" referred to individuals sharing residential space, domestic resources, and usually productive tasks but who may not share a genetic connection. It was argued that households were distinct from families but sociologically important because households reflect the structural linkages between kinship reckoning and social groups. However, it is in the family (not the household) where the necessary reproductive activities of childbearing and child rearing take place, and it was "the family" that was frequently imbued with certain affective or emotional orientations. At its extreme, the core unit of a family was defined by Ward Goodenough as primarily composed of a mother and her children but as potentially including others who are vaguely defined as "functionally significant" (Yanagisako, p. 164).

The late 1970s marked a turning point in anthropology for studies of the family. Invigorated by new ideas from both within and outside the academy, this was a time when old, embedded assumptions about the universality of the family and its sociological purposes were debated and ultimately discarded. Especially in American anthropology, the new approaches to the study of the family were influenced by two intersecting currents. First, some scholars were concerned with contributing to the debates about the possible social changes to the family brought about by the American feminist movement. At the time there was much public discussion about the potential dangers of the inevitable decline of the "American family," which opponents of the feminist movement claimed would necessarily accompany changes in women's social roles. Using cross-cultural evidence, feminist anthropologists such as Jane Collier, Michelle Rosaldo, and Sylvia Yanagisako sought to expose the unsupported assumptions that guided popular and academic discourses concerning the "ideal" composition and configuration of the family. The second intellectual influence was a discipline-wide shift in the orientation of social theory writ large. Anthropologists were moving away from the almost century-long pursuit of identifying "types" and defining human universals—necessarily etic categories—toward more nuanced analyses of cultural meanings and their relationships to particular social forms and processes.

New Directions for Family Studies

By far the most important anthropological work concerning the family to emerge in the 1970s was Yanagisako's comprehensive article "Family and Household: The Analysis of Domestic Groups" (1979). This review of almost a century of anthropological work exposed the problematic assumptions that guided studies on the family, and it set an agenda for further study. It is important to understand Yanagisako's critiques in detail as they were central in establishing theoretical approaches to the family for the next twenty years. Yanagisako grouped previous studies into two types: those concerned with identifying similarities in cross-cultural family types and household formation; and those that took a more developmental perspective focused on the evolution of particular family types over time. She found both types of studies lacking.

Yanagisako critiqued family studies that sought to identify cross-cultural universals on several fronts. First, she argued against static definitions of the family. In particular she posited that definitions that focused on the genealogical composition of a family, and especially those that reduced it to the mother-child "core," did not reflect reality but rather the Western intellectual tendency to draw unsupported parallels between the biological/natural world and the sociological. While the mother-child dyad is clearly essential for biological reproduction, cross-cultural evidence indicates that it is not the only possibility for social reproduction. Similar biological constraints do not necessarily create similar ideological or moral orientations. Not only did it become apparent that mothers do not have the same role in child rearing across cultures, but it was also clear that the nurturing of children is not done exclusively by mothers. Hence the mother-child core of the family is revealed to be only an idealized Western construct, not an ethnographic truth. Indeed, the concern for debunking the tenacious idea about the universal nature of mothering continued to be explored throughout the 1980s by scholars working in multiple disciplines. Anthropological critiques were influenced by feminist scholars outside of anthropology including Sara Ruddick and Nancy Chodorow, who refuted assumptions about the "natural" and immutable qualities of maternal love and attachment and, by extension, the universal significance of a mother's role in the family.

Second, Yanagisako argued that many family studies placed too much emphasis on categorizing families into immutable types such as nuclear, joint extended, and so on. These types were determined by examining the intersection of geneological connections and residence patterns. In addition to limiting the possibilities for family configuration to etically generated categories, this practice serves to obscure meaningful differences that may be inherent within typologies. Families that look the same structurally (joint extended, for example) may in fact behave very differently in practice, and those differences may be extremely important. Unfortunately, differences become obscured under the weight of homogenizing stereotypes about how families of any given configuration should ideally function.

The effort to categorize families into types also contributed to the second group of studies that Yanagisako critiqued, the ones oriented toward understanding the development of particular types. In particular she argued that identifying a limited range of family forms serves to reinforce (increasingly) questionable ideas about cultural evolution. The logic of the evolutionary argument is as follows. If family "types" could be shown to have consistent associations with particular subsistence strategies—the nuclear family with industrialization, the joint extended with agriculture, and so on—then family formation could be seen as an adaptation to subsistence. Hence the direction of change in family forms could even be predicted over time.

However, as Yanagisako pointed out, the problems with these studies are numerous. First, the family as a social institution, and individuals as members of them, become divested of all agency and dynamism in this model. Possibilities for both inter- and intrafamilial differences disappear. Second, the relationships between families and larger social structures and forms becomes mechanistic and unidirectional—as subsistence forms change, families will necessarily change in particular and predictable ways. Nuclear families "naturally" evolve to meet the needs of industrial capitalism, and so forth (for a critique of this idea, see Moore). Obviously this type of thinking leaves the door open for the labeling of some family "types" as abnormal when they do not mirror the established, adaptive norm. For example, as Carol Stack describes, the black, matrifocal family in America was often portrayed as deviant because it differed from the nuclear family norm. Stack, however, never fully moves away from an adaptive framework as she argues in *All Our Kin* (1974) that the matrifocal family is an adaptation to American poverty.

Finally, the focus on families as self-contained units operating in particular ecological settings denies the connections and relationships that all families have with larger social institutions and formations, including the state. Indeed, both the reification of the mother-child core bond and the focus on households as self-contained economic units serves to reinforce the mistaken notion that the domestic or private realms (in other words, families and households) exist outside of and independent from the public sphere.

In an attempt to set out an agenda for new studies of the family, Yanagisako urged researchers to move away from trying to delineate forms (and universal definitions) toward an analysis that is sensitive to the myriad activities and diverse meanings created within and by families. Mirroring David Schneider's groundbreaking work on kinship, she argued that families are "symbolic" systems laden with multiple and complex meanings. These meanings are important not only for understanding the domestic domain but because they can lead to greater understanding of broader cultural themes. Yanagisako also borrowed from gender studies, especially the work of Rosaldo, and urged a rethinking of the public (male)/private (female) split so often seen in family studies. Researchers should explore not only how women may operate in the public domain but how their domestic activities and roles impact the political. Finally, Yanagisako urged researchers to put the analysis of the family in a broader, more comprehensive framework. In particular, studies ought to include a consideration of the impacts that inequality (both societal and intrafamilial) have on family configuration and meaning and how relations of production and inequality affect domestic groups. Rather than necessarily viewing families as statically functional or adaptive institutions, intrafamilial dynamics should be explored, including tensions over the distribution of power and resources. The family should be viewed as a historically situated and dialectically responsive "ideological" unit composed of individual actors, not as a concrete thing that can be tacitly defined and described.

Putting Theory into Practice: Family Studies of the 1980s and Early 1990s

As noted above, prior to the 1980s, discussions of the family in anthropology were almost exclusively linked to larger studies of kinship, a topic that held a central position in anthropological analyses from the inception of the discipline. Kinship

studies, which suffered under similar, if not harsher, critiques as the ones for family studies, fell somewhat out of favor in the 1980s. However, that does not mean that work on the family had been abandoned. In fact, it could be argued that it was reinvigorated by its repositioning. Discussion of the family now appeared to take a more central role in social analysis in part because of its very close linkages to the important emerging theme of gender. Ethnographies were increasingly considered incomplete without a significant and meaningful discussion of women's roles, and this often meant a lengthy discussion of the family.

The following section highlights just a few of the major themes addressed in anthropology of gender in the 1980s and early 1990s, with a special emphasis on their contributions to larger theoretical concerns in relation to anthropology of the family. These themes include history and colonialism, relations of production, and intrafamilial dynamics. Each topic reflects the concerns that Yanagisako outlined above as well as those reflected in the discipline-wide shift away from formalist thinking. No clear distinctions are made here between the 1980s and the early 1990s, since work on the family during this time reflects an evolution of ideas rather than a real paradigm shift.

History, colonialism, gender, and the family. Much of anthropological writing as a whole was woefully bereft of historical contextualization. Almost from the beginning, anthropologists adopted the technique of writing in the ethnographic "present," which served to create an image of the culture under study as timeless and relatively unaffected by historical influences. That radically changed in the 1980s as anthropologists rediscovered history as an important analytic tool. This turn toward the historical included interest in private as well as public life, and the domestic world was laid open to historical reconstruction. Colonialism in particular became a pivotal theme to address, and feminist scholars, among others, concerned themselves with attempting to show how gender roles and family relations were historically, not naturally, created.

While the exact circumstances obviously vary considerably, under colonialism important economic relations changed; these impacted the ways in which families engaged in productive activities and ultimately the form and configurations of families. Under European colonial rule, land relations were altered, thereby impacting who could and could not own land. In some cases families lost all of their lands, reconfiguring family production patterns and shifting possibilities for inheritance, while in other cases women lost the ability to own land and the productive benefits that entailed. Moreover, land was often alienated from those who long worked it, changing household production from auto-production to dependence on patron-client relations or wage labor. In many parts of the world, for the first time, men, women, and children were sent from their households to work for others. Over time, households in some regions became increasingly linked to global, not domestic, economies, altering the meaning of productive work and often putting control over it, usually via wage labor, into the hands of men. In sum, researchers noted that as inheritance, division of labor, and production patterns changed, the family was transformed in unique and locally specific ways.

Along with economic changes, colonialism also brought with it important ideological shifts. European ideologies of gender and especially Christian morality toward sexuality significantly altered gender and family relations. Using Hawaii as an example, Patricia Grimshaw writes that women's lives were considerably different prior to colonialism and the work of Christian missionaries. Descent was traced through the male and female lines, adolescent female sexuality was not restrained, marriages were easily terminated, and infants were often adopted and/or reared by extended kin networks. The overall picture is one of relative freedom for at least some Hawaiian women to make choices about sexuality and marriage. Christian missionaries actively worked to expunge these ideas, and in doing so they shifted Hawaiian families toward greater control over female sexuality and ultimately toward patriarchy. Elsewhere, Christianity has been associated with the dissolution of extended family networks because it stresses individual, not group, responsibility.

Relations of production and the family.

Another area of considerable research in anthropology on the family concerns understanding the relationship between economic change, women's roles, and changes in the composition and functioning of the family. Among the themes most frequently explored by anthropologists are the impacts of incipient capitalism and the effects that the increasing penetration of the world economy has had on family roles and domestic orientations. How, for example, does unequal access to wage labor produce changes in men's and women's influence and roles within the family? How might participation in capitalism influence family configuration and intrafamilial dynamics? The evidence is plentiful, if not straightforward.

In Latin America, for example, anthropologists such as Hans Buechler and Judith-Maria Buechler have found that women who are engaged in petty commodity production or in market vending often find that their ability to support themselves and their children financially can free them from oppressive, patriarchal relationships with their husbands. Through work, entrepreneurial women have created networks beyond the family, allowing them the financial and sometimes the social freedom to reconstruct their family lives. However, access to income generation does not always translate to a drastic change in women's roles within the household. According to Florence Babb, Peruvian market women, much like their North American counterparts, often work a double day—first in the market and then at home—resulting in little real change in family relations.

What is clear from the cross-cultural evidence is that capitalism does not necessarily provide the conditions for equality within households and in fact may reinforce patriarchy. In places where wages are low and the state options for child care are very limited, women often find their abilities to access wage labor severely constrained by practical, if not ideological, considerations. Women often take the lowest-paid jobs, which offer flexibility, or they find they are unable to work except perhaps at the very margins of the informal sector. Rather than empowering women, wage labor often makes them more dependent on male wage-earners than they may have been in an agricultural setting where men and women share the productive tasks. Similarly,

families often become more patriarchal as the sole male breadwinner takes on the responsibility of "head of household." The point of interest on a theoretical level is the recognition that the effects of any particular structural or economic change, in this case the penetration of capitalism, are never uniform, and they vary not only regionally but also locally and intersect with a range of other important cultural variables.

Family dynamics.

Interest in inequality extended beyond the analysis of how social inequalities inscribe themselves on families and led some scholars to explore more deeply the ways in which inequality is manifest in intrafamilial dynamics. This was fairly new terrain for anthropologists because most studies left unquestioned the assumption that families were for the most part unified and coherent institutions. It had long been presumed that families function in a manner that implies a degree of cooperation between members and that decision making within a family involves a consideration of shared, mutual goals. Families, it was thought, were corporate groups in which hierarchy was generally unquestioned and decision making relatively smoothly enacted for the good of the family, not the individual. Yet an examination of the day-to-day lives and decision-making practices of families gives evidence that families are often far less harmonious than these functionalist theories would imply. Families, like states, are domains in which hierarchy and domination are negotiated continually, often mirroring other structural inequalities but sometimes not. The nature and content of familial conflicts, how they change over time, and the ways in which families resolve them (if at all) are important areas of scholarly concern because they reveal domains of important cultural and social tension.

One area where the conflictual role of intrafamilial dynamics has been most obviously documented is in the shifting nature of families engaged in the various forms of labor migration. One of the effects of the unequal penetration of capitalism globally has been that families must send away one or more of their members to seek wage labor. Sometimes this migration results in a rural-to-urban move of one individual or the whole family and sometimes in the international migration of one or more family members. In all of these cases families often face radical changes. Conflicts and tensions are myriad. They can appear between husbands and wives as they negotiate between urban and rural gender roles and expectations. Generational tensions can mount as young adults find themselves responsible for navigating a world their parents cannot understand. Siblings can find their worlds colliding in unexpected ways as they vie for scarce educational resources. And immigrant fathers may find their child-rearing preferences in conflict with host-country norms.

Anthropological work on the intersection of family and the global economy also contributed to our understandings of families as constructed units and not necessarily biologically based ones. For example, focusing on the Caribbean, Christine Ho discusses the emergence of what she terms "international families." International families are organized primarily around women and include kin, fictive kin, and friends who participate in mutual aid and exchange networks that span multiple cities and even continents. Ho argues that international families are responding to particular global economic inequalities, but she points out that this response is creative and dynamic and not preordained by circumstances.

The 1990s and Beyond: Reimagining Family

While gender provided the thematic focus for studies of the family in the 1980s, in the 1990s families became a focus of study in their own right. Abundant cross-cultural literature emerged in this field, but some of the most important theoretical contributions came from studies of Western families, particularly same-sex families. At the very least, the 1990s can be characterized as a period in which there existed a growing recognition of family pluralism both inside and outside the academy. The *postmodern* family, a term first used by Edward Shorter in 1975, has come to signal the many diverse, fluid, contested, and negotiated family arrangements most obviously noted in the West.

In 1990 Judith Stacey published *Brave New Families,* which made visible the improvisational and creative nature of contemporary postindustrial family life due to changes in economic realities, gender roles, and kinship conceptualizations. *Brave New Families* was read widely outside the academy and proved to be a touchstone for "family values" proponents who locate many contemporary social ills in the breakdown of the male-headed nuclear family. The resulting "family values" debate has provided fertile ground for the development of poststructuralist critiques of one of the most sacrosanct categories of Western thought, "the family." What many have called for are theories that seek to reveal the continuities as well as the shifting symbolism and creativity that people enact in the realm of kinship (Rapp). Moreover, anthropologists have turned their attention toward scrutinizing relations of power. Their interest in the "family" stems from a larger ambition to analyze family as an institution that is affected by multiple structural variables assembled in the name of both public and private well-being. These variables include legal regulation, moral ideologies, economic change, and political discourses.

Same-sex families.

At one time, same-sex families of certain configurations were inconceivable in America. However, beginning in the 1980s circumstances slowly changed and have altered the complexion of family life for gays and lesbians. Due to numerous socioeconomic changes over the last decades of the twentieth century, including the financial independence of women in lesbian families, the availability of donor sperm and the decoupling of sexuality and reproduction, and the increased acceptance of lesbians and gay men by adoption agencies and courts, planned gay and lesbian parenting is a phenomenon that has grown tremendously. However, this social transformation does not come without serious opposition. For example, in the late 1980s and early 1990s "family values" rhetoric was redirected to spotlight same-sex families, particularly childrearing by gays and lesbians (see, for example, Polikoff). The argument typically falls along the line that same-sex and transgender families threaten "the traditional American family."

Attempts in popular culture to frame same-sex families as an "exotic" other (at best) or as the "end of the American family as we know it" (at worst) were countered in the academy and elsewhere by the assertion that same-sex families are neither marginal nor exceptional but represent and illustrate a larger process of contesting dominant and sometimes oppressive concepts of the "ideal" family. While gay and lesbian parenting has sparked the ire of social critics, it has provided fertile ground for scholars in anthropology and other disciplines to reconceptualize theory.

Gay and lesbian theory.

In the 1990s gay and lesbian research moved away from issues of sexual identity to issues of the meanings of intimate relationships including romantic relationships, lesbian mothers and gay fathers, and the psychological development and social adjustment of children of lesbian and gay parents. Unfortunately, much of this work took a psychological orientation. In a review of 2,598 articles, David Demo and Katherine Allen found that while there was an important base for beginning to conceptualize how sexual orientation affects family experiences, sexist and heterosexist assumptions also underlay most of the research on same-sex families. Studies often took a "deficit model" stance in which same-sex families were compared to heterosexual nuclear families and found lacking. These studies tended to focus on individuals and outcomes rather than on gay family life as it is embedded in the broader social context.

Gay and lesbian family theory within anthropology has taken a different orientation. Gay and lesbian family theorists, most of whom are urban anthropologists in North America and Great Britain, suggest a multiplicity of theories to understand ever-increasing diversity across and within same-sex families. While little literature exists, much of gay and lesbian family theory focuses one of two themes. The first attempts to locate family within a discourse on the deconstruction of the modern heterosexual nuclear family and "family values" rhetoric. The second calls for a deconstruction of the family as a concept and a radical rethinking of how social categories become embedded. For example, the term *queer* was reclaimed by gay and lesbian activists to illustrate their resistance to hegemonic ideal constructs. Queer theory, positioned at the radical end of gay and lesbian activism, provides an important critique of family rhetoric in general. The argument proposed by queer theorists is that discussions of the family, even within the gay and lesbian movement, are predicated on certain hegemonic ideas concerning the distribution of power, division of labor, and so on. The queer movement urges a rethinking of the whole concept of family as necessarily linked to structures of power that marginalize, exclude, and oppress.

Studies that attempt to deconstruct rigid formulations of family argue that most family theories were developed with the assumption of a heterosexual orientation for all family members. The presence of same-sex families challenges that assumption. Gay and lesbian families provide a context in which to expand discussions of the relationships among gender, sexuality, and kinship. Moreover, discussions of gay and lesbian kinship reinvigorated some of the ideas set out in 1968 by David Schneider. In particular, he argued that American kinship is a symbolic system resting on two axes of contrasting but mutually dependent notions of blood and love. While blood was often discussed in the literature on families, love rarely was.

In *Families We Choose* (1991), Kath Weston argues that gay and lesbian families are a domain in which relationships are most obviously based on love rather than biological connections. According to Weston, these families are negotiating a new model of kinship ideology that repositions biology as potentially irrelevant. Weston demonstrates that gay families represent one element in a broader discourse on family whose meanings are continuously negotiated in everyday situations. Moreover, families are positioned vis-à-vis relations of power in society at large. By demonstrating the resourcefulness of many gay families as they seek to solidify and define what family means to them at a particular place and time, she acknowledges that power is not unidirectional. Her work is not merely theoretical or a cultural/historical analysis but ethnographic and therefore evocative of real experiences and real people as they attempt to negotiate "familiness" in the presence of institutions that both constrain and enable that process.

Valerie Lehr argues that queer studies offer a more radical discourse on family, one that provides an alternative to liberal, rights-based political frameworks. A rights-based approach to marriage and family does not challenge established institutions and power as much as it advocates for some gays and lesbians gaining additional power within the established social system. Rights-based approaches reinforce hegemonic symbols of family and paint the gay and lesbian "community" as a monolithic whole while denying legitimation of alternative ways to framing family. Following Lehr, Ruthann Robson argues that gay and lesbian theorists have left unproblematized the concept of family as they have shifted their focus to advocating recognition for "our" family. By not contextualizing and problematizing "functional familialism," the not-so-implicit message becomes that gay and lesbian relationships will be accorded the status of family only to the extent that they replicate the traditional husband-wife couple, a tradition based on property relations.

Theoretical discussions of family in the 1990s point to the family as an ideological construct firmly embedded in historical and material conditions of everyday life. The emergence of same-sex families as a cultural category has brought into focus the contrasting yet interdependent notions of kinship based on blood and love as well as a need for problematizing the category of "family" writ large. Moreover, as more diverse "imagined" families are created and dissolved, the legal system and social system must rethink the boundaries and meanings of "family" to accommodate the ever-shifting realities. Some relevant and urgent questions future anthropological research might address are: How do the existing structures enable or constrain how gays and lesbians imagine and construct family? Which gays and lesbians are most likely to be agents of change? How do the actions of certain people impact the production or reproduction of certain structures? At what point do these family experiences, policy positions, and incremental shifts in popular thought reach the "tipping point," the point at which difference bubbles up to a critical mass and creates change in social structure? To pose and then investigate these questions offers an opportunity to reinvigorate kinship studies by coupling them to theoretically important and timely research on gender studies, colonialism, class relations, identity, and the construction of the "other."

Conclusion

Anthropological studies of the family reflect many of the larger tensions and trends that have typified the discipline in the latter half of the twentieth century. Central anthropological arguments including those about the role of biology in social reproduction, the evolution of culture, the organization of social and cultural data, and the pervasiveness of Western ideologies have played a major role in the development of the anthropological literature on the family. Moreover, because the "family" is a social concept with very real ideological and political orientations, academic work on the family has been alternately stymied and invigorated by popular cultural assumptions, debates, and trends. In particular, since the 1970s, first feminism and then gay and lesbian studies have made important contributions in moving anthropology toward an understanding of family that is analytically sophisticated in its ability to think about heterogeneity at the same time that it reflects the on-the-ground realities of real families.

See also **Childhood and Child Rearing; Family: Modernist Anthropological Theory; Feminism; Friendship; Gay Studies; Gender Studies: Anthropology; Kinship; Motherhood and Maternity.**

BIBLIOGRAPHY

Babb, Florence E. *Between Field and Cooking Pot: The Political Economy of Marketwomen in Peru.* Austin: University of Texas Press, 1989.

Buechler, Hans, and Judith-Maria Buechler. *The World of Sofía Velasquez: The Autobiography of a Bolivian Market Vendor.* New York: Columbia University Press, 1996.

Collier, Jane, Michelle Z. Rosaldo, and Sylvia Yanagisako. "Is There a Family? New Anthropological Views." In *Rethinking the Family: Some Feminist Questions,* edited by Barrie Thorne and Marilyn Yalom, 25–39. New York: Longman, 1982.

Creed, Gerald W. "Family Values and Domestic Economies." *Annual Review of Anthropology* 29 (October 2000): 329–355.

Demo, David H., and Katherine R. Allen. "The Families of Lesbians and Gay Men: A New Frontier in Family Research." *Journal of Marriage and Family* 57 (February 1995): 111–127.

Grimshaw, Patricia. "New England Missionary Wives, Hawaiian Women, and 'The Cult of True Womanhood.' " In *Family and Gender in the Pacific: Domestic Contradictions and the Colonial Impact,* edited by Margaret Jolly and Martha Macintyre, 19–44. Cambridge, U.K., and New York: Cambridge University Press, 1989.

Ho, Christine. "The Internationalization of Kinship and the Feminization of Caribbean Migration: The Case of Afro-Trinidadian Immigrants in Los Angeles." *Human Organization* 52 (1993): 32–40.

Lehr, Valerie. *Queer Family Values: Debunking the Myth of the Nuclear Family.* Philadelphia: Temple University Press, 1999.

Moore, Henrietta L. *Feminism and Anthropology.* Cambridge, U.K.: Polity Press/Blackwell, 1988.

Polikoff, Nancy D. "Raising Children: Lesbian and Gay Parents Face the Public and the Courts." In *Creating Change,* edited by John D'Emilio, William B. Turner, and Urvashi Vaid, 305–335. New York: St. Martin's Press, 2000.

Rapp, Rayna. "Toward a Nuclear Freeze: The Gender Politics of Euro-American Kinship Analysis." In *Gender and Kinship: Essays Toward a Unified Analysis,* edited by Jane Fishburne

Collier and Sylvia Junko Yanagisako, 49–70. Stanford, Calif.: Stanford University Press, 1987.

Robson, Ruthann. "Resisting the Family: Repositioning Lesbians in Legal Theory." *Signs: Journal of Women in Culture and Society* 19 (summer 1994): 975–996.

Schneider, David. *American Kinship: A Cultural Account.* Englewood Cliffs: N.J.: Prentice Hall, 1968.

Shorter, Edward. *The Making of the Modern Family.* New York: Basic Books, 1975.

Stacey, Judith. *Brave New Families: Stories of Domestic Upheaval in Late Twentieth Century America.* New York: Basic Books, 1990.

Stack, Carol B. *All Our Kin: Strategies for Survival in a Black Community.* New York: Harper and Row, 1974.

Thorne, Barrie. "Feminist Rethinking of the Family: An Overview." In *Rethinking the Family: Some Feminist Questions,* edited by Barrie Thorne and Marilyn Yalom, 1–24. New York: Longman, 1982.

Weston, Kath. *Families We Choose: Lesbians, Gays, Kinship.* New York: Columbia University Press, 1991.

Yanagisako, Sylvia Junko. "Family and Household: The Analysis of Domestic Groups." *Annual Review of Anthropology* 8 (1979): 161–205.

Cynthia E. Foor
Ann Miles

FAMILY PLANNING.   Family planning refers to the use of modern contraception and other methods of birth control to regulate the number, timing, and spacing of human births. It allows parents, particularly mothers, to plan their lives without being overly subject to sexual and social imperatives. However, family planning is not seen by all as a humane or necessary intervention. It is an arena of contestation within broader social and political conflicts involving religious and cultural injunctions, patriarchal subordination of women, social-class formation, and global political and economic relations.

Attempts to control human reproduction is not entirely a modern phenomenon. Throughout history, human beings have engaged in both pro- and antinatalist practices directed at enhancing social welfare. In many foraging and agricultural societies a variety of methods such as prolonged breast-feeding were used to space births and maintain an equilibrium between resources and population size. But in hierarchical societies, population regulation practices did not bring equivalent or beneficial results to everyone. Anthropologists Marvin Harris and Eric Ross have shown that "As power differentials increase, the upper and lower strata may, in fact, develop different or even antagonistic systems of population regulation" (p. 19).

Being uniquely endowed with the capacity for reproduction, women of course have borne the costs of pregnancy, birth, and lactation, as well as abortion and other stressful methods of reproductive regulation. Social-class dominance over reproduction often takes place through the control of lower-class women by upper-class men. The particular forms these controls take vary across historical periods and cultures. In feudal agricultural and "plantation economies" experiencing labor shortages and short life expectancies, for example, there has

been great pressure on women to bear as many children as possible.

In the modern era of industrial capitalist development, conservative fundamentalist groups have tended to oppose abortion and reproductive choice for women on grounds of religion and tradition. They believe that abortion and contraception are inimical to the biological role of women as mothers and to the maintenance of male-dominant familial and community arrangements. In both the industrialized north and the poor countries of the south, religious fundamentalists oppose abortion and the expansion of reproductive choices for women, and sometimes they do so violently, as in the attacks in the United States against clinics and doctors providing legal abortions. The rapid spread of evangelical Christianity and militant Islam around the world further aggravate the situation.

Partly as a result of religious fundamentalist opposition, in the early twenty-first century abortion remains illegal in many countries. It is estimated that worldwide approximately 200,000 women die annually due to complications from illegal abortions. The actual figures may be higher, since only about half the countries in the world report maternal mortality statistics. Indeed, the unchallenged position of the Vatican against artificial conception and the U.S. government policy against funding for international abortions has led some to believe that illegal abortions and maternal mortality could further increase. Not only does the Bush administration refuse money for abortions, but it also prohibits medical professionals in international organizations such as International Planned Parenthood from talking about abortion if they receive U.S. government support. In the context of both the conservative religious backlash and the problems attributed to global population expansion, family planning seems an enlightened and progressive endeavor. Yet, the movement to provide modern contraception has been fraught with gender, race, and class inequalities and health and ethical problems from the outset. Efforts to reform and democratize international family planning must necessarily grapple with these concerns.

Origin and Evolution of Family Planning
The idea of modern population control is attributed to Thomas Malthus (1766–1834), who in 1798 articulated his doctrine attributing virtually all major social and environmental problems to population expansion associated with the industrial revolution. However, as a clergyman turned economist, Malthus was opposed to artificial methods of fertility control. He advocated abstinence and letting nature take its toll and allowing the poor to die.

In contrast, birth control emerged as a radical social movement led by socialists and feminists in the early twentieth century in the United States. The anarchist Emma Goldman (1869–1940) promoted birth control not only as a woman's right and worker's right, but also as a means to sexual freedom outside of conventional marriage. But soon birth control became increasingly medicalized and associated with science and corporate control as well as with the control of reproduction within marriage and conventional family life. As the radicals

Poster advocating small families, Singapore, 1972. Due to a demographic imbalance, by the mid-twentieth century countries in the southern hemisphere had a much denser population than those in the north, leading to a focus of family planning efforts in those areas. © UPI/CORBIS-BETTMANN

lost their leadership of the birth control movement to professional experts, mostly male doctors, by the 1920s birth control, which refers to voluntary and individual choice in control of reproduction, became aligned with population control, that is, a political movement by dominant groups to control the reproduction of socially subordinate groups.

During the influx of new immigrants in the 1920s and 1930s and during the depression, when the ranks of the unemployed were swelling, eugenicist (hereditary improvement) ideology and programs for immigration control and social engineering gained much ground in the United States. Even the birth-control pioneer Margaret Sanger (1879–1966) and suffragists such as Julia Ward Howe (1819–1910) and Ida Husted Harper (1851–1931) surrendered to ruling-class interests and eugenics, calling for birth control among the poor, blacks, and immigrants as a means of counteracting the declining birth rates of native-born whites. Influenced by eugenicist thinking, twenty-six states in the United States passed compulsory sterilization laws, and thousands of persons—mostly poor and black—deemed "unfit"

were prevented from reproducing. By the 1940s, eugenicist and birth-control interests in the United States were so thoroughly intertwined that they became virtually indistinguishable. In the post–World War II era, compulsory sterilization became widespread in the so-called Third World where the birth rates have been higher than in the industrialized countries (in 1995, fertility per woman was 1.9 in the more developed regions and 3.6 in the less developed regions).

In the late twentieth century, the fear of demographic imbalance again seemed to be producing differential family-planning policies for the global north and the south. This was evident in corporate-scientific development of stronger contraceptives largely for poor women of color in the south and new reproductive technologies for fertility enhancement largely for white upper-class women in the north. Some insurance companies in the United States continue to refuse to cover conception in the early twenty-first century. Countries concerned with population "implosion" in the north such as Sweden, France, and Japan are pursuing pronatalist policies encouraging women to have more children while at the same time pursuing antinatalist policies encouraging women in the south to have fewer children.

Family Planning in the Global South

Given the massive increase in population in the south hemisphere countries since World War II, much of global family-planning efforts have been directed toward those poor countries of the so-called Third World. The followers of Malthus, the neo-Malthusians, have extended his thinking, blaming global poverty, political insecurity, and environmental degradation on the "population explosion" and calling for population control as the primary solution to these problems. Their efforts have helped turn family planning into a vast establishment of governmental and nongovernmental organizations with financial, technological, and ideological power emanating from the capitals in the north toward the remote corners of the south. Within countries in the south, the hierarchical family-planning model spreads from professional elites in the cities to the poorest men and women in the villages. In India alone, there are an estimated 250,000 family-planning workers. Every year vast amounts of money are spent to promote "contraceptive acceptance" among the poor populations in the world. Contraceptive use in the "developing world" has increased from less than 10 percent of couples of reproductive age in the 1960s to more than 50 percent (42 percent excluding China) in the 1990s. The rapidly falling birth rates in the Third World are generally attributed to the "family-planning revolution" represented by expanding use of modern contraceptives.

The International Conference on Population and Development (ICPD), held in Cairo in 1994, is generally considered to have ushered in a new approach to population and development, upholding reproductive health and rights of women over meeting numerical goals for reducing fertility and population growth. Departing from earlier positions and upholding voluntary choice in family size, the ICPD Programme of Action states that demographic goals in the form of targets and quotas for the recruitment of clients should not be imposed on family-planning providers and expresses disapproval of the use of incentives and disincentives. It acknowledges the setting of demographic goals as a legitimate subject of state development strategies to be "defined in terms of unmet needs for [family-planning] information and services" (United Nations, 1994). But, as human rights activists concerned with continued abuses in family-planning programs point out, there is still a long way to go in establishing policies and ethical standards to ensure that the new health and women's rights objectives are achieved.

Notwithstanding massive spending and extensive family-planning promotion over three decades, many poor people in the Third World remain reluctant to use modern contraception in the early twenty-first century. Attitudes and the need for children among the poor are often quite different from that of family-planning enthusiasts, who are mostly middle-class professionals. Even when poor people use modern contraceptives, their continuation rates are often low due to lack of access to health care, side-effects of contraceptives, and other reasons. Given these realities and the urgency to reduce fertility, international family planning continues to rely on the use of economic incentives and disincentives as well as highly effective, provider-controlled, female methods.

Although male sterilization (vasectomy) is a much simpler operation than female sterilization (tubectomy), female sterilization is the most favored method of family planners and the most widely used method of fertility control in the world. Tubectomy is more common than vasectomy because the men in many areas refuse to have vasectomies, leaving the women little choice if they don't want more children. Female sterilization constituted about 33 percent and male sterilization 12 percent of all contraceptive use in the developing countries at the end of the 1980s. In terms of the numbers, sterilization is an increasing success, and for many women and men in the north and the south, sterilization represents a choice to be free of biological reproduction. But closer examination of conditions under which most women consent to be sterilized shows that sterilization abuse continues to be a pervasive problem for poor women.

Poverty and adverse social conditions—including lack of information and access to other methods of birth control, threats of discontinued social benefits, and economic constraints—set the conditions for abuses in family-planning programs. Targets and economic incentives/disincentives have defined the operation of many Third World family-planning programs from their inception. They have also been associated with programs directed at poor communities of color in the United States. In the early 2000s a nonprofit organization known as C.R.A.C.K. (Children Requiring A Caring Kommunity) promised a cash incentive of $200 to drug-addicted women upon verification that they had been sterilized or were using a long-term birth control method such as Norplant, Depo-Provera, or an IUD (American Public Health Association).

While targets and incentives in other realms of social policy are not necessarily wrong, the pressure to meet targets and the offer of economic incentives in family-planning programs have resulted in a highly techno-bureaucratic and monetarist approach obsessed with numbers of acceptors and financial rewards. Within such a quantitative approach, the complex psychological, sociocultural dimensions of sexuality and reproduction are easily overlooked. Not only do poor people lack much relevant information, but also, in many cases, the desperation of poverty drives them to accept contraception or sterilization in return for payments in cash or kind. In such situations, choice simply does not exist. Direct force has reportedly been used in population-control efforts in some countries, including China, India, Bangladesh, and Indonesia. But coercion does not pertain simply to the outright use of force. More subtle forms of coercion arise when individual reproductive decisions are tied to sources of survival, like the availability of food, shelter, employment, education, health care, and so on.

The "Second Contraceptive Revolution"

Claiming that the earlier contraceptive revolution was a major success, the international family-planning establishment declared the launching of a "second contraceptive revolution" and a "contraceptive 21 agenda" for the twenty-first century. This, like the earlier phase, upheld the biomedical model of mass female fertility management. In 2004 about ninety-four new contraceptive products were being pursued, of which many were variants of existing methods. Among these were four IUDs, seven hormonal implants, five hormonal injectables, five hormonal pills, six vaccines, and six methods for female sterilization.

The second contraceptive revolution also envisaged a greater role for private industry. Given the "latent demand" for new contraceptives, liberalization of trade, privatization of state-run enterprises, and other factors, contraceptive marketing in the Third World promised to be even more profitable for pharmaceutical companies than they had been in the past. The privatization of health sectors, increasing corporate mergers (such as the merger of Pharmacia Sweden and Upjohn of the United States), and the extension of intensive contraceptive promotional and marketing strategies further augmented the power and profits of transnational pharmaceutical companies in the south.

The United States Food and Drug Administration (USFDA) in the early 2000s was completely exempting more and more drugs and medical devices from review before marketing, a move that could have detrimental repercussions across the world. The ICPD and its "new" reproductive-rights agenda, however, did not address the need for strict guidelines to monitor contraceptive trials and the marketing practices of corporations. Calls for population stabilization in the context of GATT (General Agreement on Trade and Tariffs) and other "free trade" agreements, could result in further easing of protocols for contraceptive trials. Feminist activists fear increased corporate dumping of dangerous and experimental contraceptives on the bodies of poor women. Their concerns are based on the history of experimentation of contraceptives such as Depo-Provera and Norplant on poor women in the north and the south without informed consent, the use in the Third World of the Dalkon Shield IUD and other contraceptive devices banned in the United States, and other unethical and dangerous practices. The FDA has, however, been stalling on making emergency contraception available over the counter, maintaining that it needs further testing. Planned Parenthood, NOW, and NARAL, among other feminist organizations, have long urged the approval of the drug.

Health and Human Rights of Women

Modern family-planning programs have provided many poor women with contraceptives and the ability to limit family size; but they have rarely given women genuine choice, control over their bodies, or a sense of self empowerment. The focus of family planning has been on population stabilization and the meeting of targets rather than on the means or the processes to achieve its ends. Although many family planners in the early 2000s call for women's reproductive rights, population-control programs seem to be moving in authoritarian directions.

Article 16 of the Teheran Proclamation issued by the United Nations Conference on Human Rights in 1968 states that "Parents have a basic human right to determine freely and responsibly the number and spacing of their children" (United Nations, 1974). This Article represented a major victory for the population-control movement. Perhaps the term "responsibly" was the real victory because it can be interpreted in a more-or-less coercive way. Indeed, the overwhelming importance given by international donors and local governments to fertility control has led to a relative neglect of other aspects of family planning and reproductive and human rights such as the right of the poor to health and well-being, including the right to bear and sustain children. Indeed, the neglect of the survival issues by the family planners has allowed right-wing fundamentalists to appear as the only ones concerned with family and community.

The emphasis on family planning has undermined public health care and Maternal and Child Health (MCH) in many countries. In 2004, many of the new hormonal and immunological contraceptives did not protect against HIV/AIDS. In many poor communities in Africa ridden with AIDS, modern contraception was widely available while pharmaceutical drugs for AIDS were not. Target pressure and incentives continued to drive interests of health-care personnel toward population control over provision of health care. Population agencies spoke in public of integrating family planning within a broader health-care framework. But in private some have argued that family-planning programs should not be "held hostage" to strict health requirements and that maximum access to contraceptives should override safety and ethical concerns. Even when the population-control organizations have taken efforts to address public-health issues and women's social and economic rights, the population-control objective has continued to be dominant. The Safe Motherhood Initiative is an example.

The Safe Motherhood Initiative was launched by the World Bank, United Nations Development Program, United Nations Children's Fund (UNICEF), United Nations Fund for Population Activities (UNFPA) and the World Health Organization (WHO) to reduce maternal mortality. In many cases, this initiative has aimed simply to reduce childbearing; the assumption being that fewer births will cause fewer maternal deaths. A 1992 World Bank evaluation of its population-sector work admitted that its foray into broader health initiatives had been motivated by the "political sensitivity" of population control

and the need to dissipate Third World perception that "population control is really the Bank's strategic objective." The report further notes that many countries that would not accept donor support for population control would nevertheless "accept support for family health and welfare programs with family planning components" and that the likelihood of family planning getting "lost in an MCH program" was less because MCH was better accepted as a "legitimate intervention for both health and demographic reasons" (World Bank, 1992).

As Indian health researcher Malini Karkal has pointed out, the tendency to attribute maternal mortality simply to pregnancy and childbirth by the Safe Motherhood Initiative and other such programs has led to a relative neglect of causes of reproductive mortality that supercede maternal mortality. Deaths due to unsafe sterilization, hazardous contraceptives, deaths associated with sexually transmitted diseases, cancer of the reproductive organs, and unsafe treatment of infertility also account for a large proportion of reproductive mortality. Where births have been "averted" due to family-planning programs, the reproductive choices or conditions of women or of the general population, for that matter, have not increased as a result. In India, although birth rates have declined, infant mortality at about 72 per 1,000 births and maternal mortality at about 460 per 100,000 live births in 1995 continued to be relatively high. As women's-rights advocates argue, improvement of the status of women is not the consequence of family-planning programs as believed by the population planners. Rather it is a more complex outcome resulting from rise of age in marriage, education, employment, better living conditions, and general awareness, as well as family planning. Indeed, everywhere, voluntary acceptance of contraception seems to be correlated with women's access to education.

Phenomenon of "Missing Women"

In the 1980s and 1990s in several Asian countries, the proportion of girls born and living appeared to be steadily decreasing. In India, the ratio of women to men was 929 females to 1,000 males, whereas in 1901 it was 972. In China after the one-child family policy was implemented in 1979, the sex ratio became more skewed. There were 94.1 women per 100 males in the 1982 census; in the 1990 census, there were only 93.8 females per 100 males. Demographic data shows that in the early 2000s in China, India, Pakistan, Bangladesh, Nepal, West Asia, and Egypt, 100 million or more women were unaccounted for by official statistics. Further skewing of sex ratios particularly in the world's two most populous countries, India and China, are likely to create serious demographic and gender issues in the future.

One factor contributing to the problem of "missing women" is sex-selective abortions. New technologies such as amniocentesis, ultrasound, and chorionic biopsy, developed for purposes of prenatal testing for birth defects, are increasingly used for the purpose of sex determination. Sex-selection procedures are increasingly advertised in the United States as scientific advances intended to improve choice in family planning and they are likely to become routine procedures. In the patriarchal societies of China and India, where the preference for male children and the pressures to reduce family size are both very strong, abortions of female fetuses seem to be widespread. Although the use of technologies for sex selection is illegal in China, they are readily available even in rural areas. With a small bribe, parents can easily find out the sex of the embryo and abort it if it is female, thus ensuring that the only child allowed by the State's one-child-family law be a male.

In India too, sex-selective abortion is a thriving business. According to some estimates, between 1978 and 1983 alone, 78,000 female fetuses were aborted after sex-determination tests. Researchers have found that some poor districts in Uttar Pradesh, Maharashtra, and Gujarat, which do not have basic services such as potable water and electricity, have clinics doing a flourishing business in prenatal diagnostic techniques for sex selection. Even poor farmers and landless laborers were willing to pay 25 percent compound interest on loans borrowed to pay for those tests. Given extreme social pressures to produce sons, many women, not only poor uneducated women, but also educated urban women are resorting to abortion of female fetuses. Some middle-class Indian women justify these actions on grounds of choice, and some medical doctors and intellectuals have also argued that it would prevent the suffering of women and that in the long run the shortage of women would lead to their improved status in society. Nurses seeking to meet their family-planning targets actively encourage "scanning" for sex determination and abortion of female fetuses. Some doctors also promote sex-selective abortion as an effective method of population control that would allow the Indian government to achieve its population-control targets.

Female infanticide and underreporting of girls are other factors contributing to the "missing women" phenomenon. The Chinese government has either denied or condemned the practice of female infanticide, but reliable data are not available. Female infanticide does have a long tradition in patriarchal societies such as China and India. But as the demographer Terrence Hull has noted, the "behavioral and emotional setting of infanticide in contemporary China" tends to be substantially different from the traditional pattern (Hull p. 73). The resurgence of infanticide since the early 1980s, is at least partly related to the pressures of the Chinese family-planning program, and the infants killed at birth have been overwhelmingly female. Most of the abandoned infants who end up in state-run orphanages are girls. Many of these girls, as well as boys, are subjected to starvation, torture, and sexual assault. Women's rights activist Viji Srinivasan, who has studied female infanticide among poor communities in Tamil Nadu, India, has also identified the "internalization of the small family norm" due to family-planning promotion as a source of female infanticide (pp. 53–56). Her study raises questions about the ethics of aggressive population control in highly patriarchal societies and underscores the need for economic empowerment and elevation of women's status.

Family Planning and Authoritarianism

Family-planning advocates and organizations claim that the modern "contraceptive revolution" has been achieved without coercion, through "purely voluntary means" with only "minor disadvantages" to people in the Third World (UNFPA). But a closer examination of the methods of contraception and strategies of family planning reveals widespread human-rights violations and safety and ethical problems. In this regard, it is well to remember the arguments commonly put forward by influential neo-Malthusian demographers, according to whom political will and strong measures need to be used in the fight against population growth, and democratic norms may have to be sacrificed for the sake of the greater good.

Some analysts argue that neo-Malthusian family planning is a quantitative, technical, and bureaucratic approach driven by urgency and aggression to reduce the numbers of the human population in a race against the mechanical clock. Controlled by money and political influence, it has erected a vast global family-planning enterprise far removed from the broader economic needs and cultural interests of the masses whose numbers it seeks to control. Such a hierarchical and at times violent approach can reinforce existing psychosocial structures of domination and subordination; men over women (patriarchy); capital over labor (capitalism); north over south (imperialism); white over people of color (white supremacy/racism); and so on.

Dualistic thinking, the separation of self and other and of subject and object, lies at the root of neo-Malthusianism. As such, it is unable to comprehend the inherent connectedness between the self and the other. Fear of the unknown and desire for permanence and control, in this case, the control of the global masses and their reproduction, underlies this dichotomous thinking. As a fragmented, top-down, and homogeneous approach, Malthusianism leaves no room for more balanced, qualitatively oriented participatory and diverse approaches, for example, indigenous peoples' and women's approaches to reproduction. Aggression and conquest rather than compassion and caring drive the population-control establishment and the larger model of technological-capitalist development that it represents.

Indeed, understanding and empathy require patience; but, according to its advocates, population control is urgent; it cannot lose time. Thus, terminal and high-tech methods are seen as being quicker, easier, and more efficient to administer than women-controlled methods of fertility control. However, myopic vision arising out of self-interest and fear leads to dangerous policies of gender, race, and class oppression. If unchallenged and unchecked, neo-Malthusian family planning could become an even greater tool of authoritarianism and social engineering in the future than it has been in the past. A shift from population control to birth control, from external domination to greater individual control over reproduction, can only be achieved through fundamental transformation of the global political-economic order and the dominant ideologies of both religious fundamentalism and neo-Malthusianism.

Reproduction is a highly political issue and it is unlikely that in the long term either the problem of population stabilization or the global social crisis will be resolved by political repression or high technology. Questions pertaining to democracy and authoritarianism are embedded in the structures of the society. Widespread protests against forced sterilizations in India under the Emergency imposed by Indira Gandhi were a major factor in her defeat in the subsequent elections. Field researchers who have observed grassroots reactions to coercive population-control policies in India have warned that mounting dissatisfaction could again lead to conflict and violence as it did under the Emergency.

In China too, despite state authoritarianism, there have been outbursts and protests against family-planning policies, and the government has had to soften its policies on a number of occasions. Reporters who have traveled in the Chinese countryside have observed that the government's population policy has caused "a mixture of anger, support, frustration, enthusiasm, deviousness and pain" and that the "desire to procreate" stirs more emotion than any desire for political democracy (cited in Bandarage, 1997, p. 102).

Toward Democratic Reproductive Rights

A democratic and sustainable approach to human reproduction must incorporate social, ethical, and ecological criteria avoiding the dogmatism and extremism of both pronatalist right-wing religious fundamentalism and antinatalist neo-Malthusian family planning. Appropriate technology and democratic social relations must define the realm of human biological reproduction as they must the realm of economic production. Numerical targets and economic incentives must be abolished from family-planning programs in the south and they must not be extended to the north. Quality health-care services and a range of safe contraceptives that help protect people against STDS and HIV/AIDS are required. Development of safe male contraceptives is essential for greater male-female partnership in birth control and family planning. Abortion should not be used as a contraceptive method, but safe and legal abortions should be available to women who need them. Given that abortion is a painful decision for women, there must be social support and compassion for women to make their own decisions. Where needed, safe methods of infertility treatment should also be made available to poor women, not merely fertility control.

Reproductive rights cannot be realized where the basic material needs of people are not met. Education, employment, and access to other economic resources are essential if people are to make their family-planning decisions freely. Thus, the very definitions of reproduction and family planning need to be enlarged to include the material needs of individuals, families, and communities. Continued avoidance of basic health and economic survival issues will only enable religious fundamentalist groups to present themselves as the guardians of family and community. This is beginning to happen in the area of HIV/AIDS prevention, which has been relatively neglected by family planners. The powerful evangelical Christian movement in the United States is beginning to take a leadership role in international HIV/AIDS prevention with the backing of the current U.S. government. While efforts to eradicate the deadly disease need to be welcomed, it is important to recognize that the fundamentalist Christians may use the opportunity to propagate their own moral values with regard to sexuality and gender norms and to advocate abstinence over protected sex.

In many regions, poverty eradication is also falling into the hands of internationally funded religious fundamentalist groups.

Evangelical Christian groups in particular are stepping in to fill the social and economic vacuum created by privatization of state sectors and cutbacks in state social welfare accompanying economic globalization. But unlike the family planners who provide economic incentives to the poor for acceptance of sterilization or contraception, the religious proselytizers require religious conversion to their faith and the acceptance of their moral injunctions. These developments are adding further confusion and complexity to societies already torn asunder by other political-economic and cultural contradictions.

If poverty eradication is to be genuine, it must go beyond economic incentives given in exchange for contraceptive acceptance or religious conversion. In the long-term, poverty eradication calls for setting limits on corporate profit-making and on the widening gaps between the north and the south and between the rich and the poor within countries. In order to have democratic family planning, overconsumption of resources by rich families needs to be reduced and underconsumption by poor families needs to be augmented. The optimum balance between human well-being and environmental sustainability can be achieved through rational use of natural resources, sustainable economic production, and more equitable consumption.

The concepts of family and community need to be further extended, recognizing that childbirth and human reproduction are increasingly taking place outside male-headed nuclear families. It is necessary to find a more democratic approach toward reproductive rights and human liberation that transcends the extremes of both patriarchal right-wing fundamentalism and top-down authoritarian family planning. To do so, a balance needs to be struck between the traditional role of the self-sacrificing mother and the modern role of the individualist career woman. To find a middle path, women need support from men, their families, communities, work places, and the larger world. To confront the extraordinary challenges facing humanity, it is essential to create more loving and sustainable families. Family planning needs to move beyond the narrow focus of fertility control to treating humanity, if not all planetary life, as one extended family.

See also **Equality: Gender Equality; Eugenics; Feminism; Human Rights; Third World.**

BIBLIOGRAPHY
American Public Health Association. "Opposition to Coercion in Family Planning Decision Making," 01/01/2001. Available at http://www.apha.org/legislative/policy/policysearch/.
Bandarage, Asoka. "Ethnic and Religious Tension in the World: A Political-Economic Perspective." In *Global Political Economy and the Wealth of Nations,* edited by Philip O'Hara. London: Routledge, 2004.
———. "Women of Color and the Global Population Question." In *Black Woman, Globalization, and Economic Justice,* edited by Filomina Steady. Rochester, Vt.: Schenkman, 2001.
———. *Women, Population, and Global Crisis: A Political-Economic Analysis.* London: Zed Books, 1997.
Boston Women's Health Book Collective. *Our Bodies, Ourselves for the New Century: A Book by and for Women.* New York: Simon and Schuster, 1998.

Burkhalter, Holly. "The Politics of AIDS: Engaging Conservative Activists." *Foreign Affairs* 83, no.1 (Jan./Feb.2004): 8–14.

Davis, Angela Y. *Women, Race, and Class.* New York: Vintage, 1981.

Davis, Kingsley. "Wives and Work: The Sex Role Revolution and Its Consequences." *Population and Development Review* 10, no. 3 (September 1984): 397–417.

Gordon, Linda. *Woman's Body, Woman's Right: A Social History of Birth Control in America.* New York: Grossman, 1976.

Harris, Marvin, and Eric B. Ross. *Death, Sex, and Fertility: Population Regulation in Preindustrial and Developing Societies.* New York: Columbia University Press, 1987.

Hartmann, Betsy. *Reproductive Rights and Wrongs: The Global Politics of Population Control.* Boston: South End, 1995.

Hull, Terrence. "Recent Trends in Sex Ratios at Birth in China." *Population and Development Review* 16, no.1 (March 1990): 63–83.

Karkal, Malini. "Why the Cairo Document Is Flawed." *Third World Resurgence* 50 (1994): 19.

King, Maurice. "Health Is a Sustainable State." *The Lancet* 336 (15 September 1990): 664–667.

Mamdani, Mahmood. *The Myth of Population Control: Family, Caste, and Class in an Indian Village.* New York: Monthly Review, 1972.

Srinivasan, Viji. "Death to the Female: Foeticide and Infanticide in India." *Third World Resurgence* 29, no. 30 (Jan.–Feb. 1993): 53–56.

United Nations. "Proclamation of Teheran." In *United Nations Action in the Field of Human Rights.* New York: United Nations, 1974.

———. *Report of the International Conference on Population and Development (ICPD),* Cairo, 5–13 September 1994.

United Nations Fund for Population Activities (UNFPA). *State of the World Population.* New York: UNFPA, 1991.

Warwick, Donald. *Bitter Pills: Population Policies and Their Implementation in Eight Developing Countries.* Cambridge, U.K.: Cambridge University Press, 1982.

World Bank. "Population and the World Bank: Implications from Eight Case Studies." Washington, D.C.: Operations Evaluation Department, 1992.

Asoka Bandarage

FASCISM.   For the purposes of this article, fascism will be treated as a politicized and revolutionary form of ultranationalism bent on mobilizing all remaining "healthy" social and political energies to resist the perceived onslaught of decadence so as to achieve the goal of a regenerated national community. It is a project that involves the rebirth (palingenesis) of both the political system and the social and moral culture that underpins it.

In discussing fascism's place within the history of ideas two basic issues must be addressed: first its genesis as a new "generic" political force that emerged at a particular point in the evolution of Western society, and second the various ideological components that it subsumes in the individual permutations it forms, in particular in national and political contexts. It will then be possible to offer some observations about fascism's evolution since 1945, one that has led some of its contemporary variants to be arguably of more interest to the history of ideas than to conventional political analysis.

The Origins of Generic Fascism

The ideological core of fascism postulated here contains one timeless component that cannot be said to have a historical source as such, while the other component originates in a relatively specific time and place within the history of ideas. The vision of rebirth, of palingenesis, of a new cycle of regeneration and renewal growing out of what appeared to be an irreversible linear process of decay, dissolution, or death, appears to be an archetype of human mythopoeia, manifesting itself, for example, as much in the Christian faith in the Resurrection of Christ and of all true believers as in the Hindu cosmology, which computes in mathematical detail the universe's infinite cycle of creation and destruction.

Ultranationalism, on the other hand, could only appear in countries where populist notions of sovereignty as the inherent property of a national community had already firmly established themselves. Fascism was able to emerge as a modern political ideology only after nationalism had arisen as a major ideological force in an increasingly secular Europeanized world where the foundations of traditional social systems (tribal, feudal, or absolutist) had been extensively eroded. In the wake of the French Revolution, several variants were formulated by intensely patriotic ideologues who imagined the nation as a supraindividual community subject to organic processes such as decay and growth and destined to rise to greatness. Though such a concept of the nation had already been formulated in the early nineteenth century by Germans such as Johann Gottlieb Fichte (1762–1814) and Ernst Arndt (1769–1860), it was the widespread obsession in fin-de-siècle Europe with the degeneracy of liberal civilization and its urgent need for moral regeneration that first made possible the conjuncture of palingenetic myth with ultranationalism that together formed the ideal climate within which fascism was incubated.

A major contributing factor in the evolution of organic conceptions of the nation was the rise of cultural, biological, and political racism, Aryan theory, and anti-Semitism in eighteenth- and nineteenth-century Europe. These had no single source, but drew both on the widespread and highly diverse preconceptions about race first articulated by such figures as Johann Gottfried von Herder (1744–1803), Joseph-Arthur de Gobineau (1816–1882), Robert Knox (1798–1862), Richard Wagner (1813–1883), Cesare Lombroso (1836–1909), Ernst Haeckel (1834–1919), Herbert Spencer (1820–1903), Vacher de Lapouge (1854–1936), Houston Chamberlain, (1855–1927), and Friedrich Nietzsche (1844–1900), as well as on currents of humanistic, scientific, and scientist thought such as national histories, philology, physical and cultural anthropology, criminology, sociology, genetics, demography, eugenics, Social Darwinism, and vitalism. Once blended in with ultranationalism and palingenetic myth, racism could provide a pseudoscientific (scientist) rationale to the myth that a nation in decline can only fulfill its transcendent historical mission once purged of forces allegedly compromising the "purity of the race" (for example, materialism, individualism, cosmopolitanism, immorality, miscegenation, "alien" ideological elements, or some combination of these).

It was in the first decade of the twentieth century that artists and cultural commentators such as the numerous writers of

Mussolini addresses crowd from eagle-shaped podium, Turin, Italy, 1939. Fascism was born in Italy in the early twentieth century, during the regime of dictator Benito Mussolini (1883–1945). Mussolini attempted to create a corporative state, in which the working population was divided into groups representing different economic sectors. HULTON ARCHIVE/GETTY IMAGES

völkisch literature in Germany, Charles Maurras (1868–1952) and Maurice Barrès (1862–1923) in France, Giovanni Papini (1881–1956) and Gabriele D'Annunzio (1863–1938) in Italy, and Nicolae Iorga (1871–1940) in Romania provided poetic or theoretical expression to the importance of reawakening the national soul from the debilitating slumber induced by liberal modernity. Some attempts to turn these ideas into political movements were made before World War I, notably by Maurras' Action Française (1897–), the Pan-German League (1886–1914) under Heinrich Class (1868–1953), the Christian Social Party (1893–1938) founded by the Austrian anti-Semite Karl Lueger (1844–1910), and the Italian Nationalist Association (1910–1923). But it was the shattering impact of the "Great War" itself that transformed marginalized and essentially cultural movements for national rebirth into political formations with a serious revolutionary strategy based on a blend of populist rally for change, a democratic party, and an extraparliamentary paramilitary movement. It was the war that simultaneously nationalized the masses subjectively while creating localized pockets of objective political, social, and economic upheaval in many European countries, not least the collapse of the Hohenzollern, Habsburg, and Romanov dynasties and the

Russian Revolution itself, that were indispensable for new forms of revolutionary nationalism to thrive. The first of these new "militia parties" to seize power was Fascism, which conquered the Italian state in two stages, 1922–1925 (when Mussolini was head of state) and 1925–1929 (when he established a dictatorship), and it is from this movement and regime that the generic term takes its name. Since the 1920s, *fascist* has been applied by historians, political commentators, and activists to a number of dictatorial regimes that emerged in interwar Europe and in the wider Europeanized world, notably in Latin America. However, significant differences of opinion persist between experts about which regimes are embraced by the term, the inclusion of the Third Reich being especially contentious.

An Overview of the "Fascist Epoch"

The period 1918–1945 has become widely known as "the fascist epoch." Certainly by the autumn of 1941, after the recent triumph of Francisco Franco (1892–1975) in the Spanish Civil War (1936–1939) and the apparently inexorable success of Adolf Hitler's (1889–1945) Blitzkrieg in France, Scandinavia, and Poland, and with victory in Soviet Russia seemingly imminent, there were good grounds for this, however problematic the phrase may have become for later historians. By this time Benito Mussolini's (1883–1945) Partito Nazionale Fascista (PNF) and Hitler's Nationalsozialistische Deutsche Arbeiterpartei (NSDAP, whose core ideology correspond closely to the generic definition given above) had created the templates of organization and style for revolutionary nationalists to emulate all over the Europeanized world. Even democracies as stable as Switzerland, Denmark, and Iceland, or new nations still confident in their future such as the United States and Australia, hosted minute fascist parties attempting in vain to emulate the performance of mass revolutionary movements. More significant (though safely contained) fascist movements developed where the structural conditions of crisis were sufficiently strong, notably in Finland, France, Hungary, Romania, Brazil, Chile, and South Africa, and some abortive fascist movements achieved prominence under Nazi occupation, notably Vidkun Quisling's Nasjonal Samling in Norway, Léon Degrelle's Rex in Belgium, and (in 1944) Ferenc Szálasi's "Hungarist" Arrow Cross movement. Thus José Streel, a leading spokesman of the collaborationist Belgian Rex movement, had not succumbed to delusions of grandeur when he asserted in 1942 that, whether it was called "fascism," "national socialism," or "the new order," "a new force" able to "synthesize the needs of the age" was "everywhere at work giving birth to the revolution of the twentieth century" (quoted in Griffin, 1995, p. 206).

In the final analysis the fascist assault on modern history was abortive. Only two fascisms managed to conquer state power and attempt to turn their revolutionary vision into reality, and eventually both met with crushing military defeat having failed to realize their revolutionary objectives. All other fascisms were successfully marginalized by liberal democracies or fended off by conservative authoritarian states by being either crushed or absorbed. It was nevertheless a tribute to the degree to which fascism had come to be associated with the future of civilization by the 1930s that a number of authoritarian states modeled themselves on the style of fascism.

Still from the 1934 German propaganda film *Triumph of the Will*, directed by Leni Riefenstahl. Nazism, or National Socialism, was similar to Italian Fascism, with some distinctions. Nazism was based on the concepts of military authority and racial superiority, and its followers advocated a purging of those who did not adhere to certain criteria. THE KOBAL COLLECTION

A number of other authoritarian states chose to simulate the "real thing" by such ploys as organizing "from above" nationwide single parties, youth movements, and other mass organizations, proliferating nationalistic symbols, declaring the inauguration of new eras in the life of the nation or the creation of "new states," staging theatrical political events, and engineering phony leader cults. This pattern was most prominent in Franquist Spain (1938–1975), Antonio de Oliveira Salazar's Estado Novo in Portugal (1926–1974), Philippe Pétain's Vichy France (1940–1944), Ion Antonescu's National Legionary State in Romania (1940–1941), Ioannis Metaxas's dictatorship in Greece (1936–1940), Karlis Ulmanis' authoritarian Latvia (1934–1940), and Miklós Horthy de Nagybánya's authoritarian state in Hungary (1919–1944). It was equally a sign of the times that the ultimate victor was liberalism (or liberal capitalism), apparently the weakest of them all.

Spain and Portugal progressively defascistized themselves once the tide of war started to turn against the Axis powers.

Once parafascism is taken into account and with the benefit of hindsight, it is clear that interwar Europe was dominated not by fascism at all, but by a titanic struggle between liberalism, conservatism, communism, and fascism, in which fascism, which at one point looked like carrying all before it, eventually came off worst.

Non-European Fascisms

Traditionally, comparative fascist studies have focused almost exclusively on fascism as a European phenomenon. However, it should be noted that, while the emphasis on the totalitarian bid of fascism to create a new type of society distinguishes it from conservative regimes, whether traditionalist or military, there were in the "fascist epoch" a small number of non-European countries that hosted attempts to emulate the achievements of revolutionary nationalism in Italy and Germany. The most important examples are the Ossewabrandwag and the Greyshirts in South Africa, the National Socialist Movement (MNS) in Chile, and the Brazilian Integralist Action (AIB) movement that arose under Getúlio Vargas's dictatorship in Brazil (1937–1945). All of them suffered the fate of most of their European counterparts by being marginalized or crushed.

Breaking with the European pattern, two military dictatorships seem to have made a genuine bid to fascistize the nation from above rather than using fascism as a means of generating mass conformism and passivity: Chiang Kai-shek's (1887–1975) nationalist regime in China, eventually overwhelmed by Japanese imperialism, and the military dictatorship of the Grupo de Oficiales Unidos (GOU) in Argentina (1943–1946). GOU created a legacy that Juan Péron would build on after the war during his rule (1946–1955), which was in ideological and organizational terms an eclectic blend of political elements of which fascism was only a muted part.

It should also be noted that the most highly developed, dynamic, and destructive parafascist nation of all arguably emerged not in Europe but when imperial Japan entered its most totalitarian and expansionist phase between 1937 and 1945. Despite its alliance with Italian Fascism and German Nazism, it carried out its aggressive scheme of territorial expansion under a divine emperor and with its feudal social system intact rather than under a charismatic "new man" in a "reborn" nation. Nor did the defeat of Italy in 1943 and then of Germany in 1945 cause it to relent in the radicalness of its prosecution of the war, a fact that underlines the need to recognize that fascism by no means has a monopoly of right-wing totalitarian violence.

The Diversity of Individual Fascisms

We now turn to the second aspect of fascism that impinges on the history of ideas, its ideological constituents. A central premise behind the definition applied in this article is that fascism is to be treated on a par with the other major political "isms" of the modern age, such as liberalism and socialism, as an ideology in its own right with its own agenda for creating the ideal society. A corollary of this is that it can be conceived for analytic purposes as a cluster of core ("ineliminable") ideological components, which we have identified here with just two components: the conception of the people as an organic organism, and a palingenetic concept of history that envisages national decay giving way imminently or eventually to a process of regeneration and renewal. This core can become associated in particular times and places with many varied and even conflicting secondary ("adjacent" or "peripheral") concepts, with the result that fascism is externalized itself in a wide range of specific manifestations shaped by particular conjunctures of historical forces.

Another implication of this approach is that it is futile to search for the sources of generic fascism in the work of a particular thinker, such as Georges Sorel's thesis of the primacy of myth, Ernst Haeckel's organicism, Vilfredo Pareto's theory of the circulation of elites, Friedrich Nietzsche's calls for a new breed of superman, or Oswald Spengler's scheme of the decline and "Caesarist" renewal of the West, however much they may have influenced individual ideologues or movements. For the same reason it is fallacious to see all forms of fascism

drawing on the same currents of thought or driven by the same process, such as Social Darwinism, eugenics, corporatism, Marxist revisionism, modernization, or antimodernity, let alone to attribute it to generic forces such as "irrationalism," "capitalism," or "moral decline," which have minimal heuristic value as explanatory concepts.

In fact, one of fascism's outstanding traits is its eclecticism, the propensity of its numerous individual variants to accommodate or synthesize ideological components from a wide range of sources taken from any part of the left-right spectrum. Italian Fascism, for example, merged elements of right-wing politics (nationalism, imperialism, authoritarianism) with left-wing syndicalist claims of creating social justice and abolishing class conflict, and the cult of the Roman past with elements of the Futurist cult of hypermodernity. It also attracted a number of former Marxists in Italy and Germany, hosted left-wing and right-wing variants of corporatist theory, and accommodated currents of philosophical idealism and technocratic modernism; clerical Fascism and neopaganism; cultural racism (which treated patriotic Italian Jews as full members of the reborn Italy, although a more "biological" current eventually led to the adoption of anti-Semitic race laws); and the full spectrum of aesthetics from neoclassicism to futurism, from anticosmopolitan ruralism to international modernism. Even Nazism was far from homogeneous ideologically, embracing ruralist and technocratic visions of the new order, varying degrees of paganism and accommodation with Christianity, several varieties of racism, an anticapitalist ("Strasserite") current, and even a strand of promodernist aesthetics. Fascism's animus against communism and the degenerate impact of liberalism on the organic national community nevertheless makes it sensible to locate fascism within the tradition of right-wing politics rather than simply "beyond" left and right (as it sometimes claims to be).

Fascism can also manifest itself in a variety of organizational forms. It does not necessarily take the form of a properly constituted movement, let alone a full-fledged party-political movement, and has only twice formed a regime. This is why attempts to elaborate or extend the fascist minimum identified here (for example, by adding such elements as paramilitarism, the leader principle, corporatism, or territorial expansionism) severely restrict its heuristic value.

Race. Once we move from the synoptic panorama of the whole fascist epoch to consider individual fascisms in close-up, the heterogeneity of their fascist ideology emphasized here soon becomes apparent. The sense of national identity promoted by Italian Fascism, for example, was originally little more than an antiliberal version of heightened patriotism, which attempted to present the current generation as heirs of the same genius that had created the Roman Empire, the Roman Catholic Church, and the artistic and scientific Renaissance. Partly because of the powerful presence of organized Christianity in social life, "modern" biological or eugenic concepts of racial purity were relegated to a subordinate position, even if they were implicit in the demographic campaign and in the laws against miscegenation introduced in the wake of the colonization of Ethiopia. Certainly an Italian equivalent of the Nazi "euthanasia" campaign to cleanse the national community of its "hereditarily ill" was unthinkable, and though a current of anti-Semitism existed in Fascism independently of Nazism, when anti-Semitic race and citizenship laws were eventually introduced in 1938 declaring the Italians to be of Aryan stock they were widely experienced as both un-Italian and un-Fascist.

Long before coming to power, Nazism was notorious for disseminating a vision of the national community based on a concept of race that included cultural, Social Darwinian, and eugenic components. As a result, decadence was considered at least partly the product of racial decay, which in turn meant that the nation had to be purged of both ideological and physical enemies before it could be reborn. It followed from the same racial concept of the nation that its boundaries "naturally" extended to cover the whole geopolitical area in which ethnic Germans constituted a majority, and ensured that the Third Reich's plans for territorial conquest were based on a hierarchical conception of racial superiority and inferiority familiar from European imperialism overseas, but never applied before to peoples in mainland Europe.

If the abortive fascist movements are taken into account, yet more permutations of the nationalist myth come into view. The Romanian Iron Guard was viscerally anti-Semitic, elaborated its own myth of Romanian racial purity, and planned to set up an anthropological institute to build up a database on the variegated racial makeup of those living on Romanian soil. Yet its outstanding feature was its stress on the importance of Romanian Orthodox Christianity as an indicator of national and cultural identity. Other fascisms that, in contrast to the overtly neopagan Fascism and Nazism, incorporated local versions of Christianity into their concept of national belonging were the Spanish Falange, the Finnish Isänmaallinen Kansanliike (Patriotic People's Movement), and the Afrikaner Ossewabrandwag.

A different permutation of fascist racial myth again is exhibited by the ABI (the Brazilian Integralist Action), whose membership grew to 200,000 before it was outlawed by Getúlio Vargas's parafascist military regime. This highly original permutation of fascism attributed the national genius and potential for rebirth not to any one of the many ethnic groups that make up modern Brazil, but to its unique blend of peoples and cultures, a concept that precluded the pursuit of racial purity through eugenic or exterminatory policies. This avenue was also barred by the powerful presence of Catholicism in Brazil's social and political culture, though it is significant that the ABI developed an elaborate form of "political religion" for its meetings and rallies. It is also consistent with the ABI's essentially pagan conception of renewal that its leader, Plínio Salgado, published his philosophy of history according to which his movement was leading Brazilians into the "fourth era of humanity."

Economics. Although Marxists have always seen fascism as driven by a crisis of the capitalist economic system and the rise of socialism, and some non-Marxist experts identify interwar fascism with corporatism, the truth is predictably more complex. The relationship between fascism and finance capital, big business, or the bourgeoisie is far from straightforward, and

there were currents within Nazism and Fascism that were anticapitalist to the extent that they took seriously the idea of a "national socialism." Contemporary fascism contains currents that are, at least on paper, extremely hostile to (Jewish, U.S., globalizing, corporate) capitalism, notably the New Right, Third Positionism, and National Bolshevism, and some prominent "Strasserite" Third Positionists, striving to develop a stance beyond both capitalism and communism, currently use *fascist* as a pejorative term for national revolutionaries not prepared to reject capitalism.

As for corporatism, only Italian Fascism attempted to install a corporatist state, which failed in practice to fulfill the ideals of any of the rival theories of corporatism that jostled for position under Mussolini. These included a "left-wing" syndicalist current, an authoritarian nationalist strand, and a version promoted by Catholics encouraged to do so by the Catholic Church, which saw in corporatism a way of mitigating the evils of unbridled materialism and individualism. However, such was the appeal of a "third way" between laissez-faire capitalism and the Soviet planned economy that the British Union of Fascists adopted the theory of the corporatist state, and a number of interwar fascisms (e.g., in Spain, Portugal, Hungary, Brazil, and Chile) advocated a fusion of nationalism with the power of organized labor, whether it was termed "national syndicalism" or "national socialism." It should also be pointed out that the parafascist states (both Catholic countries) of Salazar and Franco retained corporatist elements in their economic systems well into the postwar period, and during the 1940s these achieved some degree of success, though at the cost of organized labor, which was forced to forfeit much of its political and economic power.

On the other hand, Nazi Germany rejected the idea of the corporatist state except in the sphere of cultural production. Nevertheless, in tune with the spirit of the age, which favored the strong state and the planned economy, the Third Reich ruthlessly applied the principle of the primacy of politics over economics that legitimized unlimited state intervention in the running of the economy. It should be added that the British strand of one of the most consistently anticapitalist forms of postwar fascism, namely Third Positionism, attempted in the 1990s to resuscitate one of the interwar "alternative" economic theories, namely distributionism, but with no prospect of practical application to date, and that many contemporary fascisms are influenced by radical Green critiques of the unsustainability of the global economy.

Culture. Fascism's relationship with modern culture is even more resistant to generalizations than its economics. One of the more unusual features of Brazil's AIB was that its ideology grew out of currents of Latin American cultural theory developed by an intelligentsia influenced by European modernism and the "revolt against positivism." In this it had parallels with Italian Fascism, which hosted a number of currents of modernism, notably futurism, whose artists believed that the innovative dynamic or conceptual dimension of their style expressed the energy that was creating the New Italy. At the same time it was possible for the experimental, anarchic, taboo-breaking thrust of modernism to be seen as embodiments of the very decadence that it was fascism's mission to banish from modern life. As a result, fascism also attracted support from those who looked to a revitalized neoclassicism, vernacular, or ruralist art to create the iconic statements of healthy values that were to be an integral part of the reborn nation. Under Mussolini both interpretations of modernism coexisted and a rich variety of aesthetics resulted. Rather than promote an official Fascist style, the regime was content to be associated with creativity under all its aspects, a principle known as "hegemonic pluralism."

In stark contrast to Brazil and Italy, in 1935 Nazi Germany launched a campaign to purge Germany of modernism, henceforth officially declared the expression of cultural and biological degeneracy. Yet even here a campaign had been fought to have expressionism classified as Aryan, and a number of artists with highly modernist temperaments, notably Gottfried Benn and Ernst Jünger, were initially attracted to the regime. The diverse subject matter of some Nazi painting, which included motorway bridges, sporting events, factories, bombing raids, and battle scenes, also underlines the need to avoid simplistic generalizations about the antimodernity of fascism or the longing to return to the idylls of peasant existence allegedly at the heart of Nazi art. It is also significant that the Nazis paid even more attention to encouraging a "healthy" national cinema industry than the Italian Fascists, hardly the sign of a compulsive antimodernity. While some films under both regimes were overtly propagandistic, the majority were made without direct state interference and dealt with the emotional and social comedies and dramas of modern Italian and German existence against the backcloth of the new order. By endorsing the values, normalcy, and modernity of fascist society they bear witness to the way the power of the film to create an aesthetic illusion of wholeness was seamlessly adapted to the new societies, thereby contributing to the routinization of the fascist revolution in the experience of "ordinary" Italians and Germans.

Architecture. The architecture of the two regimes reflected their different relationships to modernism. Despite a marked tendency toward monumentalism and the increasing use of neoclassicism for many civic buildings by the late 1930s, Fascist architects worked in a number of styles, some of them deeply indebted to the international modernism of the day. Its protagonists saw the bold use of steel and glass as reflecting the future-oriented, hypermodern dynamic of the New Italy, its urge to throw off the dead weight of tradition. This was unthinkable in Nazi Germany, where the Bauhaus was considered the symbol of "cultural Bolshevism," and the prescribed style for civic buildings was a Spartan neoclassicism whose symmetry, lack of ornament, and gargantuan proportions supposedly evoked the "purity" and heroic "will to construct" of the Aryan.

However, the Third Reich's retention of elements of modernism for such projects as bridges, factories, high-density holiday accommodation, and power stations, as well as the fact that Ludwig Mies van der Rohe tendered an unashamedly modernist design for the Dresden Bank before leaving Nazi Germany for the United States, invites a more complex reaction to its state architecture than simply dismissing it as philistine reaction. Rather, its neoclassicism is to be seen as the expression of the aesthetic correlation to the eugenics and

"racial hygiene" applied in social and demographic policy. The austere, lifeless pseudoclassical buildings and sculptures whose aesthetics it determined betoken not a nostalgia for a bygone age, but the belief in the ongoing rebirth of the German people from the quagmire of Weimar decadence. They embody in permanent plastic form the presence of "eternal values."

The anthropological revolution. When considering individual spheres of art it is important to bear in mind that art for fascists was no longer to be a separate sphere of human endeavor remote from the mainstream of political and social life in the same category as leisure or sport and prey to the forces of commercialization. For the cultural theorists of Fascism, Nazism, the British Union of Fascists, the Falange, the Iron Guard, or the AIB, whatever their stance on modernism, realism, or the celebration of rural life, art was meant to express the uncorrupted soul of the people, and made manifest the health or decadence of the entire culture. They assumed that just as the chaos and commercialism of modern art reflected the current decadence of the West, so the regenerated nation would spontaneously produce an artistic renaissance. This would come about once artists were no longer concerned with "self-expression," innovation, or experimentation; their reunion with their people and nation naturally ensured that each sculpture, film, novel, musical composition, or building expressed the values of the new age.

Art was only one of the spheres of social activity that were supposed to contribute to this ethos of palingenesis. Schools, universities, youth and leisure organizations, mass rallies, newsreels, newspapers, sporting events, national holidays, local festivals, the organization of work, business, and industry, in fact any context in which the public sphere impinged on the private became sites for the further integration of the individual into the national community. In this sense the deepest level of the fascist revolution was not political or military, but cultural. As long as fascism remained a genuinely charismatic force in Italy and Germany it was not a revolution simply imposed on society, but was fed by the spontaneous enthusiasm of many thousands of creative individuals who wanted to contribute to the transformation. This interpretation is fully consistent with recent theories of totalitarianism that place an emphasis on its bid to bring about an anthropological revolution, and on seeing the political religion that it institutes not as an exercise in collective brainwashing but as a means to transform society's political and moral culture.

This attempted anthropological revolution had particular implications for women. True to the spirit of an age that had recently experienced World War I, the interwar fascist image of the new man embraced elements of the archetypal warrior and knight, and the celebration of militarism, war, and the new order was pervaded by values that would now be recognized as male chauvinist. The corollary of this was that fascism was hostile to feminism as a force that destroyed the "natural" roles dictated by biology, and both Fascist Italy and Nazi Germany introduced legislation to remove women from the workplace, criminalize abortion, encourage big families, and glorify motherhood and domestic functions as the true vocation of women. The demographic campaign in both countries was backed up by antenatal, maternity, and childcare services that anticipated some of the best practice of the modern welfare state.

However, it is erroneous to dismiss such measures as proof of fascism's reactionary bid to turn the clock back to traditional family values. The creation of mass organizations for women of all ages and social categories, including auxiliary units for those drawn to life in the armed services, were symptomatic of an attempt to free the female population from the constraints of domesticity and motivate it into playing an active, if subordinate, role within the new national community on a par with the Soviet mobilization of women. A physically and morally healthy motherhood was celebrated as a key element in the triumph over decadence and the regeneration of the nation. A "new woman" would arise to assist the "new man" in his heroic revolutionary task. It might also be pointed out that the stereotype of women destined to breed new members of the national community is no more degrading than the stereotype that declared the destiny of men lay in their readiness to kill and be sacrificed for the sake of the new order.

A far more terrible fate than that which befell female members of the Nazi national community awaited the millions of those, male and female, adult and children, who were excluded from it on grounds of hereditary illness, asocial behavior, or membership of an inferior race, and thus were subjected to sterilization, enslavement, torture, experimentation, or extermination. It was in the fanatical persecution and mass elimination of "life unworthy of life" and "subhumans" by the Third Reich under the cover of World War II that fascism's archaic palingenetic logic of "cathartic destruction" reveals its most chilling potential for impacting on modern history.

The Survival Strategies of Postwar Fascism

The ideological definition of fascism adopted in this article leads to an interpretation of its development that sees the defeat of the Axis powers not as putting an end to fascism, but forcing it to adopt new strategies to survive in a political environment no longer characterized by the upheaval and crises that were the precondition for Fascism and Nazism to take the form of mass movements producing spectacular displays of charismatic politics. The Allied victory over fascism inaugurated the sustained recovery of liberal capitalism, which eventually outlived the state socialist experiment in creating a new order conducted by the Soviet Union and its satellites. The massive loss of life caused by World War II and the horrors committed by the Third Reich and imperial Japan in the alliance with Fascism utterly discredited the rhetoric of militarism, ultranationalism, imperialism, and new orders for all but a small, highly marginalized minority of fanatics. The mass constituency of potential trans-class support for revolutionary brands of nationalism simply evaporated (although it reemerged quickly in the chaotic conditions of post-Soviet Russia).

In such conditions any attempts to emulate the PNF or NS-DAP were doomed to have even more pathetic results than those achieved by the many abortive movements in the "fascist epoch." Even the most successful postwar fascist party, Italy's Movimento Sociale Italiano (MSI), had to dissociate itself from any paramilitary activity and strictly abide by the democratic

French presidential candidate Jean-Marie Le Pen with slogan reading "France found again," 2002. Right-wing political parties such as Le Pen's National Front (best known for its anti-immigration platform) have often tried to place what they see as the decline of society in a larger geocultural context. AP/WIDE WORLD PHOTOS

"rules of the game." This strategy put it in the position to emerge from the political ghetto reconstituted as the Alleanza Nazionale in 1994, though only after it had renounced any attachment to its revolutionary and totalitarian past.

Meanwhile, faced by the almost complete disappearance of its natural interwar habitat, "real" fascism demonstrated a remarkable capacity for adaptation. While at the level of the general public, xenophobia and anxieties over the erosion of national identity in some countries found an outlet in a new type of party, the right-wing populist party embodied in Jean–Marie Le Pen's National Front and Jörg Haider's Austrian Freedom Party, intransigent national revolutionaries could follow several tactics to keep the revolutionary vision alive. One was to concentrate on forming small cadres of fanatics dedicated to "the cause," some of whom in the 1970s and 1980s carried out a series of terroristic outrages in pursuit of what was known as the "Strategy of Tension" designed to bring down the Italian state.

A second tactic was for fascists to abandon narrow nationalism and place their concern with the decadence of society in a wider geocultural context, whether that of the white or Aryan race, or of Europe, conceived as a federation of cultural homogeneous nations or *ethnies*. A third was to withdraw from the political sphere altogether and concentrate on civic space, the realm of ideas and culture, thus turning fascism into a largely "metapolitical" force, made up not of full-fledged movements, but of numerous atomized formations known collectively as the "groupuscular right." An outstanding example of this is the pan-European vision of rebirth advocated (in conflicting terms) by the European New Right and by Third Positionism. The latter still has not abandoned political activism and the use of violence in theory (or rather in rhetoric), even if the transition to a new era has by implication been indefinitely postponed, leaving a few stoic spiritual warriors to resist the forces of cultural suicide true to the principle of "leaderless resistance." The logical consequence of this process of extreme atomization is the type of "lone wolf" terrorist act committed by Timothy McVeigh (in Oklahoma) or David Copeland (the London nail bomber), both of whom internalized and acted on the fascist critique of the state without belonging to any formal organization.

The Struggle for "Cultural Hegemony"

The most sophisticated incarnation of fascism in the "postfascist" epoch is the New Right. This is an umbrella term for a movement with a local base in a number of European countries but important international linkages, and consists of both grouspuscules and some high-profile cultural think tanks such as GRECE in France and networks of associations such as Thule-Netz in Germany. In Russia a particularly influential form of the New Right is known as "Euroasianism." In it the fascist attack on the degeneracy of liberalism as an increasingly globalized cultural and economic system combined with the call for an entirely new order has been thoroughly "metapoliticized," while the ultranationalist nostalgia for roots and organic ethnic communities has undergone extensive "Europeanization."

Many scholars, and certainly New Right intellectuals themselves, would strenuously disagree that an ideology that operates purely in the realm of ideas and has abandoned belligerent nationalism and racism can be classified as a form of fascism at all. However, the French New Right, which under the aegis of the extraordinarily prolific Alain de Benoist (b. 1943) pioneered the international movement, demonstrably grew out of a fascist milieu that by the mid-1960s despaired of seizing power through conventional political or violent means. Moreover, the war against decadence and longings for rebirth, which were the hallmarks of interwar fascism, can still be shown to form the ideological core of the sophisticated discourse of cultural criticism it has evolved since then, even if the palingenesis of the organic cultures and communities of Europe is no longer imminent.

By dedicating itself exclusively to the struggle to win "cultural hegemony" (a tactic known as "right-wing Gramscism"), the New Right has been able to exert influence on right-wing populism and neofascist activism at one stage removed. This it does by providing elaborate ideological critiques of the prevailing "system," as well as disseminating a subtle form of "differentialist" racism that preaches not racial superiority but the value of all cultures and the need to preserve them from the corrosive effects of multiculturalism, mass immigration, egalitarianism, and the "leveling" of society by cultural globalization.

The Conservative Revolution

In adapting itself so thoroughly to the prolonged "interregnum" before the next "rebirth," New Right fascism has systematically shed every external aspect of its interwar manifestations. There is no hint of charismatic leader, paramilitarism, expansionist imperialism, or theatrical politics. Yet fascism's ideological nucleus remains intact: the longing for a new order based on the restoration of organic communities, the defeat of liberalism, the transcendence of communism, materialism, chaos, and decadence, remains intact. It is no coincidence if the New Right draws extensively on the same ideologues of the Conservative Revolution, notably Friedrich Nietzsche, Ernst Jünger (1895–1998), Carl Schmitt (1888–1985), and Martin Heidegger (1889–1976), that helped prepare the way for the Nazis' war on Enlightenment values, even if one of the pioneers of the New Right, Armin Mohler (1920–2003), was careful to dissociate them from Nazism by calling them "the Trotskyites of the German Revolution" (Hitler being its Stalin).

Some thinkers of the New Right have also been influenced by the "Traditionalist" philosophy of history elaborated by the Italian "philosopher" Julius Evola (1898–1974), which posits a Hindu-like cycle of rebirth and decadence shaping human history. In his canonical diagnoses of the postwar world (which also influenced both "black" terrorism of the Strategy of Tension and contemporary Third Positionism) Fascism and Nazism are indicted with failing to inaugurate the process of rebirth, with the result that those with a sense of higher values are now condemned to stay faithful to the cause of a higher metapolitical order with no immediate prospect of inaugurating the new age. Another fruitful source of inspiration of the New Right crusade against the "decadent" Judeo-Christian, materialist, U.S.-dominated West are carefully edited liberal and far left critiques of the "totalitarianism" and metaphysical vacuousness of contemporary capitalist society. In the New Right, fascism has in a sense returned to its fin-de-siècle roots as a current of radical cultural criticism lacking any concrete political vehicle or clear strategy for gaining power other than that of taking over what one of their main spokesmen, Pierre Krebs, calls "the laboratories of thinking" (quoted in Griffin, 1995, p. 349).

The Future of Fascism

Fascists of any denomination are not alone in believing that deep structural problems threaten the sustainability of the present "hegemonic system" in the West, notably escalating ecological and resources crises, and the demographic explosion in the "two-thirds world" (often called the "third world," even though in terms of population it is far bigger than the first world). Nor can it be denied that mass immigration and globalization pose threats to established national and cultural identities. There will thus be no shortage of empirical data to convince those with a fascist mind-set that we live in an age of decadence and that "our" only hope lies, sooner or later, in a total palingenesis capable of pioneering a new type of modernity while preserving ethnic roots, cultural identity, and belonging. Given the unusual capacity of fascism for eclecticism and adaptation, it seems likely that, at least in its metapoliticized, internationalized, and groupuscularized permutations, it will continue to thrive as a permanent, though marginalized and ineffectual, part of the political and social subculture of civic society throughout an increasingly Europeanized (or Americanized) world. It will thus continue to generate a steady flow of fresh ideological specimens to occupy political scientists and historians of ideas for the foreseeable future.

See also **Authoritarianism; Communism; Eugenics; Nationalism; Propaganda; Race and Racism; Social Darwinism.**

BIBLIOGRAPHY

Bauman, Zygmunt. *Modernity and the Holocaust.* Ithaca, N.Y.: Cornell University Press, 1989.

Davies, Peter, and Derek Lynch. *Fascism and the Far Right.* London: Routledge, 2002.

Drake, Richard. *The Revolutionary Mystique and Terrorism in Contemporary Italy.* Bloomington: Indiana University Press, 1989.

Gentile, Emilio. *The Sacralization of Politics in Fascist Italy.* Cambridge, Mass.: Harvard University Press, 1996.

Griffin, Roger. "Interregnum or Endgame? The Radical Right in the 'Post-fascist' Era." In *Reassessing Political Ideologies: The Durability of Dissent,* edited by Michael Freeden. New York: Routledge, 2001.

Griffin, Roger, ed. *Fascism.* Oxford: Oxford University Press, 1995.

Kallis, Aristotle A., ed. *The Fascism Reader.* London: Routledge, 2002.

Larsen, Stein, ed. *Fascism outside Europe: The European Impulse against Domestic Conditions in the Diffusion of Global Fascism..* New York: Columbia University Press; Boulder, Colo.: Social Sciences Monographs, 2001.

Mosse, George L. *Fascist Revolution: Toward a General Theory of Fascism.* New York: Fertig, 1999.

Paxton, Robert O. *The Anatomy of Fascism.* New York: Knopf, 2004.

Payne, Stanley G. *A History of Fascism, 1914–1945.* Madison: University of Wisconsin Press, 1995.

Sternhell, Zeev. "Fascist Ideology." In *Fascism: A Reader's Guide: Analyses, Interpretations, Bibliography,* edited by Walter Laqueur. Berkeley: University of California Press, 1976.

Taylor, Brandon, and Wilfried van der Will, eds. *The Nazification of Art: Art, Design, Music, Architecture, and Film in the Third Reich.* Winchester, U.K.: Winchester Press, 1990.

Roger Griffin

FATALISM. Fatalism is the thesis that whatever happens must happen. This is not to be confused with the completely innocuous idea that whatever happens, happens. Nor is fatalism to be conflated with the proposition that, necessarily, whatever happens happens, where this assertion simply expresses the tautologous nature of the prior innocuous idea. Fatalism is a substantive thesis that claims that the occurrence of every event or state of affairs is necessary.

Elucidation of this thesis requires the articulation of the fatalist's necessity; we must know what the "must" amounts to when the fatalist tells us that whatever happens must occur. Since *fatalism* is to some measure a term of art, there are not tight a priori restrictions about how the necessity used by the fatalist is to be understood. There is, however, one criterion for any acceptable definition. Fatalism has occupied thinkers for more than two millennia primarily because its truth appears to have the consequence that we lack the power (capability, capacity) to perform any actions other than those that we actually do perform. If we perform an act, which is a type of event, and this event is necessitated, then no other act could have occurred. And, if no other act could have occurred, then we have no power to bring about any act other than the one that we, in fact,

produced. If fatalism is true, there are no alternative courses of action open to us and so the conception of ourselves as meaningful, free-willed agents who have the power to affect the constitution of the future is thoroughly compromised. Any account of fatalistic necessity worth the name needs to respect the prima facie tension between fatalism and autonomous behavior.

Virtually all philosophers construe fatalistic necessity as logical or conceptual. Steven Cahn is representative when he states that fatalism

> is the thesis that the laws of logic *alone* [his italics] suffice to prove that no man has free will, suffice to prove that the only actions which a man can perform are the actions which he does, in fact, perform, and suffice to prove that a man can bring about only those events which do, in fact, occur and can prevent only those events which do not, in fact, occur. (p. 8)

Although logical construals of fatalistic necessity meet the minimal requirement of maintaining the prima facie antagonism between fatalism and the actions of autonomous persons, they unfairly caricature the nature of some arguments that all parties deem as fatalistic. If all fatalistic arguments are conceived as containing only statements of logical laws (i.e., tautologies) as premises, it is difficult to see both how any substantive thesis could evolve and how any disagreement about the truth of fatalism could be more than merely a verbal squabble. In fact, the sophisticated fatalistic arguments of Aristotle (384–322 B.C.E.), Diodorus Cronus (d. c. 284 B.C.E.), and others demonstrate that there are implicit substantive, albeit controversial, assumptions concerning the nature of truth and time. Before examining these arguments, it is important that we distinguish between fatalism and determinism, two theses that are frequently conflated.

Fatalism and Determinism

Regardless of the exact articulation of fatalistic necessity that one accepts, virtually all agree that it should be distinguished from the necessity of determinism. This distinction is especially important since determinism can be legitimately characterized in precisely the same way as fatalism: whatever happens must happen. The necessity of determinism is causal or natural necessity; all events or states of affairs are causally determined by antecedent states of affairs and the laws of nature. Alternatively, determinism claims that it is logically necessary that given an antecedent state of the world and the laws of nature, a particular subsequent state of the world will occur. On the traditional conception of fatalism as a logical thesis, there is no reference to natural laws or causality. Presumably, logical fatalism can be true in the absence of any causality in the world.

Aristotle's Sea Battle

Aristotle's discussion in *De interpretatione,* book 9, gives rise to the following:

1. There will be a sea battle on 1 January 3000 or there will not be a sea battle on 1 January 3000.

Oedipus and the Sphinx (1808) by Jean-Auguste-Dominique Ingres. Oil on canvas. According to mythology, oracles foretold that Oedipus would kill his father, the king of Thebes. Although both father and son took measures to ensure this did not come to pass, fate could not be avoided and Oedipus did indeed take his father's life. © LOUVRE, PARIS, FRANCE/ THE BRIDGEMAN ART LIBRARY

2. If there will be a sea battle on 1 January 3000 then it was always true (it was always a fact that) there will be a sea battle on 1 January 3000; if there will not be a sea battle on 1 January 3000 then it was always true (it was always a fact that) that there will not be a sea battle on 1 January 3000.

3. If it was always true that there will be a sea battle on 1 January 3000, then there was never a time at which anyone could prevent the sea battle; if it was always true that there will not be a sea battle on 1 January 3000, then there was never a time at which anyone could bring about the sea battle.

4. Thus either no one, at any time, could prevent the sea battle or no one, at any time, could bring about the sea battle.

5. Thus, either the occurrence of the sea battle is necessary or the nonoccurrence of the sea battle is necessary.

6. The sea battle is merely an arbitrarily selected event.

7. Therefore, all events are necessitated.

8. Therefore, fatalism is true.

The necessity that this argument attaches to events is necessity of the past. That is, we are to think of our powerlessness to affect the constitution of the future as we conceive of our inability to affect the constitution of the past. Just as the past is now closed to us, so too is our future. Aristotle's radical solution was to deny that future contingent statements had truth values, and so, "there will be a sea battle" and "there will not be a sea battle" were both neither true nor false. Contemporary times have produced other reactions to the argument. Some have questioned the meaningfulness of tensing truth, of the significance of speaking of truths holding at certain times. Others have suggested that we are not powerless to affect the truth-value of some claims about the past because some of these claims represent "soft facts" and are, in part, claims about the future. The question then becomes whether a statement to the effect that it was always true that a sea battle will occur on 1 January 3000 represents a soft fact. It should be clear that a robust discussion of Aristotle's argument requires investigating foundational claims about the nature of truth and time.

Theological Fatalism

Traditional Judeo-Christian theology considers God to have omniscient infallible foreknowledge and ubiquitous providence. If God knows all that will happen in a manner that cannot be mistaken, it is difficult to understand how any event can occur differently than it actually does. And, if no event can occur differently, it appears that there are no alternative courses of action that are open to us. We seem to be impotent concerning the constitution of the future. Additionally if everything that occurs is under the control of God's will, then it appears as if every event is divinely determined and so, once again, it appears as though we do not have the power to act otherwise than we actually do.

There have been three major types of response. The Boethian solution is to conceive of God as an atemporal being, one whose beliefs and will do not occur in time. The second approach is Ockhamism, which suggests that facts about God's past beliefs (and will) are soft facts and so should not be endowed with a type of necessity of the past that precludes autonomous action. The Molinist, or "middle knowledge" solution, attempts to find space for autonomy by suggesting that God knows the contingent future by knowing "counterfactuals of freedom," statements that describe what actions persons would freely perform in every possible situation. Using this knowledge, God then creates (wills) the future.

See also ***Autonomy; Determinism; Free Will, Determinism, and Predestination; Responsibility.***

BIBLIOGRAPHY

Bernstein, Mark H. *Fatalism.* Lincoln: University of Nebraska Press, 1992.

———. "Fatalism." In *The Oxford Handbook of Free Will.* Edited by Robert Kane, pp. 65–84. New York: Oxford University Press, 2002.

Cahn, Steven M. *Fate, Logic, and Time.* New Haven, Conn.: Yale University Press, 1967.

White, Michael. *Agency and Integrality: Philosophical Themes in the Ancient Discussions of Determinism and Responsibility.* Dordrecht, Holland: Reidel, 1985.

Zagzebski, Linda. *The Dilemma of Freedom and Foreknowledge.* Oxford: Oxford University Press, 1991.

Mark H. Bernstein

FEMINISM.

This entry includes five subentries:

Overview
Africa and African Diaspora
Chicana Feminisms
Islamic Feminism
Third World U.S. Movement

OVERVIEW

Feminism may broadly be defined as a movement seeking the reorganization of the world upon the basis of sex equality, rejecting all forms of differentiation among or discrimination against individuals upon grounds of sex. It urges a worldview that rejects male-created ideologies. At another level, it is also a mode of analysis and politics, committed to freeing all women of gender-based oppressions. Literally, then, anyone who supports such an ideology can be a feminist, regardless of gender.

Since the 1980s, following women's campaigns and struggles as well as theoretical and empirical research highlighting gender discrimination pervasive in law, policy, and opportunities to work, organizations and governments around the world have begun to incorporate gender considerations into policies and programs. International agencies such as the United Nations support many women's projects globally, including World Conferences on Women (Mexico, 1975; Copenhagen, 1980; Nairobi, 1985; Beijing, 1995), bringing together thousands of women to facilitate exchange and global networks.

Any discussion of feminism must analyze not only its genesis, practices, and forms of resistance (organized women's movements) but also its writing and theorizing, which has been an important form of self-expression and indeed a conscious exercise in building a body of feminist knowledge. Since the 1980s Western feminist thought has generated newer, more nuanced understandings of such concepts as "sex," "gender," and "woman." In this entry, the term *feminism* is used inclusively to discuss facets of the women's movement as well as feminist theorizing.

Feminism (both as ideology and struggle) can hardly be discussed as a seamless narrative, for in the twenty-first century it is practiced within different social and political configurations, and women's movements flourish in diverse locations. However, it is evident that despite broad commonalities, feminist struggles are influenced by local, cultural, national, and indeed global factors that shape local polities and economies.

An overview of salient developments reveals fascinating interrogations of Western feminism by non-Western women as well as deep divisions among Western feminists based on race, class, and sexual orientation. In fact, in the early 2000s many believe that the term is valid only in its plural form, *feminisms*, to reflect its many transnational manifestations across race, class, and religion.

This entry begins with a broad chronological overview, introducing important strands within Anglo-American feminism, which occupied a "mainstream" position in scholarship until the mid-1980s, when challenges from African-American women forced major reconceptualizations. The variety of issues around which women organized created issue-based trajectories, or "schools"(cultural feminism, ecofeminism, lesbian feminism). Next, the article describes how feminist scholars drew inspiration from Marxism, psychoanalysis, and postmodernism to analyze the female subject in academia, law, and society, generating a rich variety of feminist theory. Following this is a discussion of how challenges by "Third World" feminists and documentation of feminism(s) from diverse global locations enriched feminism as a whole, offering new models for organizing across nations and cultures. Examples drawn from contexts as varied as Iran, India, Russia, China, and Latin America highlight the variety of feminist struggles and theorizing. Finally, the entry touches upon some key issues that remain the focus of feminist engagement: abortion, sexuality, legalization of prostitution, and the pressures of globalization on millions of women in developing economies.

Anglo-American Feminism

Developments in Anglo-American feminism are often characterized in terms of waves, with the "first wave" in the United States beginning with initiatives as early as the organization of the National Woman Suffrage Association in 1869 by Susan B. Anthony and other such efforts in the early decades of the twentieth century when women's liberation was seen in terms of "human" liberation. These struggles led to the passage of the Nineteenth Amendment in the U.S. Constitution, enfranchising American women in 1920.

Following this there was a comparative lull in feminist activity. Betty Friedan's *The Feminine Mystique* (1963) is widely cited as a seminal text that precipitated public dialogue in America about feminism by pointing to an inchoate sense of "something wrong lodged in the minds of countless American housewives." Kate Millett's classic text *Sexual Politics* (1970) located women's oppression in patriarchies that operated through women's most intimate sexual relationships. Anglo-American feminists of this period were also drawn to developments in French feminism, which in turn drew inspiration from early seminal texts such as Simone de Beauvoir's *The Second Sex* (1953).

The "second wave" was marked by an explosion of complicated theories borrowing from philosophy, psychoanalysis, and politics that aimed (1) to challenge patriarchal values and constructs that oppressed women and to critique such portrayals in contemporary literature and popular culture, and (2) to represent the figure of the woman as an autonomous subject, focusing on the gendered body of woman to better understand such issues as reproductive rights, sexual harassment, and violence. Consciousness-raising was seen as a key tool for furthering feminism, and oft-repeated slogans of this phase were "sisterhood is powerful" and "the personal is political."

The active entry of black women served to expose polarities within U.S. "mainstream" feminist politics. Black feminist politics, rooted in the black liberation and civil rights movements (1960s–1970s), had convinced many African-American women of the need for a politics that was both antiracist and antisexist. The Combahee River Collective (a Boston-based black feminist group founded in 1974) aimed at "struggling against racial, sexual, heterosexual, and class oppression." From these contestations emerged new practices of theorizing, most prominently articulated by bell hooks. Sisterhood, hooks asserted, required a commitment on the part of white women to examine their own complicity in white privilege, because black women's oppression was located at the intersections of race, class, and gender. Reacting to a narrowly defined feminism, the African-American writer Alice Walker coined the term *womanist* to describe a woman "committed to survival and wholeness of an entire people, male and female." Thus, responding to the reality of women's multiple identifications, feminism broadened out along issue-based trajectories.

Trajectories within Feminism

Interrogations within feminism have spawned various strands in feminist thought that have acquired labels. Although categorizations hardly do justice to the variety of complex positions, some broad explanations are possible.

Liberal feminism. Liberal feminists see the oppression of women in terms of inequality between the sexes and are concerned with equal access to opportunities for women. However, they believe that private and public domains are governed by different rules, attitudes, and behavior. Thus, in matters of family for instance, love, caring, and sensitivity come first. The National Organization for Women (NOW, 1966), an early organization of the second wave in the United States, exemplified such feminist practice.

Radical feminism. Radical feminists, on the other hand, link women's oppression to patriarchy and see its manifestations in personal relationships and sexuality. Early articulations of this position led to the celebration of women's lives and the writing of women's history. Radical feminists have founded women's newsletters, bookstores, and presses. Many radical feminists celebrate lesbianism, although all radical feminists are not lesbians.

Lesbian feminism. Lesbian feminists in the United States in the 1970s began by theorizing about how society's treatment of lesbianism reflects not only its attitudes toward homosexuality but also its attitudes toward sexuality, femininity, male power, and gender politics in general. They argued that lesbianism in turn teaches about gender politics and forces a rethinking of constructions of sexuality and female desire. Thus social lesbianism emerged as an ideology and practice that sought to transform dominant ideas of sexual roles. Disrupting hegemonic sexual roles and division of labor, lesbianism seriously calls into

question traditional attitudes toward women's roles as being primarily reproductive.

Ecofeminism. Ecofeminism links the patriarchal domination of woman with the exploitation of nature—both as forms of oppressing the "other." Their analyses involve dualisms where attributes are thought of in terms of oppositions (culture/nature, mind/body, man/woman). They campaign against racism and economic exploitation as well as the exploitation of nature. Many ecofeminists are also environment activists.

Feminist Theory and Women's Studies

From the social action of the women's movement in the United States there emerged research consciously done within a feminist context, analyzing gender issues embedded in the most familiar facets of life—family, relationships, work, education, religion, media. Thus began women's studies, in which women became "subjects" rather than "objects" of study. Women's studies centers and departments drawing scholars from disparate academic disciplines became institutionalized in the U.S. academy in the 1970s. The National Women's Studies Association (1977) and the Feminist Press (1970) were committed to the production of feminist texts in order to create a body of knowledge that could be used to teach women's studies as an academic discipline.

As feminist scholars researched and questioned women's invisibility in history and psychology, "scientific" constructions of women in medical discourses, and popular images in literature, art, and religion, there emerged feminist theory, which sought to uncover the gender bias in the production of academic knowledge. Researchers challenged the tools of analysis used in sociology, history, psychology, and economics to argue that conceptualizations excluded women and that the disciplinary models used silenced women's voices. They argued that a "method of feminist inquiry" in an academic discipline did not necessarily involve alternative methods but rather a focus on alternative origins of problematics, explanatory hypotheses, and evidence and a new prescription for the appropriate relationship between the inquirer and her or his subject of inquiry. Feminist theorizing, in its project of writing women into theory and law, thus became a strategy of resistance. Feminist scholars drew from a range of ideologies to challenge existing disciplinary paradigms.

Feminism and Other Ideologies

In analyzing the roots of women's oppression, feminist theorists were attracted to two of the central ideologies of the twentieth century—Marxism and psychoanalysis. Marxist analyses provided a framework for understanding women's economic oppression and issues of class within feminism. Psychoanalysis, with its preoccupation with sexual differences, offered a means for analyzing personality structures and object relations in the hope that individuals (i.e., women) would be freed from their unconscious conflicts. Sigmund Freud (1856–1939) became an important influence—although, while some scholars found in his theorizing important tools for their own, others attacked him for being a misogynist.

Given that by the 1980s many feminists believed that women's experience of patriarchy and male domination differed by race, class, and culture, feminist theorizing needed other theoretical tools. Those who realized the limitations of constructing theories based on generalizations about the experience of Western white middle-class women found a natural ally in postmodernism. Postmodernist critiques offered a resistance to modernist conceptions of reason and claims of scientific "neutrality." There emerged clear overlaps between the postmodernist stance and feminist positions, which had long criticized Enlightenment ideals that legitimized an autonomous self as being reflective of masculinist agendas. Constructivism and deconstruction, which challenged the positivist tradition in science and essentialist theories of a single "truth" or "reality," appealed to feminist theorists. These approaches opened up possibilities for understanding how power operates through constructions of knowledge (i.e., about women) that are perpetuated through the medium of language by those who have the power over language/knowledge (i.e., men). Feminist psychologists used constructivism to argue that theories of women's sexuality were in fact organized within particular assumptive frameworks that strengthened patriarchal controls over women's bodies and desires. Thus constructivism, with its focus on representations of gender (rather than sex difference) provided for feminist thought a germinal insight: that woman, beyond the sexual differences, is a *social* category.

Gradually a whole range of disparate concepts were inserted in feminist thought that drew not only from Freud but also Jacques Lacan (1901–1981) and Michel Foucault (1926–1984). In theorizing about difference, feminist theorists were influenced by the writings of the French philosopher Jacques Derrida (b. 1930). Foucauldian conceptualizations of power and hegemony proved useful for understanding institutionalized patriarchal power structures that subordinated women. The "postmodern turn" thus became a pressing issue for feminist scholars, although there are many diverse positions within this framework.

Anglo-American feminist theory from the 1960s into the 1980s reflected the viewpoints of white middle-class North American and western European feminist scholars who did not interrogate their own methodological legacies and failed to recognize the embeddedness of their own assumptions within a specific historical context. An example of this approach was represented by Robin Morgan's book *Sisterhood Is Global* (1984), which asserted that women in their experience of oppression "shared a common world view." These assumptions of sameness were fiercely contested for their ethnocentric bias in the 1980s.

Theoretical Challenges: Race and "Third World" Feminism

The United Nations international conferences in Mexico (1975) and Copenhagen (1980) revealed tensions between First World and Third World women. Clearly divisions along lines of nationality, race, class, caste, religion, and sexual orientation needed to be inserted into women's experiences of oppression. By the Nairobi Conference (1985) the myth of "global sisterhood" had been abandoned and feminism became as heterogeneous as the women who supported it across the globe.

The 1980s witnessed a lashing out against white middle-class feminists' universalizing and homogenizing discourses

that erased the voices of women who differed in race, class, ethnicity, or sexual orientation. Although the contestations had already been initiated by black women, an even stronger challenge came from women of color (of other ethnicities: Latina, Chicana) and Third World women from postcolonial societies in Asia and Africa. Chandra Talpade Mohanty theorized in a 1986 article about the location of Third World women "Under Western Eyes." The writings of Trinh T. Minh-ha and Gloria Anzaldúa powerfully critiqued white women's hegemony in conceptualizations of feminism and feminist struggles. Sophisticated theorizing by Gayatri Spivak, Minh-ha, and Mohanty established that women in formerly colonized societies had cast aside old lines of dependency on the "center."

These influential and groundbreaking texts on issues of race, ethnicity, region, sexuality, and class forced remappings of feminism within and beyond the United States. Henceforth, histories of women were more consciously inclusive, emphasizing multiculturalism and incorporating the experiences of African-American, Latin-American, Asian-American, and Native-American women. Thus feminism was strengthened by voices from the "margins." "Identity" and "location" became important concepts, pushing the boundaries of earlier conceptualizations to acknowledge that all oppressions are interrelated and that identity politics cannot be separated from other aspects of liberation.

Global Feminisms: Nationalism and Religion

After the mid-1980s, documentation of women's resistance movements in non-Western societies further deepened understandings of women's liberation globally. Historical reconstructions of women's movements in the nineteenth and twentieth centuries in Asia (India, Sri Lanka, China, Indonesia, Vietnam, and Japan) and elsewhere (Egypt, Turkey, and Iran) established that women had played significant roles in the national liberation and revolutionary movements of their countries. Feminist struggles had progressed along varied, sometimes interrelated trajectories, all of which contributed to the growth of feminist consciousness. This challenged the view that feminism was a "foreign" ideology being imposed upon Third World countries and asserted that, like socialism, feminism had no ethnic identity.

In the 1990s further documentations of feminist struggles in the postcolonial nations of Asia, Africa, and Latin America challenged the omissions in the existing literature. They also interrogated two other predominant Eurocentric tendencies: (1) to link women's movements with modernization and development, and (2) to assume that feminism grows out of a linear process of social change. Regional data revealed that poor women in India, Brazil, Chile, and Peru had been at the forefront of many local struggles involving issues of work, wages, and environment and that, since women's movements in India and the Philippines were stronger than in the more industrialized Japan and Russia, it could hardly be assumed that "development" and "modernity" were prerequisites for women's movements to flourish.

Thus, similarities and divergences within feminism(s) have become more starkly visible. In Africa and West Asia there appear regional similarities because feminist struggles have been intertwined with movements of national liberation and state consolidation. In Latin America, on the other hand, women's movements have been closely connected to democratization movements against authoritarian states. Women's movements in Asia, Eastern and Western Europe, and Russia are characterized by much more diversity.

Such documentation of global feminism(s) has further refined the understandings of women's movements in relation to state control and how that shapes or restricts feminist engagement, as in the cases of Russia, China, South Africa, and Palestine. For instance, although erstwhile Russia and other communist states in eastern Europe curtailed the growth of independent women's movements, they passed labor laws, legalized abortion, and created employment for women and supportive public institutions to reduce some of women's domestic work. China is one of the countries where state-affiliated women's organizations form the backbone of the women's movement. Rural women support the All-China Women's Federation (ACWF) more than they support women's groups.

Regimes of colonial domination provide important illustrations of how women's movements have had to think of race and gender simultaneously and how colonial domination facilitated women's entry into nationalist struggles and therefore into public spaces. In many postcolonial societies (India, for example), women did not have to struggle for suffrage; they gained the right to vote alongside the men when their countries were declared sovereign. Contemporary India has an active women's movement encompassing a range of issues—work, environment, ecology, civil rights, health. Abortion is legal and accessible. However, feminists are alarmed at the use of reproductive technologies (sex-determination tests) to selectively abort female fetuses despite legislation in 1994 banning such testing. Campaigns are underway to lobby for a Women's Reservation Bill, giving women 30 percent reservation in Parliament (Menon, 1999).

In the South African context, given the history of apartheid, feminism has been in intimate dialogue with the political movement. Unlike in the United States, where scholars have had to develop a feminist knowledge in the absence of a mass feminist movement, South African women have been theorizing within the context of an ongoing liberation politics—addressing apartheid as well as struggling for agency within the antiapartheid movement. In Islamic societies struggles for women's rights have involved campaigns against conservative gender-discriminatory interpretations of Islam, particularly in relation to the use of the veil, women's right to education, and for more favorable provisions in marriage and divorce laws. Women's movements in Iran and Turkey have histories of activism, and Egyptian women have made considerable progress in creating spaces for women in civil society as professionals, activists, and politicians. Even in Afghanistan and Palestine, where women have long suffered under militarization, women's groups have continued to run girls' schools and support groups to aid medical and other relief projects for victims of war and insurgency.

However, there have been destructive implications for women when ethnic and religious nationalisms have become

xenophobic. In the name of preserving a cultural national identity women have been put behind the veil by fundamentalist regimes such as the Taliban in Afghanistan. In Kashmir (India), as militancy grew in the 1980s, Muslim women felt pressured to cover their faces, although veiling was not a widespread practice in the region. Women's movements have often been challenged by caste and religious affiliations that compel women to defend oppressive cultural practices as part of asserting loyalty to religious (rather than gender) identities. Veiling in Islamic societies and female circumcision in parts of Africa are classic examples, yet it is important to appreciate regional women's viewpoints. Feminists also have been concerned about the appropriation of feminist discourse by right-wing political forces—as by the Hindu Right in India (1990s) and by neoconservative elements in U.S. politics.

However, critiques of women's status within conservative Christianity, Judaism, Islam, Hinduism, or Buddhism ultimately lead many scholars of religion to argue that while orthodox religious practices may be relentlessly misogynist, more in-depth examination can help revitalize deeper, more ancient egalitarianism in most religions. Thus feminists in the 1990s examined religious theologies pointing to both the contradictions and the spaces for subversions within religions. Such understandings can provide tools to subvert existing gender hegemonies within orthodox religions.

Some Key Issues

Theoretical dilemmas and practical issues continue to challenge the women's movement across the globe. Issues such as pornography and women's portrayal in the media have been important issues for urban women, while for millions of rural Third World women, resisting development-related policies has been critical if they are to survive the march of globalization and avoid displacement as multinational corporations appropriate their lands. Gender-discriminatory laws governing marriage and divorce in many regions and religions have generated feminist struggles for social change. Trafficking in women and children and legalization of prostitution and abortion are key issues for feminism in many countries. Feminist practices and legal strategies continue to grapple with lawmakers, state authorities, and sometimes with the conservative strands among the women's movement itself. Below is a brief discussion of some issues facing feminism(s) in the early twenty-first century, with special emphasis on the ongoing attempt within the movement to build transnational collaborations and feminist communities of solidarity that stretch beyond divisions of culture, nation, region, and privilege.

Abortion and new reproductive technologies. Abortion (the conscious decision to terminate pregnancy) has long been a contentious issue. Religion and tradition are invoked by conservative "pro-life" groups, especially within the Roman Catholic Church and some Protestant organizations. However, feminist activists the world over stress that abortion should be viewed as an issue of autonomy, constitutionality, and economic status rather than simply of ethics. There are interesting ironies: while pro-life groups in America and Europe attack abortion clinics, millions of women in ostensibly more traditional societies (China and India) have easy access to abortion.

State population control policies in these countries support a pro-choice situation.

Another critical area with regard to women's reproductive roles is the explosion of technology enabling the manipulation of genetics and reproduction, procedures collectively known as new reproductive technologies (NRTs), used for in-vitro fertilization (IVF) and surrogate motherhood. Inherent in such technologies are social consequences closely affecting women. Feminists criticize the invasive role of NRTs and the manipulation of women's bodies through powerful hormones and surgical procedures that can traumatize the system. Feminists also point out the contradiction that in America pro-life campaigners have routinely threatened abortion clinics, whereas most IVF clinics still manipulate (and often "waste") embryos for surrogate motherhood. Feminists who campaign against the use of invasive technologies argue for women's bodies to be as free from intervention as men's and not to be "plundered medically."

Globalization, feminism, and transnational collaborations.

Economic reforms undertaken by many nations in recent times have had complex implications for women and have shaped feminist agendas. With growing capitalism in China, for instance, many benefits and protections for women have been dismantled. In Russia, privatized enterprises rarely provide women the protection and maternity benefits that a strong, less democratic state did. In developing countries in Latin America and Asia, globalization and World Bank policies have rendered many women and unskilled laborers jobless. Feminists have critiqued this neoliberal globalization and U.S. policy, arguing that feminism(s) of the West must resist the cultural and economic domination of their home country over the lives of Afghans, Iraqis, Palestinians, and Israelis. Many feminists in the United States have been engaged in the effort to pluralize feminism. Zilla Einstein (2004) argues for a "polyversal feminism—multiple and connected" to express women's shared humanity. Chandra Mohanty (2003), reiterating the need to "decolonize feminism," conceptualizes transnational solidarities among women that recognize and accept difference. Such transnational "feminist communities anchored in justice and equality" aim for a feminism "without borders."

Antifeminism: The Backlash

Feminist movements the world over continue to face resistance, whether from the Catholic Church, Islamic leaders, or right-wing Hindu fundamentalists who promote restrictions on women beyond familial roles. Pro-life religious groups in Europe have been pitted against feminists lobbying for a woman's right to abortion. Resistance to feminism is manifest not only in religious fundamentalism but also in a backlash broadly termed as "antifeminism," which accuses feminism of promoting "anti-family" ideologies that threaten the well-being of children and communities. Antifeminist campaigns in the United States use Internet technology to "warn" readers about the hidden, "destructive subversions" in feminism.

Besides this issue-based resistance, it is necessary to point out that in many non-Western societies (such as Chile, India, Bangladesh, Turkey, and Iran) it is not uncommon to encounter suspicion even among women toward "feminists," who are perceived to be "man-haters" who promote "anti-family" agendas. In fact, many women who believe in broadly feminist ideals and engage in activities that promote women's rights refuse to be called "feminists." A plausible explanation for the discomfort many women feel at being called feminists may be that in its inspiration, origins, and relevance, the "ideology" of feminism is still widely perceived to be Western and bourgeois, however erroneously.

In the United States, debates continue even within feminism with regard to the goals of feminism and its successes. Conservatives within feminism argue that feminists have exaggerated the problems of workplace discrimination and violence against women and disapprove of trends in the women's movements, which they believe have hurt women by forcing them out of traditional roles. Feminists, however, argue that the women's movement is alive and well and that much ground still needs to be traversed toward achieving gender equality. They assert that in the new millennium feminism offers a politics of solidarity that, while acknowledging difference, can build feminist communities to resist many contemporary crises in the context of globalizing economies and rising fundamentalism.

See also **Antifeminism; Equality: Gender Equality; Family Planning; Feminism: Africa and African Diaspora; Feminism: Chicana Feminisms; Feminism: Islamic Feminism; Feminism: Third World U.S. Movement; Gender; Human Rights: Women's Rights; Motherhood and Maternity; Philosophies: Feminist, Twentieth-Century; Sexual Harassment; Womanism; Women and Femininity in U.S. Popular Culture; Women's History; Women's Studies.**

BIBLIOGRAPHY

Basu, Amrita, ed. *The Challenge of Local Feminisms: Women's Movements in Global Perspective.* Boulder, Colo.: Westview Press, 1995.

Beauvoir, Simon de. *The Second Sex.* Translated by H. M. Parshley. New York: Knopf, 1993. Originally published in 1953.

Daymond, Margaret J., ed. *South African Feminisms: Writing, Theory, and Criticism, 1990–1994.* New York: Garland, 1996.

Disch, Estelle. *Reconstructing Gender: A Multicultural Anthology.* 3rd ed. Boston: McGraw-Hill, 2003.

Einstein, Zilla. *Against Empire: Feminisms, Racism and the West.* London and New York: Zed Books, 2004.

Firestone, Shulasmith. *The Dialectic of Sex: The Case for Feminist Revolution.* New York: Morrow, 1970.

Harding, Sandra. *The Science Question in Feminism.* Ithaca, N.Y.: Cornell University Press, 1986.

——, ed. *Feminism and Methodology: Social Science Issues.* Bloomington: Indiana University Press, 1987.

hooks, bell. *Talking Back: Thinking Feminist, Thinking Black.* Boston: South End Press, 1989.

Jaywardena, Kumari. *Feminism and Nationalism in the Third World.* London and Totowa, N.J.: Zed Books, 1986.

Menon, Nivedita, ed. *Gender and Politics in India.* New Dehli and New York: Oxford University Press, 1999.

Mohanty, Chandra. *Feminism without Borders: Decolonizing Theory, Practicing Solidarity.* Durham, N.C., and London: Duke University Press, 2003.

Mohanty, Chandra, and G. Anzaldua, eds. *This Bridge Called My Back: Writings by Radical Women of Color.* 3rd ed. Berkeley, Calif.: Third Woman Press, 2001.

Mohanty, Chandra, Ann Russo, and Lourdes Toores, eds. *Third World Women and the Politics of Feminism.* Bloomington: Indiana University Press, 1991.

Narayan, Uma. *Dislocating Cultures: Identities, Traditions and Third-World Feminism.* New York: Routledge, 1997.

Shaw, Susan M., and Janet Lee. *Women's Voices, Feminist Visions: Classic and Contemporary Readings.* 2nd ed. Boston: McGraw-Hill, 2004.

Maina Chawla Singh

AFRICA AND AFRICAN DIASPORA

Feminism is broadly defined as the struggle for the liberation of women, and encompasses epistemologies, methodologies, theories, and modes of activism that seek to bring an end to the oppression and subordination of women by men. An individual person espousing feminism is referred to as a *feminist,* while collective mobilizations of women against the oppression of women are referred to as *feminist movements* wherever they occur. Feminist movements are defined by their relatively radical gender politics and located as a subgroup within the broader category of *women's movements.* Analysts of African women's movements have documented the mobilization of women by both military and civilian dictatorships (Abdullah; Mama) and by conservative and religious forces within civil society (Lazreg; Badran; Hale; Karam), thus contributing to the theorization of women's movements by broadening it to include mobilizations of women that may not be liberatory in the sense of bringing an end to the oppression of women.

Even so, the term *feminism* covers a diverse array of politics centered around the pursuit of more equitable gender relations; this is true of feminism in Africa. However, proper documentation and analysis of the various manifestations of feminism, and the manner in which these have changed over time in different African contexts, is hampered by the lack of access to resources and the limited opportunities for debate, networking, and scholarship grounded in continental contexts. As a result the debate around African feminism and feminism in Africa remains highly contested and difficult to define. Even in the era of nationalism, many African thinkers have rejected the word outright, considering it as "un-African" and derogating "feminists" as sexually unattractive and humorless man-haters, troublemakers, Westernized, and sexually disreputable women who pose a threat to traditional culture and society. Others have displayed varying degrees of acceptance and tolerance, generally around the emancipation and enfranchisement of women, and supporting the inclusion of women in hitherto male-dominated institutions and development. African women have devoted much effort to the redefinition of feminism evident in the plethora of publications generated under the broad rubric of gender and women's studies carried out in African contexts since the 1980s. Feminist thinkers have done much to excavate the histories of women's movements in African societies, some even going so far as to argue that Western feminism has derived much of its inspiration from Africa. Since the 1970s, Western anthropological studies of African

women have often been invoked (and at times appropriated) to provide evidence that the gender divisions of patriarchal Western societies were neither universal nor immutable, but culturally and socially constructed and therefore changeable.

Continental Feminism

African feminism draws much of its inspiration from historical, anthropological, and political evidence of African women's leadership, of women's mobilizations, and of dynamic and disparate gender relations. The diversity of contemporary African articulations of feminism can be found in a number of periodicals that have carried lengthy discussions on feminism and gender theory. Notable examples include the South African *Agenda,* "a feminist media project in Africa committed to giving women a forum, a voice and the skills to articulate their needs and interests towards transforming unequal gender relations," and the continental gender studies journal *Feminist Africa,* which "seeks to provide a platform for cutting edge, informative and provocative gender work attuned to African agendas . . . a forum for the publication and dissemination of high-quality feminist scholarship in African contexts."

These publications address the contemporary development of feminist thought in African contexts, locating it within the challenging economic, political, and cultural conditions that have given rise to a plethora of feminist struggles, ideas, and scholarship.

The conditions giving rise to feminism in Africa include the history of colonial rule and imperialism, women's involvement in nationalist struggles, and other social movements. Contemporary manifestations of feminist consciousness owe much to the particular and persistent harshness of the conditions under which most African women still live, conditions that in the early twenty-first century are widely being attributed to contemporary economic and political regimes, and the fascination with cultural restoration that many societies display when it comes to gender relations. While there are many feminist thinkers who valorize and defend aspects of African cultures, the majority are critical of the many patriarchal and abusive practices that Africans often justify in defense of "culture." Meanwhile, African cultures continue to be assailed by a complex combination of forces far more powerful than African feminist movements.

History

Feminist thinkers often draw inspiration from the history of women's leadership roles in African societies, citing examples of women who ruled kingdoms and led wars of conquest since the earliest epochs of human civilization. Most often cited are the seventh-century Berber queen known as the Kahina of the Maghreb, the ninth-century Magajiyas of Daura, the legendary sixteenth-century Queen Amina of Zazzau, the nineteenth-century Nzinga of Angola, and Nehanda of Zimbabwe. These examples illustrate that African women leaders exercised their authority—often in the distinctly feminine styles of their times—in a manner that spanned spiritual, political, and military realms, and that has served to inspire feminist ideas all over the world.

The cultural complexity and dynamism of a region in which so many cultures coexisted and interacted with one another throughout the ages has given rise to quite disparate, at times idiosyncratic, gender relations and philosophies. There is little commonality between the complex and contradictory gender cultures expressed in Yoruba, Somali, Hausa, or Egyptian oral poetry, yet all of them are African, and all are rooted in conditions and contexts that are African in the sense of having been generated and inspired on the continent.

Women's movements on the African continent reflect the gendered cultural, social, and political organization of the numerous African societies in which they are located. There is enough evidence to suggest that African history is replete with diverse examples of mobilization against women's oppression, even though these have often been omitted by historians (Zeleza). Many of these at times phenomenal movements defy a simple definition of feminism. The available evidence suggests that women's movements in Africa reflect the traditions of organization that have characterized spiritual and material life in Africa as far back as recorded history goes. Few would seriously challenge the idea that gender differentiation has been a key feature of social, cultural, and political life all over the continent as far back as records can be found. Accordingly, African women have long been organized around lineage and kinship groupings, and around women's religious, cultural, and political duties and their productive and reproductive roles. The record also shows that these existing organizations were sporadically activated to defend women's interests.

Kenyan women were organized in *mumikanda* (work parties) and in various social and welfare groups—*ngwatio* among the Kikuyu-speaking communities, and *mwethya* among the Kamba-speaking communities. In Nigeria, Igbo women were organized as in various patrilineage wives and daughters associations, and governed through women's councils. Such networks of women collectively imposed sanctions on husbands who erred (the practice of "sitting on a man"), and proved capable of instigating widespread civil disturbances when they found their interests being compromised. The early-twentieth-century example of the Nwabiola Dancing Women's Movement in colonial Igboland (Eastern Nigeria) illustrates the manner in which apparently conservative organizational forms could become militantly activist when women saw their interests being threatened (Mba). All across West Africa business has long been conducted through market women's associations and trading networks that were periodically activated in defense of women's economic interests, and at times their political interests.

As colonialism gained ground, some of the earlier women's associations and groups were redirected by missionary groups and colonial governments, often through volunteers with a degree of Western education. These modern "women's clubs" were often designed to "civilize" and "uplift" African women, usually by instilling western European ideologies of domesticity and offering training in related skills (Tranberg Hansen). Domestication notwithstanding, it is clear that African women exercised enough agency to deploy whatever skills they acquired in innovative ways that empowered them and laid the ground for future involvement in national public life. Examples of women's groups coming together as larger bodies include the Mother's Union and the Catholic Women's Clubs

of Uganda, the Federation of Nigerian Women's Societies, the National Council of Women of Kenya, and the Association of Women's Clubs in Zimbabwe. When nationalist movements gained momentum, seemingly conventional women's groups and associations—charitable and welfare groups, mother's groups, and market women's associations—often directed their energies in support of nationalist goals. The Convention People's Party led by Kwame Nkrumah was among those nationalist movements that benefited substantially from the support of women—in this case the market women of Ghana.

Many of the women who later became leading educators, activists, and politicians were initially involved in the women's clubs of the colonial era, among them Margaret Ekpo of Nigeria, Agatha Constance Cummings-John of Sierra Leone, Mable Dove-Danquah of Ghana, and Gertrude Kabwasingo of Uganda. The more radical among these women—most of whom were elite and educated women—mobilized across the class lines too, as Funmilayo Ransome-Kuti did with such success. Ransome-Kuti was a key player in the Abeokuta Women's Union, which mobilized to oust an oppressive *alake* (chief) in 1948. In the ensuing decades she became a leading national political figure identified with nationalist, socialist, and feminist causes (Johnson-Odim and Mba). Ransome-Kuti's life is illustrative of African women's vibrant and militant history of resistance to colonial rule and imperialism and highlights the key roles that women activists played in nationalist movements all over the region, long before the second wave of feminism emerged in the Western world. Well-documented examples of more overtly political women's movements include those of Egypt, Nigeria, Ghana, Kenya, Uganda, Algeria, Mozambique, and the anti-apartheid movement of South Africa.

Some were chapters for women in the existing nationalist structures (for example, SWAPO Women's League, ZANU Women's League) or women's battalions in the nationalist militia (for example, the Algerian women in the FLN, the Frelimo Women's Brigade convened by Josina Machel, the short-lived women's detachment in the National Resistance Movement [NRM], or the women fighters said to make up 30 percent of the Eritrean People's Liberation Front). Other political women's organizations derived from party organs but broke away out of frustration, at times to pursue feminist agendas more overtly, as was the case with the Egyptian Feminist Union that broke away from the Egyptian Wafdist Party under the leadership of Huda Sharaawi. In an unspecifiable number of cases, women established new kinds of organizations with varying degrees of autonomy.

Postcolonial Feminism

The relationships between women's organizations and patriarchal states has continued to present ongoing challenges for feminist thinkers. The attainment of national independence during the 1960s saw the earlier traditions of organizing continue alongside the establishment of new and more modern manifestations of feminism, both within and outside government. At critical moments in the history of feminism in Africa, these different levels of mobilization have coalesced broader movements to pursue shared goals or platforms (see below).

Overall, post-independence feminism in Africa has been characterized by an emphasis on the state, as women have directed their demands for legal and policy reforms at their governments. While this has resulted in substantial legal and policy reforms in a great many countries, to the extent that formal exclusions have largely been removed from the statute books, feminist policy analysts have found cause to be critical of a lack of serious or concerted efforts to implement and sustain these reforms.

The state has often responded to feminist demands by creating a designated bureaucratic structure, in keeping with the United Nations call on member states to set up a government machinery for women and to include gender considerations in policies and projects.

Feminist analysts have found cause to remain critical of such government initiatives, especially where governments themselves have not been legitimate or democratic. In the context of the Nigerian military dictatorship, the high-profile gender activism on behalf of the regime has been characterized as "state feminism" (Mama, 1995), or "state pseudo-feminism" (Abdullah). More broadly, the deployment of women as functionaries in untransformed state bureaucracies has been characterized as "femocratic." While this has meant a significant increase in the number of women within government in South Africa, in less-than-democratic African contexts state-driven initiatives on women have often involved the wives of the ruling elite in a manner that lacks public legitimacy, a phenomenon referred to as "first-ladyism" (Mama, 1995). First ladies who are well known for their role in mobilizing women to support and legitimize despotic regimes include Mama Ngina of Kenya, Maryam Babangida and Mariam Abacha of Nigeria, and Nana Konadu-Rawlings of Ghana.

The national machinery has taken various institutional forms, ranging from small desks within mainstream organs to whole ministries or commissions with intersectoral mandates. However, there is evidence to suggest that while state structures may have sought to co-opt women into the task of nation-statehood, they have not been as effective in pursing feminist agendas and interests even when these have been clearly and, at times assertively, articulated.

The most elaborate of these is in South Africa, where there is a complex set of structures comprising an Office on the Status of Women within the president's office, a Commission for Gender Equality, a Parliamentary Standing Committee on the Quality of Life, and Status of Women and gender desks in all major national and provincial structures. The efficacy of these has been constrained by both resource and capacity limitations. These appear to have led to a persistent gap between gender policy commitments and their realization in practice, leaving most women marginalized and subordinated. Many of the gains that might have accrued to women as a result of policy commitments to more equitable service delivery and fairer representation in the public sphere have been undermined by global shifts away from public provision of services and cutbacks in public sector employment.

Feminist Activism

Despite its diversity, feminist activism in Africa in the early twenty-first century can probably be defined by its relative autonomy from the state, and the expansion and spread of numerous kinds of organizations within and across borders. While much African feminist activism continues to focus on lobbying and making demands on the state, the limited gains in recent decades have seen many activists preferring to work from outside, rather than within the state. This explains the proliferation of organizations and networks that do not derive any support from government. The growth of feminist thinking within African universities reflects the increase in the overall numbers of women attaining higher levels of education and becoming less likely to passively accept the subordinate positions that African societies continue to arrogate to women. While there has been an increase in the number of women pursuing political careers, only a minority pursue explicitly feminist agendas, and there is a growing consensus over the need for strong autonomous women's movements to push feminist agendas in and beyond the sphere of government.

The Zimbabwean women's movement is a good example of this shift. While the new state established a women's bureau and opened up some space for legal and policy reforms, it was only a few years before key activists left government to establish independent organizations, among them the Women's Action Group and the Zimbabwe Women's Resource Centre and Network. The Women's Action Group was formed to resist the widespread victimization of women during Operation Clean-up in the early 1980s. The Zimbabwe Women's Resource Centre's key role in supporting the formation of a coalition of women's organizations to intervene in the constitutional drafting process and the Land Lobby in the 1990s is illustrative of this capacity for autonomous activism. The increasingly oppressive nature of the regime of President Robert Mugabe has also had negative effects on the women's movement and has created a new degree of reticence that did not characterize the same movement five years earlier.

In South Africa the Women's National Coalition (WNC) marked a high point in South African feminism. Formed during the negotiations that culminated in the coming to power of the African National Congress (ANC), the WNC carried out nationwide consultations and produced the National Women's Charter and ensured women a high level of participation in the emerging polity. However, the institutionalization of gender within the state apparatus has become identified as a source of concern, as independent activism has largely subsided since then, allowing for a slowing down of change, despite the proliferation of "gender desks" within government.

The uptake of gender matters within the state has seldom led to radical changes, although it has seen incremental increases in the number of women in government in many countries. Analysts frequently point to the importance of more autonomous mobilizations that can continue to lobby and advocate for change.

Despite the limits encountered within state-focused activism, the 1990s were also years of growth and diversification for feminist activism across the region, as evidenced in the number of independent organizations and networks espousing feminist causes. The best known national and subregional organizations include the Tanzania Gender Networking Programme (TGNP), the Zimbabwe Women's Resource Centre and Network, Baobab and Gender and Development Action in Nigeria, the Nairobi-based FEMNET, and the Women and Law in Southern Africa network based in Harare. Various branches of international women's organizations like the Federation of International Democratic Advocates (FIDA), the Soroptimists, and the numerous church-related and Islamic women's organizations also deserve to be mentioned.

There is also a trend toward greater specialization in organizations, as more have taken on a sectoral focus, or have been established to pursue work in a defined field. Specific organizations have addressed matters that cover the full range: domestic violence, legal rights, education, health and sexuality, reproductive rights, HIV/AIDS, militarization, peace-building, housing and land, cultural and religious practices, female genital mutilation. These are just some of the areas being addressed by women's movements in different parts of Africa.

More recently African feminists are deploying information and communication technologies in highly innovative and radical ways, as evidenced by the activism of a number of electronically-based networks, notably ISIS-WICCE, GAIN, GENNET, and the Feminist Studies Network.

However, autonomous movements of the 1980s have often been replaced or displaced by nongovernmental organizations (NGOs) primarily charged with the delivery of specific funded projects. NGOs differ from women's movements in being usually small in scale, urban-based, often sectorally specialized, and reliant on external funding. The NGO reliance on donor funding, while ensuring space for gender activism to continue in increasingly resource-starved environments, is increasingly viewed as compromising the capacity for autonomous feminist activism. Critics variously describe this as the "projectization" or "NGO-ization" of feminist movements, drawing attention to the manner in which even limited funding can have divisive and fragmenting effects, and lead to the reintroduction of conventional hierarchical structures and the neutralization of feminist agendas. It is this complicated scenario that leads African feminist Sisonke Msimang to write

> I am part of a new generation of young African feminists whose entrance into "the movement" has been marked by feminist engagement in ways that are distinctly new. Many of us are feminists by profession and our "experience" and analysis comes from having worked on projects that employ the terminology of Gender and Development. We enter the arena of activism not necessarily through struggles specifically geared towards women's liberation, but through a complicated route that often involves the technical jargon of Gender and development and human rights. (p. 54)

With the democratization of politics in many African countries, women have continued to mobilize, demanding greater

participation in political life, a concern reflected in the Beijing platform of 1995. In doing so they have also challenged the patriarchal biases of the political establishment, its militaristic culture, and the fact that large sums of money are necessary to the pursuit of political careers. Feminist politicians who have held seats in parliament have often found themselves profoundly challenged on key issues such as militarism, HIV/AIDS, land, and financial corruption, and in situations that have left them unsupported by the political mainstream. More commonly, they are simply not taken seriously by their male counterparts, as Sylvia Tamale's insightful study of women in the Ugandan parliament indicates.

Feminist Intellectuals
Well-known feminist thinkers who have played prominent roles in political and intellectual debates throughout the 1970s and 1980s include Nawal El Sadaawi (Egypt), Zenebewerke Tadesse (Ethiopia), Fatima Mernissi (Morocco), Fatou Sow (Senegal), Bolanle Awe (Nigeria), Patricia MacFadden (Swaziland), Ifi Amadiume (Nigeria), Ruth Meena (Tanzania), and Fatma Allo (Zanzibar). In terms of organizations, the establishment in 1977 of the Association of African Women for Research and Development (AAWORD) marked the growing assertiveness of African feminists. The founding workshop set out to establish a continent-wide network of scholars dedicated to undertaking research from an African and gender perspective. The declared mission of AAWORD includes two clearly feminist commitments: to analyze and transform gender relations and social conditions in Africa; and to build a powerful African women's movement linking human rights to the theory and practice of development.

During the 1980s AAWORD was joined by several other research and documentation centers, notably the Women's Research and Documentation Centre (WORDOC) at the University of Ibadan, set up by a group of Nigerian academics that included the historian Bolanle Awe, and the Women's Research and Documentation Project (WRDP) at the University of Dar Es Salaam initiated by Tanzanian academics.

The 1990s saw a continuing proliferation of documentation centers and gender and women's studies units on African campuses, as well as several new initiatives to bring these together through research and networking activities. In pursuing an initiative designed to network and strengthen the work of scholars in gender and women's studies working in African institutions, the African Gender Institute (itself formed in 1996) was able to identify as many as thirty such sites in Africa's 316 universities, with several others still being established (Boswell, 2002). The scholarly output in the field of gender studies, much of which bears the influence of feminist thinking, has also increased rapidly, as several recent reviews indicate (Mama, 1995; Lewis).

The expansion of the field appears to be continuing in the early twenty-first century, despite the apparently unfavorable context offered by Africa's beleaguered universities, most of which remain extremely resistant to the idea of feminism and offer very limited institutional support to gender and women's studies, teaching, and research (Feminist Africa). A core concern reflected in both AAWORD and the African Gender Institute is the commitment to bring critical reflection and political activism together for the benefit of women. Intellectual activism is intrinsic to feminism worldwide, but in African contexts it has raised unique challenges because of the particular salience afforded to "gender planning" and "gender mainstreaming" in the international development discourses that have such profound effects on the region.

Feminism in the African Diaspora
Diasporan feminism is rooted in the historical experience of enslavement and racism, so it challenges the oppression of women within the relations of racism that still curtail the prospects of black people located in Western contexts.

African diasporan thinkers in the United States have therefore developed feminist thinking that maintains the centrality of racism in black women's experience. In the United States these include Angela Davis's book *Woman, Race and Class* (1982) and bell hooks's *Ain't I a Woman: Black Women and the Politics of Feminism* (1982). Literary works that illustrate changing African-American feminist perspectives include the well-known work of writers such as Toni Morrison, Audre Lourde, June Jordan, Maya Angelou, and Alice Walker, all of whom have had an influence far beyond the United States.

In the European diaspora, the debate on black feminism opened up in the early 1980s with the publication of Hazel Carby's article. Caribbean and black European feminist thinkers have since produced a body of feminist thought that incorporates antiracist and anti-imperialist perspectives, while displaying a sensitivity to class oppression (Amos and Parmar; Grewal et al.). Julia Sudbury's *Other Kinds of Dreams: Black Women's Organisations and the Politics of Transformation* (1998) presents an overview of the British black feminism that emerged out of the black struggles against racism and state harassment carried out within the predominantly working-class Caribbean, African, and Asian communities during the 1980s.

The history of feminism in the Caribbean diaspora is also rooted in antislavery and antiracist movements, with its contemporary manifestations typifying postcolonial struggles around identity and difference, while pursuing feminist agendas of antiviolence activism, and responses to sexual exploitation and global economic development, to name only some of the various fronts (Reddock; Mohammed; Antrobus; Barriteau). The Caribbean Association for Feminist Research and Activism (CAFRA) and the Centre for Gender and Development Studies at the University of the West Indies have played key roles in articulating and internationalizing Caribbean feminism.

African and African diaspora women concerned with emphasizing the distinctiveness of African legacies and not always wishing to be identified with feminists in the Western world have improvised a number of alternative terms. *Womanism* is a term attributed to the African-American writer Alice Walker and adopted by some South African and Nigerian writers, while others prefer the term *motherism*. Catherine Achonulu advocates *motherism*, while Omolara Ogundipe-Leslie advocates *stiwanism*, to denote commitment to the social transformation

involving women of Africa (*stiwa*). The more pragmatic term *gender activism* has been increasingly deployed by women activists working in development organizations, where policy demands require expertise in gender, but the term *feminism* is considered too political.

While it may be hard to discern a unified and coherent feminist movement in many African countries given the complexity of gender politics and the disparate influences of the state, local, and international development agencies and diverse women's movements, it is clear that African women have been able to come together as a powerful force at key historical moments in various countries during the recent historical period. Feminist thought continues to evolve on the African continent and to maintain links with women located in various Western countries, not least because conditions on the continent ensure that continental feminists often find themselves in the diaspora.

See also **Feminism: Overview; Feminism: Islamic Feminism; Gender; Modernity: Africa; Womanism.**

BIBLIOGRAPHY
Antrobus, Peggy. *The Rise and Fall of Feminist Politics in the Caribbean Women's Movement 1975–1995: The Lucille Mathurin Mair Lecture March 2000.* Kingston, Jamaica: Centre for Gender Development Studies, University of West Indies, 2000.
Badran, Margot. *Feminists, Islam and Nation: Gender and the Making of Modern Egypt.* Princeton, N.J.: Princeton University Press, 1995.
Barriteau, V. Eudine. "Confronting Power and Politics: A Feminist Theorising of Gender in Commonwealth Caribbean Societies." *Meridians: Feminism, Race, Transnationalism* 3, no. 2 (2003): 57–92.
Boswell, B. "Gender and Women's Studies in Africa in the Year 2002: A Directory of Institutional Sites." 2003. Available at www.gwsafrica.org/directory.
Collins, Patricia Hill. *Black Feminist Thought: Knowledge, Consciousness and the Politics of Empowerment.* Boston: Unwin Hyman, 1990.
Davis, Angela Y. *Women, Race, and Class.* New York: Vintage, 1982.
Feminist Africa. "Intellectual Politics." *Feminist Africa* (2002). Available at http://www.feministafrica.org. First issue of an electronic journal.
Hale, Sondra. *Gender Politics in Sudan: Islamism, Socialism, and the State.* Boulder, Colo.: Westview, 1997.
hooks, bell. *Ain't I a Woman: Black Women and the Politics of Feminism.* Boston: South End Press, 1982.
Jayawardena, Kumari. *Feminism and Nationalism in the Third World.* London: Zed Books, 1986.
Johnson-Odim, Cheryl, and Nina Emma Mba. *For Women and Nation: Funmilayo Ransome-Kuti of Nigeria.* Urbana: University of Illinois Press, 1997.
Kabira, Wanjiku Mukabi, and Elizabeth Akinyi Nzioki. *Celebrating Women's Resistance: A Case Study of the Women's Groups Movement in Kenya.* Nairobi: African Women's Perspective, 1993.
Karam, Azza M. *Women, Islamisms, and the State: Contemporary Feminisms in Egypt.* London: Macmillan Press; New York: St. Martin's Press, 1998.
Khasiani, S. A., and E. I. Njiro, E. *The Women's Movement in Kenya.* Nairobi: African's Women's Perspective, 1993.

Lewis, Desiree, ed. *African Women's Studies: 1980–2001: A Bibliography.* Cape Town: African Gender Institute, 2003.

Mama, Amina. "Feminism or Femocracy? State Feminism and Democratisation in Nigeria." *Africa Development* 20, no. 1 (1995): 37–58.

Mba, Nina Emma. *Nigerian Women Mobilized: Women's Political Activity in Southern Nigeria, 1900–1965.* Berkeley: Institute of International Studies, University of California, 1982.

Mismang, Sisonke. "Editorial: African Feminisms Two." *Agenda* 54 (2002).

Mohammed, P. "Rethinking Caribbean Difference." *Feminist Review* 59 (1998): 6–39.

Reddock, Rhoda. "The Early Women's Movement in Trinidad and Tobago 1900–1937." In *Subversive Women: Historical Experiences of Gender and Resistance,* edited by Saskia Wieringa. London and Atlantic Highland, N.J.: Zed Books, 1995.

Sharaawi, Huda. *Harem Years: The Memoirs of an Egyptian Feminist.* Translated and introduced by Margot Badran. New York: Feminist Press, 1987.

Sudbury, Julia. *Other Kinds of Dreams: Black Women's Organisations and the Politics of Transformation.* London and New York: Routledge, 1998.

Tamale, Sylvia. 1999. *When Hens Begin To Crow: Gender and Parliamentary Politics in Uganda.* Boulder, Colo.: Westview, 1999.

Tranberg Hansen, Karen. *African Encounters with Domesticity.* New Brunswick, N.J.: Rutgers University Press, 1992.

Tsikata, D. "Gender Equality and the State in Ghana: Some Issues of Policy and Practice." In *Engendering African Social Sciences,* edited by Ayesha M. Imam, Amina Mama, and Fatou Sow. Dakar, Senegal: Council for Development of Social Science Research in Africa (CODESRIA), 1999.

Women's Studies and Studies of Women in Africa during the 1990's. CODESRIA Working Paper Series No. 5. Darkar, Senegal: Council for Development of Social Science Research in Africa (CODESRIA), 1996.

Zeleza, P. T. "Gender Biases in African Historiography.'" In *Engendering African Social Science,* edited by Ayesha M. Imam, Amina Mama, and Fatou Sow. Dakar, Senegal: Council for Development of Social Science Research in Africa (CODESRIA), 1999.

Amina Mama

CHICANA FEMINISMS

There are many definitions of feminism, and many scholars now assert that the word should be used in its plural form to encompass women's various social locations. As such, Chicana feminisms address the specific historical, economic, and social experiences of women of Mexican descent in the United States. The field of Chicana feminisms developed within the context of feminist movements in the United States, including the feminist writings of African-American, Asian-American, Native American, and white scholars. Although Chicana feminist analyses focus specifically on the condition of Chicanas, writers claim allegiance to U.S.-based as well as internationally based politically progressive movements (Saldívar-Hull).

There are four distinctive features that distinguish Chicana feminisms from other forms of feminism: history, culture, intersectionality, and political coalitions.

The Importance of History

The end of the Mexican-American War in 1848 codified in the Treaty of Guadalupe Hidalgo the colonized status of Mexico's former citizens in what became part of the U.S. southwestern states of Arizona, California, Colorado, New Mexico, and Texas. Mexicans residing in this region lost their citizen rights and saw their language and culture displaced overnight. It was this act of colonization that Chicanos in general and Chicana feminists in particular use as central in claiming a particular social and economic position in the United States that makes them different from other immigrant groups. The initial act of colonization influences even recent Mexican immigrants as they join Chicano communities in the United States that are treated differently from mainstream white communities.

During the Chicano civil rights movement of the 1960s, many Chicano writers sought to expose the suppressed history of Mexicans in the United States. Chicana feminist writers focused on highlighting the political resistance and "underground" feminisms of many important women leaders since 1848. Women of Mexican descent in the United States have a long history of resistance and political mobilization, as demonstrated by strong women leaders such as Emma Tenayuca, who was a labor leader in Texas, and *las soldaderas* (women soldiers) who fought in the Mexican Revolution of 1910. Dolores Huerta (b. 1930) followed this tradition of political leadership as she fought side-by-side with César Chávez (1927–1993) to unionize California farmworkers and continued into the twenty-first century carrying out Chávez's important political work after his untimely death in 1993.

The Importance of Culture

Chicana feminist writers agree with other feminists that patriarchy exists in most societies. However, patriarchy is manifested in culturally specific ways, and as such, Chicanas' culture and history are central to their analysis of gender in their communities. Chicana feminists have identified several cultural elements that are central in defining Chicana definitions of proper womanhood. One is the veneration of La Virgen de Guadalupe (the Virgin of Guadalupe, the national saint of Mexico); another is the figure of La Malinche, an indigenous woman who facilitated the conquest of Mexico by Hernán Cortés (1485–1547) by serving as translator and go-between in the negotiations that ultimately defeated the Aztec leader Montezuma in 1519. Both women are iconic figures of what is desirable and undesirable for Mexican women in Mexico as well as Chicanas in the United States.

The desirable aspects of Mexicana/Chicana womanhood based on La Virgen de Guadalupe are piety, dedication, humbleness, selflessness, dedication to family, and virginity. The undesirable traits, as embodied in La Malinche, are treachery, lying, deceitfulness, and sexual promiscuity. Although other cultures usually describe this distinction between women as a "virgin-whore" dichotomy, in Mexican or Chicano culture the dichotomy is tied specifically to these two figures rather than a general distinction with no cultural or historical referent. These culturally appropriate and inappropriate ways of expressing Chicana womanhood do not apply to non-Chicana

---

DOLORES HUERTA

Dolores C. Huerta, cofounder and first vice-president emeritus of the United Farm Workers of America—AFL-CIO (UFW)—played a major role in the American civil rights movement.

Dolores Huerta was born on April 10, 1930, in a small town in northern New Mexico. Her father, Juan Fernandez, was a miner, fieldworker, union activist, and state assemblyman. Dolores was raised by her mother, Alicia Chávez, after her parents divorced when she was three years old. Dolores along with her two brothers and two sisters grew up in the San Joaquin Valley in the farmworkers community of Stockton, California. Her mother was a businesswoman who owned a restaurant and a seventy-room hotel that often put up farmworkers and their families for free.

Dolores Huerta attributes her accomplishments and lifelong activism to her mother's influence and caring. Dolores was one of the first Chicanas to graduate from her high school and one of the first to receive a teaching degree from the University of the Pacific's Delta Community College. As a teacher, however, she soon realized that she could make more of a difference in her students' lives if she helped improve the lives of farmworkers—so their children did not have to attend school hungry.

Dolores began community organizing in 1955 as a founding member of the Stockton chapter of the Community Service Organization (a grassroots organization fighting social injustice). While working for the CSO, she helped create the Agricultural Workers Association (in 1960), and as a lobbyist in Sacramento in the early 1960s she was instrumental in the passage of legislation allowing voters the right to vote in Spanish and allowing individuals to take the driver's license examination in their native language. She later lobbied in Washington, D.C., for an end to the so-called *bracero* program that encouraged the use of "captive labor" from Mexico. In 1962 she joined Cesar Chávez in Delano, California, and they created the National Farm Workers Association, precursor to the United Farm Workers union.

In 1966 Huerta negotiated a farmworkers' contract with the Schenley Wine Company, marking the first time in the history of the United States that agricultural workers negotiated a labor contract with a major corporation. Her struggles on behalf of farmworkers continued into the next decades. In her seventies, she was still fighting to preserve and extend the rights of agricultural workers in the United States, working long hours and traveling to cities across North America promoting La Causa—the farmworkers' cause—and women's rights.

Huerta received a number of honorary doctorate degrees, was a board member for the Fund for the Feminist Majority (advocating for the political and equal rights for women), and president of the Dolores Huerta Foundation, with the mission of establishing Communities of Conscience focusing on community organizing and leadership training in low-income, underrepresented communities.

---

women and therefore merit a different feminist analysis from those developed by other cultural groups.

The Importance of Intersectionality

Many writers of Chicana feminisms had been active participants in the 1960s Chicano civil rights movement and in the white feminist movement. Their experience in multiple political struggles alerted them to the exclusion of gender and sexuality in ethnic mobilizations and the exclusion of social class, race, and ethnicity in feminist mobilizations. From the experience of always feeling only partially understood, Chicana feminists developed, in conjunction with other feminists of color, the concept of intersectionality. Chicana feminisms ascribe to the notion that women belong to more than one oppressed group and that through understanding the intersection of how these different social categories—sexuality, class, race, ethnicity, gender—intersect in contextually specific situations, Chicanas' multiple oppressions can be understood. For example, a poor, lesbian, immigrant, Mexican farmworker will experience patriarchy and gender subordination differently from a middle-class, heterosexual, third-generation U.S.-Chicana professor. Intersectionality immediately recognizes that not all women are the same and that social locations identified through group memberships can elucidate women's multiple sources of oppression.

A corollary to intersectionality is that the experience of multiple sources of oppression facilitates Chicanas' experiencing social reality as multilayered. That is, knowledge of more than one language and one culture allows the potential for realizing the arbitrary nature of social categories. Chicana feminist writers have identified the ability to perceive and translate different social realities as *mestiza* consciousness (Moraga and Anzaldúa), *concientización* (Castillo), and shifting consciousness (Sandoval), and have capitalized on this intellectual dexterity to capture fully the internal diversity of Chicanas in the United States and to avoid essentializing the "Chicana experience." Furthermore, the ability to communicate multiple realities has also facilitated Chicana feminist writers speaking to different constituencies through their intellectual production and addressing different sources of oppression depending on whom they are addressing (Arredondo et al.).

The Importance of Political Coalitions

Chicana feminisms do not situate the sources of women's oppression only in gender or exclusively in class, race, ethnicity, or sexuality. Their commitment to examine women's disadvantages through the lens of intersectionality allows them actively to seek political coalitions with other oppressed groups, including men of color. Chicana feminisms refuse to "rank the oppressions" (Moraga and Anzaldúa) and are committed to being self-reflexive about how everybody, regardless of their apparent powerlessness, can contribute to oppression within restricted contexts (Pérez). At the same time, Chicana feminisms see class struggles as fundamental to worldwide liberation (Saldívar-Hull).

The Future of Chicana Feminisms

Chicana feminisms are a vibrant field of study in several disciplines: American studies, anthropology, art, ethnic studies, film studies, literature, psychology, sociology, and women's studies. At the start of the twenty-first century, with Chicana feminisms as a field almost three decades old, a third generation of writers were expanding and elaborating the basic features of Chicana feminisms. Furthermore, young, educated Chicanas were embracing the political goals set out by the first generation of Chicana feminist writers and using their various professions to implement many of the ideas written about almost thirty years earlier. All of these developments, coupled with the flexibility and self-reflexivity inherent in the paradigms proposed by Chicana feminisms, make it a promising and expanding field of study as well as a potential framework for political action.

See also **Chicano Movement; Feminism: Third World U.S. Movement; Women's History.**

BIBLIOGRAPHY

Arredondo, Gabriela F., Aída Hurtado, Norma Klahn, Olga Nájera-Ramírez, and Patricia Zavella, eds. *Chicana Feminisms: A Critical Reader.* Durham, N.C.: Duke University Press, 2003. This is the most recent and comprehensive overview of the influence of Chicana feminisms on multiple disciplines.

Castillo, Ana. *Massacre of the Dreamers: Essays on Xicanisma.* Albuquerque: University of New Mexico Press, 1994. An important analysis of the historical and social influences on Chicana feminist thought.

Hurtado, Aída. *Voicing Chicana Feminisms: Young Women Speak Out on Sexuality and Identity.* New York: New York University Press, 2003. The only empirical study of young, educated Chicanas and their views on feminisms.

Moraga, Cherríe, and Gloria Anzaldúa, eds. *This Bridge Called My Back: Writings by Radical Women of Color.* Foreword by Toni Cade Bambara. Watertown, Mass.: Persephone Press, 1981. A classic in the field of Chicana feminisms.

Pérez, Emma. *The Decolonial Imaginary: Writing Chicanas into History.* Bloomington: Indiana University Press, 1999. One of the most important books in Chicana feminist thought and theorizing of their historical presence in U.S. society.

Saldívar-Hull, Sonia. *Feminism on the Border: Chicana Gender Politics and Literature.* Berkeley: University of California Press, 2000. An important exploration from a Chicana feminist perspective of creative writings by Chicanas and their connection to the U.S.-Mexican border.

Sandoval, Chela. *Methodology of the Oppressed.* Foreword by Angela Y. Davis. Minneapolis: University of Minnesota Press, 2000. The most comprehensive analysis of the connections between Chicana feminist thought and classic philosophical writings in cultural studies.

Aída Hurtado
Jessica M. Roa

ISLAMIC FEMINISM

The term *Islamic feminism* was first used in the 1990s. It is not certain who coined the term. Nor is it evident that those who first used it were aware of the explosive impact that the juxtaposition of these two words was to have. Rather than imagining and promoting a revolution in the heart of Islam, these women in Saudi Arabia, South Africa, and some Asian Muslim communities were merely describing what they and others like them were doing. They were challenging the misogyny that they saw to be essential to the projection of a newly politicized Islam.

Defining "Islamic Feminism"

To understand Islamic feminism, both words have to be examined separately and then together. The epithet "Islamic" situates a person somewhere on the continuum between a cultural identity that is Muslim and coexists easily with secularism and occasional expressions of religious observance on the one hand, and Islamist, which describes a way of life committed to fighting for the establishment of an Islamic state. "Feminist" refers to a consciousness that women are unjustly treated simply because they are women. This consciousness may, but need not, be galvanized into action to do something to change this unjust system (see introduction in Badran and Cooke).

"Islamic feminist" describes the speech, action, writing, or a way of life committed to gender justice and also an engagement with Islamic epistemology as an expansion of a faith position rather than a rejection of it. At the same time that they address themselves to this discourse and derive from it rhetorical strategies to construct a resistant identity, these women are struggling with and on behalf of all Muslim women and their right to enjoy with men full participation in a just community. Justice and citizenship, however defined, would not be borrowed, modern accretions but rather ideals integral to the spirit underlying the founding Islamic community. More recently, Islamic feminism has been described as broadening the scope of Western feminism because of its emphasis on community and belonging.

By the late 1990s, when the term *Islamic feminism* had become current, it came under scrutiny (e.g., Moghissi). What did it mean to want to be a member of a religious community considered to be patriarchal in its norms and values and, at the very same time, to demand respect for oneself as a woman with inalienable rights? Was it false consciousness to believe that such a position might be empowering?

Some Muslims and non-Muslims were writing dogmatically about Islamic feminism, calling it an oxymoron without meaning. They protested that organized religions, and particularly Islam, are unremittingly patriarchal, misogynist even. It is misguided to hope for a woman-friendly interpretation of foundational texts and laws that would allow for a transformation in attitude toward women's roles in society outside the domestic space. Some might go further to claim that proponents of Islamic feminism were merely ignorant. Either they had not read the Koran and sunna (the life of the prophet Muhammad, codified in the Traditions), or if they had, they did not understand what they had read because, despite the wide diversity of the Muslim world, "the cultural articulation of patriarchy (through structures, social mores, laws and political power) is increasingly justified by reference to Islam and Islamic doctrine" (Shaheed, p. 79).

Others, mostly Muslim women, conceded that there were women who were calling for women's empowerment within the context of a well-understood Islam, but that they were not feminists. They might look like feminists, act like feminists, but feminism would not be the right term to use. When asked for alternatives, they might come up with suggestions like "womanist" or "remaking women" (see Abu-Lughod), or they would deny the need for a single term to describe their actions and demands. Many of these women are particularly critical of non-Muslims when they describe a person, a behavior, or a language as Islamic feminist.

Clearly, there are some sensitivities involved in the word *feminism* when used to refer to the language and behavior of Muslim women. What is the problem with the term? Do Jewish, Christian, or Buddhist feminists face the same conundrum? Probably not because for them the term *feminist* is not as imbricated in recent experiences of European, colonial domination as it is for Muslims living under the yoke of the Christian civilizing mission of European colonialism. During the nineteenth century, British and French colonizers in North Africa and West and South Asia claimed to be especially concerned about the welfare of women in the societies they had invaded and occupied. Deploring barbaric practices like female genital mutilation, *sati* (Hindu women's self-immolation on their husbands' funerary pyres), veiling, and women's seclusion,

white European men made it their business to save Arab Muslim women from their men. Some scholars, such as Leila Ahmed, have pointed to these men's hypocrisy—feminists abroad, they were tyrants at home. Furthermore, they have revealed their cunning, for by pretending to protect indigenous women, they were separating them from their men. Thus, they were better able to control them and, by extension, rule their men. Feminism became deeply enmeshed in colonialism.

The Modern Era

Muslim women activists at the turn of the twentieth century were careful to distinguish their behavior, language, and appearance from those of their Western sisters. Always speaking within an observant Muslim context, they demanded education, employment opportunities, control over their lives (for example, marriage choice) and over their bodies (to veil or not to veil). They insisted that their demands were not what European women wanted. Above all, they honored their religion, their husbands, and their fathers, and all they wanted was to bring up intelligent sons. They argued that the call for unveiling indicated a desire to gain access to institutions that would make them better wives, mothers, and Muslims; it would not destroy the moral fiber of their society by encouraging promiscuity, widescale divorce, and the kind of immoral European society contemporary religious authorities were denouncing.

Many of these early activists on behalf of women's rights, such as Nazira Zayn al-Din, a Lebanese writer of the early twentieth century, prefaced their demands with claims about their qualifications to do so. They were pious Muslims, daughters of pious Muslim men (a surprising number were daughters of Islamic clerics). By the 1930s women throughout the Muslim world were gaining rights unimaginable only thirty years earlier. It became acceptable to call oneself a feminist, although the term *Islamic feminist* was never used, as though the Islamic part was assumed.

Then in 1979 a radically conservative Shiite Islamic revolution was waged and won in Iran. Bazaar, university, and women came together to expel the shah with his Western friends and worldview. The women put on veils to mark their Iranian identity, a kind of nationalist uniform. When the ayatollahs came to power, they decreed the wearing of the veil to be part of the new establishment look. Women who wanted to work in government or even only appear in public had to don the chador. Islam came to represent the restitution of authentic norms and values in a society corrupted by its overidentification with the West (a term was coined, *gharebzadeghi*, "west-toxification").

From Iran the movement to re-Islamize Muslim societies spread and encountered the Sunni thrust of Saudi Arabia. The language and symbols of a newly invigorated Islam came to dominate public space. Women were central to this transformative process. Women in public had to look and act in such a way that they confirmed the Islamicness of that space. Religious authorities issued pronouncements on what women should and should not do. The rules and regulations increased and tightened. Interpretations of foundational texts based on flimsy evidence or on proven misogynist interpretations from the early centuries of Islam, like those of Ibn Taymiyya and Ibn Jawzi, came to assume a new importance in the public practice of the religion.

Interpreting the Role of Women in Islam

By the mid-1980s women were realizing that they were going to have to assume responsibility for interpreting foundational texts if they were to hold on to rights for which their mothers had fought and that they were seeing erode under their very eyes. If they did not stop the advance of an Islamic movement that systematically targeted women's established rights and liberties, then no one would. In fact, they were wrong, because men soon joined these women. Farid Esack in South Africa raised the banner for what he called "gender jihad," and in Iran, in the heart of what was thought to be the beacon of conservative Islam, some male clerics were opposing their colleagues' antiwomen legislations.

Political and religious context, and also the Muslimness of the dominant culture, determined whether the new veiling was radical or conservative. Some women in Muslim countries like Saudi Arabia adopted the veil and strict Islamic dress codes and then called for women's rights even as they condemned Western practices and norms. They were thus able to do what before had been forbidden, namely to gather publicly in large numbers and listen to "charismatic, wealthy women, knowledgeable in religion and shari'a" (Yamani, p. 279). Other Muslim women in non-Muslim societies, such as France, put on the distinctive headscarf in order to draw attention to their religio-cultural identity. Muslim women in secular Muslim Turkey suffered the same opprobrium as their Muslim sisters in France.

The Islamization of knowledge accompanied the new veiling movement. From Indonesia to Morocco to the United States, women and men turned to the Koran, sunna, and Islamic law to collect evidence about the emancipatory nature of the religion and its founder Muhammad. The women around Muhammad were invoked as models for contemporary women: strong, intelligent, integral to the emergence of the new faith in seventh-century Arabia. His wives Khadijah and Aisha, the warrior Nusayba who saved his life in battle, his daughter Fatima, and his granddaughter Zaynab proved that from the beginning Islam was a religion unusually open to women and supportive of their rights.

Sociologists, historians, literary scholars, engineers, and physicians started to retrain themselves to become proficient in religious sciences. They studied hermeneutics and applied their new knowledge to the law and its foundations. Some, such as Amina Wadud-Muhsin, focused on the Koran and in a manner characterized by some as "textual fundamentalism," deconstructed sections word by word to produce positive meaning out of the most apparently negative passages. Others chose the Traditions, the sayings and actions of the prophet Muhammad reported by his Companions and down the generations through chains of reliable authorities. Fatima Mernissi showed how shaky was the witness of two of the most authoritative Companions, especially in what they reported the Prophet to have said about women leaders.

Teams of women collaborated on transnational projects to examine aspects of Islamic law that had negative repercussions for women. In 1982, Sisters in Islam based in Malaysia was among the first organizations to coordinate efforts on behalf of women who wanted to be good Muslims and strong, public women. Founded in 1986 by the Algerian Marie-Aimee Helie-Lucas, Women Living under Muslim Laws (WLUML) launched their Women and Law Project in 1994. Their goal was to establish a transnational feminist network that would ensure the wide dissemination of reliable information about women's rights under Islamic rule. The Iranian Mahnaz Afkhami established in 1998 the Women's Learning Partnership that produced manuals to educate women about their Islamic rights to inheritance, education, choice in marriage, choice in appearance, and protection from violence ranging from rape in marriage to honor killing. All are mobilizing on behalf of the implementation in their countries of the UN Convention on the Elimination of All Forms of Discrimination Against Women (CEDAW).

By the late 1990s this feminist labor was happening everywhere, even in the Islamic Republic of Iran. Women were studying in Tehran and Qum in women's colleges of Islamic jurisprudence and law. In Saudi Arabia women preachers were educating women in schools, colleges, and public meeting places about women's religiously guaranteed rights. They were teaching audiences how to interpret key texts for themselves in order that they not remain ignorant puppets in the hands of manipulative men. Mosques became important rallying places for women's learning circles. Feminism as a term associated with the West and its imperial projects in the lands of Islam once again became suspect. Those most opposed to its use produced a rhetoric uncannily mimetic of that of their foremothers.

However, this worldwide movement of activists struggling for the rights of women within a well-understood Islam attracted those who had not previously projected themselves as particularly religious. In Iran, journalists writing for the feminist journal *Zanan* celebrated the marriage between Islam and feminism. Far from apologizing for their use of the word *feminism,* they underscored the importance of its connections with European-American feminisms and their sociopolitical underpinnings and rigorous methodological and theoretical framing. They were proud to be both Muslim and feminists and they announced that they were Islamic feminists. This is the context in which the first Muslim woman won the Nobel Peace Prize in 2003. Shirin Ebadi, an Iranian lawyer who defended women's and children's rights throughout the toughest times of the Islamic regime, emphasized that her work had been conducted within an Islamic framework.

Ebadi is not alone in Iran or elsewhere. More and more women and men, Muslims and non-Muslims, are recognizing the dangers of a political Islam that targets Muslim women and Western institutions and then justifies this violence in religious language. They are fighting back with the goal of restoring meaning and efficacy to the word *justice* by emphasizing law. They do not see religion alone as the cause for violence and injustice, but they do believe that religion rightly understood and applied may be the key to a better future.

See also **Anticolonialism; Colonialism; Fundamentalism; Gender: Gender in the Middle East; Human Rights.**

BIBLIOGRAPHY

Abu-Lughod, Lila, ed. *Remaking Women: Feminism and Modernity in the Middle East.* Princeton, N.J.: Princeton University Press, 1998.

Afkhami, Mahnaz, ed. *Faith and Freedom: Women's Human Rights in the Muslim World.* Syracuse, N.Y.: Syracuse University Press, 1995.

Ahmed, Leila. *Women and Gender in Islam: Historical Roots of a Modern Debate.* New Haven, Conn.: Yale University Press, 1992.

Badran, Margot, and Miriam Cooke, eds. *Opening the Gates: A Century of Arab Feminist Writing.* Bloomington: Indiana University Press, 1990.

Göle, Nilüfer *The Forbidden Modern: Civilization and Veiling.* Ann Arbor: University of Michigan Press, 1996.

Mernissi, Fatima. *The Veil and the Male Elite: A Feminist Interpretation of Women's Rights in Islam.* Translated by Mary Jo Lakeland. Reading, Mass.: Addison-Wesley, 1991.

Mir-Hosseini, Ziba. *Islam and Gender: The Religious Debate in Contemporary Iran.* Princeton, N.J.: Princeton University Press, 1999.

Moghadam, Valentine. "Islamist Movements and Women's Response in the Middle East." *Gender and History* 3, no. 3 (1991): 268–283.

Moghissi, Haideh. *Feminism and Islamic Fundamentalism: The Limits of Postmodern Analysis.* London: Zed Books, 1999.

Shaheed, Farida. "Networking for Change: The Role of Women's Groups in Initiating Dialogue on Women's Issues." In *Faith and Freedom: Women's Human Rights in the Muslim World,* edited by Mahnaz Afkhami. Syracuse, N.Y.: Syracuse University Press, 1995.

Wadud-Muhsin, Amina. *Qur'an and Women.* Kuala Lumpur: Fajar Bakti, 1992.

Yamani, Mai, ed. *Feminism and Islam: Legal and Literary Perspectives.* New York: New York University Press, 1996.

Zayn al-Din, Nazira. *Al-sufur wa al-hijab* (1928). Damascus: Dar al-Mada, 1998.

Miriam Cooke

THIRD WORLD U.S. MOVEMENT

Historically, women's participation in revolutionary struggles or mass sociopolitical movements has been linked with the development of a feminist consciousness. Studies of women involved in revolutionary movements, such as the Chinese, Cuban, Mexican, and Nicaraguan revolutions, document the origins of feminist movements within the context of male-dominated nationalist struggles. Women may develop a feminist consciousness as a result of their experiences with sexism in revolutionary struggles or mass social protest movements. Such feminist consciousness represents a response to patriarchal dynamics in their respective struggles within the context of resistance to oppressive societal conditions.

Similarly, case studies of the white feminist movement in the United States during the 1960s reveal the tensions, constraints, and struggles experienced by women both in the New Left movement and in the civil rights movement. Male domination within each of these sociopolitical protest movements contributed directly to the rise of a feminist movement among white women during this time period.

African-American feminists have also traced the origins of their feminist movement to their experiences with sexism within the Black Nationalist movement. Although cultural, political, and economic constraints limited the development of a feminist consciousness and movement among Asian-American women during the early 1960s, the cross-pressures resulting from the demands of a nationalist and feminist struggle led Asian-American women in time to organize feminist organizations. Native American women also voiced their feminist agenda as they clashed with sexism demonstrated by their male counterparts in the American Indian Movement. Similarly Latina women, particularly Mexican-American women who were activists during the Chicano social protest movement El Movimiento of the 1960s and 1970s, traced the emergence of their feminist "awakening" to the internal struggles within their respective cultural nationalist movements.

Defining feminism and feminist movements represents a critical question within feminist discourse. A persistent lack of consensus reflects divergent racial/ethnic, class, sexual orientation, and other critical variables that shape the lives of women. African-American, Asian-American, Latina, and Native American women all shared the task of defining their own group's feminist ideology and political strategies. Several common themes and issues emerged over the pivotal years of the 1960s and 1970s. Women of color struggled to gain equal treatment as political activists and gain access to leadership positions within the various organizations of which they were members. Through their writings and speeches, women of color called for an end to male domination, stressing the importance of understanding the multidimensionality of oppression. They identified the multiple sources of their oppression, primarily race/ethnicity, class, and gender.

For women of color, feminism represented a movement to end sexist oppression within their own communities, political organizations, and American society in general. They understood that their feminist movement needed to go beyond women's rights to include the men of their groups, with whom they shared the experience of racial/ethnic subordination and, perhaps even more important, a commitment to build resistant movements against such oppression. Political movements among women of color in the United States represented both a cultural-nationalist and a feminist orientation.

The history of these separate political movements documents the intensity of these "feminist wars." Their male counterparts, exhibiting varying degrees of a sexist brand of cultural nationalism, challenged feminist women of color to validate their feminist political stands. For example, many Mexican-American women activists experienced dramatic ostracism. Cultural nationalists, both men and women, developed a political discourse that equated feminism with antinationalism, seeing feminism as a "white" ideology and therefore a divisive one. Feminists were labeled as "sellouts" and infiltrators whose aim was to sabotage the Chicano cultural-nationalist protest movement.

Similarly, African-American feminist women were cast as interlopers whose feminist critiques of African-American male dominance represented a dangerous departure for the civil rights and Black Power movements. Cultural nationalists argued that a feminist ideology and separatist feminist movement incited internal strife that would jeopardize the advancement of the general movement for equality and self-determination. Cultural nationalists further argued that the "woman problem" could not take center stage in the nationalist agenda; as in the Cuban revolution, the feminist agenda would be taken up once the movements succeeded in their contestation of discrimination based on race and ethnicity. Racism superseded feminism, and anyone, specifically women, who pushed for consideration of feminist concerns was labeled a traitor to the cause.

For example, Mexican-American feminist women experienced virulent attacks for adopting a so-called foreign ideology that had been introduced from the larger American society in an attempt to attack the Mexican-American community's struggle for equality and self-determination. Feminism became identified as an ideology devised to undermine the flourishing cultural renaissance emerging within Latino communities throughout the Southwest. Mexican-American feminists, like their Puerto Rican counterparts, represented a threat to their male colleagues, who argued that the attacks on male domination and sexism served only to demoralize men. Men of color developed a counterdiscourse to the emergence of a feminist one among women of color. Men of color viewed male domination or "machismo" as less an exaggerated or pernicious form of sexism and more a rational response to what they called a racist and internal colonial hegemonic control of men of color. Attacks on their manhood by all feminists—but most seriously by feminist women of color—served to reinforce the subordinate position of African-American, Asian-American, Latino, and Native American communities and others that had existed under siege by the dominant white society. Thus women of color who embraced a feminist ideology were seen as having "bought into" a dominant ideology used to suppress movements for self-determination.

Feminist women of color developed various strategies to answer these antifeminist attacks. African-American women, for example, addressed this issue by pointing to African-American history to illustrate that feminist movements had a long-standing history within their communities. They pointed to the participation of their foremothers in the antislavery movement and the role of women such as Sojourner Truth in raising women's issues within the antislavery discourse.

Similarly, Native American women relied on their specific tribal histories and traditions to underscore the vital role that their female ancestors played in resistance struggles against the tribal land encroachments and genocidal practices their communities were forced to endure. Asian-American feminists also used history to establish a link between their racial struggles and feminist struggles. Mexican-American women linked their feminist agenda to that of the Mexican women who participated in the Mexican Revolution. Puerto Rican women also fought against claims that feminism was a "foreign" ideology by stressing the critical role that women had played in nationalist struggles that had long been an issue in the territorial relations between Puerto Rico and the United States.

Interestingly, feminist women of color also reacted to their respective cultural-nationalist attacks by distancing themselves from the white feminist movement. Although women of color criticized white feminists for both subtle and overt acts of racism, they often exaggerated their separation from white feminism as a survival strategy that would lessen the impact of antifeminist attacks. Perhaps the most significant and successful technique was the argument that feminism among women of color actually strengthened the cultural-nationalist struggle by stressing the importance of women and men joining ranks in a united front to battle racism and sexism. In sum, feminist women of color struggled against the cultural-nationalist attacks but were not always successful. Nevertheless, their concerted efforts to put feminism on the agenda became a long-lasting legacy for future generations of women of color battling against multiple sources of oppression.

Not all the feminist organizations started by women of color survived, but a few continued into the twenty-first century to serve as advocacy groups for all women of color. Issues of reproductive rights, community health care delivery, immigration, poverty, and welfare policies continued to represent targets for feminist action. The decline of the cultural-nationalist period lessened but did not obliterate attacks against feminist women of color. Feminism continues to produce tensions and unresolved conflicts within communities of color in the United States; however, African-American, Asian-American, Latina, and Native American women persist in their efforts to achieve equality and social justice for themselves as women and for their communities in general.

See also **Feminism: Africa and African Diaspora; Feminism: Chicana Feminisms; Philosophies: Feminist, Twentieth-Century.**

BIBLIOGRAPHY
Allen, Paula Gunn. *The Sacred Hoop: Recovering the Feminine in American Indian Traditions.* Boston: Beacon Press, 1986.
Chow, Esther Nagan-Ling. "The Development of Feminist Consciousness among Asian American Women." *Gender and Society* 1 (1987): 284–299.
Davis, Angela Y. *Women, Race and Class.* New York: Vintage Books, 1983.
Garcia, Alma M. "The Development of Chicana Feminist Discourse: 1970–1980." *Gender and Society* 3 (1989): 217–238.

Alma M. Garcia

FETISHISM.

This entry includes two subentries:

Overview
Fetishism in Literature and Cultural Studies

OVERVIEW

Since the seventeenth century, thought about fetishism has been concerned with four overriding questions, all of them emerging in conflicts over representation that arose at the borders between cultural and historical worlds. These four questions concern the relationship between images and their referents in religious discourse; the attribution of causality and the nature of reason; the means for assessing and representing economic value; and desire and the relationship between consciousness and the material world. Although the term *fetishism* had its origins in comparative religious studies, it has become mainly associated with Marxian economic analysis on the one hand and psychoanalysis on the other.

Historical and Linguistic Origins

Most historical accounts trace the word *fetish* to the Portuguese term *feitiço* and its creoloziation as *fetisso*. Although a transliteration of the Portuguese term dominated discussion of the religious and economic practices of non-European peoples with whom merchants traded and against whom colonial powers waged wars of domination in the modern era, most of the Romance languages and English (by virtue of its residual Anglo-Norman elements) contain numerous related terms that predate this contact. These words share a Latin root meaning fabrication (*facticium*), and they are thus anchored in a historical tradition of suspicious theorizing about the human production of artifacts and artificiality. The root of *fetish* is to be found in words indicating enchantment or sorcery (*Faé, faerie,* and *faee* in Anglo-Norman; *fechiceria* in Portuguese and *hechicero* in Spanish). It is also contained in words meaning form or vessel, including that which contains spirit (*faetel* in Anglo-Norman, *feitio* in Portuguese). The same root is found in the Anglo-Norman and Middle English terms for plating or gilt, especially with gold (*faet* in this sense appears in the Anglo-Saxon saga, *Beowulf*). And, related to this, it is the root of those terms meaning to artificially enrich, as when an animal is fatted (*faeted*) in preparation for sacrifice.

If some dimension of fabrication was recognized in diverse economic and religious contexts and eras, fetish-worship was nonetheless a particularly modern accusation. As Marcel Mauss (1872–1950) observed of all magic, accusations of fetish-worship tend to be directed at religious or cultural others. Thus Christians, Jews, and Muslims, as well as Protestants and Catholics, traded accusations of fetish-worship and sorcery in the culturally contested space of the Iberian Peninsula, just as Portugal was about to embark on its imperial project along the Guinea Coast. It was there, in Africa, argues William Pietz (1985), that the multiplicity of meanings evoked by the term *feitiço* became the basis of a universalizing term, one that was not indigenous to any particular language but which seemed to travel fluidly among all. It circulated not only in the travelogues of Portuguese merchants, but also in the Dutch- and German-language reports of colonial chaplains and adventurers, wherein it was variously written as *fytys, füttise,* and *fytysi.* Apparently, the word had also entered African (especially Akan-Ashanti) vocabularies by the 1660s. Wilhelm Johann Müller's *Description of the Fetu Country, 1662–1669* (1673) not only provided na-

tive translations for what he identified as fetishes and fetish-worship, but also references the local use of the Portuguese terms *fitiso* and *fitisero* as well as a Dutch form of the word. Müller himself theorized that residents of Fetu used the term *fitisiken* to refer to their "idol-worship," because they generally rendered foreign words in a diminutive form, following the Dutch pattern. His own definition of *fitiso* included a belief in the sacred quality of natural objects, a deity demanding sacrifice, a hereditary spirit associated with the family or lineage imagined as protector, the enforcer of law, and the instrument of an oath.

Comparative Religion, Philosophy, and Fetishism

A full and comparatively oriented theory of fetishism, modeled on the concepts of animism, pantheism, and monotheism appeared a century later, when Charles de Brosses published *Du culte des dieux fétiches* (1760; On the worship of divine fetishes). On the basis of historical linguistics, de Brosses gave fetishism a meaning distinct from idolatry, with which fetish-worship had previously been conflated. He described its definitive attribute as the worship of an object per se, not as a representation of another power and hence as a confusion of a divinity with its sign, but as a material incarnation and even as a real source of power. In so describing fetishism as a carnal faith, de Brosses emphasized the arbitrariness of fetish objects, which could include plants, animals, and grander natural phenomena like oceans, mountains, and rivers, when these are treated "as Gods."

De Brosses's book not only invented a term, it initiated a critical practice whereby the identification of a seemingly "primitive" habit (in this case, random substitution) becomes the starting point for an identification of comparable qualities in the heart of so-called modern societies and institutions. He compared the putative fetish-worship of snakes in Africa to the serpent of Judah in the Book of Daniel (even contrasting fetishism with the vulgar idolatry of monotheists), while also giving to fetishism the full status of a religion (it thus constituted something like an elementary form of religious life, which Émile Durkheim [1858–1917] identified as *totemism*).

When Denis Diderot (1713–1784) included the term *fétiche* in his *Encyclopédie,* he tellingly assigned the word a modern origin but defined it only as the "name that the people of Guinea in Africa give to their divinities." By contrast, de Brosses discerned fetishism everywhere, from the Americas to Egypt, from Africa to Asia (comparative religion continues to operate on this basis). This was because fetishism was beginning to bear a more general meaning, and to connote a lack of reason whose chief symptom was a confusion of aesthetic, religious, and economic functions. Europeans conflated what they perceived to be a lack of standard measures for assessing value with what they presumed to be a capricious forging of equivalences between otherwise incommensurate things, whence emerged the possibility for the inflation and overvaluation of otherwise trivial things. This was, furthermore, associated in their minds with counterfeiting, either through the dissembling of value (as through gold-plating) or through its debasement (as through the use of alloyed gold, the latter actually being referred to as *fetiche gold*) (Pietz, 1988, pp. 110–111).

Various European philosophers found in the idea of fetishism the ideal image of Reason's other. For Immanuel Kant (1724–1804), fetishism indicated lack of judgment, an aesthetic incapacity. For Georg Wilhelm Friedrich Hegel (1770–1831), it constituted a very early if not yet fully developed form of religion within a history that he described as progressing from the perception of oneself as master of nature (associated with an unmediated magic aimed at power over single things) to the intuition of *self*-consciousness as the object of worship. Hegel observed in fetishism (and animal worship) the beginnings of a dialectical relationship, insofar as fetishism placed before the human being some kind of independent power. But he also emphasized the characteristics of contingency and arbitrariness of the fetish, and noted an aggressive relationship to the fetish, which could be destroyed and substituted with another fetish if it failed to function. Not incidentally, when writing notes on the 1871 study *The Origin of Civilisation and the Primitive Condition of Man,* by John Lubbock (1834–1913), Karl Marx (1818–1883) later reiterated this belief that fetishism is destructive of that which it venerates, when he contrasted it to idolatry as a kind of submission to objects.

The concern with substitution and (and hence, displacement) was awkwardly related to what had been an overriding interest in the affective excess posited at the heart of fetishism—and Marx's Hegelian reading of the relationship as an aggressive one was never really developed. Thus the simultaneous overattachment to an object and the capacity to destroy it was read as doubly symptomatic of irrationality and excess. Ironically, it was precisely because of this excess that Auguste Comte (1798–1857) accorded fetishism a curative function in the hyperrationalized world of his logical positivist utopia. He deemed that the rationalization of the social world could enable freedom if its principles were fully understood—hence his effort to describe that world in terms of "social statics"—but this rationalization had itself been excessive in the long but necessary development of Reason's civilization. Comte therefore advocated as corrective a "religion of Humanity." This religion would cathect people to self-sustaining values, such as an appreciation of the material and social environment, and would cultivate what he termed "universal love." It would do so through the supplementary establishment of a "Great Fetish," to which, he hoped, everyone would be spontaneously drawn. Later, Max Müller (1823–1900), whose own definitions led him to remark that neither has any religion been without fetishism, nor has fetishism ever constituted a religion unto itself, excluded Comte's Great Fetish from the very category of fetishism, on the grounds that it constituted a monotheistic deity.

Commodity Fetish

Comte was perhaps the only philosopher to advocate fetishism, but he was not the only one to identify its affective force. Nor was he alone in discovering an immanent and mimetic power in fetishism. Something of the latter is present in Marx's reading of the fetish character of the commodity, but in Marx's writing the fetish no longer grounds a strategic religion but is, rather, the conceptual basis of a strategy for reading both religion and the secular religion of capital. Significantly, Marx uses the term *fetishism* (*Fetischismus*) almost exclusively in his analyses of religion, referring to the commodity in terms of an analogous fetish-character (*Fetischcharakter*). This is an important distinction, and Marx's choice of words reflects his argument that economy had arisen in the place that religion had occupied in earlier periods, where it functioned as the institution from which law seemed naturally to emanate. Accordingly, Étienne Balibar (while overlooking the terminological distinction) argues that Marx's idea of commodity fetishism explains why, on the one hand "the capitalist mode of production . . . is the mode of production in which the economy is most easily recognized as the 'motor' of history," and, on the other, it is the mode in which "the essence of this 'economy' is unrecognized in principle" (Althusser and Balibar, p. 216). Balibar and Louis Althusser invoke the works of Marxist anthropologists to argue that in nonindustrial societies the nature of social relations is thought to be determined by extra-economic factors and institutions, which seem "natural or divine," such as the church or the monarchy. By contrast, capitalism "is the mode of production in which *fetishism* affects the economic region *par excellence*" (Althusser and Balibar, p. 179). Many anthropologists have indeed argued that in societies where there is no market economy, fetishism operates by endowing products with the qualities of the social milieu, and Michael Taussig has described the conflicts that may emerge between one regime of fetishism and another in precisely this manner. Marx, however, distinguishes between fetishism proper and an economy in which commodities possess the characteristics of the fetish.

Marx's first sustained published references to fetishism appear in his 1842 response to Karl Heinrich Hermes's newspaper article defending the Prussian state on religious grounds. In his own article, Hermes had followed Hegel in referring to fetishism as the "crudest form of religion." Marx ridiculed this argument, and Hermes's description of religion as that which raises man "above sensuous appetites." Instead, he said, fetishism is "the *religion of sensuous appetites*" (*die Religion der sinnlichen Begierde*), adding that "the fantasy of the appetites tricks the fetish worshipper into believing that an 'inanimate object' will give up its natural character to gratify his desires. The crude appetite of the fetish worshiper therefore *smashes* the fetish when the latter ceases to be its most devoted servant" (Marx, 1993, p. 22).

In the same year, Marx read several works on comparative religion, including a German translation (by Pistorius) of de Brosses's book. His investigations on the topic continued until the end of his life, and the posthumously published *Ethnological Notebooks* include several sustained passages on the topic. Nonetheless, it is the analysis of the fetish-character of commodities that has made Marx the most important single theorist of "fetishism." In *Capital,* Marx's reading of the commodity's fetish-character discloses a double substitution. First, the commodity form substitutes the objective characteristics of the products of labor for social characteristics of human labor; people are dehumanized at the same time as things appear to take on animate power and social relations are transferred from people to things. Second, the commodity form is the means by which an abstract equivalence can be posited between otherwise sensuously different objects. In this case, material difference is momentarily effaced in the fantastical image of secular transubstantiation (money appears to be capable of assuming any form) and this makes it possible for one object to substitute for another.

Marx's analysis clearly states that the fetish character of commodities arises from the social nature of production, and, at the same time, that commodities become the exclusive means by which the social character of private labor can appear. Hence, commodities seem to make possible a socialization that, in actuality, already exists by virtue of the division of labor. Thus, what reveals the social is also what hides it. Hence the fetish in Marx's analysis is what requires reading, but it is also what makes reading difficult, for it structures consciousness at a primary level. In this sense, Marxian analysis understands fetishism to be something more than excessive valorization, or overinvestment, although these attributes are not alien to it. Rather, the "the fetish-character [*Fetischcharakter*] which attaches itself to the products of labor as soon as they are produced as commodities . . . is therefore *inseparable from the production of commodities*" (1976, p. 165, my emphasis, translation modified). As Theodor Adorno (1903–1969) later summarized the point (in a dialogue with Walter Benjamin [1892–1940]), "the fetish character of the commodity is not a fact of consciousness, but dialectic in the eminent sense that it produces consciousness" (Buck-Morss, p. 121).

It is, however, when discussing the money form that Marx discerns the relationship between a misrepresentation and an overvaluation. For when money can function as the seemingly magical means by which difference can be transcended (anything can be converted into money and vice versa), and through which anything can be rendered as private property, money becomes the object of a wild desire. This desire initially fixates on money's earliest metallic forms, namely gold and silver, which leads to an aesthetic valorization of precious metals. However, in its truly abstract form (paper money, credit), the commodity makes possible an "unrestricted" desire, which Marx, in the *Grundrisse,* had specified as "greed." This greed is always greed for money—for that which can become, by purchasing, anything. Ironically, however, it is through hoarding, in which the "hoarder sacrifices the lusts of his flesh to the fetish of gold" that reserves are created and money flows regulated (Marx, 1976, p. 231). Hence, it is in the libidinous desire of the hoarder of money that capital has its origins. Fetishistic desire therefore enters Marx's analysis not as the origin but as the transformative element, the alchemical principle in capitalism's history. In a further development of this argument, Slavoj Žižek has suggested that a new stage in commodity fetishism should be recognized, namely that in which the fetish, that ostensibly sensuous object through which abstraction is made real, has been dematerialized. He identifies electronic money as the source of this dematerialization, which, he nonetheless argues, strengthens the commodity form's claims to universalizability.

Whether or not electronification does away with the sensuousness of the money fetish, much recent work shares a sense that, in the postindustrial era, commodity desire is itself productive of value and is a major stimulus for money's circula-

tion. These analyses are often indebted to the insights of Walter Benjamin, who first argued that display value was coming to displace both exchange value and use value in the marketplace of desire. Benjamin associated the emergence of a purely representational value in the era of shopping arcades with new ideological potency, as people became enthralled with what they could never possess, and were overrun by desire. Moreover, he identified this emergence with a new valuation of newness (and a corollary commodification of history), manifest most visibly in the fashion world. "Fashion prescribes the ritual according to which the commodity fetish wishes to be worshiped," he wrote (p. 153). Because fashion is also the institution in which sexual difference is deployed and cultivated, the analysis of commodity fetishism in fashion has been a staple of much feminist cultural criticism. However, this has been possible only because psychoanalysis has allowed us to see that the concept of fetishism is itself part of the organization of sexual difference, an organization that takes place in language but that is felt as an irreducibly material fact.

Psychoanalytic Interventions

Not incidentally, Sigmund Freud's (1856–1939) concept of the fetish also takes as its starting point the phenomenon of substitution. In his most direct address to the topic, the 1927 essay, "Fetishism," he argues that a fetish is a special form of penis substitute. For the boy who apprehends his mother's (and other women's) "lack" of a penis as the representation of his own possible castration, the woman's genitalia generate a "fright" (p. 154), which, Freud surmised, is universal. The woman's genitalia are henceforth an object of horror and fear for the boy, although the "normal" adult man learns to transform it into an object of desire. For some individuals, such adjustment is impossible, the trauma is too great; in the effort to overcome it, the male psyche finds a substitute, which then constitutes a "permanent memorial" to the boy's initial experience of horror. The language of memorialization is significant, and the structure of substitution as the normal (and normative) mechanism for overcoming loss recurs throughout Freud's writing. In the essay on fetishism, this substitute is the fetish: both a "token of triumph over the threat of castration *and* a safeguard against it" (p. 154, my emphasis).

At the end of the 1927 essay, Freud remarks the doubleness as well as the seeming contradictoriness of the fetish as substitute, which both "disavow[s] and . . . affirm[s]" the castration of women (p. 156). Indeed, Freud describes fetishism as a special kind of split within the subject, one that allows the male to sustain two "incompatible assertions" (p. 157). Much feminist criticism has attempted to repudiate Freud's claim that the boy naturally perceives his mother as the lacking body and as the representation of his own possible injury. Feminists have also criticized the presumption that the woman's genitalia are always already legible to the masculine subject only as lack, the negative mirroring of masculine presence. And they have suggested, in a vein ironically opened up by Jacques Lacan (1901–1981), that normative masculinity works analogously, as the substitution of the phallic symbol for the penis—not in a way that posits lack in the boy but in a manner that allows the male subject to have and to use his penis, as though by right.

Lacan had insisted that the maternal figure is phallic for the boy (she has power over him). This is possible, he says, precisely *because* she has no penis. For male subjects, the movement between having a penis, which is present, to the realm of having power can only occur in and through language, from which the Real (and hence any actual penis) is always exiled. Hence, fetishism (which is also a mode of accessing power) is a function of language, but it occurs when language is simultaneously literalized and its fully symbolic dimensions are denied. More important, it occurs as the sexual expression of a displacement made possible by this rendering of language as image (Lacan and Granoff, p. 272). Lacan makes this argument by remarking that the story on which Freud based his initial analysis, that of the young man who has an extreme and arousing affection for shiny noses, emerges from the boy's movement between languages, namely German and English. Thus, "glance on the nose" in English is linked to "*Glanz auf der Nase*" (the shine on the nose; p. 267). Here, language and, more specifically mistranslation, is the context for a substitution or "displacement," one that moves from meaning to image. Lacan and Granoff describe this displacement as one in which a person attempts to "give reality to an image" (p. 269). The resulting interstitial condition, which they believe emerges when the anxiety born of loss is linked to the guilt that is called forth by law, is one characterized by an incapacity to fully enter social relationships—those relationships mediated by the presence of another, and more particularly, a sexual other (pp. 272–273). Thus stranded, and consequently mute, "frozen in the permanent memorial" which is the fetish, the fetishist is able to find satisfaction in substitutional images. For the psychoanalytic theorist, fetishism is less an image than a kind of tableau vivant in which, as Lacan and Granoff wrote, one can find evidence for the existence of those very categories that explain fetishism as a pathology of vacillation or permanent liminality: the "symbolic, the imaginary and the real" (p. 275).

Feminist Criticism and Poststructuralist Readings

As a symptom, fetishism reveals not only the substitution through language (and its misrecognition) of one object for another, and of an object for a subject, but also the emergence of a new theory of language, one that presumes the arbitrary and unmotivated nature of the sign. However, as feminist scholars have observed, the phallus may be a signifer (or standard bearer), and even a signifer pretending to universality, but it functions by virtue of a conflation between the signifier and a material reality, to which it cannot cease referring. Jean Baudrillard links the Marxian and the Freudian analyses in order to make this point. To the extent that the money form is absolutely abstracted, its form dematerialized, it becomes a sign, operating within a code whose general principles are those of binary opposition. But this fact determines a sexual politics. Marxism fails, he suggests, because it refuses to recognize the "imposition of the law of value in the sexual domain," by which he means "the imposition of the phallus, the masculine, as the general sexual equivalent" (p. 136).

Other psychoanalytic theorists have attempted to expand the category of fetishism as part of an effort to separate the phallic from the anatomical penis. Thus, Alan Bass rereads Freud's later work and emphasizes his belief that the splitting of the ego, which fetishism incarnated and dramatized, was a general principle of all psychopathology and not just the sexual perversion of fetishism. Bass then suggests that fetishism be understood, in general, as the problem of providing "substitutes for a disturbing reality" (p. 48) and he observes that it does so in a manner that gives to consciousness a consoling concreteness while keeping unconscious what has been registered but is, nonetheless, disavowed or "defended against" (p. 51). On this ground, he goes much further than Freud to suggest that any concrete object that functions as a transitional phenomenon, as a concrete substitute for a "magical, relieving object" can provide the basis of "fetishistic formations" (pp. 207–208). The mother's breast, as much as the maternal phallus, can thus be fetishized.

This expansion of the category of fetishism may not achieve the full radicality of what Baudrillard imagined, but it addresses many feminist concerns about the tendency of the discourse on fetishism to reinscribe patriarchal narratives of phallic domination and especially those that naturalize the phallus in male anatomy. There is, of course, no single feminist analysis of fetishism. Feminist critiques have, variously, argued that sexual perversions, including fetishism, are symptoms of a conflicted effort to conform to gender stereotypes; they have noted the logical impossibility of female fetishism but also used it as a means of understanding women's and especially lesbian desire; and they have even called for a politics of fetishistic undecidability as a means of repudiating the primacy of phallic order. Such criticism has perhaps been most successful when applied to the reading of those institutional and cultural forms wherein the law of desire and the law of value, as Baudrillard would have it, are operative and mutually sustaining, namely in cinema and mass culture. Feminist film criticism, in particular, has taken up the question of cinematic spectacle, in which the woman's body is made to function as both the object of desire and of a powerful aggressivity. Laura Mulvey summarizes this long, sometimes Marxian, sometimes Freudian, analytic trajectory by identifying the "homology of structure" that allows the intensified image of the woman to cover over both the mechanics of cinematic production, and, in a double displacement, "disguises the collapse of industrial production itself" (p. 13). She asserts that the slide of signifiers characteristic of fetishism not only allows the material relations of production (and causality) to be concealed, but also it permits the tendency to conceal these relations to be itself hidden. In this process, she argues, historical analysis is lost.

Readings of fetishism are frequently, as Mulvey suggests, efforts to restore a recognition of historical materiality by attending to the ways that a seeming investment in material objects and sensuous pleasures displaces (often only partially) a true recognition of real material causes. It can, however, also entail the opposite move, namely the reading of such material investments as substitutions for the recognition of a more primary absence. Thus, Michael Taussig describes state fetishism as the conjuring of a social force that exceeds the sum powers of the individuals who constitute the social body, thereby installing a power to which people submit, and which they adore, but which exists only by virtue of such submission and adoration. Here, an object not only substitutes for a subject, it also subjects people. If there is continuity between the notion of fetishism as used by the old comparativists of religion, from de Brosses forward; the Marxian analysts of economy; the psychoanalytic descriptions of sexual perversion; and feminist critiques, then it is the sense that fetishism demands reading. This reading must entail a translation, and a recognition that, whether primitive or modern (or, as Pietz says, the product of intercultural contact in the process of modernizing colonialism), fetishism is a discourse of substitution through which the economic, erotic, and political provenance are made to converge. It is, perhaps, what the anthropologists, referring to archaic institutions of exchange, would call a "total social fact." As a modern artifact, however, it perhaps substitutes for the recognition that total social facts are no longer possible.

See also **Anthropology; Fetishism: Fetishism in Literature and Cultural Studies; Gender Studies: Anthropology; Psychoanalysis.**

BIBLIOGRAPHY

Althusser, Louis, and Étienne Balibar. *Reading "Capital."* Translated by Ben Brewster. London: Verso, 1997. First French edition 1968.

Bass, Alan. *Difference and Disavowal: The Trauma of Eros.* Stanford, Calif.: Stanford University Press, 2000.

Baudrillard, Jean. *Mirror of Production.* Translated by Mark Poster. St. Louis, Mo.: Telos, 1975.

Benjamin, Walter. "Paris, Capital of the Nineteenth Century." 1955. Reprinted in *Reflections: Essays, Aphorisms, Autobiographical Writings,"* translated by Edmond Jephcott, edited with an introduction by Peter Demetz, 146–162. New York: Schocken, 1986.

Buck-Morss, Susan. *The Dialectics of Seeing: Walter Benjamin and the Arcades Project.* Cambridge, Mass.: MIT Press, 1989.

Comte, Auguste. "Système de logique positive, ou traité de philosophie mathématique." In *Œuvres D'Auguste Comte.* Vol. 12. Paris, 1856.

de Brosses, Charles. *Du culte des dieux fétiches.* Paris: Fayard, 1760.

Freud, Sigmund. "Fetishism." In *Standard Edition of the Complete Psychological Works of Sigmund Freud* [SE], edited by James Strachey, vol. 21, 149–157. London: Hogarth, 1961. Essay originally appeared in 1927.

Grosz, Elizabeth, "Lesbian Fetishism?" In *Fetishism As Cultural Discourse,* edited by Emily Apter and William Pietz, 101–115. Ithaca, N.Y.: Cornell University Press, 1993.

Lacan, Jacques, and Wladimir Granoff. "Fetishism: The Symbolic, the Imaginary, and the Real." In *Perversions, Psychodynamics, and Therapy,* edited by Sándor Lorand, 265–276. New York: Random House, 1956.

Marx, Karl. *Capital: A Critique of Political Economy.* Vol. 1. Introduced by Ernest Mandel, translated by Ben Fowkes. London: Penguin, 1976. First German edition 1867.

———. "The Leading Article of No. 179 *Kölnische Zeitung.*" In *Karl Marx and Friedrich Engels, On Religion,* edited by Reinhold Niebuhr, 16–40. Atlanta, Ga.: Scholars, 1993. First English edition 1964.

Müller, Max. "Is Fetishism a Primitive Form of Religion?" 1878. Reprinted in *The Essential Max Müller: On Language, Mythology, and Religion,* edited by Jon R. Stone. New York: Palgrave Macmillan, 2002.

Müller, Wilhelm Johann. *Die Afrikanische auf der guineischen Gold Cust gelegene Landschafft Fetu.* 1673. Translated and reprinted as "Müller's Description of the Fetu Country, 1662–9." In *German Sources for West African History, 1599-1669,* edited by Adam Jones, 134–259. Wiesbaden: Franz Steiner Verlag, 1983.

Mulvey, Laura. *Fetishism and Curiosity.* London: British Film Institute, 1996.

Pietz, William. "The Problem of the Fetish, I." *Res* 9 (spring 1985): 5–17.

———. "The Problem of the Fetish, II." *Res* 13 (spring 1987): 23–45.

———. "The Problem of the Fetish IIIa: Bosman's Guinea and the Enlightenment Theory of Fetishism." *Res* 16 (autumn 1988): 105–123.

Taussig, Michael T. *The Devil and Commodity Fetishism in South America.* Chapel Hill: University of North Carolina Press, 1980.

———. "*Maleficium*: State Fetishism." In *Fetishism As Cultural Discourse,* edited by Emily Apter and William Pietz, pp. 217–247. Ithaca, N.Y.: Cornell University Press, 1993.

Žižek, Slavoj. *The Plague of Fantasies.* London: Verso, 1997.

Rosalind C. Morris

FETISHISM IN LITERATURE AND CULTURAL STUDIES

Fetishism is a term widely disseminated in literary and cultural studies. It carries a variety of generic meanings. Most of these derive to some degree from Marxist and psychoanalytic discourses, where the term *fetishism* has technical significance.

Commodity Fetishism

Karl Marx (1818–1883) explains his concept of fetishism in *Capital* I, where he argues that when it comes to the exchange of commodities in capitalism, a social relation between people assumes the form of a relation between things. Material objects circulated as commodities, in other words, seem to embody inherently certain characteristics that, in fact, derive from social relations. He argues that commodity fetishism originates in the social character of labor: how labor becomes value when added to what is produced by that labor. Thus work is objectified in the commodity, becoming a property of the commodity itself: its value. Marx explains the analogy with anthropological uses of the term *fetishism* in the following manner: "In order, therefore, to find an analogy, we must take flight into the misty realm of religion. There, the products of the human brain appear as autonomous figures endowed with a life of their own, which enter into relations both with each other and with the human race" (p. 165). Thus Marx associates fetishism—which he takes from a German translation of Charles de Brosses's eighteenth-century work on the cult of fetish-gods—with a religious practice that consists in anthropomorphizing objects, animating or personifying them. This is not, however, a matter of belief; it is not a matter of willfully dispelling the "mist" to which he refers. Rather, for value—the product of labor—to be understood as social and not as an objective property of products themselves, the mode of production would have to change.

History of the Fetish

According to William Pietz, who provides a historical study of the concept of the fetish that situates its use in Marx and Sigmund Freud (1856–1939), both the term and the idea of the fetish achieve new meaning and define a new problem in the cross-cultural spaces of the West African coast in the sixteenth and seventeenth centuries. He argues that the fetish comes into being at the moment of the cultural encounter between emergent capitalist modes of production and multiple noncapitalist ideologies and societies (1985, 1987); the pidgin word *Fetisso,* from the Portuguese *feitiço* (meaning, in the Middle Ages, "magical practice" or "witchcraft"), came to describe a material object that could embody a set of disparate values: religious, commercial, aesthetic, and sexual. Thus the fetish as a term comes to designate precisely the problem of value—on the contradictory cusp between materiality and abstraction—as relative and differential in circuits of exchange.

Fetishism in Psychoanalysis

As the modern European sexual perversion best known perhaps from the writings of Freud, fetishism makes its appearance in continental fin-de-siècle literary texts and in medical and psychiatric discourses of the 1880s and 1890s known as *sexology.* Freud's most extended treatment of the topic is in a relatively late essay entitled "Fetishism" (1927). Here Freud describes fetishism as a response to the refusal to acknowledge, on the part of the male child, the absence of a penis on the mother's body. This refusal occurs because to recognize its absence suggests the possibility of castration for the little boy, the possibility, in other words, that he too might lose his penis. He therefore substitutes a presence for the absence that he finds; the substitute object is often metonymically related to the area of the body where the traumatic realization would have otherwise taken place. Freud mentions that it is often the last thing seen before this moment.

Jean Laplanche and Jean-Bertrand Pontalis note that in this essay Freud seems to hesitate between two structures to describe fetishism: on the one hand, he discusses it in connection with repression; on the other—and this is the fetishistic dynamic that proves most productive as a concept in other fields—fetishism is the result of a splitting, the simultaneous denial and recognition of the absence of the woman's penis. This is the meaning of disavowal, an oscillation between two logically incompatible beliefs, captured nicely in the words of psychoanalyist Octave Mannoni's (1899–1989) patient, "I know very well, but nevertheless. . . ."

Fetishism in Feminism

According to Freud, and for obvious reasons, fetishism is a perversion restricted to men alone; however, feminist psychoanalytic and cultural theorists have also theorized the concept's broader applicability. Naomi Schor coins the term for feminism in her studies of textual instances of fetishism in the writing of Georges Sand. For Emily Apter, the combined commodity and sexual fetishism of Marx and Freud can be seen to be pastiched, parodied, and more generally deployed as a feminine phenomenon, where objects are substituted for absences and endowed with perverse, specific, "valueless" value, as illustrated in the collection of

memorabilia in, for example, the artist Mary Kelly's installation *Post-Partum Document* (1976). Elizabeth Grosz, Teresa de Lauretis, and Judith Butler have argued the applicability of notions of fetishism and the fetish for descriptions of lesbian "perverse" desire. Grosz proposes that, for women, it is not the mother's but the daughter's castration that may be disavowed (that is to say, their own). According to Grosz, in Freudian theory there are three possibilities for female fetishism. Femininity itself can be seen to be a fetish, the substitution of material signs on the woman's own body for the "missing" phallus, thereby remaking the entire body into the phallus through narcissistic self-investment. The hysteric, by contrast, invests a part of her own body with displaced sexuality. Finally, Freud's "masculinity complex" in women most closely illustrates the disavowal proper to fetishism through the substitution of an object outside of the woman (another woman's body), rather than her own or part of her own. Butler's "lesbian phallus" illustrates the potential detachability of the phallus as an idealized signifier of desire in Freudian and Lacanian theory; thus it can be transferred to and reappropriated by other kinds of bodies and subjects. De Lauretis definitively frees fetishism from its moorings in phallocentric theories (the positing of the fetish as penis or phallus substitute, the explanation of fetishism as related to horror at the sight of female genitals) by arguing that the fetish—as Sarah Kofman noted—is not the substitution for a "real" lack but is, as it were, the fetish of a fetish, the material sign of a desiring fantasy that marks both an "object" and its absence. Thus what is fetishized in lesbian desire, de Lauretis argues, is the female body itself or something that is metonymically related to it. These revisions allow feminist theorists to theorize forms of feminine desire—and especially lesbian desire—that do not correspond to heteronormative and phallocentric theories of sexuality.

Film theorists such as Metz have used the scopic specificity of the fetish—the fact that it arises in the context of a visual moment of recognition and misrecognition—to describe the workings of cinema as a medium, while feminist film theorists such as Laura Mulvey focus particularly on the fetishization of the woman's body in film (especially classic Hollywood cinema) as a way to critique the pleasures produced by narrative film for the masculine viewing subject.

Fetishism and Ideology

Combining Marx and Freudian notions of fetishism via Jacques Lacan, Slavoj Žižek has argued that ideological fantasies function according to the logic of disavowal. His studies focus on capitalism and thus on metropolitan political economies, the United States in particular. His insight is to point out that the misrecognition involved in commodity fetishism is not on the level of knowledge—that people do not know that economic exchanges are the reification of social relations—but that it is on the level of practice itself. Thus, paraphrasing Mannoni's patient's declaration, Žižek argues that individuals know very well that relations between people are behind relations between things but that they act nevertheless as though commodities embody value and thus produce social reality as fetishistic "illusion." Social reality, Žižek argues, is thus structured by an unconscious illusion that he calls ideological fantasy. This revision of Marx's commodity fetishism, combined with psychoanalytic notions of disavowal, allows Žižek to explain some of the new forms ideology takes—including cynical reason, or the perception that society is "postideological"—in postmodernity.

Fetishism and Postcolonial Studies

Following on the work of the Martinican psychoanalyst and revolutionary theorist Frantz Fanon (1925–1961), whose work sought to understand the fantasies that produce racist colonial stereotypes, postcolonial and critical race theorists use the ambivalent oscillation of fetishistic disavowal to describe how racial difference works fetishistically in colonial encounters. For Homi Bhabha, the colonial stereotype is not a static entity but a scenario that has to be continually (and anxiously) restaged as a defense and that moves between the contradictory poles of recognition and refusal of racial, cultural, and historical difference. Thus the notion of fetishism allows colonial relations to be understood as always under construction, ever ambivalent, and thus potentially open to rearticulation, resignification, and change. Anne McClintock combines the anthropological, Marxist, and psychoanalytic histories of the concept to argue that fetishism is a way to think through the displacement of social contradictions onto "impassioned objects" (p. 184) and thus that it can be usefully dislodged from Freud's Eurocentric family romance to describe the meeting points of public imperial projects and private domesticities, desire and commodity fetishism, and psychoanalysis and social history. In bringing together in a dynamically ambivalent configuration the racial and the sexual, the social and the individual, the economic and the psychic—all elements that are part of the rich historical genealogy of the concept—fetishism has proven an extraordinarily productive notion for understanding the investment of desire in objects.

See also **Body, The; Cultural Studies; Psychoanalysis.**

BIBLIOGRAPHY

Apter, Emily. *Feminizing the Fetish: Psychoanalysis and Narrative Obsession in Turn-of-the-Century France.* Ithaca, N.Y.: Cornell University Press, 1991.

Apter, Emily, and William Pietz, eds. *Fetishism as Cultural Discourse.* Ithaca, N.Y.: Cornell University Press, 1993.

Bhabha, Homi. *The Location of Culture.* New York: Routledge, 1994.

Butler, Judith. *Bodies that Matter: On the Discursive Limits of "Sex."* New York: Routledge, 1993.

De Lauretis, Teresa. *The Practice of Love: Lesbian Sexuality and Perverse Desire.* Bloomington: Indiana University Press, 1994.

Freud, Sigmund. "Fetishism." 1927. In *Sexuality and the Psychology of Love,* edited by Philip Rieff. New York: Collier, 1963.

Grosz, Elizabeth. "Lesbian Fetishism?" *Differences* 3, no. 2 (1991): 39–54.

Laplanche, J., and J.-B. Pontalis. *The Language of Psycho-Analysis.* Translated by Donald Nicholson-Smith. New York: Norton, 1973.

Mannoni, Octave. "'Je sais bien, mais quand même . . .'" In *Clefs pour l'imaginaire; ou L'autre scène,* 9–33. Paris: Seuil, 1969.

Marx, Karl. *Capital.* Vol. 1. Translated by Ben Fowkes. New York: Vintage, 1977.

McClintock, Anne. *Imperial Leather: Race, Gender, and Sexuality in the Colonial Conquest.* New York: Routledge, 1995.

Metz, Christian. *Le significant imaginaire: psychanalyse et cinéma.* Paris: Union générale d'éditions, 1977.

Mulvey, Laura. *Visual and Other Pleasures.* Basingstoke, U.K.: Macmillan, 1988.

Nye, Robert A. "The Medical Origins of Sexual Fetishism." In *Fetishism as Cultural Discourse,* edited by Emily Apter and William Pietz. Ithaca, N.Y.: Cornell University Press, 1993.

Pietz, William. "The Problem of the Fetish, I." *RES: Journal of Anthropology and Aesthetics* 9 (1985): 5–17.

———. "The Problem of the Fetish, II: The Origin of the Fetish." *RES: Journal of Anthropology and Aesthetics* 13 (1987): 23–45.

Schor, Naomi. "Fetishism." In *Feminism and Psychoanalysis: A Critical Dictionary,* edited by Elizabeth Wright. Cambridge, Mass.: Blackwell, 1992.

Žižek, Slavoj. *The Sublime Object of Ideology.* New York: Verso, 1989.

Carla Freccero

FEUDALISM, EUROPEAN. In everyday speech, *feudal* can mean "aristocratic" (in contrast to democratic), "sumptuous," "reactionary," "hierarchic" (as opposed to egalitarian), "primitive," "medieval," or simply "despotic" or "oppressive" when speaking about political, social, or economic regimes. Since the nineteenth century it has been used this way, most often as a term of opprobrium, in English, German, and the Romance languages. *Feudalism* in the sense of either a period or a regime dominated by lords or domination by people who possess financial or social power and prestige is a relatively late arrival. It first appeared in French in 1823, Italian in 1827, English in 1839, and in German only in the second half of the nineteenth century. What it refers to, however, had already appeared as *la féodalité* in the Comte de Boulainvilliers's *Histoire des anciens Parlements de France* (1737; published in English as *An Historical Account of the Antient Parliaments of France or States-General of the Kingdom,* 1739). The expression, derived from seventeenth-century legal treatises, was translated as "feodal [*sic*] government" in the English version and popularized as both "feudal government" and "the feudal system" in Adam Smith's *Wealth of Nations* (1776).

As a term of art used by historians, the adjective *feudal* and the noun *feudalism* may mean many things, most of them variants on one or more of three basic conceptions. First, they meant the legal rules, rights, and obligations that governed the holding of fiefs (*feuda* in medieval Latin), especially in the Middle Ages. This was the only meaning of *feudal* in any language before the eighteenth century. In the eighteenth and nineteenth centuries this definition was extended to encompass the nature of government at the time when fiefs were a prominent form of landholding, in particular one in which those who held fiefs exercised powers of jurisdiction and constraint either by their own customary right or by grant or usurpation from the king or emperor. In this definition such grants and usurpations are often referred to as "the privatization of public powers." Second, they meant a social economy in which landed lords dominated a subject peasantry from whom they demanded rents, labor services, and various other dues and over whom they exercised justice. This was essentially the meaning given to the term by Adam Smith and later adopted by Karl Marx. Third, they meant a form of sociopolitical organization dominated by a military class or Estate, members of which were connected to each other by ties of lordship and honorable subordination ("vassalage") and in turn dominated a subject peasantry. Lordship gave protection and defense; vassalage required service, especially service in arms. This personal relationship inseparably involved a tenurial relationship as well, the vassal holding land of his lord. Feudal domination therefore took shape within an economy where the primary source of wealth was land and its products. It was supported by a complex of religious ideas promoted by a hierarchical church that was integrated into the structure of lordship.

These three conceptions are clearly related. Modern historians may insist that one or another or some combination is the "true" or "correct" definition or may discuss one while recognizing that alternative definitions exist. German historians in the later nineteenth century invented separate terms for these different concepts: *Lehnwesen* for the first; *Feudalismus* for the second and third. British and American historians may refer to the first as *feudalism* and the second as *manorialism*, while the third may be called *feudal society*.

At the beginning of the twentieth century the English legal historian F. W. Maitland argued that "feudalism is an unfortunate word" that had been given an "impossible task" (Pollock and Maitland, vol. 1, pp. 66–67). And since the 1960s a number of historians, particularly in the United States and in England, have argued that the confusion caused by these different meanings is reason enough to ban the term from professional use. A more complex objection to the use of the term in any of its meanings has come from the difficulty historians have in reconciling the historical assumptions that lie behind all conceptions of feudalism with what they find in their detailed research into medieval social, political, and economic relationships. There has also been a shift in the academic discipline providing the tools to study medieval society. Almost all nineteenth-century and early-twentieth-century students of the subject came to it from training in the law—Roman law on the Continent and the common law in England; their accounts were shaped by legal categories. In the second half of the twentieth century, especially in the United States, anthropology increasingly influenced the conceptual framework of medievalists and therefore the way in which they read the sources. In this light, they found many legal-institutional concepts wanting, among them the concept *feudalism*.

History of the Concept

All the definitions of feudalism were born in the ideological conflicts of the Enlightenment and the French Revolution and the revolutionary politics that swept out of France across Europe in the nineteenth century. They have been shaped by the ideologies of economic liberalism, political egalitarianism, democracy, and socialism, particularly the Marxist variety. They have also been shaped by nineteenth-century philoso-

phies of history that were created in the same ideological environment. Since the eighteenth century the invidious meanings of *feudal* in popular polemical usage and the attempts by historians to give the term a technical, professional meaning have never been far apart.

The eighteenth century. On 11 August 1789, the French revolutionary National Assembly abolished the "feudal regime" (*régime féodal*). A jurist who was asked to explain to an assembly committee what exactly the act had abolished replied that it included not only rights belonging to or derived from fiefs properly speaking but all lordly rights, including rights to peasants' labor (*corvées*), crop sharing (*champart*), rents, monopolies (*banalités*), and all rights of justice "for rights of justice follow the fief and there is no fief without rights of justice."

In abolishing these lordly rights, especially those of justice, the assembly took the final logical step in a program that royal jurists had been promoting since the late sixteenth century— to establish that all rights of justice and command belonged to the state (*res publica*), were embodied in the king, and were exercised by royal commission or grant. If that were so, then all claims on the wealth or work of others, if they were not freely contracted, were likewise public powers held of the king. Once "the people," represented in the assembly, came to embody the state, they could reclaim what had once been alienated.

During the eighteenth century the two components of the "feudal regime," lordly rights over dependent tenants and lordly rights to positions of authority, had been defended by appeals to history. This is hardly surprising, for landlords pressed for funds were increasingly hiring specialists, called "feudists," to examine their ancient muniments and discover dues and rights long forgotten. Two diametrically opposed versions of the historical record emerged. One, represented notably by L'abbé Dubos in his *Histoire critique de l'établissement de la monarchie françoise dans les Gaules* (1734; Critical history of the establishment of the French monarchy in Gaul), argued that the original Frankish kings were appointed by the Roman emperors and themselves appointed the nobility to its positions and commissioned nobles to exercise their powers. Against Dubos, Boulainvilliers and, especially, Montesquieu, in his *L'esprit des lois* (1748; The spirit of laws), argued, on the contrary, that the Frankish kings and nobility with their followers had come as conquerors. The nobility, whose eminence was recognized by both grants of fiefs and participation in the assemblies that these authors believed were the precursors of the Estates, had from the beginning exercised justice over their subordinates. As they constructed their historical narratives, Boulainvilliers and Montesquieu stopped at many of the way stations that would continue to be the standard monuments of the history of feudalism in twentieth-century textbooks: the Germanic war bands described by Tacitus, the early Frankish *antrustiones* (royal followers), Carolingian oaths of fidelity, the capitulary of Quierzy, which made noble offices hereditary, and many others.

By 1789 the debate over the historical origin of noble rights had also been transformed by a dramatic change in the concept of liberty. For Boulainvilliers and Montesquieu, *liberty* meant the rights that distinguished one person or group from others, the meaning it had had since the Middle Ages. *Liberty* for them was what the modern world calls "privilege." It was in this sense that Charles Forman declared his translation of Boulainvilliers into English to be "for the instruction of . . . British lovers of liberty." For the revolutionaries of 1789, in contrast, *féodalité* was the antithesis of *liberté*, which could be realized only by equality before the law. The only distinctions the law could legitimately recognize were differences in property, excluding all those rights of exaction and justice that aristocrats had claimed as their property. Property was the realm of "private" activity; justice, taxation, and all powers of command were "public."

When combined with the earlier historical narratives, this revolutionary redefinition of liberty bequeathed two fundamental themes to all nineteenth- and twentieth-century historical accounts of "feudalism." First, feudalism involved the devolution of "public" power into "private" hands, a process that happened when the ruler granted such powers to his or her followers, or when the followers usurped them, or when the state, embodied in royal power, broke up. The historical problem became to discover exactly when and how this devolution occurred and how the "feudal state" was held together. Second, in the feudal regime all rents and obligations that were not freely contracted, whether in money, in kind, or in labor services, were the product of the political, social, and military domination of the strong over the weak, of lords over peasants. Again the historical problem was to discover how and when this developed.

The nineteenth and twentieth centuries. It was in nineteenth-century Germany that these two themes diverged, each eventually becoming the domain of an academic discipline as well as a polemical model. After the Napoleonic wars, aristocratic privileges and princely governments were partially restored in the lands of the old Holy Roman Empire. At the same time, national unity was more than ever the fervent desire of many intellectuals. Legal and constitutional historians in the developing universities sought to reconcile the two—the status quo and the desire for unity—by making "feudal government," *Lehnwesen*, the fundamental character of the old Germanic state. By defining *Lehnwesen* in a narrow technical sense as the law of fiefs (and inventing a new name for it) and at the same time universalizing it into a constitutional form, they sought to cleanse the idea of feudalism of its embarrassing polemical connotations inherited from the French Revolution. The narratives they developed were essentially variations on Montesquieu's, although they also debated whether the original German nations were unitary states of ruler and subjects (Waitz, vol. 6, pp. 357–367), or already "feudalized," as earlier historians had claimed, and if they were unitary, how and why the system of fiefs developed with its fragmentation of state power. They resolved the old debate between the "Romanist" origin of noble powers and the "Germanic" by making the "institutional" side of feudalism Roman and the "personal," Germanic.

Whatever the differences among historians, all were convinced that the "feudal state" was an organized hierarchy of fiefs and powers, from the king down to the most minor lord. The "feudal pyramid" was born. Thus they gave the German princes historical legitimacy while still asserting the existence of a "-

German constitution." William Stubbs adopted this German definition in his three-volume *Constitutional History of England* (1874–1878), asserting that William the Conqueror brought feudalism "full blown" from France. It has remained the "technical" meaning of feudalism in British historiography ever since.

Meanwhile, philosophers of history and political polemicists, most notably Karl Marx, sought to place feudalism among the stages in the historical development of human society. For Marx, the critical questions to ask in defining each stage were: Who owns the means of production? And what are the class relations to those means of production? In the stage of feudalism, landlords are the owners, and they use political and military force to extract surpluses from their peasant subjects. This conception of feudalism was the required view in the Soviet world. Since World War II it has also had a large following among western European historians. Non-Marxist or semi-Marxist "stage narratives" of the origins of feudalism have also proliferated, combining the story of the subjection of the peasantry to political and military force with various aspects of the other "technical" feudal narrative (Poly and Bournazel; Bisson).

Problems with all conceptions of feudalism have come from the discovery that before the thirteenth century fiefs had an insignificant place in aristocratic landholding; that, other than in England, peasants owed few if any labor services and in some places owned some of their land and held the rest by rental contracts; that the conception of serfdom varied widely from place to place and changed radically over time; that the relations among landholding, lordship, and fidelity likewise varied widely in space and time. Historians have questioned whether and in what ways one can speak of law and legal institutions in Europe before the revival of Roman law in the twelfth century. They have also questioned whether one can speak in any meaningful way of an early medieval state. This and much else has led some historians to argue that the concept no longer has a place in historical discourse.

See also **Bushido; Economics; History, Economic; Honor; Marxism; Monarchy.**

BIBLIOGRAPHY

Bisson, Thomas N. "The 'Feudal Revolution.'" *Past and Present* 142 (February 1994): 6–42.

Bloch, Marc Léopold Benjamin. *Feudal Society.* Translated by L. A. Manyon. Chicago: University of Chicago Press, 1961.

Brunner, Otto. "'Feudalismus,' ein Beitrag zur Begriffsgeschichte." Akademie der Wissenschaften und der Literatur in Mainz, *Abhandlungen der geistes- und sozialwissenschaftlichen Klasse* no. 10. Mainz, 1958. Translated as "Feudalism: The History of a Concept." In *Lordship and Community in Medieval Europe: Selected Readings,* edited by Fredric L. Cheyette, 32–61. New York: Holt, Rinehart, and Winston, 1968.

Cheyette, Fredric L. "Some Reflections on Violence, Reconciliation, and the Feudal Revolution." In *Conflict in Medieval Europe: Changing Perspectives on Society and Culture,* edited by Warren C. Brown and Piotr Górecki. Aldershot, U.K., and Burlington Vt.: Ashgate, 2003.

Coulborn, Rushton, comp. *Feudalism in History.* Princeton, N.J.: Princeton University Press, 1956.

Mazauric, Claude. "Note sur l'emploi de 'régime féodal' et de 'féodalité' pendant la Révolution Française." In *Sur la Révolution Française: Contributions à l'histoire de la révolution bourgeoise*, by Claude Mazauric, 119–134. Paris: Éditions sociales, 1988.

Montesquieu, Charles de Secondat, baron de. *L'esprit des lois.* Books 28–31. Paris: Bibliothèque de la Pleiade, 1958.

Pollock, Frederick, and Frederic William Maitland. *The History of English Law before the Time of Edward I.* 2nd ed. Boston: Little, Brown, 1905.

Poly, Jean-Pierre, and Éric Bournazel. *La mutation féodale, Xe–XIIe siècles.* Paris: Presses Universitaires de France, 1980.

Reynolds, Susan. *Fiefs and Vassals: The Medieval Evidence Reinterpreted.* Oxford and New York: Oxford University Press, 1994.

Stubbs, William. *Constitutional History of England.* 3 vols. Oxford: Clarendon, 1874–1878.

Waitz, Georg. *Deutsche Staats-Wörterbuch.* Vol. 6. Edited by Johann Caspar Bluntschli and Karl Brater. Stuttgart, Germany: Expedition des Staats-Wörterbuchs, 1861.

Wunder, Heide. "Einleitung." In *Feudalismus: Zehn Aufsätze,* compiled by Heide Wunder, 10–76. Munich: Nymphenburger Verlagshandlung, 1974.

Fredric L. Cheyette

FICTION. *See* **Genre.**

FIELD THEORIES. In physics, the field concept describes the distribution and propagation of effects such as magnetism and gravity through space. Field theories have helped implement the program of unifying the "forces" of nature.

Forces Propagating in Space

The discovery of a connection between electricity and magnetism is usually attributed to Hans Christian Ørsted (1777–1851), who in the winter of 1819 found that a wire carrying a current deflects a magnet. Subsequent experiments determined the dependence of the effect on the relative distance and orientation between the wire and the magnet. Ørsted had pursued his investigations because of his commitment to *Naturphilosophie* and his belief that "the same forces manifest themselves in magnetism as in electricity" and that the fundamental forces of nature were polar. Ørsted's discovery motivated numerous further investigations, by Francois Arago (1786–1853), Jean-Baptiste Biot (1774–1862), Felix Savart (1791–1841), among others, and particularly by André-Marie Ampère (1775–1836) who formulated the force law describing the interaction between two current-carrying wires. Ampère's guiding assumption was that all electrodynamic phenomena could be understood in terms of the interactions among electric charges and the currents they produce when in motion; a magnet being composed of an aggregate of electric currents.

Michael Faraday (1791–1867), prompted by analysis of Ørsted's and Ampère's investigations and of their theoretical assumptions, carried out a series of perceptive experiments. In 1821 Faraday corroborated that the force on a magnet near a current-carrying wire did not act along the line between the centers of two bodies. Following Sir Isaac Newton's (1642–1727) law of action and reaction, Faraday expected that for every effect of electricity on magnetism there should correspond an effect of magnetism on electricity. Displeased with theories of instantaneous action-at-a-distance, he sought the causes of electric and magnetic effects not only within conductors and magnets, but in the medium around them. He assumed that such effects would take time to propagate through space as "lines of force" that could interact with matter. He came to believe in the reality of these lines of force. In 1831 he found that only a *changing* current in a wire will induce a current in a nearby second wire. He came to believe that the phenomenon of the induction of a current in a wire near another that carried a time-varying current was due to its "cutting" lines of force. He also discovered that as light passes through glass near a magnet, the polarization of light rotates. Having found such connections among electricity, magnetism, and light, Faraday continued to investigate the properties of the field around ponderable bodies. His conceptualization of lines of force and of fields continued to evolve from the early 1830s through the late 1840s. Constant in this evolution was the belief that the forces between two or more electrically charged bodies were mediated by some influence—the field—that was created by each body separately, propagated in space and acted upon the other charged bodies. It is difficult to summarize Faraday's notions because contemporary language uses some of the same words as he used but with different meanings. And since Faraday did not use mathematics to describe his theoretical models, we cannot rely on that technical language to clarify his works, as in the case of later researchers. What is clear is that Faraday's notion of a *field* was entwined with his visualization of it in terms of lines of force.

In the 1840s, William Thomson (1824–1907) began to mathematically analyze Faraday's findings in terms of the deformations of a hypothetical material substance, an "ether." Drawing analogies to hydrodynamics and heat conduction, he applied the Laplace/Poisson equation to electrostatics. He showed how to represent work as spread throughout space, and described the ponderomotive force as the tendency of the field to distribute work. He represented magnetic lines of force by vortices and sought a vortex theory of ether and matter.

James Clerk Maxwell (1831–1879) developed extensively this line of research. Following Faraday, Maxwell showed that the lines of electric current and the magnetic lines were linked in a "mutual embrace." He formulated a theory with differential equations that conveyed the reciprocal embrace of constant field lines, and in 1863, for fields varying in time. The latter resulted in transverse waves in the medium, which Maxwell identified as propagating light waves. Like Thomson, Maxwell sought a mechanical account of the ether. He devised a model consisting of cellular vortices and idle wheels that transmit the motion amongst cells and represent electricity.

In Maxwell's theory, the field, which stored and conveyed energy, was fundamental and its displacements constituted charges and currents. Maxwell's theory showed a close causal connection between the separately existing electric and magnetic fields. Heinrich Rudolph Hertz (1857–1894) experimentally demonstrated the existence of invisible electromagnetic waves. Meanwhile, theorists such as Hendrik Antoon Lorentz (1853–1928) interpreted the source terms in Maxwell's equations as densities of charged particles, called electrons. Lorentz developed a theory in which ether and electrons were fundamental entities. He showed that even inside ponderable bodies, electric and magnetic effects are not merely states of matter, but of the fields within.

Fields and Subatomic Particles

In 1905, Albert Einstein (1879–1955) disposed of the concept of the mechanical ether. Electromagnetic fields propagated in vacuo with the speed of light in all inertial frames. His special theory of relativity showed that the electric and magnetic fields could be represented by one (tensor) field, such that the effects that appear in a reference system as arising from a magnetic field appear in another system moving relative to the first as a combined electric field and magnetic field, and vice versa. The theory also engendered the conception of space and time as a four-dimensional continuum. To account for gravity as a field effect, Einstein formulated the general theory of relativity in 1915. Using tensor calculus and the non-Euclidean geometry of Bernhard Riemann (1826–1866), Einstein described gravitational fields as distortions of the space-time continuum. Meanwhile, following Maxwell, some physicists attempted to construe material particles as structures of fields, places where a field is concentrated. Einstein was among them, yet in 1905 he had proposed that light is composed of particles, "photons."

In the 1920s, Werner Heisenberg (1901–1976), Erwin Schrödinger (1887–1961), Max Born (1882–1970), and others formulated quantum mechanics. Its instrumental successes suggested the possibility of describing all phenomena in terms of "elementary particles," namely electrons, protons, and photons. The components of atoms were treated as objects with constant characteristics and whose lifetimes could be considered infinite. Protons and electrons were specified by their mass, spin, and by their electromagnetic properties such as charge and magnetic moment. Particles of any one kind were assumed to be indistinguishable, obeying characteristic statistics.

Quantum mechanics originally described nonrelativistic systems with a *finite number of degrees of freedom*. Attempts to extend the formalism to include interactions of charged particles with the electromagnetic field brought difficulties connected with the quantum representation of fields—that is, systems with an infinite number of degrees of freedom. In 1927, Paul Adrien Maurice Dirac (1902–1984) gave an account of the interaction, describing the electromagnetic field as an assembly of photons. For Dirac, particles were the fundamental substance. In contradistinction, Pascual Jordan (1902–1980) argued that fields were fundamental. Jordan described the electromagnetic field by operators that obeyed Maxwell's equations and satisfied certain commutation relations. Equivalently, he could exhibit the free electromagnetic field as a superposition of harmonic oscillators, whose dynamical variables satisfied quantum commutation rules. These commutation rules implied that in any small volume of space there would be fluctuations of the electric and magnetic fields even for the vacuum state, that is even for the state in which there were no photons present, and that the root mean square value of such fluctuations diverged as the volume element probed became infinitesimally small. Jordan advocated a unitary view of nature in which both matter and radiation were described by wave fields, with particles appearing as excitations of the fields.

The creation and annihilation of particles—first encountered in the description of the emission and absorption of photons by charged particles—was a novel feature of quantum field theory (QFT). Dirac's "hole theory," the relativistic quantum theory of electrons and positrons, allowed the possibility of the creation and annihilation of matter. Dirac had recognized that the (one-particle) equation he had devised in 1928 to describe *relativistic* spin 1/2 particles, besides possessing solutions of positive energy, also admitted negative energy solutions. Unable to avoid transitions to negative energy states, Dirac eventually postulated in 1931 that the vacuum be the state in which all the negative energy states were filled. The vacuum state corresponded to the lowest energy state of the theory, and the theory now dealt with an infinite number of particles. Dirac noted that a "hole," an unoccupied negative energy state in the filled sea, would correspond to "a new kind of particle, unknown to experimental physics, having the same mass and opposite charge to an electron" (p. 62). Physicists then found evidence that positrons exist.

Beta-decay was important in the field theoretic developments of the 1930s. The process wherein a radioactive nucleus emits an electron (β-ray) had been studied extensively. In 1933, Enrico Fermi (1901–1954) indicated that the simplest model of a theory of β-decay assumes that electrons do *not* exist in nuclei before β-emission occurs, but acquire existence when emitted; in like manner as photons emitted from an atom during an electronic transition.

The discovery by James Chadwick (1891–1974) in 1932 of the neutron, a neutral particle of roughly the same mass as the proton, suggested that atomic nuclei are composed of protons and neutrons. The neutron facilitated the application of quantum mechanics to elucidate the structure of the nucleus. Heisenberg was the first to formulate a model of nuclear structure based on the interactions between the nucleons composing the nucleus. *Nucleon* was the generic name for the proton and the neutron, which aside from their differing electric charges were assumed to be identical in their nuclear interactions. Nuclear forces had to be of very short range, but strong. In 1935, Hideki Yukawa (1907–1981) proposed a field theoretic model of nuclear forces. The exchange of a meson mediated the force between neutrons and protons. In quantum electrodynamics (QED), the electromagnetic force between charged particles was conceptualized as the exchange of "virtual" photons. The massless photons implied that the range of electromagnetic forces is infinite. In Yukawa's theory, the exchanged quanta are massive. The association of interactions with exchanges of quanta is a feature of all quantum field theories.

QED, Fermi's theory of β-decay, and Yukawa's theory of nuclear forces established the model upon which subsequent developments were based. It postulated impermanent particles to account for interactions, and assumed that relativistic QFT was the proper framework for representing processes at ever-smaller distances. Yet relativistic QFTs are beset by divergence difficulties manifested in perturbative calculations beyond the lowest order. Higher orders yield infinite results. These difficulties stemmed from a description in terms of local fields, a field defined at a sharp point in space-time, and the assumption that the interaction between fields is local (that is, occurs at localized points in space-time). Local interaction terms implied that photons will couple with (virtual) electron-positron pairs of arbitrarily high momenta, and electrons and positrons will couple with (virtual) photons of arbitrary high momenta, all giving rise to divergences. Proposals to overcome these problems failed. Heisenberg proposed a fundamental unit of length, to delineate the domain where the concept of fields and local interactions would apply. His S-matrix theory, developed in the early 1940s, viewed all experiments as scattering experiments. The system is prepared in a definite state, it evolves, and its final configuration is observed afterwards. The S-matrix is the operator that relates initial and final states. It facilitates computation of scattering cross-sections and other observable quantities. The success of nonrelativistic quantum mechanics in the 1920s had been predicated on the demand that only observable quantities enter in the formulation of the theory. Heisenberg reiterated that demand that only experimentally ascertainable quantities enter quantum field theoretical accounts. Since local field operators were not measurable, fundamental theories should find new modes of representation, such as the S-matrix.

During the 1930s, deviations from the predictions of the Dirac equation for the level structure of the hydrogen atom were observed experimentally. These deviations were measured accurately in molecular beam experiments by Willis Eugene Lamb, Jr. (b. 1913), Isidor Isaac Rabi (1898–1988), and their coworkers, and were reported in 1947. Hans Albrecht Bethe (b. 1906) thereafter showed that this deviation from the Dirac equation, the Lamb shift, was quantum electrodynamical in origin, and that it could be computed using an approach proposed by Hendrik Kramers (1894–1952) using the technique that subsequently was called "mass renormalization." Kramers's insight consisted in recognizing that the interaction between a charged particle and the electromagnetic field alters its inertial mass. The experimentally observed mass is to be identified with the sum of the charged particle's mechanical mass (the one that originally appears as a parameter in the Lagrangian or Hamiltonian formulation of the theory) and the inertial mass that arises from its interaction with the electromagnetic field.

Julian Schwinger (1918–1994) and Richard P. Feynman (1918–1988) showed that all the divergences in the low orders of perturbation theory could be eliminated by re-expressing the mass and charge parameters that appear in the original Lagrangian, or in equations of motions in which QED is formulated, in terms of the actually observed values of the mass and the charge of an electron—that is, by effecting "a mass and a charge renormalization." Feynman devised a technique for visualizing in diagrams the perturbative content of a QFT, such that for a given physical process the contribution of each

diagram could be expressed readily. These diagrams furnished what Feynman called the "machinery" of the particular processes: the mechanism that explains why certain processes take place in particular systems, by the exchange of quanta. The renormalized QED accounted for the Lamb shift, the anomalous magnetic moment of the electron and the muon, the radiative corrections to the scattering of photons by electrons, pair production, and bremsstrahlung.

In 1948, Freeman Dyson (b. 1923) showed that such renormalizations sufficed to absorb all the divergences of the scattering matrix in QED to all orders of perturbation theory. Furthermore Dyson demonstrated that only for certain kinds of quantum field theories is it possible to absorb *all* the infinities by a redefinition of a *finite* number of parameters. He called such theories renormalizable. These results suggested that local QFT was the framework best suited for unifying quantum theory and special relativity. Yet experiments with cosmic rays during the 1940s and 1950s detected new "strange" particles. It became clear that meson theories were woefully inadequate to account for all properties of the new hadrons being discovered. The fast pace of new experimental findings in particle accelerators quelled hopes for a prompt and systematic transition from QED to formulating a dynamics for the strong interaction.

For some theorists, the failure of QFT and the superabundance of experimental results seemed liberating. It led to generic explorations where only general principles such as causality, cluster decomposition (the requirement that widely separated experiments have independent results), conservation of probability (unitarity), and relativistic invariance were invoked without specific assumptions about interactions. The American physicist Geoffrey Chew rejected QFT and attempted to formulate a theory using only observables embodied in the S-matrix. Physical consequences were to be extracted without recourse to dynamical field equations, by making use of general properties of the S-matrix and its dependence on the initial and final energies and momenta involved.

By shunning dynamical assumptions and instead using symmetry principles (group theoretical methods) and kinematical principles, physicists were able to clarify the phenomenology of hadrons. Symmetry became a central concept of modern particle physics. A symmetry is realized in a "normal" way when the vacuum state of the theory is invariant under the symmetry that leaves the description of the dynamics invariant. In the early 1960s, it was noted that in systems with infinite degrees of freedom, symmetries could be realized differently. It was possible to have the Lagrangian invariant under some symmetry, yet not have this symmetry reflected in the vacuum. Such symmetries are known as spontaneously broken symmetries (SBS). If the SBS is global, there will be massless spin zero bosons in the theory. If the broken symmetry is local, such bosons disappear, but the bosons associated with broken symmetries acquire mass. This is the Higgs mechanism.

The Standard Model and Beyond
In 1967 and 1968, the American nuclear physicist Steven Weinberg and the Pakistani nuclear physicist Abdus Salam independently proposed a gauge theory of the weak interactions

that unified the electromagnetic and the weak interactions using the Higgs mechanism. Their model incorporated suggestions advanced by the American theoretical physicist Sheldon Glashow in 1961 on how to formulate a gauge theory in which the weak forces were mediated by gauge bosons. Glashow's theory had been set aside because physicists doubted the consistency of gauge theories with *massive* gauge bosons, and such theories were not renormalizable. SBS offered the possibility of giving masses to the gauge bosons. The renormalizability of such theories was proved by the Dutch physicist Gerardus 't Hooft in 1972 under the guidance of Martinus Veltman. The Glashow-Weinberg-Salam theory (GWS) rose to prominence. Experiments in 1973 corroborated the existence of weak neutral currents embodied in this "electroweak" theory. The detection of the $W^{\pm}$ and of the Z_0 in 1983 gave further confirmation. Gauge theory, the mathematical framework for generating dynamics-incorporating symmetries, now plays a central role in the extension of QFT. Symmetry, gauge theories, and spontaneous symmetry breaking are the three pegs upon which modern particle physics rests.

Particles such as protons and neutrons are now understood as composed of "quarks." Quantum chromodynamics (QCD) describes the strong interactions between six quarks. Evidence for the sixth was confirmed in 1995. Quarks carry electrical charge and also a strong "color" charge, in any of three color states. QCD does not involve leptons because they have no strong interactions. It is a gauge theory involving eight massless gluons and the tricolor gauge bosons. The GWS of the weak interactions is a gauge theory involving two colors. Each quark thus carries an additional weak color (or weak charge). Four gauge bosons mediate the weak interactions between quarks. Since the 1980s, successful accounts of high energy phenomena using QCD have proliferated.

This elegant "standard model" does not accord with the known characteristics of weak interactions nor with the phenomenological properties of quarks. Local gauge invariance requires that the gauge bosons be massless, and therefore that the forces they generate be of long range. But actually, the weak force is of minute range and the masses of the W and Z bosons are large. Nor does the model accommodate quark masses. A Higgs SBS mechanism is commonly invoked to overcome such difficulties. Establishing its reality is an outstanding problem.

The work of the American physicist Kenneth Wilson and Weinberg gave support to a more restrictive view: All extant field theoretic representations of phenomena are only partial descriptions, valid in the energy domain specified by the masses of the particles that are included, and delimited by the masses of the particles that are excluded. QFTs can be viewed as low energy approximations to a more fundamental theory that is not necessarily a field theory. Such reconceptualizations have led to a hierarchical structuring of the submicroscopic realm with the dynamics in each domain described by an effective field theory. Some see it as rectifying the reductionist ideology that gripped physics. Others pursue the possibility of a more global and symmetric unification than provided by

the standard model. String theory is the only extant candidate for a consistent quantum theory to incorporate general relativity and yield a finite theory. The finiteness of the theory is the result of the fact that its fundamental entities are not point-like, but string-like, and space-time is not limited to four dimensions. Particles are then conceived as the quantum states corresponding to excitations of the basic stringlike entities.

Some theorists herald the possibility of a "final theory" that will consistently fuse quantum mechanics and general relativity and unify the four known interactions. This hope was given some credence in 1984 when superstring theory emerged as a candidate to unify all the particles and forces, including gravitation. A newer version in 1994 imagined that there is a single "big theory" with many different phases, consisting of the previously known string theories, among other things. Yet very many questions remain, including how to make contact with the experimental data explained by the standard model. Nor is it clear that such a theory—if formulated—would constitute a final theory and that no lower level might exist.

See also **Physics; Relativity; Quantum.**

BIBLIOGRAPHY

Buchwald, Jed Z. *From Maxwell to Microphysics: Aspects of Electromagnetic Theory in the Last Quarter of the Nineteenth Century.* Chicago: University of Chicago Press, 1985.

Cao, T. Yu. *Conceptual Developments of Twentieth Century Field Theories.* Cambridge, U.K.: Cambridge University Press, 1997.

Davies, Paul. ed. *The New Physics.* Cambridge, U.K.: Cambridge University Press, 1989.

Dirac, P. A. M. "Quantised Singularities in the Electromagnetic Field." *Proceedings of the Royal Society of London* Series A 133 (1931): 60–72.

Fitch, V. and Rosner, J. "Elementary Particle Physics in the Second Half of the Twentieth Century." In *Twentieth Century Physics,* edited by Laurie M. Brown, Abraham Pais, and Sir Brian Pippard. Philadelphia: American Institute of Physics, 1995.

Hoddeson, Lillian, et al., eds. *The Rise of the Standard Model: Particle Physics in the 1960s and 1970s.* Cambridge, U.K.: Cambridge University Press, 1997.

Marshak, Robert E. *Conceptual Foundations of Modern Particle Physics.* Singapore: World Scientific, 1993.

Pais, Abraham. *Inward Bound: Of Matter and Forces in the Physical World.* Oxford: Oxford University Press, 1986.

Pickering, Andrew. *Constructing Quarks: A Sociological History of Particle Physics.* Chicago: University of Chicago Press, 1984.

Purrington, Robert D. *Physics in the Nineteenth Century.* New Brunswick, N.J.: Rutgers University Press, 1997.

Schweber, Silvan S. *QED and the Men Who Made It: Dyson, Feynman, Schwinger, and Tomonaga.* Princeton, N.J.: Princeton University Press, 1994.

Weinberg, Steven. *The Quantum Theory of Fields.* 3 vols. Cambridge, U.K.: Cambridge University Press, 1995–2000.

Whittaker, E. T. *A History of the Theories of Aether and Electricity.* London: Longmans, Green, 1910. Reprint, Los Angeles: Tomash, 1989.

Alberto A. Martínez
Silvan S. Schweber

FILM. *See* **Cinema.**

FORM, METAPHYSICAL, IN ANCIENT AND MEDIEVAL THOUGHT.

The metaphysical notion of *form* (*eidos, morphe,* Gr.; *idea, forma, species,* Lat.), as it emerged in the works of Plato, must be carefully distinguished from the everyday notion from which it derived, namely, the shape or outer appearance of a thing as it presents itself to the eyes. The outer appearance of a mannequin, for instance, may be deceptively similar to that of a human being, yet, the *form* in the philosophical sense would be radically different for the two. The *form* of the thing in the philosophical sense is what determines the kind of thing it is, and so the kinds of properties it can or cannot have, and the kinds of things it can or cannot do or suffer. The mannequin, being a lifeless artifact, obviously cannot perform the characteristic operations any human being naturally can (unless prevented by some circumstance), such as walking, talking, begetting or giving birth to human offspring, and so forth. Therefore, a human being and a mannequin must have different forms. But does it follow that two individual human beings must have the *same* form? Two individual human beings are equally humans, and as such they equally have the same *sort* of characteristic operations and abilities. However, no two human beings have *numerically* the same operations and abilities. This author's activity of writing this article is not anybody else's activity, although another human being could perform exactly the same *sort* of activity. Still, the author's activity and the other person's activity are *two*, hence *numerically* distinct, activities, even if they are of the same *sort*. In the same way, the form on account of which the author has the ability to perform this activity is not numerically the same as the form on account of which another person would be able to perform the same sort of activity. So, there must be some numerically *distinct individualized* forms, namely, forms that individually determine one's essential abilities.

Forms as Universal Exemplars in Plato

Still, these individualized forms, which Plato (c. 428–348 or 347 B.C.E.) briefly recognizes in his *Phaedo* (102d–103c), are not what he would call Forms or Ideas in his Theory of Forms. Plato's Forms are rather the universal exemplars after which individualized forms are modeled. Consider, for example, any geometrical shape, say, a sphere. Any spherical thing, such as a pearl, is spherical on account of its own spherical shape (its individualized shape), but all pearls (and all billiard balls, bowling balls, etc.) are spherical because they all have the same *sort* of shape, as if each were just a copy or imitation of a common, universal model, the Form of Sphere, or Sphericity itself. To be sure, different spherical things may realize their common Form differently, say, with different diameters, and with different sorts of imperfections, but insofar as they all realize the same Form, they all constitute the same sort of objects. Indeed, imitating or participating in the same Form is precisely what Plato would take to be the reason why distinct particulars of the same kind belong to the same kind.

But how does one know about these Forms? In his *Phaedo* (73c.–75c.), Plato presents an interesting argument to show that the ability to recognize things as more or less perfect realizations of their exemplars entails people's souls' prenatal acquaintance with these exemplars. The gist of the argument can be restated as follows. Whenever one sees things that are more or less equal, the ability to recognize them as such and to judge them as being more or less perfectly equal presupposes the acquaintance with absolute, perfect Equality, the Form that all imperfectly equal things are trying to imitate with their imperfect equality. For how else would one know that an equal pair of sticks is not perfectly equal? But perfect equality can certainly never be met in one's sensory experiences. So, this acquaintance with Equality itself cannot be obtained from sensory experience. However, experiences begin with birth. Therefore, people must have their acquaintance with Equality from a prenatal form of existence, from before their souls entered their bodies at birth.

This little piece of reasoning contains all major elements of Plato's philosophical theory in a nutshell. Metaphysically, Forms are the independently existing perfect, universal standards for the perfection of any thing of any given kind. In epistemology, Forms are the source of the possibility of true universal knowledge: by recollecting one's knowledge of their universal exemplar, one has universal knowledge of all particulars that share in the same Form. Finally, in moral and political theory, the realm of Forms is that domain of pure perfection where immortal human souls belong by nature; therefore, one's task in this life is to prepare the soul for its safe return by living one's life according to the standards of perfection set by the Forms.

That the "naïve" Theory of Forms (as presented here) is inconsistent was recognized already by Plato in his *Parmenides,* where can be found the first formulation of the famous Third Man argument (132a–b), proving the inconsistency of the theory.

Consider the Form of Humanity. According to the theory, each human belongs to this species by participating in one and the same Form. But the Form itself is perfectly human, so it also belongs to the species of humans. Therefore, it should also pertain to this species by participating in the Form of Humanity. However, it cannot participate in itself, for what participates is inferior to what it participates in, and nothing can be inferior to itself. So, there has to be another Form of Humanity, which itself would also have to be human, that is, there would have to be a *Third Man,* besides the particular humans, and the first Form of Humanity. Indeed, the same reasoning could be repeated, yielding an infinite series of Forms for the species of humans. However, the theory also claims that for a species of particulars there is only a single Form in which they all participate, which is inconsistent with the infinity of Forms also implied by the claims of the theory. Therefore, the theory cannot be true as stated.

Individualized Forms in Aristotle

Moved by this and a number of other arguments, Aristotle (384–322 B.C.E.) famously rejected Plato's Forms. Hence the adage attributed to Aristotle, usually quoted in Latin: *amicus Plato sed magis amica veritas*—I love Plato, but I love the truth even more. Aristotle did not abandon, however, what has been called above the individualized forms of things. For Aristotle, it is these forms that individually determine each thing's nature, sorting them into their natural kinds, reflected in the Aristotelian system of categories.

Individualized forms are either substantial or accidental. Substantial forms are what account for the individual existence of substances, the independently existing individuals that are not properties of other individuals, such as this man. Accidental forms (or briefly, accidents) are the individualized properties of substances, such as the height or color of this man. Individual substances and accidents are classified in the system of categories into their universal kinds, their species and genera.

But how can individuals have universal knowledge concerning all individuals of the same species and genera if they cannot have the direct acquaintance with their universal exemplars presumed by Plato? Aristotle's answer is his *theory of abstraction.* In his view, the human intellect is not a merely passive recipient of "ready-made" universal information obtainable from the universal exemplars of particulars, but it is capable of actively extracting this universal information from the experience of several particulars by separating what is common to all and disregarding what is peculiar to each. The human soul, the individualized substantial form of a human body, uniquely has this ability among other living bodies, through the so-called active intellect (*nous poietikos,* Gr.; *intellectus agens,* Lat.). This unique ability of the human soul ranks it the highest in perfection among all material forms, linking it to the realm of immaterial forms or separate substances. In fact, some commentators of Aristotle, such as Averroës (Ibn Rushd; 1126–1198), interpreted Aristotle as claiming that the active intellect itself is such a separate substance. Other, more perfect separate substances are the movers of celestial spheres that by the light of the celestial bodies they hold provide the influx of energy required for the activity of the natural agents on earth (mixing the four elements, and sustaining the generation and corruption of living things). However, Aristotle argues that it is impossible to go in the series of ever more perfect movers moved by even more perfect ones to infinity. So, ultimately all are moved by a first unmoved mover, the Prime Mover, which is therefore the source of the activity of everything else.

Forms as Divine Ideas in St. Augustine

The next important step in the development of the notion form was provided by St. Augustine of Hippo's (354–430) Neoplatonic Christian conception. For Augustine, Forms are universal exemplars, just as they are for Plato, but they are not Plato's mind-independent models of various species, for they are the archetypes of creation in the Divine Mind. The Divine Ideas are the models for creatures in the eternal thought of God. Therefore, Augustine argues, a moment of understanding some eternal truth is but a glimpse into divine thought granted to humans by God in an act of illumination. Augustine's conception powerfully combined Christian teaching with elements of Platonic philosophy, but it raised a number of new questions. Especially, in epistemology, it raised the issue of why a natural capacity of the human mind, namely, the understand-

ing of "secular" eternal truths, say, in logic or mathematics, should be regarded as directly dependent on divine grace.

The Syncretic Theory of Forms of St. Thomas Aquinas

This question, and many others, received a balanced "naturalistic" answer in the Aristotelian Christian synthesis of St. Thomas Aquinas (c. 1224–1274), reconciling Christian religious doctrine and important elements of the Neoplatonic tradition with Aristotelian philosophy. For Aquinas, divine grace does not work against nature (even if it could), but through nature: *gratia non tollit naturam, sed perficit*—grace does not destroy nature, but perfects it (2SN, d. 9, q. 1, obj. 8; ST1, q. 1, a. 8, resp. 2.). Therefore, the divine light of Augustinian illumination for Aquinas becomes the same as the Aristotelian active intellect, which (pace Averroës) is not a separate substance, but a natural, although immaterial, power of the human soul. The soul itself is the Aristotelian substantial form of the human body, which, however, on account of its immaterial power, is naturally capable of surviving the death of a human person, to be supernaturally resurrected in the same body by God. The human soul thus straddles the ontological divide between material and immaterial, having access to both. The natural world of material substances, each having its natural powers on account of its characteristic substantial form, but all in need of a constant influx of energy for its natural operation, is kept in motion by the movement of heavenly spheres, in accordance with the laws of Aristotelian physics. These in turn are moved by their immaterial movers, Aristotle's subsistent forms or separate substances, which Aquinas further identifies with biblical angels. But even these immaterial forms are not pure actuality or energy (*actualitas,* Lat.; *energeia,* Gr.). Therefore, they owe their activity as well as their actual being to the Aristotelian Prime Mover, the first cause of all causes, which for Aquinas is also the creator of the universe, both material and immaterial, namely, the Judeo-Christian God, the subsistent form that is pure energy or actuality, that is, nothing but pure being: He Who Is (ST1, q. 13, a. 11; *Exodus* 3:14).

See also **Aristotelianism; Platonism.**

BIBLIOGRAPHY

PRIMARY SOURCES

Aquinas, Thomas, St. *Scriptum super libros Sententiarum.* In *S. Thomae Aquinatis Opera Omnia; ut sunt in Indice Thomistico:* additis 61 scriptis ex aliis medii aevi auctoribus. Stuttgart-Bad Cannstatt: Frommann-Holzboog, 1980.

———. *Summa Theologica.* A complete English translation, translated by the Fathers of the English Dominican Province. Westminster, Md.: Christian Classics, 1981.

A Summary of Philosophy. Translated and edited, with introduction and glossary, by Richard J. Regan, S.J. Indianapolis: Hackett, 2003. A modern translation of selected philosophical texts from Aquinas's theological masterpiece.

Aristotle. *The Complete Works of Aristotle: The Revised Oxford Translation.* 2 vols. Edited by Jonathan Barnes. Princeton, N.J.: Princeton University Press, 1984.

Augustine. *The Essential Augustine.* Edited by Vernon J. Bourke. Indianapolis,: Hackett, 1974. See especially "Divine Ideas as

Prototypes," pp. 61–62; selection from Augustine's *Eighty-three Different Questions,* q. 46, 1–2.

Plato. *Five Dialogues.* Translated by G. M. A. Grube. Revised by John M. Cooper. Indianapolis,: Hackett, 2002.

———. *Plato's Parmenides.* Translated with introduction and commentary by Samuel Scolnicov. Berkeley: University of California Press, 2003.

SECONDARY SOURCES

Davies, Brian. "Thomas Aquinas." In *Blackwell's Companion to Mediaeval Philosophy,* edited by Jorge Gracia and Timothy Noone, 643–659. Oxford: Blackwell, 2002.

Fine, Gail. *On Ideas: Aristotle's Criticism of Plato's Theory of Forms.* Oxford: Clarendon, 1993.

Klima, Gyula. "Natures: The Problem of Universals." In *The Cambridge Companion to Medieval Philosophy,* edited by Arthur Stephen McGrade, 196–207. Cambridge, U.K.: Cambridge University Press, 2003.

Vlastos, Gregory, ed. *Plato: A Collection of Critical Essays.* Notre Dame, Ind.: University of Notre Dame Press, 1978.

Gyula Klima

FORMALISM. Formalism in literary studies was not merely about formal elements of literature, though it stressed the importance of studying form. In fact, it proclaimed the unity of form and content by emphasizing that in a literary work the former cannot properly be understood when separated from the latter and vice versa. At the same time, formalism stressed the need to view literature as an autonomous verbal art, one that is oriented toward itself. Thus, formalism addressed the language of literature and established the basis for the origins and development of structuralism in literary studies.

Origins

As a movement in literary studies and a school of literary theory and analysis, formalism emerged in Russia and Poland during the 1910s. In Russia its official beginning was marked by an establishment of two organizations: the Moscow Linguistic Circle, founded in 1915 by such linguists of Moscow University as Roman Jakobson, Grigory Vinokur, and Petr Bogatyrev; and the Society for the Study of Poetic Language (or OPOYAZ, an acronym for the group's name in Russian), founded in 1916 in Petrograd (later Leningrad and then St. Petersburg—the city's original name) by literary scholars such as Osip Brik, Boris Eikhenbaum, and Viktor Shklovsky, as well as the linguist Lev Yakubinsky. A few years later the latter group was joined by the literary theorists Boris Tomashevsky and Yury Tynianov, along with some other scholars from the Petrograd State Institute of Art History.

In Poland the beginning of formalist ideas dates back to as early as the period 1911 to 1914, when Kazimierz Wóycicki, the founder of Polish formalism, wrote his first works on literary scholarship. Yet despite its early indigenous beginnings, formalism in Poland had to wait until the mid-1930s to take concrete shape as the Polish Formalist School, which had two centers: Warsaw and Wilno (present-day Vilnius, Lithuania).

Highly indebted to Russian formalism, which by 1930 had already been suppressed by Stalinist pressures, the school was formed by Manfred Kridl, who integrated the movement by drawing together his own students from the University of Wilno, notably Maria Renata Mayenowa, Maria Rzeuska, and Czesław Zgorzelski, and some other students from the University of Warsaw, including Kazmierz Budzyk, Dawid Hopensztand, and Franciszek Siedlecki.

Autonomy and "Science" of Literature

Formalism emerged as a reaction against the methods of literary scholarship of the late nineteenth and early twentieth centuries. It countered the study of literature that took an exclusive approach in which the content and ideas of literary works were embraced as faithful reflections of social and political reality. Thus formalism rejected the study of literature's background, its external conditions, its social and national tasks, and the psychology and biography of the author; instead, it proposed a focus on the literary work itself and a study of its constituent, that is, formal, components. This led to an insistence on the autonomy of both imaginative literature and of literary scholarship. Under formalism, works of literature were to be approached as artistic phenomena independent of any social, historical, ideological, or psychological circumstances. This isolation of literature from its external conditions entailed efforts to systematize and define literary scholarship. Indeed, the formalists' true concern was to reform literary study and make it a more scientific discipline. They attempted a "science" of literature by defining what the real subject of literary study is and by establishing its own methods of inquiry.

Literariness and Device

According to formalism, the background of literature and other extraliterary phenomena do not belong to literary scholarship. The proper subject matter of the discipline is not even literature itself but a phenomenon that Jakobson, in his work *Noveishaya russkaya poeziya* (1921; Recent Russian poetry), called *literaturnost'* (literariness). He declared that it is literariness that makes a given work a literary work. In other words, literariness is a feature that distinguishes literature from other human creations and is made of certain artistic techniques, or devices (*priemy*), employed in literary works. These devices became the primary object of the formalists' analyses and, as concrete structural components of the works of literature, were essential in determining the status of literary study as a science.

One of the most important devices with which the formalists dealt was the device of "defamiliarization" (*ostranenie*). As described by Shklovsky in "Iskusstvo kak priem" (1917; Art as device), defamiliarization, a typical device of all literature and art, serves to present a familiar phenomenon in an uncommon fashion for the purpose of a renewed and prolonged (the device of retardation) aesthetic perception. This kind of perception is an aim of art.

The notion of device was very seminal, as it helped the formalists do away with the traditional division of literature into form and content. They claimed that form and content are inseparable and that they constitute one unity. In place of form and content the formalists proposed to use the notions of device and material, respectively. Material stands for the raw and unorganized stuff of literature, not only themes, ideas, emotions, events, and the "outside world," but also language; device transforms material into an artistically shaped literary work of art.

Poetic Language

In their studies of the distinguishing features of literature the formalist scholars, many of whom were linguists and followers of the Polish linguist Jan Baudouin de Courtenay (1845–1929), turned to the problems of language in literature. The idea of literariness is easily embraced in terms of what differentiates literature from nonliterature. What distinguishes these is language and its particular use. The formalists juxtaposed the language of imaginative literature, especially poetry, with the language of everyday conversations to present the specific function assigned to language phenomena in literature. Colloquial language, they indicated, serves purely communicative purposes, whereas in poetry this communicative function of language is reduced to a minimum. Thus, Jakobson defined poetry as a "language in its aesthetic function" (*Noveishava russkaya poeziya*, p. 11). He also said, and Tomashevsky repeated in *Teoriya literatury: Poetika* (1925; Literary theory: Poetics), that the language of poetry is oriented toward itself and draws attention to its own properties.

To demonstrate their thesis about the aesthetic function of poetic language, the formalists turned in their early works to the study of sound and its role in poetry. The Russian scholars investigated the sound-oriented avant-garde futurist poetry, while the Polish formalists, especially Siedlecki in *Studia z metryki polskiej* (1937; Studies in Polish metrics), demonstrated that the same can be said about sound and its aesthetic use with reference to a more traditional, non–avant-garde kind of poetry. In their more mature studies the formalists investigated poetic language not only through limiting it to the sound structure but also through including its other components: syntax, vocabulary, and semantics. Wóycicki's *Forma dźwiękowa prozy polskiej i wiersza polskiego* (1912; Sound form of Polish prose and verse) and Tynianov's *Problema stikhotvornogo yazyka* (1924; The problem of verse language) serve as the best examples of formalist studies concentrated on a close correlation of sound and meaning in poetry.

What Is Literature?

In their efforts to indicate the distinguishing features of literature, the formalists did not stop at studying the use of language in poetry; they continued their inquiry with regard to prose. One of the most fundamental points of departure for the formalists was the question about the essence of literature. Indeed, they wanted to know what literature is and what makes literary works. The study of concrete prose works seemed like a valid approach in this essentialist search. It produced masterful textual analyses of narrative fiction, innovative studies in the morphology of the literary work, and new definitions of a work of literature, as well as groundbreaking inquiries into the problems of style. In such studies as "Kak sdelana *Shinel'* Gogolya" (1919; How Gogol's *The Overcoat* is made) by Eikhenbaum and *"Tristram Shendi"*

Sterna i teoriya romana (1921; Sterne's *Tristram Shandy* and the theory of the novel) and "Kak sdelan *Don Kikhot*" (1921; How *Don Quixote* is made) by Shklovsky, the formalists showed the structure, mechanisms, and laws of narrative fiction. In studying the structural components of the concrete prose works, they addressed the problems of plot composition, organizing principles of narration, and dynamism of the internal structure of the literary work. By looking into these problems the formalists were able to define the literary work in such innovative and diverse terms as a sum total of devices (Shklovsky), a uniform structure, a whole closed in itself, an organic and stylistic unity of structural components (Wóycicki), an artfully made object (Kridl), an aesthetic system (Tynianov, Wóycicki), and a dynamic structure (Tynianov, Wóycicki).

Literary Evolution

Even though the formalists, both in their theory and practice, insisted on an autonomous and intrinsic approach to literature, over time they acknowledged the importance of studying literary history and literature's connections with other spheres and "systems" of life. (In the case of the Russian formalists, this change resulted from Stalinist pressures.) Thus in its later phase, formalism introduced the notions of literary evolution and renewal and the dynamism of literary forms. These notions stood for the formalist understanding of the history of literature. It was concerned with literary change, modifications of the literary tradition, the laws of literary processes, and the development of art forms in relation to other aspects of culture. Literary change and evolution was explained in original terms of gradual shifts and reshufflings among the functions of devices, genres, works, styles, traditions, and "systems." Thus, the formalists skillfully reexamined the notion of literary history, which traditionally had been viewed as an unbound mosaic of writers and works. They showed the mechanics of continuity in the development of literature.

Suppression and Influence of Formalism

The connections of literature with other spheres and "systems," such as social conventions and other extraliterary factors, were most directly addressed in the 1928 essay "Problemy izucheniya literatury i yazyka" (Problems of the study of literature and language) by Tynianov and Jakobson. This essay, however, was only a theoretical acknowledgment by the formalists of the links between literature and social forces. These links were also presented as autonomous and separate systems governed by their own laws. Such a presentation of the problem did not spare the formalists from the attacks by Russian Marxists, who saw literature as an integral, not a separate, part of social forces. By 1930 the formalists in Russia had been silenced. Operating in a totally different environment, the Polish Formalist School, as well as the Prague Linguistic Circle in Czechoslovakia, continued the work of the Russian scholars, taking it even further, toward structuralism. The outbreak of World War II, however, finally suppressed the activity of the Polish formalists and Czech structuralists.

After the war formalism exerted a powerful influence on many trends and schools of literary criticism both in the Slavic countries and beyond. Most indebted were structuralism, considered a natural continuation of formalist theorizing, and semiotics. The Anglo-Saxon New Criticism was not influenced by formalism, but the obvious points of convergence between the two schools, comparable to the affinities among formalism, structuralism, and semiotics, clearly point to the universality, vitality, and significance of formalist ideas.

See also **Literary Criticism; Literary History; Literature; New Criticism.**

BIBLIOGRAPHY

PRIMARY SOURCES

Eikhenbaum, Boris. "How Gogol's *Overcoat* Is Made." In *Gogol from the Twentieth Century: Eleven Essays,* edited and translated by Robert A. Maguire, 269–291. Princeton, N.J.: Princeton University Press, 1974. Translation of "Kak sdelana *Shinel'* Gogolya."

———. "The Theory of the 'Formal Method.'" In *Readings in Russian Poetics: Formalist and Structuralist Views,* edited by Ladislav Matejka and Krystyna Pomorska, 3–37. Cambridge, Mass.: MIT Press, 1971. Translation of "Teoriya 'formal'nogo metoda.'"

Jakobson, Roman. *Noveishaya russkaya poeziya. Nabrosok pervyi. Velemir Khlebnikov.* Prague: "Politika," 1921.

Shklovsky, Viktor. "Art as Technique." In *Russian Formalist Criticism: Four Essays,* edited and translated by Lee T. Lemon and Marion J. Reis, 3–24. Lincoln: University of Nebraska Press, 1965. Translation of "Iskusstvo kak priem."

———. "The Making of *Don Quixote.*" In his *Theory of Prose,* translated by Benjamin Sher, 72–100. Elmwood Park, Ill.: Dalkey Archive Press, 1990. Translation of "Kak sdelan *Don Kikhot.*"

———. "Sterne's *Tristram Shandy*: Stylistic Commentary." In *Russian Formalist Criticism: Four Essays,* edited and translated by Lee T. Lemon and Marion J. Reis, 25–57. Lincoln: University of Nebraska Press, 1965. Translation of *Tristram Shendi" Sterna i teoriya romana.*

Siedlecki, Franciszek. *Studia z metryki polskiej.* Wilno: Dom Książki Polskiej, 1937.

Tomashevsky, Boris. *Teoriya literatury: Poetika.* Moscow and Leningrad: Gos. Izdatel'stvo, 1925.

Tynianov, Yury. "On Literary Evolution." In *Readings in Russian Poetics: Formalist and Structuralist Views,* edited by Ladislav Matejka and Krystyna Pomorska, 68–78. Cambridge, Mass.: MIT Press, 1971. Translation of "O literaturnoi evolutsii."

———. *The Problem of Verse Language.* Edited and translated by Michael Sosa and Brent Harvey. Ann Arbor, Mich.: Ardis, 1981. Translation of *Problema stikhotvornogo yazyka.*

Tynianov, Yury, and Roman Jakobson. "Problems in the Study of Literature and Language." In *Readings in Russian Poetics: Formalist and Structuralist Views,* edited by Ladislav Matejka and Krystyna Pomorska, 79–81. Cambridge, Mass.: MIT Press, 1971. Translation of "Problemy izucheniya literatury i yazyka."

Wóycicki, Kazimierz. *Forma dźwiękowa prozy polskiej i wiersza polskiego.* Warsaw: Wyd. Tow. Naukowego Warszawskiego, 1912.

SECONDARY SOURCES

Erlich, Victor. *Russian Formalism: History, Doctrine.* 3rd ed. New Haven, Conn.: Yale University Press, 1965.

Hansen-Löve, Aage A. *Der russische Formalismus: Methodologische Rekonstruktion seiner Entwicklung aus dem Prinzip der Verfremdung.* Vienna: Verlag der österreichischen Akademie der Wissenschaften, 1978.

Jackson, Robert Louis, and Stephen Rudy, eds. *Russian Formalism: A Retrospective Glance; A Festschrift in Honor of Victor Erlich.* New Haven, Conn.: Yale Center for International and Area Studies, 1985.

Karcz, Andrzej. *The Polish Formalist School and Russian Formalism.* Rochester, N.Y.: University of Rochester Press, 2002.

Pomorska, Krystyna. *Russian Formalist Theory and Its Poetic Ambiance.* The Hague: Mouton, 1968.

Steiner, Peter. *Russian Formalism: A Metapoetics.* Ithaca, N.Y.: Cornell University Press, 1984.

Striedter, Jurij. *Literary Structure, Evolution, and Value: Russian Formalism and Czech Structuralism Reconsidered.* Cambridge, Mass.: Harvard University Press, 1989.

Thompson, Ewa M. *Russian Formalism and Anglo-American New Criticism: A Comparative Study.* The Hague: Mouton, 1971.

Andrzej Karcz

FOUNDATIONALISM.   Knowledge is more than true belief. True beliefs that come from just lucky guesswork do not qualify as knowledge. Knowledge requires that the satisfaction of its belief condition be appropriately related to the satisfaction of its truth condition. In other words, knowledge requires a justification condition. A knower must have an adequate indication that a known proposition is true. A traditional view, suggested by Plato (c. 428–348 or 347 B.C.E.) and Immanuel Kant (1724–1804), proposes that this adequate indication consists of evidence indicating that a proposition is true. This view requires that true beliefs qualifying as knowledge be based on justifying evidence, or reasons.

When reasons are beliefs, we have inferential justification: one belief is justified on the basis of another belief. How is the latter, supporting belief itself justified? Is another supporting belief always needed? According to foundationalism, another supporting belief is not always needed.

Two-Tier Structure of Justification

Foundationalism acknowledges a two-tier structure in justification: Some justification is noninferential (that is, foundational), and all other justification is inferential (that is, nonfoundational) in that it derives ultimately from foundational justification. This view was proposed by Aristotle (384–322 B.C.E.), in *Posterior Analytics,* as a view about knowledge. It emerges too in René Descartes's *Meditationes de prima philosophia* (1641; Meditations on first philosophy), where it joins with the assumption that foundations of knowledge must be certain. Foundationalism is represented in varying forms in the writings of John Locke (1632–1704), Kant, Bertrand Russell (1872–1970), Clarence Irving Lewis (1883–1964), and Roderick M. Chisholm (1916–1999), among others. Foundationalism about evidence and justification explains a belief's (or a proposition's) having justification for a person; it does not explain one's showing that a belief has justification or is true.

Versions of foundationalism vary in explaining noninferential (foundational) justification, and in explaining how justification transmits from foundational beliefs to nonfoundational beliefs. Some philosophers have assumed that foundational beliefs must be certain (that is, indubitable or infallible). This leads to radical foundationalism, which requires that foundational beliefs be certain and that such beliefs guarantee the certainty or the truth of supported nonfoundational beliefs. Radical foundationalism faces two problems. First, very few (if any) empirical beliefs are certain. Second, beliefs that might be candidates for certainty (for instance, the belief that I am thinking) are not informative enough to guarantee the certainty or the truth of specific inferential beliefs about the external world (for example, beliefs of the sciences).

Modest foundationalism states that foundational beliefs need not possess or yield certainty and need not guarantee the truth of justified nonfoundational beliefs. A noninferentially justified, foundational belief has justification that does not derive from other beliefs, even if the causal basis of foundational beliefs includes other beliefs. Modest foundationalists have offered three influential approaches to noninferential (foundational) justification: (1) self-justification, (2) justification by nonbelief, nonpropositional experiences, and (3) justification by a reliable nonbelief origin of a belief.

Recent proponents of self-justification include Chisholm and C. J. Ducasse (1881–1969). They held that a foundational belief can justify itself, apart from evidential support from something else. Proponents of foundational justification by nonbelief experiences dissent. They hold, following Lewis, that foundational perceptual beliefs can be justified by nonbelief sensory or perceptual experiences (for example, my nonbelief experience involving seeming to see snow falling here) that either make true, are best explained by, or otherwise support those foundational beliefs (for example, the belief that snow is falling here). Advocates of foundational justification by reliable origins hold that noninferential justification depends on nonbelief belief-forming processes (such as perception, memory, and introspection) that are truth conducive, that is, they tend to produce true rather than false beliefs. Such reliabilism invokes as a justifier the reliability of a belief's nonbelief origin, whereas the previous view invokes the particular sensory experiences underlying a foundational belief. Proponents of modest foundationalism typically agree that noninferential justification for a belief can be defeated upon the acquisition of new justified beliefs, at least in most cases.

An Objection

Wilfrid Sellars and Laurence BonJour have argued against noninferential justification, on the ground that one is justified in holding a belief only if one has good reason to think that the belief is true. This ground, they suggest, implies that the justification of an alleged foundational belief will depend on an argument of this type:

1. My foundational belief that P has feature F.

2. Beliefs having feature F are likely to be true.

3. Hence, my foundational belief that P is likely to be true.

If the justification of alleged foundational beliefs depends on such an argument, these beliefs will not actually be foundational. Their justification will depend on the justification of other beliefs, namely, the beliefs represented by premises (1) and (2).

The justification of one's belief that P, however, does not require justified belief that premises (1) and (2) are true. Given such a requirement, I will be justified in believing that P only if I am justified in believing that my belief that P has feature F. Given these requirements, I will be justified in believing that (1) my belief that P has F only if I am justified in believing an additional proposition: that (4) my belief that (1) has F. In that case, we have no plausible way to preclude that similar requirements apply to the latter proposition—namely, (4)—and to each of the ensuing infinity of required justified beliefs. We do not have, however, the required infinity of increasingly complex beliefs. The conclusion is that if the justification for a belief must be accessible to a person holding the belief, that accessibility should not itself be regarded as requiring further justified belief. Some critics of foundationalism have missed this conclusion.

Current debates over internalism and externalism regarding justification concern what sort of access, if any, one must have to the justification for one's justified beliefs. Internalism incorporates an accessibility requirement of some sort on what provides justification, whereas externalism does not. Debates about internalism and externalism are prominent in contemporary epistemology and show no sign of easy resolution.

Outstanding Challenges

Proponents of foundationalism must specify the exact conditions for noninferential justification. They must also specify the exact conditions for the transmission of justification from foundational beliefs to inferentially justified (nonfoundational) beliefs. Modest foundationalism, as noted above, allows for nondeductive, merely probabilistic connections that transfer justification from foundational to nonfoundational belief. Proponents of modest foundationalism have not, however, reached consensus on the exact nature of such connections. Some proponents of modest foundationalism hold that "inference to a best explanation" underlies the transmission of justification from foundational to nonfoundational beliefs in many cases. The belief, for example, that snow is falling here can, in certain circumstances, provide a best explanation of various foundational beliefs about one's perceptual experiences (including one's seeming to see snow falling here). This, however, is a controversial matter among contemporary proponents of foundationalism.

Versions of foundationalism that restrict noninferential justification to subjective beliefs about what one seems to see, hear, feel, smell, and taste confront a special problem. These versions must explain how such subjective beliefs can yield justification for beliefs about conceiving independent physical objects (for instance, beliefs about household objects). Such subjective beliefs do not logically entail beliefs about physical objects. Given that extensive hallucination is always possible, it is possible that one's subjective beliefs are true while the pertinent beliefs about physical objects are false. This consideration challenges any version of foundationalism that includes the view that statements about physical objects can be translated, without loss of meaning, into logically equivalent statements merely about subjective states characterized by subjective beliefs. Perhaps a proponent of foundationalism will identify some nondeductive relations that explain how subjective beliefs can confer justification on beliefs about physical objects. Currently, however, no set of such relations has attracted consensus acceptance from supporters of foundationalism. Some versions of foundationalism allow for the noninferential justification of beliefs about physical objects, thereby avoiding the problem at hand.

In sum, then, foundationalism offers an influential response to questions about the nature of inferential justification. It is, however, a work in progress given its controversial features.

See also **Knowledge; Logic.**

BIBLIOGRAPHY

Alston, William P. *Epistemic Justification.* Ithaca, N.Y.: Cornell University Press, 1989.

Audi, Robert. *The Structure of Justification.* Cambridge, U.K.: Cambridge University Press, 1993.

BonJour, Laurence. *The Structure of Empirical Knowledge.* Cambridge, Mass.: Harvard University Press, 1985.

Chisholm, Roderick M. *The Foundations of Knowing.* Minneapolis: University of Minnesota Press, 1982.

Lewis, Clarence Irving. *An Analysis of Knowledge and Valuation.* La Salle, Ill.: Open Court, 1946.

Moser, Paul K. *Knowledge and Evidence.* Cambridge, U.K.: Cambridge University Press, 1989.

Moser, Paul K., and Arnold vander Nat, eds. *Human Knowledge: Classical and Contemporary Approaches.* 3rd ed. New York: Oxford University Press, 2003.

Paul K. Moser

FREEDOM. *See* **Liberty.**

FREE WILL, DETERMINISM, AND PREDESTINATION.

The concept of "free will" developed slowly. Discussions of the "will" arose only when ancient philosophical descriptions of intentional action came into contact with religious concerns about human and divine freedom. The predominant contemporary understanding of freedom as a completely undetermined choice between any two alternatives was introduced at the end of the Middle Ages. It is not clear how to reconcile free will with modern and contemporary science.

Ancient Greek Philosophy

The Greek understanding of freedom has its roots in legal codes that distinguish between intentional and nonintentional action. Socrates' (469–399 B.C.E.) understanding of human action reflects the Greek emphasis on the importance of knowledge for intentional action. Moreover, he appears to think that every agent acts for what is good, and that this good

is good both in itself and for the agent. According to Socrates, virtue is knowledge and vice is ignorance. No one acts against what he knows to be good. Plato (427?–347 B.C.E.) adopts this Socratic view, although in his later works he emphasizes that the passions have an influence on what the agent knows. The good person not only has reason, but his reason is directed toward the good.

Aristotle (384–322 B.C.E.) thinks that the Socratic account cannot explain incontinence, which is the condition in which someone does what he knows to be bad. He departs from this account by distinguishing between theoretical knowledge, which is about what cannot be changed, and practical knowledge, which is about what can be changed. The practically wise individual (*phronimos*) has that knowledge that is relevant to the action and acts upon it. Every voluntary action requires that the agent know what he is doing. An agent does not deliberate about the end, which is human happiness. Every human desires happiness. The agent deliberates only about the means that are within his power. The incontinent agent suffers from a temporary ignorance of what is good for him but always acts for the sake of something that appears to be good. For example, an incontinent person might know that chocolate cake is unhealthy, and yet his attention is drawn not to its badness but to its tastiness. He eats it not because it is unhealthy but because it is tasty.

Although Aristotle is not overly concerned with determinism, he does stress that human action requires contingency. Practical knowledge is about those events that can be changed by human action. His discussion of how future contingents are known reflects this connection and becomes important in later discussions. For Aristotle, the statement that there will be a sea battle tomorrow is neither true nor false because the event is contingent and consequently not determined by and knowable from previous events. In contrast, the Stoics believed in a strict determinism in which everything is ordered to the best. Humans cannot change the outcome of events. Nevertheless, the Stoics allowed for freedom and responsibility in that they thought that humans should understand this order and adapt themselves to it.

Jews, Christians, and Muslims

Unlike ancient philosophers, Jews and Christians believe that the whole world is contingent at least in the sense that God could have decided either to create it differently or not to create it. Everything that exists is the result of God's free choice. Moreover, the Jewish Scriptures emphasize the importance of a covenant between humans and God whereby humans freely follow its conditions. For Christians, the Epistles of Paul explain the struggle between the flesh and the spirit within a Christian. This influence of Jewish and Christian Scriptures, combined with his own moral experience, enabled Augustine of Hippo (354–430 C.E.) to develop the first explicit doctrine of the will.

Although the word *voluntas* existed previously, Augustine was the first to use it similarly to the way in which the word "will" is now used. He underwent an intellectual conversion to Christianity without at first changing his behavior. Consequently, he was compelled to reconsider the problem of incontinence. According to Augustine, the explanation of why someone is unable to do what he knows to be good is that his will is disordered. He does not use the term "free will" but "free choice" (*liberum arbitrium*). Nevertheless, he thinks that on account of their will, humans can choose to do what is right or wrong.

Although Augustine developed his understanding of the will in a primarily moral context, Greek Christians developed a parallel notion in their defense of the orthodox Christian belief that Jesus Christ has both a divine and a human will (*thelesis*). John Damascene (c. 675–c. 749) summarized the Greek teaching and emphasized that reason has its own appetite. Some later Christians base their understanding of the will as a rational appetite on his thought. Just as the senses desire what is pleasant to them, so does reason desire what it apprehends as good.

The Jewish and Christian Scriptures contributed greatly to the recognition of what we now call the will. Nevertheless, they also raised the problem of how to reconcile human wills with God's will. Although Jews and Muslims share a common belief in providence and human freedom, for the most part they have developed different approaches to explaining their compatibility. The most influential medieval Jewish position developed in response to the Muslim attempt to combine the Koran's emphasis on human freedom with the emphasis in the hadith (the body of traditions relating to Muhammad and his companions) on providence. The earliest Muslim position, namely the Mu'tazilite, distinguished between God's causality and that of human acts, for which humans are praised or blamed. God is not responsible for sin. In contrast, the Ash'arite position is that humans appropriate an act that comes from God. Although humans are responsible for their actions, they do not act independently of God. The Sunnis adopted this account, although there is no clear explanation of what this appropriation is. The greatest medieval Jewish thinker, Moses Maimonides (1135–1204), reacted strongly against the Ash'arite position. His reaction is at least partially based on the Jewish Scripture's insistence that God's covenant with the Jews requires a free response. In general, Muslims emphasize God's providence, whereas Jews emphasize human freedom.

Christians share the same difficulties as Muslims and Jews, but they also hold the doctrine of predestination, according to which God's providential decision to save some humans is prior to their response. Augustine developed this teaching in opposition to the Pelagian position that humans can obey God's commands and merit heaven without the special form of help from God that is called grace. He argued that human freedom is severely damaged by original sin and that humans are unable to perform meritorious actions on their own. Moreover, Augustine and his followers responded to a position that was later described as Semipelagian, according to which humans have the first choice in accepting or rejecting grace. The Western Church condemned Pelagianism and Semipelagianism.

Augustine's description of predestination presented many difficulties for later Christians. God moves the will, and yet the will moves freely. The agent cannot be primarily responsible for good actions, yet he is solely responsible for his bad ones. Final perseverance in grace precedes merit, although reprobates are punished only on account of their sin. Although the tension between these beliefs is most strongly felt during the early Protestant Reformation, even in the Middle Ages many thinkers emphasized some aspects of Augustine's thought at the expense of others. For example, in the early Middle Ages the Predestinarians argued that reprobation is parallel to predestination. Just as God freely wills to save some before considering their merits, so he wills to eternally punish others apart from their offenses. Predestinarianism was strongly condemned by the Western Church. Consequently, later Catholic theologians were careful to avoid Pelagianism on the one hand and predestinarianism on the other.

Scholastic Christian Thought

Thomas Aquinas (1225–1274) attempted to harmonize Augustine's account of predestination and human freedom with Aristotle's understanding of human action. Following John Damascene, Aquinas describes the will as a rational appetite. Although humans cannot choose whether to desire the ultimate end, namely happiness, they can choose between different proximate goods. He distinguishes the liberty of exercise from the liberty of specification. The liberty of specification is that freedom that has its root in reason's ability to consider alternative courses of action. The liberty of exercise rests in the will's ability to act or not to act. Scholars disagree over how significantly Aquinas's account of free choice differs from Aristotle's account of intentional action.

Like Aristotle, Aquinas thought that deliberation must be about contingent events that are not knowable as future. Unlike Aristotle, Aquinas clearly held that God is omniscient and omnipotent. How does God know future contingents? Following the early Christian writer Boethius (c. 475–525), Aquinas held that God knows future contingents not as future but as they are present to him eternally. Even God could not know them as future. How does God's providence extend to contingent events such as free human acts? God causes necessary events to happen in a necessary way and contingent events to happen in a contingent way. God is the complete universal cause of a free act, even though the agent is its complete proximate cause. Following Augustine, in his later writings Aquinas clearly states that predestination is antecedent to any foreseen merits and that original sin has made it impossible to live a fully virtuous life without grace. There is no reason on the part of the individual why God chooses to save him and allow another to sin and be damned.

Stephen Tempier, bishop of Paris, and many theologians were concerned that the reception of Aristotle's works was leading to an intellectual determinism that compromised human freedom. In particular, Franciscan theologians regarded the will as the ultimate root of human free choice, although many Dominicans followed their brother Thomas's emphasis on the intellect. Although the Franciscan John Duns Scotus (c. 1266–1308) broadly agreed with Aquinas's account of predestination and God's eternal knowledge, he had a weaker understanding of original sin and emphasized the will over the intellect. Like Aquinas, Scotus thought that the will has an inclination to the good, but he distinguishes between the inclination toward the just and the inclination toward the advantageous. Freedom results from the ability to choose between the two.

The Franciscan William of Ockham (c. 1285–c. 1349) comes much closer to the modern understanding of "free will," according to which an agent has a liberty of indifference whereby he can make any choice whatsoever. Moreover, Ockham adopts an alternative understanding of predestination according to which at least some are predestined on account of their foreseen merits. He thinks that God has knowledge of future contingents from the perspective of the past, and that both God and the agent are immediate partial causes of a free action. Consequently, God cannot internally move the will of even the great saints but must either put them in suitable circumstances or withhold his causal action when they would sin. Ockham's views on predestination were influential throughout the later medieval period, and they led to a medieval Augustinian reaction. But the greatest reaction was to occur during the Protestant Reformation.

Reformation and Counter-Reformation

Martin Luther's (1483–1546) theological education exposed him to a largely Ockhamist understanding of human freedom and predestination. He reacted strongly against this approach by denying that the human will is significantly free apart from grace and apparently by holding that predestination and reprobation are parallel. Although medieval theologians had described this position as predestinarianism, modern and contemporary scholars often call it double predestination. Subsequent Lutherans modified his position. Similarly, John Calvin (1509–1564) explicitly rejected the medieval understanding of free choice and may have adhered to double predestination. However, later Reformed theologians such as Pietro Martire Vermigli (1500–1562; also known as Peter Martyr) defended the medieval distinction between predestination and reprobation. There is not one official Reformed position on predestination. For example, Reformed theologians split over whether God's eternal decree that some will be reprobate is prior or posterior to his permission of Adam's sin. In general, later Protestant Orthodoxy permitted views on Predestination that were less severe than those of the early Protestant Reformers.

There was a variety of early Catholic responses to the Protestant Reformers, since Catholic theologians were variously Augustinian, Thomist, Scotist, and Ockhamist. Even humanists such as Erasmus (1466?–1536) were worried about the apparent denial of human freedom. The new Jesuit order reacted strongly by emphasizing a free human cooperation with grace. The Jesuit Luis de Molina (1535–1600) taught that God decides what someone will do only by foreseeing what he would do in a set of circumstances and then creating the agent and those circumstances. In general, Jesuits held an Ockhamist understanding of God's causation whereby both God and the agent contribute to the agent's action. Dominicans such as Dominic Banez (1528–1604) and John of St. Thomas (1589–1644) were the most important critics of the Jesuit positions. John held that the Protestants and Jesuits both err in thinking that a predetermination by God's grace is incompatible with

human freedom. Moreover, he thought that God wills to deprive the reprobate of grace and glory, and that this decision is prior to the permission of Adam's sin. The Dominicans claimed with some plausibility that they followed the teachings of both Augustine and Thomas Aquinas. Pope Paul V declared that the Jesuits were not to be called Semipelagians and the Dominicans were not to be called Calvinists, and they were both allowed to teach their respective positions until further notice.

Contemporary theologians and philosophers of religion still read with sympathy the works of Thomas Aquinas, William of Ockham, and Luis de Molina. Nevertheless, the Augustinian and Thomist accounts of predestination have few contemporary followers. Many now adhere to "open" theories according to which God has no complete foreknowledge of and control over human actions. Earlier Christians would have rejected such views for denying God's omnipotence and omniscience.

Modern Science and Human Freedom

In the seventeenth century modern science seemed to provide a mechanistic understanding of the world that threatened human freedom. René Descartes (1596–1650), the father of modern philosophy, held a dualistic theory whereby physical events are determined although human actions have a liberty of indifference because the soul is not material. In general, modern and contemporary philosophers have been determinists, compatibilists, or libertarians. Determinists hold that everything is physically determined and that there is no human freedom. Libertarians such as Descartes hold that human actions are free and that the free agent must have a liberty for choosing alternative possibilities that are not determined. Compatibilists such as David Hume (1711–1776) hold that human freedom is entirely compatible with physical determinism. Most compatibilists think that the indeterminacy of libertarians would only make the free actions arbitrary. Immanuel Kant (1724–1804) appeared to be a hard determinist with respect to the world of appearances and a libertarian with respect to the real world.

Contemporary philosophers still fall roughly into one of these three categories. Although a combination of chaos theory and quantum mechanics has now thrown into doubt determinist scientific theories, many philosophers think that the new science has no significant impact on debates over human freedom.

The history of ideas shows that there is no one concept of "free will." Instead, concepts of human freedom develop in response to perceived threats such as ignorance, God's omnipotence, intellectual determinism, and physical determinism.

See also **Christianity; Islam; Liberty; Reformation; Scholasticism.**

BIBLIOGRAPHY

Adams, Marilyn McCord. *William Ockham.* 2 vols. Publications in Medieval Studies 26. Notre Dame, Ind.: University of Notre Dame Press, 1987. Compares Ockham with Thomas Aquinas and Scotus.

Bourke, Vernon. *Will in Western Thought: An Historico-Critical Survey.* New York: Sheed and Ward, 1964.

Burrell, David B. *Freedom and Creation in Three Traditions.* Notre Dame, Ind.: University of Notre Dame Press, 1993. Includes a discussion of Jewish and Muslim thought.

Dihle, Albrecht. *The Theory of Will in Classical Antiquity.* Sather Classical Lectures 48. Berkeley: University of California Press, 1982.

Flint, Thomas P. *Divine Providence: The Molinist Account.* Ithaca, N.Y.: Cornell University Press, 1998.

Gallagher, David M. "Free Choice and Free Judgment in Thomas Aquinas." *Archiv für Geschichte der Philosophie* 76 (1994): 247–277.

Garrigou-Lagrange, Reginald. *Predestination.* Translated by Dom Bede Rose. St. Louis, Mo.: Herder, 1939.

Kane, Robert, ed. *The Oxford Handbook of Free Will.* Oxford: Oxford University Press, 2001.

McGrath, Alister E. *Iustitia Dei: A History of the Christian Doctrine of Justification.* 2nd ed. Cambridge, U.K.: Cambridge University Press, 1998.

Muller, Richard A. *Christ and the Decree: Christology and Predestination in Reformed Theology from Calvin to Perkins.* Studies in Historical Theology 2. Durham, N.C.: Labyrinth Press, 1986.

Rimbach, Harald. *Gnade und Erkenntnis in Calvins Prädestinationslehre: Calvin im Vergleich mit Pighius, Beza und Melancthon.* Neue Beiträge zur Historischen und Systematischen Theologie 19. Frankfurt am Main: Peter Lang, 1996.

Rist, John M. *Augustine: Ancient Thought Baptized.* Cambridge, U.K.: Cambridge University Press, 1994.

Thomas M. Osborne Jr.

Ancient Iranian relief showing two dignitaries exchanging a gesture of friendship, staircase of the Tripylon, Achaemenid period (559–330 B.C.E.) Many ancient societies placed great emphasis on male-male friendships, and some even included rituals and ceremonies to bind friends even closer together. PERSEPOLIS, IRAN. © THE ART ARCHIVE / DAGLI ORTI

FRIENDSHIP.

The visibility of "friendship" in historical writings has fluctuated over time. For the ancient Greeks and Romans, friendship was the dominant paradigm. In medieval Europe, Christian teachings subordinated human friendship to spiritual friendship. In the modern period, with its focus on impartiality, friendship was relegated to the private sphere. Toward the end of the twentieth century there was a revival of writings on friendship, with a resumption of discussions about the role of friendship in society, and debates about the politics and the ethics of friendship. Friendship, which involves close personal relations, affection, caring for and commitment to another, is intertwined with other emotions such as love, passion, patronage, spiritual love, sexual love, romance, and kinship. Different aspects and interpretations of friendship have been emphasized in different eras.

Male-Male Friendship

Anthropological evidence gives many examples of the role of friendship in different societies and cultures. For example, the Arapesh of northwestern New Guinea, the Hopi of Arizona, and the Tikopia in the Solomons created ritual or ceremonial bonds of non-kin friendship, mainly between males. Yet the traditions that focused most explicitly on friendship were the societies of classical Greece and Rome, and it is the treatises of Plato, Aristotle, and Cicero that form the linchpin around which the subsequent philosophical debate has turned or to

which it will return. Most of the classical philosophical writing on friendship presupposes a sociological context of male-male friendship. Greek writers, such as Plato and Xenophon reporting on Socrates' teaching, discuss *eros* and *philia* almost interchangeably to describe the very close relationship between men or between men and boys. Aristotle limits his concept of perfect altruistic friendship to men of virtue. The extension of friendship into a civic bond between fellow citizens is, for Aristotle, the ideal basis for politics. Cicero's accounts of friendship or *amicitia* in ancient Rome are also linked to politics and describe not only personal male heterosexual friendship, but also the concept of patronage, which sustained business and political relationships.

The ancient canon of friendship, which stresses the interests of the "other self," reciprocal consideration, and the role of friendship in contributing to a virtuous and good life, was superseded, in the medieval period, by the concept of spiritual friendship. With the rise of Christianity and hieratic religions, based on a divinity and priesthood, the relationship between man and godhead assumed prominence. The guiding emotions in religions with a supreme and omnipotent god, and especially in Christianity, were *agape*, or the love of God, and *caritas*, or charity toward others. Concepts of love and friendship were redefined by monks and theologians, as human relationships were triangulated to include God as an essential mediating force between human friendships. St. Augustine (354–430), Aethelred of Rievaulx (c. 1110–1167), and Thomas

Aquinas (1225–1274), reworking the treatises of Plato, Aristotle, and Cicero, write of spiritual friends—the need to love God in order to make possible friendships between men.

Other religious traditions also synthesize classical ideas of friendship. The Muslim theologian al-Ghazali (1058–1111) builds on the Aristotelian ideal of friendship, overlaying it with notions of the spiritual bond of Sufi brotherhood. Moses ben Maimon (Maimonides; 1135–1204) the Jewish sage, reflects both Socratic and Aristotelian ideas in advocating the importance of finding a friend.

In the modern period, few philosophers have considered friendship worthy of attention, with some notable exceptions. Francis Bacon (1561–1626) and Ralph Waldo Emerson (1803–1882) write in praise of friendship. For Michel de Montaigne (1533–1592), his friendship with the writer Étienne de La Boétie (1530–1563) represented a pure and unique experience of the finest thing in life, but was unobtainable by most men and all women. Friedrich Nietzsche (1844–1900) challenges the complaisance he sees in the thinking about friendship. He describes a friend as the "third" between I and me, with the true friend being one's best enemy. Like Aristotle and Montaigne, he considers that only "higher" forms of humans are capable of friendships. Jacques Derrida continues Nietzsche's interrogation, using the mantra "O my friend, there is no friend" to illustrate the contradictions and anomalies in the history and politics of friendship, including the omission of women in this history of friendship. The distinction between love and friendship becomes, for Derrida, submerged into ideas of "aimance" or "lovence."

Female-Male Friendship

Most philosophy, poetry, and literature discusses male-female relationships in terms of eros, romance, passion, sex, and marriage, rather than friendship. Friendship between males and females was acknowledged by some of the ancients, but almost exclusively as husband and wife. In Homer's *Odyssey,* Penelope had a role in extending *xenia* or guest friendship to various visitors to the family home in the absence of her husband, Odysseus. Her loyalty to Odysseus meant that this relationship got no closer. Lucius Annaeus Seneca (c. 4 B.C.E.–65 C.E.) and Plutarch (c. 46–after 119 C.E.) both write about the importance of friendship between husband and wife. The only philosopher of antiquity to consider women and men as equally capable of engaging in friendship was Epicurus (341–270 B.C.E.), whose Garden of Friends was open to all—men, women, and slaves.

Courtly love of the Middle Ages and the idealized relationships of the Romantic era emphasized not equal affectionate friendships, but unattainable, idealized, and exclusive male-female intimacy. It was the movement for women's equality that transformed relationships for women, both with men and with other women. The personal and political were combined in, for example, the friendships of one of the first feminists, Mary Wollstonecraft (1759–1797), during the French revolution with dissenters such as Richard Price (1723–1791) and Joseph Priestly (1733–1803), or in the bohemian literary and art circles of the

---

TERMINOLOGY

Philia: friendship

Eros: passionate/sexual love

Agape: unselfish love

Amicitia: friendship/patronage

Caritas: charity

Lovence: friendship/romance

Aimance: friendship/romance

Gyn/affection: female friendship

Xenia: guest friendship

---

early twentieth century, as with the New Zealand writer Katherine Mansfield and the Scottish painter J. D. Ferguson. Women's participation in the civil rights and the antiwar movements in the 1960s brought men and women together as friends fighting political battles. However, the concurrent sexual revolution, which endeavored to free women from the restraints of Victorian attitudes, focused on uninhibited carnal relationships rather than nonsexual friendships. The literature of heterosexual relationships became dominated by the field of psychology and includes warnings to women to avoid "love addiction" or advice about sexual enjoyment.

Female-Female Friendship

For women, whose traditional role has been in the home, social mobility meant that friendship assumed more importance as kinship ties were stretched or broken. Stories, such as the Old Testament account of Ruth and Naomi, two women related by marriage, illustrate the strength of female kinship. When friendship between women is discussed, it includes both lesbian and nonlesbian relationships. The love poems of the best-known woman writer of antiquity, Sappho (fl. c. 610–c. 580 B.C.E.), could be describing both heterosexual and lesbian relationships, but her community of women on the island of Lesbos has become the symbol of modern lesbianism.

Medieval monastic writings often portray women as a danger to men, the object of inferior emotions such as carnal desire. Suspicion was also cast upon groups of women living together in convents, especially as the nuns adopted Aethelred's notion of spiritual friendship, a companionship of souls, which sanctioned particular intimate friendships. The writings of women mystics and saints, such as Teresa of Ávila (1515–1582) Catherine of Siena (1347–1380), and Juana Inés de la Cruz, (1651–1695), expressed passionate love of the souls of their sisters.

For evidence of women's friendships, we have to rely not on the treatises written about male friendships, but on personal cor-

---

respondence, diaries, novels, and poetry. Nineteenth-century romantic friendships between women were expressed in affectionate letters to each other. The suffragettes of the late nineteenth century and early twentieth century interspersed their political communication with expressions of personal friendship.

Women's friendships with women, as well as with men, became civic bonds important for politics in the twentieth century. The second wave of feminism in the 1960s, with its slogan of "the personal is political," produced a women's network of consciousness-raising groups. Women relied on the friendship of other women for support. Janice Raymond's term "Gyn/affection" aims to describe female friendships involving not only fondness and affection, but also the sense of empowerment that female friendships can create.

Conclusion

Contemporary writings on friendship all point to a lacuna in modern literature. But toward the end of the twentieth century this gap was being addressed by various challenges, both to the impartiality of liberalism and to the objectivity of modernism by movements such as communitarianism, feminism, and postmodernism, which created a rich and ongoing scholarly debate and which resurrected some of the ideals of classical philosophy in an attempt to recognize the valuable role that can be played by friendship in the twenty-first century.

See also **Emotions; Feminism; Love, Western Notions of.**

BIBLIOGRAPHY

Badhwar, Neera Kapur, ed. *Friendship: A Philosophical Reader.* Ithaca, N.Y.: Cornell University Press, 1993.

Bell, Sandra, and Simon Coleman. *The Anthropology of Friendship.* Oxford: Berg, 1999.

Blosser, Philip, and Marshell Carl Bradley, eds. *Friendship: Philosophic Reflections on a Perennial Concern.* Lantham, New York, and Oxford: University Press of America, 1997.

Derrida, Jacques. *Politics of Friendship.* Translated by George Collins. London and New York: Verso, 1997.

Hunt, Mary E. *Fierce Tenderness: A Feminist Theology of Friendship.* New York: Crossroad, 1991.

Hutter, Horst. *Politics as Friendship: The Origins of Classical Notions of Politics in the Theory and Practice of Friendship.* Waterloo, Ont.: Wilfrid Laurier University Press, 1978.

King, Preston, and Heather Devere, eds. *The Challenge to Friendship in Modernity.* London: Frank Cass, 2000.

Leaman, Oliver, ed. *Friendship East and West: Philosophical Perspectives.* Richmond: Curzon, 1996.

Pakaluk, Michael. *Other Selves: Philosophers on Friendship.* Indianapolis: Hackett, 1991.

Raymond, Janice. *A Passion for Friends: Toward a Philosophy of Female Affection.* Boston: Beacon, 1986.

Rouner, Leroy S., ed. *The Changing Face of Friendship.* Notre Dame, Ind.: University of Notre Dame Press, 1994.

Heather Devere

FRONTIERS. *See* **Borders, Borderlands, and Frontiers, Global.**

FUNDAMENTALISM. A term used loosely to describe a reaction of (neo)traditional religion against the pressures of modernity, *fundamentalism* became a widespread topic of interest in the media and the academy during the last quarter of the twentieth century. According to many observers, fundamentalism is a worldwide phenomenon, arising in various societies with differing cultural backgrounds and experiences of modernity. The original understanding of fundamentalism, however, took shape in an American Protestant context—a context that initially informed popular and scholarly notions of fundamentalism and sometimes led to simplistic comparative interpretations. For this reason, among others, critics have questioned the viability of fundamentalism as a universal religious category, especially when applied to non-Western societies; and comparative studies of fundamentalism have been marked by self-conscious attempts to prove the existence of the phenomenon that they are presumably examining.

Origins

As a movement, fundamentalism emerged in response to the rise of liberal views within American Protestant denominations in the late nineteenth and early twentieth centuries. Liberal thinking had been influenced by evolutionary theory and German "higher criticism," a type of biblical criticism that sought to interpret the text in light of new philological and archaeological evidence, free from dogmatic and confessional assumptions. Liberals eschewed traditional theology, with its attendant belief in miracles and the supernatural, fostering instead a rational, human-centered vision of Christianity. Most offensive to fundamentalists, liberals turned accepted doctrines of faith, such as the creation story, virgin birth, atonement, and resurrection, into figurative myths, replete with meaning but devoid of historical reality. For liberals, the findings of science and the secularism of the day were fully compatible with Christianity rightly understood. Indeed, liberal theology fostered an image of Christ as immanent within the culture and thus an active force for the kind of progressive social change that modernity itself seemed to promise.

For fundamentalists, the accommodating trend of the liberals threatened to undermine both Christian faith and the moral society it had nurtured in the United States. The most coherent reply to the liberal challenge came in *The Fundamentals,* a multivolume set of essays that began publication in 1910 and lent the movement its name. While the essays did little to stem the liberal tide, they did serve to clarify the ideological rift within Protestantism. Sedate and scholarly, *The Fundamentals* appealed to an intellectual audience. The broader public, however, took notice of the doctrinal debate when the populist presidential candidate William Jennings Bryan (1860–1925) toured the country warning of the grave danger posed by liberals. The debate reached a national audience—and something of a fevered pitch—in the Scopes trial of 1925, which saw John Thomas Scopes (1900–1970), a Tennessee public school teacher, charged with breaching state law prohibiting the teaching of evolution.

Bryan, one of the prosecutors, presented the case as a referendum on the eternal truths of the Bible and their revered place in public life. The main defense attorney, Clarence Darrow, made academic freedom and separation of church and

GUSH EMUNIM IN ISRAEL

Gush Emunim or Bloc of the Faithful emerged as a faction within Israel's National Religious Party (NRP) in 1974, following the shock of the Yom Kippur War and the subsequent land concessions to Egypt in the Sinai. Gush members eventually split from the NRP, focusing their efforts on settlements and territorial expansion; but the movement's effective, sometimes militant activism for a greater Zionist state made it an important force in the nation's political debate over borders and peace. Through insightful manipulation of political divisions and popular Zionist sentiments within Israel, Gush managed to claim and build settlements upon strategic plots of land in what some regarded as the occupied territories but Gush maintained was part of Eretz Yisrael, holy ground deeded to the people of Israel in perpetuity by God in the Bible. The "ideotheology" (Sprinzak) that informed the movement traced back to the theological Zionism of Rabbi Abraham Isaac Kook (1864–1935) and the radicalization of this theology by his son, Rabbi Zvi Yehuda Kook (1891–1982). In the context of Israel's debate over its territorial future and relations with its Arab neighbors, "Kookism" (Aran) gave rise to a religious nationalist fundamentalism in which theology triumphed over policies of the secular state and compromise over territory was tantamount to a breach of God's covenant.

state the issues at stake. Clearly in violation of the law, Scopes was convicted, though the verdict was later overturned on a technicality. Bryan and the fundamentalist cause, however, emerged from the trial the real losers. Under harsh questioning from Darrow, Bryan proved incapable of offering a rational defense of biblical literalism; and news reports, especially those written by the Baltimore critic H. L. Mencken (1880–1956), portrayed fundamentalists as anti-intellectual and backward—an image from which they never fully recovered.

Political and Cultural Developments

Early detractors of fundamentalism suspected political motives behind the movement, but with few exceptions, fundamentalists avoided participation in the political arena. In fact, following the Scopes trial, fundamentalists maintained a low-key presence in the United States. By the late 1970s, however, fundamentalists had split into two distinct wings: separatists who viewed politics as a distraction from the main task of all true Christians, the salvation of individual souls; and activists who regarded social and political engagement as the best means of spreading the message of Christ. The latter returned to the public scene in force, and they began to assert their political voice in both local and national elections. Joining the fundamentalist political effort was a different, though related, group of Christian conservatives, the Evangelicals, whose numbers had grown dramatically throughout the first half of the twentieth century. This combined force came to be called the Religious Right or the New Christian Right and, as the political vector suggests, was closely linked with the concerns and candidates of the Republican Party. At work behind this conservative coalition was a cultural realignment that had been brewing for

decades. Interestingly enough, this realignment was signaled by the presidency of Jimmy Carter (1924–), a Democrat and professed born-again Southern Baptist.

The cultural agenda of Christian conservatives was shaped and broadcast by organizations such as the Moral Majority, Christian Roundtable, and, later, the Christian Coalition, whose goal was to oppose and turn back the tide of political liberalism. The United States, so these fundamentalist organizations claimed, had been founded as a Christian nation and had achieved its preeminent place in world history because of its commitment to Bible-based morality; but liberal thinking and policies had led the nation astray, and signs of decline were apparent: increasing drug use and sexual promiscuity, abortion on demand, the high rate of out-of-wedlock births and divorce, tolerance of homosexuality, absence of religion in the public schools, and court-supported attacks on public displays of faith. For fundamentalists, America's continued God-ordained prosperity depended on a return to traditional religious values and, by theological extension, a commitment to conservative political ideals, such as unwavering patriotism and anticommunism, a strong national defense, support for Israel, fiscal conservatism, and small government.

This blend of moral theology, religious nationalism, and conservative public policy had broad appeal among the electorate and helped solidify support for Ronald Reagan (1911–2004) in the 1980 presidential election. Throughout Reagan's two terms in office, fundamentalists enjoyed a measure of public attention and success that would have been hard to imagine in the aftermath of the Scopes trial. Fundamentalists basked in the glow of their newfound strength and sought to retake the cultural

BHARATIYA JANATA PARTY IN INDIA

The Bharatiya Janata Party (BJP), or Indian People's Party, was founded in 1980 after Hindu nationalists, working through the Janata Party, faired poorly in general elections against the secular Congress Party, which had ruled India since independence in 1947. The BJP drew its members from the infamous Rashtriya Swayamsevak Sangh, founded in 1925, a radical Hindu nationalist organization, one of whose former members had assassinated Mohandas K. Gandhi (1869–1948). The BJP worked to rally support for a vision of modern India that was grounded in the idea of *Hindutva* or Hindu-ness, an idea first propounded by Vinayak Damodar Savarkar (1883–1966). Hindutva portrayed India's diverse ethnic and religious factions as historical offshoots of Hinduism; and since all Indians were at base Hindus, Hindus alone were best able to express the political identity and desires of the nation. Here again, the fundamentalism at work takes the form of hyperreligious nationalism that offers citizens a cultural identity at odds with the more secular model of civic pluralism. The volatile potential of this cultural and political chauvinism manifested itself in the dispute over the Babri Masjid, which saw BJP-instigated mobs attack, in 1991, and later destroy, in 1992, a mosque at Ayodhya that Hindu nationalists claimed had been built over a temple dedicated to the god Rama. Despite the immediate political setback suffered by the BJP, the party went on to great political success, leading some to question the commonly held view that the BJP was incapable of ruling a truly democratic nation (Juergensmeyer, 1995; Hansen).

ground that they felt they had lost to liberals in the shaping of law, education, the arts, the family, and politics. Liberals, by contrast, believed that fundamentalists had, in contravention of the separation of church and state, hijacked the political process and were attempting to impose their narrow religious agenda on the country, thereby undermining the United States' civil contract of democratic pluralism. The contestation between conservatives, both political and religious, and liberals to define national identity grew so acrimonious during the 1980s that it became known as the "culture wars." It was during these wars that fundamentalism began to emerge as a comparative tool among academics, and the 1979 Islamic revolution in Iran provided the major impetus for such comparisons.

Islamic Revolution in Iran

The image of bearded clerics ruling a heretofore avowedly secular and Western-friendly Islamic country sent shock waves through the West and the Muslim world. Of particular concern among political commentators and scholars was the power of religion to contribute to the kind of revolutionary political transformation that students of history had come to associate only with modern forces like nationalism and Marxism. A revolution in the name of religion suggested to many a reassertion of premodern thinking and hence a step backward in Iran's development. Much the same view surrounded the rise to prominence of Protestant fundamentalism in the United States, which occurred against the backdrop of the 1979 Islamic revolution in Iran. Indeed, for many Western liberals, the two events had obvious dangerous parallels: a religious takeover of politics, retrograde attitudes and policies toward women, religious intolerance, and suppression of dissent. These very themes received popular treatment in Margaret Atwood's 1986 novel *The Handmaid's Tale,* which portrays the United States as a theocratic fundamentalist nation along the lines of postrevolution Iran.

To explain the revolutionary turn in Iran, scholars of the region drew on traditional social-movement theory, especially the work of Max Weber (1864–1920), whose interpretive connection to fundamentalism remained at the time unarticulated. In fact, it was in the course of analyzing the Islamic revolution in Iran, and less dramatic but equally worrying events elsewhere in the Middle East (e.g., Egypt, Algeria, and Syria), that such connections began to emerge. Scholars largely agreed (1) that the cause of the Islamic revolution lay in a crisis of cultural authenticity brought about by the Shah's failed attempts at political and social modernization; (2) that the response to this crisis was the molding of traditional Shii ideas and symbols into an ideological force for change; and (3) that the ideological formulation of Islam exhibited in the Islamic revolution was part of a larger pattern of political religion common throughout the Middle East and the larger Muslim world. Not all scholars viewed fundamentalism as a useful tool for explaining this trend, and among those who did, there were various definitions of fundamentalism proffered. Two important interrelated questions, however, informed the general debate about this trend that some called "fundamentalism." First, is it a uniquely modern phenomenon? Or is it part of a cyclic pattern of social response that can be found throughout Islamic or world history? Second, is it a progressive movement, one that will allow developing Muslim countries to move forward along the modernization path? Or is it in fact a regressive revolutionary force, one that will impede hopeful advances that had already begun to reshape Muslim societies?

> ## MUSLIM BROTHERHOOD OF EGYPT
>
> Founded in Egypt in 1928, some fifty years prior to the Islamic revolution in Iran, the Muslim Brotherhood is considered the premier Sunni Islamist organization in the Muslim world. The writings of its founder, Hassan al-Banna (1905–1949), and its main ideologue, Sayyid Qutb (1906–1966), have become standard reading for Muslim activists. Both figures were martyrs to the Islamist cause, killed by an authoritarian state that eliminated sources of authority that it could not easily control. The preaching and activism of the Brotherhood set the stage for a new kind of Muslim reformer, one who engaged society and confronted the state on a broad spectrum of issues. Indeed, through its array of clinics, schools, businesses, and mosques, the Brotherhood tried to create a mini-society that modeled the power of the Islamic alternative to Western-style modernization. This alternative included the rejection of the nation-state as a legitimate form of Muslim political organization, though some scholars believe that the Brotherhood's ultimate goal was to replace secular nationalism with religious nationalism. In either case, the Brotherhood's proposed "Islamic order"—the notion of a society and polity integrated according to Islamic cultural values and ideas—served, and continues to serve, as a challenge to the Western-leaning policies of the Egyptian government.

Scholars divided over the modern-versus-perennial question, but, like the academic debate about the nation, a consensus pointed to a modern point of origin for fundamentalism. Scholars also disagreed about fundamentalism's potential to contribute positively to the challenges of developing nations, but, once again, the tendency was to emphasize the backward-looking and thus retarding nature of the movement. Those who advocated a fundamentalist paradigm for understanding the Islamic revolution recognized that the distinction between developing and developed nations prevented direct comparisons between Iran and America. Instead, they proposed a general set of characteristics that defined fundamentalism across social and cultural boundaries, the two most common of which were a totalizing worldview—subsuming every aspect of life under religion—and scripturalism—a devotion to the inerrancy and immutability of sacred Scripture. Fundamentalists, then, rooted in the sole authority of sacred Scripture, approached the world in uncomplicated and uncompromising terms, ordering their lives and their communities (however limited or expansive based on their power) according to a strict set of God-ordained guidelines that separated the saved from the damned.

Problems with the Fundamentalist Paradigm

Fundamentalism proved a popular and important idea because it held out the promise of accounting for perceived patterns of thinking and behavior in diverse societies with differing religious and political cultures. Critics of the fundamentalist paradigm, however, saw in the patterns an inherent Western bias that created problems for meaningful comparison. For example, Protestant fundamentalists in the United States defined themselves over and against liberal trends by highlighting their scripturalist views. In the Muslim world, by contrast, the vast majority of Muslims expressed literalist attitudes toward the Koran. In fact, some scholars claimed that Muslim societies were dominated by scripturalist fundamentalism, and that their successful modernization depended on the development of a more liberal interpretive strand in Islam. Hence a supposed comparative characteristic that serves to identify and analyze a *faction* of the religious population in one context, the United States, loses this capacity in another, the Muslim world.

A similar problem arose with the pattern of a totalizing worldview. Unlike their more civic-minded and secularized fellow citizens, American Protestant fundamentalists may indeed see the private and public spheres as indivisible and necessarily religiously ordered. To speak of the same phenomenon in Muslim societies, however, is to miss the overarching role that religion has come to play in the political process. Certain groups in Muslim societies may be totalizing in their worldview, but the search for cultural authenticity has also led to a basic pattern of politicized religion among all factions. Fundamentalism, then, even if it were deemed to exist in the form of Islamism, is just a small portion of the public Islam that dominates the lives of modern Muslims. And with Islamic ideas and symbols being deployed by so many Muslim citizens with differing political agendas, how can one reasonably highlight a single faction as blending religion and politics in a distinctively different manner? For this reason, some scholars of the Muslim world avoid the term "fundamentalism," preferring instead terms like "Islamic resurgence" (Dessouki) or "Muslim politics" (Eickelman and Piscatori) to capture the multipurpose political ends to which the Islamic tradition has been put.

The above-mentioned descriptors of fundamentalism clearly contained proscriptive judgments about its rational viability. When applied to American Protestantism, totalism and scripturalism often implied that fundamentalists were out of step with modern, mainstream thinking about both Christianity and the place of religion in American public life, thus isolating the group as an aberrant form of religiosity. By contrast, when applied to entire Muslim societies, as they often were, these same descriptors leveled a more far-reaching social critique. Here fundamentalism served as a warning sign of a failure in the process of modernization, for totalism and scripturalism were thought to interfere with the kind of progressive politics and progressive religion that developing societies needed to achieve. Here too the notion of progress is clearly borrowed from a Western model, where political modernization and secularization are viewed as one, and where religions have presumably made peace with this arrangement. Not all interpretations of fundamentalism suffer from the same cultural bias, but the term has been shadowed by the uses to which it has been put.

State of the Field

Two interrelated issues have come to dominate fundamentalism as a field of study. The first relates to the shifting meaning of the phenomenon depending on whether the focus of analysis is a specific case, a regional culture, or a cross-cultural comparison. Narrowly defined examples bring out important nuances that are often glossed over when attempting to aggregate common patterns regionally or internationally. And scholars who are prepared to see a particular case in terms of fundamentalism, rightly defined, are sometimes less convinced once this case has been situated in a schema of fundamentalist types. By the 1990s, fundamentalism had become something of a cottage industry within the academy, and the result was a burgeoning number of supposed cases around the world. Typing these cases, however, has remained an elusive task, with scholars tending to select those examples that best fit their analytic agenda. In the end, the proliferation of fundamentalisms created a situation where the parameters of the field became more indistinct and fundamentalism itself more difficult to comprehend.

The other issue, and a more hopeful sign, is the growing realization that the comparative study of fundamentalism has become entangled in a global transformation of politics and culture at the end of the twentieth century. With the collapse of the Soviet Union and the declining ability of the West to impose its policies and values around the world, indigenous ethnic and religious identities—often regarded as fundamentalist—have reasserted themselves, especially in those regions that were once the object of Cold War competitive interest. For the Western academy, then, tracking the rise of fundamentalisms worldwide has been a lesson in the limits of the West. Thus what began as a study of the antimodern, antisecular "other" evolved into a study of the Western self (Marty and Appleby).

See also **Christianity; Islam; Judaism; Orthodoxy; Orthopraxy; Secularization and Secularism.**

BIBLIOGRAPHY

Appleby, R. Scott, ed. *Spokesmen for the Despised: Fundamentalist Leaders of the Middle East.* Chicago: University of Chicago Press, 1997.

Aran, Gideon. "The Father, the Son, and the Holy Land: The Spiritual Authorities of Jewish-Zionist Fundamentalism in Israel." In *Spokesmen for the Despised: Fundamentalist Leaders of the Middle East,* edited by R. Scott Appleby. Chicago: University of Chicago Press, 1997.

Bruce, Steve. *The Rise and Fall of the New Christian Right: Conservative Protestant Politics in America, 1978–1988.* Oxford: Clarendon Press, 1988.

Dekmejian, R. Hrair. *Islam in Revolution: Fundamentalism in the Arab World.* Syracuse, N.Y.: Syracuse University Press, 1985.

Dessouki, Ali E. Hillal, ed. *Islamic Resurgence in the Arab World.* New York: Praeger, 1982.

Eickelman, Dale F., and James Piscatori. *Muslim Politics.* Princeton, N.J.: Princeton University Press, 1996.

Hansen, Thomas Blom. *The Saffron Wave: Democracy and Hindu Nationalism in Modern India.* Princeton, N.J.: Princeton University Press, 1999.

Hunter, James Davison. *Culture Wars: The Struggle to Define America.* New York: Basic Books, 1991.

Huntington, Samuel P. *The Clash of Civilizations and the Remaking of World Order.* New York: Simon and Schuster, 1996.

Juergensmeyer, Mark. "Antifundamentalism." In *Fundamentalisms Comprehended.* Vol. 5. Edited by Martin E. Marty and R. Scott Appleby. Chicago: University of Chicago Press, 1995.

———. *The New Cold War? Religious Nationalism Confronts the Secular State.* Berkeley: University of California Press, 1993.

Lawrence, Bruce B. *Defenders of God: The Fundamentalist Revolt against the Modern Age.* San Francisco: Harper and Row, 1989.

Marsden, George M. *Fundamentalism and American Culture: The Shaping of Twentieth Century Evangelicalism, 1870–1925.* New York: Oxford University Press, 1980.

Marty, Martin E., and R. Scott Appleby. "The Fundamentalism Project: A User's Guide." In *Fundamentalisms Observed,* vol. 1, edited by Martin E. Marty and R. Scott Appleby. Chicago: University of Chicago Press, 1991.

Munson, Henry. *Islam and Revolution in the Middle East.* New Haven, Conn.: Yale University Press, 1988.

Nielsen, Niels C., Jr. *Fundamentalism, Mythos, and World Religions.* Albany: State University of New York Press, 1993.

Rieserbrodt, Martin. *Pious Passion: The Emergence of Modern Fundamentalism in the United States and Iran.* Translated by Don Reneau. Berkeley: University of California Press, 1993.

Sandeen, Ernest R. *The Roots of Fundamentalism: British and American Millenarianism 1800–1930.* Chicago: University of Chicago Press, 1970.

Sprinzak, Ehud. *The Ascendance of Israel's Radical Right.* New York: Oxford University Press, 1991.

Watt, William Montgomery. *Islamic Fundamentalism and Modernity.* London and New York: Routledge, 1988.

Jeffrey T. Kenney

FUTUROLOGY. Futurology is the study of the future to obtain knowledge of it on the basis of present trends. Beginning in the 1960s, it is a relatively new field of study. The word *futurology* was first used in 1943 by Ossip Flechteim, a political scientist, to describe a new scientific field of human knowledge based on a critical, systematic, and normative analysis of questions related to future. However, *future studies* (or *futures studies*), *futures research, futuristics, prognostics,* and *futurible* are also used for the term *futurology*.

Interest in the future of humanity, society, and the world in general is an age-old phenomenon. In a two-volume extensive scholarly work, Fred Polak (1961) has outlined "the close relationship between the history of images of the future and the general course of history itself" and shown that "positive images of the future, in and through their own history, have foreshadowed the outlines of the oncoming course of general events." In his study the images of future are largely those presented by the utopia. An important lesson, most relevant to futurology, drawn from his study is that the utopia "can be used by intelligent and humanitarian men as a tool for reworking society" and further that the future of society rests in human hands. This idea that man has within him the power to create a desirable future conducive to the general well-being of man and nature has guided this new field of futurology. Dramatic events, such as the successful completion of the Manhattan Project during World War II and later development in space research leading to the successful landing of a human being on the Moon, opened people's eyes to the new power of science and technology—that it can be harnessed not only to help humans determine a future desired goal, but also to achieve it in a stipulated time. Realization of this fact—that a desirable future objective can be planned and achieved—was decisive in creating this new field of futurology. It was also soon realized that human society was facing critical problems such as overpopulation, food shortages, growing economic disparities, resource depletion, worldwide energy crises, environmental pollution, threat of terrorism, and other perils, which—if unchecked—might lead to a disastrous future. It was imperative that corrective measures for such impending global dangers be taken. These afforded immediate objective for the new field of studies. In a sense, the perception of the future as a supreme resource is the driving force of futurology.

One recurrent theme appearing in the writings of the futurists characterizing the present age is what Peter Drucker refers to as the "age of discontinuity." The cleavage with the past in many important respects is brought about by the unprecedented growth in the scientific and technological knowledge, leading the world to the brink of a great transformation. The fallout of this transformation is many sided and varied, encompassing everything of human activity. What is unprecedented about this transformation is the accelerated rate of change in development, exemplified, for example, by the fact that the computer speed is doubled every eighteen months (Moore's law). Such changes have consequent impact on the nature of work, habitat, transportation, communication, and all spheres of human activity. The stress of having to cope with all the changes within a short time produces the "future shock" discussed by Alvin Toffler (1970). It is the "dizzying disorientation brought on by the premature arrival of the future," "a time phenomenon, a product of the greatly accelerated rate of change in society" (Toffler). The writings of Alvin Toffler, Arthur C. Clarke, and Buckminster Fuller have caught the imagination of the general public and generated interest in the future of human civilization.

Objectives and Characteristics

Future is to be created, as it does not yet exist. Also the events are interrelated, as changes in some components will affect the future. This indicates that there are many "futures," but the one that will finally emerge is already determined by the events of the past. Thus the emergent future comes out of all possible futures—where anything might happen. These are further limited to probable futures, which are most likely to happen and already shaped by the immediate past. Futurists would like to work for the most preferable or a desired future. Thus planning for the future presupposes importance of three factors: the interlinking of events, a vision of the future and ideas for different events that would ultimately lead to the desirable future, and time. Time is related to the importance of short-term, medium-term, and long-term planning for realization of the future. A convenient time frame for studying the future are: near-range: up to a period of one year; short-range: up to a period of five years; medium-range: from five years to twenty years; long-range: from twenty years to fifty years; and far: beyond fifty years.

Some characteristics of this new field of study as noted by Olaf Helmer (1978) are that its function is primarily predictive and not explanatory; it constructs tentative models for which no hard data about the future is available; often the intuitive judgment of the experts is the main guidance; and, most important, it is highly multidisciplinary.

However, views and perspectives about future studies differ. One view tends to project it as a way of providing "decision-makers with operationally meaningful assistance in the form of information and analysis" to facilitate better decision-making and looks upon future studies work as an "objective exploration of what future has to offer" (Helmer, p. 764). However, against this trend for confining future studies merely to forecasting in utopian areas, there are those who want future studies to lead forecasting "to planning, decision, and creative action" and require that futures research be responsive to global challenge ahead. This demands an increasingly holistic and global, more explicitly normative, and increased participation. The fundamental assumption in future studies is that interventions can change the future; this also implies assumption of responsibility for the process of changing the future. Together with its multidimensional and interdisciplinary character, creation of awareness about the desirable future, making people conscious of the effect of their action on the future, and acting as a pressure group mark the uniqueness of this field.

One common method of prediction is to extend current trends, but such interlinked and interacting systems, as futurology deals with are generally of the common adaptive type. These exhibit a range of nonadditive effects that simply cannot be summed to give the overall effect. However, even in such cases, computer-based modeling comes to help. One such mathematical modeling resulted in the widely circulated and criticized "Limits of Growth" concept published in early

1970. Methods developed since 1970 include the Delphic method, trend-impact analysis, cross-impact analysis, structural analysis, technology-sequence analysis, decision and statistical modeling, relevance trees and morphological analysis, science and technology road-mapping, scenarios and interactive scenarios, and the state of the future index method (see, for example, Glen and Gordon, 2003). In spite of such skeptics' declarations as "Futurism is dead" and that the futurist window to the world of tomorrow is just a "mirror reflecting the prejudices and preconceptions of one's own time" (Jones), futurology is going strong, with professional futurists helping their clients "draw the maps of the future and identify the obstacles (and opportunities) along the way" (Wagner). Much development in the field of ecology and sustainable development results in international cooperation in decreasing global warming and ozone hole depletion, and can be attributed to this field. Things are happening at all levels, projects like restorative development are future-inspired action plans. Rapid developments in the new field of science and technology such as NBIC (nanotechnology, biotechnology, information technology, and cognitive science) have led to a plethora of futuristic writings in these fields (see Eric Drexler [1987]; Ray Kurzweil [2000]; Rodney Brooks [2002]; John Brockman [2002]; Douglas Mulhall [2002]).

To state a truism, future begins where history ends, and it is befitting to conclude this entry with a quotation from Francis Fukuyama's much acclaimed "End of History and the Last Man":

The unfolding of modern natural science has had a uniform effect on all societies that have experienced it, for two reasons. . . . technology confers decisive military advantages on those countries that posses it, and given the continuing possibility of war in the international system of states, no states that values its independence can ignore the need for defensive modernisation. Second, modern natural science establishes a uniform horizon of economic production possibilities. Technology makes possible the limitless accumulation of wealth, and thus the satisfaction of an ever expanding set of human desires. This process guarantees an increasing homogenization of all human societies, regardless of their historical origins or cultural inheritances. All countries undergoing economic modernisation must increasingly resemble one another; they must unify nationally on the basis of the centralized state, urbanize, replace traditional forms of social organizations like tribe, sect, and family with rational ones based on function and efficiency, and provide for universal education of their citizens" (pp. xiv–xv).

See also **Cycles; History, Idea of; Science Fiction; Technology.**

BIBLIOGRAPHY

Brockman, John, ed. *The Next Fifty Years.* New York: Vintage, 2002.

Brooks, Rodney. *Flesh and Machines: How Robots Will Change Us.* New York: Pantheon Books, 2002.

Cornish, Edward. *The Study of the Future.* Bethesda, Md.: World Future Society, 1977.

Drexler, Eric. *Engines of Creation.* New York: Anchor Books, 1987.

Fukuyama, Francis. *End of History and the Last Man.* New York: Free Press, 1992.

Glenn, Jerome C., and Theodore T. Gordon. *Futures Research Methodology.* Washington, D.C.: Millennium Project/American College for the United Nations University, 2003.

Helmer, Olaf. "The Research Task before Us." In *Handbook of Future Research,* edited by Jib Fowles. London: Greenwood Press, 1978.

Jones, John. "The Amateur Prophets." Available at http://www.ensc.sfu.ca/people/faculty/jones/ENSC100/future/node4.html

Kurzweil, Ray. *The Age of Spiritual Machines: When Computers Exceed Human Intelligence.* New York: Penguin Putnam, 2000.

Mulhall, Douglas. *Our Molecular Future.* Amherst, N.Y.: Prometheus, 2002.

Polak, Fred, L. *The Image of the Future.* New York: Oceana Publications, 1961.

Toffler, Alvin. *Future Shock.* New York: Random House, 1970.

Wagner, Cindy. "Futurism Is NOT Dead" (editorial for *The Futurist*). Available at http://www.wfs.org/futurism.htm

Paramanonda Mahanta